The Cambridge Handbook of Thinking and Reasoning

The *Cambridge Handbook of Thinking and Reasoning* is the first comprehensive and authoritative handbook covering all the core topics of the field of thinking and reasoning. Written by the foremost experts from cognitive psychology, cognitive science, and cognitive neuroscience, individual chapters summarize basic concepts and findings for a major topic, sketch its history, and give a sense of the directions in which research is currently heading. The volume also includes work related to developmental, social and clinical psychology, philosophy, economics, artificial intelligence, linguistics, education, law, and medicine. Scholars and students in all these fields and others will find this to be a valuable collection.

Keith J. Holyoak is a Distinguished Professor in the Department of Psychology at the University of California, Los Angeles (UCLA). He has made a number of major contributions to the scientific understanding of human thinking and has pioneered modern work on the role of analogy in thinking.

Robert G. Morrison is president of Xunesis (www.xunesis.org), a not-for-profit company that encourages people to integrate science with their everyday lives through performance and media art that engages, entertains, and educates in both traditional and nontraditional educational settings. He received his Ph.D. in cognitive neuroscience from UCLA. His research involves understanding how the human brain implements and constrains higher cognition.

p. 173 of Stanov

– can you work out the Bayesian answer to the aids problem

5:00pm Fri

– deliver to either or both

– via email or paper

The Cambridge Handbook of Thinking and Reasoning

Edited by

Keith J. Holyoak

and

Robert G. Morrison

CAMBRIDGE UNIVERSITY PRESS
Cambridge, New York, Melbourne, Madrid, Cape Town, Singapore, São Paulo

Cambridge University Press
40 West 20th Street, New York, NY 10011-4211, USA

www.cambridge.org
Information on this title: www.cambridge.org/9780521824170

First published 2005

Printed in the United States of America

A catalog record for this publication is available from the British Library.

Library of Congress Cataloging in Publication Data

The Cambridge handbook of thinking and reasoning / edited by Keith J. Holyoak and Robert G. Morrison.

p. cm.

Includes bibliographical references.

ISBN 0-521-82417-6 (hardcover) – ISBN 0-521-53101-2 (pbk.)

1. Thought and thinking. 2. Reasoning (Psychology) I. Holyoak, Keith James, 1950– II. Morrison, Robert G., Jr., 1966– III. Title.

BF441.C265 2005
153.4′2 – dc22 2004016029

ISBN-13 978-0-521-82417-0 hardback
ISBN-10 0-521-82417-6 hardback

ISBN-13 978-0-521-53101-6 paperback
ISBN-10 0-521-53101-2 paperback

The editors gratefully dedicate this volume to
Patricia Wenjie Cheng
(from KJH)
and
Deborah Lee Morrison
(from RGM)

Contents

Preface

A few decades ago, when the science of cognition was in its infancy, the early textbooks on cognition began with perception and attention and ended with memory. So-called higher-level cognition – the mysterious, complicated realm of thinking and reasoning – was simply left out. Things have changed – any good cognitive text (and there are many) devotes several chapters to topics such as categorization, inductive and deductive reasoning, judgment and decision making, and problem solving. What has still been missing, however, is a true handbook for the field of thinking and reasoning – a book meant to be kept close "at hand" by those involved in the field. Such a book would bring together top researchers to write chapters, each of which summarizes the basic concepts and findings for a major topic, sketches its history, and provides a sense of the directions in which research is currently heading. This handbook would provide quick overviews for experts in each topic area, and more importantly for experts in allied topic areas (because few researchers can keep up with the scientific literature over the full breadth of the field of thinking and reasoning). Even more crucially, this handbook would provide an entry point into the field for the next generation of researchers by providing a text for use in classes on thinking and reasoning designed for graduate students and upper-level undergraduates.

The Cambridge Handbook of Thinking and Reasoning is intended to be this previously missing handbook. The project was first conceived at the meeting of the Cognitive Science Society in Edinburgh, Scotland, during the summer of 2001. The contents of the volume are sketched in Chapter 1. Our aim is to provide comprehensive and authoritative reviews of all the core topics of the field of thinking and reasoning, with many pointers for further reading. Undoubtedly, there are still omissions, but we have included as much as we could realistically fit in a single volume. Our focus is on research from cognitive psychology, cognitive science, and cognitive neuroscience, but we also include work related to developmental, social, and clinical psychology; philosophy; economics; artificial intelligence; linguistics; education; law; and medicine. We hope that scholars and students in all these fields and others will find this to be a valuable collection.

We have many to thank for their help in bringing this endeavor to fruition. Philip Laughlin, our editor at Cambridge University Press, gave us exactly the balance of encouragement and patience we needed. It is fitting that a handbook of thinking and reasoning should bear the imprint and indeed the name of this illustrious press, with its long history reaching back to the origins of scientific inquiry. Michie Shaw, Senior Project Manager at TechBooks, provided us with close support throughout the arduous editing process. At UCLA, Christine Vu did a great deal of organizational work in her role as our editorial assistant for the entire project. During this period, our own efforts were supported by grants R305H030141 from the Institute of Education Sciences and SES-0080375 from the National Science Foundation to KJH, and from Xunesis and National Service Research Award MH-064244 from the National Institute of Mental Health to RGM.

Then there are the authors. (It would seem a bit presumptuous to call them "our" authors!) People working on tough intellectual problems sometimes experience a moment of insight – a sense that although many laborious steps may lay ahead, the basic elements of a solution are already in place. Such fortunate people work on happily, confident that ultimate success is assured. In preparing this handbook, we also had our moment of "insight." It came when all these outstanding researchers agreed to join our project. Before the first chapter was drafted, we knew the volume was going to be of the highest quality. Along the way, our distinguished authors graciously served as each other's critics as we passed drafts around, working to make the chapters as integrated as possible, adding in pointers from one to another. Then the authors all changed hats again and went back to work revising their own chapters in light of the feedback their peers had provided. We thank you all for making our own small labors a great pleasure.

KEITH J. HOLYOAK
University of California, Los Angeles

ROBERT G. MORRISON
Xunesis, Chicago
October 2004

Contributors

John R. Anderson
Carnegie Mellon University
Department of Psychology
Pittsburgh, PA 15213-3890
ja+@cmu.edu

José F. Arocha
Department of Health Studies & Gerontology
University of Waterloo
200 University Ave. W.
Waterloo, Ontario
Canada N2L 3G1
jfarocha@healthy.uwaterloo.ca

Peter Bachman
University of California, Los Angeles
Department of Psychology
Franz Hall
Los Angeles, CA 90095-1563
bachman@psych.ucla.edu

Miriam Bassok
University of Washington
Department of Psychology
Box 351525
Seattle, WA 98195-1525
mbassok@u.washington.edu

Marc J. Buehner
School of Psychology
Cardiff University
Tower Building
Park Place
Cardiff, CF10 3AT
Wales, UK
BuehnerM@Cardiff.ac.uk

Josep Call
Max Planck Institute for Evolutionary Anthropology
Deutscher Platz 6
D-04103 Leipzig, Germany
call@eva.mpg.de

Tyrone D. Cannon
University of California, Los Angeles
Department of Psychology
Franz Hall
Los Angeles, CA 90095-1563
cannon@psych.ucla.edu

Patricia W. Cheng
University of California, Los Angeles
Department of Psychology
Franz Hall
Los Angeles, CA 90095-1563
cheng@psych.ucla.edu

Michelene T. H. Chi
University of Pittsburgh
Learning Research and Development Center
3939 O'Hara Street
Pittsburgh, PA 15260
chi@pitt.edu

Leonidas A. A. Doumas
University of California, Los Angeles
Department of Psychology
Franz Hall
Los Angeles, CA 90095-1563
adoumas@psych.ucla.edu

Kevin Dunbar
Dartmouth College
Department of Psychological & Brain Sciences
Hanover, NH 03755
kevin.n.dunbar@dartmouth.edu

Phoebe C. Ellsworth
University of Michigan
Department of Psychology
525 East University
Ann Arbor, MI 48109-1109
pce@umich.edu

Jonathan St. B. T. Evans
University of Plymouth
Centre for Thinking and Language
School of Psychology
Plymouth PL4 8AA UK
J.Evans@plymouth.ac.uk

Shane Frederick
Massachusetts Institute of Technology
Sloan School of Management
Room E56-317
38 Memorial Drive
Cambridge, MA 02142-1307
shanefre@mit.edu

Jonathan Fugelsang
Dartmouth College
Department of Psychological & Brain Sciences
Hanover, NH 03755
jonf@dartmouth.edu

Charles R. Gallistel
Rutgers University
Psychology and Rutgers Center for Cognitive Science
152 Frelinghuysen Road
Piscataway, NJ 08854-8020
galliste@ruccs.rutgers.edu

Rochel Gelman
Rutgers University
Psychology and Rutgers Center for Cognitive Science
152 Frelinghuysen Road
Piscataway, NJ 08854-8020
rgelman@ruccs.rutgers.edu

Lila Gleitman
University of Pennsylvania
Departments of Psychology and Linguistics
Institute for Research in Cognitive Science
3401 Walnut St. – 4th floor
Philadelphia, PA 19104
gleitman@cattell.psych.upenn.edu

Vinod Goel
York University
Department of Psychology
Toronto, Ontario
Canada M3J 1P3
vgoel@yorku.ca

Robert L. Goldstone
Indiana University
Psychology Department
Psychology Building
1101 E 10th St.
Bloomington, IN 47405-7007
rgoldsto@indiana.edu

Patricia M. Greenfield
University of California, Los Angeles
Department of Psychology
Franz Hall
Los Angeles, CA 90095-1563
greenfield@psych.ucla.edu

Graeme S. Halford
University of Queensland
School of Psychology
Brisbane
Queensland 4072
Australia
gsh@psy.uq.edu.au

E. Tory Higgins
Columbia University
Department of Psychology
401 D Schermerhorm
Mail Code 5501
New York, NY 10027-5501
tory@psych.columbia.edu

Keith J. Holyoak – editor
University of California, Los Angeles
Department of Psychology
Franz Hall
Los Angeles, CA 90095-1563
holyoak@lifesci.ucla.edu

John E. Hummel
University of California, Los Angeles
Department of Psychology
Franz Hall
Los Angeles, CA 90095-1563
jhummel@psych.ucla.edu

P. N. Johnson-Laird
Princeton University
Department of Psychology
3-C-3 Green Hall
Princeton, NJ 08544
phil@princeton.edu

Daniel Kahneman
Princeton University
Woodrow Wilson School
324 Wallace Hall
Princeton, NJ 08544
kahneman@princeton.edu

James C. Kaufman
California State University, San Bernardino
Department of Psychology
5500 University Parkway
San Bernardino, CA 92407
jkaufman@csusb.edu

David A. Lagnado
Department of Psychology
University College London
Gower Street
London, UK WC1E 6BT
d.lagnado@ucl.ac.uk

Robyn A. LeBoeuf
University of Florida
Warrington College of Business
Marketing Department
PO Box 117155
Gainesville, FL 32611-7155
LeBoeuf@ufl.edu

Leib Litman
Brooklyn College of CUNY
Department of Psychology
2900 Bedford Avenue
Brooklyn, NY 11210
LeibL@Brooklyn.cuny.edu

Marsha C. Lovett
Carnegie Mellon University
Department of Psychology
Pittsburgh, PA 15213-3890
lovett+@cmu.edu

Todd I. Lubart
Laboratoire Cognition et Développement
Institut de Psychologie – Université Paris 5
71, avenue Edouard Vaillant
92774 Boulogne-Billancourt cedex
France
lubart@psycho.univ-paris5.fr

Douglas L. Medin
Northwestern University
Department of Psychology
2029 Sheridan Road
Evanston, IL 60208
medin@northwestern.edu

Daniel C. Molden
Northwestern University
Department of Psychology
2029 Sheridan Road
Evanston, IL 60208
molden@northwestern.edu

Robert G. Morrison – editor
Xunesis
P.O. Box 269187
Chicago, IL 60626-9187
robertmorrison@xunesis.org

Laura R. Novick
Vanderbilt University
Department of Psychology & Human Development
Peabody College #512
230 Appleton Place
Nashville, TN 37203-5721
Laura.Novick@vanderbilt.edu

Stellan Ohlsson
University of Illinois, Chicago
Department of Psychology
Chicago, IL 60607-7137
stellan@uic.edu

Anna Papafragou
University of Pennsylvania
Institute for Research in Cognitive Science
3401 Walnut Street, Suite 400A
Philadelphia, PA 19104
anna4@linc.cis.upenn.edu

VIMLA L. PATEL
Columbia University
Department of Biomedical Informatics and Psychiatry
Vanderbilt Clinic-5 622 West 168th Street
New York, NY 10003
patel@dbmi.columbia.edu

DAVID N. PERKINS
Harvard Graduate School of Education
Project Zero
315 Longfellow Hall, Appian Way
Cambridge, MA 02138
david_perkins@harvard.edu

JEAN E. PRETZ
Department of Psychology
Illinois Wesleyan University
P.O. Box 2900
Bloomington, IL 61702-2900
jpretz@iwu.edu

ARTHUR S. REBER
Brooklyn College of CUNY
Department of Psychology
2900 Bedford Avenue
Brooklyn, NY 11210
areber@brooklyn.cuny.edu

LANCE J. RIPS
Northwestern University
Department of Psychology
2029 Sheridan Road
Evanston, IL 60208
rips@northwestern.edu

RON RITCHHART
Harvard Graduate School of Education
Project Zero
124 Mount Auburn Street
Cambridge, MA 02138
ron_ritchhart@pz.harvard.edu

TIMOTHY A. SALTHOUSE
University of Virginia
Department of Psychology
Charlottesville, VA 22904-4400
salthouse@virginia.edu

ELDAR B. SHAFIR
Princeton University
Department of Psychology and the Woodrow Wilson School of Public Affairs
Green Hall
Princeton, NJ 08544
shafir@princeton.edu

STEVEN A. SLOMAN
Brown University
Cognitive & Linguistic Sciences
Box 1978
Providence, RI 02912
Steven_Sloman@brown.edu

JI YUN SON
Indiana University
Psychology Department
Psychology Building
1101 E 10th St.
Bloomington, IN 47405-7007
jys@indiana.edu

ROBERT J. STERNBERG
PACE Center
Yale University
P.O. Box 208358
New Haven, CT 06520-8358
robert.sternberg@yale.edu

MICHAEL TOMASELLO
Max Planck Institute for Evolutionary Anthropology
Deutscher Platz 6
D-04103 Leipzig, Germany
tomas@eva.mpg.de

BARBARA TVERSKY
Stanford University
Department of Psychology
Building 420
Stanford, CA 94305-2130
bt@psych.stanford.edu

JIAJIE ZHANG
School of Health Information Sciences
University of Texas at Houston
7000 Fannin, Suite 600
Houston, TX 77030
Jiajie.Zhang@uth.tmc.edu

CHAPTER 1

Thinking and Reasoning: A Reader's Guide

Keith J. Holyoak
Robert G. Morrison

"Cogito, ergo sum," the French philosopher René Descartes famously declared, "I think, therefore I am." Every normal human adult shares a sense that the ability to think, to reason, is a part of their fundamental identity. A person may be struck blind or deaf, yet we still recognize his or her core cognitive capacities as intact. Even loss of language, the gift often claimed as the *sine qua non* of *homo sapiens*, does not take away a person's essential humanness. Unlike language ability, which is essentially unique to our species, the rudimentary ability to think and reason is apparent in nonhuman primates (see Call & Tomasello, Chap. 25); and yet it is thinking, not language, that lies closest to the core of our individual identity. A person who loses language but can still make intelligent decisions, as demonstrated by actions, is viewed as mentally intact. In contrast, the kinds of brain damage that rob an individual of the capacity to think and reason are considered the harshest blows that can be struck against a sense of personhood. *Cogito, ergo sum.*

What Is Thinking?

We can start to answer this question by looking at the various ways the word "thinking" is used in everyday language. "I think that water is necessary for life" and "George thinks the Pope is a communist" both express *beliefs* (of varying degrees of apparent plausibility), that is, explicit claims of what someone takes to be a truth about the world. "Anne is sure to think of a solution" carries us into the realm of problem solving, the mental construction of an action plan to achieve a goal. The complaint "Why didn't you think before you went ahead with your half-baked scheme?" emphasizes that thinking can be a kind of *foresight*, a way of "seeing" the possible future.[1] "What do you think about it?" calls for a *judgment*, an assessment of the desirability of an option. Then there's "Albert is lost in thought," where thinking becomes some sort of mental meadow through which a person might meander on a rainy afternoon, oblivious to the world outside.

Rips and Conrad (1989) elicited judgments from college students about how various mentalistic terms relate to one another. Using statistical techniques, the investigators were able to summarize these relationships in two diagrams, shown in Figure 1.1. Figure 1.1(A) is a hierarchy of *kinds*, or categories. Roughly, people believe planning is a kind of deciding, which is a kind of reasoning, which is a kind of conceptualizing, which is a kind of thinking. People also believe that thinking is *part of* conceptualizing, which is part of remembering, which is part of reasoning, and so on [Figure 1.1(B)]. The kinds ordering and the parts ordering are similar; most strikingly, "thinking" is the most general term in both orderings – the grand superordinate of mental activities, which permeates all the others.

It is not easy to make the move from the free flow of everyday speech to scientific definitions of mental terms, but let us nonetheless offer a preliminary definition of thinking to suggest what this book is about: *Thinking is the systematic transformation of mental representations of knowledge to characterize actual or possible states of the world, often in service of goals*. Obviously, our definition introduces a plethora of terms with meanings that beg to be unpacked, but at which we can only hint. A *mental representation* of knowledge is an internal description that can be manipulated to form other descriptions. To count as thinking, the manipulations must be *systematic* transformations governed by certain constraints. Whether a logical deduction or a creative leap, what we mean by thinking is more than unconstrained associations (with the caveat that thinking may indeed be disordered; see Bachman & Cannon, Chap. 21). The internal representations created by thinking describe states of some external world (a world that may include the thinker as an object of self-reflection) – that world might be our everyday one, or perhaps some imaginary construction obeying the "laws" of magical realism. Often (not always – the daydreamer, and indeed the night dreamer, are also thinkers), thinking is directed toward achieving some desired state of affairs, some goal that motivates the thinker to perform mental work.

Our definition thus includes quite a few stipulations, but notice also what is left out. We do not claim that thinking necessarily requires a human (higher-order primates, and perhaps some other species on this or other planets, have a claim to be considered thinkers) (see Call & Tomasello, Chap. 25) or even a sentient being. (The field of artificial intelligence may have been a disappointment in its first half-century, but we are reluctant to define it away as an oxymoron.) Nonetheless, our focus in this book is on thinking by hominids with electrochemically powered brains. Thinking often seems to be a conscious activity of which the thinker is aware (*cogito, ergo sum*); however, consciousness is a thorny philosophical puzzle, and some mental activities seem pretty much like thinking, except for being implicit rather than explicit (see Litman & Reber, Chap. 18). Finally, we do not claim that thinking is inherently rational, optimal, desirable, or even smart. A thorough history of human thinking will include quite a few chapters on stupidity.

The study of thinking includes several interrelated subfields that reflect slightly different perspectives on thinking. *Reasoning*, which has a long tradition that springs from philosophy and logic, places emphasis on the process of drawing inferences (*conclusions*) from some initial information (*premises*). In standard logic, an inference is *deductive* if the truth of the premises guarantees the truth of the conclusion by virtue of the argument form. If the truth of the premises renders the truth of the conclusion more credible but does not bestow certainty, the inference is called *inductive*.[2] *Judgment and decision making* involve assessment of the value of an option or the probability that it will yield a certain payoff (judgment) coupled with choice among alternatives (decision making). *Problem solving* involves the construction of a course of action that can achieve a goal.

Although these distinct perspectives on thinking are useful in organizing the field

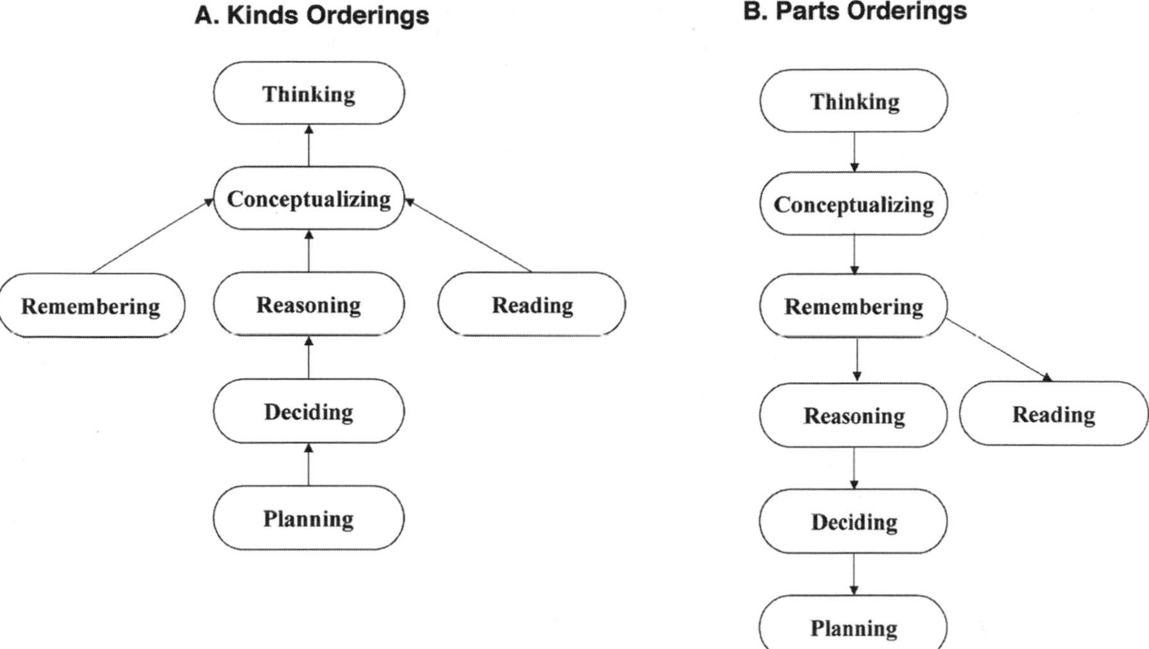

Figure 1.1. People's conceptions of the relationships among terms for mental activities. A, Ordering of "kinds." B, Ordering of "parts." (Adapted from Rips & Conrad, 1989, with permission.)

(and this volume), these aspects of thinking overlap in every conceivable way. To solve a problem, one is likely to reason about the consequences of possible actions and make decisions to select among alternative actions. A logic problem, as the name implies, is a problem to be solved (with the goal of deriving or evaluating a possible conclusion). Making a decision is often a problem that requires reasoning. These subdivisions of the field, like our preliminary definition of thinking, should be treated as guideposts, not destinations.

A Capsule History

Thinking and reasoning, long the academic province of philosophy, have over the past century emerged as core topics of empirical investigation and theoretical analysis in the modern fields known as cognitive psychology, cognitive science, and cognitive neuroscience. Before psychology was founded, the eighteenth-century philosophers Immanuel Kant (in Germany) and David Hume (in Scotland) laid the foundations for all subsequent work on the origins of causal knowledge, perhaps the most central problem in the study of thinking (see Buehner & Cheng, Chap. 7). If we were to choose one phrase to set the stage for modern views of thinking, it would be an observation of the British philosopher Thomas Hobbes, who, in 1651, in his treatise *Leviathan*, proposed, "Reasoning is but reckoning." "Reckoning" is an odd term today, but in the seventeenth century it meant *computation*, as in arithmetic calculations.[3]

It was not until the twentieth century that the psychology of thinking became a scientific endeavor. The first half of the century gave rise to many important pioneers who in very different ways laid the foundations for the emergence of the modern field of thinking and reasoning. Foremost were the Gestalt psychologists of Germany, who provided deep insights into the nature of problem solving (see Novick & Bassok, Chap. 14).

Most notable of the Gestaltists were Karl Duncker and Max Wertheimer, students of human problem solving, and Wolfgang Köhler, a keen observer of problem solving by great apes (see Call & Tomasello, Chap. 25).

The pioneers of the early twentieth century also include Sigmund Freud, whose complex and ever-controversial legacy includes the notions that forms of thought can be unconscious (see Litman & Reber, Chap. 18) and that "cold" cognition is tangled up with "hot" emotion (see Molden & Higgins, Chap. 13). As the founder of clinical psychology, Freud's legacy also includes the ongoing integration of research on normal thinking with studies of thought disorders, such as schizophrenia (see Bachman & Cannon, Chap. 21).

Other early pioneers in the early and mid-twentieth century contributed to various fields of study that are now embraced within thinking and reasoning. Cognitive development continues to be influenced by the early theories developed by the Swiss psychologist Jean Piaget (see Halford, Chap. 22) and the Russian psychologist Lev Vygotsky (see Greenfield, Chap. 27). In the United States, Charles Spearman was a leader in the systematic study of individual differences in intelligence (see Sternberg, Chap. 31). In the middle of the century, the Russian neurologist Alexander Luria made immense contributions to our understanding of how thinking depends on specific areas of the brain, anticipating the modern field of cognitive neuroscience (see Goel, Chap. 20). Around the same time, in the United States, Herbert Simon argued that the traditional rational model of economic theory should be replaced with a framework that accounted for a variety of human resource constraints such as bounded attention and memory capacity and limited time (see LeBoeuf & Shafir, Chap. 11, and Morrison, Chap. 19). This was one of the contributions that in 1978 earned Simon the Nobel Prize in Economics.

In 1943, the British psychologist Kenneth Craik sketched the fundamental notion that a mental representation provides a kind of model of the world that can be "run" to make predictions (much like an engineer might use a physical scale model of a bridge to anticipate the effects of stress on the actual bridge intended to span a river).[4] In the 1960s and 1970s, modern work on the psychology of reasoning began in Britain with the contributions of Peter Wason and his collaborator Philip Johnson-Laird (see Evans, Chap. 8).

The modern conception of thinking as computation became prominent in the 1970s. In their classic treatment of human problem solving, Allen Newell and Herbert Simon (1972) showed that the computational analysis of thinking (anticipated by Alan Turing, the father of computer science) could yield important empirical and theoretical results. Like a program running on a digital computer, a person thinking through a problem can be viewed as taking an input that represents initial conditions and a goal, and applying a sequence of operations to reduce the difference between the initial conditions and the goal. The work of Newell and Simon established computer simulation as a standard method for analyzing human thinking. Their work also highlighted the potential of production systems (see Novick & Bassok, Chap. 14), which were subsequently developed extensively as cognitive models by John Anderson and his colleagues (see Lovett & Anderson, Chap. 17).

The 1970s saw a wide range of major developments that continue to shape the field. Eleanor Rosch, building on earlier work by Jerome Bruner (Bruner, Goodnow, & Austin, 1956), addressed the fundamental question of why people have the categories they do, and not other logically possible groupings of objects (see Medin & Rips, Chap. 3). Rosch argued that natural categories often have fuzzy boundaries (a whale is an odd mammal) but nonetheless have clear central tendencies or prototypes (people by and large agree that a bear makes a fine mammal). The psychology of human judgment was reshaped by the insights of Amos Tversky and Daniel Kahneman, who identified simple cognitive strategies, or heuristics, that people use to make judgments of frequency and probability. Often quick and accurate, these strategies can in some circumstances lead to nonnormative judgments. After Tversky's death in 1996, this line of work was continued by Kahneman, who was awarded the Nobel Prize in Economics in 2002. The current view of judgment, which has emerged from 30 years of research, is summarized by Kahneman and Frederick (Chap. 12; also see LeBoeuf & Shafir, Chap. 11). (Goldstone and Son, Chap. 2, review Tversky's influential theory of similarity judgments.)

In 1982, a young vision scientist, David Marr, published a book called *Vision*. Largely a technical treatment of visual perception, the book includes an opening chapter that lays out a larger vision – a vision of how the science of mind should proceed. Marr distinguished three levels of analysis, which he termed the level of *computation*, the level of *representation and algorithm*, and the level of *implementation*. Each level, according to Marr, addresses different questions, which he illustrated with the example of a physical device, the cash register. At Marr's most abstract level, computation (not to be confused with computation of an algorithm on a computer), the basic questions are "What is the goal that the cognitive process is meant to accomplish?" and "What is the logic of the mapping from the input to the output that distinguishes this mapping from other input–output mappings?" A cash register, viewed at this level, is used to achieve the goal of calculating how much is owed for a purchase. This task maps precisely onto the axioms of addition (e.g., the amount owed should not vary with the order in which items are presented to the sales clerk, a constraint that precisely matches the commutativity property of addition). It follows that, without knowing anything else about the workings of a particular cash register, we can be sure (if it is working properly) that it will be performing addition (not division).

The level of representation and algorithm, as the name implies, deals with the questions, "What is the representation of the input and output?" and "What is the algorithm for transforming the former into the latter?" Within a cash register, addition might be performed using numbers in either decimal or binary code, starting with either the leftmost or rightmost digit. Finally, the level of implementation addresses the question, "How are the representation and algorithm realized physically?" The cash register could be implemented as an electronic calculator, a mechanical adding machine, or even a mental abacus in the mind of the clerk.

In his book, Marr stressed the importance of the computational level of analysis, arguing that it could be seriously misleading to focus prematurely on the more concrete levels of analysis for a cognitive task without understanding the goal or nature of the mental computation.[5] Sadly, Marr died of leukemia before *Vision* was published, and so we do not know how his thinking about levels of analysis might have evolved. In very different ways, Marr's conception of a computational level of analysis is reflected in several chapters in this book (see especially Doumas & Hummel, Chap. 4; Buehner & Cheng, Chap. 7; Lovett & Anderson, Chap. 17).

In the most recent quarter-century, many other springs of research have fed into the river of thinking and reasoning, including the field of analogy (see Holyoak, Chap. 6), neural network models (see Doumas & Hummel, Chap. 4; Halford, Chap. 22), and cognitive neuroscience (see Goel, Chap. 20). The chapters of this handbook collectively paint a picture of the state of the field at the dawn of the new millennium.

Overview of the Handbook

This volume brings together the contributions of many of the leading researchers in thinking and reasoning to create the most comprehensive overview of research on thinking and reasoning that has ever been available. Each chapter includes a bit of historical perspective on the topic and ends with some thoughts about where the field seems to be heading. The book is organized into seven sections.

Part I: The Nature of Human Concepts

The three chapters in Part I address foundational issues related to the representation of human concepts. Chapter 2 by **Goldstone** and **Son** reviews work on the core concept of similarity – how people assess the degree to which objects or events are alike. Chapter 3 by **Medin** and **Rips** considers research on categories and how concepts are organized in semantic memory. Thinking depends not only on representations of individual concepts, such as dogs and cats, but also on representations of the relationships among concepts, such as the fact that dogs often chase cats. In Chapter 4, **Doumas** and **Hummel** evaluate different computational approaches to the representation of relations.

Part II: Reasoning

Chapters 5 to 10 deal with varieties of the core topic of reasoning. In Chapter 5, **Sloman** and **Lagnado** set the stage by laying out the issues surrounding induction – using what is known to generate plausible, although uncertain, inferences. Then, in Chapter 6, **Holyoak** reviews the literature on reasoning by analogy, an important variety of inductive reasoning that is critical for learning. The most classic aspect of induction is the way in which humans and other creatures acquire knowledge about causal relations, which is critical for predicting the consequences of actions and events. In Chapter 7, **Buehner** and **Cheng** discuss research and theory on causal learning. Then, in Chapter 8, **Evans** reviews work on the psychology of deductive reasoning, the form of thinking with the closest ties to logic. In Chapter 9, **Johnson-Laird** describes the work that he and others have performed using the framework of mental models to deal with various reasoning tasks, both deductive and inductive. Mental models have close connections to perceptual representations that are visuospatial in Chapter 10, Barbara **Tversky** reviews work on the role of visuospatial representations in thinking.

Part III: Judgment and Decision Making

We then turn to topics related to judgment and decision making. In Chapter 11, **LeBoeuf** and **Shafir** set the stage with a general review of work on decision making. Then, in Chapter 12, **Kahneman** and **Frederick** present an overarching model of heuristic judgment. In Chapter 13, **Molden** and **Higgins** review research revealing the ways in which human motivation and emotion influence judgment.

Part IV: Problem Solving and Complex Learning

The five chapters that comprise this section deal with problem solving and allied issues concerning how people learn in problem-solving situations. In Chapter 14, **Novick** and **Bassok** provide a general overview of the field of human problem solving. Problem solving has close connections to the topic of creativity, the focus of Chapter 15 by **Sternberg, Lubart, Kaufman**, and **Pretz**. Beyond relatively routine problem solving, there are occasions when people need to restructure their knowledge in complex ways to generate deeper understanding. How such complex learning takes place is the topic of Chapter 16 by **Chi** and **Ohlsson**. In Chapter 17, **Lovett** and **Anderson** review work on thinking that is based on a particular formal approach rooted in work on problem solving, namely, production systems. Finally, in Chapter 18, **Litman** and **Reber** consider research suggesting that some aspects of thinking and learning depend on implicit mechanisms that operate largely outside of awareness.

Part V: Cognitive and Neural Constraints on Human Thought

High-level human thinking cannot be fully understood in isolation from fundamental cognitive processes and their neural substrates. In Chapter 19, **Morrison** reviews the wealth of evidence indicating that thinking and reasoning depend critically on what is known as "working memory," that is, the system responsible for short-term maintenance and manipulation of information. Current work is making headway in linking thought processes to specific brain structures such as the prefrontal cortex; in Chapter 20, **Goel** discusses the key topic of deductive reasoning in relation to its neural substrate. Brain disorders, notably schizophrenia, produce striking disruptions of normal thought processes, which can shed light on how thinking takes place in normal brains. In Chapter 21, **Bachman** and **Cannon** review research and theory concerning thought disorder.

Part VI: Ontogeny, Phylogeny, Language, and Culture

Our understanding of thinking and reasoning would be gravely limited if we restricted investigation to young adult English speakers. The six chapters in Part VI deal with the multifaceted ways in which aspects of thinking vary across the human lifespan, across species, across speakers of different languages, and across cultures. In Chapter 22, **Halford** provides an overview of the development of thinking and reasoning over the course of childhood. In Chapter 23, **Gallistel** and **Gelman** discuss mathematical thinking, a special form of thinking found in rudimentary form in nonhuman animals that undergoes development in children. In Chapter 24, **Salthouse** describes the changes in thinking and reasoning brought on by the aging process. The phylogeny of thinking – thinking and reasoning as performed by apes and monkeys – is discussed in Chapter 25 by **Call** and **Tomasello**. One of the most controversial topics in the field is the relationship between thinking and the language spoken by the thinker; in Chapter 26, **Gleitman** and **Papafragou** review the hypotheses and evidence concerning the connections between language and thought. In Chapter 27, **Greenfield** considers the ways in which modes of thinking may vary in the context of different human cultures.

Part VII: Thinking in Practice

In cultures ancient and modern, thinking is put to particular use in special cultural practices. Moreover, there are individual differences in the nature and quality of human thinking. This section includes three chapters focusing on thinking in particular practices and two chapters that deal with variations in thinking ability. In Chapter 28, **Ellsworth** reviews what is known about thinking in the field of law. In Chapter 29, **Dunbar** and **Fugelsang** discuss thinking and reasoning as manifested in the practice of science. In Chapter 30, **Patel, Arocha**, and **Zhang** discuss reasoning in a field medicine – in which accurate diagnosis and treatment are literally everyday matters of life and death. Then, in Chapter 31, **Sternberg** reviews work on the concept of intelligence as a source of individual differences in thinking and reasoning. Finally, Chapter 32 by **Ritchhart** and **Perkins** concludes the volume by reviewing one of the major challenges for education – finding ways to teach people to think more effectively.

Examples of Chapter Assignments for a Variety of Courses

This volume offers a comprehensive treatment of higher cognition. As such, it serves as an excellent source for courses on thinking and reasoning, both at the graduate level and for upper-level undergraduates. Although instructors for semester-length graduate courses in thinking and reasoning may opt to assign the entire volume as a textbook, there are a number of other possibilities (including using chapters from this volume as introductions for various topics and then supplementing with readings from the primary literature). Here are a few examples of possible chapter groupings tailored to a variety of possible course offerings:

Introduction to Thinking and Reasoning

Chapter 1	Thinking and Reasoning: A Reader's Guide
Chapter 2	Similarity
Chapter 3	Concepts and Categories: Memory, Meaning, and Metaphysics

Chapter 5 The Problem of Induction
Chapter 6 Analogy
Chapter 7 Causal Learning
Chapter 8 Deductive Reasoning
Chapter 9 Mental Models and Thought
Chapter 10 Visuospatial Reasoning
Chapter 11 Decision Making
Chapter 12 A Model of Heuristic Judgment
Chapter 14 Problem Solving
Chapter 15 Creativity
Chapter 16 Complex Declarative Learning
Chapter 18 Implicit Cognition and Thought

Development of Thinking

Chapter 2 Similarity
Chapter 3 Concepts and Categories: Memory, Meaning, and Metaphysics
Chapter 22 Development of Thinking
Chapter 23 Mathematical Thinking
Chapter 26 Language and Thought
Chapter 24 Effects of Aging on Reasoning
Chapter 25 Reasoning and Thinking in Nonhuman Primates
Chapter 19 Thinking in Working Memory
Chapter 31 Intelligence
Chapter 32 Learning to Think: The Challenges of Teaching Thinking

Modeling Human Thought

Chapter 2 Similarity
Chapter 3 Concepts and Categories: Memory, Meaning, and Metaphysics
Chapter 4 Approaches to Modeling Human Mental Representations: What Works, What Doesn't, and Why
Chapter 6 Analogy
Chapter 7 Causal Learning
Chapter 9 Mental Models and Thought
Chapter 22 Development of Thinking
Chapter 17 Thinking as a Production System

Applied Thought

Chapter 14 Problem Solving
Chapter 10 Visuospatial Reasoning
Chapter 23 Mathematical Thinking
Chapter 26 Language and Thought
Chapter 15 Creativity
Chapter 31 Intelligence
Chapter 13 Motivated Thinking
Chapter 27 Paradigms of Cultural Thought
Chapter 16 Complex Declarative Learning
Chapter 18 Implicit Cognition and Thought
Chapter 28 Legal Reasoning
Chapter 29 Scientific Thinking and Reasoning
Chapter 30 Reasoning in Medicine

Differences in Thought

Chapter 31 Intelligence
Chapter 15 Creativity
Chapter 19 Thinking in Working Memory
Chapter 21 Cognitive and Neuroscience Aspects of Thought Disorder
Chapter 22 Development of Thinking
Chapter 25 Reasoning and Thinking in Nonhuman Primates
Chapter 24 Effects of Aging on Reasoning
Chapter 26 Language and Thought
Chapter 13 Motivated Thinking
Chapter 27 Paradigms of Cultural Thought
Chapter 29 Scientific Thinking and Reasoning
Chapter 32 Learning to Think: The Challenges of Teaching Thinking

Acknowledgments

Preparation of this chapter was supported by grants R305H030141 from the Institute of Education Sciences and SES-0080375 from the National Science Foundation to Holyoak, and by Xunesis (www.xunesis.org) and a National Institute of Mental Health National Service Research Award (MH-064244) to Morrison. The authors thank Miriam Bassok and Patricia Cheng for comments on an earlier draft of this chapter.

Notes

1. Notice the linguistic connection between "thinking" and "seeing," and thought and perception, which was emphasized by the Gestalt psychologists of the early twentieth century.
2. The distinction between deduction and induction blurs in the study of the psychology of thinking, as we see in Part II of this volume.
3. There are echoes of the old meaning of "reckon" in such phrases as "reckon the cost." As a further aside, the term "dead reckoning," a procedure for calculating the position of a ship or aircraft, derives from "deductive reasoning." In an old Western movie, a hero in a tough spot might venture, "I reckon we can hold out till sun-up," illustrating how calculation has crossed over to become a metaphor for mental judgment.
4. See Johnson-Laird, Chap. 9, for a current view of thinking and reasoning that owes much to Craik's seminal ideas.
5. Indeed, Marr criticized Newell and Simon's approach to problem solving for paying insufficient attention to the computational level in his sense.

References

Bruner, J. S., Goodnow, J. J., & Austin, G. A. (1956). *A study of thinking*. New York: Wiley.

Craik, K. (1943). *The nature of explanation*. Cambridge, UK: Cambridge University Press.

Hobbes, T. (1651/1968). *Leviathan*. London: Penguin Books.

Marr, D. (1982). *Vision*. San Francisco: W. H. Freeman.

Newell, A., & Simon, H. A. (1972). *Human problem solving*. Englewood Cliffs, NJ: Prentice Hall.

Rips, L. J., & Conrad, F. G. (1989). Folk psychology of mental activities. *Psychological Review, 96*, 187–207.

Part I

THE NATURE OF HUMAN CONCEPTS

CHAPTER 2
Similarity

Robert L. Goldstone
Ji Yun Son

Introduction

Human assessments of similarity are fundamental to cognition because similarities in the world are revealing. The world is an orderly enough place that similar objects and events tend to behave similarly. This fact of the world is not just a fortunate coincidence. It is *because* objects are similar that they will tend to behave similarly in most respects. It is because crocodiles and alligators are similar in their external form, internal biology, behavior, diet, and customary environment that one can often successfully generalize from what one knows of one to the other. As Quine (1969) observed, "Similarity, is fundamental for learning, knowledge and thought, for only our sense of similarity allows us to order things into kinds so that these can function as stimulus meanings. Reasonable expectation depends on the similarity of circumstances and on our tendency to expect that similar causes will have similar effects" (p. 114). Similarity thus plays a crucial role in making predictions because similar things usually behave similarly.

From this perspective, psychological assessments of similarity are valuable to the extent that they provide grounds for predicting as many important aspects of our world as possible (Holland, Holyoak, Nisbett, & Thagard, 1986; see Dunbar & Fugelsang, Chap. 29). Appreciating the similarity between crocodiles and alligators is helpful because information learned about one is generally true of the other. If we learned an arbitrary fact about crocodiles, such as they are very sensitive to the cold, then we could probably infer that this fact is also true of alligators. As the similarity between A and B increases, so does the probability of correctly inferring that B has X upon knowing that A has X (Tenenbaum, 1999). This relation assumes we have no special knowledge related to property X. Empirically, Heit and Rubinstein (1994) showed that if we *do* know about the property, then this knowledge, rather than a one-size-fits-all similarity, is used to guide our inferences. For example, if people are asked to make an inference about an anatomical property, then anatomical similarities have more influence than behavioral similarities. Boars are anatomically but not behaviorially similar to pigs, and this difference successfully predicts that people are likely to make anatomical but not behavioral inferences from pigs to boars. The logical extreme of this line of reasoning (Goodman, 1972; Quine, 1977) is that if one has complete knowledge about the reasons why an object has a property, then general similarity is no longer relevant to generalizations. The knowledge itself completely guides whether the generalization is appropriate. Moonbeams and melons are not very similar generally speaking, but if one is told that moonbeams have the property that the word begins with Melanie's favorite letter, then one can generalize this property to melons with very high confidence.

By contrasting the cases of crocodiles, boars, and moonbeams, we can specify the benefits and limitations of similarity. We tend to rely on similarity to generate inferences and categorize objects into kinds when we do not know exactly what properties are relevant or when we cannot easily separate an object into separate properties. Similarity is an excellent example of a domain-general source of information. Even when we do not have specific knowledge of a domain, we can use similarity as a default method to reason about it. The contravening limitation of this domain generality is that when specific knowledge is available, then a generic assessment of similarity is no longer as relevant (Keil, 1989; Murphy, 2002; Murphy & Medin, 1985; Rips, 1989; Rips & Collins, 1993). Artificial laboratory experiments in which subjects are asked to categorize unfamiliar stimuli into novel categories invented by the experimenter are situations in which similarity is clearly important because subjects have little else to use (Estes, 1994; Nosofsky, 1984, 1986). However, similarity is also important in many real world situations because our knowledge does not run as deep as we think it does (Rozenblit & Keil, 2002) and because a general sense of similarity often has an influence even when more specific knowledge ought to overrule it (Allen & Brooks, 1991; Smith & Sloman, 1994).

Another argument for the importance of similarity in cognition is simply that it plays a significant role in psychological accounts of problem solving, memory, prediction, and categorization. If a problem is similar to a previously solved problem, then the solution to the old problem may be applied to the new problem (Holyoak & Koh, 1987; Ross, 1987, 1989). If a cue is similar enough to a stored memory, the memory may be retrieved (Raaijmakers & Shiffrin, 1981). If an event is similar enough to a previously experienced event, the stored event's outcome may be offered as a candidate prediction for the current event (Sloman, 1993; Tenenbaum & Griffiths, 2001). If an unknown object is similar enough to a known object, then the known object's category label may be applied to the unknown object (Nosofsky, 1986). The act of comparing events, objects, and scenes and establishing similarities between them is of critical importance for the cognitive processes we depend on.

The utility of similarity for grounding our concepts has been rediscovered in all the fields comprising cognitive science (see Medin & Rips, Chap. 3). Exemplar (Estes, 1994; Kruschke, 1992; Lamberts, 2000; Medin & Schaffer, 1978; Nosofsky, 1986), instance-based (Aha, 1992), view-based (Tarr & Gauthier, 1998), case-based (Schank, 1982), nearest neighbor (Ripley, 1996), configural cue (Gluck & Bower, 1990), and vector quantization (Kohonen, 1995) models share the underlying strategy of giving responses learned from similar, previously presented patterns to novel patterns. Thus, a model can respond to repetitions of these patterns; it can also give responses to novel patterns that are likely to be correct by sampling responses to old patterns weighted by their similarity to the novel pattern. Consistent with these models, psychological evidence suggests that people show good transfer to new stimuli in perceptual tasks to the extent that the new stimuli resemble previously learned stimuli (Kolers & Roediger, 1984; Palmeri, 1997). Another common feature of these approaches is that they represent patterns in a relatively raw, unprocessed form. This parallels the constraint described previously on the applicability of similarity. Both raw representations and generic similarity assessments are most useful as a default strategy when one does not know exactly what properties of a stimulus are important. One's best bet is to follow the principle of least commitment (Marr, 1982) and keep mental descriptions in a relatively raw form to preserve information that may be needed at a later point.

Another reason for studying similarity is that it provides an elegant diagnostic tool for examining the structure of our mental entities and the processes that operate on them. For example, one way to tell that a physicist has progressed beyond the novice stage is that he or she sees deep similarities between problems that require calculation of force even though the problems are superficially dissimilar (Chi, Feltovich, & Glaser, 1981; see Novick & Bassok, Chap. 14). Given that psychologists have no microscope with direct access to people's representations of their knowledge, appraisals of similarity provide a powerful, if indirect, lens onto representation/process assemblies (see also Doumas & Hummel, Chap. 4).

A final reason to study similarity is that it occupies an important ground between perceptual constraints and higher-level knowledge system functions. Similarity is grounded by perceptual functions. A tone of 200 Hz and a tone of 202 Hz sound similar (Shepard, 1987), and the similarity is cognitively impenetrable (Pylyshyn, 1985) – enough that there is little that can be done to alter this perceived similarity. However, similarity is also highly flexible and dependent on knowledge and purpose. By focusing on patterns of motion and relations, even electrons and planets can be made to seem similar (Gentner, 1983; Holyoak & Thagard, 1989; see Holyoak, Chap. 6). A complete account of similarity will make contact both with Fodor's (1983) isolated and modularized perceptual input devices and the "central system" in which everything a person knows may be relevant.

A Survey of Major Approaches to Similarity

There have been a number of formal treatments that simultaneously provide theoretical accounts of similarity and describe how it can be empirically measured (Hahn, 2003). These models have had a profound practical impact in statistics, automatic pattern recognition by machines, data mining, and marketing (e.g., online stores can provide "people similar to you liked the following other items . . ."). Our brief survey is organized in terms of the following models: geometric, feature based, alignment based, and transformational.

Geometric Models and Multidimensional Scaling

Geometric models of similarity have been among the most influential approaches to analyzing similarity (Carroll & Wish, 1974; Torgerson, 1958, 1965). These approaches are exemplified by nonmetric multidimensional scaling (MDS) models (Shepard, 1962a, 1962b). MDS models represent similarity relations between entities in terms of a geometric model that consists of a set of points embedded in a dimensionally organized metric space. The input to MDS routines may be similarity judgments, dissimilarity judgments, confusion matrices, correlation coefficients, joint probabilities, or any other measure of pairwise proximity. The output of an MDS routine is a geometric model of the data, with each object of the data set represented as a point in an n-dimensional space. The similarity between a pair of objects is taken to be inversely related to the distance between two objects' points in the space. In MDS, the distance between points i and j is typically computed by

$$dissimilarity(i, j) = \left[\sum_{k=1}^{n} |X_{ik} - X_{jk}|^r \right]^{\frac{1}{r}} \quad (2.1)$$

where n is the number of dimensions, X_{ik} is the value of dimension k for item i, and r is a parameter that allows different spatial metrics to be used. With $r = 2$, a standard Euclidean notion of distance is invoked, whereby the distance between two points is the length of the straight line connecting the points. If $r = 1$, then distance involves a city-block metric where the distance between two points is the sum of their distances on each dimension ("shortcut" diagonal paths are not allowed to directly connect points differing on more than one dimension). An Euclidean metric often provides a better fit to empirical data when the stimuli being compared are composed of integral, perceptually fused dimensions such as the brightness and saturation of a color. Conversely, a city-block metric is often appropriate for psychologically separated dimensions such as brightness and size (Attneave, 1950).

Richardson's (1938) fundamental insight, which is the basis of contemporary use of MDS, was to begin with subjects' judgments of pairwise object dissimilarity and work backward to determine the dimensions and dimension values that subjects used in making their judgments. MDS algorithms proceed by placing entities in an n-dimensional space such that the distances between the entities accurately reflect the empirically observed similarities. For example, if we asked people to rate the similarities [on a scale from 1 (low similarity) to 10 (high similarity)] of Russia, Cuba, and Jamaica, we might find

Similarity (Russia, Cuba) = 7
Similarity (Russia, Jamaica) = 1
Similarity (Cuba, Jamaica) = 8

An MDS algorithm would try to position the three countries in a space such that countries that are rated as being highly similar are very close to each other in the space. With nonmetric scaling techniques, only ordinal similarity relations are preserved. The interpoint distances suggested by the similarity ratings may not be simultaneously satisfiable in a given dimensional space. If we limit ourselves to a single dimension (we place the countries on a "number line"), then we cannot simultaneously place Russia near Cuba (similarity = 7) and place Russia far away from Jamaica (similarity = 1). In MDS terms, the "stress" of the one-dimensional solution would be high. We could increase the dimensionality of our solution and position the points in two-dimensional space. A perfect reconstruction of any set of proximities among a set of n objects can be obtained if a high enough dimensionality (specifically, $n - 1$ dimensions) is used.

One of the main applications of MDS is to determine the underlying dimensions comprising the set of compared objects. Once the points are positioned in a way that faithfully mirrors the subjectively obtained similarities, it is often possible to give interpretations to the axes or to rotations of the axes. In the previous example, dimensions may correspond to "political affiliation" and "climate." Russia and Cuba would have similar values on the former dimension; Jamaica and Cuba would have similar values on the latter dimension. A study by Smith, Shoben, and Rips (1974) illustrates a classic use of MDS (Figure 2.1). They obtained similarity ratings from subjects on many pairs of birds. Submitting these pairwise similarity ratings to MDS analysis, they hypothesized underlying features that were used for representing the birds. Assigning subjective interpretations to the geometric model's axes, the experimenters suggested that birds were represented in terms of their values on dimensions such as "ferocity" and "size." It is important to note that the proper psychological interpretation of a geometric representation of objects is not necessarily in terms of its Cartesian axes. In some domains, such as musical pitches, the best interpretation of objects may be in terms of their polar coordinates of angle and length (Shepard, 1982). More recent work has extended geometric representations still further, representing patterns of similarities by generalized, nonlinear manifolds (Tenenbaum, De Silva, & Lanford, 2000).

MDS is also used to create a compressed representation that conveys relative similarities among a set of items. A set of n items requires $n(n-1)/2$ numbers to express

A

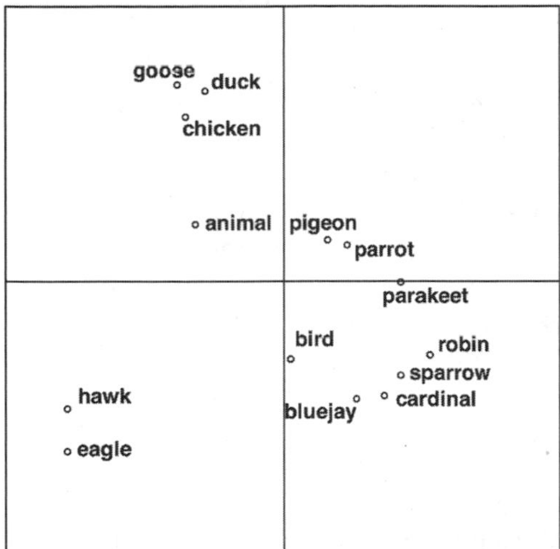

B

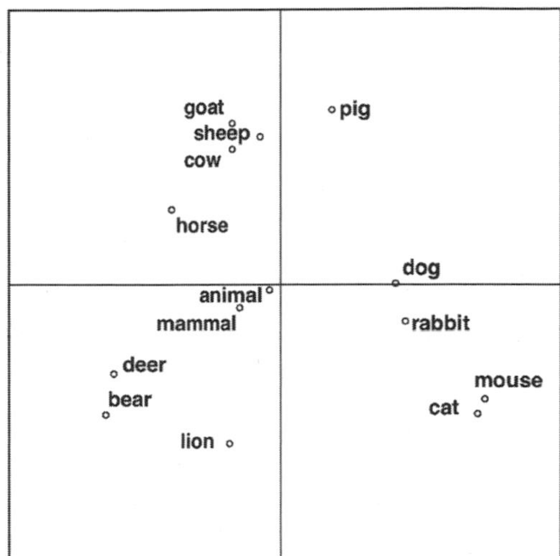

Figure 2.1. Two multidimensional scaling (MDS) solutions for sets of birds (A) and animals (B). The distances between words in the MDS space reflect their psychology dissimilarity. Once an MDS solution has been made, psychological interpretations for the dimensions may be possible. In these solutions, the horizontal and vertical dimensions may represent size and domesticity, respectively. (Reprinted from Rips, Shoben, & Smith, 1974, by permission.)

all pairwise distances among the items, if it is assumed that any object has a distance of 0 to itself and distances are symmetric. However, if an MDS solution fits the distance data well, it can allow these same distances to be reconstructed using only *ND* numbers, where *D* is the number of dimensions of the MDS solution. This compression may be psychologically very useful. One of the main goals of psychological representation is to create efficient codes for representing a set of objects. Compressed representations can facilitate encoding, memory, and processing. Shimon Edelman (1999) proposed that both people and machines efficiently code their world by creating geometric spaces for objects with much lower dimensionality than the objects' physical descriptions (see also Gardenfors, 2000).

A third use of MDS is to create quantitative representations that can be used in mathematical and computational models of cognitive processes. Numeric representations, namely coordinates in a psychological space, can be derived for stories, pictures, sounds, words, or any other stimuli for which one can obtain subjective similarity data. Once constructed, these numeric representations can be used to predict people's categorization accuracy, memory performance, or learning speed. MDS models have been successful in expressing cognitive structures in stimulus domains as far removed as animals (Smith, Shoben, & Rips, 1974), Rorschach ink blots (Osterholm, Woods, & Le Unes, 1985), chess positions (Horgan, Millis, & Neimeyer, 1989), and air flight scenarios (Schvaneveldt, 1985). Many objects, situations, and concepts seem to be psychologically structured in terms of dimensions, and a geometric interpretation of the dimensional organization captures a substantial amount of that structure.

Featural Models

In 1977, Amos Tversky brought into prominence what would become the main contender to geometric models of similarity in psychology. The reason given for proposing a feature-based model was that subjective assessments of similarity did not always satisfy the assumptions of geometric models of similarity.

PROBLEMS WITH THE STANDARD GEOMETRIC MODEL

Three assumptions of standard geometric models of similarity are

Minimality: $D(\mathrm{A,B}) \geq D(\mathrm{A,A}) = 0$
Symmetry: $D(\mathrm{A,B}) = D(\mathrm{B,A})$
Triangle Inequality: $D(\mathrm{A,B}) + D(\mathrm{B,C}) \geq D(\mathrm{A,C})$

where $D(\mathrm{A,B})$ is interpreted as the dissimilarity between items A and B. According to the minimality assumption, all objects are equally (dis)similar to themselves. Some violations of this assumption are found (Nickerson, 1972) when confusion rates or RT measures of similarity are used. First, not all letters are equally similar to themselves. For example, in Podgorny and Garner (1979), if the letter S is shown twice on a screen, subjects are faster to correctly say that the two tokens are similar (i.e., they come from the same similarity defined cluster) than if the twice-shown letter is W. By the reaction time measure of similarity, the letter S is more similar to itself than the letter W is to itself. Even more troublesome for the minimality assumption, two different letters may be more similar to each other than a particular letter is to itself. The letter C is more similar to the letter O than W is to itself, as measured by interletter confusions. In Gilmore, Hersh, Caramazza, and Griffin (1979), the letter M is more often recognized as an H ($p = .391$) than as an M ($p = .180$). This is problematic for geometric representations because the distance between a point and itself should be zero.

According to the symmetry assumption, (dis)similarity should not be affected by the ordering of items because the distance from point A to B is equal to the distance from B to A. Contrary to this presumed symmetry, similarity is asymmetric on occasion (Tversky, 1977). In one of Tversky's examples, North Korea is judged to be more similar to Red China than Red China is to North Korea. Often, a nonprominent item is more similar to a prominent item than vice versa. This is consistent with the result that people judge their friends to be more similar to themselves than they themselves are to their friends (Holyoak & Gordon, 1983), under the assumption that a person is highly prominent to him- or herself. More recently, Polk et al. (2002) found that when the frequency of colors is experimentally manipulated, rare colors are judged to be more similar to common colors than common colors are to rare colors.

According to the triangle inequality assumption (Figure 2.2), the distance/ dissimilarity between two points A and B cannot be more than the distance between A and a third point C plus the distance between C and B. Geometrically speaking, a straight line connecting two points is the shortest path between the points. Tversky and Gati (1982) found violations of this assumption when it is combined with an assumption of segmental additivity [$D(\mathrm{A,B}) + D(\mathrm{B,C}) = D(\mathrm{A,C})$, if A, B, and C lie on a straight line]. Consider three items in multidimensional space, A, B, and C, falling on a straight line such that B is between A and C. Also consider a fourth point, E, that forms a right triangle when combined with A and C. The triangle inequality assumption *cum* segmental additivity predicts that

$$D(\mathrm{A,E}) \geq D(\mathrm{A,B}) \text{ and } D(\mathrm{E,C}) \geq D(\mathrm{B,C})$$

or

$$D(\mathrm{A,E}) \geq D(\mathrm{B,C}) \text{ and } D(\mathrm{E,C}) \geq D(\mathrm{A,B})$$

Systematic violations of this prediction are found such that the path going through the corner point E is shorter than the path going through the center point B. For example, if the items are instantiated as

A = White, 3 inches
B = Pink, 4 inches
C = Red, 5 inches
E = Red, 3 inches

then people's dissimilarity ratings indicate that $D(\mathrm{A,E}) < D(\mathrm{A,B})$ and $D(\mathrm{E,C}) < D(\mathrm{B,C})$. Such an effect can be modeled by

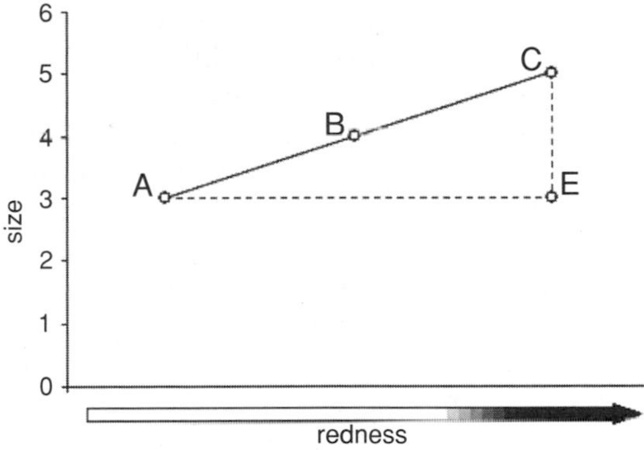

Figure 2.2. The triangle inequality assumption requires the path from A to C going through B to be shorter than the path going through E.

geometric models of similarity if r in Eq. 2.1 is given a value less than 1. However, if r is less than 1, then dissimilarity does not satisfy a power metric, which is often considered a minimal assumption for geometric solutions to be interpretable. The two assumptions of a power metric are (1) distances along straight lines are additive, and (2) the shortest path between points is a straight line.

Other potential problems with geometric models of similarity are (1) they strictly limit the number of nearest neighbors an item can have (Tversky & Hutchinson, 1986), (2) MDS techniques have difficulty describing items that vary on a large number of features (Krumhansl, 1978), and (3) standard MDS techniques do not predict that adding common features to items increases their similarity (Tversky & Gati, 1982). On the first point, MDS models consisting of two dimensions cannot predict that item X is the closest item to 100 other items. There would be no way of placing those 100 items in two dimensions such that X would be closer to all of them than any other item. For human data, a superordinate term (e.g., fruit) is often the nearest neighbor of many of its exemplars (apples, bananas, etc.), as measured by similarity ratings. On the second point, although there is no logical reason why geometric models cannot represent items of any number of dimensions (as long as the number of dimensions is less than number of items minus one), geometric models tend to yield the most satisfactory and interpretable solutions in low-dimensional space. MDS solutions involving more than six dimensions are rare. On the third point, the addition of the same feature to a pair of items increases their rated similarity (Gati & Tversky, 1984), but this is incompatible with simple MDS models. If adding a shared feature corresponds to adding a dimension in which the two items under consideration have the same value, then there will be no change to the items' dissimilarity because the geometric distance between the points remains the same. MDS models that incorporate the dimensionality of the space could predict the influence of shared features on similarity, but such a model would no longer relate similarity directly to an inverse function of inter-item distance.

One research strategy has been to augment geometric models of similarity in ways that solve these problems. One solution, suggested by Carol Krumhansl (1978), has been to model dissimilarity in terms of both inter-item distance in a multidimensional space *and* spatial density in the neighborhoods of the compared items. The more items there are in the vicinity of an item, the greater the spatial density of the item. Items are more dissimilar if they have many items surrounding them (their spatial density is high) than if they have few neighboring items. By including spatial density in an MDS analysis, violations of minimality, symmetry, and the triangle inequality can potentially be accounted for, as well as some of the influence of context on similarity. However, the empirical validity of the spatial density hypothesis is in some doubt (Corter, 1987, 1988; Krumhansl, 1988; Tversky & Gati, 1982).

Robert Nosofsky (1991) suggested another potential way to save MDS models from some of the previous criticisms. He introduces individual bias parameters in addition to the inter-item relation term. Similarity is modeled in terms of inter-item distance *and* biases toward particular items. Biases toward items may be due to attention, salience, knowledge, and frequency of items. This revision handles asymmetric similarity results and the result that a single item may be the most similar item to many other items, but it does not directly address several of the other objections.

THE CONTRAST MODEL

In light of the previous potential problems for geometric representations, Tversky (1977) proposed to characterize similarity in terms of a feature-matching process based on weighting common and distinctive features. In this model, entities are represented as a collection of features and similarity is computed by

$$S(A, B) = \theta f(A \cap B) - af(A - B) - bf(B - A) \quad (2.2)$$

The similarity of A to B is expressed as a linear combination of the measure of the common and distinctive features. The term $(A \cap B)$ represents the features that items A and B have in common. $(A - B)$ represents the features that A has but B does not. $(B - A)$ represents the features of B that are not in A. θ, a, and b are weights for the common and distinctive components. Common features, as compared with distinctive features, are given relatively more weight for verbal as opposed to pictorial stimuli (Gati & Tversky, 1984), cohesive as opposed to noncohesive stimuli (Ritov, Gati, & Tversky, 1990), similarity as opposed to difference judgments (Tversky, 1977), and entities with a large number of distinctive as opposed to common features (Gati & Tversky, 1984). There are no restrictions on what may constitute a feature. A feature may be any property, characteristic, or aspect of a stimulus. Features may be concrete or abstract (i.e., "symmetric" or "beautiful").

The contrast model predicts asymmetric similarity because a is not constrained to equal b and $f(A - B)$ may not equal $f(B - A)$. North Korea is predicted to be more similar to Red China than vice versa if Red China has more salient distinctive features than North Korea, and a is greater than b. The contrast model can also account for nonmirroring between similarity and difference judgments. The common features term $(A \cap B)$ is hypothesized to receive more weight in similarity than difference judgments; the distinctive features term receives relatively more weight in difference judgments. As a result, certain pairs of stimuli may be perceived as simultaneously being more similar to and more different from each other compared with other pairs (Tversky, 1977). Sixty-seven percent of a group of subjects selected West Germany and East Germany as more similar to each other than Ceylon and Nepal. Seventy percent of subjects also selected West Germany and East Germany as more different from each other than Ceylon and Nepal. According to Tversky, East and West Germany have more common and more distinctive features than Ceylon and Nepal. Medin, Goldstone, and Gentner (1993) presented additional evidence for nonmirroring between similarity and difference, exemplified in Figure 2.3. When two scenes share a relatively large number of relational commonalities (e.g., scenes T and B both have three objects that have the *same pattern*), but also a large number of differences on specific attributes (e.g., none of the patterns in scene T match any of the patterns in B), then the scenes tend to be judged as simultaneously very similar and very different.

A number of models are similar to the contrast model in basing similarity on features and in using some combination of the $(A \cap B)$, $(A - B)$, and $(B - A)$ components. Sjoberg (1972) proposed that similarity is defined as $f(A \cap B)/f(A \cup B)$. Eisler and Ekman (1959) claimed that similarity is proportional to $f(A \cap B)/(f(A) + f(B))$. Bush and Mosteller (1951) defined similarity as $f(A \cap B)/f(A)$. These three models can all be considered specializations of the general equation $f(A \cap B)/[f(A \cup B) + af(A - B) + bf(B - A)]$. As such, they differ from the contrast model by applying a ratio function as opposed to a linear contrast of common and distinctive features.

The fundamental premise of the contrast model, that entities can be described in terms of constituent features, is a powerful idea in cognitive psychology. Featural

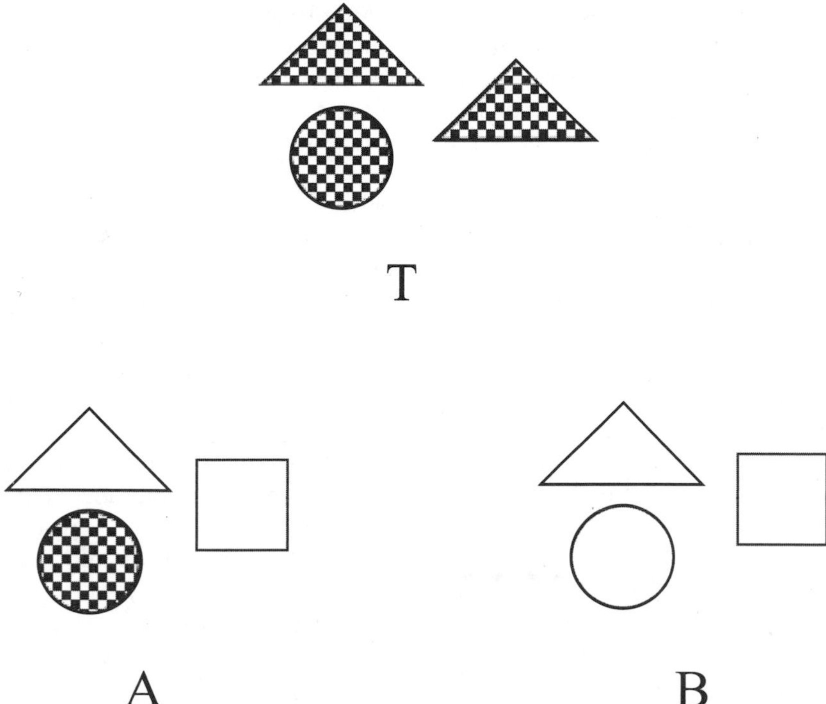

Figure 2.3. The set of objects in B is selected as both more similar to, and more different from, the set of objects in T relative to the set of objects in A. From Medin, Goldstone, and Gentner (1990). Reprinted by permission.

analyses have proliferated in domains of speech perception (Jakobson, Fant, & Halle, 1963), pattern recognition (Neisser, 1967; Treisman, 1986), perception physiology (Hubel & Wiesel, 1968), semantic content (Katz & Fodor, 1963), and categorization (Medin & Schaffer, 1978; see Medin & Rips, Chap. 3). Neural network representations are often based on features, with entities being broken down into a vector of ones and zeros, where each bit refers to a feature or "microfeature." Similarity plays a crucial role in many connectionist theories of generalization, concept formation, and learning. The notion of dissimilarity used in these systems is typically the fairly simple function "Hamming distance." The Hamming distance between two strings is simply their city-block distance; that is, it is their $(A - B) + (B - A)$ term. "1 0 0 1 1" and "1 1 1 1 1" would have a Hamming distance of 2 because they differ on two bits. Occasionally, more sophisticated measures of similarity in neural networks normalize dissimilarities by string length. Normalized Hamming distance functions can be expressed by $[(A - B) + (B - A)]/[f(A \cap B)]$.

SIMILARITIES BETWEEN GEOMETRIC AND FEATURE-BASED MODELS

Although MDS and featural models are often analyzed in terms of their differences, they also share a number of similarities. More recent progress has been made on combining both representations into a single model, using Bayesian statistics to determine whether a given source of variation is more efficiently represented as a feature or dimension (Navarro & Lee, 2003). Tversky and Gati (1982) described methods of translating continuous dimensions into featural representations. Dimensions that are sensibly described as being more or less (e.g., loud is more sound than soft, bright is more light than dim, and large is more size than small) can be represented by sequences of nested feature sets. That is, the features of B include a subset of A's features whenever B is louder, brighter, or larger than A. Alternatively, for qualitative attributes such as shape or hue (red is not subjectively "more" than blue), dimensions can be represented by chains of features such that if B is between A and C on the dimension, then $(A \cap B) \supset (A \cap C)$ and $(B \cap C) \supset (A \cap C)$. For example, if orange lies between red and yellow on the hue dimension, then this can be featurally represented if orange and red share features that orange and yellow do not share.

An important attribute of MDS models is that they create *postulated* representations, namely dimensions, that explain the systematicities present in a set of similarity data. This is a classic use of abductive reasoning; dimensional representations are hypothesized that, if they were to exist, would give rise to the obtained similarity data. Other computational techniques share with MDS the goal of discovering the underlying descriptions for items of interest but create featural rather than dimensional representations. Hierarchical cluster analysis, such as MDS, takes pairwise proximity data as input. Rather than output a geometric space with objects as points, hierarchical cluster analysis outputs an inverted-tree diagram with items at the root-level connected with branches. The smaller the branching distance between two items, the more similar they are. Just as the dimensional axes of MDS solutions are given subjective interpretations, the branches are also given interpretations. For example, in Shepard's (1972) analysis of speech sounds, one branch is interpreted as voiced phonemes, whereas another branch contains the unvoiced phonemes. In additive cluster analysis (Shepard & Arabie, 1979), similarity data are transformed into a set of overlapping item clusters. Items that are highly similar will tend to belong to the same clusters. Each cluster can be considered as a feature. More recent progress has been made on efficient and mathematically principled models that find such featural representations for large databases (Lee, 2002a, 2002b; Tenenbaum, 1996).

Another commonality between geometric and featural representations, one that motivates the next major class of similarity models that we consider, is that both use relatively unstructured representations. Entities are structured as sets of features or dimensions with no relations between these attributes. Entities such as stories, sentences, natural objects, words, scientific theories, landscapes, and faces are not simply a "grab bag" of attributes. Two kinds of structure seem particularly important: propositional and hierarchical. A proposition is an assertion about the relation between informational entities (Palmer, 1975). For example, relations in a visual domain might include *above*, *near*, *right*, *inside*, and *larger than*, which take informational entities as arguments. The informational entities might include features such as square and values on dimensions such as 3 inches. Propositions are defined as the smallest unit of knowledge that can stand as a separate assertion and have a truth value. The order of the arguments in the predicate is critical. For example, *above (triangle, circle)* does not represent the same fact as *above (circle, triangle)*. Hierarchical representations involve entities that are embedded in one another. Hierarchical representations are required to represent the fact that X is *part of* Y or that X is a *kind of* Y. For example, in Collins and Quillian's (1969) propositional networks, labeled links ("Is-a" links) stand for the hierarchical relation between *canary* and *bird*.

Some quick fixes to geometric and featural accounts of similarity are possible, but they fall short of a truly general capacity to handle structured inputs. Hierarchical clustering does create trees of features, but there is no guarantee that there are relationships, such as Is-a or Part-of, between the subtrees. However, structure might exist in terms of features that represent conjunctions of properties. For example, using the materials in Figure 2.4, 20 undergraduates were shown triads consisting of A, B, and T and were asked to say whether scene A or B was more similar to T. The strong tendency to choose A over B in the first panel suggests that

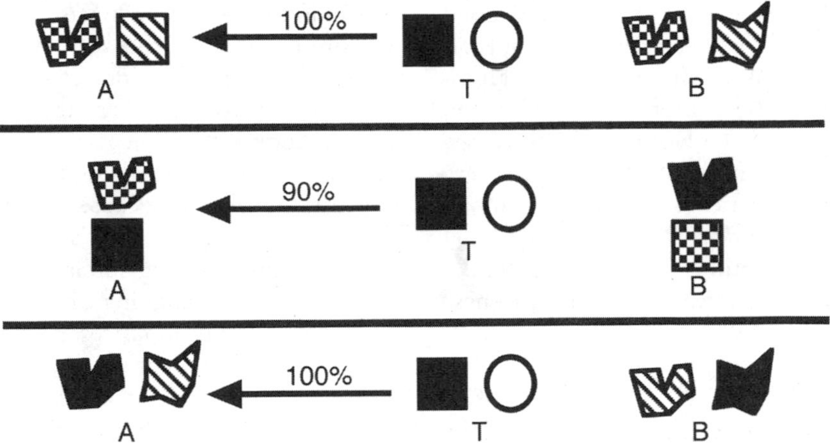

Figure 2.4. The sets of objects T are typically judged to be more similar to the objects in the A sets than the B sets. These judgments show that people pay attention to more than just simple properties such as "black" or "square" when comparing scenes.

the feature "square" influences similarity. Other choices indicated that subjects also based similarity judgments on the spatial locations and shadings of objects as well as their shapes.

However, it is not sufficient to represent the leftmost object of T as {left, square, black} and base similarity on the number of shared and distinctive features. In the second panel, A is again judged to be more similar to T than is B. Both A and B have the features "black" and "square." The only difference is that for A and T, but not B, the "black" and "square" features belong to the same object. This is only compatible with feature set representations if we include the possibility of *conjunctive features* in addition to *simple features* such as "black" and "square" (Gluck, 1991; Hayes-Roth & Hayes-Roth, 1977). By including the conjunctive feature "black-square," possessed by both T and A, we can explain, using feature sets, why T is more similar to A than B. The third panel demonstrates the need for a "black-left" feature, and other data indicate a need for a "square-left" feature. Altogether, if we want to explain the similarity judgments that people make, we need a feature set representation that includes six features (three simple and three complex) to represent the square of T.

However, there are two objects in T, bringing the total number of features required to at least two times the six features required for one object. The number of features required increases still further if we include feature triplets such as "left-black-square." In general, if there are O objects in a scene and each object has F features, then there will be OF simple features. There will be O conjunctive features that combine two simple features (i.e., *pairwise* conjunctive features). If we limit ourselves to simple and pairwise features to explain the pattern of similarity judgments in Figure 2.3, we still will require $OF(F+1)/2$ features per scene, or $OF(F+1)$ features for two scenes that are compared with one another.

Thus, featural approaches to similarity require a fairly large number of features to represent scenes that are organized into parts. Similar problems exist for dimensional accounts of similarity. The situation for these models becomes much worse when we consider that similarity is also influenced by relations between features such as "black to the left of white" and "square to the left of white." Considering only binary relations, there are O^2F^2R -OFR relations within a scene that contains O objects, F features per object, and R different types of relations between features. Although more sophisticated objections have been raised about these approaches by Hummel and colleagues (Holyoak & Hummel, 2000; Hummel, 2000, 2001; Hummel & Biederman, 1992; Hummel & Holyoak, 1997, 2003; see Doumas & Hummel, Chap. 4), at the very least, geometric and featural models apparently require an implausibly large number of attributes to account for the similarity relations between structured, multipart scenes.

Alignment-Based Models

Partly in response to the difficulties that the previous models have in dealing with structured descriptions, a number of researchers have developed alignment-based models of similarity. In these models, comparison is not just matching features but determining how elements correspond to, or align with, one another. Matching features are aligned to the extent that they play similar roles within their entities. For example, a car with a green wheel and a truck with a green hood both share the feature *green*, but this matching feature may not increase their similarity much because the car's wheel does not correspond to the truck's hood. Drawing inspiration from work on analogical reasoning (Gentner, 1983; Holyoak & Thagard, 1995; see Holyoak, Chap. 6), in alignment-based models, matching features influence similarity more if they belong to parts that are placed in correspondence, and parts tend to be placed in correspondence if they have many features in common and are consistent with other emerging correspondences (Goldstone, 1994a; Markman & Gentner, 1993a). Alignment-based models make purely relational similarity possible (Falkenhainer, Forbus, & Gentner, 1989).

Initial evidence that similarity involves aligning scene descriptions comes from Markman and Gentner's (1993a) result that when subjects are asked to determine corresponding objects, they tend to make more structurally sound choices when they have first judged the similarity of the scenes that contain the objects. For example, in Figure 2.5, subjects could be asked which object in the bottom set corresponds to the leftmost object in the top set. Subjects who had rated the similarity of the sets were more likely to choose the rightmost object – presumably because both objects were the smallest objects in their sets. Subjects who did not first assess similarity had a tendency to select the middle object because its size exactly matched the target object's size. These results are predicted if similarity judgments naturally entail aligning the elements of two scenes. Additional research has found that relational choices such as "smallest object in its set" tend to influence similarity judgments more than absolute attributes like "3 inches" when the overall amount of relational coherency across sets is high (Goldstone, Medin, & Gentner, 1991), the scenes are superficially sparse rather than rich (Gentner & Rattermann, 1991; Markman & Gentner, 1993a), subjects are given more time to make their judgments (Goldstone & Medin, 1994), the judges are adults rather than children (Gentner & Toupin, 1986), and abstract relations are initially correlated with concrete relations (Kotovsky & Gentner, 1996).

Formal models of alignment-based similarity have been developed to explain how feature matches that belong to well-aligned elements matter more for similarity than matches between poorly aligned elements (Goldstone, 1994a; Love, 2000). Inspired by work in analogical reasoning (Holyoak & Thagard, 1989), Goldstone's (1994a) SIAM model is a neural network with nodes that represent hypotheses that elements across two scenes correspond to one another. SIAM works by first creating correspondences between the features of scenes. Once features begin to be placed into correspondence, SIAM begins to place objects into correspondence that are consistent with the feature correspondences. Once objects begin to be put in correspondence, activation is fed back down to the feature (mis)matches that are consistent with the object alignments. In this way, object correspondences influence activation of feature correspondences at the same time that feature correspondences influence the activation of object correspondences. Activation between nodes spreads

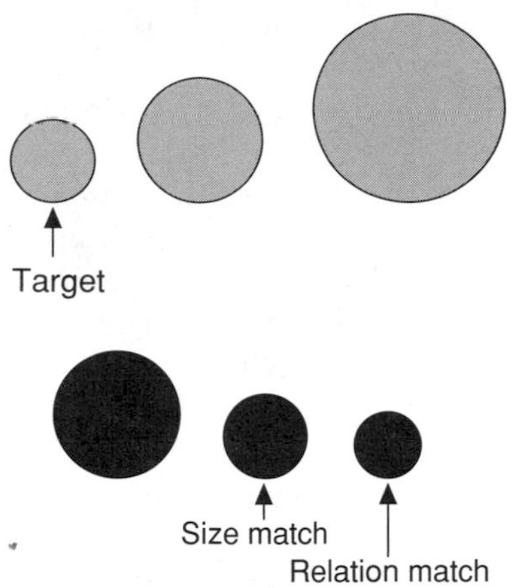

Figure 2.5. The target from the gray circles could match either the middle black object because they are the same size, or the rightmost object because both objects are the smallest objects in their sets.

in SIAM by two principles: (1) nodes that are consistent send excitatory activation to each other, and (2) nodes that are inconsistent inhibit each another (see also Holyoak, Chap. 6). Nodes are inconsistent if they create two-to-one alignments – if two elements from one scene would be placed into correspondence with one element of the other scene. Node activations affect similarity via the equation

$$similarity = \frac{\sum_{i=1}^{n} (match\ value_i^* A_i)}{\sum_{i=1}^{n} A_i}, \tag{2.3}$$

where n is the number of nodes in the system, A_i is the activation of node i, and the match value describes the physical similarity between the two features placed in correspondence according to the node i.

By this equation, the influence of a particular matching or mismatching feature across two scenes is modulated by the degree to which the features have been placed in alignment. Consistent with SIAM, (1) aligned feature matches tend to increase similarity more than unaligned feature matches (Goldstone, 1994a); (2) the differential influence between aligned and unaligned feature matches increases as a function of processing time (Goldstone & Medin, 1994); (3) this same differential influence increases with the clarity of the alignments (Goldstone, 1994a); and (4) under some circumstances, adding a poorly aligned feature match can actually decrease similarity by interfering with the development of proper alignments (Goldstone, 1996).

Another empirically validated set of predictions stemming from an alignment-based approach to similarity concerns alignable and nonalignable differences (Markman & Gentner, 1993b). Nonalignable differences between two entities are attributes of one entity that have no corresponding attribute in the other entity. Alignable differences are differences that require the elements of the entities first be placed in correspondence. When comparing a police car with an ambulance, a nonalignable difference is that police cars have weapons in them, but ambulances do not. There is no clear equivalent of weapons in the ambulance. Alignable differences include the following: police cars carry criminals to jails rather than carrying sick people to hospitals, a police car is a car whereas ambulances are vans, and police car drivers are policemen rather than emergency medical technicians. Consistent with the role of structural alignment in similarity comparisons, alignable differences influence similarity more than nonalignable differences (Markman & Gentner, 1996) and are more likely to be encoded in memory (Markman & Gentner, 1997). Alignable differences between objects also play a disproportionately large role in distinguishing between different basic-level categories (e.g., cats and dogs) that belong to the same superordinate category (e.g., animals) (Markman & Wisniewski, 1997). In short, knowing these correspondences affects not only how much a matching element increases similarity (Goldstone, 1994a), but also how much a mismatching element decreases similarity.

Thus far, much of the evidence for structural alignment in similarity has used somewhat artificial materials. Often, the systems describe how "scenes" are compared, with the underlying implication that the elements comprising the scenes are not as tightly connected as elements comprising objects. Still, if the structural alignment account proves to be fertile, it will be because it is applicable to naturally occurring materials. Toward this goal, researchers have considered structural accounts of similarity in language domains. The confusability of words depends on structural analyses to predict that "stop" is more confusable with "step" than "pest" (the "st" match is in the correct location with "step" but not "pest"), but more confusable with "pest" than "best" (the "p" match counts for something even when it is out of place). Substantial success has been made on the practical problem of determining the structural similarity of words (Bernstein, Demorest, & Eberhardt, 1994; Frisch, Broe, & Pierrehumbert, 1995). Structural alignment has also been implicated when comparing more complex language structures such as sentences (Bassok & Medin, 1997). Likewise, structural similarity has proven to be a useful notion in explaining consumer preferences of commercial products, explaining, for example, why new products are viewed more favorably when they improve over existing products along alignable rather than unalignable differences (Zhang & Markman, 1998). Additional research has shown that alignment-based models of similarity provide a better account of category-based induction than feature-based models (Lassaline, 1996). Still other researchers have applied structural accounts of similarity to the legal domain (Hahn & Chater, 1998; Simon & Holyoak, 2002). This area of application is promising because the U.S. legal system is based on cases and precedents, and cases are structurally rich and complex situations involving many interrelated parties. Retrieving a historic precedent and assessing its relevance to a current case almost certainly involves aligning representations that are more sophisticated than assumed by geometric or featural models.

Transformational Models

A final historic approach to similarity that has been more recently resuscitated is that the comparison process proceeds by transforming one representation into the other. A critical step for these models is to specify what transformational operations are possible.

In an early incarnation of a transformational approach to cognition broadly construed, Garner (1974) stressed the notion of stimuli that are transformationally equivalent and are consequently possible alternatives for each other. In artificial intelligence, Shimon Ullman (1996) argued that objects are recognized by being aligned with memorized pictorial descriptions. Once an unknown object has been aligned with all candidate models, the best match to the viewed object is selected. The alignment operations rotate, scale, translate, and topographically warp object descriptions. For rigid transformations, full alignment can be obtained by aligning three points on the object with three points on the model description. Unlike recognition strategies that require structural descriptions (e.g., Biederman, 1987; Hummel, 2000, 2001), Ullman's alignment does not require an image to be decomposed into parts.

In transformational accounts that are explicitly designed to model similarity data, similarity is usually defined in terms of transformational distance. In Wiener-Ehrlich, Bart, and Millward's (1980) generative representation system, subjects are assumed to possess an elementary set of transformations and invoke these transformations when analyzing stimuli. Their subjects saw linear pairs of stimuli such as {ABCD, DABC} or two-dimensional stimuli such as $\{\begin{smallmatrix}\text{AB}\\\text{CD}\end{smallmatrix}, \begin{smallmatrix}\text{DA}\\\text{BC}\end{smallmatrix}\}$. Subjects were required to rate the similarity of the pairs. The researchers determined transformations that accounted for each subject's ratings from the set {rotate 90 degrees, rotate 180, rotate 270, horizontal reflection, vertical reflection, positive diagonal reflection, negative diagonal reflection}. Similarity was assumed to decrease monotonically as the number of transformations required to make one sequence identical to the other increased.

Imai (1977) made a similar claim. The stimuli used were sequences such as XXOXXXOXXXOX, where Xs represent white ovals and Os represent black ovals. The four basic transformations were mirror image (XXXXXOO → OOXXXXX), phase shift (XXXXXOO → XXXXOOX), reversal (XXXXXOO → OOOOOXX), and wavelength (XXOOXXOO → XOXOXOXO). The researcher found that sequences that are two transformations removed (e.g., XXXOXXXOXXXO and OOXOOOXOOOXO require a phase shift and a reversal to be equated) are rated to be less similar than sequences that can be made identical with one transformation. In addition, sequences that can be made identical by more than one transformation (XOXOXOXO and OXOXOXOX can be made identical by mirror image, phase shift, *or* reversal transformations) are more similar than sequences that have only one identity-producing transformation.

More recent work has followed up on Imai's research and generalized it to stimulus materials, including arrangements of Lego bricks, geometric complexes, and sets of colored circles (Hahn, Chater, & Richardson, 2003). According to these researchers' account, the similarity between two entities is a function of the complexity required to transform the representation of one into the representation of the other. The simpler the transformation, the more similar they are assumed to be. The complexity of a transformation is determined in accord with Kolmogorov complexity theory (Li & Vitanyi, 1997), according to which the complexity of a representation is the length of the shortest computer program that can generate that representation. For example, the conditional Kolmogorov complexity between the sequence 1 2 3 4 5 6 7 8 and 2 3 4 5 6 7 8 9 is small because the simple instructions add 1 to each digit and subtract 1 from each digit suffice to transform one into the other. Experiments by Hahn et al. (2003) demonstrate that once reasonable vocabularies of transformation are postulated, transformational complexity does indeed predict subjective similarity ratings.

It is useful to compare and contrast alignment-based and transformational accounts of similarity. Both approaches place scene elements into correspondence. Whereas the correspondences are explicitly stated in the structural alignment method, they are implicit in transformational alignment. The transformational account often *does* produce globally consistent correspondences – for example, correspondences that obey the one-to-one mapping principle; however, this consistency is a consequent of applying a patternwide transformation and is not enforced by interactions between emerging correspondences. It is revealing that transformational accounts have been applied almost exclusively to perceptual stimuli, whereas structural accounts are most often applied to conceptual stimuli such as stories, proverbs, and scientific theories (there are also notable structural accounts in perception, i.e., Biederman, 1987; Hummel, 2000; Hummel & Biederman, 1992; Marr & Nishihara, 1978). Defining a set of constrained transformations is much more tenable for perceptual stimuli. The conceptual similarity between an atom and the solar system could possibly be discovered by transformations. As a start, a miniaturization transformation could be applied to the solar system. However, this single transformation is not nearly sufficient; a nucleus is not simply a small sun. The transformations that would turn the solar system into an atom are not readily forthcoming. If we allow transformations such as an "earth-becomes-electron" transformation, then we are simply reexpressing the structural alignment approach and its part-by-part alignment of relations and objects.

Some similarity phenomena that are well explained by structural alignment are not easily handled by transformations. To account for the similarity of "BCDCB" and "ABCDCBA" we could introduce the fairly abstract transformation "add the leftmost letter's predecessor to both sides of string." However, the pair "LMN" and "KLMNK" do not seem as similar as the earlier pair, even though the same transformation is applied. A transformation of the form "if the structure is symmetric, then add the preceding element in the series to both ends of the string" presupposes exactly the kind of analysis in defining "symmetric" and "preceding" that are the bread and butter of propositional representations and structural alignment. For this reason, one fertile research direction would be to combine alignment-based accounts' focus on representing the internal structure within individual scenes with the constraints that transformational accounts provide for establishing psychologically plausible transformations (Hofstadter, 1997; Mitchell, 1993).

Conclusions and Further Directions

To provide a partial balance to our largely historic focus on similarity, we conclude by raising some unanswered questions for the field. These questions are rooted in a desire to connect the study of similarity to cognition as a whole.

Is Similarity Flexible Enough to Provide Useful Explanations of Cognition?

The study of similarity is typically justified by the argument that so many theories in cognition depend on similarity as a theoretical construct. An account of what makes problems, memories, objects, and words similar to one another often provides the backbone for our theories of problem solving, attention, perception, and cognition. As William James put it, "This sense of Sameness is the very keel and backbone of our thinking" (James, 1890/1950, p. 459).

However, others have argued that similarity is not flexible enough to provide a sufficient account, although it may be a necessary component. There have been many empirical demonstrations of apparent dissociations between similarity and other cognitive processes, most notably categorization. Researchers have argued that cognition is frequently based on theories (Murphy & Medin, 1985), rules (Sloman, 1996; Smith & Sloman, 1994), or strategies that go beyond "mere" similarity. To take an example from Murphy and Medin (1985), consider a man jumping into a swimming pool fully clothed. This man may be categorized as drunk because we have a theory of behavior and inebriation that explains the man's action. Murphy and Medin argued that the categorization of the man's behavior does not depend on matching the man's features to the category *drunk*'s features. It is highly unlikely that the category *drunk* would have such a specific feature as "jumps into pools fully clothed." It is not the similarity between the instance and the category that determines the instance's classification; it is the fact that our category provides a theory that explains the behavior.

Developmental psychologists have argued that even young children have inchoate theories that allow them to go beyond superficial similarities in creating categories (Carey, 1985; Gelman & Markman, 1986; Keil, 1989). For example, Carey (1985) observed that children choose a toy monkey over a worm as being more similar to a human, but that when they are told that humans have spleens are more likely to infer that the worm has a spleen than that the toy monkey does. Thus, the categorization of objects into "spleen" and "no spleen" groups does not appear to depend on the same knowledge that guides similarity judgments. Adults show similar dissociations between similarity and categorization. In an experiment by Rips (1989), an animal that is transformed (by toxic waste) from a bird into something that looks like an insect is judged by subjects to be more similar to an insect but is still judged to *be* a bird. Again, the category judgment seems to depend on biological, genetic, and historic knowledge, whereas the similarity judgments seems to depend more on gross visual appearance (see also Keil, 1989; Rips & Collins, 1993).

Despite the growing body of evidence that similarity appraisals do not always track categorization decisions, there are still some reasons to be sanguine about the continued explanatory relevance of similarity. Categorization itself may not be completely flexible. People are influenced by similarity despite the subjects' intentions and the experimenters' instructions (Smith & Sloman, 1994). Allen and Brooks (1991) gave subjects an easy rule for categorizing cartoon animals into two groups. Subjects were then transferred to the animals that looked very similar to one of the training stimuli but belonged in a different category. These animals were categorized more slowly and less accurately than animals that were equally similar to an old animal but also belonged in the same category as the old animal. Likewise, Palmeri (1997) showed that even for the simple task of counting the number of dots, subjects' performances are improved when a pattern of dots is similar to a previously seen pattern with the same numerosity and worse when the pattern is similar to a previously seen pattern with different numerosity. People seem to have difficulty ignoring similarities between old and new patterns even when they know a straightforward and perfectly accurate categorization rule.

There may be a mandatory consideration of similarity in many categorization judgments (Goldstone, 1994b), adding constraints to categorization. At the same time, similarity may be more flexible and sophisticated than commonly acknowledged (Jones & Smith, 1993) and this may also serve to bridge the gap between similarity and high-level cognition. Krumhansl (1978) argued that similarity between objects decreases when they are surrounded by many close neighbors that were also presented on previous trials (also see Wedell, 1994). Tversky (1977) obtained evidence for an *extension effect* according to which features influence similarity judgments more when they vary within an entire set of stimuli. Items presented within a particular trial also influence similarity judgments. Perhaps the most famous example of this is Tversky's (1977) *diagnosticity effect* according to which features that are diagnostic for relevant classifications will have disproportionate influence on similarity judgments. More recently, Medin, Goldstone, and Gentner (1993) argued that different comparison standards are created, depending on the items that are present on a particular trial. Other research has documented intransitivities in similarity judgments situations in which A is judged to be more similar to T than is B, B is more similar to T than is C, and C is more similar to T than is A (Goldstone, Medin, & Halberstadt, 1997). This kind of result also suggests that the properties used to assess the similarity of objects are determined, in part, by the compared objects themselves.

Similarity judgments not only depend on the context established by recently exposed items, simultaneously presented items, and inferred contrast sets, but also on the observer. Suzuki, Ohnishi, and Shigemasu (1992) showed that similarity judgments depend on level of expertise and goals. Expert and novice subjects were asked to solve the Tower of Hanoi puzzle and judge the similarity between the goal and various states. Experts' similarity ratings were based on the number of moves required to transform one position to the other. Less expert subjects tended to base their judgments on the number of shared superficial features. Similarly, Hardiman, Dufresne, and Mestre (1989) found that expert and novice physicists evaluate the similarity of physics problems differently, with experts basing similarity judgments more on general principles of physics than on superficial features (see Sjoberg, 1972, for other expert/novice differences in similarity ratings). The dependency of similarity on observer-, task-, and stimulus-defined contexts offers the promise that it is indeed flexible enough to subserve cognition.

Is Similarity Too Flexible to Provide Useful Explanations of Cognition?

As a response to the skeptic of similarity's usefulness, the preceding two paragraphs could have the exact opposite of their intended effect. The skeptic might now believe that similarity is much *too* flexible to be a stable ground for cognition. In fact, Nelson Goodman (1972) put forth exactly this claim, maintaining that the notion of similarity is either vague or unnecessary. He argued that "when to the statement that two things are similar we add a specification of the property that they have in common ... we render it [the similarity statement] superfluous" (p. 445). That is, all the potential explanatory work is done by the "with respect to property Z" clause and not by the similarity statement. Instead of saying "this object belongs to category A because it is similar to A items with respect to the property 'red'," we can simplify matters by removing any notion of similarity with "this object belongs to category A because it is red."

There are reasons to resist Goodman's conclusion that "similarity tends under analysis either to vanish entirely or to require for its explanation just what it purports to explain" (p. 446). In most cases, similarity is useful precisely because we cannot flesh out the "respect to property Z" clause with just a single property. Evidence suggests that assessments of overall similarity are natural and perhaps even "primitive." Evidence from children's perception of similarity suggests that children are particularly likely to judge similarity on the basis of many integrated properties rather than analysis into dimensions. Even dimensions that are perceptually separable are treated as fused in similarity judgments (Smith & Kemler, 1978). Children younger than 5 years of age tend to classify on the basis of overall similarity and not on the basis of a single criterial attribute (Keil, 1989; Smith, 1989). Children often have great difficulty identifying the dimension along which two objects vary, even though they can easily identify that the objects are different in some way (Kemler, 1983). Smith (1989) argued that it is relatively difficult for young children to say whether two objects are identical on a particular property but relatively easy for them to say whether they are similar across many dimensions.

There is also evidence that adults often have an overall impression of similarity without analysis into specific properties. Ward (1983) found that adult subjects who tended to group objects quickly also tended to group objects like children by considering overall similarity across all dimensions instead of maximal similarity on one dimension. Likewise, Smith and Kemler (1984) found that adults who were given a distracting task produced more judgments by overall similarity than subjects who were not. To the extent that similarity is determined by many properties, it is less subject to drastic context-driven changes. Furthermore, integrating multiple sources of information into a single assessment of similarity becomes particularly important. The four approaches to similarity described in the previous section provide methods for integrating multiple properties into a single similarity judgment and, as such, go significantly beyond simply determining a single "property Z" to attend.

A final point to make about the potential overflexibility of similarity is that, although impressions of similarity can change with context and experience, automatic and "generic" assessments of similarity typically change slowly and with considerable inertia. Similarities that were once effortful and strategic become second nature to the organism. Roughly speaking, this is the process of *perceiving* what was once a *conceptual* similarity. At first, the novice mycologist explicitly uses rules for perceiving the dissimilarity between the pleasing Agaricus Bisporus mushroom and the deadly Amanita Phalloides. With time, this dissimilarity ceases to be effortful and rule based and becomes perceptual and phenomenologically direct. When this occurs, the similarity becomes generic and default and can be used as the ground for new strategic similarities. In this way, our cognitive abilities gradually attain sophistication by treating territory as level ground that once made for difficult mental climbing. A corollary of this contention is that our default impression of similarity does not typically mislead us; it is explicitly *designed* to lead us to see relations between things that often function similarly in our world. People, with good reason, expect their default similarity assessments to provide good clues about where to uncover directed, nonapparent similarities (Medin & Ortony, 1989).

Should "Similarity" Even Be a Field of Study Within Cognitive Science?

This survey has proceeded under the convenient fiction that it is possible to tell a general story for how people compare things. One reason to doubt this is that the methods used for assessing similarity have large effects on the resulting similarity viewed.

Similarity as measured by ratings is not equivalent to similarity as measured by perceptual discriminability. Although these measures correlate highly, systematic differences are found (Podgorny & Garner, 1979; Sergent & Takane, 1987). For example, Beck (1966) found that an upright T is rated as more similar to a tilted T than an upright L but that it is also more likely to be perceptually grouped with the upright Ls. Previously reviewed experiments indicate the nonequivalence of assessments that use similarity versus dissimilarity ratings, categorization versus forced-choice similarity judgments, or speeded versus leisurely judgments. In everyday discourse we talk about the similarity of two things, forgetting that this assessment depends on a particular task and circumstance.

Furthermore, it may turn out that the calculation of similarity is fundamentally different for different domains (see Medin, Lynch, & Solomon, 2000, for a thoughtful discussion of this issue). To know how to calculate the similarity of two faces, one would need to study faces specifically and the eventual account need not inform researchers interested in the similarity of words, works of music, or trees. A possible conclusion is that similarity is not a coherent notion at all. The term *similarity*, similar to the *bug* or *family values*, may not pick out a consolidated or principled set of things.

Although we sympathize with the impulse toward domain-specific accounts of similarity, we also believe in the value of studying general principles of comparison that potentially underlie many domains. Although we do not know whether general principles exist, one justification for pursuing them is the large payoff that would result from discovering these principles if they *do* exist. A historically fruitful strategy, exemplified by Einstein's search for a law to unify gravitational and electromagnetic acceleration and Darwin's search for a unified law to understand the origins of humans and other animals, has been to understand differences as parametric variations within a single model. Finding differences across tasks does not necessarily point to the incoherency of similarity. An alternative perspective would use these task differences as an illuminating source of information in developing a unified account. The systematic nature of these task differences should stimulate accounts that include a formal description not only of stimulus components but also of task components. Future success in understanding the task of comparison may depend on comparing tasks.

Acknowledgments

This research was funded by NIH grant MH56871 and NSF grant 0125287. Correspondence concerning this chapter should be addressed to rgoldsto@indiana.edu or Robert Goldstone, Psychology Department, Indiana University, Bloomington, Indiana 47405. Further information about the laboratory can be found at http://cognitrn.psych.indiana.edu

References

Aha, D. W. (1992). Tolerating noisy, irrelevant and novel attributes in instance-based learning algorithms. *International Journal of Man Machine Studies*, 36, 267–287.

Allen, S. W., & Brooks, L. R. (1991). Specializing the operation of an explicit rule. *Journal of Experimental Psychology: General*, 120, 3–19.

Attneave, F. (1950). Dimensions of similarity. *American Journal of Psychology*, 63, 516–556.

Bassok, M., & Medin, D. L. (1997). Birds of a feather flock together: Similarity judgments with semantically rich stimuli. *Journal of Memory and Language*, 36, 311–336.

Beck, J. (1966). Effect of orientation and of shape similarity on perceptual grouping. *Perception and Psychophysics*, 1, 300–302.

Bernstein, L. E., Demorest, M. E., & Eberhardt, S. P. (1994). A computational approach to analyzing sentential speech perception: Phoneme-to-phoneme stimulus/response alignment. *Journal of the Acoustical Society of America*, 95, 3617–3622.

Biederman, I. (1987). Recognition-by-components: A theory of human image understanding. *Psychological Review*, 94, 115–147.

Bush, R. R., & Mosteller, F. (1951). A model for stimulus generalization and discrimination. *Psychological Review*, 58, 413–423.

Carey, S. (1985). *Conceptual change in childhood*. Cambridge, MA: Bradford Books.

Carroll, J. D., & Wish, M. (1974). Models and methods for three-way multidimensional scaling. In D. H. Krantz, R. C. Atkinson, R. D. Luce, & P. Suppes (Eds.), *Contemporary developments in mathematical psychology* (Vol. 2, pp. 57–105). San Francisco: Freeman.

Chi, M. T. H., Feltovich, P., & Glaser, R. (1981). Categorization and representation of physics problems by experts and novices. *Cognitive Science*, 5, 121–152.

Collins, A. M., & Quillian, M. R. (1969). Retrieval time from semantic memory. *Journal of Verbal Learning and Verbal Behavior*, 8, 240–247.

Corter, J. E. (1987). Similarity, confusability, and the density hypothesis. *Journal of Experimental Psychology: General*, 116, 238–249.

Corter, J. E. (1988). Testing the density hypothesis: Reply to Krumhansl. *Journal of Experimental Psychology: General*, 117, 105–106.

Edelman, S. (1999). *Representation and recognition in vision*. Cambridge, MA: MIT Press.

Eisler, H., & Ekman, G. (1959). A mechanism of subjective similarity. *Acta Psychologica*, 16, 1–10.

Estes, W. K. (1994). *Classification and cognition*. New York: Oxford University Press.

Falkenhainer, B., Forbus, K. D., & Gentner, D. (1989). The structure-mapping engine: Algorithm and examples. *Artificial Intelligence*, 41, 1–63.

Fodor, J. A. (1983). *The modularity of mind*. Cambridge, MA: MIT Press/Bradford Books.

Frisch, S. A., Broe, M. B., & Pierrehumbert, J. B. (1995). The role of similarity in phonology: Explaining OCP-Place. In K. Elenius & P. Branderud (Eds.), *Proceedings of the 13th international conference of the phonetic sciences*, 3, 544–547.

Gardenfors, P. (2000). *Conceptual spaces: The geometry of thought*. Cambridge, MA: MIT Press.

Garner, W. R. (1974). *The processing of information and structure*. New York: Wiley.

Gati, I., & Tversky, A. (1984). Weighting common and distinctive features in perceptual and conceptual judgments. *Cognitive Psychology*, 16, 341–370.

Gelman, S. A., & Markman, E. M. (1986). Categories and induction in young children. *Cognition*, 23, 183–209.

Gentner, D. (1983). Structure-mapping: A theoretical framework for analogy. *Cognitive Science*, 7, 155–170.

Gentner, D., & Rattermann, M. J. (1991). Language and the career of similarity. In S. A. Gelman & J. P. Byrnes (Eds.), *Perspectives on language and thought interrelations in development* (pp. 225–277). Cambridge: Cambridge University Press.

Gentner, D., & Toupin, C. (1986). Systematicity and surface similarity in the development of analogy. *Cognitive Science*, 10(3), 277–300.

Gilmore, G. C., Hersh, H., Caramazza, A., & Griffin, J. (1979). Multidimensional letter similarity derived from recognition errors. *Perception and Psychophysics*, 25, 425–431.

Gluck, M. A. (1991). Stimulus generalization and representation in adaptive network models of category learning. *Psychological Science*, 2, 50–55.

Gluck, M. A., & Bower, G. H. (1990). Component and pattern information in adaptive networks. *Journal of Experimental Psychology: General*, 119, 105–109.

Goldstone, R. L. (1994a). Similarity, interactive activation, and mapping. *Journal of Experimental Psychology: Learning, Memory, and Cognition*, 20, 3–28.

Goldstone, R. L. (1994b). The role of similarity in categorization: Providing a groundwork. *Cognition*, 52, 125–157.

Goldstone, R. L. (1996). Alignment-based nonmonotonicities in similarity. *Journal of Experimental Psychology: Learning, Memory, and Cognition*, 22, 988–1001.

Goldstone, R. L., & Medin, D. L. (1994). The time course of comparison. *Journal of Experimental Psychology: Learning, Memory, and Cognition*, 20, 29–50.

Goldstone, R. L., Medin, D. L., & Gentner, D. (1991). Relational similarity and the nonindependence of features in similarity judgments. *Cognitive Psychology*, 222–263.

Goldstone, R. L., Medin, D. L., & Halberstadt, J. (1997). Similarity in context. *Memory and Cognition*, 25, 237–255.

Goodman, N. (1972). Seven strictures on similarity. In N. Goodman (Ed.), *Problems and projects* (pp. 437–446). New York: The Bobbs-Merrill Co.

Hahn, U. (2003). Similarity. In L. Nadel (Ed.), *Encyclopedia of cognitive science*. London: Macmillan.

Hahn, U., & Chater, N. (1998). Understanding similarity: A joint project for psychology, case-based reasoning and law. *Artificial Intelligence Review*, 12, 393–427.

Hahn, U., Chater, N., & Richardson, L. B. (2003). Similarity as transformation. *Cognition*, 87, 1–32.

Hardiman, P. T., Dufresne, R., & Mestre, J. P. (1989). The relation between problem categorization and problem solving among experts and novices. *Memory and Cognition*, 17, 627–638.

Hayes-Roth, B., & Hayes-Roth, F. (1977). Concept learning and the recognition and classification of exemplars. *Journal of Verbal Learning and Verbal Behavior*, 16, 321–338.

Heit, E., & Rubinstein, J. (1994). Similarity and property effects in inductive reasoning. *Journal of Experimental Psychology: Learning, Memory, and Cognition*, 20, 411–422.

Hofstadter, D. (1997). *Fluid concepts and creative analogies: Computer models of the fundamental mechanisms of thought*. New York: Basic Books.

Holland, J. H., Holyoak, K. J., Nisbett, R. E., & Thagard, P. R. (1986). *Induction: Processes of inference, learning, and discovery*. Cambridge, MA: Bradford Books/MIT Press.

Holyoak, K. J., & Gordon, P. C. (1983). Social reference points. *Journal of Personality & Social Psychology*, 44, 881–887.

Holyoak, K. J., & Hummel, J. E. (2000). The proper treatment of symbols in a connectionist architecture. In E. Dietrich & A. Markman (Eds.), *Cognitive dynamics: Conceptual change in humans and machines*. Hillsdale, NJ: Erlbaum.

Holyoak, K. J., & Koh, K. (1987). Surface and structural similarity in analogical transfer. *Memory and Cognition*, 15, 332–340.

Holyoak, K. J., & Thagard, P. (1989). Analogical mapping by constraint satisfaction. *Cognitive Science*, 13, 295–355.

Holyoak, K. J., & Thagard, P. (1995). *Mental leaps: Analogy in creative thought*. Cambridge, MA: MIT Press.

Horgan, D. D., Millis, K., & Neimeyer, R. A. (1989). Cognitive reorganization and the development of chess expertise. *International Journal of Personal Construct Psychology*, 2, 15–36.

Hubel, D. H., & Wiesel (1968). Receptive fields and functional architecture of monkey striate cortex. *Journal of Physiology*, 195, 215–243.

Hummel, J. E. (2000). Where view-based theories break down: The role of structure in shape perception and object recognition. In E. Dietrich & A. Markman (Eds.), *Cognitive dynamics: Conceptual change in humans and machines* (pp. 157–185). Hillsdale, NJ: Erlbaum.

Hummel, J. E. (2001). Complementary solutions to the binding problem in vision: Implications for shape perception and object recognition. *Visual Cognition*, 8, 489–517.

Hummel, J. E., & Biederman, I. (1992). Dynamic binding in a neural network for shape recognition. *Psychological Review*, 99, 480–517.

Hummel, J. E., & Holyoak, K. J. (1997). Distributed representations of structure: A theory of analogical access and mapping. *Psychological Review*, 104, 427–466.

Hummel, J. E., & Holyoak, K. J. (2003). A symbolic-connectionist theory of relational inference and generalization. *Psychological Review*, 110, 220–263.

Imai, S. (1977). Pattern similarity and cognitive transformations. *Acta Psychologica*, 41, 433–447.

James, W. (1890/1950). *The principles of psychology*. New York: Dover. (Original work published 1890).

Jakobson, R., Fant, G., & Halle, M. (1963). *Preliminaries to speech analysis: The distinctive features and their correlates*. Cambridge, MA: MIT Press.

Jones, S. S., & Smith, L. B. (1993). The place of perception in children's concepts. *Cognitive Development*, 8, 113–139.

Katz, J. J., & Fodor, J. (1963). The structure of semantic theory. *Language*, 39, 170–210.

Keil, F. C. (1989). *Concepts, kinds and development*. Cambridge, MA: Bradford Books/MIT Press.

Kemler, D. G. (1983). Holistic and analytic modes in perceptual and cognitive development. In T. J. Tighe & B. E. Shepp (Eds.), *Perception, cognition, and development: Interactional analyses* (pp. 77–101). Hillsdale, NJ: Erlbaum.

Kohonen, T. (1995). *Self-organizing maps*. Berlin: Springer-Verlag.

Kolers, P. A., & Roediger, H. L. (1984). Procedures of mind. *Journal of Verbal Learning and Verbal Behavior*, 23, 425–449.

Kotovsky, L., & Gentner, D. (1996). Comparison and categorization in the development of relational similarity. *Child Development*, 67, 2797–2822.

Krumhansl, C. L. (1978). Concerning the applicability of geometric models to similarity data: The interrelationship between similarity and spatial density. *Psychological Review*, 85, 450–463.

Krumhansl, C. L. (1988). Testing the density hypothesis: Comment on Corter. *Journal of Experimental Psychology: General*, 117, 101–104.

Kruschke, J. K. (1992). ALCOVE: An exemplar-based connectionist model of category learning. *Psychological Review*, 99, 22–44.

Lamberts, K. (2000). Information-accumulation theory of speeded categorization. *Psychological Review*, 107, 227–260.

Lassaline, M. E. (1996). Structural alignment in induction and similarity. *Journal of Experimental Psychology: Learning, Memory, and Cognition*, 22, 754–770.

Lee, M. D. (2002a). A simple method for generating additive clustering models with limited complexity. *Machine Learning*, 49, 39–58.

Lee, M. D. (2002b). Generating additive clustering models with limited stochastic complexity. *Journal of Classification*, 19, 69–85.

Li, M., & Vitanyi, P. (1997). *An introduction to Kolmogorov complexity and its applications* (2nd ed.). New York: Springer-Verlag.

Love, B. C. (2000). A computational level theory of similarity. *Proceeding of the Cognitive Science Society*, 22, 316–321.

Markman, A. B., & Gentner, D. (1993a). Structural alignment during similarity comparisons. *Cognitive Psychology*, 25, 431–467.

Markman, A. B., & Gentner, D. (1993b). Splitting the differences: A structural alignment view of similarity. *Journal of Memory and Language*, 32, 517–535.

Markman, A. B., & Gentner, D. (1996). Commonalities and differences in similarity comparisons. *Memory & Cognition*, 24, 235–249

Markman, A. B., and Gentner, D. (1997). The effects of alignability on memory. *Psychological Science*, 8, 363–367.

Markman, A. B., & Wisniewski, E. J. (1997). Similar and different: The differentiation of basic-level categories. *Journal of Experimental Psychology: Learning, Memory, and Cognition*, 23, 54–70.

Marr, D. (1982). *Vision*. San Francisco: Freeman.

Marr, D., & Nishihara, H. K. (1978). Representation and recognition of three dimensional shapes. *Proceedings of the Royal Society of London, Series B*, 200, 269–294.

Medin, D. L., Goldstone, R. L., & Gentner, D. (1993). Respects for similarity. *Psychological Review*, 100, 254–278.

Medin, D. L., Lynch, E. B., & Solomon, K. O. (2000). Are there kinds of concepts? *Annual Review of Psychology*, 51, 121–147.

Medin, D. L., & Ortony, A. (1989). Psychological essentialism. In S. Vosniadou & A. Ortony (Eds.), *Similarity and analogical reasoning*. Cambridge, UK: Cambridge University Press.

Medin, D. L., & Schaffer, M. M. (1978). A context theory of classification learning. *Psychological Review*, 85, 207–238.

Mitchell, M. (1993). *Analogy-making as perception: A computer model*. Cambridge, MA: MIT Press.

Murphy, G. L. (2002). *The big book of concepts*. Cambridge, MA: MIT Press.

Murphy, G. L., & Medin, D. L. (1985). The role of theories in conceptual coherence. *Psychological Review*, 92, 289–316.

Navarro, D. J., & Lee, M. D. (2003). Combining dimensions and features in similarity-based representations. In S. Becker, S. Thrun, & K. Obermayer (Eds.) Advances in Neural Information Processing Systems, 15, 67–74. MIT Press.

Neisser, U. (1967). *Cognitive psychology*. New York: Appleton-Century-Crofts.

Nickerson, R. S. (1972). Binary classification reaction time: A review of some studies of human information-processing capabilities. *Psychonomic Monograph Supplements*, 4 (whole no. 6), 275–317.

Nosofsky, R. M. (1984). Choice, similarity, and the context theory of classification. *Journal of Experimental Psychology: Learning, Memory, and Cognition*, 10, 104–114.

Nosofsky, R. M. (1986). Attention, similarity, and the identification-categorization relationship. *Journal of Experimental Psychology: General*, 115, 39–57.

Nosofsky, R. M. (1991). Stimulus bias, asymmetric similarity, and classification. *Cognitive Psychology*, 23, 94–140.

Osterholm, K., Woods, D. J., & Le Unes, A. (1985). Multidimensional scaling of Rorschach inkblots: Relationships with structured self-report. *Personality and Individual Differences*, 6, 77–82.

Palmer, S. E. (1975). Visual perception and world knowledge. In D. A. Norman & D. E. Rumelhart (Eds.), *Explorations in cognition* (pp. 279–307). San Francisco: W. H. Freeman.

Palmeri, T. J. (1997). Exemplar similarity and the development of automaticity. *Journal of Experimental Psychology: Learning, Memory, and Cognition*, 23, 324–354.

Podgorny, P., & Garner, W. R. (1979). Reaction time as a measure of inter-intraobject visual similarity: Letters of the alphabet. *Perception and Psychophysics*, 26, 37–52.

Polk, T. A., Behensky, C., Gonzalez, R., & Smith, E. E. (2002). Rating the similarity of simple perceptual stimuli: Asymmetries induced by manipulating exposure frequency. *Cognition*, 82, B75–B88.

Pylyshyn, Z. W. (1985). *Computation and cognition*. Cambridge, MA: MIT Press.

Quine, W. V. (1969). *Ontological relativity and other essays*. New York: Columbia University Press.

Quine, W. V. (1977). Natural kinds. In S. P. Schwartz (Ed.), *Naming, necessity, and natural kinds* (pp. 155–175). Ithaca, NY: Cornell University Press.

Raaijmakers, J. G. W., & Shiffrin, R. M. (1981). Search of associative memory. *Psychological Review*, 88, 93–134.

Richardson, M. W. (1938). Multidimensional psychophysics. *Psychological Bulletin*, 35, 659–660.

Ripley B. D. (1996). *Pattern recognition and neural networks*. Cambridge: Cambridge University Press.

Rips, L. J. (1989). Similarity, typicality, and categorization. In S. Vosniadu & A. Ortony (Eds.), *Similarity, analogy, and thought* (pp. 21–59). Cambridge: Cambridge University Press.

Rips, L. J., & Collins, A. (1993). Categories and resemblance. *Journal of Experimental Psychology: General*, 122, 468–486.

Rips, L. J., Shoben, E. J., & Smith, E. E. (1973). Semantic distance and the verification of semantic relations. *Journal of Verbal Learning and Verbal Behavior*, 12, 1–20.

Ritov, I., Gati, I., & Tversky, A. (1990). Differential weighting of common and distinctive components. *Journal of Experimental Psychology: General*, 119, 30.

Ross, B. H. (1987). This is like that: The use of earlier problems and the separation of similarity effects. *Journal of Experimental Psychology: Learning, Memory, and Cognition*, 13, 629–639.

Ross, B. H. (1989). Distinguishing types of superficial similarities: Different effects on the access and use of earlier problems. *Journal of Experimental Psychology: Learning, Memory, and Cognition*, 15, 456–468.

Rozenblit, L., & Keil, F. (2002). The misunderstood limits of folk science: An illusion of explanatory depth. *Cognitive Science*, 26, 521–562.

Schank, R. C. (1982). *Dynamic memory: A theory of reminding and learning in computers and people*. Cambridge: Cambridge University Press.

Schvaneveldt, R. (1985). Measuring the structure of expertise. *International Journal of Man-Machine Studies*, 23, 699–728.

Sergent, J., & Takane, Y. (1987). Structures in two-choice reaction-time data. *Journal of Experimental Psychology: Human Perception and Performance*, 13, 300–315.

Shepard, R. N. (1962a). The analysis of proximities: Multidimensional scaling with an unknown distance function. Part I. *Psychometrika*, 27, 125–140.

Shepard, R. N. (1962b). The analysis of proximities: Multidimensional scaling with an unknown distance function. Part II. *Psychometrika*, 27, 219–246.

Shepard, R. N. (1972). Psychological representation of speech sounds. In E. E. David, Jr., & P. B. Denes (Eds.), *Human communication: A unified view*, (pp. 67–111). New York: McGraw-Hill.

Shepard, R. N. (1982). Geometrical approximations to the structure of musical pitch. *Psychological Review*, 89, 305–333.

Shepard, R. N. (1987). Toward a universal law of generalization for psychological science. *Science*, 237, 1317–1323.

Shepard, R. N., & Arabie, P. (1979). Additive clustering: Representation of similarities as combinations of discrete overlapping properties. *Psychological Review*, 86, 87–123.

Simon, D., & Holyoak, K. J. (2002). Structural dynamics of cognition: From consistency theories to constraint satisfaction. *Personality and Social Psychology Review*, 6, 283–294.

Sjoberg, L. (1972). A cognitive theory of similarity. *Goteborg Psychological Reports*, 2 (10).

Sloman, S. A. (1993). Feature-based induction. *Cognitive Psychology*, 25, 231–280.

Sloman, S. A. (1996). The empirical case for two systems of reasoning. *Psychological Bulletin*, 119, 3–22.

Smith, E. E., Shoben, E. J., & Rips, L. J. (1974). Structure and process in semantic memory: A featural model for semantic decisions. *Psychological Review*, 81, 214–241.

Smith, E. E., & Sloman, S. A. (1994). Similarity-versus rule-based categorization. *Memory and Cognition*, 22, 377–386.

Smith, J. D., & Kemler, D. G. (1984). Overall similarity in adults' classification: The child in all of us. *Journal of Experimental Psychology: General*, 113, 137–159.

Smith, L. B. (1989). From global similarity to kinds of similarity: The construction of dimensions in development. In S. Vosniadou & A. Ortony (Eds.), *Similarity and analogical reasoning* (pp. 146–178). Cambridge: Cambridge University Press.

Smith, L. B., & Kemler, D. G. (1978). Levels of experienced dimensionality in children and adults. *Cognitive Psychology*, 10, 502–532.

Suzuki, H., Ohnishi, H., & Shigemasu, K. (1992). Goal-directed processes in similarity judgment. *Proceedings of the fourteenth annual conference of the Cognitive Science Society* (pp. 343–348). Hillsdale, NJ: Erlbaum.

Tarr, M. J., & Gauthier, I. (1998). Do viewpoint-dependent mechanisms generalize across members of a class? *Cognition. Special Issue: Image-Based Object Recognition in Man, Monkey, and Machine*, 67, 73–110.

Tenenbaum, J. B. (1996). Learning the structure of similarity. In G. Tesauro, D. S. Touretzky, & T. K. Leen (Eds.), *Advances in Neural Information Processing Systems* 8 (pp. 4–9). Cambridge, MA: MIT Press.

Tenenbaum, J. B. (1999). Bayesian modeling of human concept learning. In M. S. Kearns, S. A. Solla, & D. A. Cohn (Eds.), *Advances in neural information processing systems* 11 (pp. 59–68). Cambridge, MA: MIT Press.

Tenenbaum, J. B., De Silva, V., & Lanford, J. C. (2000). A global geometric framework for nonlinear dimensionality reduction. *Science*, 290, 22–23.

Tenenbaum, J. B., & Griffiths, T. L. (2001). Generalization, similarity and Bayesian inference. *Behavioral and Brain Sciences*, 24, 629–640.

Torgerson, W. S. (1958). *Theory and methods of scaling*. New York: Wiley.

Torgerson, W. S. (1965). Multidimensionsal scaling of similarity. *Psychometrika*, 30, 379–393.

Treisman, A. M. (1986). Features and objects in visual processing. *Scientific American*, 255, 106–115.

Tversky, A. (1977). Features of similarity. *Psychological Review*, 84, 327–352.

Tversky, A., & Gati, I. (1982). Similarity, separability, and the triangle inequality. *Psychological Review*, 89, 123–154.

Tversky, A., & Hutchinson, J. W. (1986). Nearest neighbor analysis of psychological spaces. *Psychological Review*, 93, 3–22.

Ullman, S. (1996). *High-level vision: Object recognition and visual cognition*. London: MIT Press.

Ward, T. B. (1983). Response tempo and separable-integral responding: Evidence for an integral-to-separable processing sequence in visual perception. *Journal of Experimental Psychology: Human Perception and Performance*, 9, 103–112.

Wedell, D. (1994). Context effects on similarity judgments of multidimensional stimuli: Inferring the structure of the emotion space. *Journal of Experimental Social Psychology*, 30, 1–38.

Wiener-Ehrlich, W. K., Bart, W. M., & Millward, R. (1980). An analysis of generative representation systems. *Journal of Mathematical Psychology*, 21 (3), 219–246.

Zhang, S., & Markman, A. B. (1998). Overcoming the early entrant advantage: The role of alignable and nonalignable differences. *Journal of Marketing Research*, 35, 413–426.

CHAPTER 3

Concepts and Categories: Memory, Meaning, and Metaphysics

Douglas L. Medin
Lance J. Rips

Introduction

The concept of concepts is difficult to define, but no one doubts that concepts are fundamental to mental life and human communication. Cognitive scientists generally agree that a concept is a mental representation that picks out a set of entities, or a category. That is, concepts *refer*, and what they refer to are categories. It is also commonly assumed that category membership is not arbitrary, but rather a principled matter. What goes into a category belongs there by virtue of some lawlike regularities. However, beyond these sparse facts, the concept CONCEPT is up for grabs. As an example, suppose you have the concept TRIANGLE represented as "a closed geometric form having three sides." In this case, the concept is a definition, but it is unclear what else might be in your triangle concept. Does it include the fact that geometry books discuss them (although some don't) or that they have 180 degrees (although in hyperbolic geometry none do)? It is also unclear how many concepts have definitions or what substitutes for definitions in ones that do not.

Our goal in this chapter is to provide an overview of work on concepts and categories in the last half-century. There has been such a consistent stream of research during this period that one reviewer of this literature, Gregory Murphy (2002), was compelled to call his monograph, *The Big Book of Concepts*. Our task is eased by recent reviews, including Murphy's aptly named one (e.g., Medin, Lynch, & Solomon, 2000; Murphy, 2002; Rips, 2001; Wisniewski, 2002). Their thoroughness gives us the luxury of writing a review focused on a single perspective or "flavor" – the relation between concepts, memory, and meaning.

The remainder of this chapter is organized as follows. In the rest of this section, we briefly describe some of the tasks or functions that cognitive scientists have expected concepts to perform. This will provide a road map to important lines of research on concepts and categories. Next, we return to developments in the late 1960s and early 1970s that raised the exciting possibility that laboratory studies could provide deep insights into both concept representations and the organization of (semantic) memory. Then we describe the sudden collapse of this optimism and the ensuing lines of research that, however intriguing and important, essentially ignored questions about semantic memory. Next, we trace a number of relatively recent developments under the somewhat whimsical heading, "Psychometaphysics." This is the view that concepts are embedded in (perhaps domain-specific) theories. This will set the stage for returning to the question of whether research on concepts and categories is relevant to semantics and memory organization. We use that question to speculate about future developments in the field. In this review, we use all caps to refer to concepts and quotation marks to refer to linguistic expressions.

Functions of Concepts

For purposes of this chapter, we collapse the many ways people can use concepts into two broad functions: categorization and communication. The conceptual function that most research has targeted is *categorization*, the process by which mental representations (concepts) determine whether some entity is a member of a category. Categorization enables a wide variety of subordinate functions because classifying something as a category member allows people to bring their knowledge of the category to bear on the new instance. Once people categorize some novel entity, for example, they can use relevant knowledge for *understanding* and *prediction*. Recognizing a cylindrical object as a flashlight allows you to understand its parts, trace its functions, and predict its behavior. For example, you can confidently infer that the flashlight will have one or more batteries, will have some sort of switch, and will normally produce a beam of light when the switch is pressed.

Not only do people categorize in order to understand new entities, but they also use the new entities to modify and update their concepts. In other words, categorization supports *learning*. Encountering a member of a category with a novel property – for example, a flashlight that has a siren for emergencies – can result in that novel property being incorporated into the conceptual representation. In other cases, relations between categories may support inference. For example, finding out that flashlights can contain sirens may lead you to entertain the idea that cell phones and fire extinguishers might also contain sirens. Hierarchical conceptual relations support both inductive and deductive reasoning. If all trees contain xylem and hawthorns are trees, then one can deduce that hawthorns contain xylem. In addition, finding out that white oaks contain phloem provides some support for the inductive inference that other kinds of oaks contain phloem. People also use categories to *instantiate goals in planning* (Barsalou, 1983). For example, a person planning to do some night fishing might create an ad hoc concept, THINGS TO BRING ON A NIGHT FISHING TRIP, which would include a fishing rod, tackle box, mosquito repellent, and flashlight.

Concepts are also centrally involved in *communication*. Many of our concepts correspond to lexical entries, such as the English word "flashlight." For people to avoid misunderstanding each other, they must have comparable concepts in mind. If A's concept of cell phone corresponds with B's concept of flashlight, it will not go well if A asks B to make a call. An important part of the function of concepts in communication is their ability to combine to create an unlimited number of new concepts. Nearly every sentence you encounter is new – one you have never heard or read before – and concepts (along with the sentence's grammar) must support your ability to understand it. Concepts are also responsible for more ad hoc uses of language. For example, from the base concepts of TROUT and FLASHLIGHT, you might create a new concept, TROUT FLASHLIGHT, which in the context of our current discussion would presumably be a flashlight used when trying to catch trout (and not a flashlight with a picture of a trout on it, although this may be the correct interpretation in some other context). A major research challenge is to understand the principles of *conceptual combination* and how they relate to communicative contexts (see Fodor, 1994, 1998; Gleitman & Papafragou, Chap. 26 ; Hampton, 1997; Partee, 1995; Rips, 1995; Wisniewski, 1997).

Overview

So far, we have introduced two roles for concepts: categorization (broadly construed) and communication. These functions and associated subfunctions are important to bear in mind because studying any one in isolation can lead to misleading conclusions about conceptual structure (see Solomon, Medin, & Lynch, 1999, for a review bearing on this point). At this juncture, however, we need to introduce one more plot element into the story we are telling. Presumably everything we have been talking about has implications for human memory and memory organization. After all, concepts are mental representations, and people must store these representations somewhere in memory. However, the relation between concepts and memory may be more intimate. A key part of our story is what we call "the semantic memory marriage," the idea that memory organization corresponds to meaningful relations between concepts. Mental pathways that lead from one concept to another – for example, from ELBOW to ARM – represent relations like IS A PART OF that link the same concepts. Moreover, these memory relations may supply the concepts with all or part of their meaning. By studying how people use concepts in categorizing and reasoning, researchers could simultaneously explore memory structure and the structure of the mental lexicon. In other words, the idea was to unify categorization, communication (in its semantic aspects), and memory organization. As we will see, this marriage was somewhat troubled, and there are many rumors about its breakup. However, we are getting ahead of our story. The next section begins with the initial romance.

A Minihistory

Research on concepts in the middle of the last century reflected a gradual easing away from behaviorist and associative learning traditions. The focus, however, remained on learning. Most of this research was conducted in laboratories using artificial categories (a sample category might be any geometric figure that is both red and striped) and directed at one of two questions: (1) Are concepts learned by gradual increases in associative strength, or is learning all or none (Levine, 1962; Trabasso & Bower, 1968)?, and (2) Which kinds of rules or concepts (e.g., disjunctive, such as RED OR STRIPED, versus conjunctive, such as RED AND STRIPED) are easiest to learn (Bourne, 1970; Bruner, Goodnow, & Austin, 1956; Restle, 1962)?

This early work tended either to ignore real world concepts (Bruner et al., 1956, represent something of an exception here) or to assume implicitly that real world concepts are structured according to the same kinds of arbitrary rules that defined the artificial ones. According to this tradition, category learning is equivalent to finding out the definitions that determine category membership.

Early Theories of Semantic Memory

Although the work on rule learning set the stage for what was to follow, two developments associated with the emergence of cognitive psychology dramatically changed how people thought about concepts.

TURNING POINT 1: MODELS OF MEMORY ORGANIZATION

The idea of programming computers to do intelligent things (artificial intelligence or AI) had an important influence on the development of new approaches to concepts. Quillian (1967) proposed a hierarchical model for storing semantic information in a computer that was quickly evaluated as a candidate model for the structure of human memory (Collins & Quillian, 1969).

Figure 3.1 provides an illustration of part of a memory hierarchy that is similar to what the Quillian model suggests.

First, note that the network follows a principle of cognitive economy. Properties true of all animals, such as eating and breathing, are stored only with the animal concept. Similarly, properties that are generally true of birds are stored at the bird node, but properties distinctive to individual kinds (e.g., being yellow) are stored with the specific concept nodes they characterize (e.g., CANARY). A property does not have to be true of all subordinate concepts to be stored with a superordinate. This is illustrated in Figure 3.1, where CAN FLY is associated with the bird node; the few exceptions (e.g., flightlessness for ostriches) are stored with particular birds that do not fly. Second, note that category membership is defined in terms of positions in the hierarchical network. For example, the node for CANARY does not directly store the information that canaries are animals; instead, membership would be "computed" by moving from the canary node up to the bird node and then from the bird node to the animal node. It is as if a deductive argument is being constructed of the form, "All canaries are birds and all birds are animals and therefore all canaries are animals."

Although these assumptions about cognitive economy and traversing a hierarchical structure may seem speculative, they yield a number of testable predictions. Assuming traversal takes time, one would predict that the time needed for people to verify properties of concepts should increase with the network distance between the concept and the property. For example, people should be faster to verify that a canary is yellow than to verify that a canary has feathers and faster to determine that a canary can fly than that a canary has skin. Collins and Quillian found general support for these predictions.

TURNING POINT 2: NATURAL CONCEPTS AND FAMILY RESEMBLANCE

The work on rule learning suggested that children (and adults) might learn concepts by trying out hypotheses until they hit on the correct definition. In the early 1970s, however, Eleanor Rosch and her associates (e.g., Rosch, 1973; Rosch & Mervis, 1975) argued that most everyday concepts are not organized in terms of the sorts of necessary and sufficient features that would form a (conjunctive) definition for a category. Instead, such concepts depend on properties that are generally true but need not hold for every member. Rosch's proposal was that concepts have a "family resemblance" structure: What determines category membership is whether an example has enough characteristic properties (is enough like other members) to belong to the category.

One key idea associated with this view is that not all category members are equally "good" examples of a concept. If membership is based on characteristic properties and some members have more of these properties than others, then the ones with more characteristic properties should better exemplify the category. For example, canaries but not penguins have the characteristic bird properties of flying, singing, and building a nest, so one would predict that canaries would be more typical birds than penguins. Rosch and Mervis (1975) found that people do rate some examples of a category to be more typical than others and that these judgments are highly correlated with the number of characteristic features an example possesses. They also created artificial categories conforming to family resemblance structures, and produced typicality effects on learning and on goodness-of-example judgments.

Rosch and her associates (Rosch, Mervis, Gray, Johnson, & Boyes-Braem, 1976) also argued that the family resemblance view has important implications for understanding concept hierarchies. Specifically, they suggested that the correlational structure of features (instances that share some features tend to share others) creates natural "chunks" or clusters of instances that correspond to what they referred to as *basic-level categories*. For example, having feathers tends to correlate with nesting in trees (among other features) in the animal

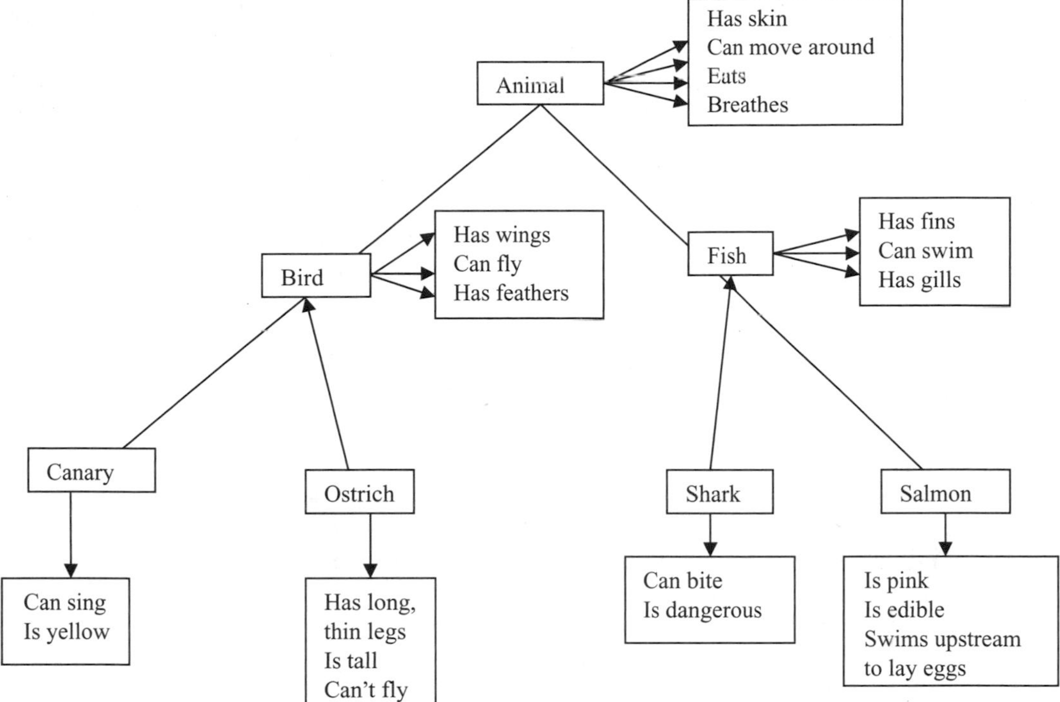

Figure 3.1. A semantic network.

kingdom, and having gills with living in water. The first cluster tends to isolate birds, whereas the second picks out fish. The general idea is that these basic-level categories provide the best compromise between maximizing within-category similarity (birds tend to be quite similar to each other) and minimizing between-category similarity (birds tend to be dissimilar to fish). Rosch et al. showed that basic-level categories are preferred by adults in naming objects, are learned first by children, are associated with the fastest categorization reaction times, and have a number of other properties that indicate their special conceptual status.

Turning points 1 and 2 are not unrelated. To be sure, the Collins and Quillian model, as initially presented, would not predict typicality effects (but see Collins & Loftus, 1975), and it was not obvious that it contained anything that would predict the importance of basic-level categories. Nonetheless, these conceptual breakthroughs led to an enormous amount of research premised on the notion that memory groups concepts according to their similarity in meaning, where similarity is imposed by correlated and taxonomic structure (see Anderson & Bower, 1973, and Norman & Rumelhart, 1975, for theories and research in this tradition, and Goldstone & Son, Chap. 2, for current theories of similarity).

Fragmentation of Semantics and Memory

Prior to about 1980, most researchers in this field saw themselves as investigating "semantic memory" – the way that long-term memory organizes meaningful information. Around 1980, the term itself became passé, at least for this same group of researchers, and the field regrouped under the banner of "Categories and Concepts" (the title of Smith & Medin's, 1981, synthesis of research in this area). At the time, these researchers may well have seen this change as a purely nominal one, but we suspect it reflected a retreat from the claim that semantic memory research had much to say about either semantics or memory. How did this change come about?

MEMORY ORGANIZATION

Initial support for a Quillian-type memory organization came from Quillian's own collaboration with Allan Collins (Collins & Quillian, 1969), which we mentioned earlier. Related evidence also came from experiments on lexical priming: Retrieving the meaning of a word made it easier to retrieve the meaning of semantically related words (e.g., Meyer & Schvanevelt, 1971). In these lexical decision tasks, participants viewed a single string of letters on each trial and decided, under reaction time instructions, whether the string was a word ("daisy") or a nonword ("raisy"). The key result was that participants were faster to identify a string as a word if it followed a semantically related item rather than an unrelated one. For example, reaction time for "daisy" was faster if, on the preceding trial, the participant had seen "tulip" rather than "steel." This priming effect is consistent with the hypothesis that activation from one concept spreads through memory to semantically related ones.

Later findings suggested, however, that the relation between word meaning and memory organization was less straightforward. For example, the typicality findings (see turning point 2) suggested that time to verify sentences of the form *An X is a Y* (e.g., "A finch is a bird") might be a function of the overlap in the information that participants knew about the meaning of *X* and *Y* rather than the length of the pathway between these concepts. The greater the information overlap – for example, the greater the number of properties that the referents of *X* and *Y* shared – the faster the time to confirm a true sentence and the slower the time to disconfirm a false one. For example, if you know a lot of common information about finches and birds but only a little common information about ostriches and birds, you should be faster to confirm the sentence "A finch is a bird" than "An ostrich is a bird." Investigators proposed several theories along these lines that made minimal commitments to the way memory organized its mental concepts (McCloskey & Glucksberg, 1979; Smith, Shoben, & Rips, 1974; Tversky, 1977). Rosch's (1978) theory likewise studiously avoided a stand on memory structure.

Evidence from priming in lexical decision tasks also appeared ambiguous. Although priming occurs between associatively related words (e.g., "bread" and "butter"), it is not so clear that there is priming between semantically linked words in the absence of such associations. It is controversial whether, for example, there is any automatic activation between "glove" and "hat" despite their joint membership in the clothing category (see Balota, 1994, for a discussion). If memory is organized on a specifically semantic basis – on the basis of word meanings – then there should be activation between semantically related words even in the absence of other sorts of associations. A meta-analysis by Lucas (2000) turned up a small effect of this type, but as Lucas noted, it is difficult to tell whether the semantically related pairs in these experiments are truly free of associations.

The idea that memory organization mimics semantic organization is an attractive one, and memory researchers attempted to modify the original Quillian approach to bring it into line with the results we have just reviewed (e.g., Collins & Loftus, 1975). The data from the sentence verification and lexical decision experiments, however, raised doubts about these theories. Later in this chapter, we consider whether newer techniques can give us a better handle on the structure of memory, but for now let's turn to the other half of the memory equals meaning equation.

SEMANTICS

Specifying the meaning of individual words is one of the goals of semantics, but only one. Semantics must also account for the meaning of phrases, sentences, and longer units of language. One problem in using a theory like Quillian's as a semantic theory is how to extend its core idea – that the meaning of a word is the coordinates of a node in memory structure – to explain how people understand meaningful phrases and sentences. Of course, Quillian's theory and its successors can tell us how we understand sentences that correspond to preexisting memory pathways. We have already seen how the model can explain our ability to confirm sentences such as "A daisy is a flower." However, what about sentences that do not correspond to preexisting connections – sentences such as "Fred placed a daisy in a lunchbox"?

The standard approach to sentence meaning in linguistics is to think of the meaning of sentences as built from the meaning of the words that compose them, guided by the sentence's grammar (e.g., Chierchia & McConnell-Ginet, 1990). We can understand sentences that we have never heard or read before, and because there are an enormous number of such novel sentences, we cannot learn their meaning as single chunks. It therefore seems quite likely that we compute the meaning of these new sentences. However, if word meaning is the position of a node in a network, it is hard to see how this position could combine with other positions to produce sentence meanings. What is the process that could take the relative network positions for FRED, PLACE, DAISY, IN, and LUNCHBOX and turn them into a meaning for "Fred placed a daisy in a lunchbox"?

If you like the notion of word meaning as relative position, then one possible solution to the problem of sentence meaning is to connect these positions with further pathways. Because we already have an array of memory nodes and pathways at our disposal, why not add a few more to encode the meaning of a new sentence? Perhaps the meaning of "Fred placed a daisy in the lunchbox" is given by a new set of pathways that interconnect the nodes for FRED, PLACE, DAISY, and so on, in a configuration corresponding to the sentence's structure. This is the route that Quillian and his successors took (e.g., Anderson & Bower, 1973; Norman & Rumelhart, 1975; Quillian, 1969), but it comes at a high price. Adding new connections changes the overall network configuration and thereby alters the meaning of the constituent terms. (Remember: Meaning is supposed to be *relative* position.) However, it is far from obvious that encoding incidental facts alters word meaning. It seems unlikely, for example, that learning the sentence about Fred changes the meaning of "daisy." Moreover, because meaning is a function of the entire network, the same incidental sentences change the meaning of all words. Learning about Fred's daisy placing shifts the meaning of seemingly unrelated words such as "hippopotamus" if only a bit.

Related questions apply to other psychological theories of meaning in the semantic memory tradition. To handle the typicality results mentioned earlier, some investigators proposed that the mental representation of a category such as daisies consists of a prototype for that category – for example, a description of a good example of a daisy (e.g., Hampton, 1979; McCloskey & Glucksberg, 1979). The meaning of "daisy" in these prototype theories would thus include default characteristics, such as growing in gardens, that apply to most, but not all, daisies. We discuss prototype theories in more detail soon, but the point for now is that prototype representations for individual words are difficult to combine to obtain a meaning for phrases that contain them. One potential way to combine prototypes – fuzzy set theory (Zadeh, 1965) – proved vulnerable to a range of counterexamples (Osherson & Smith, 1981, 1982). In general, the prototypes of constituent concepts can differ from the prototypes of their combinations in unpredictable ways (Fodor, 1994). The prototype of BIRDS THAT ARE PETS (perhaps a parakeet-like bird) may differ from the prototypes of both BIRDS and PETS (see Storms, de Boeck, van Mechelen, & Ruts, 1998, for related evidence). Thus, if word meanings are prototypes, it is hard to see how the meaning of phrases could be a compositional function of the meaning of their parts.

Other early theories proposed that category representations consist of descriptions of exemplars of the category in question. For example, the mental representation of DAISY would include descriptions of specific daisies that an individual had encoded (e.g., Hintzman, 1986; Medin & Schaffer, 1978; Nosofsky, 1986). However, these theories have semantic difficulties of their own (see Rips, 1995). For example, if by chance the only Nebraskans you have met are chiropractors and the only chiropractors you have met are Nebraskans, then exemplar models appear to mispredict that "Nebraskan" and "chiropractor" will be synonyms for you.

To recap briefly, we have found that experimental research on concepts and categories was largely unable to confirm that global memory organization (as in Quillian's semantic memory) conferred word meaning. In addition, neither the global theories that initiated this research nor the local prototype or exemplar theories that this research produced were able to provide insight into the basic semantic problem of how we understand the meaning of novel sentences. This left semantic memory theory in the unenviable position of being unable to explain either semantics or memory.

Functions and Findings

Current research in this field still focuses on categorization and communication, but without the benefit of a framework that gives a unified explanation for the functions that concepts play in categorizing, reasoning, learning, language understanding, and memory organization. In this section, we survey the state of the art, and in the following one, we consider the possibility of reuniting some of these roles.

Category Learning and Inference

One nice aspect of Rosch and Mervis's (1975) studies of typicality effects is that they used both natural language categories and artificially created categories. Finding typicality effects with natural (real world) categories shows that the phenomenon is of broad interest; finding these same effects with artificial categories provides systematic control for potentially confounding variables (e.g., exemplar frequency) in a way that cannot be done for lexical concepts. This general strategy linking the natural to the artificial has often been followed over the past few decades. Although researchers using artificial categories have sometimes been guilty of treating these categories as ends in themselves, there are enough parallels between results with artificial and natural categories that each area of research informs the other (see Medin & Coley, 1998, for a review).

PROTOTYPE VERSUS EXEMPLAR MODELS

One idea compatible with Rosch's family resemblance hypothesis is the *prototype view*. It proposes that people learn the characteristic features (or central tendency) of categories and use them to represent the category (e.g., Reed, 1972). This abstract prototype need not correspond to any experienced example. According to this theory, categorization depends on similarity to the prototypes. For example, to decide whether some animal is a bird or a mammal, a person would compare the (representation of) that animal to both the bird and the mammal prototypes and assign it to the category whose prototype it most resembled. The prototype view accounts for typicality effects in a straightforward manner. Good examples have many characteristic properties of their category and have few characteristics in common with the prototypes of contrasting categories.

Early research appeared to provide striking confirmation of the idea of prototype abstraction. Using random dot patterns as the prototypes, Posner and Keele (1968, 1970) produced a category from each prototype. The instances in a category were "distortions" of the prototype generated by moving constituent dots varying distances from their original positions. Posner and Keele first trained participants to classify examples that they created by distorting the prototypes. Then they gave a transfer test in which they presented both the old patterns and new low or high distortions that had not appeared during training. In addition, the prototypes, which the participants had never seen, were presented during transfer. Participants had to categorize these transfer patterns, but unlike the training procedure, the transfer test gave participants no feedback about the correctness of their responses. The tests either immediately followed training or appeared after a 1-week delay.

Posner and Keele (1970) found that correct classification of the new patterns decreased as distortion (distance from a category prototype) increased. This is the standard typicality effect. The most striking result was that a delay differentially affected categorization of prototypic versus old training patterns. Specifically, correct categorization of old patterns decreased over time to a reliably greater extent than performance on prototypes. In the immediate test, participants classified old patterns more accurately than prototypes; however, in the delayed test, accuracy on old patterns and prototypes was about the same. This differential forgetting is compatible with the idea that training leaves participants with representations of both training examples and abstracted prototypes but that memory, for examples, fades more rapidly than memory for prototypes. The Posner and Keele results were quickly replicated by others and constituted fairly compelling evidence for the prototype view.

However, this proved to be the beginning of the story rather than the end. Other researchers (e.g., Brooks, 1978; Medin & Schaffer, 1978) put forth an *exemplar view* of categorization. Their idea was that memory for old exemplars by itself could account for transfer patterns without the need for positing memory for prototypes. On this view, new examples are classified by assessing their similarity to stored examples and assigning the new example to the category that has the most similar examples. For instance, some unfamiliar bird (e.g., a heron) might be correctly categorized as a bird not because it is similar to a bird prototype, but rather because it is similar to flamingos, storks, and other shore birds.

In general, similarity to prototypes and similarity to stored examples will tend to be highly correlated (Estes, 1986). Nonetheless, for some category structures and for some specific exemplar and prototype models, it is possible to develop differential predictions. Medin and Schaffer (1978), for example, pitted the number of typical features against high similarity to particular training examples and found that categorization was more strongly influenced by the latter. A prototype model would make the opposite prediction.

Another contrast between exemplar and prototype models revolves around sensitivity to within-category correlations (Medin, Altom, Edelson, & Freko, 1982). A prototype representation captures what is on average true of a category, but is insensitive to within-category feature distributions. For example, a bird prototype could not represent the impression that small birds are more likely to sing than large birds (unless one had separate prototypes for large and small birds). Medin et al. (1982) found that people are sensitive to within-category correlations (see also Malt & Smith, 1984, for corresponding results with natural object categories). Exemplar theorists were also able to show that exemplar models could readily predict other effects that originally appeared to support prototype theories – differential forgetting of prototypes versus training examples, and prototypes being categorized as accurately or more accurately than training examples. In short, early skirmishes strongly favored exemplar models over prototype models. Parsimony suggested no need to posit prototypes if stored instances could do the job. Since the early 1980s, there have been a number of trends and developments in research and theory with artificially constructed categories, and we give only the briefest of summaries here.

NEW MODELS

There are now more contending models for categorizing artificial stimuli, and the early models have been extensively elaborated. For example, researchers have generalized the original Medin and Schaffer (1978) exemplar model to handle continuous dimensions (Nosofsky, 1986), to address the time course of categorization (Lamberts, 1995; Nosofsky & Palmeri, 1997a; Palmeri, 1997), to generate probability estimates in inference tasks (Juslin & Persson, 2002), and to embed it in a neural network (Kruschke, 1992).

Three new kinds of classification theories have been added to the discussion: rational approaches, decision-bound models, and neural network models. Anderson (1990, 1991) proposed that an effective approach to modeling cognition in general and categorization in particular is to analyze the information available to a person in the situation of interest and then to determine abstractly what an efficient, if not optimal, strategy might be. This approach has led to some new sorts of experimental evidence (e.g., Anderson & Fincham, 1996; Clapper & Bower, 2002) and pointed researchers more in the direction of the inference function of categories. Interestingly, the Medin and Schaffer exemplar model corresponds to a special case of the rational model, and Nosofsky (1991) discussed the issue of whether the rational model adds significant explanatory power. However, there is also some evidence undermining the rational model's predictions concerning inference (e.g., Malt, Ross, & Murphy, 1995; Murphy & Ross, 1994; Palmeri, 1999; Ross & Murphy, 1996).

Decision-bound models (e.g., Ashby & Maddox, 1993; Maddox & Ashby, 1993) draw their inspiration from psychophysics and signal detection theory. Their primary claim is that category learning consists of developing decision bounds around the category that will allow people to categorize examples successfully. The closer an item is to the decision bound the harder it should be to categorize. This framework offers a new perspective on categorization in that it may lead investigators to ask questions such as How do the decision bounds that humans adopt compare with what is optimal? and What kinds of decision functions are easy or hard to acquire? Researchers have also directed efforts to distinguish decision-bound and exemplar models (e.g., Maddox, 1999; Maddox & Ashby, 1998; McKinley & Nosofsky, 1995; Nosofsky, 1998; Nosofsky & Palmeri, 1997b). One possible difficulty with decision-bound models is that they contain no obvious mechanism by which stimulus familiarity can affect performance, contrary to empirical evidence that it does (Verguts, Storms, & Tuerlinckx, 2001).

Neural network or connectionist models are the third type of new model on the scene (see Knapp & Anderson, 1984, and Kruschke, 1992, for examples, and Doumas & Hummel, Chap. 4, for further discussion of connectionism). It may be a mistake to think of connectionist models as comprising a single category because they take many forms, depending on assumptions about hidden units, attentional processes, recurrence, and the like. There is one sense in which neural network models with hidden units may represent a clear advance on prototype models: They can form prototypes in a bottom-up manner that reflects within-category structure (e.g., Love, Medin, & Gureckis, 2004). That is, if a category comprises two distinct clusters of examples, network models can create a separate hidden unit for each chunk (e.g., large birds versus small birds) and thereby show sensitivity to within-category correlations.

MIXED MODELS AND MULTIPLE CATEGORIZATION SYSTEMS

A common response to hearing about various models of categorization is to suggest that all the models may be capturing important aspects of categorization and that research should determine in which contexts one strategy versus another is likely to dominate. One challenge to this divide and conquer program is that the predictions of alternative models tend to be highly correlated, and separating them is far from trivial. Nonetheless, there is both empirical research (e.g., Johansen & Palmeri, 2002; Nosofsky, Clark, & Shin, 1989; Reagher & Brooks, 1993) and theoretical modeling that support the idea that mixed models of categorization are useful and perhaps necessary. Current efforts combine rules and examples (e.g., Erickson & Kruschke, 1998; Nosofsky, Palmeri, & McKinley, 1994), as well as rules and decision bounds (Ashby, Alfonso-Reese, Turken, & Waldron, 1998). Some models also combine exemplars and prototypes (e.g., Homa, Sterling, & Trepel, 1981; Minda & Smith, 2001; Smith & Minda,

1998, 2000; Smith, Murray, & Minda, 1997), but it remains controversial whether the addition of prototypes is needed (e.g., Busemeyer, Dewey, & Medin, 1984; Nosofsky & Johansen, 2000; Nosofsky & Zaki, 2002; Stanton, Nosofsky, & Zaki, 2002).

The upsurge of cognitive neuroscience has reinforced the interest in multiple memory systems. One intriguing line of research by Knowlton, Squire, and associates (Knowlton, Mangels, & Squire, 1996; Knowlton & Squire, 1993; Squire & Knowlton, 1995) favoring multiple categorization systems involves a dissociation between categorization and recognition. Knowlton and Squire (1993) used the Posner and Keele dot pattern stimuli to test amnesic and matched control patients on either categorization learning and transfer or a new–old recognition task (involving five previously studied patterns versus five new patterns). The amnesiacs performed very poorly on the recognition task but were not reliably different from control participants on the categorization task. Knowlton and Squire took this as evidence for a two-system model, one based on explicit memory for examples and one based on an implicit system (possibly prototype abstraction). On this view, amnesiacs have lost access to the explicit system but can perform the classification task using their intact implicit memory.

These claims have provoked a number of counterarguments. First, Nosofsky and Zaki (1998) showed that a single system (exemplar) model could account for both types of data from both groups (by assuming the exemplar-based memory of amnesiacs was impaired but not absent). Second, investigators have raised questions about the details of Knowlton and Squire's procedures. Specifically, Palmeri and Flanery (1999) suggested that the transfer tests themselves may have provided cues concerning category membership. They showed that undergraduates who had never been exposed to training examples (the students believed they were being shown patterns subliminally) performed above chance on transfer tests in this same paradigm. The debate is far from resolved, and there are strong advocates both for and against the multiple systems view (e.g., Filoteo, Maddox, & Davis, 2001; Maddox, 2002; Nosofsky & Johansen, 2000; Palmeri & Flanery, 2002; Reber, Stark, & Squire, 1998a, 1998b). It is safe to predict that this issue will receive continuing attention.

INFERENCE LEARNING

More recently, investigators have begun to worry about extending the scope of category learning studies by looking at inference. Often, we categorize some entity to help us accomplish some function or goal. Ross (1997, 1999, 2000) showed that the category representations people develop in laboratory studies depend on use and that use affects later categorization. In other words, models of categorization ignore inference and use at their peril. Other work suggests that having a cohesive category structure is more important for inference learning than it is for classification (Yamauchi, Love, & Markman, 2002; Yamauchi & Markman, 1998, 2000a, 2000b; for modeling implications see Love, Markman, & Yamauchi, 2000; Love et al., 2004). More generally, this work raises the possibility that diagnostic rules based on superficial features, which appear so prominently in pure categorization tasks, may not be especially relevant for contexts involving multiple functions or more meaningful stimuli (e.g., Markman & Makin, 1998; Wisniewski & Medin, 1994).

FEATURE LEARNING

The final topic on our "must mention" list for work with artificial categories is feature learning. It is a common assumption in both models of object recognition and category learning that the basic units of analysis or features remain unchanged during learning. There is increasing evidence and supporting computational modeling that indicate this assumption is incorrect. Learning may increase or decrease the distinctiveness of features and may even create new features (see Goldstone, 1998, 2003; Goldstone, Lippa, & Shriffin, 2001; Goldstone & Stevyers, 2001;

Schyns, Goldstone, & Thibaut, 1998; Schyns & Rodet, 1997).

Feature learning has important implications for our understanding of the role of similarity in categorization. It is intuitively compelling to think of similarity as a causal factor supporting categorization – things belong to the same category because they are similar. However, this may have things backward. Even standard models of categorization assume learners selectively attend to features that are diagnostic, and the work on feature learning suggests that learners may create new features that help partition examples into categories. In that sense, similarity (in the sense of overlap in features) is the by-product, not the cause, of category learning. We take up this point again in discussing the theory theory of categorization later in this review.

REASONING

As we noted earlier, one of the central functions of categorization is to support reasoning. Having categorized some entity as a bird, one may predict with reasonable confidence that it builds a nest, sings, and can fly, although none of these inferences is certain. In addition, between-category relations may guide reasoning. For example, from the knowledge that robins have some enzyme in their blood, one is likely to be more confident that the enzyme is in sparrows than in raccoons. The basis for this confidence may be that robins are more similar to sparrows than to raccoons or that robins and sparrows share a lower-rank superordinate category than do robins and raccoons (birds versus vertebrates). We do not review this literature here because Sloman and Lagnado (Chap. 5) summarize it nicely.

SUMMARY

Bowing to practicalities, we have glossed a lot of research and skipped numerous other relevant studies. The distinction between artificially created and natural categories is itself artificial – at least in the sense that it has no clear definition or marker. When we take up the idea that concepts may be organized in terms of theories, we return to some laboratory studies that illustrate this fuzzy boundary. For the moment, however, we shift attention to the more language-like functions of concepts.

Language Functions

Most investigators in the concepts and categories area continue to assume that, in addition to their role in recognition and category learning, concepts also play a role in understanding language and in thinking discursively about things. In addition to determining, for example, which perceptual patterns signal the appearance of a daisy, the DAISY concept also contributes to the meaning of sentences such as our earlier example, "Fred placed a daisy in a lunchbox." We noted that early psychological research on concepts ran into problems in explaining the meaning of linguistic units larger than single words. Most early theories posited representations, such as networks, exemplars, or prototypes, that did not combine easily and, thus, complicated the problem of sentence meaning. Even if we reject the idea that sentence meanings are compositional functions of word meaning, we still need a theory of sentence meanings, and no obvious contenders are in sight. In this section, we return to the role that concepts play in language understanding to see whether new experiments and theories have clarified this relationship.

CONCEPTS AS POSITIONS IN MEMORY STRUCTURES

One difficulty with the older semantic memory view of word meaning is that memory seems to change with experience from one person to another, whereas meaning must be more or less constant. The sentences you have encoded about daisies may differ drastically from those we have encoded because your conversation, reading habits, and other verbal give and take can diverge in important ways from ours. If meaning depends on memory for these sentences, then your meaning for "daisy" should likewise differ from ours. This raises the question of how you could possibly understand the sentences in this chapter in the way we intend or how you could meaningfully disagree with us about some common topic (see Fodor, 1994).

It is possible that two people – say, Calvin and Martha – might be able to maintain mutual intelligibility as long as their conceptual networks are not too different. It is partly an empirical question as to how much their networks can vary while still allowing Calvin's concepts to map correctly into Martha's. To investigate this issue, Goldstone and Rogosky (2002) carried out some simulations that try to recover such a mapping. The simulations modeled Calvin's conceptual system as the distance between each pair of his concepts (e.g., the distance between DOG and CAT in Calvin's system might be one unit, whereas the distance between DOG and DAISY might be six units). Martha's conceptual system was represented in the same way (i.e., by exactly the same interconcept distances) except for random noise that Goldstone and Rogosky added to each distance to simulate the effect of disparate beliefs. A constraint-satisfaction algorithm then applied to Calvin's and Martha's systems that attempted to recover the original correspondence between the concepts – to map Calvin's DOG to Martha's DOG, Calvin's DAISY to Martha's DAISY, and so on. The results of the stimulations show that with 15 concepts in each system (the maximum number considered and the case in which the model performed best) and with no noise added to Martha's system, the algorithm was always able to find the correct correspondence. When the simulation added to each dimension of the interconcept distance in Martha a small random increment (drawn from a normal distribution with mean 0 and standard deviation equal to .004 times the maximum distance), the algorithm recovered the correspondence about 63% of the time. When the standard deviation increased to .006 times the maximum distance, the algorithm succeeded about 15% of the time (Goldstone & Rogosky, 2002, Figure 2).

What should one make of the Goldstone and Rogosky results? Correspondences may be recovered for small amounts of noise, but performance trailed off dramatically for larger amounts of noise. Foes of the meaning-as-relative-position theory might claim that the poor performance under the .6% noise condition proves their contention. Advocates would point to the successful part of the simulations and note that their ability to detect correct correspondences usually improved as the number of points increased (although there are some nonmonotonicities in the simulation results that qualify this finding). Clearly, this is only the beginning of the empirical side of the debate. For example, the differences between Martha and Calvin are likely to be not only random, but also systematic, as in the case in which Martha grew up on a farm and Calvin was a city kid.

CONCEPT COMBINATION

Let's look at attempts to tackle head-on the problem of how word-level concepts combine to produce the meanings of larger linguistic units. There is relatively little research in this tradition on entire sentences (see Conrad & Rips, 1986; Rips, Smith, & Shoben, 1978), but there has been a fairly steady research stream devoted to noun phrases, including adjective-noun ("edible flowers"), noun-noun ("food flowers"), and noun-relative clause combinations ("flowers that are foods"). We'll call the noun or adjective parts of these phrases *components* and distinguish the main or *head noun* ("flowers" in each of our examples) from the adjective or noun *modifier* ("edible" or "food"). The aim of the research in question is to describe how people understand these phrases and, in particular, how the typicality of an instance in these combinations depends on the typicality of the same instance in the components. How does the typicality of a marigold in the category of edible flowers depend on the typicality of marigolds in the categories of edible things and flowers? As we already noticed, this relationship is far from straightforward (parakeets are superbly typical as pet birds but less typical pets and even less typical birds).

There is an optimistic way of looking at the results of this research program and a pessimistic way as well (for more recent, mostly optimistic, reviews of this work, see Hampton, 1997; Murphy, 2002; Rips, 1995; and Wisniewski, 1997). The optimistic angle is that interesting phenomena have turned up in investigating the typicality structure of combinations. The pessimistic angle, which is a direct result of the same phenomena, is that little progress has been made in figuring out a way to predict the typicality of a combination from the typicality of its components. This difficulty is instructive – in part because all psychological theories of concept combination posit complex, structured representations, and they depict concept combination either as rearranging (or augmenting) the structure of the head noun by means of the modifier (Franks, 1995; Murphy, 1988; Smith, Osherson, Rips, & Keane, 1988) or as fitting both head and modifier into a larger relational complex (Gagné & Shoben, 1997). Table 3.1 summarizes what is on offer from these theories. Earlier models (at the top of the table) differ from later ones mainly in terms of the complexity of the combination process. Smith et al. (1988), for example, aimed at explaining simple adjective-noun combinations (e.g., "white vegetable") that, roughly speaking, refer to the intersection of the sets denoted by modifier and head (white vegetables are approximately the intersection of white things and vegetables). In this theory, combination occurs when the modifier changes the value of an attribute in the head noun (changing the value of the color attribute in VEGETABLE to WHITE) and boosts the importance of this attribute in the overall representation. Later theories attempted to account for nonintersective combinations (e.g., "criminal lawyers," who are often not both criminals and lawyers). These combinations call for more complicated adjustments – for example, determining a relation that links the modifier and head (a criminal lawyer is a lawyer whose clients are in for criminal charges) or extracting a value from the modifier that can then be assigned to the head (e.g., a panther lawyer might be one who is especially vicious or tenacious).

So why no progress? One reason is that many of the combinations that investigators have studied are familiar or, at least, have familiar referents. Some people have experience with edible flowers, for example, and know that they include nasturtiums, are sometimes used in salads, are often brightly colored, are peppery tasting, and so on. We learn many of these properties by direct or indirect observation (by what Hampton, 1987, called "extensional feedback"), and they are sometimes impossible to learn simply by knowing the meaning of "edible" and "flower." Because these properties can affect the typicality of potential instances, the typicality of these familiar combinations will not be a function of the typicality of their components. This means that if we are going to be able to predict typicality in a compositional way, we will have to factor out the contribution of these directly acquired properties. Rips (1995) refered to this filtering as the "no peeking principle" – no peeking at the referents of the combination. Of course, you might be able to predict typicality if you already know the relevant real-world facts in addition to knowing the meaning of the component concepts. The issue about understanding phrases, however, is how we are able to interpret an unlimited number of new ones. For this purpose, people need some procedure for computing new meanings from old ones that is not restricted by the limited set of facts they happened to have learned (e.g., through idiosyncratic encounters with edible flowers).

Another reason for lack of progress is that some of the combinations used in this research may be compounds or lexicalized phrases [e.g., "White House" (accent on "White") = the residence of the President] rather than modifier-head constructions [e.g., "white house" (accent on "house") = a house whose color is white]. Compounds are often idiomatic; their meaning is not an obvious function of their parts (see Gleitman & Gleitman's, 1970, distinction between phrasal and compound constructions; and Partee, 1995).

There is a deeper reason, however, for the difficulty in predicting compound typicality from component typicality. Even if we adhere to the no peeking principle and

Table 3.1. Some Theories of Concept Combination

Model	*Domain*	*Representation of Head Noun*	*Modification Process*
Hampton (1987)	Noun-Noun and Noun-Relative-Clause NPs (conjunctive NPs, e.g., *sports that are also games*)	Schemas (attribute-value lists with attributes varying in importance)	Modifier and head contribute values to combination on the basis of importance and centrality
Smith, Osherson, Rips, & Keane (1988)	Simple Adjective-Noun NPs (e.g., *red apple*)	Schemas (attribute-value lists with distributions of values and weighted attributes)	Adjective shifts value on relevant attribute in head and increases weight on relevant dimension
Murphy (1988)	Adj-Noun and Noun-Noun NPs (esp. non-predicating NPs, e.g., *corporate lawyer*)	Schemas (lists of slots and fillers)	Modifier fills relevant slot; then representation is "cleaned up" on the basis of world knowledge
Franks (1995)	Adj-Noun and Noun-Noun NPs (esp. privatives, e.g., *fake gun*)	Schemas (attribute-value structures with default values for some attributes)	Attribute-values of modifier and head are summed with modifier potentially overriding or negating head values
Gagné & Shoben (1997)	Noun-Noun NPs	Lexical representations containing distributions of relations in which nouns figure	Nouns are bound as arguments to relations (e.g., *flu virus* = virus causing flu)
Wisniewski (1997)	Noun-Noun NPs	Schemas (lists of slots and fillers, including roles in relevant events)	1. Modifier noun is bound to role in head noun (e.g., *truck soap* = soap for cleaning trucks) 2. Modifier value is reconstructed in head noun (e.g., *zebra clam* = clam with stripes) 3. Hybridization (e.g., *robin canary* = cross between robin and canary)

stick to clear modifier-head constructions, the typicality of a combination can depend on "emergent" properties that are not part of the representation of either component (Hastie, Schroeder, & Weber, 1990; Kunda, Miller, & Claire, 1990; Medin & Shoben, 1988; Murphy, 1988). For example, you may never have encountered, or even thought about, a smoky apple (so extensional feedback does not inform your conception of the noun phrase), but nevertheless it is plausible to suppose that smoky apples are not good tasting. Having a bad taste, however, is not a usual property of (and is not likely to be stored as part of a concept for) either apples or smoky things; on the contrary, many apples and smoky things (e.g., smoked meats, cheese, fish) are often quite good tasting. If you agree with our assessment that smoky apples are likely to be bad tasting, that is probably because you imagine a way in which apples could become smoky (being caught in a kitchen fire, perhaps) and you infer that under these circumstances the apple would not be good to eat. The upshot is that the properties of a combination can depend on complex inductive or explanatory inferences (Johnson & Keil, 2000; Kunda et al., 1990). If these properties affect the typicality of an instance with respect to the combination, then there is little hope of a simple model of this phenomenon. No current theory comes close to providing an adequate and general account of these processes.

INFERENTIAL VERSUS ATOMISTIC CONCEPTS

Research on the typicality structure of noun phrases is of interest for what it can tell us about people's inference and problem-solving skills. However, because these processes are quite complex – drawing on general knowledge and inductive reasoning to produce emergent information – we can not predict noun phrase typicality in other than a limited range of cases. For much the same reason, typicality structure does not appear very helpful in understanding how people construct the meaning of a noun phrase while reading or listening. By themselves, emergent properties do not rule out the possibility of a model that explains how people derive the meaning of a noun phrase from the meaning of its components. Compositionality does not require that all aspects of the noun phrase's meaning are parts of the components' meanings. It is sufficient to find some computable function from the components to the composite that is simple enough to account for people's understanding (see Partee, 1995, for a discussion of types of composition). The trouble is that if noun phrases' meanings require theory construction and problem solving, such a process is unlikely to explain the ease and speed with which we usually understand them in ongoing speech.

Of course, we have only considered the role of schemas or prototypes in concept combination, but it is worth noting that many of the same problems with semantic composition affect other contemporary theories, such as latent semantic analysis (Landauer & Dumais, 1997), which take a global approach to meaning. Latent semantic analysis takes as input a table of the frequencies with which words appear in specific contexts. In one application, for example, the items comprise about 60,000 word types taken from 30,000 encyclopedia entries, and the table indicates the frequency with which each word appears in each entry. The analysis then applies a technique similar to factor analysis to derive an approximately 300-dimensional space in which each word appears as a point and in which words that tend to co-occur in context occupy neighboring regions in the space. Because this technique finds a best fit to a large corpus of data, it is sensitive to indirect connections between words that inform their meaning. However, the theory has no clear way to derive the meaning of novel sentences. Although latent semantic analysis could represent a sentence as the average position of its component words, this would not allow it to capture the difference between, say, *The financier dazzled the movie star* versus *The movie star dazzled the financier*, which depend on sentence structure. In addition, the theory uses the distance between two words in semantic space to represent the relation between them, and so the theory has trouble with semantic relations that, unlike distances, are asymmetric. It is unclear, for example, how it could cope with the fact that *father* implies *parent* but *parent* does not imply *father*.

On the one hand, online sentence understanding is a rapid, reliable process. On the other hand, the meaning of even simple adjective-noun phrases seems to require heady inductive inferences. Perhaps we should distinguish, then, between the *interpretation* of a phrase or sentence and its *comprehension* (Burge, 1999). On this view, comprehension gives us a more or less immediate understanding of novel phrases based primarily on the word meaning of the components and syntactic/semantic structure. Interpretation, by contrast, is a potentially unlimited process relying on the result of comprehension plus inference and general knowledge. The comprehension/interpretation distinction may be more of a continuum than a dichotomy, but the focus on the interpretation end of the continuum means that research on concepts is difficult to apply to comprehension. As we have just noticed, it is hard, if not impossible, to compute the typicality structure of composites. So if we want something readily computable in order to account for comprehension, we have to look to something simpler than typicality structures (and the networks, prototypes, schemas, or theories that underlie them). One possibility (Fodor, 1994, 1998) is to consider a representation in which word meanings are mental units not much different from the words themselves, and whose semantic values derive from (unrepresented) causal connections to their referents.

GENERIC NOUN PHRASES

Even if we abandon typicality structures as accounts of comprehension, however, it does not follow that these structures are useless in explaining all linguistic phenomena. More recent research on two fronts seems to us to hold promise for interactions between psychological and linguistic theories. First, there are special constructions in English that, roughly speaking, describe default characteristics of members of a category. For example, "Lions have manes" means (approximately) that having a mane is a characteristic property of lions. Bare plural noun phrases (i.e., plurals with no preceding determiners) are one way to convey such a meaning as we have just noticed, but indefinite singular sentences ("A lion has a mane") and definite singular sentences ("The lion – *Panthera leo* – has a mane") can also convey the same idea in some of their senses. These generic sentences seem to have normative content. Unlike "Most lions have manes," generic sentences seem to hold despite the existence of numerous exceptions; "Lions have manes" seems to be true even though most lions (e.g., female and immature lions) do not have manes (see Krifka et al., 1995, for an introduction to generic sentences). There is an obvious relation between the truth or acceptability of generic sentences and the typicality structure of categories because the typical properties of a category are those that appear in true generic sentences. Of course, as Krifka et al. noted, this may simply be substituting one puzzle (the truth conditions of generic sentences) for another (the nature of typical properties), but this may be one place where linguistic and cognitive theories might provide mutual insight. Research by Susan Gelman and her colleagues (see Gelman, 2003, for a thorough review) suggests that generic sentences are a frequent way for caregivers to convey category information to children. Four-year-olds differentiate sentences with bare plurals ("Lions have manes") from those explicitly quantified by "all" or "some" in comprehension, production, and inference tasks (Gelman, Star, & Flukes, 2002; Hollander, Gelman, & Star, 2002). It would be of interest to know, however, at what age, and in what way, children discriminate generics from accidental generalizations – for example, when they first notice the difference between "Lions have manes" and "Lions frequently have manes" or "Most lions have manes."

POLYSEMY

A second place to look for linguistic-cognitive synergy is in an account of the meanings of polysemous words. Linguists (e.g., Lyons, 1977, Chap. 13) traditionally distinguish homonyms such as "mold," which have multiple unrelated meanings (e.g., a form into which liquids are poured vs. a fungus), from polysemous terms such as "line," which have multiple related meanings (e.g., a geometric line vs. a fishing line vs. a line of people, etc.). What makes polysemous terms interesting to psychologists in this area is that the relations among their meanings often possess a kind of typicality structure of their own. This is the typicality of the senses of the expression rather than the typicality of the referents of the expression and is thus a type of higher-level typicality phenomenon. Figure 3.2 illustrates such a structure for the polysemous verb "crawl," as analyzed by Fillmore and Atkins (2000). A rectangle in the figure represents each sense or use and includes both a brief label indicating its distinctive property and an example from British corpuses. According to Fillmore and Atkins, the central meanings for *crawl* have to do with people or creatures moving close to the ground (these uses appear in rectangles with darker outlines in the figure). But there are many peripheral uses – for example, time moving slowly ("The hours seemed to crawl by") and creatures teeming about ("The picnic supplies crawled with ants"). The central meanings are presumably the original ones with the peripheral meanings derived from these by a chaining process. Malt, Sloman, Gennari, Shi, and Wang (1999) observed similar instances of chaining in people's naming of artifacts, such as bottles and bowls, and it is possible that the gerrymandered naming patterns reflect the polysemy of the terms (e.g., "bottle") rather than different uses of the same meaning. As Figure 3.2 shows, it is not easy to distinguish different related meanings (polysemy) from different uses of the same meaning (contextual variation) and from different unrelated meanings (homonymy).

Some research has attacked the issue of whether people store each of the separate senses of a polysemous term (Klein & Murphy, 2002) or store only the core meaning, deriving the remaining senses as needed for comprehension (Caramazza & Grober, 1976; Franks, 1995). Conflicting evidence in this respect may be due to the fact that some relations between senses seem relatively productive and derivable (*regular* polysemy, such as the relationship between terms for animals and their food products, e.g., the animal meaning of "lamb" and its menu meaning), whereas other senses seem ad hoc (e.g., the relation between "crawl" = *moving close to the ground* and "crawl" = *teeming with people* in Figure 3.2). Multiple mechanisms are likely to be at work here.

SUMMARY

We do not mean to suggest that the only linguistic applications of psychologists' "concepts" are in dealing with interpretation, generic phrases, and polysemy – far from it. There are many areas, especially in developmental psycholinguistics, that hold the promise of fruitful interactions but that we cannot review here. Nor are we suggesting that investigators in this area give up the attempt to study the use of concepts in immediate comprehension. However, concepts for comprehension seem to have different properties from the concepts that figure in the other functions we have discussed, and researchers need to direct more attention to the interface between them.

Theories, Modules, and Psychometaphysics

We have seen, so far, some downward pressure on cognitive theories to portray human concepts as mental entities that are as simple and streamlined as possible. This pressure comes not only from the usual goal of parsimony but also from the role that concepts play in immediate language comprehension. However, there is also a great deal of upward pressure – pressure to include general knowledge about a category as part of its representation. For example, the presence of emergent properties in concept combinations suggests that people use background knowledge in interpreting these phrases. Similarly, people may bring background knowledge and theories to bear in classifying things even when they know a decision rule for the category. Consider psychodiagnostic classification. Although *DSM-IV* (the official diagnostic manual of the American Psychological Association) is atheoretical and organized in terms of rules, there is clear evidence that clinicians develop theories of disorders and, contra *DSM-IV*, weight causally central symptoms more than causally peripheral symptoms (e.g., Kim & Ahn, 2002a).

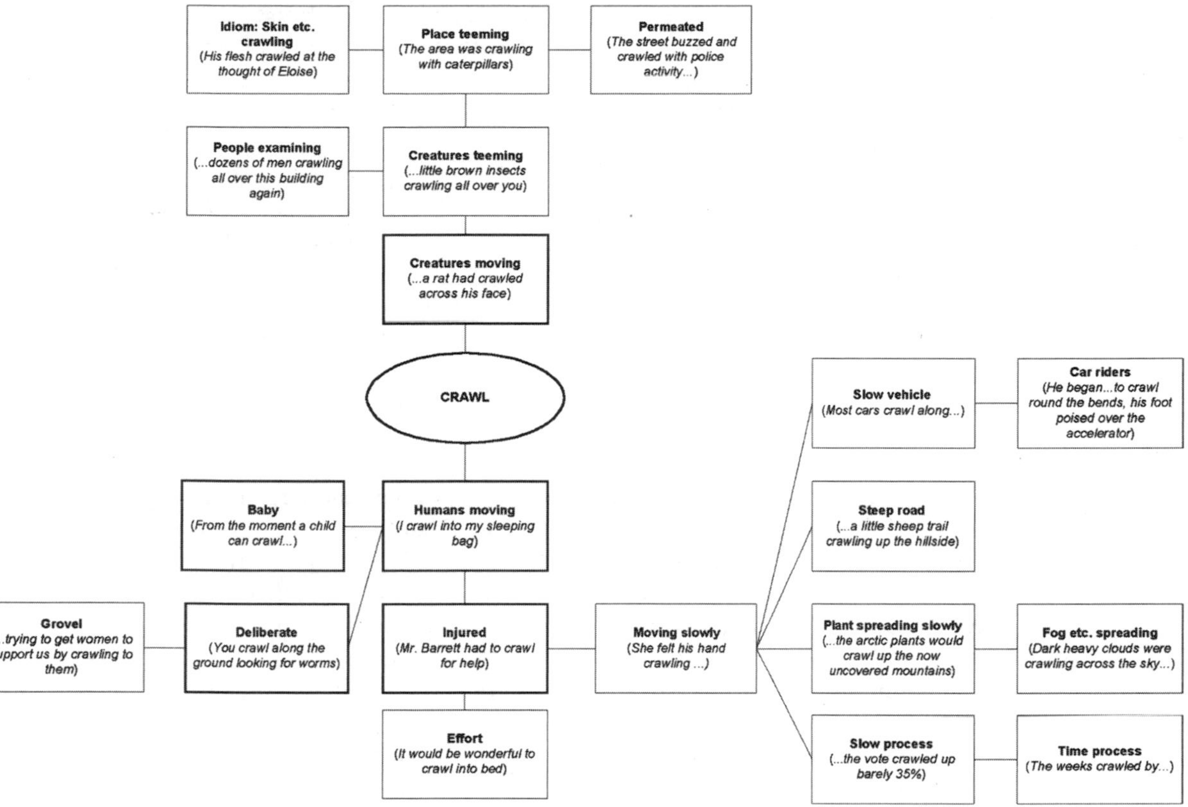

Figure 3.2. The meanings of crawl: Why it is difficult to distinguish different related meanings (polysemy) from different uses of the same meaning (contextual variation) and from different unrelated meanings (homonymy). Adapted from Fillmore & Alking (2000) by permission of Oxford University Press.

The same holds for laypersons (e.g., Furnham, 1995; Kim & Ahn, 2002b).

In this section, we examine the consequences of expanding the notion of a concept to include theoretical information about a category. In the case of the natural categories, this information is likely to be causal because people probably view physical causes as shaping and maintaining these categories. For artifacts, the relevant information may be the intentions of the person creating the object (e.g., Bloom, 1996). The issues we raise here concern the content and packaging of these causal beliefs.

The first of these issues focuses on people's beliefs about the locus of these causal forces – what we called "psychometaphysics." At one extreme, people may believe that each natural category is associated with a single source, concentrated within a category instance, that controls the nature of that instance. The source could determine, among other things, the instance's typical properties, its category membership, and perhaps even the conditions under which it comes into and goes out of existence. Alternatively, people may believe that the relevant causal forces are more like a swarm – not necessarily internal to an instance, nor necessarily emanating from a unitary spot – but shaping the category in aggregate fashion.

The second issue has to do with the cognitive divisions that separate beliefs about different sorts of categories. People surely believe that the causes that help shape daisies differ in type from those that shape teapots. Lay theories about flowers and other living things include at least crude information about specifically biological properties, whereas lay theories of teapots and other artifacts touch instead on intended and actual functions. However, how deep do these divisions go? On the one hand, beliefs about these domains could be modular (relatively clustered, relatively isolated), innate, universal, and local to specific brain regions. On the other hand, they may be free floating, learned, culturally specific, and distributed across cortical space. This issue is important to us because it ultimately affects whether we can patch up the "semantic memory" marriage.

Essentialism and Sortalism

PSYCHOLOGICAL ESSENTIALISM

What's the nature of people's beliefs about the causes of natural kinds? One hypothesis is that people think there is something internal to each member of the kind – an essence – that is responsible for its existence, category membership, typical properties, and other important characteristics (e.g., Atran, 1998; Gelman & Hirschfeld, 1999; Medin & Ortony, 1989). Of course, it is unlikely that people think that all categories of natural objects have a corresponding essence. There is probably no essence of pets, for example, that determines an animal's pet status. However, for basic-level categories, such as dogs or gold or daisies, it is tempting to think that something in the instance determines crucial aspects of its identity. Investigators who have accepted this hypothesis are quick to point out that the theory applies to people's beliefs and not to the natural kinds themselves. Biologists and philosophers of science agree that essentialism will not account for the properties and variations that real species display, in part because the very notion of species is not coherent (e.g., Ghiselin, 1981; Hull, 1999). Chemical kinds, for example, gold, may conform much more closely to essentialist doctrine (see Sober, 1980). Nevertheless, expert opinion is no bar to laypersons' essentialist views on this topic. In addition, psychological essentialists have argued that people probably do not have a fully fleshed out explanation of what the essence is. What they have, on this hypothesis, is an IOU for a theory: a belief that there must be *something* that plays the role of essence even though they can not supply a description of it (Medin & Ortony, 1989).

Belief in a hypothetical, minimally described essence may not seem like the sort of thing that could do important cognitive work, but psychological essentialists have pointed out a number of advantages that essences might afford, especially to children. The principal advantage may be induction potential. Medin (1989) suggested that essentialism is poor metaphysics but good epistemology in that it may lead people to expect that members of a kind will share numerous, unknown properties – an assumption that is sometimes correct. In short, essences have a motivational role to play in getting people to investigate kinds' deeper characteristics. Essences also explain why category instances seem to run true to type – for example, why the offspring of pigs grow up to be pigs rather than cows. They also explain the normative character of kinds (e.g., their ability to support inductive arguments and their ability to withstand exceptions and superficial changes) as well as people's tendency to view terms for kinds as well defined.

Evidence for essentialism tends to be indirect. There are results that show that children and adults do in fact hold the sorts of beliefs that essences can explain. By the time they reach first or second grade, children know that animals whose insides have been removed are no longer animals, that baby pigs raised by cows grow up to be pigs rather than cows (Gelman & Wellman, 1991), and that cosmetic surgery does not alter basic-level category membership (Keil, 1989). Research on adults also shows that "deeper" causes – those that themselves have few causes but many effects – tend to be more important in classifying than shallower causes (Ahn, 1998; Sloman, Love, & Ahn, 1998).

However, results like these are evidence for essence only if there are no better explanations for the same results, and it seems at least conceivable that children and adults make room for multiple types and sources of causes that are not yoked to an essence. According to Strevens (2000), for example, although people's reasoning and classifying suggest that causal laws govern natural kinds, it may be these laws alone, rather than a unifying essence, that are responsible for the findings. According to essentialists, people think there is something (an essence) that is directly or indirectly responsible for the typical properties of a natural kind. According to Strevens' minimalist alternative, people think that for each typical property there is something that causes it and that something may vary for different properties. It is important to settle this difference – the presence or absence of a unique central cause – if only because the essentialist claim is the stronger one.

Essentialists counter that both children and adults assume a causal structure consistent with essence (see Braisby, Franks, & Hampton, 1996; Diesendruck & Gelman, 1999; and Kalish, 1995, 2002, for debate on this issue). One strong piece of evidence for essentialism is that participants who have successfully learned artificial, family resemblance categories (i.e., those in which category members have no single feature in common) nevertheless believe that each category contained a common, defining property (Brooks & Wood, as cited by Ahn et al., 2001). Other studies with artificial "natural" kinds have directly compared essentialist and nonessentialist structures but have turned in mixed results (e.g., Rehder & Hastie, 2001). It is possible that explicit training overrides people's natural tendency to think in terms of a common cause.

In the absence of more direct evidence for essence, the essentialist-minimalist debate is likely to continue (see Ahn et al., 2001; Sloman & Malt, 2003; and Strevens, 2001, for the latest salvos in this dispute). Indeed, the authors of this chapter are not in full agreement. Medin finds minimalism too unconstrained, whereas Rips opines that essentialism suffers from the opposite problem. Adding a predisposition toward parsimony to the minimalist view seems like a constructive move, but such a move would shift minimalism considerably closer to essentialism. Ultimately, the issue boils down to determining to what extent causal understandings are biased toward the assumption of a unique, central cause for a category's usual properties.

SORTALISM

According to some versions of essentialism, an object's essence determines not only which category it belongs to but also the object's very identity. According to this view, it is by virtue of knowing that Fido is a dog that you know (in principle) how to identify Fido over time, how to distinguish Fido from other surrounding objects, and how to determine when Fido came into existence and when he will go out of it. In particular, if Fido happens to lose his dog essence, then Fido not only ceases to be a dog, but he also ceases to exist entirely. As we noted in discussing essentialism, not all categories provide these identity conditions. Being a pet, for example, doesn't lend identity to Fido because he may continue to survive in the wild as a nonpet. According to one influential view (Wiggins, 1980), the critical identity-lending category is the one that answers the question *What is it?* for an object, and because basic-level categories are sometimes defined in just this way, basic-level categories are the presumed source of the principles of identity. (Theories of this type usually assume that identity conditions are associated with just one category for each object because multiple identity conditions lead to contradictions; see Wiggins, 1980). Contemporary British philosophy tends to refer to such categories as *sortals*, however, and we adopt this terminology here.

Sortalism plays an important role in current developmental psychology because developmentalists have used children's mastery of principles of identity to decide whether these children possess the associated concept. In some well-known studies, Xu and Carey (1996) staged for infants a scene in which a toy duck appears from one side of an opaque screen and then returns behind it. A toy truck next emerges from the other side of the screen and then returns to its hidden position. Infants habituate after a number of encores of this performance, at which time the screen is removed to reveal both the duck and truck (the scene that adults expect) or just one of the objects (duck or truck). Xu and Carey reported that younger infants (e.g., 10-month-olds) exhibit no more surprise at seeing one object than at seeing two, whereas older infants (and adults) show more surprise at the one-object tableau. Xu and Carey also showed in control experiments that younger and older infants perform identically if they see a preview of the two starring objects together before the start of the performance. The investigators infer that the younger infants lack the concepts DUCK and TRUCK because they are unable to use a principle of identity for these concepts to discern that a duck cannot turn into a truck while behind the screen. Xu and Carey's experiments have sparked a controversy about whether the experimental conditions are simple enough to allow babies to demonstrate their grip on object identity (see Wilcox & Baillargeon, 1998; Xu, 2003), but for present purposes what is important is the assumption that infants' inability to reidentify objects over temporal gaps implies lack of the relevant concepts.

Sortal theories impose strong constraints on some versions of essentialism. We noted that one of essentialism's strong points is its ability to explain some of the normative properties of concepts – for example, the role concepts play in inductive inferences. However, sortalism places some restrictions on this ability. Members of sortal categories can not lose their essence without losing their existence, even in counterfactual circumstances. This means that if we are faced with a premise such as *Suppose dogs can bite through wire . . .*, we cannot reason about this supposition by assuming the essence of dogs has changed in such a way as to make dogs stronger. A dog with changed essence is not a superdog, according to sortalism, but rather has ceased to exist (see Rips, 2001). For the same reason, it is impossible to believe without contradiction both that basic-level categories are sortals and that objects can shift from one basic-level category to another.

These consequences of sortalism may be reasonable ones, but it is worth considering the possibility that sortalism – however well it fares as a metaphysical outlook – incorrectly describes people's views about object identity. Although objects typically do not survive a leap from one basic-level category to another, it may not be impossible for them to do so. Blok, Newman, and Rips (in press) and Liittschwager (1995) gave participants scenarios that described novel transformations that sometimes altered the basic-level category. In both studies, participants were more likely to agree that the transformed object was identical to the original if the transformational distance was small. However, these judgments could not always be predicted by basic-level membership.

Results from these sci-fi scenarios should be treated cautiously, but they suggest that people think individual objects have an integrity that does not necessarily line up with their basic-level category. Although this idea may be flawed metaphysics, it is not unreasonable as psychometaphysics. People may think that individuals exist as the result of local causal forces – forces that are only loosely tethered to basic-level kinds. As long as these forces continue to support the individual's coherence, it can exist even if it finds itself in a new basic-level category. Of course, not all essentialists buy into this link between sortalism and essentialism. For example, people might believe that an individual has both a category essence *and* a history and other characteristics that make it unique. Gutheil and Rosengren (1996) hypothesized that objects have two difference essences, one for membership and another for identity. Just how individual identity and kind identity play out under these scenarios could then be highly variable.

Domain Specificity

The notion of domain specificity has served to organize a great deal of research on conceptual development. For example, much of the work on essentialism has been conducted in the context of exploring children's naïve biology (see also Au, 1994; Carey, 1995; Gopnik & Wellman, 1994; Spelke, Phillips,

& Woodward, 1995). Learning in a given domain may be guided by certain skeletal principles, constraints, and (possibly innate) assumptions about the world (see Gelman, 2003; Gelman & Coley, 1990; Keil, 1981; Kellman & Spelke, 1983; Markman, 1990; Spelke, 1990). Carey's (1985) influential book presented a view of knowledge acquisition as built on framework theories that entail ontological commitments in the service of a causal understanding of real-world phenomena. Two domains can be distinguished from one another if they represent ontologically distinct entities and sets of phenomena and are embedded within different causal explanatory frameworks. These ontological commitments serve to organize knowledge into domains such as naive physics (or mechanics), naive psychology, or naive biology (e.g., see Au, 1994; Carey, 1995; Gelman & Koenig, 2001; Gopnik & Wellman, 1994; Hatano & Inagaki, 1994; Keil, 1994; Spelke et al., 1995; Wellman & Gelman, 1992). In the following, we focus on one candidate domain, naïve biology.

FOLK BIOLOGY AND UNIVERSALS

There is fairly strong evidence that all cultures partition local biodiversity into taxonomies whose basic level is that of the "generic species" (Atran, 1990; Berlin et al., 1973). Generic species often correspond to scientific species (e.g., elm, wolf, robin); however, for the large majority of perceptually salient organisms (see Hunn, 1999), such as vertebrates and flowering plants, a scientific genus frequently has only one locally occurring species (e.g., bear, oak). In addition to the spontaneous division of local flora and fauna into generic species, cultures seem to structure biological kinds into hierarchically organized groups, such as white oak/oak/tree. Folk biological ranks vary little across cultures as a function of theories or belief systems (see Malt, 1994, for a review). For example, in studies with Native American and various U.S. and Lowland Maya groups, correlations between folk taxonomies and classical evolutionary taxonomies of the local fauna and flora average $r = .75$ at the generic species level and about 0.5 with higher levels included (Atran, 1999; Bailenson et al., 2002; Medin et al., 2002). Much of the remaining variance owes to obvious perceptual biases (Itza' Maya group bats with birds in the same life form) and local ecological concerns. Contrary to received notions about the history and cross-cultural basis for folk biological classification, utility does *not* appear to drive folk taxonomies (cf. Berlin et al., 1973).

These folk taxonomies also appear to guide and constrain reasoning. For example, Coley, Medin, and Atran (1997) found that both Itza' Maya and U.S. undergraduates privilege the generic species level in inductive reasoning. That is, an inference from swamp white oak to all white oaks is little if any stronger than an inference from swamp white oak to all oaks. Above the level of oak, however, inductive confidence takes a sharp drop. In other words, people in both cultures treat the generic level (e.g., oak) as maximizing induction potential. The results for undergraduates are surprising because the original Rosch et al. (1976) basic-level studies had suggested that a more abstract level (e.g., TREE) acted as basic for undergraduates and should have been privileged in induction. That is, there is a discrepancy between results with undergraduates on basicness in naming, perceptual classification, and feature listing, on the one hand, and inductive inference, on the other hand. Coley et al. (1997) suggested that the reasoning task relies on expectations associated with labeling rather than knowledge and that undergraduates may know very little about biological kinds (see also Wolff, Medin, & Pankratz, 1999). Medin and Atran (in press) cautioned against generalizing results on biological thought from undergraduates because most have relatively little first-hand experience with nature.

INTERDOMAIN DIFFERENCES

One of the most contested domain distinctions, and one that has generated much research, is that between psychology and biology (e.g., Au & Romo, 1996, 1999; Carey, 1991; Coley, 1995; Gelman, 2003; Hatano

& Inagaki, 1996, 2001; Inagaki, 1997; Inagaki & Hatano, 1993, 1996; Johnson & Carey, 1998; Keil, 1995; Keil, Levin, Richman, G. Gutheil, 1999; Rosengren et al., 1991; Springer & Keil, 1989, 1991). Carey (1985) argued that children initially understand biological concepts such as ANIMAL in terms of folk psychology, treating animals as similar to people in having beliefs and desires. Others (e.g., Keil, 1989) argued that young children do have biologically specific theories, albeit more impoverished than those of adults. For example, Springer and Keil (1989) showed that preschoolers think biological properties are more likely to be passed from parent to child than are social or psychological properties. They argued that this implies that the children have a biology-like inheritance theory. The evidence concerning this issue is complex. On the one hand, Solomon, Johnson, Zaitchik, and Carey (1996) claimed that preschoolers do not have a biological concept of inheritance because they do not have an adult's understanding of the biological causal mechanism involved. On the other hand, there is growing cross-cultural evidence that 4- to 5-year-old children believe (like adults) that the category membership of animals and plants follows that of their progenitors regardless of the environment in which the progeny matures (e.g., progeny of cows raised with pigs, acorns planted with apple seeds) (Atran et al., 2001; Gelman & Wellman, 1991; Sousa et al., 2002). Furthermore, it appears that Carey's (1985) results on psychology versus biology may only hold for urban children who have little intimate contact with nature (Atran, et al., 2001; Ross et al., 2003). Altogether, the evidence suggests that 4- to 5-year-old children do have a distinct biology, although perhaps one without a detailed model of causal mechanisms (see Rozenbilt & Keil, 2002, for evidence that adults also only have a superficial understanding of mechanisms).

DOMAINS AND BRAIN REGIONS

Are these hypothesized domains associated with dedicated brain structure? There is intriguing evidence concerning category-specific deficits in which patients may lose their ability to recognize and name category members in a particular domain of concepts. For example, Nelson (1946) reported a patient who was unable to recognize a telephone, a hat, or a car but could identify people and other living things (the opposite pattern is also observed and is more common). These deficits are consistent with the idea that anatomically and functionally distinct systems represent living versus nonliving things (Sartori & Job, 1988). An alternative claim (e.g., Warrington & Shallice, 1984) is that these patterns of deficits are due to the fact that different kinds of information aid in categorizing different kinds of objects. For example, perceptual information may be relatively more important for recognizing living kinds and functional information more important for recognizing artifacts (see Devlin et al., 1998; Farah & McClelland, 1991, for computational implementations of these ideas). Although the weight of evidence appears to favor the kinds of information view (see Damasio et al., 1996; Forde & Humphreys, in press; Simmons & Barsalou, 2003), the issue continues to be debated (see Caramazza & Shelton, 1998, for a strong defense of the domain specificity view).

DOMAINS AND MEMORY

The issue of domain specificity returns us to one of earlier themes: Does memory organization depend on the meaning? We have seen that early research on semantic memory was problematic in this respect because many of the findings that investigators used to support meaning-based organization had alternative explanations. General-purpose decision processes could produce the same pattern of results even if the information they operated on was haphazardly organized. Of course, in those olden days, semantic memory was supposed to be a hierarchically organized network like that in Figure 3.1; the network clustered concepts through shared superordinates and properties but was otherwise undifferentiated. Modularity and domain specificity offer a new take on semantic-based memory structure – a partition of memory space into distinct theoretical domains. Can large-scale theories like these support memory organization in a more adequate fashion than homogeneous networks?

One difficulty in merging domain specificity with memory structure is that domain theories do not taxonomize categories – they taxonomize assumptions. What differentiates domains is the set of assumptions or warrants they make available for thinking and reasoning (see Toulmin, 1958, for one such theory), and this means that a particular category of objects usually falls in more than one domain. To put it another way, domain-specific theories are "stances" (Dennett, 1971) or "construals" (Keil, 1995) that overlap in their instances. Take the case of people. The naive psychology domain treats people as having beliefs and goals that lend themselves to predictions about actions (e.g., Leslie, 1987; Wellman, 1990). The naive physics domain treats people as having properties such as mass and velocity that warrant predictions about support and motion (e.g., Clement, 1983; McCloskey, 1983). The naive law school domain treats people as having properties, such as social rights and responsibilities, that lead to predictions about obedience or deviance (e.g., Fiddick, Cosmides, & Tooby, 2000). The naive biology domain (at least in the Western adult version) treats people as having properties such as growth and self-animation that lead to expectations about behavior and development. In short, each ordinary category may belong to many domains.

If domains organize memory, then long-term memory will have to store a concept in each of the domains to which it is related. Such an approach makes some of the difficulties of the old semantic memory more perplexing. Recall the issue of identifying the same concept across individuals (see "Concepts as Positions in Memory Structures"). Memory modules have the same problem, but they add to it the dilemma of identifying concepts *within* individuals. How do you know that PEOPLE in your psychology module is the same concept as PEOPLE in your physics module and PEOPLE in your law school module? Similarity is out (because the modules will not organize them in the same way), spelling is out (both concepts might be tied to the word "people" in an internal dictionary, but then fungi and metal forms are both tied to the word "mold"), and interconnections are out (because they would defeat the idea that memory is organized by domain). We can not treat the multiple PEOPLE concepts as independent either because it is important to get back and forth between them. For example, the rights and responsibilities information about people in your law school module has to get together with the goals and desires information about people in your psychology module in case you have to decide, together with your fellow jury members, whether the killing was a hate crime or was committed with malice aforethought.

It is reasonable to think that background theories provide premises or grounds for inferences about different topics, and it is also reasonable to think that these theories have their "proprietary concepts." However, if we take domain-specific modules as the basis for memory structure – as a new semantic memory – we also have to worry about nonproprietary concepts. We have argued that there must be such concepts because we can reason about the same thing with different theories. Multiple storage is a possibility if you are willing to forego memory economy and parsimony and if you can solve the identifiability problem that we discussed in the previous paragraph. Otherwise, these domain-independent concepts have to inhabit a memory space of their own, and modules can not be the whole story.

SUMMARY

We seem to be arriving at a skeptical position with respect to the question of whether memory is semantically organized, but we need to be clear about what is and what is not in doubt. What we doubt is that there is compelling evidence that long-term memory is structured in a way that mirrors lexical structure as in the original semantic memory models. We do not doubt that memory reflects meaningful relations among concepts, and it is extremely plausible that these relations depend to some extent on word meanings. For example, there may well be a relation in memory that links the concept TRUCKER with the concept BEER, and the existence of this link is probably due in part to the meaning of "trucker" and "beer." What is not so clear is whether memory structure directly reflects the sort of relations that, in linguistic theory, organizes the meaning of words (where, e.g., "trucker" and "beer" are probably not closely connected). We note, too, that we have not touched (and we do not take sides on) two related issues, which are themselves subjects of controversy.

One of these residual issues is whether there is a split in memory between (1) general knowledge and (2) personally experienced information that is local to time and place. *Semantic memory* (Tulving, 1972) or *generic memory* (Hintzman, 1978) is sometimes used as a synonym for general knowledge in this sense, and it is possible that memory is partitioned along the lines of this semantic/episodic difference, even though the semantic side is not organized by lexical content. The controversy in this case is how such a dual organization can handle learning of "semantic" information from "episodic" encounters (see Tulving, 1984, and his critics in the same issue of *Behavioral and Brain Sciences*, for the ins and outs of this debate).

The second issue that we are shirking is whether distributed brands of connectionist models can provide a basis for meaning-based memory. One reason for shirking is that distributed organization means that concepts such as DAISY and CUP are *not* stored according to their lexical content. Instead, parts of the content of each concept are smeared across memory in overlapping fashion. It is possible, however, that at a subconcept level – at the level of features or hidden units – memory has a semantic dimension, and we must leave this question open.

Conclusions and Future Directions

Part of our charge was to make some projections about the future of research on concepts. We do not recommend a solemn attitude toward our predictions. However, there are several trends that we have identified and, barring unforeseen circumstances (never a safe assumption), these trends should continue. One property our nominations share is that they uniformly broaden the scope of research on concepts. Here's our shortlist.

Sensitivity to Multiple Functions

The prototypical categorization experiment involves training undergraduates for about an hour and then giving transfer tests to assess what they have learned. This practice is becoming increasingly atypical, even among researchers studying artificially constructed categories in the lab. More recently, researchers have studied functions other than categorization, as well as interactions across functions. (See also Solomon et al., 1999.)

Broader Applications of Empirical Generalizations and Computational Models

As a wider range of conceptual functions comes under scrutiny, new generalizations emerge and computational models face new challenges (e.g., Yamauchi et al., 2002). Both developments set the stage for better bridging to other contexts and applications. This is perhaps most evident in the area of cognitive neuroscience, where computational models have enriched studies of multiple categorization and memory systems (and vice versa). Norman, Brooks, Coblenz, and Babcock (1992) provided a nice example of extensions from laboratory studies to medical diagnosis in the domain of dermatology.

Greater Interactions between Work on Concepts and Psycholinguistic Research

We have pressed the point that research on concepts has diverged from psycholinguistics because two different concepts of concepts seem to be in play in these fields. However, it cannot be true that the concepts we use in online sentence understanding are unrelated to the concepts we employ in reasoning and categorizing. There is an opportunity for theorists and experimenters here to provide an account of the interface between these functions. One possibility, for example, is to use sentence comprehension techniques to track the way that the lexical content of a word in speech or text is transformed in deeper processing (see Pinango, Zurif, & Jackendoff, 1999, for one effort in this direction). Another type of effort at integration is Wolff and Song's (2003) work on causal verbs and people's perception of cause in which they contrast predictions derived from cognitive linguistics with those from cognitive psychology.

Greater Diversity of Participant Populations

Although research with U.S. undergraduates at major universities will probably never go out of style (precedent and convenience are two powerful staying forces), we expect the recent increase to continue in the use of other populations. Work by Nisbett and his associates (e.g., Nisbett & Norenzayan, 2002; Nisbett, Peng, Choi, & Norenzayan, 2001) has called into question the idea that basic cognitive processes are universal, and categories and conceptual functions are basic cognitive functions. In much of the work by Atran, Medin, and their associates, undergraduates are the "odd group out" in the sense that their results deviate from those of other groups. In addition, cross-linguistic studies are often an effective research tool for addressing questions about the relationship between linguistic and conceptual development (e.g., Waxman, 1999).

More Psychometaphysics

An early critique of the theory theory is that it suffered from vagueness and imprecision. As we have seen in this review, however, this framework has led to more specific claims (e.g., Ahn's causal status hypothesis) and the positions are clear enough to generate theoretical controversies (e.g., contrast Smith, Jones, & Landau, 1996 with Gelman, 2000, and Booth & Waxman, 2002, in press, with Smith, Jones, Yoshida, & Colunga, 2003). It is safe to predict even greater future interest in these questions.

All of the Above in Combination

Concepts and categories are shared by all the cognitive sciences, and so there is very little room for researchers to stake out a single paradigm or subtopic and work in blissful isolation. Although the idea of a semantic memory uniting memory structure, lexical organization, and categorization may have been illusory, this does not mean that progress is possible by ignoring the insights on concepts that these perspectives (and others) provide. We may see further fragmentation in the concepts of concepts, but it will still be necessary to explore the relations among them. Our only firm prediction is that the work we will find most exciting will be research that draws on multiple points of view.

Acknowledgments

Preparation of this chapter was supported by grants NSF SBR 9983260 and NSF SES-9907424. The authors also want to thank Serge Blok, Rob Goldstone, Keith Holyoak, Ji Son, and Sandra Waxman for comments on an earlier version of the chapter.

References

Ahn, W-K. (1998). Why are different features central for natural kinds and artifacts?: The role of causal status in determining feature centrality. *Cognition, 69*, 135–178.

Ahn, W-K., Kalish, C., Gelman, S. A., Medin, D. L., Luhmann, C., Atran, S., Coley, J. D., & Shafto, P. (2001). Why essences are essential in the psychology of concepts. *Cognition, 82*, 59–69.

Anderson, J. R. (1990). *The adaptive character of thought*. Hillsdale, NJ: Erlbaum.

Anderson, J. R. (1991). Is human cognition adaptive? *Behavioral and Brain Sciences, 14*, 471–517.

Anderson, J. R., & Bower, G. H. (1973). *Human associative memory*. Hillsdale, NJ: Erlbaum.

Anderson, J. R., & Fincham, J. M. (1996). Categorization and sensitivity to correlation. *Journal of Experimental Psychology: Learning, Memory, and Cognition*, 22, 259–277.

Ashby, F. G., Alfonso-Reese, L. A., Turken, A. U., & Waldron, E. M. (1998). A neuropsychological theory of multiple systems in category learning. *Psychological Review*, 105, 442–481.

Ashby, F. G., & Maddox, W. T. (1993). Relations between prototype, exemplar, and decision bound models of categorization. *Journal of Mathematical Psychology*, 37, 372–400.

Atran, S. (1985). The nature of folk-botanical life forms. *American Anthropologist*, 87, 298–315.

Atran, S. (1990). *Cognitive foundations of natural history*. Cambridge, UK: Cambridge University Press.

Atran, S. (1998). Folk biology and the anthropology of science: Cognitive universals and cultural particulars. *Behavioral and Brain Sciences*, 21, 547–609.

Atran, S. (1999). Itzaj Maya folk-biological taxonomy. In D. Medin & S. Atran (Eds.), *Folk biology* (pp. 119–203). Cambridge, MA: MIT Press.

Atran, S., Medin, D., Lynch, E., Vapnarsky, V., Ucan Ek', E., & Sousa, P. (2001). Folkbiology doesn't come from folkpsychology; Evidence from Yukatek Maya in cross-cultural perspective. *Journal of Cognition and Culture*, 1, 3–42.

Au, T. K. (1994). Developing an intuitive understanding of substance kinds. *Cognitive Psychology*, 27, 71–111.

Au, T. K., & Romo, L. F. (1996). Building a coherent conception of HIV transmission. *Psychology of Learning and Motivation*, 35, 193–241.

Au, T. K., & Romo, L. F. (1999). Mechanical causality in children's "Folkbiology." In D. L. Medin & S. Atran (Eds.), *Folkbiology* (pp. 355–401). Cambridge, MA: MIT Press.

Bailenson, J. N., Shum, M., Atran, S., Medin, D. L., & Coley, J. D. (2002). A bird's eye view: Biological categorization and reasoning within and across cultures. *Cognition*, 84, 1–53.

Balota, D. A. (1994). Visual word recognition: A journey from features to meaning. In M. A. Gernsbacher (Ed.), *Handbook of psycholinguistics* (pp. 303–358). San Diego: Academic Press.

Barsalou, L. W. (1983). Ad-hoc categories. *Memory and Cognition*, 11, 211–227.

Berlin, B., Breedlove, D., & Raven, P. (1973). General principles of classification and nomenclature in folk biology. *American Anthropologist*, 75, 214–242.

Blok, S., Newman, G., & Rips, L. J. (in press). Individuals and their concepts. In W-K. Ahn, R. L. Goldstone, B. C. Love, A. B. Markman, & P. Wolff (Eds.), *Categorization inside and outside the lab*. Washington, DC: American Psychological Association.

Bloom, P. (1996). Intention, history, and artifact concepts. *Cognition*, 60, 1–29.

Bourne, L. E., Jr. (1970). Knowing and using concepts. *Psychological Review*, 77, 546–556.

Braosby, N., Franks, B., & Hampton, J. (1996). Essentialism, word use, and concepts. *Cognition*, 59, 247–274.

Brooks, L. R. (1978). Nonanalytic concept formation and memory for instances. In E. Rosch & B. B. Lloyd (Eds.), *Cognition and categorization* (pp. 169–211). New York: Wiley.

Bruner, J. S., Goodnow, J. J., & Austin, G. A. (1956). *A study of thinking*. New York: Wiley.

Burge, T. (1999). Comprehension and interpretation. In L. E. Hahn (Ed.), *The philosophy of Donald Davidson* (pp. 229–250). Chicago: Open Court.

Busemeyer, J. R., Dewey, G. I., & Medin, D. L. (1984). Evaluation of exemplar-based generalization and the abstraction of categorical information. *Journal of Experimental Psychology: Learning, Memory, and Cognition*, 10, 638–648.

Caramazza, A., & Grober, E. (1976). Polysemy and the structure of the subjective lexicon. In C. Raman (Ed.). *Semantics: Theory and Application* (pp. 181–206). Washington, DC: Georgetown University Press.

Caramazza, A., & Shelton, J. R. (1998). Domain specific knowledge systems in the brain. *Journal of Cognitive Neuroscience*, 10, 1–34.

Carey, S. (1985). *Conceptual change in childhood*. Cambridge, MA: MIT Press.

Corey, S. (1991). Knowledge acquisition. In S. Carey & R. Gelman (Eds.), *The epigenesis of mind* (pp. 257–291). Hillsdale, NJ: Erlbaum.

Carey, S. (1995). On the origin of causal understanding. In D. Sperber, D. Premack, & A. J. Premack (Eds.), *Causal cognition: A multidisciplinary debate* (pp. 268–308). New York: Oxford University Press.

Chierchia, G., & McConnell-Ginet, S. (1990). *Meaning and grammar: An introduction to semantics*. Cambridge, MA: MIT Press.

Clapper, J., & Bower, G. (2002). Adaptive categorization in unsupervised learning. *Journal of Experimental Psychology: Learning, Memory, and Cognition*, 28, 908–923.

Clement, J. (1983). A conceptual model discussed by Galileo and used intuitively by physics students. In D. Gentner & A. L. Stevens (Eds.), *Mental models* (pp. 325–340). Hillsdale, NJ: Erlbaum.

Coley, J. D. (1995). Emerging differentiation of folk biology and folk psychology. *Child Development*, 66, 1856–1874.

Coley, J. D., Medin, D. L., & Atran, S. (1997). Does rank have its privilege? *Cognition*, 64, 73–112.

Collins, A. M., & Loftus, E. F. (1975). A spreading activation theory of semantic processing. *Psychological Review*, 82, 407–428.

Collins, A. M., & Quillian, M. R. (1969). Retrieval time from semantic memory. *Journal of Verbal Learning and Verbal Behavior*, 8, 240–247.

Conrad, F. G., & Rips, L. J. (1986). Conceptual combination and the given/new distinction. *Journal of Memory and Language*, 25, 255–278.

Dennett, D. C. (1971). Intensional systems. *Journal of Philosophy*, 68, 87–106.

Diesendruck, G., & Gelman, S. A. (1999). Domain differences in absolute judgments of category membership. *Psychonomic Bulletin and Review*, 6, 338–346.

Erickson, M. A., & Kruschke, J. K. (1998). Rules and exemplars in category learning. *Journal of Experimental Psychology: General*, 127, 107–140.

Farah, M. J., & McClelland, J. L. (1991). A computational model of semantic memory impairment. *Journal of Experimental Psychology: General*, 120, 339–357.

Fiddick, L., Cosmides, L., & Tooby, J. (2000). No interpretation without representation: The role of domain-specific representations and inferences in the Wason selection task. *Cognition*, 77, 1–79.

Fillmore, C. J., & Atkins, B. T. S. (2000). Describing polysemy: The case of 'crawl.' In Y. Ravin & C. Leacock (Eds.), *Polysemy: Theoretical and computational approaches* (pp. 91–110). Oxford, UK: Oxford University Press.

Filoteo, J. V., Maddox, W. T., & Davis, J. D. (2001). A possible role of the striatum in linear and nonlinear categorization rule learning: Evidence from patients with Huntington's disease. *Behavioral Neuroscience*, 115, 786–798.

Fodor, J. (1994). Concepts: A potboiler. *Cognition*, 50, 95–113.

Fodor, J. (1998). *Concepts: Where cognitive science went wrong*. Oxford, UK: Oxford University Press.

Franks, B. (1995). Sense generation: A "quasi-classical" approach to concepts and concept combination. *Cognitive Science*, 19, 441–505.

Furnbam, A. (1995). Lay beliefs about phobia. *Journal of Clinical Psychology*, 51, 518–525.

Gagné, C. L., & Shoben, E. J. (1997). Influence of thematic relations on the comprehension of modifier-head combinations. *Journal of Experimental Psychology: Learning, Memory, and Cognition*, 23, 71–87.

Gelman, S. A. (2000). The role of essentialism in children's concepts. In H. W. Reese (Ed.), *Advances in child development and behavior* (Vol. 27, pp. 55–98). San Diego: Academic Press.

Gelman, S. A. (2003). *The essential child: Origins of essentialism in everyday thought*. Oxford, UK: Oxford University Press.

Gelman, S. A., & Coley, J. D. (1990). The importance of knowing a dodo is a bird: Categories and inferences in 2-year-old children. *Developmental Psychology*, 26(5), 796–804.

Gelman, S. A., & Hirschfeld, L. A. (1999). How biological is essentialism? In D. L. Medin & S. Atran (Eds.), *Folkbiology* (pp. 403–446). Cambridge, MA: MIT Press.

Gelman, S. A., & Koenig, M. A. (2001). The role of animacy in children's understanding of "move." *Journal of Child Language*, 28(3), 683–701.

Gelman, S. A., Star, J. R., & Flukes, J. E. (2002). Children's use of generics in inductive inference. *Journal of Cognition and Development*, 3, 179–199.

Gelman, S. A., & Wellman, H. M. (1991). Insides and essence: Early understandings of the non-obvious. *Cognition*, 38(3), 213–244.

Gleitman, L. R., & Gleitman, H. (1970). *Phrase and paraphrase*. New York: W. W. Norton.

Goldstone, R. L. (1998). Perceptual learning. *Annual Review of Psychology*, 49, 585–612.

Goldstone, R. L. (2003). Learning to perceive while perceiving to learn. In R. Kimchi, M. Behrmann, & C. Olson (Eds.), *Perceptual organization in vision: Behavioral and neural perspectives* (pp. 233–278). Mahwah, NJ: Erlbaum.

Goldstone, R. L., Lippa, Y., & Shiffrin, R. M. (2001). Altering object representations through category learning. *Cognition*, 78, 27–43.

Goldstone, R. L., & Rogosky, B. J. (2002). Using relations within conceptual systems to translate across conceptual systems. *Cognition*, 84, 295–320.

Goldstone, R. L., & Stevyers, M. (2001). The sensitization and differentiation of dimensions during category learning. *Journal of Experimental Psychology: General*, 130, 116–139.

Gopnik, A., & Wellman, H. M. (1994). The Theory Theory. In L. Hirschfeld & S. A. Gelman (Eds.), *Mapping the mind* (pp. 257–293). Cambridge, UK: Cambridge University Press.

Gutheil, G., & Rosengren, K. S. (1996). A rose by any other name: Preschoolers understanding of individual identity across name and appearance changes. *British Journal of Developmental Psychology*, 14, 477–498.

Hampton, J. (1979). Polymorphous concepts in semantic memory. *Journal of Verbal Learning and Verbal Behavior*, 18, 441–461.

Hampton, J. (1987). Inheritance of attributes in natural concept conjunctions. *Memory and Cognition*, 15, 55–71.

Hampton, J. (1997). Conceptual combination. In K. Lamberts & D. Shanks (Eds.), *Knowledge, concepts, and categories* (pp. 133–159). Cambridge, MA: MIT Press.

Hastie, R., Schroeder, C., & Weber, R. (1990). Creating complex social conjunction categories from simple categories. *Bulletin of the Psychonomic Society*, 28, 242–247.

Hatano, G., & Inagaki, K. (1994). Young children's naive theory of biology. *Cognition*, 50, 171–188.

Hatano, G., & Inagaki, K. (1996). Cognitive and cultural factors in the acquisition of intuitive biology. In D. Olson & N. Torrance (Eds.), *The handbook of education and human development* (pp. 638–708). Malden, MA: Blackwell.

Hintzman, D. L. (1978). *The psychology of learning and memory*. San Francisco: Freeman.

Hintzman, D. L. (1986). 'Schema abstraction' in a multiple-trace memory model. *Psychological Review*, 93, 411–428.

Hollander, M. A., Gelman, S. A., & Star, J. (2002). Children's interpretation of generic noun phrases. *Developmental Psychology*, 38, 883–894.

Homa, D., Sterling, S., & Trepel, L. (1981). Limitations of exemplar based generalization and the abstraction of categorical information. *Journal of Experimental Psychology: Human Learning and Memory*, 7, 418–439.

Inagaki, K. (1997). Emerging distinctions between naive biology and naive psychology. In H. M. Wellman & K. Inagaki (Eds.) *The emergence of core domains of thought* (pp. 27–44). San Francisco: Jossey-Bass.

Inagaki, K., & Hatano, G. (1993). Young children's understanding of the mind–body distinction. *Child Development*, 64, 1534–1549.

Inagaki, K., & Hatano, G. (1996). Young children's recognition of commonalities between animals and plants. *Child Development*, 67, 2823–2840.

Johansen, M. J. & Palmeri, T. J. (in press). Are there representational shifts in category learning? *Cognitive Psychology*.

Johnson, C., & Keil, F. (2000). Explanatory understanding and conceptual combination. In F. C. Keil & R. A. Wilson (Eds.), *Explanation and cognition* (pp. 327–359). Cambridge, MA: MIT Press.

Johnson, S. C., & Carey, S. (1998). Knowledge enrichment and conceptual change in folkbiology: Evidence from Williams syndrome. *Cognitive Psychology*, 37, 156–200.

Juslin, P., & Persson, M. (2002). Probabilities from Exemplars. *Cognitive Science*, 26, 563–607.

Kalish, C. W. (1995). Graded membership in animal and artifact categories. *Memory and Cognition*, 23, 335–353.

Kalish, C. W. (2002). Essentialist to some degree. *Memory and Cognition*, 30, 340–352.

Keil, F. C. (1989). *Concepts, Kinds, and Cognitive Development*. Cambridge, MA: MIT Press.

Keil, F. C. (1981). Constraints on knowledge and cognitive development. *Psychological Review*, 88(3), 197–227.

Keil, F. C. (1994). The birth and nurturance of concepts by domains: The origins of concepts of living things. In L. A. Hirschfeld & S. A. Gelman (Eds.), *Mapping the mind: Domain specificity in cognition and culture*. (pp. 234–254). Cambridge, UK: Cambridge University Press.

Keil, F. C. (1995). The growth of causal understanding of natural kinds. In D. Sperber, D. Premack, & A. J. Premack (Eds.), *Causal cognition* (pp. 234–262). Oxford, UK: Oxford University Press.

Keil, F. C., Levin, D. T., Richman, B. A., & Gutheil, G. (1999). Mechanism and explanation in the development of biological thought: The case of disease. In D. Medin & S. Atran (Eds.), *Folkbiology* (pp. 285–319). Cambridge, MA: MIT Press.

Kellman, P. J., & Spelke, E. S. (1983). Perception of partly occluded objects in infancy. *Cognitive Psychology*, 15, 483–524.

Kim, N. S., & Ahn, W. K. (2002a). Clinical psychologists' theory-based representations of mental disorders predict their diagnostic reasoning and memory. *Journal of Experimental Psychology: General*, 131, 451–476.

Kim, N. S., & Ahn, W. K. (2002b). The influence of naive causal theories on concepts of mental illness. *American Journal of Psychology*, 115, 33–65.

Klein, D. E., & Murphy, G. L. (2002). Paper has been my ruin: Conceptual relations of polysemous senses. *Journal of Memory and Language*, 47, 548–570.

Knapp, A. G., & Anderson, J. A. (1984). Theory of categorization based on distributed memory storage. *Journal of Experimental Psychology: Learning, Memory, and Cognition*, 10, 616–637.

Knowlton, B. J., Mangels, J. A., & Squire, L. R. (1996). A neostriatal habit learning system in humans. *Science*, 273, 1399–1402.

Knowlton, B. J., & Squire, L. R. (1993). The learning of categories: Parallel brain systems for item memory and category knowledge. *Science*, 262, 1747–1749.

Krifka, M., Pelletier, F. J., Carlson, G. N., ter Meulen, A., Link, G., & Chierchia, G. (1995). Genericity: An introduction. In G. N. Carlson & F. J. Pelletier (Eds.), *The generic book* (pp. 1–124). Chicago: University of Chicago Press.

Kruschke, J. K. (1992). ALCOVE: An exemplar based connectionist model of category learning. *Psychological Review*, 99, 22–44.

Kunda, Z., Miller, D. T., & Claire, T. (1990). Combining social concepts: The role of causal reasoning. *Cognitive Science*, 14, 551–577.

Lamberts, K. (1995). Categorization under time pressure. *Journal of Experimental Psychology: General*, 124, 161–180.

Landauer, T. K., & Dumais, S. T. (1997). A solution to Plato's problem: The latent semantic analysis theory of acquisition, induction, and representation of knowledge. *Psychological Review*, 104, 211–240.

Leslie, A. M. (1987). Pretense and representation: The origins of "theory of mind." *Psychological Review*, 94, 412–426.

Liittschwager, J. C. (1995). Children's reasoning about identity across transformations. *Dissertation Abstracts International*, 55(10), 4623B. (UMI No. 9508399).

Love, B. C., Markman, A. B., & Yamauchi, T. (2000). Modeling inference and classification learning. *The national conference on artificial intelligence (AAAI-2000)*, 136–141.

Love, B. C., Medin, D. L., & Gureckis, T. M. (2004). SUSTAIN: A network model of category learning. *Psychological Review*, 111, 309–332.

Lucas, M. (2000). Semantic priming without association. *Psychonomic Bulletin and Review*, 7, 618–630.

Lyons, J. (1977). *Semantics* (Vol. 2). Cambridge, UK: Cambridge University Press.

Maddox, W. T. (1999). On the dangers of averaging across observers when comparing decision bound models and generalized context models of categorization. *Perception and Psychophysics*, 61, 354–375.

Maddox, W. T. (2002). Learning and attention in multidimensional identification, and categorization: Separating low-level perceptual processes and high level decisional processes. *Journal of Experimental Psychology: Learning, Memory, and Cognition*, 28, 99–115.

Maddox, W. T., & Ashby, F. G. (1993). Comparing decision bound and exemplar models of categorization. *Perception & Psychophysics*, 53, 49–70.

Maddox, W. T., & Ashby, F. G. (1998). Selective attention and the formation of linear decision boundaries: Comment on McKinley and Nosofsky (1996). *Journal of Experimental Psychology: Human Perception and Performance*, 24, 301–321.

Malt, B. C. (1994). Water is not H-sub-2O. *Cognitive Psychology*, 27(1), 41–70.

Malt, B. C., Ross, B. H., & Murphy, G. L. (1995). Predicting features for members of natural categories when categorization is uncertain. *Journal of Experimental Psychology: Learning, Memory, and Cognition*, 21, 646–661.

Malt, B. C., Sloman, S. A., Gennari, S., Shi, M., & Wang, Y. (1999). Knowing vs. naming:

Similarity and the linguistic categorization of artifacts. *Journal of Memory and Language*, 40, 230–262.

Malt, B. C., & Smith, E. E. (1984). Correlated properties in natural categories. *Journal of Verbal Learning & Verbal Behavior*, 2, 250–269.

Markman, A. B., & Makin, V. S. (1998). Referential communication and category acquisition. *Journal of Experimental Psychology: General*, 127, 331–354.

Markman, E. M. (1990). Constraints children place on word meaning. *Cognitive Science*, 14, 57–77.

McCloskey, M. (1983). Naive theories of motion. In D. Gentuer & A. L. Stevens (Eds.), *Mental models* (pp. 299–324). Hillsdale, NJ: Erlbaum.

McCloskey, M., & Glucksberg, S. (1979). Decision processes in verifying category membership statements: Implications for models of semantic memory. *Cognitive Psychology*, 11, 1–37.

McKinley, S. C., & Nosofsky, R. M. (1995). Investigations of exemplar and decision bound models in large, ill defined category structures. *Journal of Experimental Psychology: Human Perception and Performance*, 21, 128–148.

Medin, D. (1989). Concepts and conceptual structures. *American Psychologist*, 45, 1469–1481.

Medin, D. L., Altom, M. W., Edelson, S. M., & Freko, D. (1982). Correlated symptoms and simulated medical classification. *Journal of Experimental Psychology: Learning, Memory, and Cognition*, 8, 37–50.

Medin, D. L., & Coley, J. D. (1998). Concepts and categorization. In J. Hochberg (Ed.), *Handbook of perception and cognition. Perception and cognition at century's end: History, philosophy, theory* (pp. 403–439). San Diego: Academic Press.

Medin, D. L., Lynch, E. B., & Solomon, K. O. (2000). Are there kinds of concepts? *Annual Review of Psychology*, 51, 121–147.

Medin, D. L., & Ortony, A. (1989). Psychological essentialism. In S. Vosniadou & A. Ortony (Eds.), *Similarity and analogical reasoning* (pp. 179–195). New York: Cambridge University Press.

Medin, D. L., Ross, N., Atran, S., Burnett, R. C., & Blok, S. V. (2002). Categorization and reasoning in relation to culture and expertise. In B. H. Ross (Ed.), *The psychology of learning and motivation: Advances in research and theory*, (pp. 1–41). San Diego: Academic Press.

Medin, D. L., & Schaffer, M. M. (1978). Context theory of classification learning. *Psychological Review*, 85, 207–238.

Medin, D. L., & Shoben, E. J. (1988). Context and structure in conceptual combination. *Cognitive Psychology*, 20, 158–190.

Meyer, D. E., & Schvaneveldt, R. W. (1971). Facilitation in recognizing pairs of words: Evidence of a dependence between retrieval operations. *Journal of Experimental Psychology*, 90, 227–234.

Minda, J. P., & Smith, J. D. (2001). Prototypes in category learning. *Journal of Experimental Psychology: Learning, Memory, & Cognition*, 27, 775–799.

Murphy, G. L. (1988). Comprehending complex concepts. *Cognitive Science*, 12, 529–562.

Murphy, G. L. (2002). *The big book of concepts*. Cambridge, MA: MIT Press.

Murphy, G. L., & Ross, B. H. (1994). Predictions from uncertain categorizations. *Cognitive Psychology*, 27, 148–193.

Nisbett, R., Peng, K., Choi, I., & Norenzayan, A. (2001). Culture and systems of thought: Holistic vs. analytic cognition. *Psychological Review*, 108, 291–310.

Nisbett, R. E., & Norenzayan, A. (2002). Culture and cognition. In H. Pashler & D. Medin (Eds.), *Strevens' handbook of experimental psychology, Vol. 2: Memory and cognitive processes* (3rd ed., pp. 561–597). New York: Wiley.

Norman, D. A., & Rumelhart, D. E. (1975). *Explorations in cognition*. San Francisco: W. H. Freeman.

Norman, G. R., Brooks, L. R., Coblentz, C. L., & Babcock, C. J. (1992). The correlation of teature identification and category judgements in diagnostic radiology. *Memory & Cognition*, 20, 344–355.

Nosofsky, R. M. (1986). Attention, similarity, and the identification–categorization relationship. *Journal of Experimental Psychology: General*, 115, 39–57.

Nosofsky, R. M. (1991). Tests of an exemplar model for relation perceptual classification and recognition in memory. *Journal of Experimental Psychology: Human Perception and Performance*, 17, 3–27.

Nosofsky, R. M. (1998). Dissociations between categorization and recognition in amnesic and normal individuals: An exemplar-based interpretation. *Psychological Science, 9*, 247–255.

Nosofsky, R. M., Clark, S. E., & Shin, H. J. (1989). Rules and exemplars in categorization, identification, and recognition. *Journal of Experimental Psychology: Learning, Memory, and Cognition, 15*, 282–304.

Nosofsky, R. M., & Johansen, M. K. (2000). Exemplar based accounts of "multiple system" phenomena in perceptual categorization. *Psychonomic Bulletin and Review, 7*, 375–402.

Nosofsky, R. M., & Palmeri, T. J. (1997a). An exemplar based random walk model of speeded classification. *Psychological Review, 104*, 266–300.

Nosofsky, R. M., & Palmeri, T. J. (1997b). Comparing exemplar retrieval and decision-bound models of speeded perceptual classification. *Perception and Psychophysics, 59*, 1027–1048.

Nosofsky, R. M., Palmeri, T. J., & McKinley, S. C. (1994). Rule-plus-exception model of classification learning. *Psychological Review, 101*, 53–79.

Nosofsky, R. M., & Zaki, S. R. (1998). Dissociations between categorization and recognition in amnesic and normal individuals: An exemplar based interpretation. *Psychological Science, 9*, 247–255.

Nosofsky, R. M., & Zaki, S. R. (2002). Exemplar and prototype models revisited: Response strategies, selective attention, and stimulus generalization. *Journal of Experimental Psychology: Learning, Memory, and Cognition, 28*, 924–940.

Osherson, D. N., & Smith, E. E. (1981). On the adequacy of prototype theory as a theory of concepts. *Cognition, 11*, 35–58.

Osherson, D. N., & Smith, E. E. (1982). Gradedness and conceptual combination. *Cognition, 12*, 299–318.

Palmeri, T. J. (1997). Exemplar similarity and the development of automaticity. *Journal of Experimental Psychology: Learning, Memory, and Cognition, 23*, 324–354.

Palmeri, T. J. (1999). Learning hierarchically structured categories: A comparison of category learning models. *Psychonomic Bulletin and Review, 6*, 495–503.

Palmeri, T. J., & Flanery, M. A. (1999). Learning about categories in the absence of training: Profound amnesia and the relationship between perceptual categorization and recognition memory. *Psychological Science, 10*, 526–530.

Palmeri, T. J., & Flanery, M. A. (2002). Memory systems and perceptual categorization. In B. H. Ross (Ed.), *The psychology of learning and motivation* (Vol. 41, pp. 141–189). San Diego: Academic Press.

Partee, B. H. (1995). Lexical semantics and compositionality. In L. R. Gleitman & M. Liberman (vol. eds.) & D. N. Osherson (series ed.), *Invitation to cognitive science (Vol. 1: Language*, pp. 311–360). Cambridge, MA: MIT Press.

Pinango, M. M., Zurif, E., & Jackendoff, R. (1999). Real-time processing implications of enriched composition at the syntax–semantics interface. *Journal of Psycholinguistics Research, 28*, 395–414.

Posner, M. I., & Keele, S. W. (1968). On the genesis of abstract ideas. *Journal of Experimental Psychology, 77*, 353–363.

Posner, M. I., & Keele, S. W. (1970). Retention of abstract ideas. *Journal of Experimental Psychology, 83*, 304–308.

Quillian, M. R. (1967). Word concepts: A theory and simulation of some basic semantic capabilities. *Behavioral Sciences, 12*, 410–430.

Quillian, M. R. (1969). The teachable language comprehender: A simulation program and theory of language. *Communications of the ACM, 12*, 459–476.

Reagher, G., & Brooks, L. R. (1993). Perceptual manifestations of an analytic structure: The priority of holistic individuation. *Journal of Experimental Psychology: General, 122*, 92–114.

Reber, P. J., Stark, C. E. L., & Squire, L. R. (1998a). Cortical areas supporting category learning identified using functional MRI. *Proceedings of the National Academy of Sciences of the USA, 95*, 747–750.

Reber, P. J., Stark, C. E. L., & Squire, L. R. (1998b). Contrasting cortical activity associated with category memory and recognition memory. *Learning and Memory, 5*, 420–428.

Reed, S. K. (1972). Pattern recognition and categorization. *Cognitive Psychology, 3*, 382–407.

Rehder, B., & Hastie, R. (2001). The essence of categories: The effects of underlying causal mechanisms on induction, categorization, and similarity. *Journal of Experimental Psychology: General*, 130, 323–360.

Restle, F. (1962). The selection of strategies in cue learning. *Psychological Review*, 69, 329–343.

Rips, L. J. (1995). The current status of research on concept combination. *Mind and Language*, 10, 72–104.

Rips, L. J. (2001). Necessity and natural categories. *Psychological Bulletin*, 127, 827–852.

Rips, L. J., Smith, E. E., & Shoben, E. J. (1978). Semantic composition in sentence verification. *Journal of Verbal Learning and Verbal Behavior*, 17, 375–401.

Rosch, E. (1973). On the internal structure of perceptual and semantic categories. In T. E. Moore (Ed.), *Cognitive development and the acquisition of language* (pp. 111–144). New York: Academic Press.

Rosch, E. (1978). Principles of categorization. In E. Rosch & B. B. Lloyd (Eds.), *Cognition and categorization* (pp. 27–48). Hillsdale, NJ: Erlbaum.

Rosch, E., & Mervis, C. B. (1975). Family resemblances: Studies in the internal structure of categories. *Cognitive Psychology*, 7, 573–605.

Rosch, E., Mervis, C. B., Gray, W. D., Johnson, D. M., & Boyes-Braem, P. (1976). Basic objects in natural categories. *Cognitive Psychology*, 8, 382–439.

Rosengren, K. S., Gelman, S. A., Kalish, G. W., & McCormick, M. (1995). As time goes by. *Child Development*, 62, 1302–1320.

Ross, B. H. (1997). The use of categories affects classification. *Journal of Memory and Language*, 37, 240–267.

Ross, B. H. (1999). Postclassification category use: The effects of learning to use categories after learning to classify. *Journal of Experimental Psychology: Learning, Memory, and Cognition*, 25, 743–757.

Ross, B. H. (2000). The effects of category use on learned categories. *Memory and Cognition*, 28, 51–63.

Ross, B. H., & Murphy, G. L. (1996). Category based predictions: Influence of uncertainty and feature associations. *Journal of Experimental Psychology: Learning, Memory, and Cognition*, 22, 736–753.

Ross, N., Medin, D., Coley, J. D., Atran, S. (2003). Cultural and experimental differences in the development of folkbiological induction. *Cognitive Development*, 18, 25–47.

Rozenblit, L., & Keil, F. (2002). The misunderstood limits of folk science: An illusion of explanatory depth. *Cognitive Science*, 26, 521–562.

Sartori, G., & Job, R. (1988). The oyster with four legs. *Cognitive Neurosychology*, 5, 105–132.

Schyns, P., Goldstone, R., & Thibaut, J. (1998). Development of features in object concepts. *Behavioral and Brain Sciences*, 21, 1–54.

Schyns, P., & Rodet, L. (1997). Categorization creates functional features. *Journal of Experimental Psychology: Learning, Memory, and Cognition*, 23, 681–696.

Simmons, W. K., & Barsalau, L. W. (2003). The similarity-in-topography principle. *Cognitive Neurosychology*, 20, 451–486.

Sloman, S. A., & Malt, B. (2003). Artifacts are not ascribed essences, nor are they treated as belonging to kinds. *Language and Cognitive Processes*, 18, 563–582.

Sloman, S. A., Love, B. C., & Ahn, W.-K. (1998). Feature centrality and conceptual coherence. *Cognitive Science*, 22(2), 189–228.

Smith, E. E., & Medin, D. L. (1981). *Categories and concepts*. Cambridge, MA: Harvard University Press.

Smith, E. E., Osherson, D. N., Rips, L. J., & Keane, M. (1988). Combining prototypes: A selective modification model. *Cognitive Science*, 12, 485–527.

Smith, E. E., Shoben, E. J., & Rips, L. J. (1974). Structure and process in semantic memory: A featural model for semantic decisions. *Psychological Review*, 81, 214–241.

Smith, J. D., & Minda, J. P. (1998). Prototypes in the mist: The early epochs of category learning. *Journal of Experimental Psychology: Learning, Memory and Cognition*, 24, 1411–1436.

Smith, J. D., & Minda, J. P. (2000). Thirty categorization results in search of a model. *Journal of Experimental Psychology: Learning, Memory, and Cognition*, 26, 3–27.

Smith, J. D., Murray, M. J., Jr., & Minda, J. P. (1997). Straight talk about linear seperability. *Journal of Experimental Psychology: Learning, Memory, and Cognition*, 23, 659–680.

Smith, L. B., Jones, S. S., & Landau, B. (1996). Naming in young children: A dumb attentional mechanism? *Cognition*, 60(2), 143–171.

Smith, L. B., Jones, S. S., Yoshida, H., & Colunga, E. (2003). Whose DAM account? Attentional learning explains Booth and Waxman. *Cognition*, 87(3), 209–213.

Sober, E. (1980). Evolution, population thinking, and essentialism. *Philosophy of Science*, 47, 350–383.

Solomon, G. E. A., Johnson, S. C., Zaitchik, D., & Carey, S. (1996). Like father like son. *Child Development*, 67, 151–171.

Solomon, K. O., Medin, D. L., & Lynch, E. B. (1999). Concepts do more than categorize. *Trends in Cognitive Science*, 3, 99–105.

Sousa, P., Atran, S., & Medin, D. (2002). Essentialism and folkbiology: Evidence from Brazil. *Journal of Cognition and Culture*, 2, 195–223.

Spelke, E. S. (1990). Principles of object perception. *Cognitive Science*, 14, 29–56.

Spelke, E. S., Phillips, A., & Woodward, A. L. (1995). Infants' knowledge of object motion and human section. In D. Sperber, D. Premack, & A. J. Premack (Eds.), *Causal Cognition* (pp. 44–78). New York: Oxford University Press.

Springer, K., & Keil, F. C. (1989). On the development of biologically specific beliefs: The case of inheritance. *Child Development*, 60, 637–648.

Springer, K., & Keil, F. C. (1991). Early differentiation of causal mechanisms appropriate to biological and nonbiological kinds. *Child Development*, 62, 767–781.

Stanton, R., Nosofsky, R. M., & Zaki, S. (2002). Comparisons between exemplar similarity and mixed prototype models using a linearly separable category structure. *Memory and Cognition*, 30, 934–944.

Storms, G., de Boeck, P., van Mechelen, I., & Ruts, W. (1998). No guppies, nor goldfish, but tumble dryers, Noriega, Jesse Jackson, panties, car crashes, bird books, and Stevie Wonder. *Memory and Cognition*, 26, 143–145.

Strevens, M. (2000). The essentialist aspect of naive theories. *Cognition*, 74, 149–175.

Strevens, M. (2001). Only causation matters. *Cognition*, 82, 71–76.

Toulmin, S. (1958). *The uses of argument*. Cambridge, UK: Cambridge University Press.

Trabasso, T., & Bower, G. H. (1968). *Attention in learning*. New York: Wiley.

Tulving, E. (1972). Episodic and semantic memory. In E. Tulving & W. Donaldson (Eds.), *Organization of memory* (pp. 381–403). New York: Academic Press.

Tulving, E. (1984). Precis of elements of episodic memory. *Behavioral and Brain Sciences*, 7, 223–268.

Tversky, A. (1977). Features of similarity. *Psychological Review*, 84, 327–352.

Verguts, T., Storms, G., & Tuerlinckx, F. (2001). Decision bound theory and the influence of familiarity. *Psychonomic Bulletin and Review*, 10, 141–148.

Wellman, H. M. (1990). *The child's theory of mind*. Cambridge, MA: MIT Press.

Wellman, H. M., & Gelman, S. A. (1992). Cognitive development: Foundational theories of core domains. *Annual Review of Psychology*, 43, 337–375.

Wiggins, D. (1980). *Sameness and substance*. Cambridge, MA: Harvard University Press.

Wilcox, T., & Baillargeon, R. (1998). Object individuation in infancy: The use of featural information in reasoning about occlusion events. *Cognitive Psychology*, 37, 97–155.

Wisniewski, E. J. (1997). When concepts combine. *Psychonomic Bulletin and Review*, 4, 167–183.

Wisniewski, E. J. (2002). Concepts and categorization. In D. L. Medin (Ed.), *Steven's handbook of experimental psychology* (3rd ed., pp. 467–532). Wiley: New York.

Wisniewski, E. J., & Medin, D. L. (1994). On the interaction of theory and data in concept learning. *Cognitive Science*, 18, 221–281.

Wolff, P., Medin, D., & Pankratz, C. (1999). Evolution and devolution of folkbiological knowledge. *Cognition*, 73, 177–204.

Wolff, P., & Song, G. (2003). Models of causation and the semantics of causal verbs. *Cognitive Psychology*, 47, 241–275.

Xu, F. (2003). The development of object individuation in infancy. In J. Fagen & H. Hayne (Eds.), *Progress in infancy research* (Vol. 3, pp. 159–192). Mahwah, NJ: Erlbaum.

Xu, F., & Carey, S. (1996). Infants' metaphysics: The case of numerical identity. *Cognitive Psychology*, 30, 111–153.

Yamauchi, T., Love, B. C., & Markman, A. B. (2002). Learning non-linearly separable categories by inference and classification. *Journal of Experimental Psychology: Learning, Memory, and Cognition*, 28(3), 585–593.

Yamauchi, T., & Markman, A. B. (1998). Category learning by inference and classification. *Journal of Memory and Language*, 39, 124–149.

Yamauchi, T., & Markman, A. B. (2000a). Inference using categories. *Journal of Experimental Psychology: Learning, Memory and Cognition*, 26, 776–795.

Yamauchi, T., & Markman, A. B. (2000b). Learning categories composed of varying instances: The effect of classification, inference and structural alignment. *Memory & Cognition*, 28, 64–78.

Zadeh, L. (1965). Fuzzy sets. *Information and Control*, 8, 338–353.

CHAPTER 4

Approaches to Modeling Human Mental Representations: What Works, What Doesn't, and Why

Leonidas A. A. Doumas
John E. Hummel

Relational Thinking

A fundamental aspect of human intelligence is the ability to acquire and manipulate relational concepts. Examples of relational thinking include our ability to appreciate analogies between seemingly different objects or events (e.g., Gentner, 1983; Gick & Holyoak, 1980, 1983; Holyoak & Thagard, 1995; see Holyoak, Chap. 6), our ability to apply abstract rules in novel situations (e.g., Smith, Langston, & Nisbett, 1992), our ability to understand and learn language (e.g., Kim, Pinker, Prince, & Prasada, 1991), and even our ability to appreciate perceptual similarities (e.g., Goldstone, Medin, & Gentner, 1991; Hummel, 2000; Hummel & Stankiewicz, 1996; Palmer, 1978; see Goldstone & Son, Chap. 2). Relational thinking is ubiquitous in human cognition, underlying everything from the mundane (e.g., the thought "the mug is on the desk") to the sublime (e.g., Cantor's use of set theory to prove that the cardinal number of the reals is greater than the cardinal number of the integers).

Relational thinking is so commonplace that it is easy to assume the psychological mechanisms underlying it are relatively simple. They are not. The capacity to form and manipulate relational representations appears to be a late evolutionary development (Robin & Holyoak, 1995) closely tied to the increase in the size and complexity of the frontal cortex in the brains of higher primates, especially humans (Stuss & Benson, 1986). Relational thinking also develops relatively late in childhood (see, e.g., Smith, 1989; Halford, Chap. 22). Along with language, the human capacity for relational thinking is the major factor distinguishing human cognition from the cognitive abilities of other animals (for reviews, see Holyoak & Thagard, 1995; Oden, Thompson, & Premack, 2001; Call & Tomasello, Chap. 25).

Relational Representations

Central to understanding human relational thinking is understanding the nature of the mental representations underlying it: How does the mind represent relational ideas such as "if every element of set A is paired with a distinct element of set B, and there are still elements of B left over, then the cardinal number of B is greater than the cardinal number of A," or even simple relations such as "John loves Mary" or "the magazine is next to the phone"? Two properties of human relational representations jointly make this apparently simple question surprisingly difficult to answer (Hummel & Holyoak, 1997): As elaborated in the next sections, human relational representations are both *symbolic* and *semantically rich*. Although these properties are straightforward to account for in isolation, accounting for both together has proven much more challenging.

RELATIONAL REPRESENTATIONS ARE SYMBOLIC

A symbolic representation is one that represents relations explicitly and specifies the arguments to which they are bound. Representing relations explicitly means having primitives (i.e., symbols, nodes in a network, neurons) that correspond specifically to relations and/or relational roles. This definition of "explicit," which we take to be uncontroversial (see also Halford et al., 1998; Holland et al., 1986; Newell, 1990), implies that relations are represented independently of their arguments (Hummel & Biederman, 1992; Hummel & Holyoak, 1997, 2003a). That is, the representation of a relation cannot vary as a function of the arguments it happens to take at a given time, and the representation of an argument cannot vary across relations or relational roles.[1]

Some well-known formal representational systems that meet this requirement include propositional notation, labeled graphs, mathematical notation, and computer programming languages (among many others). For example, the relation *murders* is represented in the same way (and means the same thing) in the proposition *murders* (Bill, Susan) as it is in the proposition *murders* (Sally, Robert), even though it takes different arguments across the two expressions. Likewise, "2" means the same thing in x^2 as in 2^x, even though its role differs across the two expressions. At the same time, relational representations explicitly specify how arguments are bound to relational roles. The relation "*murders* (Bill, Susan)" differs from "*murders* (Susan, Bill)" only in the binding of arguments to relational roles, yet the two expressions mean very different things (especially to Susan and Bill).

The claim that formal representational systems (e.g., propositional notation, mathematical notation) are symbolic is completely uncontroversial. In contrast, the claim that human mental representations are symbolic is highly controversial (for reviews, see Halford et al., 1998; Hummel & Holyoak, 1997, 2003a; Marcus, 1998, 2001). The best-known argument for the role of symbolic representations in human cognition – the argument from systematicity – was made by Fodor and Pylyshyn (1988). They observed that knowledge is systematic in the sense that the ability to think certain thoughts seems to imply the ability to think related thoughts. For example, a person who understands the concepts "John," "Mary," and "loves," and can understand the statement "John loves Mary," must surely be able to understand "Mary loves John." This property of systematicity, they argued, demonstrates that human mental representations are symbolic. Fodor and Pylyshyn's arguments elicited numerous responses from the connectionist community claiming to achieve or approximate systematicity in nonsymbolic (e.g., traditional connectionist) architectures (for a recent example, see Edelman & Intrator, 2003). At the same time, however, Fodor and Pylyshyn's definition of "systematicity" is so vague that it is difficult or impossible to evaluate these claims of "systematicity achieved or approximated" (van Gelder & Niklasson, 1994; for an example of the kind of confusion that has resulted from the attempt to approximate systematicity, see Edelman & Intrator, 2003, and the reply by Hummel, 2003). The concept of "systematicity" has arguably done more to cloud the debate over the role of symbolic representations in human cognition than to clarify it.

We propose that a clearer way to define symbolic competence is in terms of the ability to appreciate what different bindings of the same relational roles and fillers have in common and how they differ (see also Garner, 1974; Hummel, 2000; Hummel & Holyoak, 1997, 2003a; Saiki & Hummel, 1998). Under this definition, what matters is the ability to appreciate what "John loves Mary" has in common with "Mary loves John" (i.e., the same relations and arguments are involved) and how they differ (i.e., the role-filler bindings are reversed). It does not strictly matter whether you can "understand" the statements, or even whether they make any sense. What matters is that you can evaluate them in terms of the relations among their components. This same ability allows you to appreciate how "the glimby jolls the ronket" is similar to and different from "the ronket jolls the glimby," even though neither statement inspires much by way of understanding. To gain a better appreciation of the abstractness of this ability, note that the ronket and glimby may not even be organisms (as we suspect most readers initially assume they are) but may instead be machine parts, mathematical functions, plays in a strategy game, or anything else that can be named.

This definition of symbolic competence admits to more objective evaluation than does systematicity: one can empirically evaluate, for any f, x, and y, whether someone knows what $f(x, y)$ has in common with and how it differs from $f(y, x)$. It is also important because it relates directly to what we take to be the defining property of a symbolic (i.e., explicitly relational) representation: namely, as noted previously, the ability to represent relational roles independently of their arguments and to simultaneously specify which roles are bound to which arguments (see also Hummel, 2000, 2003; Hummel & Holyoak, 1997, 2003a). It is the independence of roles and fillers that allows one to appreciate that the glimby in "the glimby jolls the ronket" is the same thing as the glimby in "the ronket jolls the glimby"; and it is the ability to explicitly bind arguments to relational roles that allows one to know how the two statements differ. We take the human ability to appreciate these similarities and differences as strong evidence that the representations underlying human relational thinking are symbolic.

RELATIONAL REPRESENTATIONS ARE SEMANTICALLY RICH

The second fundamental property of human relational representations, and human mental representations more broadly, is that they are semantically rich. It means something to be a lover or a murderer, and the human mental representation of these relations makes this meaning explicit. As a result, there is an intuitive sense in which *loves* (John, Mary) is more like *likes* (John, Mary) than *murders* (John, Mary). Moreover, the meanings of various relations seem to apply specifically to individual relational *roles* rather than to relations as indivisible wholes. For example, it is easy to appreciate that the agent (i.e., killer) role of *murders* (x, y) is similar to the agent role of *attempted-murder* (x, y) even though the patient roles differ (i.e., the patient is dead in the former case but not the latter), and the patient role of *murder* (x, y) is like the patient role of *manslaughter* (x, y) even though the agent roles differ (i.e., the act is intentional in the former case but not the latter).

The semantic richness of human relational representations is also evidenced by their flexibility (Hummel & Holyoak, 1997). Given statements such as *taller-than* (Abe, Bill), *tall* (Charles), and *short* (Dave), it is easy to map Abe onto Charles and Bill onto Dave even though doing so requires the reasoner to violate the "n-ary restriction" (i.e., mapping the argument(s) and role(s) of an n-place predicate onto those of an m-place predicate, where $m \neq n$). Given *shorter-than* (Eric, Fred), it is also easy to map Eric onto Bill (and Dave) and Fred onto Abe (and Charles). These mappings are based on the semantics of individual roles, rather than, for instance, the fact that *taller-than* and *shorter-than* are logical opposites: The relation *loves* (x, y) is in some sense the opposite of *hates* (x, y) [or if you prefer, *not-loves* (x, y)] but in contrast to *taller-than* and *shorter-than* in which the first role of one relation maps to the second role of the other, the first role of *loves* (*x*, *y*) maps to the first role of *hates* (*x*, *y*) [or *not-loves* (*x*, *y*)]. The point is that the similarity and/or mappings of various relational roles are idiosyncratic and based not on the formal syntax of propositional notation, but on the semantic content of the individual roles in question. The semantics of relational roles matter and are an explicit part of the mental representation of relations.

The semantic properties of relational roles manifest themselves in numerous other ways in human cognition. For example, they influence both memory retrieval (e.g., Gentner, Ratterman, & Forbus, 1993; Ross, 1987; Wharton, Holyoak, & Lange, 1996) and our ability to discover structurally appropriate analogical mappings (Bassok, Wu, & Olseth, 1995; Krawczyk, Holyoak, & Hummel, in press; Kubose, Holyoak, & Hummel, 2002; Ross, 1987). They also influence which inferences seem plausible from a given collection of stated facts. For instance, upon learning about a culture in which nephews traditionally give their aunts a gift on a particular day of the year, it is a reasonable conjecture that there may also be a day on which nieces in this culture give their uncles gifts. This inference is based on the semantic similarity of aunts to uncles and nieces to nephews, and on the semantics of gift giving, not the syntactic properties of the *give-gift* relation.

In summary, human mental representations are both symbolic (i.e., they explicitly represent relations and the bindings of relational roles to their fillers) and semantically rich (in the sense that they make the semantic content of individual relational roles and their fillers explicit). A complete account of human thinking must elucidate how each of these properties can be achieved and how they work together. An account that achieves one property at the expense of the other is at best only a partial account of human thinking. The next section reviews the dominant approaches to modeling human mental representations, with an emphasis on how each approach succeeds or fails to capture these two properties of human mental representations. We review traditional symbolic approaches to mental representation, traditional distributed connectionist approaches, conjunctive distributed connectionist approaches (based on tensor products and their relatives), and an approach based on dynamic binding of distributed and localist connectionist representations into symbolic structures.

Approaches to Modeling Human Mental Representation

Symbol-Argument-Argument Notation

The dominant approach to modeling relational representations in the computational literature is based on propositional notation and formally equivalent systems (including varieties of labeled graphs and high-rank tensor representations). These representational systems – which we refer to collectively as symbol-argument-argument notation, or "SAA" – borrow conventions directly from propositional calculus and are commonly used in symbolic models based on production systems (see Lovett & Anderson, Chap. 17, for a review), many forms of graph matching (e.g., Falkenhainer et al., 1989; Keane et al., 1994) and related algorithms.

SAA represents relations and their arguments as explicit symbols and represents the bindings of arguments to relational roles in terms of the locations of the arguments in the relational expression. For example, in the proposition *loves* (John, Mary), John is bound to the *lover* role by virtue of appearing in the first slot after the open parenthesis, and Mary to the *beloved* by virtue of appearing in the second slot. Similarly, in a labeled graph the top node (of the local subgraph coding "John loves Mary") represents the *loves* relation, and the nodes directly below it represent its arguments with the bindings of arguments to roles captured, for example, by the order (left to right) in which those arguments are listed. These schemes, which may look different at first pass, are in fact isomorphic. In both cases, the relation is represented by a single symbol, and the bindings of arguments to relational roles are captured by the syntax of the notation (as list position within parentheses, as the locations of nodes in a directed graph, etc.).

Models based on SAA are meaningfully symbolic in the sense described previously: They represent relations explicitly (i.e., independently of their arguments), and they explicitly specify the bindings of relational roles to their arguments. This fact is no surprise, given that SAA is based on representational conventions that were explicitly designed to meet these criteria. However, the symbolic nature of SAA is nontrivial because it endows models based on SAA with all the advantages of symbolic representations. Most important, symbolic representations enable *relational generalization* – generalizations that are constrained by the relational roles that objects play, rather than simply the features of the objects themselves (see Holland et al., 1986; Holyoak & Thagard, 1995; Hummel & Holyoak, 1997, 2003a; Thompson & Oden, 2000). Relational generalization is important because, among other things, it makes it possible to define, match, and apply variablized rules. (It also makes it possible to make and use analogies, to learn and use schemas, and ultimately to learn variablized rules from examples; see Hummel & Holyoak, 2003a.) For example, with a symbolic representational system, it is possible to define the rule "if *loves* (*x*, *y*) and *loves* (*y*, *z*) and *not* [*loves* (*y*, *x*)], then *jealous* (*x*, *z*)" and apply that rule to any *x*, *y*, and *z* that match its left-hand ("if") side. As elaborated shortly, this important capacity, which plays an essential role in human relational thinking, lies fundamentally beyond the reach of models based on nonsymbolic representations (Holyoak & Hummel, 2000; Hummel & Holyoak, 2003a; Marcus, 1998).

Given the symbolic nature of SAA, it is no surprise that it has figured so prominently in models of relational thinking and symbolic cognition more generally (see Lovett & Anderson, Chap. 17). Less salient are the limitations of SAA. It has been known for a long time that SAA and related representational schemes have difficulty capturing shades of meaning and other subtleties associated with semantic content. This limitation was a central focus of the influential critiques of symbolic modeling presented by the connectionists in the mid-1980s (e.g., Rumelhart et al., 1986). A review of how traditional symbolic models have handled this problem (typically with external representational systems such as lookup tables or matrices of hand-coded "similarity" values between symbols; see Lovett & Anderson, Chap. 17) also reveals that the question of semantics in SAA is, in the very least, a thorny inconvenience (Hummel & Holyoak, 1997). However, at the same time, it is tempting to assume it is merely an inconvenience – that surely there exists a relatively straightforward way to add semantic coding to propositional notation and other forms of SAA and that a solution will be found once it becomes important enough for someone to pay attention to it. In the mean time, it is surely no reason to abandon SAA as a basis for modeling human cognition.

However, it turns out that it is more than a thorny inconvenience: As demonstrated by Doumas and Hummel (2004), it is logically impossible to specify the semantic content of relational roles within an SAA representation. In brief, SAA representations cannot represent relational roles explicitly and simultaneously specify how they come together to form complete relations. The reason for this limitation is that SAA representations specify role information only implicitly (see Halford et al., 1998). Specifying this information explicitly requires new propositions, which must be related to the original relational representation via a second relation. In SAA, this results in a new relational proposition, which itself implies role representations to which it must be related by a third relational proposition, and so forth, *ad infinitum*. In short, attempting to use SAA to link relational roles to their parent relations necessarily results in an infinite regress of nested "constituent of" relations specifying which roles belong to which relations/roles (see Doumas & Hummel, 2004 for the full argument). As a result, attempting to use SAA to specify how roles form complete relations renders any SAA system *ill-typed* (i.e., inconsistent and/or paradoxical; see, e.g., Manzano, 1996).

The result of this limitation is that SAA systems are forced to use external (i.e., non-SAA) structures to represent the meaning of symbols (or to approximate those meanings, e.g., with matrices of similarity values) and external control systems (which themselves cannot be based on SAA) to read the SAA, access the external structures, and relate the two. Thus, it is no surprise that SAA-based models rely on lookup tables, similarity matrices and so forth to specify how different relations and objects are semantically related to one another: It is not merely a convenience; it is a necessity.

This property of SAA sharply limits its utility as a general approach to modeling human mental representations. In particular, it means that the connectionist critiques of the mid-1980s were right: Not only do traditional symbolic representations fail to represent the semantic content of the ideas they mean to express, but the SAA representations on which they are based cannot even be adapted to do so. The result is that SAA is ill equipped, in principle, to address those aspects of human cognition that depend on the semantic content of relational roles and the arguments that fill them (which, as summarized previously, amounts to a substantial proportion of human cognition). This fact does not mean that models based on SAA (i.e., traditional symbolic models) are "wrong" but only that they are incomplete. SAA is at best only a shorthand (a *very short* hand) approximation of human mental representations.

Traditional Connectionist Representations

In response to limitations of traditional symbolic models, proponents of connectionist models of cognition (see, e.g., Elman et al., 1996; Rumelhart et al., 1986; St. John & McClelland, 1990; among many others) have proposed that knowledge is represented not as discrete symbols that enter into symbolic expressions but as patterns of activation distributed over many processing elements. These representations are distributed in the sense that (1) any single concept is represented as a pattern (i.e., vector) of activation over many elements ("nodes" or "units" that are typically assumed to correspond roughly to neurons or small collections of neurons), and (2) any single element will participate in the representation of many different concepts.[2] As a result, two patterns of activation will tend to be similar to the extent that they represent similar concepts: In contrast to SAA, distributed connectionist representations provide a natural basis for representing the semantic content of concepts. Similar ideas have been proposed in the context of latent semantic analysis (Landauer & Dumais, 1997) and related mathematical techniques for deriving similarity metrics from the co-occurrence statistics of words in passages of text (e.g., Lund & Burgess, 1996). In all these cases, concepts are represented as vectors, and vector similarity is taken as an index of the similarity of the corresponding concepts.

Because distributed activation vectors provide a natural basis for capturing the similarity structure of a collection of concepts (see Goldstone & Son, Chap. 2), connectionist models have enjoyed substantial success simulating various kinds of learning and generalization (see Munakata & O'Reilly, 2003): Having been trained to give a particular output (e.g., generate a specific activation vector on a collection of output units) in response to a given input (i.e., vector of activations on a collection of input units), connectionist networks tend to generalize automatically (i.e., activate an appropriate output vector, or a close approximation of it) in response to new inputs that are similar to trained inputs. In a sense, connectionist representations are much more flexible than symbolic representations based on varieties of SAA. Whereas models based on SAA require predicates to match exactly in order to treat them identically,[3] connectionist models generalize more gracefully based on the degree of overlap between trained patterns and new ones.

In another sense, however, connectionist models are substantially less flexible than symbolic models. The reason is that the distributed representations used by traditional connectionist models are not symbolic in the sense defined previously. That is, they cannot represent relational roles independently of their fillers and simultaneously specify which roles are bound to which fillers (Hummel & Holyoak, 1997, 2003a). Instead, a network's knowledge is represented as simple vectors of activation. Under this approach, relational roles (to the extent that they are represented at all) are either represented on separate units from their potential fillers (e.g., with one set of units for the *lover* role of the *loves* relation, another set for the *beloved* role, a third set for John, a fourth set for Mary, etc.), in which case the bindings of roles to their fillers is left unspecified (i.e., simply activating all four sets of units cannot distinguish "John loves Mary" from "Mary loves John" or even from a statement about a narcissistic hermaphrodite); or else units are dedicated to specific role-filler conjunctions (e.g., with one set of units for "John as lover" another for "John as beloved", etc.; e.g., Hinton, 1990), in which case the bindings are specified, but only at the expense of role-filler independence (e.g., nothing represents the *lover* or *beloved* roles, independently of the argument to which they happen to be bound). In neither case are the resulting representations truly symbolic.

Indeed, some proponents of traditional connectionist models (e.g., Elman et al., 1996) – dubbed "eliminative connectionists" by Pinker and Prince (1988; see also Marcus, 1998) for their explicit desire to eliminate the need for symbolic representations from models of cognition – are quite explicit in their rejection of symbolic representations as a component of human cognition. Instead of representing and matching symbolic "rules," eliminative (i.e., traditional) connectionist models operate by learning to associate vectors of features (where the features correspond to individual nodes in the network). As a result, they are restricted to generalizing based on the shared features in the training set and the generalization set. Although the generalization capabilities of these networks often appear quite impressive at first blush (especially if the training set is judiciously chosen to span the space of all possible input and output vectors; e.g., O'Reilly, 2001), the resulting models are not capable of relational generalization (see Hummel & Holyoak, 1997, 2003a; Marcus, 1998, 2001, for detailed discussions of this point).

A particularly clear example of the implications of this limitation comes from the story Gestalt model of story comprehension developed by St. John (1992; St. John & McClelland, 1990). In one computational experiment (St. John, 1992, simulation 1), the model was first trained with 1,000,000 short texts consisting of statements based on 136 constituent concepts. Each story instantiated a script such as "<person> decided to go to <destination>; <person> drove <vehicle> to <destination>" (e.g., "George decided to go to a restaurant; George drove a Jeep to the restaurant"; "Harry decided to go to the beach; Harry drove a Mercedes to the beach").

After the model had learned a network of associative connections based on the 1,000,000 examples, St. John tested its ability to generalize by presenting it with a text containing a new statement, such as "John decided to go to the airport." Although the statement as a whole was new, it referred to people, objects and places that had appeared in the examples used for training. St. John reported that when given a new example about deciding to go to the airport, the model would typically activate the restaurant or the beach (i.e., the destinations in prior examples of the same script) as the destination, rather than making the contextually appropriate inference that the person would drive to the airport. This type of error, which would appear quite unnatural in human comprehension, results from the model's inability to generalize relationally (e.g., if a person wants to go location x, then x will be the person's destination – a problem that requires the system to represent the variable x and its value, independently of its binding to the role of *desired location* or *destination*). As St. John noted, "Developing a representation to handle role binding proved to be difficult for the model" (1992, p. 294).

In general, although an eliminative connectionist model can make "inferences" on which it has been directly trained (i.e., the model will remember particular associations that have been strengthened by learning), the acquired knowledge may not generalize at all to novel instantiations that lie outside the training set (Marcus, 1998, 2001). For example, having learned that Alice loved Sam, Sam loved Betty, and Alice was jealous of Betty, and told that John loves Mary and Mary loves George, a person is likely to conjecture that John is likely to be jealous of George. An eliminative connectionist system would be a complete loss to make any inferences: John, Mary, and George are different people than Alice, Sam, and Betty (Holyoak & Hummel, 2000; Hummel & Holyoak, 2003a; Phillips & Halford, 1997).

A particularly simple example that reveals such generalization failures is the identity function (Marcus, 1998). Suppose, for example, that a human reasoner was trained to respond with "1" to "1," "2" to "2," and "3" to "3." Even with just these three examples, the human is almost certain to respond with "4" to "4," without any direct feedback that this is the correct output for the new case. In contrast, an eliminative connectionist model will be unable to make this obvious generalization. Such a model can be trained to give specific outputs to specific inputs (e.g., as illustrated in Figure 4.1). But when training is over, it will have learned only the input–output mappings on which it was trained (and perhaps those that can be represented by interpolating between trained examples; see Marcus, 1998): Because the model lacks the capacity to represent variables, extrapolation outside the training set is impossible. In other words, the model will simply have learned to associate "1" with "1," "2" with "2," and "3" with "3." A human, by contrast, will have learned to associate *input (x)* with *output (x)*, for any *x*; and doing so requires the capacity to bind any new number (whether it was in the training space or not) to the variable *x*. Indeed, most people are willing to generalize even beyond the world of numbers. We leave it to the reader to give the appropriate outputs in response to the following inputs: "A"; "B"; "flower."

The deep reason the eliminative connectionist model illustrated in Figure 4.1 fails to learn the identity function is that it violates variable/value (i.e., role/filler) independence. The input and output units in Figure 4.1 are intentionally mislabeled to suggest that they represent the concepts "1," "2," and so on. However, in fact, they do not represent these concepts at all. Instead, the unit labeled "1" in the input layer represents not "1," but "1 *as the input to the identity function*." That is, it represents a conjunctive binding of the value "1" to the variable "input to the function." Likewise, the unit labeled "1" in the output layer represents, not "1," but "1" as output of the identity function. Thus, counter to initial appearances, the concept "1" is not represented anywhere in the network. Neither, for that matter, is the concept "input to the identity function": Every unit in the input layer represents *some specific input* to the function; there are no units to represent *input* as a generic unbound variable.

Because of this representational convention (i.e., representing variable-value conjunctions instead of variables and values), traditional connectionist networks are forced to learn the identity function as a mapping from one set of conjunctive units (the input layer) to another set of conjunctive units (the output layer). This mapping, which to our eye resembles an approximation of the identity function, $f(x) = x$, is, to the network, just an arbitrary mapping. It is arbitrary precisely because the unit representing "1 as output of the function" bears no relation to the unit representing "1 as input to the function." Although any function specifies a mapping [e.g., a mapping from values of x to values of $f(x)$], learning a mapping is not the same thing as learning a function. Among other differences, a function can be universally quantified [e.g., $\forall x, f(x) = x$], whereas a finite mapping cannot; universal quantification permits the function to apply to numbers (and even nonnumbers) that lie well outside the "training" set. The point is that the connectionist model's failure to represent variables independently of their values (and vice versa) relegates it to (at best) approximating a subset of the

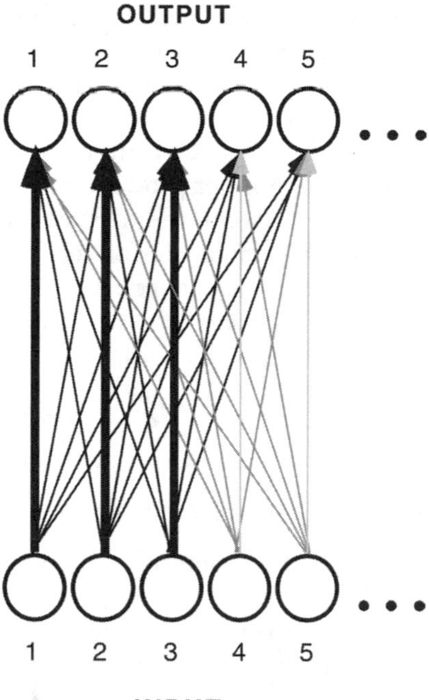

Figure 4.1. Diagram of a two-layer connectionist network for solving the identity function in which the first three units (those representing the numbers 1, 2, and 3) have been trained and the last two (those representing the numbers 4 and 5) have not. Black lines indicate already trained connections, whereas grey lines denote untrained connections. Thicker lines indicate highly excitatory connections, whereas thinner lines signify slightly excitatory or slightly inhibitory connections.

identity function as a simple, and ultimately arbitrary, mapping (see Marcus, 1998). People, by contrast, represent variables independently of their values (and vice versa) and so can recognize and exploit the decidedly nonarbitrary relation between the function's inputs and its outputs: To us, but not to the network, the function is not an arbitrary mapping at all, but rather a trivial game of "say what I say."

As these examples illustrate, the power of human reasoning and learning, most notably our capacity for sophisticated relational generalizations, is dependent on the capacity to represent relational roles (variables) and bind them to fillers (values). This is precisely the same capacity that permits composition of complex symbols from simpler ones. The human mind is the product of a symbol system; hence, any model that succeeds in eliminating symbol systems will *ipso facto* have succeeded in eliminating itself from contention as a model of the human cognitive architecture.

Conjunctive Connectionist Representations

Some modelers, recognizing both the essential role of relational representations in human cognition (e.g., for relational generalization) and the value of distributed representations, have sought to construct symbolic representations in connectionist architectures. The most common approach is based on Smolensky's (1990) tensor products (e.g., Halford et al., 1998) and its relatives, such as spatter codes (Kanerva, 1998), holographic reduced representations (HRRs; Plate, 1994), and circular convolutions (Metcalfe, 1990). We restrict our discussion to tensor products because the properties of tensors we discuss also apply to the other approaches (see Holyoak & Hummel, 2000).

A tensor product is an outer product of two or more vectors that are treated as an activation vector (i.e., rather than a matrix) for the purposes of knowledge representation (see Smolensky, 1990). In the case of a rank 2 tensor, **uv**, formed from two vectors, **u** and **v**, the activation of the *ij*th element of **uv** is simply the product of the activations of the *i*th and *j*th elements of **u** and **v**, respectively: $\mathbf{uv}_{ij} = \mathbf{u}_i\mathbf{v}_j$. Similarly, the *ijk*th value of the rank 3 tensor **uvw** is the product $\mathbf{uvw}_{ijk} = \mathbf{u}_i\mathbf{v}_j\mathbf{w}_k$, and so forth, for any number of vectors (i.e., for any rank).

Tensors and their relatives can be used to represent role-filler bindings. For example, if the *loves* relation is represented by the vector **u**, John by the vector **v**, and Mary by the vector **w**, then the proposition *loves* (John, Mary) could be represented by the tensor **uvw**; *loves* (Mary, John) would be represented by the tensor **uwv**. This procedure for representing propositions as tensors – in which the predicate is represented by one vector (here, **u**) and its argument(s) by the others (**v** and **w**) – is isomorphic with SAA (Halford et al., 1998): One entity (here, a vector) represents the relation, other entities represent its arguments, and the bindings of arguments to roles of the relation are represented spatially (note the difference between **uvw** and **uwv**). This version of tensor-based coding is SAA-isomorphic; the entire relation is represented by a single vector or symbol, and arguments are bound directly to that symbol. Consequently, it provides no basis for differentiating the semantic features of the various roles of a relation.

Another way to represent relational bindings using tensors is to represent individual relational roles as vectors, role-filler bindings as tensors, and complete propositions as sums of tensors (e.g., Tesar & Smolensky, 1994). For example, if the vector **l** represents the *lover* role of the *loves* relation, **b** the *beloved* role, **j** John and **m** Mary, then *loves* (John, Mary) would be represented by the sum **lj** + **bm**, and *loves* (Mary, John) would be the sum **lm** + **bj**.

Tensors provide a basis for representing the semantic content of relations (in the case of tensors that are isomorphic with SAA) or relational roles (in the case of tensors based on role-filler bindings) and to represent role-filler bindings explicitly. Accordingly, numerous researchers have argued that tensor products and their relatives provide an appropriate model of human symbolic representations. Halford and his colleagues also showed that tensor products based on SAA representations provide a natural account of the capacity limits of human working memory and applied these ideas to account for numerous phenomena in relational reasoning and cognitive development (see Halford, Chap. 22). Tensors are thus at least a useful approximation of human relational representations.

However, tensor products and their relatives have two properties that limit their adequacy as a general model of human relational representations. First, tensors necessarily violate role-filler independence (Holyoak & Hummel, 2000; Hummel & Holyoak, 2003a). This is true both of SAA-isomorphic tensors (as advocated by Halford and colleagues) and role-filler binding-based tensors (as advocated by Smolensky and colleagues). A tensor product is a product of two or more vectors, and so the similarity of two tensors (e.g., their inner product or the cosine of the angle between them) is equal to the *product* of the similarities of the basic vectors from which they are constructed. For example, in the case of tensors **ab** and **cd** formed from vectors **a, b, c,** and **d**:

$$\mathbf{ab} \cdot \mathbf{cd} = (\mathrm{a} \cdot \mathrm{c})(\mathrm{b} \cdot \mathrm{d}), \qquad (4.1)$$

where the "·" denotes the inner product, and

$$\cos(\mathbf{ab}, \mathbf{cd}) = \cos(\mathbf{a}, \mathbf{c})\cos(\mathbf{b}, \mathbf{d}), \qquad (4.2)$$

where cos(x, y) is the cosine of the angle between x and y.

In other words, two tensor products are similar to one another to the extent that their roles *and* fillers are similar to one another. If vectors **a** and **c** represent relations (or relational roles) and **b** and **d** represent their fillers, then the similarity of the **ab** binding to the **cd** binding is equal to the similarity of roles **a** and **c** times the similarity of fillers **b** and **d**. This fact sounds unremarkable at first blush. However, consider the case in which **a** and **c** are identical (for clarity, let us replace them both with the single vector **r**), but **b** and **d** are completely unrelated (i.e., they are orthogonal, with an inner product of zero). In this case,

$$(\mathbf{rb} \cdot \mathbf{rd}) = (\mathbf{r} \cdot \mathbf{r})(\mathbf{b} \cdot \mathbf{d}) = 0. \qquad (4.3)$$

That is, the similarity of **rb** to **rd** is zero even though both refer to the same relational role.

This result is problematic for tensor-based representations because a connectionist network (and for that matter, probably a person) will generalize learning from **rb** to **rd** to the extent that the two are similar to one another. Equation (4.3) shows that, if **b** and **d** are orthogonal, then **rb** and **rd** will be orthogonal even though they both represent bindings of different arguments to exactly the same relational role (**r**). As a result, tensor products cannot support relational generalization. The same limitation applies to all multiplicative binding schemes (i.e., representations in which the vector representing a binding is a function of the product of the vectors representing the bound elements), including HRRs, circular convolutions, and spatter codes (see Hummel & Holyoak, 2003a).

A second problem for tensor-based representations concerns the representation of the semantics of relational roles. Tensors that are SAA-isomorphic (e.g., Halford et al., 1998) fail to distinguish the semantics of different roles of the relation precisely because they are SAA-isomorphic (see Doumas & Hummel, 2004): Rather than using separate vectors to represent a relation's roles, SAA-isomorphic tensors represent the relation, as a whole, using a single vector. Role-filler binding tensors (e.g., as proposed by Smolensky and colleagues) do explicitly represent the semantic content of the individual roles of a relation. However, these representations are limited by the summing operation that is used to conjoin the separate role-filler bindings into complete propositions. The result of the summing operation is a "superposition catastrophe" (von der Malsburg, 1981) in which the original role-filler bindings – and therefore the original roles and fillers – are unrecoverable (a sum underdetermines its addends).

The deleterious effects of this superposition can be minimized by using sparse representations in a very high-dimensional space (Kanerva, 1998; Plate, 1991). This approach works because it minimizes the representational overlap between separate concepts. However, minimizing the representational overlap also minimizes the positive effects of distributed representations (which stem from the overlap between representations of similar concepts). In the limit, sparse coding becomes equivalent to localist conjunctive coding with completely separate codes for every possible conjunction of roles and fillers. In this case, there is no interference between separate bindings, but neither is there overlap between related concepts. Conversely, as the overlap between related concepts increases, so does the ambiguity of sums of separate role bindings. The ability to keep separate bindings separate thus invariably trades off against the ability to represent similar concepts with similar vectors. This trade-off is a symptom of the fact that tensors are trapped on the *implicit relations continuum* (Hummel & Biederman, 1992) – the continuum from holistic (localist) to feature-based (distributed), vector-based representations of concepts – characterizing representational schemes that fail to code relations independently of their arguments.

Role-Filler Binding by Vector Addition

What is needed is a way to both represent roles and their fillers in a distributed fashion (to capture their semantic content) and simultaneously bind roles to their fillers in a way that does not violate role-filler independence (to achieve meaningfully symbolic representation and thus relational generalization). Tensor products are on the right track in the sense that they represent relations and fillers in a distributed fashion, and they can represent role-filler bindings – just not in a way that preserves role-filler independence. Accordingly, in the search for a distributed code that preserves role-filler independence, it is instructive to consider why, mathematically, tensors violate it.

The reason is that a tensor is a product of two or more vectors, and so the value of ij^{th} element of the tensor is a function of the ith value of the role vector *and* the jth element of the filler vector. That is, a tensor is the result of a multiplicative interaction between two or more vectors. Statistically, when two or more variables do not interact – that is, when their effects are independent, as in the desired relationship between roles and their fillers – their effects are additive (rather than multiplicative). Accordingly, the way to bind a distributed vector, *r*, representing a relational role to a vector, *f*, representing its filler is not to multiply them but to add them (Holyoak & Hummel, 2000; Hummel & Holyoak, 1997, 2003a):

$$\mathbf{rf} = \mathbf{r} + \mathbf{f}, \tag{4.4}$$

where **rf** is just an ordinary vector (not a tensor).[4]

Binding by vector addition is most commonly implemented in the neural network modeling community as synchrony of neural firing (for reviews, see Hummel & Holyoak, 1997, 2003a), although it can also be realized in other ways (e.g., as systematic asynchrony for firing; Love, 1999). The basic idea is that vectors representing relational roles fire in synchrony with vectors representing their fillers and out of synchrony with other role-filler bindings. That is, at each instant in time, a vector representing a role is "added to" (fires with) the vector representing its filler.

Binding by synchrony of firing is much reviled in some segments of the connectionist modeling community. For example, Edelman and Intrator (2003) dismissed it as an "engineering convenience." Similarly, O'Reilly et al. (2003) dismissed it on the grounds that (1) it is necessarily transient [i.e., it is not suitable as a basis for storing bindings in long-term memory (LTM)], (2) it is capacity limited (i.e., it is only possible to have a finite number of bound groups simultaneously active and mutually out of synchrony; Hummel & Biederman, 1992; Hummel & Holyoak, 2003a; Hummel & Stankiewicz, 1996), and (3) bindings represented by synchrony of firing must ultimately make contact with stored conjunctive codes in LTM. These limitations do indeed apply to binding by synchrony of firing; (1) and (2) are also precisely the limitations of human working memory (WM) (see Cowan, 2000). Limitation (3) is meant to imply that synchrony is redundant: If you already have to represent bindings conjunctively in order to store them in LTM, then why bother to use synchrony? The answer is that synchrony, but not conjunctive coding, makes it possible to represent roles independently of their fillers and thus allows symbolic representations and relational generalization.

Despite the objections of Edelman and Intrator (2003), O'Reilly et al. (2003), and others, there is substantial evidence for binding by synchrony in the primate visual cortex (see Singer, 2000, for a review) and frontal cortex (e.g., Desmedt & Tomberg, 1994; Vaadia et al., 1995). It seems that evolution and the brain may be happy to exploit "engineering conveniences." This would be unsurprising given the computational benefits endowed by dynamic binding (namely, relational generalization based on distributed representations), the ease with which synchrony can be established in neural systems, and the ease with which it can be exploited (it is well known that spikes arriving in close temporal proximity have superadditive effects on the postsynaptic neuron relative to spikes arriving at very different times). The mapping between the limitations of human WM and the limitations of synchrony cited by O'Reilly et al. (2003) also constitutes indirect support for the synchrony hypothesis, as do the successes of models based on synchrony (for reviews, see Hummel, 2000; Hummel & Holyoak, 2003b; Shastri, 2003).

However, synchrony of firing cannot be the whole story. At a minimum, conjunctive coding is necessary for storing bindings in LTM and forming localist tokens of roles, objects, role-filler bindings, and complete propositions (Hummel & Holyoak, 1997, 2003a). It seems likely, therefore, that an account of the human cognitive architecture that includes both "mundane" acts (such as shape perception, which actually turns out to be relational; Hummel, 2000) and symbolic cognition (such as planning, reasoning, and problem solving) must incorporate both dynamic binding (for independent representation of roles bound to fillers in WM) and conjunctive coding (for LTM storage and token formation) and specify how they are related.

The remainder of this chapter reviews one example of this approach to knowledge representation – "LISAese," the representational format used by Hummel and Holyoak's (1992, 1997, 2003a) LISA (Learning and Inference with Schemas and Analogies) model of analogical inference and schema induction – with an emphasis on how LISAese permits symbolic representations to be composed from distributed (i.e., semantically rich) representations of roles and fillers and how the resulting representations are uniquely suited to simulate aspects

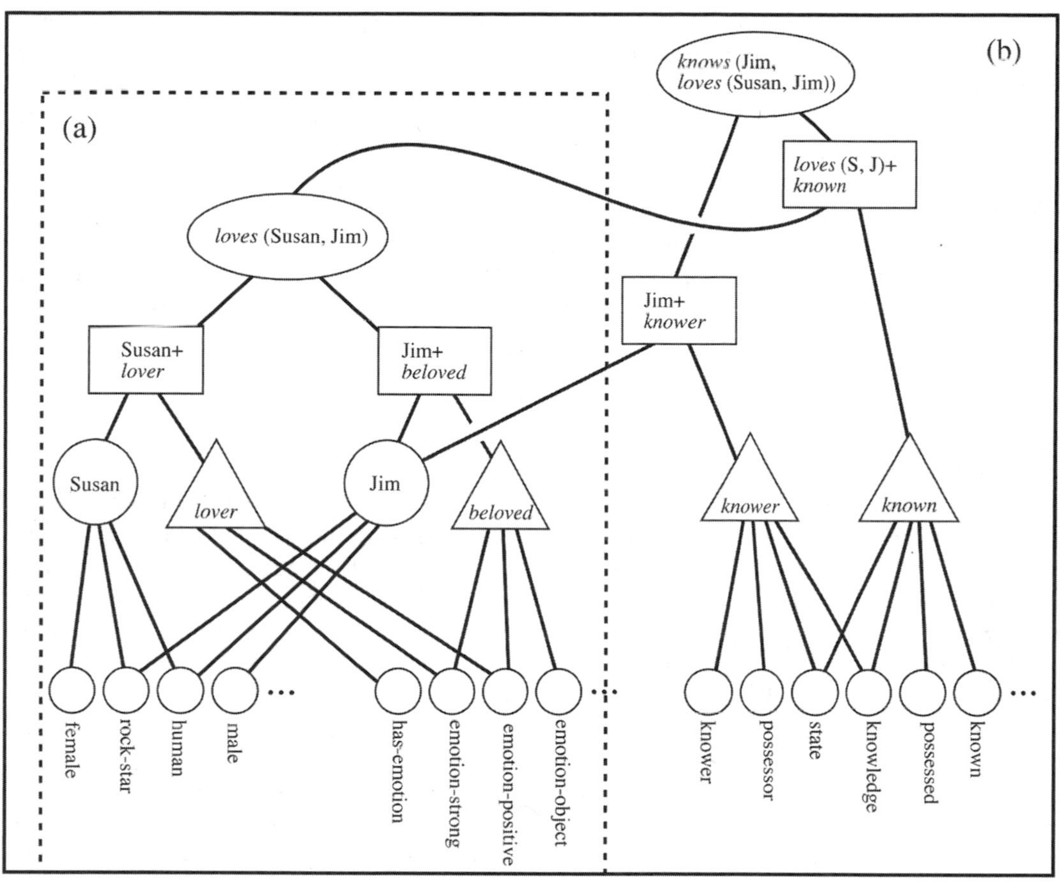

Figure 4.2. Representation of propositions in LISAese. Objects and relational roles are represented both as patterns of activation distributed over units representing semantic features (*semantic units*; small circles) and as localist units representing tokens of objects (large circles) and relational roles (triangles). Roles are bound to fillers by localist subproposition (SP) units (rectangles), and role-filler bindings are bound into complete propositions by localist proposition (P) units (ovals).
(a) Representation of *loves* (Susan, Jim). (b) Representation of *knows* [Jim, *loves* (Susan, Jim)]. When one P takes another as an argument, the lower (argument) P serves in the place of an object unit under the appropriate SP of the higher-level P unit [in this case, binding *loves* (Susan, Jim) to the SP representing what is known].

of human perception and cognition (also see Holyoak, Chap. 6).

LISAese is based on a hierarchy of distributed and localist codes that collectively represent the semantic features of objects and relational roles and their arrangement into complete propositions (Figure 4.2). At the bottom of the hierarchy, semantic units (small circles in Figure 4.2) represent objects and relational roles in a distributed fashion. For example, Jim might be represented by features such as *human*, and *male* (along with units representing his personality traits, etc.), and Susan might be represented as *human* and *female* (along with units for her unique attributes). Similarly, the *lover* and *beloved* roles of the *loves* relation would be represented by semantic units capturing their semantic content. At the next level of the hierarchy, object and predicate units (large circles and triangles in Figure 4.2) represent objects and relational roles in a localist fashion and share bidirectional excitatory connections with the corresponding semantic units. Subproposition units (SPs; rectangles in Figure 4.2) represent bindings of relational roles to their arguments [which can either be objects, as in Figure 4.2(a), or complete propositions, as in Figure 4.2(b)]. At the top of the hierarchy, separate role-filler bindings (i.e., SPs) are bound into a localist representation of the proposition as a whole via excitatory connections to a single proposition (P) unit (ovals in Figure 4.2). Representing propositions in this type of hierarchy reflects our assumption that every level of the hierarchy must be represented explicitly as an entity in its own right (see Hummel & Holyoak, 2003a). The resulting representational system is commonly referred to as a *role-filler binding* system (see Halford et al., 1998). Both relational roles and their fillers are represented explicitly, and relations are represented as linked sets of role-filler bindings. Importantly, in role-filler binding systems, relational roles, their semantics, and their bindings to their fillers are all made explicit in the relational representations themselves. As a result, role-filler binding representations are not subject to the problems inherent in SAA representations discussed previously wherein relational roles are left implicit in the larger relational structures.

A complete analog (i.e., story, situation, or event) in LISAese is represented by the collection of P, SP, predicate, object, and semantic units that code its propositional content. Within an analog, a given object, relational role, or proposition is represented by a single localist unit regardless of how many times it is mentioned in the analog [e.g., Susan is represented by the same unit in both *loves* (Susan, Jim) and *loves* (Charles, Susan)], but a given element is represented by separate localist units in separate analogs. The localist units thus represent tokens of individual objects, relations, or propositions in particular situations (i.e., analogs). A given object or relational role will tend to be connected to many of the same semantic units in all the analogs in which it is mentioned, but there may be small differences in the semantic representation, depending on context (e.g., Susan might be connected to semantics describing her profession in an analog that refers to her work and to features specifying her height in an analog about her playing basketball; see Hummel & Holyoak, 2003a). Thus, whereas the localist units represent tokens, the semantic units represent types.

The hierarchy of units depicted in Figure 4.2 represents propositions both in LISA's LTM and, when the units become active, in its WM. In this representation, the binding of roles to fillers is captured by the localist (and conjunctive) SP units. When a proposition becomes active, its role-filler bindings are also represented dynamically by synchrony of firing. When a P unit becomes active, it excites the SPs to which it is connected. Separate SPs inhibit one another, causing them to fire out of synchrony with one another. When an SP fires, it activates the predicate and object units beneath it, and they activate the semantic units beneath themselves. On the semantic units, the result is a collection of mutually desynchronized patterns of activation, one for each role binding. For example, the proposition *loves* (Susan, Jim) would be represented by two such patterns, one binding the semantic features of Susan to the features of *lover*, and the other binding Jim to *beloved*. The proposition *loves* (Jim, Susan) would be represented by the very same semantic units (as well as the same object and predicate units); only the synchrony relations would be reversed.

The resulting representations explicitly bind semantically rich representations of relational roles to representations of their fillers (at the level of semantic features, predicate and object units, and SPs) and represent complete relations as conjunctions of role-filler bindings (at the level of P units). As a result, they do not fall prey to the shortcomings of traditional connectionist representations (which cannot dynamically bind roles to their fillers), those of SAA (which can represent neither relational roles nor their semantic content explicitly), or those of tensors.

Hummel, Holyoak, and their colleagues have shown that LISAese knowledge representations, along with the operations that act on them, account for a very large number of phenomena in human relational reasoning, including phenomena surrounding memory retrieval, analogy making (Hummel & Holyoak, 1997), analogical inference, and schema induction (Hummel & Holyoak, 2003a). They provide a natural account of the limitations of human WM, ontogenetic and phylogenetic differences between individuals and species (Hummel & Holyoak, 1997), the relation between effortless ("reflexive"; Shastri & Ajjanagadde, 1993) and more effortful ("reflective") forms of reasoning (Hummel & Choplin, 2000), and the effects of frontotemporal degeneration (Morrison et al., 2004; Waltz et al., 1999) and natural aging (Viskontas et al., in press) on reasoning and memory. They also provide a basis for understanding the perceptual–cognitive interface (Green & Hummel, 2004) and how specialized cognitive "modules" (e.g., for reasoning about spatial arrays of objects) can work with the broader cognitive architecture in the service of specific reasoning tasks (e.g., transitive inference; Holyoak & Hummel, 2000) (see Hummel & Holyoak, 2003b, for a review).

Summary

An explanation of human mental representations – and the human cognitive architecture more broadly – must account both for our ability to represent the semantic content of relational roles and their fillers and for our ability to bind roles to their fillers dynamically without altering the representation of either.

Traditional symbolic approaches to cognition capture the symbolic nature of human relational representations, but they fail to specify the semantic content of roles and their fillers – a failing that, as noted by the connectionists in the 1980s, renders them too inflexible to serve as an adequate account of human mental representations, and, as shown by Doumas and Hummel (2004), appears inescapable.

Traditional distributed connectionist approaches have the opposite strengths and weaknesses: They succeed in capturing the semantic content of the entities they represent but fail to provide any basis for binding those entities together into symbolic (i.e., relational) structures. This failure renders them incapable of relational generalization.

Connectionist models that attempt to achieve symbolic competence by using tensor products and other forms of conjunctive coding as the sole basis for role-filler binding find themselves in a strange world in between the symbolic and connectionist approaches (i.e., on the implicit relations continuum) neither fully able to exploit the strengths of the connectionist approach nor fully able to exploit the strengths of the symbolic approach.

Knowledge representations based on dynamic binding of distributed representations of relational roles and their fillers (of which LISAese is an example) – in combination with a localist representations of roles, fillers, role-filler bindings, and their composition into complete propositions – can simultaneously capture both the symbolic nature and semantic richness of human mental representations. The resulting representations are neurally plausible, semantically rich, flexible, and meaningfully symbolic. They provide the basis for a unified account of human memory storage and retrieval, analogical reasoning, and schema induction, including a natural account of both the strengths, limitations, and frailties of human relational reasoning.

Acknowledgments

This work was supported by a grant from the UCLA Academic Senate. We thank Graeme Halford and Keith Holyoak for very helpful comments on an earlier draft of this chapter.

Notes

1. Arguments (or roles) may suggest different shades of meaning as a function of the roles (or fillers) to which they are bound. For example, "loves" suggests a different interpretation

in *loves* (John, Mary) than it does in *loves* (John, chocolate). However, such contextual variation does not imply in any general sense that the filler (or role) itself necessarily changes its identity as a function of the binding. For example, our ability to appreciate that the "John" in *loves (John, Mary)* is the same person as the "John" in *bites (Rover, John)* demands explanation in terms of John's invariance across the different bindings. If we assume invariance of identity with binding as the general case, then it is possible to explain contextual shadings in meaning when they occur (Hummel & Holyoak, 1997). However, if we assume lack of invariance of identity as the general case, then it becomes impossible to explain how knowledge acquired about an individual or role in one context can be connected to knowledge about the same individual or role in other contexts.

2. In the most extreme version of this account, the individual processing elements are not assumed to "mean" anything at all in isolation; rather they take their meaning only as part of a whole distributed pattern. Some limitations of this extreme account are discussed by Bowers (2002) and Page (2000).
3. For example, Falkenhainer, Forbus, and Gentner's (1989) structure matching engine (SME), which uses SAA-based representations to perform graph matching, cannot map *loves* (Abe, Betty) onto *likes* (Peter, Bertha) because *loves* and *likes* are nonidentical predicates. To perform this mapping, SME must recast the predicates into a common form, such as *has-affection-for* (Abe, Betty) and *has-affection-for* (Alex, Bertha) and then map these identical predicates.
4. At first blush, it might appear that adding two vectors where one represents a relational role and the other its filler should be susceptible to the very same problem that we faced when adding two tensors where each represented a role-filler binding, namely the superposition catastrophe. It is easy to overcome this problem in the former case, however, by simply using different sets of units to represent roles and fillers so the network can distinguish them when added (see Hummel & Holyoak, 2003a). This solution might also be applied to role-filler binding with tensors, although doing so would require using different sets of units to code different role-filler bindings. This solution would require allocating separate tensors to separate role-filler bindings, thus adding a further layer of conjunctive coding and further violating role-filler independence.

References

Bassok, M., Wu, L., & Olseth, K. L. (1995). Judging a book by its cover: Interpretive effects of content on problem-solving transfer. *Memory and Cognition*, 23, 354–367.

Bowers, J. S. (2002). Challenging the widespread assumption that connectionism and distributed representations go hand-in-hand. *Cognitive Psychology*, 45, 413–445.

Cowan, N. (2000). The magical number 4 in short-term memory: A reconsideration of mental storage capacity. *Behavioral and Brain Sciences*, 24, 87–114.

Desmedt, J., & Tomberg, C. (1994). Transient phase-locking of 40 Hz electrical oscillations in prefrontal and parietal human cortex reflects the process of conscious somatic perception. *Neuroscience Letters*, 168, 126–129.

Doumas, L. A. A., & Hummel, J. E. (2004). A fundamental limitation of symbol-argument-argument notation as a model of human relational representations. In Proceedings of the Twenty-Second Annual Conference of the Cognitive Science Society, 327–332.

Edelman, S., & Intrator, N. (2003). Towards structural systematicity in distributed, statically bound visual representations. *Cognitive Science*, 27, 73–109.

Elman, J., Bates, E., Johnson, M., Karmiloff-Smith, A., Parisi, D., & Plunkett, K. (1996). *Rethinking innateness: A connectionist perspective on development*. Cambridge, MA: MIT Press/Bradford Books.

Falkenhainer, B., Forbus, K. D., & Gentner, D. (1989). The structure mapping engine: Algorithm and examples. *Artificial Intelligence*, 41, 1–63.

Fodor, J. A., & Pylyshyn, Z. W. (1988). Connectionism and cognitive architecture. *Cognition*, 28, 3–71.

Garner, W. R. (1974). *The processing of information and structure*. Hillsdale, NJ: Erlbaum.

Gentner, D. (1983). Structure-mapping: A theoretical framework for analogy. *Cognitive Science*, 7, 155–170.

Gentner, D., Ratterman, M. J., & Forbus, K. D. (1993). The roles of similarity in transfer: Separating retrievability from inferential soundness. *Cognitive Psychology*, 25, 524–575.

Gick, M. L., & Holyoak, K. J. (1980). Analogical problem solving. *Cognitive Psychology*, 12, 306–355.

Gick, M. L., & Holyoak, K. J. (1983). Schema induction and analogical transfer. *Cognitive Psychology*, 15, 1–38.

Goldstone, R. L., Medin, D. L., & Gentner, D. (1991). Relational similarity and the nonindependence of features in similarity judgments. *Cognitive Psychology*, 23, 222–262.

Green, C. B., & Hummel, J. E. (2004). Relational perception and cognition: Implications for cognitive architecture and the perceptual-cognitive interface. In B. H. Ross (Ed.), *The psychology of learning and motivation* (Vol. 44, pp. 201–223). San Diego: Academic Press.

Halford, G. S., Wilson, W. H., & Phillips, S. (1998). Processing capacity defined by relational complexity: Implications for comparative, developmental, and cognitive psychology. *Brain and Behavioral Sciences*, 21, 803–864.

Hinton, G. E. (Ed.). (1990). *Connectionist symbol processing*. Cambridge, MA: MIT Press.

Holland, J. H., Holyoak, K. J., Nisbett, R. E., & Thagard, P. (1986). *Induction: Processes of inference, learning, and discovery*. Cambridge, MA: MIT Press.

Holyoak, K. J., & Hummel, J. E. (2000). The proper treatment of symbols in a connectionist architecture. In E. Dietrich & A. Markman (Eds.), *Cognitive dynamics: Conceptual change in humans and machines* (pp. 229–263). Hillsdale, NJ: Erlbaum.

Holyoak, K. J., & Thagard, P. (1995). *Mental leaps: Analogy in creative thought*. Cambridge, MA: MIT Press.

Hummel, J. E. (2000). Where view-based theories break down: The role of structure in shape perception and object recognition. In E. Dietrich & A. Markman (Eds.), *Cognitive dynamics: Conceptual change in humans and machines* (pp. 157–185). Hillsdale, NJ: Erlbaum.

Hummel, J. E. (2003). Effective systematicity in, effective systematicity out: A reply to Edelman & Intrator (2003). *Cognitive Science*, 27, 327–329.

Hummel, J. E., & Biederman, I. (1992). Dynamic binding in a neural network for shape recognition. *Psychological Review*, 99, 480–517.

Hummel, J. E., & Choplin, J. M. (2000). Toward an integrated account of reflexive and reflective reasoning. In *Proceedings of the twenty-second annual conference of the Cognitive Science Society*. Hillsdale, NJ: Erlbaum.

Hummel, J. E., & Holyoak, K. J. (1992). Indirect analogical mapping. *Proceedings of the 14th annual conference of the Cognitive Science Society*, 516–521.

Hummel, J. E., & Holyoak, K. J. (1997). Distributed representations of structure: A theory of analogical access and mapping. *Psychological Review*, 104, 427–466.

Hummel, J. E., & Holyoak, K. J. (2003a). A symbolic-connectionist theory of relational inference and generalization. *Psychological Review*, 110, 220–263.

Hummel, J. E., & Holyoak, K. J. (2003b). Relational reasoning in a neurally-plausible cognitive architecture: An overview of the LISA project. *Cognitive Studies: Bulletin of the Japanese Cognitive Science Society*, 10, 58–75.

Hummel, J. E., & Stankiewicz, B. J. (1996). An architecture for rapid, hierarchical structural description. In T. Inui & J. McClelland (Eds.), *Attention and performance XVI: Information integration in perception and communication* (pp. 93–121). Cambridge, MA: MIT Press.

Kanerva, P. (1998). *Sparse distributed memory*. Cambridge, MA: MIT Press.

Keane, M. T., Ledgeway, T., & Duff, S. (1994). Constraints on analogical mapping: A comparison of three models. *Cognitive Science*, 18, 387–438.

Kim, J. J., Pinker, S., Prince, A., & Prasada, S. (1991). Why no mere mortal has ever flown out to center field. *Cognitive Science*, 15, 173–218.

Krawczyk, D. C., Holyoak, K. J., & Hummel, J. E. (in press). Structural constraints and object similarity in analogical mapping and inference. *Thinking and Reasoning*.

Kubose, T. T., Holyoak, K. J., & Hummel, J. E. (2002). The role of textual coherence in incremental analogical mapping. *Journal of Memory and Language*, 47, 407–435.

Landauer, T. K., & Dumais, S. T. (1997). A solution to Plato's problem: The latent semantic analysis theory of acquisition, induction and representation of knowledge. *Psychological Review*, 104, 211–240.

Love, B. C. (1999). Utilizing time: Asynchronous binding. *Advances in Neural Information Processing Systems*, 11, 38–44.

Lund, K., & Burgess, C. (1996). Producing high-dimensional semantic spaces from lexical co-occurrence. *Behavior Research Methods, Instrumentation, and Computers*, 28, 203–208.

Manzano, M. (1996). *Extensions of first order logic*. Cambridge: Cambridge University Press.

Marcus, G. F. (1998). Rethinking eliminative connectionism. *Cognitive Psychology*, 37(3), 243–282.

Marcus, G. F. (2001). *The algebraic mind*. Cambridge, MA: MIT Press.

Metcalfe, J. (1990). Composite holographic associative recall model (CHARM) and blended memories in eyewitness testimony. *Journal of Experimental Psychology: General*, 119, 145–160.

Morrison, R. G., Krawczyk, D., Holyoak, K. J., Hummel, J. E., Chow, T., Miller, B., & Knowlton, B. J. (2004). A neurocomputational model of analogical reasoning and its breakdown in frontotemporal lobar degeneration. *Journal of Cognitive Neuroscience*, 16, 1–11.

Munakata, Y., & O'Reilly, R. C. (2003). Developmental and computational neuroscience approaches to cognition: The case of generalization. *Cognitive Studies*, 10, 76–92.

Newell, A. (1990). *Unified theories of cognition*. Cambridge, MA: Harvard University Press.

O'Reilly, R. C. (2001). Generalization in interactive networks: The benefits of inhibitory competition and Hebbian learning. *Neural Computation*, 13, 1199–1242.

O'Reilly, R. C., Busby, R. S., & Soto, R. (2003). Three forms of binding and their neural substrates: Alternatives to temporal synchrony. In A. Cleeremans (Ed.), *The unity of consciousness: Binding, integration, and dissociation* (pp. 168–192). Oxford, UK: Oxford University Press.

Oden, D. L., Thompson, R. K. R., & Premack, D. (2001). Spontaneous transfer of matching by infant chimpanzees. In D. Gentner, K. J. Holyoak, & B. N. Kokinov (Eds.), *The analogical mind* (pp. 471–497). Cambridge, MA: MIT Press.

Page, M. (2000). Connectionist modelling in psychology: A localist manifesto. *Behavioral and Brain Sciences*, 23, 443–512.

Palmer, S. E. (1978). Fundamental aspects of cognitive representation. In E. Rosch & B. B. Lloyd (Eds.), *Cognition and categorization* (pp. 259–303). Hillsdale, NJ: Erlbaum.

Phillips, S., & Halford, G. S. (1997). Systematicity: Psychological evidence with connectionist implications. In M. G. Shafto & P. Langley (Eds.), *Proceedings of the nineteenth conference of the Cognitive Science Society* (pp. 614–619). Hillsdale, NJ: Erlbaum.

Pinker, S., & Prince, A. (1988). On language and connectionism: Analysis of a parallel distributed processing model. *Cognition*, 28, 73–193.

Plate, T. (1991). Holographic reduced representations: Convolution algebra for compositional distributed representations. In J. Mylopoulos & R. Reiter (Eds.), *Proceedings of the 12th international joint conference on artificial intelligence* (pp. 30–35). San Mateo, CA: Morgan Kaufmann.

Plate, T. A. (1994). *Distributed representations and nested compositional structure*. Unpublished doctoral dissertation, Department of Computer Science, University of Toronto, Toronto, Canada.

Robin, N., & Holyoak, K. J. (1995). Relational complexity and the functions of prefrontal cortex. In M. S. Gazzaniga (Ed.), *The cognitive neurosciences* (pp. 987–997). Cambridge, MA: MIT Press.

Ross, B. (1987). This is like that: The use of earlier problems and the separation of similarity effects. *Journal of Experimental Psychology: Learning, Memory, and Cognition*, 13, 629–639.

Rumelhart, D. E., McClelland, J. L., & the PDP Research Group. (1986). *Parallel distributed processing: Explorations in the microstructure of cognition* (Vol. 1). Cambridge, MA: MIT Press.

Saiki, J., & Hummel, J. E. (1998). Connectedness and the integration of parts with relations in shape perception. *Journal of Experimental Psychology: Human Perception and Performance*, 24, 227–251.

Shastri, L. (2003). Inference in connectionist networks. *Cognitive Studies*, 10, 45–57.

Shastri, L., & Ajjanagadde, V. (1993). From simple associations to systematic reasoning: A connectionist representation of rules, variables and dynamic bindings using temporal synchrony. *Behavioral and Brain Sciences*, 16, 417–494.

Singer, W. (2000). Response synchronization, a universal coding strategy for the definition of relations. In M. S. Gazzaniga (Ed.), *The new cognitive neurosciences* (2nd ed.) (pp. 325–338). Cambridge, MA: MIT Press.

Smith, E. E., Langston, C., & Nisbett, R. E. (1992). The case for rules in reasoning. *Cognitive Science*, 16, 1–40.

Smith, L. B. (1989). From global similarities to kinds of similarities: The construction of dimensions in development. In S. Vosniadou & A. Ortoney (Eds.), *Similarity and analogical reasoning* (pp. 147–177). Cambridge, UK: Cambridge University Press.

Smolensky, P. (1990). Tensor product variable binding and the representation of symbolic structures in connectionist systems. *Artificial Intelligence*, 46, 159–216.

St. John, M. F. (1992). The story Gestalt: A model of knowledge-intensive processes in text comprehension. *Cognitive Science*, 16, 271–302.

St. John, M. F., & McClelland, J. L. (1990). Learning and applying contextual constraints in sentence comprehension. *Artificial Intelligence*, 46, 217–257.

Stuss, D., & Benson, D. (1986). *The frontal lobes*. New York: Raven Press.

Tesar, B., & Smolensky, P. (1994, August). Synchronous-firing variable binding is spatio-temporal tensor product representation. *Proceedings of the 16th annual conference of the Cognitive Science Society*, Atlanta, GA.

Thompson, R. K. R., & Oden, D. L. (2000). Categorical perception and conceptual judgments by nonhuman primates: The paleological monkey and the analogical ape. *Cognitive Science*, 24, 363–396.

Vaadia, E., Haalman, I., Abeles, M., Bergman, H., Prut, Y., Slovin, H., & Aertsen, A. (1995). Dynamics of neuronal interactions in monkey cortex in relation to behavioural events. *Nature*, 373, 515–518.

van Gelder, T. J., & Niklasson, L. (1994). On being systematically connectionist. *Mind and Language*, 9, 288–302.

Viskontas, I. V., Morrison, R. G., Holyoak, K. J., Hummel, J. E., & Knowlton, B. J. (in press). Relational integration, attention and reasoning in older adults.

von der Malsburg, C. (1981). *The correlation theory of brain function*. Internal Report 81–2. Department of Neurobiology, Max-Planck-Institute for Biophysical Chemistry, Göttingen, Germany.

Waltz, J. A., Knowlton, B. J., Holyoak, K. J., Boone, K. B., Mishkin, F. S., de Menezes Santos, M., Thomas, C. R., & Miller, B. L. (1999). A system for relational reasoning in human prefrontal cortex. *Psychological Science*, 10, 119–125.

Wharton, C. M., Holyoak, K. J., & Lange, T. E. (1996). Remote analogical reminding. *Memory and Cognition*, 24, 629–643.

Part II

REASONING

CHAPTER 5

The Problem of Induction

Steven A. Sloman
David A. Lagnado

In its classic formulation, due to Hume (1739, 1748), inductive reasoning is an activity of the mind that takes us from the observed to the unobserved. From the fact that the sun has risen every day thus far, we conclude that it will rise again tomorrow; from the fact that bread has nourished us in the past, we conclude that it will nourish us in the future. The essence of inductive reasoning lies in its ability to take us beyond the confines of our current evidence or knowledge to novel conclusions about the unknown. These conclusions may be particular, as when we infer that the next swan we see will be white, or general, as when we infer that all swans are white. They may concern the future, as in the prediction of rain from a dark cloud, or concern something in the past, as in the diagnosis of an infection from current symptoms.

Hume argued that all such reasoning is founded on the relation of cause and effect. It is this relation that takes us beyond our current evidence, whether it is an inference from cause to effect, or effect to cause, or from one collateral effect to another. Having identified the causal basis of our inductive reasoning, Hume proceeded to raise a fundamental question now known as "the problem of induction" – what are the grounds for such inductive or causal inferences? In attempting to answer this question, Hume presents both a negative and a positive argument.

In his negative thesis, Hume argued that our knowledge of causal relations is not attainable through *demonstrative* reasoning, but is acquired through past experience. To illustrate, our belief that fire causes heat, and the expectation that it will do so in the future, is based on previous cases in which one has followed the other, and not on any a priori reasoning. However, once Hume identified experience as the basis for inductive inference, he proceeded to demonstrate its inadequacy as a justification for these inferences. Put simply, any such argument requires the presupposition that past experience will be a good guide to the future, and this is the very claim we seek to justify.

For Hume, what is critical about our experience is the perceived similarity between particular causes and their effects: "From causes, which appear *similar*, we expect similar effects. This is the sum of all our experimental conclusions" (see Goldstone & Son, Chap. 2). However, this expectation cannot be grounded in reason alone because similar causes could conceivably be followed by dissimilar effects. Moreover, if one introduces hidden powers or mechanisms to explain our observations at a deeper level, the problem just gets shifted down. What guarantees that the powers or mechanisms that underlie our current experiences will do so in the future?

In short, Hume's negative argument undermines the assumption that the future will resemble the past. This assumption cannot be demonstrated a priori because it is not contradictory to imagine that the course of nature may change. However, neither can it be supported by an appeal to past experience because this would be to argue in a circle.

Hume's argument operates at two levels, both *descriptive* and *justificatory*. At the descriptive level, it suggests that there is no actual process of reflective thought that takes us from the observed to the unobserved. After all, as Hume points out, even young infants and animals make such inductions, although they clearly do not use reflective reasoning. At the justificatory level, it suggests that there is no possible line of reasoning that could do so. Thus, Hume argues both that reflective reasoning *does not* and *could not* determine our inductive inferences.

Hume's positive argument provides an answer to the descriptive question of how we *actually* pass from the unobserved to the observed but not to the justificatory one. He argues that it is custom or habit that leads us to make inferences in accordance with past regularities. Thus, after observing many cases of a flame being accompanied by heat, a novel instance of a flame creates the idea, and hence an expectation, of heat. In this way, a correspondence is set up between the regularities in the world and the expectations of the mind. Moreover, Hume maintains that this tendency is "implanted in us as an instinct" because nature would not entrust it to the vagaries of reason. In modern terms, then, we are prewired to expect past associations to hold in the future, although what is associated with what will depend on the environment we experience. This idea of a general-purpose associative learning system has inspired many contemporary accounts of inductive learning (see Buehner & Cheng, Chap. 7).

Hume's descriptive account suffers from several shortcomings. For one, it seems to assume there is an objective sense of similarity or resemblance that allows us to pass from like causes to like effects, and vice versa. In fact, a selection from among many dimensions of similarity might be necessary for a particular case. For example, to what degree and in what respects does a newly encountered object (e.g., a new type of candy bar) need to be similar to previously encountered objects for someone to expect a similar property (like a similar taste)? If we are to acquire any predictive habits, we must be able to generalize to some extent from one object to another, or to the same object at different times and contexts. How this is carried out is as much in need of a descriptive account as the problem of induction itself. Second, we might accept that no reflective reasoning can justify our inductive inferences, but this does not entail that reflective reasoning cannot be the actual cause of some of our inferences. Nevertheless, Hume presciently identified the critical role of both similarity and causality in inductive reasoning, the variables that, as we will see, are at the heart of work on the psychology of induction.

Hume was concerned with questions of both description and justification. In contrast, the logical empiricists (e.g., Carnap, 1950, 1966; Hempel, 1965; Reichenbach, 1938) focused only on justification. Having successfully provided a formal account of deductive logic (Frege, 1880; Russell & Whitehead, 1925) in which questions of deductive validity were separated from how people actually make deductive inferences (see Evans, Chap. 8), philosophers attempted to do the same for inductive inference by formulating rules for an inductive logic.

Central to this approach is the belief that inductive logic, like deductive logic, concerns the logical relations that hold between statements irrespective of their truth or falsity. In the case of inductive logic, however, these relations admit of varying strengths, a conditional probability measure reflecting the *rational* degree of belief that someone should have in a hypothesis given the available evidence. For example, the hypothesis that "all swans are white" is made probable (to degree *p*) by the evidence statement that "all swans in Central Park are white." On this basis, the logical empiricists hoped to codify and ultimately justify the principles of sound inductive reasoning.

This project proved to be fraught with difficulties, even for the most basic inductive rules. Thus, consider the rule of induction by enumeration, which states that a universal hypothesis H_1 is confirmed or made probable by its positive instances *E*. The problem is that these very same instances will also confirm a different universal hypothesis H_2 (indeed, an infinity of them), which makes an entirely opposite prediction about subsequent cases. The most notorious illustration of this point was provided by Goodman (1955) and termed "the new riddle of induction." Imagine that you have examined numerous emeralds and found them all to be colored green. You take this body of evidence *E* to confirm (to some degree) the hypothesis that "All emeralds are green." However, suppose we introduce the predicate "grue," which applies to all objects examined so far (before time *t*) and found to be green *and* to all objects not examined and blue. Given this definition and the rule that a universal hypothesis is confirmed by its positive instances, our evidence set *E* also confirms the gruesome hypothesis "All emeralds are grue." However, this is highly undesirable because each hypothesis makes an entirely different prediction as to what will happen in the future (after time *t*), when we examine a new emerald. Goodman stated this problem as one of *projectibility*: How can we justify or explain our preference to project predicates such as "green" from past to future instances, rather than predicates such as "grue"?

Many commentators object that the problem hinges on the introduction of a bizarre predicate, but the same point can be made equally well using mundane predicates or simply in terms of functions (see Hempel, 1965). Indeed, the problem of drawing a line or curve through a finite set of data points illustrates the same difficulty. Two curves C_1 and C_2 may fit the given data points equally well but diverge otherwise. According to the simple inductive rule, both are equally confirmed and yet we often prefer one curve over the other. Unfortunately, an inductive logic of the kind proposed by Carnap (1950) gives us no grounds to decide which predicate (or curve) to project.

In general, then, Goodman's (1955) problem of projectibility concerns how we distinguish projectible predicates such as "green" from nonprojectible ones such as "grue." Although he concurred with Hume's claim that induction consists of a mental habit formed by past regularities, he argued that Hume overlooked the further problem (the new riddle) of *which* past regularities are selected by this mental habit and thus projected in the future. After all, it would appear that we experience a vast range of regularities and yet are prepared to project only a small subset. Goodman himself offered a solution in terms of *entrenchment*. In short, a predicate is entrenched if it has a past history of use, where both the term itself, and the extension of the term, figure in this usage. Thus, "green" is entrenched, whereas "grue" is not because our previous history of projections involves numerous cases of the former, but none of the latter. In common with Hume, then, Goodman gave a descriptive account of inductive inference, but one grounded in the historic practices of people, and in particular their language use, rather than simply the psychology of an individual.

One shortcoming of Goodman's proposal is that it hinges on language use. Ultimately, he attempted to explain our inductive practices in terms of our linguistic practices: "the roots of inductive validity are to be found in our use of language." However, surely inductive questions, such as the problem of projectibility, arise and are solved by infants and animals without language (see Suppes, 1994). Indeed, our inductive practices may drive our linguistic practices, rather than the other way around. Moreover, Goodman ruled out, or at least overlooked, the possibility that the notions of similarity and causality are integral to the process of inductive reasoning. However, as we will see, more recent analyses suggest that these are the concepts that will give us the most leverage on the problem of induction.

In his essay, "Natural Kinds" (1970), Quine defended a simple and intuitive answer to Goodman's problem: Projectible predicates apply to members of a *kind*, a grouping formed on the basis of similarity. Thus, "green" is projectible, whereas "grue" is not because green things are more similar than grue things; that is, green emeralds form a kind, whereas grue emeralds do not. This shifts the explanatory load onto the twin notions of similarity and kind, which Quine held to be fundamental to inductive inference: "every reasonable expectation depends on similarity." For Quine, both humans and animals possess an innate standard of similarity useful for making appropriate inductions. Without this prior notion, no learning or generalization can take place.

Despite the subjectivity of this primitive similarity standard, Quine believed that its uniformity across humans makes the inductive learning of verbal behavior relatively straightforward. What guarantees, however, that our "innate subjective spacing of qualities" matches up with appropriate groupings in nature? Here, Quine appealed to an evolutionary explanation: Without such a match, and thus the ability to make appropriate inductions, survival is unlikely.

Like Hume, then, Quine proposed a naturalistic account of inductive inference, but in addition to the instinctive habit of association, he proposed an innate similarity space. Furthermore, Quine argued that this primitive notion of similarity is supplemented, as we advance from infant to adult and from savage to scientist, by ever more developed senses of "theoretical" similarity. The development of such theoretical kinds by the regrouping of things, or the introduction of entirely new groupings, arises through "trial-and-error theorizing." In Goodman's terms, novel projections on the basis of second-order inductions become entrenched if successful. Although this progress from primitive to theoretical similarity may actually engender a qualitative change in our reasoning processes, the same inductive tendencies apply throughout. Thus, whether we infer heat from a flame, or a neutrino from its path in a bubble chamber, or even the downfall of an empire from the dissatisfaction of its workers, all such inferences rest on our propensity to group kindred entities and project them into the future on this basis.

For Quine, our notions of similarity and the way in which we group things become increasingly sophisticated and abstract, culminating, he believed, in their eventual removal from mature science altogether. This conclusion seems to sit uneasily with his claims about theoretical similarity. Nevertheless, as mere humans, we will always be left with a spectrum of similarity notions and systems of kinds applicable as the context demands, which accounts for the coexistence of a variety of procedures for carrying out inductive inference, a plurality that appears to be echoed in more recent cognitive psychology (e.g., Cheng & Holyoak, 1985).

Both Goodman and Quine said little about the notion of causality. This is probably a hangover from the logical empiricist view of science that sought to avoid all reference to causal relations in favor of logical ones. Contemporary philosophical accounts have striven to reinstate the notion of causality into induction (Glymour, 2001; Lipton, 1991; Miller, 1987).

Miller (1987) and Lipton (1991) provided numerous examples of inductive inferences that depend on the supposition of, or appeal to, causal relations. Indeed, Miller proposed a definition of inductive confirmation as causal comparison: Hypotheses are confirmed by appropriate causal accounts of the data-gathering process. Armed with this notion, he claimed that Goodman's new riddle of induction is soluble. It is legitimate to project "green" but not "grue" because only "green" is consistent with our causal knowledge about color constancy and the belief that no plausible causal mechanism supports spontaneous color change. He argued that any adequate description of inductive reasoning must allow for the influence of causal beliefs. Further development of such an account, however, awaits a satisfactory theory of causality (for recent advances, see Pearl, 2000).

In summary, tracing the progress of philosophical analyses suggests a blueprint for a descriptive account of inductive reasoning – a mind that can extract relations of similarity and causality and apply them to new categories in relevant ways. In subsequent sections, we argue that this is the same picture that is emerging from empirical work in psychology.

Empirical Background

Experimental work in psychology on how people determine the projectibility of a predicate has its roots in the study of generalization in learning. Theories of learning were frequently attempts to describe the shape of a generalization gradient for a simple predicate applied to an even simpler class often defined by a single dimension. For example, if an organism learned that a tone predicts food, one might ask how the organism would respond to other tones. The function describing how a response (such as salivation) varies with the similarity of the stimulus to the originally trained stimulus is called a *generalization gradient*. Shepard (1987) argued that such functions are invariably negatively exponential in shape.

If understood as general theories of induction, such theories are necessarily reductionist in orientation. Because they only consider the case of generalization along specific dimensions that are closely tied to the senses (often spectral properties of sound or light), the assumption is, more or less explicitly, that more complex predicates can be decomposed into sets of simpler ones. The projectibility of complex predicates is thus believed to be reducible to generalization along more basic dimensions.

Reductionism of this kind is highly restrictive. It requires that there exist some fixed, fundamental set of dimensions along which all complex concepts of objects and predicates can be aligned. This requirement has been by and large rejected for many reasons. One problem is that concepts tend to arise in systems, not individually. Even a simple linguistic predicate like "is small" is construed very differently when applied to mice and when applied to elephants. Many predicates that people reason about are emergent properties whose existence depends on the attitude of a reasoning agent (consider "is beautiful" or a cloud that "looks like a mermaid"). So we cannot simply represent predicates as functions of simpler perceptual properties. Something else is needed, something that respects the information we have about predicates via the relations of objects and predicates to one another.

In the 1970s, the answer proffered was similarity (see Goldstone & Son, Chap. 2). The additional information required to project a predicate was the relative position of a category with respect to other categories; the question about one category could be decided based on knowledge of the predicate's relation to other (similar) categories (see Medin & Rips, Chap. 3). Prior to the 1970s, similarity had generally been construed as a distance in a fairly low-dimensional space (Shepard, 1980). In 1977, Tversky proposed a new measure that posited that similarity could be computed over a large number of dimensions, that both common and distinctive features were essential to determine the similarity between any pair of objects, and, critically, that the set of features used to measure similarity were context dependent. Features depended on their diagnosticity in the set of objects being compared and on the specific task used to measure similarity. Tversky's contrast model of similarity would, it was hoped, prove to have sufficient representational power to model a number of cognitive tasks, including categorization and induction.

The value of representing category structure in terms of similarity was reinforced by Rosch's (1973) efforts to construct a similarity-based framework for understanding natural categories. Her seminal work on the typicality structure of categories and on the basic level of hierarchical category structure provided the empirical basis for her arguments that categories were mentally represented in a way that carved the world at its joints. She imagined categories as clusters in a vast high-dimensional similarity space that were devised to maximize the similarity within a cluster and minimize the similarity between clusters. Her belief that the structure of this similarity space was given by the world and was not simply a matter of subjective opinion implies that the similarity space contains a lot of information that can be used for a number of tasks, including inductive inference.

Rosch (1978) suggested that the main purpose of category structure was to provide the evidential base for relating predicates to categories. She attempted to motivate the basic level as the level of hierarchical structure that maximized the usefulness of a cue for choosing a category, what she called *cue validity*, the probability of a category given a cue. Basic-level categories were presumed to maximize cue validity by virtue of being highly differentiated; members of a basic-level category have more common attributes than members of a superordinate, and they have fewer common attributes with other categories than do members of a subordinate. Murphy (1982) observed, however, that this will not work. The category with maximum probability given a cue is the most general category possible ("entity"), whose probability is 1 (or at least close to it). However, Rosch's idea can be elaborated using a measure of inductive projectibility in a way that succeeds in picking out the basic level. If the level of a hierarchy is selected by appealing to the inductive potential of the category, say by maximizing category validity, the probability of a specific feature given a category, then one is driven in the opposite direction of cue validity, namely to the most specific level. Given a particular feature, one is pretty much guaranteed to choose a category with that feature by choosing a specific object known to have the feature. By trading off category and cue validity, the usefulness of a category for predicting a feature and of a feature for predicting a category, one can arrive at an intermediate level of hierarchical structure. Jones (1983) made this suggestion, calling it a measure of "collocation." A more sophisticated information-theoretic analysis along these lines is presented in Corter and Gluck (1992) and Fisher (1987).

Another quite different but complementary line of work going on at about the same time as Rosch's, with related implications for inductive inference, was Tversky and Kahneman's (1974) development of the representativeness heuristic of probability and frequency judgment. The representativeness heuristic is essentially the idea that categorical knowledge is used to make probability judgments (see Kahneman & Frederick, Chap. 12). In that sense, it is an extension of Rosch's insights about category structure. She showed that similarity was a guiding principle in decisions about category membership; Kahneman and Tversky showed that probability judgment could, in some cases, be understood as a process of categorization driven by similarity. To illustrate, Linda is judged more likely to be a feminist bankteller than a bankteller (despite the conjunction rule of probability that disallows this conclusion) if she has characteristic feminist traits (i.e., if she seems like she is a member of the category of feminists).

In sum, the importance of similarity for how people make inductive inferences was recognized in the 1970s in the study of natural category structure and probability judgment and manifested in the development of models of similarity. Rips (1975) put these strands together in the development of a categorical induction task. He told people that all members of a particular species of animal on a small island had a particular contagious disease and asked participants to guess what proportion of other species would also have the disease. For example, if all rabbits have it, what proportion of dogs would? Rips found that judgments went up with the similarity of the two categories and with the typicality of the first (premise) category.

Relatively little work on categorical induction was performed by cognitive psychologists immediately following Rips's seminal work. Instead, the banner was pursued by developmental psychologists such as

Carey (1985). She focused on the theoretical schema that children learn through development and how they use those schema to make inductive inferences across categories. In particular, she showed that adults and 10-year-olds used general biological knowledge to guide their inductions about novel animal properties, whereas small children based their inductions on knowledge about humans. Gelman and Markman (1986) argued that children prefer to make inductive inferences using category structure rather than superficial similarity. However, it was the theoretical discussion and mathematical models of Osherson and his colleagues, discussed in what follows, that led to an explosion of interest by cognitive psychologists with a resulting menu of models and phenomena to constrain them.

Scope of Chapter

To limit the scope of this chapter, in the remainder we focus exclusively on the psychology of categorical induction: How people arrive at a statement of their confidence that a conclusion category has a predicate after being told that one or more premise categories do. As Goodman's (1955) analysis makes clear, this is a very general problem. Nevertheless, we do not address a number of issues related to induction. For example, we do not address how people go about selecting evidence to support a hypothesis (see Doherty et al., 1996; Klayman & Ha, 1987; Oaksford & Chater, 1994). We do not address how people discover hypotheses but rather focus only on their degree of certainty in a prespecified hypothesis (cf. the distinction between the contexts of discovery and confirmation; Reichenbach, 1938). This rules out a variety of work on the topic of hypothesis discovery (e.g., Klahr, 2000; Klayman, 1988). Relatedly, we do not cover the variety of work on the topic of cue learning, that is, how people learn the predictive or diagnostic value of stimuli (see Buehner & Cheng, Chap. 7).

Most of our discussion concerns the evaluation of categorical arguments, such as

Boys use GABA as a neurotransmitter.
Therefore, girls use GABA as a neurotransmitter.

that can be written schematically as a list of sentences:

$$P_1 \ldots P_n / C \qquad (5.1)$$

in which the P_i are the premises of an argument and C is the conclusion. Each statement includes a category (e.g., boys) to which is applied a predicate (e.g., use GABA as a neurotransmitter). In most of the examples discussed, the categories will vary across statements, whereas the predicate will remain constant. The general question will be how people go about determining their belief in the conclusion of such an argument after being told that the premises are true. We discuss this question both by trying to describe human judgment as a set of phenomena and by trying to explain the existence of these phenomena in terms of more fundamental and more general principles. The phenomena will concern judgments of the strength of categorical arguments or the convincingness of an argument or some other measure of belief in the conclusion once the premises are given (reviewed by Heit, 2000).

One way to represent the problem we address is in terms of conditional probability. The issue can be construed in terms of how people make judgments of the following form:

$$\text{P(Category C has some property} \mid \text{Categories } P_1 \ldots P_n \text{ have the property)}$$

Indeed, some of the tasks we discuss involve a conditional probability judgment explicitly. But even those that do not, such as argument strength, can be directly related to judgments of conditional probability.

Most of the experimental work we address attempts to restrict attention to how people use categories to reason by minimizing the role of the predicate in the reasoning process. To achieve this, arguments are usually restricted to "blank" predicates – predicates that use relatively unfamiliar terms (e.g., "use GABA as a neurotransmitter") so they do not contribute much to how people reason about the arguments (Osherson, Smith, Wilkie, López, & Shafir, 1990). They do contribute some, however. For instance, all the predicates applied to animals are obviously biological in nature, thus suggesting that the relevant properties for reasoning are biological. Lo, Sides, Rozelle, and Osherson (2002) characterized blank predicates as "indefinite in their application to given categories, but clear enough to communicate the kind of property in question" (p. 183).

Philosophers such as Carnap (1950) and Hacking (2001) have distinguished intensional and extensional representations of probability (sometimes called epistemic vs. aleatory representations). Correspondingly, in psychology we can distinguish modes of inference that depend on assessment of similarity structure and modes that depend on analyses of set structure [see Lagnado & Sloman, (2004), for an analysis of the correspondence between the philosophical and psychological distinctions]. We refer to the former as the inside view of category structure and the latter as the outside view (Sloman & Over, 2003; Tversky & Kahneman, 1983). In this chapter, we focus on induction from the inside via similarity structure. We thus neglect a host of work concerning, for example, how people make conditional probability judgments in the context of well-defined sample spaces (e.g., Johnson-Laird et al., 1999), reasoning using explicit statistical information (e.g., Nisbett, 1993), and the relative advantages of different kinds of representational format (e.g., Tversky & Kahneman, 1983).

Two Theoretical Approaches to Inductive Reasoning

A number of theoretical approaches have been taken to the problem of categorical induction in psychology. Using broad strokes, the approaches can be classified into two groups: *similarity-based induction* and *induction as scientific methodology*. We discuss each in turn. As becomes clear, the approaches are not mutually exclusive both because they overlap and because they sometimes speak at different levels of abstraction.

Similarity-Based Induction

Perhaps the most obvious and robust predictor of inductive strength is similarity. In the simplest case, most people are willing to project a property known to be true of (say) crocodiles to a very similar class, such as alligators, with some degree of confidence. Such willingness exists either because similarity is a mechanism of induction (Osherson et al., 1990) or because induction and similarity judgment have some common antecedent (Sloman, 1993). From the scores of examples of the representativeness heuristic at work (Tversky & Kahneman, 1974) through Rosch's (1973) analysis of typicality in terms of similarity, a strong correlation between probability and similarity is more the rule than the exception. The argument has been made that similarity is not a real explanation at all (Goodman, 1972; see the review in Sloman & Rips, 1998) and phenomena exist that contradict prediction based only on similarity (e.g., Gelman & Markman, 1986). Nevertheless, similarity remains the key construct in the description and explanation of inductive phenomena.

Consider the similarity and typicality phenomena (López, Atran, Coley, Medin, & Smith, 1997; Osherson et al., 1990; Rips, 1975):

Similarity
Arguments are strong to the extent that categories in the premises are similar to the conclusion category.For example,

> Robins have sesamoid bones.
> Therefore, sparrows have sesamoid bones.

is judged stronger than

> Robins have sesamoid bones.
> Therefore, ostriches have sesamoid bones.

because robins are more similar to sparrows than to ostriches.

Typicality
The more typical premise categories are of the conclusion category, the stronger

is the argument. For example, people are more willing to project a predicate from robins to birds than from penguins to birds because robins are more typical birds than penguins.

The first descriptive mathematical account of phenomena like these expressed argument strength in terms of similarity. Osherson et al. (1990) posited the similarity-coverage model that proposed that people make categorical inductions on the basis of two principles, similarity and category coverage. Category coverage was actually cashed out in terms of similarity. According to the model, arguments are deemed strong to the degree that premise and conclusion categories are similar and to the degree that premises "cover" the lowest-level category that includes both premise and conclusion categories. The idea is that the categories present in the argument elicit their common superordinate – in particular, the most specific superordinate that they share. Category coverage is determined by the similarity between the premise categories and all the categories contained in this lowest-level superordinate.

Sloman (1993) proposed a competing theory of induction that reduces the two principles of similarity and category coverage into a single principle of feature coverage. Instead of appealing to a class inclusion hierarchy of superordinates and subordinates, this theory appeals to the extent of overlap among the properties of categories. Predicates are projected from premise categories to a conclusion category to the degree that the previously known properties of the conclusion category are also properties of the premise categories – specifically, in proportion to the number of conclusion category features that are present in the premise categories. Both models can explain the similarity, typicality, and asymmetry phenomena (Rips, 1975):

Asymmetry
Switching premise and conclusion categories can lead to arguments of different strength:

Tigers have 38 chromosomes.
Therefore, buffaloes have 38 chromosomes.

is judged stronger than

Buffaloes have 38 chromosomes.
Therefore, tigers have 38 chromosomes.

The similarity-coverage model explains it by appealing to typicality. Tigers are more typical mammals than buffaloes and therefore tigers provide more category coverage. The feature-based model explains it by appealing to familiarity. Tigers are more familiar than buffaloes and therefore have more features. So the features of tigers cover more of the features of buffaloes than vice versa.

Differences between the models play out in the analysis of several phenomena. The similarity-coverage model focuses on relations among categories; the feature-based model on relations among properties. Consider diversity (Osherson et al., 1990):

Diversity
The less similar premises are to each other, the stronger the argument tends to be. People are more willing to draw the conclusion that all mammals love onions from the fact that hippos and hamsters love onions than from the fact that hippos and rhinos do because hippos and rhinos are more similar than hippos and hamsters.

The phenomenon has been demonstrated on several occasions with Western adults (e.g., López, 1995), although some evidence suggests the phenomenon does not always generalize to other groups. López et al. (1997) failed to find diversity effects among Itza' Maya. Proffitt, Coley, and Medin (2000) found that parks maintenance workers did not show diversity effects when reasoning about trees, although tree taxonomists did. Bailenson, Shum, Atran, Medin, and Coley (2002) did not find diversity effects with either Itza' Maya or bird experts. There is also some evidence that children are not sensitive to diversity (Carey, 1985; Gutheil & Gelman, 1997; López, Gelman, Gutheil, & Smith, 1992). However, using materials of greater interest to young children, Heit and Hahn (2001) did find diversity effects with 5- and 6-year-olds.

The data show only mixed support for the phenomenon. Nevertheless, it is predicted by the similarity-coverage model. Categories that are less similar will tend to cover the superordinate that includes them better than categories that are more similar. The feature-based model also predicts the phenomenon as a result of feature overlap. When categories differ, their features have relatively little overlap, and thus they cover a larger part of feature space; when categories are similar, their coverage of feature space is more redundant. As a result, more dissimilar premises are more likely to show more overlap with a conclusion category. However, this is not necessarily so and, indeed, the feature-based model predicts a boundary condition on diversity (Sloman, 1993):

Feature exclusion
A premise category that has little overlap with the conclusion category should have no effect on argument strength even if it leads to a more diverse set of premises. For example,

Fact: German Shepherds have sesamoid bones.
Fact: Giraffes have sesamoid bones.
Conclusion: Moles have sesamoid bones.

is judged stronger than

Fact: German Shepherds have sesamoid bones.
Fact: Blue whales have sesamoid bones.
Conclusion: Moles have sesamoid bones.

even though the second argument has a more diverse set of premises than the first. The feature-based model explains this by appealing to the lack of feature overlap between blue whales and moles over and above the overlap between German Shepherds and moles. To explain this phenomenon, the similarity-coverage model must make the ad hoc assumption that blue whales are not similar enough to other members of the lowest-level category, including all categories in the arguments (presumably mammals), to add more to category coverage than giraffes.

Monotonicity and Nonmonotonicity
When premise categories are sufficiently similar, adding a supporting premise will increase the strength of an argument. However, a counterexample to monotonicity occurs when a premise with a category dissimilar to all other categories is introduced:

Crows have strong sternums.
Peacocks have strong sternums.
Therefore, birds have strong sternums.

is stronger than

Crows have strong sternums.
Peacocks have strong sternums.
Rabbits have strong sternums.
Therefore, birds have strong sternums.

The similarity-coverage model explains nonmonotonicity through its coverage term. The lowest-level category that must be covered in the first argument is birds because all categories in the argument are birds. However, the lowest-level category that must be covered in the second argument is more general – animals – because rabbits are not birds. Worse, rabbits are not similar to very many animals; therefore, the category does not contribute much to argument strength. The feature-based model cannot explain this phenomenon except with added assumptions – for example, that the features of highly dissimilar premise categories compete with one another – as explanations for the predicate (see Sloman, 1993).

As the analysis of nonmonotonicities makes clear, the feature-coverage model differs from the similarity-coverage model primarily in that it appeals to properties of categories rather than instances in explaining induction phenomena and, as a result, in not appealling to the inheritance relations of a class inclusion hierarchy. That is, it assumes people will not in general infer that a category has a property because its superordinate does. Instead, it assumes that people think about categories in terms of their structural relations, in terms of property overlap and relations among properties. This is surely the explanation for the inclusion fallacy (Osherson et al., 1990; Shafir, Smith, & Osherson, 1990):

> *Inclusion Fallacy*
> Similarity relations can override categorical relations between conclusions. Most people judge
>
> All robins have sesamoid bones.
> Therefore, all birds have sesamoid bones.
>
> to be stronger than
>
> All robins have sesamoid bones.
> Therefore, all ostriches have sesamoid bones.

Of course, ostriches are birds, and so the first conclusion implies the second; therefore, the second argument must be stronger than the first. Nevertheless, robins are highly typical birds and therefore similar to other birds. Yet they are distinct from ostriches. These similarity relations determine most people's judgments of argument strength rather than the categorical relation.

An even more direct demonstration of failure to consider category inclusion relations is the following (Sloman, 1993, 1998):

> *Inclusion Similarity*
> Similarity relations can override even transparent categorical relations between premise and conclusion. People do not always judge
>
> Every individual body of water has a high number of seiches.
>
> Every individual lake has a high number of seiches.
>
> to be perfectly strong even when they agree that a lake is a body of water. Moreover, they judge
>
> Every individual body of water has a high number of seiches.
>
> Every individual reservoir has a high number of seiches.
>
> to be even weaker, presumably because reservoirs are less typical bodies of water than lakes.

These examples suggest that category inclusion knowledge has only a limited role in inductive inference. This might be related to the limited role of inclusion relations in other kinds of categorization tasks. For example, Hampton (1982) showed intransitivities in category verification using everyday objects. He found, for example, that people affirmed that "A car headlight is a kind of a lamp" and that "A lamp is a kind of furniture," but not "A car headlight is a kind of furniture."

People are obviously capable of inferring a property from a general to a more specific category. Following an explanation that appeals to inheritance is not difficult (I know naked mole rats have livers because all mammals have livers). However, the inclusion fallacy and the inclusion similarity phenomenon show that such information is not inevitably, and therefore, not automatically included in the inference process.

Gelman and Markman showed that children use category labels to mediate induction:

> *Naming effect*
> Children prefer to project predicates between objects that look similar rather than objects that look dissimilar. However, this preference is overridden when the dissimilar objects are given similar labels.

Gelman and Coley (1990) showed that children as young as 2 years old are also sensitive to the use of labels. So, on the one hand, people are extremely sensitive to the information provided by labels when making inductive inferences. On the other hand, the use of structured category knowledge for inductive inference seems to be a derivative ability, not a part of the fabric of the reasoning process. This suggests that the naming effect does not concern how people make inferences using knowledge about category structure per se, because if the use of structural knowledge is not automatic, very young children would not be expected to use it. Rather, the effect seems to be about the pragmatics of language – in particular, how people use language to mediate induction. The naming effect probably results from people's extreme sensitivity to experimenters' linguistic cues. Even young children apparently have the capacity to note that when an experimenter gives two objects similar labels, the experimenter is giving a hint, a hint that the objects should be treated similarly at least in the context of the experiment. This ability to take cues from others, and to use language to do so, may well be key mechanisms of human induction.

This is also the conclusion of cross-cultural work by Coley, Medin, and Atran (1997). Arguments are judged stronger the more specific the categories involved. If told that dalmations have an ulnar artery, people are more willing to generalize ulnar arteries to dogs than to animals (Osherson et al., 1990). Coley et al. (1997) compared people's willingness to project predicates from various levels of the hierarchy of living things to a more general level. For example, when told that a subspecific category such as "male black spider monkey" is susceptible to an unfamiliar disease, did participants think that the members of the folk-specific category "black spider monkey" were susceptible? If members of the specific category were susceptible, then were members of the folk-generic category ("spider monkey") also susceptible? If members of the generic category were susceptible, then were members of the life-form category ("mammal") also susceptible? Finally, if the life-form category displayed susceptibility, then did the kingdom ("animal")? Coley et al. found that both American college students and members of a traditional Mayan village in lowland Guatemala showed a sharp drop off at a certain point:

> *Preferred level of induction*
> People are willing to make an inductive inference with confidence from a subordinate to a near superordinate up to the folk-generic level; their willingness drops off considerably when making inferences to categories more abstract.

These results are consistent with Berlin's (1992) claim that the folk-generic level is the easiest to identify, the most commonly distinguished in speech, and serves best to distinguish categories. Therefore, one might imagine that the folk-generic level would constitute the basic-level categories that are often used to organize hierarchical linguistic and conceptual categories (Brown, 1958; Rosch et al., 1976; see Murphy, 2002, for a review). Nevertheless, the dominance of generic categories was not expected by Coley et al. (1997) because Rosch et al. (1976) had found that for the biological categories tree, fish, and bird, the life-form level was the category level satisfying a number of operational definitions of the basic level. For example, Rosch et al.'s American college students preferred to call objects they were shown "tree," "fish," or "bird" rather than "oak," "salmon," or "robin."

Why the discrepancy? Why do American college students prefer to name an object a tree over an oak, yet prefer to project a property from all red oaks to all oaks rather than from all oaks to all trees? Perhaps they simply cannot identify oaks, and therefore fall back on the much more general "tree" in order to name. However, this begs the question: If students consider "tree" to be informative and precise enough to name things, why are they unwilling to project properties to it? Coley et al.'s (1997) answer to this conundrum is that naming depends on knowledge; that is, names are chosen that are precise enough to be informative given what people know about the object being named. Inductive inference, they argued, also depends on a kind of conventional wisdom. People have learned to maximize inductive potential at a particular level of generality (the folk-generic) level because culture and linguistic convention specify that that is the most informative level for projecting properties (see Greenfield, Chap. 27). For example, language tends to use a single morpheme for naming generic level categories. This is a powerful cue that members of the same generic level have a lot in common and that therefore it is a good level for guessing that a predicate might hold across it. This idea is related to Shipley's (1993) notion of overhypotheses (cf. Goodman, 1955): that people use categorywide rules about certain kinds of properties to make some inductive inferences. For example, upon encountering a new species, people might assume members of the species will vary more in degree of obesity than in, say, skin color (Nisbett et al., 1983) despite having no particular knowledge about the species.

This observation poses a challenge to feature- and similarity-based models of induction (Heit, 1998; Osherson et al., 1990; Sloman, 1993). These models all start from the assumption that people induce new knowledge about categories from old knowledge about the same categories. However, if people make inductive inferences using not only specific knowledge about the categories at hand but also distributional knowledge about the likelihood of properties at different hierarchical levels, knowledge that is in part culturally transmitted via language, then more enters the inductive inference process than models of inductive process have heretofore allowed.

Mandler and McDonough (1998) argued that the basic-level bias comes relatively late, and demonstrated that 14-month-old infants show a bias to project properties within a broad domain (animals or vehicles) rather than at the level usually considered to be basic. This finding is not inconsistent with Coley et al.'s (1997) conclusion because the distributional and linguistic properties that they claim mediate induction presumably have to be learned, and so finding a basic-level preference only amongst adults is sufficient for their argument. Mandler and McDonough (1998) argued that infants' predilection to project to broad domains demonstrates an initial propensity to rely on "conceptual" as opposed to "perceptual" knowledge as a basis for induction, meaning that infants rely on the very abstract commonalities among animals as opposed to the perhaps more obvious physical differences among basic-level categories (pans vs. cups and cats vs. dogs). Of course, pans and cups do have physical properties in common that distinguish them from cats and dogs (e.g., the former are concave, the latter have articulating limbs). Moreover, the distinction between perceptual and conceptual properties is tenuous. Proximal and distal stimuli are necessarily different (i.e., even the eye engages in some form of interpretation), and a variety of evidence shows that beliefs about what is being perceived affects what is perceived (e.g., Gregory, 1973). Nevertheless, as suggested by the following phenomena, induction is mediated by knowledge of categories' role in causal systems; beliefs about the way the world works influence induction as much as overlap of properties does. Mandler and McDonough's data provide evidence that this is true even for 14-month-olds.

Induction as Scientific Methodology

Induction is of course not merely the province of individuals trying to accomplish everyday goals, but also one of the main activities of science. According to one common view of science (Carnap, 1966; Hempel, 1965; Nagel, 1961; for opposing views, see Hacking, 1983; Popper, 1963), scientists spend much of their time trying to induce general laws about categories from particular examples. It is natural, therefore, to look to the principles that govern induction in science to see how well they describe individual behavior (for a discussion of scientific reasoning, see Dunbar & Fugelsang, Chap. 29). Psychologists have approached induction as a scientific enterprise in three different ways.

THE RULES OF INDUCTION

First, some have examined the extent to which people abide by the normative rules of inductive inference that are generally accepted in the scientific community. One such rule is that properties that do not vary much across category instances are more projectible across the whole category than properties that vary more. Nisbett et al. (1983) showed that people are sensitive to this rule:

> *Variability/Centrality*
> People are more willing to project predicates that tend to be invariant across category instances than variable predicates. For example, people who are told that one Pacific island native is overweight tend to think it is unlikely that all natives of the island are overweight because

weight tends to vary across people. In contrast, if told the native has dark skin, they are more likely to generalize to all natives because skin color tends to be more uniform within a race.

However, sensitivity to variability does not imply that people consider the variability of predicates in the same deliberative manner that a scientist should. This phenomenon could be explained by a sensitivity to centrality (Sloman, Love, & Ahn, 1998). Given two properties A and B, such that B depends on A but A does not depend on B, people are more willing to project property A than property B because A is more causally central than B, even if A and B are equated for variability (Hadjichristidis, Sloman, Stevenson, & Over, 2004). More central properties tend to be less variable. Having a heart is more central and less variable among animals than having hair. Centrality and variability are almost two sides of the same coin (the inside and outside views, respectively). In Nisbett et al.'s case, having dark skin may be seen as less variable than obesity by virtue of being more central and having more apparent causal links to other features of people.

The diversity principle is sometimes identified as a principle of good scientific practice (e.g., Heit & Hahn, 2001; Hempel, 1965; López, 1995). Yet, Lo et al. (2002) argued against the normative status of diversity. They consider the following argument:

> House cats often carry the parasite Floxum.
> Field mice often carry the parasite Floxum.
>
> All mammals often carry the parasite Floxum.

which they compare to

> House cats often carry the parasite Floxum.
> Tigers often carry the parasite Floxum.
>
> All mammals often carry the parasite Floxum.

Even though the premise categories of the first argument are more diverse (house cats are less similar to field mice than to tigers), the second argument might seem stronger because house cats could conceivably become infected with the parasite Floxum while hunting field mice. Even if you do not find the second argument stronger, merely accepting the relevance of this infection scenario undermines the diversity principle, which prescribes that the similarity principle should be determinative for all pairs of arguments. At minimum, it shows that the diversity principle does not dominate all other principles of sound inference.

Lo et al. (2002) proved that a different and simple principle of argument strength does follow from the Bayesian philosophy of science. Consider two arguments with the same conclusion in which the conclusion implies the premises. For example, the conclusion "every single mammal carries the parasite Floxum" implies that "every single tiger carries the parasite Floxum" (on the assumption that "mammal" and "tiger" refer to natural, warm-blooded animals). In such a case, the argument with the less likely premises should be stronger. Lo et al. referred to this as the premise probability principle. In a series of experiments, they show that young children in both the United States and Taiwan make judgments that conform to this principle.

INDUCTION AS NAIVE SCIENTIFIC THEORIZING

A second approach to induction as a scientific methodology examines the contents of beliefs, what knowledge adults and children make use of when making inductive inferences. Because knowledge is structured in a way that has more or less correspondence to the structure of modern scientific theories, sometimes to the structure of old or discredited scientific theories, such knowledge is often referred to as a "naive theory" (Carey, 1985; Gopnik & Meltzoff, 1997; Keil, 1989; Murphy & Medin, 1985). One strong, contentful position (Carey, 1985) is that people are born with a small number of naive theories that correspond to a small number of domains such as physics, biology, psychology, and so on, and that all other knowledge is constructed using these original theories as a scaffolding. Perhaps, for example, other knowledge is a metaphorical extension of these original naive theories (cf. Lakoff & Johnson, 1980).

One phenomenon studied by Carey (1985) to support this position is

> *Human bias*
> Small children prefer to project a property from people rather than from other animals. Four-year-olds are more likely to agree that a bug has a spleen if told that a person does than if told that a bee does. Ten-year-olds and adults do not show this asymmetry and project as readily from nonhuman animals as from humans.

Carey argued that this transition is due to a major reorganization of the child's knowledge about animals. Knowledge is constituted by a mutually constraining set of concepts that make a coherent whole in analogy to the holistic coherence of scientific theories. As a result, concepts do not change in isolation, but instead as whole networks of belief are reorganized (Kuhn, 1962). On this view, the human bias occurs because a 4-year-old's understanding of biological functions is framed in terms of human behavior, whereas older children and adults possess an autonomous domain of biological knowledge.

A different enterprise is more descriptive; it simply shows the analogies between knowledge structures and scientific theories. For example, Gopnik and Meltzoff (1997) claimed that, just like scientists, both children and laypeople construct and revise abstract lawlike theories about the world. In particular, they maintain that the general mechanisms that underlie conceptual change in cognitive development mirror those responsible for theory change in mature science. More specifically, even very young children project properties among natural kinds on the basis of latent, underlying commonalities between categories rather than superficial similarities (e.g., Gelman & Coley, 1990). So children behave like "little scientists" in the sense that their inductive inferences are more sensitive to the causal principles that govern objects' composition and behavior than to objects' mere appearance, even though appearance is, by definition, more directly observable.

Of course, analogies between everyday induction and scientific induction have to exist. As long as both children and scientists have beliefs that have positive inductive potential, those beliefs are likely to have some correspondence to the world, and the knowledge of children and scientists will therefore have to show some convergence. If children did operate merely on the basis of superficial similarities, such things as photographs and toy cars would forever stump them. Children have no choice but to be "little scientists," merely to walk around the world without bumping into things. Because of the inevitability of such correspondences and because scientific theories take a multitude of different forms, it is not obvious that this approach, in the absence of a more fully specified model, has much to offer theories of cognition. Furthermore, proponents of this approach typically present a rather impoverished view of scientific activity, which neglects the role of social and cultural norms and practices (see Faucher et al., 2002). Efforts to give the approach a more principled grounding have begun (e.g., Gopnik et al., 2004; Rehder & Hastie, 2001; Sloman, Love, & Ahn, 1998).

Lo et al. (2002) rejected the approach outright. They argue that it just does not matter whether people have representational structures that in one way or another are similar to scientific theories. The question that they believe has both prescriptive value for improving human induction and descriptive value for developing psychological theory is whether whatever method people use to update their beliefs conforms to principles of good scientific practice.

COMPUTATIONAL MODELS OF INDUCTION

The third approach to induction as a scientific methodology is concerned with the representation of inductive structure without concern for the process by which people make inductive inferences. The approach takes its lead from Marr's (1982) analysis of the different levels of psychological analysis. Models at the highest level, those that concern themselves with a description of the goals of a cognitive system without direct description of the manner in which the mind tries to attain those goals or how the system is implemented in the brain, are computational models. Three kinds of computational models of inductive inference have been suggested, all of which find their motivation in principles of good scientific methodology.

Induction as Hypothesis Evaluation McDonald, Samuels, and Rispoli (1996) proposed an account of inductive inference that appeals to several principles of hypothesis evaluation. They argued that when judging the strength of an inductive argument, people actively construct and assess hypotheses in light of the evidence provided by the premises. They advanced three determinants of hypothesis plausibility: the scope of the conclusion, the number of premises that instantiate it, and the number of alternatives to it suggested by the premises. In their experiments, all three factors were good predictors of judged argument strength, although certain pragmatic considerations, and a fourth factor – "acceptability of the conclusion" – were also invoked to fully cover the results.

Despite the model's success in explaining some judgments, others, such as nonmonotonicity, are only dealt with by appeal to pragmatic postulates that are not defended in any detail. Moreover, the model is restricted to arguments with general conclusions. Because the model is at a computational level of description, it does not make claims about the cognitive processes involved in induction. As we see next, other computational models do offer something in place of a process model that McDonald et al.'s (1996) framework does not: a rigorous normative analysis of an inductive task.

Bayesian models of inductive inference Heit (1998) proposed that Bayes' rule provides a representation for how people determine the probability of the conclusion of a categorical inductive argument given that the premises are true. The idea is that people combine degrees of prior belief with the data given in the premises to determine a posterior degree of belief in the conclusion. Prior beliefs concern relative likelihoods that each combination of categories in the argument would all have the relevant property. For example, for the argument

$$\frac{\text{Cows can get disease X.}}{\text{Sheep can get disease X.}}$$

Heit assumes people can generate beliefs about the relative prior probability that both cows and sheep have the disease, that cows do but sheep do not, and so on. These beliefs are generated heuristically; people are assumed to bring to mind properties shared by cows and by sheep, properties that cows have but sheep do not, and so on. The prior probabilities reflect the ease of bringing each type of property to mind. Premises contribute other information as well – in this case, that only states in which cows indeed have the disease are possible. This can be used to update priors to determine a posterior degree of belief that the conclusion is true.

On the basis of assumptions about what people's priors are, Heit (1998) described a number of the phenomena of categorical induction: similarity, typicality, diversity, and homogeneity. However, the model is inconsistent with nonmonotonicity effects. Furthermore, because it relies on an extensional updating rule, Bayes' rule, the model cannot explain phenomena that are nonextensional such as the inclusion fallacy or the inclusion-similarity phenomenon.

Sanjana and Tenenbaum (2003) offered a Bayesian model of categorical inference with a more principled foundation. The model is applied only to the animal domain. They derive all their probabilities from a hypothesis space that consists of clusters of categories. The model's prediction for each argument derives from the probability that the conclusion category has the property. This reflects the probability that the conclusion category is an element of likely hypotheses – namely, that the conclusion category is in the same cluster as the examples shown (i.e., as the premise categories) and that those hypothesized clusters have high probability. The probability of each hypothesis is assumed to be inversely related to the size of the hypothesis (the number of animal types it includes) and to its complexity, the number of disjoint clusters that it includes. This model performed well in quantitative comparisons against the similarity-coverage model and the feature-based model, although its consistency with the various phenomena of induction has not been reported and is rather opaque.

The principled probabilistic foundation of this model and its good fit to data so far yield promise that the model could serve as a formal representation of categorical induction. The model would show even more promise and power to generalize, however, if its predictions had been derived using more reasonable assumptions about the structure of categorical knowledge. The pairwise cluster hierarchy Sanjana and Tenenbaum use to represent knowledge of animals is poorly motivated (although see Kemp & Tenenbaum, 2003, for an improvement), and there would be even less motivation in other domains (cf. Sloman, 1998). Moreover, if and how the model could explain fallacious reasoning is not clear.

SUMMARY OF INDUCTION AS SCIENTIFIC METHODOLOGY

Inductive inference can be fallacious, as demonstrated by the inclusion fallacy described previously. Nevertheless, much of the evidence that has been covered in this section suggests that people in the psychologist's laboratory are sensitive to some of the same concerns as scientists when they make inductive inferences. People are more likely to project nonvariable over variable predicates, they change their beliefs more when premises are a priori less likely, and their behavior can be modeled by probabilistic models constructed from rational principles.

Other work reviewed shows that people, like scientists, use explanations to mediate their inference. They try to understand why a category should exhibit a predicate based on nonobservable properties. These are valuable observations to allow psychologists to begin the process of building a descriptive theory of inductive inference. Unfortunately, current ideas and data place too few constraints on the cognitive processes and procedures that people actually use.

Conclusions and Future Directions

We have reviewed two ways that cognitive scientists have tried to describe how people make inductive inferences. We limited the scope of the problem to that of categorical induction – how people generate degrees of confidence that a predicate applies to a stated category from premises concerning other categories that the predicate is assumed to apply to. Nevertheless, neither approach is a silver bullet. The similarity-based approach has produced the most well-specified models and phenomena, although consideration of the relation between scientific methodology and human induction may prove the most important prescriptively and may in the end provide the most enduring principles to distinguish everyday human induction from ideal – or at least other – inductive processes.

A more liberal way to proceed is to accept the apparent plurality of procedures and mechanisms that people use to make inductions and to see this pluralism as a virtue rather than a vice.

The Bag of Tricks

Many computational problems are hard because the search space of possible answers is so large. Computer scientists have long used educated guesses or what are often called heuristics or rules of thumb to prune the search space, making it smaller and thus more tractable at the risk of making the problem insoluble by pruning off the best answers. The work of Kahneman and Tversky imported this notion of heuristics into the study of probability judgment (see Kahneman & Frederick, Chap. 12). They suggested that people use a set of cognitive heuristics to estimate probabilities – heuristics that were informed, that made people's estimates likely to be reasonable, but left open the possibility of systematic error in cases in which the heuristics that came naturally to people had the unfortunate consequence of leading to the wrong answer.

Kahneman and Tversky suggested the heuristics of availability, anchoring and adjustment, simulation, and causality to describe how people make probability judgments. They also suggested that people make judgments according to representativeness, the degree to which a class or event used as evidence is similar to the class or process being judged. Representativeness is a very abstract heuristic that is compatible with a number of different models of the judgment process. We understand it not so much as a particular claim about how people make probability judgments as the claim that processes of categorization and similarity play central roles in induction. This is precisely the claim of the similarity-based model outlined previously.

We believe that the bag of tricks describes most completely how people go about making inductive leaps. People seem to use a number of different sources of information for making inductive inferences, including the availability of featural information and knowledge about feature overlap, linguistic cues about the distribution of features, the relative centrality of features to one another, the relative probability of premises, and objects' roles in causal systems.

Causal Induction

Our guess is that the treasure trove for future work in categorical induction is in the development of the latter mode of inference. How do people go about using causal knowledge to make inductions? That they do is indisputable. Consider the following phenomenon due to Heit and Rubinstein (1994):

> *Relevance*
> People's willingness to project a predicate from one category to another depends on what else the two categories have in common. For example, people are more likely to project "has a liver with two chambers" from chickens to hawks than from tigers to hawks but more likely to project "prefers to feed at night" from tigers to hawks than from chickens to hawks.

More specifically, argument strength depends on how people explain why the category has the predicate. In the example, chickens and hawks are known to have biological properties in common, and therefore, people think it likely that a biological predicate would project from one to the other. Tigers and hawks are known to both be hunters and carnivores; therefore "prefers to feed at night" is more likely to project between them. Sloman (1994) showed that the strength of an argument depends on whether the premise and conclusion are explained in the same way. If the premise and conclusion have different explanations, the premise can actually reduce belief in the conclusion.

The explanations in these cases are causal; they refer to more or less well-understood causal processes. Medin, Coley, Storms, and Hayes (2003) have demonstrated five distinct phenomena that depend on causal intuitions about the relations amongst categories and predicates. For example, they showed

> *Causal asymmetry*
> Switching premise and conclusion categories will reduce the strength of an argument if a causal path exists from premise to conclusion. For example,
>
> Gazelles contain retinum.
> Lions contain retinum.
>
> is stronger than
>
> Lions contain retinum.
> Gazelles contain retinum.
>
> because the food chain is such that lions eat gazelles and retinum could be transferred in the process.

What is striking about this kind of example is the exquisite sensitivity to subtle (if mundane) causal relations that it demonstrates. The necessary causal explanation springs to mind quickly, apparently automatically, and it does so even though it depends on one fact that most people are only dimly aware of (that lions eat gazelles) among the vast number of facts that are at our disposal.

We do not interpret the importance of causal relations in induction as support for psychological essentialism, the view that people base judgments concerning categories on attributions of "essential" qualities: of a true underlying nature that confers kind identity unlike, for example, Kornblith (1993), Medin and Ortony (1989), and Gelman and Hirschfeld (1999). We rather follow Strevens (2001) in the claim that it is causal structure per se that mediates induction; no appeal to essential properties is required (cf. Rips, 2001; Sloman & Malt, 2003). Indeed, the causal relations that support inductive inference can be based on very superficial features that might be very mutable. To illustrate, the argument

Giraffes eat leaves of type X.

African tawny eagles eat leaves of type X.

seems reasonably strong only because both giraffes and African eagles can reach high leaves and both are found in Africa – hardly a central property of either species.

The appeal to causal structure is instead intended to appeal to the ability to pick out invariants and act as agents to make use of those invariants. Organisms have a striking ability to find the properties of things that maximize their ability to predict and control, and humans seem to have the most widely applicable capacity of this sort. However, prediction and control come from knowing what variables determine the values of other variables – that is, how one predicts future outcomes and knows what to manipulate to achieve an effect. This is, of course, the domain of causality. It seems only natural that people would use this talent to reason when making inductive inferences.

The appeal to causal relations is not necessarily an appeal to scientific methodology. In fact, some philosophers such as Russell (1913) argued that theories are not scientific until they are devoid of causal reference, and the logical empiricists attempted to exorcise the notion of causality from "scientific" philosophy. Of course, to the extent that scientists behave like other people in their appeal to causality, then the appeal to scientific methodology is trivial.

Normative models of causal structure have recently flowered (cf. Pearl, 2000; Spirtes, Glymour, & Scheines, 1993), and some of the insights of these models seem to have some psychological validity (Sloman & Lagnado, 2004). Bringing them to bear on the problem of inductive inference will not be trivial. However, the effort should be made because causal modeling seems to be a critical element of the bag of tricks that people use to make inductive inferences.

Acknowledgments

We thank Uri Hasson and Marc Buehner for comments on an earlier draft. This work was funded by NASA grant NCC2-1217.

References

Bailenson, J. B., Shum, M. S., Atran, S., Medin, D., & Coley, J. D. (2002). A bird's eye view: Biological categorization and reasoning within and across cultures. *Cognition*, 84, 1–53.

Berlin, B. (1992). *Ethnobiological classification: Principles of categorization of plants and animals in traditional societies*. Princeton, NJ: Princeton University Press.

Brown, R. (1958). How shall a thing be called? *Psychological Review*, 65, 14–21.

Carey, S. (1985). *Conceptual change in childhood*. Cambridge, MA: MIT Press.

Carnap, R. (1950). *The logical foundations of probability*. Chicago: University of Chicago Press.

Carnap, R. (1966). *Philosophical foundations of physics*. Ed. M. Gardner, New York: Basic Books.

Cheng, P. W., & Holyoak, K. J. (1985). Pragmatic reasoning schemas. *Cognitive Psychology*, 17, 391–416.

Coley, J. D., Medin, D. L., & Atran, S. (1997). Does rank have its privilege? Inductive inferences within folkbiological taxonomies. *Cognition*, 64, 73–112.

Corter, J. & Gluck, M. (1992). Explaining basic categories: feature predictability and information. *Psychological Bulletin*, 111, 291–303.

Doherty, M. E., Chadwick, R., Garavan, H., Barr, D., & Mynatt, C. R. (1996). On people's understanding of the diagnostic implications of probabilistic data. *Memory and Cognition, 24*, 644–654.

Faucher, L., Mallon, R., Nazer, D., Nichols, S., Ruby, A., Stich, S., & Weinberg, J. (2002). The baby in the lab coat. In P. Carruthers, S. Stich, & M. Siegal (Eds.), *The cognitive basis of science*. Cambridge, UK: Cambridge University Press.

Fisher, D. H. (1987). Knowledge acquisition via incremental conceptual clustering. *Machine Learning*, 2, 139–172.

Frege, G. W. (1880). *Posthumous writings*. Blackwell, 1979.

Gelman, S. A., & Coley, J. D. (1990). The importance of knowing a dodo is a bird: Categories and inferences in 2-year-old children. *Developmental Psychology*, 26, 796–804.

Gelman, S. A., & Hirschfeld, L. A. (1999). How biological is essentialism? In D. L. Medin & S. Atran (Eds.), *Folkbiology* (pp. 403–446). Cambridge, MA: MIT Press.

Gelman, S. A., & Markman, E. M. (1986). Categories and induction in young children. *Cognition*, 23, 183–209.

Glymour, C. (2001). *The mind's arrows: Bayes nets and graphical causal models in psychology*. Cambridge, MA: Bradford Books.

Goodman, N. (1955). *Fact, fiction, and forecast*. Cambridge, MA: Harvard University Press.

Gopnik, A., Glymour, C., Sobel, D. M., Schulz, L. E., Kushnir, T., & Danks, D. (2004). A theory of causal learning in children: Causal maps and Bayes nets. *Psychological Review*, 111, 1–31.

Gopnik, A., & Meltzoff, A. N. (1997). *Words, thoughts, and theories*. Cambridge, MA: MIT Press.

Gregory, R. L. (1973). *The intelligent eye*. New York: McGraw-Hill.

Gutheil, G., & Gelman, S. A. (1997). The use of sample size and diversity in category-based induction. *Journal of Experimental Child Psychology*, 64, 159–174.

Hacking, I. (1983). *Representing and intervening: Introductory topics in the philosophy of natural science*. Cambridge, UK: Cambridge University Press.

Hacking, I. (2001). *An introduction to probability and inductive logic*. Cambridge, UK: Cambridge University Press.

Hadjichristidis, C., Sloman, S. A., Stevenson, R. J., & Over D. E. (2004). Feature centrality and property induction. *Cognitive Science*, 28, 45–74.

Hampton, J. A. (1982). A demonstration of intransitivity in natural categories. *Cognition*, 12, 151–164.

Heit, E. (1998). A Bayesian analysis of some forms of inductive reasoning. In M. Oaksford & N. Chater (Eds.), *Rational models of cognition* (pp. 248–274). Oxford, UK: Oxford University Press.

Heit, E. (2000). Properties of inductive reasoning. *Psychonomic Bulletin and Review*, 7, 569–592.

Heit, E., & Hahn, U. (2001). Diversity-based reasoning in children. *Cognitive Psychology*, 47, 243–273.

Heit, E., & Rubinstein, J. (1994). Similarity and property effects in inductive reasoning. *Journal of Experimental Psychology: Learning, Memory, and Cognition*, 20, 411–422.

Hempel, C. (1965). *Aspects of scientific explanation*. New York: Free Press.

Hume, D. (1739). *A treatise of human nature*. Ed. D. G. C. Macnabb. London: Collins.

Hume, D. (1748). *An enquiry concerning human understanding*. Oxford, UK: Clarendon.

Johnson-Laird, P. N., Legrenzi, P., Girotto, V., Legrenzi, M., & Caverni, J-P. (1999). Naive probability: a mental model theory of extensional reasoning. *Psychological Review*, 106, 62–88.

Jones, G. (1983). Identifying basic categories. *Psychological Bulletin*, 94, 423–428.

Keil, F. C. (1989). *Concepts, kinds, and cognitive development*. Cambridge, MA: MIT Press.

Kemp, C., & Tenenbaum, J. B. (2003). Theory-based induction. *Proceedings of the twenty-fifth annual conference of the Cognitive Science Society*, Boston, MA.

Klahr, D. (2000). *Exploring science: The cognition and development of discovery processes*. Cambridge, MA: MIT Press.

Klayman, J., & Ha, Y-W. (1987). Confirmation, disconfirmation, and information in hypothesis testing. *Psychological Review*, 94, 211–228.

Klayman, J. (1988). Cue discovery in probabilistic environments: Uncertainty and experimentation. *Journal of Experimental Psychology: Learning, Memory, and Cognition*, 14, 317–330.

Kornblith, H. (1993). *Inductive inference and its natural ground*. Cambridge: MIT Press.

Kuhn, T. (1962). *The structure of scientific revolutions*. Chicago: University of Chicago Press.

Lagnado, D., & Sloman, S. A., (2004). Inside and outside probability judgment. In D. J. Koehler & N. Harvey (Eds.), *Blackwell handbook of judgment and decision making* (pp. 157–176). Oxford, UK: Blackwell Publishing.

Lakoff, G. & Johnson, M. (1980). *Metaphors we live by*. Chicago: University of Chicago Press.

Lipton, P. (1991). *Inference to the best explanation*. New York: Routledge.

Lo, Y., Sides, A., Rozelle, J., & Osherson, D. (2002). Evidential diversity and premise probability in young children's inductive judgment. *Cognitive Science, 26*, 181–206.

Lopez, A. (1995). The diversity principle in the testing of arguments. *Memory and Cognition, 23*, 374–382.

López, A., Atran, S., Coley, J. D., Medin, D. L., & Smith E. E. (1997). The tree of life: Universal and cultural features of folkbiological taxonomies and inductions. *Cognitive Psychology, 32*, 251–295.

Lopez, A., Gelman, S. A., Gutheil, G., & Smith, E. E. (1992). The development of category-based induction. *Child Development, 63*, 1070–1090.

Mandler, J. M., & McDonough, L. (1998). Studies in inductive inference in infancy. *Cognitive Psychology, 37*, 60–96.

Marr, D. (1982). *Vision*. New York: W. H. Freeman and Co.

McDonald, J., Samuels, M., & Rispoli, J. (1996). A hypothesis-assessment model of categorical argument strength. *Cognition, 59*, 199–217.

Medin, D. L., Coley, J. D., Storms, G., & Hayes, B. (2005). A relevance theory of induction. *Psychonomic Bulletin and Review, 10*, 517–532.

Medin, D. L., & Ortony, A. (1989). Psychological essentialism. In S. Vosniadou & A. Ortony (Eds.), *Similarity and analogical reasoning* (pp. 179–195). New York: Cambridge University Press.

Miller, R. W. (1987). *Fact and method*. Princeton, NJ: Princeton University Press.

Murphy, G. L. (1982). Cue validity and levels of categorization. *Psychological Bulletin, 91*, 174–177.

Murphy, G. L. (2002). *The big book of concepts*. Cambridge, MA: MIT Press.

Murphy, G. L. & Medin, D. L. (1985). The role of theories in conceptual coherence. *Psychological Review, 92*, 289–316.

Nagel, E. (1961). *The structure of science: Problems in the logic of scientific explanation*. New York: Harcourt, Brace and World.

Nisbett, R. E. (Ed.) (1993). *Rules for reasoning*. Hillsdale, NJ: Erlbaum.

Nisbett, R. E., Krantz, D. H., Jepson, D. H., & Kunda, Z. (1983). The use of statistical heuristics in everyday inductive reasoning. *Psychological Review*, 90, 339–363.

Oaksford, M., & Chater, N. (1994). A rational analysis of the selection task as optimal data selection. *Psychological Review, 101*, 608–631.

Osherson, D. N., Smith, E. E., Wilkie, O., López, A., & Shafir, E. (1990). Category-based induction. *Psychological Review, 97*, 185–200.

Pearl, J. (2000). *Causality*. Cambridge, MA: Cambridge University Press.

Popper, K. (1963). *Conjectures and refutations*. London: Routledge.

Proffitt, J. B., Coley, J. D., & Medin, D. L. (2000). Expertise and category-based induction. *Journal of Experimental Psychology: Learning, Memory, and Cognition, 26*, 811–828.

Quine, W. V. (1970). Natural kinds. In N. Rescher (Ed.), *Essays in honor of Carl G. Hempel* (pp. 5–23). Dordrecht: D. Reidel.

Rehder, B., & Hastie, R. (2001). Causal knowledge and categories: The effects of causal beliefs on categorization, induction, and similarity. *Journal of Experimental Psychology: General, 130*, 323–360.

Reichenbach, H. (1938). *Experience and prediction*. Chicago: University of Chicago Press.

Rips, L. J. (1975). Inductive judgements about natural categories. *Journal of Verbal Learning and Verbal Behavior, 14*, 665–681.

Rips, L. (2001). Necessity and natural categories. *Psychological Bulletin, 127*, 827–852.

Rosch, E. H. (1973). Natural categories. *Cognitive Psychology, 4*, 328–350.

Rosch, E., Mervis, C. B., Gray, W. D., Johnson, D. M., & Boyes-Braem, P. (1976). Basic objects in natural categories. *Cognitive Psychology, 8*, 382–439.

Rosch, E. (1978). Principles of categorization. In E. Rosch & B. B. Lloyd (Eds.). *Cognition and categorization* (pp. 27–48), Hillsdale, NJ: Erlbaum.

Russell, B. (1913). On the notion of cause. *Proceedings of the Aristotelian Society, 13*, 1–26.

Russell, B., & Whitehead, A. N. (1925). *Principia mathematica*. Cambridge, UK: Cambridge University Press.

Sanjana, N. E., & Tenenbaum, J. B. (2003). Bayesian models of inductive generalization. In Becker, S., Thrun, S., & Obermayer, K. (Eds.), *Advances in Neural Processing Systems 15*. Cambridge, MA: MIT Press.

Shafir, E., Smith, E. E., & Osherson, D. N. (1990). Typicality and reasoning fallacies. *Memory and Cognition, 18*, 229–239.

Shepard, R. N. (1980). Multidimensional scaling, tree-fitting, and clustering. *Science, 210*, 390–398.

Shepard, R. N. (1987). Towards a universal law of generalization for psychological science. *Science, 237*, 1317–1323.

Shipley, E. F. (1993). Categories, hierarchies, and induction. In D. L. Medin (Ed.), *The psychology of learning and motivation*, 30, pp. 265–301. San Diego: Academic Press.

Sloman, S. A. (1993). Feature based induction. *Cognitive Psychology, 25*, 231–280.

Sloman, S. A. (1994). When explanations compete: The role of explanatory coherence on judgments of likelihood. *Cognition, 52*, 1–21.

Sloman, S. A. (1998). Categorical inference is not a tree: The myth of inheritance hierarchies. *Cognitive Psychology, 35*, 1–33.

Sloman, S. A., & Lagnado, D. A. (2004). Causal invariance in reasoning and learning. In B. Ross (Ed.), *Handbook of learning and motivation, 44*, 287–325.

Sloman, S. A., Love, B. C., & Ahn, W. (1998). Feature centrality and conceptual coherence. *Cognitive Science, 22*, 189–228.

Sloman, S. A., & Malt, B. C. (2003). Artifacts are not ascribed essences, nor are they treated as belonging to kinds. *Language and Cognitive Processes, 18*, 563–582.

Sloman, S. A., & Over, D. (2003). Probability judgment from the inside and out. In D. Over (Ed.), *Evolution and the psychology of thinking: The debate* (pp. 145–169). New York: Psychology Press.

Sloman, S. A., & Rips, L. J. (1998). Similarity as an explanatory construct. *Cognition, 65*, 87–101.

Spellman, B. A., López, A., & Smith, E. E. (1999). Hypothesis testing: Strategy selection for generalizing versus limiting hypotheses. *Thinking and Reasoning, 5*, 67–91.

Spirtes, P., Glymour, C., & Scheines, R. (1993). *Causation, prediction, and search*. New York: Springer-Verlag.

Strevens, M. (2001). The essentialist aspect of naive theories. *Cognition, 74*, 149–175.

Suppes, P. (1994). *Learning and projectibility*. In D. Stalker (Ed.), *Grue: The new riddle of induction* (pp. 263–272). Chicago: Open Court.

Tversky, A., & Kahneman, D. (1974). Judgment under uncertainty: Heuristics and biases. *Science, 185*, 1124–1131.

Tversky, A. & Kahneman, D. (1983). Extension versus intuitive reasoning: The conjunction fallacy in probability judgment. *Psychological Review, 90*, 293–315.

CHAPTER 6

Analogy

Keith J. Holyoak

Analogy is a special kind of similarity (see Goldstone & Son, Chap. 2). Two situations are analogous if they share a common pattern of relationships among their constituent elements even though the elements themselves differ across the two situations. Typically, one analog, termed the *source* or *base*, is more familiar or better understood than the second analog, termed the *target*. This asymmetry in initial knowledge provides the basis for analogical transfer, using the source to generate inferences about the target. For example, Charles Darwin drew an analogy between breeding programs used in agriculture to select more desirable plants and animals and "natural selection" for new species. The well-understood source analog called attention to the importance of variability in the population as the basis for change in the distribution of traits over successive generations and raised a critical question about the target analog: What plays the role of the farmer in natural selection? (Another analogy, between Malthus' theory of human population growth and the competition of individuals in a species to survive and reproduce, provided Darwin's answer to this question.) Analogies have figured prominently in the history of science (see Dunbar & Fugelsang, Chap. 29) and mathematics (Pask, 2003) and are of general use in problem solving (see Novick & Bassok, Chap. 14). In legal reasoning, the use of relevant past cases (legal precedents) to help decide a new case is a formalized application of analogical reasoning (see Ellsworth, Chap. 28). Analogies can also function to influence political beliefs (Blanchette & Dunbar, 2001) and to sway emotions (Thagard & Shelley, 2001). Analogical reasoning goes beyond the information initially given, using systematic connections between the source and target to generate plausible, although fallible, inferences about the target. Analogy is thus a form of inductive reasoning (see Sloman & Lagnado, Chap. 5).

Figure 6.1 sketches the major component processes in analogical transfer (see Carbonell, 1983; Gentner, 1983; Gick & Holyoak, 1980, 1983; Novick & Holyoak, 1991). Typically, a target situation serves as a retrieval cue for a potentially useful source analog. It is then necessary to establish a *mapping*, or a set of systematic correspondences that serve to align the

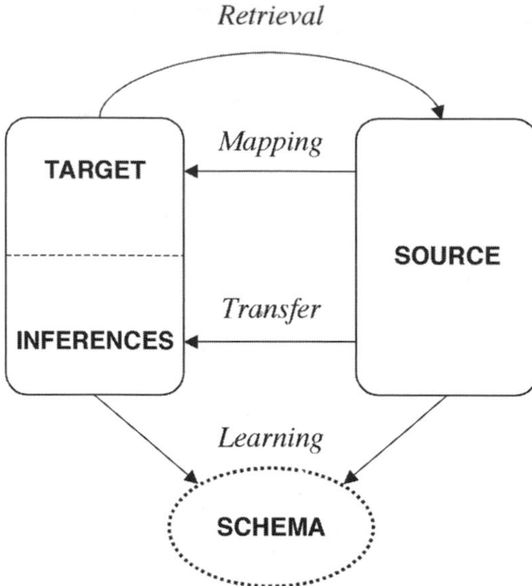

Figure 6.1. Major components of analogical reasoning.

elements of the source and target. On the basis of the mapping, it is possible to derive new inferences about the target, thereby elaborating its representation. In the aftermath of analogical reasoning about a pair of cases, it is possible that some form of relational generalization may take place, yielding a more abstract schema for a class of situations, of which the source and target are both instances. For example, Darwin's use of analogy to construct a theory of natural selection ultimately led to the generation of a more abstract schema for a selection theory, which in turn helped to generate new specific theories in many fields, including economics, genetics, sociobiology, and artificial intelligence. Analogy is one mechanism for effecting conceptual change (see Chi & Ohlsson, Chap. 16).

A Capsule History

The history of the study of analogy includes three interwoven streams of research, which respectively emphasize analogy in relation to psychometric measurement of intelligence, metaphor, and the representation of knowledge.

Psychometric Tradition

Work in the psychometric tradition focuses on four-term or "proportional" analogies in the form A:B::C:D, such as HAND: FINGER :: FOOT: ?, where the problem is to infer the missing D term (TOE) that is related to C in the same way B is related to A (see Sternberg, Chap. 31). Thus A:B plays the role of source analog and C:D plays the role of target. Proportional analogies were discussed by Aristotle (see Hesse, 1966) and in the early decades of modern psychology became a centerpiece of efforts to define and measure intelligence. Charles Spearman (1923, 1927) argued that the best account of observed individual differences in cognitive performance was based on a general or *g* factor, with the remaining variance being unique to the particular task. He reviewed several studies that revealed high correlations between performance in solving analogy problems and the *g* factor. Spearman's student John C. Raven (1938) developed the Raven's Progressive Matrices Test (RPM), which requires selection of a geometric figure to fill an empty cell in a two-dimensional matrix (typically 3×3) of such figures. Similar to a geometric proportional analogy, the RPM requires participants to extract and apply information based on visuospatial relations. (See Hunt, 1974, and Carpenter, Just, & Shell, 1990, for analyses of strategies for solving RPM problems.) The RPM proved to be an especially pure measure of *g*.

Raymond Cattell (1971), another student of Spearman, elaborated his mentor's theory by distinguishing between two components of *g*: *crystallized* intelligence, which depends on previously learned information or skills, and *fluid* intelligence, which involves reasoning with novel information. As a form of inductive reasoning, analogy would be expected to require fluid intelligence. Cattell confirmed Spearman's (1946) observation that analogy tests and the RPM provide sensitive measures of *g*, clarifying that

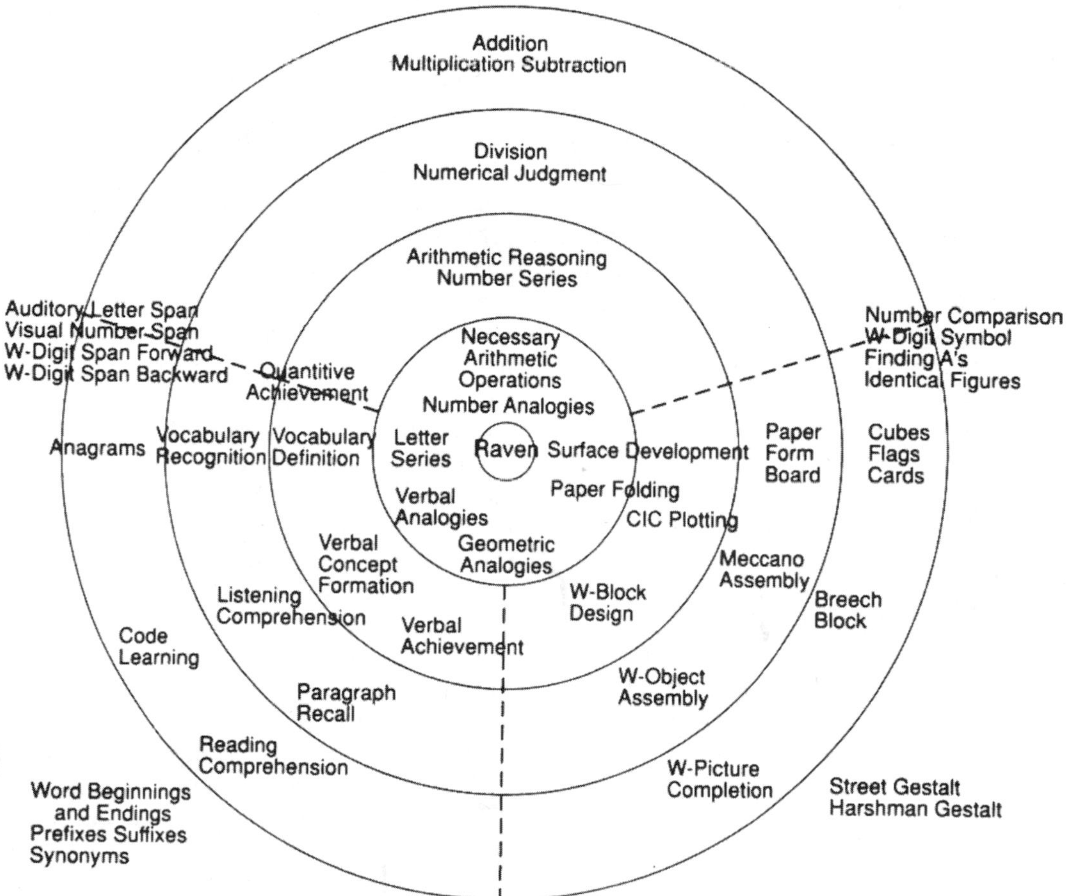

Figure 6.2. Multidimensional scaling solution based on intercorrelations among the Raven's Progressive Matrices test, analogy tests, and other common tests of cognitive function. (From Snow, Kyllonen, & Marshalek, 1984, p. 92. Reprinted by permission.)

they primarily measure fluid intelligence (although verbal analogies based on difficult vocabulary items also depend on crystallized intelligence). Figure 6.2 graphically depicts the centrality of RPM performance in a space defined by individual differences in performance on various cognitive tasks. Note that numeric, verbal, and geometric analogies cluster around the RPM at the center of the figure.

Because four-term analogies and the RPM are based on small numbers of relatively well-specified elements and relations, it is possible to manipulate the complexity of such problems systematically and analyze performance (based on response latencies and error rates) in terms of component processes (e.g., Mulholland, Pellegrino, & Glaser, 1980; Sternberg, 1977). The earliest computational models of analogy were developed for four-term analogy problems (Evans, 1968; Reitman, 1965). The basic components of these models were elaborations of those proposed by Spearman (1923), including encoding of the terms, accessing a relation between the A and B terms, and evoking a comparable relation between the C and D terms.

More recently, four-term analogy problems and the RPM have figured prominently in neuropsychological and neuroimaging studies of reasoning (e.g., Bunge, Wendelken, Badre & Wagner, 2004; Kroger et al., 2002; Luo et al., 2003; Prabhakaran et al., 1997; Waltz et al., 1999; Wharton et al., 2000). Analogical reasoning depends on working memory (see Morrison, Chap. 19). The neural basis of working memory includes the dorsolateral prefrontal cortex, an area of the brain that becomes increasingly activated as the complexity of the problem (measured in terms of number of relations relevant to the solution) increases. It has been argued that this area underlies the fluid component of Spearman's *g* factor in intelligence (Duncan et al., 2000), and it plays an important role in many reasoning tasks (see Goel, Chap. 20).

Metaphor

Analogy is closely related to metaphor and related forms of symbolic expression that arise in everyday language (e.g., "the evening of life," "the idea blossomed"), in literature (Holyoak, 1982), the arts, and cultural practices such as ceremonies (see Holyoak & Thagard, 1995, Chap. 9). Similar to analogy in general, metaphors are characterized by an asymmetry between target (conventionally termed "tenor") and source ("vehicle") domains (e.g., the target/tenor in "the evening of life" is life, which is understood in terms of the source/vehicle of time of day). In addition, a mapping (the "grounds" for the metaphor) connects the source and target, allowing the domains to interact to generate a new conceptualization (Black, 1962). Metaphors are a special kind of analogy in that the source and target domains are always semantically distant (Gentner, 1982; Gentner, Falkenhainer, & Skorstad, 1988), and the two domains are often blended rather than simply mapped (e.g., in "the idea blossomed," the target is directly described in terms of an action term derived from the source). In addition, metaphors are often combined with other symbolic "figures" – especially metonymy (substitution of an associated concept). For example, "sword" is a metonymic expression for weaponry, derived from its ancient association as the prototypical weapon – "Raising interests rates is the Federal Reserve Board's sword in the battle against inflation" extends the metonymy into metaphor.

Fauconnier and Turner (1998; Fauconnier, 2001) analyzed complex conceptual blends that are akin to metaphor. A typical example is a description of the voyage of a modern catamaran sailing from San Francisco to Boston that was attempting to beat the speed record set by a clipper ship that had sailed the same route over a century earlier. A magazine account written during the catamaran's voyage said the modern boat was "barely maintaining a 4.5 day lead over the ghost of the clipper *Northern Light*. . . . " Fauconnier and Turner observed that the magazine writer was describing a "boat race" that never took place in any direct sense; rather, the writer was blending the separate voyages of the two ships into an imaginary race. The fact that such conceptual blends are so natural and easy to understand attests to the fact that people can readily comprehend novel metaphors.

Lakoff and Johnson (1980; also Lakoff & Turner, 1989) argued that much of human experience, especially its abstract aspects, is grasped in terms of broad conceptual metaphors (e.g., events occurring in time are understood by analogy to objects moving in space). Time, for example, is understood in terms of objects in motion through space as in expressions such as "My birthday is fast approaching" and "The time for action has arrived." (See Boroditsky, 2000, for evidence of how temporal metaphors influence cognitive judgments.) As Lakoff and Turner (1989) pointed out, the course of a life is understood in terms of time in the solar year (youth is springtime; old age is winter). Life is also conventionally conceptualized as a journey. Such conventional metaphors can still be used in creative ways, as illustrated by Robert Frost's famous poem, "The Road Not Taken":

> Two roads diverged in a wood, and I –
> I took the one less traveled by,
> And that has made all the difference.

According to Lakoff and Turner, comprehension of this passage depends on our implicit knowledge of the metaphor that life is a journey. This knowledge includes understanding several interrelated correspondences (e.g., person is a traveler, purposes are destinations, actions are routes, difficulties in life are impediments to travel, counselors are guides, and progress is the distance traveled).

Psychological research has focused on demonstrations that metaphors are integral to everyday language understanding (Glucksberg, Gildea, & Bookin, 1982; Keysar, 1989) and debate about whether metaphor is better conceptualized as a kind of analogy (Wolff & Gentner, 2000) or a kind of categorization (Glucksberg & Keysar, 1990; Glucksberg, McClone, & Manfredi, 1997). A likely resolution is that novel metaphors are interpreted by much the same process as analogies, whereas more conventional metaphors are interpreted as more general schemas (Gentner, Bowdle, Wolff, & Boronat, 2001).

Knowledge Representation

The most important influence on analogy research in the cognitive science tradition has been concerned with the representation of knowledge within computational systems. Many seminal ideas were developed by the philosopher Mary Hesse (1966), who was in turn influenced by Aristotle's discussions of analogy in scientific classification and Black's (1962) interactionist view of metaphor. Hesse placed great stress on the purpose of analogy as a tool for scientific discovery and conceptual change and on the close connections between causal relations and analogical mapping. In the 1970s, work in artificial intelligence and psychology focused on the representation of complex knowledge of the sort used in scientific reasoning, problem solving, story comprehension, and other tasks that require structured knowledge. A key aspect of structured knowledge is that elements can be flexibly *bound* into the roles of relations. For example, "dog bit man" and "man bit dog" have the same elements and the same relation, but the role bindings have been reversed, radically altering the meaning. How the mind and brain accomplish role binding is thus a central problem to be solved by any psychological theory of structured knowledge, including any theory of analogy (see Doumas & Hummel, Chap. 4).

In the 1980s, a number of cognitive scientists recognized the centrality of analogy as a tool for discovery and its close connection with theories of knowledge representation. Winston (1980), guided by Minsky's (1975) treatment of knowledge representation, built a computer model of analogy that highlighted the importance of causal relations in guiding analogical inference. Other researchers in artificial intelligence also began to consider the use of complex analogies in reasoning and learning (Kolodner, 1983; Schank, 1982), leading to an approach to artificial intelligence termed *case-based reasoning* (see Kolodner, 1993).

Around 1980, two research projects in psychology began to consider analogy in relation to knowledge representation and eventually integrate computational modeling with detailed experimental studies of human analogical reasoning. Gentner (1982, 1983; Gentner & Gentner, 1983) began working on mental models and analogy in science. She emphasized that in analogy, the key similarities lie in the *relations* that hold within the domains (e.g., the flow of electrons in an electrical circuit is analogically similar to the flow of people in a crowded subway tunnel), rather than in features of individual objects (e.g., electrons do not resemble people). Moreover, analogical similarities often depend on *higher-order* relations – relations *between* relations. For example, adding a resistor to a circuit *causes* a decrease in flow of electricity, just as adding a narrow gate in the subway tunnel would decrease the rate at which people pass through (where *causes* is a higher-order relation). In her structure-mapping theory, Gentner proposed that analogy entails finding a structural alignment, or mapping, between domains. In this theory, alignment between two representational structures is characterized by structural parallelism (consistent, one-to-one correspondences between mapped elements) and systematicity – an implicit preference for deep, interconnected systems of relations governed by higher-order relations, such as causal, mathematical, or functional relations.

Holyoak (1985; Gick & Holyoak, 1980, 1983; Holyoak & Koh, 1987) focused on the role of analogy in problem solving with a strong concern for the role of pragmatics in analogy – that is, how causal relations that impact current goals and context guide the interpretation of an analogy. Holyoak and Thagard (1989a, 1995) developed an approach to analogy in which several factors were viewed as jointly constraining analogical reasoning. According to their multiconstraint theory, people tend to find mappings that maximize *similarity* of corresponding elements and relations, *structural* parallelism (i.e., isomorphism, defined by consistent, one-to-one correspondences), and *pragmatic* factors such as the importance of elements and relations for achieving a goal. Gick and Holyoak (1983) provided evidence that analogy can furnish the seed for forming new relational categories by abstracting the relational correspondences between examples into a schema for a class of problems. Analogy was viewed as a central part of human induction (Holland, Holyoak, Nisbett, & Thagard, 1986; see Sloman & Lagnado, Chap. 5) with close ties to other basic thinking processes, including causal inference (see Buehner & Cheng, Chap. 7), categorization (see Medin & Rips, Chap. 3), deductive reasoning (see Evans, Chap. 8), and problem solving (see Novick & Bassok, Chap. 14).

Analogical Reasoning: Overview of Phenomena

This section provides an overview of the major phenomena involving analogical reasoning that have been established by empirical investigations. This review is organized around the major components of analogy depicted in Figure 6.1. These components are inherently interrelated, so the connections among them are also discussed. The retrieval and mapping components are first considered followed by inference and relational generalization.

Retrieval and Mapping

A PARADIGM FOR INVESTIGATING ANALOGICAL TRANSFER

Gick and Holyoak (1980, 1983) introduced a general laboratory paradigm for investigating analogical transfer in the context of problem solving. The general approach was first to provide people with a source analog in the guise of some incidental context, such as an experiment on "story memory." Later, participants were asked to solve a problem that was in fact analogous to the story they had studied earlier. The questions of central interest were (1) whether people would spontaneously notice the relevance of the source analog and use it to solve the target problem, and (2) whether they could solve the analogy once they were cued to consider the source. Spontaneous transfer of the analogous solution implies successful retrieval and mapping; cued transfer implies successful mapping once the need to retrieve the source has been removed.

The source analog used by Gick and Holyoak (1980) was a story about a general who is trying to capture a fortress controlled by a dictator and needs to get his army to the fortress at full strength. Because the entire army could not pass safely along any single road, the general sends his men in small groups down several roads simultaneously. Arriving at the same time, the groups join together and capture the fortress.

A few minutes after reading this story under instructions to read and remember it (along with two other irrelevant stories), participants were asked to solve a tumor problem (Duncker, 1945), in which a doctor has to figure out how to use rays to destroy a stomach tumor without injuring the patient in the process. The crux of the problem is that it seems that the rays will have the same effect on the healthy tissue as on the tumor – high intensity will destroy both, whereas low intensity will destroy neither. The key issue is to determine how the rays can be made to impact the tumor selectively while sparing the surrounding tissue. The source analog, if it can be retrieved and mapped, can be used to generate a "convergence" solution to the tumor problem, one that parallels the general's military strategy: Instead of using a single high-intensity ray, the doctor could administer several low-intensity rays at once from different directions. In that way, each ray would be at low intensity along its path, and hence, harmless to the healthy tissue, but the effects of the rays would sum to achieve the effect of a high-intensity ray at their focal point, the site of the tumor.

When Gick and Holyoak (1980) asked college students to solve the tumor problem, without a source analog, only about 10% of them produced the convergence solution. When the general story had been studied, but no hint to use it was given, only about 20% of participants produced the convergence solution. In contrast, when the same participants were then given a simple hint that "you may find one of the stories you read earlier to be helpful in solving the problem," about 75% succeeded in generating the analogous convergence solution. In other words, people often fail to notice superficially dissimilar source analogs that they could readily use.

This gap between the difficulty of retrieving remote analogs and the relative ease of mapping them has been replicated many times, both with adults (Gentner, Rattermann, & Forbus, 1993; Holyoak & Koh, 1987; Spencer & Weisberg, 1986) and with young children (Chen, 1996; Holyoak, Junn, & Billman, 1984; Tunteler & Resing, 2002). When analogs must be cued from long-term memory, cases from a domain similar to that of the cue are retrieved much more readily than cases from remote domains (Keane, 1987; Seifert, McKoon, Abelson, & Ratcliff, 1986). For example, Keane (1987) measured retrieval of a convergence analog to the tumor problem when the source analog was studied 1 to 3 days prior to presentation of the target radiation problem. Keane found that 88% of participants retrieved a source analog from the same domain (a story about a surgeon treating a brain tumor), whereas only 12% retrieved a source from a remote domain (the general story). This difference in ease of access was dissociable from the ease of postaccess mapping and transfer because the frequency of generating the convergence solution to the radiation problem once the source analog was cued was high and equal (about 86%), regardless of whether the source analog was from the same or a different domain.

DIFFERENTIAL IMPACT OF SIMILARITY AND STRUCTURE ON RETRIEVAL VERSUS MAPPING

The main empirical generalization concerning retrieval and mapping is that similarity of individual concepts in the analogs has a relatively greater impact on retrieval, whereas mapping is relatively more sensitive to relational correspondences (Gentner et al., 1993; Holyoak & Koh, 1987; Ross, 1987, 1989). However, this dissociation is not absolute. Watching the movie *West Side Story* for the first time is likely to trigger a reminding of Shakespeare's *Romeo and Juliet* despite the displacement of the characters in the two works over centuries and continents. The two stories both involve young lovers who suffer because of the disapproval of their respective social groups, causing a false report of death, which in turn leads to tragedy. It is these structural parallels between the two stories that make them analogous rather than simply that both stories involve a young man and woman, a disapproval, a false report, and a tragedy.

Experimental work on story reminding confirms the importance of structure, as well as similarity of concepts, in retrieving analogs from memory. Wharton and his colleagues (Wharton et al., 1994; Wharton, Holyoak, & Lange, 1996) performed a series of experiments in which college students tried to find connections between stories that overlapped in various ways in terms of the actors and actions and the underlying themes. In a typical experiment, the students first studied about a dozen "target" stories presented in the guise of a study of story understanding. For example, one target story exemplified a theme often called "sour grapes" after one of Aesop's fables. The theme in this story is that the protagonist tries to achieve a goal, fails, and then retroactively decides the goal had not really been desirable after all. More specifically, the actions involved someone trying unsuccessfully to get accepted to an Ivy League college. After a delay, the students read a set of different cue stories and were asked to write down any story or stories from the first session of which they were reminded. Some stories (far analogs) exemplified the same theme, but with very different characters and actions (e.g., a "sour grapes" fairy tale about a unicorn who tries to cross a river but is forced to turn back). Other stories were far "disanalogs" formed by reorganizing the characters and actions to represent a distinctly different theme (e.g., "self-doubt" – the failure to achieve a goal leads the protagonist to doubt his or her own ability or merit). Thus, neither type of cue was similar to the target story in terms of individual elements (characters and actions); however, the far analog maintained structural correspondences of higher-order causal relations with the target story, whereas the far disanalog did not.

Besides varying the relation between the cue and target stories, Wharton et al. (1994) also varied the number of target stories that were in some way related to a single cue. When only one target story in a set had been studied ("singleton" condition), the probability of reminding was about equal, regardless of whether the cue was analogous to the target. However, when two target stories had been studied (e.g., both "sour grapes" and "self-doubt," forming a "competition" condition), the analogous target was more likely to be retrieved than the disanalogous one. The advantage of the far analog in the competition condition was maintained even when a week intervened between initial study of the target stories and presentation of the cue stories (Wharton et al., 1996).

These results demonstrate that structure does influence analogical retrieval, but its impact is much more evident when multiple memory traces, each somewhat similar to the cue, must compete to be retrieved. Such retrieval competition is likely typical of everyday analogical reminding. Other evidence indicates that having people generate case examples, as opposed to simply asking them to remember cases presented earlier, enhances structure-based access to source analogs (Blanchette & Dunbar, 2000).

THE "RELATIONAL SHIFT" IN DEVELOPMENT

Retrieval is thus sensitive to structure and direct similarity of concepts. Conversely, mapping is sensitive to direct similarity and structure (e.g., Reed, 1987; Ross, 1989). Young children are particularly sensitive to direct similarity of objects; when asked to identify corresponding elements in two analogs, their mappings are dominated by object similarity when semantic and structural constraints conflict (Gentner & Toupin, 1986). Younger children are particularly likely to map on the basis of object similarity when the relational response requires integration of multiple relations, and hence, is more dependent on working memory resources (Richland, Morrison, & Holyoak, 2004). The developmental transition toward greater reliance on structure in mapping has been termed the "relational shift" (Gentner & Rattermann, 1991). Greater sensitivity to relations with age appears to arise owing to a combination of incremental accretion of knowledge about relational concepts and stage-like increments in working memory capacity (Halford, 1993; Halford & Wilson, 1980). (For reviews of developmental research on analogy, see Goswami, 1992, 2001; Halford, Chap. 22 ; Holyoak & Thagard, 1995).

GOAL-DIRECTED MAPPING

Mapping is guided not only by relational structure and element similarity but also by the goals of the analogist (Holyoak, 1985). People draw analogies not to find a pristine isomorphism for its own sake but to make plausible inferences that will achieve their goals. Particularly when the mapping is inherently ambiguous, the constraint of pragmatic centrality – relevance to goals – is critical (Holyoak, 1985). Spellman and Holyoak (1996) investigated the impact of processing goals on the mappings generated for inherently ambiguous analogies. In one experiment, college students read two science fiction stories about countries on two planets. These countries were interrelated by various economic and military alliances. Participants first made judgments about individual countries based on either economic or military relationships and were then asked mapping questions about which countries on one planet corresponded to which on the other. Schematically, planet 1 included three countries, such that "Afflu" was economically richer than "Barebrute," whereas the latter was militarily stronger than "Compak." Planet 2 included four countries, with "Grainwell" being richer than "Hungerall" and "Millpower" being stronger than "Mightless." The critical aspect of this analogy problem is that Barebrute (planet 1) is both economically weak (like Hungerall on planet 2) and militarily strong (like Millpower) and therefore, has two competing mappings that are equally supported by structural and similarity constraints.

Spellman and Holyoak (1996) found that participants whose processing goal led them to focus on economic relationships tended to map Barebrute to Hungerall rather than Millpower, whereas those whose processing goal led them to focus on military relationships had the opposite preferred mapping. The variation in pragmatic centrality of the information thus served to decide between the competing mappings. One interpretation of such findings is that pragmatically central propositions tend to be considered earlier and more often than those that are less goal relevant and hence, dominate the mapping process (Hummel & Holyoak, 1997).

COHERENCE IN ANALOGICAL MAPPING

The key idea of Holyoak and Thagard's (1989a) multiconstraint theory of analogy is that several different kinds of constraints – similarity, structure, and purpose – all interact to determine the optimal set of correspondences between source and target. A good analogy is one that appears *coherent* in the sense that multiple constraints converge on a solution that satisfies as many different constraints as possible (Thagard, 2000). Everyday use of analogies depends on the human ability to find coherent mappings – even when source and target are complex and the mappings are ambiguous. For example, political debate often makes use of analogies between prior situations and some current controversy (Blanchette & Dunbar, 2001, 2002). Ever since World War II, politicians in the United States and elsewhere have periodically argued that some military intervention was justified because the current situation was analogous to that leading to World War II. A commonsensical mental representation of World War II, the source analog, amounts to a story figuring an evil villain, Hitler; misguided appeasers, such as Neville Chamberlain; and clear-sighted heroes, such as Winston Churchill and Franklin Delano Roosevelt. The countries involved in World War II included the villains, Germany and Japan; the victims, such as Austria, Czechoslovakia, and Poland; and the heroic defenders, notably Britain and the United States.

A series of American presidents have used the World War II analog as part of their argument for American military intervention abroad (see Khong, 1992). These include Harry Truman (Korea, 1950), Lyndon Johnson (Vietnam, 1965), George Bush senior (Kuwait and Iraq, 1991), and his son George W. Bush (Iraq, 2003). Analogies to World War II have also been used to support less aggressive responses. Most notably, during the Cuban missile crisis of 1962, President John F. Kennedy decided against a surprise attack on Cuba in part because he did not want the United States to behave in a way that could be equated to Japan's surprise attack on Pearl Harbor.

The World War II situation was, of course, very complex and is never likely to map perfectly onto any new foreign policy problem. Nonetheless, by selectively focusing on goal-relevant aspects of the source and target and using multiple constraints in combination, people can often find coherent mappings in situations of this sort. After the Iraqi invasion of Kuwait in 1990, President George H. W. Bush argued that Saddam Hussein, the Iraqi leader, was analogous to Adolf Hitler and that the Persian Gulf crisis in general was analogous to events that had led to World War II a half-century earlier. By drawing the analogy between Hussein and Hitler, President Bush encouraged a reasoning process that led to the construction of a coherent system of roles for the players in the Gulf situation. The popular understanding of World War II provided the source, and analogical mapping imposed a set of roles on the target Gulf situation by selectively emphasizing the most salient relational parallels between the two situations. Once the analogical correspondences were established (with Iraq identified as an expansionist dictatorship like Germany, Kuwait as its first victim, Saudi Arabia as the next potential victim, and the United States as the main defender of the Gulf states), the clear analogical inference was that both self-interest and moral considerations required immediate military intervention by the United States. Aspects of the Persian Gulf situation that did not map well to World War II (e.g., lack of democracy in Kuwait) were pushed to the background.

Of course, the analogy between the two situations was by no means perfect. Similarity at the object level favored mapping the United States of 1991 to the United States of World War II simply because it was the same country, which would in turn support mapping Bush to President Roosevelt. However, the United States did not enter World War II until it was bombed by Japan, well after Hitler had marched through much of Europe. One might therefore argue that the United States of 1991 mapped to Great Britain of World War II and that Bush mapped to Winston Churchill, the British Prime Minister (because Bush, similar to Churchill, led his nation and Western allies in early opposition to aggression). These conflicting pressures made the mappings ambiguous. However, the pressure to maintain structural consistency implies that people who mapped the United States to Britain should also tend to map Bush to Churchill, whereas those who mapped the United States to the United States should instead map Bush to Roosevelt.

During the first 2 days of the U.S.-led counterattack against the Iraqi invasion of Kuwait, Spellman and Holyoak (1992) asked a group of American undergraduates a few questions to find out how they interpreted the analogy between the then-current situation in the Persian Gulf and World War II. The undergraduates were asked to suppose that Saddam Hussein was analogous to Hitler. Regardless of whether they believed the analogy was appropriate, they were then asked to write down the most natural match in the World War II situation for Iraq, the United States, Kuwait, Saudi Arabia, and George Bush. For those students who gave evidence that they knew the basic facts about World War II, the majority produced mappings that fell into one of two patterns. Those students who mapped the United States to itself also mapped Bush to Roosevelt; these same students also tended to map Saudi Arabia to Great Britain. Other students, in contrast, mapped the United States to Great Britain and Bush to Churchill, which in turn (so as to maintain one-to-one correspondences) forced Saudi Arabia to map to some country other than Britain. The mapping for Kuwait (which did not depend on the choice of mappings for Bush, the United States, or Saudi Arabia) was usually to one or two of the early victims of Germany in World War II (usually Austria or Poland).

The analogy between the Persian Gulf situation and World War II thus generated a "bistable" mapping: People tended to provide mappings based on either of two coherent but mutually incompatible sets of correspondences. Spellman and Holyoak (1992) went on to perform a second study, using a different group of undergraduates, to show that people's preferred mappings could be pushed around by manipulating their knowledge of the source analog, World War II. Because many undergraduates were lacking in knowledge about the major participants and events in World War II, it proved possible to "guide" them to one or the other mapping pattern by having them first read a slightly biased summary of events in World War II. The various summaries were all historically "correct," in the sense of providing only information taken directly from history books, but each contained slightly different information and emphasized different points. Each summary began with an identical passage about Hitler's acquisition of Austria, Czechoslovakia, and Poland and the efforts by Britain and France to stop him. The versions then diverged. Some versions went on to emphasize the personal role of Churchill and the national role of Britain; other versions placed greater emphasis on what Roosevelt and the United States did to further the war effort. After reading one of these summaries of World War II, the undergraduates were asked the same mapping questions as had been used in the previous study. The same bistable mapping patterns emerged as before, but this time the summaries influenced which of the two coherent patterns of responses students tended to give. People who read a "Churchill" version tended to map Bush to Churchill and the United States to Great Britain, whereas those who read a "Roosevelt" version tended to map Bush to Roosevelt and the United States to the United States. It thus appears that even when an analogy is messy and ambiguous, the constraints on analogical coherence produce predictable interpretations of how the source and target fit together.

Achieving analogical coherence in mapping does not, of course, guarantee that the source will provide a clear and compelling basis for planning a course of action to deal with the target situation. In 1991, President Bush considered Hussein enough of a Hitler to justify intervention in Kuwait but not enough of one to warrant his removal from power in Iraq. A decade later his son, President George W. Bush, reinvoked the World War II analogy to justify a preemptive invasion of Iraq itself. Bush claimed (falsely, as was later revealed) that Hussein was acquiring biological and perhaps nuclear weapons that posed an imminent threat to the United States and its allies. Historical analogies can be used to obfuscate as well as to illuminate.

Figure 6.3. An example of a pair of pictures used in studies of analogical mapping with arrows added to indicate featural and relational responses. (From Tohill & Holyoak, 2000, p. 31. Reprinted by permission.)

WORKING MEMORY IN ANALOGICAL MAPPING

Analogical reasoning, because it depends on manipulating structured representations of knowledge, would be expected to make critical use of working memory. The role of working memory in analogy has been explored using a picture-mapping paradigm introduced by Markman and Gentner (1993). An example of stimuli similar to those they used is shown in Figure 6.3. In their experiments, college students were asked to examine the two pictures and then decide (for this hypothetical example) what object in the bottom picture best goes with the man in the top picture. When this single mapping is considered in isolation, people often indicate that the boy in the bottom picture goes with the man in the top picture based on perceptual and semantic similarity of these elements. However, when people are asked to match not just one object but three (e.g., the man, dog, and the tree in the top picture to objects in the bottom picture), they are led to build an integrated representation of the relations among the objects and of higher-order relations between relations. In the top picture, a man is unsuccessfully trying to restrain a dog, which then chases the cat. In the bottom picture, the tree is unsuccessful in restraining the dog, which then chases the boy. Based on these multiple interacting relations, the preferred match to the man in the top picture is not the boy in the lower scene but the tree. Consequently, people who map three objects at once are more likely to map the man to the tree on the basis of their similar relational roles than are people who map the man alone.

Whereas Markman and Gentner (1993) showed that the number of objects to be mapped influences the balance between the impact of element similarity versus relational structure, other studies using the picture-mapping paradigm have demonstrated that manipulations that constrict working memory resources have a similar impact. Waltz, Lau, Grewal, and Holyoak (2000) asked college students to map pictures while performing a secondary task designed to tax working memory (e.g., generating random digits). Adding a dual task diminished relational responses and increased similarity-based responses (see Morrison, Chap. 19). A manipulation that increases people's anxiety level (performing mathematical calculations under speed pressure prior to the mapping task) yielded a similar shift in mapping responses (Tohill & Holyoak, 2000). Most dramatically, degeneration of the frontal lobes radically impairs relation-based mapping (Morrison et al., 2004). In related work using complex story analogs, Krawczyk, Holyoak, and Hummel (2004) demonstrated that mappings (and inferences) based on element similarity versus relational structure were made about equally often when the element similarities were salient and the relational structure was highly complex. All these findings support the hypothesis that mapping on the basis of relations requires adequate working memory to represent and manipulate role bindings (Hummel & Holyoak, 1997).

Inference and Relational Generalization

COPY WITH SUBSTITUTION AND GENERATION

Analogical inference – using a source analog to form a new conjecture, whether it be a step toward solving a math problem (Reed, Dempster, & Ettinger, 1985; see Novick & Bassok, Chap. 14), a scientific hypothesis (see Dunbar & Fugelsang, Chap. 29), a diagnosis for puzzling medical symptoms (see Patel, Arocha, & Zhang, Chap. 30), or a basis for deciding a legal case (see Ellsworth, Chap. 28) – is the fundamental purpose of analogical reasoning. Mapping serves to highlight correspondences between the source and target, including "alignable differences" (Markman & Gentner, 1993) – the distinct but corresponding elements of the two analogs. These correspondences provide the input to an inference engine that generates new target propositions. The basic form of analogical inference has been called "copy with substitution and generation" (CWSG; Holyoak et al., 1994). CWSG involves constructing target analogs of unmapped source propositions by substituting the corresponding target element, if known, for each source element, and if no corresponding target element exists, postulating one as needed. This procedure gives rise to two important corollaries concerning inference errors. First, if critical elements are difficult to map (e.g., because of strong representational asymmetries such as those that hinder mapping a discrete set of elements to a continuous variable; Bassok & Holyoak, 1989; Bassok & Olseth, 1995), then no inferences can be constructed. Second, if elements are mismapped, predictable inference errors will result (Holyoak et al., 1994; Reed, 1987).

All major computational models of analogical inference use some variant of CWSG (e.g., Falkenhainer et al., 1989; Halford et al., 1994; Hofstadter & Mitchell, 1994; Holyoak et al., 1994; Hummel & Holyoak, 2003; Keane & Brayshaw, 1988; Kokinov & Petrov, 2001). CWSG is critically dependent on variable binding and mapping; hence, models that lack these key computational properties (e.g., traditional connectionist models) fail to capture even the most basic aspects of analogical inference (see Doumas & Hummel, Chap. 4).

Athough all analogy models use some form of CWSG, additional constraints on this inference mechanism are critical (Clement & Gentner, 1991; Holyoak et al., 1994; Markman, 1997). If CWSG were unconstrained, then *any* unmapped source proposition would generate an inference about the target. Such a loose criterion for inference generation would lead to rampant errors whenever the source was not isomorphic to a subset of the target, and such isomorphism will virtually never hold for problems of realistic complexity. Several constraints on CWSG were demonstrated in a study by Lassaline (1996; also see Clement & Gentner, 1991; Spellman & Holyoak, 1996). Lassaline had college students read analogs describing properties of hypothetical animals and then rate various possible target inferences for the probability that the conclusion would be true given the information in the premise. Participants rated potential inferences as more probable when the source and target analogs shared more attributes, and hence, mapped more strongly. In addition, their ratings were sensitive to structural and pragmatic constraints. The presence of a higher-order linking relation in the source made an inference more credible. For example, if the source and target animals were both described as having an acute sense of smell, and the source animal was said to have a weak immune system that "develops before" its acute sense of smell, then the inference that the target animal also has a weak immune system would be bolstered relative to stating only that the source animal had an acute sense of smell "and" a weak immune system. The benefit conveyed by the higher-order relation was increased if the relation was explicitly causal (e.g., in the source animal, a weak immune system "causes" its acute sense of smell), rather than less clearly causal ("develops before"). (See Hummel & Holyoak, 2003, for a simulation of this and other inference results using a CWSG algorithm.)

An important question is when analogical inferences are made and how inferences generated by CWSG relate to facts about the target analog that are stated directly. One extreme possibility is that people only make analogical inferences when instructed to do so and that inferences are carefully "marked" as such so they will never be confused with known facts about the target. At the other extreme, it is possible that some analogical inferences are triggered when the target is first processed (given that the source has been activated) and that such inferences are then integrated with prior knowledge of the target. One paradigm for addressing this issue is based on testing for false "recognition" of potential inferences in a subsequent memory test. The logic of the recognition paradigm (Bransford, Barclay, & Franks, 1972) is that if an inference has been made and integrated with the rest of the target analog, then later the reasoner will falsely believe that the inference had been directly presented.

Early work by Schustack and Anderson (1979) provided evidence that people sometimes falsely report that analogical inferences were actually presented as facts. Blanchette and Dunbar (2002) performed a series of experiments designed to assess when analogical inferences are made. They had college students (in Canada) read a text describing a current political issue, possible legalization of marijuana use, which served as the target analog. Immediately afterward, half the students read, "The situation with marijuana can be compared to . . . ", followed by an additional text describing the period early in the twentieth century when alcohol use was prohibited. Importantly, the students in the analogy condition were not told how prohibition mapped onto the marijuana debate, nor were they asked to draw any inferences. After a delay (1 week in one experiment, 15 minutes in another), the students were given a list of sentences and were asked to decide whether each sentence had actually been presented in the text about marijuana use. The critical items were sentences such as "The government could set up agencies to control the quality and take over the distribution of marijuana." These sentences had never been presented; however, they could be generated as analogical inferences by CWSG based on a parallel statement contained in the source analog ("The government set up agencies to control the quality and take over the distribution of alcohol"). Blanchette and Dunbar found that students in the analogy condition said "yes" to analogical inferences about 50% of the time, whereas control subjects who had not read the source analog about prohibition said "yes" only about 25% of the time. This tendency to falsely "recognize" analogical inferences that had never been read was obtained both after long and short delays and with both familiar and less familiar materials.

It thus appears that when people notice the connection between a source and target, and they are sufficiently engaged in an effort to understand the target situation, analogical inferences will be generated by CWSG and then integrated with prior knowledge of the target. At least sometimes, an analogical inference becomes accepted as a stated fact. This result obviously has important implications for understanding analogical reasoning, such as its potential for use as a tool for persuasion.

RELATIONAL GENERALIZATION

In addition to generating local inferences about the target by CWSG, analogical reasoning can give rise to relational generalizations – abstract schemas that establish an explicit representation of the commonalities between the source and the target. Comparison of multiple analogs can result in the induction of a schema, which in turn will facilitate subsequent transfer to additional analogs. The induction of such schemas has been demonstrated in both adults (Catrambone & Holyoak, 1989; Gick & Holyoak, 1983; Loewenstein, Thompson, & Gentner, 1999; Ross & Kennedy, 1990) and young children (Brown, Kane, & Echols, 1986; Chen & Daehler, 1989; Holyoak et al., 1984; Kotovsky & Gentner, 1996). People are able to induce schemas by comparing just two analogs to one another (Gick & Holyoak, 1983). Indeed, people will form schemas simply as a side effect of applying one solved source problem to an unsolved target problem (Novick & Holyoak, 1991; Ross & Kennedy, 1990).

In the case of problem schemas, more effective schemas are formed when the goal-relevant relations are the focus rather than incidental details (Brown et al., 1986; Brown, Kane, & Long, 1989; Gick & Holyoak, 1983). In general, any kind of processing that helps people focus on the underlying causal structure of the analogs, thereby encouraging learning of more effective problem schemas, will improve subsequent transfer to new problems. For example, Gick and Holyoak (1983) found that induction of a "convergence" schema from two disparate analogs was facilitated when each story stated the underlying solution principle abstractly: "If you need a large force to accomplish some purpose, but are prevented from applying such a force directly, many smaller forces applied simultaneously from different directions may work just as well." In some circumstances, transfer can also be improved by having the reasoner generate a problem analogous to an initial example (Bernardo, 2001). Other work has shown that abstract diagrams that highlight the basic idea of using multiple converging forces can aid in schema induction and subsequent transfer (Beveridge & Parkins, 1987; Gick & Holyoak, 1983) – especially when the diagram uses motion cues to convey perception of forces acting on a central target (Pedone, Hummel, & Holyoak, 2001; see Figure 6.4, top).

Although two examples can suffice to establish a useful schema, people are able to incrementally develop increasingly abstract schemas as additional examples are provided (Brown et al., 1986, 1989; Catrambone & Holyoak, 1989). However, even with multiple examples that allow novices to start forming schemas, people may still fail to transfer the analogous solution to a problem drawn from a different domain if a substantial delay intervenes or if the context is changed (Spencer & Weisberg, 1986). Nonetheless, as novices continue to develop

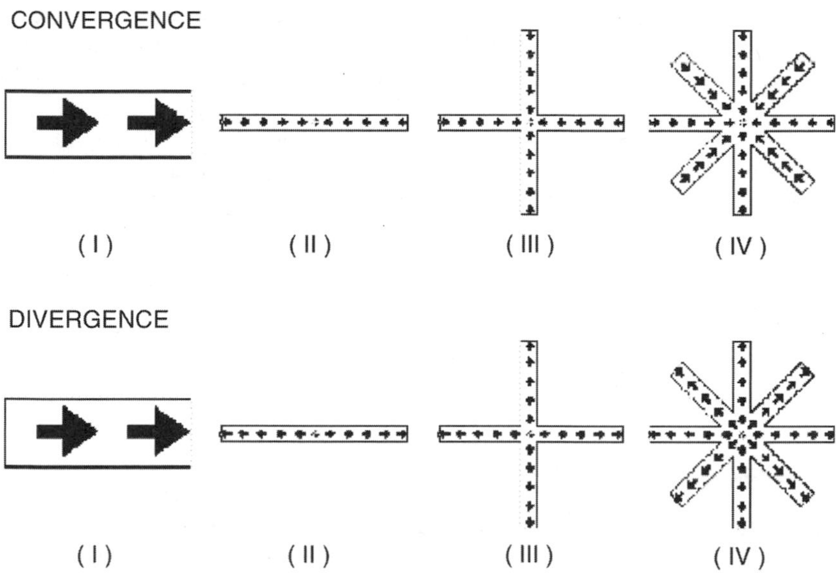

Figure 6.4. Sequence of diagrams used to convey the convergence schema by perceived motion. Top: sequence illustrating convergence (arrows appear to move inward in II–IV). Bottom: control sequence in which arrows diverge instead of converge (arrows appear to move outward in II–IV). (From Pedone, Holyoak, & Hummel, 2001, p. 217. Reprinted by permission.)

more powerful schemas, long-term transfer in an altered context can be dramatically improved (Barnett & Koslowski, 2002). For example, Catrambone and Holyoak (1989) gave college students a total of three convergence analogs to study, compare, and solve. The students were first asked a series of detailed questions designed to encourage them to focus on the abstract structure common to two of the analogs. After this abstraction training, the students were asked to solve another analog from a third domain (not the tumor problem), after which they were told the convergence solution to it (which most students were able to generate themselves). Finally, 1 week later, the students returned to participate in a different experiment. After the other experiment was completed, they were given the tumor problem to solve. More than 80% of participants came up with the converging rays solution without any hint. As the novice becomes an expert, the emerging schema becomes increasingly accessible and is triggered by novel problems that share its structure. Deeper similarities have been constructed between analogous situations that fit the schema. As schemas are acquired from examples, they in turn guide future mappings and inferences (Bassok, Wu, & Olseth, 1995).

Computational Models of Analogy

From its inception, work on analogy in relation to knowledge representation has involved the development of detailed computational models of the various components of analogical reasoning typically focusing on the central process of structure mapping. The most influential early models included SME (Structure Mapping Engine; Falkenhainer, Forbus, & Gentner, 1989), ACME (Analogical Mapping by Constraint Satisfaction; Holyoak & Thagard, 1989a), IAM (Incremental Analogy Model; Keane & Brayshaw, 1988), and Copycat (Hofstadter & Mitchell, 1994). More recently, models of analogy have been developed based on knowledge representations constrained by neural mechanisms (Hummel & Holyoak,

1992). These efforts included an approach based on the use of tensor products for variable binding, the STAR model (Structured Tensor Analogical Reasoning; Halford et al., 1994; see Halford, Chap. 22), and another based on neural synchrony, the LISA model (Learning and Inference with Schemas and Analogies; Hummel & Holyoak, 1997, 2003; see Doumas & Hummel, Chap. 4). (For a brief overview of computational models of analogy, see French, 2002.) Three models are sketched to illustrate the general nature of computational approaches to analogy.

Structure Mapping Engine (SME)

SME (Falkenhainer et al., 1989) illustrates how analogical mapping can be performed by algorithms based on partial graph matching. The basic knowledge representation for the inputs is based on a notation in the style of predicate calculus. If one takes a simple example based on the World War II analogy as it was used by President George Bush in 1991, a fragment might look like

SOURCE:
Führer-of (Hitler, Germany)
occupy (Germany, Austria)
evil (Hitler)
cause [evil (Hitler), occupy (Germany, Austria)]
prime-minister-of (Churchill, Great Britain)
cause [occupy (Germany, Austria), counterattack (Churchill, Hitler)]

TARGET:
president-of (Hussein, Iraq)
invade (Iraq, Kuwait)
evil (Hussein)
cause [evil (Hussein), invade (Iraq, Kuwait)]
president-of (Bush, United States)

SME distinguishes objects (role fillers, such as "Hitler"), attributes (one-place predicates, such as "evil" with its single role filler), first-order relations (multiplace predicates, such as "occupy" with its two role fillers), and higher-order relations (those such as "cause" that take at least one first-order relation as a role filler). As illustrated in Figure 6.5, the predicate-calculus notation is equivalent to a graph structure. An analogical mapping can then be viewed as a set of correspondences between partially matching graph structures.

The heart of the SME algorithm is a procedure for finding graph matches that satisfy certain criteria. The algorithm operates in three stages, progressing in a "local-to-global" direction. First, SME proposes local matches between all identical predicates and their associated role fillers. It is assumed similar predicates (e.g., "Führer-of" and "president-of"; "occupy" and "invade") are first transformed into more general predicates (e.g.,"leader-of"; "attack") that reveal a hidden identity. (In practice, the programmer must make the required substitutions so similar but nonidentical predicates can be matched.) The resulting matches are typically inconsistent in that one element in the source may match multiple elements in the target (e.g., Hitler might match either Hussein or Bush because all are "leaders"). Second, the resulting local matches are integrated into structurally consistent clusters or "kernels" (e.g., the possible match between Hitler and Bush is consistent with that between Germany and the United States, and so these matches would form part of a single kernel). Third, the kernels are merged into a small number of sets that are maximal in size (i.e., that include matches between the greatest number of nodes in the two graphs), while maintaining correspondences that are structurally consistent and one to one. SME then ranks the resulting sets of mappings by a structural evaluation metric that favors "deep" mappings (ones that include correspondences between higher-order relations). For our example, the optimal set will respectively map Hitler, Germany, Churchill, and Great Britain to Hussein, Iraq, Bush, and the United States because of the support provided by the mapping between the higher-order "cause" relations involving "occupy/invade." Using this optimal mapping, SME applies a CWSG algorithm to generate inferences about the target based on unmapped propositions in the source. Here, the final "cause" relation

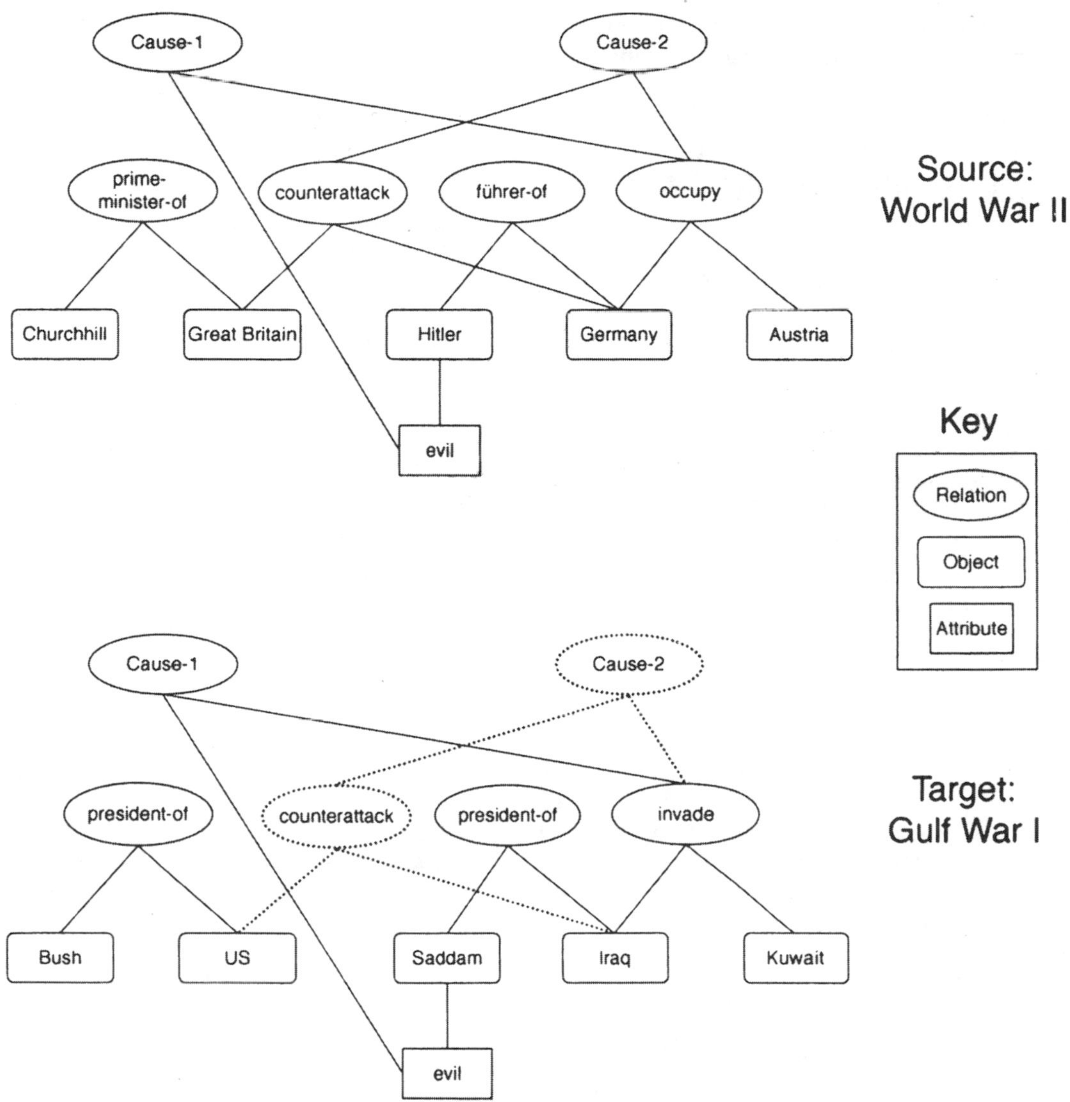

Figure 6.5. SME's graphical representation of a source and target analog.

in the source will yield the analogical inference, *cause [attack (Iraq, Kuwait), counterattack (Bush, Hussein)]*.

SME thus models the mapping and inference components of analogical reasoning. A companion model, MACFAC ("Many Are Called but Few Are Chosen"; Forbus, Gentner, & Law, 1995) deals with the initial retrieval of a source analog from long-term memory. MACFAC has an initial stage ("many are called") in which analogs are represented by *content vectors*, which code the relative number of occurrences of a particular predicate in the corresponding structured representation. (Content vectors are computed automatically from the underlying structural representations.) The content vector for the target is then matched to vectors for all analogs stored in memory, and the dot product for each analog pair is calculated as an index of similarity. The source analog with the highest dot product, plus other stored analogs with relatively high dot products, are marked as retrieved. In its second stage, MACFAC uses SME to assess the degree of the structural overlap between the target and each possible source, allowing the program to identify a smaller number of potential sources that have the highest degrees of structural parallelism with the target ("few are chosen"). As the content vectors used in the first stage of MACFAC do not code role bindings, the model provides a qualitative account of why the retrieval stage of analogy is less sensitive to structure than is the mapping stage.

Analogical Mapping by Constraint Satisfaction (ACME)

The ACME model (Holyoak, Novick, & Melz, 1994; Holyoak & Thagard, 1989a) was directly influenced by connectionist models based on parallel constraint satisfaction (Rumelhart, Smolensky, McClelland, & Hinton, 1986; see Doumas & Hummel, Chap. 4). ACME takes as input symbolic representations of the source and target analogs in essentially the same form as those used in SME. However, whereas SME focuses on structural constraints, ACME instantiates a multiconstraint theory in which structural, semantic, and pragmatic constraints interact to determine the optimal mapping. ACME accepts a numeric code for degree of similarity between predicates, which it uses as a constraint on mapping. Thus, ACME, unlike SME, can match similar predicates (e.g., "occupy" and "invade") without explicitly recoding them as identical. In addition, ACME accepts a numeric code for the pragmatic importance of a possible mapping, which is also used as a constraint.

ACME is based on a constraint satisfaction algorithm, which proceeds in three steps. First, a connectionist "mapping network" is constructed in which the units represent hypotheses about possible element mappings and the links represent specific instantiations of the general constraints (Figure 6.6). Second, an interactive-activation algorithm operates to "settle" the mapping network in order to identify the set of correspondences that collectively represent the "optimal" mapping between the analogs. Any constraint may be locally violated to establish optimal global coherence. Third, if the model is being used to generate inferences and correspondences, CWSG is applied to generate inferences based on the correspondences identified in the second step.

ACME has a companion model, ARCS (Analog Retrieval by Constraint Satisfaction; Thagard, Holyoak, Nelson, & Gochfeld, 1990) that models analog retrieval. Analogs in long-term memory are connected within a semantic network (see Medin & Rips, Chap. 3); this network of concepts provides the initial basis by which a target analog activates potential source analogs. Those analogs in memory that are identified as having semantic links to the target (i.e., those that share similar concepts) then participate in an ACME-like constraint satisfaction process to select the optimal source. The constraint network formed by ARCS is restricted to those concepts in each analog that have semantic links; hence, ARCS shows less sensitivity to structure in retrieval than does ACME in mapping. Because constraint satisfaction algorithms are inherently competitive, ARCS can model the finding that analogical access is more sensitive to structure when similar source analogs in long-term memory compete to be retrieved (Wharton et al., 1994, 1996).

Learning and Inference with Schemas and Analogies (LISA)

Similar to ACME, the LISA model (Hummel & Holyoak, 1997, 2003) is based on the principles of the multiconstraint theory of analogy; unlike ACME, LISA operates within psychologically and neurally realistic constraints on working memory (see Doumas & Hummel, Chap. 4; Morrison, Chap. 19). The models discussed previously include at most localist representations of the meaning of concepts (e.g., a semantic network in the case of ARCS), and most of their processing is performed on propositional representations unaccompanied by any more detailed level of conceptual representation (e.g., neither

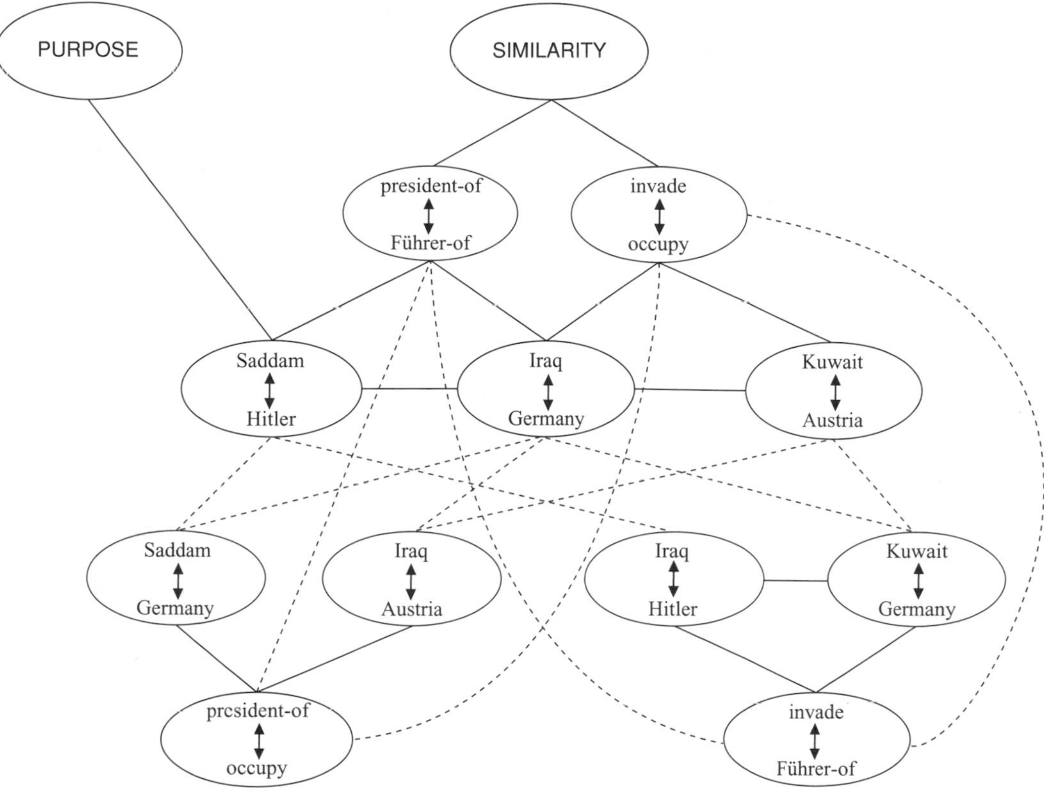

Figure 6.6. A constraint-satisfaction network in ACME.

ACME nor SME includes any representation of the meaning of concepts). LISA also goes beyond previous models in that it provides a unified account of all the major components of analogical reasoning (retrieval, mapping, inference, and relational generalization).

LISA represents propositions using a hierarchy of distributed and localist units (see Figure 4.1 in Doumas & Hummel, Chap. 4). LISA includes both a long-term memory for propositions and concept meanings and a limited-capacity working memory. LISA's working memory representation, which uses neural synchrony to encode role-filler bindings, provides a natural account of the capacity limits of working memory because it is only possible to have a finite number of bindings simultaneously active and mutually *out* of synchrony.

Analog retrieval is accomplished as a form of guided pattern matching. Propositions in a target analog generate synchronized patterns of activation on the semantic units, which in turn activate propositions in potential source analogs residing in long-term memory. The resulting coactivity of source and target elements, augmented with a capacity to learn which structures in the target were coactive with which in the source, serves as the basis for analogical mapping. LISA includes a set of *mapping connections* between units of the same type (e.g., object, predicate) in separate analogs. These connections grow whenever the corresponding units are active simultaneously and thereby permit LISA to learn the correspondences between structures in separate analogs. They also permit correspondences learned early in mapping to influence the correspondences learned later. Augmented with a simple algorithm for self-supervised learning, the mapping algorithm serves as the basis for analogical inference by CWSG. Finally, augmented with a simple algorithm for intersection discovery, self-supervised relational learning serves as the basis for schema induction. LISA has been used to simulate a wide range of data on analogical reasoning (Hummel & Holyoak, 1997, 2003), including both behavioral and neuropsychological studies (Morrison et al., 2004).

Conclusions and Future Directions

When we think analogically, we do much more than just compare two analogs based on obvious similarities between their elements. Rather, analogical reasoning is a complex process of retrieving structured knowledge from long-term memory, representing and manipulating role-filler bindings in working memory, performing self-supervised learning to form new inferences, and finding structured intersections between analogs to form new abstract schemas. The entire process is governed by the core constraints provided by isomorphism, similarity of elements, and the goals of the reasoner (Holyoak & Thagard, 1989a). These constraints apply in all components of analogical reasoning: retrieval, mapping, inference, and relational generalization. When analogs are retrieved from memory, the constraint of element similarity plays a large role, but relational structure is also important – especially when multiple source analogs similar to the target are competing to be selected. For mapping, structure is the most important constraint but requires adequate working memory resources; similarity and purpose also contribute. The success of analogical inference ultimately depends on whether the purpose of the analogy is achieved, but satisfying this constraint is intimately connected with the structural relations between the analogs. Finally, relational generalization occurs when schemas are formed from the source and target to capture those structural patterns in the analogs that are most relevant to the reasoner's purpose in exploiting the analogy.

Several current research directions are likely to continue to develop. Computational models of analogy, such as LISA (Hummel & Holyoak, 1997, 2003), have begun to connect behavioral work on analogy with research in cognitive neuroscience (Morrison et al., 2004). We already have some knowledge of the general neural circuits that underlie analogy and other forms of reasoning (see Goel, Chap. 20). As more sophisticated noninvasive neuroimaging methodologies are developed, it should become possible to test detailed hypotheses about the neural mechanisms underlying analogy, such as those based on temporal properties of neural systems.

Most research and modeling in the field of analogy has emphasized quasilinguistic knowledge representations, but there is good reason to believe that reasoning in general has close connections to perception (e.g., Pedone et al., 2001). Perception provides an important starting point for grounding at least some "higher" cognitive representations (Barsalou, 1999). Some progress has been made in integrating analogy with perception. For example, the LISA model has been augmented with a Metric Array Module (MAM; Hummel & Holyoak, 2001), which provides specialized processing of metric information at a level of abstraction applicable to both perception and quasispatial concepts. However, models of analogy have generally failed to address evidence that the difficulty of solving problems and transferring solution methods to isomorphic problems is dependent on the difficulty of perceptually encoding key relations. The ease of solving apparently isomorphic problems (e.g., isomorphs of the well-known Tower of Hanoi) can vary enormously, depending on perceptual cues (Kotovsky & Simon, 1990; see Novick & Bassok, Chap. 14).

More generally, models of analogy have not been well integrated with models of problem solving (see Novick & Bassok, Chap. 14), even though analogy clearly affords an important mechanism for solving problems. In its general form, problem solving requires sequencing multiple operators, establishing subgoals, and using combinations of rules to solve related but nonisomorphic problems. These basic requirements are beyond the capabilities of virtually all computational models of analogy (but see Holyoak & Thagard, 1989b, for an early although limited effort to integrate analogy within a rule-based problem-solving system). The most successful models of human problem solving have been formulated as production systems (see Lovett & Anderson, Chap. 17), and Salvucci and Anderson (2001) developed a model of analogy based on the ACT-R production system. However, this model is unable to solve reliably any analogy that requires integration of multiple relations – a class that includes analogies within the grasp of young children (Halford, 1993; Richland et al., 2004; see Halford, Chap. 22). The integration of analogy models with models of general problem solving remains an important research goal.

Perhaps the most serious limitation of current computational models of analogy is that their knowledge representations must be hand-coded by the modeler, whereas human knowledge representations are formed autonomously. Closely related to the challenge of avoiding hand-coding of representations is the need to flexibly rerepresent knowledge to render potential analogies perspicuous. Concepts often have a close conceptual relationship with more complex relational forms (e.g., Jackendoff, 1983). For example, causative verbs such as *lift* (e.g., "John lifted the hammer") have very similar meanings to structures based on an explicit higher-order relation, *cause* (e.g., "John caused the hammer to rise"). In such cases, the causative verb serves as a "chunked" representation of a more elaborate predicate-argument structure. People are able to "see" analogies even when the analogs have very different linguistic forms (e.g., "John lifted the hammer in order to strike the nail" might be mapped onto "The Federal Reserve used an increase in interest rates as a tool in its efforts to drive down inflation"). A deeper understanding of human knowledge representation is a prerequisite for a complete theory of analogical reasoning.

Acknowledgments

Preparation of this chapter was supported by grants R305H030141 from the Institute of Education Sciences and SES-0080375 from the National Science Foundation. Kevin Dunbar and Robert Morrison provided valuable comments on an earlier draft.

References

Barnett, S. M., & Koslowski, B. (2002). Solving novel, ill-defined problems: Effects of type of experience and the level of theoretical understanding it generates. *Thinking & Reasoning*, 8, 237–267.

Barsalou, L. W. (1999). Perceptual symbol systems. *Behavioral and Brain Sciences*, 22, 577–660.

Bassok, M., & Holyoak, K. J. (1989). Interdomain transfer between isomorphic topics in algebra and physics. *Journal of Experimental Psychology: Learning, Memory, and Cognition*, 15, 153–166.

Bassok, M., & Olseth, K. L. (1995). Object-based representations: Transfer between cases of continuous and discrete models of change. *Journal of Experimental Psychology: Learning, Memory, and Cognition*, 21, 1522–1538.

Bassok, M., Wu, L. L., & Olseth, K. L. (1995). Judging a book by its cover: Interpretative effects of content on problem-solving transfer. *Memory & Cognition*, 23, 354–367.

Bernardo, A. B. I. (2001). Principle explanation and strategic schema abstraction in problem solving. *Memory & Cognition*, 29, 627–633.

Beveridge, M., & Parkins, E. (1987). Visual representation in analogical problem solving. *Memory & Cognition*, 15, 230–237.

Black, M. (1962). *Models and metaphors*. Ithaca, NY: Cornell University Press.

Blanchette, I., & Dunbar, K. (2000). Analogy use in naturalistic settings: The influence of audience, emotion, and goal. *Memory & Cognition*, 29, 730–735.

Blanchette, I., & Dunbar, K. (2001). How analogies are generated: The roles of structural and superficial similarity. *Memory & Cognition*, 28, 108–124.

Blanchette, I., & Dunbar, K. (2002). Representational change and analogy: How analogical inferences alter target representations. *Journal of Experimental Psychology: Learning, Memory, and Cognition*, 28, 672–685.

Boroditsky, L. (2000). Metaphoric structuring: Understanding time through spatial metaphors. *Cognition*, 75, 1–28.

Bransford, J. D., Barclay, J. R., & Franks, J. J. (1972). Sentence memory: A constructive versus interpretive approach. *Cognitive Psychology*, 3, 193–209.

Brown, A. L., Kane, M. J., & Echols, C. H. (1986). Young children's mental models determine analogical transfer across problems with a common goal structure. *Cognitive Development*, 1, 103–121.

Brown, A. L., Kane, M. J., & Long, C. (1989). Analogical transfer in young children: Analogies as tools for communication and exposition. *Applied Cognitive Psychology*, 3, 275–293.

Bunge, S. A., Wendelken, C., Badre, D., & Wagner, A. D. (2004). Analogical reasoning and prefrontal cortex: Evidence for separable retrieval and integration mechanisms. *Cerebral Cortex, x*.

Carbonell, J. G. (1983). Learning by analogy: Formulating and generalizing plans from past experience. In R. S. Michalski, J. G. Carbonell, & T. M. Mitchell (Eds.), *Machine learning: An artificial intelligence approach* (pp. 137–161). Palo Alto, CA: Tioga.

Carpenter, P. A., Just, M. A., & Shell, P. (1990). What one intelligence test measures: A theoretical account of the processing in the Raven Progressive Matrices test. *Psychological Review*, 97, 404–431.

Catrambone, R., & Holyoak, K. J. (1989). Overcoming contextual limitations on problem-solving transfer. *Journal of Experimental Psychology: Learning, Memory, and Cognition*, 15, 1147–1156.

Cattell, R. B. (1971). *Abilities: Their structure, growth, and action*. Boston, MA: Houghton-Mifflin.

Chen, Z. (1996). Children's analogical problem solving: The effects of superficial, structural, and procedural similarity. *Journal of Experimental Child Psychology*, 62, 410–431.

Chen, Z., & Daehler, M. W. (1989). Positive and negative transfer in analogical problem solving by 6-year-old children. *Cognitive Development*, 4, 327–344.

Clement, C. A., & Gentner, D. (1991). Systematicity as a selection constraint in analogical mapping. *Cognitive Science*, 15, 89–132.

Duncan, J., Seitz, R. J., Kolodny, J., Bor, D., Herzog, H., Ahmed, A., Newell, F. N., & Emslie, H. (2000). A neural basis for general intelligence. *Science*, 289, 457–460.

Duncker, K. (1945). On problem solving. *Psychological Monographs*, 58 (Whole No. 270).

Evans, T. G. (1968). A program for the solution of geometric-analogy intelligence test questions. In M. Minsky (Ed.), *Semantic information processing* (pp. 271–353). Cambridge, MA: MIT Press.

Falkenhainer, B., Forbus, K. D., & Gentner, D. (1989). The structure-mapping engine: Algorithm and examples. *Artificial Intelligence*, 41, 1–63.

Fauconnier, G. (2001). Conceptual blending and analogy. In D. Gentner, K. J. Holyoak, & B. N. Kokinov (Eds.), *The analogical mind: Perspectives from cognitive science* (pp. 255–285). Cambridge, MA: MIT Press.

Fauconnier, G., & Turner, M. (1998). Conceptual integration networks. *Cognitive Science*, 22, 133–187.

Forbus, K. D., Gentner, D., & Law, K. (1995). MAC/FAC: A model of similarity-based retrieval. *Cognitive Science*, 19, 141–205.

French, R. M. (2002). The computational modeling of analogy-making. *Trends in Cognitive Science*, 6, 200–205.

Gentner, D. (1982). Are scientific analogies metaphors? In D. S. Miall (Eds.), *Metaphor: Problems and perspectives* (pp. 106–132). Brighton, UK: Harvester Press.

Gentner, D. (1983). Structure-mapping: A theoretical framework for analogy. *Cognitive Science*, 7, 155–170.

Gentner, D., Bowdle, B., Wolff, P., & Boronat, C. (2001). Metaphor is like analogy. In D. Gentner, K. J. Holyoak, & B. N. Kokinov (Eds.), *The analogical mind: Perspectives from cognitive science* (pp. 199–253). Cambridge, MA: MIT Press.

Gentner, D., Falkenhainer, B., & Skorstad, J. (1988). Viewing metaphor as analogy. In D. H. Helman (Eds.), *Analogical reasoning: Perspectives of artificial intelligence, cognitive science, and philosophy* (pp. 171–177). Dordrecht, The Netherlands: Kluwer.

Gentner, D., & Gentner, D. R. (1983). Flowing waters or teeming crowds: Mental models of electricity. In D. Gentner & A. L. Stevens (Eds.), *Mental models* (pp. 99–129). Hillsdale, NJ: Erlbaum.

Gentner, D., & Rattermann, M. (1991). Language and the career of similarity. In S. A. Gelman & J. P. Byrnes (Eds.), *Perspectives on thought and language: Interrelations in development* (pp. 225–277). Cambridge, UK: Cambridge University Press.

Gentner, D., Rattermann, M., & Forbus, K. (1993). The roles of similarity in transfer: Separating retrievability from inferential soundness. *Cognitive Psychology*, 25, 524–575.

Gentner, D., & Toupin, C. (1986). Systematicity and surface similarity in the development of analogy. *Cognitive Science*, 10, 277–300.

Gick, M. L., & Holyoak, K. J. (1980). Analogical problem solving. *Cognitive Psychology*, 12, 306–355.

Gick, M. L., & Holyoak, K. J. (1983). Schema induction and analogical transfer. *Cognitive Psychology*, 15, 1–38.

Glucksberg, S., Gildea, P., & Bookin, H. (1982). On understanding nonliteral speech: Can people ignore metaphors? *Journal of Verbal Learning and Verbal Behaviour*, 21, 85–98.

Glucksberg, S., & Keysar, B. (1990). Understanding metaphorical comparisons: Beyond similarity. *Psychological Review*, 97, 3–18.

Glucksberg, S., McClone, M. S., & Manfredi, D. (1997). Property attribution in metaphor comprehension. *Journal of Memory and Language*, 36, 50–67.

Goswami, U. (1992). *Analogical reasoning in children*. Hillsdale, NJ: Erlbaum.

Goswami, U. (2001). Analogical reasoning in children. In D. Gentner, K. J. Holyoak, & B. N. Kokinov (Eds.), *The analogical mind: Perspectives from cognitive science* (pp. 437–470). Cambridge, MA: MIT Press.

Halford, G. S. (1993). *Children's understanding: The development of mental models*. Hillsdale, NJ: Erlbaum.

Halford, G. S., & Wilson, W. H. (1980). A category theory approach to cognitive development. *Cognitive Psychology*, 12, 356–411.

Halford, G. S., Wilson, W. H., Guo, J., Gayler, R. W., Wiles, J., & Stewart, J. E. M. (1994). Connectionist implications for processing capacity limitations in analogies. In K. J. Holyoak & J. A. Barnden (Eds.), *Advances in connectionist and neural computation theory, Vol. 2: Analogical connections* (pp. 363–415). Norwood, NJ: Ablex.

Hesse, M. (1966). *Models and analogies in science*. Notre Dame, IN: Notre Dame University Press.

Hofstadter, D. R., & Mitchell, M. (1994). The Copycat project: A model of mental fluidity and analogy-making. In K. J. Holyoak & J. A. Barnden (Eds.), *Analogical connections. Advances in connectionist and neural computation theory* (Vol. 2, pp. 31–112). Norwood, NJ: Ablex.

Holland, J. H., Holyoak, K. J., Nisbett, R. E., & Thagard, P. (1986). *Induction: Processes of inference, learning, and discovery*. Cambridge, MA: MIT Press.

Holyoak, K. J. (1982). An analogical framework for literary interpretation. *Poetics*, 11, 105–126.

Holyoak, K. J. (1985). The pragmatics of analogical transfer. In G. H. Bower (Ed.), *The psychology of learning and motivation* (Vol. 19, pp. 59–87). New York: Academic Press.

Holyoak, K. J., Junn, E. N., & Billman, D. O. (1984). Development of analogical problem-solving skill. *Child Development*, 55, 2042–2055.

Holyoak, K. J., & Koh, K. (1987). Surface and structural similarity in analogical transfer. *Memory & Cognition*, 15, 332–340.

Holyoak, K. J., Novick, L. R., & Melz, E. R. (1994). Component processes in analogical transfer: Mapping, pattern completion, and adaptation. In K. J. Holyoak & J. A. Barnden (Eds.), *Advances in connectionist and neural computation theory, Vol. 2: Analogical connections* (pp. 113–180). Norwood, NJ: Ablex.

Holyoak, K. J., & Thagard, P. (1989a). Analogical mapping by constraint satisfaction. *Cognitive Science*, 13, 295–355.

Holyoak, K. J., & Thagard, P. (1989b). A computational model of analogical problem solving. In S. Vosniadou & A. Ortony (Eds.), *Similarity and analogical reasoning* (pp. 242–266). New York: Cambridge University Press.

Holyoak, K. J., & Thagard, P. (1995). *Mental leaps: Analogy in creative thought*. Cambridge, MA: MIT Press.

Hummel, J. E., & Holyoak, K. J. (1992). Indirect analogical mapping. In *Proceedings of the Forteenth Annual Conference of the Cognitive Science Society* (pp. 516–521). Hillsdale, NJ: Erlbaum.

Hummel, J. E., & Holyoak, K. J. (1997). Distributed representations of structure: A theory of analogical access and mapping. *Psychological Review*, 104, 427–466.

Hummel, J. E., & Holyoak, K. J. (2001). A process model of human transitive inference. In M. L. Gattis (Ed.), *Spatial schemas in abstract thought* (pp. 279–305). Cambridge, MA: MIT Press.

Hummel, J. E., & Holyoak, K. J. (2003). A symbolic-connectionist theory of relational inference and generalization. *Psychological Review, 110*, 220–263.

Hunt, E. B. (1974). Quote the raven? Nevermore! In L. W. Gregg (Ed.), *Knowledge and cognition* (pp. 129–157). Hillsdale, NJ: Erlbaum.

Jackendoff, R. (1983). *Semantics and cognition*. Cambridge, MA: MIT Press.

Keane, M. T. (1987). On retrieving analogues when solving problems. *Quarterly Journal of Experimental Psychology, 39A*, 29–41.

Keane, M. T., & Brayshaw, M. (1988). The incremental analogical machine: A computational model of analogy. In D. Sleeman (Ed.), *European working session on learning* (pp. 53–62). London: Pitman.

Keysar, B. (1989). On the functional equivalence of literal and metaphorical interpretations in discourse. *Journal of Memory and Language, 28*, 375–385.

Khong, Y. F. (1992). *Analogies at war: Korea, Munich, Dien Bien Phu, and the Vietnam decisions of 1965*. Princeton, NJ: Princeton University Press.

Kokinov, B. N., & Petrov, A. A. (2001). Integration of memory and reasoning in analogy-making: The AMBR model. In D. Gentner, K. J. Holyoak, & B. N. Kokinov (Eds.), *The analogical mind: Perspectives from cognitive science* (pp. 59–124). Cambridge, MA: MIT Press.

Kolodner, J. L. (1983). Reconstructive memory: A computer model. *Cognitive Science, 7*, 281–328.

Kolodner, J. L. (1993). *Case-based reasoning*. San Mateo, CA: Morgan Kaufmann.

Kotovsky, K., & Simon, H. A. (1990). What makes some problems really hard? Explorations in the problem space of difficulty. *Cognitive Psychology, 22*, 143–183.

Kotovsky, L., & Gentner, D. (1996). Comparison and categorization in the development of relational similarity. *Child Development, 67*, 2797–2822.

Krawczyk, D. C., Holyoak, K. J., & Hummel, J. E. (2004). Structural constraints and object similarity in analogical mapping and inference. *Thinking & Reasoning, 10*, 85–104.

Kroger, J. K., Saab, F. W., Fales, C. L., Bookheimer, S. Y., Cohen, M. S., & Holyoak, K. J. (2002). Recruitment of anterior dorsolateral prefrontal cortex in human reasoning: A parametric study of relational complexity. *Cerebral Cortex, 12*, 477–485.

Lakoff, G., & Johnson, M. (1980). *Metaphors we live by*. Chicago: University of Chicago Press.

Lakoff, G., & Turner, M. (1989). *More than cool reason: A field guide to poetic metaphor*. Chicago: University of Chicago Press.

Lassaline, M. E. (1996). Structural alignment in induction and similarity. *Journal of Experimental Psychology: Learning, Memory, and Cognition, 22*, 754–770.

Loewenstein, J., Thompson, L., & Gentner, D. (1999). Analogical encoding facilitates knowledge transfer in negotiation. *Psychonomic Bulletin and Review, 6*, 586–597.

Luo, Q., Perry, C., Peng, D., Jin, Z., Xu, D., Ding, G., & Xu, S. (2003). The neural substrate of analogical reasoning: An fMRI study. *Cognitive Brain Research, 17*, 527–534.

Markman, A. B. (1997). Constraints on analogical inference. *Cognitive Science, 21*, 373–418.

Markman, A. B., & Gentner, D. (1993). Structural alignment during similarity comparisons. *Cognitive Psychology, 23*, 431–467.

Minsky, M. (1975). A framework for representing knowledge. In P. Winston (Ed.), *The psychology of computer vision* (pp. 211–281). New York: McGraw-Hill.

Morrison, R. G., Krawczyk, D. C., Holyoak, K. J., Hummel, J. E., Chow, T. W., Miller, B. L., & Knowlton, B. J. (2004). A neurocomputational model of analogical reasoning and its breakdown in frontotemporal lobar degeneration. *Journal of Cognitive Neuroscience, 16*, 260–271.

Mulholland, T. M., Pellegrino, J. W., & Glaser, R. (1980). Components of geometric analogy solution. *Cognitive Psychology, 12*, 252–284.

Novick, L. R., & Holyoak, K. J. (1991). Mathematical problem solving by analogy. *Journal of Experimental Psychology: Learning, Memory, and Cognition, 17*, 398–415.

Pask, C. (2003). Mathematics and the science of analogies. *American Journal of Physics, 71*, 526–534.

Pedone, R., Hummel, J. E., & Holyoak, K. J. (2001). The use of diagrams in analogical problem solving. *Memory & Cognition, 29*, 214–221.

Prabhakaran, V., Smith, J. A. L., Desmond, J. E., Glover, G. H., & Gabrieli, J. D. E. (1997). Neural substrates of fluid reasoning: An fMRI study of neocortical activation during performance of the Raven's Progressive Matrices Test. *Cognitive Psychology*, 33, 43–63.

Raven, J. C. (1938). *Progressive matrices: A perceptual test of intelligence, individual form*. London: Lewis.

Reed, S. K. (1987). A structure-mapping model for word problems. *Journal of Experimental Psychology: Learning, Memory, and Cognition*, 13, 124–139.

Reed, S. K., Dempster, A., & Ettinger, M. (1985). Usefulness of analogical solutions for solving algebra word problems. *Journal of Experimental Psychology: Learning, Memory, and Cognition*, 11, 106–125.

Reitman, W. (1965). *Cognition and thought*. New York: Wiley.

Richland, L. E., Morrison, R. G., & Holyoak, K. J. (2004). Working memory and inhibition as constraints on children's development of analogical reasoning. In K. Forbus, D. Gentner & T. Regier (Eds.), *Proceedings of the Twenty-sixth Annual Conference of the Cognitive Science Society*. Mahwah, NJ: Erlbaum.

Ross, B. (1987). This is like that: The use of earlier problems and the separation of similarity effects. *Journal of Experimental Psychology: Learning, Memory, and Cognition*, 13, 629–639.

Ross, B. (1989). Distinguishing types of superficial similarities: Different effects on the access and use of earlier problems. *Journal of Experimental Psychology: Learning, Memory, and Cognition*, 15, 456–468.

Ross, B. H., & Kennedy, P. T. (1990). Generalizing from the use of earlier examples in problem solving. *Journal of Experimental Psychology: Learning, Memory, and Cognition*, 16, 42–55.

Rumelhart, D. E., Smolensky, P., McClelland, J. L., & Hinton, G. E. (1986). Schemata and sequential thought processes in PDP models. In J. L. McClelland, D. E. Rumelhart, & the PDP Research Group (Eds.), *Parallel distributed processing: Explorations in the microstructure of cognition* (Vol. 2). Cambridge, MA: MIT Press.

Salvucci, D. D., & Anderson, J. R. (2001). Integrating analogical mapping and general problem solving: The path-mapping theory. *Cognitive Science*, 25, 67–110.

Schank, R. C. (1982). *Dynamic memory*. New York: Cambridge University Press.

Schustack, M. W., & Anderson, J. R. (1979). Effects of analogy to prior knowledge on memory for new information. *Journal of Verbal Learning and Verbal Behavior*, 18, 565–583.

Seifert, C. M., McKoon, G., Abelson, R. P., & Ratcliff, R. (1986). Memory connections between thematically similar episodes. *Journal of Experimental Psychology: Learning, Memory, and Cognition*, 12, 220–231.

Snow, R. E., Kyllonen, C. P., & Marshalek, B. (1984). The topography of ability and learning correlations. In R. J. Sternberg (Ed.), *Advances in the psychology of human intelligence* (pp. 47–103). Hillsdale, NJ: Erlbaum.

Spearman, C. (1923). *The nature of intelligence and the principles of cognition*. London, UK: Macmillan.

Spearman, C. (1927). *The abilities of man*. New York: Macmillan.

Spearman, C. (1946). Theory of a general factor. *British Journal of Psychology*, 36, 117–131.

Spellman, B. A., & Holyoak, K. J. (1992). If Saddam is Hitler then who is George Bush?: Analogical mapping between systems of social roles. *Journal of Personality and Social Psychology*, 62, 913–933.

Spellman, B. A., & Holyoak, K. J. (1996). Pragmatics in analogical mapping. *Cognitive Psychology*, 31, 307–346.

Spencer, R. M., & Weisberg, R. W. (1986). Context-dependent effects on analogical transfer. *Memory & Cognition*, 14, 442–449.

Sternberg, R. J. (1977). Component processes in analogical reasoning. *Psychological Review*, 84, 353–378.

Thagard, P. (2000). *Coherence in thought and action*. Cambridge, MA: MIT Press.

Thagard, P., Holyoak, K. J., Nelson, G., & Gochfeld, D. (1990). Analog retrieval by constraint satisfaction. *Artificial Intelligence*, 46, 259–310.

Thagard, P., & Shelley, C. (2001). Emotional analogies and analogical inference. In D. Gentner, K. J. Holyoak, & B. N. Kokinov (Eds.), *The analogical mind: Perspectives from cognitive science* (pp. 335–362). Cambridge, MA: MIT Press.

Tohill, J. M., & Holyoak, K. J. (2000). The impact of anxiety on analogical reasoning. *Thinking & Reasoning*, 6, 27–40.

Tunteler, E., & Resing, W. C. M. (2002). Spontaneous analogical transfer in 4-year-olds: A microgenetic study. *Journal of Experimental Child Psychology*, 83, 149–166.

Waltz, J. A., Knowlton, B. J., Holyoak, K. J., Boone, K. B., Mishkin, F. S., de Menezes Santos, M., Thomas, C. R., & Miller, B. L. (1999). A system for relational reasoning in human prefrontal cortex. *Psychological Science, 10*, 119–125.

Waltz, J. A., Lau, A., Grewal, S. K., & Holyoak, K. J. (2000). The role of working memory in analogical mapping. *Memory & Cognition, 28*, 1205–1212.

Wharton, C. M., Grafman, J., Flitman, S. S., Hansen, E. K., Brauner, J., Marks, A., & Honda, M. (2000). Toward neuroanatomical models of analogy: A positron emission tomography study of analogical mapping. *Cognitive Psychology, 40*, 173–197.

Wharton, C. M., Holyoak, K. J., Downing, P. E., Lange, T. E., Wickens, T. D., & Melz, E. R. (1994). Below the surface: Analogical similarity and retrieval competition in reminding. *Cognitive Psychology, 26*, 64–101.

Wharton, C. M., Holyoak, K. J., & Lange, T. E. (1996). Remote analogical reminding. *Memory & Cognition, 24*, 629–643.

Winston, P. H. (1980). Learning and reasoning by analogy. *Communications of the ACM, 23*, 689–703.

Wolff, P., & Gentner, D. (2000). Evidence for role-neutral initial processing of metaphors. *Journal of Experimental Psychology: Leaning, Memory, and Cognition, 26*, 529–541.

CHAPTER 7

Causal Learning

Marc J. Buehner
Patricia W. Cheng

Introduction

This chapter is an introduction to the psychology of causal inference using a computational perspective with the focus on causal discovery. It explains the nature of the problem of causal discovery and illustrates the goal of the process with everyday and hypothetical examples. It reviews two approaches to causal discovery, a purely statistical approach and an alternative approach that incorporates causal hypotheses in the inference process. The latter approach provides a coherent framework within which to answer different questions regarding causal inference. The chapter ends with a discussion of two additional issues – the level of abstraction of the candidate cause and the temporal interval between the occurrence of the cause and the occurrence of the effect – and a sketch of future directions for the field.

The Nature of the Problem and a Historical Review: Is Causality an Inscrutable Fetish or the Cement of the Universe?

Imagine a world in which we could not reason about causes and effects. What would it be like? Typically, reviews about causal reasoning begin by declaring that causal reasoning enables us to predict and control our environment and by stating that causal reasoning allows us to structure an otherwise chaotic flux of events into meaningful episodes. In other words, without causal inference, we would be unable to learn from the past and incapable of manipulating our surroundings to achieve our goals. Let us see how a noncausal world would be grim and the exact role causal inference plays for adaptive intelligence. We illustrate the noncausal world by intuitive examples as well as by what is predicted by associative and other purely statistical models – models that do not go through an intermediate step of positing hypotheses about causal relations in the world rather than just in the head.

We want to see the goals of causal reasoning; we also want to see what the givens are, so we can step back and see what the problem of causal learning is. One way of casting this problem is to ask, "What minimal set of processes would one endow an artificial system, so that when put on Planet Earth and given the types of information humans receive, it will evolve to represent the world as they do?" For example, what process must the system have so it would know that exposure to the sun causes tanning in skin but bleaching in fabrics? These causal facts are unlikely to be innate in humans. The learning process would begin with noncausal observations. For both cases, the input would be observations on various entities (people and articles of clothing, respectively) with varying exposures to sunlight and, in one case, the darkness of skin color and, in the other, the darkness of fabric colors. Consider another example: Suppose the system is presented with observations that a rooster in a barn crowed soon before sunrise and did not crow at other times during the day when the sun did not rise. What process must the system have so it would predict that the sun would soon rise when informed that the rooster had just spontaneously crowed but would *not* predict the same when informed that the rooster had just been deceived into crowing by artificial lighting? Neither would the system recommend starting a round-the-clock solar energy enterprise even if there were reliable ways of making roosters crow. Nor would it, when a sick rooster is observed not to crow, worry about cajoling it into crowing to ensure that the sun will rise in the morning. In a noncausal world, such recommendations and worries would be natural (also see Sloman & Lagnado, Chap. 5).

Our examples illustrate that by keeping track of events that *covary* (i.e., vary together, are statistically associated), one would be able to predict a future event from a covariation provided that causes of that event remained unperturbed. However, one might be unable to predict the consequences of actions (e.g., exposure to the sun, deceiving the rooster into crowing). Causation, and only causation, licenses the prediction of the consequences of actions. Both kinds of predictions are obviously helpful (e.g., we appreciate weather reports), but the latter is what allows (1) goal-directed behaviors to achieve their goals and (2) maladaptive recommendations that accord with mere correlations to be dismissed. The examples also illustrate that only causation supports explanation (Woodward, 2003). Whereas one would explain that one's skin is tanned because of exposure to the sun, one would not explain that the sun rises because the rooster crows, despite the reliable predictions that one can make in each case. Understanding what humans do when they reason about causation is a challenge, and the ability to build a system that accomplishes what humans accomplish is a test of one's understanding of that psychological process.

We see that even when there is temporal information so one can reliably predict an event from an earlier observation (e.g., sunrise from a rooster's crowing, a storm from a drop in the barometric reading), correlation need not imply causation. One might think that intervention (i.e., action, manipulation) is what differentiates between covariation and causation: When the observations are obtained by intervention, by oneself or others, the covariations are causal; otherwise, they are not necessarily causal. A growing body of research is dedicated to the role of intervention in causal learning, discovery, and reasoning (e.g., Gopnik et al., 2004; Lagnado & Sloman, 2004; Steyvers, Tenenbaum, Wagenmakers, & Blum, 2003). Indeed, the general pattern reported is that observations based on intervention allow causal inferences that are not possible with mere observations. However, although intervention generally allows causal inference, it does not guarantee it. Consider a food allergy test that introduces samples of food into the body by needle punctures on the skin. The patient may react with hives on all punctured spots, and yet one may not know whether the patient is allergic to any of the foods. Suppose the patient's skin is allergic to needle punctures so hives also appear on punctured spots without food. In this example, there is an intervention, but no causal inference regarding food allergy seems warranted (Cheng, 1997). What then are the conditions that allow causal discovery? Note that in this example the intervention was suboptimal because two interventions occurred concurrently (adding allergens into the bloodstream and puncturing the skin), resulting in confounding.

Historically, causality has been the domain of philosophers, from Aristotle through to Hume and Kant, to name just a few. The fundamental challenge since Hume (1739/1888) that has been occupying scholars in this area is that causality per se is not directly in the input. This issue fits well in the framework of creating an artificial reasoning system – causal knowledge has to emerge from noncausal input. Nothing in the evidence available to our sensory system can ensure someone of a causal relation between, say, flicking a switch and the hallway lights turning on. Yet, we regularly and routinely have strong convictions about causality. David Hume made a distinction between analytic and empirical knowledge. Moreover, he pointed out that causal knowledge is empirical, and that of this kind of knowledge, we can only be certain of the states of observable events or objects (e.g., the presence of an event of interest and its magnitude) and the temporal and spatial relations between them. Any impression of causality linking two constituent events, he argued, is a mental construct.

Psychologists entered the arena to study the exact nature and determinants of such mental constructs. Michotte (1946/1963) investigated the perceptual processing of causal events (mostly impact of one moving object on another object, the "launching effect"). Many researchers since then have argued that such perception of causality is modular or encapsulated (for an overview, see Scholl & Tremoulet, 2000) and not subject to conscious inference. To some, the encapsulation puts the process outside the scope of this chapter. Within our framework, however, the problem has the same general core: How would an intelligent system transform noncausal input into a causal relation as its output? That problem remains, despite the additional innate or learned spatiotemporal constraints (see, Cheng, 1993, for an inductive analysis of the launching effect, and Scholl & Nakayama, 2002, for a demonstration of inductive components of the visual system's analysis of launching events).

Causal discovery is not the only process with which one would endow the artificial reasoning system. Many psychologists have addressed a related but distinct issue of updating and applying prior causal knowledge. Once causal knowledge is acquired, it would be efficient to apply it to novel situations involving events of like kind. We are all familiar with such applications of causal knowledge transmitted culturally or acquired on our own. A number of researchers have proposed Bayesian accounts of the integration of prior causal knowledge and current information (Anderson, 1990; Tenenbaum & Griffiths, 2002). It may seem that there is a ready answer to the updating and application problem. What may not be straightforward, however, is the determination of "events of like kind," the variables in a causal relation. The application of causal knowledge therefore highlights an issue that has been mostly neglected in the research on causal discovery: What determines which categories are formed and the level of abstraction at which they are formed (see Medin & Rips, Chap. 3; Rosch, 1978)? Similarly, what determines which events are regarded as analogous (see Holyoak, Chap. 6)? The "cause" categories in causal learning experiments were typically predefined by the experimenter in terms of a variable with a single causal value and do not have the structure of natural categories (see Lien & Cheng, 2000, for an exception). If the relations inferred have no generality, they cannot be applied to novel but similar events, thus failing to fulfill a primary function of causal inference.

It is perhaps the segregation of research on category formation and on causal learning that has engendered the *mechanism* view, which pits top-down and bottom-up causal reasoning against each other. It has been argued that inferring a causal connection is *contingent* on insight into the mechanism (i.e., a network of intervening causal relations) by which the candidate cause brings about its effect (e.g., Ahn, Kalish, Medin, & Gelman, 1995). A commonly used research paradigm involved providing participants with current information concerning the covariation between potential causes and effects at some designated level of abstraction but manipulating whether a (plausible) causal mechanism was presented (Ahn, Kalish, Medin, & Gelman, 1995; Bullock, Gelman, & Baillargeon, 1982; Shultz, 1982; White, 1995), with the causal mechanism implying more reliable covariation information at a different, more abstract, level. The common finding from these studies was that participants deemed knowledge about causal power or force as more significant than what was designated as covariational information. Studies in this "causal power" tradition are valuable in that they demonstrate the role of abduction and coherence: People indeed strive to link causes and effects mentally by postulating the (perhaps hypothetical) presence of some known causal mechanism that connects them in an attempt to create the most coherent explanation encompassing multiple relevant pieces of knowledge (see Holland, Holyoak, Nisbett, & Thagard, 1986, on abduction; see Thagard, 1989, for accounts of coherence). This work shows that coherence plays a key role in the application of causal knowledge (also see Lien & Cheng, 2000; coherence also plays a role in causal discovery, see Cheng, 1993). However, the argument that inferring a causal relation is contingent on belief in an underlying causal network is circular – it simply pushes the causal discovery question one step back. How was knowledge about the links in the causal network discovered in the first place?

Rather than pitting covariation and prior causal knowledge against each other, Thagard (2000) offered a complementary view of covariation, prior causal knowledge, and a general causal framework in scientific explanation. Illustrating with cases in medical history (e.g., the bacterial theory of ulcers), he showed that inferring a causal connection is not contingent on insight into an intervening mechanism, but is bolstered by it. The inferred causal networks subsequently explain novel instances when the networks are instantiated by information on the instances. Maximizing explanatory coherence might be a process closely intertwined with causal discovery, but nonetheless separate from it, that one would incorporate in an artificial reasoning system.

In the rest of this chapter, we review the main computational accounts of causal discovery. We first review statistical models, then problems with the statistical approach, problems that motivate a causal account that incorporates assumptions involving alternative causes. We follow these accounts with a review of new empirical tests of the two approaches. We then broaden our scope to consider the possible levels of abstraction of a candidate cause and the analogous problem of the possible temporal lag of a causal relation. These issues have implications for category formation. We end the chapter with a sketch of future research directions from a computational perspective.

Information Processing Accounts

A Statistical Approach

OVERVIEW

Some computational accounts of causal discovery are only concerned with statistical information (e.g., Allan & Jenkins, 1980; Chapman & Robbins, 1990; Jenkins & Ward, 1965; Rescorla & Wagner, 1972), ignoring hypotheses regarding unobservable causal relations (see Gallistel's, 1990, critique of these models as being unrepresentational). Such accounts not only adopt Hume's (1739/1888) problem but also his solution. To these theorists, causality is nothing more than a mental habit, a fictional epiphenomenon floating unnecessarily on the surface of indisputable facts.[1] After all, causal relations are unobservable. In fact, Karl Pearson, one of the fathers of modern statistics, subscribed to a positivist view and concluded that calculating correlations is the ultimate and only meaningful transformation of evidence at our disposal: "Beyond such discarded fundamentals as 'matter' and 'force' lies still another fetish amidst the inscrutable arcana of modern science, namely, the category of cause and effect" (Pearson, 1892/1957). Correlation at least enables one to make predictions based on observations even when the predictions are not accompanied by causal understanding.

Psychological work in this area was pioneered by social psychologists, most notably Kelley (1973), who studied causal attributions in interpersonal exchanges. His ANOVA model specifies a set of inference rules that indicate, for instance, whether a given outcome arose owing to particular aspects of the situation, the involved person(s), or both.

Around the same time in a different domain (Pavlovian and instrumental conditioning), prediction based on observations was also the primary concern. Predictive learning in conditioning, often involving nonhuman animals, and causal reasoning in humans showed so many parallels (Rescorla, 1988) that associative learning theorists were prompted to apply models of conditioning to explain causal reasoning. Explaining causal learning with associative theories implies a mapping of causes to cues (or CSs) and effects to outcomes (or USs). In a detailed review, Shanks and Dickinson (1987; see Dickinson, 2001, for a more recent review) noted that the two cornerstones of associative learning, *cue-outcome contingency* and *temporal contiguity*, also drive human causal learning (also see Miller & Matute, 1996). To a first approximation, association matters: The more likely that a cause will be followed by an effect, the stronger participants believe that they are causally related. However, if this probability stays constant, but the probability with which the effect occurs in the absence of the cause increases, causal judgments tend to decrease; in other words, it is contingency that matters

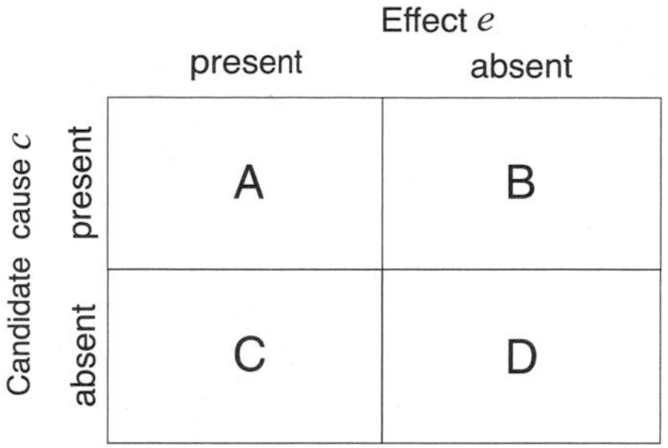

Figure 7.1. A standard 2 × 2 contingency table. A through D are labels for the frequencies of event types resulting from a factorial combination of the presence and absence of cause *c* and effect *e*.

(see Rescorla, 1968, for a parallel demonstration of the role of contingency in rats). As for temporal contiguity, Shanks, Pearson, and Dickinson (1989) showed that separating cause and effect in time tends to decrease impressions of causality (see also Buehner & May, 2002, 2003, 2004). This pattern of results, Shanks and Dickinson argued, parallels well-established findings from conditioning studies involving nonhuman animals.

Contingency and temporal contiguity are conditions that enable causal learning. A robust feature of the resultant acquisition of causal knowledge is that it is gradual and can be described by a negatively accelerated learning curve with judgments reaching an equilibrium level under some conditions after sufficient training (Shanks, 1985a, 1987).

A Statistical Model for Situations with One Varying Candidate Cause For situations involving only one varying candidate cause, an influential decision rule for almost four decades has been the ΔP rule:

$$\Delta P = p(e \mid c) - P(e \mid \bar{c}) \qquad \text{(Eq. 7.1)}$$

according to which the strength of the relation between a binary cause c and effect e is determined by their *contingency* or *probabilistic contrast* – the difference between the probabilities of e in the presence and absence of c (see, e.g., Allan & Jenkins, 1980; Jenkins & Ward, 1965). ΔP is estimated by relative frequencies. Figure 7.1 displays a *contingency table* where A and B represent the frequencies of occurrence of e in the presence and absence of c, respectively, and C and D represent the frequencies of nonoccurrence of e in the presence and absence of c, respectively. $P(e|c)$ is estimated by $\frac{A}{A+B}$, and $P(e|\bar{c})$ is estimated by $\frac{C}{C+D}$.

If ΔP is positive, then c is believed to produce e; if it is negative, then c is believed to prevent e; and if ΔP is zero, then c and e are not believed to be causally related to each other. Several modifications of the ΔP rule have been discussed (e.g., Anderson & Sheu, 1995; Mandel & Lehman, 1998; Perales & Shanks, 2003; Schustack & Sternberg, 1981; White, 2002). All these modifications parameterize the original rule in one way or another and thus, by allowing extra degrees of freedom, manage to fit certain aspects of human judgment data better than the original rule. What is common across all these models, however, is that they take covariational information contained in the contingency table as input and transform it into a measure of causal strength as output without any consideration of the influence of alternative causes. Whenever there is confounding by an alternative cause (observed or unobserved), the ΔP rule fails.

A Statistical Model for Situations Involving Multiple Varying Candidate Causes Predictive learning, of course, is the subject of associative learning theory. An appeal of this approach is that it is sometimes capable of explaining inference involving multiple causes. The most influential such theory (Rescorla & Wagner, 1972, and all its variants since) is based on an algorithm of error correction driven by a discrepancy between the expected and actual outcomes. For each learning trial where the cue was presented, the model specifies

$$\Delta V_{CS} = \alpha_{CS}\beta_{US}(\lambda - \Sigma V) \qquad \text{(Eq. 7.2)}$$

where ΔV is the change in the strength of a given CS–US association on a given trial (CS = conditioned stimulus, e.g., a tone; US = unconditioned stimulus, e.g., a footshock); α and β represent learning rate parameters reflecting the saliencies of the CS and US, respectively; λ stands for the actual outcome of each trial (usually 1.0 if it is present and 0 if it is absent); and ΣV is the expected outcome defined as the sum of all associative strengths of all CSs present on that trial. Each time a cue is followed by an outcome, the association between them is strengthened (up to the maximum strength US can support, λ); each time the cue is presented without the outcome, the association weakens (again within certain boundaries, $-\Sigma V$, to account for preventive cues).

For situations involving only one varying cue, its mean weight at equilibrium according to the RW algorithm has been shown to equal ΔP if the value of β remains the same when the US is present and when it is absent (for the λ values just mentioned; Chapman & Robbins, 1990). In other words, this simple and intuitive algorithm elegantly explains why causal learning is a function of contingency. It also explains a range of results for designs involving multiple cues such as *blocking* (see "Blocking: Illustrating an Associationist Explanation" section), *conditioned inhibition*, *overshadowing*, and *cue validity* (Miller, Barnet, & Grahame, 1995). For some of these designs, the mean weight of a cue at equilibrium has been shown to equal ΔP conditional on the constant presence of other cues that occur in combination with that cue (see Cheng, 1997; Danks, 2003). Danks derived the mean equilibrium weights for a larger class of designs.

BLOCKING: ILLUSTRATING AN ASSOCIATIONIST EXPLANATION

Beyond the cornerstones, the parallels between conditioning and human causal learning are manifested across numerous experimental designs often called paradigms in the literature. One parallel involves the blocking paradigm. Using a Pavlovian conditioning paradigm, Kamin (1969) established cue B as a perfect predictor for an outcome (B+, with "+" representing the occurrence of the outcome). In a subsequent phase, animals were presented with a compound consisting of B and a new, redundant cue A. The AB compound was also always followed by the outcome (AB+), yet A received little conditioning; its conditioning was *blocked* by

B. According to RW, B initially acquires the maximum associative strength supported by the stimulus. Because the association between B and the outcome is already at asymptote when A is introduced, there is no error left for A to explain. In other words, the outcome is already perfectly predicted by B, and nothing is left to be predicted by A, which accounts for the lack of conditioning to cue A. Shanks (1985b) replicated the same finding in a causal reasoning experiment with human participants, although the human responses seem to reflect uncertainty of the causal status of A rather than certainty that it is noncausal (e.g., Waldmann & Holyoak, 1992).

FAILURE OF THE RW ALGORITHM TO TRACK COVARIATION WHEN A CUE IS ABSENT

The list of similarities between animal conditioning and human causal reasoning seemed to grow, prompting the interpretation that causal learning is nothing more than associative learning. However, Shanks' (1985b) results also revealed evidence for backward blocking; in fact, there is evidence for backward blocking even in young children (Gopnik et al., 2004). In this procedure, the order of learning phases is simply reversed; participants first learn about the perfect relation between AB and the outcome (AB+) and subsequently learn that B by itself is also a perfect predictor (B+). Conceptually, forward and backward blocking are identical – at least from a causal perspective. A causal explanation might go: If one knows that A and B together always produce an effect, and one also knows that B by itself also always produ- ces the effect, one can infer that B is a strong cause. A, however, could be a cause, even a strong one, or noncausal; its causal status is unclear. Typically, participants express such uncertainty with low to medium ratings relative to ratings from control cues that have been paired with the effect an equal number of times (see Cheng, 1997, for a review).

Beyond increasing susceptibility to attention and memory biases (primacy and recency, cf. for example, Dennis & Ahn, 2001), there is no reason why the temporal order in which knowledge about AB and B is acquired should play a role under a causal learning perspective. This is not so under an associative learning perspective, however. The standard assumption here is that the strength of a cue can only be updated when that cue is present. In the backward blocking paradigm, however, participants *retrospectively* alter their estimate of A on the B+ trials in phase 2. In other words, the ΔP of A, conditional on the presence of B, decreases over a course of trials in which A is actually absent, and the algorithm fails to track the covariation for A.

Several modifications of RW have been proposed to allow the strengths of absent cues to be changed, for instance, by setting the learning parameter α negative on trials where the cue is absent (see Dickinson & Burke, 1996; Van Hamme & Wasserman, 1994). Such modifications can explain backward blocking and some other findings showing retrospective revaluation (see, e.g., Larkin, Aitken, & Dickinson, 1998; for an extensive review of modifications to associative learning models applicable to human learning, see De Houwer & Beckers, 2002). However, they also oddly predict that one will have difficulty learning that there are multiple sufficient causes of an effect. For example, if one sometimes drinks both tea and lemonade, then learning that tea alone can quench thirst will cause one to unlearn that lemonade can quench thirst. They also fail when two steps of retrospective revaluation are required. Macho and Burkart (2002) demonstrated that humans are capable of *iterative retrospective revaluation*, a backward process whereby the causal strength of a target cause is disambiguated by evaluating another cause, which in turn is evaluated by drawing on information about a third cause (see also Lovibond, Been, Mitchell, Bouton, & Frohardt, 2003, for further evidence that blocking in human causal reasoning is inferential, and De Houwer, 2002, for a demonstration that even forward blocking recruits retrospective inferences). In these cases, ΔP with other cues controlled coincides with causal intuitions, but associative models fail to track conditional ΔP.

Causal Inference Goes Beyond Covariation Tracking

PREDICTIONS BY THE STATISTICAL VIEW AND THE CAUSAL MECHANISM VIEW ON SOME INTUITIVE EXAMPLES

Even successfully tracked covariation, however, does not equal causation, as we illustrated earlier and as every introductory statistics text warns. None of these cases can be explained by the ΔP rule in Eq. (7.1). For example, even if the ΔP for rooster crowing is 1, nobody would claim that the crowing *caused* the sun to rise. Although the candidate cause, crowing, covaries perfectly with the effect, sunrise, there is an alternative cause that covaries with the candidate: Whenever the rooster crows, the Earth's rotation is just about to bring the farm toward the sun. Our intuition would say that because there is confounding, one cannot draw any causal conclusion. This pattern of information fits the *overshadowing* design. If crowing is the more salient of the two confounded cues, then RW would predict that crowing causes sunrise.

Let us digress for a moment to consider what the causal mechanism view predicts. Power theorists might argue that the absence of a plausible mechanism whereby a bird could influence the motion of stellar objects, rather than anything that has to do with covariation, is what prevents us from erroneously inducing a causal relation. In this example, in addition to the confounding by the Earth's rotation, there happens to be prior causal knowledge, specifically, of the noncausality of a bird's crowing with respect to sunrise. Tracing the possible origin of that knowledge, however, we see that we do have covariational information that allows us to arrive at the conclusion that the relation is noncausal. If we view crowing and sunrise at a more general level of abstraction, namely, as sound and the movement of large objects, we no longer have the confounding we noted at the specific level of crowing and sunrise. We have observed that sounds, when manipulated at will so alternative causes *do* occur independently of the candidate, thus allowing causal inference, do not move large objects. Consequently, crowing belongs to a category that does not cause sunrise (and does not belong to any category that does cause sunrise), and the confounded covariation between crowing and sunrise is disregarded as spurious.

Our consideration shows that, contrary to the causal mechanism view, prior knowledge of noncausality neither precludes nor refutes observation-based causal discovery. Thagard (2000) gave a striking historic illustration of this fact. Even though the stomach had been regarded as too acidic an environment for viruses to survive, a virus was inferred to be a cause of stomach ulcer. Prior causal knowledge may render a novel candidate causal relation more or less plausible but cannot rule it out definitively. Moreover, prior causal knowledge is often stochastic. Consider a situation in which one observes that insomia results whenever one drinks champagne. Now, there may be a straightforward physiological causal mechanism linking cause and effect, but it is also plausible that the relation is not causal; it could easily be that drinking and insomnia are both caused by a third variable – for example, attending parties (cf. Gopnik et al., 2004).

Returning to the pitfall of statistical and associative models, besides the confounding problem, we find that there is the overdetermination problem, where two or more causes covary with an effect, and each cause by itself would be sufficient to produce the effect. The best-known illustration of overdetermination is provided by Mackie (1974): Imagine two criminals who both want to murder a third person who is about to cross a desert; unaware of each other's intentions, one criminal puts poison in the victim's water bottle, while the other punctures the bottle. Each action on its own covaries perfectly with the effect, death, and would have been sufficient to bring the effect about. However, in the presence of the alternative cause of death (a given fact in this example), so that there is no confounding, varying each candidate cause in this case makes no difference; for instance, the ΔP for poison with respect to death, conditional on the presence of the puncturing of the water canteen, is 0! So, Mackie's puzzle goes, which of the two criminals should be called the murderer? Presumably, a lawyer could defend each criminal by arguing that their respective deed made no difference to the victim's ultimate fate – he would have died anyway as a result of the other action (but see Katz, 1989; also see Ellsworth, Chap. 28; Pearl, 2000; and Wright, 1985, on actual causation). Mackie turned to the actual manner of death (by poison or by dehydration) for a solution. But, suppose the death is discovered too late to yield useful autopsy information. Would the desert traveler then have died without a cause? Surely our intuition says no: The lack of covariation in this case does not imply the lack of causation (see Ellsworth, Chap. 28; Spellman & Kincannon, 2001, for studies on intuitive judgments in situations involving multiple sufficient causes). What matters is the prediction of the consequences of actions, such as poisoning, which may or may not be revealed in the covariation observed in a particular context.

Empirical Findings on Humans and Rats

The observed distinction between covariation and causation in the causal learning literature corroborates intuitive judgment in the rooster and desert traveler examples. It is no wonder that Pearson's condemnation of the concept of causality notwithstanding, contemporary artificial intelligence has wholeheartedly embraced causality (see, for example, Pearl, 2000). We now review how human causal reasoning capacities exceed the mere tracking of stimulus–outcome associations.

THE DIRECTION OF CAUSALITY

As mentioned earlier, correlations and associations are bidirectional (for implications of the bidirectional nature of associations on conditioning, see, e.g., Miller & Barnet, 1993; and Savastano & Miller, 1998) and thus cannot represent directed causal information. However, the concept of causality is fundamentally directional (Reichenbach, 1956) in that causes produce effects, but effects cannot produce causes. This directionality constrains the pool of possible candidate causes of an effect. A straightforward demonstration that humans are sensitive to the direction of the causal arrow was provided by Waldmann and Holyoak (1992).

A corollary of the directional nature of the causal arrow, Waldmann and Holyoak (1992) reasoned, is that only causes, but not effects, should "compete" for explanatory power. Let us first revisit the blocking paradigm with a causal interpretation. If B is a perfect *cause* of an outcome O, and A is only presented in conjunction with B, one has no basis of knowing to what extent, if at all, A actually produces O. Consequently, the predictiveness of A should be depressed relative to B in a predictive situation. However, if B is a consistent *effect* of O, there is no reason why A cannot also be an equally consistent effect of O. Alternative causes need to be kept constant to allow causal inference, but alternative effects do not. Consequently, the predictiveness of A should *not* be depressed in a diagnostic situation.

This asymmetric prediction was tested using scenarios to manipulate whether a variable is interpreted as a candidate cause or an effect without changing the associations between variables. For example, participants had to learn the relation between several light buttons and the state of an alarm system. The instructions introduced the buttons as causes for the alarm in the *predictive* condition but as potential consequences of the state of the alarm system in the *diagnostic* condition.

As predicted: There was blocking in the predictive condition, but not in the diagnostic condition. These results reveal that humans are sensitive to, and make use of, the direction of the causal arrow.

Associationists in fact have no reason for objecting to using temporal information. Unlike causal relations, temporal ordering is observable. To address the problem raised by Waldmann and Holyoak (1992), associationist models can specify that, when applied to explain causal learning, candidate causes can precede their effects, but not vice versa, and that the temporal ordering that counts is that of the actual occurrence of events rather than that of the recount of events to the reasoner. Previous associationist models, however, have not made a distinction between occurrence and presentation order. Therefore, by default, they treat the buttons, for which information was presented first, as cues and the alarm, for which information was presented second, as an outcome, and hence, predict equal amounts of cue competition in both scenarios.

Instead of amending associationist models to treat the order of actual occurrence as critical, which would be natural under a computational approach, researchers criticized Waldmann and Holyoak's (1992) findings on technical grounds (Matute, Arcediano, & Miller, 1996; Shanks & Lopez, 1996). Follow-up work from Waldmann's lab (Waldmann, 2000, 2001; Waldmann & Holyoak, 1997), however, has demonstrated that the asymmetry in cue competition is indeed a robust finding (Waldmann, 2001).

CEILING EFFECTS AND PEOPLE'S SENSITIVITY TO PROPER EXPERIMENTAL DESIGN

A revealing case of the distinction between covariation and causation has to do with what is known in experimental design as a ceiling effect. This case does not involve any confounding. We illustrate it with the preventive version of the effect, which is never covered in courses on experimental design – the underlying intuition is so powerful it needs no instructional augmentation. Imagine that a scientist conducts an experiment to find out whether a new drug cures migraine. She follows the usual procedure and administers the drug to an experimental group of patients, while an equivalent control group receives a placebo. At the end of the study, the scientist discovers that none of the patients in the experimental group, but also none of the patients in the control group, suffered from migraine. If we enter this information into the ΔP rule, we see that $P(e|c) = 0$ and $P(e|\bar{c}) = 0$, yielding $\Delta P = 0$. According to the ΔP rule and RW, this would indicate that there is no causal relation; that is, the drug does not cure migraine. Would the scientist really conclude that? No, the scientist would instead recognize that she has conducted a poor experiment. For some reason, her sample suffered from a preventive version of the ceiling effect – the effect never occurred, regardless of the manipulation. If the effect never occurs in the first place, how can a preventive intervention be expected to prove its effectiveness?

Even rats seem to appreciate this argument. When an inhibitory cue, that is, one with negative associative strength, is repeatedly presented without the outcome so that the actual outcome is 0 whereas the expected outcome is negative, associative models would predict that the cue reduces its strength toward 0. That is, in a noncausal world, we would unlearn our preventive causes whenever they are not accompanied by a generative cause. For example, when we inoculate child after child with polio vaccine in a country and there is no occurrence of polio in that country, we would come to believe that the polio vaccine does not function anymore (rather than merely that it is not needed). To the contrary, even for rats, the inhibitory cue retains its negative strength (Zimmerhart-Hart & Rescorla, 1974). In other words, when an outcome in question never occurred, both when a conditioned inhibitory cue was present and when it was not, the rats apparently treated the zero ΔP value as uninformative and retained the inhibitory status of the cue. In this case, in spite of a discrepancy between the expected and actual outcomes, there is no revision of causal strength. We are not aware of any modification of associative algorithms that can accomodate this finding.

Notice that in the hypothetical migraine experiment, one can in fact conclude that the drug *does not cause* migraine. Thus, given the exact same covariation, one's conclusion differs depending on the direction of influence under evaluation (generative vs. preventive). Wu and Cheng (1999) conducted an experiment that showed that beginning college students, just like experienced scientists, refrain from making causal inferences in the generative and preventive ceiling effects situations. People's preference to refrain from causal judgment in such situations is at odds with purely covariational or associative accounts. What must the process of human causal induction involve so it will reflect people's unwillingness to engage in causal inference in such situations? More generally, what must this process involve so it will distinguish causation from mere covariation?

A Causal Network Approach

A solution to the puzzle posed by the distinction between covariation and causation is to test hypotheses involving causal structures (Cheng, 1997; Novick & Cheng, 2004; Pearl, 1988, 2000; Spirtes, Glymour, & Scheines, 1993/2000). Pearl (2000) and Spirtes et al. (1993/2000) developed a formal framework for causal inference based on causal Bayesian networks. In this framework, causal structures are represented as directed acyclic graphs, graphs with nodes connected by arrows. The nodes represent variables, and each arrow represents a direct causal relation between two variables. "Acyclic" refers to the constraint that the chains formed by the arrows are never loops. The graphs are assumed to satisfy the Markov condition, which states that for any variable X in the graph, for any set S of variables in the graph not containing any direct or indirect effects of X, X is jointly independent of the variables in S conditional on any set of values of the set of variables that are direct causes of X (see Pearl, 1988, 2000; Spirtes et al., 1993/2000). An effect of X is a variable that has (1) an arrow directly from X pointing into it or (2) a pathway of arrows originating from X pointing into it. Gopnik et al. (2004) proposed that people are able to assess patterns of conditional independence using the Markov assumption and infer entire causal networks from the patterns. Cheng (1997) proposed instead that people (and perhaps other species) evaluate one causal relation in a network at a time while taking into consideration other relations in the network. Clearcut evidence discriminating between these two variants is still unavailable.

A COMPUTATIONAL-LEVEL THEORY OF CAUSAL INDUCTION

Cheng (1997)'s power PC theory (short for a causal power theory of the probabilistic contrast model) starts with the Humean constraint that causality can only be inferred using observable evidence (in the form of covariations and temporal and spatial information) as input to the reasoning process. She combines that constraint with Kant's (1781/1965) postulate that reasoners have an a priori notion that types of causal relations exist in the universe. This unification can best be illustrated with an analogy. According to Cheng, the relation between a causal relation and a covariation is like the relation between a scientific theory and a model. Scientists postulate theories (involving unobservable entities) to explain models (i.e., observed regularities or laws); the kinetic theory of gases, for example, is used to explain Boyle's law. Boyle's law describes an observable phenomenon, namely that pressure × volume = constant (under certain boundary conditions), and the kinetic theory of gases explains in terms of unobservable entities why Boyle's law holds (gases consist of small particles moving at a speed proportional to their temperature, and pressure is generated by the particles colliding with the walls of the container). Likewise, a causal relation is the unobservable entity that reasoners hope to infer in order to explain observable regularities between events (Cheng, 1997).

This distinction between a causal relation as a distal, postulated entity and covariation as an observable, proximal stimulus implies that there can be situations in which there is observable covariation but causal inference is not licensed. Computationally, this means that causality is represented as an *unbound* variable (cf. Doumas & Hummel, Chap. 4; Holyoak & Hummel, 2000) represented separately and not bound to covariation, allowing situations in which covariation has a definite value (e.g., 0, as in the ceiling effect) but causal power has no value. Traditional models (Allan & Jenkins, 1980; Anderson & Sheu, 1995; Jenkins & Ward, 1965; Mandel & Lehman, 1998; Schustack & Sternberg, 1981; White, 2002; and Rescorla & Wagner,

1972), which are purely covariational, do not represent causality as a separate variable. Hence, whenever there is observed covariation, they will always compute a definite causal strength. In an analogy to perception, one could say that such models never go beyond describing features of the proximal stimulus (observable evidence – covariation or image on the retina) and fail to infer features of the distal stimulus (causal power that produced the covariation or object in the 3D world that produced retinal images).

How then does the power PC theory (Cheng, 1997) go beyond the proximal stimulus and explain the various ways in which covariation does not imply causation? The first step in the solution is the inclusion of unobservable entities, including the desired unknown, the distal causal relation, in the equations. The theory partitions all (observed and unobserved) causes of effect *e* into the candidate cause in question, *c*, and *a*, a composite of all alternative causes of *e*. The unobservable probability with which *c produces e* (in other words, the probability that *e* occurs *as a result of c*'s occurring) is termed the *generative* power of *c*, represented by q_c here. When $\Delta P \geq 0$, q_c is the desired unknown. Likewise, when $\Delta P \leq 0$, the preventive power of *c* is the desired unknown. Two other relevant theoretical unknowns are q_a, the probability with which *a* produces *e* when it occurs, and P(*a*), the probability with which *a* occurs. The composite *a* may include unknown and therefore unobservable causes. Because any causal power may have a value of 0, or even no value at all, these variables are merely hypotheses – they do not presuppose that *c* and *a* indeed have causal influence on *e*. The idea of a cause producing an effect and the idea of a cause preventing an effect are primitives in the theory.

On the assumption that *c* and *a* influence *e* independently, the power PC theory explains the two conditional probabilities defining ΔP as follows:

$$P(e \mid c) = q_c + P(a \mid c) \cdot q_a - q_c \cdot P(a \mid c) \cdot q_a \quad \text{(Eq. 7.3)}$$

$$P(e \mid \bar{c}) = P(a \mid \bar{c}) \cdot q_a \quad \text{(Eq. 7.4)}$$

Equation (7.3) "explains" that, given that *c* has occurred, *e* is produced by *c* or by the composite *a*, nonexclusively (*e* is jointly produced by both with a probability that follows from the independent influence of *c* and *a* on *e*). Equation (7.4) "explains" that given that *c* did not occur, *e* is produced by *a* alone.

It follows from Eqs. (7.3) and (7.4) that

$$\Delta P_c = q_c + P(a \mid c) \cdot q_a - q_c \cdot P(a \mid c) \cdot q_a - P(a \mid \bar{c}) \cdot q_a \quad \text{(Eq. 7.5)}$$

From Eq. (7.5), it can be seen that unless *c* and *a* occur independently, there are four unknowns: $-q_c$, q_a, $P(a \mid c)$, and $P(a \mid \bar{c})$; it follows that, in general, despite ΔP's having a definite value, there is no unique solution for q_c. This failure corresponds to our intuition that covariation need not imply causation – an intuition that purely covariational models are incapable of explaining.

In the special case in which *a* occurs independently of *c* (e.g., when alternative causes are held constant), Eq. (7.5) simplifies to Eq. (7.6),

$$q_c = \frac{\Delta P}{1 - P(e \mid \bar{c})} \quad \text{(Eq. 7.6)}$$

in which all variables besides q_c are observable. In this case, q_c can be solved. Being able to solve for q_c only under the condition of *independent occurrence* explains why manipulation by free will encourages causal inference (the principle of *control* in experimental design and everyday reasoning). When one manipulates a variable, that decision by free will is likely to occur independently of alternative causes of that variable. At the same time, the condition of independent occurrence explains why causal inferences resulting from interventions are not always correct. Alternative causes are unlikely to covary with one's decision to manipulate, but sometimes they may, as the food allergy example illustrates. Note that the principle of "no confounding" is a result in this theory, rather than an unexplained axiomatic assumption, as it is in current scientific methodology (also see Dunbar & Fugelsang, Chap. 29).

An analogous explanation yields p_c, the power of c to prevent e

$$p_c = \frac{-\Delta P}{P(e \mid \bar{c})} \qquad \text{(Eq. 7.7)}$$

Now it is also obvious how the power PC theory can explain why the ceiling effects block causal inference (even when there is no confounding) and do so under different conditions. In the generative case, e always occurs, regardless of the manipulation; hence, $P(e \mid c) = P(e \mid \bar{c}) = 1$, leaving q_c in Eq. (7.6) with an undefined value. In contrast, in the preventive case, e never occurs again regardless of the manipulation; therefore, $P(e \mid c) = P(e \mid \bar{c}) = 0$, leaving p_c in Eq. (7.7) with an undefined value.

Although the theory distinguishes between generative and preventive causal powers, this distinction does not constitute a free parameter. Which of the two equations applies readily follows from the value of ΔP. On occasions where $\Delta P = 0$, both equations apply and make the same prediction, namely, that causal power should be 0 except in ceiling effect situations. Here, the reasoner has to make a pragmatic decision on whether he or she is evaluating the evidence to assess a preventive or generative relation, and whether the evidence at hand is meaningful or not for that purpose.

Most causes are complex, involving not just a single factor but a conjunction of factors operating in concert. In other words, the assumption made by the power PC theory that c and a influence e independently is false most of the time. When this assumption is violated, if an alternative cause (part of a) is observable, the independent influence assumption can be given up for that cause, and progressively more complex causes can be evaluated using the same distal approach that represents causal powers. This approach has been extended to evaluate conjunctive causes involving two factors (see Novick & Cheng, 2004). Even if alternative causes are not observable, however, Cheng (2000) showed that as long as they occur with about the same probability in the learning context as in the generalization context, predictions according to simple causal power involving a single factor will hold. That is, under that condition, it does not matter what the reasoner assumes about the independent influence of c and a on e.

EXPERIMENTAL TESTS OF A COMPUTATIONAL CAUSAL POWER APPROACH

The predictions made by the power PC theory and by noncausal accounts differ in diverse ways. We review three of these differences in this section. The first concerns a case in which covariation does not equal causation. The second concerns a qualitative pattern of the influence of $P(e \mid \bar{c})$, the *base rate of e*, for candidate causes with the same ΔP. The third concerns the flexible and coherent use of causal power to make causal predictions.

More Studies on Covariation and Causation We have already mentioned Wu and Cheng's (1999) study on ceiling situations, showing that they distinguish covariation from causation. Lovibond et al. (2003) reported a further test of this distinction. Their experiments are not a direct test of the power PC theory because they do not involve binary variables only. They do, however, test the same fundamental idea underlying a distal approach. That is, to account for the distinction between covariation and causation, there must be an explicit representation of unobservable causal relations.

Lovibond et al. (2003) tested human subjects on "backward blocking" and on "release from overshadowing," when the outcome (an allergic reaction to some food) occurred at what the subjects perceived as the "ceiling" level for one condition and at an intermediate level for another condition. The release-from-overshadowing condition involved a retrospective design, and differed from the backward blocking condition only in that, when the blocking cue B (the cue that did appear by itself) appeared, the outcome did *not* occur. Thus, considering the effect of cue A, the cue that never appeared by itself, with cue B held constantly present, one sees that introducing A made a difference to the occurrence of the outcome. This nonzero ΔP implies causality, regardless of whether the outcome occurred (given the compound) at a ceiling or nonceiling level.

The critical manipulation was a "pretraining compound" phase during which one group of subjects, the *ceiling* group, saw that a combination of two allergens produced an outcome at the same level ("an allergic reaction") as a single allergen (i.e., the ceiling level). In contrast, the *nonceiling* group saw that a combination of two allergens produced a stronger reaction ("a STRONG allergic reaction") than a single allergen ("an allergic reaction"). Following this pretraining phase, all subjects were presented with information regarding various cues and outcomes according to their assignment to the backward-blocking or release-from-overshadowing groups. Critically, the outcome in this main training phase always only occurred at the intermediate level ("an allergic reaction") for both the *ceiling* and *nonceiling* groups. Ingeniously, as a result of pretraining, subjects' perception of the level of the outcome in the main phase would be expected to differ. For the exact same outcome, "an allergic reaction," the only form of the outcome then, whereas the *ceiling* group would perceive it to occur at the ceiling level, the *nonceiling* group would perceive it to occur at an intermediate level. For the backward-blocking condition for both groups, cue A made no difference to the occurrence of the outcome (holding B constant, there was always a reaction whether or not A was there). However, as explained by the power PC theory, whereas a ΔP of 0 implies noncausality (i.e., a causal rating of 0) when the outcome occurred at a nonceiling level, the same value does not allow causal inference when the outcome occurred at a ceiling level. In support of this interpretation, the mean causal rating for cue A was reliably lower for the *nonceiling* group than for the *ceiling* group. In contrast, recovery from overshadowing was not dependent on whether or not the outcome was perceived to occur at a ceiling level.

Why does the level at which the outcome was perceived to occur lead to different responses in the backward-blocking condition but not in the release-from-overshadowing condition? This result adds to the challenges for associative accounts. Both designs involved retrospective revaluation, but even modifications of associative models that explain retrospective revaluation cannot explain this difference. In contrast, a simple and intuitive answer follows from a causal account.

Base Rate Influence on Conditions with Identical ΔP Several earlier studies on human contingency judgment have reported that, although ΔP clearly influences causal ratings (e.g., Allan & Jenkins, 1980; Wasserman, Elek, Chatlosh, & Baker, 1993), for a given level of ΔP, causal ratings diverge from ΔP as the base rate of the effect e, $P(e \mid \bar{c})$ increases. If we consider Eq. (7.6) (the power PC theory) for any constant positive ΔP, causal ratings should increase as $P(e \mid \bar{c})$ increases. Conversely, according to Eq. (7.7), preventive causal ratings should decrease as $P(e \mid \bar{c})$ increases for the same negative ΔP. Zero contingencies, however, regardless of the base rate of e, should be judged as noncausal (except when judgment should be withheld due to ceiling effects). No other current model of causal learning predicts this qualitative pattern of the influence of the base rate of e, although some covariational or associative learning models can explain one or another part of this pattern given felicitous parameter values. For example, in the RW, if $\beta_{\mathrm{US}} > \beta_{\overline{\mathrm{US}}}$, causal ratings will always increase as base rate increases, whereas the opposite trend would be obtained if the parameter ordering were reversed. Another prominent associative learning model, Pearce's (1987) model of stimulus generalization, can likewise account for opposite base rate influences in positive and negative contingencies if the parameters are set accordingly, but this model would then additionally predict a base rate influence on noncontingent conditions.

Figure 7.2 illustrates the intuitiveness of a rating that deviates from ΔP. The reasoning is counterfactual. $P(e \mid \bar{c})$ estimates the "expected" probability of e in the *presence* of c if c had been absent so that only

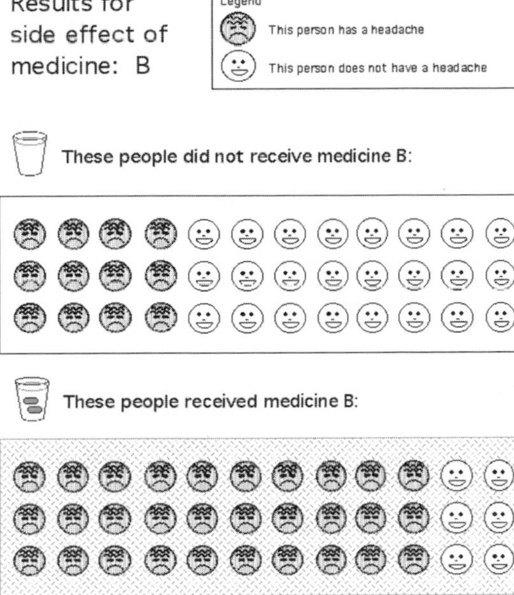

Figure 7.2. Examples of stimulus materials from a condition in Buehner et al. (2003).

causes other than *c* exerted an influence on *e*. A deviation from this counterfactual probability indicates that *c* is a simple cause of *e*. Under the assumption that the patients represented in the figure were randomly assigned to the two groups, one that received the drug and another that did not, one would reason that about one-third of the patients in the "drug" group would be expected to have headaches if they had not received the drug. The drug then would be the sole cause of headaches among the two-thirds who did not already have headaches caused by other factors. In this subgroup, headaches occurred in three-fourths of the patients. One might therefore reason, although $\Delta P = 1/2$, that the probability the drug will produce headaches is three-fourths.

The initial attempts to test the power PC theory yielded mixed results. Buehner and Cheng (1997; see Buehner, Cheng, & Clifford, 2003 for a more detailed report) varied the base rate of *e* for conditions with the same value of ΔP using a sequential trial procedure and demonstrated that base rate indeed influences the evaluation of positive and negative contingencies in the way that power PC predicts. However, contrary to the predictions of the power PC theory, Buehner and Cheng (1997) also found that base rate did not only influence contingent conditions with equal ΔP values but also influenced noncontingent conditions (in which $\Delta P = 0$). The latter, a robust result (see Shanks 1985a; 1987; and Shanks, Holyoak & Mediu, 1996, for a review) seems nonsensical if ΔP had in fact been 0 in the input to the reasoner. Furthermore, they also found that comparisons between certain conditions where causal power [as defined in Eqs. (7.6) and (7.7)] was constant but ΔP varied showed variations in the direction of ΔP, as predicted by the RW and Pearce model.

Many researchers treated Buehner and Cheng's (1997) and similar results (Lober & Shanks, 2000) as a given and regarded the findings that deviated from the predictions of the power PC theory as refutations of it. Lober and Shanks (2000) concluded that these results fully support RW, even though they had to use opposite parameter orderings of β_{US} and $\beta_{\overline{US}}$ for generative candidates, as was the case for preventive candidates, to fit the data. Similarly, Tenenbaum and Griffiths (2001) concluded that these results support their Bayesian *causal support* model, which evaluates how confident one is that *c* causes *e*. It does so by comparing the posterior probabilities of two causal networks, both of which have a background cause that is constantly present in the learning context, differing only in that one network has an arrow between *c* and *e*. When the posterior probability of the network with the extra arrow is greater than that without the arrow, then one decides that *c* causes *e*. Otherwise, one decides that *c* does not cause *e*. Support is defined as the log of the ratio of the two posterior probabilities.

DEVIATIONS FROM NORMATIVITY AND AMBIGUOUS EXPERIMENTS

Buehner et al.'s (2003) attempts to test the qualitative pattern of causal strengths predicted by the power PC theory illustrate a *modular* approach to psychological research. This approach attempts to study the mind rather than behavior as it happens to be observed. It attempts to isolate the influence of a mental process under study, even though tasks in our everyday life typically involve confounded contributions from multiple cognitive processes (e.g., comprehension and memory). An analysis of the experimental materials in Buehner and Cheng (1997) suggests that the deviations from the power PC theory are due to factors extraneous to the causal inference process (Buehner et al., 2003). First, the typical dependent variable used to measure causal judgments is highly ambiguous. Participants are typically asked to indicate how strongly they think *c* causes or prevents *e*. The question may be interpreted to ask how confident one is that *c* causes *e*, rather than how strongly *c* causes *e*. Also, it may be interpreted to refer to either the current learning context or a counterfactual context in which there are no other causes.

Notably, the distal approach allows formulations of coherent answers to each of these interpretations (see Buehner et al., 2003; Tenenbaum & Griffiths, 2001). It seems plausible that people are capable of answering a variety of causal questions. Moreover, they may be able to do so coherently, in which case models of answers to the various questions would be complementary if they are logically consistent.

Answers to the various questions (regarding the same conditions), however, may form different patterns. Testing the power PC theory directly requires removing both ambiguities. To do so, Buehner et al. (2003) adopted a counterfactual question: for example, "Imagine 100 patients who do not suffer from headaches. How many would have headaches if given the medication?" To minimize memory demands, Buehner et al. presented the trials simultaneously. They found that causal ratings using the counterfactual question and simultaneous trials were perfectly in line with causal power as predicted by the power PC theory. Berry (2003) corroborated Buehner et al.'s findings with a nonfrequentist counterfactual question.

Buehner et al. (2003) explained how the ambiguity of earlier causal questions can lead to confounded results that show an influence of ΔP on conditions with identical causal power. However, it cannot account for the base rate influence on noncontingent conditions. But, given the memory demands in typical sequential trial experiments, it is inevitable that some participants would erroneously misperceive the contingencies to be nonzero, in which case Eqs. (7.6) and (7.7) would predict an influence of base rate. These equations explain why the misperceptions do not cancel each other out, as one might expect if they were random. Instead, for the same absolute amount of misperception, a positive misperception that occurs at a higher base rate would imply a higher generative power, and a negative misperception (leading to a negative causal rating) that occurs at a lower base rate would imply a more negative preventive power. In both cases, causal ratings for objectively noncontingent candidates would increase as base rate increases. Thus, the base-rate influence for noncontingent candidates may reflect an interaction between memory and causal reasoning.

Buehner et al. (2003) confirmed this interpretation in two ways. First, when learning trials were presented simultaneously, thereby eliminating the possibility of misperceiving a zero contingency to be nonzero, participants no longer exhibited a base rate influence in noncontingent conditions. Second, they showed that in an experiment involving sequential trials, every judgment that deviated from 0 was indeed traceable to the subject's misperception of the zero contingency. All accurately perceived ΔP of 0 was rated as noncausal. Not a single subject did what all nonnormative accounts predict – differentially weighing an accurately perceived ΔP of 0 to result in a nonzero causal rating.

In sum, earlier deviations form the power PC theory's predictions were the result of confounding due to comprehension and memory processes. Once these extraneous problems were curtailed, as motivated by a modular approach, causal ratings followed exactly the pattern predicted by power PC. The complex pattern of results observed cannot be accounted for by any current associationist model, regardless of how its parameters are set. In contrast, the power PC theory explains the results without any parameters.

FLEXIBILITY AND COHERENCE

A general goal of inference is that it is both flexible and coherent. We mentioned earlier that a distal approach allows a coherent formulation of answers to different questions. These questions may concern confidence in the existence of a causal relation (Tenenbaum & Griffiths, 2001); conjunctive causation (Novick & Cheng, 2004); prediction under a change in context, enabling conditions rather than causes (Cheng & Novick, 1991; Goldvarg & Johnson-Laird, 2001); and interventions (e.g., Cheng, 1997; Gopnik et al., 2004; Lagnado & Sloman, 2004; Steyvers et al., 2003). The approach also provides an explanation of iterative retrospective revaluation (Macho & Burkart, 2002).

Iterative Retrospective Revaluation If an equation in several variables characterizes the operation of a system, the equation can potentially be used flexibly to solve for each variable when given the values of other variables, and the solutions would all be logically consistent. Evidence suggests that the equations in the power PC theory are used this way.

Macho and Burkart (2002, Experiment 2) presented trials in two phases: In the first, two pairs of candidate causes (TC and CD) were presented with the outcome e sometimes occurring, with the same relative frequency for both combinations; in the second phase, a single disambiguiting candidate, D, was presented. Two experimental groups differed only with respect to whether e always or never occurred with D in the second phase. For these groups, despite the fact that for both groups T and C were equally absent in the critical second phase, the mean causal ratings for T were higher than for C in one group, but lower in the other group. Consider what one would infer about T and C when D was always accompanied by e in the second phase (without D, e did not occur; therefore, D causes e). Holding D constantly present, because e occurred less often when C was there than when it was not, C prevents e, and its preventive power can be estimated. Instantiating Eq. (7.7) for this design, p_c is estimable as just mentioned, and $P(e \mid \text{TC})$ is given in phase 1; therefore, $P(e \mid \text{T not-C})$, the only unknown in the equation, can be solved. Once this unknown is solved, one can next use it to apply Eq. (7.6) to T, which has a positive ΔP: together with the information that $p(e \mid \text{not-T not-C}) = 0$ given in both phases, a positive generative power of T results. T and C are therefore generative and preventive, respectively. An analogous sequence of inference can be made when D is never accompanied by e, resulting in reversed causal powers for T and C (preventive and generative, respectively). Associative models either cannot predict any retrospective revaluation or erroneously predict that

C and T acquire weights in the same direction in phase 2 for each condition, because these cues are equally absent in the phase 2 when their weights are adjusted.

These results on iterative revaluations show that the use of Eqs. (7.6) and (7.7) in Cheng's (1997) power PC theory is more flexible than she originally discussed. In her paper, she interpreted the causal power variables on the left-hand side (LHS) as the desired unknowns. What Macho and Burkart (2002) showed is that, when given the value of the variables on the LHS, people are able to treat a variable on the right-hand side as the desired unknown and solve for it.

Intervention. The advantage of intervention over observation is most readily appreciated when trying to establish which of several competing hypotheses underlies a complex data structure. We explained this abstractly earlier in terms of the likely satisfaction of the independent occurrence condition. Let us non consider as an example the often reported correlation between teenage aggression, consumption of violent television or movies, and poor school performance. A correlation between these three variables could be due to either a common-cause structure: AGGRESSION ← TV → SCHOOL, where violent television would be the cause for both poor school performance and increased aggression, or a chain structure: AGGRESSION → TV → SCHOOL, where increased aggression would lead to increased consumption of violent TV, which in turn results in poor school performance. Without temporal information, these competing causal models cannot be distinguished by observation limited to the three-node network alone. However, if one were to *intervene* on the TV node, the two structures make different predictions: According to the former, restrictions on access to violent TV should lead to both improved school performance and decreased aggression; according to the latter, the same restriction would still improve school performance but would have no effect on aggressive behavior. Note that the intervention on TV effectively turned what was a three-node network into a four-node network: The amount of TV is controlled by an external agent, which was not represented in the simple three-node network. When the amount of TV is manipulated under free will, the external node would occur independently of aggression in the causal chain structure, because aggression and the external agent are alternative causes (of consumption of violent TV) in the causal chain structure, but not in the common cause structure. As mentioned earlier, one is likely to assume that alternative causes of an outcome remain constant while that outcome is manipulated under free will. This assumption, along with the independent occurrence condition, together explain why manipulation allows differentiation between the two structures.

An Enabling Condition. When asked "What caused the forest fire?" investigators are unlikely to reply, "The oxygen in the air." Rather, they are likely to reserve the title of cause to to such factors as "lightning," "arson," or the "dryness of the air." To explain the distinction between causes and enabling conditions, a number of theorists argued that a causal question invariably implies computation within a selected set of events in which a component cause is constantly present (e.g., Mackie, 1974). On this view, the forest fire question can be understood as "What made the difference between this occasion in the forest on which there was a fire and other occasions in the forest on which there was no fire?" Note that the selected set of events in the expanded question does not include all events in one's knowledge base that are related to fire. In particular, it does not include events in which oxygen is absent, even though such events (at least in an abstract form) are in a typical educated person's knowledge base. The power PC theory explains the distinction between causes, enabling conditions, and irrelevant factors the same way as Cheng and Novick (1992) do, except that now there is a justification for conditions that allow causal inference. A varying candidate cause is a cause if it covaries with the target effect in the current set of events, the set specified by the expanded question, in which other causes and causal-factors are constant. A candidate cause is an enabling condition if it is constantly present in the current set of events but is a cause according to another subset of events. Finally, a candidate cause is irrelevant if its covariation with the effect is not noticeably different from 0 in any subset of events that allows causal inference. (See Goldvarg & Johnson-Laird, 2001, for a similar explanation.)

Causal Inference and Category Formation: What Is the Level of Abstraction at Which ΔP Should Be Computed?

Cheng (1993) noted the problem of the level of abstraction at which covariations should be calculated. Consider the problem of evaluating whether smoking causes lung cancer. The candidate cause "smoking" can be viewed at various levels of abstraction, for instance, "smoking a particular brand of cigarettes" or "inhaling fumes". If one were to compute ΔP for smoking with respect to lung cancer, one would obtain lower values for both the narrower and the more abstract conceptions of the cause than for "smoking cigarettes." For example, if one adopted the more abstract conception "inhaling fumes," $P(e \mid \bar{c})$ would remain unchanged, but one would lower $P(e \mid c)$ because now other noncarcinogenic fumes (e.g., steam) contribute to the estimate of this probability. The more abstract exception would result in a smaller overall probability of c to produce e.

Causes and effects (like all events, see Vallacher & Wegner, 1987) can be conceptualized at various levels of abstraction. Cheng (1993) hypothesized that to evaluate a causal relation, people represent the relation at the level of abstraction at which ΔP, with alternative causes held constant, is maximal. Lien and Cheng (2000) showed that people indeed are sensitive to this idea. In a completely novel situation, where participants could not possibly recruit background knowledge (unlike in the smoking/lung cancer example), stimuli varied along two dimensions, color and shape, such that variations could be described at various levels of abstraction (e.g., cool vs. warm colors, red vs. orange, or particular shades of red). Participants in Lien and Cheng's experiments spontaneously represented the causal relation they learned at the level of abstraction at which ΔP was maximal.

Computing ΔP at an optimal level is consistent with an approach to causal learning that does not begin with well-defined candidate causes. In contrast, the current default assumption in the psychological literature is that causal discovery depends on the definition of the entities among which relations are to be discovered; categorization therefore precedes causal discovery. The opposite argument can be made, however. Causal discovery could be the driving force underlying our mental representation of the world – not only in the sense that we need to know how things influence each other but also in the sense that causal relations define what should be considered *things* in our mental universe (Lewis, 1929). Lien and Cheng (2000) provided evidence that the definition of an entity and the discovery of a causal relation operate as a single process in which optimal causal discovery is the driving force. Causal discovery therefore has direct implications for the formation of categories instead of requiring well-defined candidate causes as givens.

Time and Causal Inference: The Time-Frame of Covariation Assessment

We have concentrated on theoretical approaches that specify how humans take the mental leap from covariation to causation. Irrespective of any differences in theoretical perspective, all these approaches assume covariation can be readily assessed. This assumption is reflected in the experimental paradigms most commonly used. Typically, participants are presented with evidence structured in the form of discrete, simultaneous, or sequential learning trials in which each trial contains observations on whether the cause occurred and whether the effect occurred. In other words, in these tasks it is always perfectly clear whether a cause is followed by an effect on a given occasion. Such tasks grossly oversimplify the complexities of causal induction in some situations outside experimental laboratories: Some events have immediate outcomes; others do not reveal their consequences until much later. Before an organism can evaluate whether a specific covariation licenses causal conjecture, the covariation needs to be detected and parsed in the first place.

So far, little research effort has been directed toward this problem. The scarce evidence that exists comes from two very different theoretical approaches. One is associative learning, and the other is perception of causality. Using an instrumental learning paradigm, Shanks, Pearson, and Dickinson (1989) instructed participants to monitor whether pressing a key caused a triangle to light up on a computer screen. The apparatus was programmed to illuminate the triangle 75% of the time the key was pressed and never when the key was not pressed. However, participants were also told that sometimes the triangle might "light up on its own." This actually never happened in any of the experimental conditions but only in a set of yoked control conditions during which the apparatus played back an outcome pattern produced in the previous experimental condition. In other words, in these control conditions, participants' key presses were without any consequences whatsoever. Participants could distinguish reliably between experimental and control conditions (i.e., they noticed whether their key presses were causally effective). However, when Shanks et al. inserted a delay between pressing the key and the triangle's illumination, the distinction became considerably harder. In fact, when the delay was longer than 2 seconds, participants could no longer distinguish between causal and noncausal conditions, even though their key presses were still effective 75% of the time. Shanks et al. interpreted this finding as supporting an associative account of causal judgment.

Perceptual causality (see beginning of chapter) refers to the instant impression of causality that arises from certain stimulus displays. The most prominent phenomenon is the launching effect. An object A moves toward a stationary object B until it collides with B. Immediately after the collision, B moves along the same trajectory as A, while A becomes stationary. Nearly all perceivers report that such displays look as if A "launched" B or "made B move" (Michotte, 1946/1963; for a recent overview, see Scholl & Tremoulet, 2000). However, if a temporal gap of more than 150 ms is inserted between the collision of A and B and the onset of B's motion, the impression of causality disappears and observers report two distinct, unrelated motions.

From a computational perspective, it is easy to see why delays would produce decrements in causal reasoning performance. Contiguous event pairings are less demanding on attention and memory. They are also much easier to parse. When there is a temporal delay and there are no constraints on how the potential causes and effects are bundled, as in Shanks et al. (1989), the basic question on which contingency depends no longer has a clear answer: Should this particular instance of *e* be classified as occurring in the presence of *c* or in its absence? Each possible value of temporal lag results in a different value of contingency. The problem is analogous to that of the possible levels of abstractions of the candidate causes and the effects at which to evaluate contingency (and may have an analogous solution). Moreover, for a given *e*, when alternative intervening events occur, the number of hypotheses to be considered multiply. The result is a harder, more complex inferential problem – one with a larger search space. One might think that keeping track of outcome rates and changes in these rates conditional on the presence and absence of other events would solve the problem (Gallistel & Gibbon, 2000). Measuring outcome rates, however, would not help in Shanks et al.'s (1989) situation. Unless there are additional constraints (e.g., discrete entities in which *c* may or may not occur at any moment, but once it occurs for an entity, *c* can be considered "present" for that entity, even when it is no longer occurring), the parsing problem remains, as does the proliferation of candidate causes that precede an outcome.

Until now, we have focused on situations in which there is no prior causal knowledge. We digress here to discuss a case in which there is such knowledge. When the search space is large, constraints provided by prior knowledge of types of causal relations become increasingly important. Assessing maximal covariation among the set of hypotheses may be impractical given the large search space, or at least inefficient given the existence of prior knowledge. When there is prior knowledge, why not use it? Some evidence suggests, however, that children are unable to integrate prior temporal knowledge with frequency observations. Schlottmann (1999) showed that 5- to 7-year-old children, although able to learn about and understand delayed causal mechanisms perfectly, when presented with a choice between a delayed and immediate cause, always preferred the immediate, contiguous cue, even when they explicitly *knew* that the causal relation in question involved a delay. Schlottmann interpreted her findings to indicate that temporal contiguity is a powerful cue to causality. Because young children fail to integrate two kinds of evidence (knowledge of a delayed mechanism and contingency evaluated at the hypothesized delay), they discard the knowledge cue and focus exclusively on temporal contiguity.

Adult reasoners, in contrast, can most likely integrate the two kinds of evidence. If the reasoner anticipates that a causal relation might involve a delay, its discovery and assessment should be considerably easier. According to Einhorn and Hogarth's (1986) *knowledge mediation hypothesis*, people make use of their prior causal knowledge about the expected length of the delay to reduce the complexity of the inference problem. They focus on the expected delay for a type of causal relation and evaluate observations with respect to it. In Bayesian terms, they evaluate likelihoods, the probability of the observations resulting from a hypothesis. Both Shanks et al.'s (1989) and Michotte's (1946/1963) findings are consistent with Einhorn and Hogarth's (1986) hypothesis. However, these findings cannot be cited as unequivocally demonstrating that adults use prior causal knowledge as a basis for event parsing because the inductive problem gets increasingly difficult as the delay increases, and an account based on problem difficulty alone would predict the same qualitative pattern of results.

Hagmayer and Waldmann (2002) showed that people use prior knowledge of temporal intervals in causal relations to classify evidence about the presence and absence of *c* and *e* in continuous time accordingly. Participants in their Experiment 1 were presented with longitudinal information concerning the occurrence of mosquito plagues over a 20-year period in two adjacent communities. They were told that one community relied on insecticides, whereas the other employed biological means (planting a flower that mosquito larvae-eating beetles need to breed). Although the instructions never mentioned the time frame of the causal mechanisms in question explicitly, Hagmayer and Waldmann assumed the insecticide instructions would create expectations of immediate causal agency, whereas mentioning the biological mechanism would create expectation of a delay. Data were presented in tabular form showing for each of the 20 years whether the intervention had taken place (insecticide delivered, plants planted) and whether there was a plague in that year. The data were constructed to yield a moderately negative contingency between intervention and plague when considered within the same year but a positive contingency when considered over a 1-year delay. Participants' evaluation of the same covariational data varied as a function of the instructions in line with a knowledge-mediation account. These results illustrate that people in principle can and do use temporal knowledge to structure evidence into meaningful units.

Buehner and May (2002, 2003, 2004) further showed that adults are able to reduce the otherwise detrimental influence of delay on causal relations elapsing in real time also by making use of expectations about the time frame of the causal relation in question. Buehner and May instructed participants at the outset of the experiment about potential delays. They did this in a number of ways and found that both explicit and implicit instructions about potential delays improved the assessment of delayed causal relationships. The use of prior temporal knowledge raises the question of how that knowledge might have been acquired. Causal discovery without prior temporal knowledge may be difficult (e.g., longitudinal studies are expensive, even though they have more constraints for limiting the search space than in Shanks et al.'s situation), but it is possible given computational resources.

Summary and Future Directions

Our chapter has taken a computational perspective – in particular, one of constructing an artificial intelligence system capable of causal learning given the types of noncausal observations available to the system. We have reviewed arguments and empirical results showing that an approach that interprets observable events in terms of a hypothetical causal framework explains why covariation need not imply causation and how one can go beyond predicting future observations to predicting the consequences of interventions. An additional appeal of this approach is that it allows one to address multiple research questions within a coherent framework. We compared this framework with an associative framework in our review of previous theoretical and empirical research, which focused on the estimation of causal strength. There are many other interesting causal questions that remain to be addressed under this framework. Some of these are

- How do people evaluate their confidence in whether a causal relation exists? Tenenbaum and Griffiths (2001) proposed a model of this process and began to evaluate it. The assessment of confidence, unlike causal strength, can give rise to the observed gradual acquisition curves.
- How do people evaluate how much an outcome that is known to have occurred is attributable to a candidate cause (see Ellsworth, Chap. 28; Spellman, 2000)? This issue is important in legal decision making. Can a causal power approach overcome the difficulty in cases involving overdetermination?
- What determines the formation of the categories? Does it matter whether the variables are linked by a causal relation? What demarcates an event given that events occur in continuous time? Does a new category form in parallel as a new causal relation is inferred?
- What determines the level of abstraction at which a causal relation is inferred? What determines the choice of the temporal interval between a cause and an effect for probabilistic causal relations?
- Do people make use of prior causal knowledge in a Bayesian way (Tenenbaum & Griffiths, 2002)? Are various kinds of prior causal knowledge (e.g., temporal, mechanistic) integrated with current information in the same way? What role, if any, does coherence play? All models of causal learning in principle allow the use of prior causal knowledge, regardless of whether they are Bayesian. If a comparison among these models involves a situation in which the reasoner has prior knowledge, then the default assumption would be to equate the input to the models, for example, by supplying the data on which prior causal knowledge is based in the input supplied to the non-Bayesian models. They would not be alternative models with respect to the last two questions, for example. It seems to us that including the use of prior knowledge would not make a difference at Marr's computational level with respect to the issue of what is computed in the process but would concern issues of

representation and algorithm. In Bayesian models, there is explicit representation of the prior probability of a causal hypothesis.

- Are people able to make use of patterns of conditional independence as Bayesian network models do (Gopnik et al., 2004) to infer entire causal networks, rather than infer individual causal relations link by link as assumed by most current associative and causal accounts?

Acknowledgments

Preparation of this chapter was supported by grant MH64810 from the National Institute of Mental Health to Cheng. We also thank Steve Sloman for detailed and helpful comments on an earlier version of this chapter.

Note

1. Ulrike Hahn provided this interpretation.

References

Ahn, W.-K., Kalish, C. W., Medin, D. L., & Gelman, S. A. (1995). The role of covariation vs. mechanism information in causal attribution. *Cognition*, 54, 299–352.

Allan, L. G., & Jenkins, H. M. (1980). The judgment of contingency and the nature of response alternatives. *Canadian Journal of Psychology*, 34(1), 1–11.

Anderson, J. R. (1990). *The adaptive character of thought*. Hillsdale, NJ: Erlbaum.

Anderson, J. R., & Sheu, C. F. (1995). Causal inferences as perceptual judgments. *Memory and Cognition*, 23(4), 510–524.

Berry, C. J. (2003). *Conformity to the power PC theory of causal induction: The influence of a counterfactual probe.* London, UK: University College London.

Buehner, M. J., & Cheng, P. W. (1997). Causal induction: The power PC theory versus the Rescorla–Wagner model. In M. G. Shafto & P. Langley (Eds.), *Proceedings of the nineteenth annual conference of the Cognitive Science Society* (pp. 55–60). Hillsdale, NJ: Erlbaum.

Buehner, M. J., Cheng, P. W., & Clifford, D. (2003). From covariation to causation: A test of the assumption of causal power. *Journal of Experimental Psychology: Learning, Memory, and Cognition*, 29(6), 1119–1140.

Buehner, M. J., & May, J. (2002). Knowledge mediates the timeframe of covariation assessment in human causal induction. *Thinking and Reasoning*, 8(4), 269–295.

Buehner, M. J., & May, J. (2003). Rethinking temporal contiguity and the judgment of causality: Effects of prior knowledge, experience, and reinforcement procedure. *Quarterly Journal of Experimental Psychology Section A – Human Experimental Psychology*, 56*A*(5), 865–890.

Buehner, M. J., & May, J. (2004). Abolishing the effect of reinforcement delay on human causal learning. *Quarterly Journal of Experimental Psychology Section B – Comparative and Physiological Psychology*, 57*B*(2), 179–191.

Bullock, M., Gelman, R., & Baillargeon, R. (1982). The development of causal reasoning. In W. J. Friedman (Ed.), *The developmental psychology of time* (pp. 209–254). New York: Academic Press.

Chapman, G. B., & Robbins, S. J. (1990). Cue interaction in human contingency judgment. *Memory and Cognition*, 18(5), 537–545.

Cheng, P. W. (1993). Separating causal laws from casual facts: Pressing the limits of statistical relevance. In D. L. Medin (Ed.), *The psychology of learning and motivation. Advances in research and theory* (Vol. 30, pp. 215–264). San Diego, CA: Academic Press.

Cheng, P. W. (1997). From covariation to causation: A causal power theory. *Psychological Review*, 104(2), 367–405.

Cheng, P. W. (2000). Causality in the mind: Estimating contextual and conjunctive causal power. In F. Keil & R. Wilson (Eds.), *Cognition and explanation* (pp. 227–253). Cambridge, MA: MIT Press.

Cheng, P. W., & Novick, L. R. (1991). Causes versus enabling conditions. *Cognition*, 40, 83–120.

Cheng, P. W., & Novick, L. R. (1992). Covariation in natural causal induction. *Psychological Review*, 99(2), 365–382.

Danks, D. (2003). Equilibria of the Rescorla–Wagner model. *Journal of Mathematical Psychology*, 47(2), 109–121.

De Houwer, J. (2002). Forward blocking depends on retrospective inferences about the presence of the blocked cue during the elemental phase. *Memory and Cognition*, 30(1), 24–33.

De Houwer, J., & Beckers, T. (2002). A review of recent developments in research and theories on human contingency learning. *Quarterly Journal of Experimental Psychology: Comparative and Physiological Psychology*, 55*B*(4), 289–310.

Dennis, M. J., & Ahn, W.-K. (2001). Primacy in causal strength judgments: The effect of initial evidence for generative versus inhibitory relationships. *Memory and Cognition*, 29(1), 152–164.

Dickinson, A. (2001). Causal learning: An associative analysis. *Quarterly Journal of Experimental Psychology Section B – Comparative and Physiological Psychology*, 54(1), 3–25.

Dickinson, A., & Burke, J. (1996). Within-compound associations mediate the retrospective revaluation of causality judgements. *Quarterly Journal of Experimental Psychology: Comparative and Physiological Psychology*, 49*B*(1), 60–80.

Einhorn, H. J., & Hogarth, R. M. (1986). Judging probable cause. *Psychological Bulletin*, 99(1), 3–19.

Gallistel, C. R. (1990). *The organization of learning*. Cambridge, MA: MIT Press.

Gallistel, C. R., & Gibbon, J. (2000). Time, rate, and conditioning. *Psychological Review*, 107(2), 289–344.

Goldvarg, Y., & Johnson-Laird, P. N. (2001). Naive causality: A mental model theory of causal meaning and reasoning. *Cognitive Science*, 25, 565–610.

Gopnik, A., Glymour, C., Sobel, D. M., Schulz, L. E., Kushnir, T., & Danks, D. (2004). A theory of causal learning in children: Causal maps and Bayes nets. *Psychological Review*, *111*(1), 3–32.

Hagmayer, Y., & Waldmann, M. R. (2002). How temporal assumptions influence causal judgments. *Memory & Cognition*, 30(7), 1128–1137.

Holland, J. H., Holyoak, K. J., Nisbett, R. N., & Thagard, P. (1986). *Induction: Processes of inference, learning, and discovery*. Cambridge, MA: MIT Press.

Holyoak, K. J., & Hummel, J. E. (2000). The proper treatment of symbols in a connectionist architecture. In E. Dietrich & A. Markman (Eds.), *Cognitive dynamics: Conceptual change in humans and machines* (pp. 229–263). Mahwah, NJ: Erlbaum.

Hume, D. (1739/1888). A treatise of human nature. In L. A. Selby-Bigge (Ed.), *Hume's treatise of human nature*. Oxford, UK: Clarendon Press.

Jenkins, H., & Ward, W. (1965). Judgment of contingencies between responses and outcomes. *Psychological Monographs*, 7, 1–17.

Kamin, L. J. (1969). Predictability, surprise, attention and conditioning. In B. A. Campbell & R. M. Church (Eds.), *Punishment and aversive behavior*. New York: Appleton-Century-Crofts.

Kant, I. (1781/1965). *Critique of pure reason*. London: Macmillan.

Katz, L. (1989). *Bad acts and guilty minds*. Chicago: The University of Chicago Press.

Kelley, H. H. (1973). The processes of causal attribution. *American Psychologist*, 28(2), 107–128.

Lagnado, D., & Sloman, S. (2004). The advantage of timely intervention. *Journal of Experimental Psychology: Learning, Memory and Cognition*, 30(4), 856–876.

Larkin, M. J. W., Aitken, M. R. F., & Dickinson, A. (1998). Retrospective revaluation of causal judgments under positive and negative contingencies. *Journal of Experimental Psychology: Learning, Memory, and Cognition*, 24(6), 1331–1352.

Lewis, C. I. (1929). *Mind and the world order*. New York: Scribner.

Lien, Y. W., & Cheng, P. W. (2000). Distinguishing genuine from spurious causes: A coherence hypothesis. *Cognitive Psychology*, 40(2), 87–137.

Lober, K., & Shanks, D. R. (2000). Is causal induction based on causal power? Critique of Cheng (1997). *Psychological Review*, 107(1), 195–212.

Lovibond, P. F., Been, S. L., Mitchell, C. J., Bouton, M. E., & Frohardt, R. (2003). Forward and backward blocking of causal judgment is enhanced by additivity of effect magnitude. *Memory and Cognition*, 31 (1), 133–142.

Macho, S., & Burkart, J. (2002). Recursive retrospective revaluation of causal judgments. *Journal of Experimental Psychology: Learning, Memory, and Cognition*, 28(6), 1171–1186.

Mackie, J. L. (1974). *The cement of the universe: A study on causation*. Oxford, UK: Clarendon Press.

Mandel, D. R., & Lehman, D. R. (1998). Integration of contingency information in judgments of cause, covariation, and probability. *Journal of Experimental Psychology: General*, 127(3), 269–285.

Matute, H., Arcediano, F., & Miller, R. R. (1996). Test question modulates cue competition between causes and between effects. *Journal of Experimental Psychology: Learning, Memory, and Cognition*, 22(1), 182–196.

Michotte, A. E. (1946/1963). *The perception of causality* (T. R. Miles, Trans.). London, UK: Methuen & Co.

Miller, R. R., & Barnet, R. C. (1993). The role of time in elementary associations. *Current Directions in Psychological Science*, 2(4), 106–111.

Miller, R. R., Barnet, R. C., & Grahame, N. J. (1995). Assessment of the Rescorla–Wagner model. *Psychological Bulletin*, 117, 363–386.

Miller, R. R., & Matute, H. (1996). Animal analogues of causal judgment. In D. R. Shanks, K. J. Holyoak, & D. L. Medin (Eds.), *The psychology of learning and motivation – Causal learning*, Vol. 34: (pp. 133–166). San Diego, CA: Academic Press.

Novick, L. R., & Cheng, P. W. (2004). Assessing interactive causal influence. *Psychological Review*, 111(2), 455–485.

Pearce, J. M. (1987). A model for stimulus generalization in Pavlovian conditioning. *Psychological Review*, 94(1), 61–73.

Pearl, J. (1988). *Probabilistic reasoning in intelligent systems*. San Mateo, CA: Morgan Kaufmann.

Pearl, J. (2000). *Causality: Models, reasoning, and inference*. Cambridge, UK: Cambridge University Press.

Pearson, K. (1892/1957). *The Grammar of Science*. New York: Meridian Books.

Perales, J. C., & Shanks, D. R. (2003). Normative and descriptive accounts of the influence of power and contingency on causal judgments. *Quarterly Journal of Experimental Psychology Section A – Human Experimental Psychology*, 56*A*(6), 977–1007.

Reichenbach, H. (1956). *The direction of time*. Berkeley & Los Angeles: University of California Press.

Rescorla, R. A. (1968). Probability of shock in the presence and absence of CS in fear conditioning. *Journal of Comparative and Physiological Psychology*, 66, 1–5.

Rescorla, R. A. (1988). Pavlovian conditioning: It's not what you think it is. *American Psychologist*.

Rescorla, R. A., & Wagner, A. R. (1972). A theory of Pavlovian conditioning: Variations in the effectiveness of reinforcement and nonreinforcement. In A. H. Black & W. F. Prokasy (Eds.), *Classical conditioning II: Current theory and research* (pp. 64–99). New York: Appleton-Century-Crofts.

Rosch, E. (1978). Principles of categorization. In E. Rosch & B. Lloyd (Eds.), *Cognition and categorization* (pp. 27–48). Hillsdale, NJ: Erlbaum.

Savastano, H. I., & Miller, R. R. (1998). Time as content in Pavlovian conditioning. *Behavioural Processes*, 44(2), 147–162.

Schlottmann, A. (1999). Seeing it happen and knowing how it works: How children understand the relation between perceptual causality and underlying mechanism. *Developmental Psychology*, 35(5), 303–317.

Scholl, B. J., & Nakayama, K. (2002). Causal capture: Contextual effects on the perception of collision events. *Psychological Science*, 13(6), 493–498.

Scholl, B. J., & Tremoulet, P. D. (2000). Perceptual causality and animacy. *Trends in Cognitive Sciences*, 4(8), 299–309.

Schustack, M. W., & Sternberg, R. J. (1981). Evaluation of evidence in causal inference. *Journal of Experimental Psychology: General*, 110, 101–120.

Shanks, D. R. (1985a). Continuous monitoring of human contingency judgment across trials. *Memory and Cognition*, 13(2), 158–167.

Shanks, D. R. (1985b). Forward and backward blocking in human contingency judgement. *Quarterly Journal of Experimental Psychology: Comparative and Physiological Psychology*, 37*B*(1), 1–21.

Shanks, D. R. (1987). Acquisition functions in contingency judgment. *Learning and Motivation*, 18(2), 147–166.

Shanks, D. R., & Dickinson, A. (1987). Associative accounts of causality judgment. In G. H. Bower (Ed.), *The Psychology of learning and motivation – Advances in research and theory* (Vol. 21, pp. 229–261). San Diego, CA: Academic Press.

Shanks, D. R., Holyoak, K. J., & Media, D. L. (Eds.) (1996). *The Psychology of Learning and Motivation – Causal learning* (Vol. 34) San Diego, CA: Academic Press.

Shanks, D. R., & Lopez, F. J. (1996). Causal order does not affect cue selection in human associative learning. *Memory and Cognition*, 24(4), 511–522.

Shanks, D. R., Pearson, S. M., & Dickinson, A. (1989). Temporal contiguity and the judgment of causality by human subjects. *Quarterly Journal of Experimental Psychology Section B – Comparative and Physiological Psychology*, 41(2), 139–159.

Shultz, T. R. (1982). Rules of causal attribution. *Monographs of the Society for Research in Child Development*, 47(1), 1–51.

Spellman, B., & Kincannon, A. (2001). The relation between counterfactual ("But for") and causal reasoning: Experimental findings and implications for jurors' decisions. *Law and contemporary problems*, 64, 241–264.

Spirtes, P., Glymour, C., & Scheines, R. (1993/2000). *Causation, prediction and search* (2nd ed.). Boston, MA: MIT Press.

Steyvers, M., Tenenbaum, J. B., Wagenmakers, E-J., & Blum, B. (2003). Inferring causal networks from observations and interventions. *Cognitive Science*, 27, 453–489.

Tenenbaum, J. B., & Griffiths, T. L. (2001). Structure learning in human causal induction. In T. K. Leen, T. G. Dietterich, & V. Tresp (Eds.), *Advances in neural processing systems* (Vol. 13, pp. 59–65). Cambridge, MA: MIT Press.

Thagard, P. (1989). Explanatory coherence. *Behavioral and Brain Sciences*, 12, 435–467.

Thagard, P. (2000). Explaining disease: Correlations, causes, and mechanisms. In F. Keil & R. Wilson (Eds.), *Cognition and explanation* (pp. 227–253). Cambridge, MA: MIT Press.

Vallacher, R. R., & Wegner, D. M. (1987). What do people think they're doing? Action identification and human behavior. *Psychological Review*, 94(1), 3–15.

Van Hamme, L. J., & Wasserman, E. A. (1994). Cue competition in causality judgments: The role of nonpresentation of compound stimulus elements. *Learning and Motivation*, 25(2), 127–151.

Waldmann, M. R. (2000). Competition among causes but not effects in predictive and diagnostic learning. *Journal of Experimental Psychology: Learning, Memory, and Cognition*, 26(1), 53–76.

Waldmann, M. R. (2001). Predictive versus diagnostic causal learning: Evidence from an overshadowing paradigm. *Psychonomic Bulletin and Review*, 8, 600–608.

Waldmann, M. R., & Holyoak, K. J. (1992). Predictive and diagnostic learning within causal models: Asymmetries in cue competition. *Journal of Experimental Psychology: General*, 121(2), 222–236.

Waldmann, M. R., & Holyoak, K. J. (1997). Determining whether causal order affects cue selection in human contingency learning: Comments on Shanks and Lopez (1996). *Memory and Cognition*, 25(1), 125–134.

Wasserman, E. A., Elek, S. M., Chatlosh, D. L., & Baker, A. G. (1993). Rating causal relations: Role of probability in judgments of response-outcome contingecy. *Journal of Experimental Psychology:Learning, Memory, and Cognition*, 19, 174–188.

White, P. A. (1995). Use of prior beliefs in the assignment of causal roles: Causal powers versus regularity-based accounts. *Memory and Cognition*, 23(2), 243–254.

White, P. A. (2002). Causal attribution from covariation information: The evidential evaluation model. *European Journal of Social Psychology*, 32(5), 667–684.

Woodward, J. (2003). *Making things happen: A theory of causal explanation*. Oxford, UK: Oxford University Press.

Wright, R. W. (1985). Causation in tort law. *California Law Review*, 73, 1735–1828.

Wu, M., & Cheng, P. W. (1999). Why causation need not follow from statistical association: Boundary conditions for the evaluation of generative and preventive causal powers. *Psychological Science*, 10(2), 92–97.

Zimmerhart & Rescorla (1974): Zimmer-Hart, C. L., & Rescorla, R. A. (1974). Extinction of Pavlovian conditioned inhibition. *Journal of Comparative and Physiological Psychology*, 86, 837–845.

CHAPTER 8

Deductive Reasoning

Jonathan St. B. T. Evans

The study of deductive reasoning has been a major field of cognitive psychology for the past 40 years or so (Evans, 2002; Evans, Newstead, & Byrne, 1993; Manktelow, 1999). The field has its origins in philosophy, within the ancient discipline of logic, and reflects the once influential view known as logicism in which logic is proposed to be the basis for rational human thinking. This view was prevalent in the 1960s when psychological study of deductive reasoning became an established field in psychology, especially reflecting the theories of the great developmental psychologist Jean Piaget (e.g., Inhelder & Piaget, 1958). Logicism was also influentially promoted to psychologists studying reasoning in a famous paper by Henle (1962). At this time, rationality was clearly tied to logicality.

So what exactly is deductive logic? (See Sloman & Lagnado, Chap. 5, for a contrast with induction.) As a model for human reasoning, it has one great strength but several serious weaknesses. The strength is that an argument deemed valid in logic guarantees that if the premises are true, then the conclusion will also be true. Consider a syllogism (an old form of logic devised by Aristotle) with the following form:

All C are B.
No A are B.
Therefore, no A are C.

This is valid argument and will remain so no matter what terms we substitute for A, B, and C. For example,

All frogs are reptiles.
No cats are reptiles.
Therefore, no cats are frogs.

has two true premises and a true conclusion. Unfortunately, the argument is equally valid if we substitute terms as follows:

All frogs are mammals.
No cats are mammals.
Therefore, no cats are frogs.

A valid argument can allow a true conclusion to be drawn from false premises, as previously, which would make it seem a nonsense to most ordinary people (that is, not logicians). This is one weakness of logic in describing everyday reasoning, but there are others. The main limitation is that deductive reasoning does not allow you to learn anything new at all because all logical argument depends on assumptions or suppositions. At best, deduction may enable you to draw out conclusions that were only implicit in your beliefs, but it cannot add to those beliefs. There are also severe limitations in applying logic to real world arguments where premises are uncertain and conclusions may be made provisionally and later withdrawn (Evans & Over, 1996; Oaksford & Chater, 1998).

Although these limitations are nowadays widely recognized, the ability of people to reason logically (or the lack of it) was considered an important enough issue in the past for the use of the deduction paradigm to become well established. The standard paradigm consists of giving people premises and asking them to draw conclusions. There are two key instructions that make this a deductive reasoning task. First, people must be told to assume the premises are true and (usually) are told to base their reasoning only on these premises. Second, they must only draw or endorse a conclusion that *necessarily* follows from the premises.

An example of a large deductive reasoning study was that more recently reported by Evans, Handley, Harper, and Johnson-Laird (1999) using syllogistic reasoning. Syllogisms have four kinds of statement as follows:

Universal	All A are B.
Particular	Some A are B.
Negative universal	No A are B.
Negative particular	Some A are not B.

Because a syllogism comprises two premises and a conclusion, there are 64 possible *moods* in which each of the three statements can take each of the four forms. In addition, there are four *figures* produced by changing the order of reference to the three linked terms, A, B, and C, making 256 logically distinct syllogisms. For example, the following syllogisms have the same mood but different figures:

No C are B. Some A are B. Therefore, some A are not C.	(1)	No C are B. Some B are A. Therefore, some C are not A.	(2)

Although these arguments look very similar, (1) is logically valid and (2) is invalid. Like most invalid arguments, the conclusion to (2) is *possible* given the premises, but not necessary. Hence, it is a fallacy. Here is a case in which a syllogism in form (2) seems persuasive because it has true premises and a true conclusion:

No voters are under 18 years of age.
Some film stars are under 18 years of age.
Therefore, some voters are not film stars.

However, we can easily construct a *counterexample* case. A counterexample proves an argument to be invalid by showing that you could have true premises but a false conclusion, such as

No bees are carnivores.
Some animals are carnivores.
Therefore, some bees are not animals.

Evans et al. (1999) actually gave participants all 64 possible combinations of syllogistic premises and asked them to decide in one group whether each of the four possible conclusions followed necessarily from these premises in line with standard deductive reasoning instructions (in this study, all problem materials were abstract, using capital letters for the terms). A relatively small number of syllogisms have necessary (valid) conclusions or impossible (determinately false) conclusions. Most participants accepted the former and rejected the latter in accord with logic. The interesting cases are the potential fallacies like (2), where the conclusion could be true but does not have to be. In accordance with previous research, Evans et al. found that fallacies were frequently endorsed, although with an interesting qualification to which we return. They ran a second group who were instructed to endorse conclusions that could be true (that is possible) given their premises. The results suggested that ordinary people have a poor understanding of logical necessity. Possibility instructions should have selectively increased acceptance of conclusions normally marked as fallacies. In fact, participants in the possibility groups accepted conclusions of all kinds more frequently, regardless of the logical argument.

Rule- Versus Model-Based Accounts of Reasoning

Logical systems can be described using a syntactic or semantic approach, and psychological theories of deductive reasoning can be similarly divided. In the syntactic approach, reasoning is described using a set of abstract inference rules that can be applied in sequence. The approach is algebraic in that one must start by recovering the logical form of an argument and discarding the particular content or context in which it is framed. In standard propositional logic, for example, several inference rules are applied to conditional statements of the form *if p then q*. These rules can be derived from first principles of the logic and provide a short-cut method of deductive reasoning. Here are some examples:

Modus Ponens (MP)	*Modus Tollens* (MT)
If *p* then *q*	If *p* then *q*
p	not-*q*
Therefore *q*	Therefore, not-*p*

For example, suppose we know that "if the switch is down then the light is on." If I notice that the switch is down, then I can obviously deduce that the light is on (MP). If I see that the light is off, I can also validly infer that the switch is not down (MT). One of the difficulties with testing people's logical ability with such arguments, however, is that they can easily imagine counterexample cases that block such valid inferences (Evans et al., 1993). For example, if the light bulb has burned out, neither MP not MT will deliver a true conclusion. That is why the instruction to assume the truth of the premises should be part of the deduction experiment. It also shows why deductive logic may have limited application in real world reasoning, where most rules – such as conditional statements – do have exceptions.

Some more complex rules involve suppositions. In suppositional reasoning, you add a temporary assumption to those given that is later deleted. An example is conditional proof (CP), which states that if by assuming *p* you can derive *q*, then it follows that *if p then q*, a conclusion that no longer depends on the assumption of *p*. Suppose the following information is given:

> If the car is green, then it has four-wheel drive.
>
> The car has either four-wheel drive or power steering, but not both.

What can you conclude? If you make the supposition that the car is in fact green, then you can draw the conclusion, in two steps, that it does not have power steering. Now you do not know if the car is actually green, but the CP rule allows you to draw the conclusion, "If the car is green then it does not have power steering."

Some philosophers described inference rule systems as "natural logics," reflecting the idea that ordinary people reason by applying such rules. This has been developed by modern psychologists into sophisticated psychological theories of rule-based reasoning, often described as "mental logics." The best-developed systems are those of Rips (1994) and Braine and O'Brien (1998). According to these accounts, people reason by abstracting the underlying logical structure of arguments and then applying inference rules. Direct rules of inferences, such as MP, are applied immediately and effortlessly. Indirect, suppositional rules such as CP are more difficult and error prone. Although MT is included as a standard rule in propositional logic, mental logicians do not include this as a direct rule of inference for the simple reason that people find it difficult. Here is an MT argument:

> If the card has an A on the left, then it has a 3 on the right.
>
> The card does not have a 3 on the right.
>
> Therefore, the card does not have an A on the left.

Table 8.1. Truth Table Analysis

Possibility	*First premise if A then 3*	*Second premise not-3*	*Conclusion not-A*
A, 3	True	False	False
A, not-3	False	True	False
Not-A, 3	True	False	True
Not-A, not-3	True	True	True

Whereas MP is made nearly 100% of the time with such abstract materials, MT rates are quite variable but typically around 70% to 75% (Evans et al., 1993). Mental logicians therefore propose that it depends on an indirect suppositional rule known as reductio ad absurdum (RAA). This rule states that if a supposition leads to a contradiction, then the negation of the supposition is a valid conclusion. With the previous, we make the supposition that the card has an A on the left. Hence, it follows that there is a 3 on the right (MP). However, we are told that there is not a 3 on the right, which gives us a contradiction. Contradictions are not logically possible, and so the supposition from which it followed must be false. Hence, the conclusion given must be true.

A powerful rival account of deductive reasoning is given by the mental model theory (Johnson-Laird, 1983; Johnson-Laird & Byrne, 1991, 2002; see Johnson-Laird, Chap. 9), which is based on the semantic logical approach. The semantic method proves arguments by examining logical possibilities. In this approach, for example, the previous MT argument could be proved by *truth table analysis*. This involves writing down a line in the truth table for each possibility and evaluating both premises and conclusions. An argument is valid if there is not a line in the table where the premises are true and the conclusion false. A truth table analysis for the previous argument is shown in Table 8.1.

It should be noted that the previous analysis, in accord with standard propositional logic, assumes the conditional statement "if p then q" conveys a logical relationship called *material implication*. Severe doubts have been expressed in both the philosophical and psychological literatures that the ordinary conditional of everyday discourse could be a material conditional (Edgington, 1995; Evans, Handley, & Over, 2003; Evans & Over, 2004). However, this distinction does not affect the validity of the arguments discussed here. In the previous example, because there is no case in which true premises can lead to a false conclusion, the argument is valid. Let us contrast this with one of the classical fallacies of conditional reasoning known as affirmation of the consequent (AC). Suppose we are tempted to argue from the previous conditional that if the letter on the right is known to be a 3, then the letter on the left must be an A. See Table 8.2 for the truth table.

The analysis exposes the argument as a fallacy because there is a state of affairs – a card that does not have an A on the left but has a 3 on the right – in which the premises would both be true but the conclusion false.

Just as the mental logic approaches do not simply adopt the inference rules of standard logic to account for human reasoning, so the mental models approach does not endorse truth table analysis either (Johnson-Laird, Byrne, 1991; 2002). Mental models do represent logical possibilities, but the model theory adds psychological proposals about how people construct and reason with such models. First, according to the *principle of truth*, people normally represent only true possibilities. Hence, the theory proposes that the full meaning of a "basic conditional" is the explicit set of true possibilities:

$$\{pq, \neg pq, \neg p\neg q\}$$

where ¬ means "not." Second, owing to working memory limitations, people form

Table 8.2. Truth Table Analysis

Possibility	*First premise if A then 3*	*Second premise 3*	*Conclusion A*
A, 3	True	True	True
A, not-3	False	False	True
Not-A, 3	True	True	False
Not-A, not-3	True	False	False

incomplete initial representations. Thus the conditional *if p then q* is normally represented as

$$[p]q$$
$$\ldots$$

where "..." is a mental footnote to the effect that there may be other possibilities, although they are not explicitly represented. Like the mental logic theory, mental model theory gives an account of why MP is easier than MT. The square brackets around p in the model for the pq possibility indicate that p is exhaustively represented with respect to q (that is, it must be present in all models that include q). Hence, when the premise p is presented, there is no need to flesh out any other possibilities and the conclusion q can be drawn right away (MP). When the MT argument is presented, however, the second premise is not-q, which is not represented in any explicit model. Consequently, some people will say that "nothing follows."

Successful MT reasoners, according to this theory, flesh out the explicit models for the conditional:

$$pq$$
$$\neg pq$$
$$\neg p\neg q$$

The second premise eliminates the first two models, leaving only the possibility $\neg p\neg q$. Hence, the conclusion not-p must follow. With regard to the MT problem presented earlier, this means that people must decide that if there is not a 3 on right of the card, the only possibility consistent with the conditional is that the card does not have an A on the left either.

The model theory was originally developed to account for syllogistic reasoning of the kind considered earlier (Johnson-Laird & Bara, 1984). In this version, it was argued that people formed a model of the premises and formulated a provisional conclusion consistent with this model. It was further proposed that people made an effort at deduction by searching for a counterexample case, that is, a model that agrees with the premises and not with the conclusion. This involves the same semantic principle as truth table analysis: An argument is valid if there is no counterexample to it in which the premises hold and the conclusion does not. Although this accounts for deductive competence, the main finding on syllogistic reasoning is that people in fact endorse many fallacies. By analyzing the nature of the fallacies that people make and those they avoid, Evans et al. (1999) were able to provide strong evidence that people do *not* normally search for counterexample cases during syllogistic reasoning. Some fallacies are made as frequently as valid inferences and some as infrequently as on syllogisms where the conclusion is impossible. This strongly suggests that people consider only a single model of the premises, endorsing the fallacy if this model happens to include the conclusion. This issue has also been addressed in more recent papers by Newstead, Handley, and Buck (1999) and by Bucciarelli & Johnson-Laird (1999).

Both the mental logic and mental models theories described here provide abstract, general-purpose systems that can account for human deductive competence across any domain, but that also allow for error. There has been a protracted – and in my view, inconclusive – debate between advocates of the two theories with many claims and counterclaims that one side or the other had found decisive empirical evidence (for review and discussion, see Evans et al., 1993, Chap. 3; Evans & Over, 1996, 1997). It is important to note that these two theories by no means exhaust the major theoretical attempts to account for the findings in reasoning experiments, although other theorists are less concerned with providing a general account of deductive competence. Other approaches include theories framed in terms of content-specific rules such as pragmatic reasoning schemas (Cheng & Holyoak, 1985; Holyoak & Cheng, 1995) or Darwinian algorithms (Cosmides, 1989; Fiddick, Cosmides, & Tooby, 2000), which were designed to account for content and context effects in reasoning discussed in the next section. The heuristic-analytic theory of Evans

(1984, 1989) was intended to given an account of biases in deductive reasoning tasks to which we now turn.

Biases in Deductive Reasoning

I have already mentioned that people are very prone to making fallacies in syllogistic reasoning and that they do not always succeed in drawing valid inferences such as MT in conditional reasoning. In fact, people make many logical errors generally on deductive reasoning tasks. These errors are not necessarily random but often systematic, leading to description by term *bias*. We should note at this point that a bias is by definition a regular deviation from the logic norm and defer for the time being the question of whether biases should be taken to indicate irrationality.

One of the earliest known biases in conditional reasoning was that of "negative conclusion bias" (Evans, 1982), which affects several conditional inferences, including MT (Schroyens, Schaeken, & d'Ydewalle, 2001). I gave an example of an MT inference earlier, with an affirmative conditional statement, and said that people solve this about 75% of the time. Consider a subtly changed version of the earlier problem:

> If the card does not have an A on the left, then it has a 3 on the right.
>
> The card does not have a 3 on the right.
>
> Therefore, the card has an A on the left.

The difference is that a negative has been introduced into the first part of the conditional and the conclusion is now affirmative. This argument is still MT and valid, but now only around 40% to 50% of the time do people succeed in making it – a very large and reliable difference across many studies. The most likely account of this bias is a double negation effect. Reasoning by RAA on the previous problem will, following discovery of the contradiction, lead one to conclude that the supposition that the card does not have an A on the left must be false. However, this is a double negative from which one must then work out that this means that A must be on the left. The double negation effect can also be given an interpretation within mental model theory (Evans, Clibbens, & Rood, 1995).

Introducing negatives into conditional statements can also cause an effect known as *matching bias* (Evans, 1998). This is best illustrated in a problem known as the Wason selection task (Wason, 1966). Although not strictly a deductive reasoning task, the selection task involves the logic of conditionals and is considered part of the literature on the deduction. In a typical abstract version of the problem, participants are shown four cards lying on a table and told that each has a capital letter on one side and a single figure number on the other. The visible sides are

B L 2 9

They are told that the following rule applies to these four cards and may be true or false:

> If a card has a B on one side, then it has a 2 on the other side.

The task is to decide which cards need to be turned over in order to check whether the rule is true or false. Wason argued that the correct choice is B and 9 because only a card with a B on one side and a number other than 2 on the other side could disprove the rule. Most subsequent researchers have accepted this normative analysis, although some argue against it on the assumption that people interpret the task as having to do with categories rather than specific cards (Oaksford & Chater, 1994). In any event, only around 10% of university students typically choose the B and 9. The most common choices are B and 2, or just B. Wason originally argued that this provided evidence of a confirmation bias in reasoning (Wason & Johnson-Laird, 1972). That is, participants were trying to discover the confirming combination of B and 2 rather than the disconfirming combination of B and 9.

Wason later abandoned this account, however, in light of the evidence of Evans and Lynch (1973). These authors argued that with an affirmative conditional the verifying cards are also the matching cards in other words, those that match the values specified in the rule. By introducing negative components, it is possible to separate the two accounts. For example, suppose the rule was

> If a card has a B on one side, then it does NOT have a 2 on the other side.

Now the matching choice of B and 2 is also the correct choice because a card with a B on one side and a 2 on the other side could disprove the rule. Nearly everyone gets the task right with this version – a curious case of a negative making things a lot easier. In fact, when the presence of negatives is systematically rotated, the pattern of findings strongly supports matching bias in both the Evans and Lynch (1973) study and a number of replication experiments reported later in the literature (Evans, 1998).

What then is the cause of this matching bias? There is strong evidence that it reflects difficulty in processing implicit negation. Evans, Clibbens, and Rood (1996) presented descriptions of the cards in place of the actual cards. In the materials of the example given previously, their descriptions for an implicit and explicit negation group were as follows:

Implicit negation	*Explicit negation*
The letter on the card is a B.	The letter on the card is a B.
The letter on the card is an L.	The letter on the card is not a B.
The number on the card is a 2.	The number on the card is a 2.
The number on the card is a 9.	The number on the card is not a 9.

The presence of negations was also varied in the conditionals in order to provide the standard method of testing for matching bias. Whereas the implicit negation group showed normal strong matching bias, there was *no matching bias at all* in the explicit negation group. However, this group did not perform more logically. They simply picked more of the mismatching cards that would normally have been suppressed, regardless of whether they were logically appropriate. Of course, in the explicit negation group, the negative cases really still match because they refer to the letter and number in the conditional statement. In spite of this strong evidence, an alternative theory of matching bias has been promoted by Oaksford and Chater (1994) based on expected information gain (negative statements convey less information). Yama (2001) more recently reported experiments trying to separate the two accounts with somewhat ambivalent findings.

One of the most important biases investigated in the deductive reasoning literature is the belief bias effect, which is typically but inaccurately described as a tendency to endorse the validity of arguments when you agree with their conclusions. I consider the belief bias effect in the following section on content and context effects. First, I briefly discuss the implications of reasoning biases for the debate about human rationality. Cohen (1981) was one of the first critics to launch an attack on research in this field, as well as the related "heuristic and biases" program of work on probability judgment (Gilovich, Griffin, & Kahneman, 2002; Kahneman, Slovic, & Tversky, 1982; see Kahneman & Frederick, Chap. 12). Cohen argued that evidence of error and bias in experiments on reasoning and judgment should *not* be taken as evidence of human irrationality. Cohen's arguments fall into three categories that have also been reflected in writings of subsequent authors: the *normative system problem*, the *interpretation problem*, and the *external validity problem* (Evans, 1993).

The first issue is that people can only be judged to be in error relative to some normative system that may well be disputable. For example, philosophers have proposed alternative logics, and the standard propositional logic for deductive reasoning can be seen as mapping poorly to real world reasoning, which allows for uncertainty and the withdrawal of inferences in light of new evidence (Evans & Over, 1996; Oaksford & Chater, 1998). The interpretation problem is that correctness of inference is judged on the assumption that the participant understands the task as the experimenter intended. This is also a pertinent criticism. As I (Evans, 2002, p. 991) previously put it:

> *The interpretation problem is a very serious one indeed for traditional users of the deduction paradigm who wish to assess logical accuracy. To pass muster, participants are required not only to disregard problem content but also any prior beliefs they have relevant to it. They must translate the problem into a logical representation using the interpretation of key terms that accord with a textbook (not supplied) of standard logic... whilst disregarding the meaning of the same terms in everyday discourse.*

The external validity argument is that the demonstration of cognitive biases and illusions in the psychological laboratory does not necessarily tell us anything about the real world. This one I have much less sympathy with. The laws of psychology apply in the laboratory, as well as everywhere else, and many of the biases that have been discovered have been shown to also affect expert groups. For example, base rate neglect in statistical reasoning has been shown many times in medical and other expert groups (Koehler, 1996), and there are numerous real world studies of heuristics and biases (Fischhoff, 2002).

One way of dealing with the normative system problem is to distinguish between normative and personal rationality (Anderson, 1990; Evans & Over, 1996). Logical errors on deductive reasoning tasks violate normative rationality because the instructions require one to assume the premises and draw necessary conclusions. Whether they violate personal rationality is moot, however, because we may have little use for deductive reasoning in everyday life and carry over inappropriate but normally useful procedures instead (Evans & Over, 1996). A different distinction is that between individual and evolutionary rationality (Stanovich, 1999; Stanovich & West, 2000, 2003). Stanovich argues that what serves the interests of the genes does not always serve the interests of the individual. In particular, the tendency to contextualize all problems against background belief and knowledge (see the next section) may prevent us from the kind of abstract reasoning that is needed in a modern technological society, so different from the world in which we evolved.

Content and Context Effects

Once thematic materials are introduced into deductive reasoning experiments, especially when some kind of context – however minimal – is given, participants' responses become heavily influenced by pragmatic factors. This has led paradoxically to claims both that familiar problem content can facilitate logical reasoning and that such familiarity can be cause of bias! The task on which facilitation is usually claimed is the deontic selection task that we examine first.

The Deontic Selection Task

It has been known for many years that "realistic" versions of the Wason selection task can facilitate correct card choices, although it was not immediately realized that most of these versions change the logic of the task from one of indicative reasoning to one of deontic reasoning. An indicative conditional, of the type used in the standard abstract task discussed earlier, makes an assertion about the state of the world that may be true or false. Deontic conditionals concern rules and regulations and are often phrased using the terms "may" or "must," although these may be implicit. A rule such as "if you are driving on the highway then you must keep your speed under 70 mph" cannot be true or false. It may or may not be in force, and it may or may not be obeyed.

A good example of a facilitatory version of the selection task is the drinking age problem (Griggs & Cox, 1982). Participants are told to imagine that they are police officers observing people drinking in a bar and making sure that they comply with the following law:

> If a person is drinking in a bar, then that person must be over 19 years of age

(The actual age given depends on which population group is being presented with the task and normally corresponds to the local law it knows.) They are told that each card represents a drinker and has on one side the beverage being drunk and on the other side the age of the drinker. The visible sides of the four cards show:

Drinking beer	Drinking coke	22 years of age	16 years of age

The standard instruction is to choose those cards that could show that the rule is being violated. The correct choice is the drinking beer and 16 year old, and most people choose this. Compared with the abstract task, it is very easy. However, the task has not simply been made realistic. It is a deontic task and one in which the context makes not only the importance of violation salient but also makes it very easy to identify the violating case. There have been many replications and variations of such tasks (see Evans et al., 1993, and Manktelow, 1999, for reviews). It has been established that real world knowledge of the actual rule is not necessary to achieve facilitation (see, for example, Cheng & Holyoak, 1985). Rules that express permission or obligation relationships in plausible settings usually lead people to the appropriate card choices.

Most of the elements of presentation of the drinking age problem as originally devised by Griggs and Cox need to be in place, however. Removing the deontic orientation of the violation instructions greatly weakens the effect (see Evans et al., 1993), and removing the minimal context about the police officer blocks most of the facilitation (Pollard & Evans, 1987). Hence, it is important to evoke pragmatic processes of some kind that introduce prior knowledge into the reasoning process. These factors can override the actual syntax of the conditional rule. Several authors discovered independently that the perspective given to the participant in the scenario can change card choices (Gigerenzer & Hug, 1992; Manktelow & Over, 1991; Politzer & Nguyen-Xuan, 1992). For example, imagine that a big department store, struggling for business, announces the following rule:

> If a customer spends more than $100, then he or she may take a free gift.

The four cards represent customers showing the amount spent on one side and whether they received a gift on the other: "spent $120," "spent $75," "received gift," "did not take gift." If participants are given the perspective of a store detective looking for cheating customers, they turn over cards 2 and 3 because a cheater would be taking the gift without spending $100. If they are given the perspective of a customer checking that the store is keeping its promise, however, they turn cards 1 and 4 because a cheating store would not provide the gift to customers who spent the required amount.

There are several theoretical accounts of the deontic selection task in the literature. One of the earliest was the pragmatic reasoning schema theory of Cheng and Holyoak (1985). These authors proposed that people retrieve and apply a *permission schema* comprising a set of production rules. For example, on the drinking age problem, you need to fulfil the precondition of being older than 19 years of age in order to have permission to drink beer in a bar. Once these elements are recognized and encoded as "precondition" and "action," the abstract rules of the schema can be applied, leading to appropriate card choices. This theory does not suppose that some general process of logical reasoning is being facilitated. The authors later added an obligation schema to explain the perspective shift effect discussed previously (Holyoak & Cheng, 1995). The rules of the obligation schema change the pattern of card choices, and the perspective determines which schema is retrieved and applied.

A well-known but somewhat controversial theory is that choices on the deontic selection task are determined by Darwinian algorithms for social contracts, leading to cheater detection, or else by an innate hazard avoidance module (Cosmides, 1989; Fiddick et al., 2000). The idea is that such modules would have been useful in the evolving environment, although that does not in itself constitute evidence for them (Fodor,

2000). Although influential in philosophy and environmental biology, this work has been subject to a number of criticisms in the psychological literature (Cheng & Holyoak, 1989; Evans & Over, 1996; Sperber, Cara, & Girotto, 1995; Sperber & Girotto, 2002). One criticism is that the responses that are predicted are those that would be adaptive in contemporary society and so could be accounted for by social learning in the lifetime of the individual; another is that the effects to which the theory is applied can be accounted for by much more general cognitive processes. These include theories that treat the selection task as a decision task in which people make choices in accord with expected utility (Evans & Over, 1996; Manktelow & Over, 1991; Oaksford & Chater, 1994), as well as a theory applying principles of pragmatic relevance (Sperber et al., 1995).

Regardless of which – if any – of these accounts may be correct, it is clear that pragmatic process heavily influences the deontic selection task. I have more to say about this in a later section of the chapter when discussing "dual process" theory.

Biasing Effects of Content and Context

In contrast with the claims of facilitation effects on the Wason selection task, psychologists have produced evidence that introducing real world knowledge may bias responses to deductive reasoning tasks. It is known, for example, that certain logically valid inferences that people normally draw can be suppressed when people introduce background knowledge (see Evans et al., 1993, pp. 55–61). Suppose you give people the following problem:

> If she meets her friend, she will go to a play.
> She meets her friend.
> What follows?

Nearly everyone will say, that she will go to the play. This is a very simple and, of course, valid argument known in logic as MP. Many participants will also make the MT inference if the second premise is changed to "she does not go to the play," inferring that "she does not meet her friend." These inferences are easily defeated by additional information, however, a process known technically as defeasible inference (Elio & Pelletier, 1997; Oaksford & Chater, 1991). Suppose we add an extra statement:

> If she meets her friend, she will to go a play.
> If she has enough money, she will go to a play.
> She meets her friend.
> What follows?

In one study (Byrne, 1989), 96% of participants gave the conclusion "she goes to the play" for the first MP problem, but only 38% for the second problem. In standard logic, an argument that follows from some premises must still follow if you add new information. What is happening psychologically in the second case is that the extra conditional statement introduces doubt about the truth of the first. People start to think that, even though she wants to go to the play with her friend, she might not be able to afford it, and the lack of money will prevent her. The same manipulation inhibits the MT inference.

This work illustrates the difficulty of using the term "bias" in deductive reasoning research. Because a valid inference has been suppressed, the effect is technically a bias. However, the reasoning of the participants in this experiment seems perfectly reasonable and indeed more adaptive to everyday needs than a strictly logical answer would have been. A related finding is that, even though people may be told to assume the premises of arguments are true, they are reluctant to draw conclusions if they personally do not believe the premises. In real life, of course, it makes perfect sense to base your reasoning only on information that you believe to be true.

In logic, there is a distinction drawn between a valid inference and a sound inference. A valid inference may lead to a false conclusion, if at least one premise is false, as in the following syllogism:

All students are lazy.
No lazy people pass examinations.
Therefore, no students pass examinations.

The falsity of the previous conclusion is more immediately evident than that of either of the premises. However, the argument is valid, and so at least one premise must be false. A *sound* argument is a valid argument based on true premises and has the merit of guaranteeing a true conclusion. Because the standard deductive reasoning task includes instructions to assume the premises, as well as to draw necessary conclusions, psychologists generally assume they have requested their participants to make validity judgments. However, there is evidence that when familiar problem content is used, people respond as though they had been asked to judge soundness instead (Thompson, 2001). This might well account for the suppression of MP. The inference is so obvious that it can hardly reflect a failure in reasoning.

People are also known to be influenced by the believability of the conclusion of the argument presented, reliably (and usually massively) preferring to endorse the validity of arguments with believable rather than unbelievable conclusions, the so-called "belief bias" effect. The standard experiment uses syllogisms and independently manipulates the believability of the conclusion and the validity of the argument. People accept both more valid arguments (logic effect) and more believable conclusions (belief effect), and the two factors normally interact (Evans, Barston, & Pollard, 1983). This is because the belief bias effect is much stronger on invalid than valid arguments. The effect is really misnamed, however, because as we saw in our earlier discussion, people tend to endorse many fallacies when engaged in abstract syllogistic reasoning. When belief-neutral content is included in belief bias experiments, the effect of belief is shown to be largely negative: Unbelievable conclusions cause people to withhold fallacies that they would otherwise have made (Evans, Handley, & Harper, 2001). So we might as well call it belief debias!

Could people's preference for sound arguments explain the belief bias effect? Many experiments in the literature have failed to control for the believability of premises. However, this can be done by introducing nonsense linking terms, as in the following syllogism:

All fish are phylones.
All phylones are trout.
Therefore, all fish are trout.

Because no one knows what a phylone is, he or she can hardly be expected to have any prior belief about either premise. However, the conclusion is clearly unbelievable, and the same technique can be made to render believable conclusions. Newstead, Pollard, Evans, and Allen (1992) found substantial belief bias effects with such syllogisms. However, it could still be the case that people resist arguments with false conclusions because such arguments must *by definition* be unsound. As we observed earlier, if the argument is valid and the conclusion false, at least one premise must be false, even if we cannot tell which one. For further discussion of this and related issues, see Evans et al. (2001) and Klauer, Musch, and Naumer (2000).

Dual-Process Theory

The deductive reasoning paradigm has yielded a wealth of psychological data over the past 40 years or so. Understanding the issues involved has been assisted by more recent developments in dual-process theories of reasoning (Evans, 2003; Evans & Over, 1996; Sloman, 1996; Stanovich, 1999), which have gradually evolved from much earlier proposals in the reasoning literature (Evans, 1984; Wason & Evans, 1975) and has been linked with research on implicit learning (see Litman & Reber, Chap. 18; Dienes & Perner, 1999; Reber, 1993) and intuitive judgment (Gilovich & Griffin,

2002; Kahneman & Frederick, 2002; see Kahneman & Frederick, Chap. 12). The idea is that there are two distinct cognitive systems with different evolutionary histories. System 1 (to use Stanovich's terminology) is the ancient system that relies on associative learning through distributed neural networks and may also reflect the operation of innate modules. It is really a bundle of systems that most theorists regarded as implicit, meaning that only the final products of such a process register in consciousness, and they may stimulate actions without any conscious reflection. System 2, in contrast, is evolutionarily recent and arguably unique to humans. This system requires use of central working memory resources and is therefore slow and sequential in nature. System 2 function relates to general measures of cognitive ability such as IQ, whereas system 1 function does not (Reber, 1993; Stanovich, 1999). However, system 2 allows us to engage in abstract reasoning and hypothetical thinking. There is more recent supporting evidence of a neuropsychological nature for this theory. When resolving belief–logic conflicts in the belief bias paradigm, the response that dominates correlates with distinct areas of brain activity (Goel, Buchel, Rith, & Olan, 2000; see Goel, Chap. 20).

Dual-process theory can help us make sense of much of the research on deductive reasoning that we have been discussing. It seems that the default mode of everyday reasoning is pragmatic, reflecting the associative processes of system 1. Deductive reasoning experiments, however, include instructions that require a conscious effort at deduction and often require the suppression of pragmatic processes because we are asked to disregard relevant prior belief and knowledge. Hence, reasoning tasks often require strong system 2 intervention if they are to be solved. In support of this theory, Stanovich (1999) reviewed a large research program in which it was consistently shown that participants with high SAT scores (a measure of general cognitive ability) produced more normative solutions than those with lower scores on a wide range of reasoning, decision, and judgment problems. This clearly implicates system 2.

Consider the Wason selection task, for example. The abstract indicative version, which defeats most people, contains no helpful pragmatic cues and thus requires abstract logical reasoning for its solution. Stanovich and West (1998) accordingly showed that the small numbers who solve it have significantly higher SAT scores. However, they also showed *no* difference in SAT scores between solvers and nonsolvers of the deontic selection task. This makes sense because the pragmatic processes that account for the relative ease of this task are of the kind attributed in the theory to system 1. However, this does call into question whether the deontic selection task really requires a process that we would want to call *reasoning*. The solution appears to be provided automatically, without conscious reflection.

If the theory is right, then system 2 intervention occurs mostly because of the use of explicit instructions requiring an effort at deduction. We know that the instructions used have a major influence on the response people make (Evans, Allen, Newstead, & Pollard, 1994; George, 1995; Stevenson & Over, 1995). The more instructions emphasize logical necessity, the more logical the responding; when instructions are relaxed and participants are asked if a conclusion follows, responses are much more strongly belief based. The ability to resist belief in belief–logic conflict problems when instructed to reason logically is strongly linked to measures of cognitive ability (Stanovich & West, 1997), and the same facility is known to decline sharply in old age (Gilinsky & Judd, 1994; see Salthouse, Chap. 24). This provides strong converging evidence for dual systems of reasoning (see also Sloman, 2002).

Conclusions and Future Directions

Research on deductive reasoning was originally stimulated by the traditional interest in logicism – the belief that logic provided the rational basis for human thinking. This rationale has been considerably undermined over the past 40 years because many psychologists have abandoned logic, first as a descriptive and later as a normative system for human reasoning (Evans, 2002). Research with the deduction paradigm has also shown, as indicated in this chapter, that pragmatic processes have a very large influence once realistic content and context are introduced. Studying such processes using the paradigm necessarily defines them as biases because the task requires one to assume premises and draw necessary conclusions. However, it is far from clear that such biases should be regarded as evidence of irrationality, as discussed earlier.

The deductive reasoning field has seen discussion and debate of a wide range of theoretical ideas, a number of which have been described here. This includes the long-running debate over whether rule-based mental logics or mental model theory provides the better account of basic deductive competence, as well as the development of accounts based on content-specific reasoning, such as pragmatic reasoning schemas, relevance theory, and Darwinian algorithms. It has been a major focus for the development of dual-process theories of cognition, even though these have a much wider application. It has also been one of the major fields (alongside intuitive and statistical judgment) in which cognitive biases have been studied and their implications for human rationality debated at length.

So where does the future of the deduction paradigm lie? I have suggested (Evans, 2002) that we should use a much wider range of methods for studying human reasoning, especially when we are interested in investigating the pragmatic reasoning processes of system 1. In fact, there is no point at all in instructing people to make an effort at deduction unless we are interested in system 2 reasoning or want to set the two systems in conflict. However, this conflict is of both theoretical and practical interest and will undoubtedly continue to be studied using the deduction paradigm. It is important, however, that we understand that this is what we are doing. It is no longer appropriate to equate performance on deductive reasoning tasks with rationality or to assume that logic provides an appropriate normative account of everyday, real world reasoning.

References

Anderson, J. R. (1990). *The adaptive character of thought*. Hillsdale, NJ: Erlbaum.

Braine, M. D. S., & O'Brien, D. P. (Eds). (1998). *Mental logic*. Mahwah, NJ: Erlbaum.

Bucciarelli, M., & Johnson-Laird, P. N. (1999). Strategies in syllogistic reasoning. *Cognitive Science, 23*, 247–303.

Byrne, R. M. J. (1989). Suppressing valid inferences with conditionals. *Cognition, 31*, 61–83.

Cheng, P. W., & Holyoak, K. J. (1985). Pragmatic reasoning schemas. *Cognitive Psychology, 17*, 391–416.

Cheng, P. W., & Holyoak, K. J. (1989). On the natural selection of reasoning theories. *Cognition, 33*, 285–314.

Cohen, L. J. (1981). Can human irrationality be experimentally demonstrated? *Behavioral and Brain Sciences, 4*, 317–370.

Cosmides, L. (1989). The logic of social exchange: Has natural selection shaped how humans reason? *Cognition, 31*, 187–276.

Dienes, Z., & Perner, J. (1999). A theory of implicit and explicit knowledge. *Behavioral and Brain Sciences, 22*, 735–808.

Edgington, D. (1995). On conditionals. *Mind, 104*, 235–329.

Elio, R., & Pelletier, F. J. (1997). Belief change as propositional update. *Cognitive Science, 21*, 419–460.

Evans, J. St. B. T. (1982). *The psychology of deductive reasoning*. London: Routledge.

Evans, J. St. B. T. (1984). Heuristic and analytic processes in reasoning. *British Journal of Psychology, 75*, 451–468.

Evans, J. St. B. T. (1989). *Bias in human reasoning: Causes and consequences*. Hove, UK: Erlbaum.

Evans, J. St. B. T. (1993). Bias and rationality. In K. I. Manktelow & D. E. Over (Eds.), *Rationality: Psychological and philosophical perspectives* (pp. 6–30). London: Routledge.

Evans, J. St. B. T. (1998). Matching bias in conditional reasoning: Do we understand it after 25 years? *Thinking and Reasoning*, 4, 45–82.

Evans, J. St. B. T. (2002). Logic and human reasoning: An assessment of the deduction paradigm. *Psychological Bulletin*, 128, 978–996.

Evans, J. St. B. T. (2003). In two minds: Dual process accounts of reasoning. *Trends in Cognitive Sciences*, 7, 454–459.

Evans, J. St. B. T., Allen, J. L., Newstead, S. E., & Pollard, P. (1994). Debiasing by instruction: The case of belief bias. *European Journal of Cognitive Psychology*, 6, 263–285.

Evans, J. St. B. T., Barston, J. L., & Pollard, P. (1983). On the conflict between logic and belief in syllogistic reasoning. *Memory and Cognition*, 11, 295–306.

Evans, J. St. B. T., Clibbens, J., & Rood, B. (1995). Bias in conditional inference: Implications for mental models and mental logic. *Quarterly Journal of Experimental Psychology*, 48A, 644–670.

Evans, J. St. B. T., Clibbens, J., & Rood, B. (1996). The role of implicit and explicit negation in conditional reasoning bias. *Journal of Memory and Language*, 35, 392–409.

Evans, J. St. B. T., Handley, S. H., & Harper, C. (2001). Necessity, possibility and belief: A study of syllogistic reasoning. *Quarterly Journal of Experimental Psychology*, 54A, 935–958.

Evans, J. St. B. T., Handley, S. J., Harper, C., & Johnson-Laird, P. N. (1999). Reasoning about necessity and possibility: A test of the mental model theory of deduction. *Journal of Experimental Psychology: Learning, Memory and Cognition*, 25, 1495–1513.

Evans, J. St. B. T., Handley, S. H., & Over, D. E. (2003). Conditionals and conditional probability. *Journal of Experimental Psychology: Learning, Memory and Cognition*, 29, 321–355.

Evans, J. St. B. T., & Lynch, J. S. (1973). Matching bias in the selection task. *British Journal of Psychology*, 64, 391–397.

Evans, J. St. B. T., Newstead, S. E., & Byrne, R. M. J. (1993). *Human reasoning: The psychology of deduction*. Hove, UK: Erlbaum.

Evans, J. St. B. T., & Over, D. E. (1996). *Rationality and reasoning*. Hove, UK: Psychology Press.

Evans, J. St. B. T., & Over, D. E. (2004). *If*. Oxford, UK: Oxford University Press.

Fiddick, L., Cosmides, L., & Tooby, J. (2000). No interpretation without representation: The role of domain-specific representations and inferences in the Wason selection task. *Cognition*, 77, 1–79.

Fischhoff, B. (2002). Heuristics and biases in application. In T. Gilovich, D. Griffin, & D. Kahneman (Eds.), *Heuristics and biases: The psychology of intuitive judgement* (pp. 730–748). Cambridge, UK: Cambridge University Press.

Fodor, J. (2000). Why we are so good at catching cheaters? *Cognition*, 75, 29–32.

George, C. (1995). The endorsement of the premises: Assumption-based or belief-based reasoning. *British Journal of Psychology*, 86, 93–111.

Gigerenzer, G., & Hug, K. (1992). Domain-specific reasoning: Social contracts, cheating and perspective change. *Cognition*, 43, 127–171.

Gilinsky, A. S., & Judd, B. B. (1994). Working memory and bias in reasoning across the life-span. *Psychology and Aging*, 9, 356–371.

Gilovich, T., & Griffin, D. (2002). Introduction – Heuristics and biases: Then and now. In T. Gilovich, D. Griffin, & A. Kahneman (Eds.), *Heuristics and biases: The psychology of intuitive judgment* (pp. 1–18). Cambridge, UK: Cambridge University Press.

Gilovich, T., Griffin, D., & Kahneman, D. (2002). *Heuristics and biases: The psychology of intuitive judgement*. Cambridge, UK: Cambridge University Press.

Goel, V., Buchel, C., Rith, C., & Olan, J. (2000). Dissociation of mechanisms underlying syllogistic reasoning. *NeuroImage*, 12, 504–514.

Griggs, R. A., & Cox, J. R. (1982). The elusive thematic materials effect in the Wason selection task. *British Journal of Psychology*, 73, 407–420.

Henle, M. (1962). On the relation between logic and thinking. *Psychological Review*, 69, 366–378.

Holyoak, K., & Cheng, P. (1995). Pragmatic reasoning with a point of view. *Thinking and Reasoning*, 1, 289–314.

Inhelder, B., & Piaget, J. (1958). *The growth of logical thinking*. New York: Basic Books.

Johnson-Laird, P. N. (1983). *Mental models*. Cambridge, UK: Cambridge University Press.

Johnson-Laird, P. N., & Bara, B. G. (1984). Syllogistic inference. *Cognition*, 16, 1–61.

Johnson-Laird, P. N., & Byrne, R. M. J. (1991). *Deduction*. Hove, UK: Erlbaum.

Johnson-Laird, P. N., & Byrne, R. M. J. (2002). Conditionals: A theory of meaning, pragmatics and inference. *Psychological Review*, 109, 646–678.

Kahneman, D., & Frederick, S. (2002). Representativeness revisited: Attribute substitution in intuitive judgement. In T. Gilovich, D. Griffin, & D. Kahneman (Eds.), *Heuristics and biases: The psychology of intuitive judgement* (pp. 49–81). Cambridge, UK: Cambridge University Press.

Kahneman, D., Slovic, P., & Tversky, A. (1982). *Judgment under uncertainty: Heuristics and biases*. Cambridge, UK: Cambridge University Press.

Klauer, K. C., Musch, J., & Naumer, B. (2000). On belief bias in syllogistic reasoning. *Psychological Review*, 107, 852–884.

Koehler, J. J. (1996). The base rate fallacy reconsidered: Descriptive, normative and methodological challenges. *Behavioral and Brain Sciences*, 19, 1–53.

Manktelow, K. I. (1999). *Reasoning and thinking*. Hove, UK: Psychology Press.

Manktelow, K. I., & Over, D. E. (1991). Social roles and utilities in reasoning with deontic conditionals. *Cognition*, 39, 85–105.

Newstead, S. E., Handley, S. H., & Buck, E. (1999). Falsifying mental models: Testing the predictions of theories of syllogistic reasoning. *Journal of Memory and Language*, 27, 344–354.

Newstead, S. E., Pollard, P., Evans, J. St. B. T., & Allen, J. L. (1992). The source of belief bias effects in syllogistic reasoning. *Cognition*, 45, 257–284.

Oaksford, M., & Chater, N. (1991). Against logicist cognitive science. *Mind and Language*, 6, 1–38.

Oaksford, M., & Chater, N. (1994). A rational analysis of the selection task as optimal data selection. *Psychological Review*, 101, 608–631.

Oaksford, M., & Chater, N. (1998). *Rationality in an uncertain world*. Hove, UK: Psychology Press.

Politzer, G., & Nguyen-Xuan, A. (1992). Reasoning about conditional promises and warnings: Darwinian algorithms, mental models, relevance judgements or pragmatic schemas? *Quarterly Journal of Experimental Psychology*, 44, 401–412.

Pollard, P., & Evans, J. St. B. T. (1987). On the relationship between content and context effects in reasoning. *American Journal of Psychology*, 100, 41–60.

Reber, A. S. (1993). *Implicit learning and tacit knowledge*. Oxford, UK: Oxford University Press.

Rips, L. J. (1994). *The psychology of proof*. Cambridge, MA: MIT Press.

Schroyens, W., Schaeken, W., & d'Ydewalle, G. (2001). The processing of negations in conditional reasoning: A meta-analytic study in mental models and/or mental logic theory. *Thinking and Reasoning*, 7, 121–172.

Sloman, S. A. (1996). The empirical case for two systems of reasoning. *Psychological Bulletin*, 119, 3–22.

Sloman, S. A. (2002). Two systems of reasoning. In T. Gilovich, D. Griffin, & D. Kahneman (Eds.), *Heuristics and biases: The psychology of intuitive judgment* (pp. 379–398). Cambridge, UK: Cambridge University Press.

Sperber, D., Cara, F., & Girotto, V. (1995). Relevance theory explains the selection task. *Cognition*, 57, 31–95.

Sperber, D., & Girotto, V. (2002). Use or misuse of the selection task? Rejoinder to Fiddick, Cosmides and Tooby. *Cognition*, 85, 277–290.

Stanovich, K. E. (1999). *Who is rational? Studies of individual differences in reasoning*. Mahwah, NJ: Erlbaum.

Stanovich, K. E., & West, R. F. (1997). Reasoning independently of prior belief and individual differences in actively open-minded thinking. *Journal of Educational Psychology*, 89, 342–357.

Stanovich, K. E., & West, R. F. (1998). Cognitive ability and variation in selection task performance. *Thinking and Reasoning*, 4, 193–230.

Stanovich, K. E., & West, R. F. (2000). Individual differences in reasoning: Implications for the rationality debate. *Behavioral and Brain Sciences*, 23, 645–726.

Stanovich, K. E., & West, R. F. (2003). Evolutionary versus instrumental goals: How evolutionary psychology misconceives human rationality. In D. Over (Ed.), *Evolution and the psychology of thinking* (pp. 171–230). Hove, UK: Psychology Press.

Stevenson, R. J., & Over, D. E. (1995). Deduction from uncertain premises. *The Quarterly*

Journal of Experimental Psychology, *48A*, 613–643.

Thompson, V. A. (2001). Reasoning from false premises: The role of soundness in making logical deductions. *Canadian Journal of Experimental Psychology*, 50, 315–319.

Wason, P. C. (1966). Reasoning. In B. M. Foss (Ed.), *New horizons in psychology I* (pp. 106–137). Harmondsworth: Penguin.

Wason, P. C., & Evans, J. St. B. T. (1975). Dual processes in reasoning? *Cognition*, 3, 141–154.

Wason, P. C., & Johnson-Laird, P. N. (1972). *Psychology of reasoning: Structure and content*. London: Batsford.

Yama, H. (2001). Matching versus optimal data selection in the Wason selection task. *Thinking and Reasoning*, 7, 295–311.

CHAPTER 9

Mental Models and Thought

P. N. Johnson-Laird

How do we think? One answer is that we rely on *mental models*. Perception yields models of the world that lie outside us. An understanding of discourse yields models of the world that the speaker describes to us. Thinking, which enables us to anticipate the world and to choose a course of action, relies on internal manipulations of these mental models. This chapter is about this theory, which it refers to as the *model* theory, and its experimental corroborations. The theory aims to explain all sorts of thinking about propositions, that is, thoughts capable of being true or false. There are other sorts of thinking – the thinking, for instance, of a musician who is improvising. In daily life, unlike the psychological laboratory, no clear demarcation exists between one sort of thinking and another. Here is a protocol of a typical sequence of everyday thoughts:

> *I had the book in the hotel's restaurant, and now I've lost it. So, either I left it in the restaurant, or it fell out of my pocket on the way back to my room, or it's somewhere here in my room. It couldn't have fallen from my pocket – my pockets are deep and I walked slowly back to my room – and so it's here or in the restaurant.*

Embedded in this sequence is a logical deduction of the form:

A or B or C.
Not B.
Therefore, A or C.

The conclusion is *valid:* It must be true given that the premises are true. However, other sorts of thinking occur in the protocol (e.g., the inference that the book could not have fallen out of the protagonist's pocket).

A simple way to categorize thinking about propositions is in terms of its effects on semantic information (Johnson-Laird, 1993). The more possibilities an assertion rules out, the greater the amount of semantic information it conveys (Bar-Hillel & Carnap, 1964). Any step in thought from current premises to a new conclusion therefore falls into one of the following categories:

- The premises and the conclusion eliminate the same possibilities.

- The premises eliminate at least one more possibility over those the conclusion eliminates.
- The conclusion eliminates at least one more possibility over those the premises eliminate.
- The premises and conclusion eliminate disjoint possibilities.
- The premises and conclusion eliminate overlapping possibilities.

The first two categories are deductions (see Evans, Chapter 11). The third category includes all the traditional cases of induction, which in general is definable as any thought yielding such an increase in semantic information (see Sloman & Lagnado, Chap. 3). The fourth category occurs only when the conclusion is inconsistent with the premises. The fifth case occurs when the conclusion is consistent with the premises but refutes at least one premise and adds at least one new proposition. Such thinking goes beyond induction. It is associative or creative (see Sternberg, Chap. 13).

The model theory aims to explain all propositional thinking, and this chapter illustrates its application to the five preceding categories. The chapter begins with the history of the model theory. It then outlines the current theory and its account of deduction. It reviews some of the evidence for this account. It shows how the theory extends to probabilistic reasoning. It then turns to induction, and it describes the unconscious inferences that occur in understanding discourse. It shows how models underlie causal relations and the creation of explanations. Finally, it assesses the future of the model theory.

The History of Mental Models

In the seminal fifth chapter of his book, *The Nature of Explanation*, Kenneth Craik (1943) wrote:

> *If the organism carries a "small-scale model" of external reality and of its own possible actions within its head, it is able to try out various alternatives, conclude which is the best of them, react to future situations before they arise, utilize the knowledge of past events in dealing with the present and the future, and in every way to react in a much fuller, safer, and more competent manner to the emergencies which face it.*

This same process of internal imitation of the external world, Craik wrote, is carried out by mechanical devices such as Kelvin's tidal predictor. Craik died in 1945, before he could develop his ideas. Several earlier thinkers had, in fact, anticipated him (see Johnson-Laird, 2003). Nineteenth-century physicists, including Kelvin, Boltzmann, and Maxwell, stressed the role of models in thinking. In the twentieth century, physicists downplayed these ideas with the advent of quantum theory (but cf. Deutsch, 1997).

One principle of the modern theory is that the parts of a mental model and their structural relations correspond to those which they represent. This idea has many antecedents. It occurs in Maxwell's (1911) views on diagrams, in Wittgenstein's (1922) "picture" theory of meaning, and in Köhler's (1938) hypothesis of an isomorphism between brain fields and the world. However, the nineteenth-century grandfather of the model theory is Charles Sanders Peirce.

Peirce coinvented the main system of logic known as *predicate* calculus, which governs sentences in a formal language containing idealized versions of negation, sentential connectives such as "and" and "or," and quantifiers such as "all" and "some." Peirce devised two diagrammatic systems of reasoning, not to improve reasoning, but to display its underlying mental steps (see Johnson-Laird, 2002). He wrote:

> *Deduction is that mode of reasoning which examines the state of things asserted in the premisses, forms a diagram of that state of things, perceives in the parts of the diagram relations not explicitly mentioned in the premisses, satisfies itself by mental experiments upon the diagram that these relations would always subsist, or at least would do so in a certain proportion of cases, and concludes their necessary, or probable,*

truth (Peirce, 1.66; this standard notation refers to paragraph 66 of Volume 1 of Peirce, 1931–1958).

Diagrams can be *iconic*, in other words, have the same structure as what they represent (Peirce, 4.447). It is the inspection of an iconic diagram that reveals truths other than those of the premises (2.279, 4.530). Hence, Peirce anticipates Maxwell, Wittgenstein, Köhler, and the model theory. Mental models are as iconic as possible (Johnson-Laird, 1983, pp. 125, 136).

A resurgence of mental models in cognitive science began in the 1970s. Theorists proposed that knowledge was represented in mental models, but they were not wed to any particular structure for models. Hayes (1979) used the predicate calculus to describe the naive physics of liquids. Other theorists in artificial intelligence proposed accounts of how to envision models and use them to simulate behavior (de Kleer, 1977). Psychologists similarly examined naive and expert models of various domains, such as mechanics (McCloskey, Caramazza, & Green, 1980) and electricity (Gentner & Gentner, 1983). They argued that vision yields a mental model of the three-dimensional structure of the world (Marr, 1982). They proposed that individuals use these models to simulate behavior (e.g., Hegarty, 1992; Schwartz & Black, 1996). They also studied how models develop (e.g., Vosniadou & Brewer, 1992; Halford, 1993), how they serve as analogies (e.g., Holland, Holyoak, Nisbett, & Thagard, 1986; see Holyoak, Chap. 6), and how they help in the diagnosis of faults (e.g., Rouse & Hunt, 1984). Artifacts, they argued, should be designed so users easily acquire models of them (e.g., Ehrlich, 1996; Moray, 1990, 1999).

Discourse enables humans to experience the world by proxy, and so another early hypothesis was that comprehension yields models of the world (Johnson-Laird, 1970). The models are iconic in these ways: They contain a token for each referent in the discourse, properties corresponding to the properties of the referents, and relations corresponding to the relations among the referents. Similar ideas occurred in psycholinguistics (e.g., Bransford, Barclay, & Franks, 1972), linguistics (Karttunen, 1976), artificial intelligence (Webber, 1978), and formal semantics (Kamp, 1981). Experimental evidence corroborated the hypothesis, showing that individuals rapidly forget surface and underlying syntax (Johnson-Laird & Stevenson, 1970), and even the meaning of individual sentences (Garnham, 1987). They retain only models of who did what to whom. Psycholinguists discovered that models are constructed from the meanings of sentences, general knowledge, and knowledge of human communication (e.g., Garnham, 2001; Garnham & Oakhill, 1996; Gernsbacher, 1990; Glenberg, Meyer, & Lindem, 1987).

Another early discovery was that content affects deductive reasoning (Wason & Johnson-Laird, 1972; see Evans, Chap. 8), which was hard to reconcile with the then dominant view that reasoners depend on *formal* rules of inference (Braine, 1978; Johnson-Laird, 1975; Osherson, 1974–1976). Granted that models come from perception and discourse, they could be used to reason (Johnson-Laird, 1975): An inference is *valid* if its conclusion holds in all the models of the premises because its conclusion must be true granted that its premises are true. The next section spells out this account.

Models and Deduction

Mental models represent entities and persons, events and processes, and the operations of complex systems. However, what is a mental model? The current theory is based on principles that distinguish models from linguistic structures, semantic networks, and other proposed mental representations (Johnson-Laird & Byrne, 1991). The first principle is

> *The principle of* iconicity: *A mental model has a structure that corresponds to the known structure of what it represents.*

Visual images are iconic, but mental models underlie images. Even the rotation of mental images implies that individuals rotate three-dimensional models (Metzler & Shepard, 1982), and irrelevant images impair reasoning (Knauff, Fangmeir, Ruff, & Johnson-Laird, 2003; Knauff & Johnson-Laird, 2002). Moreover, many components of models cannot be visualized.

One advantage of iconicity, as Peirce noted, is that models built from premises can yield new relations. For example, Schaeken, Johnson-Laird, and d'Ydewalle (1996) investigated problems of temporal reasoning concerning such premises as

John eats his breakfast before he listens to the radio.

Given a problem based on several premises with the form:

A before B.

B before C.

D while A.

E while C.

reasoners can build a mental model with the structure:

A	B	C
D		E

where the left-to-right axis is time, and the vertical axis allows different events to be contemporaneous. Granted that each event takes roughly the same amount of time, reasoners can infer a new relation:

D before E.

Formal logic less readily yields the conclusion. One difficulty is that an infinite number of conclusions follow validly from any set of premises, and logic does not tell you *which* conclusions are useful. From the previous premises, for instance, this otiose conclusion follows:

A before B, *and* B before C.

Possibilities are crucial, and the second principle of the theory assigns them a central role:

The principle of possibilities: *Each mental model represents a possibility.*

Table 9.1. The Truth Table for Exclusive Disjunction

A	*B*	*A or else B, but not both*
True	True	False
True	False	True
False	True	True
False	False	False

This principle is illustrated in *sentential* reasoning, which hinges on negation and such sentential connectives as "if" and "or." In logic, these connectives have idealized meanings: They are *truth-functional* in that the truth-values of sentences formed with them depend solely on the truth-values of the clauses that they connect. For example, a disjunction of the form: *A or else B but not both* is true if *A* is true and *B* is false, and if *A* is false and *B* is true, but false in any other case. Logicians capture these conditions in a truth table, as shown in Table 9.1. Each row in the table represents a different possibility (e.g., the first row represents the possibility in which both *A* and *B* are true), and so here the disjunction is false.

Naive reasoners do not use truth tables (Osherson, 1974–1976). *Fully explicit* models of possibilities, however, are a step toward psychological plausibility. The fully explicit models of the exclusive disjunction, *A or else B but not both*, are shown here on separate lines:

A	¬B
¬A	B

where "¬" denotes negation. Table 9.2 presents the fully explicit models for the main sentential connectives. Fully explicit models correspond exactly to the true rows in the truth table for each connective. As the table shows, the conditional *If A then B* is treated in logic as though it can be paraphrased as *If A then B, and if not-A then B or not-B*. The paraphrase does not do justice to the varied meanings of everyday conditionals (Johnson-Laird & Byrne, 2002). In fact, no connectives in natural language are truth

Table 9.2. Fully Explicit Models and Mental Models of Possibilities Compatible with Sentences Containing the Principal Sentential Connectives

Sentences	*Fully Explicit Models*		*Mental Models*	
A and B:	A	B	A	B
Neither A nor B:	¬A	¬B	¬A	¬B
A or else B but not both:	A	¬B	A	
	¬A	B		B
A or B or both:	A	¬B	A	
	¬A	B		B
	A	B	A	B
If A then B:	A	B	A	B
	¬A	B	. . .	
	¬A	¬B		
If, and only if A, then B:	A	B	A	B
	¬A	¬B	. . .	

functional (see the section on implicit induction and the modulation of models).

Fully explicit models yield a more efficient reasoning procedure than truth tables. Each premise has a set of fully explicit models, for example, the premises:

1. A or else B but not both.
2. Not-A.

have the models:

(Premise 1)		(Premise 2)
A	¬B	¬A
¬A	B	

Their conjunction depends on combining each model in one set with each model in the other set according to two main rules:

- A contradiction between a pair of models yields the null model (akin to the empty set).
- Any other conjunction yields a model of each proposition in the two models.

The result is:

Input from (1)		Input from (2)	Output	
A	¬B	¬A	null model	
¬A	B	¬A	¬A	B

or in brief:

¬A   B

Because an inference is valid if its conclusion holds in all the models of the premises, it follows that: *B*. The same rules are used recursively to construct the models of compound premises containing multiple connectives.

Because infinitely many conclusions follow from any premises, computer programs for proving validity generally evaluate conclusions given to them by the user. Human reasoners, however, can draw conclusions for themselves. They normally abide by two constraints (Johnson-Laird & Byrne, 1991). First, they do not throw semantic information away by adding disjunctive alternatives. For instance, given a single premise, *A*, they never spontaneously conclude, *A or B or both*. Second, they draw novel conclusions that are parsimonious. For instance, they never draw a conclusion that merely conjoins the premises, even though such a deduction is valid. Of course, human performance rapidly degrades with complex problems, but the goal of parsimony suggests that intelligent programs should draw conclusions that succinctly express all the information in the premises. The model theory yields an algorithm that draws such conclusions (Johnson-Laird & Byrne, 1991, Chap. 9).

Fully explicit models are simpler than truth tables but place a heavy load on working memory. *Mental* models are still simpler because they are limited by the third principle of the theory:

> *The principle of* truth: *A mental model represents a true possibility, and it represents a clause in the premises only when the clause is true in the possibility.*

The simplest illustration of the principle is to ask naive individuals to list what is possible for a variety of assertions (Barrouillet & Lecas, 1999; Johnson-Laird & Savary, 1996). Given an exclusive disjunction, *not-A or else B*, they list two possibilities corresponding to the mental models:

¬A	
	B

The first mental model does not represent *B*, which is false in this possibility; and the second mental model does not represent *not-A*, which is false in this possibility, in other words, *A* is true. Hence, people tend to neglect these cases. Readers might assume that the principle of truth is equivalent to the representation of the propositions *mentioned* in the premises. However, this assumption yields the same models of *A* and *B* regardless of the connective relating them. The right way to conceive the principle is that it yields pared-down versions of fully explicit models, which in turn map into truth tables. As we will see, the principle of truth predicts a striking effect on reasoning.

Individuals can make a mental footnote about what is false in a possibility, and these footnotes can be used to flesh out mental models into fully explicit models. However, footnotes tend to be ephemeral. The most recent computer program implementing the model theory operates at two levels of expertise. At its lowest level, it makes no use of footnotes. Its representation of the main sentential connectives is summarized in Table 9.2. The mental models of a conditional, *if A then B*, are

A	B
. . .	

The ellipsis denotes an *implicit* model of the possibilities in which the antecedent of the conditional is false. In other words, there are alternatives to the possibility in which *A* and *B* are true, but individuals tend not to think explicitly about what holds in these possibilities. If they retain the footnote about what is false, then they can flesh out these mental models into fully explicit models. The mental models of the biconditional, *If, and only if, A then B*, as Table 9.2 shows, are identical to those for the conditional. What differs is that the footnote now conveys that both *A* and *B* are false in the implicit model. The program at its higher level uses fully explicit models and so makes no errors in reasoning.

Inferences can be made with mental models using a procedure that builds a set of models for a premise and then updates them according to the other premises. From the premises,

> A or else B but not both.
> Not-A.

the disjunction yields the mental models

A	
	B

The categorical premise eliminates the first model, but it is compatible with the second model, yielding the valid conclusion, *B*. The rules for updating mental models are summarized in Table 9.3.

The model theory of deduction began with an account of reasoning with quantifiers as in *syllogisms* such as:

> Some actuaries are businessmen.
> All businessmen are conformists.
> Therefore, some actuaries are conformists.

A plausible hypothesis is that people construct models of the possibilities compatible with the premises and draw whatever conclusion, if any, holds in all of them. Johnson-Laird (1975) illustrated such an account with Euler circles. A premise of the form, *Some A are B*, however, is compatible with four distinct possibilities, and the previous premises are compatible with 16 distinct possibilities. Because the inference is easy, reasoners may fail to consider

Table 9.3. The procedures for forming a conjunction of a pair of models. Each procedure is presented with an accompanying example. Only mental models may be implicit and therefore call for the first two procedures

1: The conjunction of a pair of implicit models yields the implicit model:
. . . and . . . yield . . .

2: The conjunction of an implicit model with a model representing propositions yields the null model (akin to the empty set) by default, for example,
. . . and B C yield nil.

But, if none of the atomic propositions (B C) is represented in the set of models containing the implicit model, then the conjunction yields the model of the propositions, for example,
. . . and B C yield B C.

3: The conjunction of a pair of models representing respectively a proposition and its negation yield the null model, for example,
A ¬B and ¬A yield nil.

4: The conjunction of a pair of models in which a proposition, B, in one model is not represented in the other model depends on the set of models of which this other model is a member. If B occurs in at least one of these models, then its absence in the current model is treated as negation, for example,
A B and A yields nil.

However, if B does not occur in one of these models (e.g., only its negation occurs in them), then its absence is treated as equivalent to its affirmation, and the conjunction (following the next procedure) is
A B and A yields A B.

5: The conjunction of a pair of fully explicit models free from contradiction update the second model with all the new propositions from the first model, for example,
¬A B and ¬A C yield ¬A B C.

all the possibilities (Erickson, 1974), or they may construct models that capture more than one possibility (Johnson-Laird & Bara, 1984). The program implementing the model theory accordingly constructs just one model for the previous premises:

actuary	[businessman]	conformist
actuary		
	[businessman]	conformist
	. . .	

where each row represents a different sort of individual, the ellipsis represents the possibility of other sorts of individual, and the square brackets represent that the set of businessmen has been represented exhaustively – in other words, no more tokens representing businessmen can be added to the model. This model yields the conclusion that *Some actuaries are conformists*. There are many ways in which reasoners might use such models, and Johnson-Laird and Bara (1984) described two alternative strategies. Years of tinkering with the models for syllogisms suggest that reasoning does not rely on a single deterministic procedure. The following principle applies to thinking in general but can be illustrated for reasoning:

> *The principle of strategic variation: Given a class of problems, reasoners develop a variety of strategies from exploring manipulations of models (Bucciarelli & Johnson-Laird, 1999).*

Stenning and his colleagues anticipated this principle in an alternative theory of syllogistic reasoning (e.g., Stenning & Yule, 1997). They proposed that reasoners focus on individuals who necessarily exist given the premises (e.g., given the premise *Some A are B*, there must be an *A* who is *B*). They implemented this idea in three different algorithms that all yield the same inferences. One algorithm is based on Euler circles supplemented with a notation for necessary individuals, one is based on tokens of individuals in line with the model theory, and one is based on verbal rules, such as

If there are two existential premises, that is, that contain "some", then respond that there is no valid conclusion.

Stenning and Yule concluded from the equivalence of the outputs from these algorithms that a need exists for data beyond merely the conclusions that reasoners draw, and they suggested that reasoners may develop different representational systems, depending on the task. Indeed, from Störring (1908) to Stenning (2002), psychologists have argued that some reasoners may use Euler circles and others may use verbal procedures.

The *external* models that reasoners constructed with cut-out shapes corroborated the principle of strategic variation: Individuals develop various strategies (Bucciarelli & Johnson-Laird, 1999). They also overlook possible models of premises. Their search may be organized toward finding necessary individuals, as Stenning and Yule showed, but the typical representations of premises included individuals who were not necessary; for example, the typical representation of *Some A are B* was

A B
A B
A

A focus on necessary individuals is a particular strategy. Other strategies may call for the representation of other sorts of individuals, especially if the task changes – a view consistent with Stenning and Yule's theory. For example, individuals readily make the following sort of inference (Evans, Handley, Harper, & Johnson-Laird, 1999):

Some A are B.

Some B are C.

Therefore, it is possible that Some A are C.

Such inferences depend on the representation of possible individuals.

The model theory has been extended to some sorts of inference based on premises containing more than one quantifier (Johnson-Laird, Byrne, & Tabossi, 1989). Many such inferences are beyond the scope of Euler circles, although the general principles of the model theory still apply to them. Consider, for example, the inference (Cherubini & Johnson-Laird, 2004):

There are four persons: Ann, Bill, Cath, and Dave.

Everybody loves anyone who loves someone.

Ann loves Bill.

What follows?

Most people can envisage this model in which arrows denote the relation of *loving*:

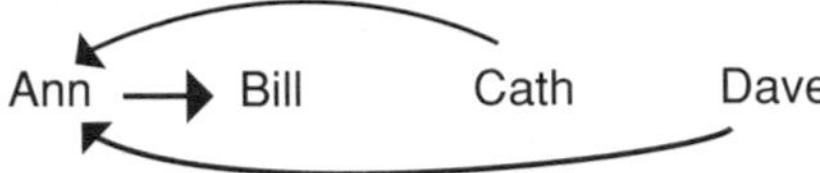

Hence, they infer that everyone loves Ann. However, if you ask them whether it follows that Cath loves Dave, they tend to respond "no." They are mistaken, but the inference calls for using the quantified premise again. The result is this model (strictly speaking, all four persons love themselves, too):

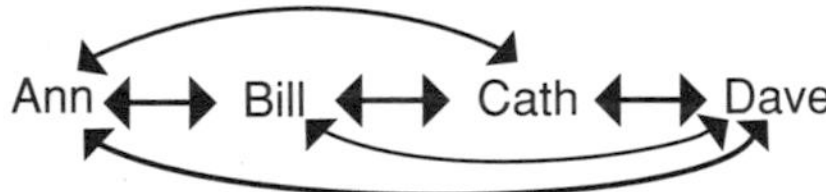

It follows that Cath loves Dave, and people grasp its validity if it is demonstrated with diagrams. No complete model theory exists for inferences based on quantifiers and connectives (cf. Bara, Bucciarelli, & Lombardo, 2001). However, the main principles of the theory should apply: iconicity, possibilities, truth, and strategic variation.

Experimental Studies of Deductive Reasoning

Many experiments have corroborated the model theory (for a bibliography, see the Web page created by Ruth Byrne: www.tcd.ie/Psychology/People/Ruth_Byrnelmental_

models/). This section outlines the corroborations of five predictions.

Prediction 1: The fewer the models needed for an inference, and the simpler they are, the less time the inference should take and the less prone it should be to error. Fewer entities do improve inferences (e.g., Birney & Halford, 2002). Likewise, fewer models improve spatial and temporal reasoning (Byrne & Johnson-Laird, 1989; Carreiras & Santamaría, 1997; Schaeken, Johnson-Laird, & d'Ydewalle, 1996; Vandierendonck & De Vooght, 1997). Premises yielding one model take less time to read than corresponding premises yielding multiple models; however, the difference between two and three models is often so small that it is unlikely that reasoners construct all three models (Vandierendonck, De Vooght, Desimpelaere, & Dierckx, 2000). They may build a single model with one element represented as having two or more possible locations.

Effects of number of models have been observed in comparing one sort of sentential connective with another and in examining batteries of such inferences (see Johnson-Laird & Byrne, 1991). To illustrate these effects, consider the "double disjunction" (Bauer & Johnson-Laird, 1993):

> *Ann is in Alaska or else Beth is in Barbados, but not both.*
> *Beth is in Barbados or else Cath is in Canada, but not both.*
> *What follows?*

Reasoners readily envisage the two possibilities compatible with the first premise, but it is harder to update them with those from the second premise. The solution is

Ann in Alaska		Cath in Canada
	Beth in Barbados	

People represent the spatial relations: Models are not made of words. The two models yield the conclusion: *Either Ann is in Alaska and Cath is in Canada or else Beth is in Barbados.* An increase in complexity soon overloads working memory. This problem defeats most people:

> *Ann is in Alaska or Beth is in Barbados, or both.*
> *Beth is in Barbados or Cath is in Canada, or both.*
> *What follows?*

The premises yield five models, from which it follows: *Ann is in Alaska and Cath is in Canada, or Beth is in Barbados, or all three.* When the order of the premises reduces the number of models to be held in mind, reasoning improves (García-Madruga, Moreno, Carriedo, Gutiérrez, & Johnson-Laird, 2001; Girotto, Mazzocco, & Tasso, 1997; Mackiewicz & Johnson-Laird, 2003).

Because one model is easier than many, an interaction occurs in *modal* reasoning. It is easier to infer that a situation is possible (one model of the premises suffices as an example) than that it is *not* possible (all the models of the premises must be checked for a counterexample to the conclusion). In contrast, it is easier to infer that a situation is *not* necessary (one counterexample suffices) than that it is necessary (all the models of the premises must be checked as examples). The interaction occurs in both accuracy and speed (Bell & Johnson-Laird, 1998; see also Evans et al., 1999).

Prediction 2: Reasoners should err as a result of overlooking models of the premises. Given a double disjunction (such as the previous one), the most frequent errors were conclusions consistent with just a single model of the premises (Bauer & Johnson-Laird, 1993). Likewise, given a syllogism of the form,

> None of the A is a B.
> All the B are C.

reasoners infer: *None of the A is a* C (Newstead & Griggs, 1999). They overlook the possibility in which Cs that are not Bs are *A*s, and so the valid conclusion is

> *Some of the* C *are not A*.

They may have misinterpreted the second premise, taking it also to mean that *all the* C *are* B (Newstead & Griggs, 1999), but many errors with syllogisms appear to arise because individuals consider only a single model (Bucciarelli & Johnson-Laird, 1999; Espino, Santamaría, & García-Madruga, 2000). Ormerod proposed a "minimal completion" hypothesis according to which reasoners construct only the minimally necessary models (see Ormerod, Manktelow, & Jones, 1993; Richardson & Ormerod, 1997). Likewise, Sloutsky postulated a process of "minimalization" in which reasoners tend to construct only single models for all connectives, thereby reducing them to conjunctions (Morris & Sloutsky, 2002; Sloutsky & Goldvarg, 1999). Certain assertions, however, do tend to elicit more than one model. As Byrne and her colleagues showed (e.g., Byrne, 2002; Byrne & McEleney, 2000; Byrne & Tasso, 1999), counterfactual conditionals such as

If the cable hadn't been faulty then the printer wouldn't have broken

tend to elicit models of both what is factually the case, that is,

cable faulty   printer broken

and what holds in a counterfactual possibility

¬ cable faulty   ¬ printer broken

Prediction 3: Reasoners should be able to refute invalid inferences by envisaging counterexamples (i.e., models of the premises that refute the putative conclusion). There is no guarantee that reasoners will find a counterexample, but, where they do succeed, they *know* that an inference is invalid (Barwise, 1993). The availability of a counterexample can suppress fallacious inferences from a conditional premise (Byrne, Espino, & Santamaría, 1999; Markovits, 1984; Vadeboncoeur & Markovits, 1999). Nevertheless, an alternative theory based on mental models has downplayed the role of counterexamples (Polk & Newell, 1995), and reasoners' diagrams have sometimes failed to show their use (e.g., Newstead, Handley, & Buck, 1999). However, when reasoners had to construct external models (Bucciarelli & Johnson-Laird, 1999), they used counterexamples (see also Neth & Johnson-Laird, 1999; Roberts, in press).

There are two sorts of invalid conclusions. One sort is invalid because the conclusion is disjoint with the premises; for example,

A or B or both.
B or else C but not both.
Therefore, not-A and C.

The premises have three fully explicit models:

A	¬ B	C
¬ A	B	¬ C
A	B	¬ C

The conclusion is inconsistent with the premises because it conflicts with each of their models. But, another sort of invalid conclusion is consistent with the premises but does not follow from them such as the conclusion *A and not*-C from the previous premises. It is consistent with the premises because it corresponds to their third model, but it does not follow from them because the other two models are counterexamples. Reasoners usually establish the invalidity of the first sort of conclusion by detecting its inconsistency with the premises, but they refute the second sort of conclusion with a counterexample (Johnson-Laird & Hasson, 2003). An experiment using functional magnetic resonance imaging showed that reasoning based on numeric quantifiers, such as *at least five* – as opposed to arithmetical calculation based on the same premises – depended on the right frontal hemisphere. A search for counterexamples appeared to activate the right frontal pole (Kroger, Cohen, & Johnson-Laird, 2003).

Prediction 4: Reasoners should succumb to *illusory* inferences, which are compelling but invalid. They arise from the principle of truth and its corollary that reasoners neglect what is false. Consider the problem:

> *Only one of the following assertions is true about a particular hand of cards:*
>
> *There is a king in the hand or there is an ace, or both.*
>
> *There is a queen in the hand or there is an ace, or both.*
>
> *There is a jack in the hand or there is a ten, or both.*
>
> *Is it possible that there is an ace in the hand?*

Nearly everyone responds, "yes" (Goldvarg & Johnson-Laird, 2000). They grasp that the first assertion allows two possibilities in which an ace occurs, so they infer that an ace is possible. However, it is impossible for an ace to be in the hand because both of the first two assertions would then be true, contrary to the rubric that only one of them is true. The inference is an illusion of possibility: Reasoners infer wrongly that a card is possible. A similar problem to which reasoners tend to respond "no" and thereby commit an illusion of impossibility is created by replacing the two occurrences of "there is an ace" in the problem with, "there is not an ace." When the previous premises were stated with the question

> Is it possible that there is a jack?

the participants nearly all responded "yes," again. They considered the third assertion, and its mental models showed that there could be a jack. However, this time they were correct: The inference is valid. Hence, the focus on truth does not always lead to error, and experiments have accordingly compared illusions with matching control problems for which the neglect of falsity should not affect accuracy.

The computer program implementing the theory shows that illusory inferences should be sparse in the set of all possible inferences. However, experiments have corroborated their occurrence in reasoning about possibilities, probabilities, and causal and deontic relations. Table 9.4 illustrates some different illusions. Studies have used remedial procedures to reduce the illusions (e.g., Santamaría & Johnson-Laird, 2000). Yang taught participants to think explicitly about what is true and what is false. The difference between illusions and control problems vanished, but performance on the control problems fell from almost 100% correct to around 75% correct (Yang & Johnson-Laird, 2000). The principle of truth limits understanding, but it does so without participants realizing it. They were highly confident in their responses, no less so when they succumbed to an illusion than when they responded correctly to a control problem.

The rubric, "one of these assertions is true and one of them is false," is equivalent to an exclusive disjunction between two assertions: *A or else B, but not both*. This usage leads to compelling illusions that seduce novices and experts alike, for example,

> If there is a king then there is an ace, or else if there isn't a king then there is an ace.
>
> There is a king.
>
> What follows?

More than 2000 individuals have tackled this problem (see Johnson-Laird & Savary, 1999), and nearly everyone responded, "there is an ace." The prediction of an illusion depends not on logic but on how other participants interpreted the relevant connectives in simple assertions. The preceding illusion occurs with the rubric: *One of these assertions is true and one of them is false* applying to the conditionals. That the conclusion is illusory rests on the following assumption, corroborated experimentally: If a conditional is false, then one possibility is that its antecedent is true and its consequent is false. If skeptics think that the illusory responses are correct, then how do they explain the effects of a remedial procedure? They should then say that the remedy produced illusions. Readers may suspect that the illusions arise from the artificiality of the problems, which

Table 9.4. Some illusory inferences in abbreviated form, with percentages of illusory responses. Each study examined other sorts of illusions and matched control problems

Premises	*Illusory responses*	*Percentages of illusory responses*
1. If A then B or else B. A.	B.	100
2. Either A and B, or else C and D. A.	B.	87
3. If A then B or else if C then B. A and B.	Possibly both are true.	98
4. A or else not both B and C. A and not B.	Possibly both are true.	91
5. One true and one false: not-A or not-B, or neither. Not-C and not-B.	Possibly not-C and not-B.	85
6. Only one is true: At least some A are not B. No A are B.	Possibly No B are A.	95
7. If one is true so is the other: A or else not B. A.	A is more likely than B.	95
8. If one is true so is the other: A if and only if B. A.	A is equally likely as B.	90

Note: 1 is from Johnson-Laird and Savary (1999), 2 is from Walsh and Johnson-Laird (2003), 3 is from Johnson-Laird, Legrenzi, Girotto, and Legrenzi (2000), 4 is from Legrenzi, Girotto, and Johnson-Laird (2003), 5 is from Goldvarg and Johnson-Laird (2000), 6 is from Experiment 2, Yang and Johnson-Laird (2000), and 7 and 8 are from Johnson-Laird and Savary (1996).

never occur in real life and therefore confuse the participants. The problems may be artificial, although analogs do occur in real life (see Johnson-Laird & Savary, 1999), and artificiality fails to explain the correct responses to the controls or the high ratings of confidence in both illusory and control conclusions.

Prediction 5: Naive individuals should develop different reasoning strategies based on models. When they are tested in the laboratory, they start with only rough ideas of how to proceed. They can reason, but not efficiently. With experience but no feedback about accuracy, they spontaneously develop various strategies (Schaeken, De Vooght, Vandierendonck, & d'Ydewalle, 1999). Deduction itself may be a strategy (Evans, 2000), and people may resort to it more in Western cultures than in East Asian cultures (Peng & Nisbett, 1999). However, deduction itself leads to different strategies (Van der Henst, Yang, & Johnson-Laird, 2002). Consider a problem in which each premise is *compound*, that is, contains a connective:

A if and only if B.
Either B or else C, but not both.
C if and only if D.
Does it follow that if not A then D?

where A, B, ... refer to different colored marbles in a box. Some individuals develop a strategy based on suppositions. They say, for example,

> Suppose *not A. It follows from the first premise that not B. It follows from the second premise that C. The third premise then implies D. So, yes, the conclusion follows.*

Some individuals construct a chain of conditionals leading from one clause in the conclusion to the other – for example: *If D then C, If C then not B, If not B then not A*. Others develop a strategy in which they enumerate the different possibilities compatible with the premises. For example, they draw a horizontal line across the page and write down the possibilities for the premises:

```
A     B
-------------------
            C     D
```

When individuals are taught to use this strategy, as Victoria Bell showed in unpublished studies, their reasoning is faster and more accurate. The nature of the premises and the conclusion can bias reasoners to adopt a predictable strategy (e.g., conditional premises encourage the use of suppositions, whereas disjunctive premises encourage the enumeration of possibilities) (Van der Henst et al., 2002).

Reasoners develop diverse strategies for relational reasoning (e.g., Goodwin & Johnson-Laird, in press; Roberts, 2000), suppositional reasoning (e.g., Byrne & Handley, 1997), and reasoning with quantifiers (e.g., Bucciarelli & Johnson-Laird, 1999). Granted the variety of strategies, there remains a robust effect: Inferences from one mental model are easier than those from more than one model (see also Espino, Santamaría, Meseguer, & Carreiras, 2000). Different strategies could reflect different mental representations (Stenning & Yule, 1997), but those so far discovered are all compatible with models. Individuals who have mastered logic could make a strategic use of formal rules. Given sufficient experience with a class of problems, individuals begin to notice some formal patterns.

Probabilistic Reasoning

Reasoning about probabilities is of two sorts. In *intensional* reasoning, individuals use heuristics to infer the probability of an event from some sort of index, such as the availability of information. In *extensional* reasoning, they infer the probability of an event from a knowledge of the different ways in which it might occur. This distinction is due to Nobel laureate Daniel Kahneman and the late Amos Tversky, who together pioneered the investigation of heuristics (Kahneman, Slovic, & Tversky, 1982; see Kahneman & Frederick, Chap. 12). Studies of extensional reasoning focused at first on "Bayesian" reasoning in which participants try to infer a conditional probability from the premises. These studies offered no account of the foundations of extensional reasoning. The model theory filled the gap (Johnson-Laird, Legrenzi, Girotto, Legrenzi, & Caverni, 1999), and the present section outlines its account.

Mental models represent the extensions of assertions (i.e., the possibilities to which they refer). The theory postulates

> *The principle of* equiprobability*: Each mental model is assumed to be equiprobable, unless there are reasons to the contrary.*

The probability of an event accordingly depends on the proportion of models in which it occurs. The theory also allows that models can be tagged with numerals denoting probabilities or frequencies of occurrence, and that simple arithmetical operations can be carried out on them. Shimojo and Ichikawa (1989) and Falk (1992) proposed similar principles for Bayesian reasoning. The present account differs from theirs in that it assigns equiprobability, not to actual events, but to mental models. And equiprobability applies only by default. An analogous principle of "indifference" occurred in classical probability theory, but it is problematic because it applies to events (Hacking, 1975).

Consider a simple problem such as

> In the box, there is a green ball or a blue ball or both.
>
> What is the probability that both the green and the blue ball are there?

The premise elicits the mental models:

green	
	blue
green	blue

Naive reasoners follow the equiprobability principle, and infer the answer, "1/3." An experiment corroborated this and other predictions based on the mental models for the connectives in Table 9.2 (Johnson-Laird et al., 1999).

Conditional probabilities are on the borderline of naive competence. They are difficult because individuals need to consider several fully explicit models. Here is a typical Bayesian problem:

> *The patient's PSA score is high. If he doesn't have prostate cancer, the chances of such a value is 1 in 1000. Is he likely to have prostate cancer?*

Many people respond, "yes." However, they are wrong. The model theory predicts the error: Individuals represent the conditional probability in the problem as one explicit model and one implicit model tagged with their chances:

¬ prostate cancer	high PSA	1
. . .		999

The converse conditional probability has the same mental models, and so people assume that if the patient has a high PSA the chances are only 1 in 1000 that he does not have prostate cancer. Because the patient has a high PSA, then he is highly likely to have prostate cancer (999/1000). To reason correctly, individuals must envisage the complete partition of possibilities and chances. However, the problem fails to provide enough information. It yields only:

¬ prostate cancer	high PSA	1
¬ prostate cancer	¬ high PSA	999
prostate cancer	high PSA	?
prostate cancer	¬ high PSA	?

There are various ways to provide the missing information. One way is to give the base rate of prostate cancer, which can be used with Bayes's theorem from the probability calculus to infer the answer. However, the theorem and its computations are beyond naive individuals (Kahneman & Tversky, 1973; Phillips & Edwards, 1966). The model theory postulates an alternative:

> *The* subset *principle: Given a complete partition, individuals infer the conditional probability, P(A | B), by examining the subset of B that is A and computing its proportion (Johnson-Laird* et al., 1999*).*

If models are tagged with their absolute frequencies or chances, then the conditional probability equals their value for the model of *A and B* divided by their sum for all the models containing *B*. A complete partition for the patient problem might be

¬ prostate cancer	high PSA	1
¬ prostate cancer	¬ high PSA	999
prostate cancer	high PSA	2
prostate cancer	¬ high PSA	0

The subset of chances of prostate cancer within the two possibilities of a high PSA (rows 1 and 3) yields the conditional probability: P(prostate cancer | high PSA) = 2/3. It is high, but far from 999/1000.

Evolutionary psychologists postulate that natural selection led to an innate "module" in the mind that makes Bayesian inferences from naturally occurring frequencies. It follows that naive reasoners should fail the patient problem because it is about a unique event (Cosmides & Tooby, 1996; Gigerenzer & Hoffrage, 1995). In contrast, as the model theory predicts, individuals cope with problems about unique or repeated events provided they can use the subset principle and the arithmetic is easy (Girotto & Gonzalez, 2001).

The model theory dispels some common misconceptions about probabilistic reasoning. It is *not* always inductive. Extensional reasoning can be deductively valid, and it need not depend on a tacit knowledge of the probability calculus. It is not always correct because it can yield illusions (Table 9.4).

Induction and Models

Induction is part of everyday thinking (see Sloman & Lagnado, Chap. 5). Popper (1972) argued, however, that it is not part of scientific thinking. He claimed that science is based on explanatory conjectures, which observations serve only to falsify. Some scientists agree (e.g., Deutsch, 1997, p. 159). However, many astronomical, meteorological, and medical observations are not tests of hypotheses. Everyone makes inductions in daily life. For instance, when the starter will not turn over the engine, your immediate thought is that the battery is dead. You are likely to be right, but there is no guarantee. Likewise, when the car ferry, *Herald of Free Enterprise*, sailed from Zeebrugge on March 6, 1987, its master made the plausible induction that the bow doors had been closed. They had always been closed in the past, and there was no evidence to the contrary. However, they had not been closed, the vessel capsized and sank, and many people drowned. Induction is a common but risky business.

The textbook definition of induction – alas, all too common – is that it leads from the particular to the general. Such arguments are indeed inductions, but many inductions such as the preceding examples are inferences from the particular to the particular. That is why the "Introduction" offered a more comprehensive definition: Induction is a process that increases semantic information. As an example, consider again the inference:

The starter won't turn.
Therefore, the battery is dead.

Like all inductions, it depends on knowledge and, in particular, on the true conditional:

If the battery is dead, then the starter won't turn.

It is consistent with the possibilities:

battery dead	¬ starter turn
¬ battery dead	¬ starter turn
¬ battery dead	starter turn

The premise of the induction eliminates the third possibility, but the conclusion goes beyond the information given because it eliminates the second of them. The availability of the first model yields an intensional inference of a high probability, but its conclusion rejects a real possibility. Hence, it may be false. Inductions are vulnerable because they increase semantic information.

Inductions depend on knowledge. As Kahneman and Tversky (1982) showed, various heuristics constrain the use of knowledge in inductions. The *availability* heuristic, illustrated in the previous example, relies on whatever relevant knowledge is available (e.g., Tversky & Kahneman, 1973). The *representativeness* heuristic yields inferences dependent on the representative nature of the evidence (e.g., Kahneman & Frederick, 2002; also see Kahneman & Frederick, Chap. 12). The present account presupposes these heuristics but examines the role of models in induction. Some inductions are *implicit:* They are rapid, involuntary, and unconscious (see Litman & Reber, Chap. 18). Other inductions are *explicit:* They are slow, voluntary, and conscious. This distinction is familiar (e.g., Evans & Over, 1996; Johnson-Laird & Wason, 1977, p. 341; Sloman, 1996; Stanovich, 1999). The next part considers implicit inductions, and the part thereafter considers explicit inductions and the resolution of inconsistencies.

Implicit Induction and the Modulation of Models

Semantics is central to models, and the content of assertions and general knowledge can modulate models. Psychologists have proposed many theories about the mental representation of knowledge, but knowledge is about what is possible, and so the model theory postulates that it is represented in fully explicit models (Johnson-Laird & Byrne, 2002). These models, in turn, modulate the mental models of assertions according to

> *The principle of* modulation: *The meanings of clauses, coreferential links between them, general knowledge, and knowledge of context, can modulate the models of an assertion. In the case of inconsistency, meaning and knowledge normally take precedence over the models of assertions.*

Modulation can add information to mental models, prevent their construction, and flesh them out into fully explicit models. As an illustration of semantic modulation, consider the following conditional:

If it's a game, then it's not soccer.

Its fully explicit models (Table 9.2), if they were unconstrained by coreference and semantics, would be

game	¬ soccer
¬ game	¬ soccer
¬ game	soccer

The meaning of the noun *soccer* entails that it is a game, and so an attempt to construct the third model fails because it would yield an inconsistency. The conditional has only the first two models.

The pragmatic effects of knowledge have been modeled in a computer program, which can be illustrated using the example

If the match is struck properly, then it lights.
The match is soaking wet and it is struck properly.
What happens?

In logic, it follows that the match lights, but neither people nor the program draws this conclusion. Knowledge that wet matches do not light overrides the model of the premises. The program constructs the mental model of the premises:

match wet   match struck   match lights   [the model of the premises]

If a match is soaking wet, it does not light, and the program has a knowledge base containing this information in fully explicit models:

match wet	¬ match lights
¬ match wet	¬ match lights
¬ match wet	match lights

The second premise states that the match is wet, which triggers the matching possibility in the preceding models:

match wet   ¬ match lights

The conjunction of this model with the model of the premises would yield a contradiction, but the program follows the principle of modulation and gives precedence to knowledge yielding the following model:

match wet   match struck   ¬ match lights

and so the match does not light. The model of the premises also triggers another possibility from the knowledge base:

¬ match wet   match lights

This possibility and the model of the premises are used to construct a counterfactual conditional:

If it had not been the case that match wet *and given* match struck, *then it might have been the case that* match lights.

Modulation is rapid and automatic, and it affects comprehension and reasoning (Johnson-Laird & Byrne, 2002; Newstead, Ellis, Evans, & Dennis, 1997; Ormerod & Johnson-Laird, in press). In logic, connectives such as conditionals and disjunctions are *truth functional*, and so the truth value of a sentence in which they occur can be determined solely from a knowledge of the truth values of the clauses they interconnect. However, in natural language, connectives are not truth functional: It is always necessary to check whether their content and context modulate their interpretation.

Explicit Induction, Abduction, and the Creation of Explanations

Induction is the use of knowledge to increase semantic information: Possibilities are eliminated either by adding elements to a mental model or by eliminating a mental model altogether. After you have stood in line to no avail at a bar in Italy, you are likely to make an explicit induction:

In Italian bars with cashiers, you pay the cashier first and then take your receipt to the bar to make your order.

This induction is a general description. You may also formulate an explanation:

The barmen are too busy to make change, and so it is more efficient for customers to pay a cashier.

Scientific laws are general descriptions of phenomena (e.g., Kepler's third law describes the elliptical orbits of the planets). Scientific theories explain these regularities in terms of more fundamental considerations (e.g., the general theory of relativity explains planetary orbits as the result of the sun's mass curving space-time). Peirce (1903) called thinking that leads to explanations *abduction*. In terms of the five categories of the "Introduction," abduction is creative when it leads to the revision of beliefs.

Consider the following problem:

If a pilot falls from a plane without a parachute, the pilot dies. This pilot did not die, however. Why not?

Most people respond, for example, that

The plane was on the ground.
The pilot fell into a deep snow drift.

Only a minority draws the logically valid conclusion:

The pilot did not fall from the plane without a parachute.

Hence, people prefer a causal explanation repudiating the first premise to a valid deduction, albeit they may presuppose that the antecedent of the conditional is true. Granted that knowledge usually takes precedence over contradictory assertions, the explanatory mechanism should dominate the ability to make deductions.

In daily life, the propensity to explain is extraordinary, as Tony Anderson and this author discovered when they asked participants to explain the inexplicable. The participants received pairs of sentences selected *at random* from separate stories:

John made his way to a shop that sold TV sets.
Celia had recently had her ears pierced.

In another condition, the sentences were modified to make them coreferential:

Celia made her way to a shop that sold TV sets.
She had recently had her ears pierced.

The participants' task was to explain what was going on. They readily went beyond the given information to account for what was happening. They proposed, for example, that Celia was getting reception in her earrings and wanted the TV shop to investigate, that she wanted to see some new earrings on closed circuit TV, that she had won a bet by having her ears pierced and was spending the money on a TV set, and so on. Only rarely were the participants stumped for an explanation. They were almost as equally ingenious with the sentences that were not coreferential.

Abduction depends on knowledge, especially of causal relations, which according to the model theory refer to temporally ordered sets of possibilities (Goldvarg & Johnson-Laird, 2001; see Cheng & Buehner, Chapter 5.). An assertion of the form C *causes* E is compatible with three fully explicit possibilities:

$$\begin{array}{ll} C & E \\ \neg C & E \\ \neg C & \neg E \end{array}$$

with the temporal constraint that *E* cannot precede C. An "enabling" assertion of the form C *allows* E is compatible with the three possibilities:

$$\begin{array}{ll} C & E \\ C & \neg E \\ \neg C & \neg E \end{array}$$

This account, unlike others, accordingly distinguishes between the meaning and logical consequences of causes and enabling conditions (pace, e.g., Einhorn & Hogarth, 1978; Hart & Honoré, 1985; Mill, 1874). It also treats causal relations as determinate rather than probabilistic (pace, e.g., Cheng, 1997; Suppes, 1970). Experiments support both these claims: Participants listed the previous possibilities, and they rejected other cases as impossible, contrary to probabilistic accounts (Goldvarg & Johnson-Laird, 2001). Of course, when individuals induce a causal relation from a series of observations, they are influenced by relative frequencies. However, on the present account, the meaning of any causal relation that they induce is deterministic.

Given the cause from a causal relation, there is only one possible effect, as the previous models show; however, given the effect, there is more than one possible cause. Exceptions do occur (Cummins, Lubart, Alksnis, & Rist, 1991; Markovits, 1984), but the principle holds in general. It may explain why inferences from causes to effects are more plausible than inferences from effects to causes. As Tversky and Kahneman (1982) showed, conditionals in which the antecedent is a cause such as

A girl has blue eyes if her mother has blue eyes.

are judged as more probable than conditionals in which the antecedent is an effect:

The mother has blue eyes if her daughter has blue eyes.

According to the model theory, when individuals discover inconsistencies, they try to construct a model of a cause and effect that resolves the inconsistency. It makes possible the facts of the matter, and the belief that the causal assertion repudiates is taken to be a counterfactual possibility (in a comparable way to the modulation of models by knowledge). Consider, for example, the scenario:

If the trigger is pulled then the pistol will fire. The trigger is pulled, but the pistol does not fire. Why not?

Given 20 different scenarios of this form (in an unpublished study carried out by Girotto, Legrenzi, & Johnson-Laird), most explanations were causal claims that repudiated the conditional. In two further experiments with the scenarios, the participants rated the statements of a cause and its effect as the most probable explanations; for example,

A prudent person had unloaded the pistol and there were no bullets in the chamber.

The cause alone was rated as less probable, but as more probable than the effect alone, which in turn was rated as more probable than an explanation that repudiated the categorical premise; for example,

The trigger wasn't really pulled.

The greater probability assigned to the conjunction of the cause and effect than to either of its clauses is an instance of the "conjunction" fallacy in which a conjunction is in error judged to be more probable than its constituents (Tversky & Kahneman, 1983).

Abductions that resolve inconsistencies have been implemented in a computer program that uses a knowledge base to create causal explanations. Given the preceding example, the program constructs the mental models of the conditional:

trigger pulled	pistol fires
. . .	

The conjunction of the categorical assertion yields

trigger pulled	pistol fires	[the model of the premises]

That the pistol did not fire is inconsistent with this model. The theory predicts that individuals should tend to abandon their belief in the conditional premise because its one explicit mental model conflicts with the fact that the pistol did not fire (see Girotto, Johnson-Laird, Legrenzi, & Sonino, 2000, for corroborating evidence). Nevertheless, the conditional expresses a useful idealization, and so the program treats it as the basis for a counterfactual set of possibilities:

trigger pulled	¬pistol fires	[the model of the facts]
trigger pulled	pistol fires	[the models of counterfactual possibilities]
. . .		

People know that a pistol without bullets does not fire, and so the program has in its knowledge base the models:

¬ bullets in pistol	¬ pistol fires
bullets in pistol	¬ pistol fires
bullets in pistol	pistol fires

The model of the facts triggers the first possibility in this set, which modulates the model of the facts to create a possibility:

¬ bullets in pistol	trigger pulled	¬ pistol fires

The new proposition in this model triggers a causal antecedent from another set of models in the knowledge base, which explains the inconsistency: A person emptied the pistol and so it had no bullets. The counterfactual possibilities yield the claim: If the person had not emptied the pistol, then it would have had bullets, and . . . it would have fired. The fact that the pistol did not fire has been used to reject the conditional premise, and available knowledge has been used to create an explanation and to modulate the conditional premise into a counterfactual. There are, of course, other possible explanations.

In sum, reasoners can resolve inconsistencies between incontrovertible evidence and the consequences of their beliefs. They use their available knowledge – in the form of explicit models – to try to create a causal scenario that makes sense of the facts. Their reasoning may resolve the inconsistency, create an erroneous account, or fail to yield any explanation whatsoever.

Conclusions and Further Directions

Mental models have a past in the nineteenth century. The present theory was developed in the twentieth century. In its application to deduction, as Peirce anticipated, if a conclusion holds in all the models of the premises, it is necessary given the premises. If it holds in a proportion of the models, then, granted that they are equiprobable, its probability is equal to that proportion. If it holds in at least one model, then it is possible. The theory also applies to inductive reasoning – both the rapid implicit inferences that underlie comprehension and the deliberate inferences yielding generalizations. It offers an account of the creation of causal explanations. However, if Craik was right, mental models underlie all thinking with a propositional content, and so the present theory is radically incomplete.

What of the future of mental models? The theory is under intensive development and intensive scrutiny. It has been corroborated in many experiments, and it is empirically distinguishable from other theories. Indeed, there are distinguishable variants of the theory itself (see, e.g., Evans, 1993; Ormerod, Manktelow, & Jones, 1993; Polk & Newell, 1995). The most urgent demands for the twenty-first century are the extension of the theory to problem solving, decision making, and strategic thinking when individuals compete or cooperate.

Acknowledgments

This chapter was made possible by a grant from the National Science Foundation (Grant BCS 0076287) to study strategies in reasoning. The author is grateful to the editor, the community of reasoning researchers, and his colleagues, collaborators, and students – many of their names are found in the "References" section.

References

Bar-Hillel, Y., & Carnap, R. (1964). An outline of a theory of semantic information. In Y. Bar-Hillel (Ed.), *Language and information processing*. Reading, MA: Addison-Wesley.

Bara, B. G., Bucciarelli, M., & Lombardo, V. (2001). Model theory of deduction: A unified computational approach. *Cognitive Science*, 25, 839–901.

Barrouillet, P., & Lecas, J-F. (1999). Mental models in conditional reasoning and working memory. *Thinking and Reasoning*, 5, 289–302.

Barsalou, L. W. (1999). Perceptual symbol systems. *Behavioral and Brain Sciences*, 22, 577–660.

Barwise, J. (1993). Everyday reasoning and logical inference. *Behavioral and Brain Sciences*, 16, 337–338.

Bauer, M. I., & Johnson-Laird, P. N. (1993). How diagrams can improve reasoning. *Psychological Science*, 4, 372–378.

Bell, V., & Johnson-Laird, P. N. (1998). A model theory of modal reasoning. *Cognitive Science*, 22, 25–51.

Birney, D., & Halford, G. S. (2002). Cognitive complexity of suppositional reasoning: An application of relational complexity to the knight-knave task. *Thinking and Reasoning*, 8, 109–134.

Braine, M. D. S. (1978). On the relation between the natural logic of reasoning and standard logic. *Psychological Review*, 85, 1–21.

Bransford, J. D., Barclay, J. R., & Franks, J. J. (1972). Sentence memory: A constructive versus an interpretive approach. *Cognitive Psychology*, 3, 193–209.

Bucciarelli, M., & Johnson-Laird, P. N. (1999). Strategies in syllogistic reasoning. *Cognitive Science*, 23, 247–303.

Bucciarelli, M., & Johnson-Laird, P. N. (in press). Naïve deontics: A theory of meaning, representation, and reasoning. *Cognitive Psychology*.

Byrne, R. M. J. (2002). Mental models and counterfactual thoughts about what might have been. *Trends in Cognitive Sciences*, 6, 426–431.

Byrne, R. M. J., Espino, O., & Santamaría, C. (1999). Counterexamples and the suppression of inferences. *Journal of Memory and Language*, 40, 347–373.

Byrne, R. M. J., & Handley, S. J. (1997). Reasoning strategies for suppositional deductions. *Cognition*, 62, 1–49.

Byrne, R. M. J., & Johnson-Laird, P. N. (1989). Spatial reasoning. *Journal of Memory and Language*, 28, 564–575.

Byrne, R. M. J., & McEleney, A. (2000). Counterfactual thinking about actions and failures to act. *Journal of Experimental Psychology: Learning, Memory, and Cognition*, 26, 1318–1331.

Byrne, R. M. J., & Tasso, A. (1999). Deductive reasoning with factual, possible, and counterfactual conditionals. *Memory and Cognition*, 27, 726–740.

Carreiras, M., & Santamaría, C. (1997). Reasoning about relations: Spatial and nonspatial problems. *Thinking and Reasoning*, 3, 191–208.

Cheng, P. W. (1997). From covariation to causation: A causal power theory. *Psychological Review*, 104, 367–405.

Cherubini, P., & Johnson-Laird, P. N. (2004). Does everyone love everyone? The psychology of iterative reasoning. *Thinking and Reasoning*, 10, 31–53.

Cosmides, L., & Tooby, J. (1996). Are humans good intuitive statisticians after all? Rethinking some conclusions from the literature on judgment under uncertainty. *Cognition*, 58, 1–73.

Craik, K. (1943). *The nature of explanation*. Cambridge: Cambridge University Press.

Cummins, D. D., Lubart, T., Alksnis, O., & Rist, R. (1991). Conditional reasoning and causation. *Memory and Cognition*, 19, 274–282.

de Kleer, J. (1977). Multiple representations of knowledge in a mechanics problem-solver. *International Joint Conference on Artificial Intelligence*, 299–304.

Deutsch, D. (1997). *The fabric of reality: The science of parallel universes – and its implications*. New York: Penguin Books.

Ehrlich, K. (1996). Applied mental models in human–computer interaction. In J. Oakhill & A. Garnham (Eds.), *Mental models in cognitive science*. Mahwah, NJ: Erlbaum.

Einhorn, H. J., & Hogarth, R. M. (1978). Confidence in judgment: Persistence of the illusion of validity. *Psychological Review*, 85, 395–416.

Erickson, J. R. (1974). A set analysis theory of behaviour in formal syllogistic reasoning tasks. In R. Solso (Ed.), *Loyola symposium on cognition* (Vol. 2). Hillsdale, NJ: Erlbaum.

Espino, O., Santamaría, C., & García-Madruga, J. A. (2000). Activation of end terms in syllogistic reasoning. *Thinking and Reasoning*, 6, 67–89.

Espino, O., Santamaría, C., Meseguer, E., & Carreiras, M. (2000). Eye movements during syllogistic reasoning. In J. A. García-Madruga, N. Carriedo, & M. J. González-Labra (Eds.), *Mental models in reasoning* (pp. 179–188). Madrid: Universidad Nacional de Educación a Distancia.

Evans, J. St. B. T. (1993). The mental model theory of conditional reasoning: Critical appraisal and revision. *Cognition*, 48, 1–20.

Evans, J. St. B. T. (2000). What could and could not be a strategy in reasoning. In W. S. Schaeken, G. De Vooght, A. Vandierendonck, & G. d'Ydewalle (Eds.), *Deductive reasoning and strategies*. (pp. 1–22) Mahwah, NJ: Erlbaum.

Evans, J. St. B. T., Handley, S. J., Harper, C. N. J., & Johnson-Laird, P. N. (1999). Reasoning about necessity and possibility: A test of the mental model theory of deduction. *Journal of Experimental Psychology: Learning, Memory, and Cognition*, 25, 1495–1513.

Evans, J. St. B. T., & Over, D. E. (1996). *Rationality and reasoning*. Hove, East Sussex: Psychology Press.

Falk, R. (1992). A closer look at the probabilities of the notorious three prisoners. *Cognition*, 43, 197–223.

Forbus, K. (1985). Qualitative process theory. In D. G. Bobrow (Ed.), *Qualitative reasoning about physical systems*. Cambridge, MA: MIT Press.

García-Madruga, J. A., Moreno, S., Carriedo, N., Gutiérrez, F., & Johnson-Laird, P. N. (2001). Are conjunctive inferences easier than disjunctive inferences? A comparison of rules and models. *Quarterly Journal of Experimental Psychology, 54A*, 613–632.

Garnham, A. (1987). *Mental models as representations of discourse and text*. Chichester, UK: Ellis Horwood.

Garnham, A. (2001). *Mental models and the interpretation of anaphora*. Hove, UK: Psychology Press.

Garnham, A., & Oakhill, J. V. (1996). The mental models theory of language comprehension. In B. K. Britton & A. C. Graesser (Eds.), *Models of understanding text* (pp. 313–339). Hillsdale, NJ: Erlbaum.

Gentner, D., & Gentner, D. R. (1983). Flowing waters or teeming crowds: Mental models of electricity. In D. Gentner & A. L. Stevens (Eds.), *Mental models*. Hillsdale, NJ: Erlbaum.

Gernsbacher, M. A. (1990). *Language comprehension as structure building*. Hillsdale, NJ: Erlbaum.

Gigerenzer, G., & Hoffrage, U. (1995). How to improve Bayesian reasoning without instruction: Frequency format. *Psychological Review, 102*, 684–704.

Girotto, V., & Gonzalez, M. (2001). Solving probabilistic and statistical problems: A matter of question form and information structure. *Cognition, 78*, 247–276.

Girotto, V., Johnson-Laird, P. N., Legrenzi, P., & Sonino, M. (2000). Reasoning to consistency: How people resolve logical inconsistencies. In J. A. García-Madruga, N. Carriedo, & M. González-Labra (Eds.), *Mental models in reasoning* (pp. 83–97). Madrid: Universidad Naciónal de Educacion a Distanzia.

Girotto, V., Legrenzi, P., & Johnson-Laird, P. N. (Unpublished studies).

Girotto, V., Mazzocco, A., & Tasso. A. (1997). The effect of premise order in conditional reasoning: A test of the mental model theory. *Cognition, 63*, 1–28.

Glasgow, J. I. (1993). Representation of spatial models for geographic information systems. In N. Pissinou (Ed.), *Proceedings of the ACM Workshop on Advances in Geographic Information Systems* (pp. 112–117). Arlington, VA: Association for Computing Machinery.

Glenberg, A. M., Meyer, M., & Lindem, K. (1987). Mental models contribute to foregrounding during text comprehension. *Journal of Memory and Language, 26*, 69–83.

Goldvarg, Y., & Johnson-Laird, P. N. (2000). Illusions in modal reasoning. *Memory and Cognition, 28*, 282–294.

Goldvarg, Y., & Johnson-Laird, P. N. (2001). Naïve causality: A mental model theory of causal meaning and reasoning. *Cognitive Science, 25*, 565–610.

Goodwin, G., & Johnson-Laird, P. N. (in press). Reasoning about the relations between relations.

Hacking, I. (1975). *The emergence of probability*. Cambridge, UK: Cambridge University Press.

Halford, G. S. (1993). *Children's understanding: The development of mental models*. Hillsdale, NJ: Erlbaum.

Hart, H. L. A., & Honoré, A. M. (1985). *Causation in the law* (2nd ed.). Oxford, UK: Clarendon Press. (First edition published in 1959.)

Hayes, P. J. (1979). *Naive physics I – Ontology for liquids*. Mimeo, Centre pour les études Semantiques et Cognitives, Geneva. (Reprinted in Hobbs, J., & Moore, R. (Eds.). (1985). *Formal theories of the commonsense world*. Hillsdale, NJ: Erlbaum.)

Hegarty, M. (1992). Mental animation: Inferring motion from static diagrams of mechanical systems. *Journal of Experimental Psychology: Learning, Memory, and Cognition, 18*, 1084–1102.

Holland, J. H. (1998). *Emergence: From chaos to order*. Reading, MA: Perseus Books.

Holland, J. H., Holyoak, K. J., Nisbett, R. E., & Thagard, P. R. (1986). *Induction: Processes of inference, learning, and discovery*. Cambridge, MA: MIT Press.

Johnson-Laird, P. N. (1970). The perception and memory of sentences. In J. Lyons (Ed.), *New horizons in linguistics* (pp. 261–270). Harmondsworth: Penguin Books.

Johnson-Laird, P. N. (1975). Models of deduction. In R. Falmagne (Ed.), *Reasoning: Representation and process*. Springdale, NJ: Erlbaum.

Johnson-Laird, P. N. (1983). *Mental models: Towards a cognitive science of language, inference and consciousness*. Cambridge: Cambridge

University Press; Cambridge, MA: Harvard University Press.

Johnson-Laird, P. N. (1993). *Human and machine thinking*. Hillsdale, NJ: Erlbaum.

Johnson-Laird, P. N. (2002). Peirce, logic diagrams, and the elementary operations of reasoning. *Thinking and Reasoning*, 8, 69–95.

Johnson-Laird, P. N. (in press). The history of mental models. In K. Manktelow (Ed.), *Psychology of reasoning: Theoretical and historical perspectives*. London: Psychology Press.

Johnson-Laird, P. N., & Bara, B. G. (1984). Syllogistic inference. *Cognition*, 16, 1–61.

Johnson-Laird, P. N., & Byrne, R. M. J. (1991). *Deduction*. Hillsdale, NJ: Erlbaum.

Johnson-Laird, P. N., & Byrne, R. M. J. (2002). Conditionals: A theory of meaning, pragmatics, and inference. *Psychological Review*, 109, 646–678.

Johnson-Laird, P. N., Byrne, R. M. J., & Tabossi, P. (1989). Reasoning by model: The case of multiple quantification. *Psychological Review*, 96, 658–673.

Johnson-Laird, P. N., & Hasson, U. (2003). Counterexamples in sentential reasoning. *Memory and Cognition*, 31, 1105–1113.

Johnson-Laird, P. N., Legrenzi, P., Girotto, P., & Legrenzi, M. S. (2000). Illusions in reasoning about consistency. *Science*, 288, 531–532.

Johnson-Laird, P. N., Legrenzi, P., Girotto, V., Legrenzi, M., & Caverni, J.-P. (1999). Naive probability: A mental model theory of extensional reasoning. *Psychological Review*, 106, 62–88.

Johnson-Laird, P. N., & Savary, F. (1996). Illusory inferences about probabilities. *Acta Psychologica*, 93, 69–90.

Johnson-Laird, P. N., & Savary, F. (1999). Illusory inferences: A novel class of erroneous deductions. *Cognition*, 71, 191–229.

Johnson-Laird, P. N., & Stevenson, R. (1970). Memory for syntax. *Nature*, 227, 412.

Johnson-Laird, P. N., & Wason, P. C. (Eds.). (1977). *Thinking*. Cambridge, UK: Cambridge University Press.

Kahneman, D., & Frederick, S. (2002). Representativeness revisited: Attribute substitution in intuitive judgment. In T. Gilovich, D. Griffin, & D. Kahneman (Eds.), *Heuristics of intuitive judgment: Extensions and applications*. New York: Cambridge University Press.

Kahneman, D., Slovic, P., & Tversky, A. (Eds.). (1982). *Judgment under uncertainty: Heuristics and biases*. Cambridge, UK: Cambridge University Press.

Kahneman, D., & Tversky, A. (1973). On the psychology of prediction. *Psychological Review*, 80, 237–251.

Kamp, H. (1981). A theory of truth and semantic representation. In J. A. G. Groenendijk, T. M. V. Janssen, & M. B. J. Stokhof (Eds.), *Formal methods in the study of language* (pp. 277–322). Amsterdam: Mathematical Centre Tracts.

Karttunen, L. (1976). Discourse referents. In J. D. McCawley (Ed.), *Syntax and semantics, vol. 7: Notes from the linguistic underground*. New York: Academic Press.

Knauff, M., Fangmeir, T., Ruff, C. C., & Johnson-Laird, P. N. (2003). Reasoning, models, and images: Behavioral measures and cortical activity. *Journal of Cognitive Neuroscience*, 4, 559–573.

Knauff, M., & Johnson-Laird, P. N. (2002). Imagery can impede inference. *Memory and Cognition*, 30, 363–371.

Köhler, W. (1938). *The place of value in a world of facts*. New York: Liveright.

Kroger, J. K., Cohen, J. D., & Johnson-Laird, P. N. (2003). A double dissociation between logic and mathematics. Unpublished MS.

Kuipers, B. (1994). *Qualitative reasoning: Modeling and simulation with incomplete knowledge*. Cambridge, MA: MIT Press.

Legrenzi, P., Girotto, V., & Johnson-Laird, P. N. (2003). Models of consistency. *Psychological Science*, 14, 131–137.

Mackiewicz, R., & Johnson-Laird, P. N. (in press). Deduction, models, and order of premises.

Markovits, H. (1984). Awareness of the "possible" as a mediator of formal thinking in conditional reasoning problems. *British Journal of Psychology*, 75, 367–376.

Marr, D. (1982). *Vision*. San Francisco: Freeman.

Maxwell, J. C. (1911). Diagram. *The Encyclopaedia Britannica, Vol. XVIII*. New York: Encylopaedia Britannica Co.

McCloskey, M., Caramazza, A., & Green, B. (1980). Curvilinear motion in the absence of external forces: Naïve beliefs about the motions of objects. *Science*, 210, 1139–1141.

Metzler, J., & Shepard, R. N. (1982). Transformational studies of the internal representations of three-dimensional objects. In R. N. Shepard & L. A. Cooper (Eds.), *Mental images and their transformations* (pp. 25–71). Cambridge, MA: MIT Press. (Originally published in Solso, R. L. (Ed.). (1974). *Theories in cognitive psychology: The Loyola Symposium*. Hillsdale, NJ: Erlbaum).

Mill, J. S. (1874). *A system of logic, ratiocinative and inductive: Being a connected view of the principles of evidence and the methods of scientific evidence* (8th ed.). New York: Harper. (First edition published 1843.)

Moray, N. (1990). A lattice theory approach to the structure of mental models. *Philosophical Transactions of the Royal Society of London B*, 327, 577–583.

Moray, N. (1999). Mental models in theory and practice. In D. Gopher & A. Koriat (Eds.), *Attention & performance XVII: Cognitive regulation of performance: Interaction of theory and application* (pp. 223–258). Cambridge, MA: MIT Press.

Morris, B. J., & Sloutsky, V. (2002). Children's solutions of logical versus empirical problems: What's missing and what develops? *Cognitive Development*, 16, 907–928.

Neth, H., & Johnson-Laird, P. N. (1999). The search for counterexamples in human reasoning. *Proceedings of the twenty first annual conference of the Cognitive Science Society*, 806.

Newstead, S. E., Ellis, M. C., Evans, J. St. B. T., & Dennis, I. (1997). Conditional reasoning with realistic material. *Thinking and Reasoning*, 3, 49–76.

Newstead, S. E., & Griggs, R. A. (1999). Premise misinterpretation and syllogistic reasoning. *Quarterly Journal of Experimental Psychology*, 52A, 1057–1075.

Newstead, S. E., Handley, S. J., & Buck, E. (1999). Falsifying mental models: Testing the predictions of theories of syllogistic reasoning. *Memory and Cognition*, 27, 344–354.

Ormerod, T. C., & Johnson-Laird, P. N. (in press). How pragmatics modulates the meaning of sentential connectives.

Ormerod, T. C., Manktelow, K. I., & Jones, G. V. (1993). Reasoning with three types of conditional: Biases and mental models. *Quarterly Journal of Experimental Psychology*, 46A, 653–678.

Osherson, D. N. (1974–1976) *Logical abilities in children, vols. 1–4*. Hillsdale, NJ: Erlbaum.

Peirce, C. S. (1903). Abduction and induction. In J. Buchler (Ed.), *Philosophical writings of Peirce*. New York: Dover, 1955.

Peirce, C. S. (1931–1958). *Collected Papers of Charles Sanders Peirce*. 8 vols. Hartshorne, C., Weiss, P., & Burks, A. (Eds.) Cambridge, MA: Harvard University Press.

Peng, K., & Nisbett, R. E. (1999). Culture, dialectics, and reasoning about contradiction. *American Psychologist*, 54, 741–754.

Phillips, L., & Edwards, W. (1966). Conservatism in a simple probability inference task. *Journal of Experimental Psychology*, 72, 346–354.

Polk, T. A., & Newell, A. (1995). Deduction as verbal reasoning. *Psychological Review*, 102, 533–566.

Popper, K. R. (1972). *Objective knowledge*. Oxford, UK: Clarendon.

Richardson, J., & Ormerod, T. C. (1997). Rephrasing between disjunctives and conditionals: Mental models and the effects of thematic content. *Quarterly Journal of Experimental Psychology*, 50A, 358–385.

Roberts, M. J. (2000). Strategies in relational inference. *Thinking and Reasoning*, 6, 1–26.

Roberts, M. J. (in press). Falsification and mental models: It depends on the task. In W. Schaeken, A. Vandierendonck, W. Schroyens, & G. d'Ydewalle (Eds.), *The mental models theory of reasoning: Refinement and extensions*. Mahwah, NJ: Erlbaum.

Rouse, W. B., & Hunt, R. M. (1984). Human problem solving in fault diagnosis tasks. In W. B. Rouse (Ed.), *Advances in man–machine systems research*. Greenwich, CT: JAI Press.

Santamaría, C., & Johnson-Laird, P. N. (2000). An antidote to illusory inferences. *Thinking and Reasoning*, 6, 313–333.

Schaeken, W. S., De Vooght, G., Vandierendonck, A., & d'Ydewalle, G. (Eds.). (1999). *Deductive reasoning and strategies*. Mahwah, NJ: Erlbaum.

Schaeken, W. S., Johnson-Laird, P. N., & d'Ydewalle, G. (1996). Mental models and temporal reasoning. *Cognition*, 60, 205–234.

Schwartz, D., & Black, J. B. (1996). Analog imagery in mental model reasoning: Depictive models. *Cognitive Psychology*, 30, 154–219.

Shimojo, S., & Ichikawa, S. (1989). Intuitive reasoning about probability: Theoretical and experimental analyses of the 'problem of three prisoners'. *Cognition*, 32, 1–24.

Sloman, S. A. (1996). The empirical case for two systems of reasoning. *Psychological Bulletin, 119*, 3–22.

Sloutsky, V. M., & Goldvarg, Y. (1999). Effects of externalization on representation of indeterminate problems. In M. Hahn & S. Stones (Eds.), *Proceedings of the 21st annual conference of the Cognitive Science Society* (pp. 695–700). Mahwah, NJ: Erlbaum.

Stanovich, K. E. (1999). *Who is rational? Studies of individual differences in reasoning.* Mahwah, NJ: Erlbaum.

Stenning, K. (2002). *Seeing reason: Image and language in learning to think.* Oxford: Oxford University Press.

Stenning, K., & Yule, P. (1997). Image and language in human reasoning: A syllogistic illustration. *Cognitive Psychology, 34*, 109–159.

Stevenson, R. J. (1993). *Language, thought and representation.* New York: Wiley.

Störring, G. (1908). Experimentelle Untersuchungen über einfache Schlussprozesse. *Archiv für die gesamte Psychologie, 11*, 1–27.

Suppes, P. (1970). *A probabilistic theory of causality.* Amsterdam: North-Holland.

Tversky, A., & Kahneman, D. (1973). Availability: A heuristic for judging frequency and probability. *Cognitive Psychology, 5*, 207–232.

Tversky, A., & Kahneman, D. (1982). Causal schemas in judgements under uncertainty. In D. Kahneman, P. Slovic, & A. Tversky (Eds), *Judgement under uncertainty: Heuristics and biases* (pp. 117–128). Cambridge, Cambridge University Press.

Tversky, A., & Kahneman, D. (1983). Extensional versus intuitive reasoning: The conjunction fallacy in probability judgment. *Psychological Review, 90*, 292–315.

Vadeboncoeur, I., & Markovits, H. (1999). The effect of instructions and information retrieval on accepting the premises in a conditional reasoning task. *Thinking and Reasoning, 5*, 97–113.

Van der Henst, J-B., Yang, Y., & Johnson-Laird, P. N. (2002). Strategies in sentential reasoning. *Cognitive Science, 26*, 425–468.

Vandierendonck, A., & De Vooght, G. (1997). Working memory constraints on linear reasoning with spatial and temporal contents. *Quarterly Journal of Experimental Psychology, 50A*, 803–820.

Vandierendonck, A., De Vooght, G., Desimpelaere, C., & Dierckx, V. (1999). Model construction and elaboration in spatial linear syllogisms. In W. S. Schaeken, G. De Vooght, A. Vandierendonck, & G. d'Ydewalle (Eds.), *Deductive reasoning and strategies* (pp. 191–207). Mahwah, NJ: Erlbaum.

Vosniadou, S., & Brewer, W. F. (1992). Mental models of the earth: A study of conceptual change in childhood. *Cognitive Psychology, 24*, 535–585.

Walsh, C. R., & Johnson-Laird, P. N. (2004). Coreference and reasoning. *Memory and Cognition, 32*, 96–106.

Wason, P. C., & Johnson-Laird, P. N. (1972). *The psychology of reasoning.* Cambridge, MA: Harvard University Press.

Webber, B. L. (1978). Description formation and discourse model synthesis. In D. L. Waltz (Ed.), *Theoretical issues in natural language processing* (vol. 2). New York: Association for Computing Machinery.

Wittgenstein, L. (1922). *Tractatus logico-philosophicus.* London: Routledge & Kegan Paul.

Yang, Y., & Johnson-Laird, P. N. (2000). How to eliminate illusions in quantified reasoning. *Memory and Cognition, 28*, 1050–1059.

CHAPTER 10

Visuospatial Reasoning

Barbara Tversky

Visuospatial reasoning is not simply a matter of running to retrieve a fly ball or wending a way through a crowd or plotting a path to a destination or stacking suitcases in a car trunk. It is a matter of determining whether gears will mesh (Schwartz & Black, 1996a), understanding how a car brake works (Heiser & Tversky, 2002), discovering how to destroy a tumor without destroying healthy tissue (Duncker, 1945; Gick & Holyoak, 1980, 1983), and designing a museum (Suwa & Tversky, 1997). Perhaps more surprising, it is also a matter of deciding whether a giraffe is more intelligent than a tiger (Banks & Flora, 1977; Paivio, 1978), whether one event is later than another (Boroditsky, 2000), and whether a conclusion follows logically from its premises (Barwise & Etchemendy, 1995; Johnson-Laird, 1983). All these abstract inferences, and more, appear to be based on spatial reasoning. Why is that? People begin to acquire knowledge about space and the things in it probably before they enter the world. Indeed, spatial knowledge is critical to survival and spatial inference critical to effective survival. Perhaps because of the (literal) ubiquity of spatial reasoning, perhaps because of the naturalness of mapping abstract elements and relations to spatial ones, spatial reasoning serves as a basis for abstract knowledge and inference. The prevalence of spatial figures of speech in everyday talk attests to that: We feel close to some people and remote from others; we try to keep our spirits up, to perform at the peak of our powers, to avoid falling into depressions, pits, or quagmires; we enter fields that are wide open, struggling to stay on top of things and not get out of depth. Right now, in this section, we establish fuzzy boundaries for the current field of inquiry.

Reasoning

Before the research, a few words about the words are in order. The core of *reasoning* seems to be, as Bruner put it years ago, going beyond the information given (Bruner, 1973). Of course, nearly every human activity requires going beyond the information given. The simplest recognition or generalization task, as well as the simplest action, requires going beyond the information given, for, according to a far more ancient saying, you never step into the same river twice. Yet many of these tasks and actions do not feel cognitive, do not feel like reasoning. However, the border between perceptual and cognitive processes may be harder to establish than the borders between countries in conflict. Fortunately, psychology is typically free of territorial politics, and so establishing boundaries between perception and cognition is not essential. There seems to be a tacit understanding as to what counts as perceptual and what as cognitive, although for these categories just as for simpler ones, such as chairs and cups, the centers of the category enjoy more consensus than the borders. Invoking principles or requirements for the boundaries between perception and cognition – consciousness, for example – seems to entail more controversy than the separation into territories.

How do we go beyond the information given? Going beyond the information given does not necessarily mean adding information. One way to go beyond the information given is to transform the information given. This is the concern of the earlier part of the manuscript. Going beyond the information given can also mean transforming the given information, sometimes according to rules, as in deductive reasoning. Another way to go beyond the information given is to make inferences or judgments from it. Inference and judgment are the concerns of the later part of the manuscript. Now some more distinctions regarding the *visuospatial* portion of the title are made.

Representations and Transformations

Truths are hard to come by in science, but useful fictions and approximate truths abound. One of these is the distinction between representations and transformations, between information and processes, between data and the operations performed on data. Representations place limits on transformations as they select and structure the information captured from the world or the mind. Distinguishing representations and transformations, even under direct observation of the brain, is another distinction fraught with complexity and controversy. Evidence brought to bear for one can frequently be reinterpreted as evidence for the other (e.g., Anderson, 1978). Both representations and transformations themselves can each be decomposed into representations and transformations. Despite these complications, the distinction has been a productive way to think about psychological processes. In fact, it is a distinction that runs deep in human cognition, captured in language as subject and predicate and in behavior as agent/object and action. The distinction will prove useful here more than as a way of organizing the literature (for related discussion, see Doumas & Hummel, Chap. 4).

It has been argued that the very establishment of representations entails inferential operations. A significant example is the Gestalt principles of perceptual organization – grouping by similarity, proximity, common fate, and good continuity – that contribute to scene segmentation and representation. These are surely a form of visuospatial inference. Representations are internal translations of external stimuli (or internal data); as such, they not only eliminate information from the external world – they also add to it and distort it in the service of interpretation or behavior. Thus, if inference is to be understood in terms of operating on or manipulating information to draw new conclusions, then it begins in the periphery of the sensory systems with leveling and sharpening and feature detection and organization. Nevertheless, the field has accepted a level of description of representations and transformations – one higher than the levels of sensory and perceptual processing; that level is reflected here.

Visuospatial

What makes visuospatial representations visuospatial? Visuospatial transformations visuospatial? First and foremost, visuospatial representations capture visuospatial properties of the world. They do this in a way that preserves, at least in part, the spatial–structural relations of that information (see Johnson-Laird, 1983; Pierce in Houser & Kloesel, 1992). This means that visuospatial properties that are close or above or below in the world preserve those relations in the representations. Visual includes static properties of objects, such as shape, texture, and color, or between objects and reference frames, such as distance and direction. It also includes dynamic properties of objects such as direction, path, and manner of movement. By this account, visuospatial transformations are those that change or use visuospatial information. Many of these properties of static and dynamic objects and of spatial relations between objects are available from modalities other than vision. This may explain why well-adapted visually impaired individuals are not disadvantaged at many spatial tasks (e.g., Klatzky, Golledge, Cicinelli, & Pellegrino, 1995). Visuospatial representations are regarded as contrasting with other forms of representation – notably linguistic. The similarities (e.g., Talmy, 1983, 2001) and differences between visuospatial and linguistic representations provide insights into both.

Demonstrating properties of internal representations and transformations is tricky for another reason; representations are many steps from either (controlled) input or (observed) output. For these reasons, the study of internal representations and processes was eschewed not only by behaviorists but also by experimentalists. It was one of the first areas to flourish after the so-called Cognitive Revolution of the 1960s with a flurry of innovative techniques to demonstrate form and content of internal representations and the transformations performed on them. It is to that research that we now turn.

Representations and Transformations

Visuospatial reasoning can be approached bottom-up by studying the elementary representations and processes that presumably form the building blocks for more complex reasoning. It can also be approached top-down by studying complex reasoning that has a visuospatial basis. Both approaches have been productive. We begin with elements.

Imagery as Internalized Perception

The major research tradition studying visuospatial reasoning from a bottom-up perspective has been the *imagery* program pioneered by Shepard (see Finke & Shepard, 1986; Shepard & Cooper, 1982; Shepard & Podgorny, 1978, for overviews) and Kosslyn (1980, 1994b), which has aimed to demonstrate parallels between visual perception and visual imagery. There are two basic tenets of the approach, one regarding representations and the other regarding operations on representations: that mental images resemble percepts and that mental transformations on images resemble observable changes in things in the world, as in mental rotation, or perceptual processes performed on things in the world, as in mental scanning. Kosslyn (1994b) has persisted in these aims, more recently demonstrating that many of the same neural structures are used for both. Not the demonstrations per se, but the interpretations of them have met with controversy (e.g., Pylyshyn, 1978, 1981). In attempting to demonstrate the similarities between imagery and perception, the imagery program has focused both on properties of objects and on characteristics of transformations on objects – the former, representations, and the latter, operations or transformations. The thrust of the research programs has been to demonstrate that images are like internalized perceptions and transformations of images like transformations of things in the world.

REPRESENTATIONS

In the service of demonstrating that images preserve characteristics of perceptions, Shepard and his colleagues brought evidence from similarity judgments as support. They demonstrated "second-order isomorphisms," similarity spaces for perceived and imagined stimuli that have the same structure, that is, are fit by the same underlying multidimensional space (Shepard & Chipman, 1970). For example, similarity judgments of shapes of cutouts of states conform to the same multidimensional space as similarity judgments of imagined shapes of states. The same logic was used to show that color is preserved in images, as well as configurations of faces (see Gordon & Hayward, 1973; Shepard, 1975). Similar reasoning was used to demonstrate qualitative differences between pictorial and verbal representations in a task requiring sequential same–different judgments on pairs of schematic faces and names (Tversky, 1969). The pictorial and verbal similarity of the set of faces was orthogonal so the "different" responses were a clue to the underlying representation; times to respond "different" were faster when more features between the pairs differ. These times indicated that when participants expected the target (second) stimulus would be a picture, they encoded the first stimulus pictorially, whether it had been a picture of a face or its name. The converse also held: When the target stimulus was expected to be a name, participants coded the first stimulus verbally irrespective of its presented modality.

To demonstrate that mental images preserve properties of percepts, Kosslyn and his colleagues presented evidence from studies of reaction times to detect features of imagined objects. One aim is to show that properties that take longer to verify in percepts take longer to identify in images. For example, when participants were instructed to construct images of named animals in order to judge whether the animal had a particular part, they verified large parts of animals, such as the back of a rabbit, faster than small but highly associated ones, such as the whiskers of a rat. When participants were not instructed to use imagery to make judgments, they verified small associated parts faster than large ones. When not instructed to use imagery, participants used their general world knowledge to make judgments (Kosslyn, 1976). Importantly, when the participants explicitly used imagery, they took longer to verify parts, large or small, than when they relied on world knowledge. Additional support for the claim that images preserve properties of percepts comes from tasks requiring construction of images. Constructing images takes longer when there are more parts to the image, even when the same figure can be constructed from more or fewer parts (Kosslyn, 1980).

The imagery-as-internalized-perception has proved to be too narrow a view of the variety of visuospatial representations. In accounting for syllogistic reasoning, Johnson-Laird (1983) proposed that people form mental models of the situations described by the propositions (see Johnson-Laird, Chap. 9). Mental models contrast with classic images in that they are more schematic than classical images. Entities are represented as tokens, not as likenesses, and spatial relations are approximate, almost qualitative. A similar view was developed to account for understanding text and discourse, then listeners and readers construct schematic models of the situations described (e.g., Kintsch & van Dijk, 1983; Zwaan & Radvansky, 1998). As is seen, visuospatial mental representations of environments, devices, and processes are often schematic, even distorted, rather than detailed and accurate internalized perceptions.

TRANSFORMATIONS

Here, the logic is the same for most research programs and in the spirit of Shepard's notion of second-order isomorphisms: to demonstrate that the times to make particular visuospatial judgments in memory increase with the times to observe or perform the transformations in the world. The dramatic first demonstration was mental rotation (Shepard & Metzler, 1971): time to judge whether two figures in different orientations (Figure 10.1) are the same or mirror images correlate linearly with the angular distance between the orientations of the figures. The linearity of the relationship – 12 points on a straight line – suggests smooth, continuous mental transformation. Although linear functions have been obtained for the original stimuli, strings of 10 cubes with two bends, monotonic, but not

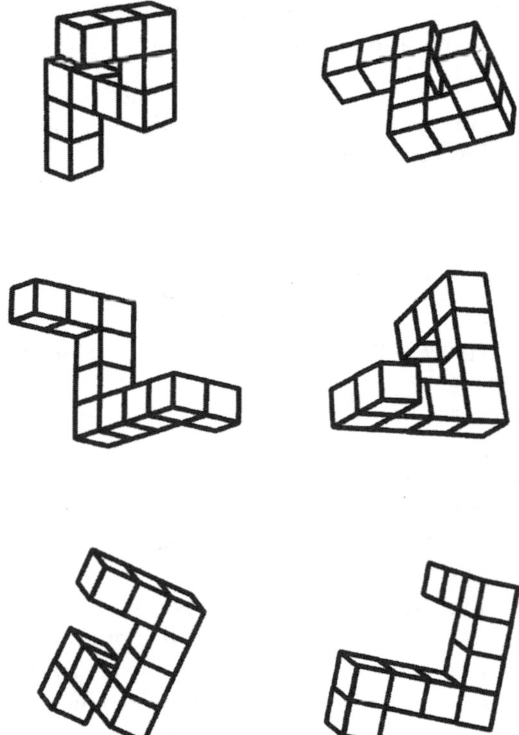

Figure 10.1. Mental rotation task of Shepard and Metzler (1971). Participants determine whether members of each pair can be rotated into congruence.

linear, functions are obtained for other stimuli such as letters (Shepard & Cooper, 1982). There are myriad possible mental transformations, only a few of which have been studied in detail. They may be classified into mental transformations on other objects and individuals, and mental transformations on oneself. In both cases, the transformations may be global, wholistic, or of the entire entity – the transformations may be operations on parts of entities.

Mental Transformations on Objects. Rotation is not the only transformation that objects in the world undergo. They can undergo changes of size, shape, color, internal features, position, combination, and more. Mental performance of some of these transformations has been examined. The time to mentally compare the shapes of two rectangles differing in size increases as the actual size difference between them increases (Bundesen, Larsen, & Farrell, 1981; Moyer, 1973). New objects can be constructed in imagery, which is a skill presumably related to design and creativity (e.g., Finke, 1990, 1993). In a well-known example, Finke, Pinker, and Farah (1989) asked students to imagine a capital letter J centered under an upside-down grapefruit half. Students reported "seeing" an umbrella. Even without instructions to image, certain tasks spontaneously encourage formation of visual images. For example, when participants are asked whether a described spatial array, such as *star above plus*, matches a depicted one, response times indicate that they transform the description into a depiction when given sufficient time to mentally construct the situation (Glushko & Cooper, 1978; Tversky, 1975).

In the cases of mental rotation, mental movement, and mental size transformations, objects or object parts undergo imagined transformations. There is also evidence that objects can be mentally scanned in a continuous manner. In a popular task introduced by Kosslyn and his colleagues, participants memorize a map of an island with several landmarks such as a well and a cave. Participants are then asked to conjure an image of the map and to imagine looking first at the well and then mentally scanning from the well to the cave. The general finding is that mental scanning between two imagined landmarks increases linearly as the distance between them increases (Denis & Kosslyn, 1999; Kosslyn, Ball, & Rieser, 1978; Figure 10.2). The phenomenon holds for spatial arrays established by description rather than depiction – again, under instructions to form and use images (Denis, 1996). Mental scanning occurs for arrays in depth and for flat perspectives on 3D arrays (Pinker, 1980). In the previous studies, participants were trained to mentally scan and directed to do so, leaving open the question of whether it occurs spontaneously. It seems to do so in a task requiring direction judgments on remembered arrays. Participants first saw an array of dots. After the dots disappeared, an arrow appeared on the screen. The task was to say whether the arrow pointed to the previous location of a dot. Reaction times increased with distance of the arrow to the likely dot, suggesting that participants mentally scan from the arrow to answer the question (Finke & Pinker, 1982, 1983). Mental scanning may be part of catching or hitting the ball in baseball, tennis, and other sports.

Applying Several Mental Transformations. Other mental transformations on objects are possible – for example, altering the internal configuration of an object. To solve some problems, such as geometric analogies, people need to apply more than one mental transformation to a figure to obtain the answer. In most cases, the order of applying the transformations is optional; that is, first rotating and then moving a figure yield the same answer as first moving and then rotating. Nevertheless, people have a preferred order for performing a sequence of mental transformations, and when this order is violated, both errors and performance time increase (Novick & Tversky, 1987). What accounts for the preferred order? Although the mental transformations are performed in working memory, the determinants of order do not seem to be related to working memory demands. *Move* is one of the least demanding transformations, and it is typically performed first, whereas *rotate* is one of the most difficult transformations and is performed second. Then transformations of intermediate difficulty are performed. What correlates with the order of applying successive mental transformations is the order of drawing. *Move* determines where the pencil is to be put on the paper, the first act of drawing. *Rotate* determines the direction in which the first stroke should be taken, and it is the next transformation. The next transformations to be applied are those that determine the size of the figure and its internal details (*remove, add part, change size, change shading, add part*). Although the mental transformations have been tied to perceptual processes, the ordering of performing them appears to be tied to a motor process, the act of drawing or constructing a figure. This finding presaged later work showing that complex visuospatial reasoning has not only perceptual, but also motor, foundations.

Mental Transformations of Self. That mental imagery is both perceptual and motor follows from broadening the basic tenets of the classical account for imagery. According to that account, mental processes are internalizations of external or externally driven processes – perceptual ones according to the classic view (e.g., in the chapter title of Shepard & Podgorny, 1978, "Cognitive processes that resemble perceptual processes"). The acts of drawing a figure or constructing an object entail both perceptual and motor processes working in concert as do many other activities performed in both real and virtual worlds, from shaking hands to wayfinding.

Evidence for mental transformations of self, or motor imagery, rather than or in addition to visual imagery has come from a variety of tasks. The time taken to judge whether a depicted hand is right or left correlates with the time taken to move the hand into the depicted orientation as if participants were mentally moving their hands in order to make the right/left decision (Parsons, 1987b; Sekiyama, 1982). Mental reorientation of one's body has been used to account for reaction times to judge whether a left or right arm is extended in pictures of bodies in varying orientations from upright (Parsons, 1987a). In those studies, reaction times depend on the angle of rotation and the degree of rotation. For some orientations, notably the picture plane, the degree of rotation from upright has no effect. This allows dissociating mental transformations of other, in this case, mental rotation from mental transformations of self, in this case, perspective transformations, for the latter do yield increases in reaction times with degree of rotation from upright (Zacks, Mires, Tversky, & Hazeltine, 2000; Zacks & Tversky, in press). Imagining oneself interacting with a familiar object such as a ball or a razor selectively activates left inferior parietal and sensorimotor cortex, whereas imagining another interacting with the same objects selectively activates right inferior parietal,

Figure 10.2. Mental scanning. Participants memorize map and report time to mentally scan from one feature to another (after Kosslyn, Ball, & Rieser, 1978).

precuneus, posterior cingulated, and frontopolar cortex (Ruby & Decety, 2001).

There have been claims that visual and motor imagery, or as we have put it, mental transformations of object and of self, share the same underlying mechanisms (Wexler, Kosslyn, & Berthoz, 1998; Wolschlager & Wolschlager, 1998). For example, performing clockwise physical rotations facilitates performing clockwise mental rotations but interferes with performing counterclockwise mental rotations. However, this may be because planning, performing, and monitoring the physical rotation require both perceptual and motor imagery. The work of Zacks and collaborators (Zacks et al., 2000; Zacks & Tversky, in press) and Ruby and Decety (2001) suggests that these two classes of mental transformations are dissociable. Other studies directly comparing the two systems support their dissociability: The consequences of using one can be different from the consequences of using the other (Schwartz, 1999; Schwartz & Black, 1999; Schwartz & Holton, 2000). When people imagine wide and narrow glasses filled to the same level and are asked which would spill first when tilted, they are typically incorrect from visual imagery. However, if they close their eyes and imagine tilting each glass until it spills, they correctly tilt a wide glass less than a narrow one (Schwartz & Black, 1999). Think of turning a car versus turning a boat. To imagine making a car turn right, you must imagine rotating the steering wheel to the right; however, to imagine making a boat turn right, you must imagine moving the rudder lever left. In mental rotation of left and right hands, the shortest motor path accounts for the reaction times better than the shortest visual path (Parsons, 1987b). Mental enactment also facilitates memory, even for actions described verbally (Englekamp, 1998). Imagined motor transformations presumably underlie mental practice of athletic and musical routines – techniques known to benefit performance (e.g., Richardson, 1967).

The reasonable conclusion, then, is that both internalized perceptual transformations and internalized motor transformations can serve as bases for transformations in mental imagery. Perceptual and motor imagery can work in concert in imagery, just as perceptual and motor processes work in concert in conducting the activities of life.

ELEMENTARY TRANSFORMATIONS

The imagery-as-internalized-perception approach has provided evidence for myriad mental transformations. We have reviewed evidence for a number of mental perceptual transformations: scanning, changing orientation, location, size, shape, color; constructing from parts; and rearranging parts. Then we have motor transformations: motions of bodies, wholes, or parts. This approach has the potential to provide a catalog of elementary mental transformations that are simple inferences and that can combine to enable complex inferences.

The work on inference, judgment, and problem solving will suggest transformations that have yet to be explored in detail. Here, we propose a partial catalog of candidates for elementary properties of representations and transformations, expanding from the research reviewed:

- *Determining static properties of entities:* figure/ground, symmetry, shape, internal configuration, size, color, texture, and more
- *Determining relations between static entities*:
  - With respect to a frame of reference: location, direction, distance, and more
  - With respect to other entities, comparing size, color, shape, texture, location, orientation, similarity, and other attributes
- *Determining relations of dynamic and static entities*:
  - With respect to other entities or to a reference frame: direction, speed, acceleration, manner, intersection/collision
- *Performing transformations on entities:* change location (scanning); change perspective, orientation, size, shape; moving wholes; reconfiguring parts; zooming; enacting
- *Performing transformations on self:* change of perspective, change of location, change of size, shape, reconfiguring parts, enacting

INDIVIDUAL DIFFERENCES

Yes, people vary in spatial ability. However, spatial ability does not contrast with verbal ability; in other words, someone can be good or poor at both, as well as good in one and poor in the other. In addition, spatial ability (like verbal ability) is not a single, unitary ability. Some of the separate spatial abilities differ qualitatively; that is, they map well onto the kinds of mental transformations they require. A meta-analysis of a number of factor analyses of spatial abilities yielded three recurring factors (Linn & Peterson, 1986): spatial perception, spatial visualization, and mental rotation. Rod-and-frame and water-level tasks load high on spatial perception; this factor seems to reflect choice of frame of reference, within an object or extrinsic. Performance on embedded figures, finding simple figures in more complex ones, loads high on spatial visualization, and performance on mental rotation tasks naturally loads high on the mental rotation factor. As frequently as they are found, these three abilities do not span the range of spatial competencies. Yet another partially independent visuospatial ability is visuospatial memory, remembering the layout of display (e.g., Betrancourt & Tversky, in press). The number of distinct spatial abilities as well as their distinctness remain controversial (e.g., Carroll, 1993; Hegarty & Waller, in press).

More recent work explores the relations of spatial abilities to the kinds of mental transformations that have been distinguished – for example, imagining an object rotate versus imagining changing one's own orientation. The mental transformations, in turn, are often associated with different brain regions (e.g., Zacks, Mires, Tversky, & Hazeltine, 2000; Zacks, Ollinger, Sheridan, & Tversky, 2002; Zacks & Tversky, in press). Kozhevniikov, Kosslyn, and Shepard (in press) proposed that spatial visualization and mental rotation correspond respectively to the two major visual pathways in the brain – the ventral "what" pathway underlying object recognition and the dorsal "where" pathway underlying spatial location. Interestingly, scientists and engineers score relatively high on mental rotation and artists score relatively high on spatial visualization. Similarly, architects and designers score higher than average on embedded figure tasks but not on mental rotation (Suwa & Tversky, 2003). Associating spatial ability measures to mental transformations and brain regions are promising directions toward a systematic account of spatial abilities.

Inferences

Inferences from Observing Motion in Space

To ensure effective survival, in addition to perceiving the world as it is we need to also anticipate the world that will be. This entails inference – inferences from visuospatial information. Some common inferences, such as determining where to intersect a flying object – in particular, a fly ball (e.g., McBeath, Shaffer, & Kaiser, 1995) – or what moving parts belong to the same object (e.g., Spelke, Vishton, & von Hofsten, 1995) are beyond the scope of the chapter. From simple, abstract motions of geometric figures, people, even babies, infer causal impact and basic ontological categories – notably, inanimate and animate. A striking demonstration of perception of causality comes from the work of Michotte (1946/1963; see Buehner & Cheng, Chap. 7). Participants watch films of a moving object, A, coming into contact with a stationary object, B. When object B moves immediately, continuing the direction of motion suggested by object A, people perceive A as launching B, A as causing B to move. When A stops so both A and B are stationary before B begins to move, the perception of a causal connection between A's motion and B's is lost; their movements are seen as independent events. This is a forceful demonstration of immediate perception of causality from highly abstract actions, as well as of the conditions for perception of causality. What seems to underlie the perception of causality is the perception that object A *acts on* object B. Actions on objects turn out to be the basis for segmenting events into parts (Zacks, Tversky, & Iyer, 2001).

In Michotte's (1946/1963) demonstrations, the timing of the contact between the initially moving object and the stationary object that begins to move later is critical. If A stops moving considerably before B begins to move, then B's motion is perceived to be independent of A's. B's movement in this case is seen as self-propelled. Self-propelled movement is possible only for animate agents, or, more recently in the history of humanity, for machines. Possible paths and trajectories of animate motion differ from those for inanimate motion. Preschool children can infer which motion paths are appropriate for animate and inanimate motion, and even for abstract stimuli; they also offer sensible explanations for their inferences (Gelman, Durgin, & Kaufman, 1995).

From abstract motion paths, adults can make further inferences about what generated the motion. In point-light films, the only thing visible is the movement of lights placed at motion junctures of, for example, the joints of people walking or along branches of bushes swaying. From point-light films, people can determine whether the motion is walking, running, or dancing, of men or of women, of friends (Cutting & Kozlowski, 1977; Johannson, 1973; Kozlowski & Cutting, 1977), of bushes or trees (Cutting, 1986). Surprisingly, from point-light displays of action, people are better at recognizing their own movements than those of friends, suggesting that motor experience contributes to perception of motion (Prasad, Loula, & Shiffrar, 2003). Even abstract films of movements of geometric figures in sparse environments can be interpreted as complex social interactions, such as chasing and bullying, when they are especially designed for that (Heider & Simmel, 1944; Martin & Tversky, 2003; Oatley & Yuill, 1985) or playing hide-and-seek, but interpreting these as intentional actions is not immediate; rather, it requires repeated exposure and possibly instructions to interpret the actions (Martin & Tversky, 2003).

Altogether, simply from abstract motion paths or animated point-light displays, people can infer several basic ontological categories: causal action, animate versus inanimate motion, human motion, motion of males or females and familiar individuals, and social interactions.

Mental Spatial Inferences

INFERENCES IN REAL ENVIRONMENTS

Every kid who has figured out a short-cut, and who has not, has performed a spatial inference (for a more recent overview of kids, see Newcombe & Huttenlocher, 2000). Some of these inferences turn out to be easier than others, often surprisingly. For example, in real environments, inferences about where objects will be in relationship to oneself after imagined movement in the environment turn out to be relatively accurate when the imagined movement is a translation, that is, movement forward or backward aligned with the body. However, if the imagined movement is rotational, a change in orientation, updating is far less accurate (e.g., Presson & Montello, 1994; Reiser, 1989). When asked to imagine walking forward a certain distance, turning, walking forward another distance, and then pointing back to the starting point, participants invariably err by not taking into account the turn in their pointing (Klatzky, Loomis, Beall, Chance, & Golledge, 1998). If they actually move forward, turn, and continue forward, but blindfolded, they point correctly. Spatial updating in real environments is more accurate after translation than after rotation, and updating after rotation is selectively facilitated by physical rotation. This suggests a deep point about spatial inferences and possibly other inferences: that in inference, mental acts interact with physical acts.

GESTURE

Interaction of mind and body in inference is also revealed in gesture. When people describe space but are asked to sit on their hands to prevent gesturing, their speech falters (Rauscher, Krauss, & Chen, 1996), suggesting that the acts of gesturing promote spatial reasoning. Even blind children gesture as they describe spatial layouts (Iverson & Goldin-Meadow, 1997).

The nature of spontaneous gestures suggests how this happens. When describing continuous processes, people make smooth, continuous gestures; when describing discrete ones, people make jagged, discontinuous ones (Alibali, Bassok, Solomon, Syc, & Goldin-Meadow, 1999). For space, people tend to describe environments as if they were traveling through them or as if they were viewing them from above. The plane of their gestures differs in each case in correspondence with the linguistic perspective they adopt (Emmorey, Tversky, & Taylor, 2000). Earlier, mental transformations that appear to be internalized physical transformations, such as those underlying handedness judgments, were described. Here, we also see that actual motor actions affect and reflect the character of mental ones.

INFERENCES IN MENTAL ENVIRONMENTS

The section on inference opened with spatial inferences made in real environments. Often, people make inferences about environments they are not currently in, for example, when they tell a friend how to get to their house and where to find the key when they arrive. For familiar environments, people are quite competent at these sorts of spatial inferences. The mental representations and processes underlying these inferences have been studied for several kinds of environments – notably the immediately surrounding visible or tangible environment and the environment too large to be seen at a glance. These two situations, the space around the body, and the space the body navigates, seem to function differently in our lives, and consequently, to be conceptualized differently (Tversky, 1998).

Spatial updating for the space around the body was first studied using language alone to establish the environments (Franklin & Tversky, 1990). It is significant that language alone, with no specific instructions to form images, was sufficient to establish mental environments that people could update easily and without error. In the prototypical *spatial framework* task, participants read a narrative that describes themselves in a 3D spatial scene, such as a museum or hotel lobby (Franklin & Tversky, 1990; Figure 10.3). The narrative locates and describes objects appropriate to the scene beyond the observer's head, feet, front, back, left, and right (locations chosen randomly). After participants have learned the scenes described by the narratives, they turn to a computer that describes them as turning in the environment so they are now facing a different object. The computer then cues them with direction terms, *front, back, head*, and so on, to which the participants respond with the name of the object now in that direction. Of interest are the times to respond, depending on the direction from the body. The classical imagery account would predict that participants will imagine themselves in

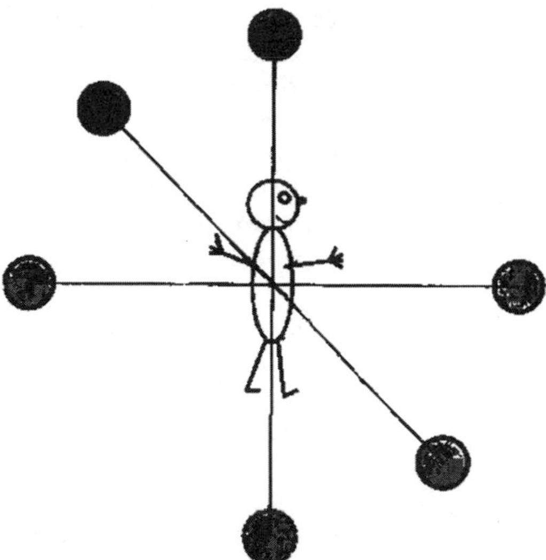

Figure 10.3. Spatial framework situation. Participants read a narrative describing objects around an observer (after Bryant, Tversky, & Franklin, 1992).

the environment facing the selected object and then imagine themselves turning to face each cued object in order to retrieve the object in the cued direction. The imagery account predicts that reaction times should be fastest to the object in front, then to the objects 90 degrees away from front, that is, left, right, head, and feet, and slowest to objects 180 degrees from front, that is, objects to the back. Data from dozens of experiments fail to support that account.

Instead, the data conform to the *spatial framework theory* according to which participants construct a mental spatial framework from extensions of three axes of the body: head/feet, front/back, and left/right. Times to access objects depend on the asymmetries of the body axes as well as the asymmetries of the axes of the world. The front/back and head/feet axes have important perceptual and behavioral asymmetries that are lacking in the left/right axis. The world also has three axes, only one of which is asymmetric, the axis conferred by gravity. For the upright observer, the head/feet axis coincides with the axis of gravity, and so responses to head and feet should be fastest, and they are. According to the spatial framework account, times should be next fastest to the front/back axis and slowest to the left/right axis, the pattern obtained for the prototypical situation. When narratives describe observers as reclining in the scenes, turning from back to side to front, then no axis of the body is correlated with gravity; thus, times depend on the asymmetries of the body, and the pattern changes. Times to retrieve objects in front and back are then fastest because the perceptual and behavioral asymmetries of the front/back axis are most important. This is, the axis that separates the world that can be seen and manipulated from the world that cannot be seen or manipulated.

By now, dozens of experiments have examined patterns of response times to systematic changes in the described spatial environment (e.g., Bryant, Tversky, & Franklin, 1992; Franklin, Tversky, & Coon, 1992). In one variant, narratives described participants at an oblique angle outside the environment looking onto a character (or two!) inside the environment; in that case, none of the axes of the observer's body is correlated with axes of the characters in the narrative, and the reaction times to all directions are equal (Franklin et al., 1992). In another variant, narratives described the scene, a special space house constructed by NASA, as rotating around the observer instead of the observer's turning in the scene (Tversky, Kim, & Cohen, 1999). That condition proved difficult for participants. They took twice as long to update the environment when the environment moved than when the observer moved – a case problematic for pure propositional accounts of mental spatial transformations. Once participants had updated the environment, retrieval times corresponded to the spatial framework pattern.

Yet other experiments have varied the way the environment was conveyed, comparing description, diagram, 3D model, and life (Bryant & Tversky, 1999; Bryant, Tversky, & Lanca, 2001). When the scene is conveyed by narrative, life, or a 3D model, the standard spatial framework pattern obtains. However, when the scene is conveyed by a diagram, participants spontaneously adopt an external perspective on the environment.

Their response times are consonant with performing a mental rotation of the entire environment rather than performing a mental change of their own perspective with respect to a surrounding environment (Bryant & Tversky, 1999). Which viewpoint participants adopt, and consequently which mental transformation they perform, can be altered by instructions. When instructed to do so, participants will adopt the internal perspective embedded in the environment in which the observer turns from a diagram or the external perspective from a model in which the entire environment is rotated with the predicted changes in patterns of retrieval times. Similar findings have been reported by Huttenlocher and Presson (1979), Wraga, Creem, and Proffitt (2000), and Zacks et al. (in press).

ROUTE AND SURVEY PERSPECTIVES

When people are asked to describe environments that are too large to be seen at a glance, they do so from one of two perspectives (Taylor & Tversky, 1992a, 1996). In a *route* perspective, people address the listener as "you," and take "you" on a tour of the environment, describing landmarks relative to your current position in terms of your *front*, *back*, *left*, and *right*. In a *survey* perspective, people take a bird's eye view of the environment and describe locations of landmarks relative to one another in terms of *north*, *south*, *east*, and *west*. Speakers (and writers) often mix perspectives, contrary to linguists who argue that a consistent perspective is needed both for coherent construction of a message and for coherent comprehension (Taylor & Tversky, 1992, 1996; Tversky, Lee, & Mainwaring, 1999). In fact, construction of a mental model is faster when perspective is consistent, but the effect is small and disappears quickly during retrieval from memory (Lee & Tversky, in press). In memory for locations and directions of landmarks, route and survey statements are verified equally quickly and accurately regardless of the perspective of learning, provided the statements are not taken verbatim from the text (Taylor & Tversky, 1992b). For route perspectives, the mental transformation needed to understand the location information is a transformation of self, an egocentric transformation of one's viewpoint in an environment. For survey perspectives, the mental transformation needed to understand the location information is a transformation of other, a kind of mental scanning of an object.

The prevalence of these two perspectives in imagery, the external perspective viewing an object or something that can be represented as an object and the internal perspective viewing an environment from within, is undoubtedly associated with their prevalence in the experience of living. In life, we observe changes in the orientation, size, and configuration of objects in the world and scan them for those changes. In life, we move around in environments, updating our position relative to the locations of other objects in the environment. We are adept at performing the mental equivalents of these actual transformations. There is a natural correspondence between the internal and external perspectives and the mental transformations of self and other, but the human mind is flexible enough to apply either transformation to either perspective. Although we are biased to take an external perspective on objects and mentally transform them and biased to take an internal perspective on environments and mentally transform our bodies with respect to them, we can take internal perspectives on objects and external perspectives on events. The mental world allows perspectives and transformations, whereas the physical world does not. Indeed, conceptualizing a 3D environment that surrounds us and is too large to be seen at once as a small flat object before the eyes, something people, even children, have done for eons whenever they produce a map, is a remarkable feat of the human mind (cf. Tversky, 2000a).

EFFECTS OF LANGUAGE ON SPATIAL THINKING

Speakers of Dutch and other Western languages use both route and survey perspectives. Put differently, they can use either a relative spatial reference system or an absolute (extrinsic) spatial reference system to describe locations of objects in space. Relative systems use the spatial relations "left," "right," "front," and "back" to locate objects; absolute or extrinsic systems use terms equivalent to "north," "south," "east," and "west." A smattering of languages dispersed around the world do not describe locations using "left" and "right" (Levinson, 2003). Instead, they rely on an absolute system, so a speaker of those languages would refer to your coffee cup as the "north" cup rather than the one on "your right." Talk apparently affects thought. Years of talking about space using an absolute spatial reference system have had fascinating consequences for thinking about space. For example, speakers of absolute languages reconstruct a shuffled array of objects relative to extrinsic directions in contrast to speakers of Dutch, who reconstruct the array relative to their own bodies. What's more, when speakers of languages with only extrinsic reference systems are asked to point home after being driven hither and thither, they point with impressive accuracy, in contrast to Dutch speakers, who point at random. The view that the way people talk affects how they think has naturally aroused controversy (see Gleitman & Papafragou, Chap. 26), but is receiving increasing support from a variety of tasks and languages (e.g., Boroditsky, 2001; Boroditsky, Ham, & Ramscar, 2002). If we take a broader perspective, the finding that language affects thought is not as startling. Language is a tool, such as measuring instruments or arithmetic or writing; learning to use these tools also has consequences for thinking.

Judgments

Complex visuospatial thinking is fundamental to a broad range of human activity, from providing directions to the post office and understanding how to operate the latest electronic device to predicting the consequences of chemical bonding or designing a shopping center. Indeed, visuospatial thinking is fundamental to the reasoning processes described in other chapters in this handbook, as discussed in the chapters on similarity (see Goldstone & Son, Chap. 2), categorization (see Medin & Rips, Chap. 3), induction (see Sloman & Lagnado, Chap. 5), analogical reasoning (see Holyoak, Chap. 6), causality (see Buehner & Cheng, Chap. 7), deductive reasoning (see Evans, Chap. 8), mental models (see Johnson-Laird, Chap. 9), and problem solving (see Novick & Bassok, Chap. 14). Fortunately for both reader and author, there is no need to repeat those discussions here.

Distortions as Clues to Reasoning

Another approach to revealing visuospatial reasoning has been to demonstrate the ways that visuospatial representations differ systematically from situations in the world. This approach, which can be called the *distortions* program, contrasts with the classical imagery approach. The aim of the distortions approach is to elucidate the processes involved in constructing and using mental representations by showing their consequences. The distortions approach has focused more on relations between objects and relations between objects and reference frames, as these visuospatial properties seem to require more constructive processes than those for establishing representations of objects. Some systematic distortions have also been demonstrated in representations of objects.

REPRESENTATIONS

Early on, the Gestalt psychologists attempted to demonstrate that memory for figures got distorted in the direction of good figures (see Riley, 1962). This claim was contested and countered by increasingly sophisticated empirical demonstrations. The dispute faded in a resolution: visual stimuli are interpreted, sometimes as good figures; memory tends toward the interpretations. So if o – o is interpreted as "eyeglasses," participants later draw the connection curved, whereas if it is interpreted as "barbells," they do not (Carmichael, Hogan, & Walter,

1932). Little noticed is that the effect does not appear in recognition memory (Prentice, 1954). Since then, and relying on the sophisticated methods developed, there has been more evidence for shape distortion in representations. Shapes that are nearly symmetric are remembered or judged as more symmetric than they actually are, as if people code nearly symmetric objects as symmetric (Freyd & Tversky, 1984; McBeath, Schiano, & Tversky, 1997; Tversky & Schiano, 1989). Given that many of the objects and beings that we encounter are symmetric, but are typically viewed at an oblique angle, symmetry may be a reasonable assumption, although one that is wrong on occasion. Size is compressed in memory (Kerst & Howard, 1978). When portions of objects are truncated by picture frames, the objects are remembered as more complete than they actually were (Intraub, Bender, & Mangels, 1992).

REPRESENTATIONS AND TRANSFORMATIONS: SPATIAL CONFIGURATIONS AND COGNITIVE MAPS

The Gestalt psychologists also produced striking demonstrations that people organize the visual world in principled ways, even when that world is a meaningless array (see Hochberg, 1978). Entities in space, especially ones devoid of meaning, are difficult to understand in isolation but easier to grasp in context. People group elements in an array by proximity or similarity or good continuation. One inevitable consequence of perceptual organizing principles is distorted representations.

Many of the distortions reviewed here have been instantiated in memory for perceptual arrays that do not stand for anything. They have also been illustrated in memory for cognitive maps and for environments. As such, they have implications for how people reason in navigating the world, a visuospatial reasoning task that people of all ages and parts of the world need to solve. Even more intriguing, many of these phenomena have analogs in abstract thought.

For the myriad spatial distortions described here (and analyzed more fully in Tversky, 1992, 2000b, 2000c), it is difficult to clearly attribute error to either representations or processes. Rather the errors seem to be consequences of both, of schematized, hence distorted, representations constructed ad hoc in order to enable specific judgments, such as the direction or distance between pairs of cities. When answering such questions, it is unlikely that people consult a library of "cognitive maps." Rather, it seems that they draw on whatever information they have that seems relevant, organizing it for the question at hand. The reliability of the errors under varying judgments makes it reasonable to assume erroneous representations are reliably constructed. Some of the organizing principles that yield systematic errors are reviewed in the next section.

Hierarchical Organization. Dots that are grouped together by good continuation, for example, parts of the same square outlined in dots, are judged to be closer than dots that are actually closer but parts of separate groups (Coren & Girgus, 1980). An analogous phenomenon occurs in judgments of distance between buildings (Hirtle & Jonides, 1985): Residents of Ann Arbor think that pairs of university (or town) buildings are closer than actually closer pairs of buildings that belong to different groups, one to the university and the other to the town. Hierarchical organization of essentially flat spatial information also affects accuracy and time to make judgments of direction. People incorrectly report that San Diego is west of Reno. Presumably this error occurs because people know the states to which the cities belong and use the overall directions of the states to infer the directions between cities in the states (Stevens & Coupe, 1978). People are faster to judge whether one city is east or north of another when the cities belong to separate geographic entities than when they are actually farther but part of the same geographic entity (Maki, 1981; Wilton, 1979).

A variant of hierarchical organization occurs in locating entities belonging to a bounded region. When asked to remember the location of a dot in a quadrant, people place it closer to the center of the quadrant, as if they were using general information about the area to locate the entity contained in it (Huttenlocher, Hedges, & Duncan, 1991; Newcombe & Huttenlocher, 2000).

Amount of Information. That representations are constructed on the fly in the service of particular judgments seems to be the case for other distance estimates. Distances between A and B, say two locations within a town, are greater when there are more cross streets or more buildings or more obstacles or more turns on the route (Newcombe & Liben, 1982; Sadalla & Magel, 1980; Sadalla & Staplin, 1980a, 1980b; Thorndyke, 1981), as if people mentally construct a representation of a path from A to B from that information and use the amount of information as a surrogate for the missing exact distance information. There is an analogous visual illusion: A line appears longer if bisected and longer still with more tick marks (at some point of clutter, the illusion ceases or reverses).

Perspective. Steinberg regaled generations of readers of the *New Yorker* and denizens of dormitory rooms with his maps of views of the world. In the each view, the immediate surroundings are stretched and the rest of the world shrunk. The psychological reality of this genre of visual joke was demonstrated by Holyoak and Mah (1982). They asked students in Ann Arbor to imagine themselves on either coast and to estimate the distances between pairs of cities distributed more or less equally on an east–west axis across the states. Regardless of imagined perspective, students overestimated the near distances relative to the far ones.

Landmarks. Distance judgments are also distorted by landmarks. People judge the distance of an undistinguished place to be closer to a landmark than vice versa (McNamara & Diwadkar, 1997; Sadalla, Burroughs, & Staplin, 1980). Landmark asymmetries violate elementary metric assumptions, assumptions that are more or less realized in real space.

Figure 10.4. Alignment. A significant majority of participants think the incorrect lower map is correct. The map has been altered so the United States and Europe and South American and Africa are more aligned (after Tversky, 1981).

Alignment. Hierarchical, perspective, and landmark effects can all be regarded as consequences of the Gestalt principle of grouping. Even groups of two equivalent entities can yield distortion. When people are asked to judge which of two maps is correct, a map of North and South America in which South America has been moved westward to overlap more with North America, or the actual map, in which the two continents barely overlap, the majority of respondents prefer the former (Tversky, 1981; Figure 10.4). A majority of observers also prefer an incorrect map of the Americas and Europe/Africa/Asia in which the Americas are moved northward so the United States and Europe and South America and Africa are more directly east–west. This phenomenon has been called *alignment*; it occurs when people group two spatial entities and then remember them more in correspondence than they actually are. It appears not only in judgments of maps of the world but also in judgments of directions between cities in memory for artificial maps and in memory for visual blobs.

Spatial entities cannot be localized in isolation; they can be localized with respect to other entities or to frames of reference. When they are coded with respect to another entity, alignment errors are likely. When entities are coded with respect to a frame of reference, rotation errors, described in the next section, are likely.

Rotation. When people are asked to place a cutout of South America in a north–south east–west frame, they upright it. A large spatial object, such as South America, induces its own coordinates along an axis of elongation and an axis parallel to that one. The actual axis of elongation of South America is tilted with respect to north–south, and people upright it in memory. Similarly, people incorrectly report that Berkeley is east of Stanford when it is actually slightly west. Presumably this occurs because they upright the Bay Area, which actually runs at an angle with respect to north–south. This error has been called *rotation*; it occurs when people code a spatial entity with respect to a frame of reference (Tversky, 1981; Figure 10.5). As for rotation, it appears in memory for artificial maps and uninterpreted blobs, as well as in memory for real environments. Others have replicated this error in remembered directions and in navigation (e.g., Glicksohn, 1994; Lloyd & Heivly, 1987; Montello, 1991; Presson & Montello, 1994).

Are Spatial Representations Incoherent? This brief review has brought evidence for distortions in memory and judgment for shapes of objects, configurations of objects, and distances and directions between objects that are a consequence of the organization of the visuospatial information. These are not errors of lack of knowledge; even experienced taxi drivers make them (Chase & Chi, 1981). Moreover, many of these biases have parallels in abstract domains, such as judgments about members of one's own social or political groups relative to judgments about members of other groups (e.g., Quattrone, 1986).

What might a representation that captures all these distortions look like? It would look like nothing that can be sketched on a sheet of paper, that is, is coherent in two dimensions. Landmark asymmetries alone disallow that. It does not seem likely that people make these judgments by retrieving a coherent prestored mental representation, a "cognitive map," and reading the direction or distance from it. Rather, it seems that people construct representations on the fly, incorporating only the information needed for that judgment, the relevant region, the specific entities within it. Some of the information may be visuospatial from experience or from maps; some may be linguistic. For these reasons, "cognitive collage" seems a more apt metaphor than "cognitive map" for whatever representations underlie spatial judgment and memory (Tversky, 1993). Such representations are schematic; they leave out much information and simplify others. Schematization occurs for at least two reasons. More exact information may not be known and therefore cannot be represented. More exact information may not even be needed because the situation on the ground may fill it in. More information may overload working memory, which is notoriously limited. Not only must the representation be constructed in working memory, but a judgment must also be made on the representation. Schematization may hide incoherence, or it may not be noticed. Schematization necessarily entails systematic error.

Why do Errors Persist? It is reasonable to wonder why so many systematic errors persist. Some reasons for the persistence of error have already been discussed – that there may be correctives on the ground, that some errors are a consequence of the schematization processes that are an inherent part of memory and information processing. Yet another reason is that the correctives are specific – now I know that Rome is north of Philadelphia – and do not affect or even make contact with the general information organizing principle that generated the error and that serves us well in many situations (e.g., Tversky, 2003a).

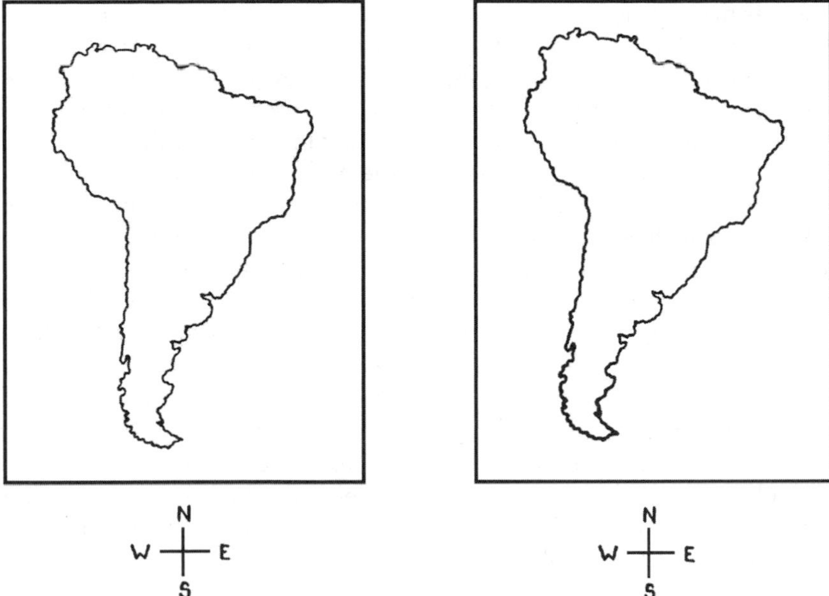

Figure 10.5. Rotation. When asked to place a cutout of South America in a NSEW framework, most participants upright it, as in the left example (after Tversky, 1981).

From Spatial to Abstract Reasoning

Visuospatial reasoning does not only entail visuospatial transformations on visuospatial information. Visuospatial reasoning also includes making inferences from visuospatial information, whether that information is in the mind or in the world. An early demonstration was the *symbolic distance effect* (e.g., Banks & Flora, 1977; Moyer, 1973; Paivio, 1978). The time to judge which of two animals is more intelligent or pleasant is faster when the entities are farther on the dimension than when they are closer – as if people were imagining the entities arrayed on a line corresponding to the abstract dimension. It is easier, hence faster, to discriminate larger distances than smaller ones. Note that a subjective experience of creating and using an image does not necessarily accompany making these and other spatial and abstract judgments. Spatial thinking can occur regardless of whether thinkers have the sensation of using an image. So many abstract concepts have spatial analogs (for related discussion, see Holyoak, Chap. 6).

Indeed, spatial reasoning is often studied in the context of graphics, maps, diagrams, graphs, and charts. External representations bear similarities to internal representations if only because they are creations of the human mind that is cognitive tools to increase the power of the human mind. They also bear formal similarities in that both internal and external representations are mappings between elements and relations. External representations are constrained by a medium and unconstrained by working memory; for this reason, inconsistencies, ambiguities, and incompleteness may be reduced in external representations.

Graphics: Elements

The readiness with which people map abstract information onto spatial information is part of the reason for the widespread use of diagrams to represent and convey abstract information from the sublime – the harmonies of the spheres rampant in religions spanning the globe – to the mundane corporate charts and statistical graphs.

Graphics, such as these, consist of elements and spatial relations among the elements. In contrast to written (alphabetic) languages, both elements and use of space in graphics can convey meaning rather directly (e.g., Bertin, 1967/1983; Pinker, 1994; Tversky, 1995, 2001; Winn, 1989). Elements may consist of likenesses, such as road signs depicting picnic tables, falling rocks, or deer. Elements may also be figures of depiction, similar to figures of speech: synecdoche, where a part represents a whole, common in ideographic writing, for example, using a ram's horns to represent a ram; or metonomy, where an association represents an entity or action, which is common in computer menus, such as scissors to denote *cut* text or a trashcan to allow deletion of files.

Graphics: Relations

Relations among entities preserve different levels of information. The information preserved is reflected in the mapping to space. In some cases, the information preserved is simply categorical; space is used to separate entities belonging to different categories. The spaces between words, for example, indicate that one set of letters belongs to one meaning and another set to another meaning. Space can also be used to represent ordinal information, for example, listing historic events in their order of occurrence, groceries by the order of encountering them in the supermarket, and companies by their profits. Space can be used to represent interval or ratio information, as in many statistical graphs, where the spatial distances among entities reflect their distances on some other dimension.

SPONTANEOUS USE OF SPACE TO REPRESENT ABSTRACT RELATIONS

Even preschool children spontaneously use diagrammatic space to represent abstract information (e.g., diSessa, Hammer, Sherin, & Kolpakowski, 1991; Tversky, Kugelmass, & Winter, 1991). In one set of studies (Tversky et al., 1991), children from three language communities were asked to place stickers on paper to represent spatial, temporal, quantitative, and preference information, for example, to place stickers for TV shows they loved, liked, or disliked. Almost all the preschoolers put the stickers on a line, preserving ordinal information. Children in the middle school years were able to represent interval information, but representing more than ordinal information was unusual for younger children, despite strong manipulations to encourage them. Not only did children (and adults) spontaneously use spatial relations to represent abstract relations, but children also showed preferences for the direction of increases in abstract dimensions. Increases were represented from right to left or left to right (irrespective of direction of writing for quantity and preference) or down to up. Representing increasing time or quantity from up to down was avoided. Representing increases as upward is especially robust; it affects people's ability to make inferences about second-order phenomena such as rate, which is spontaneously mapped to slope, from graphs (Gattis, 2002; Gattis & Holyoak, 1996). The correspondence of upward to more, better, and stronger appears in language – on top of the world, rising to higher levels of platitude – and in gesture – thumbs up, high five – as well as in graphics. These spontaneous and widespread correspondences between spatial and abstract relations suggest they are cognitively natural (e.g., Tversky, 1995a, 2001).

The demonstrations of spontaneous use of spatial language and diagrammatic space to represent abstract relations suggests that spatial reasoning forms a foundation for more abstract reasoning. In fact, children used diagrammatic space to represent abstract relations earlier for temporal relations than for quantitative ones, and earlier for quantitative relations than for preference relations (Tversky et al., 1991). Corroborative evidence comes from simple spatial and temporal reasoning tasks, such as judging whether one object or person is before another. In many languages, words for spatial and temporal relations, such as *before, after*, and *in between*, are shared. That spatial terms are the foundation for the temporal comes from research showing priming of temporal perspective from spatial perspective but not vice versa (Boroditsky, 2000). More support for the primacy of spatial thinking for abstract thought comes from studies of problem solving (Carroll, Thomas, & Mulhotra, 1980). One group of participants was asked to solve a spatial problem under constraints, arranging offices to facilitate communication among key people. Another group was asked to solve a temporal analog, arranging processes to facilitate production. The solutions to the spatial analog were superior to those to the temporal analog. When experimenters suggested using a diagram to yet another group solving the temporal analog, their success equaled that of the spatial analog group.

DIAGRAMS FACILITATE REASONING

Demonstrating that using a spatial diagram facilitates temporal problem solving also illustrates the efficacy of diagrams in thinking – a finding amply supported, even for inferences entailing complex logic, such as double disjunctions, although to succeed, diagrams have to be designed with attention to the ways that space and spatial entities are used to make inferences (Bauer & Johnson-Laird, 1993). Middle school children studying science were asked to put reminders on paper. Those children who sketched diagrams learned the material better than those who did not (Rode & Stern, in press).

DIAGRAMS FOR COMMUNICATING

Many maps, charts, diagrams, and graphs are meant to communicate clearly for travelers, students, and scholars, whether they are professionals or amateurs. To that end, they are designed to be clear and easy to comprehend, and they meet with varying success. Good design takes account of human perceptual and cognitive skills, biases, and propensities. Even ancient Greek vases take account of how they will be seen. Because they are curved round structures, creating a veridical appearance requires artistry. The vase "Achilles and Ajax playing a game" by the Kleophrades Painter in the Museum of Metropolitan Art in New York City (Art. 65.11.12, ca. 500–480 B.C.) depicts a spear that appears in one piece from the desired viewing angle, but in three pieces when viewed straight on (J. P. Small, personal communication, May 27, 2003).

The perceptual and cognitive processes and biases that people bring to graphics include the catalog of mental representations and transformations that was begun earlier. In that spirit, several researchers have developed models for graph understanding, notably Pinker (1990), Kosslyn (1989, 1994a), and Carpenter and Shah (1998) (see Shah 2003/2004, for an overview). These models take account of the particular perceptual or imaginal processes that need to be applied to particular kinds of graphs to yield the right inferences. Others have taken account of perceptual and cognitive processing in the construction of guidelines for design. (e.g., Carswell & Wickens, 1990; Cleveland, 1985; Kosslyn, 1994a; Tufte, 1983, 1990, 1997; Wainer, 1984, 1997). In some cases the design principles are informed by research, but in most they are informed by the authors' educated sensibilities and/or rules of thumb from graphic design.

Inferences from Diagrams: Structural and Functional. The existence of spontaneous mapping of abstract information onto spatial does not mean that the meanings of diagrams are transparent and can be automatically and easily extracted (e.g., Scaife & Rogers, 1995). Diagrams can support many different classes of inferences, notably, structural and functional (e.g., Mayer & Gallini, 1990). Structural inferences, or inferences about qualities of parts and the relations among them, can be readily made from inspection of a diagram. Distance, direction, size, and other spatial qualities and properties can be "read off" a diagram (Larkin & Simon, 1987), at least with some degree of accuracy. "Reading off" entails using the sort of mental transformations discussed earlier, mental scanning, mental distance, size, shape, or direction judgments or comparisons. Functional inferences, or inferences about the behavior of entities, cannot be readily made from inspection of a diagram in the absence of additional knowledge or assumptions that are often a consequence of expertise. Spatial information may provide clues to functional information, but it is not sufficient for concepts such as force, mass, and friction. Making functional inferences requires linking perceptual information to conceptual information; it entails both knowing how to "read" a diagram, that is, what visuospatial features and relations to inspect or transform, and knowing how to interpret that visuospatial information.

Structural and functional inferences respectively correspond to two senses of *mental model* prevalent in the field. In both cases, *mental model* contrasts with *image*. In one sense, a mental model contrasts with an image in being more skeletal or abstract. This is the sense used by Johnson-Laird in his book, *Mental Models* (1983), in his explication of how people solve syllogisms (see Johnson-Laird, Chap. 9, and Evans, Chap. 8). Here, a mental model captures the structural relations among the parts of a system. In the other sense, a mental model contrasts with an image in having moving parts, in being "runnable" to derive functional or causal inferences (for related discussion on causality, see Buehner and Cheng, Chap. 7, and on problem solving, see Chi and Ohlsson, Chap. 16). This is the sense used in another book also titled *Mental Models* (Gentner & Stevens, 1983). One goal of diagrams is to instill mental models in the minds of their users. To that end, diagrams abstract the essential elements and relations of the system they are meant to convey. As is seen, conveying structure is more straightforward than conveying function.

What does it mean to say that a mental model is "runnable?" One example comes from research on pulley systems (Hegarty, 1992). Participants were timed to make two kinds of judgments from diagrams of three-pulley systems. For true-false judgments of structural questions, such as "The upper left pulley is attached to the ceiling," response times did not depend on which pulley in the system was queried. For judgments of functional questions, such as "The upper left pulley goes clockwise," response times did depend on the order of that pulley in the mechanics of the system. To answer functional questions, it is as if participants mentally animate the pulley system in order to generate an answer. Mental animation, however, does not seem to be a continuous process in the same way as physical animation. Rather, mental animation seems to be a sequence of discrete steps – for example, the first pulley goes clockwise, and the rope goes under the next pulley to the left of it, so it must go counterclockwise. That continuous events are comprehended as sequences of steps is corroborated by research on segmentation and interpretation of everyday events, such as making a bed (Zacks, Tversky, & Iyer, 2001).

It has long been known that domain experts are more adept at functional inferences from diagrams than novices. Experts can "see" sequences of organized chess moves in a midgame display (Chase & Simon, 1973; De Groot, 1965). Similarly, experts in Go (Reitman, 1976), electricity (Egan & Schwartz, 1979), weather (Lowe, 1989), architecture (Suwa & Tversky, 1997), and more make functional inferences with ease from diagrams in their domain. Novices are no different from experts in structural inferences.

Inferences from Diagrams of Systems. The distinction between structural and functional inferences is illustrated by work on production and comprehension of diagrams for mechanical systems, such as a car brake, a bicycle pump, or a pulley system (Heiser & Tversky, 2002; Figure 10.6). Participants were asked to interpret a diagram of one of the systems. On the whole, their interpretations were structural, that is, they described the relations among the parts of the system. Another set of participants was given the same diagrams enriched by arrows indicating the sequence of action in the systems. Those participants gave functional descriptions; that is, they described the step-by-step operation of the system. Reversing the tasks, other groups of participants read structural or functional descriptions of the systems and produced diagrams of them. Those who

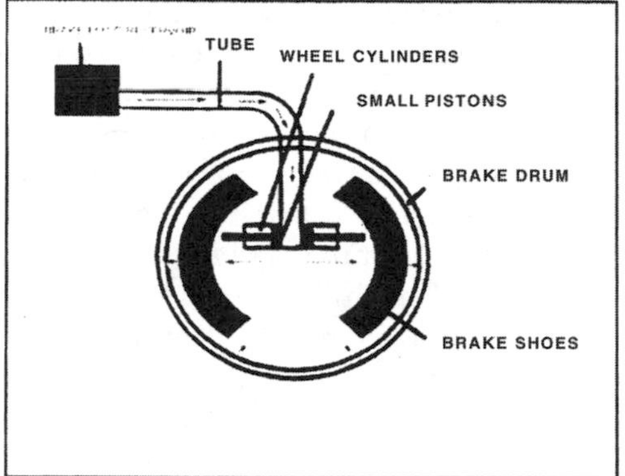

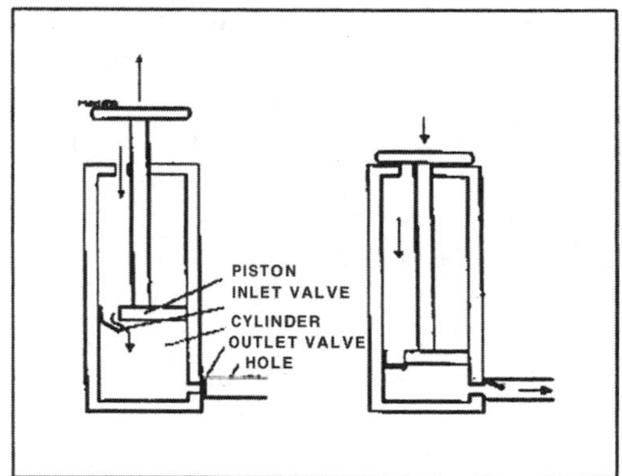

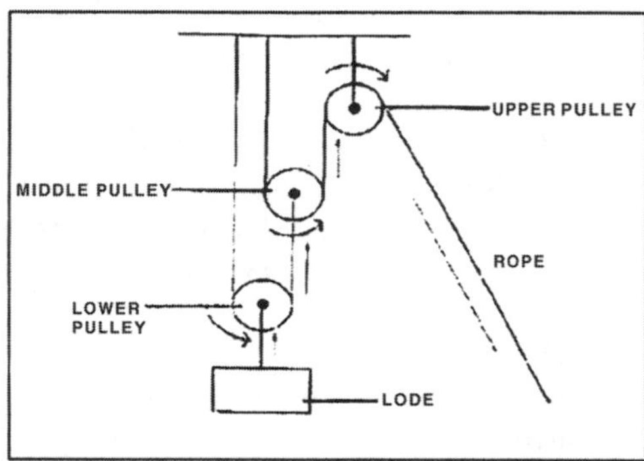

Figure 10.6. Diagrams of a car brake and a bicycle pump (both after Mayer & Gallini, 1990), and a pulley system (after Hegarty, 1992). Diagrams without arrows encouraged structural descriptions and diagrams with arrows yielded functional descriptions (Heiser and Tversky, in press).

read functional descriptions used arrows in their diagrams far more than those who read structural descriptions. Arrows are an extrapictorial device that have many meanings and functions in diagrams, such as pointing, indicating temporal sequence, causal sequence, and path and manner of motion (Tversky, 2001).

Expertise came into play in a study of learning rather than interpretation. Participants learned one of the mechanical systems from a diagram with or without arrows or from structural or functional text. They were later tested on both structural and functional information. Participants high in expertise/ability (self-assessed) were able to infer both structural and functional information from either diagram. In contrast, participants low in expertise/ability could derive structural but not functional information from the diagrams. Those participants were able to infer functional information from functional text. This finding suggests that people with high expertise/ability can form unitary diagrammatic mental models of mechanical systems that allow spatial and functional inferences with relative ease, but people with low expertise/ability have and use diagrammatic mental models for structural information but rely on propositional representations for functional information.

Enriching Diagrams to Facilitate Functional Inferences. As noted, conveying spatial or structural information is relatively straightforward in diagrams. Diagrams can use space to represent space in direct ways that are readily interpreted, as in maps and architectural sketches. Conveying information that is not strictly spatial, such as change over time, forces, and kinematics, is less straightforward. Some visual conventions for conveying information about dynamics or forces have been developed in comics and in diagrams (e.g., Horn, 1998; Kunzle, 1990; McCloud, 1994), and many of these conventions are cognitively compelling. Arrows are a good example. As lines, arrows indicate a relationship, a link. As asymmetric lines, they indicate an asymmetric relationship. The arrowhead is compelling as an indicator of the direction of the asymmetry because of its correspondence to arrowheads common as weapons in the world or its correspondence to Vs created by paths of downward moving water. A survey of diagrams in science and engineering texts shows wide use of extrapictorial diagrammatic devices, such as arrows, lines, brackets, and insets, although not always consistently (Tversky, Heiser, Lozano, MacKenzie, & Morrison, in press). As a consequence, these devices are not always correctly interpreted. Some diagrams of paradigmatic processes, such as the nitrogen cycle in biology or the rock cycle in geology, contain the same device, typically an arrow, with multiple senses, pointing or labeling, indicating movement path or manner, suggesting forces or sequence, in the same diagram. Of course, there is ambiguity in many words that appear commonly in scientific and other prose, words that parallel these graphic devices, such as *line* and *relationship*. Nevertheless, the confusion caused by multiple senses of diagrammatic devices in interpreting diagrams suggests that greater care in design is worthwhile.

An intuitive way to visualize change over time is by animations. After all, an animation uses change over time to convey change over time, a cognitively compelling correspondence. Despite the intuitive appeal, a survey of dozens of studies that have compared animated graphics to informationally comparable static graphics in teaching a wide variety of concepts, physical, mechanical, and abstract, did not find a single example of superior learning by animations (Tversky, Morrison, & Betrancourt, 2002). Animations may be superior for purposes other than learning, for example, in maintaining perspective or in calling attention to a solution in problem solving. For example, a diagram containing many arrows moving toward the center of a display was superior to a diagram with static arrows in suggesting the solution to the Duncker radiation problem of how to destroy a tumor without destroying healthy tissue (Pedone, Hummel, & Holyoak, 2001; see Holyoak, Chap. 6, Figure 6.4). The failure of animations to improve learning itself becomes intuitive on further reflection. For one thing, animations are often complex, so it is difficult for a viewer to know where to look and to make sense of the timing of many moving components. However, even simple animations, such as the path of a single moving circle, are not superior to static graphics (Morrison & Tversky, in press). The second reason for the lack of success of animations is one reviewed earlier. If people think of dynamic events as sequences of steps rather than continuous animations, then presenting change over time as sequences of steps may make the changes easier to comprehend.

Diagrams for Insight

Maps for highways and subways, diagrams for assembly and biology, graphs for economics and statistics, and plans for electricians and plumbers are designed to be concise and unambiguous, although they may not always succeed. Their inventors want to communicate clearly and without error. In contrast are graphics created to be ambiguous, to allow reinterpretation and discovery. Art falls into both those categories. Early design sketches are meant to be ambiguous, to commit the designer to only those aspects of the design that are likely not to change, and to leave open other aspects. One reason for this is fixation; it is hard to "think out of the box." Visual displays express, suggest, more than what they display. That expression, in fact, came from solution attempts to the famous nine-dot problem (see Novick & Bassok, Chap. 14, Fig. 14.4). Connect all nine dots in a 3 × 3 array using four straight lines without lifting the pen from the paper. The solution that is hard to see is to extend the lines beyond the "box" suggested

Figure 10.7. A sketch by an architect designing a museum. Upon reinspection, he made an unintentional discovery (Suwa, Tversky, Gero, & Purcell, 2001).

by the 3 × 3 array. The Gestalt psychologists made us aware of the visual inferences the mind makes without reflection, grouping by proximity, similarity, good continuation, and common fate.

INFERENCES FROM SKETCHES

Initial design sketches are meant to be ambiguous for several reasons. In early stages of design, designers often do not want to commit to the details of a solution, only the general outline, leaving open many possibilities; gradually, they will fill in the details. Perhaps more important, skilled designers are able to get new ideas by reexamining their own sketches, by having a conversation with their sketches, bouncing ideas off them (e.g., Goldschmidt, 1994; Schon, 1983; Suwa & Tversky, 1997; Suwa, Tversky, Gero, & Purcell, 2001). They may construct sketches with one set of ideas in mind, but on later reexamination they see new configurations and relations that generate new design ideas. The productive cycle between reexamining and reinterpreting is revealed in the protocol of one expert architect. When he saw a new configuration in his own design, he was more likely to invent a new design idea; similarly, when he invented a new design idea, he was more likely to see a new configuration in his sketch (Suwa et al., 2001; Figure 10.7).

Underlying these unintended discoveries in sketches is a cognitive skill termed *constructive perception*, which consists of two independent processes: a perceptual one, mentally reorganizing the sketch, and a conceptual one, relating the new organization to some design purpose (Suwa & Tversky, 2003). Participants adept at generating multiple interpretations of ambiguous sketches excelled at the perceptual ability of finding hidden figures and at the cognitive ability of finding remote meaningful associations, yet these two abilities were uncorrelated.

Expertise affects the kinds of inferences designers are able to make from their sketches. Novice designers are adept at perceptual inferences, such as seeing proximity and similarity relations. Expert designers are also adept at functional inferences, such as "seeing" the flow of traffic or the changes in light from sketches (Suwa & Tversky, 1997).

Conclusions and Future Directions

Starting with the elements of visuospatial representations in the mind, we end with visuospatial representations created by the mind. Like language, graphics serve to express and clarify individual spatial and abstract concepts. Graphics have an advantage over language in expressiveness (Stenning & Oberlander, 1995); graphics use elements and relations in graphic space to convey elements and relations in real or metaphoric space. As such, they allow inference based on the visuospatial processing that people have become expert in as a part of their everyday interactions with space (Larkin & Simon, 1997). As cognitive tools, graphics facilitate reasoning, both by externalizing, thus offloading memory and processing, and by mapping abstract reasoning onto spatial comparisons and transformations. Graphics organize and schematize spatial and abstract information to highlight and focus the essential information. Like language, graphics serve to convey spatial and abstract concepts to others. They make private thoughts public to a community that can then use and revise those concepts collaboratively.

Of course, graphics and physical and mental transformations on them are not identical to visuospatial representations and reasoning; they are an expression of it. Talk about space and actions in it were probably among the first uses of language, telling others how to find their way and what to look for when they get there. Cognitive tools to promote visuospatial reasoning were among the first to be invented from tokens for property counts, believed to be the precursor of written language (Schmandt-Besserat, 1992), to trail markers to maps in the sand. Spatial thought, spatial language, and spatial graphics reflect the importance and prevalence of visuospatial reasoning in our lives, from knowing how to get home to knowing how to design a house, from explaining how to find the freeway to explaining how the judicial system works, from understanding basic science to inventing new conceptions of the origins of the universe. Where do we go from here? Onward and upward!

Acknowledgments

I am grateful to Phil Johnson-Laird and Jeff Zacks for insightful suggestions on a previous draft. Preparation of this chapter and some of the research reported were supported by Office of Naval Research, Grant Numbers NOOO14-PP-1-O649, N000140110717, and N000140210534 to Stanford University.

References

Alibali, M. W., Bassok, M., Solomon, K. O., Syc, S. E., & Goldin-Meadow, S. (1999). Illuminating mental representations through speech and gesture. *Psychological Science*, 10, 327–333.

Anderson, J. R. (1978). Arguments concerning representations for mental imagery. *Psychological Review*, 85, 249–277.

Banks, W. P., & Flora, J. (1977). Semantic and perceptual processes in symbolic comparisons. *Journal of Experimental Psychology: Human Perception and Performance*, 3, 278–290.

Barwise, J., & Etchemendy. (1995). In J. Glasgow, N. H. Naryanan, & G. Chandrasekeran (Eds.), *Diagrammatic reasoning: Cognitive and computational perspectives* (pp. 211–234). Cambridge, MA: MIT Press.

Bauer, M. I., & Johnson-Laird, P. N. (1993). How diagrams can improve reasoning. *Psychological Science*, 6, 372–378.

Bertin, J. (1967/1983). *Semiology of graphics: Diagrams, networks, maps*. (Translated by W. J. Berg.) Madison: University of Wisconsin Press.

Betrancourt, M., & Tversky, B. (in press). Simple animations for organizing diagrams. *International Journal of Human-Computer Studies*.

Beveridge, M., & Parkins, E. (1987). Visual representation in analogical problem solving. *Memory and Cognition*, 15, 230–237.

Boroditsky, L. (2000). Metaphoric structuring: Understanding time through spatial metaphors. *Cognition*, 75, 1–28.

Boroditsky, L. (2001). Does language shape thought?: Mandarin and English speakers' conceptions of time. *Cognitive Psychology*, 43, 1–23.

Boroditsky, L., Ham, W., & Ramscar, M. (2002). What is universal in event perception? Comparing English and Indonesian speakers. In

W. D. Gray & C. D. Schunn (Eds.), *Proceedings of the 24th annual meeting of the Cognitive Science Society* (pp. 136–1441). Mahwah, NJ: Erlbaum.

Bruner, J. S. (1973). *Beyond the information given: Studies in the psychology of knowing.* Oxford, UK: Norton.

Bryant, D. J., & Tversky, B. (1999). Mental representations of spatial relations from diagrams and models. *Journal of Experimental Psychology: Learning, Memory, and Cognition*, 25, 137–156.

Bryant, D. J., Tversky, B., & Franklin, N. (1992). Internal and external spatial frameworks for representing described scenes. *Journal of Memory and Language*, 31, 74–98.

Byrant, D. J., Tversky, B., & Lanca, M. (2001). Retrieving spatial relations from observation and memory. In E. van der Zee & U. Nikanne (Eds.), *Conceptual structure and its interfaces with other modules of representation* (pp. 116–139). Oxford, UK: Oxford University Press.

Bundesen, C., & Larsen, A. (1975). Visual transformation of size. *Journal of Experimental Psychology: Human Perception and Performance*, 1, 214–220.

Bundesen, C., Larsen, A., & Farrell, J. E. (1981). Mental transformations of size and orientation. In A. Baddeley & J. Long (Eds.), *Attention and performance IX* (pp. 279–294). Hillsdale, NJ: Erlbaum.

Carmichael, R., Hogan, H. P., & Walter, A. A. (1932). An experimental study of the effect of language on the reproduction of visually perceived forms. *Journal of Experimental Psychology*, 15, 73–86.

Carpenter, P. A., & Shah, P. (1998). A model of the perceptual and conceptual processes in graph comprehension. *Journal of Experimental Psychology: Applied*, 4, 75–100.

Carroll, J. (1993). *Human cognitive abilities: A survey of factor-analytical studies*. New York: Cambridge University Press.

Carroll, J. M., Thomas, J. C., & Malhotra, A. (1980). Presentation and representation in design problem solving. *British Journal of Psychology*, 71, 143–153.

Carswell, C. M. (1992). Reading graphs: Interaction of processing requirements and stimulus structure. In B. Burns (Ed.), *Percepts, concepts, and categories* (pp. 605–645). Amsterdam: Elsevier.

Carswell, C. M., & Wickens, C. D. (1990). The perceptual interaction of graphic attributes: Configurality, stimulus homogeneity, and object integration. *Perception and Psychophysics*, 47, 157–168.

Chase, W. G., & Chi, M. T. H. (1981). Cognitive skill: Implications for spatial skill in large-scale environments. In J. H. Harvey (Ed.), *Cognition, social behavior, and the environment* (pp. 111–136). Hillsdale, NJ: Erlbaum.

Chase, W. G., & Simon, H. A. (1973). The mind's eye in chess. In W. G. Chase (Ed.), *Visual information processing*. New York: Academic Press.

Cleveland, W. S. (1985). *The elements of graphing data*. Monterey, CA: Wadsworth.

Coren, S., & Girgus, J. S. (1980). Principles of perceptual organization and spatial distortion: The Gestalt illusions. *Journal of Experimental Psychology: Human Performance and Perception*, 6, 404–412.

Cutting, J. E. (1986). *Perception with an eye for motion*. Cambridge, MA: Bradford Books/MIT Press.

Cutting J. E., & Kozlowski L. T. (1977). Recognizing friends by their walk: Gait perception without familiarity cues. *Bulletin of the Psychonomic Society*, 9, 353–356.

De Groot, A. D. (1965). *Thought and choice in chess*. The Hague: Mouton.

Denis, M. (1996). Imagery and the description of spatial configurations. In M. de Vega & M. Marschark (Eds.), *Models of visuospatial cognition* (pp. 128–1197). New York: Oxford University Press.

Denis, M., & Kosslyn, S. M. (1999). Scanning visual mental images: A window on the mind. *Cahiers de Psychologie Cognitive*, 18, 409–465.

diSessa, A. A., Hammer, D., Sherin, B., & Kolpakowski, T. (1991). Inventing graphing: Meta-representational expertise in children. *Journal of Mathematical Behavior*, 10, 117–160.

Duncker, K. (1945). On problem solving. *Psychological Monographs*, 58, (Whole No. 270).

Egan, D. E., & Schwartz, B. J. (1979). Chunking in recall of symbolic drawings. *Memory and Cognition*, 7, 149–158.

Emmorey, K., Tversky, B., & Taylor, H. A. (2000). Using space to describe space: Perspective in speech, sign, and gesture. *Journal of Spatial Cognition and Computation*, 2, 157–180.

Englekamp, J. (1998). *Memory for action*. Hove, UK: Psychology Press.

Finke, R. A. (1990). *Creative imagery*. Hillsdale, NJ: Erlbaum.

Finke, R. A. (1993). Mental imagery and creative discovery. In B. Roskos-Evoldsen, M. J. Intons-Peterson, & R. E. Anderson (Eds.), *Imagery, creativity, and discovery*. Amsterdam: North-Holland.

Finke, R. A., & Pinker, S. (1982). Spontaneous imagery scanning in mental extrapolation. *Journal of Experimental Psychology: Learning, Memory, and Cognition*, 8, 142–147.

Finke, R. A., & Pinker, S. (1983). Directional scanning of remembered visual patterns. *Journal of Experimental Psychology: Learning, Memory, and Cognition*, 9, 398–410.

Finke, R. A., Pinker, S., & Farah, M. J. (1989). Reinterpreting visual patterns in mental imagery. *Cognitive Science*, 12, 51–78.

Finke, R., & Shepard, R. N. (1986). Visual functions of mental imagery. In K. R. Boff, L. Kaufman, & J. P. Thomas (Eds.), *Handbook of perception and human performance* (vol. II, pp. 19–55). New York: Wiley.

Franklin, N., & Tversky, B. (1990). Searching imagined environments. *Journal of Experimental Psychology: General*, 119, 63–76.

Franklin, N., Tversky, B., & Coon, V. (1992). Switching points of view in spatial mental models acquired from text. *Memory and Cognition*, 20, 507–518.

Freyd, J., & Tversky, B. (1984). The force of symmetry in form perception. *American Journal of Psychology*, 97, 109–126.

Gattis, M. (2002). Structure mapping in spatial reasoning. *Cognitive Development*, 17, 1157–1183.

Gattis, M., & Holyoak, K. J. (1996). Mapping conceptual to spatial relations in visual reasoning. *Journal of Experimental Psychology: Learning, Memory, and Cognition*, 22, 1–9.

Gelman, R., Durgin, F., & Kaufman, L. (1995). Distinguishing between animates and inanimates: Not by motion alone. In D. Sperber, D. Premack, & A. J. Premack (Eds.), *Causal cognition: A multidisciplinary debate* (pp. 150–184). Oxford, UK: Clarendon Press.

Gentner, D., & Stevens, A. (1983). *Mental models*. Hillsdale, NJ: Erlbaum.

Gick, M. L., & Holyoak, K. J. (1980). Analogical problem solving. *Cognitive Psychology*, 12, 306–355.

Gick, M. L., & Holyoak, K. J. (1983). Schema induction and analogical transfer. *Cognitive Psychology*, 15, 1–28.

Glicksohn, J. (1994). Rotation, orientation, and cognitive mapping. *American Journal of Psychology*, 107, 39–51.

Glushko, R. J., & Cooper, L. A. (1978). Spatial comprehension and comparison processes in verification tasks. *Cognitive Psychology*, 10, 391–421.

Goldschmidt, G. (1994). On visual design thinking: The vis kids of architecture. *Design Studies*, 15, 158–174.

Gordon, I. E., & Hayward, S. (1973). Second-order isomorphism of internal representations of familiar faces. *Perception and Psychophysics*, 14, 334–336.

Hegarty, M. (1992). Mental animation: Inferring motion from static displays of mechanical systems. *Journal of Experimental Psychology: Learning, Memory, and Cognition*, 18, 1084–1102.

Hegarty, M., & Waller, D. (in press). Individual differences in spatial abilities. In P. Shah & A. Miyake (Eds.), *Handbook of higher-level visuospatial thinking and cognition*. Cambridge, UK: Cambridge University Press.

Heider, F., & Simmel, M. (1944). An experimental study of apparent behavior. *American Journal of Psychology*, 57, 243–259.

Heiser, J., & Tversky, B. (2002). Diagrams and descriptions in acquiring complex systems. *Proceedings of the meetings of the Cognitive Science Society*.

Heiser, J., Tversky, B., Agrawala, M., & Hanrahan, P. (2003). Cognitive design principles for visualizations: Revealing and instantiating. In *Proceedings of the Cognitive Science Society meetings*.

Hirtle, S. C., & Jonides, J. (1985). Evidence of hierarchies in cognitive maps. *Memory and Cognition*, 13, 208–217.

Hochberg, J. (1978). *Perception*. Englewood Cliffs, NJ: Prentice-Hall.

Holyoak, K. J., & Mah, W. A. (1982). Cognitive reference points in judgments of symbolic magnitude. *Cognitive Psychology*, 14, 328–352.

Horn, R. E. (1998). *Visual language*. Bainbridge Island, WA: MacroVu, Inc.

Houser, N., & Kloesel, C. (1992). *The essential Pierce, Vol. 1 and Vol. 2*. Bloomington: Indiana University Press.

Huttenlocher, J., Hedges, L. V., & Duncan, S. (1991). Categories and particulars: Prototype effects in estimating spatial location. *Psychological Review*, 98, 352–376.

Huttenlocher, J., Newcombe, N., & Sandberg, E. H. (1994). The coding of spatial location in young children. *Cognitive Psychology*, 27, 115–147.

Huttenlocher, J., & Presson, C. C. (1979). The coding and transformation of spatial information. *Cognitive Psychology*, 11, 375–394.

Intraub, H., Bender, R. S., & Mangels, J. A. (1992). Looking at pictures but remembering scenes. *Journal of Experimental Psychology: Learning, Memory, and Cognition*, 18, 180–191.

Iverson, J., & Goldin-Meadow, S. (1997). What's communication got to do with it? Gesture in children blind from birth. *Developmental Psychology*, 33, 453–467.

Johansson, G. (1973). Visual perception of biological motion and a model for its analysis. *Perception and Psychophysics*, 14, 201–211.

Johnson-Laird, P. N. (1983). *Mental models*. Cambridge, MA: Harvard University Press.

Kerst, S. M., & Howard, J. H. (1978). Memory psychophysics for visual area and length. *Memory and Cognition*, 6, 327–335.

Kieras, D. E., & Bovair, S. (1984). The role of a mental model in learning to operate a device. *Cognitive Science*, 11, 255–273.

Klatzky, R. L., Golledge, R. G., Cicinelli, J. G., & Pellegrino, J. W. (1995). Performance of blind and sighted persons on spatial tasks. *Journal of Visual Impairment and Blindness*, 89, 70–82.

Klatzky, R. L., Loomis, J. M., Beall, A. C., Chance, S. S., & Golledge, R. G. (1998). Spatial updating of self-position and orientation during real, imagined, and virtual locomotion. *Psychological Science*, 9, 293–298.

Kosslyn, S. M. (1976). Can imagery be distinguished from other forms of internal representation? *Memory and Cognition*, 4, 291–297.

Kosslyn, S. M. (1980). *Image and mind*. Cambridge, MA: Harvard University Press.

Kosslyn, S. M. (1989). Understanding charts and graphs. *Applied Cognitive Psychology*, 3, 185–223.

Kosslyn, S. M. (1994a). *Elements of graph design*. New York: Freeman.

Kosslyn, S. M. (1994b). *Image and brain: The resolution of the imagery debate*. Cambridge, MA: MIT Press.

Kosslyn, S. M., Ball, T. M., & Rieser, B. J. (1978). Visual images preserve metric spatial information: Evidence from studies of image scanning. *Journal of Experimental Psychology: Human Perception and Performance*, 4, 47–60.

Kozhevnikov, M., Kosslyn, S., & Shepard, J. (in press). Spatial versus object visualizers: A new characterization of visual cognitive style. *Memory and Cognition*.

Kozlowski, L. T., & Cutting, J. E. (1977). Recognizing the sex of a walker from a dynamic point light display. *Perception and Psychophysics*, 21, 575–580.

Kunzle, D. (1990). *The history of the comic strip*. Berkeley: University of California Press.

Lakoff, G., & Johnson, M. (1980). *Metaphors we live by*. Chicago: University of Chicago Press.

Larkin, J. H., & Simon, H. A. (1987). Why a diagram is (sometimes) worth ten thousand words. *Cognitive Science*, 11, 65–99.

Lee, P. U., & Tversky, B. (in press). Costs to switch perspective in acquiring but not in accessing spatial information.

Levinson, S. C. (2003). *Space in language and cognition: Explorations in cognitive diversity*. Cambridge, UK: Cambridge University Press.

Linn, M. C., & Petersen, A. C. (1986). A meta-analysis of gender differences in spatial ability: Implications for mathematics and science achievement. In J. S. Hyde & M. C. Linn (Eds.), *The psychology of gender: Advances through metaanalysis* (pp. 67–101). Baltimore: Johns Hopkins University Press.

Lowe, R. K. (1989). Search strategies and inference in the exploration of scientific diagrams. *Educational Psychology*, 9, 27–44.

Maki, R. H. (1981). Categorization and distance effects with spatial linear orders. *Journal of Experimental Psychology: Human Learning and Memory*, 7, 15–32.

Martin, B., & Tversky, B. (2003). Segmenting ambiguous events. *Proceedings of the Cognitive Science Society meeting*, Boston.

Mayer, R. E. (1998). Instructional technology. In F. Durso (Ed.), *Handbook of applied cognition*. Chichester, UK: Wiley.

Mayer, R. E., & Gallini, J. K. (1990). When is an illustration worth ten thousand words? *Journal of Educational Psychology*, 82, 715–726.

McBeath, M. K., Schiano, D. J., & Tversky, B. (1997). Three-dimensional bilateral symmetry bias in judgments of figural identity and orientation. *Psychological Science*, 8, 217–223.

McBeath, M. K., Shaffer, D. M., & Kaiser, M. K. (1995). How baseball outfielders determine where to run to catch fly balls. *Science*, 268(5210), 569–573.

McCloud, S. (1994). *Understanding comics*. New York: HarperCollins.

McNamara, T. P., & Diwadkar, V. A. (1997). Symmetry and asymmetry of human spatial memory. *Cognitive Psychology*, 34, 160–190.

Michotte, A. E. (1946/1963). *The perception of causality*. New York: Basic Books.

Milgram, S., & Jodelet, D. (1976). Psychological maps of Paris. In H. Proshansky, W. Ittelson, & L. Rivlin (Eds.), *Environmental psychology* (2nd edition, pp. 104–124). New York: Holt, Rinehart and Winston.

Montello, D. R. (1991). Spatial orientation and the angularity of urban routes: A field study. *Environment and Behavior*, 23, 47–69.

Montello, D. R., & Pick, H. L., Jr. (1993). Integrating knowledge of vertically-aligned large-scale spaces. *Environment and Behavior*, 25, 457–484.

Morrison, J. B., & Tversky, B. (in press). Failures of simple animations to facilitate learning.

Moyer, R. S. (1973). Comparing objects in memory: Evidence suggesting an internal psychophysics. *Perception and Psychophysics*, 13, 180–184.

Newcombe, N., & Huttenlocher, J. (2000). *Making space*. Cambridge, MA: MIT Press.

Newcombe, N., Huttenlocher, J., Sandberg, E., Lee, E., & Johnson, S. (1999). What do misestimations and asymmetries in spatial judgment indicate about spatial representation? *Journal of Experimental Psychology: Learning, Memory, and Cognition*, 25, 986–996.

Newcombe, N., & Liben, L. S. (1982). Barrier effects in the cognitive maps of children and adults. *Journal of Experimental Child Psychology*, 34, 46–58.

Novick, L. R., & Tversky, B. (1987). Cognitive constraints on ordering operations: The case of geometric analogies. *Journal of Experimental Psychology: General*, 116, 50–67.

Oatley, K., & Yuill, N. (1985). Perception of personal and inter-personal action in a cartoon film. *British Journal of Social Psychology*, 24, 115–124.

Paivio, A. (1978). Mental comparisons involving abstract attributes. *Memory and Cognition*, 6, 199–208.

Parsons, L. M. (1987a). Imagined spatial transformation of one's body. *Journal of Experimental Psychology: General*, 116, 172–191.

Parsons, L. M. (1987b). Imagined spatial transformations of one's hands and feet. *Cognitive Psychology*, 19, 192–191.

Pedone, R., Hummel, J. E., & Holyoak, K. J. (2001). The use of diagrams in analogical problem solving. *Memory and Cognition*, 29, 214–221.

Pinker, S. (1980). Mental imagery and the third dimension. *Journal of Experimental Psychology: General*, 109, 354–371.

Pinker, S. (1990). A theory of graph comprehension. In R. Freedle (Ed.), *Artificial intelligence and the future of testing* (pp. 73–126). Hillsdale, NJ: Erlbaum.

Pinker, S., Choate, P., & Finke, R. A. (1984). Mental extrapolation in patterns constructed from memory. *Memory and Cognition*, 12, 207–218.

Pinker, S., & Finke, R. A. (1980). Emergent two-dimensional patterns in images rotated in depth. *Journal of Experimental Psychology: Human Perception and Performance*, 6, 224–264.

Prasad, S., Loula, F., & Shiffrar, M. (2003). Who's there? Comparing recognition of self, friend, and stranger movement. *Proceedings of the Object Perception and Memory meeting*.

Prentice, W. C. H. (1954). Visual recognition of verbally labeled figures. *American Journal of Psychology*, 67, 315–320.

Presson, C. C., & Montello, D. (1994). Updating after rotational and translational body movements: Coordinate structure of perspective space. *Perception*, 23, 1447–1455.

Pylyshyn, Z. W. (1973). What the mind's eye tells the mind's brain: A critique of mental imagery. *Psychological Bulletin*, 80, 1–24.

Pylyshyn, Z. W. (1979). The rate of "mental rotation" of images: A test of a holistic analogue hypothesis.. *Memory and Cognition*, 7, 19–28.

Pylyshyn, Z. W. (1981). The imagery debate: Analogue media versus tacit knowledge. *Psychological Review*, 88, 16–45.

Quattrone, G. A. (1986). On the perception of a group's variability. In S. Worchel & W. Austin (Eds.), *The psychology of intergroup relations* (pp. 25–48). New York: Nelson-Hall.

Rauscher, F. H., Krauss, R. M., & Chen, Y. (1996). Gesture, speech, and lexical access: The role of lexical movements in speech production. *Psychological Science*, 7, 226–231.

Reitman, W. (1976). Skilled perception in GO: Deducing memory structures from interresponse times. *Cognitive Psychology, 8*, 336–356.

Richardson, A. (1967). Mental practice: A review and discussion. *Research Quarterly, 38*, 95–107.

Rieser, J. J. (1989). Access to knowledge of spatial structure at novel points of observation. *Journal of Experimental Psychology: Learning, Memory, and Cognition, 15*, 1157–1165.

Riley, D. A. (1967). Memory for form. In L. Postman (Ed.), *Psychology in the making* (pp. 402–465). New York: Knopf.

Rode, C., & Stern, E. (in press). Diagrammatic tool use in male and female secondary school students. *Learning and Instruction*.

Ruby, P., & Decety, J. (2001). Effect of subjective perspective taking during simulation of action: A PET investigation of agency. *Nature Neuroscience, 4*, 546–550.

Sadalla, E. K., Burroughs, W. J., & Staplin, L. J. (1980). Reference points in spatial cognition. *Journal of Experimental Psychology: Human Learning and Memory, 5*, 516–528.

Sadalla, E. K., & Magel, S. G. (1980). The perception of traversed distance. *Environment and Behavior, 12*, 65–79.

Sadalla, E. K., & Montello, D. R. (1989). Remembering changes in direction. *Environment and Behavior, 21*, 346–363.

Sadalla, E. K., & Staplin, L. J. (1980a). An information storage model or distance cognition. *Environment and Behavior, 12*, 183–193.

Sadalla, E. K., & Staplin, L. J. (1980b). The perception of traversed distance: Intersections. *Environment and Behavior, 12*, 167–182.

Scaife, M., & Rogers, Y. (1996). External cognition: How do graphical representations work? *International Journal of Human-Computer Studies, 45*, 185–213.

Schiano, D., & Tversky, B. (1992). Structure strategy in viewing simple graphs. *Memory and Cognition, 20*, 12–20.

Schmandt-Besserat, D. (1992). *Before writing, volume 1: From counting to cuneiform*. Austin: University of Texas Press.

Schon, D. A. (1983). *The reflective practitioner*. New York: Harper Collins.

Schwartz, D. L. (1999). Physical imagery: Kinematic vs. dynamic models. *Cognitive Psychology, 38*, 433–464.

Schwartz, D. L., & Black, J. B. (1996a). Analog imagery in mental model reasoning: Depictive models. *Cognitive Psychology, 30*, 154–219.

Schwartz, D., & Black, J. B. (1996b). Shuttling between depictive models and abstract rules: Induction and feedback. *Cognitive Science, 20*, 457–497.

Schwartz, D. L., & Black, T. (1999). Inferences through imagined actions: Knowing by simulated doing. *Journal of Experimental Psychology: Learning, Memory, and Cognition, 25*, 116–136.

Schwartz, D. L., & Holton, D. L. (2000). Tool use and the effect of action on the imagination. *Journal of Experimental Psychology: Learning, Memory, and Cognition, 26*, 1655–1665.

Sekiyama, K. (1982). Kinesthetic aspects of mental representations in the identification of left and right hands. *Perception and Psychophysics, 32*, 89–95.

Shah, P., & Carpenter, P. A. (1995). Conceptual limitations in comprehending line graphs. *Journal of Experimental Psychology: General, 124*, 43–61.

Shah, P., Freedman, E. O., & Vekiri, I. (2003/2004). Graphical displays. In P. Shah & A. Miyake (Eds.), *Handbook of higher-level visuospatial thinking and cognition*. Cambridge, UK: Cambridge University Press.

Shah, P., & Miyake, A. (Eds.). (2003/2004). *Handbook of higher-level visuospatial thinking and cognition*. Cambridge, UK: Cambridge University Press.

Shepard, R. N. (1975). Form, formation, and transformation of internal representations. In R. Solso (Ed.), *Information processing and cognition: The Loyola symposium*. Hillsdale, NJ: Erlbaum.

Shepard, R. N., & Chipman, S. F. (1970). Second-order isomorphism of internal representations: Shapes of states. *Cognitive Psychology, 1*, 1–17.

Shepard, R. N., & Cooper, L. (1982). *Mental images and their transformation*. Cambridge, MA: MIT Press.

Shepard, R. N., & Feng, C. (1972). A chronometric study of mental paper folding. *Cognitive Psychology, 3*, 228–243.

Shepard, R. N., & Metzler, J. (1971). Mental rotation of three-dimensional objects. *Science, 171*, 701–703.

Shepard, R. N., & Podgorny, P. (1978). Cognitive processes that resemble perceptual processes. In W. K. Estes (Ed.), *Handbook of learning and cognitive processes* (Vol. 5, pp. 189–237). Hillsdale, NJ: Erlbaum.

Shiffrar, M., & Freyd, J. J. (1990). Apparent motion of the human body. *Psychological Science*, *1*, 257–264.

Spelke, E. P., Vishton, P. M., & von Hofsten, C. (1995). Object perception, object-directed action, and physical knowledge in infancy. In M. S. Gazzaniga (Ed.), *The cognitive neurosciences* (pp. 275–340). Cambridge, MA: MIT Press.

Stenning, K., & Oberlander, J. (1995). A cognitive theory of graphical and linguistic reasoning: Logic and implementation. *Cognitive Science*, *19*, 97–140.

Stevens, A., & Coupe, P. (1978). Distortions in judged spatial relations. *Cognitive Psychology*, *10*, 422–437.

Suwa, M., & Tversky, B. (1997). What architects and students perceive in their sketches: A protocol analysis. *Design Studies*, *18*, 385–403.

Suwa, M., & Tversky, B. (2003). Constructive perception: A skill for coordinating perception and conception. In *Proceedings of the Cognitive Science Society meeting*.

Suwa, M., Tversky, B., Gero, J., & Purcell, T. (2001). Seeing into sketches: Regrouping parts encourages new interpretations. In J. S. Gero, B. Tversky, & T. Purcell (Eds.), *Visual and spatial reasoning in design* (pp. 207–219). Sydney, Australia: Key Centre of Design Computing and Cognition.

Talmy, L. (1983). How language structures space. In H. L. Pick, Jr., & L. P. Acredolo (Eds.), *Spatial orientation: Theory, research and application* (pp. 225–282). New York: Plenum.

Talmy, L. (2001). *Toward a cognitive semantics. Vol. 1: Concept-structuring systems. Vol. 2: Typology and process in concept structuring.* Cambridge, MA: MIT Press.

Taylor, H. A., & Tversky, B. (1992a). Descriptions and depictions of environments. *Memory and Cognition*, *20*, 483–496.

Taylor, H. A., & Tversky, B. (1992b). Spatial mental models derived from survey and route descriptions. *Journal of Memory and Language*, *31*, 261–282.

Taylor, H. A., & Tversky, B. (1996). Perspective in spatial descriptions. *Journal of Memory and Language*, *35*, 371–391.

Thorndyke, P. (1981). Distance estimation from cognitive maps. *Cognitive Psychology*, *13*, 526–550.

Tufte, E. R. (1983). *The visual display of quantitative information*. Chesire, CT: Graphics Press.

Tufte, E. R. (1990). *Envisioning information*. Cheshire, CT: Graphics Press.

Tufte, E. R. (1997). *Visual explanations*. Cheshire, CT: Graphics Press.

Tversky, B. (1969). Pictorial and verbal encoding in short-term memory. *Perception and Psychophysics*, *5*, 275–287.

Tversky, B. (1975). Pictorial encoding in sentence-picture comparison. *Quarterly Journal of Experimental Psychology*, *27*, 405–410.

Tversky, B. (1981). Distortions in memory for maps. *Cognitive Psychology*, *13*, 407–433.

Tversky, B. (1985). Categories and parts. In C. Craig & T. Givon (Eds.), *Noun classes and categorization* (pp. 63–75). Philadelphia: John Benjamins.

Tversky, B. (1991). Spatial mental models. In G. H. Bower (Ed.), *The psychology of learning and motivation: Advances in research and theory* (Vol. 27, pp. 109–145). New York: Academic Press.

Tversky, B. (1992). Distortions in cognitive maps. *Geoforum*, *23*, 131–138.

Tversky, B. (1993). Cognitive maps, cognitive collages, and spatial mental models. In A. U. Frank & I. Campari (Eds.), *Spatial information theory: A theoretical basis for GIS* (pp. 14–24). Berlin: Springer-Verlag.

Tversky, B. (1995a). Cognitive origins of graphic conventions. In F. T. Marchese (Ed.), *Understanding images* (pp. 29–53). New York: Springer-Verlag.

Tversky, B. (1995b). Perception and cognition of 2D and 3D graphics. *Human factors in computing systems*. New York: ACM.

Tversky, B. (1998). Three dimensions of spatial cognition. In M. A. Conway, S. E. Gathercole, & C. Cornoldi (Eds.), *Theories of memory II* (pp. 259–275). Hove, UK: Psychological Press.

Tversky, B. (2000a). Some ways that maps and diagrams communicate. In C. Freksa, W. Brauer, C. Habel, & K. F. Wender (Eds.), *Spatial cognition II: Integration abstract theories, empirical studies, formal models, and powerful applications* (pp. 72–79). Berlin: Springer-Verlag.

Tversky, B. (2000b). Levels and structure of cognitive mapping. In R. Kitchin & S. M. Freundschuh (Eds.), *Cognitive mapping: Past, present and future* (pp. 24–43). London: Routledge.

Tversky, B. (2000c). Remembering spaces. In E. Tulving & F. I. M. Craik (Eds.), *Handbook of memory* (pp. 363–378). New York: Oxford University Press.

Tversky, B. (2001). Spatial schemas in depictions. In M. Gattis (Ed.), *Spatial schemas and abstract thought* (pp. 79–111). Cambridge, MA: MIT Press.

Tversky, B. (2003a). Navigating by mind and by body. In C. Freksa (Ed.), *Spatial cognition III* (pp. 1–10). Berlin: Springer-Verlag.

Tversky, B. (2003b). Structures of mental spaces: How people think about space. *Environment and Behavior*, 35, 66–80.

Tversky, B. (in press). Functional significance of visuospatial representations. In P. Shah & A. Miyake (Eds.), *Handbook of higher-level visuospatial thinking*. Cambridge, UK: Cambridge University Press.

Tversky, B., Heiser, J., Lozano, S., MacKenzie, R., & Morrison, J. B. (in press). Enriching animations. In R. Lowe & W. Schwartz (Eds.), *Leaving with animals: Research and Innovation Design*. New York: Cambridge University Press.

Tversky, B., & Hemenway, K. (1984). Objects, parts, and categories. *Journal of Experimental Psychology: General*, 113, 169–193.

Tversky, B., Kim, J., & Cohen, A. (1999). Mental models of spatial relations and transformations from language. In C. Habel & G. Rickheit (Eds.), *Mental models in discourse processing and reasoning* (pp. 239–258). Amsterdam: North-Holland.

Tversky, B., Kugelmass, S., & Winter, A. (1991). Cross-cultural and developmental trends in graphic productions. *Cognitive Psychology*, 23, 515–557.

Tversky, B., & Lee, P. U. (1998). How space structures language. In C. Freksa, C. Habel, & K. F. Wender (Eds.), *Spatial cognition: An interdisciplinary approach to representation and processing of spatial knowledge* (pp. 157–175). Berlin: Springer-Verlag.

Tversky, B., & Lee, P. U. (1999). Pictorial and verbal tools for conveying routes. In C. Freksa & D. M. Mark (Eds.), *Spatial information theory: Cognitive and computational foundations of geographic information science* (pp. 51–64). Berlin: Springer-Verlag.

Tversky, B., Lee, P. U., & Mainwaring, S. (1999). Why speakers mix perspectives. *Journal of Spatial Cognition and Computation*, 1, 399–412.

Tversky, B., Morrison, J. B., & Betrancourt, M. (2002). Animation: Does it facilitate? *International Journal of Human-Computer Studies*, 57, 247–262.

Tversky, B., Morrison, J. B., & Zacks, J. (2002). On bodies and events. In A. Meltzoff & W. Prinz (Eds.), *The imitative mind: Development evolution, and brain bases* (pp. 221–232). Cambridge, UK: Cambridge University Press.

Tversky, B., & Schiano, D. (1989). Perceptual and conceptual factors in distortions in memory for maps and graphs. *Journal of Experimental Psychology: General*, 118, 387–398.

Ullman, S. (1996). *High-level vision: Object recognition and visual cognition*. Cambridge, MA: MIT Press.

van Dijk, T. A., & Kintsch, W. (1983). *Strategies of discourse comprehension*. New York: Academic Press.

Wainer, H. (1984). How to display data badly. *The American Statistician*, 38, 137–147.

Wainer, H. (1997). *Visual revelations. Graphical tales of fate and deception from Napoleon Bonaparte to Ross Perot*. New York: Springer-Verlag.

Wexler, M., Kosslyn, S. M., & Berthoz, A. (1998). Motor processes in mental rotation. *Cognition*, 68, 77–94.

Wilton, R. N. (1979). Knowledge of spatial relations: The specification of information used in making inferences. *Quarterly Journal of Experimental Psychology*, 31, 133–146.

Winn, W. (1989). The design and use of instructional graphics. In H. Mandl & J. R. Levin (Eds.), *Knowledge acquisition from text and pictures* (pp. 125–143). Amsterdam: Elsevier.

Wohlschlager, A., & Wolschlager, A. (1998). Mental and manual rotation. *Journal of Experimental Psychology: Human Perception and Performance*, 24, 37–412.

Wraga, M., Creem, S. H., & Proffitt, D. R. (2000). Updating displays after imagined object and viewer rotations. *Journal of Experimental Psychology: Learning, Memory, and Cognition*, 151–168.

Zacks, J. M., Mires, J., Tversky, B., & Hazeltine, E. (2000). Mental spatial transformations of objects and perspective. *Journal of Spatial Cognition and Computation*, 2, 315–332.

Zacks, J. M., Ollinger, J. M., Sheridan, M., & Tversky, B. (2002). A parametric study of mental spatial transformations of bodies. *Neuroimage*, 16, 857–872.

Zacks, J. M., & Tversky, B. (in press). Multiple systems for spatial imagery: Transformations of objects and perspective.

Zacks, J., Tversky, B., & Iyer, G. (2001). Perceiving, remembering and communicating structure in events. *Journal of Experimental Psychology: General*, 136, 29–58.

Zwaan, R. A., & Radvansky, G. A. (1998). Situation models in language comprehension and memory. *Psychological Bulletin*, 123, 162–185.

Part III

JUDGMENT AND DECISION MAKING

CHAPTER 11

Decision Making

Robyn A. LeBoeuf
Eldar B. Shafir

Introduction

People make countless decisions every day, ranging from ones that are barely noticed and soon forgotten ("What should I drink with lunch?" "What should I watch on TV?"), to others that are highly consequential ("How should I invest my retirement funds?" "Should I marry this person?"). In addition to having practical significance, decision making plays a central role in many academic disciplines: Virtually all the social sciences – including psychology, sociology, economics, political science, and law – rely on models of decision-making behavior. This combination of practical and scholarly factors has motivated great interest in how decisions are and should be made. Although decisions can differ dramatically in scope and content, research has uncovered substantial and systematic regularities in how people make decisions and has led to the formulation of general psychological principles that characterize decision-making behavior. This chapter provides a selective review of those regularities and principles. (For further reviews and edited collections, see, among others, Hastie & Dawes, 2001; Goldstein & Hogarth, 1997; Kahneman & Tversky, 2000.)

The classical treatment of decision making, known as the "rational theory of choice" or the "standard economic model," posits that people have orderly preferences that obey a few simple and intuitive axioms. When faced with a choice problem, decision makers are assumed to gauge each alternative's "subjective utility" and to choose the alternative with the highest. In the face of uncertainty about whether outcomes will obtain, decision makers are believed to calculate an option's subjective *expected* utility, which is the sum of its subjective utilities over all possible outcomes weighted by these outcomes' estimated probabilities of occurrence. Deciding then is simply a matter of choosing the option with the greatest expected utility; indeed, choice is believed to *reveal* a person's subjective utility functions and, hence, his or her underlying preferences (e.g., Keeney & Raiffa, 1976; Savage, 1954; von Neumann & Morgenstern, 1944).

Although highly compelling in principle, the standard view has met with persistent critiques addressing its inadequacy as a description of how decisions are actually made. For example, Simon (1955) suggested replacing the rational model with a framework that accounted for a variety of human resource constraints, such as bounded attention and memory capacity, as well as limited time. According to this bounded rationality view, it was unreasonable to expect decision makers to exhaustively compute options' expected utilities.

Other critiques have focused on systematic violations of even the most fundamental requirements of the rational theory of choice. According to the theory, for example, preferences should remain unaffected by logically inconsequential factors such as the precise manner in which options are described, or the specific procedure used to elicit preferences (Arrow, 1951, 1988; Tversky & Kahneman, 1986). However, compelling demonstrations emerged showing that choices failed to obey simple consistency requirements and were, instead, affected by nuances of the decision context that were not subsumed by the normative accounts (e.g., Lichtenstein & Slovic, 1971, 1973; Tversky & Kahneman, 1981). In particular, preferences appeared to be constructed, not merely revealed, in the making of decisions (Slovic, 1995), and this, in turn, was shown to lead to significant and systematic departures from normative predictions.

The mounting evidence has forced a clear division between normative and descriptive treatments. The rational model remains the normative standard against which decisions are often judged, both by experts and by novices (cf. Stanovich, 1999). At the same time, substantial multidisciplinary research has made considerable progress in developing models of choice that are descriptively more faithful. Descriptive accounts as elegant and comprehensive as the normative model are not yet (and may never be) available, but research has uncovered robust principles that play a central role in the making of decisions. In what follows, we review some of these principles, and we consider the fundamental ways in which they conflict with normative expectations.

Choice Under Uncertainty

In the context of some decisions, the availability of options is essentially certain (as when choosing items from a menu or cars at a dealer's lot). Other decisions are made under uncertainty: They are "risky" when the probabilities of the outcomes are known (e.g., gambling or insurance) or, as with most real world decisions, they are "ambiguous," in that precise likelihoods are not known and must be estimated by the decision maker. When deciding under uncertainty, a person must consider both the desirability of the potential outcomes and their likelihoods; much research has addressed the manner in which these factors are estimated and combined.

Prospect Theory

When facing a choice between a risky prospect that offers a 50% chance to win \$200 (and a 50% chance to win nothing) versus an alternative of receiving \$100 for sure, most people prefer the sure gain over the gamble, although the two prospects have the same expected value. (The expected value is the sum of possible outcomes weighted by their probabilities of occurrence. The expected value of the gamble above is .50 * \$200 + .50 * 0 = \$100.) Such preference for a sure outcome over a risky prospect of equal expected value is called *risk aversion*; people tend to be risk averse when choosing between prospects with positive outcomes. The tendency toward risk aversion can be explained by the notion of diminishing sensitivity first formalized by Daniel Bernoulli (1738/1954). Bernoulli proposed that preferences are better described by expected utility than by expected value and suggested that "the utility resulting from a fixed small increase in wealth will be inversely proportional to the quantity of goods previously possessed," thus effectively predicting a concave utility function (a function is concave if a line joining two points

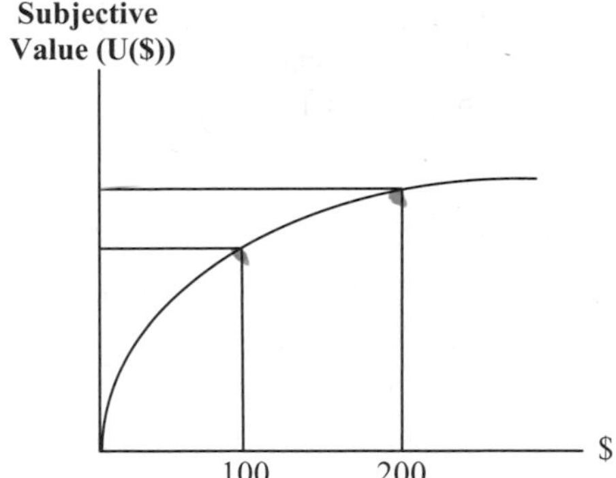

Figure 11.1. A concave function for gains.

on the curve lies below the curve). The expected *utility* of a gamble offering a 50% chance to win $200 (and 50% nothing) is .50 * *u*($200), where *u* is the person's utility function (*u*(0) = 0). As illustrated in Figure 11.1, diminishing sensitivity and a concave utility function imply that the subjective value attached to a gain of $100 is more than one-half of the value attached to a gain of $200 (*u*(100) > .5**u*(200)), which entails preference for the sure $100 gain and, hence, risk aversion.

However, when asked to choose between a prospect that offers a 50% chance to lose $200 (and a 50% chance of nothing) versus losing $100 for sure, most people prefer the risky gamble over the certain loss. This is because diminishing sensitivity applies to negative as well as to positive outcomes: The impact of an initial $100 loss is greater than that of an additional $100, which implies a convex value function for losses. The expected utility of a gamble offering a 50% chance to lose $200 is thus greater (i.e., less negative) than that of a sure $100 loss: (.50**u*(−$200) > *u*(−$100)). Such preference for a risky prospect over a sure outcome of equal expected value is described as *risk seeking*. With the exception of prospects that involve very small probabilities, risk aversion is generally observed in choices involving gains, whereas risk seeking tends to hold in choices involving losses.

These insights led to the S-shaped value function that forms the basis for prospect theory (Kahneman & Tversky, 1979; Tversky & Kahneman, 1992), a highly influential descriptive theory of choice. The value function of prospect theory, illustrated in Figure 11.2, has three important properties: (1) it is defined on gains and losses rather than total wealth, capturing the fact that people normally treat outcomes as departures from a current reference point (rather than in terms of final assets, as posited by the rational theory of choice); (2) it is steeper for losses than for gains; thus, a loss of $X is more aversive than a gain of $X is attractive, capturing the phenomenon of *loss aversion;* and (3) it is concave for gains and convex for losses, predicting, as described previously, risk aversion in the domain of gains and risk seeking in the domain of losses.

In addition, according to prospect theory, probabilities are not treated linearly; instead, people tend to overweight small probabilities and to underweight large ones (Gonzalez & Wu, 1999; Kahneman & Tversky, 1979; Prelec, 2000). This, among other things, has implications for the attractiveness of gambling and of insurance (which typically involve low-probability events), and it yields substantial discontinuities at the endpoints, where the passage from impossibility to possibility and from high likelihood to certainty can have inordinate impact (Camerer, 1992; Kahneman & Tversky, 1979). Furthermore, research has suggested that the weighting of probabilities can be influenced by factors such as the decision

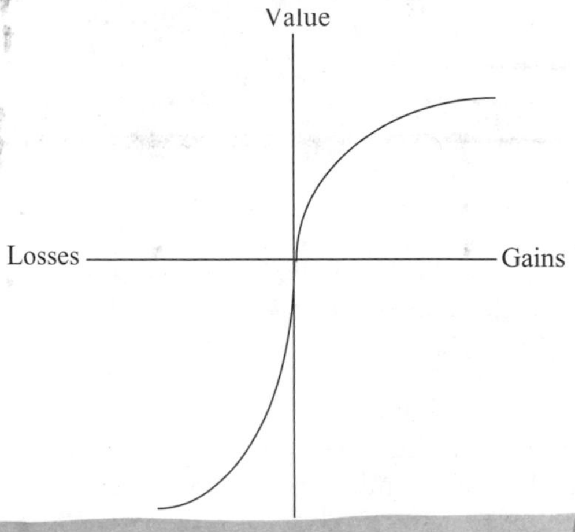

Figure 11.2. Prospect theory's value function.

maker's feeling of competence in a domain (Heath & Tversky, 1991), or by the level of affect engulfing the options under consideration (Rottenstreich & Hsee, 2001). Such attitudes toward value and chance entail substantial sensitivity to contextual factors when making decisions, as discussed further in the next section.

The Framing of Risky Decisions

The previously described attitudes toward risky decisions appear relatively straightforward, and yet, they yield choice patterns that conflict with normative standards. Perhaps the most fundamental are "framing effects" (Tversky & Kahneman, 1981, 1986): Because risk attitudes differ when outcomes are seen as gains as opposed to losses, the same decision can be framed to elicit conflicting risk attitudes. In one example, respondents were asked to assume themselves $300 richer and to choose between a sure gain of $100 or an equal chance to win $200 or nothing. Alternatively, they were asked to assume themselves $500 richer and to choose between a sure loss of $100 and an equal chance to lose $200 or nothing. The two problems are identical in terms of final assets: Both amount to a choice between $400 for sure versus an even chance at $300 or $500 (Tversky & Kahneman, 1986). People, however, tend to "accept" the provided frame and consider the problem as presented, failing to reframe it from alternate perspectives. As a result, most people choosing between "gains" show a risk-averse preference for the certain ($400) outcome, whereas most of those choosing between "losses" express a risk-seeking preference for the gamble. This pattern violates the normative requirement of "description invariance," according to which logically equivalent descriptions of a decision problem should yield the same preferences (see Kühberger, 1995; Levin, Schneider, & Gaeth, 1998, for reviews).

The acceptance of the problem frame, combined with the nonlinear weighting of probabilities and, in particular, with the elevated impact of perceived "certainty," has a variety of normatively troubling consequences. Consider, for example, the following choice between gambles (Tversky & Kahneman, 1981, p. 455):

> *A. A 25% chance to win $30*
> *B. A 20% chance to win $45*

Faced with this choice, the majority (58%) of participants preferred option B. Now, consider the following extensionally equivalent problem:

> *In the first stage of this game, there is a 75% chance to end the game without winning anything, and a 25% chance to move into the second stage. If you reach the second stage, you have a choice between:*
>
> C. *A sure win of $30*
> D. *An 80% chance to win $45*

The majority (78%) of participants now preferred option C over option D, even though, when combined with the "first stage" of the problem, options C and D are equivalent to A and B, respectively. Majority preference thus reverses as a function of a supposedly irrelevant contextual variation. In this particular case, the reversal is due to the impact of apparent certainty (which renders option C more attractive) and to another important factor, namely, people's tendency to contemplate decisions from a "local" rather than a "global" perspective. Note that a combination of the two stages in the last problem would have easily yielded the same representation as that of the preceding version. However, rather than amalgamating across events and decisions, as is often assumed in normative analyses, people tend to contemplate each decision separately, which can yield conflicting attitudes across choices. We return to the issue of local versus global perspectives in a later section.

As a further example of framing, it is interesting to note that, even within the domain of losses, risk attitudes can reverse depending on the context of decision. Thus, participants actually tend to prefer a sure loss to a risky prospect when the sure loss is described as "insurance" against a low-probability, high-stakes loss (Hershey & Schoemaker, 1980). The insurance context brings to the forefront a social norm, making the insurance premium appear more like an investment than a loss, with the low-probability, high-stakes loss acquiring the character of a neglected responsibility rather than a considered risk (e.g., Hershey & Schoemaker, 1980; Kahneman & Tversky, 1979; Slovic, Fischhoff, & Lichtenstein, 1988).

The framing of certainty and risk also impacts people's thinking about financial transactions through inflationary times, as illustrated by the following example. Participants were asked to imagine that they were in charge of buying computers (currently priced at $1000) that would be delivered and paid for 1 year later, by which time, due to inflation, prices were expected to be approximately 20% higher (and equally likely to be above or below the projected 20%). All participants essentially faced the same choice: They could agree to pay either $1200 (20% more than the current price) upon delivery next year, or they could agree to pay the going market price in 1 year, which would depend on inflation. Reference points were manipulated to make one option appear certain while the other appeared risky: Half the participants saw the contracts framed in nominal terms so the $1200 price appeared certain, whereas the future nominal market price (which could be more or less than $1200) appeared risky. Other participants saw the contracts framed in real terms, so the future market price appeared appropriately indexed, whereas precommitting to a $1200 price, which could be lower or higher than the actual future market price, seemed risky. As predicted, in both conditions respondents preferred the contract that appeared certain, preferring the fixed price in the nominal frame and the indexed price in the "real" frame (Shafir, Diamond, & Tversky, 1997). As with many psychological tendencies, the preference for certainty can mislead in some circumstances, but it may also be exploited for beneficial ends, such as when the certainty associated with a particular settlement is highlighted to boost the chance for conflict resolution (Kahneman & Tversky, 1995).

Riskless Choice

Not all decisions involve risk or uncertainty. For example, when choosing between items in a store, we can be fairly confident that the displayed items are available. (Naturally, there could be substantial uncertainty about one's eventual satisfaction with the choice, but we leave those considerations aside for the moment.) The absence of uncertainty, however, does not eliminate preference malleability, and many of the principles discussed previously continue to exert an impact even on riskless decisions. Recall that outcomes can be framed as gains or as losses relative to a reference point, that losses typically "loom larger" than comparable gains, and that people tend to accept the presented frame. These factors, even in the absence of risk, can yield normatively problematic decision patterns.

Loss Aversion and the Status Quo

A fundamental fact about the making of decisions is loss aversion: According to loss aversion, the pain associated with giving up a good is greater than the pleasure associated with obtaining it (Tversky & Kahneman, 1991). This yields "endowment effects," wherein the mere possession of a good (such that parting with it is rendered a loss) can lead to higher valuation of the good than if it were not in one's possession. A classic experiment illustrates this point (Kahneman, Knetsch, & Thaler, 1990). Participants were arbitrarily assigned to be *sellers* or *choosers*. The sellers were each given an attractive mug, which they could keep, and were asked to indicate the lowest amount for which they would sell the mug. The *choosers* were not given a mug but were instead asked to indicate the amount of money that the mug was worth to them. Additional procedural details were designed to promote truthful estimates; in short, an official market price, $X, was to be revealed; all those who valued the mug at more than $X received a mug, whereas those who valued the mug below $X received $X. All participants, whether sellers or choosers, essentially faced the same task of determining a price at which they would prefer money over the mug. Because participants were randomly assigned to be sellers or choosers, standard expectations are that the two groups would value the mugs similarly. Loss aversion, however, suggests that the sellers would set a higher price (for what they were about to "lose") than the choosers. Indeed, sellers' median asking price was twice that of choosers.

Another manifestation of loss aversion is a general reluctance to trade, illustrated in a study in which one-half of the subjects were given a decorated mug, whereas the others were given a bar of Swiss chocolate (Knetsch, 1989). Later, each subject was shown the alternative gift and offered the opportunity to trade his or her gift for the other. Because the initial allocation of gifts was arbitrary and transaction costs minimal, economic theory predicts that about one-half the participants would exchange their gifts. Loss aversion, however, predicts that most participants would be reluctant to give up a gift in their possession (a loss) to obtain the other (a gain). Indeed, only 10% of the participants chose to trade. This contrasts sharply with standard analysis in which the value of a good does not change when it becomes part of one's endowment.

Loss aversion thus promotes stability rather than change. It implies that people will not accept an even chance to win or lose $X, because the loss of $X is more aversive than the gain of $X is attractive. In particular, it predicts a strong tendency to maintain the status quo because the disadvantages of departing from it loom larger than the advantages of its alternative (Samuelson & Zeckhauser, 1988). A striking tendency to maintain the status quo was observed in the context of insurance decisions when New Jersey and Pennsylvania both introduced the option of a limited right to sue, entitling automobile drivers to lower insurance rates. The two states differed in what they offered consumers as the default option: New Jersey motorists had to acquire the full right to sue (transaction costs were minimal: a signature), whereas in Pennsylvania, the full right was the default, which could be forfeited in favor of the limited alternative. Whereas only about 20% of New Jersey drivers chose to acquire the full right to sue, approximately 75% of Pennsylvania drivers chose to retain it. The difference in adoption rates resulting from the alternate defaults had financial repercussions estimated at nearly $200 million (Johnson, Hershey, Meszaros, & Kunreuther, 1993). Another naturally occurring "experiment" was more recently observed in Europeans' choices to be potential organ donors (Johnson & Goldstein, 2003). In some European nations drivers are by default organ donors unless they elect not to be, whereas in other European nations they are, by default, not donors unless they choose to be. Observed rates of organ donors are almost 98% in the former nations and about 15% in the latter, a remarkable difference given the low transaction costs and the significance of the decision.

For another example, consider two candidates, Frank and Carl, who are running for election during difficult times and have announced target inflation and unemployment figures. Frank proposes a 42% yearly inflation rate and 15% unemployment, whereas Carl envisions 23% inflation and 22% unemployment. When Carl's figures represent the status quo, Frank's plans entail greater inflation and diminished unemployment, whereas when Frank's figures are the status quo, Carl's plan entails lower inflation and greater unemployment. As predicted, neither departure from the "current" state was endorsed by the majority of respondents, who preferred whichever candidate was said to represent the status quo (Quattrone & Tversky, 1988).

The status quo bias can affect decisions in domains as disparate as job selection (Tversky & Kahneman, 1991), investment allocation (Samuelson & Zeckhauser, 1988), and organ donation (Johnson & Goldstein, 2003), and it can also hinder the negotiated resolution of disputes. If each disputant sees the opponent's concessions as gains but its own concessions as losses, agreement will be hard to reach because each will perceive itself as relinquishing more than it stands to gain. Because loss aversion renders foregone gains more palatable than comparable losses (cf. Kahneman, 1992), an insightful mediator may do best to set all sides' reference points low, thus requiring compromises over outcomes that are mostly perceived as gains.

Semantic Framing

The tendency to adopt the provided frame can lead to "attribute-framing" effects (Levin, Schneider, & Gaeth, 1998). A package of ground beef, for example, can be described as 75% lean or else as 25% fat. Not surprisingly, it tends to be evaluated more favorably under the former description than the latter (Levin, 1987; see also Levin, Schnittjer, & Thee, 1988). Similarly, a community with a 3.7% crime rate tends to be allocated greater police resources than one described as 96.3% "crime free" (Quattrone & Tversky, 1988). Attribute-framing effects are not limited to riskless choice; for example, people are more favorably inclined toward a medical procedure when its chance of success, rather than failure, is highlighted (Levin et al., 1988).

Attribute-framing manipulations affect the perceived quality of items by changing their descriptions. Part of the impact of such semantic factors may be due to spreading activation (Collins & Loftus, 1975), wherein positive words (e.g., "crime-free") activate associated positive concepts, and negative words activate negative concepts. The psychophysical properties of numbers also contribute to these effects. A 96.3% "crime free" rate, for example, appears insubstantially different from 100% and suggests that "virtually all" are law abiding. The difference between 0% and 3.7%, in contrast, appears more substantial and suggests the need for intervention (Quattrone & Tversky, 1988). Like the risk attitudes previously described, such perceptual effects often seem natural and harmless in their own right but can generate preference inconsistencies that appear perplexing, especially given the rather mild and often unavoidable manipulations (after all, things need to be described one way or another) and the trivial computations often required to translate from one frame to another.

Conflict and Reasons

Choices can be hard to make. People often approach difficult decisions by looking for a compelling rationale for choosing one option over another. At times, compelling rationales are easy to come by and to articulate, whereas other times no compelling rationale presents itself, rendering the conflict between options hard to resolve. Such conflict can be aversive and can lead people to postpone the decision or to select a "default" alternative. The tendency to rely on compelling rationales that help minimize conflict appears benign; nonetheless, it can generate preference patterns that are fundamentally different from those predicted by normative accounts based on value maximization.

Decisional Conflict

One way to avoid conflict in choice is to opt for what appears to be no choice at all, namely, the status quo. In one example (Tversky & Shafir, 1992a), participants who were purportedly looking to buy a CD player were presented with a Sony player that was on a 1-day sale for $99, well below the list price. Two-thirds of the participants said they would buy such a CD player. Another group was presented with the same Sony player and also with a top-of-the-line Aiwa player for $159. In the latter case, only 54% expressed interest in buying either option, and a full 46% preferred to wait until they learned more about the various models. The addition of an attractive option increased conflict and diminished the number who ended up with either player, despite the fact that most preferred the initial alternative to the status quo. This violates what is known as the regularity condition, according to which the "market share" of an existing option – here, the status quo – cannot be increased by enlarging the offered set (see also Tversky & Simonson, 1993).

A related pattern was documented using tasting booths in an upscale grocery store, where shoppers were offered the opportunity to taste any of 6 jams in one condition, or any of 24 jams in the second (Iyengar & Lepper, 2000). In the 6-jams condition, 40% of shoppers stopped to have a taste and, of those, 30% proceeded to purchase a jam. In the 24-jam condition, a full 60% stopped to taste, but only 3% purchased. Presumably, the conflict between so many attractive options proved hard to resolve. Further studies found that those choosing goods (e.g., chocolate) from a larger set later reported lower satisfaction with their selections than those choosing from a smaller set. Conflict among options thus appears to make people less happy about choosing, as well as less happy with their eventual choices.

Decisional conflict tends to favor default alternatives, much as it advantages the status quo. In one study, 80 students agreed to fill out a questionnaire in return for $1.50. Following the questionnaire, one-half of the respondents were offered the opportunity to exchange the $1.50 (the default) for one of two prizes: a metal Zebra pen, or a pair of plastic Pilot pens. The remaining subjects were only offered the opportunity to exchange the $1.50 for the Zebra. The pens were shown to subjects, who were informed that each prize regularly costs just over $2.00. The results were as follows. Twenty-five percent opted for the payment over the Zebra when Zebra was the only alternative, but a reliably greater 53% chose the payment over the Zebra or the Pilot pens when both options were offered (Tversky & Shafir, 1992a). Whereas the majority of subjects took advantage of the opportunity to obtain a valuable alternative when only one was offered, the availability of competing valuable alternatives increased the tendency to retain the default option.

Related effects have been documented in decisions made by expert physicians and legislators (Redelmeier & Shafir, 1995). In one scenario, neurologists and neurosurgeons were asked to decide which of several patients awaiting surgery ought to be operated on first. Half the respondents were presented with two patients, a woman in her early fifties and a man in his seventies. Others saw the same two patients along with a third, a woman in her early fifties highly comparable to the first, so it was difficult to think of a rationale for choosing either woman over the other. As predicted, more physicians (58%) chose to operate on the older man in the latter version, where the two highly comparable women presented decisional conflict, than in the former version (38%), in which the choice was between only one younger woman and the man.

The addition of some options can generate conflict and increase the tendency to refrain from choosing. Other options, however, can lower conflict and increase the likelihood of making a choice. *Asymmetric dominance* refers to the fact that in a choice between options A and B, a third option, A′, can be added that is clearly inferior to A (but not to B), thereby increasing the choice likelihood of A (Huber, Payne, & Puto, 1982). For example, a choice between $6 and an elegant pen presents some conflict for participants. However, when a less attractive pen is added to the choice set, the superior pen clearly dominates the inferior pen. This dominance provides a rationale for choosing the elegant alternative and leads to an increase in the percentage of those choosing the elegant pen over the cash. Along related lines, the *compromise effect* occurs when the addition of a third, extreme option makes a previously available option appear as a reasonable compromise, thus increasing its popularity (Simonson, 1989; Simonson & Tversky, 1992).

Standard normative accounts do not deny conflict, nor, however, do they assume any direct influence of conflict on choice. (For people who maximize utility, there does not appear to be much room for conflict: Either the utility difference is large and the decision is easy, or it is small and the decision is of little import.) In actuality, people are concerned with making the "right" choice, which can render decisional conflict influential beyond mere considerations of value. Conflict is an integral aspect of decision making, and the phenomenology of conflict, which can be manipulated via the addition or removal of alternatives, yields predictable and systematic violations of standard normative predictions.

Reason-Based Choice

The desire to make the "right" choice often leads people to look for good reasons when making decisions, and such reliance on reasons helps make sense of phenomena that appear puzzling from the perspective of value maximization (Shafir, Simonson, & Tversky, 1993). Relying on good reasons seems like sound practice: After all, the converse, making a choice without good reason, seems unwise. At the same time, abiding by this practice can be problematic because the reasons that come to mind are often fleeting, are limited to what is introspectively accessible, and are not necessarily those that guide, or ought to guide, the decision. For example, participants who were asked to analyze *why* they felt the way that they did about a set of jams showed less agreement with "expert" ratings of the jams than did those who merely stated their preferences (Wilson & Schooler, 1991). A search for reasons can alter preference in line with reasons that come readily to mind, but those reasons may be heavily influenced by salience, availability, or momentary context. A heavy focus on a biased set of temporarily available reasons can cause one to lose sight of one's (perhaps more valid) initial feelings (Wilson, Dunn, Kraft, & Lisle, 1989).

Furthermore, a wealth of evidence suggests that people are not always aware of their reasons for acting and deciding (see Nisbett & Wilson, 1977). In one example, participants presented with four identical pairs of stockings and asked to select one showed a marked preference for the option on the right. However, despite this evidence that choice was governed by position, no participant mentioned position as the reason for the choice. Respondents easily generated "reasons" (in which they cited attributes, such as stocking texture), but the reasons they provided bore little resemblance to those that actually guided choice (Nisbett & Wilson, 1977).

Finally, and perhaps most normatively troubling, a reliance on reasons can induce preference inconsistencies because nuances in decisional context can render certain reasons more or less apparent. In one study (Tversky & Shafir, 1992b), college students were asked to imagine that they had just taken and passed a difficult exam and now had a choice for the Christmas holidays: They could buy an attractive vacation package at a low price, they could forego the vacation package, or they could pay a $5 fee to defer the decision by a day. The majority elected to buy the vacation package, and less than one-third elected to delay the decision. A second group was asked to imagine that they had taken the exam and failed and would need to retake it after the Christmas holidays. They were then presented with the same choice and, as before, the majority elected to buy the vacation package; less than one-third preferred to defer. However, when a third group of participants was to imagine they did not know whether they had passed or failed the exam, the majority preferred to pay to defer the decision until the next day, when the exam result would be known, and only a minority was willing to commit to the trip without knowing. Apparently, participants were comfortable booking the trip when they had clear reasons for the decision – celebrating when they passed the exam or recuperating when they had failed – but were reluctant to commit when their reasons for the trip were uncertain. This pattern, which violates the sure thing principle (Savage, 1954), has been documented in a variety of contexts, including gambling and strategic interactions (e.g., prisoner's dilemmas; see also Shafir, 1994; Shafir & Tversky, 1992).

The tendency to delay decision for the sake of further information can have a significant impact on the ensuing choice.

Consider the following scenario (Bastardi & Shafir, 1998):

> *For some time, you have considered adding a compact disc (CD) player to your stereo system. You now see an ad for a week-long sale offering a very good CD player for only $120, 50% off the retail price. Recently, however, your amplifier broke. You learn that your warranty has expired and that you have to pay $90 for repairs.*

One group (the "simple" condition) was asked whether they would buy the CD player during the sale, and the vast majority (91%) said they would. Another ("uncertain") group was presented with the same scenario, but was told that they would not know until the next day whether the warranty covered the $90 repairs. They could wait until the following day (when they would know about the warranty) to decide whether to buy the CD player; 69% elected to wait. Those who chose to wait then learned that the warranty had expired and would not cover repairs; upon receiving the news, the majority decided not to buy the CD player. Note that this contrasts sharply with the unequivocal choice to buy the CD player when the $90 repair costs were a given. Although they faced the same decision, only 55% (including those who waited and those who did not) chose to buy the CD player in the uncertain condition, when they did not know but could pursue information about the repair costs, compared with 91% in the certain condition, when repair costs were known from the start. The decision to pursue information can focus attention on the information obtained and thereby trigger emergent rationales for making the choice, ultimately distorting preference (Bastardi & Shafir, 1998). Similar patterns have been replicated in a variety of contexts, including one involving professional nurses in a renal failure ward, more of whom expressed willingness to donate a kidney (to a hypothetical relative) when they had purportedly been tested and learned that they were eligible than when they had known they were eligible from the start (Redelmeier, Shafir, & Aujla, 2001). A reliance on reasons in choice leaves decision makers susceptible to a variety of contextual and procedural nuances that render alternative potential reasons salient and thus may lead to inconsistent choices.

Processing of Attribute Weights

Choices can be complex, requiring the evaluation of multiattribute options. Consider, for example, a choice between two job candidates: One candidate did well in school but has relatively unimpressive work experience and moderate letters of recommendation, whereas the other has a poor scholastic record but better experience and stronger letters. To make this choice, the decision maker must somehow combine the attribute information, which requires determining not only the quality or value of each attribute, but also the extent to which a shortcoming on one attribute can be compensated for by strength on another.

Attribute evaluation may be biased by a host of factors known to hold sway over human judgment (for a review, see Kahneman & Frederick, Chap. 12). Moreover, researchers have long known that people have limited capacity for combining information across attributes. Because of unreliable attribute weights in human judges, simple linear models tend to yield normatively better predictions than the very judges on whom the models are based (Dawes, 1979; Dawes, Faust, & Meehl, 1989). In fact, people's unreliable weighting of attributes makes them susceptible to a host of manipulations that alter attribute weights and yield conflicting preferences (see Shafir & LeBoeuf, 2004, for a further discussion of multiattribute choice).

Compatibility

Options can vary on several dimensions. Even simple monetary gambles, for example, differ on payoffs and the chance to win. Respondents' preferences among such gambles can be assessed in different but logically equivalent, ways (see Schkade & Johnson,

1989, for a review). For example, participants may be asked to choose among the gambles or, alternatively, they may estimate their maximum willingness to pay for each gamble. Notably, these procedures, although logically equivalent, often result in differential weightings of attributes and, consequently, in inconsistent preferences.

Consider two gambles: One offers an eight-in-nine chance to win $4 and the other a one-in-nine chance to win $40. People typically choose the high-probability gamble but assign a higher price to the high-payoff gamble, thus expressing conflicting preferences (Grether & Plott, 1979; Lichtenstein & Slovic, 1971, 1973; Tversky, Slovic, & Kahneman, 1990). This pattern illustrates the principle of *compatibility*, according to which an attribute's weight is enhanced by its compatibility with the response mode (Slovic, Griffin, & Tversky, 1990; Tversky, Sattath, & Slovic, 1988). In particular, a gamble's potential payoff is weighted more heavily in pricing, where both the price and the payoff are in the same monetary units, than in choice, where neither attribute maps onto the response scale (Schkade & Johnson, 1989). As a consequence, the high-payoff gamble is valued more in pricing relative to choice.

For another type of response compatibility, imagine having to choose or, alternatively, having to reject, one of two options. Logically speaking, the two tasks are interchangeable: If people prefer one option, they will reject the second, and vice versa. However, people tend to focus on the relative strengths of options (more compatible with choosing) when they choose, and on weaknesses (compatible with rejecting) when they reject. As a result, options' positive features (the pros) loom larger in choice, whereas their negative features (the cons) are weighted relatively more during rejection. In one study, respondents were presented with pairs of options – an enriched option, with various positive and negative features, and an impoverished option, with no real positive or negative features (Shafir, 1993). For example, consider two vacation destinations: one with a variety of positive and negative attributes, such as gorgeous beaches and great sunshine but cold water and strong winds, and another that is neutral in all respects. Some respondents were asked which destination they preferred; others decided which to forego. Because positive features are weighed more heavily in choice and negative features matter relatively more during rejection, the enriched destination was most frequently chosen and rejected. Overall, its choice and rejection rates summed to 115%, significantly more than the impoverished destination's 85%, and more than the 100% expected if choice and rejection were complementary (see also Downs & Shafir, 1999; Wedell, 1997).

Separate Versus Comparative Evaluation

Decision contexts can facilitate or hamper attribute evaluation, and this can alter attribute weights. Not surprisingly, an attribute whose value is clear can have greater impact than an attribute whose value is vague. The effects of ease of evaluation, referred to as "evaluability," occur, for example, when an attribute proves difficult to gauge in isolation but easier to evaluate in a comparative setting (Hsee, 1996; Hsee, Loewenstein, Blount, & Bazerman, 1999). In one study, subjects were presented with two second-hand music dictionaries: one with 20,000 entries but a slightly torn cover, and the other with 10,000 entries and an unblemished cover. Subjects had only a vague notion of how many entries to expect in a music dictionary; when they saw these one at a time, they were willing to pay more for the dictionary with the new cover than for the one with a cover that was slightly torn. When the dictionaries were evaluated concurrently, however, the number-of-entries attribute became salient: Most subjects obviously preferred the dictionary with more entries, despite the inferior cover.

For another example, consider a job that pays $80,000 a year at a firm where one's peers receive $100,000, compared with a job that pays $70,000 while coworkers are paid $50,000. Consistent with the fact that most people prefer higher incomes, a majority of second-year MBA students who compared the two options preferred the job with the higher absolute – despite the lower relative – income. When the jobs are contemplated separately, however, the precise merits of one's own salary are hard to gauge, but earning less than comparable others renders the former job relatively less attractive than the latter, where one's salary exceeds one's peers'. Indeed, the majority of MBA students who evaluated the two jobs separately anticipated higher satisfaction in the job with the lower salary but the higher relative position, obviously putting more weight on the latter attribute in the context of separate evaluation (Bazerman, Schroth, Shah, Diekmann, & Tenbrunsel, 1994).

In the same vein, decision principles that are hard to apply in isolated evaluation may prove decisive in comparative settings, producing systematic fluctuations in attribute weights. Kahneman and Ritov (1994), for example, asked participants about their willingness to contribute to several environmental programs. One program was geared toward saving dolphins in the Mediterranean Sea; another funded free medical checkups for farm workers at risk for skin cancer. When asked which program they would rather support, the vast majority chose the medical checkups for farm workers, presumably following the principle that human lives come before those of animals. However, when asked separately for the largest amount they would be willing to pay for each intervention, respondents, moved by the animals' vivid plight, were willing to pay more for the dolphins than for workers' checkups. In a similar application, potential jurors awarded comparable dollar amounts to plaintiffs who had suffered either physical or financial harm, as long as the cases were evaluated separately. However, in concurrent evaluation, award amounts increased dramatically when the harm was physical as opposed to financial, affirming the notion that personal harm is the graver offense (Sunstein, Kahneman, Schkade, & Ritov, 2001).

Attribute weights, which are normatively assumed to remain stable, systematically shift and give rise to patterns of inconsistent preferences. Notably, discrepancies between separate versus concurrent evaluation have profound implications for intuition and for policy. Outcomes in life are typically experienced one at a time: A person lives through one scenario or another. Normative intuitions, however, typically arise from concurrent introspection: We entertain a scenario along with its alternatives. When an event triggers reactions that stem from its being experienced in isolation, important aspects of the experience will be misconstrued by intuitions that arise from concurrent evaluation (see Shafir, 2002).

Local Versus Global Perspectives

Many of the inconsistency patterns described previously would not have arisen were decisions considered from a more global perspective. The framing of decisions, for instance, would be of little consequence were people to go beyond the provided frame to represent the decision outcomes in a canonical manner that is description independent. Instead, people tend to accept the decision problem as it is presented, largely because they may not have thought of other ways to look at the decision, and also because they may not expect their preferences to be susceptible to presumably incidental alterations. (Note that even if they were to recognize the existence of multiple perspectives, people may still not know how to arrive at a preference independent of a specific formulation; cf. Kahneman, 2003). In this final section, we review several additional decision contexts in which a limited or myopic approach is seen to guide decision making, and inconsistent preferences arise as a result of a failure to adopt a more "global" perspective. Such a perspective requires one to ignore momentarily salient features of the decision in favor of other, often less salient, considerations that have long-run consequences.

Repeated Decisions

Decisions that occur on a regular basis are often more meaningful when evaluated "in the long run." For example, the choice to diet or to exercise makes little difference on any one day and can only be carried out under a long-term perspective that trumps the person's short-term preferences for cake over vegetables or for sleeping late rather than going to the gym early. People, however, often do not take this long-term perspective when evaluating instances of a recurring choice; instead, they tend to treat each choice as an isolated event.

In one study, participants were offered a 50% chance to win $2000 and a 50% chance to lose $500. Although most participants refused to play this gamble once, the majority were eager to play the gamble five times, and, when given the choice, preferred to play the gamble six times rather than five. Apparently, fear of possibly losing the single gamble is compensated for by the high likelihood of ending up ahead in the repeated version. Other participants were asked to imagine that they had already played the gamble five times (outcome as yet unknown) and were given the option to play once more. In this formulation, a majority of participants rejected the additional play. Although participants preferred to play the gamble six times rather than five, once they had finished playing five, the additional opportunity was immediately "segregated" and treated as a single instance, which – as we know from the single gamble version – participants preferred to avoid (Redelmeier & Tversky, 1992).

In a related vein, consider physicians, who can think of their patients "individually" (i.e., patient by patient) or "globally" (e.g., as groups of patients with similar problems). In several studies, Redelmeier and Tversky (1990) found that physicians were more likely to take "extra measures," such as ordering an expensive medical test or recommending an in-person consultation, when they considered the treatment of an individual patient than when they considered a larger group of similarly afflicted patients. Personal concerns loomed larger when patients were considered individually than when "patients in general" were considered, with the latter group more likely to highlight efficiency concerns. Because physicians tend to see patients one at a time, this predicts a pattern of individual decisions that is inconsistent with what these physicians would endorse from a more global perspective. For a more mundane example, people report greater willingness to wear a seatbelt – and to support proseatbelt legislation – when they are shown statistics concerning the lifetime risk of being in a fatal accident instead of the dramatically lower risk associated with any single auto trip (Slovic et al., 1988).

Similar patterns prompted Kahneman and Lovallo (1993) to argue that decision makers often err by treating each decision as unique rather than categorizing it as one in a series of similar decisions made over a lifetime (or, in the case of corporations, made by many workers). They distinguish an "inside view" of situations and plans, characterized by a focus on the peculiarities of the case at hand, from an "outside view," guided by an analysis of a large number of similar cases. Whereas an outside view, based, for example, on base rates, typically leads to a more accurate evaluation of the current case, people routinely adopt an inside view, which typically overweighs the particulars of the given case at the expense of base-rate considerations. Managers, for example, despite knowing that past product launches have routinely run over budget and behind schedule, may convince themselves that this time will be different because the team is excellent or the product exceptional. The inside view can generate overconfidence (Kahneman & Lovallo, 1993), as well as undue optimism, for example, regarding the chances of completing projects by early deadlines (e.g., the planning fallacy; Buehler, Griffin, & Ross, 1994). The myopia that emerges from treating repeated decisions as unique leads to overly bold predictions and to the neglect of considerations that ought to matter in the long run.

Mental Accounting

Specific forms of myopia arise in the context of "mental accounting," the behavioral equivalent of accounting done by firms wherein people reason about and make decisions concerning matters such as income, spending, and savings. Contrary to the assumption of "fungibility," according to which money in one account, or from one source, is a perfect substitute for money in another, it turns out that the labeling of accounts and the nature of transactions have a significant impact on people's decisions (Thaler, 1999). For one example, people's reported willingness to spend $25 on a theater ticket is unaffected by having incurred a $50 parking ticket but is significantly lowered when $50 is spent on a ticket to a sporting event (Heath & Soll, 1996). Respondents apparently bracket expenses into separate accounts so spending on entertainment is impacted by a previous entertainment expense in a way that it is not if that same expense is "allocated" to, say, travel. Along similar lines, people who had just lost a $10 bill were happy to buy a $10 ticket for a play but were less willing to buy the ticket if, instead of the money, they had just lost a similar $10 ticket (Tversky & Kahneman, 1981). Apparently, participants were willing to spend $10 on a play even after losing $10 cash but found it aversive to spend what was coded as $20 on a ticket.

Finally, consider the following scenario, which respondents saw in one of two versions:

> *Imagine that you are about to purchase a jacket for $125 [$15] and a calculator for $15 [$125]. The calculator salesman informs you that the calculator you want to buy is on sale for $10 [$120] at the other branch of the store, located 20 minutes drive away. Would you make the trip to the other store? (Tversky & Kahneman, 1981, p. 457)*

Faced with the opportunity to save $5 on a $15 calculator, a majority of respondents agreed to make the trip. However, when the calculator sold for $125, only a minority was willing to make the trip for the same $5 savings. A global evaluation of either version yields a 20-minute voyage for $5 savings; people, however, seem to make decisions based on what has been referred to as "topical" accounting (Kahneman & Tversky, 1984), wherein the same $5 saving is coded as a substantial ratio in one case and as quite negligible in the other.

Specific formulations and contextual details are not spontaneously reformulated or translated into more comprehensive or canonical representations. As a consequence, preferences prove highly labile and dependent on what are often theoretically, as well as practically, unimportant and accidental details. An extensive literature on mental accounting, as well as behavioral finance, forms part of the growing field of behavioral economics (see, e.g., Camerer, Loewenstein, & Rabin, 2004; Thaler 1993, 1999).

Temporal Discounting

A nontrivial task is to decide how much weight to give to outcomes extended into the distant future. Various forms of uncertainty (regarding nature, one's own tastes, and so on) justify some degree of discounting in calculating the present value of future goods. Thus, $1000 received next year is typically worth less than $1000 received today. As it turns out, observed discount rates tend to be unstable and often influenced by factors, such as the size of the good and its temporal distance, that are not subsumed under standard normative analyses (see Ainslie, 2001; Frederick, Loewenstein, & Donoghue, 2002; Loewenstein & Thaler, 1989, for review). For example, although some people prefer an apple today over two apples tomorrow, virtually nobody prefers one apple in 30 days over two apples in 31 days (Thaler, 1981). Because discount functions are nonexponential (see also Loewenstein & Prelec, 1992), a 1-day delay has greater impact when that day is near than when it is far. Similarly, when asked what amount of money in the future would be comparable to receiving a specified amount today, people require about $60 in 1 year to match $15 now, but they are satisfied with $4000 in a year instead of $3000 today. This implies discount rates of 300% in the first case and of 33% in the second. To the extent that one engages in a variety of transactions throughout time, imposing wildly disparate discount rates on smaller versus larger amounts ignores the fact that numerous small amounts will eventually add up to be larger, yielding systematic inconsistency.

Excessive discounting turns into myopia, which is often observed in people's attitudes toward future outcomes (see, e.g., Elster, 1984; Elster & Loewenstein, 1992). Loewenstein and Thaler (1989) discussed a West Virginia experiment in which the high school dropout rate was reduced by one-third when dropouts were threatened with the loss of their driving privileges. This immediate consequence apparently had a significantly greater impact than the far more serious but more distant socioeconomic implications of failing to graduate from high school. These authors also mention physicians' typical lament that warning about the risk of skin cancer from excessive sun exposure has less effect than the warning that such exposure can cause large pores and acne. In fact, "quit smoking" campaigns have begun to stress the immediate benefits of quitting (quick reduction in the chance of a heart attack, improved ability to taste foods within 2 days, and such) even more prominently than the long-term benefits (American Lung Association, 2003). Similar reasoning applies in the context of promoting safe sex practices and medical self-examinations, where immediate gratification or discomfort often trumps much greater, but temporally distant, considerations. Schelling (1980, 1984) thought about similar issues of self-control in the face of immediate temptation as involving multiple "selves"; it is to related considerations of alternate frames of mind that we turn next.

Frames of Mind

Myopic decisions can occur when highly transient frames of mind are momentarily triggered, highlighting values and desires that may not reflect the decision maker's more global preferences. Because choices often involve delayed consumption, failure to anticipate the labile nature of preferences may lead to the selection of later-disliked alternatives.

PRIMING

At the most basic level, transient mindsets arise when specific criteria are made momentarily salient. Grocery shopping while very hungry, for example, is likely to lead to purchases that would not have been made under normal circumstances (cf. Loewenstein, 1996). In a study of the susceptibility to temporary criterion salience, participants first received a "word perception test" in which either creativity, reliability, or a neutral topic was primed. Participants then completed an ostensibly unrelated "product impression task" that gauged their opinions of various cameras. Cameras advertised for their creative potential were rated as more attractive by those primed for creativity than by those exposed to words related to reliability or a neutral topic (Bettman & Sujan, 1987). Momentary priming thus impacted ensuing preferences, rendering more salient criteria that had not previously been considered important, despite the fact that product consumption was likely to occur long after such momentary criterion salience dissipated (see Mandel & Johnson, 2002; Verplanken & Holland, 2002; Wright & Heath, 2000).

IDENTITIES

At a broader level, preferences fluctuate along with momentarily salient identities. A working woman, for example, might think of herself primarily as a mother when in the company of her children but may see herself primarily as a professional while at work. The list of potential identities can be extensive (Turner, 1985) with some of a person's identities (e.g., "mother") conjuring up strikingly different values and ideals from others (e.g., "CEO"). Although choices are typically expected to reveal stable and coherent preferences that correspond to the wishes of the self as a whole, in fact, choice often fluctuates in accord with happenstance fluctuations in identity salience. In one study, college students whose "academic" identities had been triggered were more likely to opt for more academic periodicals (e.g., *The Economist*) than were those whose "socialite" identities had been made salient. Similarly, Chinese Americans whose American identities were evoked adopted more stereotypically American preferences (e.g., for individuality and competition over collectivism and cooperation) compared with when their Chinese identities had been triggered (LeBoeuf, 2002; LeBoeuf & Shafir, 2004). Preference tends to align with currently salient identities, yielding systematic tension anytime there is a mismatch between the identity that does the choosing and the one likely to do the consuming, as when a parent commits to a late work meeting only to regret missing her child's soccer game once back at home.

EMOTIONS AND DRIVES

Emotions can have similar effects, influencing the momentary evaluation of outcomes, and thus choice. The anticipated pain of a loss is apparently greater for people in a positive mood than for those in a negative mood; this leads to greater risk aversion among those in a good mood as they strive for "mood maintenance" (e.g., Isen, Nygren, & Ashby, 1988). Furthermore, risk judgments tend to be more pessimistic among people in a negative than a positive mood (e.g., Johnson & Tversky, 1983). However, valence is not the sole determinant of an emotion's influence: Anger, a negative emotion, seems to increase appraisals of individual control, leading to optimistic risk assessment and to risk seeking, whereas fear, also a negative emotion, is not associated with appraisals of control and promotes risk aversion (Lerner & Keltner, 2001).

Emotions, or affect, also influence the associations or images that come to mind in decision making. Because images can be consulted quickly and effortlessly, an "affect heuristic" has been proposed with affective assessments sometimes guiding decisions (Slovic, Finucane, Peters, & MacGregor, 2002). Furthermore, "anticipatory emotions" (e.g., emotional reactions to being in a risky situation) can influence the cognitive appraisal of decision situations and can affect choice (Loewenstein, Weber, Hsee, & Welch, 2001) just as drives and motivations can influence reasoning more generally (see Molden & Higgins, Chap. 13). Emotion and affect thus influence people's preferences; however, because these sentiments are often transient, such influence contributes to reversals of preference as momentary emotions and drives fluctuate.

Inconsistency thus often arises because people do not realize that their preferences are being momentarily altered by situationally induced sentiments. Evidence suggests, however, that even when people *are* aware of being in the grip of a transient drive or emotion, they may not be able to "correct" adequately for that influence. For example, respondents in one study were asked to predict whether they would be more bothered by thirst or by hunger if trapped in the wilderness without water or food. Some answered right before exercising (when not especially thirsty), whereas others answered immediately after exercising (thus, thirsty). Postexercise, 92% indicated that they would be more troubled by thirst than by hunger in the wilderness, compared with 61% preexercise (Van Boven & Loewenstein, 2003). Postexercise, people could easily attribute their thirst to the exercise. Nonetheless, when imagining how they would feel in another, quite different and distant situation, people projected their current thirst. More generally, people tend to exhibit "empathy gaps," wherein they underestimate the degree to which various contextual changes will impact their drives, emotions, and preferences (e.g., Van Boven, Dunning, & Loewenstein, 2000; see also Gilbert, Pinel, Wilson, Blumberg, & Wheatley, 1998). This can further contribute to myopic decision making, for people honor present feelings and inclinations not fully appreciating the extent to which these may be attributable to fairly incidental factors that thus may soon dissipate.

Conclusions and Future Directions

A review of the behavioral decision-making literature shows peoples' preferences to be highly malleable and systematically affected by a host of factors not subsumed under the compelling and popular normative theory of choice. People's preferences are heavily shaped, among other things, by particular perceptions of risk and value, by multiple influences on attribute weights, by the tendency to avoid decisional conflict and to rely on compelling reasons for choice, by salient identities and emotions, and by a general tendency to accept decision situations as they are described, rarely reframing them in alternative, let alone canonical, ways.

It is tempting to attribute many of the effects to shallow processing or to a failure to consider the decision seriously (see, e.g., Grether & Plott, 1979; Smith, 1985; see also Shafir & LeBoeuf, 2002, for further review of critiques of the findings). After all, it seems plausible that participants who consider a problem more carefully might notice that it can be framed in alternate ways. This would allow a consideration of the problem from multiple perspectives and perhaps lead to a response unbiased by problem frame or other "inconsequential" factors (cf. Sieck & Yates, 1997). Evidence suggests, however, that the patterns documented previously cannot be attributed to laziness, inexperience, or lack of motivation. The same general effects are observed when participants are provided greater incentives (Grether & Plott, 1979; see Camerer & Hogarth, 1999, for a review), when they are asked to justify their choices (Fagley & Miller, 1987; LeBoeuf & Shafir, 2003; Levin & Chapman, 1990), when they are experienced or expert decision makers (Camerer, Babcock, Loewenstein, & Thaler, 1997; McNeil, Pauker, Sox, & Tversky, 1982; Redelmeier & Shafir, 1995; Redelmeier, Shafir, & Aujla, 2001), or when they are the types (e.g., "high need for cognition") who naturally think more deeply about problems (LeBoeuf & Shafir, 2003; Levin, Gaeth, Schreiber, & Lauriola, 2002). These findings suggest that many of the attitudes triggered by specific choice problem frames are at least somewhat entrenched, with extra thought or effort only serving to render the dominant perspective more compelling, rather than highlighting the need for debiasing (Arkes, 1991; LeBoeuf & Shafir, 2003; Thaler, 1991).

Research in decision making is active and growing. Among interesting current developments, several researchers have argued for a greater focus on emotion as a force guiding decisions (Hsee & Kunreuther, 2000; Loewenstein et al., 2001; Rottenstreich & Hsee, 2001; Slovic et al., 2002). Others are investigating systematic dissociations between *experienced* utility, that is, the hedonic experience an option actually brings, from *decision* utility, the utility implied by the decision. Such investigations correctly point out that, in addition to exhibiting consistent preferences, one would also want decision makers to choose those options that will maximize the quality of experience (Kahneman, 1994). As it turns out, misprediction of experienced utility is common, in part because people misremember the hedonic qualities of past events (Kahneman, Fredrickson, Schreiber, & Redelmeier, 1993), and in part because they fail to anticipate how enjoyment may be impacted by factors such as mere exposure (Kahneman & Snell, 1992), the dissipation of satiation (Simonson, 1990), and the power of adaptation, even to dramatic life changes (Gilbert et al., 1998; Schkade & Kahneman, 1998).

An accurate description of human decision making needs to incorporate those and other tendencies not reviewed in this chapter, including a variety of other judgmental biases (see Kahneman & Frederick, Chap. 12), as well as people's sensitivity to considerations such as fairness (Kahneman, Knetsch, & Thaler, 1986a, 1986b; Rabin, 1993) and sunk costs (Arkes & Blumer, 1985; Gourville & Soman, 1998). A successful descriptive model must allow for violations of normative criteria, such as procedure and description invariance, dominance, regularity, and, occasionally, transitivity. It must also allow for the eventual incorporation of other psychological processes that might impact choice. For example, it has been suggested that taking aspiration levels into account may sometimes predict risky decision making better than does prospect theory's reliance only on reference points (Lopes & Oden, 1999). The refinement of descriptive theories is an evolving process; however, the product that emerges continuously seems quite distant from the elegant and optimal normative treatment. At the same time, acknowledged departures from the normative theory need not weaken that theory's normative force. After all, normative theories are themselves empirical projects, capturing what people consider ideal: As we improve our understanding of how decisions are made, we may be able to formulate prescriptive procedures to guide decision makers, in light of their limitations, to better capture their normative wishes.

Of course, there are instances in which people have very clear preferences that no amount of subtle manipulation will alter (cf. Payne, Bettman, & Johnson, 1992). At other times, we appear to be at the mercy of factors that we would often like to consider inconsequential. This conclusion, well accepted within psychology, is becoming increasingly influential not only in decision research, but also in the social sciences more generally, with prominent researchers in law, medicine, sociology, and economics exhorting their fields to pay attention to findings of the sort reviewed here in formulating new ways of thinking about and predicting behavior. Given the academic, personal, and practical import of decision making, such developments may prove vital to our understanding of why people think, act, and decide as they do.

References

Ainslie, G. (2001). *Breakdown of will.* New York: Cambridge University Press.

American Lung Association. (2003). What are the benefits of quitting smoking? Available: http://www.lungusa.org/tobacco/quit_ben.html.

Arkes, H. R. (1991). Costs and benefits of judgment errors: Implications for debiasing. *Psychological Bulletin,* 110, 486–498.

Arkes, H. R., & Blumer, C. (1985). The psychology of sunk cost. *Organizational Behavior and Human Decision Processes,* 35, 124–140.

Arrow, K. J. (1951). Alternative approaches to the theory of choice in risk-taking situations. *Econometrica,* 19, 404–437.

Arrow, K. J. (1988). Behavior under uncertainty and its implications for policy. In D. E. Bell, H. Raiffa, & A. Tversky (Eds.), *Decision making: Descriptive, normative, and prescriptive interactions* (pp. 497–507). Cambridge, UK: Cambridge University Press.

Bastardi, A., & Shafir, E. (1998). On the pursuit and misuse of useless information. *Journal of Personality and Social Psychology,* 75, 19–32.

Bazerman, M. H., Schroth, H. A., Shah, P. P., Diekmann, K. A., & Tenbrunsel, A. E. (1994). The inconsistent role of comparison with others and procedural justice in reactions to hypothetical job descriptions: Implications for job acceptance decisions. *Organizational Behavior and Human Decision Processes,* 60, 326–352.

Bernoulli, D. (1738/1954). Exposition of a new theory on the measurement of risk. *Econometrica,* 22, 23–36.

Bettman, J. R., & Sujan, M. (1987). Effects of framing on evaluation of comparable and non-comparable alternatives by expert and novice consumers. *Journal of Consumer Research,* 14, 141–154.

Buehler, R., Griffin, D., & Ross, M. (1994). Exploring the "planning fallacy:" Why people underestimate their task completion times. *Journal of Personality and Social Psychology,* 67, 366–381.

Camerer, C. (1992). Recent tests of generalizations of expected utility theories. In W. Edwards (Ed.), *Utility theories: Measurement and applications* (pp. 207–251). Dordrecht: Kluwer.

Camerer, C., Babcock, L., Loewenstein, G., & Thaler, R. (1997). Labor supply of New York City cabdrivers: One day at a time. *The Quarterly Journal of Economics,* 112, 407–441.

Camerer, C. F., & Hogarth, R. M. (1999). The effects of financial incentives in experiments: A review and capital-labor-production framework. *Journal of Risk and Uncertainty,* 19, 7–42.

Camerer, C. F., Loewenstein, G., & Rabin, M. (2004). *Advances in behavioral economics.* Princeton, NJ: Princeton University Press.

Collins, A. M., & Loftus, E. F. (1975). A spreading-activation theory of semantic processing. *Psychological Review*, 82, 407–428.

Dawes, R. M. (1979). The robust beauty of improper linear models in decision making. *American Psychologist*, 34, 571–582.

Dawes, R. M., Faust, D., & Meehl, P. E. (1989). Clinical verus actuarial judgment. *Science*, 243, 1668–1674.

Downs, J. S., & Shafir, E. (1999). Why some are perceived as more confident and more insecure, more reckless and more cautious, more trusting and more suspicious, than others: Enriched and impoverished options in social judgment. *Psychonomic Bulletin and Review*, 6, 598–610.

Elster, J. (1984). *Studies in rationality and irrationality*. Revised edition. Cambridge, UK: Cambridge University Press.

Elster, J., & Loewenstein, G. (Eds.). (1992). *Choice over time*. New York: Russell Sage Foundation.

Fagley, N. S., & Miller, P. M. (1987). The effects of decision framing on choice of risky vs. certain options. *Organizational Behavior and Human Decision Processes*, 39, 264–277.

Frederick, S., Loewenstein, G., & Donoghue, T. (2002). Time discounting and time preference: A critical review. *Journal of Economic Literature*, 40, 351–401.

Gilbert, D. T., Pinel, E. C., Wilson, T. D., Blumberg, S. J., & Wheatley, T. P. (1998). Immune neglect: A source of durability bias in affective forecasting. *Journal of Personality and Social Psychology*, 75, 617–638.

Goldstein, W. M., & Hogarth, R. M. (Eds.). (1997). *Research on judgment and decision making: Currents, connections, and controversies*. New York: Cambridge University Press.

Gonzalez, R., & Wu, G. (1999). On the shape of the probability weighting function. *Cognitive Psychology*, 38, 129–166.

Gourville, J. T., & Soman, D. (1998). Payment depreciation: The behavioral effects of temporally separating payments from consumption. *Journal of Consumer Research*, 25, 160–174.

Grether, D., & Plott, C. (1979). Economic theory of choice and the preference reversal phenomenon. *American Economic Review*, 69, 623–638.

Hastie, R., & Dawes, R. M. (2001). *Rational choice in an uncertain world: The psychology of judgement and decision making*. Thousand Oaks: Sage.

Heath, C., & Soll, J. B. (1996). Mental budgeting and consumer decisions. *Journal of Consumer Research*, 23, 40–52.

Heath, C., & Tversky, A. (1991). Preference and belief: Ambiguity and competence in choice under uncertainty. *Journal of Risk and Uncertainty*, 4, 5–28.

Hershey, J. C., & Schoemaker, P. J. H. (1980). Risk taking and problem context in the domain of losses: An expected utility analysis. *The Journal of Risk and Insurance*, 47, 111–132.

Hsee, C. K. (1996). The evaluability hypothesis: An explanation of preference reversals between joint and separate evaluations of alternatives. *Organizational Behavior and Human Decision Processes*, 67, 247–257.

Hsee, C. K., & Kunreuther, H. C. (2000). The affection effect in insurance decisions. *Journal of Risk and Uncertainty*, 20, 141–159.

Hsee, C. K., Loewenstein, G. F., Blount, S., & Bazerman, M. H. (1999). Preference reversals between joint and separate evaluations of options: A review and theoretical analysis. *Psychological Bulletin*, 5, 576–590.

Huber, J., Payne, J. W., & Puto, C. (1982). Adding asymmetrically dominated alternatives: Violations of regularity and the similarity hypothesis. *Journal of Consumer Research*, 9, 90–98.

Isen, A. M., Nygren, T. E., & Ashby, F. G. (1988). Influence of positive affect on the subjective utility of gains and losses: It is just not worth the risk. *Journal of Personality and Social Psychology*, 55, 710–717.

Iyengar, S. S., & Lepper, M. R. (2000). When choice is demotivating: Can one desire too much of a good thing? *Journal of Personality and Social Psychology*, 79, 995–1006.

Johnson, E. J., & Goldstein, D. (2003). Do defaults save lives? *Science*, 302, 1338–1339.

Johnson, E. J., Hershey, J., Meszaros, J., & Kunreuther, H. (1993). Framing, probability distortions, and insurance decisions. *Journal of Risk and Uncertainty*, 7, 35–51.

Johnson, E. J., & Tversky, A. (1983). Affect, generalization, and the perception of risk. *Journal of Personality and Social Psychology*, 45, 20–31.

Kahneman, D. (1992). Reference points, anchors, and mixed feelings. *Organizational Behavior and Human Decision Processes*, 51, 296–312.

Kahneman, D. (1994). New challenges to the rationality assumption. *Journal of Institutional and Theoretical Economics, 150*, 18–36.

Kahneman, D. (2003). A perspective on judgment and choice: Mapping bounded rationality. *American Psychologist, 58*, 697–720.

Kahneman, D., Fredrickson, B. L., Schreiber, C. A., & Redelmeier, D. A. (1993). When more pain is preferred to less: Adding a better end. *Psychological Science, 4*, 401–405.

Kahneman, D., Knetsch, J. L., & Thaler, R. H. (1986a). Fairness and the assumptions of economics. *Journal of Business, 59*, s285–s300.

Kahneman, D., Knetsch, J. L., & Thaler, R. H. (1986b). Fairness as a constraint on profit seeking: Entitlements in the market. *American Economic Review, 76*, 728–741.

Kahneman, D., Knetsch, J. L., & Thaler, R. (1990). Experimental tests of the endowment effect and the Coase theorem. *Journal of Political Economics, 98*, 1325–1348.

Kahneman, D., & Lovallo, D. (1993). Timid choices and bold forecasts: A cognitive perspective on risk taking. *Management Science, 39*, 17–31.

Kahneman, D., & Ritov, I. (1994). Determinants of stated willingness to pay for public goods: A study in the headline method. *Journal of Risk and Uncertainty, 9*, 5–38.

Kahneman, D., & Snell, J. (1992). Predicting a changing taste: Do people know what they will like? *Journal of Behavioral Decision Making, 5*, 187–200.

Kahneman, D., & Tversky, A. (1979). Prospect theory: An analysis of decision under risk. *Econometrica, 47*, 263–291.

Kahneman, D., & Tversky, A. (1984). Choices, values, and frames. *American Psychologist, 39*, 341–350.

Kahneman, D., & Tversky, A. (1995). Conflict resolution: A cognitive perspective. In K. J. Arrow, R. H. Mnookin, L. Ross, A. Tversky, & R. B. Wilson (Eds.), *Barriers to conflict resolution* (pp. 45–60). New York: W. W. Norton.

Kahneman, D., & Tversky, A. (Eds.). (2000). *Choices, values, and frames*. Cambridge, UK: Cambridge University Press.

Keeney, R. L., & Raiffa, H. (1976). *Decisions with multiple objectives: Preferences and value tradeoffs*. Cambridge, UK: Cambridge University Press.

Knetsch, J. L. (1989). The endowment effect and evidence of nonreversible indifference curves. *American Economic Review, 79*, 1277–1284.

Kühberger, A. (1995). The framing of decisions: A new look at old problems. *Organizational Behavior and Human Decision Processes, 62*, 230–240.

LeBoeuf, R. A. (2002). *Alternating selves and conflicting choices: Identity salience and preference inconsistency*. Unpublished doctoral dissertation, Princeton University, Princeton, NJ.

LeBoeuf, R. A., & Shafir, E. (2003). Deep thoughts and shallow frames: On the susceptibility to framing effects. *Journal of Behavioral Decision Making, 16*, 77–92.

LeBoeuf, R. A., & Shafir, E. (2004). *Alternating selves and conflicting choices: Identity salience and preference inconsistency*. Manuscript under review.

Lerner, J. S., & Keltner, D. (2001). Fear, anger, and risk. *Journal of Personality and Social Psychology, 81*, 146–159.

Levin, I. P. (1987). Associative effects of information framing. *Bulletin of the Psychonomic Society, 25*, 85–86.

Levin, I. P., & Chapman, D. P. (1990). Risk taking, frame of reference, and characterization of victim groups in AIDS treatment decisions. *Journal of Experimental Social Psychology, 26*, 421–434.

Levin, I. P., Gaeth, G. J., Schreiber, J., & Lauriola, M. (2002). A new look at framing effects: Distribution of effect sizes, individual differences, and independence of types of effects. *Organizational Behavior and Human Decision Processes, 88*, 411–429.

Levin, I. P., Schneider, S. L., & Gaeth, G. J. (1998). All frames are not created equal: A typology and critical analysis of framing effects. *Organizational Behavior and Human Decision Processes, 76*, 149–188.

Levin, I. P., Schnittjer, S. K., & Thee, S. L. (1988). Information framing effects in social and personal decisions. *Journal of Experimental Social Psychology, 24*, 520–529.

Lichtenstein, S., & Slovic, P. (1971). Reversals of preference between bids and choices in gambling decisions. *Journal of Experimental Psychology, 89*, 46–55.

Lichtenstein, S., & Slovic, P. (1973). Response-induced reversals of preferences in gambling:

An extended replication in Las Vegas. *Journal of Experimental Psychology, 101*, 16–20.

Loewenstein, G. (1996). Out of control: Visceral influences on behavior. *Organizational Behavior and Human Decision Processes, 65*, 272–292.

Loewenstein, G., & Prelec, D. (1992). Anomalies in intertemporal choice: Evidence and an interpretation. *The Quarterly Journal of Economics, 107*, 573–597.

Loewenstein, G., & Thaler, R. H. (1989). Intertemporal choice. *Journal of Economic Perspectives, 3*, 181–193.

Loewenstein, G. F., Weber, E. U., Hsee, C. K., & Welch, N. (2001). Risk as feelings. *Psychological Bulletin, 127*, 267–286.

Lopes, L. L., & Oden, G. C. (1999). The role of aspiration level in risky choice: A comparison of cumulative prospect theory and SP/A theory. *Journal of Mathematical Psychology, 43*, 286–313.

Mandel, N., & Johnson, E. J. (2002). When Web pages influence choice: Effects of visual primes on experts and novices. *Journal of Consumer Research, 29*, 235–245.

McNeil, B. J., Pauker, S. G., Sox, H. C., & Tversky, A. (1982). On the elicitation of preferences for alternative therapies. *New England Journal of Medicine, 306*, 1259–1262.

Nisbett, R. E., & Wilson, T. D. (1977). Telling more than we can know: Verbal reports on mental processes. *Psychological Review, 84*, 231–259.

Payne, J. W., Bettman, J. R., & Johnson, E. J. (1992). Behavioral decision research: A constructive processing perspective. *Annual Review of Psychology, 43*, 87–131.

Prelec, D. (2000). Compound invariant weighting functions in prospect theory. In D. Kahneman & A. Tversky (Eds.), *Choices, values, and frames* (pp. 67–92). New York: Cambridge University Press.

Quattrone, G. A., & Tversky, A. (1988). Contrasting rational and psychological analyses of political choice. *American Political Science Review, 82*, 719–736.

Rabin, M. (1993). Incorporating fairness into game theory and economics. *American Economic Review, 83*, 1281–1302.

Redelmeier, D., Shafir, E., & Aujla, P. (2001). The beguiling pursuit of more information. *Medical Decision Making, 21*, 376–381.

Redelmeier, D. A., & Shafir, E. (1995). Medical decision making in situations that offer multiple alternatives. *Journal of the American Medical Association, 273*, 302–305.

Redelmeier, D. A., & Tversky, A. (1990). Discrepancy between medical decisions for individual patients and for groups. *New England Journal of Medicine, 322*, 1162–1164.

Redelmeier, D. A., & Tversky, A. (1992). On the framing of multiple prospects. *Psychological Science, 3*, 191–193.

Rottenstreich, Y., & Hsee, C. K. (2001). Money, kisses, and electric shocks: On the affective psychology of risk. *Psychological Science, 12*, 185–190.

Samuelson, W., & Zeckhauser, R. (1988). Status quo bias in decision making. *Journal of Risk and Uncertainty, 1*, 7–59.

Savage, L. J. (1954). *The foundations of statistics*. New York: Wiley.

Schelling, T. (1980). The intimate contest for self-command. *Public Interest, 60*, 94–118.

Schelling, T. (1984). Self-command in practice, in policy, and in theory of rational choice. *American Economic Review, 74*, 1–11.

Schkade, D. A., & Johnson, E. J. (1989). Cognitive processes in preference reversals. *Organizational Behavior and Human Decision Processes, 44*, 203–231.

Schkade, D. A., & Kahneman, D. (1998). Does living in California make people happy? A focusing illusion in judgments of life satisfaction. *Psychological Science, 9*, 340–346.

Shafir, E. (1993). Choosing versus rejecting: Why some options are both better and worse than others. *Memory and Cognition, 21*, 546–556.

Shafir, E. (1994). Uncertainty and the difficulty of thinking through disjunctions. *Cognition, 50*, 403–430.

Shafir, E. (2002). Cognition, intuition, and policy guidelines. In R. Gowda & J. C. Fox (Eds.), *Judgments, decisions, and public policy* (pp. 71–88). New York: Cambridge University Press.

Shafir, E., Diamond, P., & Tversky, A. (1997). Money illusion. *Quarterly Journal of Economics, 112*, 341–374.

Shafir, E., & LeBoeuf, R. A. (2002). Rationality. *Annual Review of Psychology, 53*, 491–517.

Shafir, E., & LeBoeuf, R. A. (2004). Context and conflict in multiattribute choice. In D. Koehler & N. Harvey (Eds.), *Blackwell handbook of judgment and decision making* (pp. 341–359). Oxford, UK: Blackwell.

Shafir, E., Simonson, I., & Tversky, A. (1993). Reason-based choice. *Cognition*, 49, 11–36.

Shafir, E., & Tversky, A. (1992). Thinking through uncertainty: Nonconsequential reasoning and choice. *Cognitive Psychology*, 24, 449–474.

Sieck, W., & Yates, J. F. (1997). Exposition effects on decision making: Choice and confidence in choice. *Organizational Behavior and Human Decision Processes*, 70, 207–219.

Simon, H. A. (1955). A behavioral model of rational choice. *Quarterly Journal of Economics*, 69, 99–118.

Simonson, I. (1989). Choice based on reasons: The case of attraction and compromise effects. *Journal of Consumer Research*, 16, 158–174.

Simonson, I. (1990). The effect of purchase quantity and timing on variety seeking behavior. *Journal of Marketing Research*, 27, 150–162.

Simonson, I., & Tversky, A. (1992). Choice in context: Tradeoff contrast and extremeness aversion. *Journal of Marketing Research*, 29, 289–295.

Slovic, P. (1995). The construction of preference. *American Psychologist*, 50, 364–371.

Slovic, P., Finucane, M., Peters, E., & MacGregor, D. G. (2002). The affect heuristic. In T. Gilovich, D. Griffin, & D. Kahneman (Eds.), *Heuristics and biases: The psychology of intuitive judgment* (pp. 397–420). New York: Cambridge University Press.

Slovic, P., Fischhoff, B., & Lichtenstein, S. (1988). Response mode, framing, and information-processing effects in risk assessment. In D. E. Bell, H. Raiffa, & A. Tversky (Eds.), *Decision making: Descriptive, normative, and prescriptive interactions* (pp. 152–166). Cambridge, UK: Cambridge University Press.

Slovic, P., Griffin, D., & Tversky, A. (1990). Compatibility effects in judgment and choice. In R. M. Hogarth (Ed.), *Insights in decision making: A tribute to Hillel J. Einhorn* (pp. 5–27). Chicago: University of Chicago Press.

Smith, V. L. (1985). Experimental economics: Reply. *American Economic Review*, 75, 265–272.

Stanovich, K. E. (1999). *Who is rational? Studies of individual differences in reasoning*. Mahwah, NJ: Erlbaum.

Sunstein, C. R., Kahneman, D., Schkade, D., & Ritov, I. (2001). *Predictably incoherent judgments*. Unpublished working paper, The University of Chicago Law School, Chicago, IL.

Thaler, R. H. (1981). Some empirical evidence on dynamic inconsistency. *Economic Letters*, 8, 201–207.

Thaler, R. H. (1991). The psychology of choice and the assumptions of economics. In R. H. Thaler (Ed.), *Quasi-rational economics* (pp. 137–166). New York: Russell Sage Foundation.

Thaler, R. H. (1993). *Advances in behavioral finance*. New York: Russell Sage Foundation.

Thaler, R. H. (1999). Mental accounting matters. *Journal of Behavioral Decision Making*, 12, 183–206.

Turner, J. C. (1985). Social categorization and the self-concept: A social cognitive theory of group behavior. In E. J. Lawler (Ed.), *Advances in group processes* (Vol. 2, pp. 77–121). Greenwich, CT: JAI Press.

Tversky, A., & Kahneman, D. (1981). The framing of decisions and psychology of choice. *Science*, 211, 453–458.

Tversky, A., & Kahneman, D. (1986). Rational choice and the framing of decisions. *Journal of Business*, 59, S251–S278.

Tversky, A., & Kahneman, D. (1991). Loss aversion in riskless choice: A reference dependent model. *Quarterly Journal of Economics*, 106, 1039–1061.

Tversky, A., & Kahneman, D. (1992). Advances in prospect theory: Cumulative representation of uncertainty. *Journal of Risk and Uncertainty*, 5, 297–323.

Tversky, A., Sattath, S., & Slovic, P. (1988). Contingent weighting in judgment and choice. *Psychological Review*, 95, 371–384.

Tversky, A., & Shafir, E. (1992a). Choice under conflict: The dynamics of deferred decision. *Psychological Science*, 3, 358–361.

Tversky, A., & Shafir, E. (1992b). The disjunction effect in choice under uncertainty. *Psychological Science*, 3, 305–309.

Tversky, A., & Simonson, I. (1993). Context-dependent preferences. *Management Science*, 39, 1178–1189.

Tversky, A., Slovic, P., & Kahneman, D. (1990). The causes of preference reversal. *American Economic Review*, 80, 204–217.

Van Boven, L., Dunning, D., & Loewenstein, G. (2000). Egocentric empathy gaps between owners and buyers: Misperceptions of the endowment effect. *Journal of Personality and Social Psychology, 79*, 66–76.

Van Boven, L., & Loewenstein, G. (2003). Social projection of transient drive states. *Personality and Social Psychology Bulletin, 29*, 1159–1168.

Verplanken, B., & Holland, R. W. (2002). Motivated decision making: Effects of activation and self-centrality of values on choices and behavior. *Journal of Personality and Social Psychology, 82*, 434–447.

von Neumann, J., & Morgenstern, O. (1944). *Theory of games and economic behavior*. Princeton, NJ: Princeton University Press.

Wedell, D. H. (1997). Another look at reasons for choosing and rejecting. *Memory and Cognition, 25*, 873–887.

Wilson, T. D., Dunn, D. S., Kraft, D., & Lisle, D. J. (1989). Introspection, attitude change, and attitude consistency: The disruptive effects of explaining why we feel the way we do. In L. Berkowitz (Ed.), *Advances in experimental and social psychology* (pp. 123–205). San Diego: Academic Press.

Wilson, T. D., & Schooler, J. W. (1991). Thinking too much: Introspection can reduce the quality of preferences and decisions. *Journal of Personality and Social Psychology, 60*, 181–192.

Wright, J., & Heath, C. (2000, November). *Identity-based choice: Who I am determines what I choose*. Paper presented at the annual meeting of the Society for Judgment and Decision Making, New Orleans, LA.

CHAPTER 12

A Model of Heuristic Judgment

Daniel Kahneman
Shane Frederick

The program of research now known as the heuristics and biases approach began with a study of the statistical intuitions of experts, who were found to be excessively confident in the replicability of results from small samples (Tversky & Kahneman, 1971). The persistence of such systematic errors in the intuitions of experts implied that their intuitive judgments may be governed by fundamentally different processes than the slower, more deliberate computations they had been trained to execute.

From its earliest days, the heuristics and biases program was guided by the idea that intuitive judgments occupy a position – perhaps corresponding to evolutionary history – between the automatic parallel operations of perception and the controlled serial operations of reasoning. Intuitive judgments were viewed as an extension of perception to judgment objects that are not currently present, including mental representations that are evoked by language. The mental representations on which intuitive judgments operate are similar to percepts. Indeed, the distinction between perception and judgment is often blurry: The *perception* of a stranger as menacing entails a *prediction* of future harm.

The ancient idea that cognitive processes can be partitioned into two main families – traditionally called intuition and reason – is now widely embraced under the general label of dual-process theories (Chaiken & Trope, 1999; Evans and Over, 1996; Hammond, 1996; Sloman, 1996, 2002; see Evans, Chap. 8). Dual-process models come in many flavors, but all distinguish cognitive operations that are quick and associative from others that are slow and governed by rules (Gilbert, 1999).

To represent intuitive and deliberate reasoning, we borrow the terms "system 1" and "system 2" from Stanovich and West (2002). Although suggesting two autonomous homunculi, such a meaning is not intended. We use the term "system" only as a label for collections of cognitive processes that can be distinguished by their speed, their controllability, and the contents on which they operate. In the particular dual-process model we assume, system 1 quickly proposes intuitive answers to judgment problems as they arise, and system 2 monitors the quality of these proposals, which it may endorse, correct, or override. The judgments that are eventually expressed are called intuitive if they retain the hypothesized initial proposal with little modification.

The effect of concurrent cognitive tasks provides the most useful indication of whether a given mental process belongs to system 1 or system 2. Because the overall capacity for mental effort is limited, effortful processes tend to disrupt each other, whereas effortless processes neither cause nor suffer much interference when combined with other tasks (Kahneman, 1973; Pashler, 1998). It is by this criterion that we assign the monitoring function to system 2: People who are occupied by a demanding mental activity (e.g., attempting to hold in mind several digits) are much more likely to respond to another task by blurting out whatever comes to mind (Gilbert, 1989). By the same criterion, the acquisition of highly skilled performances – whether perceptual or motor – involves the transformation of an activity from effortful (system 2) to effortless (system 1). The proverbial chess master who strolls past a game and quips, "White mates in three" is performing intuitively (Simon & Chase, 1973).

Our views about the two systems are similar to the "correction model" proposed by Gilbert (1989, 1991) and to other dual-process models (Epstein, 1994; Hammond, 1996; Sloman, 1996; see also Shweder, 1977). We assume system 1 and system 2 can be active concurrently, that automatic and controlled cognitive operations compete for the control of overt responses, and that deliberate judgments are likely to remain anchored on initial impressions. We also assume that the contribution of the two systems in determining stated judgments depends on both task features and individual characteristics, including the time available for deliberation (Finucane et al., 2000), mood (Bless et al., 1996; Isen, Nygren, & Ashby, 1988), intelligence (Stanovich & West, 2002), cognitive impulsiveness (Frederick, 2004), and exposure to statistical thinking (Agnoli, 1991; Agnoli & Krantz, 1989; Nisbett et al., 1983).

In the context of a dual-system view, errors of intuitive judgment raise two questions: "What features of system 1 created the error?" and "Why was the error not detected and corrected by system 2?" (cf. Kahneman & Tversky, 1982). The first question is more basic, of course, but the second is also relevant and ought not be overlooked. Consider, for example, the paragraph that Tversky and Kahneman (1974; p. 3 in Kahneman, Slovic, & Tversky, 1982) used to introduced the notions of heuristic and bias:

> *The subjective assessment of probability resembles the subjective assessment of physical quantities such as distance or size. These judgments are all based on data of limited validity, which are processed according to heuristic rules. For example, the apparent distance of an object is determined in part by its clarity. The more sharply the object is seen, the closer it appears to be. This rule has some validity, because in any given scene the more distant objects are seen less sharply than nearer objects. However, the reliance on this rule leads to systematic errors in the estimation of distance. Specifically, distances are often overestimated when visibility is poor because the contours of objects are blurred. On the other hand, distances are often underestimated when visibility is good because the objects are seen sharply. Thus the reliance on clarity as an indication leads to common biases. Such biases are also found in intuitive judgments of probability.*

This statement was intended to extend Brunswik's (1943) analysis of the perception of distance to the domain of intuitive thinking and to provide a rationale for using biases to diagnose heuristics. However, the analysis of the effect of haze is flawed: It neglects the fact that an observer looking at a distant mountain possesses two relevant cues, not one. The first cue is the blur of the contours of the target mountain, which is positively correlated with its distance, when all else is equal. This cue should be given positive weight in a judgment of distance, and it is. The second relevant cue, which the observer can readily assess by looking around, is the ambient or general haziness.

In an optimal regression model for estimating distance, general haziness is a suppressor variable, which must be weighted negatively because it contributes to blur but is uncorrelated with distance. Contrary to the argument made in 1974, using blur as a cue does not inevitably lead to bias in the judgment of distance – the illusion could just as well be described as a failure to assign adequate negative weight to ambient haze. The effect of haziness on *impressions* of distance is a failing of system 1: The perceptual system is not designed to correct for this variable. The effect of haziness on *judgments* of distance is a separate failure of system 2. Although people are capable of consciously correcting their impressions of distance for the effects of ambient haze, they commonly fail to do so. A similar analysis applies to some of the judgmental biases we discuss later, in which errors and biases only occur when both systems fail.

In the following section, we present an attribute-substitution model of heuristic judgment, which assumes that difficult questions are often answered by substituting an answer to an easier one. This elaborates and extends earlier treatments of the topic (Kahneman & Tversky, 1982; Tversky & Kahneman, 1974, 1983). Following sections introduce a research design for studying attribute substitution, as well as discuss the controversy over the representativeness heuristic in the context of a dual-system view that we endorse. The final section situates representativeness within a broad family of prototype heuristics, in which properties of a prototypical exemplar dominate global judgments concerning an entire set.

Attribute Substitution

The early research on judgment heuristics was guided by a simple and general hypothesis: When confronted with a difficult question, people may answer an easier one instead and are often unaware of the substitution. A person who is asked "What proportion of long-distance relationships break up within a year?" may answer as if she had been asked "Do instances of failed long-distance relationships come readily to mind?" This would be an application of the availability heuristic. A professor who has heard a candidate's job talk and now considers the question "How likely is it that this candidate could be tenured in our department?" may answer the much easier question: "How impressive was the talk?". This would be an example of one form of the representativeness heuristic.

The heuristics and biases research program has focused primarily on representativeness and availability – two versatile attributes that are automatically computed and can serve as candidate answers to many different questions. It has also focused principally on thinking under uncertainty. However, the restriction to particular heuristics and to a specific context is largely arbitrary. Kahneman and Frederick (2002) argued that this process of *attribute substitution* is a general feature of heuristic judgment; that whenever the aspect of the judgmental object that one intends to judge (the *target attribute*) is less readily assessed than a related property that yields a plausible answer (the *heuristic attribute*), individuals may unwittingly substitute the simpler assessment. For an example, consider the well-known study by Strack, Martin, and Schwarz (1988) in which college students answered a survey that included these two questions: "How happy are you with your life in general?" and "How many dates did you have last month?" The correlation between the two questions was negligible when they occurred in the order shown, but rose to .66 if the dating question was asked first. We suggest that the question about dating frequency automatically evokes an evaluation of one's romantic satisfaction and that this evaluation lingers to become the heuristic attribute when the global happiness question is subsequently encountered.

To further illustrate the process of attribute substitution, consider a question in a study by Frederick and Nelson (2004): "If a sphere were dropped into a open cube, such that it just fit (the diameter of the sphere is the same as the interior width of the cube), what proportion of the volume of the cube would the sphere occupy?" The target attribute in this judgment (the volumetric relation between a cube and sphere) is simple enough to be understood but complicated enough to accommodate a wide range of estimates as plausible answers. Thus, if a relevant simpler computation or perceptual impression exists, respondents will have no strong basis for rejecting it as their "final answer." Frederick and Nelson (2004) proposed that the areal ratio of the respective cross-sections serves that function; that is, that respondents answer *as if* they were asked the simpler two-dimensional analog of this problem ("If a *circle* were drawn inside a *square*, what proportion of the *area* of the square does the circle occupy?"). As evidence, they noted that the mean estimate of the "sphere inside cube" problem (74%) is scarcely different from the mean estimate of the "circle inside square" problem (77%) and greatly exceeds the correct answer (52%) – a correct answer that most people, not surprisingly, are surprised by.

Biases

Whenever the heuristic attribute differs from the target attribute, the substitution of one for the other inevitably introduces systematic biases. In this treatment, we are mostly concerned with *weighting biases,* which arise when cues available to the judge are given either too much or too little weight. Criteria for determining optimal weights can be drawn from several sources. In the classic lens model, the optimal weights associated with different cues are the regression weights that optimize the prediction of an external criterion, such as physical distance or the grade point average that a college applicant will attain (Brunswik, 1943; Hammond, 1955). Our analysis of weighting biases applies to such cases, but it also extends to attributes for which no objective criterion is available, such as an individual's overall happiness or the probability that a particular patient will survive surgery. Normative standards for these attributes must be drawn from the constraints of ordinary language and are often imprecise. For example, the conventional interpretation of *overall happiness* does not specify how much weight ought to be given to various life domains. However, it certainly does require that substantial weight be given to every important domain of life and that no weight at all be given to the current weather or to the recent consumption of a cookie. Similar rules of common sense apply to judgments of probability. For example, the statement "John is more likely to survive a week than a month" is clearly true, and, thus, implies a rule that people would want their probability judgments to follow. Accordingly, neglect of duration in assessments of survival probabilities would be properly described as a weighting bias, even if there were no way to establish a normative probability for individual cases (Kahneman & Tversky, 1996).

For some judgmental tasks, information that could serve to supplement or correct the heuristic is not neglected or underweighted but simply lacking. If asked to judge the relative frequency of words beginning with K or R (Tversky & Kahneman, 1973) or to compare the population of a familiar foreign city with one that is unfamiliar (Gigerenzer & Goldstein, 1996), respondents have little recourse but to base their judgments on ease of retrieval or recognition. The necessary reliance on these heuristic attributes renders such judgments susceptible to biasing factors (e.g., the amount of media coverage). However, unlike weighting biases, such biases of insufficient information cannot be described as errors of judgment because there is no way to avoid them.

Accessibility and Substitution

The intent to judge a target attribute initiates a search for a reasonable value. Sometimes this search ends quickly because the required value can be read from a stored memory (e.g., the answer to the question "How tall are you?") or a current experience (e.g., the answer to the question "How much do you like this cake?"). For other judgments, however, the target attribute does not readily come to mind, but the search for it evokes other attributes that are conceptually and associatively related. For example, a question about overall happiness may retrieve the answer to a related question about satisfaction with a particular aspect of life upon which one is currently reflecting.

We adopt the term *accessibility* to refer to the ease (or effort) with which particular mental contents come to mind (see, e.g., Higgins, 1996; Tulving & Pearlstone, 1966). The question of why thoughts become accessible – why particular ideas come to mind at particular times – has a long history in psychology and encompasses notions of stimulus salience, associative activation, selective attention, specific training, and priming. In the present usage, *accessibility* is determined jointly by the characteristics of the cognitive mechanisms that produce it and by the characteristics of the stimuli and events that evoke it, and it may refer to different aspects and elements of a situation, different objects in a scene, or different attributes of an object.

Attribute substitution occurs when a relatively inaccessible target attribute is assessed by mapping a relatively accessible and related heuristic attribute onto the target scale. Some attributes are permanent candidates for the heuristic role because they are routinely evaluated as part of perception and comprehension and therefore always accessible (Tversky & Kahneman, 1983). These *natural assessments* include physical properties such as size and distance and more abstract properties such as similarity (e.g., Tversky & Kahneman, 1983; see Goldstone & Son, Chap. 2), cognitive fluency in perception and memory (e.g., Jacoby & Dallas, 1991; Schwarz & Vaughn, 2002; Tversky & Kahneman, 1973), causal propensity (Heider, 1944; Kahneman & Varey, 1990; Michotte, 1963), surprisingness (Kahneman & Miller, 1986), mood (Schwarz & Clore, 1983), and affective valence (e.g., Bargh, 1997; Cacioppo, Priester, & Berntson, 1993; Kahneman, Ritov, & Schkade, 1999; Slovic et al., 2002; Zajonc, 1980, 1997).

Because affective valence is a natural assessment, it is a candidate for attribute substitution in a wide variety of affect-laden judgments. Indeed, the evidence suggests that a list of major general-purpose heuristics should include an *affect heuristic* (Slovic et al., 2002). Slovic and colleagues (2002) show that a basic affective reaction governs a wide variety of more complex evaluations such as the cost–benefit ratio of various technologies, the safe level of chemicals, or even the predicted economic performance of various industries. In the same vein, Kahneman and Ritov (1994) and Kahneman, Ritov, and Schkade (1999) proposed that an automatic affective valuation is the principal determinant of willingness to pay for public goods, and Kahneman, Schkade, and Sunstein (1998) interpreted jurors' assessments of punitive awards as a mapping of outrage onto a dollar scale of punishments.

Attributes that are not naturally assessed can become accessible if they have been recently evoked or primed (see, e.g., Bargh et al., 1986; Higgins & Brendl, 1995). The effect of temporary accessibility is illustrated by the "romantic satisfaction heuristic" for judging happiness. The mechanism of attribute substitution is the same, however, whether the heuristic attribute is chronically or temporarily accessible.

There is sometimes more than one candidate for the role of heuristic attribute. For an example that we borrow from Anderson (1991), consider the question "Are more deaths caused by rattlesnakes or bees?" A respondent who has recently read about someone who died from a snakebite or bee sting may use the relative availability of instances of the two categories as a heuristic. If no instances come to mind, that person might consult his or her impressions of the "dangerousness" of the typical snake or bee, an application of representativeness. Indeed, it is possible that the question initiates both a search for instances and an assessment of dangerousness, and that a contest of accessibility determines the role of the two heuristics in the final response. As Anderson observed, it is not always possible to determine a priori which heuristic will govern the response to a particular problem.

The original list of heuristics (Tversky & Kahneman, 1974) also included an "anchoring heuristic." An anchoring effect, however, does not involve the substitution of a heuristic attribute for a target attribute: It is due to the temporary salience of a particular value of the target attribute. However, anchoring and attribute substitution are both instances of a broader family of *accessibility effects* (Kahneman, 2003). In attribute substitution, a highly accessible attribute controls the evaluation of a less accessible one. In anchoring, a highly accessible *value* of the target attribute dominates its judgment. This conception is compatible with more recent theoretical treatments of anchoring (see, e.g., Chapman & Johnson, 1994, 2002; Mussweiler & Strack 1999; Strack & Mussweiler, 1997).

Cross-Dimensional Mapping

The process of attribute substitution involves the mapping of the heuristic attribute of the judgment object onto the scale of the target attribute. Our notion of cross-dimensional mapping extends Stevens' (1975) concept of cross-modality matching. Stevens postulated that intensive attributes (e.g., brightness, loudness, the severity of crimes) can be mapped onto a common scale of sensory strength, allowing direct matching of intensity across modalities – permitting, for example, respondents to match the loudness of sounds to the severity of crimes. Our conception allows other ways of comparing values across dimensions, such as matching relative positions (e.g., percentiles) in the frequency distributions or ranges of different attributes (Parducci, 1965). An impression of a student's position in the distribution of aptitude may be mapped directly onto a corresponding position in the distribution of academic achievement and then translated into a letter grade. Note that cross-dimensional matching is inherently nonregressive: A judgment or prediction is just as extreme as the impression mapped onto it. Ganzach and Krantz (1990) applied the term "univariate matching" to a closely related notion.

Cross-dimensional mapping presents special problems when the scale of the target attribute has no upper bound. Kahneman, Ritov, and Schkade (1999) discussed two situations in which an attitude (or affective valuation) is mapped onto an unbounded scale of dollars: when respondents in surveys are required to indicate how much money they would contribute for a cause, and when jurors are required to specify an amount of punitive damages against a negligent firm. The mapping of attitudes onto dollars is a variant of direct scaling in psychophysics, where respondents assign numbers to indicate the intensity of sensations (Stevens, 1975). The normal practice of direct scaling is for the experimenter to provide a *modulus* – a specified number that is to be associated with a standard stimulus. For example, respondents may be asked to assign the number 10 to the loudness of a standard sound and judge the loudness of other sounds relative to that standard. Stevens (1975) observed that when the experimenter fails to provide a modulus, respondents spontaneously adopt one. However, different respondents may pick moduli that differ greatly (sometimes varying by a factor of 100 or more); thus, the variability in judgments of particular stimuli is dominated by arbitrary individual differences in the choice of modulus. A similar analysis applies to situations in which respondents are required to use the dollar scale to express affection for a species or outrage toward a defendant. Just as Stevens' observers had no principled way to assign a number to a moderately loud sound, survey participants and jurors have no principled way to scale affection or outrage into dollars. The analogy of scaling without a modulus has been used to explain the notorious variability of dollar responses in surveys of willingness to pay and in jury awards (Kahneman, Ritov, & Schkade, 1999; Kahneman, Schkade, & Sunstein, 1998).

System 2: The Supervision of Intuitive Judgments

Our model assumes that an intuitive judgment is expressed overtly only if it is endorsed by system 2. The Stroop task illustrates this two-system structure. Observers who are instructed to report the color in which words are printed tend to stumble when the word is the name of another color (e.g., the word BLUE printed in green ink). The difficulty arises because the word is automatically read, and activates a response ("blue" in this case) that competes with the required response ("green"). Errors are rare in the Stroop test, indicating generally successful monitoring and control of the overt response, but the conflict produces delays and hesitations. The successful suppression of erroneous responses is effortful, and its efficacy is reduced by stress and distraction.

Gilbert (1989) described a correction model in which initial impulses are often wrong and normally overridden. He argued that people initially believe whatever they are told (e.g., "Whitefish love grapes") and that it takes some time and mental effort to "unbelieve" such dubious statements. Here again, cognitive load disrupts the controlling operations of system 2, increasing the rate of errors and revealing aspects of intuitive thinking that are normally suppressed. In an ingenious extension of this approach, Bodenhausen (1990) exploited natural temporal variability in alertness. He found that "morning people" were substantially more susceptible to a judgment bias (the conjunction fallacy) in the evening and that "evening people" were more likely to commit the fallacy in the morning.

Because system 2 is relatively slow, its operations can be disrupted by time pressure. Finucane et al. (2000) reported a study in which respondents judged the risks and benefits of various products and technologies (e.g., nuclear power, chemical plants, cellular phones). When participants were forced to respond within 5 seconds, the correlations between their judgments of risks and their judgments of benefits were strongly negative. The negative correlations were much weaker (although still pronounced) when respondents were given more time to ponder a response. When time is short, the same affective evaluation apparently serves as a heuristic attribute for assessments of both benefits and risks. Respondents can move beyond this simple strategy, but they need more than 5 seconds to do so. As this example illustrates, judgment by heuristic often yields simplistic assessments, which system 2 sometimes corrects by bringing additional considerations to bear.

Attribute substitution can be prevented by alerting respondents to the possibility that their judgment could be contaminated by an irrelevant variable. For example, although sunny or rainy weather typically affects reports of well-being, Schwarz and Clore (1983) found that weather has no effect if respondents are asked about the weather just before answering the well-being question. Apparently, this question reminds respondents that their current mood (a candidate heuristic attribute) is influenced by a factor (current weather) that is irrelevant to the requested target attribute (overall well-being). Schwarz (1996) also found that asking people to describe their satisfaction with some particular domain of life *reduces* the weight this domain receives in a subsequent judgment of overall well being. As these examples illustrate, although priming typically increases the weight of that variable on judgment (a system 1 effect), this does not occur if the prime is a sufficiently explicit reminder that brings the self-critical operations of system 2 into play.

We suspect that system 2 endorsements of intuitive judgments are granted quite casually under normal circumstances. Consider the puzzle "A bat and a ball cost $1.10 in total. The bat costs $1 more than the ball. How much does the ball cost?" Almost everyone we ask reports an initial tendency to answer "10 cents" because the sum $1.10 separates naturally into $1 and 10 cents, and 10 cents is about the right magnitude. Many people yield to this immediate impulse. Even among undergraduates at elite institutions, about half get this problem wrong when it is included in a short IQ test (Frederick, 2004). The critical feature of this problem is that anyone who reports 10 cents has obviously not taken the trouble to check his or her answer. The surprisingly high rate of errors in this easy problem illustrates how lightly system 2 monitors the output of system 1: People are often content to trust a plausible judgment that quickly comes to mind. (The correct answer, by the way, is 5 cents.)

The bat and ball problem elicits many errors, although it is not really difficult and certainly not ambiguous. A moral of this example is that people often make quick intuitive judgments to which they are not deeply committed. A related moral is that we should be suspicious of analyses that explain apparent errors by attributing to respondents a bizarre interpretation of the question. Consider someone who answers a question about happiness by reporting her satisfaction with her romantic life. The respondent is surely not committed to the absurdly narrow interpretation of happiness that her response seemingly implies. More likely, at the time of answering, she thinks that she *is* reporting happiness: A judgment comes quickly to mind and is not obviously mistaken – end of story. Similarly, we propose that respondents who judge probability by representativeness do not seriously believe that the questions "How likely is X to be a Y?" and "How much does X resemble the stereotype of Y?" are synonymous. People who make a casual intuitive judgment normally know little about how their judgment came about and know even less about its logical entailments. Attempts to reconstruct the meaning of intuitive judgments by interviewing respondents (see, e.g., Hertwig & Gigerenzer, 1999) are therefore unlikely to succeed because such probes require better introspective access and more coherent beliefs than people normally muster.

Identifying a Heuristic

Hypotheses about judgment heuristics have most often been studied by examining weighting biases and deviations from normative rules. However, the hypothesis that one attribute is substituted for another in a judgment task – for example, representativeness for probability – can also be tested more directly. In the *heuristic elicitation* design, one group of respondents provides judgments of a target attribute for a set of objects and another group evaluates the hypothesized heuristic attribute for the same objects. The substitution hypothesis implies that the judgments of the two groups, when expressed in comparable units (e.g., percentiles), will be identical. This section examines several applications of heuristic elicitation.

Eliciting Representativeness

Figure 12.1 displays the results of two experiments in which a measure of representativeness was elicited. These results were published long ago, but we repeat them here because they still provide the most direct evidence for both attribute substitution and the representativeness heuristic. For a more recent application of a similar design, see Bar-Hillel and Neter (1993).

The object of judgment in the study from which Figure 12.1(a) is drawn (Kahneman & Tversky, 1973; p. 127 in Kahneman, Slovic, & Tversky, 1982) was the following description of a fictitious graduate student, which was shown along with a list of nine fields of graduate specialization:

> *Tom W. is of high intelligence, although lacking in true creativity. He has a need for order and clarity and for neat and tidy systems in which every detail finds its appropriate place. His writing is rather dull and mechanical, occasionally enlivened by somewhat corny puns and by flashes of imagination of the sci-fi type. He has a strong drive for competence. He seems to have little feel and little sympathy for other people and does not enjoy interacting with others. Self-centered, he nonetheless has a deep moral sense.*

Participants in a *representativeness* group ranked the nine fields of specialization by the degree to which Tom W. "resembles a typical graduate student." Participants in the *probability* group ranked the nine fields according to the likelihood of Tom W.'s specializing in each. Figure 12.1(a) plots the mean judgments of the two groups. The correlation between representativeness and

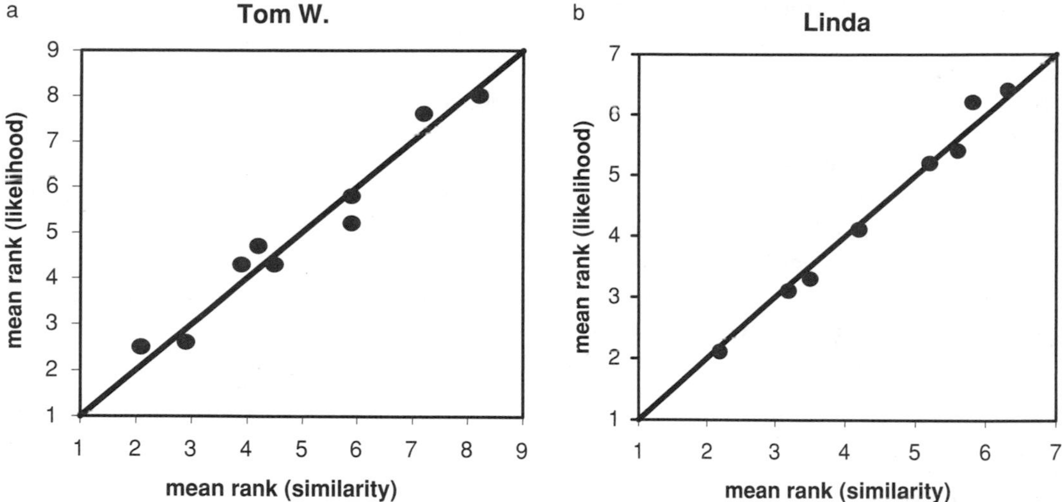

Figure 12.1. (a) Plot of average ranks for nine outcomes for Tom W. ranked by probability and by similarity to stereotypes of graduate students in various fields. (b) Plot of average ranks for eight outcomes for Linda ranked by probability and by representativeness.

probability is nearly perfect (.97). No stronger support for attribute-substitution could be imagined. However, interpreting representativeness as the heuristic attribute in these judgments does require two additional plausible assumptions – that representativeness is more accessible than probability, and that there is no third attribute that could explain both judgments.

The Tom W. study was also intended to examine the effect of the base rates of outcomes on categorical prediction. For that purpose, respondents in a third group estimated the proportion of graduate students enrolled in each of the nine fields. By design, some outcomes were defined quite broadly, whereas others were defined more narrowly. As intended, estimates of base rates varied markedly across fields, ranging from 3% for Library Science to 20% for Humanities and Education. Also by design, the description of Tom W. included characteristics (e.g., introversion) that were intended to make him fit the stereotypes of the smaller fields (library science, computer science) better than the larger fields (humanities and social sciences).[1] As intended, the correlation between the average judgments of representativeness and of base rates was strongly negative (−.65).

The logic of probabilistic prediction in this task suggests that the ranking of outcomes by their probabilities should be intermediate between their rankings by representativeness and by base rate frequencies. Indeed, if the personality description is taken to be a poor source of information, probability judgments should stay quite close to the base rates. The description of Tom W. was designed to allow considerable scope for judgments of probability to diverge from judgments of representativeness, as this logic requires. Figure 12.1 (a) shows no such divergence. Thus, the results of the Tom W. study simultaneously demonstrate the substitution of representativeness for probability and the neglect of known (but not explicitly mentioned) base rates.

Figure 12.1 (b) is drawn from an early study of the Linda problem, the best-known and most controversial example in the representativeness literature (Tversky & Kahneman, 1982) in which a woman named Linda was described as follows:

> *Linda is 31 years old, single, outspoken and very bright. She majored in philosophy. As a student she was deeply concerned with issues of discrimination and social justice and also participated in antinuclear demonstrations.*

As in the Tom W. study, separate groups of respondents were asked to rank a set of eight outcomes by representativeness and probability. The results are shown in Figure 12.1(b). Again the correlation between these rankings was almost perfect (.99).[1]

Six of the eight outcomes that subjects were asked to rank were fillers (e.g., elementary school teacher, psychiatric social worker). The two critical outcomes were #6 (bank teller) and the so-called conjunction item #8 (bank teller and active in the feminist movement). Most subjects ranked the conjunction higher than its constituent, both in representativeness (85%) and probability (89%). The observed ranking of the two items is quite reasonable for judgments of similarity, but not for probability: Linda may resemble a feminist bank teller more than she resembles a bank teller, but she cannot be more likely to be a feminist bank teller than to be a bank teller. In this problem, reliance on representativeness yields probability judgments that violate a basic logical rule. As in the Tom W. study, the results make two points: They support the hypothesis of attribute substitution and also illustrate a predictable judgment error.

The Representativeness Controversy

The experiments summarized in Figure 12.1 provided direct evidence for the representativeness heuristic and two concomitant biases: neglect of base rates and conjunction errors. In the terminology introduced by Tversky and Kahneman (1983), the design of these experiments was "subtle": Adequate information was available for participants to avoid the error, but no effort was made to call their attention to that information. For example, participants in the Tom W. experiment had general knowledge of the relative base rates of the various fields of specialization, but these base rates were not explicitly mentioned in the problem. Similarly, both critical items in the Linda experiment were included in the list of outcomes, but they were separated by a filler so respondents would not feel compelled to compare them. In the anthropomorphic language used here, system 2 was given a chance to correct the judgment but was not prompted to do so.

In view of the confusing controversy that followed, it is perhaps unfortunate that the articles documenting base rate neglect and conjunction errors did not stop with subtle tests. Each article also contained an experimental flourish – a demonstration in which the error occurred in spite of a manipulation that called participants' attention to the critical variable. The engineer–lawyer problem (Kahneman & Tversky, 1973) included special instructions to ensure that respondents would notice the base rates of the outcomes. The brief personality descriptions shown to respondents were reported to have been drawn from a set containing descriptions of 30 lawyers and 70 engineers (or vice versa), and respondents were asked "What is the probability that this description belongs to one of the 30 lawyers in the sample of 100?" To the authors' surprise, base rates were largely neglected in the responses, despite their salience in the instructions. Similarly, the authors were later shocked to discover that more than 80% of undergraduates committed a conjunction error even when asked point blank whether Linda was more likely to be "a bank teller" or "a bank teller who is active in the feminist movement" (Tversky & Kahneman, 1983). The novelty of these additional direct or "transparent" tests was the finding that respondents continued to show the biases associated with representativeness even in the presence of strong cues pointing to the normative response. The errors that people make in transparent judgment problems are analogous to observers' failure to allow for ambient haze in estimating distances: A correct response is within reach, but not chosen, and the failure involves an unexpected weakness of the corrective operations of system 2.

Discussions of the heuristics and biases approach have focused almost exclusively on the direct conjunction fallacy and on the engineer–lawyer problems. These are also the only studies that have been extensively replicated with varying parameters. The amount of critical attention is remarkable because the studies were not, in fact, essential to the authors' central claim. In terms of the present treatment, the claim was that intuitive prediction is an operation of system 1, which is susceptible to both base rate neglect and conjunction fallacies. There was no intent to deny the possibility of system 2 interventions that would modify or override intuitive predictions. Thus, the articles in which these studies appeared would have been substantially the same, although far less provocative, if respondents had overcome base rate neglect and conjunction errors in transparent tests.

To appreciate why the strong forms of base rate neglect and of the conjunction fallacy sparked so much controversy, it is useful to distinguish two conceptions of human rationality (Kahneman, 2000b). *Coherence rationality* is the strict conception that requires the agent's entire system of beliefs and preferences to be internally consistent and immune to effects of framing and context. For example, an individual's probability *p* ("Linda is a bank teller") should be the sum of the probabilities *p* ("Linda is a bank teller and a feminist"), and *p* ("Linda is a bank teller and not a feminist"). A subtle test of coherence rationality could be conducted by asking individuals to assess these three probabilities on separate occasions under circumstances that minimize recall. Coherence can also be tested in a between-groups design. If random assignment is assumed, the sum of the average probabilities assigned to the two component events should equal the average judged probability of "Linda is a bank teller." If this prediction fails, then at least some individuals are incoherent. Demonstrations of incoherence present a significant challenge to important models of decision theory and economics, which attribute to agents a very strict form of rationality (Tversky & Kahneman, 1986). Failures of perfect coherence are less provocative to psychologists, who have a more realistic view of human capabilities.

A more lenient concept, *reasoning rationality*, only requires an ability to reason correctly about the information currently at hand without demanding perfect consistency among beliefs that are not simultaneously evoked. The best known violation of reasoning rationality is the famous "four card" problem (Wason, 1960). The failure of intelligent adults to reason their way through this problem is surprising because the problem is "easy" in the sense of being easily understood once explained. What everyone learns, when first told that intelligent people fail to solve the four-card problem, is that one's expectations about human reasoning abilities had not been adequately calibrated. There is, of course, no well-defined metric of reasoning rationality, but whatever metric one uses, the Wason problem calls for a downward adjustment. The surprising results of the Linda and engineer–lawyer problems led Tversky and Kahneman to a similar realization: The reasoning of their subjects was less proficient than they had anticipated. Many readers of the work shared this conclusion, but many others strongly resisted it.

The implicit challenge to reasoning rationality was met by numerous attempts to dismiss the findings of the engineer–lawyer and the Linda studies as artifacts of ambiguous language, confusing instructions, conversational norms, or inappropriate normative standards. Doubts have been raised about the proper interpretation of almost every word in the conjunction problem, including "bank teller," "probability," and even "and" (see, e.g., Dulany & Hilton, 1991; Hilton & Slugoski, 2001). These claims are not discussed in detail here. We suspect that most of them have some validity and that they identified mechanisms that may have made the results in the engineer–lawyer and Linda studies exceptionally strong. However, we note a significant weakness shared by all these critical discussions: They provide no explanation of the essentially perfect consistency of the judgments observed in direct tests of the conjunction rule and in three other types of experiments: subtle comparisons, between-Ss comparisons, and most important, judgments of representativeness (see also Bar-Hillel & Neter, 1993). Interpretations of the conjunction fallacy as an artifact implicitly dismiss the results of Figure 12.1(b) as a coincidence (for an exception, see Ayton, 1998). The story of the engineer-lawyer problem is similar. Here again, multiple demonstrations in which base rate information was used (see Koehler, 1996, for a review) invited the inference that there is no general problem of base rate neglect. Again, the data of prediction by representativeness in Figure 12.1(a) (and related results reported by Kahneman & Tversky, 1973) were ignored.

The demonstrations that under some conditions people avoid the conjunction fallacy in direct tests, or use explicit base rate information, led some scholars to the blanket conclusion that judgment biases are artificial and fragile and that there is no need for judgment heuristics to explain them. This position was promoted most vigorously by Gigerenzer (1991). Kahneman and Tversky (1996) argued in response that the heuristics and biases position does not preclude the possibility of people's performing flawlessly in particular variants of the Linda and the engineer–lawyer problems. Because laypeople readily acknowledge the validity of the conjunction rule and the relevance of base rate information, the fact that they sometimes obey these principles is neither a surprise nor an argument against the role of representativeness in routine intuitive prediction. However, the study of conditions under which errors are avoided can help us understand the capabilities and limitations of system 2. We develop this argument further in the next section.

Making Biases Disappear: A Task for System 2

Much has been learned over the years about variables and experimental procedures that reduce or eliminate the biases associated with representativeness. We next discuss conditions under which errors of intuition are successfully overcome and some circumstances under which intuitions may not be evoked at all.

STATISTICAL SOPHISTICATION

The performance of statistically sophisticated groups of respondents in different versions of the Linda problem illustrates the effects of both expertise and research design (Tversky & Kahneman, 1983). Statistical expertise provided no advantage in the eight-item version in which the critical items were separated by a filler and were presumably considered separately. In the two-item version, in contrast, respondents were effectively compelled to compare "bank teller" with "bank teller and is active in the feminist movement." The incidence of conjunction errors remained essentially unchanged among the statistically naive in this condition but dropped dramatically for the statistically sophisticated. Most of the experts followed logic rather than intuition when they recognized that one of the categories contained the other. In the absence of a prompt to compare the items, however, the statistically sophisticated made their predictions in the same way as everyone else does – by representativeness. As Stephen Jay Gould (1991, p. 469) noted, knowledge of the truth does not dislodge the feeling that Linda is a feminist bank teller: "I know [the right answer], yet a little homunculus in my head continues to jump up and down, shouting at me – 'but she can't just be a bank teller; read the description.'"

INTELLIGENCE

Stanovich (1999) and Stanovich and West (2002) observed a generally negative correlation between conventional measures of intelligence and susceptibility to judgment biases. They used transparent versions of the problems, which include adequate cues to the correct answer and therefore provide a test of reasoning rationality. Not surprisingly, intelligent people are more likely to possess the relevant logical rules and also to recognize the applicability of these rules in particular situations. In the terms of the present analysis, high-IQ respondents benefit from relatively efficient system 2 operations that enable them to overcome erroneous intuitions when adequate information is available. (However, when a problem is too difficult for everyone, the correlation may reverse because the more intelligent respondents are more likely to agree on a plausible error than to respond randomly, as discussed in Kahneman, 2000b.)

FREQUENCY FORMAT

Relative frequencies (e.g., 1 in 10) are more vividly represented and more easily understood than equivalent probabilities (.10) or percentages (10%). For example, the emotional impact of statements of risk is enhanced by the frequency format: "1 person in 1000 will die" is more frightening than a probability of .001 (Slovic et al., 2002). The frequency representation also makes it easier to visualize partitions of sets and detect that one set is contained in another. As a consequence, the conjunction fallacy is generally avoided in direct tests in which the frequency format makes it easy to recognize that feminist bank tellers are a subset of bank tellers (Gigerenzer & Hoffrage, 1995; Tversky & Kahneman, 1983). For similar reasons, some base rate problems are more easily solved when couched in frequencies than in probabilities or percentages (Cosmides & Tooby, 1996). However, there is little support for the more general claims about the evolutionary adaptation of the mind to deal with frequencies (Evans et al., 2000). Furthermore, the ranking of outcomes by predicted relative frequency is very similar to the ranking of the same outcomes by representativeness (Mellers, Hertwig, & Kahneman, 2001). We conclude that the frequency format affects the corrective operations of system 2, not the intuitive operations of system 1. The language of frequencies improves respondents' ability to impose the logic of set inclusion on their considered judgments but does not reduce the role of representativeness in their intuitions.

MANIPULATIONS OF ATTENTION

The weight of neglected variables can be increased by drawing attention to them, and experimenters have devised many ingenious ways to do so. Schwarz et al. (1991) found that respondents pay more attention to base rate information when they are instructed to think as statisticians rather than clinical psychologists. Krosnick, Li, and Lehman (1990) exploited conversational conventions about the sequencing of information and confirmed that the impact of base rate information was enhanced by presenting that information *after* the personality description rather than before it. Attention to the base rate is also enhanced when participants observe the drawing of descriptions from an urn (Gigerenzer, Hell, & Blank, 1988) perhaps because watching the drawing induces conscious expectations that reflect the known proportions of possible outcomes. The conjunction fallacy can also be reduced or eliminated by manipulations that increase the accessibility of the relevant rule, including some linguistic variations (Macchi, 1995), and practice with logical problems (Agnoli, 1991; Agnoli & Krantz, 1989).

The interpretation of these attentional effects is straightforward. We assume most participants in judgment studies know, at least vaguely, that the base rate is relevant and that the conjunction rule is valid (Kahneman & Tversky, 1982). Whether they apply this knowledge to override an intuitive judgment depends on their cognitive skills (education, intelligence) and on formulations that make the applicability of a rule apparent (frequency format) or a relevant factor more salient (manipulations of attention). We assume intuitions are less sensitive to these factors and that the appearance or disappearance of biases mainly reflects variations in the efficacy of corrective operations. This conclusion would be circular, of course, if the corrective operations were both inferred from the observation of correct performance and used to explain that performance. Fortunately, the circularity can be avoided because the role of system 2 can be verified – for example, by using manipulations of time pressure, cognitive load, or mood to interfere with its operations.

WITHIN-SUBJECTS FACTORIAL DESIGNS

The relative virtues of between-subjects and within-subject designs in studies of judgment are a highly contentious issue. Factorial designs have their dismissive critics (e.g., Poulton, 1989) and their vigorous defenders (e.g., Birnbaum, 1999). We do not attempt to adjudicate this controversy here. Our narrower point is that between-subjects designs are more appropriate for the study of heuristics of judgment. The following arguments favor this conclusion:

- Factorial designs are transparent. Participants are likely to identify the variables that are manipulated, especially if there are many trials and especially in a fully factorial design in which the same stimulus attributes are repeated in varying combinations. The message that the design conveys to the participants is that the experimenter expects to find effects of every factor that is manipulated (Bar-Hillel & Fischhoff, 1981; Schwarz, 1996).
- Studies that apply a factorial design to judgment tasks commonly involve schematic and impoverished stimuli. The tasks are also highly repetitive. These features encourage participants to adopt simple mechanical rules that will allow them to respond quickly without forming an individuated impression of each stimulus. For example, Ordóñez and Benson (1997) required respondents to judge the attractiveness of gambles on a 100-point scale. They found that under time pressure many respondents computed or estimated the expected values of the gambles and used the results as attractiveness ratings (e.g., a rating of 15 for a 52% chance to win $31.50).
- Factorial designs often yield judgments that are linear combinations of the manipulated variables. This is a central conclusion of a massive research effort conducted by Anderson (1996), who observed that people often average or add where they should multiply.

In summary, the factorial design is not appropriate for testing hypotheses about biases of neglect because it effectively guarantees that no manipulated factor is neglected. Figure 12.2 illustrates this claim by several examples of an *additive extension effect* that we discuss further in the next section. The experiments summarized in the different panels share three important features: (1) In each case, the quantitative variable plotted on the abscissa was completely neglected in similar experiments conducted in a between-subjects or subtle design; (2) in each case, the quantitative variable combines additively with other information; (3) in each case, a compelling normative argument can be made for a quasimultiplicative rule in which the lines shown in Figure 12.2 should fan out. For example, Figure 12.2(c) presents a study of categorical prediction (Novemsky & Kronzon, 1999) in which respondent 5 judged the relative likelihood that a person was a member of one occupation rather than another (e.g., computer programmer vs. flight attendant) on the basis of short personality sketches (e.g., "shy, serious, organized, and sarcastic") and one of three specified base rates (10%, 50%, or 90%). Representativeness and base rate were varied factorially within subjects. The effect of base rate is clearly significant in this design (see also Birnbaum & Mellers, 1983). Furthermore, the effects of representativeness and base rate are strictly additive. As Anderson (1996) argued, averaging (a special case of additive combination) is the most obvious way to combine the effects of two variables that are recognized as relevant (e.g., "She looks like a bank teller, but the base-rate is low."). Additivity is not normatively appropriate in this case – any Bayes-like combination would produce curves that initially fan out from the origin and converge again at high values. Similar considerations apply to the other three panels of Figure 12.2 discussed later. Between-subjects and factorial designs often yield different results in studies of intuitive judgment. Why should we

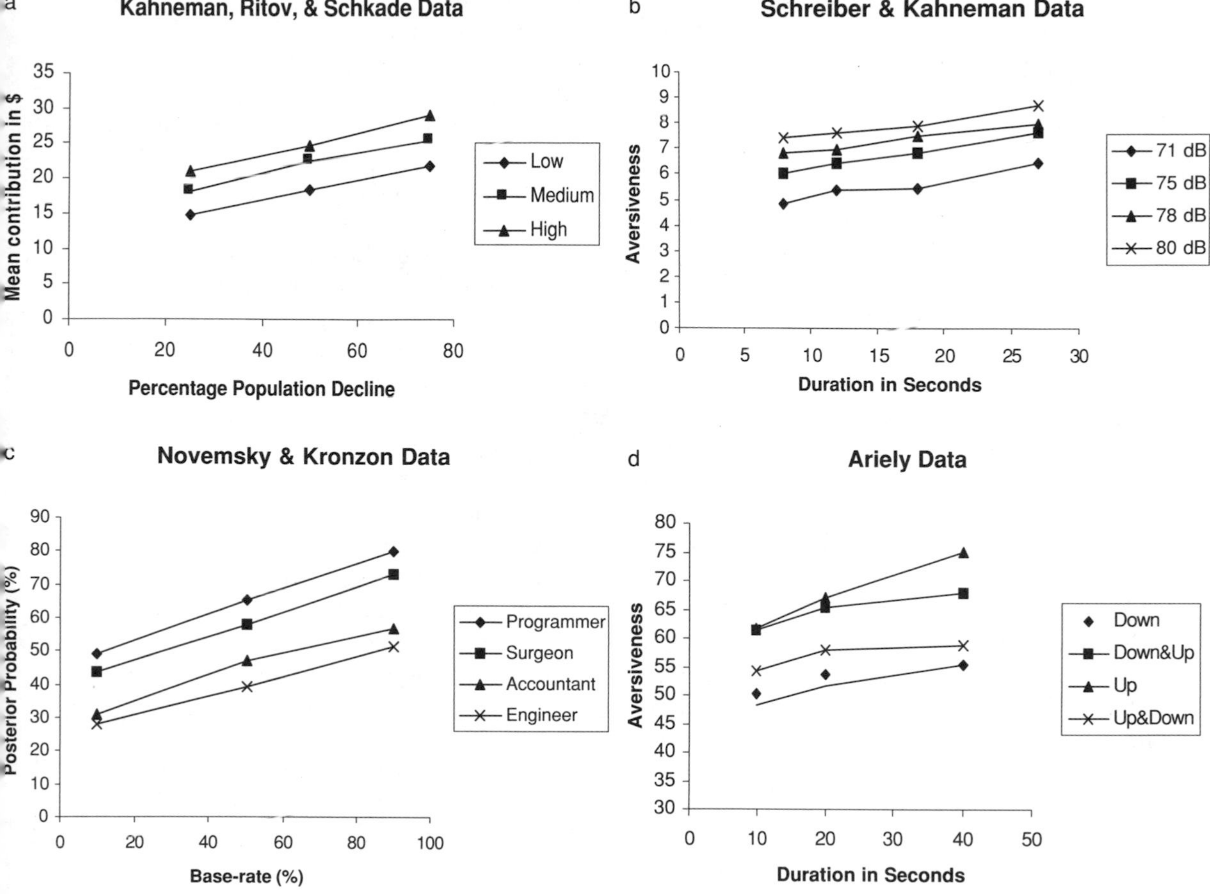

Figure 12.2. (a) Willingness to pay to restore damage to species that differ in popularity as a function of the damage they have suffered (from Kahneman, Ritov, & Schkade 2000); (b) global evaluations of aversive sounds of different loudness as a function of duration for subjects selected for their high sensitivity to duration (from Schreiber & Kahneman, 2000); (c) ratings of probability for predictions that differ in representativeness as a function of base rate frequency (from Novemsky & Kronzon, 1999); (d) global evaluations of episodes of painful pressure that differ in temporal profile as a function of duration (Ariely, 1998).

believe one design rather than the other? The main argument against the factorial design is its poor ecological validity. Encountering multiple judgment objects in rapid succession in a rigidly controlled structure is unique to the laboratory, and the solutions that they evoke are not likely to be typical. Direct comparisons among concepts that differ in only one variable – such as bank teller and feminist bank tellers – also provide a powerful hint and a highly unusual opportunity to overcome intuitions. The between-subjects design, in contrast, mimics the haphazard encounters in which most judgments are made and is more likely to evoke the casually intuitive mode of judgment that governs much of mental life in routine situations (e.g., Langer, 1978).

Prototype Heuristics and the Neglect of Extension

In this section, we offer a common account of three superficially dissimilar judgmental tasks: (1) categorical prediction (e.g., "*In a set of 30 lawyers and 70 engineers, what is the probability that someone described as 'charming, talkative, clever, and cynical' is one of the lawyers?*"); (2) summary evaluations of past events (e.g., "*Overall, how aversive was it to be exposed for 30 minutes to your neighbor's car alarm?*"); and (3) economic valuations of public goods (e.g., "*What is the most you would be willing to pay to prevent 200,000 migrating birds from drowning in uncovered oil ponds?*"). We propose that a generalization of the representativeness heuristic accounts for the remarkably similar biases that are observed in these diverse tasks.

The original analysis of categorical prediction by representativeness (Kahneman & Tversky 1973; Tversky & Kahneman, 1983) invoked two assumptions in which the word "representative" was used in different ways: (1) A prototype (a *representative* exemplar) is used to represent categories (e.g., bank tellers) in the prediction task, and (2) the probability that the individual belongs to a category is judged by the degree to which the individual resembles (is *representative* of) the category stereotype. Thus, categorical prediction by representativeness involves two separate acts of substitution – the substitution of a representative exemplar for a category and the substitution of the heuristic attribute of representativeness for the target attribute of probability. Perhaps because they share a label, the two processes have not been distinguished in discussions of the representativeness heuristic. We separate them here by describing *prototype heuristics* in which a prototype is substituted for its category, but in which representativeness is not necessarily the heuristic attribute.

The target attributes to which prototype heuristics are applied are *extensional*. An extensional attribute pertains to an aggregated property of a set or category for which an extension is specified – the probability that a set of 30 lawyers includes Jack, the overall unpleasantness of a set of moments of hearing a neighbor's car alarm, and the personal dollar value of saving a certain number of birds from drowning in oil ponds. Normative judgments of extensional attributes are governed by a general principle of conditional adding, which dictates that each element of the set adds to the overall judgment an amount that depends on the elements already included. In simple cases, conditional adding is just regular adding – the total weight of a collection of chairs is the sum of their individual weights. In other cases, each element of the set contributes to the overall judgment, but the combination rule is not simple addition and is most typically subadditive. For example, the economic value of protecting X birds should be increasing in X, but the value of saving 2000 birds is for most people less than twice as large as the value of saving 1000 birds.

The logic of categorical prediction entails that the probability of membership in a category should vary with its relative size, or base rate. In prediction by representativeness, however, the representation of outcomes by prototypical exemplars effectively discards base rates because the prototype of a category (e.g., lawyers) contains no information about the size of its membership. Next, we show that phenomena analogous to the neglect of *base rate* are observed in other prototype heuristics: The monetary value attached to a public good is often insensitive to its *scope*, and the global evaluation of a temporally extended experience is often insensitive to its *duration*. These various instantiations of *extension neglect* (neglect of base rates, scope, and duration) have been discussed in separate literatures, but all can be explained by the two-part process that defines prototype heuristics: (1) A category is represented by a prototypical exemplar, and (2) a (nonextensional) property of the prototype is then used as a heuristic attribute to evaluate an extensional target attribute of the category. As might be expected from the earlier discussion of base rate neglect, extension neglect in all its forms is most likely to be observed in between-subjects experiments. Within-subject factorial designs consistently yield the *additive extension effect* illustrated in Figure 12.2.

Scope Neglect in Willingness to Pay

The contingent valuation method (CVM) was developed by resource economists (see Mitchell & Carson, 1989) as a tool for assessing the value of public goods for purposes of litigation or cost–benefit analysis. Participants in contingent valuation (CV) surveys are asked to indicate their willingness to pay (WTP) for specified public goods, and their responses are used to estimate the total amount that the community would pay to obtain these goods. The economists who design contingent valuation surveys interpret WTP as a valid measure of economic value and assume that statements of WTP conform to the extensional logic of consumer theory. The relevant logic has been described by a critic of CVM (Diamond, 1996), who illustrates the conditional adding rule by the following example: In the absence of income effects, WTP for saving X birds should equal WTP for saving $(X - k)$ birds, plus WTP to save k birds, where the last value is contingent on the costless prior provision of safety for $(X - k)$ birds.

Strict adherence to Bayes' rule may be an excessively demanding standard for intuitive predictions; similarly, it would be too much to ask for WTP responses that strictly conform to the "add-up rule." In both cases, however, it seems reasonable to expect *some* sensitivity to extension – to the base rate of outcomes in categorical prediction and to the scope of the good in WTP. In fact, several studies have documented nearly complete neglect of scope in CV surveys. The best-known demonstration of scope neglect is an experiment by Desvouges et al. (1993), who used the scenario of migratory birds that drown in oil ponds. The number of birds said to die each year was varied across groups. The WTP responses were completely insensitive to this variable; the mean WTPs for saving 2000, 20,000, or 200,000 birds were $80, $78, and $88, respectively.

A straightforward interpretation of this result involves the two acts of substitution that characterize prototype heuristics. The deaths of numerous birds are first represented by a prototypical instance – perhaps an image of a bird soaked in oil and drowning. The prototype automatically evokes an affective response, and the intensity of that emotion is then mapped onto the dollar scale – substituting the readily accessible heuristic attribute of affective intensity for the more complex target attribute of economic value. Other examples of radical insensitivity to scope lend themselves to a similar interpretation. Among others, Kahneman (1986) found that Toronto residents were willing to pay almost as much to clean up polluted lakes in a small region of Ontario as to clean up all the polluted lakes in Ontario, and McFadden and Leonard (1993) reported that residents in four western states were willing to pay only 28% more to protect 57 wilderness areas than to protect a single area (for more discussion of scope insensitivity, see Frederick & Fischhoff, 1998).

The similarity between WTP statements and categorical predictions is not limited to such demonstrations of almost complete extension neglect. The two responses also yield similar results when extension and prototype information are varied factorially within subjects. Figure 12.2(a) shows the results of a study of WTP for programs that prevented different levels of damage to species of varying popularity (Ritov & Kahneman, unpublished observations, cited in Kahneman, Ritov, & Schkade, 1999). As in the case of base rate [Figure 12.2(c)], extensional information (levels of damage) combines additively with nonextensional information. This rule of combination is unreasonable; in any plausible theory of value, the lines would fan out.

Finally, the role of the emotion evoked by a prototypical instance was also examined directly in the same experiment, using the heuristic elicitation paradigm introduced earlier: Some respondents were asked to imagine that they saw a television program documenting the effect of adverse ecological circumstances on individual members of different species. The respondents indicated, for each species, how much concern they expected to feel while watching such a documentary. The correlation between this measure of affect and willingness to pay, computed across species, was .97.

Duration Neglect in the Evaluation of Experiences

We next discuss experimental studies of the global evaluation of experiences that extend over some time, such as a pleasant or a horrific film clip (Fredrickson & Kahneman, 1993), a prolonged unpleasant noise (Schreiber & Kahneman, 2000), pressure from a vise (Ariely, 1998), or a painful medical procedure (Redelmeier & Kahneman, 1996). Participants in these studies provided a continuous or intermittent report of hedonic or affective state, using a designated scale of momentary affect (Figure 12.3). When the episode had ended, they indicated a global evaluation of "the *total* pain or discomfort" associated with the entire episode.

We first examine the normative rules that apply to this task. The global evaluation of a temporally extended outcome is an extensional attribute, which is governed by a distinctive logic. The most obvious rule is temporal monotonicity: There is a compelling intuition that adding an extra period of pain to an episode of discomfort can only make it worse overall. Thus, there are two ways of making a bad episode worse – making the discomfort more intense or prolonging it. It must therefore be possible to trade off intensity against duration. Formal analyses have identified conditions under which the total utility of an episode is equal to the temporal integral of a suitably transformed measure of the instantaneous utility associated with each moment (Kahneman, 2000a; Kahneman, Wakker, & Sarin, 1997).

Next, we turn to the psychology. Fredrickson and Kahneman (1993) proposed a "snapshot model" for the retrospective evaluation of episodes, which again involves two acts of substitution: First, the episode is represented by a prototypical moment; next, the affective value attached to the representative moment is substituted for the extensional target attribute of global evaluation. The snapshot model was tested in an experiment in which participants provided continuous ratings of their affect while watching plotless films that varied in duration and affective value (e.g., fish swimming in coral reefs, pigs being beaten to death with clubs), and later reported global evaluations of their experiences. The central finding was that the retrospective evaluations of these observers were predicted with substantial accuracy by a simple average of the peak affect recorded during a film and the end affect reported as the film was about to end. This has been called the peak/end rule. However, the correlation between retrospective evaluations and the duration of the films was negligible – a finding that Fredrickson and Kahneman labeled *duration neglect*. The resemblance of duration neglect to the neglect of scope and base rate is striking and unlikely to be accidental. In this analysis, all three are manifestations of extension neglect caused by the use of a prototype heuristic.

The peak/end rule and duration neglect have both been confirmed on multiple occasions. Figure 12.3 presents raw data from a study reported by Redelmeier and Kahneman (1996), in which patients undergoing colonoscopy reported their current level of pain every 60 seconds throughout the procedure. Here again, an average of peak and end pain quite accurately predicted subsequent global evaluations and choices. The duration of the procedure varied considerably among patients (from 4 to 69 minutes), but these differences were not reflected in subsequent global evaluations in accord with duration neglect. The implications of these psychological rules of evaluation are paradoxical. In Figure 12.3, for example, it appears evident that patient B had a worse colonoscopy than patient A (on the assumption they used the scale similarly). However, it is also apparent that the peak/end average was worse for patient A, whose procedure ended at a moment of relatively intense pain. The peak/end rule prediction for these two profiles is that patient A would evaluate the procedure more negatively than patient B and would be more likely to prefer to undergo a barium enema rather than a repeat colonoscopy. The prediction was correct for these two individuals and confirmed by the data of a large group of patients.

The effects of substantial variations of duration remained small (although statistically robust) even in studies conducted in a factorial design. Figure 12.2(d) is drawn from a study of responses to ischemic pain (Ariely, 1998), in which duration varied by a factor of 4. The peak/end average accounted for 98%

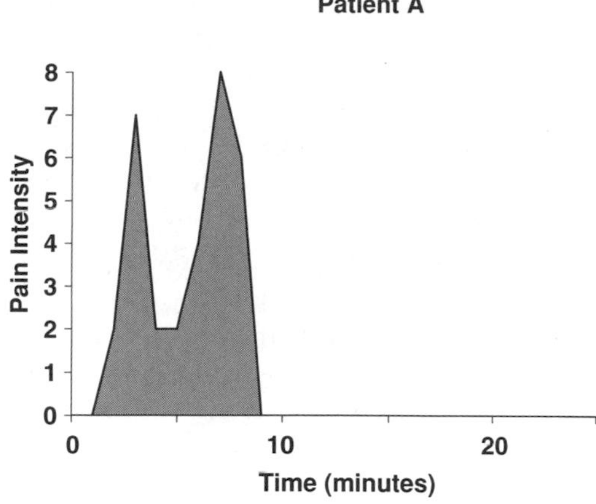

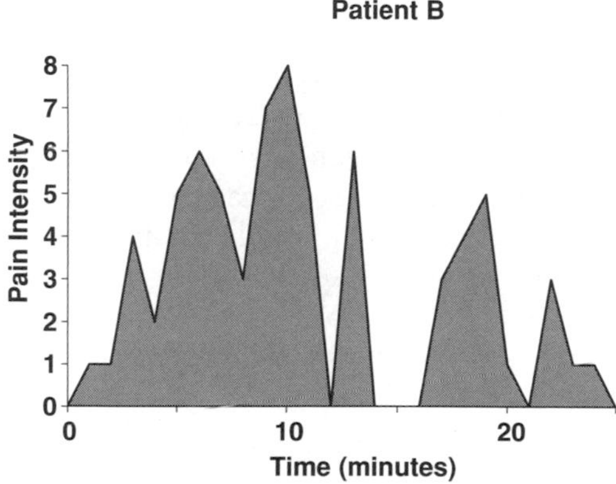

Figure 12.3. Pain intensity reported by two colonoscopy patients.

of the systematic variance of global evaluations in that study and for 88% of the variance in a similar factorial study of responses to loud unpleasant sounds [Schreiber & Kahneman, 2000, Figure 12.2(b)]. Contrary to the normative standard for an extensional attribute, the effects of duration and of other determinants of evaluation were additive [Figures 12.2(b) and 12.2(d)].

The participants in these studies were well aware of the relative duration of their experiences and did not consciously decide to ignore duration in their evaluations. As Fredrickson and Kahneman (1993) noted, duration neglect is an attentional phenomenon:

> *...duration neglect does not imply that duration information is lost, nor that people believe that duration is unimportant... people may be aware of duration and consider it important in the abstract [but] what comes most readily to mind in evaluating episodes are the salient moments of those episodes and the affect associated with those moments. Duration neglect might be overcome, we suppose, by drawing attention more explicitly to the attribute of time. (p. 54)*

This comment applies equally well to other instances of extension neglect: The neglect of base rate in categorical prediction, the neglect of scope in willingness to pay, the neglect of sample size in evaluations of evidence (Griffin & Tversky, 1992; Tversky & Kahneman, 1971), and the neglect of probability of success in evaluating a program of species preservation (DeKay & McClelland, 1995). More generally, inattention plays a similar role in any situation in which the intuitive judgments generated by system 1 violate rules that would be accepted as valid by the more deliberate reasoning that we associate with system 2. As we noted earlier, the responsibility for these judgmental mishaps is properly shared by the two systems: System 1 produces the initial error, and system 2 fails to correct it, although it could.

Violations of Dominance

The conjunction fallacy observed in the Linda problem is an example of a dominance violation in judgment: Linda must be at least as likely to be a bank teller as to be a feminist bank teller, but people believe the opposite. Insensitivity to extension (in this case, base rate) effectively guarantees the existence of such dominance violations. For another illustration, consider the question: "How many murders were there last year in [Detroit/Michigan]?" Although there cannot be more murders in Detroit than in Michigan, because Michigan contains Detroit, the word "Detroit" evokes a more violent image than the word "Michigan" (except of course for people who immediately think of Detroit when Michigan is mentioned). If people use an impression of violence as a heuristic and neglect geographic extension, their estimates of murders in the city may exceed their estimates for the state. In a large sample of University of Arizona students, this hypothesis was confirmed – the median estimate of the number of murders was 200 for Detroit and 100 for Michigan.

Violations of dominance akin to the conjunction fallacy have been observed in several other experiments involving both indirect (between-subjects) and direct tests. In a clinical experiment reported by Redelmeier, Katz, and Kahneman (2001), half of a large group of patients ($N = 682$) undergoing a colonoscopy were randomly assigned to a condition that made the actual experience strictly worse. Unbeknownst to the patient, the physician deliberately delayed the removal of the colonoscope for approximately 1 minute beyond the normal time. The instrument was not moved during the extra period. For many patients, the mild discomfort of the added period was an improvement relative to the pain than they had just experienced. For these patients, of course, prolonging the procedure reduced the peak/end average of discomfort. As expected, retrospective evaluations were less negative in the experimental group, and a 5-year follow-up showed that participants in that group were also somewhat more likely to comply with recommendations to undergo a repeat colonoscopy (Redelmeier, Katz, & Kahneman, 2001).

In an experiment that is directly analogous to the demonstrations of the conjunction fallacy, Kahneman et al. (1993) exposed participants to two cold-pressor experiences, one with each hand: a "short" episode (immersion of one hand in 14 °C water for 60 seconds), and a "long" episode (the short episode, plus an additional 30 seconds during which the water was gradually warmed to 15 °C). The participants indicated the intensity of their pain throughout the experience. When they were later asked which of the two experiences they preferred to repeat, a substantial majority chose the long trial. These choices violate dominance, because after 60 seconds in cold water anyone will prefer the immediate experience of a warm towel to 30 extra seconds of slowly diminishing pain. In a replication, Schreiber and Kahneman (2000, experiment 2) exposed participants to pairs of unpleasant noises in immediate succession. The participants listened to both sounds and chose one to be repeated at the end of the session. The "short" noise lasted 8 seconds at 77 db. The "long" noise consisted of the short noise plus an extra period (of up to 24 seconds) at 66 db (less aversive, but still unpleasant and certainly worse than silence). Here again, the longer noise was preferred most of the time, and this unlikely preference persisted over a series of five choices.

The violations of dominance in these direct tests are particularly surprising because the situation is completely transparent. The participants in the experiments could easily retrieve the durations of the two experiences between which they had to choose, but the results suggest that they simply ignored duration. A simple explanation is that the results reflect "choosing by liking" (see Frederick, 2002). The participants in the experiments simply followed the normal strategy of choice: "When choosing between two familiar options, consult your retrospective evaluations and choose the one that you like most (or dislike least)." Liking and disliking are products of system 1, which do not conform to the rules of extensional logic. System 2 could have intervened, but in these experiments it generally did not. Kahneman et al. (1993) described a participant in their study, who chose to repeat the long cold-pressor experience. Soon after the choice was recorded, the participant was asked which of the two experiences was longer. As he correctly identified the long trial, the participant was heard to mutter "the choice I made doesn't seem to make much sense." Choosing by liking is a form of mindlessness (Langer, 1978), which illustrates the casual governance of system 2.

Like the conjunction fallacy in direct tests, which we discussed earlier, violations of temporal monotonicity in choices should be viewed as an expendable flourish. Because the two aversive experiences occurred within a few minutes of each other and respondents could accurately recall the duration of the two events, system 2 had enough information to override choosing by liking. Its failure to do so is analogous to the failures observed in direct tests of the Linda problem. In both cases, the violations of dominance tell us nothing new about system 1; they only illustrate an unexpected weakness of system 2. Just as the theory of intuitive categorical prediction would have remained intact if the conjunction fallacy had not "worked" in a direct test, the model of evaluation by moments would have survived even if violations of dominance had been eliminated in highly transparent situations. The same methodological issues arise in both contexts. Between-subjects experiments or subtle tests are most appropriate for studying the basic intuitive evaluations of system 1, and also most likely to reveal complete extension neglect. Factorial designs in which extension is manipulated practically guarantee an effect of this variable, and almost guarantee that it will be additive, as in Figures 12.2(b) and 12.2(d) (Ariely, 1998; Ariely, Kahneman, & Loewenstein, 2000; Schreiber & Kahneman, 2000). Finally, although direct choices sometimes yield systematic violations of dominance, these violations can be avoided by manipulations that prompt system 2 to take control.

In our view, the similarity of the results obtained in diverse contexts is a compelling argument for a unified interpretation, and a significant challenge to critiques that pertain only to selected subsets of this body of evidence. A number of commentators have offered competing interpretations of base rate neglect (Cosmides & Tooby, 1996; Koehler, 1996), insensitivity to scope in WTP (Kopp, 1992), and duration neglect (Ariely & Loewenstein, 2000). However, these interpretations are generally specific to a particular task and would not carry over to analogous findings in other domains. Similarly, the various attempts to explain the conjunction fallacy as an artifact do not explain analogous violations of dominance in the cold-pressor experiment. The account we have offered is, in contrast, equally applicable to all three contexts and possibly others (see also Kahneman, Ritov, & Schkade, 1999). We attribute extension neglect and violations of dominance to a lazy system 2, and to a prototype heuristic that combines two processes of system 1: the representation of categories by prototypes and the substitution of a nonextensional heuristic attribute for an extensional target attribute. We also propose that people have some appreciation of the role of extension in the various judgment tasks. Consequently, they will incorporate extension in their judgments when their attention is drawn to this factor – most reliably in factorial experiments, and sometimes (although not always) in direct tests. The challenge for competing interpretations is to provide a unified account of the diverse phenomena that have been considered in this section.

Conclusions and Future Directions

The original goal of the heuristics and biases program was to understand intuitive judgment under uncertainty. Heuristics were described as a collection of disparate cognitive procedures, related only by their common function in a particular judgmental domain – choice under uncertainty. It now appears, however, that judgment heuristics are applied in a wide variety of domains and share a common process of *attribute substitution*, in which difficult judgments are made by substituting conceptually or semantically related assessments that are simpler and more readily accessible.

The current treatment explicitly addresses the conditions under which intuitive judgments are modified or overridden. Although attribute substitution provides an initial input into many judgments, it need not be the sole basis for them. Initial impressions are often supplemented, moderated, or overridden by other considerations, including the recognition of relevant logical rules and the deliberate execution of learned algorithms. The role of these supplemental or alternative inputs depends on characteristics of the judge and the judgment task.

Our use of the dual-process terminology does not entail a belief that every mental operation (including each postulated heuristic) can be definitively assigned to one system or the other. The placement of dividing lines between "systems" is arbitrary because the bases by which we characterize mental operations (difficulty of acquisition, accessibility to introspection, and disruptability) are all continua. However, this does not make distinctions less meaningful; there is broad agreement that mental operations range from rapid, automatic, perception-like impressions to deliberate computations that apply explicit rules or external aids.

Many have questioned the usefulness of the notion of heuristics and biases by pointing to inconsistencies in the degree to which illusions are manifested across different studies. However, there is no mystery here to explain. Experimental studies of "the same" cognitive illusions can yield different results for two reasons: (1) because of variation in factors that determine the accessibility of the intuitive illusion, and (2) because they vary in factors that determine the accessibility of the corrective thoughts that are associated with system 2. Both types of variation can often be anticipated because of the vast amount of psychological knowledge that has accumulated about the different sets of factors that determine the ease with which thoughts come to mind – from principles of grouping in perception to principles that govern transfer of training in rule learning (Kahneman, 2003). Experimental surprises will occur, of course, and should lead to refinements in the understanding of the rules of accessibility.

The argument that system 1 will be expressed unless it is overridden by system 2 sounds circular, but it is not, because empirical criteria can be used to test whether a particular characterization of the two systems is accurate. For example, a feature of the situation will be associated with system 2 if it is shown to influence judgments only when attention is explicitly directed to it (through, say, a within-subjects design). In contrast, a variable will be associated with system 1 if it can be shown to influence even those judgments that are made in a split second. Thus, one need not be committed, a priori, to assigning a process to a particular system; the data will dictate the best characterization.

The two-system model is a framework that combines a set of empirical generalizations about cognitive operations with a set of tests for diagnosing the types of cognitive operations that underlie judgments in specific situations. The generalizations and the specific predictions are testable and can be recognized as true or false. The framework itself will be judged by its usefulness as a heuristic for research.

Acknowledgments

This chapter is a modified version of a chapter by Kahneman and Frederick (2002). Preparation of this chapter was supported by grant SES-0213481 from the National Science Foundation.

Note

1. The entries plotted in Figure 12.1 are averages of multiple judgments, and the correlations are computed over a set of judgment objects. It should be noted that correlations between averages are generally much higher than corresponding correlations within the data of individual respondents (Nickerson, 1995). Indeed, group results may even be unrepresentative if they are dominated by a few individuals who produce more variance than others and have an atypical pattern of responses. Fortunately, this particular hypothesis is not applicable to the experiments of Figure 12.1, in which all responses were ranks.

References

Agnoli, F. (1991). Development of judgmental heuristics and logical reasoning: Training counteracts the representativeness heuristic. *Cognitive Development*, 6, 195–217.

Agnoli, F., & Krantz, D. H. (1989). Suppressing natural heuristics by formal instruction: The case of the conjunction fallacy. *Cognitive Psychology, 21*, 515–550.

Anderson, N. H. (1991). *Contributions to information integration theory. Vol. I: cognition*. Hillsdale, NJ: Erlbaum.

Anderson, N. H. (1996). *A functional theory of cognition*. Mahwah, NJ: Erlbaum.

Ariely, D. (1998). Combining experiences over time: The effects of duration, intensity changes and on-line measurements on retrospective pain evaluations. *Journal of Behavioral Decision Making, 11*, 19–45.

Ariely, D. (2001). Seeing sets: Representation by statistical properties. *Psychological Science, 12*(2), 157–162.

Ariely, D., Kahneman, D., & Loewenstein, G. (2000). Joint comment on "When does duration matter in judgment and decision making?" (Ariely & Loewenstein, 2000). *Journal of Experimental Psychology: General, 129*, 524–529.

Ariely, D., & Loewenstein, G. (2000). When does duration matter in judgment and decision making. *Journal of Experimental Psychology: General, 129*, 508–523.

Ayton, P. (1998). How bad is human judgment? In G. Wright & P. Goodwin (Eds.), *Forecasting with judgment*. West Sussex, UK: Wiley.

Bargh, J. A. (1997). The automaticity of everyday life. In R. S. Wyer, Jr. (Ed.), *Advances in social cognition* (Vol. 10). Mahwah, NJ: Erlbaum.

Bargh, J. A., Bond, R. N., Lombardi, W. J., & Tota, M. E. (1986). The additive nature of chronic and temporary sources of construct accessibility. *Journal of Personality and Social Psychology, 50*(5), 869–878.

Bar-Hillel, M., & Fischhoff, B. (1981). When do base-rates affect predictions? *Journal of Personality and Social Psychology, 41*(4), 671–680.

Bar-Hillel, M., & Neter, E. (1993). How alike is it versus how likely is it: A disjunction fallacy in probability judgments. *Journal of Personality and Social Psychology, 41*(4), 671–680.

Begg, I., Anas, A., & Farinacci, S. (1992). Dissociation of processes in belief: Source recollection, statement familiarity, and the illusion of truth. *Journal of Experimental Psychology: General, 121*(4), 446–458.

Begg, I., & Armour, V. (1991). Repetition and the ring of truth: Biasing comments. *Canadian Journal of Behavioural Science, 23*, 195–213.

Birnbaum, M. H. (1999). How to show that 9 > 221: Collect judgments in a between-subjects design. *Psychological Methods, 4*(3), 243–249.

Birnbaum, M. H., & Mellers, B. A. (1983). Bayesian inference: Combining base rates with opinions of sources who vary in credibility. *Journal of Personality and Social Psychology, 45*, 792–804.

Bless, H., Clore, G. L., Schwarz, N., Golisano, V., Rabe, C., & Wolk, M. (1996). Mood and the use of scripts: Does a happy mood really lead to mindlessness? *Journal of Personality and Social Psychology, 71*(4), 665–679.

Bodenhausen, G. V. (1990). Stereotypes as judgmental heuristics: Evidence of circadian variations in discrimination. *Psychological Science, 1*(5), 319–322.

Brunswik, E. (1943). Organismic achievement and environmental probability. *Psychological Review, 50*, 255–272.

Cacioppo, J. T., Priester, J. R., & Berntson, G. G. (1993). Rudimentary determinants of attitudes: II. Arm flexion and extension have differential effects on attitudes. *Journal of Personality and Social Psychology, 65*, 5–17.

Chaiken, S., & Trope, Y. (1999). *Dual-process theories in social psychology*. New York: Guilford Press.

Chapman, G., & Johnson, E. (2002). Incorporating the irrelevant: Anchors in judgments of belief and value. In T. Gilovich, D. Griffin, & D. Kahneman (eds.), *Heuristics and biases: The psychology of intuitive judgment* (pp. 120–138). New York: Cambridge University Press.

Chase, W. G., & Simon, H. A. (1973). Perception in chess. *Cognitive Psychology, 4*, 55–81.

Cohen, J. (1969). *Statistical power analysis for the behavioral sciences*. San Diego: Academic Press.

Cohen, J. (1992). A power primer. *Psychological Bulletin, 112*(1), 155–159.

Cosmides L., & Tooby J. (1996). Are humans good intuitive statisticians after all? Rethinking some conclusions from the literature on judgment under uncertainty. *Cognition, 58*(1), 1–73.

DeKay, M. L., & McClelland, G. H. (1995). Probability and utility components of endangered species preservation programs. *Journal of Experimental Psychology: Applied, 2*, 60–83.

Desvouges, W. H., Johnson, F., Dunford, R., Hudson, S., Wilson, K., & Boyle, K. (1993). Measuring resource damages with contingent valuation: Tests of validity and reliability.

In *Contingent valuation: A critical assessment*. Amsterdam: North Holland.

Diamond, P. (1996). Testing the internal consistency of contingent valuation surveys. *Journal of Environmental Economics and Management*, 28, 155–173.

Dulany, D. E. & Hilton, D. J. (1991). Conversational implicature, conscious representation, and the conjunction fallacy. *Social Cognition*, 9, 85–110.

Epstein, S. (1994). Integration of the cognitive and the psychodynamic unconscious. *American Psychologist*, 49(8), 709–724.

Evans, J., Handley, S. J., Perham, N., Over, D. E., & Thompson, V. A. (2000). Frequency versus probability formats in statistical word problems. *Cognition*, 77, 197–213.

Evans, J. St. B. T., & Over, D. E. (1996). *Rationality and reasoning*. Hove, UK: Psychology Press.

Finucane, M. L., Alhakami, A., Slovic, P., & Johnson, S. M. (2000). The affect heuristic in judgments of risks and benefits. *Journal of Behavioral Decision Making*, 13, 1–17.

Frederick, S. W. (2002). Automated choice heuristics. In T. Gilovich, D. Griffin, & D. Kahneman (eds.), *Heuristics and biases: The psychology of intuitive judgment* (pp. 548–558). New York: Cambridge University Press.

Frederick, S. W. (2004). *(Im)patient, (un)-adventurous, (in)sensitive, and (im)moral: Cognitive (in)ability as a predictor of time preference, risk preference, magnitude sensitivity, and cheating*. Working paper, Massachusetts Institute of Technology, Cambridge, MA.

Frederick, S. W., & Fischhoff, B. (1998). Scope (in)sensitivity in elicited valuations. *Risk, Decision, and Policy*, 3, 109–123.

Frederick, S. W., & Nelson, L. (2004). *Attribute substitution in physical judgments*, Working paper, Massachusetts Institute of Technology, Cambridge, MA.

Fredrickson, B. L., & Kahneman, D. (1993). Duration neglect in retrospective evaluations of affective episodes. *Journal of Personality and Social Psychology*, 65(1), 45–55.

Ganzach, Y., & Krantz, D. H. (1990). The psychology of moderate prediction: I. Experience with multiple determination. *Organizational Behavior and Human Decision Processes*, 47, 177–204.

Gigerenzer, G. (1991). How to make cognitive illusions disappear: Beyond "heuristics and biases." In W. Stroebe & M. Hewstone (Eds.), *European review of social psychology* (Vol. 2, pp. 83–115). Chichester, UK: Wiley.

Gigerenzer, G., Czerlinski, J., & Martignon, L. (2002). How good are fast and frugal heuristics? In T. Gilovich, D. Griffin, & D. Kahneman (Eds.), *Heuristics and biases: The psychology of intuitive judgment* (pp. 559–581). New York: Cambridge University Press.

Gigerenzer, G., & Goldstein, D. G. (1996). Reasoning the fast and frugal way: Models of bounded rationality. *Psychological Review*, 103(4), 650–669.

Gigerenzer, G., Hell, W., & Blank, H. (1988). Presentation and content – The use of base rates as a continuous variable. *Journal of Experimental Psychology – Human Perception and Performance*, 14(3), 513–525.

Gigerenzer, G., & Hoffrage, U. (1995). How to improve Bayesian reasoning without instruction: Frequency formats. *Psychological Review*, 102, 684–704.

Gigerenzer, G., Todd, P. M., & the ABC Group. (1999). *Simple heuristics that make us smart*. New York: Oxford University Press.

Gilbert, D. (1989). Thinking lightly about others: Automatic components of the social inference process. In J. Uleman & J. A. Bargh (Eds.), *Unintended thought* (pp. 189–211). New York: Guilford Press.

Gilbert, D. (1991). How mental systems believe. *American Psychologist*, 46(2), 107–119.

Gilbert, D. (1999). What the mind's not. In S. Chaiken & Y. Trope (Eds.), *Dual-process theories in social psychology* (pp. 3–11). New York: Guilford Press.

Gould, S. J. (1991). *Bully for brontosaurus. Reflections in natural history*. New York: Norton.

Griffin, D., & Tversky, A. (1992). The weighing of evidence and the determinants of confidence. *Cognitive Psychology*, 24(3), 411–435.

Hammond, K. R. (1955). Probabilistic functioning and the clinical method. *Psychological Review*, 62, 255–262.

Hammond, K. R. (1996). *Human judgment and social policy*. New York: Oxford University Press.

Heider, F. (1944). Social perception and phenomenal causality. *Psychological Review*, 51, 358–374.

Hertwig, R., & Gigerenzer, G. (1999). The 'conjunction fallacy' revisited: How intelligent inferences look like reasoning errors. *Journal of Behavioral Decision Making*, 12(4), 275–305.

Higgins, E. T., & Brendl, C. M. (1995). Accessibility and applicability: Some "activation rules" influencing judgment. *Journal of Experimental Social Psychology, 31*, 218–243.

Hilton, D. J., & Slugoski, B. R. (2001). Conversational processes in reasoning and explanation. In A. Tesser & N. Schwarz (Eds.), *Blackwell handbook of social psychology. Vol. 1: Intraindividual processes* (pp. 181–206). Oxford, UK: Blackwell.

Isen, A. M., Nygren, T. E., & Ashby, F. G. (1988). Influence of positive affect on the subjective utility of gains and losses – It is just not worth the risk. *Journal of Personality and Social Psychology, 55*(5), 710–717.

Jacoby, L. L., & Dallas, M. (1981). On the relationship between autobiographical memory and perceptual learning. *Journal of Experimental Psychology: General, 3*, 306–340.

Kahneman, D. (1986). Valuing environmental goods: An assessment of the contingent valuation method. In R. Cummings, D. Brookshire, & W. Schulze (Eds.), *Valuing environmental goods: An assessment of the contingent valuation method*. Totowa, NJ: Rowman and Allanheld.

Kahneman, D. (2000a). Experienced utility and objective happiness: A moment-based approach. In D. Kahneman & A. Tversky (Eds.), *Choices, values, and frames*. New York: Cambridge University Press and the Russell Sage Foundation.

Kahneman, D. (2000b). A psychological point of view: Violations of rational rules as a diagnostic of mental processes (commentary on Stanovich and West). *Behavioral and Brain Sciences, 23*, 681–683.

Kahneman, D. (2003). A perspective on judgment and choice: Mapping bounded rationality. *American Psychologist, 58*, 697–720.

Kahneman, D., & Frederick, (2002). In T. Gilovich, D. Griffin, & D. Kahneman (Eds.), *Heuristics of intuitive judgment*. New York: Cambridge University Press.

Kahneman, D., Fredrickson, D. L., Schreiber, C. A., & Redelmeier, D. A. (1993). When more pain is preferred to less: Adding a better end. *Psychological Science, 4*, 401–405.

Kahneman, D., & Miller, D. T. (1986). Norm theory: Comparing reality with its alternatives. *Psychological Review, 93*, 136–153.

Kahneman, D., & Ritov, I. (1994). Determinants of stated willingness to pay for public goods: A study in the headline method. *Journal of Risk and Uncertainty, 9*, 5–38.

Kahneman, D., Ritov, I., & Schkade, D. (1999). Economic preferences or attitude expressions? An analysis of dollar responses to public issues. *Journal of Risk and Uncertainty, 19*, 203–235.

Kahneman, D., Schkade, D. A., & Sunstein, C. R. (1998). Shared outrage and erratic awards: The psychology of punitive damages. *Journal of Risk and Uncertainty, 16*, 49–86.

Kahneman, D., Slovic, P., & Tversky, A. E. (1982). *Judgment under uncertainty: Heuristics and biases*. New York: Cambridge University Press.

Kahneman, D., & Tversky, A. (1972). Subjective probability: A judgment of representativeness. *Cognitive Psychology, 3*, 430–454.

Kahneman, D., & Tversky, A. (1973). On the psychology of prediction. *Psychological Review, 80*, 237–251.

Kahneman, D., & Tversky, A. (1982). On the study of statistical intuitions. *Cognition, 11*, 123–141.

Kahneman, D., & Tversky, A. (1996). On the reality of cognitive illusions: A reply to Gigerenzer's critique. *Psychological Review, 103*, 582–591.

Kahneman, D., & Varey, C. A. (1990). Propensities and counterfactuals: The loser that almost won. *Journal of Personality and Social Psychology, 59*(6), 1101–1110.

Kahneman, D., Wakker, P. P., & Sarin, R. (1997). Back to Bentham? Explorations of experienced utility. *Quarterly Journal of Economics, 112*, 375–405.

Keysar, B. (1989). On the functional equivalence of literal and metaphorical interpretations in discourse. *Journal of Memory and Language, 28*, 375–385.

Koehler, J. (1996). The base-rate fallacy reconsidered: Descriptive, normative, and methodological challenges. *Behavioral and Brain Sciences, 19*, 1–53.

Kopp, R. (1992). Why existence value should be used in cost–benefit analysis. *Journal of Policy Analysis and Management, 11*, 123–130.

Krosnick, J. A., Li, F., & Lehman, D. R. (1990). Conversational conventions, order of information acquisition, and the effect of base rates and individuating information on social judgment. *Journal of Personality and Social Psychology, 59*, 1140–1152.

Langer, E. J. (1978). Rethinking the role of thought in social interaction. In Harvey, Ickes,

& Kidd (Eds.), *New directions in attribution research* (Vol. 2). Potomac, MD: Erlbaum.

Macchi, L. (1995). Pragmatic aspects of the base-rate fallacy. *Quarterly Journal of Experimental Psychology, 48A*, 188–207.

Mandler, G., Hamson, C., & Dorfman, J. (1990). Tests of dual process theory – Word priming and recognition. *Quarterly Journal of Experimental Psychology*, 42(4), 713–739.

Margolis, H. (1987). *Patterns, thinking & cognition*. Chicago: University of Chicago Press.

McFadden, D., & Leonard, G. K. (1993). Issues in the contingent valuation of environmental goods: Methodologies for data collection and analysis. In Hausman (Ed.), *Contingent valuation. A critical assessment*. Amsterdam: North-Holland.

Mellers, B., Hertwig, R., & Kahneman, D. (2001). Do frequency representations eliminate conjunction effects? An exercise in adversarial collaboration. *Psychological Science*, 12, 269–275.

Michotte, A. (1963). *The perception of causality*. New York: Basic Books.

Mitchell, R., & Carson, R. (1989). *Using surveys to value public goods: The contingent valuation method*. Washington, DC: Resources for the Future.

Nickerson, C. (1995). Does willingness-to-pay reflect the purchase of moral satisfaction? A reconsideration of Kahneman and Knetsch. *Journal of Environmental Economics and Management*, 28, 126–133.

Nisbett, R. E., Krantz, D. H., Jepson, C., & Kunda, Z. (1983). The use of statistical heuristics in everyday inductive reasoning. *Psychological Review*, 90(4), 339–363.

Novemsky, N., & Kronzon, S. (1999). How are base-rates used, when they are used: A comparison of Bayesian and additive models of base-rate use. *Journal of Behavioral Decision Making*, 12, 55–69.

Ordóñez, L., & Benson, L., III. (1997). Decisions under time pressure: How time constraint affects risky decision making. *Organizational Behavior and Human Decision Processes*, 71(2), 121–140.

Parducci, A. (1965). Category judgment: A range-frequency model. *Psychological Review*, 72, 407–418.

Pashler, H. E. (1998). *The psychology of attention*. Cambridge, MA: MIT Press.

Poulton, (1989). *Bias in quantifying judgments*. London: Erlbaum.

Redelmeier, D., Katz, J., & Kahneman, D. (2001). Memories of colonoscopy: A randomized trial.

Redelmeier, D., & Kahneman, D. (1996). Patients' memories of painful medical treatments: Real-time and retrospective evaluations of two minimally invasive procedures. *Pain*, 66, 3–8.

Schreiber, C., & Kahneman, D. (2000). Determinants of the remembered utility of aversive sounds. *Journal of Experimental Psychology: General*, 129, 27–42.

Schwarz, N. (1996). *Cognition and communication: Judgmental biases, research methods, and the logic of conversation*. Mahwah, NJ: Erlbaum.

Schwarz, N., Bless, H., Strack, F., Klumpp, G., Rittenauer-Schatka, H., & Simons, A. (1991). Ease of retrieval as information: Another look at the availability heuristic. *Journal of Personality and Social Psychology*, 61, 195–202.

Schwarz, N., & Clore, G. L. (1983). Mood, misattribution, and judgments of well-being: Informative and directive functions of affective states. *Journal of Personality and Social Psychology*, 45(3), 513–523.

Schwarz, N., Strack, F., Hilton, D., & Naderer, G. (1991). Base rates, representativeness, and the logic of conversation: The contextual relevance of "irrelevant" information. *Social Cognition*, 9, 67–84.

Schwarz, N., & Vaughn, L. A. (2002). The availability heuristic revisited: Ease of recall and content of recall as distinct sources of information. In T. Gilovich, D. Griffin, & D. Kahneman (Eds.), *Heuristics & biases: The psychology of intuitive judgment* (pp. 103–119). New York: Cambridge University Press.

Shweder, R. (1977). Likeness and likelihood in everyday thought – Magical thinking in judgments about personality. *Current Anthropology*, 18(4), 637–658.

Simon, H. A., & Chase, W. G. (1973). Skill in chess. *American Scientist*, 61, 394–403.

Sloman, S. A. (1996). The empirical case for two systems of reasoning. *Psychological Bulletin*, 119, 3–22.

Sloman, S. A. (2002). Two systems of reasoning. In T. Gilovich, D. Griffin, & D. Kahneman (Eds.), *Heuristics & biases: The psychology of intuitive judgment* (pp. 379–396). New York: Cambridge University Press.

Slovic, P., Finucane, M., Peters, E., & MacGregor, D. G. (2002). The affect heuristic. In T. Gilovich, D. Griffin, & D. Kahneman (Eds.),

Heuristics & biases: The psychology of intuitive judgment (pp. 397–420). New York: Cambridge University Press.

Stanovich, K. E. (1999). *Who is rational?: Studies of individual differences in reasoning*. Mahwah, NJ: Erlbaum.

Stanovich, K. E., & West, R. (2002). Individual differences in reasoning: Implications for the rationality debate? In T. Gilovich, D. Griffin, & D. Kahneman (Eds.), *Heuristics & biases: The psychology of intuitive judgment* (pp. 421–440). New York: Cambridge University Press.

Stevens, S. S. (1957). On the psychophysical law. *Psychological Review*, 64, 153–181.

Stevens, S. S. (1975). *Psychophysics: Introduction to its perceptual, neural, and social prospects*. New York: Wiley.

Strack, F., Martin, L. L., & Schwarz, N. (1988). Priming and communication: The social determinants of information use in judgments of life-satisfaction. *European Journal of Social Psychology*, 18, 429–442.

Tversky, A., & Kahneman, D. (1971). Belief in the law of small numbers. *Psychological Bulletin*, 76, 105–110.

Tversky, A., & Kahneman, D. (1973). Availability: A heuristic for judging frequency and probability. *Cognitive Psychology*, 5(2), 207–232.

Tversky, A., & Kahneman, D. (1974). Judgment under uncertainty: Heuristics and biases. *Science*, 185(4157), 1124–1131.

Tversky, A., & Kahneman, D. (1982). Judgments of and by representativeness. In D. Kahneman, P. Slovic, & A. Tversky (Eds.), *Judgment under uncertainty: Heuristics and biases* (pp. 84–98). New York: Cambridge University Press.

Tversky, A., & Kahneman, D. (1983). Extensional vs. intuitive reasoning: The conjunction fallacy in probability judgment. *Psychological Review*, 90, 293–315.

Tversky, A., & Kahneman, D. (1986). Rational choice and the framing of decisions. *Journal of Business*, 59, S251–S278.

Wason, P. C. (1960). On the failure to eliminate hypotheses in a conceptual task. *Quarterly Journal of Experimental Psychology*, 12, 129–140.

Zajonc, R. B. (1980). Feeling and thinking: Preferences need no inferences. *American Psychologist*, 35(2), 151–175.

Zajonc, R. B. (1997). Emotions. In D. T. Gilbert, S. T. Fiske, & G. Lindzey (Eds.), *Handbook of social psychology* (4th ed., pp. 591–632). New York: Oxford University Press.

CHAPTER 13

Motivated Thinking

Daniel C. Molden
E. Tory Higgins

At one time or another, every one of us has engaged in "wishful thinking," or "let our hearts influence our heads." That is, every one of us has felt the effects of our motivations on our thought processes. Given this common everyday experience, it is not surprising that an essential part of early psychological research was the idea that drives, needs, desires, motives, and goals can profoundly influence judgment and reasoning. More surprising is that motivational variables play only a small role in current theories of reasoning. Why might this be?

One possible explanation is that since the cognitive revolution in the 1960s and 1970s, researchers studying motivational and cognitive processes have been speaking somewhat different languages. That is, there has been a general failure to connect traditional motivational concepts, such as *drives* or *motives*, to information processing concepts, such as *expectancies* or *spreading activation*, which form the foundation for nearly all contemporary research on thinking and reasoning. For a time, this led not only to misunderstanding but also to conflict between motivational and cognitive perspectives on judgment. More recently however, there has been a sharp increase in attempts to achieve a marriage between these two viewpoints in a wide variety of research areas. The primary objective of this chapter is to review these attempts and to demonstrate how it is not only possible, but also desirable, to reintroduce motivational approaches to the study of basic thought processes. We begin by providing some historical background on such approaches.

A Brief History of Motivated Thinking

Motivational perspectives on thought and reasoning originated most prominently with Freud's (1905) clinical theorizing on the psychodynamic conflicts created by unconscious drives and urges. These perspectives quickly spread to other areas of psychology. Early pioneers of experimental social psychology gave primary emphasis to motivational variables such as drives, goals, and aspirations (e.g., Allport, 1920; Lewin, 1935). The study of personality came to involve the identification and classification of different types of needs and motives (e.g., Murray, 1938). Even research on sensory and perceptual processes was influenced by a motivational approach with the emergence of the "New Look" school (e.g., McGinnies, 1949).

After this early period of growth and expansion, however, research and theory on motivated thinking became quite controversial. With the ascendance of cognitive perspectives on thinking and reasoning in the 1960s and 1970s, many supposed instances of motivated reasoning were recast as merely a product of imperfect information processing by imperfect perceivers (compare Bruner, 1957, with McGinnies, 1949; Festinger, 1957, with Bem, 1967; Bradley, 1978, with Nisbett & Ross, 1980). The various "motivation versus cognition" debates that subsequently developed continued off and on for years before they were declared not only unwinnable but also counterproductive. An uneasy armistice was declared (Tetlock & Levi, 1982) that effectively quieted the public conflict but did nothing to reconcile the deep conceptual differences that still remained between researchers favoring cognitive or motivational perspectives.

Following this period of conflict, enthusiasm for questions concerning motivational influences on thinking was dampened in the 1970s and early 1980s. Beginning in the late 1980s, however, there was a resurgence of interest in this area (for recent reviews and overviews, see, Dunning, 1999; Gollwitzer & Bargh, 1996; Higgins & Molden, 2003; Kruglanski, 1996; Kunda, 1990; Sorrentino & Higgins, 1986). One reason for this new life is that instead of revisiting debates about the workings of motivational versus cognitive processes, researchers began to examine the important interactions between these two processes. Thus, more recent investigations have focused on the identification of principles that describe the *interface* between motivation and cognition, and the implications of this interface for thinking, reasoning, and judgment (see Kruglanski, 1996; Kunda, 1990; Higgins & Molden, 2003).

This chapter provides an overview of this "second generation" of research on motivated thinking and discusses some of the larger principles that have emerged from the study of the motivation/cognition interface. We consider two general classes of motivational influences; the first involves people's desires for reaching certain types of *outcomes* in their judgments, and the second involves people's desires to use certain types of *strategies* while forming their judgments. In so doing, we adopt a rather broad focus and discuss several different varieties of motivated thinking. Given space constraints, this broad focus necessitates being selective in the phenomena to be described. We have chosen those programs of research that we believe are representative of the larger literature and are especially relevant not only to the study of reasoning but also to other areas in cognitive psychology.[1] After reviewing the separate influences on thinking of outcome- and strategy-based motivations, we conclude by suggesting potential directions for future research, giving special attention to circumstances in which multiple sources of motivation might operate simultaneously.

Outcome-Motivated Thinking

The most prominent approach to motivated reasoning, in both classic and contemporary perspectives, has been to examine the influence on people's thought processes of their needs, preferences, and goals to reach desired outcomes (or avoid undesired outcomes). Although the types of preferred outcomes that have been studied are highly diverse, they can be divided into two general classes: *directional* outcomes and *nondirectional* outcomes (see Kruglanski, 1996; Kunda, 1990). Individuals who are motivated by directional outcomes are interested in reaching specific desired conclusions, such as impressions of themselves as intelligent, caring, and worthy people (e.g., Dunning, 1999; Pyszczynski & Greenberg, 1987), or positive beliefs about others whom they find likeable or to whom they are especially close (e.g., Murray, 1999).

In contrast, individuals who are motivated by nondirectional outcomes have more general concerns, such as reaching the most accurate conclusion possible (e.g., Fiske & Neuberg, 1990) or making a clear and concise decision (e.g., Kruglanski & Webster, 1996), whatever this conclusion or decision may be.

Whether outcome motivation is directional or nondirectional, however, this motivation has been conceptualized as affecting thought and reasoning in the same way: by directing people's cognitive processes (e.g., their recall, information search, or attributions) in ways that help to ensure they reach their desired conclusions. That is, individuals' preferences for certain outcomes are believed to often shape their thinking so as to all but guarantee that they find a way to believe, decide, and justify whatever they like. In this section, we review several programs of research that have more closely examined the specific mechanisms by which this can occur – first in relation to motivations for directional outcomes and then in relation to motivations for nondirectional outcomes. Following this, we discuss several limitations of the effects of outcome motivation on reasoning and identify circumstances in which these motivations are most likely to have an impact.

Influences of Directional Outcome Motivation

Overall, the kinds of phenomena that have been studied most extensively in research on motivated thinking involve directional outcome preferences (i.e., individuals' desires to reach specific conclusions about themselves and others; for reviews, see Dunning, 1999; Kunda, 1990; Murray, 1999; Pyszczynski & Greenberg, 1987). Although a variety of outcomes have been investigated, people's well-documented preference for viewing themselves, and those close to them, in a generally positive manner (see Baumeister, 1998) has, by far, received the most attention. This outcome is the primary focus here.[2] In the next sections, we review several effects of desires for positive self-evaluation involving many different cognitive processes, including attribution, evaluation of evidence, information search, recall and knowledge activation, and the organization of concepts in memory.

EFFECTS ON ATTRIBUTION

Some of the first evidence for the effects on reasoning of motivations for positive self-evaluation grew out of work on attribution (see Kelley, 1973). Early attributional research found that when people were explaining their performance on tasks measuring important abilities they tended to take responsibility for their success (i.e., cite internal and stable causes, such as "I'm good at this task") and to deny responsibility for their failure (i.e., cite external and unstable causes, such as "I was unlucky"). Such findings were typically described as stemming from desires for positive beliefs about the self (for a review, see Bradley, 1978).

The motivational nature of these findings was questioned, however. Several researchers (e.g., Nisbett & Ross, 1980) argued that although one's attributions may sometimes be biased, this does not necessarily imply that motivational forces are at work (e.g., previous expectancies for success could lead people to label an unexpected failure as unusual or unlucky). Yet, subsequent research has found that, although people's expectancies do play a role in these attributional effects, there is substantial evidence that motivation plays an important role as well (see Kunda, 1990; Pyszczynski & Greenberg, 1987).

One type of evidence for the role of motivation in self-serving attributions is that, independent of expectancies from prior success or failure, the more personally important a success is in any given situation, the stronger is the tendency to claim responsibility for this success but to deny responsibility for failure (Miller, 1976). Another type of evidence is that people's attributions become increasingly self-serving when success or failure feedback is experienced as highly arousing. For instance, Gollwitzer, Earle, and Stephan (1982) had participants first complete an intelligence test, then vigorously ride a stationary bicycle while the test was being scored (increasing their arousal), and finally, receive feedback about succeeding or failing on the test. Feedback was given 1 minute, 5 minutes, or 9 minutes after riding the bicycle. Both those receiving feedback after 9 minutes, who were no longer aroused, and those receiving feedback after 1 minute, who were aroused but still associated this arousal with the exercise, showed only small attributional differences following success versus failure feedback. In contrast, those receiving feedback after 5 minutes, who were still aroused but no longer associated this with the exercise, misattributed their arousal to the feedback concerning the test and showed a strong tendency to credit their ability for success and blame bad luck for failure (see also Stephan & Gollwitzer, 1981).

EFFECTS ON EVIDENCE EVALUATION

Similar to these attribution effects, more recent research has found that motivations for positive self-evaluations also influence the way in which people evaluate information that either supports or contradicts these positive self-evaluations. In general, individuals tend to (1) give more credence to, and be more optimistic about, the validity of information that supports or confirms their standing as kind, competent, and healthy people; and (2) be more skeptical and cautious about information that threatens this standing.

An example of the first type of influence can be found in a study by Ditto, Scepansky, Munro, Apanovitch, and Lockhart (1998). Individuals were "tested" for the presence of a fictitious enzyme in the body, TAA, and everyone was told that they had tested positive. Half of the people were informed that this had positive health consequences, and half were informed that this had negative health consequences. Those who believed TAA had negative health consequences were largely dismissive of the test when told it was slightly unreliable (i.e., had a 10% false-positive rate) and judged the result to be only somewhat more valid when told the test was highly reliable (i.e., had a .05% false-positive rate). Those who believed TAA had positive health consequences, however, judged the test to be highly valid regardless of its reliability (see also Doosje, Spears, & Koomen, 1995).

An example of the second type of influence can be found in a study by Kunda (1987). Participants read a scientific article reporting that caffeine consumption was related to serious health problems in women. Afterward, women (but not men) who were heavy caffeine consumers reported that the article was less convincing than women who were light caffeine consumers. In a follow-up study in which people read a similar article that revealed caffeine caused only mild health problems, there was no relation between their evaluation of the article and their caffeine consumption. Because, in both studies, people's reasoning was altered only when there was a significant threat to the self, this demonstrates the motivational nature of these results (see also Beauregard & Dunning, 1998; Ditto et al., 1998).

Similar effects of people's desire to view themselves positively have also been demonstrated in domains that do not directly involve health consequences. For instance, people who encounter scientific research that appears to support their cherished attitudes describe this research as being better conducted, and its conclusions as being more valid, than those who encounter the same research but believe it to be in conflict with their cherished attitudes (e.g., Lord, Ross, & Lepper, 1979). In addition, people have been shown to engage in considerable counterfactual thinking (i.e., mentally undoing the present state of affairs by imagining "if only..."; see Roese, 1997) when evidence supporting predictions from a preferred theory or worldview fails to materialize. Such counterfactual thinking allows them to generate ways in which they were almost correct. However, when evidence is consistent with their theories, these same individuals do not engage in counterfactual thinking, which would force them to generate ways in which they were almost wrong (Tetlock, 1998).

EFFECTS ON INFORMATION SEARCH

The motivational influences discussed thus far center on the *quality* of people's information processing during reasoning (e.g., biased attributions, more or less critical evaluations). However, desires for positive self-evaluations also affect the *quantity* of people's information processing (Kruglanski, 1996). Specifically, such desires motivate decreased processing and quick acceptance of favorable evidence and increased processing and hesitant acceptance of unfavorable evidence. As one example, Ditto and colleagues (Ditto & Lopez, 1992; Ditto et al., 1998) demonstrated that, compared with evaluating favorable evidence, when people evaluate unfavorable evidence they spend a greater amount of time examining this evidence and spontaneously generate more alternate hypotheses about why it might be unreliable (see also Pyszczynski & Greenberg, 1987). Moreover, they have also shown that individuals who are prevented from putting this extra cognitive effort into the examination of unfavorable evidence (e.g., participants who are placed under *cognitive load*) return evaluations that are substantially less critical.

Additional evidence of increased information processing of information that is inconsistent with preferred conclusions comes from Chaiken and colleagues (Giner-Sorolla & Chaiken, 1997; Liberman & Chaiken, 1992). In one experiment, for example, people read scientific reports claiming that there was either a strong link or a weak link between caffeine consumption and significant health risks similar to the Kunda (1987) studies discussed earlier. As before, the group of women who were the most threatened by this information were the least convinced by the reports. In addition, the study found that the most threatened group of participants also expended the most effort to find flaws in the studies described and identified the most weaknesses.

EFFECTS ON RECALL AND KNOWLEDGE ACTIVATION

In addition to affecting the appraisal and encoding of new information, people's desires for positive views of themselves (and certain well-liked others) have also been found to influence their use of stored knowledge in memory such as the selective activation of concepts and recall of events that support these views. These phenomena are exemplified in a series of studies by Santioso, Kunda, and Fong (1990). Participants in these studies read fictitious articles revealing that either introverts or extroverts tend to have more academic and professional success. Following this, individuals who believed that introversion was linked to success were more likely to recall, and were faster to recall, autobiographical instances of introverted behaviors than extroverted behaviors. The opposite pattern of results was found for individuals who believed that extroversion was linked to success.

More recent work has demonstrated that, in addition to creating selective recall, directional outcome motivation can also lead to the *reconstruction* of previous memories. For instance, McDonald and Hirt (1997) showed people a videotape of a fellow college student who was portrayed as either likeable or unlikable. They then provided some additional information about the target, including his midterm scores in several classes. Later, when the target's scores on his final exams were revealed, those who found the target likeable remembered some of the target's midterm scores as lower than they actually were in order to make the final scores more consistent with improvement. In contrast, those who found the target unlikable remembered some of the midterm scores as *higher* than they actually were in order to make the final scores more consistent with decline (see also Conway & Ross, 1984).

Finally, besides influencing explicit recall, motivations to reach specific preferred conclusions also influence more implicit processes, such as knowledge activation and accessibility. In one demonstration of this (Sinclair & Kunda, 1999), individuals either received positive or negative feedback from a person who was a member of multiple social categories. One of these social categories (doctor) was associated with mostly positive stereotypes and another (African

American) was associated with mostly negative stereotypes. Those who had received positive feedback from the other person were faster than baseline to identify doctor-related words and slower than baseline to identify African American–related words on a lexical-decision task. Those who had received negative feedback showed a reverse pattern of activation (see also Spencer, Fein, Wolfe, Hodgson, & Dunn, 1998; for a reversal of these effects when people are motivated by *egalitarian* rather than self-serving outcomes, see Moskowitz, Gollwitzer, Wasel, & Schaal, 1999).

EFFECTS ON ORGANIZATION OF CONCEPTS IN MEMORY

Finally, beyond affecting the activation of knowledge from memory, motivation for directional outcomes can also influence the way in which people come to organize this knowledge. The most widely studied example of this concerns how desires for positive self-evaluation lead people to form stronger associations between their self-concepts and attributes that they feel are praiseworthy or related to success. Three primary strategies by which people accomplish this have been identified: (1) altering one's self-concept to include attributes that are believed to bring about successful outcomes (e.g., Klein & Kunda, 1992; Kunda & Santioso, 1989); (2) coming to view the attributes that one already possesses as essential for successful outcomes (Dunning, Leuenberger, & Sherman, 1995; Dunning, Perie, & Story, 1991; Kunda, 1987); and (3) redefining the criteria that must be met before one can be considered successful or in possession of particular positive and negative qualities (Beauregard & Dunning, 1998; Dunning & Cohen, 1992; see also Alicke, LoSchiavo, Zerbst, & Zhang, 1997).

The second two strategies are of particular relevance to the issue of knowledge organization. Use of the second strategy can clearly be seen in a program of research by Dunning and his colleagues (Dunning et al., 1995; Dunning et al., 1991). In one study, people who considered themselves either more *goal-oriented* or more *people-oriented* rated only those traits that were central to their own orientation (e.g., *determined* in the former case versus *dependable* in the latter) as more prototypical of successful leaders (see also Kunda, 1987). In another study, individuals rated their own characteristics as more prototypical of positive qualities such as intelligence but as less prototypical of negative qualities such as aloofness.

Use of the third strategy can be seen in another series of experiments by Dunning and his colleagues (Beauregard & Dunning, 1998; Dunning & Cohen, 1992; see also Alicke et al., 1997). Participants in these experiments were asked to judge the abilities of others in several domains (e.g., math, athletics). When participants themselves were highly skilled in the domain they were considering or had just experienced a relevant personal success, they set higher performance standards for others. That is, to distinguish their own superiority, they judged others as less successful. However, when participants themselves were not highly skilled in the domain they were considering or had just experienced a relevant personal failure, they set lower performance standards for others. That is, to cast those outperforming them as relatively high achievers, they judged them as more successful.

In sum, motivations for directional outcomes can affect basic cognitive processes and influence thinking in several profound ways. These types of motivations affect not only how people search for, evaluate, and explain information in the world around them but also how they activate, access, and organize their knowledge about themselves and others. The next section reviews research indicating that motivations for nondirectional outcomes can be equally important.

Influences of Nondirectional Outcome Motivation

Although less research exists concerning the cognitive effects of nondirectional outcome motivation, several varieties have been considered in some depth (e.g., Cacioppo, Petty, Feinstein, & Jarvis, 1996; Fiske & Neuberg, 1990; Kruglanski & Webster, 1996; Lerner &

Tetlock, 1999). Among these, the two most prominent are desires for *accuracy* (Fiske & Neuberg, 1990) and desires for clarity and conciseness, or *closure* (Kruglanski & Webster, 1996). Here, we consider the effects of these two motivations (which, as will be discussed, often have opposing effects on information processing) on many of the same cognitive processes examined in the previous section.

Before beginning, however, it should be noted that both accuracy and closure motivation have been operationalized in multiple ways. For example, motivations for accuracy have been studied in terms of wanting to know as much as possible about a person on whom one is going to be dependent (Neuberg & Fiske, 1987), feelings of accountability for one's judgments (e.g., Tetlock, 1983), a "fear of invalidity" (e.g., Kruglanski & Freund, 1983), and simple desires to be as correct as possible (e.g., Neuberg, 1989). Motivations for closure have been examined in terms of feelings of time pressure (Kruglanski & Freund, 1983), a desire to quickly complete judgment tasks that are dull and unattractive (Webster, 1993), and desires to escape noisy environments (Kruglanski, Webster, & Klem, 1993; see Kruglanski & Webster, 1996). In the initial discussion presented, each of these varieties of accuracy or closure motivation are treated as equivalent; some important differences among the effects of these various operationalizations are considered at the end.

EFFECTS ON ATTRIBUTION

In addition to self-serving biases that occur when people explain their own performance, as described previously, research on attribution has also identified more general biases. For example, there is the tendency for people to fixate on one particular cause for some action or event and then fail to adequately consider alternative causes that are also possible (see Gilbert & Malone, 1995; see also Buehner & Cheng, Chap. 7; Kahneman & Frederick, Chap. 12). Although these attributional biases have been largely considered from a purely cognitive standpoint, there is evidence to suggest that they can also be influenced by accuracy and closure motivations.

In one study, Tetlock (1985) had participants read an essay either supporting or opposing affirmative action that had ostensibly been written by someone from a previous experiment. They were then informed that the author of the essay had been assigned to take this position by the experimenter and asked to judge the extent to which the arguments presented in the essay reflected the author's own attitude. People who were not provided with any additional motivations displayed the typical fixation on a single cause. These individuals reported that the position taken in the supportive essay could be explained by the positive attitude of the author toward affirmative action, whereas the position taken in the opposing essay could be explained by the negative attitude of the author toward affirmative action despite knowing that both essays had been largely coerced by the experimenter. However, people who were motivated to make accurate judgments (by informing them that they would later be discussing the reasons for their impressions with the experimenter) did consider the alternative cause represented by the experimenter's coercion. These individuals judged the attitude of the author to be neutral regardless of which essay they read. A study by Webster (1993) using a similar paradigm showed that, in contrast, when participants' motivation for closure was increased, the typical fixation on a single cause became even *more* pronounced. Thus, a need for accuracy and a need for closure appear to have opposite effects on people's considerations of alternate causes during attribution (see Kruglanski & Freund, 1983; Kruglanski & Webster, 1996).

EFFECTS ON EVIDENCE EVALUATION AND INFORMATION SEARCH

As discussed earlier, research on directional outcome motivation has demonstrated that people engage in increased evidence evaluations and prolonged information search when encountering evidence unfavorable to their preferred self-views and reduced evidence evaluation and information search when encountering evidence favorable to their preferred self-views. In contrast, accuracy motivation produces prolonged information search, and closure motivation produces reduced information search, regardless of the circumstances.

This consequence of accuracy motivation is evident in a study by Neuberg (1989), where people were asked to conduct a telephone interview with a peer but were given unfavorable expectations concerning the interviewee. Those participants who were instructed to "form the most accurate impressions possible" of the other person spent more time listening and provided more opportunities for the interviewee to elaborate his or her opinions. This in turn prevented their unfavorable expectations from creating negative final impressions of the interviewee, which is what occurred with those participants who were not given any special instructions for the interview.

Similar consequences of accuracy motivation are also seen in research by Chaiken and colleagues (for reviews, see Chen & Chaiken, 1999; Eagly & Chaiken, 1993). For example, in one study by Maheswaran and Chaiken (1991), participants evaluated a product based on a detailed review that described this product more favorably or less favorably than similar products. Participants who were high in accuracy motivation, because they believed their evaluations would have important consequences generated more thoughts about the strengths and weaknesses of the specific product-quality arguments that were listed in the review than did those who were low in accuracy motivation. This again attenuated any effects of people's prior expectations on their final evaluations.

The consequences of closure motivation on evidence evaluation and information search has been shown in several studies by Kruglanski et al. (1993). People were paired with someone else for a discussion about the verdict of a mock trial. Before the discussion, everyone received a summarized legal analysis of the case which, unbeknownst to the participants in the study, supported a different verdict for each member of the pair. Participants with high (versus low) closure motivation attempted to bring about a quick end to the discussion. Moreover, when asked before the discussion, they expressed a strong preference for a partner who could be easily persuaded to their existing viewpoint, and once the discussion began, they stubbornly attempted to convince their partner to see things their way rather than considering alternative arguments.

EFFECTS ON EVALUATION COMPLEXITY

In addition to affecting the length of people's analysis and evaluation of evidence, nondirectional outcome motivation can also influence the complexity of this analysis. Accuracy-motivated individuals form judgments that show greater consideration of conflicting opinions and evidence, whereas closure-motivated individuals form judgments that show less of this type of consideration. Tetlock and colleagues demonstrated these effects in experiments in which participants were asked to write down their thoughts about topics such as affirmative action, American foreign policy, and the causes of certain historical events (for a review, see Lerner & Tetlock, 1999). Responses were then coded for their *integrative complexity*, which was defined in terms of the degree to which multiple perspectives on an issue were both identified and then integrated into a framework that included complex connections between them. Findings with people who were both novices and experts on the issues they were analyzing (i.e., college students and professional historians, respectively) indicated that those with increased accuracy motivation provided a more integratively complex analysis (e.g., Tetlock, 1983), whereas those with increased closure motivation provided a less integratively complex analysis (Tetlock, 1998).

EFFECTS ON RECALL AND KNOWLEDGE ACTIVATION

Whereas directional outcome motivation was seen earlier to have qualitative effects on recall and knowledge activation, nondirectional outcome motivation has largely quantitative effects. Once again, accuracy motivation and closure motivation have opposite influences.

In an investigation of accuracy motivation on recall during impression formation, Berscheid and colleagues found that when people observed interviews involving individuals with whom they might later be paired, they paid more attention to the interview and remembered more information about the interviewees than when they did not expect any future interactions (Berscheid, Graziano, Monson, & Dermer, 1976; see also Srull, Lichtenstein, & Rothbart, 1985). However, in studies of closure motivation and impression formation, individuals with chronically high (versus low) need for closure spent less time reading different pieces of behavioral information they were given about a target and later recalled fewer of these behaviors (Dijksterhuis, van Knippenberg, Kruglanski, & Schaper, 1996). There is also evidence that people with high (versus low) accuracy motivation activate more pieces of individuating trait and behavioral information when forming impressions of others (Kruglanski & Freund, 1983; Neuberg & Fiske, 1987), whereas people with high (versus low) need for closure display an increased tendency to rely solely on categorical information during impression formation (Dijksterhuis et al., 1996; Kruglanski & Freund, 1983; see also Moskowitz, 1993).

Similar effects are found for the use of highly accessible knowledge structures or attitudes in judgment. In typical circumstances, concepts or attitudes that have been recently or frequently activated will lead people to assimilate their judgments to this highly accessible information without considering any additional information (see Fazio, 1995; Higgins, 1996). Increased accuracy motivation can attenuate assimilation effects by increasing the activation of alternative interpretations, whereas increased closure motivation can exacerbate assimilation effects by decreasing the activation of alternative interpretations. For example, when evaluating the behavior of a target person who was ambiguously adventurous or reckless, participants based their evaluations on whichever one of these concepts was most accessible to a greater extent when their closure motivation was high but to a lesser extent when their accuracy motivation was high (Ford & Kruglanski, 1995; Thompson et al., 1994). These effects have been found both when people are making online judgments (Kruglanski & Freund, 1983; Schuette & Fazio, 1995) and when they are reconsidering previously encountered information (Sanbonmatsu & Fazio, 1990; Thompson et al., 1994).

Overall, then, motivations for nondirectional outcomes can also affect basic cognitive processes and profoundly influence thinking. Whereas motivations for directional outcomes were earlier shown to alter *how* people activate, evaluate, and explain information during reasoning, motivations for nondirectional outcomes (at least in terms of the accuracy and closure motivations reviewed here) instead alter *how much* activation, evaluation, or explanation, in fact, occurs. Furthermore, as the findings presented here illustrate, such quantitative differences in thought can often affect the outcomes of people's judgments and decisions just as much as the qualitative differences described previously.[3]

Limits to Outcome-Motivated Thinking

Although, so far, people have been shown to have an impressive array of cognitive mechanisms at their disposal when attempting to reach desired conclusions, limits do exist concerning when these mechanisms are applied. These limits are first described for directional outcome-motivated thinking and then for nondirectional outcome-motivated thinking.

REALITY CONSTRAINTS ON MOTIVATIONS FOR DIRECTIONAL OUTCOMES

Although there are often specific outcomes, such as positive self-views, that people have some preference for during judgment, most individuals still acknowledge there is some kind of "objective reality" about whatever information they are considering.

That is, motivated thinking related to directional outcomes operates within what Kunda (1990) has called *reality constraints* (see also Pyszczynski & Greenberg, 1987; cf. Kruglanski, 1999). Therefore, although there is a degree to which people adjust their definitions of success, engage in selective recall, or seek to criticize unfavorable evidence, this does not make them entirely unresponsive to world around them, except perhaps in extreme circumstances (see Bachman & Cannon, Chap. 21).

Indeed, evidence for this principle of reality constraints has been repeatedly found in the context of the research previously described. For example, a study using a paradigm discussed earlier, in which participants first learned that introverts or extroverts were generally more successful before rating themselves on these traits, was performed using participants who had been preselected as having high trait levels of either introversion or extroversion (Santioso et al., 1990). Although beliefs that one trait was more beneficial than the other increased everyone's self-ratings concerning that trait, demonstrating motivated reasoning, there was also a large effect of people's chronic dispositions. Introverts' ratings of themselves, were always more introverted than extroverts' ratings of themselves, no matter how beneficial the introverts believed the trait of extroversion to be. That is, regardless of how desirable it would have been, introverts did not suddenly believe themselves to be extroverts and vice versa.

Another example of the influence of reality constraints is that people's thinking is guided by their preferred outcomes to a much greater extent in situations of uncertainty (e.g., Dunning, Meyerowitz, & Holtzberg, 1989; Hsee, 1995). When there is more potential for constructing idiosyncratic criteria for a certain judgment (e.g., judging whether one possess somewhat vague traits such as sensibility or insecurity), then people use this opportunity to select criteria that allow them to reach their desired conclusion. However, when there is less potential for this construction (e.g., judging whether one possesses more precise traits such as punctuality or gullibility), people engage in less motivated reasoning (Dunning et al., 1989). Overall, these results suggest that thinking and reasoning inspired by directional outcomes do not so much lead people to ignore the sometimes disappointing reality they face because it inspires them to exploit the uncertainties that exist in this reality to their favor.

COGNITIVE-RESOURCE CONSTRAINTS ON ACCURACY MOTIVATION

Virtually all the effects of accuracy motivation reviewed here involve increases in the total amount of information processing that people perform during judgment. Therefore, in circumstances in which one's ability to engage in this information processing is constrained, the effects of increased accuracy motivation should be minimal (Fiske & Neuberg, 1990). One demonstration of this was provided by Pendry and Macrae (1994). As described earlier, accuracy-motivated individuals who were forming an impression of a target displayed an increased use of individuating trait and behavioral information when they possessed their full information processing resources (see Neuberg & Fiske, 1987). However, accuracy-motivated individuals whose processing resources were depleted based their impression primarily on categorical information in the same way as those who had little accuracy motivation (see also Kruglanski & Freund, 1983). In addition, Sanbonmatsu and Fazio (1990) showed that the influence of accuracy motivation in reducing people's assimilation of their judgments to highly accessible attitudes disappears when people are placed under time pressure, which prevents extended information processing.

DOES MOTIVATION FOR ACCURACY RESULT IN ACCURATE REASONING?

Another important consideration of the effects of accuracy motivation on thinking and reasoning is that even when people high in accuracy motivation are free to engage in extended information processing this does not guarantee that they will arrive at more accurate judgments. One obvious example of this situation is finding that evidence beyond what is immediately and effortlessly available does not exist or has faded from memory (see, e.g., Thompson et al., 1994). In an another manifestation, people are affected by certain biases outside their awareness or are aware of such biases but unaware of what the proper strategy is to correct them. In all these circumstances, although accuracy motivation might increase information search, recall, and consideration of multiple interpretations, it would not be expected to eliminate judgment errors (Fischhoff, 1982), and might even increase them (Pelham & Neter, 1995; Tetlock & Boettger, 1989).

DISTINCTIONS AMONG CIRCUMSTANCES THAT LEAD TO ACCURACY MOTIVATION

As alluded to earlier, the different types of accuracy motivation inductions reviewed here are not always equivalent and can have markedly different effects. For example, although having one's outcomes dependent on another person can increase desires for accuracy in diagnosing that person's true character (e.g., Neuberg & Fiske, 1987), in other cases such circumstances can produce a desire to see a person that one is going to be depending on in the best possible light (e.g., Berscheid et al., 1976; Klein & Kunda, 1992; see Kruglanski, 1996). As another example, although believing that one's judgment has important consequences may motivate an accurate consideration of all the relevant evidence, it could also motivate a more general need to increase elaborative thinking that is not necessarily focused on accuracy (see Footnote 3; Petty & Wegener, 1999). Finally, although justifying one's judgments to an audience can motivate accuracy when the opinion of the audience is unknown, it can also lead to more directional outcome motivation, such as ingratiation toward this audience, when the opinion of the audience is known (Tetlock, 1983; see Lerner & Tetlock, 1999). Therefore, when attempting to anticipate the effects of accuracy motivation on reasoning in a particular situation, it is important to consider both the current source of this motivation and the larger context in which it exists.

THE INFLUENCE OF INFORMATION AVAILABILITY ON CLOSURE MOTIVATION

Certain qualifications must also be noted in the effects of closure motivation. All the findings discussed so far have involved the tendency for people with increased closure motivation to quickly assimilate their judgments to readily available or highly accessible information, leading to an early "freezing" of their information search. However, in situations in which little information is available, high closure motivation may inspire efforts to find something clear and concise to "seize" upon and *increase* information search (see Kruglanski & Webster, 1996). For example, in the Kruglanski et al. (1993) studies described previously that involved partners discussing the verdict of a mock trial, people with high closure motivation preferred easily persuadable partners and were unwilling to consider alternative arguments only when they had enough information at their disposal (i.e., a summarized legal analysis) to form a clear initial impression. When these same individuals were not provided with the legal analysis and did not begin the discussion with a clear opinion, they expressed a desire to be paired with someone who was highly *persuasive* and shifted toward their partner's point of view.

Conclusions on Outcome-Motivated Thinking

Recent research has uncovered many potential routes by which people's desires for particular judgment outcomes can affect their thinking and reasoning. To summarize, both directional outcome motivations, where people have a specific preferred conclusion they are trying to reach, and nondirectional outcome motivations, where people's preferred conclusions are more general, alter many basic cognitive processes during reasoning. These include (1) the explanation of events and behaviors; (2) the organization, recall, and activation of knowledge in memory; and (3) the pursuit and evaluation of evidence relevant to decision making. Outcome motivation effects involve both how such cognitive processes are initiated and directed as well as how thoroughly these processes are implemented. Moreover, in any given situation the specific cognitive processes influenced by outcome motivation are typically those that aid the gathering and interpretation of information supporting the favored outcome. In this self-fulfilling way, then, people's outcome-motivated reasoning often successfully brings about their desired conclusions.

Strategy-Motivated Thinking

Although outcome-motivated thinking has been the most widely studied form of motivated reasoning, other varieties of motivational influences on cognition are also possible. One alternate perspective that has more recently emerged and complements an outcome-based view proposes that people are motivated not only with respect to the outcomes of their judgments but also with respect to the manner in which they go about making these judgments. That is, not only do people have preferred conclusions, but they also have *preferred strategies* for reaching their conclusions (Higgins & Molden, 2003; cf. Tyler & Blader, 2000). Therefore, independent of whatever outcome holds the most interest for them, people may be motivated to reach these outcomes using strategies that "feel right" in terms of, and allow them to sustain, their current motivational orientation (e.g., eagerly gathering evidence that might support a positive self-view or facilitate cognitive closure versus vigilantly suppressing evidence that could undermine a positive self-view or threaten cognitive closure).

Several lines of research have examined how motivations for particular judgment strategies can also influence people's basic cognitive processes. In the vast majority of these studies, strategic motivations were measured and manipulated in terms of people's *regulatory focus* (see Higgins, 1997). Regulatory focus theory distinguishes between two basic motivational orientations: a *promotion focus* involving concerns with advancement and approaching gains versus avoiding nongains, and a *prevention focus* involving concerns with security and approaching nonlosses versus avoiding losses. Because it centers on the presence and absence of positive outcomes, a promotion focus has been found to create preferences for *eager* judgment strategies that emphasize advancement (or, to use signal detection terminology, finding *hits*) and ensure against overlooking something that might be important (or, to again use signal detection terminology, avoiding *errors of omission*). In contrast, because it centers on the presence and absence of negative outcomes, a prevention focus has been found to engender preferences for *vigilant* judgment strategies that emphasize protection (or making *correct rejections*) and ensure against committing to something that might be a mistake (or avoiding *errors of commission*; see Higgins & Molden, 2003). Therefore, even in circumstances in which individuals are pursuing the same outcome, they may show marked differences in their pursuit of this outcome depending upon whether they are currently promotion focused or prevention focused. The studies reviewed here are intended to illustrate the effects of eager or vigilant strategic motivation on several types of thought processes similar to those found to be influenced by outcome motivation (for a larger overview, see Higgins & Molden, 2003).

EFFECTS ON THE CONSIDERATION OF ALTERNATIVE HYPOTHESES

Considering alternative hypotheses is a fundamental component of many varieties of thinking (see Sloman & Lagnado, Chap. 5). How might eager versus vigilant strategic preferences influence this process? In general, an eager strategy of considering alternatives would involve attempting to attain hits and to ensure against errors of omission by generating and selecting any plausible hypotheses that could *remotely* be correct. However, a vigilant strategy of considering alternatives would involve attempting to make correct rejections and to ensure against errors of commission by generating and selecting only the most probable hypotheses that seem *likely* to be correct. Therefore people in a promotion focus would be expected to consider a greater number of alternatives during thinking and reasoning than people in a prevention focus.

This question was addressed in several studies by Liberman, Molden, Idson, and Higgins (2001). One important instance of considering alternatives occurs when people form hypotheses about what they are perceiving (see Tversky, Chap. 10). Therefore, Liberman et al. (2001) examined the effects of people's strategic preferences on a task where people identified vague and distorted objects in a series of photographs. Across several studies in which a promotion or prevention focus was both measured as an individual differences variable and induced experimentally, results indicated that those in a promotion focus generated a greater number of alternatives for the identity of the objects than those in a prevention focus (see also Crowe & Higgins, 1997).

In addition to examining the effects of strategic preferences on generating alternative hypotheses for object perception, Liberman et al. (2001) also investigated whether similar effects occurred for social perception. Participants read a scenario describing the helpful behavior of a target person and were asked to evaluate several equally plausible alternative explanations for this behavior. Consistent with the results described previously, participants in a promotion focus again selected a greater number of alternative explanations than participants in a prevention focus. Moreover, these effects were also found to influence the general impressions people formed of the target. After selecting their reasons for the target's helpful behavior, participants predicted how helpfully he or she would behave in the future. Those in a promotion focus, because they were considering more interpretations of a target's behavior, formed more equivocal impressions and showed relatively little generalization about the target's behavior as compared with those in a prevention focus (see Kelley, 1973).

Finally, additional research by Molden and Higgins (2004) has more recently demonstrated similar effects for eager versus vigilant strategic preferences on the generation and selection of alternatives during basic categorization processes. People were given vague descriptions of a target person from which it was not clear how to categorize him or her correctly, and a number of alternatives could all have been possible. As before, participants with either a chronic or experimentally induced promotion focus generated more possible categories for the target than those with either a chronic or experimentally induced prevention focus.

Overall, then, people's eager versus vigilant strategic preferences play a significant role in their generation of alternatives during a number of important thought processes. Moreover, it is important to note that in all the studies described in this section, everyone was pursuing the exact same outcome (identifying an object, explaining behaviors) and did not have motivations for any specific conclusion or end-state. Furthermore, measures of people's motivations for more general outcomes such as accuracy and closure were also taken, and these factors were statistically removed from all analyses. Therefore, the observed effects of promotion or prevention motivational orientations are distinct from the outcome motivation effects reviewed earlier and can be attributed to the influences of these orientations on people's strategic preferences.

EFFECTS ON COUNTERFACTUAL THINKING

Besides generating and evaluating hypotheses, another way in which people consider alternatives during reasoning is in their use of counterfactuals. As briefly mentioned, earlier counterfactual thinking involves mentally undoing the present state of affairs and imagining alternative realities "if only" different decisions had been made or actions been taken (Roese, 1997). Several different varieties of counterfactual thinking have been identified. One broad distinction that has been made is between thoughts that concern the reversal of a previous inaction (e.g., if only I had acted, things might have gone better), or *additive* counterfactuals, and thoughts that concern the reversal of a previous action (e.g., if only I hadn't acted, things wouldn't be so bad), or *subtractive* counterfactuals.

Because additive counterfactuals simulate the correction of a past error of omission, this type of thinking represents a more eager strategy of considering alternative realities. In contrast, because subtractive counterfactuals simulate the correction of a past error of commission, this type of thinking represents a more vigilant strategy of considering alternate realities. Therefore, a promotion focus should increase the generation of additive counterfactuals, and a prevention focus should increase the generation of subtractive counterfactuals. In line with this, Roese, Hur, and Pennington (1999) found that, both when analyzing hypothetical examples and when describing particular instances of their own behavior, participants who considered promotion-related setbacks (i.e., nongains and missed opportunities for advancement) offered a greater number of additive counterfactuals, whereas participants who considered prevention-related setbacks (i.e., losses and missed opportunities to prevent mistakes) offered a greater number of subtractive counterfactuals. In the literature that exists on counterfactual thinking, it has been traditionally assumed that subtractive counterfactuals are more common than additive counterfactuals and that failures associated with action inspire more regret than failures associated with inaction (Roese, 1997). However, the results of these studies demonstrate that, in some cases, people's strategic preferences can result in additive counterfactuals being more common and perhaps being associated with greater regret (see also Camacho, Higgins, & Lugar, 2003).

It is important to note that care was taken to make sure the outcomes that participants were considering in these studies did not differ across any important dimensions such as how painful they were imagined to be or how much regret they inspired (see Roese et al., 1999). Therefore, the results can again only be explained in terms of differences in strategic motivation.

EFFECTS ON FAST VERSUS ACCURATE INFORMATION PROCESSING

A major focus across many areas of psychology has been when and why people choose to emphasize either speed or accuracy in their thinking and decision making (e.g., Josephs & Hahn, 1995; Zelaznik, Mone, McCabe, & Thaman, 1988). Förster, Higgins, and Bianco (2003) more recently investigated whether promotion preferences for strategic eagerness would result in faster information processing and a higher *quantity* of output in a search for possible hits, whereas prevention preferences for strategic vigilance would result in more accurate information processing and a higher *quality* of output in an effort to avoid mistakes.

Participants were given a task involving four pictures taken from a children's "connect the dots" drawing book. For each picture, the objective was to connect sequentially numbered dots within a given time period in order to complete the outline of an image. Participants' speed on each picture was assessed by the highest number dot they reached by the end of the time period for that picture, and their accuracy on each picture was assessed by the number of dots they skipped (i.e., that were not connected). Across two studies where participants' promotion or prevention focus was both measured and experimentally induced, promotion-focused individuals were faster and produced a higher quantity of responses, whereas prevention-focused individuals were more accurate and produced a higher quality of responses over the entire task. Moreover, both of these tendencies increased in intensity as people moved closer to goal completion, resulting in stronger effects of strategic preferences toward the end of a task than toward the beginning of a task (i.e., the "goal looms larger" effect in which motivation increases as one's distance to the completion of a goal decreases; Lewin, 1935). This provides strong support that people's motivations for different judgment strategies can alter their concerns with different aspects of information processing (e.g., speed versus accuracy).

EFFECTS ON KNOWLEDGE ACTIVATION AND RECALL

Analogous to the selective recall and activation of information from memory that occurs in the presence of motivations for directional outcomes, another influence of strategic preferences on thinking is to increase sensitivities to, and recall of, information that that is particularly relevant to these preferences. A study by Higgins, Roney, Crowe, and Hymes (1994) demonstrated this by having participants read an essay about the life of a hypothetical target person in which two different types of situations were encountered. In one type of situation, the target used eager strategies that were advancement oriented (e.g., waking up early in order to be on time for a favorite class), whereas in the other type of situation, the target used vigilant strategies that were more protection oriented (e.g., being careful not to sign up for a class whose schedule conflicted with a desired activity). Individuals who had chronic promotion orientations showed a stronger sensitivity for information related to advancement versus protection strategies and later showed greater recall for these episodes, whereas individuals who had chronic prevention orientations showed the reverse effect.

Another study by Higgins and Tykocinski (1992), which again had people read an essay about the life of a hypothetical target person, extends these findings. In this study, the target person experienced situations that either involved the presence or absence of gains (finding $20 on the street or missing a movie that he or she wanted to see, respectively) or the presence or absence of losses (being stuck in a crowded subway for an extended period of time or getting a day off from a particularly arduous class schedule, respectively). Similar to the previous study, individuals who were chronically promotion focused showed a stronger sensitivity and recall for gain-related information that is more meaningful in the context of eager strategic preferences, whereas individuals who were chronically prevention-focused showed a stronger sensitivity and recall for loss-related information that is more meaningful in the context of vigilant strategic preferences.

Strategic Preferences and Regulatory Fit

Although the studies presented thus far have demonstrated how people's motivational orientations can lead them to prefer and choose certain judgment strategies, situations may exist in which they may be more or less able to follow these preferences. For example, some situations may generally require greater use of eager strategies of pursuing gains or vigilant strategies of preventing mistakes such as when supervisors demand either innovative and creative practices of all their employees in search of advancement or cautious and responsible practices in hope of preventing losses. What might be the consequences of making judgments and decisions in a way that either suits one's current strategic preferences (i.e., promotion-focused individuals using eager strategies and prevention-focused individuals using vigilant strategies) or does not suit one's preferences (i.e., promotion-focused individuals using vigilant strategies and prevention-focused individuals using eager strategies)?

Higgins and colleagues have examined this question and investigated how the *regulatory fit* between one's motivational orientation and the means one uses during goal pursuit affects thinking and reasoning (e.g., Camacho et al., 2003; Freitas & Higgins 2002; Higgins, Idson, Freitas, Spiegel, & Molden, 2003). Although space limitations prohibit a more thorough review of this work here (see Higgins, 2000a; Higgins & Molden, 2003), the general findings have been that that the primary consequence of regulatory fit is to increase the perceived value of the goal one is pursuing. That is, regulatory fit (as compared with nonfit) leads people to "feel right" about their goal pursuit, which then leads them to (1) feel good while pursuing these goals (i.e., what *feels* right *feels* good; see Freitas & Higgins, 2002); (2) experience the outcomes they are striving for as having more value or worth (i.e., what *feels* right *is* good; see Higgins et al., 2003); and (3) believe the strategies they are using are inherently right (i.e., what *feels* right *is* right; see Camacho et al., 2003). Therefore, another avenue for future research on how people's motivations to use certain judgment strategies can affect their thought processes is the further refinement and elaboration of the process of regulatory fit.

Conclusions on Strategy-Motivated Thinking

In sum, several emerging programs of research are beginning to demonstrate that, beyond the effects on reasoning of people's desires for particular judgment outcomes, there are additional effects on reasoning of people's desires to use particular judgment strategies. For example, preferences for eager judgment strategies, shown by those with promotion concerns, versus preferences for vigilant judgment strategies, shown by those with prevention concerns, alter many basic cognitive processes during reasoning. These include (1) the generation and testing of hypotheses, (2) the use of counterfactual thinking, (3) an emphasis on fast versus accurate processing of information, and (4) knowledge activation and recall. Strategy motivation effects include whether cognitive processes are implemented in order to advance the right decision and avoid errors of omission in judgment or to protect against the wrong decision and avoid errors of commission in judgment. They also include whether such implementation fits or does not fit one's current motivational orientation. The implementation of cognitive processes for either of these strategic reasons or for regulatory fit influences what pieces of information are considered during judgment and how much this information is valued in a final decision. In this way, then, people's strategic motivations have important effects on their thinking and reasoning above and beyond their outcome motivations.

General Conclusions and Future Directions

The sheer number and diversity of the studies reviewed here is a testament to the return of motivational perspectives on cognition to the vanguard of psychology. The richness and consistency of the findings emerging from these studies is also a testament to the utility of this perspective in the study of thinking and reasoning. We optimistically forecast a further expansion of research informed by motivational perspectives and, in conclusion, briefly outline two general directions we believe should be priorities for the future.

The first direction involves expanding current conceptualizations of the ways in which motivational and cognitive processes interact during judgment. Although there is still much to be learned from examining the effects on thinking of people's motivations for certain outcomes (either directional or nondirectional), there may potentially be other important sources of motivated thought as well. In this chapter, we reviewed our own initial research on one of these possible sources – people's motivations for employing preferred strategies during judgment. We expect that further study will lead to the development of additional perspectives on the interface of motivation and cognition that go beyond both motivated outcomes and motivated strategies.

The second direction involves moving past research that examines different varieties of motivated thinking in isolation from one another (i.e., studying situations in which people are only motivated to achieve positive self-views or only motivated to be accurate). There is a need to consider how multiple goals, desires, and motives interact to influence the thought process – that is, the effects of patterns of motivational forces. For instance, it has been noted for some time now that people possess many potential objectives when processing information (e.g., Chen & Chaiken, 1999). Although it is certainly the case that, at times, objectives such as accuracy, ingratiation, or self-enhancement may be predominant (Kruglanski, 1999), it is also true that there are many instances in which several of these objectives are pursued simultaneously. What happens when people not only want to be accurate but also want to please others or boost their own self-esteem? Studies addressing these questions are just beginning to appear, and early findings are indicating that important interactions can occur (Lundgren & Prislin, 1998; Nienhuis, Manstead, & Spears, 2001; Ruscher, Fiske, & Schnake, 2000).

Similarly, although we have made a distinction between outcome- and strategy-motivated thinking and discussed their effects independently, there are situations in which these two sources of motivation operate in concert. One of these situations has been the focus of recent studies by Molden and Higgins (2004). These studies examined how preferences for eager versus vigilant decision strategies influence people's generation of alternative explanations for their own success and failure. In addition to replicating both the previously discussed self-serving pattern of attributions for performance (an outcome-motivated effect) and the selection of a greater number of alternative attributions by those preferring eager strategies over vigilant strategies (a strategy-motivated effect), these studies showed that self-serving and strategic motivations interacted to determine the extent to which people generalized their current experiences to their future performance. Individuals using eager strategies, because they tended to consider multiple attributions, including both internal and external causes, showed only moderate generalization after both success and failure. In contrast, individuals using vigilant strategies, because they tended to consider only a few attributions, including primarily internal causes following success but external causes following failure, showed strong generalizations following success and almost no generalization after failure. These results demonstrate the importance of considering the effects of multiple sources of motivated reasoning simultaneously (see also Förster, Higgins, & Strack, 2000).

One final way in which investigating the cognitive effects of interacting motivational forces could be fruitfully expanded is by synthesizing work on how motivation influences reasoning with work on how affect influences reasoning (see Forgas, 2000; Martin & Clore, 2001). Great strides have been made in determining the mechanisms by which affective and emotional states can alter people's judgments. Many of the changes in the quality and quantity of information processing found in this research bear a striking resemblance to the motivational effects reviewed here. For example, positive moods have generally been found to support less thorough and complex information processing, similar to closure motivation, whereas negative moods have generally been found to support more thorough and complex information processing, similar to accuracy motivation (for a review, see Schwarz & Clore, 1996). This is not to say, however, that the effects reviewed here are actually just due to changes in emotion, because many of the studies discussed carefully controlled for affective influences and continued to find independent effects. Therefore, it would be fruitful to investigate how affective thinking may give rise to motivational thinking (e.g., Erber & Erber, 2000), and how motivational thinking may give rise to affective thinking (e.g., Higgins, 2000b), in order to develop a better understanding of how these two factors are related and what their combined and separate consequences might be.

In conclusion, this chapter reviewed research that displays the broad applicability of emerging motivational perspectives to the study of thinking and reasoning. Through this review, we attempted to convey the potential utility of these perspectives and to advocate a greater incorporation of principles of outcome- and strategy-based motivation in future research. The further refinement and elaboration of these principles, we believe, will benefit not only the study of thinking but also cognitive science in general.

Acknowledgments

Preparation of this chapter was supported by NIMH grants F31 MH-65772-01 and MH39429. The authors want to thank Phoebe Ellsworth for her helpful comments on an earlier draft.

Notes

1. One area of study that is notably absent in this review concerns affective and emotional influences on reasoning. This important and extensive literature certainly enjoys a central place in the study of motivated thinking. However, the topic of affect and cognition has recently been the subject of several entire handbooks on its own (see Forgas, 2000; Martin & Clore, 2001). Therefore, rather than attempt an extremely limited overview of this major topic alongside the other topics mentioned previously, we instead refer the interested reader to these other sources. The larger relation between research on emotional thinking and the research described here is discussed briefly below.
2. It is important to note that, although a wealth of studies have demonstrated people's broad and robust desires for positive self-evaluation, these studies have almost exclusively been performed on members of Western, and generally more *individualistic* cultures (Baumeister, 1998). In contrast, recent evidence collected from Eastern, and generally more *collectivist* cultures, has demonstrated that, in these populations, such desires for self-evaluation are often considerably less and that some of the effects described here are thereby weaker (see Greenfield, Chap. 27). Yet, this should *not* be taken to mean that the general effects of outcome-motivated thinking are necessarily culture specific or only apply to Western cultures. Instead, this indicates that, if general principles of this type of motivated thinking are to be revealed, future investigations of outcome-motivated thinking in different cultures should take care to identify *which specific outcomes* are culturally desirable in those contexts (e.g., proper fulfillment of one's social duties to others, high social status relative to others; see, e.g., Endo, Heine, & Lehman, 2000).
3. Another type of nondirectional outcome motivation that has been the focus of considerable study is the *need for cognition*, or a general desire for elaborative thinking and increased cognitive activity (Cacioppo et al., 1996). At times, the need for cognition has been considered equivalent to accuracy motivation (Chen & Chaiken, 1999). Consistent with this, research has shown that an increased need for cognition can affect thinking in the same way as heightened accuracy motivation, reducing biases during attribution (D'agostino & Fincher-Kiefer, 1992), increasing recall (Srull et al., 1985), lessening assimilation to highly accessible attitudes (Florack, Scarabis, & Bless, 2001), and increasing information search (Verplanken, 1993; see Cacioppo et al., 1996). However, at times the effects of the need for cognition differ from those of accuracy motivation. Accuracy motivation, because it inspires a thorough consideration of *all* available evidence, weakens the tendency to base judgments on early superficial impressions (i.e., primacy effects; Kruglanski & Freund, 1983). In contrast, the need for cognition, because it simply inspires cognitive elaboration even if this involves only part of the available evidence, can lead to increased rumination on one's early superficial impressions and *strengthen* primacy effects (see Petty & Wegener, 1999). Given these conceptual and empirical distinctions, we have not included research on need for cognition in our larger review of the effects of accuracy motivation and consider it a separate form of nondirectional outcome motivation (for a review of need for cognition effects, see Cacioppo et al., 1996).

References

Alicke, M. D., LoSchiavo, F. M., Zerbst, J. I., & Zhang, S. (1997). The person who outperforms me is a genius: Maintaining perceived competence in upward social comparison. *Journal of Personality and Social Psychology*, 73, 781–789.

Allport, F. H. (1920). The influence of the group upon association and thought. *Journal of Experimental Psychology*, 3, 159–182.

Baumeister, R. F. (1998). The self. In D. Gilbert, S. Fiske, & G. Lindzey (Eds.), *The handbook of social psychology* (4th ed., Vol. 1, pp. 680–740). New York: McGraw-Hill.

Beauregard, K. S., & Dunning, D. (1998). Turning up the contrast: Self-enhancement motives prompt egocentric contrast effects in social judgment. *Journal of Personality and Social Psychology*, 74, 606–621.

Bem, D. J. (1967). Self-perception: An alternative interpretation of cognitive dissonance phenomena. *Psychological Review*, 74, 183–200.

Berscheid, E., Graziano, W., Monson, T., & Dermer, M. (1976). Outcome dependency: Attention, attribution, and attraction. *Journal of Personality and Social Psychology*, 34, 978–989.

Bradley, G. W. (1978). Self-serving biases in the attribution process: A reexamination of the fact or fiction question. *Journal of Personality and Social Psychology*, 18, 68–88.

Bruner, J. S. (1957). On perceptual readiness. *Psychological Review*, 64, 123–152.

Cacioppo, J. T., Petty, R. E., Feinstein, J. A., & Jarvis, W. B. G. (1996). Dispositional differences in cognitive motivation: The life and times of individuals varying in need for cognition. *Psychological Bulletin*, 119, 197–253.

Camacho, C. J., Higgins, E. T., & Lugar, L. (2003). Moral value transfer from regulatory fit: What feels right *is* right and what feels wrong *is* wrong. *Journal of Personality and Social Psychology*, 84, 498–510.

Chen S., & Chaiken, S. (1999). The heuristic-systematic model in its broader context. In S. Chaiken & Y. Trope (Eds.), *Dual-process theories in social psychology* (pp. 73–96). New York: Guilford.

Conway, M., & Ross, M. (1984). Getting what you want by revising what you had. *Journal of Personality and Social Psychology*, 47, 738–748.

Crowe, E., & Higgins, E. T. (1997). Regulatory focus and strategic inclinations: Promotion and prevention in decision-making. *Organizational Behavior and Human Decision Processes*, 69, 117–132.

D'agostino, P. R., & Fincher-Kiefer, R. (1992). Need for cognition and the correspondence bias. *Social Cognition*, 10, 151–163.

Dijksterhuis, A., van Knippenberg, A., Kruglanski, A. W., & Schaper, C. (1996). Motivated social cognition: Need for closure effects on memory and judgment. *Journal of Experimental Social Psychology*, 32, 254–270.

Ditto, P. H., & Lopez, D. F. (1992). Motivated skepticism: Use of differential decision criteria for preferred and non-preferred conclusions. *Journal of Personality and Social Psychology*, 63, 569–584.

Ditto, P. H., Scepansky, J. A., Munro, G. D., Apanovitch, A. M., & Lockhart, L. K. (1998). Motivated sensitivity to preference-inconsistent information. *Journal of Personality and Social Psychology*, 75, 53–69.

Doosje, B., Spears, R., & Koomen, W. (1995). When bad isn't all bad: Strategic use of sample information in generalization and stereotyping. *Journal of Personality and Social Psychology*, 69, 642–655.

Dunning, D. (1999). A newer look: Motivated social cognition and the schematic representation of social concepts. *Psychological Inquiry*, 10, 1–11.

Dunning, D., & Cohen, G. L. (1992). Egocentric definitions of traits and abilities in social judgment. *Journal of Personality and Social Psychology*, 63, 341–355.

Dunning, D., Leuenberger, A., & Sherman, D. A. (1995). A new look at motivated inference: Are self serving theories of success a product of motivational forces? *Journal of Personality and Social Psychology*, 69, 58–68.

Dunning, D., Meyerowitz, J. A., & Holtzberg, A. D. (1989). Ambiguity and self-evaluation: The role of idiosyncratic trait definitions in self-serving assessments of ability. *Journal of Personality and Social Psychology*, 57, 1082–1090.

Dunning, D. A., Perie, M., & Story, A. L. (1991). Self-serving prototypes of social categories. *Journal of Personality and Social Psychology*, 61, 957–968.

Eagly, A. H., & Chaiken, S. (1993). *The psychology of attitudes*. New York: Harcourt Brace College.

Endo, Y., Heine, S. J., & Lehman, D. R. (2000). Culture and positive illusions in close relationships: How my relationships are better than yours. *Personality and Social Psychology Bulletin*, 26, 1571–1586.

Erber, M. W., & Erber, R. (2000). The role of motivated social cognition in the regulation of affective states. In J. P. Forgas (Ed.), *Handbook of affect and social cognition* (pp. 275–292). Mahwah, NJ: Erlbaum.

Fazio, R. H. (1995). Attitudes as object-evaluation associations: Determinants, consequences, and correlates of attitude accessibility. In R. E. Petty & J. A. Krosnick (Eds.), *Attitude strength: Antecedents and consequences* (pp. 247–282). Mahwah, NJ: Erlbaum.

Festinger, L. (1957). *A theory of cognitive dissonance*. Stanford, CA: Stanford University Press.

Fischhoff, B. (1982). "Debiasing." In D. Kahneman, P. Slovic, & A. Tversky (Eds.), *Judgment under uncertainty* (pp. 237–262). Cambridge, MA: Cambridge University Press.

Fiske, S. T., & Neuberg, S. L. (1990). A continuum of impression formation, from category-based to individuating processes: Influences of information and motivation on attention and interpretation. In M. P. Zanna (Ed.), *Advances in experimental social psychology* (Vol. 23, pp. 1–74). New York: Academic Press.

Florack, A., Scarabis, M., & Bless, H. (2001). When do associations matter? The use of automatic associations toward ethnic groups in person judgments. *Journal of Experimental Social Psychology, 37*, 518–524.

Ford, T. E., & Kruglanski, A. W. (1995). Effects of epistemic motivations on the use of accessible constructs in social judgment. *Personality and Social Psychology Bulletin, 21*, 950–962.

Forgas, J. P. (Ed.). (2000). *Handbook of affect and social cognition*. Mahwah, NJ: Erlbaum.

Förster, J., Higgins, E. T., & Bianco, A. T. (2003). Speed/accuracy decisions in task performance: Built in trade-off of separate strategic concerns. *Organization Behavior and Human Decision Processes, 90*, 148–164.

Förster, J., Higgins, E. T., & Strack, F. (2000). When stereotype disconfirmation is a personal threat: How prejudice and prevention focus moderate incongruency effects. *Social Cognition, 18*, 178–197.

Freitas, A. L., & Higgins, E. T. (2002). Enjoying goal-directed action: The role of regulatory fit. *Psychological Science, 13*, 1–6.

Freud, S. (1905). Fragments of an analysis of a case of hysteria. In J. Strachey (Ed.), "The Standard Edition of the Complete Psychological Works of Sigmund Freud." *Standard edition, vol. 7*. Macmillan: Hogarth, 1964.

Gilbert, D. T., & Malone, P. S. (1995). The correspondence bias. *Psychological Bulletin, 117*, 21–38.

Giner-Sorolla, R., & Chaiken, S. (1997). Selective use of heuristic and systematic processing under defense motivation. *Personality and Social Psychology Bulletin, 23*, 84–97.

Gollwitzer, P. M., & Bargh, J. A. (Eds.). (1996). *The psychology of action: Linking cognition and motivation to behavior*. New York: Guilford Press.

Gollwitzer, P. M., Earle, W. B., & Stephan, W. G. (1982). Affect as a determinant of egotism: Residual excitation and performance attributions. *Journal of Personality and Social Psychology, 43*, 702–709.

Higgins, E. T. (1996). Knowledge activation: Accessibility, applicability, and salience. In E. T. Higgins & A. W. Kruglanski (Eds.), *Social psychology: Handbook of basic principles* (pp. 133–168). New York: Guilford Press.

Higgins, E. T. (1997). Beyond pleasure and pain. *American Psychologist, 52*, 1280–1300.

Higgins, E. T. (2000a). Making a good decision: Value from "fit." *American Psychologist, 55*, 1217–1230.

Higgins, E. T. (2000b). Promotion and prevention experiences: Relating emotions to non-emotional motivational states. In J. P. Forgas (Ed.), *Handbook of affect and social cognition* (pp. 186–211). Mahwah, NJ: Erlbaum.

Higgins, E. T., Idson, L. C., Freitas, A. L., Spiegel, S., & Molden, D. C. (2003). Transfer of value from fit. *Journal of Personality and Social Psychology, 84*, 1140–1153.

Higgins, E. T., & Molden, D. C. (2003). How strategies for making judgments and decisions affect cognition: Motivated cognition revisited. In G. V. Bodenhausen & A. J. Lambert (Eds.), *Foundations of social cognition: A festschrift in honor of Robert S Wyer, Jr.* (pp. 211–236). Mahwah, NJ: Erlbaum.

Higgins, E. T., Roney, C., Crowe, E., & Hymes, C. (1994). Ideal versus ought predilections for approach and avoidance: Distinct self-regulatory systems. *Journal of Personality and Social Psychology, 66*, 276–286.

Higgins, E. T., & Tykocinski, O. (1992). Self-discrepancies and biographical memory: Personality and cognition at the level of psychological situations. *Personality and Social Psychology Bulletin, 18*, 527–535.

Hsee, C. K. (1995). Elastic justification: How tempting but task-irrelevant factors influence decisions. *Organizational Behavior and Human Decision Processes, 62*, 330–337.

Josephs, R. A., & Hahn, E. D. (1995). Bias and accuracy in estimates of task duration. *Organizational Behavior and Human Decision Processes, 61*, 202–213.

Kelley, H. H. (1973). The process of causal attribution. *American Psychologist, 28*, 107–128.

Klein, W. M., & Kunda, Z. (1992). Motivated person perception: Constructing justifications for desired beliefs. *Journal of Experimental Social Psychology, 28*, 145–168.

Kruglanski, A. W. (1996). Motivated social cognition: Principles of the interface. In E. T. Higgins & A. W. Kruglanski (Eds.), *Social psychology: Handbook of basic principles* (pp. 493–520). New York: Guilford Press.

Kruglanski, A. W. (1999). Motivation, cognition, and reality: Three memos for the next generation of research. *Psychological Inquiry, 10*, 58.

Kruglanski, A. W., & Freund, T. (1983). The freezing and unfreezing of lay inferences: Effects on impression primacy, ethnic stereotyping and numerical anchoring. *Journal of Experimental Social Psychology, 19*, 448–468.

Kruglanski, A. W., & Webster, D. M. (1996). Motivated closing of the mind: "Seizing" and "freezing." *Psychological Review, 103*, 263–283.

Kruglanski, A. W., Webster, D. M., & Klem, A. (1993). Motivated resistance and openness to persuasion in the presence of absence of prior information. *Journal of Personality and Social Psychology, 65*, 861–876.

Kunda, Z. (1987). Motivated inference: Self-serving generation and evaluation of causal theories. *Journal of Personality and Social Psychology, 53*, 636–647.

Kunda, Z. (1990). The case for motivated reasoning. *Psychological Bulletin, 108*, 480–498.

Kunda, Z., & Santioso, R. (1989). Motivated change in the self-concept. *Journal of Experimental Social Psychology, 25*, 272–285.

Lerner, J. S., & Tetlock, P. E. (1999). Accounting for the effects of accountability. *Psychological Bulletin, 125*, 255–275.

Lewin, K. (1935). *A dynamic theory of personality*. New York: McGraw-Hill.

Liberman, A., & Chaiken, S. (1992). Defensive processing of personally relevant health messages. *Personality and Social Psychology Bulletin, 18*, 669–679.

Liberman, N., Molden, D. C., Idson, L. C., & Higgins, E. T. (2001). Promotion and prevention focus on alternative hypotheses: Implications for attributional functions. *Journal of Personality and Social Psychology, 80*, 5–18.

Lord, C. G., Ross, L., & Lepper, M. R. (1979). Biased assimilation and attitude polarizations: The effects of prior theories on subsequently considered evidence. *Journal of Personality and Social Psychology, 37*, 2098–2109.

Lundgren, S. R., & Prislin, R. (1998). Motivated cognitive processing and attitude change. *Personality and Social Psychology Bulletin, 24*, 715–726.

Maheswaran, D., & Chaiken, S. (1991). Promoting systematic processing in low-motivation settings: Effect of incongruent information on processing and judgment. *Journal of Personality and Social Psychology, 61*, 13–25.

Martin, L., & Clore, G. C. (Eds.). (2001). *Theories of mood and cognition*. Mahwah, NJ: Erlbaum.

McDonald, H. E., & Hirt, E. R. (1997). When expectancy meets desire: Motivational effects in reconstructive memory. *Journal of Personality and Social Psychology, 72*, 5–23.

McGinnies, E. (1949). Emotionality and perceptual defense. *Psychological Review, 56*, 244–251.

Miller, D. T. (1976). Ego involvement and attributions for success and failure. *Journal of Personality and Social Psychology, 34*, 901–906.

Molden, D. C., & Higgins, E. T. (2004). *Preferred strategies for self-attribution: Motivated inference beyond self-serving biases*. Manuscript under review.

Molden, D. C., & Higgins, E. T. (2004). Categorization under uncertainty: Resolving vagueness and ambiguity with eager versus vigilant strategies. *Social Cognition, 22*, 248–277.

Moskowitz, G. B. (1993). Individual differences in social categorization: The influence of personal need for structure on spontaneous trait inferences. *Journal of Personality and Social Psychology, 65*, 132–142.

Moskowitz, G. B., Gollwitzer, P. M., Wasel, W., & Schaal, B. (1999). Preconscious control of stereotype activation through chronic egalitarian goals. *Journal of Personality and Social Psychology, 77*, 167–184.

Murray, H. A. (1938). *Explorations in personality*. New York: Oxford University Press.

Murray, S. L. (1999). The quest for conviction: Motivated cognition in romantic relationships. *Psychological Inquiry, 10*, 23–34.

Neuberg, S. L. (1989). The goal of forming accurate impressions during social interactions: Attenuating the impact of negative expectancies.

Journal of Personality and Social Psychology, 56, 374–386.

Neuberg, S. L., & Fiske, S. T. (1987). Motivational influences on impression formation: Dependency, accuracy-driven attention, and individuating information. *Journal of Personality and Social Psychology, 53*, 431–444.

Nienhuis, A. E., Manstead, A. S. R., & Spears, R. (2001). Multiple motives and persuasive communication: Creative elaboration as a result of impression motivation and accuracy motivation. *Personality and Social Psychology Bulletin, 27*, 118–132.

Nisbett, R. E., & Ross, L. (1980). *Human inference: Strategies and shortcomings of social judgment*. Englewood Cliffs, NJ: Prentice-Hall.

Pelham, B. W., & Neter, E. (1995). The effect of motivation on judgment depends on the difficulty of the judgment. *Journal of Personality and Social Psychology, 68*, 581–594.

Pendry, L. F., & Macrae, C. N. (1994). Stereotypes and mental life: The case of the motivated but thwarted tactician. *Journal of Experimental Social Psychology, 30*, 303–325.

Petty, R. E., & Wegener, D. T. (1999). The elaboration likelihood model: Current status and controversies. In S. Chaiken & Y. Trope (Eds.), *Dual-process theories in social psychology* (pp. 41–72). New York: Guilford Press.

Pyszczynski, T., & Greenberg, J. (1987). Toward an integration of cognitive and motivational perspectives on social inference: A biased hypothesis testing model. In L. Berokowitz (Ed.), *Advances in experimental social psychology* (Vol. 20, pp. 297–340). New York: Academic Press.

Roese, N. J. (1997). Counterfactual thinking. *Psychological Bulletin, 121*, 133–148.

Roese, N. J., Hur, T., & Pennington, G. L. (1999). Counterfactual thinking and regulatory focus: Implications for action versus inaction and sufficiency versus necessity. *Journal of Personality and Social Psychology, 77*, 1109–1120.

Ruscher, J. B., Fiske, S. T., & Schnake, S. B. (2000). The motivated tactician's juggling act: Compatible vs. incompatible impression goals. *British Journal of Social Psychology, 39*, 241–256.

Sanbonmatsu, D. M., & Fazio, R. H. (1990). The role of attitudes in memory-based decision making. *Journal of Personality and Social Psychology, 59*, 614–622.

Santioso, R., Kunda, Z., & Fong, G. T. (1990). Motivated recruitment of autobiographical memories. *Journal of Personality and Social Psychology, 59*, 229–241.

Schuette, R. A., & Fazio, R. H. (1995). Attitude accessibility and motivation as determinants of biased processing: A test of the MODE model. *Personality and Social Psychology Bulletin, 21*, 704–710.

Schwarz, N., & Clore, G. L. (1996). Feelings and phenomenal experiences. In E. T. Higgins & A. W. Kruglanski (Eds.), *Social psychology: Handbook of basic principles* (pp. 433–465). New York: Guilford Press.

Sinclair, L., & Kunda, Z. (1999). Reactions to a black professional: Motivated inhibition and activation and conflicting stereotypes. *Journal of Personality and Social Psychology, 77*, 885–904.

Sorrentino, R. M., & Higgins, E. T. (Eds.). (1986). *Handbook of motivation and cognition, vols. 1–3*. New York: Guilford Press.

Spencer, S. J., Fein, S., Wolfe, C., Hodgson, H. L., & Dunn, M. A. (1998). Stereotype activation under cognitive load: The moderating role of self-image threat. *Personality and Social Psychology Bulletin, 24*, 1139–1152.

Srull, T. K., Lichtenstein, M., & Rothbart, M. (1985). Associative storage and retrieval processes in person memory. *Journal of Experimental Psychology: Learning, Memory, and Cognition, 11*, 316–345.

Stephan, W. F., & Gollwitzer, P. (1981). Affect as a mediator of attributional egotism. *Journal of Experimental Social Psychology, 17*, 443–458.

Tetlock, P. E. (1983). Accountability and complexity of thought. *Journal of Personality and Social Psychology, 45*, 74–83.

Tetlock, P. E. (1985). Accountability: A social check on the fundamental attribution error. *Social Psychology Quarterly, 48*, 227–236.

Tetlock, P. (1998). Close-call counterfactuals and belief-system defense: I was not almost wrong but I was almost right. *Journal of Personality and Social Psychology, 75*, 639–652.

Tetlock, P. E., & Boettger, R. (1989). Accountability: A social magnifier of the dilution effect. *Journal of Personality and Social Psychology, 57*, 388–398.

Tetlock, P. E., & Levi, A. (1982). Attribution bias: On the inconclusiveness of the cognition-motivation debate. *Journal of Experimental Social Psychology, 18*, 68–88.

Thompson, E. P., Roman, R. J., Moskowitz, G. B., Chaiken, S., & Bargh, J. A. (1994). Systematic processing and the debasing of covert primacy effects in impression formation: Unshackling the motivated perceiver from constraints of accessibility. *Journal of Personality and Social Psychology*, 66, 474–489.

Tyler, T. R., & Blader, S. L. (2000). *Cooperation in groups: Procedural justice, social identity, and behavioral engagement*. Philadelphia: Psychology Press.

Webster, D. M. (1993). Motivated augmentation and reduction of the over-attribution bias. *Journal of Personality and Social Psychology*, 65, 261–271.

Verplanken, B. (1993). Need for cognition and external information search: Responses to time pressure during decision-making. *Journal of Research in Personality*, 27, 238–252.

Zelaznik, H. N., Mone, S., McCabe, G. P., & Thaman, C. (1988). Role of temporal and spatial precision in determining the nature of the speed-accuracy trade-off in aimed-hand movement. *Journal of Experimental Psychology: Human Perception and Performance*, 14, 221–230.

Part IV

PROBLEM SOLVING AND COMPLEX LEARNING

CHAPTER 14

Problem Solving

Laura R. Novick
Miriam Bassok

Introduction

People are confronted with problems on a daily basis such as extracting a broken light bulb from a socket, multiplying eight times seven, finding the roots of a quadratic equation, planning a family vacation, and deciding whom to vote for in a presidential election. Although these examples differ in many ways, they share a common core: "A problem arises when a living creature has a goal but does not know how this goal is to be reached. Whenever one cannot go from the given situation to the desired situation simply by action [i.e., by the performance of obvious operations], then there has to be recourse to thinking" (Duncker, 1945, p. 1). Consider the broken light bulb. The obvious operation – holding the glass part of the bulb with one's fingers while unscrewing the base from the socket – is prevented by the fact that the glass is broken. Thus, there must be "recourse to thinking" – for example, one might try mounting half a potato on the broken bulb.

A little thought concerning the light bulb situation, as well as our other examples, reveals that what constitutes a problem for one person may not be a problem for another person, or for that same person at another point in time. For example, the second time one has to remove a broken light bulb from a socket, the solution likely can be retrieved from memory; there is no problem. Similarly, 8×7 would generally be considered a problem for 8-year-olds but not for readers of this chapter. Of course, age here is just a proxy for prior knowledge, for there are 6-year-olds for whom this question does not constitute a problem because they know the standard multiplication table. Given that a problem has been identified, the nature of people's background knowledge pertaining to that problem has important implications for the solution-related thinking they do. To understand this thinking, it is important to distinguish (1) the solver's representation of the problem (i.e., the solver's understanding of the underlying nature of the problem) and (2) the sequence of steps the solver takes to get from the given situation to the goal.

A problem representation is a model of the problem constructed by the solver to summarize his or her understanding of the problem's essential nature. Ideally, this model includes information about the goal, the objects and their interrelations, the operations that can be applied (i.e., the steps that can be taken) to solve the problem, and any constraints on the solution process. Consider, for example, Posner's (1973, pp. 150–151) trains and bird problem:

> *Two train stations are fifty miles apart. At 2 P.M. one Saturday afternoon two trains start toward each other, one from each station. Just as the trains pull out of the stations, a bird springs into the air in front of the first train and flies ahead to the front of the second train. When the bird reaches the second train it turns back and flies toward the first train. The bird continues to do this until the trains meet. If both trains travel at the rate of twenty-five miles per hour and the bird flies at a hundred miles per hour, how many miles will the bird have flown before the trains meet?*

Figure 14.1 shows two different representations of this problem that imply different solution methods. Solver A [Figure 14.1(a)] represents the problem as one concerning the ongoing flight path of the bird, which is the focus of the problem as presented. This perspective yields a problem that would be difficult for most people to solve (e.g., a series of differential equations). In contrast, solver B [Figure 14.1(b)] represents the problem from the perspective of the paths of the trains. This perspective yields a relatively easy distance-rate-time problem. To take another example, the problem 14 × 8 might be represented as 8 *groups of* 14 or as 10 *groups of* 8 *plus* 4 *groups of* 8 (or in a variety of other ways).

For some problems, the primary work of solution is to find the best representation; for other problems, there is little uncertainty about the representation, and the primary work is to discover a solution path (or the best solution path) from the *initial state* of the problem (the situation as initially presented to the solver) to the *goal state*. Consider, for example, the Tower of Hanoi problem: There are three pegs mounted on a base. On the leftmost peg, there are three disks of differing sizes. The disks are arranged in order of size with the largest disk on the bottom and the smallest disk on the top. The disks may be moved one at a time, but only the top disk on a peg may be moved, and at no time may a larger disk be placed on a smaller disk. The goal is to move the three-disk tower from the leftmost peg to the rightmost peg. Figure 14.2 shows all the possible legal arrangements of disks on pegs. The arrows indicate transitions between states that result from moving a single disk. The shortest path that connects the initial state to the goal state (i.e., the optimum solution) is indicated by the thicker grey arrows.

Researchers who study problem solving present people with various types of problems for which those people do not have a prestored solution in memory and attempt

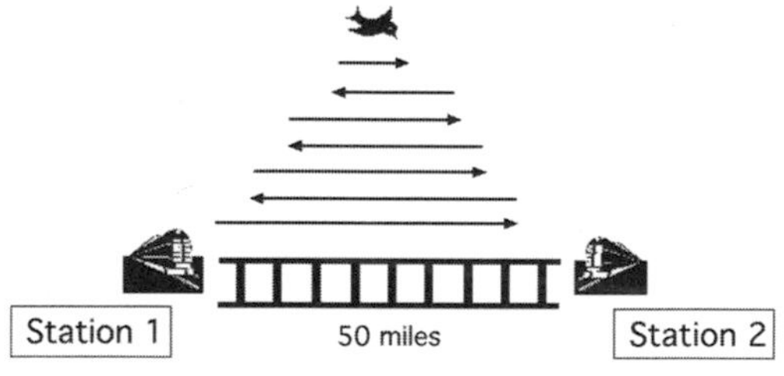

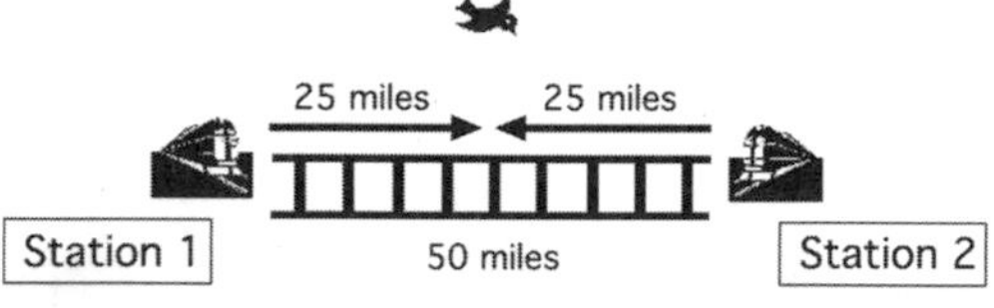

Figure 14.1. Alternative representations of Posner's (1973) trains and bird problem. (From "Transferring symbolic representations across non-isomorphic problems," by L. R. Novick & C. E. Hmelo, 1994, *Journal of Experimental Psychology: Learning, Memory, and Cognition*, 20, p. 1297. Copyright 1994 by the American Psychological Association. Adapted with permission.)

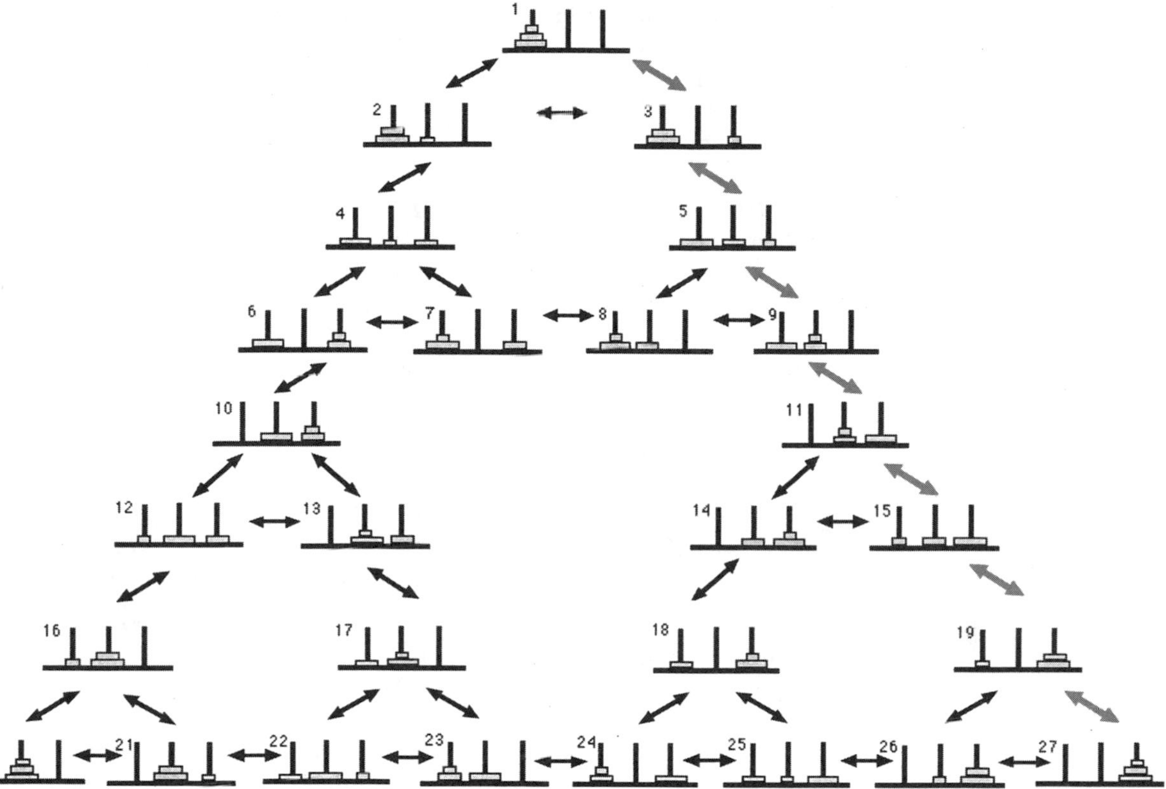

Figure 14.2. All possible problem states for the three-disk Tower of Hanoi problem. The thicker grey arrows show the optimum solution path connecting the initial state (state #1) to the goal state (state #27).

to find regularities in the resulting problem-solving behavior. For example, Greeno (1978) distinguished problems of inducing structure [e.g., proportional analogies such as those found on standardized tests – for example, *bird:fly::snake:??* (solution is *slither*)], transformation (e.g., the Tower of Hanoi), and arrangement [e.g., anagrams – for example, unscramble *dnsuo* to form an English word (solution is *sound*)], and discussed the processes required to solve problems of each type. Regardless of the specific problem type, problem-solving behavior involves an inherent interaction between constructing a representation and generating a solution. However, some researchers are most interested in factors that affect the way solvers represent problems, whereas others look for regularities in the way solvers apply operators to get from the initial state to the goal state. Based on their main focus of interest, researchers devise or select problems that are likely to induce distinct representations (e.g., the trains and bird problem, problems of inducing structure) or to require repeated selection and application of operators within a particular problem representation (e.g., the Tower of Hanoi and other problems of transformation, problems of arrangement). This division of labor, with its distinct historic antecedents and research traditions, has led to many interesting findings. We review the main findings from each tradition and then review results from studies that highlight the interaction between how people understand problems and how they derive problem solutions.

The remainder of this chapter is organized into five sections. First, we provide a brief historic perspective on problem-solving research. Next, we summarize research on the step-by-step process of generating problem solutions. In the third section, we describe a variety of factors that affect problem representation. Fourth, we consider the interplay between constructing a representation and generating a solution. Finally, we draw some conclusions and consider directions for future research. Our review focuses on general findings that pertain to a wide variety of problems. Research on specific types of processes that are involved in problem solving and on problem solving in particular content domains may be found elsewhere in this volume: induction (see Sloman & Lagnado, Chap. 5); analogy (see Holyoak, Chap. 6); causal learning (see Buehner & Cheng, Chap. 7); deductive reasoning (see Evans, Chap. 8); and problem solving in law (see Ellsworth, Chap. 28), science (see Dunbar & Fugelsang, Chap. 29), and medicine (see Patel, Arocha, & Zhang, Chap. 30).

A Brief History

Research on human problem solving has its origins in Gestalt psychology, an influential approach in European psychology during the first half of the twentieth century. (Behaviorism was the dominant perspective in American psychology at this time.) Karl Duncker published a book on the topic in his native German in 1935, which was subsequently translated into English and published 10 years later as the monograph "On problem-solving" (Duncker, 1945). Max Wertheimer also published a book on the topic in 1945, titled "Productive thinking." An enlarged edition published posthumously includes previously unpublished material (Wertheimer, 1959). Interestingly, 1945 seems to have been a watershed year for problem solving, for mathematician George Polya's book, "How to solve it," also appeared then. (A second edition was published 12 years later; Polya, 1957.) Extending the organizational principles of perception to the domain of problem solving, the Gestalt psychologists emphasized the importance of problem representation – how people view, interpret, or organize the given information – distinguishing the formation of a representation from the process of generating a solution. The Gestalt psychologists documented the impact of changes in perspective on problem difficulty as well as the effects of extraneous assumptions and prior knowledge on the way people understand problems and, therefore, generate problem solutions.

The psychological study of human problem solving faded into the background after the demise of the Gestalt tradition, and problem solving was investigated only sporadically until 1972, when Allen Newell and Herbert Simon's "Human problem solving" (Newell & Simon, 1972) sparked a flurry of research on this topic. In contrast to the Gestalt psychologists, Newell and Simon emphasized the step-by-step process of searching for a solution path connecting the initial state to the goal state. Their research goal was to identify general-purpose strategies that humans use to solve a variety of problems. Newell and Simon and their colleagues were heavily influenced by the information-processing approach to cognitive psychology and by work in computer science on artificial intelligence. These influences led them to construct the General Problem Solver (GPS), a computer program that modeled human problem solving (Ernst & Newell, 1969; Newell & Simon, 1972). A great strength of GPS was its ability to solve problems as different as the Tower of Hanoi problem and the construction of logic proofs with a single general-purpose strategy (means-ends analysis, which we discuss in "Generating Problem Solutions").

In the mid- to late 1970s, the role of background knowledge became an important research topic in cognitive psychology, particularly in the area of text comprehension (e.g., Anderson, Reynolds, Schallert, & Goetz, 1977; Bransford & McCarrell, 1974). In the field of problem solving, researchers recognized that a fundamental weakness of GPS was its lack of domain knowledge. For every problem type, the general-purpose strategy had to be supplemented with domain-specific knowledge. Moreover, research on expertise in knowledge-rich academic domains, such as mathematics, physics, and political science, especially during the late 1970s and early 1980s, made clear the necessity of taking domain knowledge into account for understanding problem solving. This research on expertise (e.g., Chi, Feltovich, & Glaser, 1981; Silver, 1979, 1981) provided empirical evidence for assertions first made by Duncker decades earlier: In his discussion of expertise differences in the domain of mathematics, Duncker (1945, p. 110) noted that "with 'poor' mathematicians, the thought-material is from the very beginning more thoroughly imbued with perceptual functions. For the 'good' mathematician, on the other hand, there remains a more abstract stratum ... in which only the specific mathematical properties still exist" (italics removed).

It is perhaps inevitable that the two traditions in problem-solving research – one emphasizing representation and the other emphasizing the process of generating a solution – would eventually come together. Although no single publication can be credited for the rapprochement, one impetus for a blending of the two traditions was the realization that background knowledge plays a critical role in problem solving. In particular, differences in background knowledge called attention to the interdependence between the representation constructed and the solution method employed, for solvers who constructed different representations were observed to generate the solution in different ways. Figure 14.1 provides a clear example of this interdependence for the trains and bird problem. To take another example, the 8-year-old son of one of the authors mentally represented the verbally stated multiplication problem "sixty-seven times ninety-five" as $(60 \times 95) + (7 \times 95)$ and then proceeded to mentally execute the indicated arithmetic operations to get the answer. In contrast, most people would represent this problem as 67 *groups of* 95 and turn to paper and pencil to compute the answer using the standard multiplication algorithm (given the absence of a calculator). The structure of this chapter aims to capture the evolution of research in the field of problem solving: from research on general principles of representation and solution that transcend domains to the importance of domain-specific knowledge, and from research that separates issues of representation and solution generation to a focus on their interaction.

Generating Problem Solutions

Algorithmic Versus Heuristic Solution Strategies

The step-by-step solution process is the sequence of actions solvers take to find and execute a procedure for generating a solution to the problem as they understand it. Researchers who study solution processes have made a distinction between algorithmic and heuristic strategies.

An *algorithm* is a procedure that is guaranteed to yield the solution. One type of algorithm is a mathematical formula. For example, multiplying the length of the base of a rectangle times its height is guaranteed to yield the rectangle's area. Similarly, the formula

$$X = \frac{-b \pm \sqrt{b^2 - 4ac}}{2a} \qquad \text{(Eq. 14.1)}$$

is guaranteed to provide the roots of the quadratic equation

$$aX^2 + bX + c = 0. \qquad \text{(Eq. 14.2)}$$

We discuss mathematical problem solving in some detail in "The Interplay Between Representation and Solution" (also see Gallistel & Gelman, Chap. 23).

Another type of algorithm – *exhaustive search* – involves checking every possible move. For example, one could solve the Tower of Hanoi problem by exhaustively considering every possible move in Figure 14.2. Similarly, one could solve a four-letter anagram (e.g., *idrb*) by systematically evaluating the 24 possible permutations of the given letters (the solution is *bird*). For problems with a large number of possible states, however, exhaustive search is impractical or impossible. For example, if the task is to find all possible solutions of a five-letter anagram (e.g., *ebrda* forms *bread*, *beard*, *bared*, and *debar*), exhaustive search would require examination of 120 letter orders. More strikingly, consider the game of chess (Holding, 1985): White has 20 possible opening moves, to which black can respond in any of 20 ways. Thus, on the second turn, white may be confronted with any of 400 possible board positions. After white's third move, there are 7.5 million possible board positions; after black's third move, there are 225 million possible positions. For a game of average length, the number of possible positions is approximately 10^{117}.

Clearly, some method is needed to prune the number of possible moves to be considered. Such pruning is necessary for human solvers owing to the limited capacity of working memory; it is also necessary for computers when, as in chess, the number of possible states is extremely large. *Heuristics* are problem-solving strategies that accomplish this goal. Although heuristics do not guarantee solution, they are highly likely to lead to success. For example, a good heuristic for solving anagrams, especially those with five or more letters (e.g., *dsyha*), is to consider letter pairs that commonly begin words of the given length (e.g., Ronning, 1965). This heuristic is useful because, by definition, most words begin with common letter pairs. Application of this heuristic to the example should quickly lead to the solution, *shady*. That considering common initial letter pairs is a heuristic rather than an algorithm is nicely illustrated by a second anagram, *uspyr*, which cannot be solved by this strategy because it begins with an uncommon letter pair (the solution, *syrup*, is the only five-letter word in English that begins with *sy*; Novick & Sherman, 2004).

A large body of literature has examined the heuristics that people use to generate problem solutions. Much of this research has focused on puzzle-like problems, such as the Tower of Hanoi, that require little domain-specific knowledge. These problems are useful because they enable researchers to focus their attention primarily on the process of generating solutions. Newell and Simon (1972) were the pioneers in this area of research. In the next section, we discuss their view that problem solving can be described as a process of heuristic search within a specific type of representation, and we consider in some detail two important search heuristics: hill climbing and means-ends analysis.

Problem Solving as Search Through a Problem Space

Newell and Simon (1972) wrote a magnum opus detailing their theory of problem solving and presenting several lines of supporting evidence. Because their goal was to develop a theory to encompass all human problem solving, they emphasized what is common across the diversity of problems and problem solvers. Their fundamental proposal was that problem solving could be conceptualized as a process of searching through a problem space for a path connecting the initial state of knowledge (the solver's understanding of the given information) to the goal state (the desired solution).

Problem space is the term Newell and Simon (1972) coined to refer to the solver's representation of the task as presented (also see Simon, 1978). Briefly, a problem space consists of a set of knowledge states (the initial state, the goal state, and various possible intermediate states), a set of operators that allow movement from one knowledge state to another, and local information about the path one is taking through the space (e.g., the current knowledge state and how one got there). For the three-disk Tower of Hanoi problem, the initial state is illustrated at the top of Figure 14.2 (state #1), and the goal state is illustrated at the bottom right of that figure (state #27). All other knowledge states shown in the figure are possible intermediate states. The current knowledge state is the one at which the solver is located at any given point in the solution process. For example, the current state for a solver who has made three moves along the optimum solution path would be state #9. The solver presumably would know that he or she arrived at this state from state #5. This knowledge allows the solver to recognize a move that involves backtracking. Finally, the three operators in this problem are moving each of the three disks from one peg to another. These operators are subject to the constraint that a larger disk may not be placed on a smaller disk.

Newell and Simon's (1972) primary focus of investigation was the strategies solvers use to find a path connecting the initial state to the goal state. That is, they sought to discover regularities in how solvers *search* through a problem space. In a nutshell, search is a serial method for making incremental progress toward the goal by applying operators to move from one knowledge state to another adjacent knowledge state. Newell and Simon discovered that, for a wide variety of problems, solvers' search is guided by a small number of heuristics.

To investigate these heuristics, Newell and Simon (1972) relied on two primary methodologies – think-aloud protocols (also see Duncker, 1945) and computer simulation. Solvers were required to say out loud everything they were thinking as they solved the problem – that is, everything that went through verbal working memory. Subjects' verbalizations – their *think-aloud protocols* – were tape-recorded and then transcribed verbatim for analysis. This method is advantageous for studying problem solving because it provides a detailed record of the solver's ongoing solution process. An important caveat that must be kept in mind while interpreting a subject's verbalizations is that "a protocol is relatively reliable only for what it positively contains, but not for that which it omits" (Duncker, 1945, p. 11). The use of think-aloud protocols to study problem solving was popularized by Newell and Simon. Ericsson and Simon (1980) provided an in-depth discussion of the conditions under which this method is valid (but see Russo, Johnson, & Stephens, 1989, for an alternative perspective). To test their interpretation of a subject's verbal protocol, Newell and Simon created a *computer simulation* that was intended to solve the problem the same way the subject did. To the extent that the computer simulation provided a close approximation of the solver's step-by-step solution process, the interpretation may be judged useful. Lovett and Anderson (Chap. 17) provide an in-depth treatment of computer models of thinking.

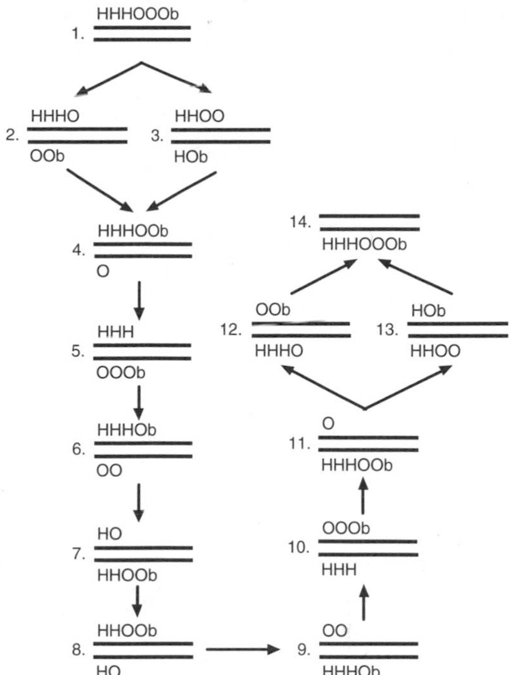

Figure 14.3. Problem states on the solution path for the Hobbits and Orcs problem. Each H represents a Hobbit, each O represents an Orc, and the b represents the boat. The two horizontal lines indicate the banks of the river. State #1 is the initial state, and state #14 is the goal state.

HILL CLIMBING

Hill climbing is a heuristic in which, at each step, the solver applies the operator that yields a new state that appears to be most similar to the goal state. This heuristic can be used whenever solvers can define an evaluation function that yields information about the similarity of the problem state generated by a candidate operator to the goal state. For example, Chronicle, MacGregor, and Ormerod (2004) found evidence that subjects use hill climbing to solve various problems in which a set of coins has to be rearranged from one configuration to another. We illustrate this heuristic using an example of a river-crossing problem (Figure 14.3), one of the classic problem types in the field: There are three Hobbits, three Orcs, and a boat on one side of a river (state #1). The goal is to use the boat, which has a capacity of only two creatures, to ferry all the creatures across the river (state #14). At no time may Orcs outnumber Hobbits on either side of the river because they will eat the Hobbits. The solution path for this problem is essentially linear, as shown in Figure 14.3.

From the initial state, there are two legal moves available – ferrying two Orcs or one Orc and one Hobbit across the river. Both moves yield new states that are equally similar to the goal state, and so either may be chosen. Use of the hill-climbing heuristic proceeds smoothly for the most part until the solver reaches state #7 in which there is one Hobbit and one Orc on the original side of the river; the boat and the remaining creatures are on the other (goal) side. The correct move at this point, in fact the only nonbacktracking move, is for one Hobbit and one Orc to take the boat back to the original side of the river. Thomas (1974) and Greeno (1974) found that solvers have particular difficulty moving from state #7 to state #8: Both the probability of making an incorrect move and the time taken to make a move are quite large for this transition compared with other transitions. According to Wickelgren (1974), this difficulty occurs for either of two reasons. For solvers who evaluate their progress one move at a time, this transition is problematic because one must detour more than usual by taking two creatures back to the original side of the river (logically, only one creature is needed to get the boat back to the original side). For solvers who evaluate their progress two moves at a time (i.e., round trips of the boat from the original side back to the original side), this transition is problematic because it results in no net progress toward the goal compared with state #6.

The difficulty solvers encounter in moving from state #7 to state #8 illustrates the primary drawback of the hill-climbing heuristic: Sometimes one needs to move either backward or laterally to move forward. Climbing a mountain can rarely be accomplished solely by following the strategy of taking the largest uphill step at all times. Sometimes one needs to walk downhill for a while to achieve the ultimate goal of reaching the mountain top.

MEAN-ENDS ANALYSIS

Means-ends analysis is a more sophisticated heuristic than hill climbing because it does not depend on simple similarity to the goal. This heuristic consists of the following steps:

1. Identify a difference between the current state and the goal (or subgoal) state.
2. Find an operator that will remove (or reduce) the difference.

3a. If the operator can be directly applied, do so, or

3b. If the operator cannot be directly applied, set a subgoal to remove the obstacle that is preventing execution of the desired operator.

4. Repeat steps 1 to 3 until the problem is solved.

We illustrate this heuristic with the Tower of Hanoi problem. A key difference between the initial state and the goal state (Figure 14.2) is that the large disk is on the wrong peg (step 1). The move-large-disk operator is required to remove this difference (step 2). However, this operator cannot be applied because of the presence of the medium and small disks on top of the large disk. Therefore, the solver may set a subgoal to move that two-disk tower to the middle peg (step 3b), thereby leaving the right peg free for the large disk. A key difference between the initial state and this new subgoal state is that the medium disk is on the wrong peg. Because application of the move-medium-disk operator is blocked, the solver sets another subgoal to move the small disk to the right peg. This subgoal can be satisfied immediately by applying the move-small-disk operator (step 3a), generating state #3. The solver then returns to the previous subgoal – moving the tower consisting of the small and medium disks to the middle peg. The differences between the current state (#3) and the subgoal state (#9) can be removed by applying first the move-medium-disk operator (yielding state #5) and then the move-small-disk operator (yielding state #9). Finally, the move-large-disk operator is no longer blocked. The solver takes that action, moving the large disk to the right peg, yielding state #11. Notice that the subgoals are stacked up in the order in which they are generated so they pop up in the order of last in first out. Given the first subgoal in our example, repeated application of the means-ends analysis heuristic will yield the shortest-path solution indicated by the thick grey arrows.

The key difference between hill climbing and mean-ends analysis is the online generation of subgoals in the latter heuristic. Adding new subgoals during problem solving greatly increases the power of heuristic search. Subgoals provide direction, and to the extent that they are appropriate, they can be expected to prune the space of possible states. Moreover, by assessing progress toward a required subgoal rather than the final goal, solvers may be able to make moves that otherwise seem unwise. To take a concrete example, consider the transition from state #1 to state #3 in Figure 14.2. Comparing the initial state with the goal state, we find that this move seems unwise because it places the small disk on the bottom of the right peg, whereas it ultimately needs to be at the top of the tower on that peg. However, if one compares the initial state with the solver-generated subgoal state of having the medium disk on the middle peg, this is exactly where the small disk needs to go. More generally, generating subgoals allows solvers to plan several moves ahead. (Duncker, 1945, also talked about the importance of subgoals.)

As we noted in our brief historic review, means-ends analysis is the heuristic that GPS used to successfully model human problem solving across a wide variety of tasks (Ernst & Newell, 1969; Newell & Simon, 1972). A large body of research has found that mean-ends analysis tends to be people's preferred solution method for novel problems that are relatively free of specialized content and for which a definite goal is given (Greeno & Simon, 1988) – for example, the Tower of Hanoi problem as opposed to the problem of finding the roots of a quadratic equation or of unscrambling an anagram.

Some Conclusions from Research on Problem Solving as Search

Newell and Simon's (1972) goal was to discover general problem-solving strategies that are common across problem solvers and across problems. One important contribution of their work concerns the methods they adopted for studying this issue. Duncker (1945) was an early advocate of collecting think-aloud protocols, and he used this methodology very successfully to study problem solving. With the rise to dominance of behaviorism and the fall of the Gestalt approach to psychology, however, this methodology fell into disfavor. Newell and Simon (1972) brought a high degree of scientific rigor to the collection of verbal protocols, enabling this methodology to gain a degree of acceptance in the field that it did not previously enjoy. In addition, Newell and Simon were among the early pioneers in the use of computer simulation as a tool for testing theories of psychological processes. Both of these methods are now seen as ordinary rather than exotic means of investigating problem solving (as well as other cognitive processes).

Newell and Simon's (1972) goal of uncovering general problem-solving strategies necessitated a focus on the solution of puzzles such as the Tower of Hanoi and Hobbits and Orcs, which are relatively uncontaminated by domain knowledge that necessarily varies across individuals. This focus was much like Ebbinghaus' strategy of investigating general principles of memory by studying nonsense syllables. Using this strategy, Newell and Simon and their colleagues made important contributions to the field of problem solving: Means-ends analysis and other heuristics are very flexible and general strategies that people frequently use to successfully solve a large variety of problems.

Nevertheless, the view of problem solving as search through a problem space does not provide a complete understanding of how people solve problems. Although people rely on general-purpose search heuristics when they encounter novel problems, because these heuristics are weak and fallible, they abort them as soon as they acquire some knowledge about the particular problem space. At that point, they switch to more specialized strategies (e.g., Anzai & Simon, 1979). In general, whenever solvers have some relevant background knowledge, they tend to use stronger, albeit more narrowly applicable, domain-specific methods. The impact of learning and domain knowledge on strategy use led problem-solving researchers to turn their attention from the solution of knowledge-lean puzzles and riddles to problems that made connections to solvers' background knowledge. This shift is analogous to memory and comprehension researchers' switch from studying nonsense syllables to studying words, paragraphs, and stories in order to understand the role of prior knowledge in memory and comprehension. As we noted in the introduction, background knowledge plays an important role in determining the representation a solver constructs for a problem, which, in turn, affects the processes the solver uses to generate a solution. In the next two sections, we focus on problem representation and the interplay between representation and solution, respectively.

Problem Representation

Overview

In problems such as the Tower of Hanoi and Hobbits and Orcs, all the problem components – the initial conditions, the goal, the means for generating and evaluating the solution, and the constraints – are well defined in the problem as presented. In most real-world problems, however, the solver has to define one or more of the problem components. For example, a person's desire to cook a tasty dinner, a student's aspiration to write a term paper that will earn a grade of "A," and a young executive's need to find suitable housing are all examples of *ill-defined problems* (Reitman, 1965). In these problems, the goal is not well defined, nor is it clear how to determine that the goal has been accomplished. For example, what constitutes a tasty dinner, and how does one decide that a particular recipe is tasty enough? It seems obvious that a cook's definition of the goal state will depend on his or her background knowledge. A poor graduate student might picture homemade pizza, a parent of young children might imagine lasagna, an Indian couple without children might think of spicy lamb vindaloo, and a gourmet cook might visualize beef Wellington. The tasty dinner problem is ill defined in other ways as well. The cook has to define the given information (only ingredients found at home or also those at the grocery store?), the operators (e.g., to bake or stir fry or simmer on the stove), and the constraints (e.g., time, cost, the differing tastes of adults and children).

As we noted earlier, the Gestalt psychologists focused their attention on the factors that affect how people define, understand, or represent problems. Greeno (1977), in specific counterpoint to Newell and Simon's (1972) focus on problem solving as search, also highlighted the central importance of representation. More recently, researchers who have studied problem solving in particular knowledge domains (e.g., mathematics, physics, medical diagnosis) have also emphasized the critical role of representation in successful problem solving. Their investigations have shown that various aspects of the problem situation, as well as people's background knowledge, affect how people represent problems and, in turn, how they generate problem solutions. The trains and bird problem we discussed at the outset (Figure 14.1) provides an anecdotal example of the importance of the representation constructed for the ultimate success of one's solution attempt.

We stated informally at the outset that a problem representation is a model of the problem constructed by solvers to summarize their understanding of the problem's essential nature. More specifically, a representation has four components (Markman, 1999): (1) a represented world – in this case, the description of the problem to be solved,

(2) a representing world – the set of elements to be used to depict the objects and relations in the represented world, (3) a set of rules that map elements of the represented world to elements of the representing world, and (4) a process that uses the information in the representing world – in this case, to solve the problem. This last component highlights the link between representation and solution: Without some process that uses the information in the representation for some purpose, the so-called representation has no symbolic meaning (i.e., it does not serve a representational function).

The representation a solver uses to support and guide problem solving can be either internal (residing in working memory) or external (e.g., drawn on paper). In either case, the elements of the representing world may follow a variety of different formats. Some representations are best described as verbal or propositional or declarative. Others are pictorial or diagrammatic, such as a drawing of a pulley system, a matrix or network, and a bar or line graph (see Hegarty, Carpenter, & Just, 1991, for a discussion of types of diagrammatic representations). Finally, some representations are "runnable" mental models (e.g., a mental abacus – Stigler, 1984; a system of interlocking gears – Schwartz & Black, 1996).

In the previous section of this chapter, we highlighted how solvers generate problem solutions, leaving in the background the question of how they represent the information in the problem. In this section, we take the opposite perspective, highlighting the problem representations that solvers construct and leaving in the background the methods by which those representations are used to generate the solution. We consider solution only as a dependent measure (i.e., accuracy and/or solution time), illustrating that differences in problem representation affect problem solution. Our discussion of research in this area is organized around two classes of factors that have been found to affect the representation that solvers select or construct for the problem at hand – problem context and solver's knowledge. In the next section of the chapter, we consider the interplay between representation and solution, focusing there on studies showing that the representation one constructs for a problem affects *how* one generates the solution.

The Importance of Problem Context

A number of studies have found that various aspects of the problem context have a strong influence on the representations solvers construct. In this section, we describe three such studies, which illustrate three different types of problem context effects. The first study illustrates an effect of the perceptual form of the problem, the second study shows an effect of semantic interpretation based on how objects are used, and the third study demonstrates an effect of the story content of the problem.

PERCEPTUAL FORM

Problems that are presented as visual displays or diagrams may provide information about configuration that solvers deem relevant to the solution and include in their problem representation. This effect is nicely illustrated by Maier's (1930) nine-dot problem: Nine dots are arrayed in a 3 × 3 grid, and the task is to connect all the dots by drawing four straight lines without lifting one's pencil from the paper. People have difficulty solving this problem because their initial representations generally include a constraint, inferred from the configuration of dots, that the lines cannot go outside the boundary of the imaginary square formed by the outer dots. With this constraint implied by the perceptual form of the dots, the problem cannot be solved (but see Adams, 1979). Without this constraint, the problem may be solved as shown in Figure 14.4.

The nine-dot problem is a classic *insight* problem. According to the Gestalt view (e.g., Duncker, 1945; Maier, 1931; see Ohlsson, 1984a, for a review), the solution to an insight problem appears suddenly, accompanied by an "aha!" sensation, immediately following the sudden restructuring of one's understanding of the problem: "The decisive points in thought-processes, the moments of sudden comprehension, of the 'Aha!,' of the new, are always at the same time moments in which such a sudden restructuring of the thought-material takes place" (Duncker, 1945, p. 29). For the nine-dot problem, one view of the required restructuring is that the solver relaxes the constraint implied by the perceptual form of the problem and realizes that the lines in fact may extend past the boundary of the imaginary square.

To test this view, in one experiment Weisberg and Alba (1981) compared the performance of control subjects who were given 20 attempts to solve the nine-dot problem with that of other subjects who received 10 attempts before a restructuring hint, followed by 10 attempts after the hint. The restructuring hint involved telling subjects that they had exhausted all possibilities inside the square, and so they had to go outside the square to solve the problem. No subject in either condition solved the problem in the first 10 tries, and no subject in the control condition ever solved the problem (excluding those who had seen the problem before). However, 20% of the restructuring hint group solved the problem in the second 10 tries. A follow-up study that gave subjects many more solution attempts replicated these results. Interestingly, solution was neither quick nor direct following the restructuring hint in either study, for subjects generally required 5 to 11 solution attempts after the hint before solving the problem. Moreover, 75% to 80% of the subjects failed to solve the problem despite the hint. Thus, restructuring, as provided by Weisberg and Alba's hint, appears to be necessary but not sufficient for solution. We reconsider the nature of insight in "The Interplay Between Representation and Solution."

OBJECT-BASED INFERENCES

In addition to making inferences from the perceptual form of a presented figure, solvers may draw inferences from the specific entities that appear in a problem, and these inferences may likewise affect the constructed problem representation. A classic example of such inferences is the phenomenon of *functional fixedness* introduced by Duncker (1945): If an object has been used for one purpose, or is habitually used for a certain purpose, it is difficult to see that object as having properties that would enable it to be used for a dissimilar purpose. Duncker's basic experimental paradigm involved two conditions that varied in terms of whether the object that was crucial for solution was initially used for a function other than that required for solution.

Consider the candles problem, the most well-known of the five problems Duncker (1945) investigated. Three candles are to be mounted at eye height on a door. On the table for use in completing this task are some tacks and three boxes. The solution is to tack the three boxes to the door to serve as platforms for the candles. In the control condition, the three boxes were presented to subjects empty. In the functionally fixed condition, the three boxes were filled with candles, tacks, and matches. Thus, in the latter condition, the boxes initially served the function of container, whereas the solution requires that they serve the function of platform. The results showed that 100% of the subjects who received empty boxes solved the candles problem compared with only 43% of subjects who received filled boxes. Every one of the five problems showed a difference favoring the control condition over the functionally fixed condition with average solution rates across the five problems of 97% and 58%, respectively. In "The Interplay between Representation and Solution" we discuss additional examples of object-based inferences that link semantic content to representation and then to the method of solution adopted.

STORY CONTENT

In our earlier discussion of the trains and bird problem, we mentioned that the text is written such that it invites the solver to focus on the motion of the bird [Figure 14.1(a)] rather than of the trains [Figure 14.1(b)]. In general, the story content and phrasing of the problem text may affect how the solver represents the problem. Hayes and Simon (1977; also see Kotovsky, Hayes, & Simon,

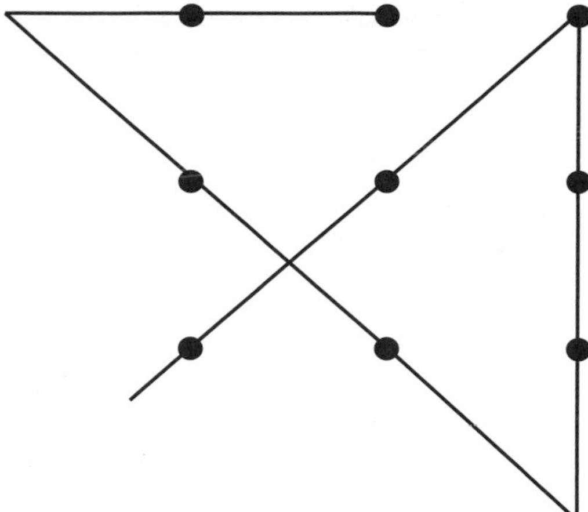

Figure 14.4. A solution to the nine-dot problem.

1985) provided empirical evidence that differences in the descriptions of the operators in two isomorphic (i.e., structurally equivalent) problems yielded quite different representations with important consequences for the problems' relative difficulty. They used several variants of the Tower of Hanoi problem that concerned monsters and globes that came in three sizes: small, medium, and large. We discuss one "transfer" variant and one "change" variant used in Hayes and Simon's research. For both variants, the initial state had the small monster holding the large globe, the medium-size monster holding the small globe, and the large monster holding the medium-size globe. The goal was for each monster to have a globe proportionate to its own size. Both variants can be mapped onto the Tower of Hanoi problem states shown in Figure 14.2. If we map the small, medium, and large monsters onto the left, center, and right pegs, respectively, and map increasing globe size onto decreasing disc size, both monster variants are equivalent to the task of getting from state #12 to state #5 in Figure 14.2.

The only difference between the two monsters and globes isomorphs concerned the description of the operators. In the transfer variant, subjects were told that the monsters could transfer the globes from one to another as long as they followed three rules: (1) Only one globe may be transferred at a time; (2) if a monster is holding multiple globes, only the larger globe may be transferred; and (3) a globe cannot be transferred to a monster that is holding a larger globe. In the change variant, subjects were told that the monsters could shrink and expand themselves according to the following rules: (1) Only one monster may change size at a time; (2) if two monsters are the same size, only the one holding the larger globe may change size; and (3) a monster may not change size so it becomes the same size as another monster that is holding a larger globe.

Because these two problems are structurally identical, they can be solved by making the same sequence of moves in the same problem space. However, the subjects did not translate the problems to a common representation. Rather, they accepted the cover story as given and, depending on the variant they received, proceeded to either move globes or change monster sizes. The different representations and operators adopted were apparent in the written notations produced by subjects as they solved the problem (Hayes & Simon, 1977). Importantly, the representation constructed had a large effect on solution time: The transfer variant took about 14 minutes to solve compared with about 29 minutes for the change variant. The greater difficulty of the change variant is due to an additional step needed to check that the operator constraints have been satisfied.

The Importance of Solvers' Knowledge

In the previous section, we discussed problem factors that affect the representations solvers construct. However, the extent to which solvers respond to various problem factors depends on their prior experience and background knowledge. Consider, for example, the following mathematical word problem: "Susan has 12 cookies and three boxes. How many cookies should she place in each box in order to divide them up fairly?" A child who has sufficient experience with solving such problems is likely to represent this problem in terms of its mathematical structure – simple division. In contrast, a child who has never encountered such problems might try to understand it in terms of human motivation and behavior. This child might consider the size of the cookies and the boxes, or wonder who Susan is and why she wants to put the cookies in the boxes. In general, solvers' background knowledge affects whether and to what extent they focus their attention on problem aspects that are or are not relevant to determining the solution. In this section, we discuss three types of background knowledge that pertain to solvers' understanding of the problem at hand. First, we consider solvers' prior experience with a structurally similar or analogous problem. Second, we consider their generalized schemas for types of solution procedures as well as types of common representational tools (e.g., matrices). Third, we consider differences in problem representation that are due to differences in solvers' domain expertise.

EXPERIENCE WITH A STRUCTURALLY SIMILAR OR ANALOGOUS PROBLEM

A large body of research has examined people's use of specific examples of problems to help them understand and solve a current problem. An example can be helpful for solving a novel problem only if the two problems have a similar underlying structure because a problem's structure is what determines appropriate solution methods (e.g., division for the cookie problem). The example will not be helpful if the problems only share a similar cover story and involve similar objects (e.g., a person, cookies, and boxes) but differ in their underlying structure (e.g., in the example Susan distributes cookies among boxes, but in the novel problem Leah removes one cookie from each box). Research on analogical problem solving (also referred to as analogical transfer) shows that solvers' understanding, or representation, of a novel problem can be facilitated by prior experience with an analogous (i.e., structurally equivalent) problem. However, people may fail to retrieve an analogous problem from memory, or fail to apply an analogous solution, if they focus their attention on the solution-irrelevant differences between the example and the novel problem. Holyoak (Chap. 6) provides an in-depth treatment of research on analogy. Here, we describe in detail only a single, now classic, study (Gick & Holyoak, 1980) that illustrates this line of research.

Gick and Holyoak (1980) used Duncker's (1945) radiation problem as their target (novel) problem. This problem involves finding a way to use some rays to destroy a patient's stomach tumor, without harming the patient. At sufficiently high intensity, the rays will destroy the tumor. However, at that intensity they will also destroy the healthy tissue surrounding the tumor. At lower intensity, the rays will not harm the healthy tissue, but they also will not destroy the tumor. The desired solution is to project multiple low-intensity rays at the tumor from several points around the patient. The rays will converge on the tumor, where their individual intensities will sum to a level sufficient to destroy the tumor. Baseline use of this *convergence* solution is quite low – about 10% (Gick & Holyoak, 1980). Gick and Holyoak examined whether solvers' understanding of the radiation problem, as indexed by their use of the convergence solution, might be facilitated by prior exposure to an analogous situation. To this end, they had subjects attempt to solve the radiation problem after having previously read a story that described the following analogous situation: A general was trying to capture a fortress controlled by a dictator. Multiple roads led to the fortress from all directions. However, the roads were mined in such a way that large groups of soldiers could not travel on them. The general decided to send a separate small group of soldiers down each of the various roads so the full army would converge at the fortress. In this way, he was able to overthrow the evil dictator and capture the fortress.

Gick and Holyoak (1980) found that subjects generally did not spontaneously notice that the story about the fortress was relevant to solving the radiation problem: Only about 20% provided the convergence solution to that problem after having read the fortress story. However, when these same subjects were subsequently given a simple hint indicating that one of the stories they had read earlier might be helpful for solving the radiation problem, about 75% generated the convergence solution. These results indicate that solvers may fail to spontaneously notice the relevance of problems stored in memory for understanding and solving a current problem, although they are able to use the prior problem appropriately when its relevance is highlighted.

An important factor that mediates spontaneous retrieval and use of analogous solutions is people's understanding of the learned example. Chi, Bassok, Lewis, Reimann, and Glaser (1989) investigated this issue in the domain of physics, using problems from elementary mechanics. They found that learners who understood the logic of textbook examples spontaneously applied the example problems' solutions to analogous test problems that differed from the learned examples in many respects. However, poor learners failed to recognize the structural similarity between the examples and the novel problems. People's ability to exploit analogous solutions also depends on their domain expertise. We discuss expertise differences in problem representation after considering schematic knowledge. Then, in "The Interplay Between Representation and Solution" we consider the implications of expertise differences for analogical transfer.

GENERAL SCHEMAS IN MEMORY

In addition to knowledge of specific problems encountered in the past, solvers also have in memory abstract schemas for types of problems, types of solution procedures, and types of representations. These schemas are abstract in the sense that they include information that is common to multiple problems of a particular type but exclude information that is idiosyncratic to the individual problems over which the abstraction has occurred. For example, an abstract schema for the convergence solution would specify that multiple, low-intensity forces converge from different directions on a central target, but it would not specify that the forces are soldiers (or rays) or that the target is a fortress (or a tumor). A number of studies have shown that schemas for solution procedures can be induced by comparing two or more analogous problems (with their solutions) or by successfully solving one problem by analogy to another (solved) problem, and such schema induction in turn facilitates understanding and solution of subsequent analogous problems (e.g., Bassok & Holyoak, 1989; Gick & Holyoak, 1983; Novick & Holyoak, 1991; Ross & Kennedy, 1990). Research on solution schemas is discussed in more detail by Holyoak (Chap. 6).

In the remainder of this section, we discuss some of the recent research on representation schemas (Hurley & Novick, 2004; Novick, 2001; Novick, Hurley, & Francis, 1999). This research shows that college students possess abstract schemas for three spatial diagrams – matrices, networks, and hierarchies – that are important tools for understanding and solving problems from a variety of domains (see Tversky, Chap. 10, for a general review of visuospatial reasoning). These schemas presumably were induced over the course of students' in-school and out-of-school experiences with concrete instances of these diagrams in use (Novick, 2001). For example, matrices are used for multiplication tables, time schedules, grade books, and seating charts. The spatial diagram schemas seem to be at an intermediate level of generality (Novick et al., 1999): Each type of diagram is best suited for a particular type of relational structure, regardless of the content domain in which that structure is embedded. For example, a matrix is appropriate whenever (1) all possible combinations of items across two sets must be considered, (2) the relation between items is associative (i.e., nondirectional), and (3) it is important to be able to distinguish between items that are related and those that are not (Novick & Hurley, 2001). The abstract representation schemas are more useful than are specific relevant example problems for understanding the structures of novel problems (Novick et al., 1999).

To measure problem understanding, Novick et al. (1999) asked subjects to select the most appropriate type of spatial diagram to represent the structure of each of 12 story problems. (Solving these problems would have required using analytical or mathematical reasoning.) In one experiment, some subjects participated in a specific example condition, whereas other subjects participated in a general category condition. The initial task in the specific example condition provided subjects with three example problems, each illustrating the use of a different one of the three spatial diagrams. Subjects spent 6 minutes solving each example problem using the diagrammatic representation given. In contrast, the initial task in the general category condition was designed to cue the abstract schemas that subjects were hypothesized to have in memory. Subjects were shown (one at a time) an abstract (empty) hierarchy, matrix, and network. Above each diagram was a short phrase naming the type of diagram (e.g., "a network or system of paths"). Subjects saw the abstract diagrams for 20 seconds each and were asked to familiarize themselves with the diagrams so they would have clearly in mind what each one is like for the next task.

If college students possess at least rudimentary abstract schemas for the three spatial diagrams, then the brief (20-second) study times for the abstract diagrams presented in the general category condition should have been sufficient to cue those schemas. Abstract schemas provide a more reliable source of knowledge for understanding new problems than do specific example problems because the schemas do not contain specific story content (Holyoak, 1985). In contrast, example problems do contain specific content, and this content must be ignored when it mismatches that of the novel problems. Given this difference between abstract schemas and concrete examples, Novick et al. (1999) predicted that subjects in the general category condition would be more successful than those in the specific example condition at selecting the most appropriate type of representation for the test problems that required spatial diagram representations. The results strongly supported this prediction: Cueing subjects' prior knowledge by having them think about each abstract diagram for 20 seconds greatly facilitated understanding of the test problems compared with spending 6 minutes studying and successfully solving each of the relevant example problems.

EXPERTISE

The studies discussed in the previous two sections examined the effects of background knowledge on problem representation among typical college students. It has also proved to be especially interesting to investigate problem representation among people who differ with respect to their expertise in the domain under investigation. Duncker (1945) was perhaps the first psychologist to note that experts and novices in a domain focus their attention on different aspects of that domain, leading them to construct problem representations that are quite different: Whereas experts' representations tend to highlight solution-relevant structural features (in particular, meaningful causal relations among the objects in the problem), novices' representations tend to highlight solution-irrelevant superficial features (e.g., the particular objects themselves or how the question is phrased). Evidence for these representational differences has been found using a wide variety of experimental tasks and procedures.

A number of studies have found that experts' attention is quickly captured by meaningful configurations within a presented stimulus, a result that calls to mind the Gestalt view that problem solving is related to perception. In contrast, novices' attention is focused on isolated components of the stimulus. Perhaps the earliest research investigating this issue comes from the domain of chess (Chase & Simon, 1973; de Groot, 1966). In the typical study, subjects view 20 or more chess pieces arranged on a chess board for 5 seconds and then have to immediately reconstruct what they saw on a new chess board. The arrangement of chess pieces is either from the middle of a real game or is random. When the arrangement comes from a real game, recall improves dramatically as a function of expertise, from about 5 pieces for novices to about 20 pieces for players at the level of International Master or above (Gobet & Simon, 1996). Recall also improves with expertise for random positions, although the effect is much smaller (from about 2.6 to 5.3 pieces; Gobet & Simon, 1996). These expertise differences can be explained by the hypothesis that expert chess players have stored in memory meaningful groups (chunks) of chess pieces. Chase and Simon (1973) found evidence for such chunks based on an analysis of the latencies between recall of consecutive pieces. Better recall of structured or meaningful stimuli by experts than by novices has been found in many other domains as well: Circuit diagrams (Egan & Schwartz, 1979), computer programming (McKeithen, Reitman, Rueter, & Hirtle, 1981), medicine (Coughlin & Patel, 1987; Myles-Worsley, Johnston, & Simons, 1988), basketball and field hockey (Allard & Starkes, 1991), and figure skating (Deakin & Allard, 1991).

Evidence for representational differences between experts and novices also comes from studies in which subjects were asked to sort problems into groups based on how they would be solved. In one of the early studies using this methodology, Chi et al. (1981) asked students to group physics (mechanics) word problems into categories of related problems. They found that advanced physics graduate students tended to group the problems according to the physics principles required for solution (e.g., conservation of energy). In contrast, undergraduates who had successfully completed an introductory physics course tended to group the problems according to the types of objects presented (e.g., springs versus pulleys versus inclined planes).

Comparable results have been found in the domains of mathematics and computer programming using measures based on both problem sorting and free recall (Adelson, 1981; McKeithen et al., 1981; Silver, 1979, 1981; Weiser & Shertz, 1983). These knowledge-based differences in problem representations are not restricted to mathematical domains. For example, Kindfield (1993/1994) analyzed the chromosome diagrams produced by subjects who varied in their degree of formal training in genetics as they reasoned about the process of meiosis. She found that the more expert subjects produced more abstract chromosome diagrams that highlighted the features that were biologically relevant to the problem at hand. In contrast, the diagrams of the less advanced subjects more literally resembled chromosome appearance under a light microscope, including aspects such as dimensionality and shape that have no bearing on the process of meiosis.

Similar findings also have emerged from research involving geometric analogies, a problem type that does not seem to involve detailed domain knowledge. Schiano, Cooper, Glaser, and Zhang (1989) asked high school students who had received very low or very high scores on a standardized geometric analogy test to sort proportional analogies (of the form A:A′::B:B′) involving geometric figures into groups of related problems. They found that the low-scoring students tended to sort the problems according to superficial perceptual similarities. For example, they put the problems involving circles and those involving partially shaded hexagons into separate piles. In contrast, the high-scoring students tended to sort the problems according to the abstract, transformational relations underlying solution. For example, they put the problems involving rotations and those involving size transformations into separate piles.

It is important to note that these representational differences between experts and novices (or between people who are highly skilled versus less skilled in a domain) are a matter of emphasis and degree. With increasing expertise/knowledge, there is a gradual change in the focus of attention and in the problems that are seen as related, and the extremes are not quite as extreme as summaries of the differences often suggest (e.g., Deakin & Allard, 1991; Hardiman, Dufresne, & Mestre, 1989;

McKeithen et al., 1981; Myles-Worsley et al., 1988; Schoenfeld & Herrmann, 1982; Silver, 1981).

The Interplay Between Representation and Solution

So far, we have considered problem representation and the process of generating problem solutions separately. We noted at the outset, however, that these topics are inherently interrelated: The representation one constructs is likely to affect how one goes about generating a solution. A classic example comes from Wertheimer (1959). Students are generally taught how to compute the area of a parallelogram as shown in Figure 14.5(a). Wertheimer distinguished two groups of students based on their representations of the solution method. Some students constructed what we might call today a procedural representation. They were able to compute the area by rote application of the learned formula. The representations of other students reflected good conceptual understanding of the solution method, namely that a triangle can be cut off from one side of the geometric figure and pasted onto the other side to create a rectangle to which the learned formula then obviously applies. Wertheimer found that students who represented the problem as one of converting the parallelogram into a rectangle were able to find the area of the quadrilateral in Figure 14.5(b) and that of the irregularly shaped geometric figure in Figure 14.5(c) by similar conversion of those figures into rectangles as shown by the superimposed dashed lines. In contrast, students who represented the parallelogram problem in terms of the appropriate formula to apply were stumped by the problems presented in Figures 14.5(b) and 14.5(c), because the formula is not applicable to those problems as presented (because the figures are not parallelograms). These results demonstrate that structural understanding (exemplified by the convert-to-rectangle solution method) enables solvers to recognize similarity between problems that differ in appearance.

In this section, we review research that highlights this interplay between representation and solution generation. The first part of our review focuses on problem solving in mathematics. As suggested by our initial example from Wertheimer (1959), this is a domain in which the interplay between representation and solution generation is easy to see. We show how the effects on representation of several of the solver and problem factors identified in the previous section have consequences for the solution method employed. In the second part of our review, we revisit the nature of insight problem solving, a topic that is currently receiving much attention. The research on this topic aims to sort out the inherent interplay between representation and solution generation.

Mathematical Problem Solving

DOMAIN KNOWLEDGE

Wertheimer (1959) found that structural understanding helps solvers to see important similarities between problems that differ in appearance. Research reviewed in the representation section showed that experts (i.e., people with high domain knowledge) better understand the structure of problems within their domain of expertise than do novices (i.e., people with low domain knowledge). It therefore seems reasonable to predict that the expertise-related differences in problem representation would affect the methods that experts and novices attempt to use to solve novel problems. We review two studies by Novick (1988) on mathematical problem solving by analogy that provide evidence for such a link between representation and solution.

In one experiment, Novick (1988) reasoned that arithmetic experts (i.e., people who are highly skilled at arithmetic) would be more likely than novices (i.e., people who are less skilled at arithmetic) to apply a learned procedure to an analogous test problem with a different cover story, because only experts would construct similar

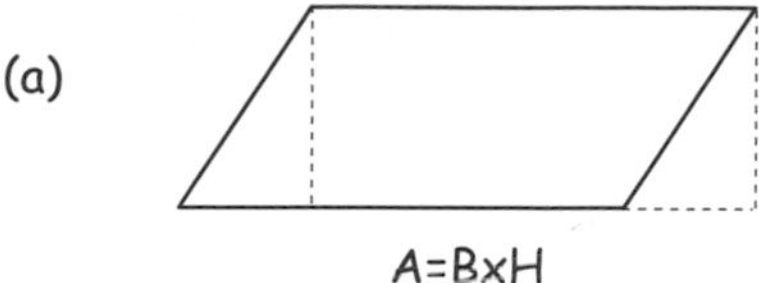

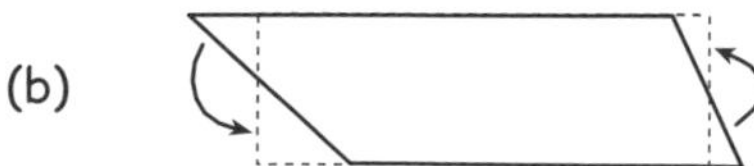

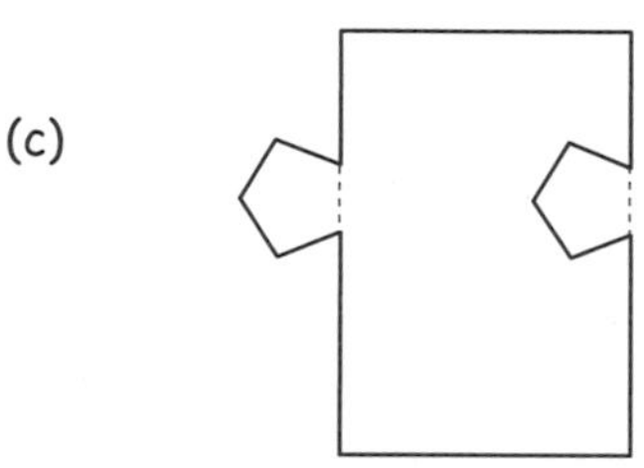

Figure 14.5. Finding the area of (a) a parallelogram, (b) a quadrilateral, and (c) an irregularly shaped geometric figure. The solid lines indicate the geometric figures whose areas are desired. The dashed lines show how to convert the given figures into rectangles (i.e., they show solutions with understanding).

representations for the two problems. The example problem concerned purchasing plants for a vegetable garden. The test problem concerned arranging members of a marching band into rows and columns. In the control condition, subjects attempted to solve the band problem after having been taught how to solve three unrelated problems. In the experimental condition, one of the unrelated problems was replaced by the vegetable garden problem. The learned solution procedure for this problem was based on finding the lowest common multiple (LCM) of three numbers and then examining multiples of the LCM to find a number that fit certain constraints. This solution procedure is also appropriate for the band problem. Alternatively, the band problem can be solved by examining multiples of the individual numbers given in the problem. The data strongly supported Novick's hypothesis of differential transfer for experts and novices: Among the novice group, 6% of subjects in each condition used the LCM procedure to solve the marching band problem. Among the experts, in contrast, 56% of subjects in the experimental condition used the more efficient LCM procedure, compared with only 6% of subjects in the control condition. Consistent with these results, Dunbar (2001) reported that when scientists attempted to resolve puzzles in their own work, they generally retrieved analogies on the basis of shared relational structure.

Novick's (1988) first experiment focused on the beneficial consequences of experts' structurally based representations. Another experiment focused on potential negative consequences of novices' superficially based representations. All subjects were initially taught to solve three problems. One problem was the vegetable garden problem, which is similar in structure but dissimilar in story content to the marching band problem. A second problem concerned seating people in rows and columns on an auditorium stage. Despite its similarity in story content to the band problem, the auditorium problem required a different solution procedure (i.e., the problems were structurally dissimilar). (Because the auditorium problem's solution procedure is inappropriate for the band problem, control subjects almost never try to use that procedure to solve the band problem.) The third problem was unrelated to the band problem. Thus, when subjects received the band problem to solve, they could choose to use the LCM procedure from the analogous vegetable garden problem, the incorrect procedure from the superficially similar auditorium problem, or some other solution method. As predicted, novices were more likely than experts to attempt to apply the incorrect procedure from the auditorium problem to the band problem, and they were more persistent in their attempts to use this procedure. As many intermediates as novices tried to use the incorrect procedure, but fewer tried to do so more than once. Thus, superficial features play a decreasing role in analogical problem solving as expertise increases (also see Dunbar, 2001). Replicating the results of the initial experiment, experts were more likely than subjects in the other two groups to use the LCM procedure to solve the band problem.

LEARNING ABOUT PROBLEM SUBGOALS REVISITED

As we discussed earlier in connection with means-ends analysis and the Tower of Hanoi problem, solvers often generate subgoals when they are unable to directly apply a desired operator. Subgoals also have been identified as components of task structure that can be taught to learners (Catrambone, 1998). For example, in a statistics class, the task of computing a statistic for testing a hypothesis concerning central tendency can be divided into three subgoals: calculate the observed value, the hypothesized value, and the appropriate standard error. Subgoals in this sense decompose the problem into conceptually distinct and meaningful parts. Identifying the right subgoals thus implies that one has a good understanding of the structure of the problem, that is, a good representation.

Catrambone (1996, 1998) investigated the consequences for problem solving of instructional manipulations that affect subgoal learning. He found that manipulating solvers' opportunity to learn an important subgoal influenced their ability to solve probability problems involving the Poisson distribution and to adapt the learned procedure to solve slightly altered problems. In one experiment, Catrambone (1996) manipulated subjects' representations by varying whether the solution to the example problem provided a label for the subgoal of finding the total number of objects of type X. Then he gave subjects several problems to solve, some of which were isomorphic to the example problem and some of which provided somewhat different information about the objects relevant to the subgoal. He found that all subjects were highly successful at solving the isomorphic problems, which required the same solution method as the example problem. However, for the test problems that required a different method for finding the total number of objects of type X, subjects who had learned the subgoal performed much better than those who had not (80% vs. 49% correct, respectively). That is, when solvers had good conceptual understanding of the numeric quantity they needed to compute, they were better able to devise a new method for finding that quantity when the expected information was not provided in the problem. This result is reminiscent of Wertheimer's (1959) findings with the parallelogram problem and related area problems (Figure 14.5).

OBJECT-BASED INFERENCES FROM STORY CONTENT

In the section on problem representation, we described Hayes and Simon's (1977) study in which differences in the texts of the transfer and change monsters and globes problems led to differences in the representations solvers constructed for those two problem isomorphs. We also described Duncker's (1945) candles problem, in which the given objects (boxes) evoked inferences pertaining to their functional role (containers). In related work, Bassok and her colleagues have found that the objects in the texts of mathematical word problems affect (1) how people represent the described problem situation (i.e., the *situation model* they construct) and, accordingly, (2) which mathematical solution, or *mathematical model*, they select or construct (for a review, see Bassok, 2001).

One set of studies varied the objects in mathematically isomorphic word problems involving constant change (Alibali, Bassok, Solomon, Syc, & Goldin-Meadow, 1999; Bassok & Olseth, 1995). The objects were chosen to evoke situation models involving either discrete or continuous change (e.g., constant change in the number of books per shelf on consecutive shelves of a bookcase or constant change in the amount of air pressed per minute into a hot air balloon, respectively). In Alibali et al.'s (1999) study, subjects had to describe the problems to a confederate and solve the problems. Subjects' internal representations of the manner of change (i.e., their situation models) for each problem were coded from their speech and, separately, from their gestures. The solution method a subject used for each problem was categorized as either the sum strategy or the average strategy, which are compatible, respectively, with a representation of change as a set of discrete events or as a single event. The results indicated that when subjects were judged to have constructed a situation model involving discrete change (based on both speech and gesture), they were most likely to use the discrete sum strategy for solution. In contrast, when they constructed a situation model involving continuous change, they were most likely to use the continuous sum strategy for solution.

Another set of studies varied the semantic symmetry between object pairs in mathematical word problems and found that people's solutions of these problems tended to have a corresponding mathematical symmetry. Bassok, Chase, and Martin (1998) proposed that the objects in a problem (e.g., tulips, vases) activate semantic and pragmatic knowledge that evokes relational inferences (e.g., the "contain" relation), which people include in their representations of the described situation. These situation models, in turn, guide the selection of structurally analogous mathematical solutions. In the tulips and vases example, because the inferred containment relation between the objects is asymmetric (tulips are in vases rather than vice versa), people select a mathematically asymmetric solution (e.g., the division operation, which is asymmetric because $a \div b \neq b \div a$). In a complementary way, objects from the same taxonomic category (e.g., tulips, roses) evoke a symmetric semantic relation (both tulips and roses are flowers), and the semantically symmetric situation model leads people to select a mathematically symmetric solution (e.g., the addition operation, which is symmetric because $a + b = b + a$). Bassok et al. refer to this two-stage process as *semantic alignment*.

Semantic alignments affect how students solve novel mathematical word problems. For example, Bassok, Wu, and Olseth (1995) asked college students to solve unfamiliar permutation problems that involved random assignment of three objects from one set to another set. They used two sets of mathematically identical problems that varied with respect to the objects in the set of assignees (m) and those in the assigned set (n). Most subjects who attempted to solve these novel problems arrived at incorrect solutions that revealed systematic effects of semantic alignment. When the problems involved assignment of semantically asymmetric sets (e.g., m computers assigned to n secretaries), the solutions of most subjects placed the numbers representing the two sets in mathematically asymmetric structural roles (e.g., $m^3/n!$ or $m/3n$); however, when the problems involved assignment of semantically symmetric sets (e.g., m doctors from one hospital assigned to n doctors from another hospital), the solutions of most subjects placed the numbers representing the two sets in mathematically symmetric structural roles [e.g., $(m + n)/(mn)^3$, $3/(m + n)!$]. That is, the incorrect solutions students generated to the permutation problems were structurally analogous to the semantic relation evoked by the paired sets.

Semantic alignments also determine the relative difficulty of mathematically isomorphic problems. Martin and Bassok (in press) asked middle school, high school, and college students to solve simple division word problems, such as the following: "At a certain university, there are 3,450 students. There are 6 times as many students as professors. How many professors are there?" In this example, the semantic relation between the described sets is asymmetric (professors teach students) and therefore semantically aligned with the correct (asymmetric) division operation. In other problems, the semantic relation between the described sets was symmetric and therefore misaligned with the correct (asymmetric) division operation. For example: "On a given day, a certain factory produces 3,450 nails. It produces 6 times as many nails as screws. How many screws does it produce?" Students at all grade levels were more successful at solving the aligned than the misaligned problems, although the difference was most pronounced in middle school: 80% of seventh graders solved the students and professors problem, but only 40% solved the nails and screws problem.

Guthormsen, Bassok, Osterhout, and Inoue (2002) found evidence from electrophysiological data that semantic alignments occur very early in the solution process, when solvers read mathematical problems. People had to solve mathematically aligned problems, such as 3 *tulips* + 5 *daisies* =, and mathematically misaligned problems, such as 3 *tulips* + 5 *vases* =. Their event-related potentials (ERPs) revealed a significantly larger response of a certain specific type (the N400 response, a negative electrical response occurring approximately 400 ms after the event) to the misaligned target word (vases) than to the aligned target word (daisies). This pattern is consistent with other evidence that N400 is evoked by detection of semantic anomalies.

Insight Problem Solving Revisited

OVERVIEW

We introduced the notion of insight in our discussion of perceptual factors affecting solvers' representations of the nine-dot problem. As we mentioned, the Gestalt view (e.g., Duncker, 1945; Maier, 1931; see Ohlsson, 1984a, for a review) is that insight problem solving is characterized by an initial work period during which no progress toward solution is made (i.e., an impasse), a sudden restructuring of one's problem representation to a more suitable form, followed immediately by the sudden appearance of the solution. Thus, solving insight problems is all about representation with essentially no role for a step-by-step process of generating the solution. Although subsequent and contemporary researchers concur with the Gestalt view that getting the right representation is crucial, this view does not provide a complete understanding of the nature of insight solutions because the solution does not necessarily arise suddenly or full-blown following restructuring (e.g., Weisberg & Alba, 1981). Kershaw and Ohlsson (2004) argued that insight problems are difficult because the key behavior required for solution may be hindered by perceptual factors (this is the Gestalt perspective), background knowledge, and/or process factors (e.g., the amount of mental look-ahead required to find the solution). A full understanding of insight problem solving, like non-insight problem solving, requires attention to both representation and process. The interplay between these two factors is illustrated in the two subsections that follow in which we consider (1) whether insight solutions arise full blown and (2) what explains the initial impasse and its resolution.

DO INSIGHT SOLUTIONS ARISE FULL BLOWN?

We noted in our earlier discussion of Weisberg and Alba's (1981) research that solution of the nine-dot problem was neither quick nor direct following the restructuring hint. For example, subjects who solved the problem generally required 5 to 11 solution attempts after the hint to achieve success. Multiple solution attempts were needed because the required restructuring of one's problem representation – realizing that (1) the lines may extend outside the imaginary square boundary formed by the dots, and (2) they may intersect at points in space that do not contain dots (Kershaw & Ohlsson, 2004) – suggests a new problem space, with alternative operators, through which the solver can search for the correct solution (Lung & Dominowski, 1985; Ohlsson, 1984b; Weisberg & Alba, 1981).

For other problems, the required restructuring "brings the goal state within the horizon of mental look-ahead" (Ohlsson, 1984b, p. 124), yielding insight in the traditional sense of sudden understanding of the solution. For example, explain the following situation (Durso, Rea, & Dayton, 1994, p. 95): "A man walks into a bar and asks for a glass of water. The bartender points a shotgun at the man. The man says 'Thank you,' and walks out." The solution to this problem typically pops into mind suddenly and fully intact, accompanied by an irresistible feeling of "aha!" Moreover, the solver has no awareness of incremental progress toward the goal such as that which accompanies search solutions. (The solution to the barroom puzzle is that the man had the hiccups. The bartender scared him with the gun, which cured him.) Anagrams are also known to yield such "pop-out" solutions (e.g., Mendelsohn & O'Brien, 1974), especially among highly skilled anagram solvers (Novick & Sherman, 2003a).

For problems that yield pop-out solutions – that is, for which solvers have the phenomenological experience of insight – the question remains as to whether the solutions arise full blown or through the gradual accumulation of relevant partial information as for the nine-dot problem and noninsight problems (e.g., simplifying algebra equations to solve for X). Durso et al. (1994) investigated this issue using the barroom puzzle. In one experiment, they collected similarity ratings for 12 pairs of concepts at several points during subjects' solution attempts – before and after reading the puzzle, every 10 minutes until the puzzle was solved, and immediately after the solution. The concept pairs included two insight pairs (*surprise/remedy* and *relieved/thank you*) that the results of an initial experiment showed were connected in the conceptual networks of solvers but not nonsolvers. The results suggested that the key restructuring required for solution did not arise full-blown contrary to the Gestalt view of insight: The two insight pairs that were critical for solution were seen as dissimilar at the first two time points, moderately similar at the next two time points, and highly similar after solution. In contrast, the unrelated pairs (e.g., *pretzel/shotgun*) were seen as dissimilar and the related pairs (e.g., *shotgun/loaded*) as similar at all time points.

Novick and Sherman (2003a) noted, however, that having to repeatedly rate the similarity of concepts that were critical for solution may have changed subjects' solution strategies. This possibility led them to provide an additional test of the hypothesis using anagrams. The accrual of partial information was tested using a solvability judgment task in which subjects had to indicate whether letter strings (e.g., *nrtai*, *botda*) could be unscrambled to form an English word (only the first of the two examples is solvable – *train*). A deadline procedure forced subjects to make their yes/no judgments based on any partial information that had accrued prior to the deadline. On average, subjects' responses were made within approximately 650 or 1130 ms after the onset of the letter string. By testing highly skilled and less skilled anagram solvers on anagrams that were known to yield pop-out solutions (for experts) or not, Novick and Sherman were able to assess whether pop-out solutions arise full blown or are preceded by the gradual accumulation of partial information (outside awareness). Consistent with Durso et al.'s (1994) results, and contrary to the Gestalt view, they found that pop-out solutions arise gradually through the accumulation of relevant partial information (also see Bowden & Jung-Beeman, 2003).

Despite this important similarity between insight and noninsight solutions, phenomenologically, the two types of solutions are different. The solver is aware of the accumulation of partial information for noninsight solutions – for example, consider the Hobbits and Orcs problem or the problem of simplifying an algebra equation to solve for X – but that accumulation occurs outside awareness for insight solutions (e.g., the barroom puzzle, anagrams). Novick and Sherman (2003a, 2003b) hypothesized that pop-out solutions to anagrams, which are characteristic of experts, may result from a parallel constraint satisfaction process; in contrast, nonpop-out anagram solutions result from a conscious process of serially testing and rejecting hypotheses (e.g., Mendelsohn & O'Brien, 1974).

THE IMPASSE AND ITS RESOLUTION

As discussed by Knoblich, Ohlsson, Haider, and Rhenius (1999), theories of insight problem solving need to explain two phenomena concerning the interplay between representation and solution generation: (1) why solvers initially reach an impasse in solving a problem for which they have the necessary knowledge to generate the solution, and (2) what enables them to break out of the impasse. Two recent theories have attempted to account for these phenomena – MacGregor, Ormerod, and Chronicle's (2001) progress monitoring theory, and Knoblich et al.'s representational change theory.

According to the progress monitoring theory, solvers use hill climbing (see "Problem Solving as Search through a Problem Space") in their solution attempts for insight as well as noninsight problems. Solvers are hypothesized to monitor their progress toward solution using a criterion generated from the problem's current state. For the nine-dot problem, for example, this criterion is the number of dots through which lines have been drawn relative to the number of dots remaining. If solvers reach criterion failure, they seek alternative solutions by trying to relax one or more problem constraints. The nine-dot problem is difficult, according to this theory, because criterion failure is not reached until the fourth move (recall that the problem must be solved in four moves). MacGregor et al. (2001) found support for this theory using several variants of the nine-dot problem (also see Ormerod, MacGregor, & Chronicle, 2002).

According to Knoblich et al.'s (1999) representational change theory, insight problems are highly likely to evoke initial representations in which solvers place inappropriate constraints on their solution attempts. Impasses are resolved by revising one's representation of the problem. They tested this theory using Roman numeral matchstick arithmetic problems in which solvers must move one stick to a new location to change a false numeric statement (e.g., VI = VIII + III) into a statement that is true. According to Knoblich et al.'s theory, rerepresentation may happen through either of two mechanisms – constraint relaxation or chunk decomposition. *Constraint relaxation* involves deactivating some knowledge element that has constrained the operators being considered, thereby allowing application of new operators: For example, changing II + to III – requires relaxation of the value constraint (numeric values do not change except by applying an operation that produces a compensating change in some other value). *Chunk decomposition* involves breaking the bonds that link components of a meaningful unit in the problem: For example, changing II + to III – requires decomposition of the plus sign. (The solution to the this problem is to break apart the first V and change it to an X, yielding XI = VIII + III). Knoblich et al. found good support for their theory using solution rate and solution time as their dependent measures. Knoblich, Ohlsson, and Raney (2001) found additional support using eye fixation data.

Jones (2003) attempted to distinguish the progress monitoring and representational change theories using eye fixation data as subjects solved the car park problem. In this problem, the goal is to maneuver a taxi out of a car park. Other cars need to be moved out of the way, and there are constraints on how cars may be moved. Jones' results supported predictions from both theories, although the effects of the experimental manipulations suggested that the representational change theory is a better predictor of performance. Based on his data, Jones argued that the two theories should be combined into a single theory. This makes sense because Knoblich et al.'s (1999) theory focuses more on the representational aspect of problem solution, whereas MacGregor et al.'s (2001) theory focuses more on the step-by-step solution process. Jones noted that the progress monitoring theory provides an account of the solution process up to the point that the impasse is reached and representational change is sought. The representational change theory picks up at this point and explains how insight may be achieved.

Conclusions and Directions for Future Research

In this chapter, we examined two broad components of the problem-solving process – representation and solution generation. Although it is possible to focus one's research on one or the other of these components, a full understanding of problem solving requires an integration of the two, for the representation one constructs for a problem determines (or at least constrains) how one goes about trying to generate a solution. This interplay is obvious for mathematical problem solving, as we discussed in the previous section. Consideration of both representation and solution generation also seems to be behind the resurgence of interest in insight problem solving. This new strategy for investigating insight seems to be yielding progress in understanding this fascinating phenomenon that is at the core of human creative endeavors. We believe the interplay between representation and solution generation will lead to significant progress in understanding the full range of activities considered to be problem solving. Elevating this interplay to the status of a core assumption, we want to suggest three directions for future research.

First, we would stress the importance of conducting educationally relevant research. Students spend a considerable amount of time both solving problems and learning how to solve problems. Society expects that the problem-solving lessons learned in school – from how to solve math problems to how to design and execute a science fair project to how to analyze literature – will transfer to students' adult lives for the betterment of the world. We believe that a two-pronged effort is needed here: (1) It is important to gain a better understanding of students' contributions to problem solving. What are their goals, beliefs, strategies, and conceptions? How do they construct meaning and infer structure? (2) At the same time, there is an objective reality to problems, messy though they may sometimes be. The nature of a problem's underlying structure places constraints on the types of representations that will be useful or appropriate, which in turn determine the types of solution methods that will be effective and efficient. It is important, therefore, to understand the factors that facilitate or hinder a student's ability to represent a problem's structure as well as to investigate methods for helping students to succeed in this endeavor. The National Council of Teachers of Mathematics (2000) similarly promotes the importance of teaching students how to create and use a variety of different types of representations to model phenomena in the world. Effective problem solving and reasoning, as well as creative invention, all require appropriate models as their starting point.

Second, the trend toward examining more complex, knowledge-intensive problems should continue. Although the available evidence suggests that many of the conclusions about problem solving drawn from research on well-defined problems are applicable to ill-defined problems, messy, knowledge-intensive, real-world problems may not be simply scaled-up versions of laboratory tasks or of tasks practiced in school. The critical problems of the day, at any given point in history, are always ill defined in some way. Investigation of such problems (e.g., in science, medicine, and technology) is likely to yield both theoretical and practical payoffs.

Finally, we come full circle and end where we began. The last direction is suggested by the definition of a problem given by Karl Duncker, arguably the father of research on problem solving. He defined a problem as a situation in which a desired goal cannot be attained by direct application of known operators, and so "there has to be recourse to thinking" (Duncker, 1945, p. 1). Our review of problem-solving research in this chapter has been rather narrow – focusing on puzzles (e.g., Hobbits and Orcs, Tower of Hanoi, anagrams, the nine-dot problem) and on mathematical problems. However, Duncker's reference to thinking is quite broad. By Duncker's definition, humans engage in problem solving when they pursue the following goal-directed activities: (1) placing objects into categories and making inferences based on category membership, (2) making inductive inferences from multiple instances, (3) reasoning by analogy, (4) identifying the causes of events, (5) deducing logical implications of given information, (6) making legal judgments, and (7) diagnosing medical conditions from historical and laboratory data. Much of the material included in the chapters on these topics in the present volume arguably could have appeared in our chapter on problem solving. Rather than engaging in a turf battle, we would suggest that research on problem solving be integrated with research in these other areas of thinking, or that research in these other areas be informed by insights gained from research on what has more traditionally been identified as problem solving.

References

Adams, J. L. (1979). *Conceptual blockbusting: A guide to better ideas* (2nd ed.). New York: Norton.

Adelson, B. (1981). Problem solving and the development of abstract categories in programming languages. *Memory and Cognition*, 9, 422–433.

Alibali, M. W., Bassok, M., Solomon, K. O., Syc, S. E., & Goldin-Meadow, S. (1999). Illuminating mental representations through speech and gesture. *Psychological Science*, 10, 327–333.

Allard, F., & Starkes, J. L. (1991). Motor-skill experts in sports, dance, and other domains. In K. A. Ericsson & J. Smith (Eds.), *Toward a general theory of expertise: Prospects and limits* (pp. 126–152). New York: Cambridge University Press.

Anderson, R. C., Reynolds, R. E., Schallert, D. L., & Goetz, E. T. (1977). Frameworks for comprehending discourse. *American Educational Research Journal*, 14, 367–381.

Anzai, Y., & Simon, H. A. (1979). The theory of learning by doing. *Psychological Review*, 86, 124–140.

Bassok, M. (2001). Semantic alignments in mathematical word problems. In D. Gentner, K. J. Holyoak, & B. N. Kokinov (Eds.), *The analogical mind: Perspectives from cognitive science* (pp. 401–433). Cambridge, MA: MIT Press.

Bassok, M., Chase, V. M., & Martin, S. A. (1998). Adding apples and oranges: Alignment of semantic and formal knowledge. *Cognitive Psychology*, 35, 99–134.

Bassok, M., & Holyoak, K. J. (1989). Interdomain transfer between isomorphic topics in algebra and physics. *Journal of Experimental Psychology: Learning, Memory, and Cognition*, 15, 153–166.

Bassok, M., & Olseth, K. L. (1995). Object-based representations: Transfer between cases of continuous and discrete models of change. *Journal of Experimental Psychology: Learning, Memory, and Cognition*, 21, 1522–1538.

Bassok, M., Wu, L., & Olseth, L. K. (1995). Judging a book by its cover: Interpretative effects of content on problem solving transfer. *Memory and Cognition*, 23, 354–367.

Bowden, E. M., & Jung-Beeman, M. (2003). Aha! Insight experience correlates with solution activation in the right hemisphere. *Psychonomic Bulletin and Review*, 10, 730–737.

Bransford, J. D., & McCarrell, N. S. (1974). A sketch of a cognitive approach to comprehension: Some thoughts about understanding what it means to comprehend. In W. B. Weimer & D. S. Palermo (Eds.), *Cognition and the symbolic processes* (pp. 189–229). Hillsdale, NJ: Erlbaum.

Catrambone, R. (1996). Generalizing solution procedures learned from examples. *Journal of Experimental Psychology: Learning, Memory, and Cognition*, 22, 1020–1031.

Catrambone, R. (1998). The subgoal learning model: Creating better examples so that students can solve novel problems. *Journal of Experimental Psychology: General*, 127, 355–376.

Chase, W. G., & Simon, H. A. (1973). Perception in chess. *Cognitive Psychology*, 4, 55–81.

Chi, M. T. H., Bassok, M., Lewis, M. W., Reimann, P., & Glaser, R. (1989). Self-explanations: How students study and use examples in learning to solve problems. *Cognitive Science*, 13, 145–182.

Chi, M. T. H., Feltovich, P. J., & Glaser, R. (1981). Categorization and representation of physics problems by experts and novices. *Cognitive Science*, 5, 121–152.

Chronicle, E. P., MacGregor, J. N., & Ormerod, T. C. (2004). What makes an insight problem? The roles of heuristics, goal conception, and solution recoding in knowledge-lean problems. *Journal of Experimental Psychology: Learning, Memory, and Cognition*, 30, 14–27.

Coughlin, L. D., & Patel, V. L. (1987). Processing of critical information by physicians and medical students. *Journal of Medical Education*, 62, 818–828.

Deakin, J. M., & Allard, F. (1991). Skilled memory in expert figure skaters. *Memory and Cognition*, 19, 79–86.

de Groot, A. D. (1966). Perception and memory versus thought: Some old ideas and recent findings. In B. Kleinmuntz (Ed.), *Problem solving: Research, method, and theory* (pp. 19–50). New York: Wiley.

Dunbar, K. (2001). The analogical paradox: Why analogy is so easy in naturalistic settings, yet so difficult in the psychological laboratory. In D. Gentner, K. J. Holyoak, & B. Kokinov (Eds.), *Analogy: Perspectives from cognitive science* (pp. 313–362). Cambridge, MA: MIT Press.

Duncker, K. (1945). On problem-solving (L. S. Lees, Trans.). *Psychological Monographs*, 58 (Whole No. 270). (Original work published 1935.)

Durso, F. T., Rea, C. B., & Dayton, T. (1994). Graph-theoretic confirmation of restructuring during insight. *Psychological Science*, 5, 94–98.

Egan, D. E., & Schwartz, B. J. (1979). Chunking in the recall of symbolic drawings. *Memory and Cognition*, 7, 149–158.

Ericsson, K. A., & Simon, H. A. (1980). Verbal reports as data. *Psychological Review*, 87, 215–251.

Ernst, G. W., & Newell, A. (1969). *GPS: A case study in generality and problem solving*. New York: Academic Press.

Gick, M. L., & Holyoak, K. J. (1980). Analogical problem solving. *Cognitive Psychology*, 12, 306–355.

Gick, M. L., & Holyoak, K. J. (1983). Schema induction and analogical transfer. *Cognitive Psychology*, 15, 1–38.

Gobet, F., & Simon, H. (1996). Recall of rapidly presented random chess positions is a function of skill. *Psychonomic Bulletin and Review*, 3, 159–163.

Greeno, J. G. (1974). Hobbits and orcs: Acquisition of a sequential concept. *Cognitive Psychology*, 6, 270–292.

Greeno, J. G. (1977). Process of understanding in problem solving. In N. J. Castellan, Jr., D. B. Pisoni, & G. R. Potts (Eds.), *Cognitive theory* (Vol. 2, pp. 43–83). Hillsdale, NJ: Erlbaum.

Greeno, J. G. (1978). Natures of problem-solving abilities. In W. K. Estes (Ed.), *Handbook of learning and cognitive processes* (Vol. 5, pp. 239–270). Hillsdale, NJ: Erlbaum.

Greeno, J. G., & Simon, H. A. (1988). Problem solving and reasoning. In R. C. Atkinson, R. J. Herrnstein, G. Lindzey, & R. D. Luce (Eds.), *Stevens' handbook of experimental psychology* (2nd ed., Vol. 2, pp. 589–672). New York: Wiley.

Guthormsen, A., Bassok, M., Osterhout, L., & Inoue, K. (2002, November). *ERP as a measure of alignment between mathematical and semantic relations*. Paper presented at the 43rd annual meeting of the Psychonomic Society, Kansas City, MO.

Hardiman, P. T., Dufresne, R., & Mestre, J. P. (1989). The relation between problem categorization and problem solving among experts and novices. *Memory and Cognition*, 17, 627–638.

Hayes, J. R., & Simon, H. A. (1977). Psychological differences among problem isomorphs. In N. J. Castellan, D. B. Pisoni, & G. R. Potts (Eds.), *Cognitive theory* (Vol. 2, pp. 21–44). Hillsdale, NJ: Erlbaum.

Hegarty, M., Carpenter, P. A., & Just, M. A. (1991). Diagrams in the comprehension of scientific texts. In R. Barr, M. L. Kamil, P. Mosenthal, & P. D. Pearson (Eds.), *Handbook of reading research* (Vol. 2, pp. 641–668). New York: Longman.

Holding, D. H. (1985). *The psychology of chess skill*. Hillsdale, NJ: Erlbaum.

Holyoak, K. J. (1985). The pragmatics of analogical transfer. In G. H. Bower (Ed.), *The psychology of learning and motivation* (Vol. 19, pp. 59–87). New York: Academic Press.

Hurley, S. M., & Novick, L. R. (2004). *Context and structure: The nature of students' knowledge about three spatial diagram representations*. Manuscript under review.

Jones, G. (2003). Testing two cognitive theories of insight. *Journal of Experimental Psychology: Learning, Memory, and Cognition*, 29, 1017–1027.

Kershaw, T. C., & Ohlsson, S. (2004). Multiple causes of difficulty in insight: The case of the nine-dot problem. *Journal of Experimental Psychology: Learning, Memory, and Cognition*, 30, 3–13.

Kindfield, A. C. H. (1993/1994). Biology diagrams: Tools to think with. *Journal of the Learning Sciences*, 3, 1–36.

Knoblich, G., Ohlsson, S., Haider, H., & Rhenius, D. (1999). Constraint relaxation and chunk decomposition in insight problem solving. *Journal of Experimental Psychology: Learning, Memory, and Cognition*, 25, 1534–1555.

Knoblich, G., Ohlsson, S., & Raney, G. E. (2001). An eye movement study of insight problem solving. *Memory and Cognition*, 29, 1000–1009.

Kotovsky, K., Hayes, J. R., & Simon, H. A. (1985). Why are some problems hard? Evidence from Tower of Hanoi. *Cognitive Psychology*, 17, 248–294.

Lung, C.-T., & Dominowski, R. L. (1985). Effects of strategy instructions and practice on nine-dot problem solving. *Journal of Experimental Psychology: Learning, Memory, and Cognition, 11*, 804–811.

MacGregor, J. N., Ormerod, T. C., & Chronicle, E. P. (2001). Information processing and insight: A process model of performance on the nine-dot and related problems. *Journal of Experimental Psychology: Learning, Memory, and Cognition, 27*, 176–201.

Maier, N. (1930). Reasoning in humans. I. On direction. *Journal of Comparative Psychology, 10*, 15–43.

Maier, N. (1931). Reasoning in humans. II. The solution of a problem and its appearance in consciousness. *Journal of Comparative Psychology, 12*, 181–194.

Markman, A. B. (1999). *Knowledge representation*. Mahwah, NJ: Erlbaum.

Martin, S. A., & Bassok, M. (in press). Effects of semantic cues on mathematical modeling: Evidence from word-problem solving and equation construction tasks. *Memory and Cognition*.

McKeithen, K. B., Reitman, J. S., Rueter, H. H., & Hirtle, S. C. (1981). Knowledge organization and skill differences in computer programmers. *Cognitive Psychology, 13*, 307–325.

Mendelsohn, G. A., & O'Brien, A. T. (1974). The solution of anagrams: A reexamination of the effects of transition letter probabilities, letter moves, and word frequency on anagram difficulty. *Memory and Cognition, 2*, 566–574.

Myles-Worsley, M., Johnston, W. A., & Simons, M. A (1988). The influence of expertise on X-ray image processing. *Journal of Experimental Psychology: Learning, Memory, and Cognition, 14*, 553–557.

National Council of Teachers of Mathematics. (2000). *Principles and standards for school mathematics*. Reston, VA: Author.

Newell, A., & Simon, H. A. (1972). *Human problem solving*. Englewood Cliffs, NJ: Prentice-Hall.

Novick, L. R. (1988). Analogical transfer, problem similarity, and expertise. *Journal of Experimental Psychology: Learning, Memory, and Cognition, 14*, 510–520.

Novick, L. R. (2001). Spatial diagrams: Key instruments in the toolbox for thought. In D. L. Medin (Ed.), *The psychology of learning and motivation* (Vol. 40, pp. 279–325). San Diego: Academic Press.

Novick, L. R., & Hmelo, C. E. (1994). Transferring symbolic representations across nonisomorphic problems. *Journal of Experimental Psychology: Learning, Memory, and Cognition, 20*, 1296–1321.

Novick, L. R., & Holyoak, K. J. (1991). Mathematical problem solving by analogy. *Journal of Experimental Psychology: Learning, Memory, and Cognition, 17*, 398–415.

Novick, L. R., & Hurley, S. M. (2001). To matrix, network, or hierarchy: That is the question. *Cognitive Psychology, 42*, 158–216.

Novick, L. R., Hurley, S. M., & Francis, M. (1999). Evidence for abstract, schematic knowledge of three spatial diagram representations. *Memory and Cognition, 27*, 288–308.

Novick, L. R., & Sherman, S. J. (2003a). On the nature of insight solutions: Evidence from skill differences in anagram solution. *The Quarterly Journal of Experimental Psychology, 56A*, 351–382.

Novick, L. R., & Sherman, S. J. (2003b). *The effects of superficial and structural information on on-line problem solving as a function of expertise*. Manuscript under revision.

Novick, L. R., & Sherman, S. J. (2004). Type-based bigram frequencies for five-letter words. *Behavior Research Methods, Instruments, and Computers*.

Ohlsson, S. (1984a). Restructuring revisited I. Summary and critique of the Gestalt theory of problem solving. *Scandinavian Journal of Psychology, 25*, 65–78.

Ohlsson, S. (1984b). Restructuring revisited II. An information processing theory of restructuring and insight. *Scandinavian Journal of Psychology, 25*, 117–129.

Ormerod, T. C., MacGregor, J. N., & Chronicle, E. P. (2002). Dynamics and constraints in insight problem solving. *Journal of Experimental Psychology: Learning, Memory, and Cognition, 28*, 791–799.

Polya, G. (1957). *How to solve it* (2nd ed.). Princeton, NJ: Princeton University Press.

Posner, M. I. (1973). *Cognition: An introduction*. Glenview, IL: Scott, Foresman and Company.

Reitman, W. R. (1965). *Cognition and thought*. New York: Wiley.

Ronning, R. R. (1965). Anagram solution times: A function of the "ruleout" factor. *Journal of Experimental Psychology, 69*, 35–39.

Ross, B. H., & Kennedy, P. T. (1990). Generalizing from the use of earlier examples in problem solving. *Journal of Experimental Psychology: Learning, Memory, and Cognition, 16*, 42–55.

Russo, J. E., Johnson, E. J., & Stephens, D. L. (1989). The validity of verbal protocols. *Memory and Cognition, 17*, 759–769.

Schiano, D., Cooper, L. A., Glaser, R., & Zhang, H. C. (1989). Highs are to lows as experts are to novices: Individual differences in the representation and solution of standardized figural analogies. *Human Performance, 2*, 225–248.

Schoenfeld, A. H., & Herrmann, D. J. (1982). Problem perception and knowledge structure in expert and novice mathematical problem solvers. *Journal of Experimental Psychology: Learning, Memory, and Cognition, 8*, 484–494.

Schwartz, D. L., & Black, J. B. (1996). Shuttling between depictive models and abstract rules: Induction and fallback. *Cognitive Science, 20*, 457–497.

Silver, E. A. (1979). Student perceptions of relatedness among mathematical verbal problems. *Journal for Research in Mathematics Education, 10*, 195–210.

Silver, E. A. (1981). Recall of mathematical problem information: Solving related problems. *Journal for Research in Mathematics Education, 12*, 54–64.

Simon, H. A. (1978). Information-processing theory of human problem solving. In W. K. Estes (Ed.), *Handbook of learning and cognitive processes* (Vol. 5, pp. 271–295). Hillsdale, NJ: Erlbaum.

Stigler, J. W. (1984). "Mental abacus": The effect of abacus training on Chinese children's mental calculation. *Cognitive Psychology, 16*, 145–176.

Thomas, J. C., Jr. (1974). An analysis of behavior in the hobbits-orcs problem. *Cognitive Psychology, 6*, 257–269.

Weisberg, R. W., & Alba, J. W. (1981). An examination of the alleged role of "fixation" in the solution of several "insight" problems. *Journal of Experimental Psychology: General, 110*, 169–192.

Weiser, M., & Shertz, J. (1983). Programming problem representation in novice and expert programmers. *International Journal of Man-Machine Studies, 19*, 391–398.

Wertheimer, M. (1959). *Productive thinking* (enlarged ed.). Chicago: The University of Chicago Press.

Wickelgren, W. A. (1974). *How to solve problems*. San Francisco: Freeman Press.

CHAPTER 15

Creativity

Robert J. Sternberg
Todd I. Lubart
James C. Kaufman
Jean E. Pretz

Creativity is the ability to produce work that is novel (i.e., original, unexpected), high in quality, and appropriate (i.e., useful, meets task constraints) (Lubart, 1994; Ochse, 1990; Sternberg, 1988a, 1999c; Sternberg & Lubart, 1995, 1996). Creativity is a topic of wide scope that is important at both the individual and societal levels for a wide range of task domains. At an individual level, creativity is relevant, for example, when solving problems on the job and in daily life. At a societal level, creativity can lead to new scientific findings, new movements in art, new inventions, and new social programs. The economic importance of creativity is clear because new products or services create jobs. Furthermore, individuals, organizations, and societies must adapt existing resources to changing task demands to remain competitive.

This chapter attempts to provide readers with a basic understanding of the literature on creativity. It first reviews alternative approaches to understanding creativity. Then it reviews alternative approaches to understanding kinds of creative work. Finally, it draws some conclusions.

Creativity may be viewed as taking place in the interaction between a person and the person's environment (Amabile, 1996; Csikszentmihalyi, 1996, 1999; Feldman, 1999; Feldman, Csikszentmihalyi, & Gardner, 1994; Sternberg, 1985a; Sternberg & Lubart, 1995). According to this view, the essence of creativity cannot be captured just as an intrapersonal variable. Thus, we can characterize a person's cognitive processes as more or less creative (Finke, Ward, & Smith, 1992; Rubenson & Runco, 1992; Weisberg, 1986), or the person as having a more or less creative personality (Barron, 1988; Feist, 1999). We further can describe the person as having a motivational pattern that is more or less typical of creative individuals (Hennessey & Amabile, 1988), or even as having background variables that more or less dispose that person to think creatively (Simonton, 1984, 1994). However, we cannot fully judge that person's creativity independent of the field and the temporal context in which the person works.

For example, a contemporary artist might have thought processes, personality, motivation, and even background variables similar to those of Monet, but that artist, painting today in the style of Monet or of Impressionism in general, probably would not be judged to be creative in the way Monet was. Artists, including Monet, have experimented with Impressionism, and unless the contemporary artist introduced some new twist, he or she might be viewed as imitative rather than creative.

The importance of context is illustrated by the difference, in general, between creative discovery and rediscovery. For example, BACON and related programs of Langley, Simon, Bradshaw, and Zytkow (1987) rediscover important scientific theorems that were judged to be creative discoveries in their time. The processes by which these discoveries are made via computer simulation are presumably not identical to those by which the original discoverers made their discoveries. One difference derives from the fact that contemporary programmers can provide, in their programming of information into computer simulations, representations and particular organizations of data that may not have been available to the original creators. However, putting aside the question of whether the processes are the same, a rediscovery might be judged to be creative with respect to the rediscoverer but would not be judged to be creative with respect to the field at the time the rediscovery is made. Ramanujan, the famous Indian mathematician, made many such rediscoveries. A brilliant thinker, he did not have access in his early life to much of the recent literature on mathematics and so unwittingly regenerated many discoveries that others had made before him.

Alternative Approaches to Creativity

Mystical Approaches to the Study of Creativity

The study of creativity has always been tinged – some might say tainted – with associations to mystical beliefs. Perhaps the earliest accounts of creativity were based on divine intervention. The creative person was seen as an empty vessel that a divine being would fill with inspiration. The individual would then pour out the inspired ideas, forming an otherworldly product.

In this vein, Plato argued that a poet is able to create only that which the Muse dictates, and even today, people sometimes refer to their own Muse as a source of inspiration. In Plato's view, one person might be inspired to create choral songs, another, epic poems (Rothenberg & Hausman, 1976). Often, mystical sources have been suggested in creators' introspective reports (Ghiselin, 1985). For example, Rudyard Kipling referred to the "Daemon" that lives in the writer's pen: "My Daemon was with me in the Jungle Books, Kim, and both Puck books, and good care I took to walk delicately, lest he should withdraw.... When your Daemon is in charge, do not think consciously. Drift, wait, and obey" (Kipling, 1985, p. 162).

The mystical approaches to the study of creativity have probably made it harder for scientists to be heard. Many people seem to believe, as they believe for love (see Sternberg, 1988b, 1988c), that creativity is something that just does not lend itself to scientific study because it is a more spiritual process. We believe it has been hard for scientific work to shake the deep-seated view of some that, somehow, scientists are treading where they should not.

Pragmatic Approaches

Equally damaging for the scientific study of creativity, in our view, has been the takeover of the field, in the popular mind, by those who follow what might be referred to as a pragmatic approach. Those taking this approach have been concerned primarily with developing creativity, secondarily with understanding it, but almost not at all with testing the validity of their ideas about it.

Perhaps the foremost proponent of this approach is Edward De Bono, whose work on *lateral thinking* – seeing things broadly and from varied viewpoints – as well as other aspects of creativity has had what appears to be considerable commercial success (e.g., De

Bono, 1971, 1985, 1992). DeBono's concern is not with theory, but with practice. Thus, for example, he suggests using a tool such as "Positive-Minus-Interesting" (PMI) to focus on the aspects of an idea that are pluses, minuses, and interesting. Or he suggests using the word "po," derived from hypothesis, suppose, possible, and poetry, to provoke rather than to judge ideas. Another tool, that of "thinking hats," has individuals metaphorically wear different hats, such as a white hat for data-based thinking, a red hat for intuitive thinking, a black hat for critical thinking, and a green hat for generative thinking, in order to stimulate seeing things from different points of view.

DeBono is not alone in this enterprise. Osborn (1953), based on his experiences in advertising agencies, developed the technique of brainstorming to encourage people to solve problems creatively by seeking many possible solutions in an atmosphere that is constructive rather than critical and inhibitory. Gordon (1961) developed a method called synectics, which involves primarily seeing analogies, also for stimulating creative thinking.

More recently, authors such as Adams (1974, 1986) and von Oech (1983) suggested that people often construct a series of false beliefs that interfere with creative functioning. For example, some people believe that there is only one "right" answer and that ambiguity must be avoided whenever possible. People can become creative by identifying and removing these mental blocks. Von Oech (1986) also suggested that to be creative we need to adopt the roles of explorer, artist, judge, and warrior in order to foster our creative productivity.

These approaches have had considerable public visibility, and they may well be useful. From our point of view as psychologists, however, most of these approaches lack any basis in serious psychological theory as well as serious empirical attempts to validate them. Of course, techniques can work in the absence of psychological theory or validation. However, the effect of such approaches is often to leave people associating a phenomenon with commercialization and to see it as less than a serious endeavor for psychological study.

The Psychodynamic Approach

The psychodynamic approach can be considered the first of the major twentieth-century theoretical approaches to the study of creativity. On the basis of the idea that creativity arises from the tension between conscious reality and unconscious drives, Freud (1908/1959) proposed that writers and artists produce creative work as a way to express their unconscious desires in a publicly acceptable fashion. These unconscious desires may concern power, riches, fame, honor, or love (Vernon, 1970). Case studies of eminent creators, such as Leonardo da Vinci (Freud, 1910/1964), were used to support these ideas.

Later, the psychoanalytic approach introduced the concepts of adaptive regression and elaboration for creativity (Kris, 1952). *Adaptive regression*, the primary process, refers to the intrusion of unmodulated thoughts in consciousness. Unmodulated thoughts can occur during active problem solving but often occur during sleep, intoxication from drugs, fantasies or daydreams, or psychoses. *Elaboration*, the secondary process, refers to the reworking and transformation of primary process material through reality-oriented, ego-controlled thinking. Other theorists (e.g., Kubie, 1958) emphasized that the preconscious, which falls between conscious reality and the encrypted unconscious, is the true source of creativity because thoughts are loose and vague but interpretable. In contrast to Freud, Kubie claimed that unconscious conflicts actually have a negative effect on creativity because they lead to fixated, repetitive thoughts. More recent work has recognized the importance of both primary and secondary processes (Noy, 1969; Rothenberg, 1979; Suler, 1980; Werner & Kaplan, 1963).

Although the psychodynamic approach may have offered some insights into creativity, psychodynamic theory was not at the center of the emerging scientific psychology.

The early twentieth-century schools of psychology, such as structuralism, functionalism, and behaviorism, were devoting practically no resources at all to the study of creativity. The Gestaltists studied a portion of creativity – insight – but their study never went much beyond labeling, as opposed to characterizing the nature of insight.

Further isolating creativity research, the psychodynamic approach and other early work on creativity relied on case studies of eminent creators. This methodology has been criticized historically because of the difficulty of measuring proposed theoretical constructs (e.g., primary process thought), and the amount of selection and interpretation that can occur in a case study (Weisberg, 1993). Although there is nothing a priori wrong with case study methods, the emerging scientific psychology valued controlled, experimental methods. Thus, both theoretical and methodological issues served to isolate the study of creativity from mainstream psychology.

Psychometric Approaches

When we think of creativity, eminent artists or scientists such as Michelangelo or Einstein immediately come to mind. However, these highly creative people are quite rare and difficult to study in the psychological laboratory. In his American Psychological Association address, Guilford (1950) noted that these problems had limited research on creativity. He proposed that creativity could be studied in everyday subjects using paper-and-pencil tasks. One of these was the Unusual Uses Test, in which an examinee thinks of as many uses for a common object (e.g., a brick) as possible. Many researchers adopted Guilford's suggestion, and "divergent thinking" tasks quickly became the main instruments for measuring creative thinking. The tests were a convenient way of comparing people on a standard "creativity" scale.

Building on Guilford's work, Torrance (1974) developed the Torrance Tests of Creative Thinking. These tests consist of several relatively simple verbal and figural tasks that involve divergent thinking plus other problem-solving skills. The tests can be scored for fluency (total number of relevant responses), flexibility (number of different categories of relevant responses), originality (the statistical rarity of the responses), and elaboration (amount of detail in the responses). Some of the subtests from the Torrance battery include

1. Asking questions: The examinee writes out all of the questions he or she can think of based on a drawing of a scene.
2. Product improvement: The examinee lists ways to change a toy monkey so children will have more fun playing with it.
3. Unusual uses: The examinee lists interesting and unusual uses of a cardboard box.
4. Circles: The examinee expands empty circles into different drawings and titles them.

A number of investigators have studied the relationship between creativity and intelligence – at least as measured by IQ. Three basic findings concerning creativity and conventional conceptions of intelligence are generally agreed upon (see, e.g., Barron & Harrington, 1981; Lubart, 1994). First, creative people tend to show above-average IQs – often above 120 (see Renzulli, 1986). This figure is not a cutoff but rather an expression of the fact that people with low or even average IQs do not seem to be well represented among the ranks of highly creative individuals. Cox's (1926) geniuses had an estimated average IQ of 165. Barron estimated the mean IQ of his creative writers to be 140 or higher based on their scores on the Terman Concept Mastery Test (Barron, 1963, p. 242). It should be noted that the Concept Mastery Test is exclusively verbal and thus provides a somewhat skewed estimate of IQ. The other groups in the Institute for Personality Assessment (IPAR) studies, that is, mathematicians and research scientists, were also above average in intelligence. Anne Roe (1952, 1972), who did similarly thorough assessments of eminent scientists before the IPAR group was set up, estimated IQs for her participants ranged between 121 and 194, with medians between 137 and 166, depending on whether the IQ test was verbal, spatial, or mathematical.

Second, an IQ above 120, does not seem to matter as much to creativity as it does when an IQ is below 120. In other words, creativity may be more highly correlated with IQ below an IQ of 120, but only weakly or not at all correlated with it above an IQ of 120. [This relationship is often called the threshold theory. See the contrast with Hayes's (1989) certification theory discussed below.] In the architects' study, in which the average IQ was 130 (significantly above average), the correlation between intelligence and creativity was −.08, not significantly different from zero (Barron, 1969, p. 42). However, in the military officer study, in which participants were of average intelligence, the correlation was .33 (Barron, 1963, p. 219). These results suggest that extremely highly creative people often have high IQs, but not necessarily that people with high IQs tend to be extremely creative (see also Getzels & Jackson, 1962).

Some investigators (e.g., Simonton, 1994; Sternberg, 1996) have suggested that very high IQ may actually interfere with creativity. Those who have very high IQs may be so highly rewarded for their IQ-like (analytical) skills that they fail to develop the creative potential within them, which may then remain latent.

Third, the correlation between IQ and creativity is variable, usually ranging from weak to moderate (Flescher, 1963; Getzels & Jackson, 1962; Guilford, 1967; Herr, Moore, & Hasen, 1965; Torrance, 1962; Wallach & Kogan, 1965; Yamamoto, 1964). The correlation depends in part on what aspects of creativity and intelligence are being measured, how they are being measured, and in what field the creativity is manifested. The role of intelligence is different in art and music, for instance, than it is in mathematics and science (McNemar, 1964).

An obvious drawback to the tests used and assessments done by Roe and Guilford is the time and expense involved in administering them, as well as the subjective scoring of them. In contrast, Mednick (1962) produced a 30-item, objectively scored, 40-minute test of creative ability called the Remote Associates Test (RAT). The test is based on his theory that the creative thinking process is the "forming of associative elements into new combinations which either meet specified requirements or are in some way useful. The more mutually remote the elements of the new combination, the more creative the process or solution" (Mednick, 1962). Because the ability to make these combinations and arrive at a creative solution necessarily depends on the existence of the combinations (i.e., the associative elements) in a person's knowledge base, and because the probability and speed of attainment of a creative solution are influenced by the organization of the person's associations, Mednick's theory suggests that creativity and intelligence are very related; they are overlapping sets.

Moderate correlations of .55, .43, and .41 have been shown between the RAT and the WISC (Wechsler Intelligence Scale for Children), the SAT verbal, and the Lorge-Thorndike Verbal intelligence measures, respectively (Mednick & Andrews, 1967). Correlations with quantitative intelligence measures were lower ($r = .20 - .34$). Correlations with other measures of creative performance have been more variable (Andrews, 1975).

This psychometric approach for measuring creativity had both positive and negative effects on the field. On the positive side, the tests facilitated research by providing a brief, easy to administer, objectively scorable assessment device. Furthermore, research was now possible with "everyday" people (i.e., noneminent samples). However, there were also some negative effects. First, some researchers criticized brief paper-and-pencil tests as trivial, inadequate measures of creativity; larger productions such as actual drawings or writing samples should be used instead. Second, other critics suggested that no fluency, flexibility, originality, or elaboration scores captured the concept of creativity. In fact, the definition and criteria for creativity are a matter of ongoing debate, and relying on the objectively defined statistical rarity of a response with regard to all of the responses of a subject population is only one of many options. Other possibilities include using the social consensus of judges (see Amabile, 1983). Third, some researchers were less enchanted by the assumption that noneminent samples could shed light on eminent levels of creativity, which was the ultimate goal for many studies of creativity (e.g., Simonton, 1984). Thus, a certain malaise developed and continues to accompany the paper-and-pencil assessment of creativity. Some psychologists, at least, avoided this measurement quagmire in favor of less problematic research topics.

Cognitive Approaches

The cognitive approach to creativity seeks understanding of the mental representations and processes underlying creative thought (see Lubart, 2000–2001). By studying perception or memory, one would already be studying the bases of creativity; thus, the study of creativity would merely represent an extension, and perhaps not a very large one, of work that is already being done under another guise. For example, in the cognitive area, creativity was often subsumed under the study of intelligence (see Sternberg, Chap. 31). We do not argue with the idea that creativity and intelligence are related to each other (Lubart, 2003; Sternberg & O'Hara, 1999). However, the subsumption has often been so powerful that researchers such as Wallach and Kogan (1965), among others, had to write at length on why creativity and intelligence should be viewed as distinct entities. In more recent cognitive work, Weisberg (1986, 1988, 1993, 1999) has proposed that creativity involves essentially ordinary cognitive processes yielding extraordinary products. A similar point has been made by Perkins (1981). Weisberg attempted to show that the insights depend on subjects using conventional cognitive processes (e.g., analogical transfer) applied to knowledge already stored in memory. He did so through the use of case studies of eminent creators and laboratory research, such as studies with Duncker's (1945) candle problem. This problem requires participants to attach a candle to a wall using only objects available in a picture (candle, box of tacks, and book of matches). Langley et al. (1987) made a similar claim about the ordinary nature of creative thinking.

As a concrete example of this approach, Weisberg and Alba (1981) had people solve the notorious nine-dot problem. In this problem, people are asked to connect all of the dots, which are arranged in the shape of a square with three rows of three dots each, using no more than four straight lines, never arriving at a given dot twice, and never lifting their pencil from the page. The problem can be solved only if people allow their line segments to go outside the periphery of the dots. Typically, solution of this task had been viewed as hinging upon the insight that one had to go "outside the box." Weisberg and Alba showed that even when people were given that insight, they still had difficulty in solving the problem. In other words, whatever is required to solve the nine-dot problem, it is not just some kind of extraordinary insight.

There have been studies with both human subjects and computer simulations of creative thought. Approaches based on the study of human subjects are perhaps prototypically exemplified by the work of Finke, Ward, and Smith (1992) (see also contributions to Smith, Ward, & Finke, 1995; Sternberg & Davidson, 1994; Ward, Smith, & Finke, 1999). Finke and his colleagues have proposed what they call the *Geneplore model*, according to which there are two main processing phases in creative thought – a generative phase and an exploratory phase. In the generative phase, an individual constructs mental representations referred to as preinventive structures, which have properties promoting creative discoveries. In the exploratory phase, these properties are used to come up with creative ideas. A number of mental processes may enter into these phases of creative invention, such as retrieval, association, synthesis, transformation (see Tversky, Chap. 10), analogical transfer (see Holyoak, Chap. 6), and categorical reduction (i.e., mentally reducing objects or elements to more primitive categorical descriptions). In a typical experimental test based on the model (Finke & Slayton, 1988), participants will be shown parts of objects, such as a circle, a cube, a parallelogram, and a cylinder. On a given trial, three parts will be named, and participants will be asked to imagine combining the parts to produce a practical object or device. For example, participants might imagine a tool, a weapon, or a piece of furniture. The objects thus produced are then rated by judges for their practicality and originality. Morrison and Wallace (2002) found that judged creativity on such a task correlated strongly with the individuals' perceived imagery vividness.

In work on convergent creative thinking that required participants to think in unusual ways, we presented 80 individuals with novel kinds of reasoning problems that had a single best answer. For example, they might be told that some objects are green and others blue, whereas still other objects might be grue, meaning green until the year 2000 and blue thereafter, or bleen, meaning blue until the year 2000 and green thereafter. Or they might be told about four kinds of people on the planet Kyron, blens, who are born young and die young; kwefs, who are born old and die old; balts, who are born young and die old; and prosses, who are born old and die young (Sternberg, 1981, 1982; Tetewsky & Sternberg, 1986). Their task was to predict future states from past states, given incomplete information. In another set of studies, 60 people were given more conventional kinds of inductive reasoning problems, such as analogies, series completions, and classifications. However, the problems had premises preceding them that were either conventional (dancers wear shoes) or novel (dancers eat shoes). The participants had to solve the problems as though the counterfactuals were true (Sternberg & Gastel, 1989a, 1989b).

In these studies, we found that correlations with conventional kinds of tests depended on how novel or nonentrenched the conventional tests were. The more novel the items, the higher the correlations of our tests with scores on successively more novel conventional tests. Thus, the components isolated for relatively novel items would tend to correlate more highly with more unusual tests of fluid abilities than with tests of crystallized abilities. We also found that when response times on the relatively novel problems were componentially analyzed, some components better measured the creative aspect of intelligence than did others. For example, in the "grue-bleen" task mentioned previously, the information processing component requiring people to switch from conventional green-blue thinking to grue-bleen thinking, and then back to green-blue thinking again, was a particularly good measure of the ability to cope with novelty.

Computer simulation approaches, reviewed by Boden (1992, 1999), have as their goal the production of creative thought by a computer in a manner that simulates what people do. Langley, Simon, Bradshaw, and Zytkow (1987), for example, developed a set of programs that rediscover basic scientific laws. These computational models rely on heuristics – problem-solving guidelines – for searching a data set or conceptual space and finding hidden relationships between input variables. The initial program, called BACON, uses heuristics such as "if the value of two numeric terms increase together, consider their ratio" to search data for patterns. One of BACON's accomplishments has been to examine observational data on the orbits of planets available to Kepler and to rediscover Kepler's third law of planetary motion. This program is unlike creative functioning, however, in that the problems are given to it in a structured form, whereas creative functioning is largely about figuring out what the problems are (see Runco, 1994). Further programs have extended the search heuristics, the ability to transform data sets, and the ability to reason with qualitative data and scientific concepts. There are also models concerning an artistic domain. For example, Johnson-Laird (1988) developed a jazz improvisation program in which novel deviations from the basic jazz chord sequences are guided by harmonic constraints (or tacit principles of jazz) and random choice when several allowable directions for the improvisation exist.

Social-Personality and Social-Cognitive Approaches

Developing in parallel with the cognitive approach, work in the social-personality approach has focused on personality variables, motivational variables, and the sociocultural environment as sources of creativity. Researchers such as Amabile (1983), Barron (1968, 1969), Eysenck (1993), Gough (1979), MacKinnon (1965), and others noted that certain personality traits often characterize creative people. Through correlational studies and research contrasting high and low creative samples (at both eminent and everyday levels), a large set of potentially relevant traits has been identified (Barron & Harrington, 1981; Feist, 1999). These traits include independence of judgment, self-confidence, attraction to complexity, aesthetic orientation, openness to experience, and risk taking.

Proposals regarding self-actualization and creativity can also be considered within the personality tradition. According to Maslow (1968), boldness, courage, freedom, spontaneity, self-acceptance, and other traits lead a person to realize his or her full potential. Rogers (1954) described the tendency toward self-actualization as having motivational force and being promoted by a supportive, evaluation-free environment. These ideas, however, seem at odds with the many studies that have linked creativity and mental illness (e.g., Kaufman, 2001a, 2001b; Kaufman & Baer, 2002; Ludwig, 1995). If full creative potential is truly linked with self-acceptance and other positive traits, then one would not expect to find so many eminent creative individuals to have such maladjusted and poor coping strategies (Kaufman, 2002; Kaufman & Sternberg, 2000).

Focusing on motivation for creativity, a number of theorists have hypothesized the relevance of intrinsic motivation (Amabile, 1983, 1996; Crutchfield, 1962; Golann, 1962), need for order (Barron, 1963), need for achievement (McClelland, Atkinson, Clark, & Lowell, 1953), and other motives. Amabile (1983, 1996; Hennessey & Amabile, 1988) and her colleagues conducted seminal research on intrinsic and extrinsic motivation. Studies using motivational training and other techniques have manipulated these motivations and observed effects on creative performance tasks, such as writing poems and making collages.

Finally, the relevance of the social environment to creativity has also been an active area of research. At the societal level, Simonton (1984, 1988, 1994, 1999) conducted numerous studies in which eminent levels of creativity over large spans of time in diverse cultures have been statistically linked to environmental variables. These variables include, among others, cultural diversity, war, availability of role models, availability of resources (e.g., financial support), and number of competitors in a domain. Cross-cultural comparisons (e.g., Lubart, 1990) and anthropological case studies (e.g., Maduro, 1976; Silver, 1981) have demonstrated cultural variability in the expression of creativity. Moreover, they have shown that cultures differ simply in the amount that they value the creative enterprise.

The social-cognitive and social-personality approaches have each provided valuable insights into creativity. However, if you look for research that investigates both social-cognitive and social-personality variables at the same time, you would find only a handful of studies. The cognitive work on creativity has tended to ignore the personality and social system, and the social-personality approaches tended to have little or nothing to say about the mental representations and processes underlying creativity.

Looking beyond the field of psychology, Wehner, Csikszentmihalyi, and Magyari-Beck (1991) examined 100 more recent doctoral dissertations on creativity. They found a "parochial isolation" of the various studies concerning creativity. There were relevant dissertations from psychology, education, business, history, history of science, and other fields, such as sociology and political science. However, the different fields tended to use different terms and focus on different aspects of what seemed to be the same basic phenomenon. For example, business dissertations used the term "innovation" and tended to look at the organizational level, whereas psychology dissertations used the term "creativity" and looked at the level of the individual. Wehner, Csikszentmihalyi, and Magyari-Beck (1991) described the situation with creativity research in terms of the fable of the blind men and the elephant. "We touch different parts of the same beast and derive distorted pictures of the whole from what we know: 'The elephant is like a snake,' says the one who only holds its tail; 'The elephant is like a wall,' says the one who touches its flanks" (p. 270).

Evolutionary Approaches to Creativity

The evolutionary approach to creativity was instigated by Donald Campbell (1960), who suggested that the same kinds of mechanisms that have been applied to the study of the evolution of organisms could be applied to the evolution of ideas. This idea has been enthusiastically picked up by a number of investigators (Simonton, 1995, 1998, 1999).

The basic idea underlying this approach is that there are two basic steps in the generation and propagation of creative ideas. The first is *blind variation*, by which the creator generates an idea without any real idea of whether the idea will be successful (selected for) in the world of ideas. Indeed, Dean Simonton (1996) argued that creators do not have the slightest idea as to which of their ideas will succeed. As a result, their best bet for producing lasting ideas is to go for a large quantity of ideas. The reason is that their hit rate remains relatively constant through their professional life span. In other words, they have a fixed proportion of ideas that will succeed. The more ideas they have in all, the more ideas they have that will achieve success.

The second step is *selective retention*. In this step, the field in which the creator works either retains the idea for the future or lets it die out. Those ideas that are selectively retained are the ones that are judged to be novel and of value, that is, creative. This process, as well as blind generation, are described further by Cziko (1998).

Does an evolutionary model really adequately describe creativity? Robert Sternberg (1997, 2003) argued that it does not, and David Perkins (1998) also had doubts. Sternberg argued that it seems utterly implausible that great creators such as Mozart, Einstein, or Picasso were using nothing more than blind variation to come up with their ideas. Good creators, like experts of any kind, may or may not have more ideas than other people have, but they have better ideas, ones that are more likely to be selectively retained. The reason they are more likely to be selectively retained is that they were not produced in a blind fashion. This debate is by no means resolved, however, and is likely to continue into the future for some time to come.

Perkins (1995, 1998) argued that the analogy between biological evolution and creativity is oversimplified. In particular (Perkins, 1998), biological evolution relies on massive parallel search for mutations (millions of bacteria, for example, are mutating every second), whereas humans do not. At the same time, humans can do fairly extensive searches, such as when they seek out new antibiotics.

Were it the case that an understanding of creativity required a multidisciplinary approach, the result of a unidisciplinary approach might be that we would view a part of the whole as the whole. At the same time, though, we would have an incomplete explanation of the phenomenon we are seeking to explain, leaving dissatisfied those who do not subscribe to the particular discipline doing the explaining. We believe that traditionally this has been the case for creativity. More recently, theorists have begun to develop confluence approaches to creativity, which we now discuss.

Confluence Approaches to the Study of Creativity

Many more recent works on creativity hypothesize that multiple components must converge for creativity to occur (Amabile, 1983; Csikszentmihalyi, 1988; Gardner, 1993; Gruber, 1989; Gruber & Wallace, 1999; Lubart, 1994, 1999; Lubart, Mouchiroud, Tordjman, & Zenasni, 2003; Mumford & Gustafson, 1988; Perkins, 1981; Simonton, 1988; Sternberg, 1985b; Sternberg & Lubart, 1991, 1995, 1996; Weisberg, 1993; Woodman & Schoenfeldt, 1989). Sternberg (1985b), for example, examined laypersons' and experts' conceptions of the creative person. People's implicit theories contain a combination of cognitive and personality elements, such as "connects ideas," "sees similarities and differences," "has flexibility," "has aesthetic taste," "is unorthodox," "is motivated," "is inquisitive," and "questions societal norms."

At the level of explicit theories, Amabile (1983, 1996; Collins & Amabile, 1999) described creativity as the confluence of intrinsic motivation, domain-relevant knowledge and abilities, and creativity-relevant skills. The creativity-relevant skills include

1. a cognitive style that involves coping with complexities and breaking one's mental set during problem solving;
2. knowledge of heuristics for generating novel ideas, such as trying a counterintuitive approach; and
3. a work style characterized by concentrated effort, an ability to set aside problems, and high energy.

Gruber (1981, 1989) and Gruber and Davis (1988) proposed a developmental *evolving-systems model* for understanding creativity. A person's knowledge, purpose, and affect grow over time, amplify deviations that an individual encounters, and lead to creative products. Developmental changes in the knowledge system have been documented in cases such as Charles Darwin's thoughts on evolution. Purpose refers to a set of interrelated goals, which also develop and guide an individual's behavior. Finally, the affect or mood system notes the influence of joy or frustration on the projects undertaken.

Csikszentmihalyi (1988, 1996; Feldman, Csikszentmihalyi, & Gardner, 1994) took a different "systems" approach and highlighted the interaction of the individual, domain, and field. An individual draws upon information in a domain and transforms or extends it via cognitive processes, personality traits, and motivation. The field, consisting of people who control or influence a domain (e.g., art critics and gallery owners), evaluates and selects new ideas. The domain, a culturally defined symbol system such as alphabetic writing, mathematical notation, or musical notation, preserves and transmits creative products to other individuals and future generations. Gardner (1993; see also Policastro & Gardner, 1999) conducted case studies that suggest that the development of creative projects may stem from an anomaly within a system (e.g., tension between competing critics in a field) or moderate asynchronies between the individual, domain, and field (e.g., unusual individual talent for a domain). In particular, Gardner (1993) analyzed the lives of seven individuals who made highly creative contributions in the twentieth century with each specializing in one of the multiple intelligences (Gardner, 1983): Sigmund Freud (intrapersonal), Albert Einstein (logical-mathematical), Pablo Picasso (spatial), Igor Stravinsky (musical), T. S. Eliot (linguistic), Martha Graham (bodily-kinesthetic), and Mohandas Gandhi (interpersonal). Charles Darwin would be an example of someone with extremely high naturalist intelligence. Gardner pointed out, however, that most of these individuals actually had strengths in more than one intelligence and that they also had notable weaknesses in others (e.g., Freud's weaknesses may have been in spatial and musical intelligences).

Although creativity can be understood in terms of uses of the multiple intelligences to generate new and even revolutionary ideas, Gardner's (1993) analysis goes well beyond the intellectual. For example, Gardner pointed out two major themes in the behavior of these creative giants. First, they tended to have a matrix of support at the time of their creative breakthroughs. Second, they tended to drive a "Faustian bargain," whereby they gave up many of the pleasures people typically enjoy in life to attain extraordinary success in their careers. However, it is not clear that these attributes are intrinsic to creativity, per se; rather, they seem to be associated with those who have been driven to exploit their creative gifts in a way that leads them to attain eminence.

Gardner (1993) further followed Csikszentmihalyi (1988, 1996) in distinguishing between the importance of the domain (the body of knowledge about a particular subject area) and the field (the context in which this body of knowledge is studied and elaborated, including the persons working with the domain, such as critics, publishers, and other "gatekeepers"). Both are important to the development, and, ultimately, the recognition of creativity.

A final confluence theory considered here is Sternberg and Lubart's (1991, 1995) *investment theory of creativity*. According to this theory, creative people are ones who are willing and able to "buy low and sell high" in the realm of ideas (see also Lubart & Runco, 1999; Rubenson & Runco, 1992, for use of concepts from economic theory). Buying low means pursuing ideas that are unknown or out of favor but that have growth potential. Often, when these ideas are first presented, they encounter resistance. The creative individual persists in the face of this resistance, and eventually sells high, moving on to the next new or unpopular idea.

Preliminary research within the investment framework has yielded support for this model (Lubart & Sternberg, 1995). This research has used tasks such as

1. writing short stories using unusual titles (e.g., "the octopus' sneakers"),
2. drawing pictures with unusual themes (e.g., "the earth from an insect's point of view"),
3. devising creative advertisements for boring products (e.g., cufflinks), and
4. solving unusual scientific problems (e.g., how we could tell if someone had been on the moon within the past month?).

This research showed creative performance to be moderately domain specific and to be predicted by a combination of six distinct but interrelated resources: intellectual abilities, knowledge, styles of thinking, personality, motivation, and environment.

Concerning the confluence of components, creativity is hypothesized to involve more than a simple sum of a person's level on each component. First, there may be thresholds for some components (e.g., knowledge), below which creativity is not possible regardless of the levels on other components. Second, partial compensation may occur in which a strength on one component (e.g., motivation) counteracts a weakness on another component (e.g., environment). Third, interactions may also occur between components, such as intelligence and motivation, in which high levels on both components could multiplicatively enhance creativity.

In general, confluence theories of creativity offer the possibility of accounting for diverse aspects of creativity (Lubart, 1994). For example, analyses of scientific and artistic achievements suggest that the median-rated creativity of work in a domain tends to fall toward the lower end of the distribution and the upper – high creativity – tail extends quite far. This pattern can be explained through the need for multiple components of creativity to co-occur in order for the highest levels of creativity to be achieved. As another example, the partial domain specificity of creativity that is often observed can be explained through the mixture of some relatively domain-specific components for creativity, such as knowledge, and other more domain-general components, such as, perhaps, the personality trait of perseverance. Creativity, then, is largely something that people show in a particular domain.

Alternate Approaches to Understanding Kinds of Creative Contributions

Generally, we think of creative contributions as being of a single kind. However, a number of researchers on creativity have questioned this assumption. There are many ways of distinguishing among types of creative contributions. It is important to remember, though, that creative contributions can be viewed in different ways at different times. At a given time, the field can never be sure of whose work will withstand the judgments of the field over time (e.g., that of Mozart) and whose work will not (e.g., that of Salieri) (Therivel, 1999).

Theorists of creativity and related topics have recognized that there are different types of creative contributions (see reviews in Ochse, 1990; Sternberg, 1988c; Weisberg, 1993). For example, Kuhn (1970) distinguished between normal and revolutionary science. Normal science expands upon or otherwise elaborates upon an already existing paradigm of scientific research, whereas revolutionary science proposes a new paradigm (see Dunbar & Fugelsang, Chap. 29). The same kind of distinction can be applied to the arts and letters.

Gardner (1993, 1994) also described different types of creative contributions individuals can make. They include

1) the solution of a well-defined problem,
2) the devising of an encompassing theory,
3) the creation of a "frozen work,"
4) the performance of a ritualized work, and
5) a "high-stakes" performance. Each type of creativity has as its result a different kind of creative product.

Other bases for distinguishing among types of creative contributions also exist. For example, psychoeconomic models such as those of Rubenson and Runco (1992) and Sternberg and Lubart (1991, 1995, 1996) can distinguish different types of contributions in terms of the parameters of the models. In the Sternberg–Lubart model, contributions might differ in the extent to which they "defy the crowd" or in the extent to which they redefine how a field perceives a set of problems.

Simonton's (1997) model of creativity also proposes parameters of creativity, and various kinds of creative contributions might be seen as differing in terms of the extent to which they vary from other contributions and the extent to which they are selected for recognition by a field of endeavor (see also Campbell, 1960; Perkins, 1995; Simonton, 1997). However, in no case were these models intended explicitly to distinguish among types of creative contributions.

Maslow (1967) distinguished more generally between two types of creativity, which he referred to as primary and secondary. Primary creativity is the kind of creativity a person uses to become self-actualized – to find fulfillment in him- or herself and his or her life. Secondary creativity is the kind of creativity with which scholars in the field are more familiar – the kind that leads to creative achievements recognized by a field.

Ward, Smith, and Finke (1999) noted that there is evidence to favor the roles of both focusing (Bowers et al., 1990; Kaplan & Simon, 1990) and exploratory thinking (Bransford & Stein, 1984; Getzels & Csikszentmihalyi, 1976) on creative thinking. In focusing, one concentrates on pursuing a single problem-solving approach, whereas in exploratory thinking one considers many such approaches. A second distinction made by Ward and his colleagues is between domain specific (Clement, 1989; Langley, Simon, Bradshaw, & Zytkow, 1987; Perkins, 1981; Weisberg, 1986) and universal (Finke, 1990, 1995; Guilford, 1968; Koestler, 1964) creativity skills. Finally, Ward and his colleagues distinguish between unstructured (Bateson, 1979; Findlay & Lumsden, 1988; Johnson-Laird, 1988) and structured or systematic (Perkins, 1981; Ward, 1994; Weisberg, 1986) creativity, where the former is displayed in systems with relatively few rules, and the latter, in systems with many rules.

There are tens of thousands of artists, musicians, writers, scientists, and inventors today. What makes some of them stand out from the rest? Why will some of them become distinguished contributors in the annals of their field and others be forgotten? Although many variables may contribute to who stands out from the crowd, certainly creativity is one of them. The standouts are often those who are doing particularly creative work in their line of professional pursuit. Are these highly creative individuals simply doing more highly creative work than their less visible counterparts, or does the creativity of their work also differ in quality? One possibility is that creative contributors make different *decisions* regarding *how* to express their creativity. This section describes a propulsion theory of creative contributions (Sternberg, 1999b; Sternberg, Kaufman, & Pretz, 2002) that addresses this issue of how people decide to invest their creative resources. The basic idea is that creativity can be of different kinds, depending on how it propels existing ideas forward. When developing creativity in children, we can foster different kinds of creativity, ranging from minor replications to major redirections in their thinking.

Creative contributions differ not only in their amounts but also in the types of creativity they represent. For example, both Sigmund Freud and Anna Freud were highly creative psychologists, but the nature of their contributions seems in some way or ways to have been different. Sigmund Freud proposed a radically new theory of human thought and motivation, and Anna Freud largely elaborated on and modified Sigmund Freud's theory. How do creative contributions differ in quality and not just in quantity of creativity?

The type of creativity exhibited in a creator's works can have at least as much of an effect on judgments about that person and his or her work as does the amount of creativity exhibited. In many instances, it may have more of an effect on these judgments.

Given the importance of purpose, creative contributions must always be defined in some context. If the creativity of an individual is judged in a context, then it will help to understand how the context interacts with how people are judged. In particular, what are the types of creative contributions a person can make within a given context? Most theories of creativity concentrate on attributes of the individual (see Sternberg, 1999b). However, to the extent that creativity depends on the interaction of person with context, we would also need to concentrate on the attributes of the individual and the individual's work relative to the environmental context.

A taxonomy of creative contributions needs to deal with the question not just of in what domain a contribution is creative but of what the type of creative contribution is. What makes one work in biology more creative or creative in a different way from another work in biology, or what makes its creative contribution different from that of a work in art? Thus, a taxonomy of domains of work is insufficient to elucidate the nature of creative contributions. A field needs a basis for scaling how creative contributions differ quantitatively and, possibly, qualitatively. For instance,

1. *Replication*. The contribution is an attempt to show that the field is in the right place. The propulsion keeps the field where it is rather than moving it. This type of creativity is represented by stationary motion, as of a wheel that is moving but staying in place.
2. *Redefinition*. The contribution is an attempt to redefine where the field is. The current status of the field thus is seen from different points of view. The propulsion leads to circular motion such that the creative work leads back to where the field is but as viewed in a different way.
3. *Forward Incrementation*. The contribution is an attempt to move the field forward in the direction it already is going. The propulsion leads to forward motion.
4. *Advance Forward Incrementation*. The contribution is an attempt to move the field forward in the direction it is already going, but by moving beyond where others are ready for it to go. The propulsion leads to forward motion that is accelerated beyond the expected rate of forward progression.
5. *Redirection*. The contribution is an attempt to redirect the field from where it is toward a different direction. The propulsion thus leads to motion in a direction that diverges from the way the field is currently moving.
6. *Reconstruction/Redirection*. The contribution is an attempt to move the field back to where it once was (a reconstruction of the past) so it may move onward from that point, but in a direction different from the one it took from that point onward.

The propulsion thus leads to motion that is backward and then redirective.

7. *Reinitiation*. The contribution is an attempt to move the field to a different as yet unreached starting point and then to move from that point. The propulsion is thus from a new starting point in a direction that is different from that the field previously has pursued.
8. *Integration*. The contribution is an attempt to integrate two formerly diverse ways of thinking about phenomena into a single way of thinking about a phenomenon. The propulsion thus is a combination of two different approaches that are linked together.

The eight types of creative contributions described previously are largely qualitatively distinct. Within each type, however, there can be quantitative differences. For example, a forward incrementation can represent a fairly small step forward or a substantial leap. An initiation can restart a subfield (e.g., the work of Leon Festinger on cognitive dissonance) or an entire field (e.g., the work of Einstein on relativity theory). Thus, the theory distinguishes contributions both qualitatively and quantitatively.

Conclusions and Future Directions

In sum, creativity, which has often been viewed as beyond study, is anything but. Creativity can be understood about as well as any psychological construct, if appropriate methods are brought to bear upon its investigations. The history of creativity theory and research is long and interesting. It represents a diversity of attempts to understand the phenomenon. More recently, scholars have recognized that creativity can be of multiple kinds and have tried to understand these different kinds. A full account of creativity would need to take into account not just differing amounts of creativity but differing kinds. These kinds would include creativity that accepts current paradigms, creativity that rejects them, and creativity that synthesizes them into a new whole.

Author Notes

Preparation of this article was supported by Grant No. REC-9979843 from the National Science Foundation and by a grant under the Javits Act Program (Grant No. R206R000001) as administered by the Institute of Education Sciences, U.S. Department of Education. Grantees undertaking such projects are encouraged to express freely their professional judgment. This article, therefore, does not necessarily represent the position or policies of the National Science Foundation, Office of Educational Research and Improvement, or the U.S. Department of Education, and no official endorsement should be inferred.

References

Adams, J. L. (1974). *Conceptual blockbusting: A guide to better ideas*. San Francisco: Freeman Press.

Adams, J. L. (1986). *The care and feeding of ideas: A guide to encouraging creativity*. Reading, MA: Addison-Wesley.

Amabile, T. M. (1983). *The social psychology of creativity*. New York: Springer–Verlag.

Amabile, T. M. (1996). *Creativity in context*. Boulder, CO: Westview.

Andrews, F. M. (1975). Social and psychological factors which influence the creative process. In I. A. Taylor & J. W. Getzels (Eds.), *Perspectives in creativity* (pp. 117–145). Chicago: Aldine.

Barron, F. (1963). *Creativity and psychological health*. Princeton, NJ: D. Van Nostrand.

Barron, F. (1968). *Creativity and personal freedom*. New York: Van Nostrand.

Barron, F. (1969). *Creative person and creative process*. New York: Holt, Rinehart & Winston.

Barron, F. (1988). Putting creativity to work. In R. J. Sternberg (Ed.), *The nature of creativity* (pp. 76–98). New York: Cambridge University Press.

Barron, F., & Harrington, D. M. (1981). Creativity, intelligence, and personality. *Annual Review of Psychology*, 32, 439–476.

Bateson, G. (1979). *Mind and nature*. London: Wildwood House.

Boden, M. (1992). *The creative mind: Myths and mechanisms*. New York: Basic Books.

Boden, M. A. (1999). Computer models of creativity. In R. J. Sternberg (Ed.), *Handbook of creativity* (pp. 351–372). New York: Cambridge University Press.

Bowers, K. S., Regehr, G., Balthazard, C., & Parker, K. (1990). Intuition in the context of discovery. *Cognitive Psychology, 22*, 72–109.

Bransford, J. D., & Stein, B. (1984). *The IDEAL problem solver*. New York: Freeman Press.

Campbell, D. T. (1960). Blind variation and selective retention in creative thought and other knowledge processes. *Psychological Review, 67*, 380–400.

Clement, J. (1989). Learning via model construction and criticism: Protocol evidence on sources of creativity in science. In G. Glover, R. Ronning, & C. Reynolds (Eds.), *Handbook of creativity* (pp. 341–381). New York: Plenum.

Collins, M. A., & Amabile, T. M. (1999). Motivation and creativity. In R. J. Sternberg (Ed.), *Handbook of creativity* (pp. 297–312). New York: Cambridge University Press.

Cox, C. M. (1926). *The early mental traits of three hundred geniuses*. Stanford, CA: Stanford University Press.

Crutchfield, R. (1962). Conformity and creative thinking. In H. Gruber, G. Terrell, & M. Wertheimer (Eds.), *Contemporary approaches to creative thinking* (pp. 120–140). New York: Atherton Press.

Csikszentmihalyi, M. (1988). Society, culture, and person: A systems view of creativity. In R. J. Sternberg (Ed.), *The nature of creativity* (pp. 325–339). New York: Cambridge University Press.

Csikszentmihalyi, M. (1996). *Creativity: Flow and the psychology of discovery and invention*. New York: Harper Collins.

Csikszentmihalyi, M. (1999). Implications of a systems perspective for the study of creativity. In R. J. Sternberg (Ed.), *Handbook of creativity* (pp. 313–335). New York: Cambridge University Press.

Cziko, G. A. (1998). From blind to creative: In defense of Donald Campbell's selectionist theory of human creativity. *Journal of Creative Behavior, 32*, 192–208.

De Bono, E. (1971). *Lateral thinking for management*. New York: McGraw-Hill.

De Bono, E. (1985). *Six thinking hats*. Boston: Little, Brown.

De Bono, E. (1992). *Serious creativity: Using the power of lateral thinking to create new ideas*. New York: Harper Collins.

Duncker, K. (1945). On problem solving. *Psychological Monographs*, 68(5), whole no. 270.

Eysenck, H. J. (1993). Creativity and personality: A theoretical perspective. *Psychological Inquiry, 4*, 147–178.

Feist, G. J. (1999). The influence of personality on artistic and scientific creativity. In R. J. Sternberg (Ed.), *Handbook of creativity* (pp. 273–296). New York: Cambridge University Press.

Feldman, D. H. (1999). The development of creativity. In R. J. Sternberg (Ed.), *Handbook of creativity* (pp. 169–186). New York: Cambridge University Press.

Feldman, D. H., Csikszentmihalyi, M., & Gardner, H. (1994). *Changing the world: A framework for the study of creativity*. Westport, CT: Praeger Publishers.

Findlay, C. S., & Lumsden, C. J. (1988). The creative mind: Toward an evolutionary theory of discovery and invention. *Journal of Social and Biological Structures, 11*, 3–55.

Finke, R. (1990). *Creative imagery: Discoveries and inventions in visualization*. Hillsdale, NJ: Erlbaum.

Finke, R. (1995). A. Creative insight and preinventive forms. In R. J. Sternberg & J. E. Davidson (Eds.), *The nature of insight* (pp. 255–280). Cambridge, MA: MIT Press.

Finke, R. A., & Slayton, K. (1988). Explorations of creative visual synthesis in mental imagery. *Memory and Cognition, 16*(3), 252–257.

Finke, R. A., Ward T. B., & Smith, S. M. (1992). *Creative cognition: Theory, research, and applications*. Cambridge, MA: MIT Press.

Flescher, I. (1963). Anxiety and achievement of intellectually gifted and creatively gifted children. *Journal of Psychology, 56*, 251–268.

Freud, S. (1908/1959). The relation of the poet to day-dreaming. In S. Freud (Ed.), *Collected papers* (Vol. 4, pp. 173–183). London: Hogarth Press.

Freud, S. (1910/1964). *Leonardo da Vinci and a memory of his childhood*. New York: Norton. (Original work published in 1910).

Gardner, H. (1983). *Frames of mind: The theory of multiple intelligences*. New York: Basic Books.

Gardner, H. (1993). *Multiple intelligences: The theory in practice*. New York: Basic Books.

Gardner, H. (1994). The stories of the right hemisphere. In W. D. Spaulding (Ed.), *Integrative views of motivation, cognition, and emotion. Nebraska symposium on motivation* (Vol. 41, pp. 57–69). Lincoln: University of Nebraska Press.

Getzels, J., & Csikszentmihalyi, M. (1976). *The creative vision: A longitudinal study of problem finding in art*. New York: Wiley-Interscience.

Getzels, J. W., & Jackson, P. W. (1962). *Creativity and intelligence: Explorations with gifted students*. New York: Wiley.

Ghiselin, B. (Ed.). (1985). *The creative process: A symposium*. Berkeley: University of California Press.

Golann, S. E. (1962). The creativity motive. *Journal of Personality*, 30, 588–600.

Gough, H. G. (1979). A creativity scale for the adjective check list. *Journal of Personality and Social Psychology*, 37, 1398–1405.

Gordon, W. J. J. (1961). *Synectics: The development of creative capacity*. New York: Harper & Row.

Gruber, H. (1981). *Darwin on man: A psychological study of scientific creativity* (2nd ed.). Chicago: University of Chicago Press. (Original work published 1974.)

Gruber, H. E. (1989). The evolving systems approach to creative work. In D. B. Wallace & H. E. Gruber (Eds.), *Creative people at work: Twelve cognitive case studies* (pp. 3–24). New York: Oxford University Press.

Gruber, H. E., & Davis, S. N. (1988). Inching our way up Mount Olympus: The evolving-systems approach to creative thinking. In R. J. Sternberg (Ed.), *The nature of creativity* (pp. 243–270). New York: Cambridge University Press.

Gruber, H. E., & Wallace, D. B. (1999). The case study method and evolving systems approach for understanding unique creative people at work. In R. J. Sternberg (Ed.), *Handbook of creativity* (pp. 93–115). New York: Cambridge University Press.

Guilford, J. P. (1950). Creativity. *American Psychologist*, 5, 444–454.

Guilford, J. P. (1967). *The nature of human intelligence*. New York: McGraw-Hill.

Guilford, J. P. (1968). Intelligence has three facets. *Science*, 160(3828), 615–620.

Hayes, J. R. (1989). Cognitive processes in creativity. In J. A. Glover, R. R. Ronning, & C. R. Reynolds (Eds.), *Handbook of creativity* (pp. 135–145). New York: Plenum.

Hennessey, B. A., & Amabile, T. M. (1988). The conditions of creativity. In R. J. Sternberg (Ed.), *The nature of creativity* (pp. 11–38). New York: Cambridge University Press.

Herr, E. L., Moore, G. D., & Hasen, J. S. (1965). Creativity, intelligence, and values: A study of relationships. *Exceptional Children*, 32, 114–115.

Johnson-Laird, P. N. (1988). Freedom and constraint in creativity. In R. J. Sternberg (Ed.), *The nature of creativity* (pp. 202–219). New York: Cambridge University Press.

Kaplan, C. A., & Simon, H. A. (1990). In search of insight. *Cognitive Psychology*, 22, 374–419.

Kaufman, J. C. (2001a). Genius, lunatics, and poets: Mental illness in prize-winning authors. *Imagination, Cognition, and Personality*, 20(4), 305–314.

Kaufman, J. C. (2001b). The Sylvia Plath effect: Mental illness in eminent creative writers. *Journal of Creative Behavior*, 35(1), 37–50.

Kaufman, J. C. (2002). Creativity and confidence: Price of achievement? *American Psychologist*, 57, 375–376.

Kaufman, J. C., & Baer, J. (2002). I bask in dreams of suicide: Mental illness and poetry. *Review of General Psychology*, 6(3), 271–286.

Kaufman, J. C., & Sternberg, R. J. (2000). Are there mental costs to creativity? *Bulletin of Psychology and the Arts*, 1(2), 38.

Kipling, R. (1985). Working-tools. In B. Ghiselin (Ed.), *The creative process: A symposium* (pp. 161–163). Berkeley: University of California Press. (Original article published 1937.)

Koestler, A. (1964). *The act of creation*. New York: Dell.

Kris, E. (1952). *Psychoanalytic exploration in art*. New York: International Universities Press.

Kubie, L. S. (1958). *The neurotic distortion of the creative process*. Lawrence: University of Kansas Press.

Kuhn, T. S. (1970). *The structure of scientific revolutions* (2nd ed.). Chicago: University of Chicago Press.

Langley, P., Simon, H. A., Bradshaw, G. L., & Zytkow, J. M. (1987). *Scientific discovery: Computational explorations of the creative processes*. Cambridge, MA: MIT Press.

Lubart, T. I. (1990). Creativity and cross-cultural variation. *International Journal of Psychology*, 25, 39–59.

Lubart, T. I. (1994). Creativity. In R. J. Sternberg (Ed.), *Thinking and problem solving* (pp. 290–332). San Diego: Academic Press.

Lubart, T. I. (1999). Componential models of creativity. In M. A. Runco & S. Pritzer (Eds.), *Encyclopedia of creativity* (pp. 295–300). New York: Academic Press.

Lubart, T. I. (2000–2001). Models of the creative process: Past, present and future. *Creativity Research Journal*, 13(3–4), 295–308.

Lubart, T. I. (2003). In search of creative intelligence. In R. J. Sternberg, J. Lautrey, & T. I. Lubart (Eds.), *Models of intelligence for the next millennium* (pp. 279–292). Washington, DC: American Psychological Association.

Lubart, T. I., Mouchiroud, C., Tordjman, S., & Zenasni, F. (2003). *Psychologie de la créativité [Psychology of creativity]*. Paris: Colin.

Lubart, T. I., & Runco, M. A. (1999). Economic perspective on creativity. In M. A. Runco & S. Pritzer (Eds.), *Encyclopedia of creativity* (pp. 623–627). New York: Academic Press.

Lubart, T. I., & Sternberg, R. J. (1995). An investment approach to creativity: Theory and data. In S. M. Smith, T. B. Ward, & R. A. Finke (Eds.), *The creative cognition approach* (pp. 269–302). Cambridge, MA: MIT Press.

Ludwig, A. M. (1995). *Price of greatness*. New York: Guilford Press.

MacKinnon, D. W. (1965). Personality and the realization of creative potential. *American Psychologist*, 20, 273–281.

Maduro, R. (1976). *Artistic creativity in a Brahmin painter community*. Research monograph 14. Berkeley: Center for South and Southeast Asia Studies, University of California.

Maslow, A. (1967). The creative attitude. In R. L. Mooney & T. A. Rasik (Eds.), *Explorations in creativity* (pp. 43–57). New York: Harper & Row.

Maslow, A. (1968). *Toward a psychology of being*. New York: Van Nostrand.

McClelland, D. C., Atkinson, J. W., Clark, R. A., & Lowell, E. L. (1953). *The achievement motive*. New York: Irvington Publishing.

McNemar, Q. (1964). Lost: Our intelligence? Why? *American Psychologist*, 19, 871–882.

Mednick, M. T., & Andrews, F. M. (1967). Creative thinking and level of intelligence. *Journal of Creative Behavior*, 1, 428–431.

Mednick, S. A. (1962). The associative basis of the creative process. *Psychological Review*, 69, 220–232.

Morrison, R. G., & Wallace, B. (2002). Imagery vividness, creativity, and the visual arts. *Journal of Mental Imagery*, 25, 135–152.

Mumford, M. D., & Gustafson, S. B. (1988). Creativity syndrome: Integration, application, and innovation. *Psychological Bulletin*, 103, 27–43.

Noy, P. (1969). A revision of the psychoanalytic theory of the primary process. *International Journal of Psychoanalysis*, 50, 155–178.

Ochse, R. (1990). *Before the gates of excellence*. New York: Cambridge University Press.

Osborn, A. F. (1953). *Applied imagination* (rev. ed.). New York: Charles Scribner's Sons.

Perkins, D. N. (1981). *The mind's best work*. Cambridge, MA: Harvard University Press.

Perkins, D. N. (1995). Insight in minds and genes. In R. J. Sternberg & J. E. Davidson (Eds.), *The nature of insight* (pp. 495–534). Cambridge, MA: MIT Press.

Perkins, D. N. (1998). In the country of the blind an appreciation of Donald Campbell's vision of creative thought. *Journal of Creative Behavior*, 32(3), 177–191.

Policastro, E., & Gardner, H. (1999). From case studies to robust generalizations: An approach to the study of creativity. In R. J. Sternberg (Ed.), *Handbook of creativity* (pp. 213–225). New York: Cambridge University Press.

Renzulli, J. S. (1986). The three-ring conception of giftedness: a developmental model for creative productivity. In R. J. Sternberg & J. E. Davidson (Eds.), *Conceptions of giftedness* (pp. 53–92). New York: Cambridge University Press.

Roe, A. (1952). *The making of a scientist*. New York: Dodd, Mead.

Roe, A. (1972). Patterns of productivity of scientists. *Science*, 176, 940–941.

Rogers, C. R. (1954). Toward a theory of creativity. *ETC: A Review of General Semantics*, 11, 249–260.

Rothenberg, A. (1979). *The emerging goddess*. Chicago: University of Chicago Press.

Rothenberg, A., & Hausman, C. R. (Eds.). (1976). *The creativity question*. Durham, NC: Duke University Press.

Rubenson, D. L., & Runco, M. A. (1992). The psychoeconomic approach to creativity. *New Ideas in Psychology*, 10, 131–147.

Runco, M. A. (Ed.). (1994). *Problem finding, problem solving, and creativity*. Norwood, NJ: Ablex.

Silver, H. R. (1981). Calculating risks: The socioeconomic foundations of aesthetic innovation in an Ashanti carving community. *Ethnology*, 20(2), 101–114.

Simonton, D. K. (1984). *Genius, creativity, and leadership*. Cambridge, MA: Harvard University Press.

Simonton, D. K. (1988). *Scientific genius*. New York: Cambridge University Press.

Simonton, D. K. (1994). *Greatness: Who makes history and why?* New York: Guilford Press.

Simonton, D. K. (1995). Foresight in insight: A Darwinian answer. In R. J. Sternberg & J. E. Davidson (Eds.), *The nature of insight* (pp. 495–534). Cambridge, MA: MIT Press.

Simonton, D. K. (1996). Creative expertise: A life-span developmental perspective. In K. A. Ericsson (Ed.), *The road to excellence* (pp. 227–253). Mahwah, NJ: Erlbaum.

Simonton, D. K. (1997). Creative productivity: A predictive and explanatory model of career trajectories and landmarks. *Psychological Review*, 104, 66–89.

Simonton, D. K. (1998). Donald Campbell's model of the creative process: Creativity as blind variation and selective retention. *The Journal of Creative Behavior*, 32, 153–158.

Simonton, D. K. (1999). Talent and its development: An emergenic and epigenetic mode. *Psychological Review*, 106, 435–457.

Smith, S. M., Ward, T. B., & Finke, R. A. (Eds.). (1995). *The creative cognition approach*. Cambridge, MA: MIT Press.

Sternberg, R. J. (1981). Intelligence and nonentrenchment. *Journal of Educational Psychology*, 73, 1–16.

Sternberg, R. J. (1982). Natural, unnatural, and supernatural concepts. *Cognitive Psychology*, 14, 451–488.

Sternberg, R. J. (1985a). *Beyond IQ: A triarchic theory of human intelligence*. New York: Cambridge University Press.

Sternberg, R. J. (1985b). Implicit theories of intelligence, creativity, and wisdom. *Journal of Personality and Social Psychology*, 49(3), 607–627.

Sternberg, R. J. (1988a). *The triarchic mind: A new theory of human intelligence*. New York: Viking.

Sternberg, R. J. (1988b). Mental self-government: A theory of intellectual styles and their development. *Human Development*, 31, 197–224.

Sternberg, R. J. (Ed.). (1988c). *The nature of creativity: Contemporary psychological perspectives*. New York: Cambridge University Press.

Sternberg, R. J. (1996). For whom does the Bell Curve toll? It tolls for you. *Journal of Quality Learning*, 6(1), 9–27.

Sternberg, R. J. (1997). *Successful intelligence*. New York: Plume.

Sternberg, R. J. (Ed.). (1999a). *Handbook of creativity*. New York: Cambridge University Press.

Sternberg, R. J. (1999b). A propulsion model of creative contributions. *Review of General Psychology*, 3, 83–100.

Sternberg, R. J. (2003). *WICS: A theory of wisdom, intelligence, and creativity, synthesized*. New York: Cambridge University Press.

Sternberg, R. J., & Davidson, J. E. (Eds.). (1994). *The nature of insight*. Cambridge, MA: MIT Press.

Sternberg, R. J., & Gastel, J. (1989a). Coping with novelty in human intelligence: An empirical investigation. *Intelligence*, 13, 187–197.

Sternberg, R. J., & Gastel, J. (1989b). If dancers ate their shoes: Inductive reasoning with factual and counterfactual premises. *Memory and Cognition*, 17, 1–10.

Sternberg, R. J., Kaufman, J. C., & Pretz, J. E. (2002). *The creativity conundrum: A propulsion model of kinds of creative contributions*. New York: Psychology Press.

Sternberg, R. J., & Lubart, T. I. (1991). An investment theory of creativity and its development. *Human Development*, 34(1), 1–31.

Sternberg, R. J., & Lubart, T. I. (1995). *Defying the crowd: Cultivating creativity in a culture of conformity*. New York: Free Press.

Sternberg, R. J., & Lubart, T. I. (1996). Investing in creativity. *American Psychologist*, 51 (7), 677–688.

Sternberg, R. J., & O'Hara, L. (1999). Creativity and intelligence. In R. J. Sternberg (Ed.), *Handbook of creativity* (pp. 251–272). New York: Cambridge University Press.

Suler, J. R. (1980). Primary process thinking and creativity. *Psychological Bulletin*, 88, 555–578.

Tetewsky, S. J., & Sternberg, R. J. (1986). Conceptual and lexical determinants of nonentrenched thinking. *Journal of Memory and Language*, 25, 202–225.

Therivel, W. A. (1999). Why Mozart and not Salieri? *Creativity Research Journal*, 12, 67–76.

Torrance, E. P. (1962). *Guiding creative talent*. Englewood Cliffs, NJ: Prentice-Hall.

Torrance, E. P. (1974). *Torrance tests of creative thinking*. Lexington, MA: Personnel Press.

Vernon, P. E. (Ed.). (1970). *Creativity: Selected readings* (pp. 126–136). Baltimore: Penguin Books.

von Oech, R. (1983). *A whack on the side of the head*. New York: Warner.

von Oech, R. (1986). *A kick in the seat of the pants*. New York: Harper & Row.

Wallach, M., & Kogan, N. (1965). *Modes of thinking in young children*. New York: Holt, Rinehart, & Winston.

Ward, T. B. (1994). Structured imagination: The role of conceptual structure in exemplar generation. *Cognitive Psychology*, 27, 1–40.

Ward, T. B., Smith, S. M., & Finke, R. A. (1999). Creative cognition. In R. J. Sternberg (Ed.), *Handbook of creativity* (pp. 189–212). New York: Cambridge University Press.

Wehner, L., Csikszentmihalyi, M., & Magyari-Beck, I. (1991). Current approaches used in studying creativity: An exploratory investigation. *Creativity Research Journal*, 4(3), 261–271.

Weisberg, R. W. (1986). *Creativity, genius and other myths*. New York: Freeman Press.

Weisberg, R. W. (1988). Problem solving and creativity. In R. J. Sternberg (Ed.), *The nature of creativity* (pp. 148–176). New York: Cambridge University Press.

Weisberg, R. W. (1993). *Creativity: Beyond the myth of genius*. New York: Freeman Press.

Weisberg, R. W. (1999). Creativity and knowledge: A challenge to theories. In R. J. Sternberg (Ed.), *Handbook of creativity* (pp. 226–250). New York: Cambridge University Press.

Weisberg, R. W., & Alba, J. W. (1981). An examination of the alleged role of "fixation" in the solution of several "insight" problems. *Journal of Experimental Psychology: General*, 110, 169–192.

Werner, H., & Kaplan, B. (1963). *Symbol formation*. Hillsdale, NJ: Erlbaum.

Woodman, R. W., & Schoenfeldt, L. F. (1989). Individual differences in creativity: An interactionist perspective. In J. A. Glover, R. R. Ronning, & C. R. Reynolds (Eds.), *Handbook of creativity* (pp. 77–91). New York: Plenum.

Yamamoto, K. (1964). Creativity and sociometric choice among adolescents. *Journal of Social Psychology*, 64, 249–261.

CHAPTER 16

Complex Declarative Learning

Michelene T. H. Chi
Stellan Ohlsson

Introduction

How do people acquire a complex body of knowledge, such as the history of the Panama Canal, the structure of the solar system, or the explanation for how the human circulatory system works? Complex learning takes longer than a few minutes and requires processes that are more complicated than the associative processes needed to memorize pairs of words. The materials that support complex learning – such as texts, illustrations, practice problems, and instructor feedback presented in classrooms and elsewhere – are often difficult to understand and might require extensive processing. For example, learning about the human circulatory system requires many component processes, such as integrating information from several sources, generating inferences, connecting new information with existing knowledge, retrieving appropriate analogies, producing explanations, coordinating different representations and perspectives, abandoning or rejecting prior concepts that are no longer useful, and so forth. Many of these component processes are still poorly understood so we have even less understanding of the complex process of learning a large body of knowledge.

Complex knowledge can be partitioned into two types: declarative knowledge and procedural knowledge (see Lovett & Anderson, Chap. 17). Declarative knowledge has traditionally been defined as knowledge of facts or knowing *that*, whereas procedural knowledge is knowing *how* (Anderson, 1976; Winograd, 1975). Declarative knowledge is descriptive and use independent. It embodies concepts, principles, ideas, schemas, and theories (Ohlsson, 1994, 1996). Examples of declarative knowledge are the laws of the number system, Darwin's theory of evolution, and the history of the Panama Canal. The sum total of a person's declarative knowledge is his or her understanding of the way the world, or some part or aspect of the world, works, independently of the particular tasks the person undertakes.

Procedural knowledge, such as how to operate and troubleshoot a machine, how to solve a physics problem, or how to use a computer text editor, is prescriptive and use specific. It consists of associations between goals, situations, and actions. Research in cognitive neuroscience supports the reality of this distinction between declarative and procedural knowledge (Squire, 1987).

The acquisition of complex procedural knowledge has been extensively investigated in laboratory studies of skill acquisition, problem solving, and expertise (Ericsson, 1996; Feltovich, Ford, & Hoffman, 1997; see Novick & Bassok, Chap. 14), and in field studies of practitioners (Hutchins, 1995; Keller & Keller, 1996). Issues that have been explored include the role of perceptual organization in expert decision making, the breakdown of goals into subgoals, the effect of ill-defined goals, the nature of search strategies, choices between competing strategies, the conditions of transfer of problem-solving strategies from one problem context to another, the effect of alternative problem representations, the role of collaboration in complex tasks, and so on. As is obvious in this chapter, the issues relevant to the study of complex procedural learning are different from those relevant to the study of complex declarative learning. Because the acquisition of procedural knowledge has been researched so extensively in the past few decades, there are several recent reviews (Lovett, 2002; VanLehn, 1989; see Novick & Bassok, Chap. 14). Therefore, this chapter focuses primarily on the acquisition of a body of declarative knowledge.

The study of complex declarative learning is still in its infancy and has not yet produced a unified theory or paradigmatic framework. The organization of this chapter is meant to suggest one form that such a framework might take. In the first section, we describe basic characteristics of complex declarative knowledge. In the second section, we classify the different types of changes that occur in declarative knowledge as one learns. This classification is the main contribution of the chapter. The third section is a brief treatment of the so-called learning paradox (Bereiter, 1985). We end with a few concluding remarks.

Basic Characteristics of Declarative Knowledge

Size of Knowledge Base

The most basic observation one can make about declarative knowledge is that humans have a lot of it. There are no precise estimates of the amount of knowledge a person possesses, but two attempts at an estimate seem well grounded. The first is an estimate of the size of the mental lexicon. The average college-educated adult knows between 40,000 and 60,000 words (Miller, 1996, pp. 136–138). The total number of words in the English language is larger than 100,000. Because concepts only constitute a subset of declarative knowledge, this represents a lower bound on the size of a person's declarative knowledge base. Second, Landauer (1986) estimated how much information, measured in bits, people can remember from a lifetime of learning. His estimate is 2 × 10^9 bits by age 70. It is not straightforward to convert bits to concepts or pieces of knowledge, but even very fast computers use only 32 or 64 bits to encode one basic instruction. If we make the conservative assumption that it requires 1000 bits to encode one piece of knowledge, Landauer's estimate implies that a person's declarative knowledge base eventually approximates 1 million pieces of knowledge.

These estimates apply to the size of the knowledge base as a whole. At the level of individual domains, estimates of the size of domain-specific knowledge bases tend to result in numbers that are comparable to estimates of the mental lexicon. For example, Simon and Gilmartin (1973) estimated the number of chess piece configurations – chunks or patterns – known by master players to be between 10,000 and 100,000. We do not know whether this is a coincidence or a symptom of some deeper regularity.

In short, even without a precise definition of what is to count as a unit of knowledge, the average person's declarative knowledge base must be measured in tens of thousands, or more likely hundreds of thousands, of units. How all this knowledge – the raw material for reasoning and thinking – is acquired is clearly a nontrivial, but under-researched, question.

Organization

Knowledge does not grow as a set of isolated units but in some organized fashion. To capture the organization of the learners' declarative knowledge, cognitive scientists operate with three distinct representational constructs: semantic networks, theories, and schemas (Markman, 1999).

The key claim behind *semantic networks* is that a person's declarative knowledge base can be thought of as a gigantic set of nodes (concepts) connected by links (relations). All knowledge is interrelated, and cognitive processes, such as retrieval and inferencing, operate by traversing the links. Early computer simulations of long-term memory for declarative knowledge explored variants of this network concept (Abelson, 1973; Anderson & Bower, 1973; Norman & Rumelhart, 1975; Quillian, 1968; Schank, 1972; see Medin & Rips, Chap. 3).

Because the distance between two nodes in a semantic network is determined by the number of relations one must traverse to reach from one to the other, semantic networks implicitly claim that declarative knowledge is *grouped by domain*. We use the term "domain" to refer to both informal areas of knowledge, such as home decorating, eating at a restaurant, and watching sports, and formal disciplines, such as botany, linguistics, and physics. Pieces of knowledge that belong to the same domain are similar in meaning and therefore cluster together functionally. Consistent with this notion, membership in the same domain tends to produce higher similarity ratings, stronger priming effects, and other quantitative behavioral consequences; descriptions of these well-known effects can be found in textbooks in cognitive psychology (e.g., Ashcraft, 2002; Reisberg, 2001).

The structure of any domain representation depends on the dominant relations of that domain. If the dominant relation is set inclusion, the representation is organized as a *hierarchy*. The standard taxonomies for animals and plants are prototypical examples. In contrast, relations such as *cause–effect* and *before–after* produce chain-like structures. In general, the representations of domains are *locally structured* by their dominant relations.

The semantic network idea claims that all knowledge is interrelated, but it does not propose any single, overarching structure for the network as a whole. Concepts and assertions are components of domains, but domains are not components of a yet higher level of organization. Domains relate to each other in a contingent rather than systematic way. Informal observations support this notion. We have one concept hierarchy for *tools* and another for *furniture*, but the node *lamp* appears in both. Home decorating is not a subset of cooking, or vice versa, but the two share the *kitchen*. The concept of *tangled hierarchies* (Hofstadter, 1999) describes one aspect of local, unsystematic contact points between internally structured domains. These comments are somewhat speculative because there is little cognitive research aimed at elucidating the structure of the declarative knowledge base as a whole.

Domains can also be represented as *theories*. Theories are "deep" representations (borrowing a term from social psychologists, see Rokeach, 1970) in the sense of having well-articulated *center-periphery* structures. That is, a theory is organized around a small set of core concepts or principles – big ideas – on which the rest of the elements in the domain are dependent. The core knowledge elements are typically fundamental and abstract, whereas the peripheral ones are based on, derived from, or instances of the core ones. The most pristine examples of center-periphery structures are the formal axiomatic systems of mathematics and logic in which a small set of chosen axioms provide a basis for the proofs of all other theorems in a particular formal theory, and natural science theories, such as Newton's theory of mechanical motion, Darwin's theory of biological evolution, and the atomic theory of chemical reactions. These theories are obviously experts' and novices' representations of those same domains and may or may not exhibit a similar structure, indicating that change in structure is one dimension of complex learning. For example, DiSessa (1988, 1993) argued that novice knowledge of mechanical motion is not theory-like at all but is better thought of as an irregular collection of fragments (see Smith, DiSessa, & Roschelle, 1995, for a modified version of this view).

Other cognitive scientists, however, prefer to represent the novices' understandings of the natural world as *intuitive theories* in deliberate analogy with the explicit and codified theories of scientists and mathematicians (Gopnik & Meltzoff, 1997; Gopnik & Wellman, 1994; McCloskey, 1983; Wiser & Carey, 1983). By referring to someone's naive representation as a theory, one implies specifically that the representation shares certain characteristics with explicit theories; most prominently that it has a center-periphery structure.[1]

A well-developed center-periphery structure is often the hallmark of an expert's representation of a domain, and a comparison between novices' and experts' representations of the same domain often reveals differences in the "depth" of their representations. However, one can raise the question of whether "depth" should also be construed as a characteristic of the domain itself. That is, are some domains intrinsically "deep" whereas others not, so that a center-periphery structure is not an appropriate representation for some domains? If so, we would expect neither experts nor novices to construct "deep" representations of those domains. For example, in informal everyday domains such as *home decorating* or *eating at a restaurant*, the center-periphery structure is certainly less salient. (However, even if an everyday domain such as *entertaining* might not have a principled theory, its subdomain of *formal table setting* does; Bykofsky & Fargis, 1995, pp. 144–146; Tuckerman & Dunnan, 1995, pp. 176–177.) Moreover, even for informal domains such as *cooking* for which we as novices might claim to lack deep principles, many professional chefs would disagree. Thus, to what extent is the pervasive striving for a center-periphery structure with increasing expertise a law of mental representation, and to what extent is it an adaptation to the objective structure of domains, remains an open question.

The network concept codifies the intuition that everything is related to everything else, and the theory concept codifies the intuition that some knowledge elements are more important than others. The concept of a *schema*, however, codifies the intuition that much of our declarative knowledge represents recurring patterns in experience (see Holyoak, Chap. 6). Although the term "schema" has never been formally defined, the key strands in this construct are nevertheless clear. To a first approximation, a schema is a set of relations among a set of slots or attributes, where the slots can be thought of as variables that can take values within a specified range (Bobrow & Collins, 1975; Brewer & Nakamura, 1984; Marshall, 1995; Minsky, 1975; Norman & Rumelhart, 1975; Thorndyke, 1984). Take the concept of "cousin" as an example. A cousin can be defined by a schema containing slots such as children, parents, and siblings along with a collection of relations such as parent-of and sibling-of:

$$\text{(cousin-of y w)} = \text{def[(parent-of x y)} \times \text{(sibling-of z x)(parent-of z w)]} \quad \text{(Eq. 16.1)}$$

To say that a person understands that Steve (slot y) and Bob (slot w) are cousins is to say that he or she knows that Steve (slot y) is the son of Carl (slot x), Carl is the brother of John (slot z), and John is the father of Bob (slot w). The slots are associated with ranges of appropriate values. Being a child, Steve must be younger than Carl; thus, slot y might have an age range of 1 to 50 years old, and slot x might have an age range of 21 to 85 years old. Similarly, slot y can have the values of being either a male (a son) or a female (a daughter).

Schemas are bounded units of knowledge, and it is essential to their hypothesized function that they are retrieved or activated as units. That is, if one part of a schema (relation or slot) is activated, there is a high probability that the rest of the schema will also be retrieved. Schemas are typically abstract precisely because they represent recurring patterns in experience. Level of abstraction can vary (Ohlsson, 1993a).

There are many variants of the schema idea in the cognitive literature. In the classic chess studies of deGroot (1965) and Chase and Simon (1973), chess experts were found to know by heart thousands of board patterns (each pattern consisting of a few chess pieces arranged in a meaningful configuration), and these familiar patterns altered their perception of the board to suggest promising moves. Similar findings regarding the power of perceptual patterns to influence high-level cognition can be seen in a physician's ability to read X-rays (Lesgold et al., 1988) and a fire fighter's ability to size up a fire (Klein, 1998). Similarly, there is evidence to show that experts' programming knowledge includes frame-like structures called *plans* (Soloway & Erhlich, 1984), which are stereotypical situations that occur frequently in programming: looping, accumulating values, and so forth. These basic plans not only serve as the building blocks when writing programs, but they are also necessary for comprehension of programs. *Scripts* are higher-order knowledge structures that represent people's knowledge of informal or everyday events such as eating in a restaurant or visting the dentist's office (Schank & Abelson, 1977). *Explanation patterns* are schemas for how to construct explanations of particular types (Kitcher, 1993; Ohlsson, 2002; Ohlsson & Hemmerich, 1999; Schank, 1986). Yet other schema-like constructs have been proposed (e.g., Collins & Ferguson, 1993; Keegan, 1989; Machamer & Woody, 1992). Chunks, explanation patterns, frames, plans, and scripts are variants of the basic idea that much declarative knowledge consists of representations of recurring patterns. For simplicity, we use the term *schema* throughout this chapter to refer to all these constructs.

Although the three constructs of networks, theories, and schemas appear side by side in the cognitive literature, the relations between them are unclear. First, it is not clear how a schema should be understood within the larger notion of a semantic network. For a schema to be a distinct representational entity, there has to be a well-defined boundary between the schema and the rest of the knowledge network. (If not, activation will spread evenly across the nodes and links in the schema and the nodes and links that are not in the schema, which contradicts the central claim of schema theory that the probability of spreading from one node within the schema to another node within the schema is higher than spreading to a node outside the schema.) However, the concept of a network does not provide any obvious way to explain what would constitute such a boundary other than to assume that links among nodes within a schema are more strongly connected than links among nodes between schemas (Chi & Ceci, 1987; Rumelhart, Smolensky, McClelland, & Hinton, 1986). The differentiation in the strength of linkages can create clusters that can be conceived of as schemas (Chi & Koeske, 1983).

The relations between a schema and a theory are equally unclear. One can conceptualize a schema as a tool for organizing information, but it is not obvious whether a schema makes assertions or claims about the world. In this conception, schemas are not theories, but people obviously have theories. Finally, any explication of the relation between networks and theories must specify how the center-periphery structure that is intrinsic to theories can be embedded within networks.

In this chapter, we take the stance that networks, theories, and schemas are three partially overlapping but distinct theoretical constructs. Different aspects of the organization of declarative knowledge are best understood with the help of one or the other of these constructs, or with some mixture of the three.

In summary, declarative knowledge bases are very large and they exhibit complex organization. The notion of semantic networks captures the fact that every part of a person's knowledge is related, directly or indirectly, to every other part. Representations of particular domains vary in "depth," that is, the extent to which they are characterized by a central set of fundamental ideas or principles to which other, more peripheral knowledge units are related. Declarative knowledge also represents recurring patterns in experience with schemas, small packets of abstract structural information that are retrieved as units and used to organize information. These three types of organization cannot easily be reduced to each other, and explanations of change in complex knowledge draw upon one or the other of these constructs or on some mixture of the three.

Types of Changes

The purpose of this section is to describe different types of changes in the knowledge base as one learns a body of declarative knowledge. There exists no widely accepted taxonomy of changes in a body of declarative knowledge. We chose to characterize changes as potentially occurring along seven dimensions. Presumably, different cognitive mechanisms are responsible for changes along different dimensions, but the field has not specified with any precision learning mechanisms for every dimension. In each section here, we specify a dimension of change, summarize some relevant empirical evidence, and describe the cognitive processes and mechanisms, if any, that have been proposed to explain change along that dimension.

Larger Size

Cumulative growth in size is a basic dimension of change in a body of declarative knowledge. Adults obviously know more about the world in general than do children (Chi, 1976), and thus children are often referred to as universal novices (Brown & DeLoache, 1978). Similarly, experts obviously know more about their domains of expertise than novices (Chi, Glaser, & Farr, 1988). People routinely accumulate additional facts about the world from sources such as news programs, texts, pictures, and conversations. These sources present people with some factual information that they did not know before, and some of those facts are retained. The declarative knowledge base continues to grow in size throughout the life span, albeit perhaps at a slower rate as a person ages (Rosenzweig, 2001). Rumelhart and Norman (1978) referred to this type of cumulative addition of pieces of knowledge as *accretion*.

For adults, cumulative acquisition of individual pieces of knowledge – facts – must be pervasive and account for a large proportion of all learning. There is little mystery as to the processes of acquisition. People acquire them via perception and observation, via comprehension of oral and written discourse, and via inductive (see Sloman & Lagnado, Chap. 5) and deductive (see Evans, Chap. 8) reasoning (i.e., by inferring new facts from prior knowledge, or by integrating new facts with old knowledge and making further inferences from the combination).

A particularly interesting property of accretion is that it is self-strengthening. Many psychology studies have confirmed that what is encoded, comprehended, and inferred depends on the individual learner's prior knowledge. For example, Spilich, Vesonder, Chiesi, and Voss (1979) presented a passage describing a fictitious baseball game. Not only was the amount of recall of the individuals with high prior baseball knowledge greater (suggesting that the information was properly encoded), but the pattern of recall also differed. The high-knowledge individuals recalled more information directly related to the goal structure of the game (Spilich et al., 1979) as well as the actions of the game and the related changes in the game states (Voss, Vesonder, & Spilich, 1980), whereas the low-knowledge individuals recalled the teams, the weather, and other less important events and confused the order of the actions. Moreover, high-knowledge individuals were better than low-knowledge individuals at integrating a sequence of sentences (Chiesi, Spilich, & Voss, 1979, exp. V). In short, prior knowledge leads to more effective accretion, which in turn generates more prior knowledge.

Although encoding, comprehending, and inference processes augment the knowledge base, they do not necessarily cause deep changes in prior knowledge. Consider once again a baseball fan reading a newspaper article about a game. He or she will acquire facts that are obviously new – the score in the eighth inning cannot have been known before the game has been played – but the facts about past games are not altered, and he or she is unlikely to acquire a new and different conception of the game itself, although additional facts about baseball games per se may be acquired. The key characteristic that makes this an instance of accretion is that the learner already has a schema for a baseball game, which presumably has slots for the basic actions (throwing the ball), the highest-level goal (winning the game), and other aspects of the game (Soloway, 1978). Once that schema has been acquired, to become increasingly knowledgeable is largely to acquire more knowledge that fits into those slots, as well as knowledge of subgoals and relations between the basic actions and the goal (Means & Voss, 1985). Similarly, readers of narratives might acquire facts about some fictional events, but they are unlikely to change their conceptions of causality, time, or human motivation, arguably three central schemas in comprehending narratives (Graesser, Singer, & Trabasso, 1994; Kintsch, 1998).

These observations imply that we need to distinguish between two levels of learning. Comprehension as normally understood results in the construction of a specific instance of a schema or the accretion of schema-relevant facts. New information is *assimilated* to existing schemas. This is the basic mechanism of accretion. The size of the relevant declarative knowledge base increases without fundamental changes in structure.

Deeper learning, however, results in some structural modification of the learner's prior schema. The same distinction can easily be expressed within the other two theoretical frameworks that we use in this chapter. In network terms, accretion adds nodes and links without deleting or altering any prior ones, while deeper learning requires a reorganization of the network. In terms of intuitive theories, cumulative growth might develop the relations between the core principles and peripheral knowledge items, while deeper learning either develops the core principles or replaces or alters one or more of the core principles. We discuss deeper learning processes later in this chapter.

Denser Connectedness

In network terms, *connectedness* can be defined as the density of relations between the knowledge elements. We would expect the density of connections in a representation to increase as the learner acquires more knowledge. This implication was supported by a study in which we compared the node-link representation of a single child's knowledge of 20 familiar dinosaurs with his representation of 20 less familiar dinosaurs (Chi & Koeske, 1983; Figures 16.1 and 16.2). The nodes and relations of the network were captured from the child's generation protocols of dinosaurs and their attributes. The representation of the 20 more familiar dinosaurs was better connected into meaningful clusters in that it had more links relating the dinosaurs that belonged to the same family, as well as relating the dinosaurs with their attributes of diet and habitat. The representation of the 20 less familiar dinosaurs had fewer links within clusters, and thus the cluster were less densely connected, so they appear less differentiated and more diffused. In short, the better learned materials were more densely connected in an organized way, even though, overall, the two networks represented the same number of nodes and links.

A special case of connectedness is the mapping between layers. Layers can be defined in different ways in different domains. For example, in the context of computer programming we can conceive of the specification (the goals) as the highest layer, and the implementation (the data structures and primitive actions of the program) as the lowest level. Designing and comprehending a program requires building a bridge between the specification and the implementation

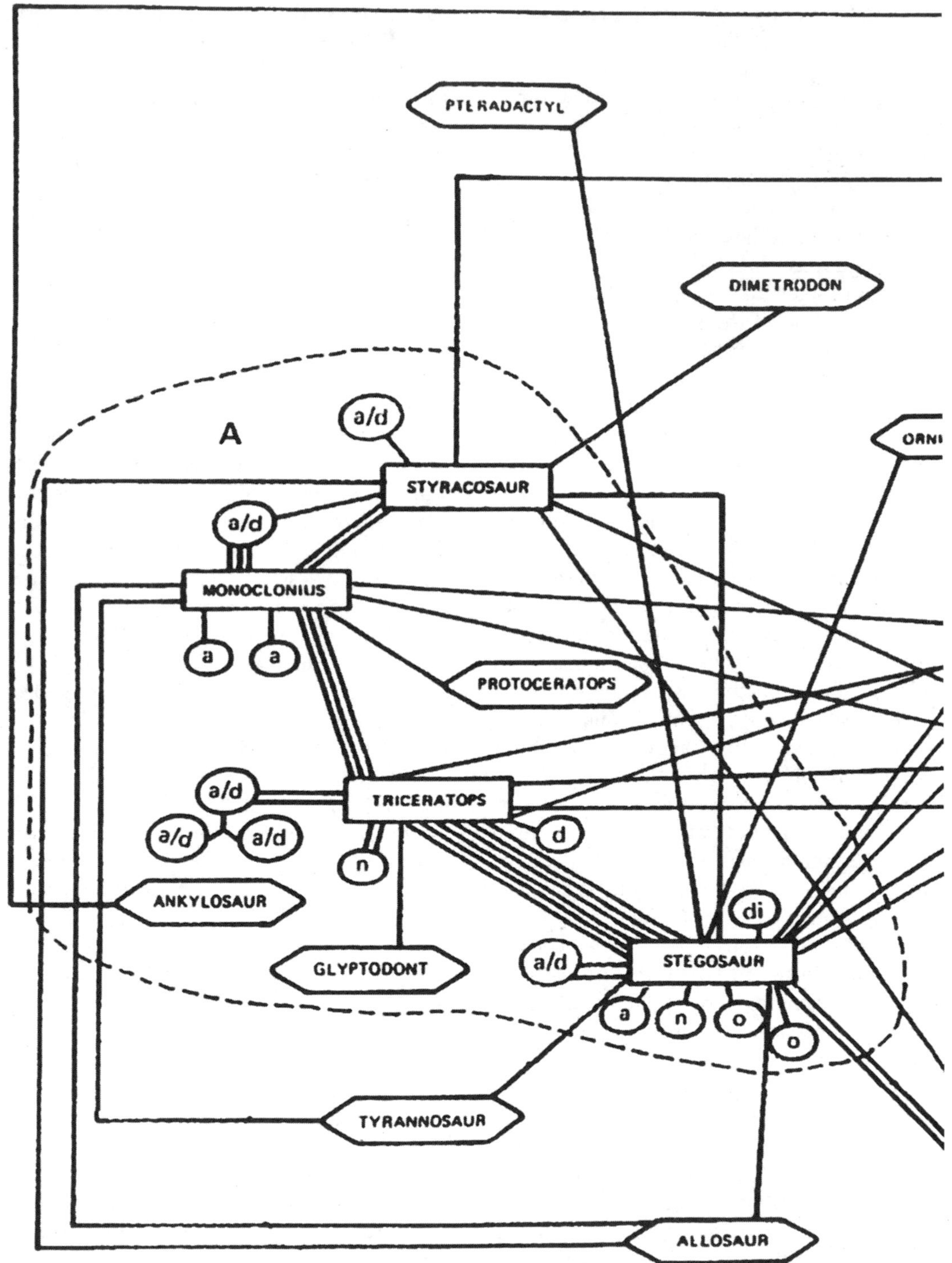

Figure 16.1. A child's representation of 20 familiar dinosaurs. (From Chi & Koeske, 1983.)

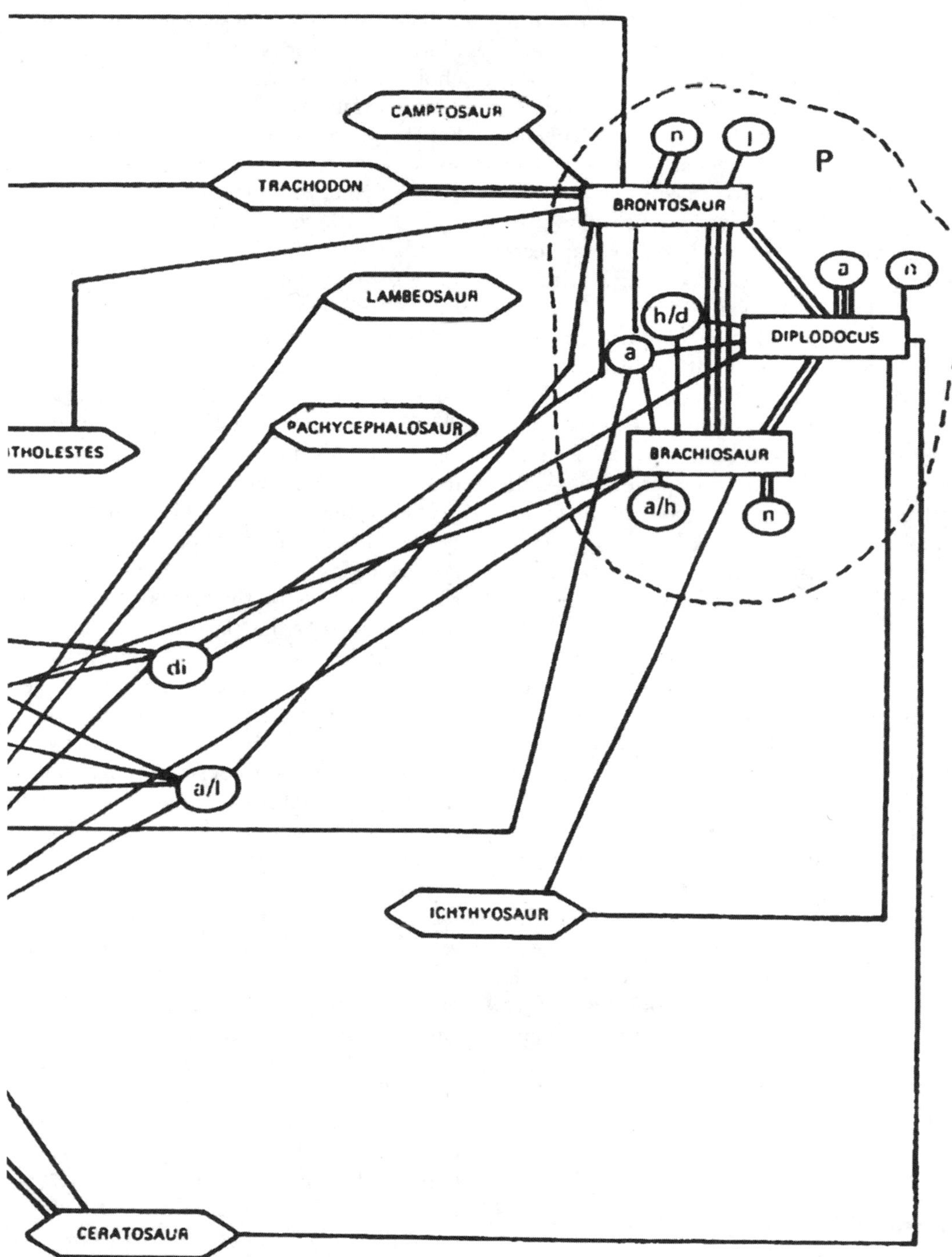
CAMPTOSAUR
TRACHODON
BRONTOSAUR
P
LAMBEOSAUR
h/d
a
DIPLODOCUS
PACHYCEPHALOSAUR
THOLESTES
BRACHIOSAUR
a/h
n
di
a/l
ICHTHYOSAUR
CERATOSAUR

(Brooks, 1983). This bridge maps the implementation to the specification through a series of layers. Expert programmers are skilled at linking high-level goals to specific segments of programming code, whereas less skilled programmers are more likely to link program goals to triggers like variable names (Pennington, 1987). Once again, we see that a person's knowledge base appears to become more densely connected with increased knowledge acquisition.

Another special case of connectedness is between the conditions (declarative knowledge) and the actions (procedural knowledge). For example, experienced and inexperienced pilots knew equivalent numbers of facts, but the inexperienced pilots failed to apply them in the context of actions (Stokes, Kemper, & Kite, 1997). One can interpret this to mean that the facts that the inexperienced pilots knew were not connected to their actions.

Although the cited studies involved highly domain-specific relations, there are many types of connections that play central roles in declarative knowledge bases. For example, causal relations play a central role in the comprehension of narratives (see Buehner & Cheng, Chap. 7; Trabasso & van den Broek, 1985) and scientific theories (see Dunbar & Fugelsang, Chap. 29), and hierarchical relations such as set–subset relations form the backbone of taxonomic or classificatory knowledge structures (see Medin & Rips, Chap. 3). The general point is that, as knowledge acquisition proceeds in a domain, the learner's representation of that domain will increase in connectedness in a meaningful way.

Increased Consistency

The *consistency* of a knowledge representation refers to the degree to which the multiple assertions embedded in an intuitive theory can, in fact, be true at the same time. A person who claims that the Earth is round but who refuses to sail on the ocean for fear of falling over the edge is inconsistent in this sense.

The concept of consistency has been explored for decades in many areas of psychology, philosophy, and education. Social psychologists investigated the consistency of belief systems in the 1950s and 1960s (Abelson et al., 1968; Festinger, 1962/1957; Fishbein & Ajzen, 1975; Heider, 1944; McGuire, 1968), and it remains an area of active research (Eagly & Chaiken, 1993; Harmon-Jones & Mills, 1999). In the wake of Thomas Kuhn's influential book *The Structure of Scientific Revolutions* (Kuhn, 1970), the philosophical debate about theory change in science came to focus on how scientists react to inconsistencies (anomalies) between theory and data, and this perspective carried over into contemporary approaches to science education (Hewson & Hewson, 1984; Posner, Strike, Hewson, & Gertzog, 1982; Strike & Posner, 1985). Education researchers were already primed for this focus by the traditional concern in the Piagetian tradition with contradictions and inconsistencies as driving forces for cognitive development (Piaget, 1985). Unfortunately, the social, philosophical, educational, and developmental literatures on cognitive consistency are not as tightly integrated as they ought to be in light of the nearly identical ideas that drive research in these fields.

It is reasonably certain that people prefer consistent over inconsistent beliefs, at least locally, and that the discovery of local inconsistency (or conflict; Ames & Murray, 1982) triggers cognitive processes that aim to restore consistency, just as Piaget, Festinger, Kuhn, and others have hypothesized. For example, Thagard (1989, 2000) explored a computational network model called ECHO in which consistency is defined as the lack of contradictions between assertions and hypotheses. ECHO has successfully predicted human data from a variety of situations, including the evaluation of scientific theories in light of data (Thagard, 1992a) and the outcome of court cases (Thagard, 1992b).

However, the relation between experienced inconsistency and cognitive change is complex. Several investigators suggested that conflict triggers efforts to restore

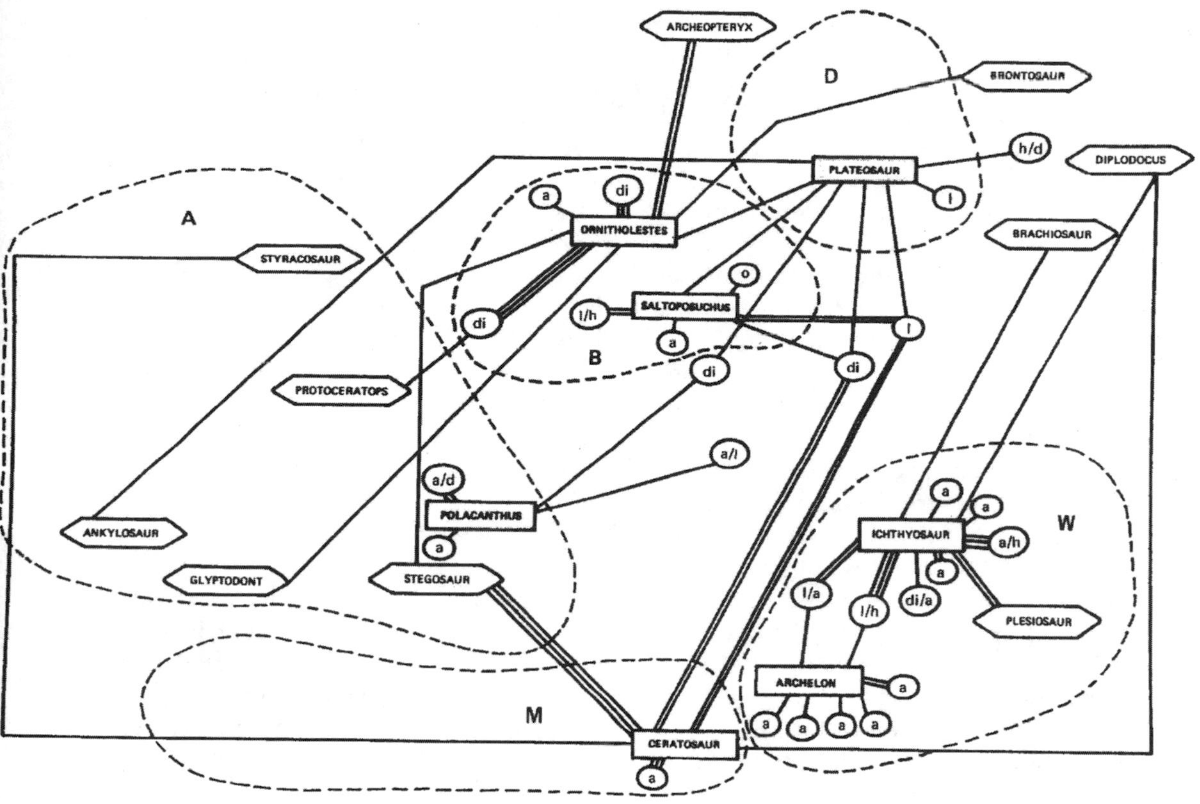

Figure 16.2. A child's representation of 20 less familiar dinosaurs (From Chi & Koeske, 1983.)

consistency only when the conflict is recognized by the learner him- or herself through reflection (Chi, 2000; Ohlsson, 1999; Strike & Posner, 1992). When learners are alerted to inconsistencies and conflicts by an external source, they are more likely to either assimilate or dismiss them (Chinn & Brewer, 1993). Contradiction highlighted by an external source is likely to trigger change processes only if the learner is dissatisfied with his or her current conception (Posner et al., 1982). Furthermore, there are many ways to respond to inconsistency (Chinn & Brewer, 1993; Darden, 1992; Kelman & Baron, 1968), and not all modes of response increase consistency (as opposed to bypassing the problem); we return to this topic in "The Learning Paradox: Monotonic and Nonmonotonic Change."

Consistency should not be confused with veridicality. It is possible for a knowledge representation to be locally consistent and yet be inaccurate. For example, we have argued that the naive conception of the circulatory system as a single-loop system is flawed but nevertheless constrained by a consistent set of identifiable yet inaccurate principles. The learner can use such a flawed conception systematically to generate incorrect explanations. (Chi, 2000). Historically, the Ptolemian epicycle theory of the solar system was as internally consistent as the Keplerian theory, but obviously not as accurate.

Consistency should also not be confused with level of expertise. A more knowledgeable person does not necessarily have a more consistent domain representation than someone who knows less. Ability to operate with inconsistency has often been proposed as a sign of intellectual sophistication, whereas insistence on total consistency has long been associated with dogmatism and lack of intellectual flexibility (Ehrlich & Leed, 1969; Rokeach, 1960). A famous historic example is the resolution – or lack of resolution – within quantum mechanics between the wave and particle models of photons. These annoying entities insist on behaving as both waves and particles, and since the time of Niels Bohr physicists have been content to let them be that way.

Consistency is sometimes used synonymously with the term *coherence*, as in Thagard's (1992a) use of the term *explanatory coherence* to refer to the consistency between a hypothesis and evidence and other hypotheses. However, consistency is distinct from coherence in that, as a measure of a representation, coherence can be used to refer to the more well-defined connectedness in a semantic representation in which the notion of contradiction or conflict is not an issue (Chi & Koeske, 1983). There is not enough evidence or agreement about the concept of coherence to warrant discussing it as a separate dimension of change.

In summary, increased consistency is an important type of change in a declarative knowledge base, but it is distinct from the concepts of higher veridicality, more advanced knowledge, and coherence.

Finer Grain of Representation

Reality is not simple, and almost any aspect of it can be described or represented at different levels of grain. As one learns more about something, one often comes to understand it at a finer grain. For example, learning how the human circulatory system works involves learning the components of the system, such as the heart, the lungs, blood, and blood vessels, and the relation that the contraction of the heart sends blood to different parts of the body.

Given this level of representation, one can then ask, *how does the heart contract?* To answer this question, one would have to learn about the constituents of the heart: the properties of contractive muscle fibers, the role of ventricle pressure, and so on. The learner might push yet toward another level by asking how individual muscle fibers contract. At each level the system is understood in terms of its constituent parts, and further knowledge acquisition expands each component into its constituent parts. This type of process expands the knowledge base, but in a particular way: It moves along *part-of* links (as opposed to *kind-of* links). In network terms, what was formerly a single node is expanded downward into an entire subtree.

Miyake (1986) collected protocol data that illustrated this type of change. She showed that dyads, in attempting to understand how a sewing machine works, would move to lower and lower levels when they recognized that they had not understood the mechanism. For example, in figuring out how a stitch is made, one can understand it by explaining that the needle pushes a loop of the upper thread through the material to the underside so the upper thread loops entirely around the lower thread. However, to understand how this looping mechanism works, one has to explain the mechanism at a yet finer level – namely, in terms of how the bottom thread goes through the loop of the upper thread.

Knowledge expansion via finer grain of representation is quite common in the sciences. The ultimate example is perhaps the reduction by chemists of material substances to molecules, described in terms of atoms, which in turn are re-represented by physicists in terms of elementary particles. We should keep in mind though that it is the experts' representations of these domains that are refined, and novices' representations do not necessarily follow suit.

In analyzing biological systems such as the circulatory system and machines such as the sewing machine, the parts are objects of the *same kind* as the system itself so they embody the *part-of* relations. In these examples, valves and veins are of the same kind and are both parts of the cardiovascular system, and thread and a stitch are of the same kind and are both parts of the sewing process. The link between the behavior of the parts and the behavior of the whole can often be understood in terms of direct cause and effect, or in terms of mechanical constraints that force movement in one direction rather than another, such as the valves in the veins.

However, there are systems in which the relation between the finer and coarser levels of analysis is not of the same kind and the behavior of the system is *emergent* (Chi, in press; Wilensky & Resnick, 1999). A traffic jam is an example. A traffic jam is a gridlock of cars such that cars can no longer move at normal speed. However, the cars are not of the same kind as the traffic jam. In this kind of system, the (often) observable macrolevel behavior (the traffic jam) can be represented independently of the microlevel objects (the moving cars). Each individual car may be following the same simple rule, which is to accelerate if there is no car in front within a certain distance and to slow down when there is another car within that distance. However, the jam itself can move backward even though the individual cars move forward. Thus, the behavior of the individual cars in a jam is independent of the jam. Nevertheless, the macrolevel pattern (the jam) arises from local interactions among the microlevel individual cars.

Learning about systems of this kind does not necessarily proceed by unpacking parts into yet smaller parts but might more often occur by acquiring the two representations of the system separately and then linking them. This type of learning process re-represents the macro in terms of the relationship between the micro- and the macrolevels to explain the macrolevel phenomenon (Chi, in press; Chi & Hausmann, 2003).

It is not clear how often people are driven to expand their representations downward to a finer grain of analyses. In everyday life, people do not always feel the necessity to connect phenomena at one level to phenomena at more fine-grained levels. For example, people appear content to understand the weather at the level of wind, temperature, clouds, humidity, rain, and snow, without re-representing them at the finer levels of molecular phenomena available to the professional meteorologist (Wilson & Keil, 2000). We do not yet understand the factors and processes that drive people to expand, but the possibility of such expansion is one important dimension of change in declarative knowledge.

Greater Complexity

A distinct type of change in the knowledge structure is needed when the learner's current concepts are not sufficient to represent the phenomenon or system as a whole. The thing to be understood cannot be assimilated within any schema the learner has available. The learner can respond by creating a more complex schema (see Halford, Chap. 22). Although little is known about how more complex schemas are developed, one plausible hypothesis is that they are created by combining or assembling several existing schemas (Ohlsson & Hemmerich, 1999; Ohlsson & Lehtinen, 1997).

The creation of the theory of evolution by natural selection is a case in point. In the nineteenth century, many biologists knew that there were variations within species and that many species produce more offspring than survive into adult (reproductive) age, and the fact (as opposed to the explanation) of inheritance was of course commonly accepted. The theory of evolution is the result of assembling or combining these three schemas in a very particular way into a new, more complex schema. The change process here does not move along either *kind-of* or *part-of* relations, and it does not refine the grain of representation. Instead, it moves to greater complexity. The resulting schema is more complex than either of the prerequisite schemas. Such a move does not necessarily require a higher level of abstraction (see the next section). The prior principles of intraspecies variation, inheritance, and differential survival were already abstract, and there is no significant increase in abstraction in the theory that combines them.

The assembly process can be prompted. In one study, Ohlsson and Regan (2001) studied a laboratory version of the problem of the structure of DNA. Based on published historic accounts of the discovery of DNA, we extracted eight different component concepts that had to be combined to represent the double-helix structure. These turned out to be concepts that most educated adults can be expected to possess (e.g., parallel, pairwise, inverse, complement). We found a linear relationship between the proportion of these eight concepts that were primed by exercises prior to problem solving and the time it took undergraduate students to solve the laboratory version of the DNA problem.

The assembly process can be understood as a combination of schemas. The key step in combining schemas must be to align the slots of one schema to those of another. A natural selection schema does not work unless the species that exhibits variation is also the species that is subject to selective pressure. The assembly process might share features with *conceptual combination*, although the latter process refers to single lexical concepts consisting of unfamiliar noun-noun or adjective-noun pairs, such as *pet fish* (Costello & Keane, 2000; Hampton, 1997; Medin & Shoben, 1988; Smith, Osherson, Rips, & Keane, 1988; see Medin & Rips, Chap. 3). We know little about the frequency and prevalence of moves toward creating greater complexity at either the single concept or schema levels, and less about the conditions that prompt people to engage in such moves.

Higher Level of Abstraction

The concept of abstraction, in terms of where it comes from or how it is derived, continues to be controversial after two millennia of scholarship. Besides the issue of how abstractions are formed, there is a second, frequently overlooked meaning of moving toward higher abstraction: Given a preexisting set of abstractions, it is possible to re-represent an object or a domain at a higher level of abstraction. For example, Chi, Feltovich, and Glaser (1981) showed that physicists represented routine physics problems in terms of the deep principles that would be needed to construct a solution, whereas physics novices (those who have taken one course in college with an A grade) tended to represent the same problems according to their concrete surface components, such as pulleys and inclined planes. The point is that one and the same problem tends to be represented at these different levels of abstraction by two groups *both of whom know the relevant principles*. The novices in the Chi et al. (1981) study knew the relevant principles in the sense that they could both state them and use them. However, they did not spontaneously represent problems in terms of those principles instead of concrete properties. Somewhere along the path to expertise, the physicists came to do so (see Novick & Bassok, Chap. 14).

Re-representing at a higher level of abstraction (using already acquired abstractions) is an interesting dimension of change, but relevant empirical studies are scarce. As is the case with most other types of changes, we lack knowledge of the conditions that prompt people to move along this dimension and the exact nature of the relevant cognitive mechanism.

Shifted Vantage Point

Changing the level of abstraction is closely related to, but different from, the process that we in normal parlance call *change of perspective*. A classic study by Anderson and Pichert (1978) demonstrates that this phrase does not merely refer to a metaphor but to a concrete psychological process. They gave subjects a text to read that described a home. They instructed subjects to take the perspective of either a burglar or a prospective home buyer. The results showed that the instructions led the subjects to remember different details, even when the perspective-taking instructions were given *after* the subjects had read the text.

Shifting one's point of view can facilitate problem solving. For example, Hutchins and Levin (1981) used the occurrence of deictic verbs, such as "come," "go," "take," "send," and "bring," and place adverbs, such as "here," "there," and "across," in think-aloud protocols to determine the point of view of subjects solving the Missionaries and Cannibals problem. They found that problem solvers shift perspective as they solve the problem. Initially, they view the river that the Missionaries and Cannibals have to cross from the left bank. Later in the problem-solving process, they view the river from the right bank. One of their most interesting findings was that when solvers were in an impasse after having two nonprogressive moves out of their current problem-solving state, they could resolve the impasse if they shifted their point of view. In short, the somewhat mysterious process of "taking" a particular perspective should not be understood as purely metaphorical; this form of re-representation has real consequences for cognitive processing.

In the cases discussed, the perspective shift was transient. There is some evidence to suggest that children become more able to shift perspective as they grow older (see Halford, Chap. 22). For example, Shatz and Gelman (1973) showed that young 2-year-olds could not adjust their speech to the age of the listener, whereas 4-year-olds did adjust their speech, depending on whether they were speaking to another peer or an adult. This suggests that older (but not younger) children are capable of shifting their perspectives to that of the listeners. Similarly, Piaget and Inhelder (1956) showed that older but not younger children are capable of understanding what another viewer might see, when the other person views it from another perspective. One might assume that as children mature they acquire more knowledge that enables them to shift perspective, and another study confirms this interpretation because it manipulated knowledge directly. We gave high school students opportunities to play with a computer simulation that allows them to take different roles in a business context, such as being the vice president of a bank. Students were much more able to take the perspective of the client after playing with the simulation, whereas they were only able to take the perspective of the bank before playing with the simulation (Jeong, Taylor, & Chi, 2000).

In another series of studies, we attempted to teach first-grade children about the shape of the Earth (Johnson, Moher, Ohlsson, & Gillingham, 1999; Johnson, Moher, Ohlsson, & Leigh, 2001; Ohlsson, Moher, & Johnson, 2000). Deep understanding of this topic requires that a person can coordinate the normal – we call it *ego-centered* – perspective of a person walking around on the Earth with an *exo-centered* perspective from a hypothetical (and physically unattainable) vantage point in space. Such perspective coordinations can be very complex. For example, consider sunsets. What in the ego-centered perspective appears as the sun disappearing behind the horizon appears in the exo-centered perspective as movement of the border between light and shadow across the surface of the Earth owing to the latter's rotation. Clearly, the mapping between these two views of the event is far from natural, simple, or direct, and it requires considerable learning and instruction to develop the exo-centered perspective and to link it to everyday perception.

These and related studies demonstrate the occurrence of shifting vantage points and document the advantages they bring. This type of change must be an important dimension of growth of declarative knowledge.

Discussion

We suggest that a complex body of declarative knowledge over time moves along multiple dimensions of change: size, connectedness, consistency, grain, complexity, abstraction, and vantage point. Undoubtedly, there are other dimensions along which declarative knowledge also changes during learning, such as coherence, but each of these has at least some support in empirical studies.

Although we separate these seven dimensions analytically for purposes of this chapter, we do not suggest that a cognitive change typically moves along a single dimension. Most complex knowledge acquisition processes will involve simultaneous movement along more than one dimension. For example, learning about chemistry involves thinking of material substances as *solids*, *liquids*, and *gases*, instead of, for example, *iron*, *water*, and *air*; this is a move toward higher abstraction. At the same time, the chemistry student acquires a finer-grained analysis of material substances in terms of atoms and molecules and a large number of previously unknown isolated facts about such substances (e.g., their melting points). He or she might have to assemble a new schema such as *dynamic equilibrium*, which involves shifting the vantage point between the atomic level (where there are continuous processes) and the emergent macrolevel (where there is, nevertheless, stability). A year of high school chemistry is likely to require movement along all seven of these dimensions. We suggest that this is typical in the acquisition of complex declarative knowledge.

Given that a representation can change in all the ways we have described previously, research on the acquisition of complex declarative knowledge encounters a particular difficulty – how to assess the effects of different learning scenarios and training procedures. The study of declarative knowledge contrasts in this respect with the study of procedural knowledge. Learning of procedural knowledge such as problem solving can be assessed relatively straightforwardly by measuring the degree to which a learner's representation of the procedure approximates the correct solution procedure in terms of the rules and strategies. Learning of declarative knowledge, however, must be measured in light of the seven dimensions mentioned previously. This is perhaps the most important methodological problem in the study of complex declarative knowledge.

Although we understand the character of these seven dimensions relatively well, we know little about what triggers people to move along one or the other dimension. What are the factors that trigger someone to move to a finer grain or to another level of abstraction? Under what conditions will a learner move to an alternative vantage point? Similarly, we do not fully understand the nature of the processes that bring about the changes in each dimension. Empirical research has been focused on documenting the psychological reality of each type of change and has not sufficiently pursued the questions of triggering conditions and the processes of change.

The seven types of changes discussed so far expand the learner's prior knowledge base in a *monotonic* way in that the prior knowledge need not be rejected or overwritten. It is possible to move toward larger size, denser connectedness, finer grain of representation, greater complexity, higher abstraction, and a different vantage point without rejecting or replacing one's prior knowledge representation. The one exception is a move toward increased consistency. To achieve increased consistency, one might have to reject or abandon some prior knowledge or belief. The next section discusses such *nonmonotonic* changes.

The Learning Paradox: Monotonic and Nonmonotonic Change

It is tempting to think of a novice as primarily lacking knowledge. The learning process is then naturally seen as a process of accretion – filling a void or adding information. Some of the types of changes described in the previous sections, such as increased connectedness and moves toward finer grain of representation, also have this cumulative nature because they significantly extend prior knowledge. However, several of the other types of changes, such as greater complexity, higher level of abstraction, and shifting vantage point, do not have this cumulative nature. Rather, they go further in that they re-represent the domain rather than merely add to it. However, in either the cumulative cases or the re-representation cases, the changes do not require that prior knowledge be rejected or replaced. For example, re-representing something at a higher level of abstraction does not require rejection of the prior representation because abstract and concrete representations of the same thing are not mutually incompatible. We can switch back and forth between conceptualizing something as a *hammer* and as a *tool* without any need to make a permanent choice between these two concepts. Thus, in these types of re-representation process, the old and the new representation can coexist, as well as the re-representing of two component concepts or schemas into a more complex concept or schema via assembly. The representations for the original concepts remain. In short, these types of cumulative and re-representational changes are *monotonic*.

However, there are learning scenarios in which (1) the learner has a well-developed intuitive theory of the target domain, and (2) the subject matter to be acquired directly contradicts one or more of the core principles or beliefs of that intuitive theory. Successful learning in scenarios with these properties requires that the learner go beyond mutually compatible representations. The learner has to re-represent the domain in the more fundamental sense of abandoning or rejecting (i.e., stop believing) what he or she believed before, and replacing it with something else. We refer to this as *nonmonotonic* change.

Science education provides numerous examples of prior conceptions that must be abandoned. Research on so-called misconceptions has documented that people have complex and rich conceptions about domains in which they have not received explicit instruction, but for which everyday experience provides raw material for intuitive theory formation (Confrey, 1990). Research on such spontaneous science theories has focused on physics, chemistry, and biology, although social science and nonscience domains have also been investigated (Limon, 2002). (The older social psychology work on belief systems focused primarily on intuitive theories of society and religion; see, e.g., Abelson et al, 1968; Rokeach, 1970.)

Mechanics (forces and motion) is by far the most investigated domain. The dominant misconception in this domain is that motion implies force (Clement, 1982; DiSessa, 1983, 1988; Halloun & Hestenes, 1985; McCloskey, 1983; Minstrel, 1982). Students assume that when an object is in motion, the motion is caused by a force being applied to the object, the object's motion is in the direction of the force, an object will move with constant velocity as long as it is under the influence of a constant force, and the velocity of an object is proportional to the magnitude of the applied force. When there is no force, an object will either slow down, if it is moving, or remain at rest. Motion is thus misconceived as being produced by force, as opposed to the more accurate view that motion is a natural (i.e., equilibrium) state that will continue indefinitely unless some force interferes with it. Students' intuitive theory is more like the impetus theory held by Jean Buridan and other fourteenth-century thinkers (Robin & Ohlsson, 1989) than like the inertia principle that is central to the Newtonian theory. Misconceptions about other topics, such as biological evolution, are also well documented (Bishop & Anderson, 1990; Brumby, 1984; Demasters, Settlage, & Good, 1995; Ferrari & Chi, 1998; Lawson & Thompson, 1988).

The empirical findings not only show that novices possess well-developed misconceptions about many domains (Reiner, Slotta, Chi, & Resnick, 2000) but that these misconceptions persist in the face of instruction and other innovate kinds of intervention. For example, many science misconceptions in Newtonian mechanics are robust and remain after instruction, even at very selective academic institutions (DiSessa, 1982; Caramazza, McCloskey, & Green, 1980). With respect to mechanics, innovative instructional interventions include using carefully chosen analogies (Clement, Brown, & Zietsman, 1989; Driver, 1987), deliberately invoking cognitive conflict (Posner et al., 1982), engaging in deliberate confrontation (Licht, 1987), or using a succession of increasingly sophisticated models (White & Frederiksen, 1990). Although it is difficult to evaluate the outcomes of such interventions, it appears that students at best acquire the scientific conception, perhaps in an encapsulated form, while maintaining their initial intuitive conception (Johsua & Dupin, 1987), which is not quite the intended outcome. There are at least three reasons (presented in the next section) why misconceptions are so resistant to instruction that nonmonotonic change often fails.

Distortion via Assimilation

As was mentioned earlier, in learning, new information is typically assimilated to existing schemas. Thus, one reason that misconceptions persist is that, when an instructor states the more veridical theory so it contradicts the learner's prior misconceived knowledge, the new information is typically distorted in the process of being assimilated to the prior misconceived knowledge. To illustrate, consider a young child who believes that the Earth is as flat as it looks to the unaided eye. What happens if he or she is told that the Earth is round? Nussbaum (1979; 1985), Nussbaum and Novak (1976), Vosniadou (1994a, 1994b), and Vosniadou and Brewer (1992) observed two intuitive schemas that we are tempted to interpret as consequences of distortion by assimilation. Some children draw the Earth as a flat entity with a circular periphery (like a pancake); others claim that the Earth is spherical but hollow and half-filled with dirt (thus providing a flat surface for people to walk on). In both cases, the Earth is both flat and round. Instruction to the effect that the Earth is round was thus assimilated to a prior flat-Earth conception without any significant changes in the latter.

Evasion of Conflicts

Distortion via assimilation is most plausible when the learner is unaware of the conflict between his or her prior knowledge and new information. The previous example involving the shape of the Earth illustrates this well; the young child is not aware that he or she is interpreting the adjective "round" in a different way than that intended by the adult speaker. This type of distortion can be reliably triggered in the laboratory by deliberately creating texts that violate a normal reader's worldview (Graesser, Kassleer, Kreuz, & Mclain-Allen, 1998).

However, even if the conflict between prior knowledge and new information is detected, it does not necessarily trigger productive change processes. Social psychologists (Abelson et al., 1968) and cognitive researchers (Chinn & Brewer, 1993; Darden, 1992) have converged on very similar lists of potential modes of response to inconsistency. They agree that inconsistency often triggers evasive maneuvers that dismiss the inconsistency in some other way than by revising the relevant knowledge. The most basic mode of response is *abeyance*, that is, to postpone dealing with a contradiction on the grounds that not enough information is available to decide what, if anything, follows. One step removed from doing nothing is *bolstering*: The person who encounters information that contradicts some concept or belief X hastens to seek out supporting or confirming evidence that supports X. Festinger (1962/1957) and others hypothesized that the need to reduce an inconsistency is proportional to the ratio of supporting to contradicting pieces of information. Thus, by drowning the contradicting piece of information in a flood of confirming ones, it is possible to lower the need to resolve the contradiction and hence to keep going without altering one's knowledge. Another process with a similar outcome is *recalibration*, that is, to lower the importance one attaches to the conflicting thoughts, thus making the conflict itself less important and easier to ignore. (A student might decide that he or she is not interested in science after all, so it does not matter what they teach in science courses.) These processes constitute evasive modes of response to inconsistent information, but they are not *learning* processes because there is no constructive change in the person's knowledge.

Lack of Computational Power

In describing the seven dimensions of changes, we sometimes speculated on the processes of change. What would happen if the inconsistent information triggered one or more of the learning processes that we proposed in previous sections? Take the process of creating greater complexity via assembly as example. In that process, a more complex representation is created by combining two or more existing representations. It is doubtful whether this process could lead to a new, more veridical theory. Each of the assembled representations will presumably be consistent with the learner's prior intuitive theory, so they will lack veridicality. One cannot combine two nonveridical representations to create a third, veridical representation. For example, learners' naive conception of heat and temperature, when combined, do not add up to the correct scientific conception of heat (Wiser & Carey, 1983), nor can teleological and Lamarckian ideas combine to form the principle of natural selection.

Although we do not spell out each argument here, a similar case could be made regarding the processes responsible for each of the seven types of changes discussed in the previous section. None of them has the computational power to create a new conception that goes beyond its own conceptual inputs because, by definition, they are nonmonotonic changes.

In summary, the mere presence of contradictory information is not sufficient to trigger productive cognitive change of the nonmonotonic kind. A conflict between prior knowledge and new information might go undetected, in which case the learner might blithely assimilate the new information to prior knowledge, probably distorting it in the process. Even if the learner detects the conflict, he or she might hold the new information in abeyance rather than respond to it. If he or she feels a need to deal with the contradiction, there is a repertoire of evasive maneuvers, including bolstering and recalibration of subjective importance, that will make the contradiction less disturbing without any revisions in prior knowledge. Finally, the productive learning processes discussed previously do not have the computational power to create a new conception that goes beyond the conceptual inputs to those processes. The prevalence of these three kinds of responses to encounters with contradictory information – distortion via assimilation, evading conflicts, and lacking computational power – raises the question of how an intuitive theory can ever be replaced. That is, how can a truly new theory or idea that is not an extension of old theories or ideas ever be acquired? Bereiter (1985) referred to this as the *learning paradox*.

Conclusions and Future Directions

Despite the prevalence of distortion via assimilation to prior knowledge, evasion of conflicts, and lack of computational power, nonmonotonic change does happen.

Children do replace their childhood conceptions with adult ones, some physics students do succeed in learning Newtonian mechanics, and scientists do sometimes replace even their most fundamental theories in the face of anomalous data. Thus, there must be cognitive mechanisms and processes that can overcome the learning paradox. A theory of complex learning should explain both why nonmonotonic change has such a low probability of occurring, and how, by what processes, it happens when it does happen.

The study of such noncumulative learning processes is as yet in its infancy. In this section, we offer a small number of speculative proposals about how nonmonotonic learning processes can occur. These brief proposals are intended to serve as inspiration for further research.

Pathways to Nonmonotonic Change?

We describe below four mechanisms, along with some empirical support. We then consider whether each of them can potentially achieve nonmonotonic change.

TRANSFORMATION VIA BOOTSTRAPPING

One hypothetical path to a new theory is to edit or revise one's existing theory piece by piece until the theory says something significantly different from what it said originally. We can conceptualize such a bootstrapping process as a series of *local repairs* of a knowledge structure. Local repairs require simple mechanisms such as adding links, deleting links, reattaching links, and so forth. The critical condition for local repairs is that the student recognize that the repairs are needed by reflecting on the differences between his or her existing knowledge and new knowledge. We have some evidence that the accumulation of local repairs can lead to a significant transformation of a person's mental model of the circulatory system from a flawed single-loop model to the correct double-loop model (Chi, 2000).

As a second example of bootstrapping, Thagard (1992a) analyzed the changes in the French chemist Lavoiser's conception of matter during the critical years of the development of the oxygen theory of combustion. Thagard shows how Lavoiser's conception of combustion can be modeled by a semantic network, and how that network is gradually transformed over several years as the scientist is reflecting on the outcomes of empirical experiments. By adding and deleting nodes and redrawing links, Thagard depicts Lavoisier's knowledge network as undergoing a gradual transformation such that its initial state represents the phlogiston theory of combustion, but its final state represents the oxygen theory.

How much can transformation via local repairs explain? There are multiple explanations for why local repairs succeed in the case of the circulatory system. One reason is that the transformation from a single-loop model to a double-loop model crosses no ontological categories (Chi & Roscoe, 2002). Another reason might be the relative lack of "depth" of this domain in the sense that it cannot be represented by a center-periphery structure. The single-loop principle does not deductively imply the other relevant facts about the circulatory system in the manner in which Newton's three laws of motion imply more peripheral statements within the domain of motion. The looser connection between center and periphery might make the single-loop principle easy to tinker with. Finally, there is a question of commitment (Ohlsson, 1999). Although students believe that there is a single circulatory loop, this is not one of their most cherished beliefs and they probably do not experience it as important to their worldview. Tinkering even with the core principle of this domain might therefore come easier than in domains with a stronger center-periphery structure and deeper commitment to the core principles. Rokeach (1970) presented evidence from other than scientific domains that knowledge elements are more resistant to change the more central they are. It is plausible that transformation via bootstrapping a sequence of local repairs is less applicable the "deeper" the domain, at least as long as the change has to encompass the core principles to be complete. So perhaps this bootstrapping process cannot be considered a true nonmonotonic change mechanism.

REPLACEMENT

If stepwise revisions can only go so far to explain nonmonotonic change, what alternative is there? Knowledge structures can be *replaced*. That is, an alternative representation of a domain is constructed in parallel with a prior one through processes that do not use the prior one as input. The old and the new representations then compete for the control of discourse and behavior in the course of question answering, explanation, reasoning, and problem solving. The new, presumably more veridical representation frequently wins, and the old one eventually fades from disuse.

Bottom-up Replacement. Replacement can proceed either bottom-up or top-down. First, consider a new representation built bottom-up. This might occur when the new knowledge is encountered in a context that does not necessarily evoke the conflicting prior knowledge. For example, students might experience science instruction as so distant from everyday experience that they build representations of what is taught in class that are independent from, and unconnected to, the former. The outcome of such encapsulated knowledge is an ability to solve textbook problems without enriched understanding of relevant phenomena encountered in other contexts (everyday experience, news reports, etc.). Owing to the compartmentalization of contexts, the conflict between the prior intuitive theory and the new theory is not salient to the learner, and the construction of the new theory can proceed without interference from prior knowledge.

If matters remain in this state, it is doubtful whether this can be considered successful nonmonotonic learning. The crucial question is whether the new theory, once constructed, can migrate into and usurp the territory of the prior intuitive conception. Successful nonmonotonic learning requires that a phenomenon previously understood within the intuitive theory begin to be understood within the new theory instead.

Top-Down Replacement. Consider the po–ssibility of top-down generation of a new knowledge structure. An abstract schema might be acquired in an alternative domain and transferred wholesale to a new domain. An example of this hypothetical process is provided by more recent attempts to understand the operation of the immune system in Darwinian terms. Philosophers and theoretical biologists have attempted to formalize Darwin's theory of evolution (Thompson, 1989), and the resulting abstract schema has been applied to the question of how the immune system could produce antibodies for a wide variety of antigens. The Darwinian answer is that the immune system continually generates more or less random antibodies. High fit between antibodies and antigens triggers increased production of the former; thus, the antigens themselves function as an environment that selects for the antibodies that fight them (Gazzaniga, 1992). The accuracy of this theory of the immune system is not the issue here. It is an example of a process in which a complex abstract schema was transferred as a whole to provide a cognitive template for a novel theory of a physiological process far removed from the evolutionary processes of speciation and adaptation for which the schema was originally constructed.

This top-down process is limited in that it relies on the prior existence of an appropriate abstract schema, which raises the question of where abstractions originate. This issue has remained controversial for more than two millennia. The standard suggestions include induction over exemplars (see Medin & Rips, Chap. 3) and social interaction (see Greenfield, Chap. 27). Because the topic of abstraction is discussed elsewhere in this volume, we do not intend to answer this question here.

Side-stepping the issue of where an abstract schema comes from in the first place, we first need to know whether top-down replacement is possible, given that an abstract schema exists. To test the feasibility of this top-down replacement process, we are instructing students about a domain-general abstract schema that might serve as a template for understanding multiple concepts in many domain. One example is the schema of emergence (Chi, in press), which has applications in biology, chemistry, and physics. It is plausible that direct instruction of this sort results in the de novo construction of an alternative conception, as opposed to gradual transformation of a prior conception.

TRANSFER VIA ANALOGY

Existence of an abstract schema may not be a necessary requisite for the top-down process to work. A concrete schema from another domain might serve as template if the two domains are easy enough to align that the transfer process can operate via analogy (see Holyoak, Chap. 6). In this hypothetical process, the learner acquires a schema in some source domain S; later, he or she is learning about some target domain T for which he or she already has an intuitive theory. The new information about T contradicts his or her prior intuitive theory about T but is analogous to what is known about S. If the learner creates a new representation for T based on what is known about S instead of building directly on his or her current intuitive theory of T, then he or she might avoid distortion by assimilation.

We tested the reality of this *transfer of concrete schema* process in a virtual reality-based scenario for teaching children that the Earth is round (Johnson et al., 1999, 2001; Ohlsson et al., 2000). We created a virtual planet that was small enough so the consequences of sphericality were immediately perceivable. For example, even minor movement through the virtual world made objects visibly "appear" or "disappear" over the horizon. Having acquired a notion of living on a spherical planet in the context of this fictional asteroid (about which the children were not expected to have any distorting prior views), we then supported, via a one-on-one dialogue, the analogical transfer of that schema to the context of the Earth. Pre- to posttest comparisons between the treatment and a dialogue-only control group showed that the effect of prior learning in the virtual environment was positive (albeit small in magnitude). We infer that the schema for the virtual asteroid to some extent served as template for the new conception of the Earth that we tried to teach them. Hence, the learning paradox was overcome by stimulating the children to build a representation of what life on a sphere is like independent of their prior knowledge of the Earth, and then encouraging the use of that representation as a template for building a new representation of the Earth.

ONTOLOGICAL SHIFT

Ontological categories refer to a set of categories to which people partition the world in terms of its most fundamental features (as opposed to characteristic and defining features; Chi, 1997). For example, two high-level categories that people are likely to partition the different types of entities in the world into are substances and processes. Each type of entity is conceptualized as having certain fundamental properties. For example, substances such as sand can be contained in a box, but processes such as a baseball game, cannot; however, processes can last for 2 hours, but substances cannot. Misconceptions are miscategorizations of entities into wrong ontological categories. For example, students typically misconceive heat or electricity as a substance that can move from one location to another (Chi, Slotta, & de Leeuw, 1994). Continued study of some entity that is initially believed as belonging to category X might reveal properties that are not consistent with its ontological status. In those cases, successful learning requires that the learner re-represent the entity as belonging to another ontological category, such as from a kind of substance to a kind of process (Slotta, Chi, & Joram, 1995).

This kind of ontological shift replaces a prior conception with a new conception in terms of an entity's ontological status. Thus, this process of ontological shift may qualify as a kind of a nonmonotonic mechanism.

Toward a Theory of Learning

In 1965, Robert M. Gagné published *The Conditions of Learning,* which summarized what was known about learning at the time. His approach was the unusual one of assuming that there are multiple, distinct types of learning processes distinguishable with respect to their prerequisites, processes, and results. He presented these in order of increasing complexity, beginning with "signal learning" (simple conditioning) and ending with "problem solving" (Gagné, 1965). The most noteworthy feature of his approach is signaled by the book's title: For each type of learning, Gagné asked under which conditions that type of learning might occur.

In our efforts to summarize what is known about the acquisition of complex declarative knowledge, we, too, have been led to present a list of different types of learning. In the realm of monotonic learning, we distinguish between seven different dimensions of change: size, connectedness, consistency, grain, complexity, abstraction, and vantage point. In the realm of nonmonotonic change, we have specified numerous non-learning modes of response to contradictory information such as assimilation and evasive processes of abeyance, bolstering, recalibration, and explained why many of the learning mechanisms cannot in principle produce true nonmonotonic learning. Finally, even our proposals with respect to nonmonotonic learning break down into multiple processes such as transformation via local repairs, bottom-up compartmentalized replacement, top-down replacement with the help of abstract schemas, transfer of concrete schema via analogies, and ontological shift. It seems likely that, as the study of complex learning progresses, cognitive scientists will further our understanding of these replacement processes.

However, as Gagné clearly saw 40 years ago, a list of learning processes is by itself an incomplete theory of learning. One would expect such a theory to support explanation of learning outcomes, to allow us to say why one subject matter is more difficult to acquire than another, to predict the success rate of particular instructional scenarios, and so on. However, to accomplish these and other theoretical tasks, we need to know when, under which circumstances, one or the other learning process is likely to occur. A predictive science of complex learning requires that we can specify the *when* and *wherefore* of the many process hypotheses that spring from the imagination of the cognitive scientist. Nowhere is this more obvious than in the case of nonmonotonic learning. This, we suggest, is the research front in the study of complex declarative learning.

Note

1. In social cognition research, intuitive theories are called *belief systems* (Fishbein & Ajzen, 1975; Rokeach, 1960, 1970). Although the two constructs of intuitive theory and belief system are essentially identical, this connection between social and cognitive psychology has been overlooked on both sides (but see Schultz & Lepper, 1996).

Acknowledgments

Preparation of this chapter was supported in part by Grant 200100305 from the Spencer Foundation and in part by Grant Number 9720359 from the National Science Foundation (for the Center for Interdisciplinary Research on Constructive Learning Environments, CIRCLE, http://www.pitt.edu/~circle) to the first author, and Grant BCS-9907839 from the National Science Foundation to the second author.

References

Abelson, R. P. (1973). The structure of belief systems. In R. C. Schank & K. M. Colby (Eds.), *Computer models of thought and language* (pp. 287–339). San Francisco: Freeman.

Abelson, R. P., Aronson, E., McGuire, W. J., Newcomb, T. M., Rosenberg, M. J., & Tannenbaum, P. H. (Eds.). (1968). *Theories of cognitive consistency: A sourcebook*. Chicago: Rand McNally.

Ames, G. J., & Murray, F. B. (1982). When two wrongs make a right: Promoting cognitive change by social conflict. *Developmental Psychology*, 18, 894–897.

Anderson, J. R. (1976). *Language, memory, and thought*. Hillsdale, NJ: Erlbaum.

Anderson, J. R., & Bower, G. H. (1973). *Human associative memory*. New York: Wiley.

Anderson, R. C., & Pichert, J. (1978). Recall of previously unrecallable information following a shift in perspective. *Journal of Verbal Learning and Verbal Behavior*, 17, 1–12.

Ashcraft, M. H. (2002). *Cognition* (3rd ed.). Upper Saddle River, NJ: Prentice-Hall.

Bereiter, C. (1985). Toward a solution of the learning paradox. *Review of Educational Research*, 55(2), 201–226.

Bishop, B., & Anderson, C. (1990). Student conceptions of natural selection and its role in evolution. *Journal of Research in Science Teaching*, 27, 415–427.

Bobrow, D. G., & Collins, A. (1975). *Representation and understanding: Studies in cognitive science*. New York: Academic Press.

Brewer, W. F., & Nakamura, G. V. (1984). The nature and functions of schemas. In R. Wyer, & T. Srull (Eds.), *Handbook of social cognition* (pp. 119–160). Hillsdale, NJ: Erlbaum.

Brooks, R. (1983). Towards a theory of the comprehension of computer programs. *International Journal of Man-Machine Studies*, 18, 543–554.

Brown, A. L., & DeLoache, J. S. (1978). Skills, plans and self-regulation. In R. S. Siegler (Ed.), *Children's thinking: What develops?* (pp. 3–35). Hillsdale, NJ: Erlbaum.

Brumby, M. (1984). Misconceptions about the concept of natural selection by medical biology students. *Science Education*, 68, 493–503.

Bykofsky, S., & Fargis, P. (1995). *The big book of life's instructions*. New York: Galahad.

Caramazza, A., McCloskey, M., & Green, B. (1980). Naive beliefs in "sophisticated" subjects: Misconceptions about trajectories of objects. *Cognition*, 9, 117–123.

Chase, W. G., & Simon, H. A. (1973). Perception in chess. *Cognitive Psychology*, 4, 55–81.

Chi, M. T. H. (1976). Short-term memory limitations in children: Capacity or processing deficits? *Memory and Cognition*, 4, 559–572.

Chi, M. T. H. (1992). Conceptual change within and across ontological categories: Examples from learning and discovery in science. In R. N. Giere (Ed.), *Cognitive models of science* (pp. 129–186). Minneapolis: University of Minnesota Press.

Chi, M. T. H. (1997). Creativity: Shifting across ontological categories flexibly. In T. B. Ward, S. M. Smith, & J. Vaid (Eds.), *Conceptual structures and processes: Emergence, discovery and change* (pp. 209–234). Washington, DC: American Psychological Association.

Chi, M. T. H. (2000). Self-explaining: The dual processes of generating inferences and repairing mental models. In R. Glaser (Ed.), *Advances in instructional psychology* (pp. 161–237). Mahwah, NJ: Erlbaum.

Chi, M. T. H. (in press). Common sense conceptions of emergent processes. *Journal of the Learning Sciences*.

Chi, M. T. H., & Ceci, S. J. (1987). Content knowledge: Its role, representation, and restructuring in memory development. In H. S. Reese (Ed.), *Advances in child development and behavior* (Vol. 20, pp. 91–142). New York: Academic Press.

Chi, M. T. H., Feltovich, P., & Glaser, R. (1981). Categorization & representation of physics problems by experts and novices. *Cognitive Science*, 5, 121–152. (citation classic)

Chi, M. T. H., Glaser, R., & Farr, M. (1988). *The nature of expertise*. Hillsdale, NJ: Erlbaum.

Chi, M. T. H., & Hausmann, R. G. M. (2003). Do radical discoveries require ontological shifts? In L. V. Shavinina (Ed.), *International handbook on innovation* (pp. 430–444). Oxford, UK: Elsevier.

Chi, M. T. H., & Koeske, R. D. (1983). Network representation of a child's dinosaur knowledge. *Developmental Psychology*, 19, 29–39.

Chi, M. T. H., & Roscoe, R. D. (2002). The processes and challenges of conceptual change. In M. Limon & L. Mason (Eds.), *Reconsidering conceptual change: Issues in theory and practice* (pp. 3–27). Netherlands, Dordrecht: Kluwer Academic.

Chi, M. T. H., Slotta, J. D., & de Leeuw, N. (1994). From things to processes: A theory of conceptual change for learning science concepts. *Learning and Instruction*, 4, 27–43.

Chiesi, H. L., Spilich, G. J., & Voss, J. F. (1979). Acquisition of domain-related information in relation to high and low domain knowledge. *Journal of Verbal Learning and Verbal Behavior*, 18, 257–274.

Chinn, C. A., & Brewer, W. F. (1993). The role of anomalous data in knowledge acquisition: A theoretical framework and implications for science instruction. *Review of Educational Research*, 63, 1–49.

Clement, J. (1982). Students' preconceptions introductory mechanics. *American Journal of Physics*, 50, 66–71.

Clement, J., Brown, D., & Zietsman, A. (1989). Not all preconceptions are misconceptions: Finding anchoring conceptions for grounding instruction on students' intuitions. *International Journal of Science Education*, 11, 554–565.

Collins, A., & Ferguson, W. (1993). Epistemic forms and epistemic games: Structures and strategies to guide inquire. *Educational Psychologist*, 28, 25–42.

Confrey, J. (1990). A review of the research on student cnceptions in mathematics, science, and programming. In C. B. Cazden (Ed.), *Review of research in education* (Vol. 1, pp. 3–56). Washington, DC: American Educational Research Association.

Costello, F. J., & Keane, M. T. (2000). Efficient creativity: Constraint-guided conceptual combination. *Cognitive Science*, 24, 299–349.

Darden, L. (1992). Strategies for anomaly resolution. In R. Giere (Ed.), *Cognitive models of science* (pp. 251–273). Minneapolis: University of Minnesota Press.

deGroot, A. D. (1965). *Thought and choice in chess*. The Hague, Netherlands: Mouton.

Demasters, S., Settlage, J., & Good, R. (1995). Students' conceptions of natural selection and its role in evolution: Cases of replication and comparison. *Journal of Research in Science Teaching*, 32, 535–550.

diSessa, A. (1982). Unlearning Aristotelian physics: A study of knowledge-based learning. *Cognitive Science* 6, 37–75.

diSessa, A. (1983). Phenomenology and the evolution of intuition. In D. Gentner & A. L. Stevens (Eds.), *Mental models* (pp. 15–33). Hillsdale, NJ: Erlbaum.

diSessa, A. (1988). Knowledge in pieces. In G. Forman & P. Pufall (Eds.), *Constructivism in the computer age* (pp. 49–70). Hillsdale, NJ: Erlbaum.

diSessa, A. (1993). Toward an epistemology of physics. *Cognition and Instruction*, 10, 101–104.

Driver, R. (1987). Promoting conceptual change in classroom settings: The experience of the children's learning in science project. In J. D. Novak (Ed.), *Proceeding of the second international seminar on misconceptions and educational strategies in science and mathematics* (Vol. II, pp. 97–107). Ithaca, NY: Department of Education, Cornell University.

Eagly, A. H., & Chaiken, S. (1993). *The psychology of attitudes*. Ft. Worth, TX: Harcourt, Brace & Jovanovich.

Ehrlich, H. J., & Leed, D. (1969). Dogmatism, learning, and resistance to change: A review and a new paradigm. *Psychological Bulletin*, 71, 249–260.

Ericsson, K. A. (1996). *The road to excellence*. Mahwah, NJ: Erlbaum.

Feltovich, P. J., Ford, K. M., & Hoffman, R. R. (1997). *Expertise in context*. Menlo Park, CA: AAAI Press.

Ferrari, M., & Chi, M. T. H. (1998). The nature of naïve explanations of natural selection. *International Journal of Science Education*, 20, 1231–1256.

Festinger, L. (1962/1957). *A theory of cognitive dissonance*. Stanford, CA: Stanford University Press.

Fishbein, M., & Ajzen, I. (1975). *Belief, attitude, intention and behavior*. Reading, MA: Addison-Wesley.

Gagné, R. M. (1965). *The conditions of learning*. New York: Holt, Rinehart & Winston.

Gazzaniga, M. S. (1992). *Nature's mind*. New York: Basic Books.

Gopnik, A., & Meltzoff, A. N. (1997). *Words, thoughts, and theories*. Cambridge, MA: MIT Press.

Gopnik, A., & Wellman, H. M. (1994). The theory theory. In L. A. Hirschfeld & S. A. Gelman (Eds.), *Mapping the mind: Domain specificity in cognition and culture* (pp. 255–293). Cambridge, UK: Cambridge University Press.

Graesser, A., Kassleer, M. A., Kreuz, R. J., & Mclain-Allen, B. (1998). Verification of statements about story worlds that deviate from normal conceptions of time: What is true about Einstein's dreams. *Cognitive Psychology*, 35, 246–301.

Graesser, A., Singer, M., & Trabasso, T. (1994). Constructing inferences during narrative text comprehension. *Psychological Review*, 101, 186–209.

Halloun, I. A., & Hestenes, D. (1985). Common sense concepts about motion. *American Journal of Physics*, 53, 1056–1065.

Hampton, J. A. (1997). Emergent attributes in combined concepts. In T. Ward, S. M. Smith, & J. Vaid (Eds.), *Creative thought: An investigation of conceptual structures and processes* (pp. 83–110). Washington, DC: American Psychological Association.

Harmon-Jones, E., & Mills, J. (1999). *Cognitive dissonance: Progress on a pivotal theory in social psychology*. Washington, DC: American Psychological Association.

Heider, F. (1944). Social perception and phenomenal causality. *Psychological Review*, 51, 358–374.

Hewson, P. W., & Hewson, M. G. A. (1984). The role of conceptual conflict in conceptual change and the design of science instruction. *Instructional Science*, 13, 1–13.

Hofstadter, D. (1999). *Godel, Escher, Bach – An eternal golden braid*. New York: Basic Books.

Hutchins, E. (1995). *Cognition in the wild*. Cambridge, MA: MIT Press.

Hutchins, E. L., & Levin, J. A. (1981). *Point of view in problem solving*. CHIP Tech. Rep. No. 105, University of California at San Diego.

Jeong, H., Taylor, R., & Chi, M. T. H (2000). Learning from a computer workplace simulation. *Proceedings of the 22nd annual meeting of the Cognitive Science Society* (pp. 705–710). Mahwah, NJ: Erlbaum.

Johnson, A., Moher, T., Ohlsson, S., & Gillingham, M. (1999). The Round Earth

Project – Collaborative VR for conceptual learning. *IEEE Computer Graphics and Applications*, 19(6), 60–69.

Johnson, A., Moher, T., Ohlsson, S., & Leigh, J. (2001). Exploring multiple representations in elementary school science education. In *Proceedings of IEEE VR 2001* (pp. 201–208). Yokohama, Japan, Mar 13–17.

Johsua, S., & Dupin, J. J. (1987). Taking into account student conceptions in instructional strategy: An example in physics. *Cognition and Instruction*, 4(2), 117–135.

Keegan, R. T. (1989). How Charles Darwin became a psychologist. In D. B. Wallace & H. E. Gruber (Eds.), *Creative people at work: Twelve cognitive case studies* (pp. 107–125). New York: Oxford University Press.

Keller, C. M., & Keller, J. D. (1996). *Cognition and tool use: The blacksmith at work*. Cambridge, UK: Cambridge University Press.

Kelman, H. C., & Baron, R. M. (1968). Determinants of modes of resolving inconsistency dilemmas: A functional analysis. In R. P. Abelson, E. Aronson, W. J. McGuire, T. M. Newcomb, M. J. Rosenberg, & P. H. Tannenbaum (Eds.), *Theories of cognitive consistency: A sourcebook* (pp. 670–683). Chicago: Rand McNally.

Kintsch, W. (1998). *Comprehension*. Cambridge, UK: Cambridge University Press.

Kitcher, P. (1993). *The advancement of science*. New York: Oxford University Press.

Klein, G. (1998). *Sources of power: How people make decisions*. Cambridge, MA: MIT Press.

Kuhn, T. (1970). *The structure of scientific revolutions*. Chicago: University of Chicago Press.

Landauer, T. K. (1986). How much do people remember? Some estimates of the quantity of learned information in long-term memory. *Cognitive Science*, 10, 477–493.

Lawson, A., & Thompson, L. (1988). Formal reasoning ability and misconceptions concerning genetics and natural selection. *Journal of Research in Science Teaching*, 25, 733–746.

Lesgold, A., Rubinson, H., Feltovich, P., Glaser, R., Klopfer, D., & Wang, Y. (1988). Expertise in a complex skill: Diagnosing x-ray pictures. In M. Chi, R. Glaser, & M. Farr (Eds.), *The nature of expertise* (pp. 311–342). Hillsdale, NJ: Erlbaum.

Licht, P. (1987). A strategy to deal with conceptual and reasoning problems in introductory electricity education. In J. Novak (Ed.), *Proceedings of the 2nd international seminar "Misconceptions and Educational Strategies in Science and Mathematics"* (Vol. II, pp. 275–284). Ithaca, NY: Cornell University.

Limon, M. (2002). Conceptual change in history. In M. Limon & L. Mason (Eds.), *Reconsidering conceptual change: Issues in theory and practice* (pp. 259–289). Amsterdam: Kluwer Academic.

Lovett, M. C. (2002). Problem solving. In H. Pashler & D. Medin (Eds.), *Stevens' handbook of experimental psychology, volume 2: Memory and cognitive processes* (pp. 317–362). New York: Wiley.

Machamer, P., & Woody, A. (1992). Models of intelligibility in science: Using the balance as a model for understanding the motion of bodies. In S. Hills (Ed.), *The history and philosophy of science in science education* (Vol. 2, pp. 95–111). Kingston, Ontario: Queen's University.

Markman, A. B. (1999). *Knowledge representation*. Mahwah, NJ: Erlbaum.

Marshall, S. P. (1995). *Schemas in problem solving*. Cambridge, UK: Cambridge University Press.

McCloskey, M. (1983). Naïve theories of motion. In D. Gentner & A. L. Stevens (Eds.), *Mental models* (pp. 299–323). Hillsdale, NJ: Erlbaum.

McGuire, W. J. (1968). Theory of the structure of human thought. In R. P. Abelson, E. Aronson, W. J. McGuire, T. M. Newcomb, M. J. Rosenberg, & P. H. Tannenbaum (Eds.), *Theories of cognitive consistency: A sourcebook* (pp. 140–162). Chicago: Rand McNally.

Means, M. L., & Voss, J. F. (1985). Star wars: A developmental study of expert and novice knowledge structures. *Journal of Memory and Language*, 24, 746–757.

Medin, D. L., & Shoben, E. J. (1988). Context and structure in conceptual combination. *Cognitive Psychology*, 20, 158–190.

Miller, G. A. (1996). *The science of words*. New York: Scientific American Library.

Minsky, M. A. (1975). A framework for the representation of knowledge. In P. Winston (Ed.), *The psychology of computer vision*. New York: McGraw-Hill.

Minstrel, J. (1982). Explaining the "at rest" condition of an object. *The Physics Teacher*, January, 10–14.

Miyake, N. (1986). Constructive interaction and the iterative process of understanding, *Cognitive Science*, 10, 151–177.

Norman, D. A., & Rumelhart, D. E. (1975). *Explorations in cognition*. San Francisco: Freeman.

Nussbaum, J. (1979). Children's conception of the Earth as a cosmic body: A cross-age study. *Science Education*, 63, 83–93.

Nussbaum, J. (1985). The Earth as a cosmic body. In R. Driver, E. Guesne, & A. Tiberghien (Eds.), *Children's ideas in science* (pp. 170–192). Milton Keynes, UK: Open University Press.

Nussbaum, J., & Novak, J. D. (1976). An assessment of children's concepts of the Earth utilizing structured interviews. *Science Education*, 60, 535–550.

Ohlsson, S. (1993a). Abstract schemas. *Educational Psychologist*, 28, 51–66.

Ohlsson, S. (1993b). The interaction between knowledge and practice in the acquisition of cognitive skills. In A. Meyrowitz & S. Chipman (Eds.), *Foundations of knowledge acquisition: Cognitive models of complex learning* (pp. 147–208). Norwell, MA: Kluwer Academic.

Ohlsson, S. (1994). Declarative and procedural knowledge. In T. Husen & T. Neville-Postlethwaite (Eds.), *The international encyclopedia of education* (Vol. 3, 2nd ed., pp. 1432–1434). London, UK: Pergamon Press.

Ohlsson, S. (1996). Learning from performance errors. *Psychological Review*, 103, 241–262.

Ohlsson, S. (1999). Theoretical commitment and implicit knowledge: Why anomalies do not trigger learning. *Science and Education*, 8, 559–574.

Ohlsson, S. (2002). Generating and understanding qualitative explanations. In J. Otero, J. A. Leon, & A. C. Graesser (Eds.), *The psychology of science text comprehension* (pp. 91–128). Mahwah, NJ: Erlbaum.

Ohlsson, S., & Hemmerich, J. (1999). Articulating an explanation schema: A preliminary model and supporting data. In M. Hahn & S. Stones (Eds.), *Proceedings of the twenty first annual conference of the Cognitive Science Society* (pp. 490–495). Mahwah, NJ: Erlbaum.

Ohlsson, S., & Lehtinen, E. (1997). Abstraction and the acquisition of complex ideas. *International Journal of Educational Research*, 27, 37–48.

Ohlsson, S., Moher, T. G., & Johnson, A. (2000). Deep learning in virtual reality: How to teach children that the Earth is round. In L. R. Gleitman & A. K. Joshi (Eds.), *Proceedings of the twenty-second annual conference of the Cognitive Science Society* (pp. 364–368). Mahwah, NJ: Erlbaum.

Ohlsson, S., & Regan, S. (2001). A function for abstract ideas in conceptual learning and discovery. *Cognitive Science Quarterly*, 1, 23–277.

Pennington, N. (1987). Comprehension strategies in programming. In G. M. Olson, S. Sheppard, & E. Soloway (Eds.), *Empirical studies of programmers: Second workshop* (pp. 100–113). Norwood, MJ: Ablex.

Piaget, J. (1985). *The equilibration of cognitive structures*. Chicago: University of Chicago Press.

Piaget, J., & Inhelder, B. (1956). *The child's conception of space*. London: Routledge and Kegan Paul.

Posner, G. J., Strike, K. A., Hewson, P. W., & Gertzog, W. A. (1982). Accommodation of a scientific conception: Toward a theory of conceptual change. *Science Education*, 66, 211–227.

Quillian, M. R. (1968). Semantic memory. In M. Minsky (Ed.), *Semantic information processing* (pp. 227–270). Cambridge, MA: MIT Press.

Reiner, M., Slotta, J. D., Chi, M. T. H., & Resnick, L. B. (2000). Naive physics reasoning: A commitment to substance-based conceptions. *Cognition and Instruction*, 18(1), 1–34.

Reisberg, D. (2001). *Cognition: Exploring the science of the mind* (2nd ed.). New York: Norton.

Rips, L., & Medin, D. (in press). Concepts and categories: Memory, meaning and metaphysics. In K. J. Holyoak & B. G. Morrison (Eds.), *Cambridge handbook of thinking and reasoning*. New York: Cambridge University Press.

Robin, N., & Ohlsson, S. (1989). Impetus then and now: A detailed comparison between Jean Buridan and a single contemporary subject. In D. E. Herget (Ed.), *The history and philosophy of science in science teaching* (pp. 292–305). Tallahassee: Florida State University.

Rokeach, M. (1960). *The open and closed mind*. New York: Basic Books.

Rokeach, M. (1970). *Beliefs, attitudes, and values: A theory of organization and change*. San Francisco: Jossey-Bass.

Rosenzweig, M. R. (2001). Learning and neural plasticity over the life span. In P. E. Gold & W. T. Greenough (Eds.), *Memory consolidation* (pp. 275–294). Washington, DC: American Psychological Association.

Rumelhart, D. E., & Norman, D. A. (1978). Accretion, tuning and restructuring: Three modes of learning. In J. W. Cotton & R. Klatzky (Eds.), *Semantic factors in cognition* (pp. 37–54). Hillsdale, NJ: Erlbaum.

Rumelhart, D. E., Smolensky, P., McClelland, J. L., & Hinton, G. E. (1986). Schemata and sequential thought processes in PDG models. In J. McClelland & D. E. Rumbelhart (Eds.), *Parallel distributed processing: Explorations in the microstructure of cognition* (Vol. 2, pp. 7–57). Cambridge, MA: MIT Press.

Schank, R. (1972). Conceptual dependency: A theory of natural language understanding. *Cognitive Psychology*, 3, 552–631.

Schank, R. (1986). *Explanation patterns*. Hillsdale, NJ: Erlbaum.

Schank, R. C., & Abelson, R. P. (1977). *Scripts, plans, goals, and understanding: An inquiry into human knowledge structures.* Hillsdale, NJ: Erlbaum.

Schultz, T. R., & Lepper, M. R. (1996). Cognitive dissonance reduction as constraint satisfaction. *Psychological Review*, 103, 219–240.

Shatz, M., & Gelman, R. (1973). *The development of communication skills: Modifications in the speech of young children as a function of listener.* Monographs of the Society for Research in Child Development, Serial number 152, 38(5).

Simon, H. A., & Gilmartin, K. (1973). A simulation of memory for chess positions. *Cognitive Psychology*, 5, 29–46.

Slotta, J. D., Chi, M. T. H., & Joram, E. (1995). Assessing students' misclassifications of physics concepts: An ontological basis for conceptual change. *Cognition and Instruction*, 13(3), 373–400.

Smith, E. E., Osherson, D. N., Rips, L. J., & Keane, M. (1988). Combining prototypes: A selective modification model. *Cognitive Science*, 12, 485–527.

Smith, J. P., III, DiSessa, A. A., & Roschelle, J. (1995). Misconceptions reconceived: A constructivist analysis of knowledge in transition. *The Journal of the Learning Sciences*, 3, 115–163.

Soloway, E., & Erhlich, K. (1984). Empirical studies of programming knowledge. *IEEE Transactions on Software Engineering*, 10, 595–609.

Soloway, E. M. (1978). *Learning = interpretation + generalization: A case study in knowledge-directed learning.* Unpublished doctoral dissertation. Amherst: University of Massachusetts.

Spilich, G. J., Vesonder, G. T., Chiesi, H. L., & Voss, J. F. (1979). Test processing of domain-related information for individuals with high and low domain knowledge. *Journal of Verbal Learning and Verbal Behavior*, 18, 275–290.

Squire, L. R. (1987). *Memory and brain.* New York: Oxford University Press.

Stokes, A. F., Kemper, K., & Kite, K. (1997). Aeronautical decision making, cue recognition, and expertise under time pressure. In C. E. Zsambok & G. Klein (Eds.), *Naturalistic decision making. Expertise: Research and applications* (pp. 183–196). Mahwah, NJ: Erlbaum.

Strike, K. A., & Posner, G. J. (1985). A conceptual change view of learning and understanding. In L. West & L. Pines (Eds.), *Cognitive structure and conceptual change* (pp. 211–231). New York: Academic Press.

Strike, K. A., & Posner, G. J. (1992). A revisionist theory of conceptual change. In R. A. Duschl & R. J. Hamilton (Eds.), *Philosophy of science, cognitive psychology, and educational theory and practice* (pp. 147–176). New York: State University of New York Press.

Thagard, P. (1989). Explanatory coherence. *Behavioral and Brain Sciences*, 12, 435–467.

Thagard, P. (1992a). *Conceptual revolutions.* Princeton, NJ: Princeton University Press.

Thagard, P. (1992b). Adverserial problem solving: Modeling an opponent using explanatory coherence. *Cognitive Science*, 16, 123–149.

Thagard, P. (2000). *Coherence in thought and action.* Cambridge, MA: MIT Press.

Thompson, P. (1989). *The structure of biological theories.* New York: State University of New York Press.

Thorndyke, P. W. (1984). Applications of schema theory in cognitive research. In J. R. Anderson & S. M. Kosslyn (Eds.), *Tutorials in learning and memory* (pp. 167–192). San Francisco: Freeman.

Trabasso, T., & van den Broek, P. (1985). Causal thinking and the representation of narrative events. *Journal of Memory and Language*, 24, 612–630.

Tuckerman, N., & Dunnan, N. (1995). *The Amy Vanderbilt complete book of etiquette.* New York: Doubleday.

VanLehn, K. (1989). Problem solving and cognitive skill acquisition. In M. I. Posner (Ed.), *Foundations of cognitive science* (pp. 527–579). Cambridge, MA: MIT Press.

Vosniadou, S. (1994a). Capturing and modeling the process of conceptual change. *Learning and Instruction*, 4, 45–69.

Vosniadou, S. (1994b). Universal and culture-specific properties of children's mental models of the earth. In L. Hirschfeld & S. Gelman

(Eds.), *Mapping the mind* (pp. 412–430). Cambridge, MA: Cambridge University Press.

Vosniadou, S., & Brewer, W. F. (1992). Mental models of the earth: A study of conceptual change in childhood. *Cognitive Psychology*, 24, 535–585.

Voss, J. F., Vesonder, G. T., & Spilich, G. J. (1980). Text generation and recall by high-knowledge and low-knowledge individuals. *Journal of Verbal Learning and Verbal Behavior*, 19, 651–667.

White, B., & Frederiksen, J. (1990). Causal model progressions as a foundation for intelligent learning environments. *Artificial Intelligence*, 42, 99–157.

Wilensky, U., & Resnick, M. (1999). Thinking in levels: A dynamic systems perspective to making sense of the world. *Journal of Science Education and Technology*, 8, 3–19.

Wilson, R. A., & Keil, F. C. (2000). The shadows and shallows of explanation. In F. C. Keil & R. A. Wilson (Eds.), *Explanation and cognition* (pp. 137–159). Cambridge, MA: MIT Press.

Winograd, T. (1975). Frame representations and the declarative/procedural controversy. In D. Bobrow & A. Collins (Eds.), *Representation and understanding: Studies in cognitive science* (pp. 185–210). New York: Academic Press.

Wiser, M., & Carey, S. (1983). When heat and temperature were one. In D. Gentner & A. Stevens (Eds.), *Mental models* (pp. 267–297). Hillsdale, NJ: Erlbaum.

CHAPTER 17

Thinking as a Production System

Marsha C. Lovett
John R. Anderson

Thinking as a Production System

Since their birth (ca. late 1960s), production systems have been developed as a formal tool not only for describing but for explaining how humans think. Indeed, "to advance our understanding of how humans think" is the stated goal of Newell and Simon's classic book, *Human Problem Solving* (1972), in which the first body of work on production-system models of human thought was presented (see Novick & Bassok, Chap. 14). The main goal for production systems in psychological research has changed little in the intervening years, and yet the state of the art has advanced dramatically. The aim of this chapter is to present a contemporary production-systems approach to open questions in problem solving, reasoning, analogy, and language. We highlight the ways in which today's production systems allow for more flexibility, stochasticity, and sensitivity than their predecessors. Besides demonstrating that production systems can offer insight into current questions and add to our understanding of human thinking, we discuss our view of production systems in future research.

Background on Production Systems

A production system is a set of *production rules* – each of which represents a contingency for action – and a set of mechanisms for matching and applying production rules. Because the production rule is the fundamental unit of this formalism, it is worth giving a few examples. Table 17.1 presents four sample production rules written in English. Note that each is divided into two parts by the word "then": The first part of each production rule (before the "then") specifies the conditions under which that production rule is applicable, and the second part specifies the actions to be applied. Conditions may reflect an aspect of the external world (e.g., it is dark) or an internal, mental state (e.g., my current goal is to reach a particular location, or I can retrieve a particular fact). Likewise, actions may transform a feature in the real world (e.g., flip the light switch) or an internal, mental state (e.g., change my current goal, or add a fact to memory).

Table 17.1. Illustrative examples of production rules, written in English

Number	*Specification of Production Rule*
1	When my current goal involves navigating in a dark room, then I flip the light switch in that room.
2	When my current goal is to go to a location that is more than 300 miles away, then I set a subgoal to go to the local airport.
3	When my current goal is to answer an arithmetic problem of the form D1 + D2, then I change the goal to try retrieving the sum of D1 and D2 from memory.
4	When my current goal is to answer an arithmetic problem of the form D1 + D2, then I hold up D2 fingers and change the goal to count them starting with the number after D1.

To operate, a production system requires a *dynamic memory* that represents the current state of the system and is used to match against production rules' conditions. For example, when dynamic memory includes the goal "to get to San Francisco," the second production rule in Table 17.1 would match for someone in Pittsburgh, Pennsylvania. This *pattern matching* of production rules to dynamic memory leads to a set of potentially applicable production rules called the *conflict set*. However, not all production rules in the conflict set are applied. The process of *conflict resolution* specifies which production rules from the conflict set will *execute* their actions or *fire*. These actions are likely to change the external and/or internal state of the system reflected in a change to dynamic memory. Then, a potentially different set of production rules may comprise the conflict set, and the cycle continues.

One way to view how production rules operate is by analogy to stimulus–response associations; that is, when a particular stimulus is present, an associated response is triggered. This fits with the notion that a production rule cannot be directly verbalized but rather is observable through behavior. This analogy to stimulus–response associations emphasizes the fact that production systems do not operate via a homunculus interpreting production rules as programming code. Instead, each production rule – when it matches dynamic memory – has the potential to fire and change the current state, thus setting other production rules into action.

This discussion leads to the question of what it means to model thinking as a production system: What are the theoretical implications associated with representing knowledge as production rules? The following are four features commonly attributed to production-rule representations:

1. *Production rules are modular.* Each production rule represents a well-circumscribed unit of knowledge such that any production rule can be added, refined, or deleted independently of other production rules in the system. Moreover, each production rule is atomic such that it would be added, refined, and deleted as whole unit. It is important to note, however, that this modularity does *not* preclude production rules from interacting with each other extensively in a running system. Indeed, adding a new production rule to an existing set can – and often does – completely change the functioning of the system because of the way production rules' actions impact each

others' firing. Early production-system modelers (Klahr & Wallace, 1976; Young & O'Shea, 1981) took advantage of this feature by adding or deleting production rules to explicitly test how that change would impact the system's behavior. More recently, production systems have been developed with autonomous learning mechanisms that enable the system's production rules to change based on experience. In these systems, modularity is achieved because these learning mechanisms create and modify individual production rules independently of other rules.

2. *Production rules are asymmetric.* Each production rule is a unidirectional contingency for action. This means that the production rule "When I want to type the letter 'j', then I punch my right index finger" is different from "When I punch my right index finger, then I type the letter 'j'". Moreover, asymmetry and modularity imply that, if these two production rules were in the same system, adding, deleting, or refining the former would not directly change the latter. That is, practicing typing would exercise the first production rule, strengthening the index-finger response when "j" is the desired letter, but it would not strengthen one's knowledge that "j" appears when touch-typing with that finger. For expert touch-typists, this asymmetry is quite noticeable: Without looking at a keyboard, try to identify the letter that is typed with your left index finger. Tough, isn't it? Typing the word "frog" would have been easier. Such asymmetry has been documented in many contexts (see Singley & Anderson, 1989, for a review).

3. *Production rules can be abstract.* Production rules allow for generalization because their conditions may be represented as templates that match to a wide range of patterns. These conditions specify the relationship(s) between items without specifying the items themselves (e.g., "When *A* is taller than *B* and *B* is taller than C, then say *A* is taller than C" is true for any values of *A*, *B*, and C). The capability to represent abstract relationships allows for transfer of learning across different situations as long as they fit within the conditions of the given production rule. For example, the first production rule in Table 17.1 could match to a dark dining room, living room, or office, meaning that experience at flipping the light switch in any of these rooms would transfer to the others. Likewise, the third production rule in Table 17.1 could match to any two-addend addition problem.

4. *Production rules cannot be directly verbalized.* This feature is based on the notion that each production rule represents knowledge about a contingency for action that is not directly accessible to verbalization. A good example of this occurs when someone knows how to drive a standard transmission car but cannot explain it verbally. It is important to note that, while this feature implies that knowledge represented in production-rule form cannot be accessed directly, it does not imply that one cannot use other techniques to talk about performance knowledge. For example, when changing gears in a standard transmission car, it is possible to observe one's own performance and verbally describe these observations. Also, knowledge about how to perform a task may be represented in multiple forms – some that can be verbalized and some that cannot.

This last point confronts a common misconception about production systems – namely, that knowledge *about* rules or procedures is necessarily represented *as* production rules. Whereas knowledge about rules and procedures can be represented in production-rule form, it is not the content of knowledge that determines how it is represented. Instead, the four features listed previously serve as a set of necessary conditions for knowledge to be considered as being represented in production-rule form. To illustrate the distinction between knowledge contents and representational form, Table 17.2 shows that the same knowledge content (either column) can be represented in a production-rule form (top entry) or not

Table 17.2. Examples Illustrating that the Form (Rows) and Content (Columns) of Knowledge Are Independent

	Knowledge Contents	
Representational Form	*Rulelike*	*Factlike*
Production rule	When I want to type a letter and I know its finger move, then make that move	When I want to type the letter "j," then I punch with my right index finger on the home row
Declarative fact	To touch-type, one must make the finger move corresponding to the currently desired letter	The letter "j" goes with the right index finger in home-row position

(bottom entry as a declarative fact). So, when considering what it means for knowledge to be represented in production-rule form, the key is not in *what* knowledge is being represented but rather in *how*.

Production Systems, Then and Now

The first production systems set out to establish a mechanistic account of how human adults perform relatively short, moderately difficult, symbolic tasks (Newell & Simon, 1972). Besides demonstrating that production systems could solve these tasks, the main goal was to connect the system's processing steps to human problem-solving steps. Several features distinguish these early production systems from their current-day progeny. First, early production systems tended to focus on demonstrating human-like *performance;* current models rely heavily on learning mechanisms to derive predictions about *learning and performance* across time. Second, early models focused on reproducing qualitatively the processing steps of *individual* problem solvers, whereas more recent models have been submitted to both quantitative analyses of fit to aggregate data (e.g., average reaction times for various conditions) and qualitative analyses (e.g., whether the model demonstrates the same errors as people).[1] Third, the role of noise processes has increased drastically from early models that avoided stochastic processes completely to current day models in which stochasticity plays an important role (Lebiere, Anderson, & Bothell, 2002; Lebiere et al., 2003). Fourth, early models focused on the "cognitive" layer of processing and eschewed integrating receptors and effectors into models. In contrast, current production systems incorporate and emphasize perception and action in their frameworks (Anderson & Lebiere, 1998; Meyer & Kieras, 1997). Finally, the fifth feature that distinguishes early and recent production systems is so strongly linked to the early models that it has sometimes been considered a defining feature of production systems. This is the symbolic nature of early production systems. However, almost all modern production systems take a *hybrid* view by positing symbolic representations as important conceptual units and acknowledging graded representations as a valuable additional layer (e.g., associating continuously valued quantities with each production rule).

Current Production Systems in Context

This section provides a brief overview of four production systems currently being used in a variety of cognitive modeling situations. The systems to be described are ACT-R (Anderson & Lebiere, 1998), EPIC (Meyer & Kieras, 1997), Soar (Laird, Newell, & Rosenbloom, 1991), and 4-CAPS (Just, Carpenter, & Varma, 1999). ACT-R emphasizes the notion of a *cognitive modeling architecture* in which the same set of mechanisms and representational schemes are used to capture human learning and performance across tasks. Recently, this has been extended to map various ACT-R mechanisms and modules to particular brain regions for comparison with neuroimaging data. EPIC has focused on capturing the connections among the cognitive, perceptual, and motor systems. Recently, EPIC has been used to make quantitative predictions about perception-to-action loops in multiple-task situations and across the adult age span. Soar was originally developed to address issues in both psychology and artificial intelligence. Recently, it has been particularly successful in simulating multiagent, dynamic interactions with real world application (e.g., Jones, et al., 1999). The 4-CAPS architecture, like its predecessor 3-CAPS (Just & Carpenter, 1992), focuses on individual differences.

To delineate the space of current production systems, we next highlight the dimensions along which these systems differ. First, they differ with regard to their degree of processing parallelism. Toward one end of the spectrum, ACT-R posits that only a single production rule can fire at a time. However, ACT-R allows for parallelism in other ways: asynchronous parallelism among its perceptual and motor modules[2], parallel retrieval of information from declarative memory, and parallel production-rule matching and selection. Soar similarly posits serial processing in that a single operator is chosen in each decision phase, but this is preceded by an elaboration phase that allows parallel production firing. 4-CAPS allows parallel firing of production rules for all cycles, but this parallelism is subject to a capacity limitation such that the more production rules firing, the less rapidly each of them is executed. EPIC is the only system with fully parallel production-rule firing. To manage its multiply threaded central cognition, EPIC uses task-coordination strategies that impose ordering constraints when necessary.

Another dimension along which the systems differ is the degree of modularity they propose. Soar is at one end of this spectrum because of its unitary structure – a single set of production rules representing long-term memory. 4-CAPS posits a number of distinct sets of production rules connected to each other. In ACT-R and EPIC, multiple modules correspond to separate perceptual and motor modalities and to "central cognition." These modules are considered encapsulated, independent processors with their interactions handled by the production system.

Although all four systems produce quantitative predictions that match well to performance data, ACT-R and Soar have particularly focused on production-rule *learning* as well. Yet another dimension in which these architectures differ is their commitment to hybridization with Soar committed to a purely symbolic account whereas ACT-R and 4-CAPS postulate continuously varying quantities that drive the processing of symbolic units. EPIC does have continuously varying parameters associated with various modules but does not appear to have information-laden nonsymbolic quantities in its theory of central cognition.

Finally, production systems differ in the role that noise processes play in their processing. In Soar, their role is minimal (i.e., when a "tie" between production rules arises, one of them is chosen at random). In ACT-R and 4-CAPS, noise processes are assumed added to the various continuously varying computations that influence system performance. In EPIC, noise is used more to represent variability in system parameters (e.g., rate parameter in Fitt's law governing motor movements) than to represent a generic nondeterminism of the system.

Organization of the Remainder of the Chapter

Our own research has involved the ACT-R system and slight variants. In this chapter, we describe six ACT-R models with which we are familiar that address different aspects of cognition. We do not focus on the ACT-R details of these models but rather on how they illustrate the general trends in production-system models toward softer, more flexible, and highly detailed characterizations of human cognition. We place each model in the multidimensional space described previously by highlighting the following features: Does the model include both performance *and* learning mechanisms? Does the model make use of symbolic (rule-based) *and* other continuously varying computations? Does the model draw upon multiple processing modules beyond a central production-rule memory? We use the template in Table 17.3 to summarize how each model fits into this three-dimensional space in terms of its use

Table 17.3. Template for Describing the Knowledge Structures and Mechanisms Involved in Each ACT-R Model

	Performance Mechanisms		*Learning Mechanisms*	
	Symbolic	*Subsymbolic*	*Symbolic*	*Subsymbolic*
Declarative chunks	Knowledge (usually facts) that can be directly verbalized	Relative activation of declarative chunks affects retrieval	Adding new declarative chunks to the set	Changing activation of declarative chunks and changing strength of links between chunks
Production rules	Knowledge for taking particular actions in particular situations	Relative utility of production rules affects choice	Adding new production rules to the set	Changing utility of production rules

of various ACT-R representations and mechanisms. In addition, we comment on how each model makes use of parallelism and noise processes, as appropriate.

We use the term "subsymbolic" to refer to the numerical values and computations associated with each symbolic unit. In this sense, the prefix "sub" refers to a level of description *below* the symbolic units and that determines those symbolic units' access in competition with other symbols. The use of the term subsymbolic from a connectionist perspective often refers to the fact that symbols may be represented in a distributed fashion, with the prefix sub referring to the pieces of the pattern that constitute a symbol. For instance, Smolensky (1988, p. 3) writes, "The name subsymbolic paradigm is intended to suggest cognitive descriptions built up of entities that correspond to *constituents* of the symbols used in the symbolic paradigm; these fine-grained constituents could be called *subsymbols*, and they are the activities of individual processing units in connectionist networks." It is an interesting question whether these two views are really in contradiction. The subsymbolic values discussed in this chapter are updated and used only locally, but at the same time have a global impact on the system's processing, just as the activations of units in a connectionist system do. As an example of this, consider the utility values associated with production rules: When multiple production rules match the current situation, the one with the highest utility value succeeds in firing. This competition occurs among the individual units themselves without any explicit selection by a controlling homunculus and without any conscious access to the utility values. Another important kind of numerical quantity in our subsymbolic representation is similarities between symbols. With these quantities, a production rule can partially match against a symbol similar to the one specified in its condition, allowing the system to realize soft constraints. This fact further blurs the difference between the two senses of "subsymbolic." Work exploring a connectionist implementation of the ACT-R architecture (Lebiere & Anderson, 1993) suggests that symbolic units represented in a distributed fashion can yield the behavior of a symbolic system that has continuously valued quantities influencing the access and use of its symbols.

Choice

One of the perennial questions in problem-solving research involves how solvers make choices: choices of the next step, of an appropriate solution strategy, and of whether to use weak (domain-general) versus strong (domain-specific) methods. Indeed, around the time when production systems were first developed, Newell and Simon introduced the idea that the very process of problem

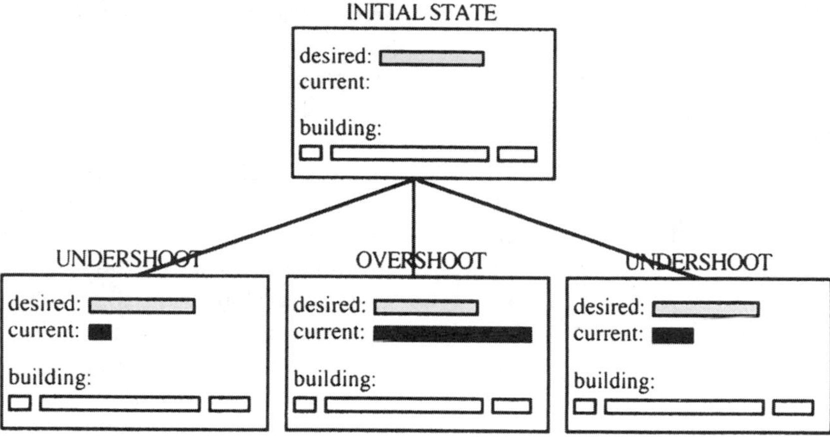

Figure 17.1. Initial state and three possible subsequent problem states from the Building Sticks Task.

solving could be viewed as search in a problem space, which equates problem solving with a series of choices. Research then addressed the question, "How do solvers make choices?" by focusing on cases in which solvers have little or no domain knowledge. Production-rule models representing various problem-solving heuristics predicted performance and established links between heuristics and human data. Current research asks, "How do solvers make choices?" but focuses on cases in which solvers have prior, relevant experience. This is, at its heart, a question about learning, so production systems that learn from their experience may offer additional insight.

In a set of studies by Lovett (Lovett & Anderson, 1996; Lovett, 1998), participants' choice learning in the Building Sticks Task (BST) was studied and modeled within ACT-R. The BST is an isomorph of the water jars task (Luchins, 1942) such that, in each problem, solvers must add and subtract the lengths of three building sticks to equal the length of a goal stick (see top of Figure 17.1). Solvers face a choice between two strategies (see bottom row of Figure 17.1): *overshoot*, which involves starting with the longest building stick and shortening it by the others, and *undershoot*, which involves starting with the short or medium building stick and then lengthening it. In these studies, participants encountered the BST for the first time and solved a sequence of problems in which the proportion of problems that could be solved by each of the two strategies was manipulated (e.g., 30% overshoot-only problems and 70% undershoot-only problems or vice versa). The results can be summarized in three main findings:

1. Participants' choices initially followed a hill-climbing heuristic with little bias toward undershoot or overshoot.
2. With experience, participants gradually learned to prefer the more successful strategy for their condition.
3. Changes in strategy choice were sensitive to recent experiences in that participants were more likely to choose the strategy that had been successful on the previous (or even second-previous) problem.

The model that was built for this task has since been applied in various forms to account for choice learning in several other tasks (see Lovett, 1998). Here we describe the BST model specifically. The model was initially endowed with production rules that implement two domain-general heuristics, hill-climbing and guessing, for the particulars of this task. For example, the *guess–overshoot* production rule makes the first overshoot move regardless of the details of the problem, and *guess–undershoot* does this for undershoot. These productions represent an uninformed guess that their action will lead to a solution and match to any BST problem. In addition, the *hillclimb–overshoot* production makes the first overshoot move but only matches when this move takes the initial state closest to the goal state; *hillclimb–undershoot* does the same for undershoot. These productions represent knowledge for taking the action that looks best according to a hill-climbing metric. Note that three of these four production rules will match to each BST problem's initial state – both guess production rules and one hillclimb production rule, whichever matches the stick lengths of the problem (e.g., *hillclimb–undershoot* in Figure 17.1). Note also that, although three production rules match to an initial stimulus, two of them produce the same response but on the basis of different knowledge (i.e., two separate production rules). This emphasizes that production rules are not simply stimulus–response associations but represent additional information in their conditions, which defines the (potentially different) scopes over which they apply.

Beyond the task-specific composition of its production rules, this model's most important features come from ACT-R's general, subsymbolic computations for production-rule *utility* values. Each production rule has an associated utility – learned by experience – that represents a combined estimate of how successful and costly that production rule is likely to be. Whenever the model is faced with multiple matching production rules, there is a noisy selection process that fires the production rule with the highest subsymbolic utility value. This noise process serves to lead the model *generally* to choose the production rule that has been most useful in past experience, but to do so a proportion of the time consistent with that production rule's utility relative to the competing production rules' utility (e.g., competing production rules with very close utility values are selected virtually at random). These utility values are learned from experience according to a prespecified mechanism: Specifically, each production rule's utility is computed arithmetically as a time-weighted average of its past success rate combined with a (negated) time-weighted average of its past costs, where cost is measured in time the production rule "spends" when fired.

In the case of the BST model, learned utility values average in new experiences of success and failure across trials, allowing the model to gradually increase the utility value for production rules that have had greater success and lower cost, and hence to gradually increase the likelihood of firing more useful production rules. Thus, the model shows the same gradual preference for the more successful BST strategy, as do participants. In addition, because this updating mechanism includes a time-weighted decay, the impact of recent successes and costs on a production rule's overall utility value is greater, leading the model – like participants – to change strategy choice with greater sensitivity to recent experiences.

Summary

This production-system model of problem-solving choice specifies a set of fairly generic production rules to represent the heuristics of guessing and hill-climbing and then draws on ACT-R's pre-existing production-rule mechanisms to learn to solve problems by experience. The major claim, then, is that strategy-choice learning is strongly guided by problem-solving experiences of success and cost associated with using those strategies and that strategies are effectively represented as production rules. More specifically, the model posits that choices in problem solving are governed by an implicit competition among production rules based on their utility values (a subsymbolic performance mechanism) and that these utilities are updated naturally based on experience (a subsymbolic learning mechanism). The corresponding two subsymbolic, production-rule cells have checks in Table 17.4. Although this model does not address how production rules specific to this task are acquired (i.e., there is no symbolic production-rule learning), its initial production rule set is composed mainly of general heuristics that have been adapted only slightly to the context of the particular task. In other words,

Table 17.4. Knowledge Structures and Mechanisms Used in a Production-Systems Model of Choice

	Performance Mechanisms		*Learning Mechanisms*	
	Symbolic	*Subsymbolic*	*Symbolic*	*Subsymbolic*
Declarative chunks	√			
Production rules	√	√		√

for this relatively knowledge-lean task, it is reasonable to suspect that participants and the model can manage without acquiring many new, task-specific production rules. It is also interesting that, in this task, production rules – with their somewhat broad conditions of applicability – largely determine the behavior of the system; although declarative knowledge is involved, it is not involved critically in the explanation of the phenomena. This representational bias is supported by the relatively broad, within-task transfer that problem solvers show in carrying over their strategic preferences from trained BST problems to novel BST problems.

Analogy

Analogy, the process of finding and using correspondences between concepts, plays a fundamental and ubiquitous role in human cognition (see Holyoak, Chap. 6). From mathematical problem solving (Novick & Holyoak, 1991) to computer programming (Anderson & Thompson, 1989) to creative discovery (Holyoak & Thagard, 1995), analogy facilitates better understanding of old knowledge and the formation and inference of new knowledge. The critical step in analogy is finding a mapping from objects and relations in the *source* or known domain, where pre-existing knowledge forms the base of the analogy, to objects and relations in the *target* or novel domain, where knowledge from the source domain will be applied. Numerous researchers have proposed theories that describe how analogical mapping takes place (Gentner, 1983, 1989; Hofstadter & Mitchell, 1994; Holyoak & Thagard, 1989; Hummel & Holyoak, 1997; Keane, Ledgeway, & Duff, 1994; Kokinov, 1998). A common feature of these theories is that they require a mixture of symbolic and subsymbolic processes. The symbolic processes are required to reason about the structure of the domains, but the softness of subsymbolic processes is required to stretch the analogy in semantically plausible ways.

Given the requirement of a mixture of symbolic and subsymbolic processes, modern production systems would seem well designed to model analogy. Salvucci & Anderson (2001) describe a relatively successful application of the ACT-R theory to modeling results in the analogy literature. Before reviewing it, we would like to highlight the value added by such a theory. Although the model incorporates many of the insights of the other theories, it is not just a matter of implementing these theories in ACT-R. As a complete theory of cognition, the model contributes three factors lacking in these other models. First, it naturally maps these processes onto precise predictions about real world metrics of latency and correctness, rather than the more qualitative and ordinal predictions that have typified other theories. Second, it integrates the process of analogy with the rest of cognition and thus makes predictions about how processes such as eye movements are interleaved with the analogy process. Third, it shows that the mechanisms underlying analogy are the same as the mechanisms underlying other aspects of cognitive processing.

Figure 17.2 illustrates the representation of the famous solar system analogy (Gentner, 1983) in the Salvucci and Anderson system. Analogs are represented as higher-order structures built up of three components: objects, relations, and roles. The first two components, objects and relations (represented as ovals in Figure 17.2) serve the same purpose as in other theories of analogy: Objects are the semantic primitives of the analogs, whereas relations link objects or relations together according to their function. The solar-system domain contains the two objects ss-sun and ss-planet, along with the three relations ss-causes, ss-attracts, and ss-revolves. Similarly, the atom domain contains the two objects at-nucleus and at-electron and the three relations at-causes, at-attracts, and at-revolves. The boxes in Figure 17.2 represent the third component of an analog structure – roles, which serve to link objects and relations to form higher-order conceptual structures. Each role comprises five components:

parent: a pointer to the parent relation
parent-type: the semantic type of the parent relation
slot: the relation slot that the object fills in the relation
child: a pointer to the child object or relation
child-type: the semantic type of the child object or relation.

For example, in the case of the ss-attractor role, ss-attracts is the parent, attracts is the parent-type, attractor is the slot, ss-sun is the child, and sun is the child-type.

Salvucci and Anderson (2001) describe a path-mapping process by which the structure in the source is made to correspond to the structure in the analog. This mapping process is achieved by production rules that essentially walk through these graphs looking for correspondences. The critical step in this mapping is retrieving roles from the target domain to map onto roles in the source domain. This is achieved by the partial matching process in ACT-R that selects the most similar role. Similarity between the source and target role is determined based on the similarities among the parent-type, slot, and child-type components of the roles. One of the consequences is that the model can be misled to select inappropriate analogs on the basis of surface similarity between the components of a source and target. For instance, the model successfully simulated the results from Ross (1989) that showed role confusions in probability problems based on surface similarities between examples. One limitation of the path-mapping process built into this model is that it only considers one proposition at at time. For that reason, the model cannot solve analogies that require the consideration of multiple propositions in parallel, whereas people and other models can (e.g., Hummel & Holyoak, 1997).

On the other hand, the production system control structure leads to other predictions. Since the model goes from the source to the target, it has a preference for many-to-one mappings over one-to-many mappings. This enables the model to successfully predict the results of Experiment 2 in Spellman and Holyoak (1996). They presented subjects with two stories involving countries on different planets and asked subjects to map countries on one planet to those on the other. The story relations can be summarized as follows:

Story 1	*Story 2*
richer (Afflu, Barebrute)	richer (Grainwell, Hungerall)
stronger (Barebrute, Compak)	stronger (Millpower, Mightless)

The relations include an ambiguous mapping – namely, the mapping of Barebrute to either Hungerall or Millpower. Subjects were divided into two conditions: In the 1–2 condition, subjects mapped objects from story 1 to those in story 2; in the 2–1 condition, subjects mapped objects from story 2 to story 1. In both conditions, subjects had the option of including any, all, or no objects in their mapping, thus allowing the possibility of a one-to-one, one-to-many, or many-to-one mapping, if so desired. Spellman and Holyoak found that subjects rarely produced one-to-many mappings (fewer than 2% of subjects), whereas they frequently produced many-to-one mappings (more than 30% of subjects).

In addition to reproducing these results in the literature, Salvucci and Anderson had subjects try to determine the analogies between two stories and collected their eye

SOURCE

ss-causes
ss-cause
causes
cause
attracts
ss-effect
causes
effect
revolves
ss-attracts
ss-revolves
ss-attractor
attracts
attractor
sun
ss-attracted
attracts
attracted
planet
ss-revolver
revolves
revolver
planet
ss-center
revolves
center
sun
ss-sun
ss-planet

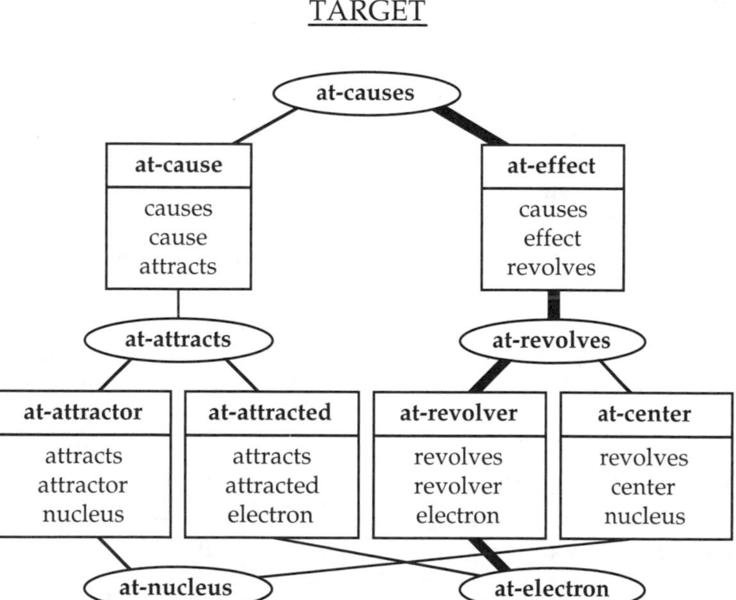

Figure 17.2. Sample analogs for the solar-system and atom domains.

movements while they were doing so. The data showed that subjects moved their eyes back and forth between the two stories as they read them and searched for the analogs. The Salvucci and Anderson model was able to predict the eye movement transitions. This is a critical study because it shows how analogy is dynamically integrated with cognition and how it can control – and be determined by – processes such as eye movements.

Summary

This production-system model of analogy specifies a set of production rules that

Table 17.5. Knowledge Structures and Mechanisms Used in a Production-Systems Model of Analogy Making

	Performance Mechanisms		*Learning Mechanisms*	
	Symbolic	*Subsymbolic*	*Symbolic*	*Subsymbolic*
Declarative chunks	√	√		
Production rules	√			

implement a path-mapping process through declaratively represented source and target structures. That is, the model posits that analogies are made and used via an explicit process of path mapping that is influenced by the relative activation levels of the elements to be mapped. The subsymbolic mechanisms governing declarative retrieval specify which parts of those declarative structures will be retrieved and when. In this way, the model makes specific, quantitative predictions about the results of analogy making and its time course (as observed through eye movement data). Although analogy making is a process that produces new knowledge – the mapping, which in turn can be used to produce new inferences – the process of analogy usually occurs in a single trial without much learning. Thus, Table 17.5 highlights that this model of analogy making draws on three of the four performance mechanisms in ACT-R.

Working Memory

Just as the previous section's model of analogy makes heavy use of declarative knowledge and corresponding mechanisms, so does this section's model of working memory. Working memory has been implicated in the performance of such diverse tasks as verbal reasoning and prose comprehension (Baddeley & Hitch, 1974), sentence processing (Just & Carpenter, 1992), free recall learning (Baddeley & Hitch, 1977), prospective memory (Marsh & Hicks, 1998), and note-taking and writing (Engle, 1994). This research has suggested that working-memory resources are limited because, as working-memory demands of a task increase, participants' performance declines. Moreover, working-memory limitations appear to differ across people such that some people show a more striking decrease in performance as a function of task demands than others (see also Morrison, Chap. 19).

Each of the four production systems discussed thus far has an account for the impact of working-memory demands on cognitive processing (see Miyake & Shah, 1999). EPIC implements Baddeley's articulatory loop via production rules acting on the auditory store and vocal/motor processor. These production rules implement strategies for rehearsal and recall and are constrained by the processing features of the modules they engage (e.g., all-or-none decay of items from the auditory store and time to re-read an item by the vocal/motor processor). In contrast, Soar assumes no a priori limit to working memory through its dynamic memory.[3] Rather, limitations arise when multiple levels of processing are necessary to establish multiple subgoals to handle a sequence of impasses. In the CAPS architecture(s), working-memory limitations are captured through a limitation in the amount of activation that can propagate through the system: When less activation is available, production-rule firing takes more processing cycles. CAPS has been used to model different patterns of sensitivity to working-memory demands among groups of individuals with low, medium, and high capacity (e.g., Just & Carpenter, 1992).

In ACT-R, working-memory limitations are imposed via a limitation to the amount of attention that can be focused on the current goal. This attentional activation (also called source activation) serves to maintain elements of the goal as highly active, activate above their resting levels any goal-relevant facts in declarative memory, and suppress below their resting levels any facts negatively associated with the current goal. Although they sound similar, the CAPS and ACT-R limitations in activation are quite different. CAPS directly limits total activation in the system, whereas ACT-R limits the ability to differentially activate goal-relevant information above goal-irrelevant information. In other words, greater source activation in ACT-R is akin to having a better signal-to-noise ratio for retrieving facts. It is worth noting that the working-memory limitations in both ACT-R and CAPS are imposed as constraints on a particular model parameter, whereas in other working-memory accounts (e.g., SOAR) the connectionist system LISA (Hummel & Holyoak, 1997) and, to some degree EPIC, these limitations emerge as a natural consequence of general processing.

In this section, we demonstrate how implementation of working memory in ACT-R can be used to estimate individuals' working-memory capacity from performance on one task (call it Task A) and then make accurate zero-parameter predictions of those individuals' performance on other tasks – B, C, and so on. Task A is a Modified Digit Span task (MODS) designed as an isomorph of the reading span (Daneman & Carpenter, 1980) and the operation span (Turner & Engle, 1989). In this task, participants perform dual tasks of reading various presented characters and memorizing the exact order of digits only. Figure 17.3 shows a sample MODS trial in which the participant would read "a j 2 b i e 6 c f 8" and then recall the digits *in order* (2 6 8). Because the task is fast paced (there is little time for idiosyncratic strategies), it draws on skills that are highly practiced (there is little chance for skill or knowledge differences), and both aspects of the task are monitored (there is little opportunity for different levels of task compliance), most of the variation in performance on this task should be attributable to differences in participants' fundamental processing capacities. For our modeling purposes, we take this to be variation in source activation.

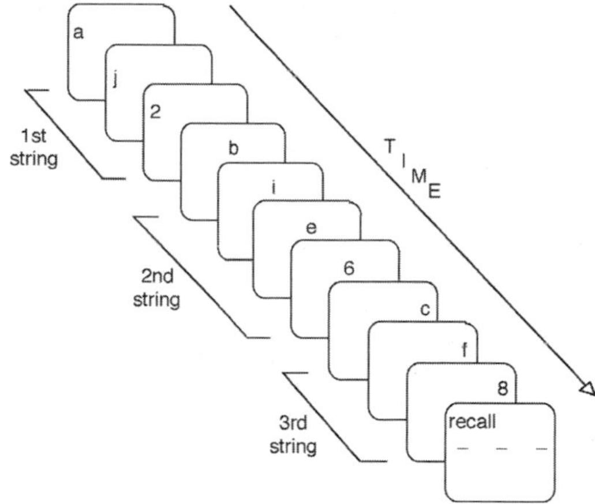

Figure 17.3. Graphic illustration of a Modified Digit Span task trial with a memory set of size 3. The differences in the positions of the characters on-screen have been exaggerated for clarity.

An ACT-R model of the MODS task successfully fits individual participant's data as a function of set size (Figure 17.4) and as a function of serial position for the set size six trials (Figure 17.5) by only varying the source-activation parameter (Daily, Lovett, & Reder, 2001). This suggests that source activation presents a reasonable implementation of working memory that can explain the variation in individuals' MODS performance. Moreover, because source activation plays the same role in all ACT-R models, this allows for predictions to be made for the same participants on other tasks by plugging each participant's estimated source-activation parameter into the other task models. In Lovett, Daily, and Reder (2000), this is accomplished for the n-back task. Specifically, individual participant estimates of source activation were derived from their MODS task performance and then used to make zero-parameter, individual participant predictions on the n-back task.

The n-back task is a continuous trial paradigm in which, for a given block of trials, participants are asked to respond to whether each letter stimulus is a repeat of the stimulus "n" trials back (e.g., Braver et al., 1997; Cohen et al., 1994). For example, suppose

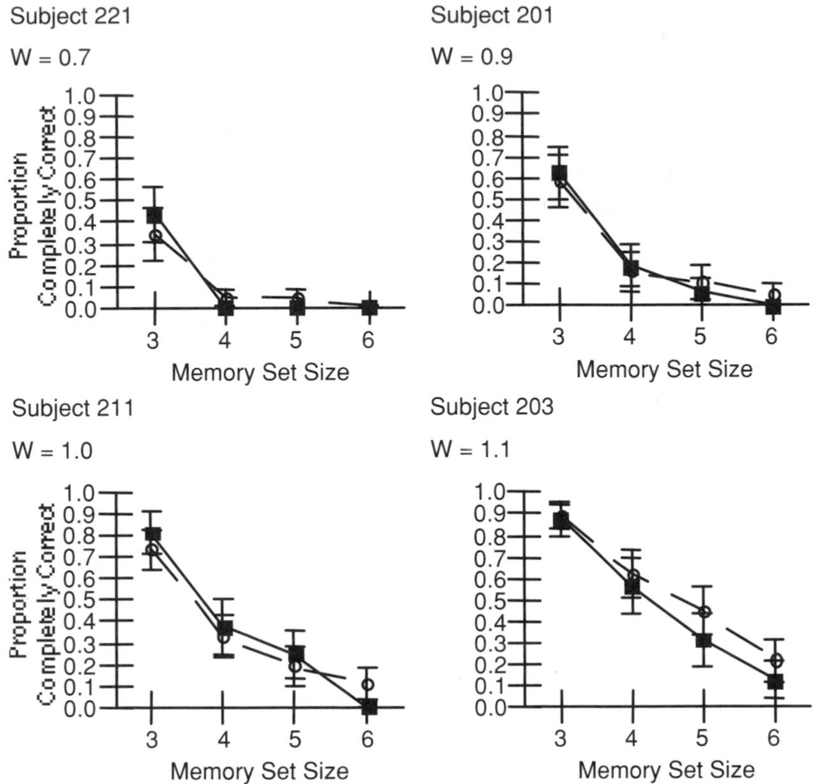

Figure 17.4. Model fits for four representative subjects from Daily et al. (1999). Filled symbols are subject data; open symbols are the model's predictions.

the participant saw the stimuli "U E E R E K L L". In a "1-back" block, a participant should say "yes" to the third and last stimulus and "no" elsewhere, whereas in a "2-back" block, the participant should say "yes" to the fifth stimulus and "no" elsewhere. As "n" increases, the working memory demands of the task increase and, not suprisingly, performance degrades. Figure 17.6 shows high-fidelity modeling fits at the individual participant level in the n-back task by using the individualized source activation parameter values that were estimated from the same participants' MODS performance.

Summary

This model of working memory includes production rules to perform the various tasks studied. Across all tasks, the ACT-R architecture provides a single theory of working memory in which working-memory limitations are represented by a fixed amount of source activation, propagated from the current focus of attention to increase the activation of goal-relevant items and to decrease the activation of goal-irrelevant items. The larger this source activation for a given individual, the greater the degree of facilitation (suppression) of goal-relevant (irrelevant) items. This leads to direct performance implications as a function of source activation, plus there are indirect effects in the model (e.g., more rehearsals are possible because of faster retrievals with high source activation) that can further the implications. In sum, this working-memory model relies most heavily on the relative activation levels of declarative chunks (both those that are part of the initial model and those that are newly acquired as part of task performance); this is highlighted by the check marks filling the declarative chunks row in Table 17.6.

Table 17.6. Knowledge Structures and Mechanisms Used in a Production-Systems Model of Working Memory

	Performance Mechanisms		*Learning Mechanisms*	
	Symbolic	*Subsymbolic*	*Symbolic*	*Subsymbolic*
Declarative chunks	√	√	√	
Production rules	√	√		

Categorization

Research on human category learning has a history that extends back at least to Hull's (1920) study of learning to categorize Chinese symbols and his conclusions in favor of an associative learning proposal. It was an important domain early in the cognitive revolution during which theorists argued for various hypothesis-testing theories (e.g., Trabasso & Bower, 1964; Levine, 1975). The hypothesis-testing theories were based on research with stimuli that had a very simple, often one-dimensional categorical structure. The 1970s saw a renewed interest in more complex, fuzzy categories and proposals for

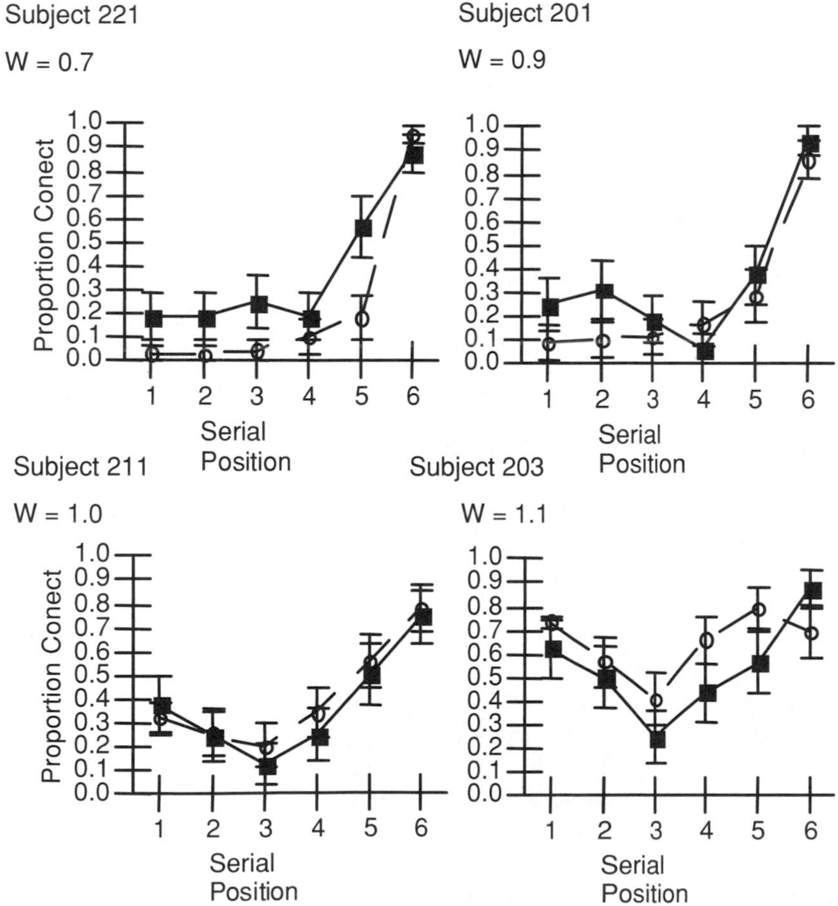

Figure 17.5. Fits to the serial position data (largest set size only) for four typical subjects. Filled symbols are subject data; open symbols are the model's predictions.

prototype theories (Reed, 1972; Rosch, 1975) and exemplar theories (e.g., Medin & Schaffer, 1978). The rise of connectionist models resulted in the proposal of associative theories (e.g., Gluck & Bower, 1988) not that different from the original Hull proposal. Whereas the original research focused on accuracy data, new emphasis has been on latency data to help choose among theories (e.g., Lamberts, 1998; Nosofsky & Palmeri, 1997). Recently, neuro-imaging and other cognitive neuroscience data have been recruited to try to decide among alternative theories (e.g., Ashby, et al., 1998; Smith, Patalano, & Jonides, 1998). Impressive growth has been attained in the characterizations of the phenomena in category learning (see Medin and Rips, Chap. 3). However, the field does not seem any closer to coming to consensus regarding what "the" mechanism of category learning is.

Anderson and Betz (2001) produced a production system model that reflected the belief that this contest of theories was misplaced and that different mechanisms were being used to different degrees in different experiments. In particular, they implemented two alternative models in ACT-R that have been advanced for categorization – Nosofsky, Palmeri, and McKinley's (1994) rule-plus-exception (RULEX) model and Nosofsky and Palmeri's (1997) exemplar-based random-walk (EBRW) model. The first model proposes that subjects store explicit rules for category membership and possible exceptions. The EBRW model proposes that subjects retrieve instances that are similar to the test stimulus and assign the stimulus to the category that has the most retrieved exemplars after exceeding a particular threshold. Whereas the original models are mathematical characterizations of participants' behavior, the ACT-R model is a computational system that actually performs the task. Production rules provide the control structure for how the ACT-R model approaches the task (e.g., whether it employs a RULEX- or EBRW-based approach), whereas declarative memory stores the rules, exceptions, and examples used and strengthened by each approach. The subsymbolic components of the architecture determine which production rules and declarative structures are retrieved at any time.

The component of the model incorporating an EBRW approach retrieves past instances from memory as a function of their similarity to the current stimulus. This depends critically on the ability of the ACT-R system to retrieve partially matching traces. Specifically, the probability of retrieving a memory in ACT-R is a function of how similar it is to the memory probe. Anderson and Betz (2001) show that this retrieval function yields a similar, but not identical, selection rule to that used in the original Nosfosky and Palmeri formulation. In addition, the ACT-R mechanism for chunk strengthening favors the retrieval of more frequently presented items and therefore produces a speed increase similar to that in EBRW (which uses multiple traces and a Logan (1988) race process). Although the original EBRW and the ACT-R implementation are not identical, they prove largely indistinguishable in their predictions. This near-equivalence is strongly dependent on the pre-existing subsymbolic processes built into ACT-R.

The component of the ACT-R model implementing a RULEX approach depends more on the symbolic production-level system because the actual logic of hypothesis testing in RULEX is quite complex (e.g., different rules specify when to settle on a hypothesis, when to switch from single dimension to multiple dimension rules, and when and how to form exceptions). Nevertheless, the subsymbolic level of ACT-R, which governs the selection among production rules based on their ever-changing utility values, is essential for this model component to capture the randomness of RULEX. Indeed, this noisy selection process enables this model component to reproduce the wide variety of hypotheses that subjects display.

The Anderson and Betz effort is a relatively successful integration of the two models. Moreover, the effort adds value over the two original models. First, it establishes that the two theories are not necessarily

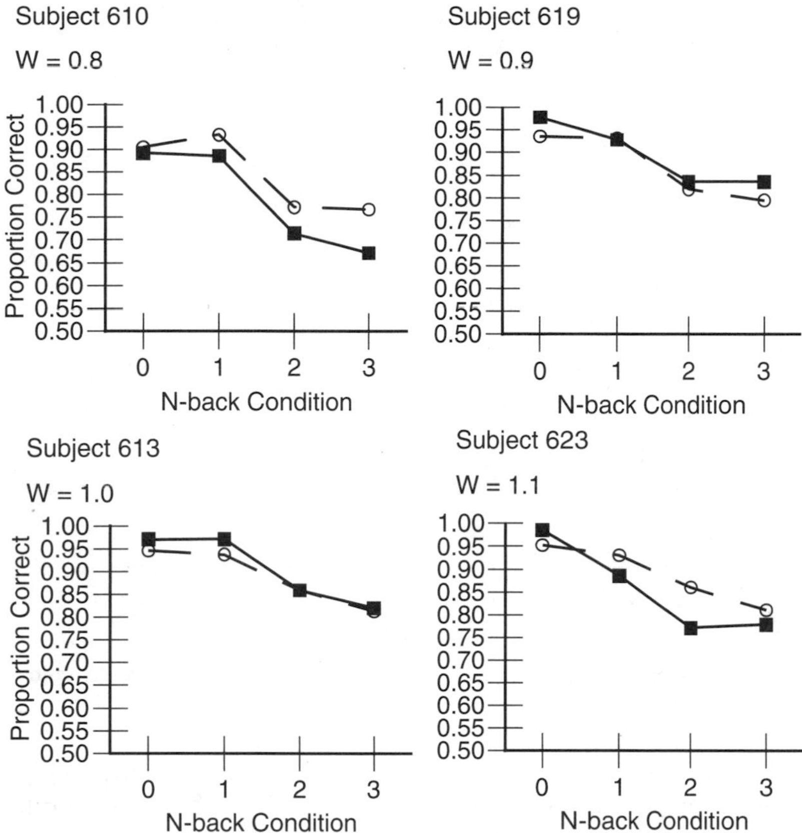

Figure 17.6. N-back performance and model predictions for individual participants where parameter estimates of individuals' working-memory capacities were derived from performance on the Modified Digit Span task.

in opposition and in fact reflect the same underlying subsymbolic processes but with different symbolic control. Moreover, those subsymbolic processes are the same ones that can be used to model other, very different domains of human cognition. Also, because both categorization mechanisms are able to sit within the same architecture, Anderson and Betz were able to address the issue of choice between the two mechanisms. This depends on the relative utility of these two mechanisms. Anderson and Betz show that the mixture of the two strategies is able to account for phenomena that cannot be accounted for by either strategy alone. They also show a natural tendency for this mixture of strategies to evolve from being dominated by rule-based classification to being dominated by instance-based classification because the latter is more efficient. Figure 17.7 shows the tendency for exemplar use to increase in two of the models reported by Anderson & Betz. This increased exemplar use is consistent with reported results of a strategy shift with extensive practice (Johansen & Palmeri, 2002).

Summary

This contemporary production-system model of categorization integrates two approaches (implemented as different sets of cohabitating production rules) and chooses between them (based on the production rules' learned utility values). In one approach, production rules are the conduit for creating and accessing exemplars (implemented as declarative chunks) in a

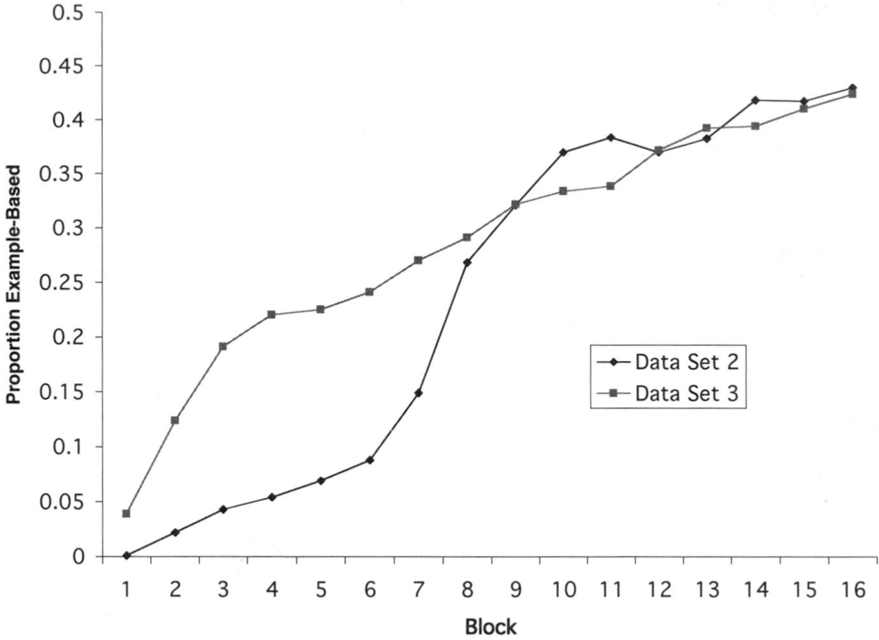

Figure 17.7. Proportion exemplar use across blocks in two data sets modeled in Anderson and Betz (2001).

context-sensitive and frequency-sensitive way. In the other approach, production rules create and manipulate declarative rules for categorizing items. In all cases, the ACT-R subsymbolic learning mechanisms for production rules and declarative chunks govern how these kinds of knowledge are used. Table 17.7 highlights this (see checks in the right column) as well as the fact that this model employs ACT-R's symbolic learning mechanism for declarative chunks.

Skill Learning

Research into skill learning can be roughly divided into two categories. One category focuses on how skills are learned in the first place (e.g., Catrambone, 1996; Chi et al., 1989; VanLehn & Jones, 1993). The other focuses on how skills are refined to achieve domain expertise (see also Novick & Bassok, Chap. 14). Research in the former category has addressed issues of learning from instruction, transfer, and induction. Research in the latter category has addressed issues of generalization, specialization, and automaticity. A unified approach merges these issues into a single explanation. Production-systems models – particularly those that address the question of production-rule learning – hold the promise of offering such an explanation.

Among production-systems models, Soar holds the most parsimonious view of skill learning, with its single mechanism,

Table 17.7. This Model of Categorization Relies on Three Out of Four of ACT-R's Learning mechanisms

	Performance Mechanisms		*Learning Mechanisms*	
	Symbolic	*Subsymbolic*	*Symbolic*	*Subsymbolic*
Declarative chunks	√	√	√	√
Production rules	√	√		√

Table 17.8. Two Parent Production Rules and the Learned Child Production Rule

Production A	*Production B*	*Production C*
When the goal is to add the numbers *x* and *y*, then try to retrieve the sum of *x* and *y*	When the goal is to add the numbers *x* and *y* and the sum of *x* and *y* has been retrieved as *z*, then update the goal with *z* as the answer	When the goal is to add 2 to 5, then update the goal with 7 as the answer

chunking. Chunking is invoked whenever the system encounters an impasse (i.e., when existing production rules do not directly specify the next step). At this point, the system creates a subgoal to solve the impasse by applying domain-general production rules. Solving the impasse creates a new rule specialized for that situation. A similar rule-learning process is employed by Cascade, a model of skill acquisition that incorporates both the impasse-repair-reflect cycle and analogical problem solving (VanLehn, 1999). After the new rule is learned, when Cascade subsequently encounters the same (or a related) situation, it can apply the new rule directly and avoid the extra processing. These models employ specialization – making a new rule that is a specific version of its parents – and composition – combining multiple production rules into one new rule.

ACT-R also has a production-rule learning mechanism. This mechanism combines *composition* – merging two production rules that fire in sequence – and *proceduralization* – creating a new version of an existing production rule in which the new version avoids fact retrieval by instantiating necessary information directly into the new rule. For example, consider a pair of production rules that solve addition problems of the form x + y = ? by first retrieving the relevant addition fact from memory and then using this fact to make a response (A and B in Table 17.8). When these production rules are applied to the problem 2 + 5 = ?, a single production rule is learned (C in Table 17.8) that combines the two steps into one but is specific to the case of 2 = 5. This mechanism treats skill learning as a ubiquitous process of building more specific, more powerful, and less explicit problem-solving knowledge. Greater power comes from the knowledge's being faster, no longer subject to retrieval failures, and incurring lower working-memory load. Less explicitness comes from the fact that the new rule transforms a fully inspectable, declarative fact into the body of a production rule, where knowledge is not open to inspection.

We exemplify ACT-R's production-rule learning in the context of an experimental paradigm in which rule-like knowledge is learned in many different forms (Anderson & Fincham, 1994; Anderson, Fincham, and Douglass, 1997). This paradigm involves teaching participants a number of sports facts such as "Hockey was played on Saturday at 3 PM and then on Monday at 1 PM." After committing these sports facts to memory, participants are told that each one conveys a particular pattern or rule for the game times for that sport (e.g., Hockey's second game time is always two days later and two hours earlier than its first). Participants are then given practice at using these sports facts to solve new problems in which either the first or second time is given and the other must be predicted. Figure 17.8a shows the speed-up in performance from Anderson & Fincham (1994) as participants practiced this over three days (each "bump" occurred at the beginning of a new day). Figure 17.8a also shows the predictions of an ACT-R simulation (Taatgen and Wallach, 2002) that involves four representations of the sports-fact knowledge.

Figure 17.8b tracks the contribution of these four sources of knowledge over the three days. The initial representation was simply the set of eight studied sports facts represented as declarative facts (see first row of Table 17.9). Specifically, each

Table 17.9. Model's Different Representations of the Sports Facts from Anderson and Fincham (1994)

Knowledge Type	*Declarative vs. Production*	*How Generated*	*Sports*	*No. of Steps Required*
Original sports fact components	Declarative	Original study	4	≈20
General relationships	Declarative	Analogy on original sports fact components	2	≈10
Procedural relation	Production rule	Production compilation on relationships	4	≈6
Studied instance	Declarative	Result of previous (& often repeated) example	2 for each example	2

sports fact was represented in terms of four interrelated chunks to capture the two days and two times for that sport (e.g., "Hockey's first event day was Saturday", "Hockey's first event time was 3", "Hockey's second event day was Monday", "Hockey's second event time was 1"). To solve problems using these facts, the model was endowed with a set of production rules representing the weak methods of direct retrieval (applicable for the original facts) and analogy.

From this initial knowledge base, the model generated the other three representations of the sports-fact knowledge. The first of these represents the rule-like relationships of each original sports fact as two declarative chunks (e.g., "Hockey's day relationship is +2", and "Hockey's time relationship is −2"). The model produces this declaratively represented generalization as a byproduct of the analogizing process (see second row of Table 17.9). Once these generalized relationships are derived, applying them to a new problem is much simpler than solving by analogy. The second new representation of knowledge comes in true production-rule form. Specifically, a new production rule is learned that merges the steps involved in applying the declarative generalizations just mentioned. Note that this production rule is specialized to the sport and direction (time 1 → time 2 or vice versa) under which it was generated. Such a directional production rule should show faster performance for problems in the practiced direction, and Anderson and Fincham showed that such asymmetry develops with extensive practice.

The third new representation is a specific instance representing the solution to a particular previous (and often repeated) problem. This knowledge can complete a new problem in just two steps (one each for the day and time). However, it is specific to a particular problem and is only generated after the preceding forms of knowledge have paved its way. It predicts that participants will be faster on frequently repeated problems, and Anderson, Fincham, and Douglass (1997) provide evidence for such item-specific learning.

Summary

The most noteworthy aspect of this production-systems model of skill learning is that it posits multiple, overlapping stages in the development of a new skill, some of which represent the new skill knowledge in production-rule form and some of which do not. Because of the acquisition of new production rules and new declarative chunks, the model relies on both symbolic learning mechanisms in ACT-R. In addition, these new knowledge representations are refined and strengthened through experience, drawing on ACT-R's subsymbolic learning mechanisms. Finally, the model chooses among the different knowledge representations via the subsymbolic performance mechanisms:

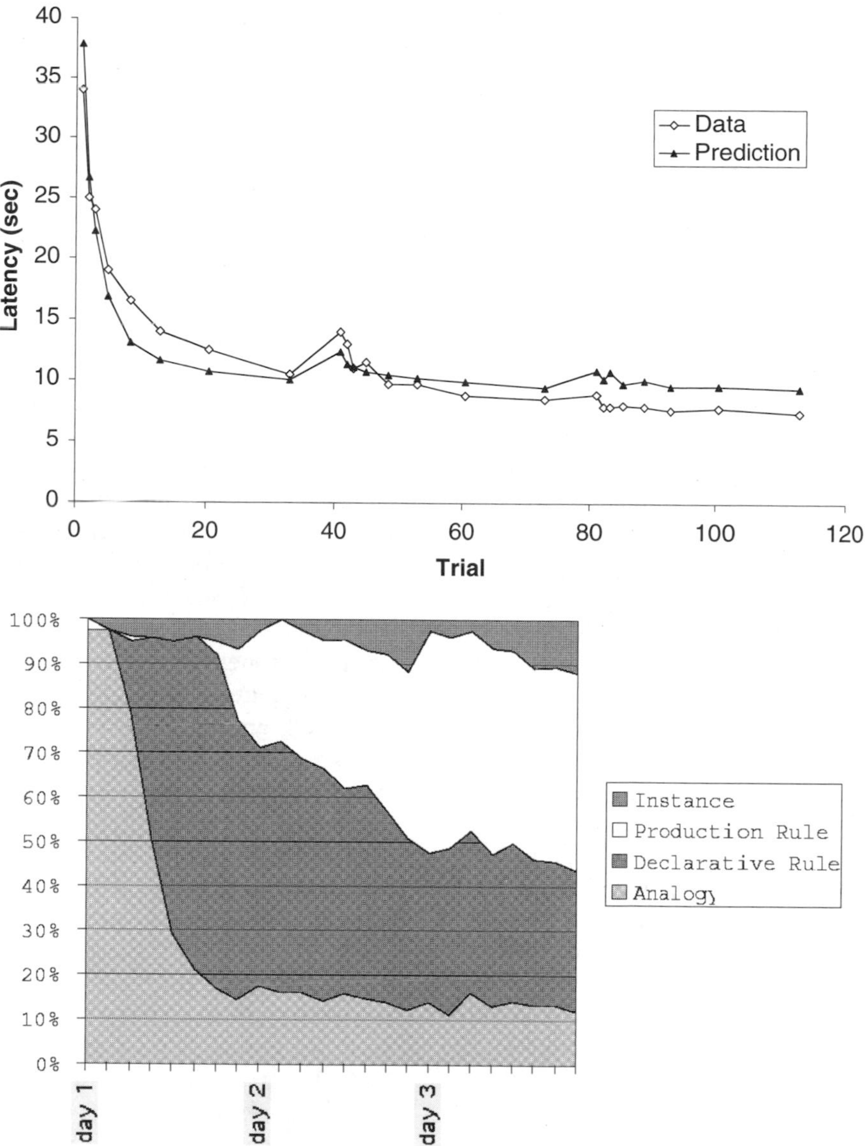

Figure 17.8. Latency to respond across trials in each session in Anderson and Fincham, 1994 (panel a), and proportion of simulation runs in which particular knowledge representations were used across trials in Taatgen and Wallach, 2002 (panel b).

As declarative representations are strengthened through use, those with higher activation will tend to get retrieved, and as new production rules are used and are successful, those with higher utilities will tend to get chosen (over more generic production rules that employ declarative representations). In sum, this model draws on all eight mechanisms presented in Table 17.10.

Language Learning: Past Tense

The learning of the English past tense is another domain in which symbolic and subsymbolic models have clashed. The appearance of over-regularization errors in children's past tense (e.g., go–goed as opposed to go–went) had been originally taken as evidence (e.g., Brown, 1973) that children

Table 17.10. Knowledge Structures and Mechanisms Used in Production-Systems Model of Skill Learning

	Performance Mechanisms		*Learning Mechanisms*	
	Symbolic	*Subsymbolic*	*Symbolic*	*Subsymbolic*
Declarative chunks	√	√	√	√
Production rules	√	√	√	√

were acquiring abstract rules. However, Rumelhart and McClelland (1987) showed that by learning associations between the phonological representations of stems and past tense it was possible to produce a model that made overgeneralizations without building any rules into it. It was able to account for the U-shaped learning function demonstrated by children by which they first do not produce such overgeneralization, then do, and finally, gradually eliminate the overgeneralizations. This attracted a great many critiques and, although the fundamental demonstration of generalization without rules stands, it is acknowledged by all to be seriously flawed as a model of the process of past-tense generation by children. Many more recent and more adequate connectionist models (some reviewed in Elman et al., 1996) have been proposed, and many of these have tried to use the backpropogation learning algorithm.

This would seem like an appropriate domain for production-system models, and Taatgen and Anderson (2002) have produced a successful model of these phenomena. Significantly, they show that one can account for past-tense learning with a similar dual mechanism model like that of Anderson and Betz (2001). The model posits that children initially approach the task of past-tense generation with two strategies. Given a particular word like "give," they can either try to retrieve the past tense for that word or they can try to retrieve some other example of a past tense (e.g., live–lived) and try to apply this by analogy to the current case. In the case of analogy, previously encountered present–past tense pairs serve as potential sources, and a source that has a present tense form similar to the target's present tense form will be retrieved. Then, the transformation driving the past-tense form in the retrieved source is applied to the target. Eventually, through the production-rule learning mechanisms in ACT-R, the analogy process will be converted into a production rule that generatively applies the past-tense rule. Once the past-tense rule is learned, the generation of past tenses will be determined largely by a competition between the general rule and retrieval of specific cases. Thus, ACT-R has basically a dual-route model of past-tense generation in which both routes are implemented by production rules. The rule-based approach depends on general production rules whereas the exemplar approach depends on the retrieval of declarative chunks by production rules that implement an instance-based strategy.

Figure 17.9 graphically displays the variety of ways this model can generate the past tense. Although all of these options are implemented in ACT-R production rules, only the two rightmost options represent the application of general past-tense rules (e.g., add "ed"). The second and third options initiate procedures for retrieving a memory trace that can then be applied directly or by analogy to the current situation.

The general past-tense rule, once discovered by analogy, gradually enters the competition as the system learns that this new rule is widely applicable. This gradual entry, which depends on ACT-R's subsymbolic utility-learning mechanisms, is responsible for the onset of overgeneralization. Although this onset is not all-or-none in either the model or the data, it is a relatively rapid transition in both model and data and corresponds to the first turn in the U-shaped function. However, as this is happening, the ACT-R model is encountering and strengthening the declarative representations of

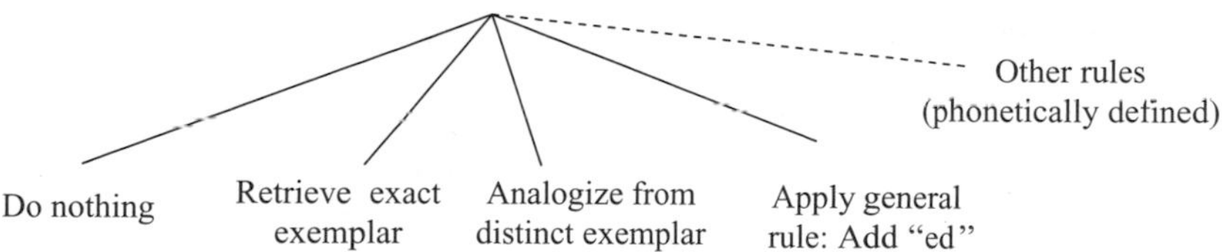

Figure 17.9. Different choices the model can make in generating the past tense. Each option is executed by the firing of a production rule, but only the two rightmost options actually implement a generalized rule. ACT-R's production-rule competition and learning mechanisms govern the model's selection among these options.

exceptions to the general rule. Retrieval of the exceptions comes to counteract the overgeneralizations. Retrieval of exceptions is preferred because they tend to be shorter and phonetically more regular (Burzio, 2002) than regular past tenses. Growth in this retrieval process corresponds to the second turn in the U-shaped function and is much more gradual – again, both in model and data.

Note that the Taatgen model, unlike many other past-tense models, does not make artificial assumptions about frequency of exposure but learns given a presentation schedule of words (both from the environment and its own generations) like that actually encountered by children. Its ability to reproduce the relatively rapid onset of overgeneralization and slow extinction depends critically on both its symbolic and subsymbolic learning mechanisms. Symbolically, it is learning general production rules and declarative representations of exceptions. Subsymbolically, it is learning the utility of these production rules and the activation strengths of the declarative chunks.

Beyond just reproducing the U-shaped function, the ACT-R model explains why exceptions should be high-frequency words. There are two aspects to this explanation. First, only high-frequency words develop enough base-level activation to be retrieved. Indeed the theory predicts how frequent a word has to be to maintain an exception. Less obviously, the model explains why so many high-frequency words actually end up as exceptions. This is because the greater phonological efficiency of the irregular form promotes its adoption according to the utility calculations of ACT-R. Indeed, in another model that basically invents its own past-tense grammar without input from the environment, Taatgen showed that it will develop one or more past-tense rules for low-frequency words but will tend to adopt more efficient irregular forms for high-frequency words. In the ACT-R economy the greater phonological efficiency of the irregular form justifies its maintenance in declarative memory if it is of sufficiently high frequency.

Note that the model receives no feedback on the past tenses it generates unlike most models but in apparent correspondence with the facts about child language learning. However, it receives input from the environment in the form of the past tenses it hears, and this input influences the base-level activation of the past-tense forms in declarative memory. The model also uses its own past-tense generations as input to declarative memory and can learn its own errors (a phenomenon also noted in cognitive arithmetic by Siegler, 1988). The amount of overgeneralization displayed by the model is sensitive to the ratio of input it receives from the environment to its own past-tense generations.

Summary

Although this model of past-tense generation fully depends on the existence (and emergence) of rules and symbols, it also critically depends on the subsymbolic properties of ACT-R to produce the observed graded effects. Table 17.11 highlights the fact that this model relies on learning of both declarative and procedural knowledge at both the symbolic and subsymbolic level. This eclectic position enables the model to achieve a number of other features not attained by many other models:

1. It does not have to rely on artificial assumptions about presentation frequency.
2. It does not need corrective feedback on its own generations.
3. It explains why irregular forms tend to be high frequency and why high-frequency words tend to be irregular.
4. It correctly predicts that novel words will receive regular past tenses.
5. It predicts the gradual onset of overgeneralization and its much more gradual extinction.

Conclusions and Future Directions

This chapter describes six production-systems models accounting for six different areas of cognition: problem-solving choice, analogy making, working memory, categorization, skill learning, and past-tense learning. In some cases, an important contribution of the model lies in specifying a production system that implements a fairly general reasoning strategy (e.g., analogy making and categorization). The analogy model specifies a path-mapping process as a set of production rules. The categorization model specifies two processes for categorization – by rules (with exceptions) and by retrieving multiple category exemplars – both implemented as sets of production rules that cohabit a single production system. In both models, it is not only the production rules that govern model behavior but also subsymbolic quantities that influence how the production rules do their work. In the analogy model, subsymbolic activation levels associated with different declarative chunks influence which parts of the analogy will get mapped and when; in the categorization model, subsymbolic utility levels associated with different production rules influence which categorization approach will be chosen and when.

Another contribution made by several of the models is specifying how multiple strategic approaches to a given task can be integrated. Indeed, a common but often underemphasized feature of high-level cognitive tasks is that people can approach them in so many ways. The problem-solving model addresses this issue of choice directly and illustrates a modern interpretation of production-rule conflict resolution. Specifically, this model (along with the categorization, skill-learning, and past-tense–learning models) demonstrates that a noisy selection of the production rule with highest utility (where utility is naturally learned through experience by the system) works well to choose among different strategies.

A related contribution made by some of these models is making clear that rule-like thinking is not always best represented in terms of production rules. The categorization, skill-learning, and past-tense–learning models all use multiple strategic approaches; in the latter two models, one of the approaches is based on production-rule representations of knowledge and another is *not* based on production-rule representations of knowledge. Together, the two representational forms complement each other in a way that accounts for the variability in people's behavior. Accounting for variability is probably the most notable contribution of the working-memory model given that it posits a theory of working-memory limitations that can be used to estimate individuals' working-memory capacities and then predict other task performance on that basis.

What is most striking about these models as a whole, however, is that they make use of the same set of mechanisms for learning and using knowledge across such a disparate set of tasks and that they use the same two kinds of knowledge representations – production rules and declarative chunks. Although each model emphasizes a somewhat different subset of mechanisms (compare Tables 17.4–17.7, 17.10, and 17.11), they all fit together in a unified architecture, just as the many processes of human cognition all must fit together in the human brain. Likewise, modern productions systems offer an

Table 17.11. This Model of Past-Tense Generation Relies on All Four of ACT-R's Learning mechanisms

	Performance Mechanisms		*Learning Mechanisms*	
	Symbolic	*Subsymbolic*	*Symbolic*	*Subsymbolic*
Declarative chunks	√	√	√	√
Production rules	√	√	√	√

understanding of how the many components of cognition are integrated.

Production Systems into the Future

Given the progress represented by the relatively few models presented here, it is worthwhile to speculate how production systems will continue to be involved in future research on cognition. Two areas in which production systems have ventured in the past few years are already showing initial levels of success and promise to play a large role in future developments in modeling.

One of these areas involves the development of production-system models that can handle complex tasks. Complexity can arise in many dimensions, but one involves the dynamic qualities of the task. Air-traffic control is a dynamic task in that it requires continuous attention to changing stimuli and changing task demands. It is complex in that it requires the integration of multiple areas of knowledge (e.g., different skills to handle the different situations) and the integration of perceptual, motor, and cognitive processing (e.g., actually working with a graphical and keyboard interface akin to what real air-traffic controllers use). A modeling competition to account for human data of various sorts on an air-traffic-control task called AMBR (Agent-Based Modeling and Behavior Representation) set the bar high with regard to modeling a complex, dynamic task (Gluck & Pew, 2001). Several production-system models, including one built within ACT-R (Lebiere, Anderson, and Bothell, 2001) and one built within an EPIC–Soar combination (Chong and Wray, 2002), took on the challenge and demonstrated success in accounting for the number and type of errors of human controllers and, in the case of ACT-R, similar levels of variability in performance among human controllers. Similar successes are beginning to arise in real world applications of production-systems models. For instance, there is the Soar model that managed to fly 50 Air Force training missions (Jones et al., 1999), and other examples of production-systems models used in industry and military applications will likely become more the rule than the exception (pardon the pun!). Some of these will likely come in the form of cognitive agents (e.g., Best, Lebiere, and Scarpinatto, 2002) that act in virtual worlds (e.g., for training purposes with humans) or real environments (e.g., in coordination with robotic systems).

Another area of current growth in production-systems modeling that promises to expand is the integration of production-systems models (i.e., their components and their predictions) with neuroimaging work. With the growth of functional neuroimaging as a means of studying cognition (see Goel, Chap. 20), the field of cognitive modeling has another dependent measure for testing models' predictions. To take advantage of this additional constraint, however, the model must posit some mapping between model output and neuroimaging results. A direct approach is to map brain locations to model functions and then predict localization of activation on the basis of model functions. This basic approach can be elaborated to account for the time course of brain activity either at a coarse-grain size (e.g., predicting differential localization of activity early versus late in the task or between conditions) or at a fine-grain size (e.g., within a single trial). Both of these approaches have been used in tasks ranging from language processing (Just, Carpenter, and Varma, 1999) to equation solving (Anderson, et al., in press), to planning (Fincham et al., 2002) to task switching (Sohn et al., 2000). The goal of this work is to improve our understanding of brain function and also of the mapping to production-system models of thought. Whereas production systems have tended to describe cognitive processes at a high level of abstraction, the trend has been toward more and more fine-grained models, so it is now becoming appropriate to consider the neural processing implications of many of the issues in production-system models.

Acknowledgments

The authors thank Stacey Becker, Norma Chang, and Niels Taatgen for comments on an earlier draft. This work was partially sponsored by the Department of the Navy, Office of Naval Research. Any opinions, findings, and conclusions, or recommendations expressed in this material, are those of the authors and do not necessarily reflect the views of the Office of Naval Research.

Notes

1. Interestingly, recent production-system models have returned to embrace an individual participant approach with quantitative analyses (e.g., Daily, Lovett, & Reder, 2001; Lovett, Daily, & Reder, 2000).
2. Asynchronous parallelism means that each perceptual/motor module can work in parallel with others in such a way that the actions of each need not be synchronized with actions of the others.
3. However, Young and Lewis (1999) have posited that no more than two items with the same type of coding (e.g., phonological or syntactic) can be stored in dynamic memory at a time.

References

Anderson, J. R., & Betz, J. (2001). A hybrid model of categorization. *Psychonomic Bulletin and Review*, 8(4), 629–647.

Anderson, J. R., & Fincham, J. M. (1994). Acquisition of procedural skills from examples. *Journal of Experimental Psychology: Learning, Memory, and Cognition*, 20, 1322–1340.

Anderson, J. R., Fincham, J. M, & Douglass, S. (1997). The role of examples and rules in the acquisition of a cognitive skill. *Journal of Experimental Psychology: Learning, Memory, and Cognition*, 22, 259–277.

Anderson, J. R., & Lebiere, C. (1998). *The Atomic Components of Thought*. Mahwah, NJ: Erlbaum.

Anderson, J. R., Qin, Y., Sohn, M-H., Stenger, V. A. & Carter, C. S. (in press). An information-processing model of the BOLD response in symbol manipulation tasks. *Psychonomic Bulletin and Review*.

Anderson, J. R., & Thompson, R. (1989). Use of analogy in a production system architecture. In S. Vosniadou & A. Ortony (Eds.), *Similarity and Analogy*, (pp. 367–397). New York: Cambridge University Press.

Ashby, F., Alfonso-Reese, L., Turken, A., & Waldron, E. (1998). A neuropsychological theory of multiple systems in category learning. *Psychological Review*, 105(3), 442–481.

Baddeley, A. D., & Hitch, G. (1974). Working memory. In G. H. Bower (Ed.), *The Psychology of Learning and Motivation*, 8. New York: Academic Press.

Baddeley, A. D., & Hitch, G. (1977). Recency reexamined. In S. Dornic (Ed.), *Attention and performance VI*. Hillsdale, NJ: Erlbaum.

Best, B., Lebiere, C., & Scarpinatto, C. (2002). A model of synthetic opponents in MOUT training simulations using the ACT-R cognitive architecture. In Proceedings of the Eleventh Conference on Computer Generated Forces and Behavior Representation. Orlando, FL.

Braver, T. S., Cohen, J. D., Nystrom, L. E., Jonides, J., Smith, E. E., & Noll, D. C. (1997). A parametric study of prefrontal cortex involvment in human working memory. *Neuroimage*, 5, 49–62.

Brown, R. (1973). *A first language: The early stages* Cambridge, MA: Harvard University Press.

Budiu, R. (2001) The role of background knowledge in sentence processing. *Doctoral Dissertation, Department of Computer Science, Carnegie Mellon University*. Pittsburgh, PA.

Burzio, L. (2002). Missing players: Phonology and the past-tense debate. *Lingua*, 112, 157–199.

Catrambone, R. (1996). Generalizing solution procedures learned from examples. *Journal of Experimental Psychology: Learning, Memory, and Cognition*, 22, 1020–1031.

Chi, M. T. H., Bassok, M., Lewis, M., Reimann, P., & Glaser, R. (1989). Self-explanations: How students study and use examples in learening to solve problems. *Cognitive Science*, 13, 145–182.

Chong, R. S., & Wray, R. E. (2002). An EPIC-Soar model of concurrent performance on a category learning and a simplified air traffic control task. In W. D. Gray & C. D. Schunn (Eds.) *Proceedings of the 20th Annual Conference of the Cognitive Science Society* (pp. 21–22). Mahwah, NJ: Erlbaum.

Cohen, J. D., Forman, S. D., Braver, T. S., Casey, B. J., Servan-Schreiber, D., & Noll, D. C. (1994). Activation of prefrontal cortex in a non-spatial working memory task with functional MRI. *Human Brain Mapping*, 1, 293–304.

Daily, L. Z., Lovett, M. C., & Reder, L. M. (2001). Modeling individual differences in working memory performance: A source activation account in ACT-R. *Cognitive Science*, 25, 315–353.

Daneman, M., & Carpenter, P. (1980). Individual differences in working memory and reading. *Journal of Verbal Learning and Verbal Behavior*, 19, 450–466.

Elman, J. L., Bates, E. A., Johnson, M. H., & Karmiloff-Smith, A. (1996). *Rethinking Innateness: A Connectionist Perspective on Development*. Cambridge, MA: MIT Press.

Fincham, J. M., Carter, C. S., van Veen, V., Stenger, V. A., & Anderson, J. R. (2002). Neural mechanisms of planning: A computational analysis using event-related fMRI. *Proceedings of the National Academy of Sciences*, 99(5), 3346–3351.

Engle, R. W. (1994). Individual differences in memory and implications for learning. In R. Sternberg (Ed.), *Encyclopedia of Intelligence.* New York: Macmillan.

Gentner, D. (1983). Structure-mapping: A theoretical framework for analogy. *Cognitive Science*, 7, 155–170.

Gentner, D. (1989). The mechanisms of analogical learning. In S. Vosniadou & A. Ortony (Eds), *Similarity and Analogical Reasoning* (pp. 199–241). Cambridge, UK: Cambridge University Press.

Gluck, M. A., & Bower, G. H. (1988). From conditioning to category learning: An adaptive network model. *Journal of Experimental Psychology: General*, 117, 225–244.

Gluck, K. A., & Pew, R. W. (2001). Overview of the agent-based modeling and behavior representation (AMBR) model comparison project. To appear in the *Proceedings of the Tenth Conference on Computere Generated Forces and Behavior Representation*. Norfolk, VA.

Hofstadter, D. R., & Mitchell, M. (1994). An overview of the Copycat project. In K. J. Holyoak & J. A. Barnden (Eds.), *Advances in Connectionist and Neural Computation Theory. Vol 2 : Analogical Connections* (pp. 31–112). Hillsdale, NJ: Erlbaum.

Holyoak, K. J., & Thagard, P. R. (1989). Analogical mapping by constraint satisfaction. *Cognitive Science*, 13, 295–355.

Holyoak, K. J., & Thagard, P. R. (1995). *Mental Leaps: Analogy in Creative Thought*. Cambridge, MA: MIT Press.

Hull, C. (1920). Quantitative aspects of the evolution of concepts. *Psychological Monographs*, 28(1), 1–86.

Hummel, H. E., & Holyoak, K. J. (1997). Distributed representations of structure: A theory of analogical access and mapping. *Psychological Review*, 104, 427–466.

Johansen, M. K., & Palmeri, T. J. (2002). Are there representational shifts during category learning? *Cognitive Psychology*, 45, 482–553.

Jones, R. M., Laird, J. E., Nielsen, P. E., Coulter, K. J., Kenny, P. G., & Koss, F. V. (1999). Automated intelligent pilots for combat flight simulation. *AI Magazine*, 20(1), 27–41.

Just, M. A., & Carpenter, P. N. (1992) A capacity theory of comprehension: Individual differences in working memory. *Psychological Review*, 99, 122–149.

Just, M. A., Carpenter, P. A., & Varma, S. (1999). Computational modeling of high-level cognition and brain function. *Human Brain Mapping*, 8, 128–136.

Kahneman, D., Slovic, P., & Tversky, A. (1982). *Judgment under Uncertainty: Heuristics and Biases*. New York: Cambridge University Press.

Kaplan, C. A., & Simon, H. A. (1990). In search of insight. *Cognitive Psychology*, 22, 374–419.

Keane, M. T., Ledgeway, T., & Duff, S. (1994). Constraints on analogical mapping: A comparison of three models. *Cognitive Science*, 18, 387–438.

Klahr, D. & Wallace, J. G. (1976). *Cognitive Development: An Information Processing View*. Hillsdale, NJ: Erlbaum.

Kokinov, B. N. (1998). Analogy is like cognition: Dynamic, emergent, and context-sensitive. In K. J. Holyoak, D. Gentner, & B. Kokinov (Eds.), *Advances in Analogy Research: Integration of Theory and Data Form the Cognitive, Computational, and Neural Sciences*. Sofia, Bulgaria: NBU Press.

Laird, J. E., Newell, A., & Rosenbloom, P. S. (1991). Soar: An architecture for general intelligence. *Artificial Intelligence*, 47, 289–325.

Lamberts, K. (1998). The time course of categorization. *Journal of Experimental Psychology: Learning, Memory, and Cognition*, 24, 695–711.

Lebiere, C., & Anderson, J. R. (1993). A connectionist implementation of the ACT-R production system. In *Proceedings of the Fifteenth Annual Meeting of the Cognitive Science Society*, (pp. 635–640). Hillsdale, NJ: Erlbaum.

Lebiere, C., Anderson, J. R., & Bothell, D. (2001). Multi-tasking and cognitive workload in an ACT-R model of a simplified air traffic control task. To appear in the *Proceedings of the Tenth Conference on Computere Generated Forces and Behavior Representation*. Norfolk, VA.

Lebiere, C., Gray, R., Salvucci, D., & West, R. (2003). Choice and learning under uncertainty: A case study in baseball batting. Proceedings of the 25*th Annual Conference of the Cognitive Science Society*. Mahwah, NJ: Erlbaum.

Levine, M. (1975). *A Cognitive Theory of Learning*. Hillsdale, NJ: Erlbaum.

Lewis, R. L. (1993). An Architecturally-based Theory of Human Sentence Comprehension. Ph.D. thesis, Carnegie Mellon University. *Computer Science Technical Report* CMU-CS-93-226.

Logan, G. (1988). Toward an instance theory of automatization. *Psychological Review*, 95, 492–527.

Lovett, M. C. (1998). Cognitive task analysis in service of intelligent tutoring systems design: A case study in statistics. In B. P. Goettl, H. M. Halff, C. L. Redfield, & V. J. Shute (Eds.) *Intelligent Tutoring Systems, Lecture Notes in Computer Science, Vol.* 1452 (pp. 234–243). New York: Springer–Verlag.

Lovett, M. C., & Anderson, J. R. (1996). History of success and current context in problem solving: Combined influences on operator selection. *Cognitive Psychology*, 31, 168–217.

Lovett, M. C., Daily, L. Z., & Reder, L. M. (2000). A source activation theory of working memory: Cross-task prediction of performance in ACT-R. *Cognitive Systems Research*, 1, 99–118.

Luchins, A. S. (1942). Mechanization in problem solving. *Psychological Monographs*, 54, 248.

Marsh, R. L., & Hicks, J. L. (1998). Event-based prospective memory and executive control of working memory. *Journal of Experimental Psychology: Learning, Memory, and Cognition*, 24, 336–349.

Medin, D. L., & Schaffer, M. M. (1978). Context theory of classification learning. *Psychological Review*, 85, 207–238.

Meyer, D. E., & Kieras, D. E. (1997). A computational theory of executive cognitive processes and multiple-task performance: Part 1. Basic mechanisms. *Psychological Review*, 104, 3–65.

Miyake, A. & Shah, P. (1999). *Models of Working Memory: Mechanisms of Active Maintenance and Executive Control*. New York: Cambridge University Press.

Newell, A. (1990). *Unified Theories of Cognition*. Cambridge, UK: Cambridge University Press.

Newell, A., & Simon, H. A. (1972). *Human Problem Solving*. Englewood Cliffs, NJ: Prentice-Hall.

Nosofsky, R. M., & Palmeri, T. J. (1997). An exemplar-based random walk model of speeded classification. *Psychological Review*, 104, 266–300.

Nosofsky, R., Palmeri, T., & McKinley, S. (1994). Rule-plus-exception model of classification learning. *Psychological Review*, 101 (1), 53–79.

Novick, L. R., & Holyoak, K. J. (1991). Mathematical problem solving by analogy. *Journal of Experimental Psychology: Learning, Memory, and Cognition*, 17, 398–415.

Reed, S. K. (1972). Pattern recognition and categorization. *Cognitive Psychology*, 3, 382–407.

Rosch, E. (1975). Cognitive representations of semantic categories. *Journal of Experimental Psychology: General*, 104, 192–233.

Ross, B. H. (1989). Distinguishing types of superficial similarities: Different effects on the access and use of earlier problems. *Journal of Experimental Psychology: Learning, Memory, and Cognition*, 15, 456–468.

Rumelhart, D. E., & McClelland, J. L. (1987). Learning the past tenses of English verbs: Implicit rules or parallel distributed processing?

In B. MacWhinney (Ed.) *Mechanisms of Language Acquisition* (pp. 195–248). Hillsdale, NJ: Erlbaum.

Salvucci, D. D., & Anderson, J. R. (2001). Integrating analogical mapping and general problem solving: The path-mapping theory. *Cognitive Science*, 25, 67–110.

Siegler, R. S. (1988). Individual differences in strategy choices: Good students, not-so-good students, and perfectionists. *Child Development*, 59, 833–851.

Singley, Mark K. & Anderson, J. R. (1989). *The Transfer of Cognitive Skill.* Cambridge, MA: Harvard University Press.

Smith, E., Patalano, A., & Jonides, J. (1998). Alternative strategies of categorization. *Cognition*, 65, 167–196.

Smolensky, P. (1988). On the proper treatment of connectionism. *Behavioral and Brain Sciences*, 11, 1–74.

Sohn, M. H., Ursu, S., Anderson, J. R., Stenger, V. A., & Carter, C. S. (2000). The role of prefrontal cortex and posterior parietal cortex in task-switching. *Proceedings of National Academy of Science USA*, 97(24), 13448–13453.

Spellman, B. A., & Holyoak, K. J. (1996). Pragmatics in analogical mapping. *Cognitive Psychology*, 31, 307–346.

Taatgen, N. A. & Anderson, J. R. (2002). Why do children learn to say "broke"? A model of learning the past tense without feedback. *Cognition*, 86(2), 123–155.

Taatgen, N., & Wallach, D. (2002). Whether skill acquisition is rule or instance based is determined by the structure of the task. *Cognitive Science Quarterly* 2, 163–204.

Trabasso, T., & Bower, G. (1964). Memory in concept identification. *Psychonomic Science*, 1, 133–134.

Turner, M. L., & Engle, R. W. (1989). Is working memory capacity task dependent? *Journal of Memory and Language*, 28, 127–154.

VanLehn, K. (1999). Rule-learning events in the acquisition of a complex skill: An evaluation of cascade. *Journal of the Learning Sciences*, 8, 71–125.

VanLehn, K., & Jones, R. M. (1993). Learning by explaining examples to oneself: A computational model. In S. Chipman & A. L. Meyrowitz (Eds.), *Foundations of Knowledge Acquisition: Cognitive Models of Complex Learning* (pp. 25–82). Boston: Kluwer Academic.

Young, R. M., & Lewis, R. L. (1999). The SOAR cognitive architecture and human working memory. In A. Miyake, & P. Shah (Eds.), *Models of Working Memory: Mechanisms of Active Maintenance and Executive Control.* New York: Cambridge University Press.

Young, R. M. & O'Shea, T. (1981). Errors in children's subtraction. *Cognitive Science*, 5, 153–177.

CHAPTER 18

Implicit Cognition and Thought

Leib Litman
Arthur S. Reber

Introduction

The debate about the existence of an unconscious mental life is as old as psychology itself. An overview of the contemporary opinions about the nature of the unconscious shows that, despite countless studies, the opinions expressed by the researchers working in this field are as diverse today as they were when the debates began. The spectrum of opinions range from a profound conviction that a significant aspect of mental life is embodied in the unconscious (Erdelyi, 1985; Pyszczynski, Greenberg, & Solomon, 1999; Reber, 1993) to opinions that stress that the very idea of a complex and abstract unconscious mental life is virtually a contradiction of terms (Perruchet & Vinter, 2003; Shanks & St. John, 1994). Despite the divergence in the range of opinions, findings such as the following certainly suggest that the notion of unconscious thought has to be taken seriously, even by the most skeptical.

- Subjects learn to differentiate seemingly nonsensical sequences of letters that follow complex rules from those that violate the rules despite being unaware of the nature or even the existence of the rules (Reber, 1967, 1993).
- Participants display analogic transfer from one complex problem to another without awareness of the commonalities in the two sets of conditions (Schunn & Dunbar, 1996).
- Infants show a similar ability to discriminate rule-governed patterns of phonetic and visual elements from those that violate the rules (Gomez & Gerken, 1999, 2000; Saffran, Aslin, & Newport, 1996).
- fMRI data show that brain areas that normally process particular stimuli are activated even when the words are presented subliminally (Naccache & Dehaene (2001).
- Amnesiacs, who have lost the ability to form conscious memories, display improved performance on a variety of tasks over time, suggesting that the past experiences are unconsciously represented and are influencing thoughts and behavior (Glisky & Schacter, 1986).

- Patients show residual knowledge for words that were read to them while under anesthesia (Kihlstrom et al., 1990).
- Subjects with neurological disorders that limit their ability to perceive certain areas of the visual field nevertheless respond to stimuli that are presented in those areas (Weiskrantz, 1986).

No one of these findings is in itself conclusive. Arguments have been made that attack the assumptions and techniques used in each case. In a recent exchange, Perruchet and Vinter (2003) debate these and other issues with upwards of three dozen commentators and critics.

Here, we present an overview of the basic findings that support the existence of a sophisticated cognitive system that operates largely independent of consciousness, discuss the criticisms mounted against these findings, and outline the various approaches that have been taken in an attempt to overcome those critiques. Included in our overview are areas such as implicit learning and memory, subliminal perception, the role of attention, and the impact implicit processes have on problem solving and creativity. Rather than providing a thorough review of the findings in any one of these areas, our focus is on developing a conceptual theme that subsumes the diverse field of the studies involved in investigating implicit cognition.

What *Implicit* Implies

What, exactly, do we mean by *implicit* and *explicit thought*? Traditionally the terms "implicit" and "explicit" have been treated as synonyms of the terms "conscious" and "unconscious." Implicit knowledge is defined as being: "unconscious, covert, tacit, hence of a process that takes place largely outside of the awareness of the individual; the term is used in this sense to characterize cognitive processes that operate independently of consciousness" (Reber & Reber, 2001). The use of the terms implicit and explicit in this context refers to *states* of consciousness. To say that something is explicitly or consciously represented in memory, for example, is to say that it can be consciously recalled or recognized. When someone explicitly recalls a friend's name, that name, at the time of recall, is consciously represented.

Implicit thought on the other hand is unconscious, and the content of a memory is considered to be implicit when it exerts its influence on thought or action even though it cannot be recalled. Claparède (1911/1951) described the classic case of an amnesic patient whom he pricked with a concealed needle in his palm. The patient, of course, forgot what happened almost immediately after the incident in the sense that she no longer had explicit memory for the event or even, for that matter, Claparède. However, when he attempted to shake the patient's hand some days later she, surprisingly, refused exclaiming, "One never knows what people carry around in their hands." Experience with this patient, as well as hundreds of others (Cohen & Squire, 1980; Schacter, 1987; Scollville & Milner, 1957), shows that memory for events can influence both thought and behavior even when that memory is no longer available for conscious inspection.

Describing implicit and explicit thought merely in terms of subjective states, however, is hardly sufficient to capture the distinctions between them. Implicit representations are, at least in some ways, not only unconscious, but are also thought of, at least by some theorists (e.g. Perruchet & Vinter, 2003), as being of a different form than conscious representations.

Implicit knowledge may be stored in a different form from when it appears in consciousness. Here's an argument put forward by Perruchet and Vinter (2003): imagine a computer representation of a pencil. When a picture of the pencil is presented on the computer screen the entire pencil is represented. However, off the screen, there is only a bit-wise representation that in no way resembles its on-screen form. Inside the computer you will not find a picture of a pencil as such. The bits representing the pencil might exist in very different parts of the hard drive and, when taken together, will look nothing like the picture of the pencil when it is processed and brought up to the screen. By analogy, tacit knowledge may not contain a full representation of objects – this can only happen in consciousness – that is, on the screen. This position is consistent with the Lockean notion that true mental representations are only possible in consciousness.

Most computational models, in one way or another, have endorsed the perspective that unconscious representations are not identical to conscious ones. In Anderson's ACT-R model, implicit memory represents subsymbolic information that operates by controlling access to explicit declarative knowledge (Anderson & Lebiere, 2003; Lovett & Anderson, Chap, 17). Various other models that are built on connectionist architectures (Dienes, 1992; Cleeremans, 1993; Servan-Shreiber, Cleeremans, & McClelland, 1991) share the notion that implicit knowledge is nonrule based and nonsymbolic.

The one thing that is clear here is that there is no consensus as to whether implicit knowledge can be symbolic. Our position is that it can. We will have more to say about the nature of the representations of implicit knowledge later. For now, keep in mind these two nuanced entailments of *implicit*: the conscious quality of knowledge and the extent to which the knowledge is symbolically represented. Although often used interchangeably, the two senses do not perfectly overlap. When processes such as rule use and symbol manipulation are discussed they are typically assumed to be conscious, top-down operations. However, there is no a priori reason to conclude that the unconscious cannot manipulate symbols and use predefined rules. We favor the notion that implicit thought can be based on abstract representations and that such knowledge is not only possible but is responsible for much of the complexity and adaptiveness of human behavior (Lovett & Anderson, Chap. 17). However, much evidence has been presented both for and against this view, and in what follows we provide an overview of this research.

Some Thoughts on Methodology

How can we know exactly when a mental process is unconscious? In examining this question it is useful to make a distinction between two stages of information processing: encoding and retrieval. The importance of this distinction is that a suitable methodology for demonstrating the implicitness at one point is not applicable at another. Consider research with amnesiacs in which the evidence for tacitly held knowledge is found at the retrieval stage (i.e., a patient performs better over time but does not remember the training session) but not at encoding (i.e., amnesiac patients are consciously aware of what they are learning while they are learning it). Demonstrating that memory is not used consciously at the time of retrieval entails a different methodology than that used to demonstrate that the encoding process was unconscious. For encoding, it is necessary to demonstrate that at the moment of the presentation of the stimulus, the subject's awareness of that stimulus was deficient.

It turns out that demonstrating a lack of awareness at encoding is deeply problematic. How do we know that the stimulus was really not consciously perceived in some, perhaps minimal, way? Because the decision as to whether the subject consciously perceived the stimulus relies on one or another form of subjective self-report, we are stuck with having to rely on nonverifiable measurement.

Accessibility and Availability

Imagine a typical subliminal perception experiment in which subjects are given brief or masked exposure to objects or words. Later, knowledge of the target is assessed either by direct tests (what word did you see?) or by indirect tests (changes in response times over time). Note that there are actually two constructs here: the *accessibility* of the information at encoding and the *availability* of the stored knowledge sometime after presentation. Some (Brody, 1989; Eriksen, 1959) maintain that unconscious perception can only be reliably established if the accessibility of the stimulus at the time of encoding is zero. In other words, there should be no difference in accessibility of a stimulus between the subject and a blind person. This criterion is very difficult (if not impossible) to achieve because it is always possible that something was perceived consciously and chance performance is attributable to subjects' not being sufficiently confident to make a response based on what little they did see.

Alternatively, as suggested by Erdelyi (1986, 2004), we can require that the availability of the stimulus to consciousness be greater than the extent to which that stimulus was consciously accessible at the time of encoding. This approach has an important advantage in that it reveals a critical but often unrecognized fact: the impact of unconscious knowledge on behavior is a continuum and not an either/or issue.

The Implicit/Explicit Continuum

It is erroneous to say that a behavior has to be explained in its entirety by either conscious or unconscious input. Most cognitive tasks, including perception, memory, problem solving, and creativity are products of the influences of both conscious and unconscious processes. The existence of conscious factors does not in any way preclude the further influence of unconscious ones. The findings of two important experiments help make this point.

In the first, Mathews et al. (1989) had experimental subjects engage in an implicit learning task over a four-day period. The study used what is known as an artificial grammar (AG). An example of a typical AG is given in Figure 18.1 along with several letter strings that it can generate and a number of nongrammatical or not well-formed strings that contain a single letter violation. It is apparent that the system is complex and, as Mathews et al., found, not easy to describe. In the canonical AG learning study, subjects memorize a number (perhaps 15 or 20) of exemplary letter strings and then, using what knowledge they acquired from the learning phase, attempt to distinguish whether new letter strings are "well-formed" or not – that is, whether or not they conform to the rules that generated the original set.

The clever twist that Mathews and his colleagues used was to stop their participants from time to time during the "well-formedness" phase and ask them to explicate, in as much detail as possible, what they knew and how they were making their decisions. Transcripts of their responses were then given to four different yoked-control groups who, without having any learning experience, were asked to classify the same strings. If subjects were consciously aware of the knowledge they had acquired and could communicate it, the yoked subjects should perform at the same level as the experimental participants.

Mathews et al. found that their experimental subjects could make reliable decisions on the very first day of the study but were remarkably inept in communicating what they had learned – yoked subjects working with the Day 1 transcripts performed at chance. However, as the experiment progressed, the experimental subjects' ability to verbalize their knowledge improved dramatically. In fact, the yoked subjects who received the Day 4 transcripts made decisions nearly as well as the experimental participants. Interestingly, the experimental subjects' performance on the primary task didn't improve significantly after the second day although their ability to explicate what they knew did. This is an example of how knowledge is encoded implicitly but over time becomes explicit and can then be retrieved consciously. Another implication of Mathews teams' study is that the implicit and the explicit are bound up in a delicate synergy and we would be wise to refrain from all-or-none distinctions.

In the second study, Knowlton and Squire (1994) showed that even when conscious knowledge is fully available (i.e. in Erdelyi's [1986] terms, accessibility equals availability) it doesn't mean that it is necessarily being utilized at all times. They found that amnesic patients' performance was indistinguishable from normal controls on a standard AG learning task, as described

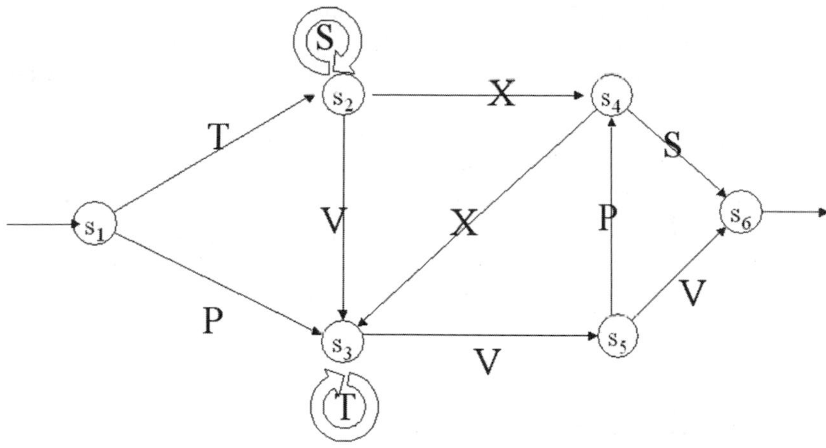

Well-Formed Strings	Strings with a single-letter violation
PVPXVPS	**PTTVVPS**
TSSXXVPS	**TXXTXPS**
TSXS	**TSSXV**
PTVPXVV	**VTTVV**
PTTTVV	**TSSTVV**
PVPXVPXVV	**PTTTVPV**

Figure 18.1. A typical artificial grammar used in many studies of implicit learning. The grammar generates letter strings by following the arrows from the input state (S_1) to the terminal state (S_6). Several examples of "well-formed" strings are presented along with others that contain a violation of the grammar.

previously, suggesting that representations of knowledge need not be held in a conscious form to be used to make decisions. However, when both groups were encouraged to make decisions by utilizing any similarities between the test stimuli and those used during learning, the two groups differed. The normal controls showed a small but significant improvement, whereas the patient group's performance, perhaps not surprisingly, actually diminished.

There are two implications of these studies. First, in these tasks, normal subjects possess a delicate balance of implicit and explicit knowledge and how each is manifested depends as much on the task demands as on the accessibility of conscious knowledge. Second, amnesic patients, whose neurological injuries have compromised their ability to form consciously accessible long-term memories, can still carry out complex implicit learning tasks. The balanced synergy is largely missing in this population, but the implicit system appears to be relatively intact.

In short, it is both theoretically sounder and methodologically more plausible to look at the impact of implicit knowledge as operating along a continuum. Rather than ask whether or not a particular task was implicitly or explicitly performed, one should examine the extent to which both implicit and explicit factors are playing a role in the behavior in question. With this framework in mind, let's explore the several domains in which unconscious mechanisms have been examined.

Consciousness at Encoding

DIVERTED ATTENTION

One interesting aspect of attention, at least for the purposes of implicit processes, is that attention and consciousness are highly correlated. When something is being attended to, for example, the words of this sentence, the object in the focus of attention becomes conscious. Of course, because of the limits on attention, some, if not most, of the sensorial events in the outside world are not within the focus of our attention. When reading a book, we "tune out" much of the outside world such as conversations and, traffic. Indeed, we ignore most of the events that are outside of the attentional focus. The question that almost asks itself is, What effect do the unattended, nonconscious events in our environment have on us? Do they get registered unconsciously in some fashion without our awareness, or are the effects of unattended events trivial and only become important when and if they are consciously attended to?

The effects of diverting attention from the stimulus at encoding are usually studied in the context of a dual-task paradigm in which attention is diverted by a secondary stimulus (Morrison, Chap. 19). For example, in the classic dichotic-listening task two different messages are played, one to each ear. One message is attended to, the other not – although the secondary message often contains important information. Afterwards, a simple memory or priming task is used to discover the effects of diverted attention.

The initial findings here suggested that, when attention is diverted from a stimulus, the effect of that stimulus is greatly reduced (Broadbent, 1958; Cherry, 1953; Moray, 1959). For example, Johnson and Wilson (1980) presented ambiguous words like "sock" to one ear while a disambiguating word ("foot" or "punch") was presented in the other. They found that the amount of attention allocated to the encoded stimulus was critical. When the instructions were to attend to both channels, the word "foot" facilitated the interpretation of the ambiguous homophone "sock." But when attention was directed to the channel in which the target words were presented, items in the unattended channel did not influence the perceived meaning of the targets.

Later studies, however, questioned this conclusion. Eich (1984) presented subjects with homophones such as "fare/fair" in one ear and a modifier of the less frequent meaning (e.g., "taxi") in the other. Subjects were then given a recognition test for the modifiers and were asked to spell the target words ("fare" or "fair"). Eich found a clear impact of implicit memory. Despite being virtually at chance on the recognition task, subjects showed a strong tendency to spell the test words according to their primed, but less common, meaning. Similar findings were reported in a series of studies by Mulligan (1997, 1998) in which subjects memorized word lists while their attention was diverted by a secondary task involving repeating strings of digits of varying lengths. Attentional load was manipulated by varying the length of the digit string from three to seven. Mulligan found that increasing the attentional load impaired explicit memory performance for the original words (using cued recall) but had essentially no effect on implicit memory (as measured by stem completion). It seems therefore that at-encoding stimuli have an impact on subsequent performance even when they are not consciously perceived.

UNDER ANESTHESIA

Although diverting attention certainly reduces the likelihood of the stimuli's being consciously encoded, Kihlstrom et al. (1990) made quite certain that their input stimuli were not being attended to. Their participants were surgical patients who were presented with a repeating list of stimulus items while completely anesthetized. After surgery, although patients had no explicit memory for the material, an implicit, free-association test showed that information presented during anesthesia was encoded. Shanks and St. John (1994) criticized these and other studies on the grounds that they produced mixed findings and often used questionable methodology. However, recently, Merikle and Daneman (1996) conducted a meta-analysis of 44 studies with several thousand participants and concluded that, taken as a whole, these studies support the argument that items presented during anesthesia can have an impact on postsurgical tests. Questions still remain however with regard to the possibility that at least some of the subjects were partially conscious during stimulus presentation.

SUBLIMINAL PERCEPTION

Historically, subliminal perception studies have been controversial. They have ranged from the embarrassing "eat popcorn – drink coke" hoax that was foisted on the public a half-century ago by an overzealous advertising agent (Pratkanis, 1992) to the vigorously debated use of subliminal messages in psychotherapeutic settings (Silverman, 1983; Weinberger, 1992). Admittedly, much of the early work was suspect and has been vigorously criticized (Eriksen, 1959; Holender, 1986; Shanks & St. John, 1994), and, as we noted earlier, there are numerous methodological traps that await the unwary. However, the impact of subliminally presented material on subsequent behavior has now been replicated in literally hundreds of experiments and the evidence appears to be convincing. Subliminal presentation can have an effect on emotional preferences (Kunst-Wilson & Zajonc, 1980; Murphy & Zajonc, 1993) and produce semantic priming (Draine & Greenwald, 1998). Moreover, similarly undetectable stimuli have been shown to activate appropriate brain regions – emotionally charged stimuli activate the amygdala (Elliot & Dolan, 1998; Whalen et al., 1998) and numerical presentations produce parietal activity (Naccache & Dehaene, 2001).

The studies with which we are most comfortable are those that follow Erdelyi's (1986, 2004) advice cited previously. Ensure that there are separate and reliable measures of accessible and available knowledge – with the critical inequality being those situations in which knowledge that is "accessible" by consciousness is less than knowledge that is "available" and can be shown to have some (indirect or implicit) impact on behavior. (For more on the issues of measuring unconscious knowledge, see Merikle and Reingold, 1992.) Two classic studies that appear to satisfy this condition (Marcel, 1983 and Kunst-Wilson & Zajonc, 1980) are worth a closer look.

In an extended series of experiments, Marcel (1983) showed that graphic (what the word looks like) and semantic (what the word means) information of subliminally presented words can affect choice behavior. One of Marcel's standard protocols involved presenting subjects with two words, one subliminally and the other supraliminally. After each presentation, subjects were asked whether or not they saw a word. After the pair was presented, they were asked whether the two words were physically and semantically related. By systematically varying the sub/supra-liminality of the stimuli, Marcel was able to explore the manner in which implicitly and explicitly encoded stimuli affected subjects' choices. The key finding was a threshold effect whereby subjects were at chance in determining the presence or absence of the subliminally presented word but could reliably report whether the two words were semantically and graphically similar. Marcel's conclusion, based on the full series of experiments, was that although there is a gradual effect of awareness on performance, importantly, a complete lack of awareness does not entirely remove that effect.

In Kunst-Wilson and Zajonc's (1980) classic study, subjects were subliminally presented with a set of irregular octagons. They were then shown pairs of octagons supraliminally, one of which was from the set previously presented and one of which was new. Subjects were asked both to select the item they thought was presented before and to pick the one they preferred. Kunst-Wilson and Zajonc found that, despite being at chance on the recognition task, subjects showed a preference for the subliminally presented octagons over the novel ones, demonstrating that affective preferences can be influenced by events that were not consciously noticed (Kunst-Wilson & Zajonc, 1980; Murphy and Zajonc, 1993).

Elliot and Dolan (1998) extended this "subliminal mere exposure" effect and showed that, in addition to preferring the previously presented items, different brain regions were activated when old and novel stimuli were later presented supraliminally. This finding is consistent with a large number of fMRI studies that suggest that implicit and explicit memory retrieval involves the activation of distinct brain regions (for a review see Cabeza & Nyberg (2000). Whalen et al. (1998) have also demonstrated that subliminally presented faces displaying fearful emotions activated the amygdala despite a lack of subjective awareness of ever having seen those faces. Happy faces presented for identical time periods had no effect on these structures.

Finally, Naccache and Dehaene (2001) presented evidence of abstract representation in subliminal priming. Subjects were asked to decide whether a target number was bigger or smaller than 5. Each target was preceded by a subliminal prime that was either spelled out (six) or presented in numeric form (6). Subjects displayed faster reaction times when the prime and target were the same number – regardless of the number's form. In addition, fMRI data revealed that the subliminal primes elicited the same parietal lobe activity as the supraliminal targets, suggesting similar cortical processing.

All of the studies above are open to the critique that some awareness of the stimuli might have contaminated the procedure (Holender, 1986; Shanks & St. John, 1994). To counter this criticism, Debner and Jacoby (1994) used the process-dissociation procedure (Jacoby, 1991). In their study, words (e.g. MOTEL) were first presented subliminally. During testing, subjects were asked to complete word stems such as MOT with the restriction that they not use any word they thought might have been used in the subliminal presentation phase. The logic here is clever. If the word was consciously perceived, the subjects should have been able to refrain from using that word to complete the word-stem. However if they did not see the word, then the subliminally presented word should have been used as often as the others. The results showed that subjects were typically not able to follow this instruction and tended to use the subliminal primes.

In summary, the suggestion that attention and consciousness is needed for the encoding of complex, semantically sensitive events (Perruchet & Vinter, 2003; Shanks & St. John, 1994) is probably unwarranted. These studies, although not uniform in their conclusions, suggest that fairly sophisticated information about complex stimulus displays can be picked up under severe attentional load, when the material is presented subliminally and, possibly, under anesthesia. They also support the notion that this information is not simply logged in some inert form but has an impact on memorial representations, choice behavior, and decision making.

Memory

Virtually every complex living organism has the ability to store the products of experience to be accessed at some later time. People's ability to store a seemingly endless array of episodes, facts, motor skills, and linguistic and social knowledge and to retrieve the appropriate information rapidly and appropriately are remarkable phenomena – and one that still remains something of a mystery. Cognitive investigations of memory revealed early on that human memory is not a single, unified phenomenon. There are different kinds of memories and each is instantiated in a variety of ways. Our concern here is the extent to which memory processes are modulated by conscious intentions or are implicit and operate outside the spotlight of consciousness.

Conscious or explicit memory has traditionally been studied using direct tests in which participants are asked to consciously recall or recognize previously memorized items. The original assumption was that a failure to recall or an inability to recognize an item is diagnostic of that item having been forgotten. However, as we noted earlier, just because people cannot recall something does not necessarily mean the memory no longer exists. In some ways, it is surprising that it took cognitive psychologists so long to appreciate this aspect of human memory. Early reports by neurologists such as Claparède and Korsakoff implicated implicit representational systems and, lest we forget, Freudian psychoanalysis was founded on the existence of nonretrievable memories that play a role in human behavior (Erdelyi, 1985).

The renewed interest in implicit memory was largely attributable to the discovery that amnesiac patients, despite being compromised in their ability to form new explicit knowledge, can nevertheless acquire new information implicitly. The laying down of consciously retrievable, long-term memories has been compellingly shown to be dependent on structures in the medial temporal lobes (MTL), specifically the hippocampus (Squire, 1995). When the hippocampus and its associated areas are damaged or destroyed, it becomes difficult and, in extreme cases impossible, for new explicit memories to be formed. The discovery of the critical role the MTL structures play here was made in the case of HM, the first neurological patient to have his hippocampus surgically removed (see Corkin, 1968; Milner, 1962; Milner, Corkin, & Teuber, 1968; Squire, 1992; Warrington & Weiskrantz, 1968). HM suffered from severe, intractable epilepsy, the neural focal point of which was in the MTL. To alleviate his multiple, daily seizures surgeons extirpated bilaterally the affected brain regions. Although the surgery was successful in stopping the seizures, HM emerged from the procedure with profound, chronic anterograde amnesia.

The standard interpretation of HM, based on the now rather large number of patients with similar neurological damage (see Squire, 1992 for a review), is that such people do not suffer from a learning deficit, per se, but rather from an inability to consolidate new explicit, or declarative, knowledge. Patients with MTL damage show no diminished ability to recall episodes that occurred prior to the trauma, they present a nearly normal short-term memory profile, and, importantly from our perspective, they show relatively intact implicit learning and memory. Indeed, a large literature has accumulated in recent years showing that the performance of anterograde amnesiacs is virtually indistinguishable from that of normals on a wide variety of memory tasks including word-stem completion (Warrington & Weiskrantz, 1968; 1974), fragment completion (Tulving, Hayman, & MacDonald, 1991), context sensitive memory (Schacter & Graf, 1986), memory for letter strings generated by an AG (Knowlton, Ramus, & Squire, 1992; Knowlton & Squire, 1994), and recall of dot patterns (Knowlton & Squire, 1994). As Seger (1994) argued, amnesiac patients provide the best empirical support for the proposition that knowledge that is not consciously accessible can still have a profound influence on ongoing behavior.

These discoveries gave rise to a number of significant advances in our understanding of memory, both implicit and explicit. Reber (1992a,b), Schacter (1987) and Squire (1992) all argued that the human memorial system can be fruitfully viewed as though there were two distinct information-processing systems – one declarative or explicit, the other procedural or implicit. The explicit system was theorized to include declarative, conscious knowledge of episodes, facts, and events, whereas the implicit system was assumed to be operating largely outside of consciousness and to include implicit learning and memory, conditioning, and learning various skills and habits (sensorimotor learning). Although this distinction is probably a useful one in that it draws attention to the ways in which implicit and explicit functions can be dissociated, it is probably not the best stance to take from a functionalist point of view. As Reber (1993) argued, we need to be wary of falling into a "polarity" fallacy in which we treat two distinguishable systems that lie at the poles of a continuum as though they were ontologically separate and distinct. It is almost certainly the case that virtually everything interesting that human beings entails a delicate synergy between the implicit and the explicit, the conscious and declarative, and the unconscious and procedural. If the implicit and the explicit systems ultimately are shown to be based on neuroanatomically distinct structures (as we suspect will be done), it will still be virtually impossible to find functionally pure instantiations of them.

In addition, Reber (1992a,b) argued that because human consciousness and its accompanying functions are late arrivals on the evolutionary scene, there should be particular patterns of dissociation between these two systems. The key predictions of the model for this discussion are:

(a) Storage and retrieval systems that serve the implicit system should be more robust and relatively undisturbed by insult and injury that compromise explicit functions.
(b) There should be relatively little in the way of developmental and life-span changes in implicit compared with explicit functions. This two-system model has garnered significant support over the past decade (see Reber, Allen, & Reber, 1999 and Squire & Knowlton, 2000 for reviews).

Taken together, this literature paints a clear picture. Human memory has distinct systems with distinct evolutionary histories and separate, although only partly understood, neurological underpinnings that map, on one hand, into conscious, subjective experience and, on the other, into a nexus of encoding, storage, and retrieval systems that function largely independently of awareness and consciousness. However, this picture is still incomplete, and appreciating the manner in which it operates in complex human thinking requires a deeper look at the topic of learning – specifically implicit learning in which knowledge about the complexities of the environment is acquired without benefit of consciously controlled processes.

Learning

Implicit learning is the process whereby organisms acquire knowledge about the regularities of complex environments without intending to do so and largely independently of conscious awareness of the nature of what was learned (Stadler & Frensch, 1998; Reber, 1967; Reber, 1993). The complex environments include virtually every facet of human life, including language learning, trait knowledge, categorization, acculturation, and the development of aesthetic preferences. The claim we are making is that people extract information about the world more often than they are aware and that this knowledge exists in a tacit form, influencing thought and behavior while itself remaining mostly concealed from conscious awareness.

IMPLICIT LEARNING IN INFANTS

By the second month of life, infants can already distinguish between utterances spoken in their native language and those spoken in foreign languages. Infants can do this although they don't understand what the sentences mean in either language. Interestingly, this effect disappears when the sentences are presented backwards (Dehaene-Lambertz, & Houston, 1998; Mehler et al., 1988; Ramus et al., 1999). The implications here are that, despite not understanding the sentences backwards or forwards, the infants have become attuned to the natural flow of language. This natural flow is violated when the sentence is reversed. This sensitivity to the structure of linguistic sounds which seems to be the first stage of language acquisition, takes place implicitly and recruits brain regions similar to those of adults as shown by fMRI studies (Dehaene-Lambertz, Dehaene, & Hertz-Pannier, 2002).

Within a surprisingly short time, infants extract the phonetic regularities of their linguistic surroundings and can differentiate between sound sequences that are well formed and those that are not. The backwards sentences sound ill-formed to the infants because their sequential structure is discoordinate with the infant's experience and therefore seem as ill-formed as sentences in a foreign language. Note the similarity of this to the standard implicit learning procedure in Artificial Grammar studies discussed below.

These kinds of effects are not restricted to natural languages. Rovee-Collier and her colleagues (see Rovee-Collier, 1990 for a review) report that infants rapidly pick up the relationships between their own motor actions and the impact that they have on the external world. Haith, Wentworth, and Canfield (1993) showed that babies make anticipatory eye movements to regularities in the spatial patterns of visual displays. Saffran and her colleagues reported that infants as young as 8 months show a similar sensitivity to the arbitrary statistical nature of auditory patterns and can learn the rules governing artificial word segmentation (Saffran, & Aslin, & Newport, 1996). Interestingly, in Saffran's studies, the infants performed as well as a group of adults, a result that supports Reber's (1992b) prediction that implicit learning systems are present at a very early age and undergo little developmental change. Similarly, Gomez and Gerken (1999, 2000), using the AG learning procedure, showed that not only do one-year-olds learn the structural characteristics of these rather complex systems, they also transfer this knowledge to novel stimulus domains.

To date, this research has been restricted largely to sensorimotor, perceptual, and cognitive tasks. Surprisingly, little empirical work has been carried out on behaviors that are more reflective of social learning. However, given the existing database, we suspect that when processes of socialization are examined from this perspective, they will reveal a parallel set of operations in which infants gradually become inculcated with the social mores and ethical codes of their culture without conscious awareness of what has been learned and with little in the way of top-down control of the process.

IMPLICIT LEARNING IN ADULTS

In recent years, a rather impressive array of specific tasks have been discovered to have dissociative elements in that either direct and indirect tests distinguish between implicit and explicit memorial systems, or various patient populations manifest distinct patterns of loss of explicit acquisitional functions while maintaining those based on the implicit processes. Included here are studies on motor learning (P.J. Reber & Squire, 1998), AG learning (Knowlton & Squire, 1994, 1996; Reber, 1967, 1989), category learning (Knowlton & Squire, 1993; Squire & Knowlton, 1996), Pavlovian conditioning (Daum & Ackerman, 1994; Gabrieli et al., 1995), decision making in social settings (Lewicki, 1986a; any of several contributions to Uleman & Bargh, 1989), the sequential reaction time task (see Hsiao & Reber, 1998 for a review), the hidden covariation task (Lewicki, 1986b), preference formation (Gordon & Holyoak, 1983; Manza, Zizak, & Reber, 1998), the production control task (Berry & Broadbent, 1988), and dot pattern classification (P.J. Reber, Stark, & Squire, 1998). The various chapters in Stadler and Frensch's (1998) edited volume *Handbook of Implicit Learning* are a good resource for a more detailed discussion.

These many reports are supplemented by additional findings that show that patients with damage to primary visual cortex learn to respond to objects in their blind fields (Weiskrantz, 1986), prosopagnosiacs who cannot consciously recognize the faces of family members show virtually normal implicit facial memory (De Haan, Young, & Newcombe, 1991), patients with neglect respond to the meaning of stimuli that they are unaware of processing (Berti & Rizzolatti, 1992), amnesic patients show improvement in solving problems (Winter et al., 2001) and learn to operate complex equipment (Glisky, Schacter, & Tulving, 1986) despite no conscious memory of the earlier training phases of the studies. Issues of the mechanisms underlying disordered thought are pursued in detail elsewhere in this volume by Bachman and Cannon (see Chap. 21).

The model that has emerged from this literature characterizes implicit learning as a mechanism the primary function of which is to monitor the environment for reliable relationships between events and to encode those patterns of covariation. In all likelihood, the underlying neurological mechanisms are diffuse neural nets that are linked to the modality of input of the stimulus display (Ungerleider, 1995). The underlying representations that are established are probably not as flexible or abstract as those that are under conscious control simply because the top-down modulation that comes with consciousness allows for deliberative shifts in representation and use of knowledge. However, this issue is a highly contentious one and we have more to say on it subsequently.

In addition, implicit acquisitional mechanisms appear early in life, well before conscious awareness has developed. They show relatively little change over the life span compared with explicit cognitive functions (Howard & Howard, 1992, 1997) and relatively little in the way of individual-to-individual variation (Reber & Allen, 2000). As noted previously in several places, the implicit system demonstrates a rather remarkable robustness and continues to function effectively in the face of a wide variety of neurological and psychiatric disorders that severely compromise functions based on explicit, consciously modulated mechanisms. It seems clear that the implicit system is the critical mental component that enables the infant and child to learn to navigate the world. Virtually all the essential knowledge of the perceptual, sensorimotor, linguistic and social patterns, that make up the environment and eventually become the epistemic foundations of adulthood is acquired through this nondeclarative, procedural mechanism. This is, indeed, how we learn about the world around us. For further explorations of this and related developmental mechanisms, see Halford (this volume).

Although these aspects of implicit thought are fairly well established, there are two issues that remain deeply problematical and need to be addressed: First, are (or better, perhaps, *can*) these implicitly formed representations be regarded as abstract? Second, what role might they play in complex cognitive processes such as problem solving that have been generally regarded as largely, if not completely, explicit and under conscious control?

Abstraction and Implicit Thought

One possibility might be that these unconscious, perceptual, and motoric representations are not themselves anything like conscious thoughts in terms of their underlying form. Thinking consciously about the world involves forming abstract mental "pictures." We can be thinking about *a* tree and not necessarily be looking at or remembering any *specific* tree. We can know an abstract rule such as "if A > B and B > C, then A > C" that can be applied to any set of objects that can be ranked along a single dimension like height or weight. This kind of abstract memorial code feels very natural to us. We freely think about legal decisions (guilt or innocence), geometry (all plane triangles have 180 degrees), artistic expressions, drama, poetry, aesthetics, politics, and so on. When we do, we have an ineffable sense of manipulating abstract and flexible representations, ones that feel loose and unconstrained by particular settings or features.

Our personal, introspective experiences with these daily activities are so compelling that, historically, consciousness was often viewed as though it were *the* defining feature of human thought. The philosophical traditions that have had the strongest influence on psychology are those of Locke and Descartes, and while these two didn't agree on much, the one proposition they shared was that cognitive states are transparent to introspection. If it's cognitive, it's conscious – and by cognitive states they meant those that are semantic, flexible in function and representationally abstract. In fact, the notion that there is anything truly cognitive about any unconscious process – that an implicit mechanism could result in abstract mental representations is, according to this perspective, self-contradictory nonsense (Dennett, 1987).

In the next two sections we explore related questions like: Is unconscious, tacit knowledge in any way like conscious knowledge in its complexity? Are implicit representations flexible? Can they be characterized as abstract? Do they play a role in the computations of problem solving? Or is unconscious knowledge more like low-level perceptual processes – rigid, inflexible, and concrete and playing virtually no role in higher-level functions such as problem solving and creativity?

Perceptual and Conceptual Representations

Perceptual representation involves capturing surface features of objects without necessarily understanding what the objects are. A picture taken by a computer scanner is an example of a perceptual but not a conceptual representation. A scanner can take a picture of an object and store it in memory, while having no semantics and not representing anything meaningfully. The meaningful representation of objects involves, among other things, the ability to categorize and form mental representations of the categories abstractly. It has been proposed by a variety of researchers that many of the phenomena discussed in this chapter so far such as priming, lexical decision making, word fragment completion, artificial grammar learning, and dot pattern classification are tapping perceptual – not conceptual – processes (e.g., Perruchet & Vinter, 1998, 2003; Shanks & St. John, 1994). From this perspective, the unconscious acts as a purely perceptual system capable, in some ways like a scanner or a camera, of capturing the perceptual or auditory properties of the world. The unconscious, according to this perspective, is not particularly smart, and does not contain any real representations at least not those that are "about" something.

Exploring these considerations has become a virtual cottage industry. Toth and Reingold (1996) present an overview of the work using priming, and Kirsner (1998) provides a review of the implicit memory literature. Both suggest that, although the issues are complex, implicitly encoded material shows both abstract and instance-based representations. Here we review a topic that focuses directly on the issue, transfer in AG learning. Unlike the study of implicit memory using priming or stem completion in which the stimulus materials tend to be common words and objects, the AG experiments use novel, arbitrary stimulus displays, affording the opportunity to examine the representational form of knowledge that was acquired in a controlled setting.

The original claim (Reber, 1967, 1969) was that the representations established while memorizing exemplars from an AG like that shown in Figure 18.1 are based on the rules of the grammar and, hence, are abstract and independent of the surface features of the stimuli. This claim did not go uncontested. Brooks and Vokey (1991), Dulany, Carlson and Dewey (1984), Perruchet and Pacteau (1991), and Shanks and St. John (1994) all argued that subjects' performance in these experiments is also consistent with representations based on the micro components of the exemplar strings. That is, a well-formed sequence like PTVPS is not necessarily represented as an instance of a complex rule but may be captured by a concrete instantiation. Some (e.g., Perruchet & Pacteau, 1994; Servan-Schreiber & Anderson, 1990) argued for an encoding based on small chunks like bi- and trigrams (PT, TV, VPS). Others (Brooks & Vokey, 1991) argued for a more holistic instantiation of the specific stimulus input, but eschew the possibility that the implicit memorial forms are abstract.

The key studies that speak to this issue are those that use a transfer protocol. That is, subjects learn an AG instantiated in one symbol set but are switched to stimuli made up using a different symbol set at some point in the experiment. The argument is that, if subjects' implicit memorial forms, are based on concrete representations then transfer to a novel letter set should seriously compromise their ability to function. If the representations are abstract in nature, the subjects should be comfortable with the transfer condition.

In the first of these studies Reber (1969) asked subjects to memorize letter strings from an AG over 12 trial blocks. After the sixth block, either the letters used to instantiate the AG were changed, or the AG itself was changed. Switching letter sets was surprisingly benign. So long as the rules that governed letter order were left intact, subjects were able to work with novel letter sets with little difficulty. However, changing the rules for letter order disrupted subjects' ability to encode and store the materials.

This study was followed up by a parallel series of experiments in which subjects memorized letter strings from an AG and then had to judge how well novel strings instantiated using new letters had been formed. Subjects learn about the underlying regularities of an AG by memorizing strings like TSSVVPS but then have to judge the grammaticality of strings like BXXMMRX. Thus, the surface features of the stimuli differ from learning to testing, but the deep structure remains the same. Using this technique, numerous studies have found successful transfer (Altmann, Dienes, & Goode, 1995; Brooks & Vokey, 1991; Gomez & Schvaneveldt, 1994; Knowlton & Squire, 1996; Manza & Reber, 1997; Mathews et al., 1989; Shanks, Johnstone, & Staggs, 1997; Vokey & Brooks, 1992; Whittlesea & Dorken, 1993).

Although it is generally agreed that the transfer effect is real (Perruchet & Vinter, 2003; Redington & Chater, 1998), there is still no consensus on interpretation. Although the effect would seem to implicate an abstract representational form, Brooks and Vokey (1991; Vokey & Brooks, 1992) have pointed out that transfer could also be a product of the physical similarity between the grammatical strings and the transformed test strings. For example, what makes the two sequences given above "similar" is that they both consist of seven letters, they both contain two repeats after the first letter, and they end with one of those repeating letters. They called this a "relational" or "abstract analogy" for the sequences. According to this view, subjects are not learning the deep structure of the grammar that can be applied to any domain; they have learned a specific set of facts about individual exemplars.

Brooks and Vokey tested their theory by controlling for the physical similarity and the grammaticality of the test items and found evidence for both forms of encoding. That is, about half the explainable variance in subjects' decision making could be traced to an underlying abstract representation based upon the rules of the AG and about half was shown to be dependent on abstract analogical representations that were linked to the physical forms of the input stimuli.

Of course, these studies still leave open the question of the actual memorial form of the representations. As noted previously, representations could be based not on whole items but on more molecular "chunks." There is evidence both in favor of and against this chunking interpretation. On one hand, Knowlton and Squire (1994) replicated Brooks and Vokey's findings, but when they controlled for "chunk strength" (stimuli had equal numbers of common bigrams) they found little effect of overall similarity. On the other, simply encoding the chunking characteristics of an AG cannot be all that is learned in these experiments. "Chunk-trained" subjects who never learn full strings perform reasonably well on the grammaticality task (Perruchet & Pacteau, 1990), but they do not show transfer (Manza & Reber, 1997).

What seems to be emerging from this line of research is that there is no "default" representational form (Whittlesea & Dorken, 1993). Rather, representational form is dictated by context effects and task demands. Manza and Reber (1997) included a condition that supports this functionalist position. One group memorized letter strings instantiated in one letter set. Another group learned structurally identical strings, but half of them were instantiated using a second letter set. Both groups were tested using strings made up of both old and new letter sets. The second group showed better transfer on the items instantiated with a novel letter set. Training with the two distinct instantiations encouraged a more abstract representational form that assisted the subjects when they confronted yet another surface form.

Finally, several researchers have demonstrated another hallmark of abstract representation – cross-modality transfer. Altmann, Dienes, and Goode (1995), Howard and Ballas (1982), and Manza and Reber (1997) have all shown that subjects can learn visual sequences and make judgments about the well-formedness of auditory sequences and vice versa. Taken together these findings suggest that abstraction is an important factor in AG learning. Whether or not this conclusion ultimately applies to all forms of tacit knowledge is yet to be determined. Our best guess is that virtually all forms of implicit learning will yield some memorial representations that are abstract but that Whittlesea and Dorken's message is likely correct. The degree to which the underlying memorial code is abstract or concrete and what its detailed form will look like is going to have a good deal to do with the processing constraints placed on individuals in particular settings. The manner in which representations get established is critical in determining which relational generalizations can be formed from multiple examples (Holyoak, Chap. 6).

Creativity and Problem Solving

We began our exploration of implicit, unconscious process in human thought with the "simpler" functions of perception and memory. We'll end with a quick look at the more complex topics of problem solving and creativity (see Novick & Bassok, Chap. 14; Sternberg et al., Chap. 15). Although there hasn't been much recent study of unconscious influence on these functions, the notion that tacit knowledge affects the creative process was a central theme in the Gestalt approach (Köhler, 1925; Wertheimer, 1945), which assumed three main elements of unconscious thought: intuition, or the feeling of directionality of the unconscious process; incubation, or the tacit processing of information that eventually leads to problem solving; and insight, the "aha" experience in which the implicit processes become conscious (Kihlstrom 1999; Dorfman, Shames, & Kihlstrom, 1996).

In the now classic test of this model, Maier (1931) asked subjects to tie together two strings hanging from the ceiling. The strings were too far apart to grab one string while still holding on to the other. One solution was to tie a small object, strategically placed in the room, to one of the strings and to swing it like a pendulum. Maier found that subjects were much more likely to solve this problem after the experimenter casually brushed against one of the strings, producing the swinging motion. Interestingly, Maier's subjects did not report having consciously noticed the manipulation. Judson, Cofer, and Gelfand (1956) found similar facilitation if subjects memorized word lists that contained items related to the problem's solution such as *swing*, *string* or *pendulum*. Recently, Knoblich and Wartenberg (1998) reported a similar effect when the priming words were presented subliminally.

Most modern approaches to these issues invoke the notion of *spreading activation* – an important theoretical mechanism in many contemporary models of human cognition. The notion is that experience registers in specific cortical areas and "spreads" to other "nodes" that are associatively linked with the input. Meyer and Schvaneveldt (1971) showed that the encoding process influences the subsequent processing of related words on indirect tests such as the lexical decision task. For example, subjects presented with words like "bread" respond more rapidly to "butter" than to "nurse" – although the reverse applies if the prime is "doctor." The argument is that the initial prime initiates a spread of activation and related representations in the semantic network are affected. The question that interests us here is whether such a process can take place unconsciously. Are processes like intuition, insight, and creativity facilitated by the activity engendered in semantically related but tacitly represented memories that are not part of our conscious experience?

Yaniv and Meyer (1987) examined this possibility by looking at the influence of inaccessible material on reaction time in a lexical decision task. Subjects were first read definitions of rare words and asked to provide the word and, when they could not, to rate their feeling of knowing the word. In the subsequent lexical decision task, subjects showed faster reaction times for words that they could not recall than for control words and, interestingly, the "feeling of knowing" was positively related to the reaction times. A kind of metacognition appears to be operating in this situation in which subjects are sensitive to the contents of tacit knowledge even though the actual material is not available for conscious recall. In an extension of this idea, Shames, Kihlstrom, and Forster (1994) presented subjects with a list of three words such as: "goat," "pass," and "green" and asked them to generate an associate that all three have in common. They found that in cases in which subjects could not provide the correct answer to the triad ("mountain"), the reaction time to the correct answer was faster on a lexical decision task than an unrelated word. These experiments, along with the Gestalt problem-solving studies, suggest that the initial experience of trying to solve a problem, retrieve a rare word, or find the common element in a word-triad seems to set in motion a spread of activation process which, intriguingly, is engaged effectively even with knowledge that is tacit and unavailable for conscious recall.

Additional recent evidence of unconscious influences in problem solving is seen in complex problems that do not require top-down control such as the balls and boxes puzzle (P. J. Reber & Kotovsky, 1997). In these studies subjects sit in front of a computer screen displaying five boxes, each of which is associated with one of five balls. Initially all the balls sit outside the boxes and the goal is to place all the balls inside the boxes. The rule for moving balls in or out of boxes is as follows: "The rightmost ball can always move; other balls can be moved if the ball immediately to the right is in its box and all other balls to the right are out of their boxes." The results showed that participants frequently solved the puzzle while being unaware of the rule system that governed it. The following is a telling conversation between the experimenter and one of the participants immediately following the first completion of the puzzle.

Experimenter: Now I want to ask you about the puzzle you just solved, how it worked, what you did.

Participant: No idea

E: No idea?

P: No idea. It was very painful. (Laughs)

E: You did get it, right?

P: Yeah, but it was basically luck . . . that I got it.

E: You had no idea what you were doing?

P: Not really.

E: Suppose somebody else was going to do the puzzle who had never seen it before and you had to give them some hints, tell them how to solve it.

P: Well, let's see. I don't know what to say . . . but, I guess (garbled) the puzzle . . . the good part was that there usually wasn't any more than like one or two choices. I think there was one choice was there any more than one choice? I don't know. But I had (garbled). Which is why I kept ending up back where I started from, which was frustrating. I would tell them, I would tell them, good luck. That's all.

In spite of being unaware of the rules, this participant's overall performance was quite good. In fact, as Reber and Kotovsky reported, "Immediately after giving this fairly uninformative description of his process of solving the puzzle he . . . solved the puzzle in 21 moves (the minimum). . . . superior to most of the other participants."

Recent experiments provide similar findings with regard to creativity. Marsh, Bink, and Hicks (1999) demonstrated the possible influence of previously encountered events, which are not necessarily consciously remembered, on creative expression and thought. Participants were asked to spend a period of twenty minutes drawing space creatures from their imagination. Before beginning they were shown three pictures of fictitious space creatures presented as examples of other participants' drawings. Each of these creatures had fangs, spikes, or weapons, all objects which are oriented around one theme – hostility. Participants were then asked to draw any type of creature that they wanted as long as they did not copy any aspect of the creatures shown. The results were intriguing and reminiscent of the work of Jacoby and his colleagues with the process-dissociation procedure discussed earlier. Although subjects were explicitly told not to include any of the exemplar characteristics, the core concept around which these characteristics revolved, hostility, could be seen in most of their creative work.

Importantly, little influence of the actual characteristics of the exemplars could be seen in the creative works of the participants. The elements that made the exemplar creatures hostile (fangs, spikes, and weapons) were virtually never depicted by the participants in their novel drawings. Rather it was the underlying theme, the shared qualities of the exemplars that were influencing the participants' drawings. In a post-experimental interview, only 4 of the 142 participants described the original three samples as displaying hostility. These effects were not limited to visual displays. Subjects who initially worked with scrambled sentences exhibiting a mild hostility-related theme produced similar data. These results are consistent with the spreading activation perspective in that the creative process is facilitated by previously encountered, and unconsciously detected, themes in one's environment.

Taken together, these studies suggest that complex processes such as problem solving or creative invention can be influenced by previously encountered experiences that are not, at the critical time of the task, consciously available. There are relatively few studies that have looked directly at this issue and, of course, we are not suggesting that these experiments are process pure. It is possible that subjects in these situations, to some extent, have been consciously aware of the previously provided material (see Jacoby, Lindsay, & Toth, 1992). Nevertheless, the work is provocative and is coordinate with the converging lines of evidence cited previously. See Sternberg (Chap. 31) for additional approaches to the issue of creativity.

Conclusions and Future Directions

Unhappily, we don't feel as though we have presented more than a dollop of the literature. We never got to discussing work on such intriguing topics as the implicit cognitive factors in sensorimotor skills (Weiss, Reber, & Owen, in review), various formal models of implicit learning (Cleeremans, 1993; Keele, Ivry, et al., 2003), the role that implicit processes play in aesthetics (Zizak & Reber, 2004), social intuition (Lieberman, 2000), moral judgment (Haidt, 2001), creativity (Polanyi, 1958; Reber, 1993), the time course of memory consolidation and sleep (Litman & Reber, 2002), the patterns of lost and preserved functions in a variety of developmental disorders (Don et al., 2003; Smith, 2003), the issue of life-span changes and individual differences (Reber & Allen, 2000), implicit acquisition of fear and other emotions (Phelps, 2004) and the influence of unconscious thought on psychological well-being (Pyszczynski, Greenberg, & Solomon, 1999).

Over the past several decades, it has become increasingly clear that implicit processes, those that operate largely outside of the spotlight of consciousness, play a significant role in most of the interesting things that human beings do. We can only hope that the coming decades will produce a better understanding of these mechanisms, their underlying cortical pathways, and the manner in which they are integrated into the complex synergistic interplay of the top-down and the bottom-up that makes up human cognitive functioning.

Acknowledgment

Preparation of this chapter was supported by NSF Grant No. 0113025 to Arthur S. Reber.

References

Altmann, G., Dienes, Z., & Goode, A. (1995). On the modality independence of implicitly learned grammatical knowledge. *Journal of Experimental Psychology: Learning, Memory, and Cognition*, 21, 899–912.

Anderson, J. R., & Lebiere, L. (2003). The Newell test for a theory of mind. *Behavioral and Brain Sciences*, 26(5), 587–640.

Berry, D., & Broadbent, D. (1988). Interactive tasks and the implicit-explicit distinction. *British Journal of Psychology*, 79, 251–272.

Berti, A., & Rizzolatti, G. (1992). Visual processing without awareness: Evidence from unilateral neglect, *Journal of Cognitive Neuroscience*, 4, 45–351.

Broadbent, D. E. (1958). *Perception and Communication*. New York: Pergamon Press.

Brody, H. (1989). Unconscious learning of rules: Comment on Reber's analysis of implicit learning. *Journal of Experimental Psychology: General*, 118, 236–238.

Brooks, L. R., & Vokey, J. R. (1991). Abstract analogies and abstracted grammars: A Comment on Reber, and Mathews et al. *Journal of Experimental Psychology: General*, 120, 316–323.

Cabeza, R., & Nyberg, L. (2000). Imaging cognition II: An empirical review of 275 PET and fMRI studies. *Journal of Cognitive Neuroscience*, 12, 1–47

Cherry, E. C. (1953). Some experiments on the recognition of speech with one or two ears. *Journal of the Acoustical Society of America*, 25, 975–979.

Claparède, E. (1951). Recognition and "me-ness" (E. Rapaport, Trans.). In D. Rapaport (Ed.), *Organisation and pathology of thought*. New York: Columbia University Press. (Original work published 1911.)

Cleeremans, A. (1993). *Mechanisms of implicit learning: Connectionist Models of Sequence Processing*. Cambridge, MA: MIT Press.

Cohen N. J., & Squire L. R. (1980). Preserved learning and retention of pattern-analyzing skill in amnesia: Dissociation of knowing how and knowing that. *Science*, 210, 207–210.

Corkin, S. (1968). Acquisition of motor skill after bilateral medial temporal-lobe excision. *Neuropsychologia*, 6, 225–264.

Daum, I., & Ackermann, H. (1994). Frontal-type memory impairment associated with thalamic damage. *International Journal of Neuroscience*, 77, 187–198.

De Haan, E. H. F., Young, A. W., & Newcombe, F. (1991). Covert and overt recognition in prosopagnosia. *Brain*, 114, 2575–2591.

Debner, J. A., & Jacoby, L. L. (1994). Unconscious perception: attention, awareness, and control. *Journal of Experimental Psychology: Learning, Memory and Cognition*, 20, 304–317.

Dehaene-Lambertz, G, & Houston, D. (1998). Faster orientation latency toward native language in two-month-old infants. *Language and Speech*, 41, 21–43.

Dehaene-Lambertz, G., Dehaene, S., & Hertz-Pannier, L. (2002). Functional neuroimaging of speech perception in infants. *Science*, 298, 2013–2015.

Dennett, D. C. (1987). Consciousness. In G. L. Gregory (Ed.), *The Oxford Companion to the Mind* (pp. 161–164). New York: Oxford University Press.

Dienes, Z. (1992). Connectionist and memory array models of artificial grammar learning. *Cognitive Science*, 16, 41–79.

Don, A. J., Schellenberg, E. G., Reber, A. S., DiGirolamo, D. M., & Wang, P. P. (2003). Implicit learning in individuals with Williams Syndrome. *Developmental Neuropsychology*, 73 (1–2), 201–775.

Dorfman, J., Shames, V. A., & Kihlstrom, J. F. (1996). Intuition, incubation, and insight: Implicit cognition in problem solving. In G. Underwood (Ed.), *Implicit Cognition* (pp. 257–296). Oxford, UK: Oxford University Press.

Draine, S. C., & Greenwald, A. G. (1998). Replicable unconscious semantic priming. *Journal of Experimental Psychology: General*, 127, 286–303.

Dulany, D. E., Carlson, R., & Dewey, G. (1984). A case of syntactical learning and judgment: How concrete and how abstract? *Journal of Experimental Psychology: General*, 113, 541–555.

Eich, E. (1984). Memory for unattended events: Remembering with and without awareness. *Memory and Cognition*, 12, 105–111.

Elliot, R., & Dolan, J. R. (1998). Neural response during preference and memory judgments for subliminally presented stimuli: A functional neuroimaging study. *The Journal of Neuroscience*, 18, 4697–4704.

Erdelyi, M. H. (1985). *Psychoanalysis: Freud's Cognitive Psychology*. New York: Freeman Press.

Erdelyi, M. H. (1986). Experimental indeterminacies in the dissociation paradigm. *Behavioral and Brain Sciences*, 9, 30–31.

Erdelyi, M. H. (2005). Subliminal perception and its cognates: Theory, indeterminacy, and time. *Consciousness and Cognition*, 13(1), 73–91.

Eriksen, C. W., Unconscious Processes (1959): In M. R. Jones (Ed.), *Nebraska Symposium on Motivation (1958)* (Vol. 6, pp 169–277). Lincoln: University of Nebraska Press.

Gabrieli, J. D. E., Fleischman D. A., Keane M. M., Reminger S. L., Morrell F. (1995). Double dissociation between memory systems underlying explicit and implicit memory in the human brain. *Psychological Science*, 6, 76–82.

Glisky, E. L., Schacter, D. L., & Tulving, E. (1986). Computer learning by memory-impaired patients: Acquisition and retention of complex knowledge. *Neuropsychologia*, 24, 313–328.

Glisky, E. L., Schacter, D. L., & Tulving, E. (1986). Learning and retention of computer related vocabulary in memory-impaired patients: Method of vanishing cues. *Journal of Clinical and Experimental Neuropsychology*, 8, 292–312.

Gomez, R. L., & Gerken, L. (1999). Artificial grammar learning by 1-year-olds leads to specific and abstract knowledge. *Cognition*, 70, 109–135.

Gomez, R. L., & Gerken, L. (2000). Infant artificial language learning and language acquisition. *Trends in Cognitive Sciences*, 4, 178–187.

Gomez, R. L., & Schvaneveldt, R. W. (1994). What is learned from artificial grammars? Transfer of simple associations. *Journal of Experimental Psychology: Learning Memory and Cognition*, 20, 396–410.

Gordon, P. C., & Holyoak, K. J. (1983). Implicit learning and generalization of the "Mere Exposure" effect. *Journal of Personality and Social Psychology*, 45, 492–500.

Haith, M. M., Wentworth, N., & Canfield, R. L. (1993). The formation of expectations in early infancy. In C. Rovee-Collier & L. P. Lipsitt (Eds.), *Advances in Infancy Research*. Norwood, NJ: Ablex.

Haidt, J. (2001). The emotional dog and its rational tail: A social intuitionist approach to moral judgment. *Psychological Review*, 108, 814–834.

Holender, D. (1986). Semantic activation without conscious identification in dichotic listening, parafoveal vision, and visual masking: A survey and appraisal. *Behavioral and Brain Sciences*, 9, 1–23.

Howard, D. V., & Howard, J. H., Jr. (1992). Adult age differences in the rate of learning serial patterns: Evidence from direct and indirect tests. *Psychology and Aging*, 7, 232–241.

Howard, J. H., Jr., & Howard, D. V. (1997). Learning and memory. In A. D. Fisk & W. A. Rogers (Eds.). *Handbook of human factors and the older adult* (pp. 7–26). New York: Academic Press.

Howard, J. H., & Ballas, J. A. (1982). Acquisition of acoustic pattern categories by exemplar observation. *Organisational Behaviour and Human Performance*, 30, 157–173.

Hsiao, A., & Reber, A. S. (1998). The role of attention in implicit sequence learning: exploring the limits of the cognitive unconscious. In M. Stadler & P. French (Eds) *Handbook of implicit learning*. Sage.

Hsiao, A., & Reber, A. S. (2001). The role of attention in the serial reaction time task: Fine tuning the timing. *Psychonomic Bulletin and Review*, 8, 336–342.

Jacoby, L. L. (1991). A process dissociation framework: Separating automatic from intentional uses of memory. *Journal of Memory and Language*, 30, 513–41.

Jacoby, L. L., Lindsay, D. S., & Toth, J. P. (1992). Unconscious processes revealed: A question of control. *American Psychologist*, 47, 802–809.

Johnson, W. A., & Wilson, J. (1980). Perceptual processing of non-targets in an attention task. *Memory and Cognition*, 8, 372–377.

Judson, A. J., Cofer, C. N., & Gelfand, S. (1956). Reasoning as an associative process II: "Direction" in problem solving as a function of reinforcement of relevant responses. *Psychological Reports*, 2, 501–507.

Keele, S. W., Ivry, R., & Mayr, U. (2003). The cognitive and neural architecture of sequence representation. *Psychological Review*, 110, 316–339.

Kihlstrom, J. F. (1999). Conscious versus unconscious cognition. In R. J. Sternberg, *The Nature of Cognition*. Cambridge, MA: MIT Press.

Kihlstrom, J. F., Schacter, D. L., Cork, R. C., Hurt, C. A., & Behr, S. E. (1990). Implicit and explicit memory following surgical anesthesia. *Psychological Science*, 1, 303–306.

Kirsner, K. (1998). Implicit memory. In K. Kirsner, C. Speelman, M. Mayberry, A. O'Brien-Malone, M. Anderson, & C. MacLeod (Eds.) *Implicit and Explicit Mental Processes*. Mahwah, NJ: Erlbaum.

Knoblich, G., & Wartenberg, F. (1998). Unbemerkte Lösungshinweise erleichern Repräsentationswechsel beim Problemlösen. (Unnoticed hints facilitate representational change in problem solving.) *Zeitschrift für Psychologie*, 206, 207–234.

Knowlton, B. J., Ramus, S. J., & Squire, L. R. (1992). Intact artificial grammar learning in amnesia: Dissociation of classification learning and explicit memory for specific instances *Psychological Science*, 3, 172–179.

Knowlton, B. J., & Squire, L. R. (1993). The learning of categories: Parallel brain systems for item memory and category knowledge. *Science*, 262, 1747–49.

Knowlton, B. J., & Squire, L. R. (1994). The information acquired in artificial grammar learning. *Journal of Experimental Psychology: Learning, Memory and Cognition*, 20, 79–91.

Knowlton, B. J., & Squire, L. R. (1996). Artificial grammar learning depends on implicit acquisition of both rule-based and exemplar-specific information. *Journal of Experimental Psychology: Learning, Memory, and Cognition*, 22, 169–181.

Köhler, W. (1925). *The Mentality of Apes*. (E. Winter, trans.). New York: Harcourt, Brace.

Kunst-Wilson, W. R., & Zajonc, R. B. (1980). Affective discrimination of stimuli that cannot be recognized. *Science*, 207, 557–558.

Lewicki, P. (1986a). *Nonconscious Social Information Processing*. New York: Academic Press.

Lewicki, P. (1986b). Processing information about covariations that cannot be articulated. *Journal of Experimental Psychology: Learning, Memory, and Cognition*, 12, 135–146.

Lieberman, M. D. (2000). Intuition: A social cognitive neuroscience approach. *Psychological Bulletin*, 126, 109–137.

Litman, L., & Reber, A. S. (2002). On the temporal course of consolidation of implicit knowledge. *Evolution and Cognition*, 8, 145–155.

Maier, N. (1931). Reasoning in humans II: The solution of a problem and its appearance in consciousness. *Journal of Comparative Psychology*, 12, 181–194.

Manza, L., & Reber, A. S. (1997). Representing artificial grammars: Transfer across stimulus forms and modalities. In D. C. Berry (Ed.), *How implicit is implicit learning?* Oxford, UK: Oxford University Press.

Manza, L., Zizak, D., & Reber, A. S. (1998). Artificial grammar learning and the mere exposure effect: Emotional preference tasks and the implicit learning process. In M. A. Stadler & P. A. Frensch (Eds.), *Handbook of implicit learning*. Thousand Oaks, CA: Sage.

Marcel, A. J. (1983). Conscious and unconscious perception: Experiments on visual masking and word recognition. *Cognitive Psychology*, 15, 197–237.

Marsh, R. L., Bink, M. L., & Hiks, J. L. (1999). Conceptual priming in a generative problem-solving task. *Memory and Cognition*, 27, 355–363.

Mathews, R. C., Buss, R. R., Stanley, W. B., Blanchard-Fields, F., Cho, J. R., & Bruhan, B. (1989). Role of implicit and explicit processes of learning from examples: A synergistic effect. *Journal of Experimental Psychology: Learning, Memory, and Cognition*, 15, 1083–1100.

Mehler, J., Jusczyk, P., Lambertz, G., Halsted, N., Bertoncini, J., & Amiel-Tison, C. (1988). A precursor of language acquisition in young infants. *Cognition*, 29, 143–178.

Merikle, P., & Reingold, E. (1992). Measuring unconscious perceptual processes. In R. Bornstein and T. Pittman (Eds.), *Perception without awareness: Cognitive, clinical, and social perspectives*. NY: Guilford Press.

Merikle, P. M., & Daneman, M. (1996). Memory for unconsciously perceived events: Evidence from anesthetized patients. *Consciousness and Cognition*, 5, 525–541.

Meyer, D. E., & Schvaneveldt, R. W. (1971). Facilitation in recognizing words: Evidence of a dependence upon retrieval operations. *Journal of Experimental Psychology*, 90, 227–234.

Moray, N. (1959). Attention in dichotic listening: Affective cues and the influence of instructions. *Quarterly Journal of Experimental Psychology*, 11, 56–60.

Milner B., Corkin, S., & Teuber, H. L., (1968). Alteration of perception and memory in man: Reflections on methods. In L. Weiskrantz (Ed.), *Analysis of Behavioral Change*. New York: Harper & Row.

Milner, B. (1962). Les troubles de la memoire accompagnant des lesions hippocampiques bilaterales [Disorders of memory accompanying bilateral hippocampal lesions], *Physiologiede l'hippocampe*. Paris: Centre National de la Recherche Scientifique.

Mulligan, N. (1997). Attention and implicit memory tests: The effects of varying attentional load on conceptual priming. *Memory and Cognition*, 25, 11–17.

Mulligan, N. (1998). The role of attention during encoding in implicit and explicit memory. *Journal of Experimental Psychology: Learning, Memory, and Cognition*, 24, 27–47.

Murphy, S. T., & Zajonc, R. B. (1993). Affect, cognition and awareness: Affective priming with optimal and suboptimal stimulus exposures.

Journal of Personality and Social Psychology, 64, 723–739.

Naccache, L., & Dehaene, S. (2001). The priming method: Imaging unconscious repetition priming reveals an abstract representation of number in the parietal lobes. *Cerebral Cortex, 11*, 966–974.

Naccache, L., Blandin, E., & Dehaene, S. (2002). Unconscious masked priming depends on temporal attention. *Psychological Science, 13*, 416–424.

Perruchet, P., & Pacteau, C. (1990). Synthetic grammar learning: Implicit rule abstraction or explicit fragmentary knowledge? *Journal of Experimental Psychology: General, 119*, 264–275.

Perruchet, P., & Pacteau, C. (1991). The implicit acquisition of abstract knowledge about artificial grammar: Some methodological and conceptual issues. *Journal of Experimental Psychology: General, 120*, 112–116.

Perruchet, P., & Vinter, A. (1998). PARSER: A model for word segmentation. *Journal of Memory and Language, 39*, 246–263.

Perruchet, P., & Vinter, R. (2003). The self-organizing consciousness. *Behavioral and Brain Sciences, 25*(3), 297–388.

Phelps, E. A. (2004). The human amygdala and awareness: Interactions between emotion and cognition. In M.S. Gazzaniga (Ed.), *The cognitive neurosciences*, (3rd ed.). Cambridge, MA: MIT Press.

Polanyi, M. (1958). *Personal Knowledge: Towards a Post-critical Philosophy*. Chicago: University of Chicago Press.

Pratkanis, A. R. (1992). The cargo-cult science of subliminal persuasion. *Skeptical Inquirer, 16*, 260–272.

Pyszczynski, T., Greenberg, J., & Solomon, S. (1999). A dual process model of defense against conscious and unconscious death-related thoughts: An extension of terror management theory. *Psychological Review, 106*, 835–845.

Ramus, F., Nespor, M., & Mehler, J. (1999). Correlates of linguistic rhythm in the speech signal. *Cognition, 73*, 265–292.

Reber, A. S. (1967). Implicit learning of artificial grammars. *Journal of Verbal Learning and Verbal Behavior, 5*, 855–863.

Reber, A. S. (1969). Implicit learning of artificial grammars. *Journal of Verbal Learning and Verbal Behavior, 6*, 855–863.

Reber, A. S. (1989). Implicit learning and tacit knowledge. *Journal of Experimental Psychology: General, 118*, 219–235

Reber, A. S. (1992a). An evolutionary context for the cognitive unconscious. *Philosophical Psychology, 5*, 33–51.

Reber, A, S. (1992b). The cognitive unconscious: An evolutionary perspective. *Consciousness and Cognition, 1*, 93–133.

Reber, A. (1993). *Implicit Learning and Tacit Knowledge*. New York: Oxford University Press.

Reber, A. S., & Allen, R. (2000) Individual differences in implicit learning. In R. G. Kunzendorf & B. Wallace (Eds.), *Individual differences in conscious experience*. Philadelphia: John Benjamins.

Reber, A. S., Allen, R., & Reber, P. J. (1999). Implicit and explicit learning. In R. Steinberg (Ed.), *The Nature of cognition*. Cambridge, MA: MIT Press.

Reber, A. S., & Reber, E. S. (2001). *Dictionary of psychology*, (3rd ed.). London: Penguin Books, Ltd.

Reber, P. J., & Kotovsky, K. (1997). Implicit learning in problem solving: The role of working memory capacity. *Journal of Experimental Psychology: General, 126*, 178–203.

Reber, P. J., & Squire, L. R. (1998). Encapsulation of implicit and explicit memory in sequence learning. *Journal of Cognitive Neuroscience, 10*, 248–263.

Reber, P. J., Stark, C. E. L., & Squire, L. R. (1998). Cortical areas supporting category learning identified using functional magnetic resonance imaging. *Proceedings of the National Academy of Sciences, 95*, 747–750.

Redington, M., Chater, N., & Finch, S. (1998). Distributional information: A powerful cue for acquiring syntactic categories. *Cognitive Science, 22*, 425–469.

Roberts, P. (1998). Implicit knowledge and connectionism: What is the connection? In K. Kirsner, C. Speelman, M. Mayberry, A. O'Brien-Malone, M. Anderson, & C. MacLeod (Eds.), *Implicit and explicit mental processes*. Mahwah, NJ: Erlbaum.

Rovee-Collier, C. (1990). The "memory system" of prelinguistic infants. *Annals of the New York Academy of Sciences, 608*, 517–536.

Saffran, J. R., Aslin, R. N., & Newport, E. L. (1996). Statistical learning by 8-month-old infants. *Science, 274*, 1926–1928.

Saffran, J. R., Newport, E. L., & Aslin, R. N. (1996). Word segmentation: The role of distributional cues. *Journal of Memory and Language, 35*, 606–621.

Schacter, D. L., & Sherry, D. F. (1987). The evolution of multiple memory systems. *Psychological Review, 94*, 439–454.

Schacter, D. L., & Graf, P. (1986). Preserved learning in amnesic patients: Perspectives from research on direct priming. *Journal of Clinical Experimental Neuropsychology, 8*, 727–743.

Scolville, W. B., & Milner, B. (1957). Loss of recent memory after bilateral hippocampal lesions. *Journal of Neurobiology, Neurosurgery and Psychiatry, 20*, 11–21.

Schunn, C. D., & Dunbar, K. (1996). Priming, analogy, and awareness in complex reasoning. *Memory and Cognition, 24*, 271–284.

Searle, J. (1992). *The rediscovery of the mind.* Cambridge, MA: MIT Press.

Seger, C. A. (1994). Implicit learning. *Psychological Bulletin, 115*, 163–196.

Servan-Schreiber, E., & Anderson, J. R. (1990). Learning artificial grammars with competitive chunking. *Journal of Experimental Psychology: Learning, Memory, and Cognition, 16*, 592–608.

Servan-Schreiber, D., Cleeremans, A., & McClelland, J. L. (1991).Graded state machines: The representation of temporal contingencies in simple recurrent networks. *Machine Learning, 7*, 161–193.

Shames, V. A., Kihlstrom, J. F., & Forster, K. I. (1994). An implicit test of problem-solving. Paper presented at the annual meeting of the American Psychological Society, Washington, D.C.

Shanks, D. R., & St. John, M. F. (1994). Characteristics of dissociable human learning systems. *Behavioral and Brain Sciences, 17*, 367–447.

Shanks, D. R., Johnstone, T., & Staggs, L. (1997). Abstraction processes in artificial grammar learning. *Quarterly Journal of Experimental Psychology, 50*, 216–252.

Silverman, L. H. (1983). The subliminal psychodynamic activation method: Overview and comprehensive listing of studies. In J. Masling (Ed.), *Empirical studies of psychoanalytic theories*. Hillsdale, NJ: Erlbaum.

Smith, C. (2003). Intact implicit learning in a population with autistic spectrum disorder – provided the stimuli are non-social. Unpublished doctoral dissertation. City University of New York, NY.

Squire, L. R. (1992). Memory and the hippocampus: A synthesis from findings with rats, monkeys, and humans. *Psychological Review, 2*, 195–231.

Squire, L. R. (1995). Biological foundation of accuracy and inaccuracy in memory. In D. L. Schacter (Ed.), *Memory Distortion: How Minds, Brains, and Societies Reconstruct the Past.* Cambridge, MA: Harvard University Press.

Squire, L. R., & Knowlton, B. J. (1995). Memory, hippocampus, and brain systems. In M. S. Gazzaniga (Ed.), *The Cognitive Neurosciences*. Cambridge, MA: MIT Press.

Squire, L. R., & Knowlton, B. J. (2000). In M. S. Gazzaniga (Ed.)., *The New Cognitive Neurosciences*. Cambridge, MA: MIT Press.

Stadler, M. A., & Frensch, P. A. (Eds.), (1998), *Handbook of implicit learning*. Thousand Oaks, CA: Sage.

Toth, J. P., & Reingold, E. M. (1996). Beyond perception: Conceptual contributions to unconscious influences of memory. In G. Underwood (Ed.), *Implicit cognition*. New York: Oxford University Press.

Tulving E., Hayman C. A. G., & MacDonald, C. (1991). Long-lasting perceptual priming and semantic learning in amnesia: A case experiment. *Journal of Experimental Psychology: Learning Memory and Cognition, 17*, 595–617.

Uleman, J. S., & Bargh, J. A. (Eds). (1989). *Unintended Thought*. New York: Guilford Press.

Ungerleider, L. G. (1995). Functional brain imaging studies of cortical mechanisms for memory. *Science, 270*, 769–775.

Vokey, J. R., & Brooks, L. R. (1992). Salience of item knowledge in learning artificial grammars. *Journal of Experimental Psychology: Learning, Memory, and Cognition, 18*, 328–344.

Warrington, E. K., & Weiskrantz, L. (1968). New method of testing long-term retention with special reference to amnesic patients. *Nature, 217*, 972–974.

Warrington, E. K., & Weiskrantz, L. (1974). The effect of prior learning on subsequent retention in amnesic patients. *Neuropsychologia, 12*, 419–428.

Weinberger, N. M. (1992). Beyond neuronal excitability: Receptive field analysis reveals that association specifically modifies the representation of auditory information. In L. R.

Squire & N. Butters (Eds.), *Neuropsychology of memory* (2nd ed.). New York: Guilford Press.

Weiskrantz, L. (1986). *Blindsight*. Oxford, UK: Oxford University Press.

Weiss, S. M., Reber, A. S., & Owen, D. R. (in review). The locus of focus: Attentional strategies in the acquisition of sensorimotor skills.

Wertheimer, M. (1945). *Productive Thinking*. New York: Harper & Row.

Whalen, P. J., Rauch, S. L., Etcoff, N. L., McInerney, S. C., Lee, M. B., & Jenike, M. A. (1998). Masked presentations of emotional facial expressions modulate amygdala activity without explicit knowledge. *Journal of Neuroscience*, 18, 411–418.

Whalen, P. J. (1998). Fear, vigilance, and ambiguity: Initial neuroimaging studies of the human amygdala. *Current Directions in Psychological Science*, 7, 177–188.

Whittlesea, B. W. A., & Dorken, M. D. (1993). Incidentally, things in general are particularly determined: An episodic-processing account of implicit learning. *Journal of Experimental Psychology: General*, 122, 227–248.

Winter, W., Broman, M., Rose, A., & Reber, A. S. (2001). Assessment of cognitive procedural learning in amnesia: Why the Tower of Hanoi has fallen down. *Brain and Cognition*, 45, 79–96.

Yaniv, I., & Meyer, D. M. (1987). Activation and metacognition of inaccessible stored information: Potential bases for incubation effects in problem solving. *Journal of Experimental Psychology: Learning, Memory, and Cognition*, 13, 187–205.

Zajonc, (1980). Feeling and thinking: Preferences need no inferences. *American Psychologist*, 35, 151–175.

Zizak, D., & Reber, A. R. (2004). The structural mere exposure effect: dual role of familiarity. *Consciousness and Cognition*, 13(2), 336–362.

Part V

COGNITIVE AND NEURAL CONSTRAINTS ON HUMAN THOUGHT

CHAPTER 19

Thinking in Working Memory

Robert G. Morrison

Introduction

It is not an accident that this discussion of working memory is positioned near the center of a volume on thinking and reasoning. Central to higher-level cognitive processes is the ability to form and manipulate mental representations (see Doumas & Hummel, Chap. 4). Working memory is the cognitive construct responsible for the maintenance and manipulation of information and therefore is neccessary for many of the types of complex thought described in this book. Likewise, the development and failures of working memory are critical to understanding thought changes with development (see Halford, Chap. 22) and aging (see Salthouse, Chap. 24) as well as many types of higher-level cognitive impairments (see Bachman & Cannon, Chap. 21). In spite of its obvious importance for thinking and reasoning, working memory's role in complex thought is just beginning to be understood. In this chapter, we review several dominant models of working memory, viewing them from different methodological perspectives, including dual-task experiments, individual differences, and cognitive neuroscience.

Multiple Memory Systems?

Although the idea of separate primary memory is credited to William James (1890), Waugh and Norman (1965) and Atkinson and Shiffrin (1968) developed the idea of distinct primary (i.e., short-term) and secondary (i.e., long-term) memory components into defined models of the human memory system. These multicomponent models of memory were supported by observations from many different studies during the 1950s and 1960s. Perhaps the most familiar justification for separate short-term and long-term memory systems is the serial position effect (e.g., Murdock, 1962). During list learning, the most recently studied items show an advantage when tested immediately – an advantage that goes away quickly with a delay in test provided that participants are prevented from rehearsing. This *recency effect* is presumably the result

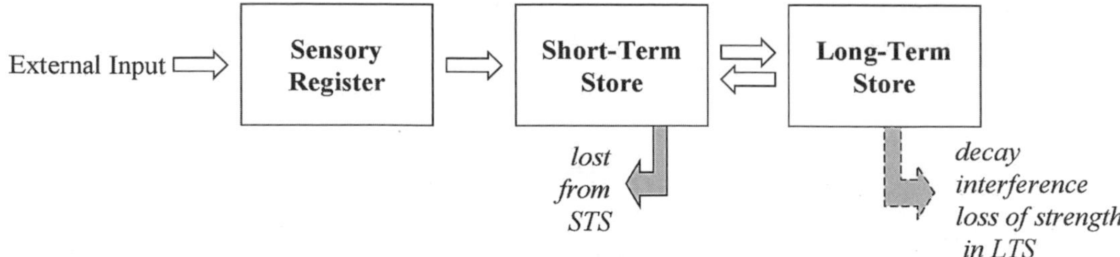

Figure 19.1. Atkinson and Shiffrin's (1968) multicomponent memory model.

of quickly unloading short-term memory at test. In contrast, the first items in the list show an advantage that withstands a delay period. This *primacy effect* presumably occurs because these initial items have been stored in long-term memory through practice. Conrad (1964) provided another important finding justifying distinct systems when he observed that errors in short-term remembering were usually phonological whereas long-term memory was dominated by semantic coding. This suggested that rehearsal or storage systems were different between the two types of memory. Yet another important finding was that, although the capacity of long-term memory was seemingly limitless, short-term memory as observed in a simple digit-span task was of limited capacity (Miller, 1956) – a finding confirmed using many other experimental paradigms. Lastly, around this same era, neuropsychological evidence began to emerge suggesting that at least parts of the short- and long-term memory systems were anatomically distinct. Milner's (1966) famous amnesic patient, HM, with his long-term memory deficits but preserved short-term digit span, and Shallice and Warrington's (1970) patient, KF, with his intact long-term memory but grossly impaired digit span, presented a double dissociation favoring at least partially distinct short- and long-term memory systems. Atkinson and Shiffrin's (1968) memory model was typical of models from the late 1960s with distinct sensory, short-term, and long-term memory stores (Figure 19.1). Short-term memory was viewed as a short-term buffer for information that was maintained by active rehearsal. It was also believed to be the mechanism by which information was stored in long-term memory.

A Multi-component Working Memory Model

While exploring the issues described in the previous section, Baddeley and Hitch (1974) proposed a model that expanded short-term memory into the modern concept of *working memory* – a term that has been used in several different contexts in psychology.[1] Baddeley (1986) defined working memory as "a system for the temporary holding and manipulation of information during the performance of a range of cognitive tasks such as comprehension, learning, and reasoning" (Ref. 3, p. 34). In a recent description of his working-memory model, Baddeley (2000) proposed a four-component model (Figure 19.2), including the *phonological loop*, the *visuospatial sketchpad*, the *central executive*, and the model's most recent addition, the *episodic*

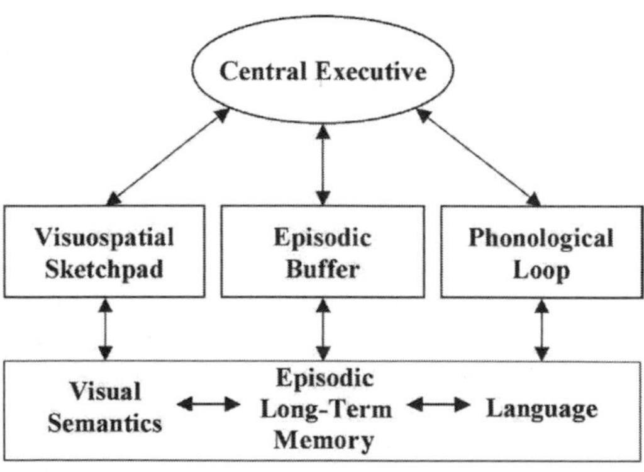

Figure 19.2. Baddeley's (2000) four-component working memory model.

buffer. This model has primarily been conceptualized based on results from behavioral dual-task paradigms and neuropsychology. For instance, using behavioral methods, Baddeley and Hitch (1974) reasoned that they could identify the separable elements of working memory by looking for task interference. If you assume the various components of working memory are capacity limited, then if the simultaneous performance of a secondary task degrades performance of a primary task, these two tasks must tap a common limited resource – particularly if there exists another primary task that is unaffected by performance of the secondary task and is affected by a different secondary task that does not affect the first primary task. Likewise, neuropsychological evidence such as the existence of patients with selectively disabled verbal (e.g., patient KF, Shallice & Warrington, 1970) and visual (e.g., de Renzi & Nichelli, 1975) digit span suggested that verbal and visual working-memory systems are somewhat separable as well.

Using this type of methodology, Baddeley has suggested that the phonological loop and visuospatial sketchpad are modality-specific *slave systems* that are responsible for maintaining information over short periods of time. The phonological loop is responsible for the maintenance and rehearsal of information that can be coded verbally (e.g., the digits in a digit-span task). It is phonemically sensitive (e.g., Ted and Fred are harder to remember than Ted and Bob), and its capacity is approximately equal to the amount of information that can be subvocally cycled in approximately 2 seconds. Baddeley (1986) argues that these two characteristics of verbal working memory are best explained by two components: (1) a *phonological store* that holds all of the information that is currently active and is sensitive to phonemic interference effects and (2) an *articulatory loop* that is used to refresh the information via a process of time-limited subvocal cycling. The articulatory loop is specifically disrupted by the common phonological loop secondary task, *articulatory suppression* (i.e., repeating a word or

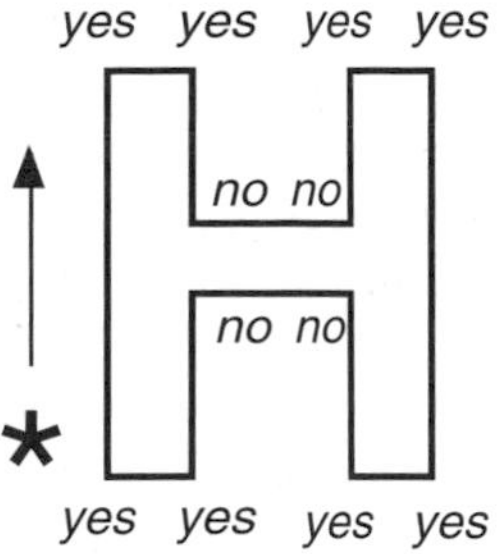

Figure 19.3. The Brooks (1968) letter task. Participants are to image a block letter and then decide whether each corner of the letter is an outside edge.

number vocally). Thus, verbal span is constrained by both the amount of information to be maintained and the time that it takes to rehearse it. In contrast to the phonological loop, the visuospatial sketchpad has been more difficult to describe. In a dual-task experiment, Baddeley (1986) asked subjects to simultaneously perform a pursuit rotor task (i.e., track a spot of light that followed a circular path with a stylus) while performing either a verbal or spatial memory task previously developed by Brooks (1968; Figure 19.3). The verbal task required subjects to remember a sentence (e.g., "A bird in hand is not in the bush") and scan through each word deciding whether it was a noun or not. The correct pattern of output for this example would be: NO, YES, NO, YES, NO, NO, NO, NO, YES. In the visual memory task, participants are first shown a block letter with one corner marked with an asterisk (Figure 19.3). They are then asked to imagine the letter and, beginning at the marked corner, judge whether each corner is an outside corner or not. Thus, in both the verbal and visual memory tasks, participants are required to hold a modality-specific object in memory and inspect it, answering yes or no to questions about their inspection. Baddeley found that the visual memory task, but not the verbal memory task, seriously degraded pursuit rotor tracking performance.

Logie (1995) has argued for a visual similarity effect analogous to the phonemic similarity effect used to support the phonological store. Participants were visually presented strings of upper- and lowercase letters (e.g., "KcPs" or "gBrQ"). Letters were chosen based on the similarity of their lower and uppercase characters. Thus Kk, Cc, Pp, Ss were visually similar while Gg, Bb, Rr, Qq were visually dissimilar. To discourage use of the phonological loop to perform the task, participants performed simultaneous articulatory suppression. After a retention period, participants had to write down the letter sequence in correct order and case. Logie found that participants made significantly more errors when the letter cases were visually similar. This finding suggests the existence of a visual store analogous to the phonological store in the phonological loop. It is possible that a visual rehearsal loop analogous to the articulatory loop exists; however, to date evidence is limited to introspective accounts of mnemonics. What is clear is that both visual and spatial qualities of stimuli can be stored in the short term; however, the independence of systems responsible for visual and spatial memory is the topic of much debate (see Logie, 1995).

The third component of Baddeley's working memory model, the central executive, was initially a catch-all for the working-memory-processes necessary for certain cognitive abilities that did not fit cleanly into the phonological loop or visuospatial sketchpad. This category included many of the cognitive abilities discussed in this book, including reasoning, problem solving, and language. For instance, Shallice and Warrington's (1970) patient KF had a drastically degraded verbal span (i.e., two letters) with relatively intact language comprehension. Believing that both of these abilities required working memory, Baddeley and Hitch (1974) reasoned that verbal span and language comprehension must use separate working-memory modules. To test this hypothesis, they devised a short-term memory load task that balanced maintenance load and time (Baddeley & Hitch, 1974). For instance, a low-load condition might require participants to remember three numbers, outputting them every 2 seconds, while a high-load condition might require participants to remember six numbers, outputting them every 4 seconds. Participants performed this secondary task while simultaneously performing a primary task involving auditory language comprehension. They found that language comprehension only suffered at high concurrent memory load and not under lower memory load conditions. At low memory load, participants had sufficient resources to carry out the comprehension task; however, at high memory load there were insufficient resources for language comprehension. Adding the results of this study to many other similar experiments and the neuropsychological evidence from patients like KF, Baddeley and Hitch postulated that comprehension and digit span utilizes separate modules of working memory that taps a common resource pool.

Given the amorphous nature of the cognitive tasks for which the central executive was necessary, Baddeley (1986) initially embraced Norman and Shallice's (1980; 1986) concept of a *Supervisory Attentional System* as a model for the central executive. Norman and Shallice suggested that most well-learned cognitive functions operate via *schemata*, or sets of actions that run automatically. Although many schemata may be shared by most individuals (e.g., driving a car, dialing a telephone, composing a simple sentence, etc.), additional schemata may be acquired through the development of specific expertise (e.g., writing lines of computer code, swinging a golf club, etc.). At many times during an ordinary day, we must perform more than one of these schemata concurrently (e.g., talking while driving). Norman and Shallice suggest that when we must perform multiple schemata, their coordination or prioritization is accomplished via the semi-automatic *Contention Scheduler* and the strategically controlled Supervisory Attentional System. The Contention Scheduler uses priorities and environmental cues (e.g., a car quickly pulls in front of me), whereas the Supervisory Attentional System tends to follow larger goals (e.g., convincing my wife that I'm a good driver). Thus, when the car rapidly pulled in front of me, I pressed the brake on the car and then proceeded to tell my wife how attentive I am while on the road. One important characteristic of the Supervisory Attentional System as a model of the central executive was that it was sensitive to capacity limits. According to Norman and Shallice, capacity limits constrain thinking and action during (1) complex cognitive processes such as reasoning or decision making; (2) novel tasks that have not developed schemata; (3) life-threatening or single, difficult tasks; and (4) functions that require the suppression of habitual responses.

Baddeley (1986) suggested that the Supervisory Attentional System provided a useful framework for understanding random generation, a task frequently associated with the central executive. In random generation, a participant is asked to generate a series of random responses from a predetermined list (e.g., integers from 0 to 9, for instance: 1,8,4,6,0,7,6, 8,4,5,6,1,2). Response patterns from this task usually exhibit two characteristics: (1) certain responses appear at much lower frequencies than others (e.g, 3 or 9 did not appear whereas 1,4,6, and 8 appeared repeatedly) and (2) stereotyped responses (e.g., 4,5,6 or 1,2) are much more common than other equally likely two- or three-number sequences (Baddeley, 1966). Baddeley suggested that the higher-order goal of randomness is at odds with the dominant schemata for the production of numbers (i.e., counting). Thus, random generation potently requires the services of the Supervisory Attentional System to override or inhibit the dominant schemata. When random number generation is performed with another working-memory–intensive task, the resources available to the Supervisory Attentional System (i.e., central executive) are in even more demand and responses become more stereotyped (Baddeley et al., 1998).

Although the Supervisory Attentional System describes an important ability that underlies complex cognitive processes such as language comprehension and problem solving, it fails to offer a tenable account of how, short of a homunculus, this direction would occur. Acknowledging this problem, Baddeley's current model of the central executive fractionates the central executive in the hope that by understanding precisely what the central executive does we might learn how it does it. Baddeley (1996) suggested four arguably distinct central executive functions: "(1) the capacity to coordinate performance on two separate tasks, (2) the capacity to switch retrieval strategies as reflected in random generation, (3) the capacity to attend selectively to one stimulus and inhibit the disrupting effect of others, and (4) the capacity to hold and manipulate information in long-term memory, as reflected in measures of working memory span" (Ref. 4, p. 5). Thus, Baddeley argued that the central executive is important for task switching, inhibition of internal representations or prepotent responses, and the activation of information in long-term memory during an activity that requires the active manipulation of material. In comparison to the slave systems, relatively little attention has been paid to the central executive utilizing dual-task methodologies.

The last and most recently added component of Baddeley's working-memory model is the episodic buffer. One problem encountered by a modal working-memory model is the need for integration. How can a complex problem requiring the integration of information across modalities be solved if all the information is being held in separate distinct buffers? This binding problem, whether it is binding information within a modality or across modalities, is one of the central challenges for a working-memory system capable of high-level cognition (see Doumas & Hummel, Chap. 4). To address this issue, Baddeley (2000) has proposed a third type of buffer that uses a multidimensional code. Thus, this buffer can maintain information from several modalities that has been bound together by the central executive. Fuster, Bodner, and Kroger (2000) have found evidence of the existence of neurons in prefrontal cortex that seem to be responsible for this type of function. Another important function of the episodic buffer is serving as a scratchpad for the development of new mental representations during complex problem solving. There are many examples of situations requiring the functions ascribed to the episodic buffer, but the methods for studying such a resource utilizing the task-interference paradigm are still under development.

Embedded-Processes Working-Memory Model

Although Baddeley's multi-component working-memory model has dominated the field for much of the past thirty years, there are alternative conceptions of working memory. Cowan (1988, 1995) has proposed a model that tightly integrates short- and long-term memory systems with attention. In his Embedded-Processes working-memory model (Figure 19.4), Cowan defines working memory as the set of cognitive processes that keep mental representations in an easily accessible state. Within this system, information can either be within the *focus of attention*, which Cowan believes is capacity limited, or in *active memory*, which Cowan suggests is time limited. The focus of attention is similar to James's (1890) concept of primary memory and is equated to the information that is currently in conscious awareness. In contrast, active memory, a concept similar to Hebb's (1949) cell assemblies or Ericsson and Kintsch's (1995) long-term working memory, refers to information that has higher activation either from recently being in the focus of attention or through some type of automatic activation (e.g., priming). In the Embedded-Processes model, a central executive, somewhat similar to Norman and Shallice's (1980, 1986) Supervisory Attention System, is responsible for bringing information into the focus of attention while an automatic recruitment of attention mechanism can bring information into active memory without previously having been in the focus of attention.

A critical distinction between Cowan's Embedded-Processes model and Baddeley's multi-component model is how the two models deal with the topic of maintenance of information. As previously discussed, Baddeley hypothesizes modality-specific buffers for the short-term storage of information that coordinate with the Episodic Buffer, which is responsible for storing integrated information. In contrast, Cowan suggests that information is maintained in working memory simply by activating its representations in long-term memory via short-term – specific neurons in the prefrontal or parietal cortices. This latter view suggests that information from different modalities will behave differently to the extent that they are coded differently in long-term memory, a view somewhat at odds with findings of phonological errors in short-term memory tasks and semantic errors in long-term memory tasks. Cowan counters this objection by noting that different codes are used in the storage of information in long-term memory and, depending on the nature of the task, different codes are likely to be more important. Likewise, Baddeley has argued that short-term and long-term memory systems are distinct based on neuropsychological evidence suggesting that short-term and long-term systems can be dissociated and therefore must be distinct systems. This argument, however, relies to some extent on the belief that the individual short- and long-term systems are anatomically unitary, an assumption that seems unlikely given recent evidence from cognitive neuroscience. Fuster has argued, based on results from single-cell recording in nonhuman primates, that neurons in prefrontal cortex are responsible for maintaining information in working memory (Fuster & Alexander 1971); however, disrupting circuits between this area and more posterior or inferior regions associated with long-term storage of information can also result in working-memory deficits (Fuster, 1997). Recent evidence from electrophysiology in humans seems to confirm that areas in prefrontal cortex and areas associated with long-term storage of information are temporally coactive during working-memory tasks (see Ruchkin et al., 2003, for a review).

A second important distinction between Baddeley's multi-component working-memory model and Cowan's

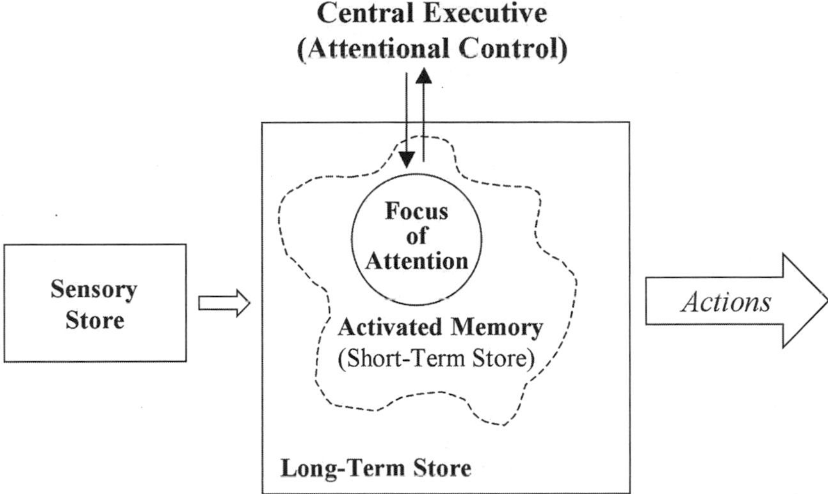

Figure 19.4. Simplified diagram of Cowan's (1988) Embedded-Processes Model.

Embedded-Processs model is modality specificity. Specifically, Baddeley has proposed independent modules within working memory for maintaining information from different modalities (e.g., visual or verbal). In contrast, Cowan suggests only a domain-general central executive that, in turn, can activate networks for various modalities of information stored in long-term memory. Baddeley also proposes a domain-general central executive, so the main distinction between the models is whether information to be maintained in working memory is loaded into domain-specific buffers or whether it is simply activated in long-term memory. From our earlier discussion, there seems to be no doubt that it is easier to maintain a certain quantity of information across several modalities than to maintain the same amount of information within just a single modality. Although this observation does not necessitate independent buffers, it does suggest that capacity limitations may be somewhat domain-specific.

Reasoning and Working Memory: Using the Task-Interference Paradigm

Although the task-interference paradigm has been very useful in exploring working memory slave systems, relatively little has been done using this technique to study high-level cognition or the central executive. Central to high-level cognitive processes is the ability to form and manipulate mental representations. Review of the functions of the central executive in either Baddeley or Cowan's models suggests that the central executive should be critical for thinking and reasoning – a hypothesis that has been confirmed in several studies. In their seminal work on working memory Baddeley and Hitch (1974) asked participants to perform a reasoning task in which they read a simple sentence containing information about the order of two abstract terms (i.e., A and B). Their task was to judge whether a letter sequence presented after the sentence reflected the order of the terms in the statement. For instance, a TRUE statement would be "A not preceded by B" followed by AB (Ref. 7, p. 50). Baddeley and Hitch varied the statements with respect to statement voicing (i.e., active or passive), negation, and verb type (i.e., precedes or follows). They found that low concurrent memory loads (i.e., one to two items to remember) had no effect on reasoning accuracy or response time; however, high concurrent memory load (i.e., six items to remember) had a reliable effect on response time. Depending on the emphasis of the instructions used, they found that the decrement in performance was either in the reasoning task or the memory task. There was no statistical interaction between concurrent memory and the reasoning task difficulty.

Several other researchers have investigated how working memory is important for deductive reasoning. Gilhooly et al. (1993), utilizing methods similar to Baddeley and Hitch, asked participants to perform verbal syllogisms (Evans, Chap. 8, for a description of syllogistic reasoning) of varying levels of complexity. In a first experiment, participants either viewed the premises of the syllogisms visually, all at once, or heard the premises read one at a time. Gilhooly et al. hypothesized that verbal presentation would result in a higher working-memory load because participants would have to maintain the content of the premises before they were able to solve the problem. They found this result: Participants made more errors in the verbal condition than in the visual condition. An error analysis indicated that the errors made were the result of not remembering the premises correctly, not errors made in the process of integration of information between premises. In a second experiment, they had participants perform the syllogism task visually while performing one of three different secondary tasks. They found that only random number generation interfered with performance of syllogisms. Gilhooly et al. concluded that the central executive is critical for relational reasoning and the phonological loop (as interfered with by articulatory suppression) may be involved to a lesser extent. They also concluded that the visuospatial sketchpad, as interfered with by spatial tapping (i.e., tapping a fixed pattern with the fingers), was not important for performing verbal syllogisms and thus argued against models of reasoning that are at least in principle dependent on involvement of visual working memory (e.g., Kirby & Kosslyn, 1992; Johnson-Laird, 1983). In a similar study, Toms, Morris, and Ward (1993) found no evidence that a variety of secondary tasks loading on either the phonological loop or visuospatial sketchpad had any effect on either reasoning accuracy or latency. Of the secondary tasks they used, only a high concurrent memory load (i.e., six digits) affected reasoning performance, and this effect appeared to be limited to difficult syllogisms.

Klauer, Stegmaier, and Meiser (1997) had participants perform syllogisms and spatial reasoning tasks that involved transitive inference (see Halford, Chap. 22, for a description of transitive inference tasks). The spatial reasoning problems varied in complexity from simple transitive inference (e.g., "The circle is to the right of the triangle. The square is to the left of the triangle." See Ref. 44, p. 13) to more complicated transitive inference problems that required greater degrees of relational integration. Klauer et al. had participants perform a visual tracking task (i.e., follow one object on a screen filled with distractor objects) while listening to the premises of the reasoning problems. They found that this visuospatial secondary task interfered with spatial reasoning but had little effect on syllogism performance. In another experiment, Klauer et al. presented syllogisms or spatial reasoning problems either auditorally (as in the previous experiment) or visually on a computer screen. While performing these primary tasks, participants performed random generation either verbally or spatially, by pressing keys in a random pattern. They found that both forms of random generation affected both syllogism and spatial reasoning performance; however, spatial random generation caused somewhat less interference than verbal random generation – a finding consistent with Baddeley et al.'s (1998) extensive study of random generation. In their final experiment, Klauer et al. found that articulatory suppression (i.e., counting repeatedly from 1 to 5) had a mild effect on syllogism and spatial reasoning latencies. Overall, Klauer et al. found evidence for involvement of the central executive (as interfered with by random generation) and somewhat less interference by slave system tasks consistent with the modality of the reasoning task.

Unlike the examples of deductive and spatial reasoning we discussed previously, analogical reasoning frequently requires the extensive retrieval of semantic information in addition to the relational processing characteristic of all types of reasoning (see Holyoak, Chap. 6, for a detailed discussion of analogical reasoning). Waltz et al. (2000) had participants perform an analogical reasoning task while performing one of several secondary tasks. In the analogical reasoning task (adapted from Markman & Gentner, 1993), participants studied pairs of pictures of scenes with multiple objects (see Figure 6.3 in Holyoak, Chap. 6). For instance, one problem showed a boy trying to walk a dog in one picture while the companion picture showed a dog failing to be restrained by a leash tied to a tree. Participants were asked to study each picture and pick one object in the second picture that "goes with" a target object in the first picture. In the example problem in Figure 6.3, the man in the first picture is a *featural* match to the boy in the second picture while using an analogy the boy is a *relational* match to the tree in the second picture. Participants were simply asked to select one object; they were thus free to complete the task based on either featural similarity or make an analogical mapping and inference, answering based on relational similarity. Waltz et al. found that participants who maintained a concurrent memory load or performed verbal random number generation or articulatory suppression (i.e., saying the word "the" once each second) gave fewer relational responses than a control group not performing a dual task. In a recent extension with this task, my lab replicated Waltz et al.'s articulatory suppression finding (i.e., saying the English nonword "zorn" once each second) and also found a similar effect for a visuospatial working-memory dual task (manually tapping a simple spatial pattern).

In the previous studies, the extent of interference with the analogy task was similar for both central executive (concurrent memory load and verbal random number generation) and slave system (articulatory suppression and spatial tapping) dual tasks. One explanation of these results is that analogical reasoning is more resource demanding than the deductive and spatial reasoning tasks previously discussed, and thus even the slave system tasks cause significant interference. Another possibility is that analogical reasoning places greater demands specifically on the modality-specific slave systems of working memory than other forms of relational reasoning. To investigate this issue, Morrison, Holyoak, and Truong (2001) had participants perform either a verbal or visual analogy task, while performing articulatory suppression (i.e., saying the nonword "zorn" once a second), spatial tapping (i.e., touching one of four red dots each second in a predetermined pattern), or verbal random number generation. In the verbal analogy task, participants verified verbal analogies, such as BLACK:WHITE::NOISY:QUIET, answering either TRUE or FALSE via a floor pedal. In the visual analogy task, participants performed Sternberg's (1977) People Pieces analogy task. In this task, participants verify whether the relational pattern of characteristics between two cartoon characters is the same or different than between a second pair of characters. Morrison, Holyoak, and Truong found that, for verbal analogies, articulatory suppression and verbal random number generation resulted in an increase in analogy error rate, whereas only verbal random number generation increased analogy response time for correct responses. Spatial tapping had no reliable effect on verbal analogy performance. In contrast, for visual analogy, both spatial tapping and verbal random number generation resulted in more analogy errors, whereas only random generation increased analogy response time. Articulatory suppression had no reliable effect on visual analogy performance. Thus, there seems to be a modality-specific role for working memory in analogical reasoning.

In summary, all of the reasoning tasks described in the previous section are interfered with by dual tasks considered to tap the central executive (e.g., random number generation or concurrent memory load). The deductive reasoning tasks reported require the manipulation and the alignment of premises that are provided in the problem. In addition to these operations, analogical reasoning may require the reasoner to retrieve information from semantic memory (e.g., the relations that bind the terms in the analogy) and then map the resulting relational statements (and in some cases make an inference that requires retrieving a term that completes the analogy).

To evaluate the extent that working-memory resources are necessary for semantic memory retrieval and relational binding, my lab went on to examine the component processes in working memory is necessary for analogical reasoning. We wondered whether working memory is necessary for the simple process of relational binding or only becomes necessary when multiple relations need to be maintained and compared during the analogical mapping process. To address this question, we used the stimuli from the verbal analogy task but simply asked participants to verify relational statements instead of comparing two of them as in the analogy task. Thus, participants would respond TRUE to a statement like "black is the opposite of white" and FALSE to the statement "noisy is the opposite of noisier." As in the verbal analogy task, articulatory suppression and verbal random number generation affected performance with spatial tapping also having a smaller, but reliable effect. Thus, relational binding, not just maintenance and mapping, require use of the working-memory system, including the modality-specific slave systems.

Individual Differences in Working Memory

An alternative to Baddeley's dual-task methodology uses individual differences to study working memory. Daneman and Carpenter (1980) first used this approach to investigate how working memory was involved in language comprehension. They developed a reading span task that required subjects to read several sentences and then later recall the last word of each sentence in the correct order. The participant's span is typically defined as the maximum-sized trial with perfect performance. This measure correlated relatively well with individuals' reading comprehension ability. Unlike a simple short-term memory-span task, the working-memory–span task required the subjects to do a more complex task while also remembering a list of items. In this way, the span task is believed to tap both the maintenance (slave system) and manipulation (central executive and episodic buffer) aspects of working memory. Other span tasks have been developed to vary the nature of the task that participants perform and what they maintain. For example, Turner and Engle (1989) asked participants to solve simple arithmetic problems and then remember a word presented at the end of each problem. In the n-back task (Figure 19.5; Smith & Jonides, 1997 for a complete description), the manipulation task is changed to having to continuously update the set of items. Using this approach, researchers have found working-memory capacity to be an important predictor of performance in a broad range of higher cognitive tasks, including reading comprehension (Daneman & Carpenter, 1980), language comprehension (Just & Carpenter, 1992), following directions (Engle, Carullo, & Collins, 1991), reasoning (Carpenter, Just, & Shell, 1990; Kyllonen & Christal, 1990), and memory retrieval (Conway & Engel, 1994).

Researchers using working-memory-span measures typically measure participants' working-memory span using one or more measures and then use this to predict performance on another task. A high correlation suggests that working memory is an important target for the task. More sophisticated studies collect a variety of other measures of information processing ability (e.g., processing speed or short-term memory span) and use either multiple regression or structural equation modeling to determine whether these various abilities are separable with respect to the target task. Engle and his collaborators (Engle, Kane, & Tuholski, 1999; Kane & Engle, 2003b; see also

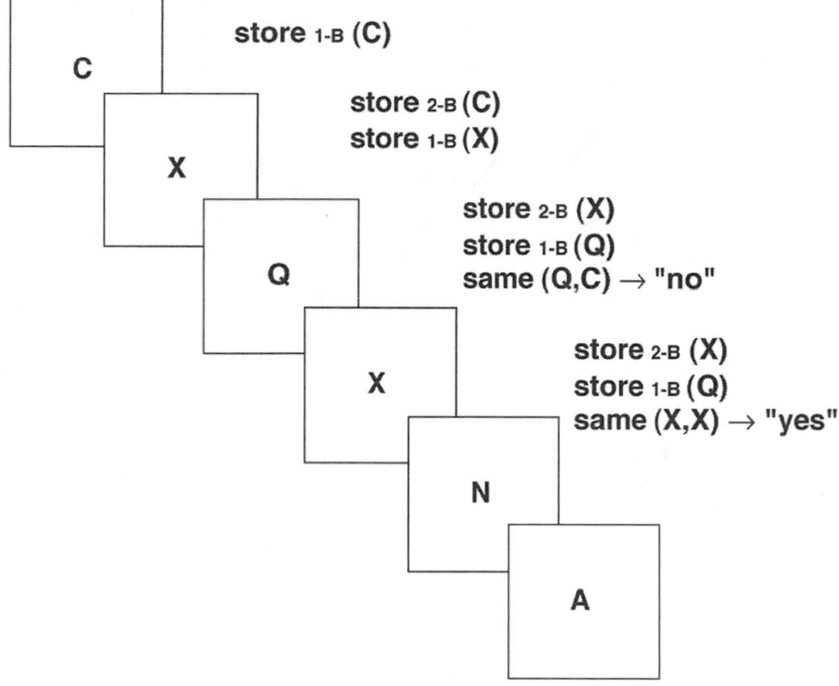

Figure 19.5. The n-back task. Participants see a stream of letters, numbers, or symbols and have to continuously answer whether the current item was the same as the item presented "n-back" in the stream. This task requires maintenance of the current in-set item and continuous updating of this set – an ability considered to be manipulation of the set.

Salthouse, Chap. 24) have used this approach to argue that, although working-memory-span and short-term-memory-span tasks share much variance, it is working-memory capacity that best predicts higher cognitive performance as measured by tasks such as the Ravens Progressive Matrices (see Figure 19.6).

Kane and Engle believe that the ability measured by a working-memory-span task once simple maintenance is stripped away is best described as controlled attention. They have argued that working-memory capacity is a good predictor of task performance in tasks that (a) require maintenance of task goals, (b) require scheduling competing actions or responses, (c) involve response competition or (d) involve inhibiting information irrelevant to the task (Engle, Kane, & Tuholski, 1999). This list is very similar to the functions that Baddeley (1996) attributes to the central executive. Obviously, these are the types of cognitive processes that are omnipresent in high-level cognition. They are also the types of cognitive abilities necessary to perform traditional tests of fluid or analytical intelligence such as the Ravens Progressive Matricies (1938), leading researchers to hypothesize that working-memory capacity is the critical factor that determines analytical intelligence (see Kane & Engle, 2003a; Sternberg, Chap. 31).

The Where, What, and How of Working Memory and Thought

So far, we have suggested that there are at least two important aspects of working memory for human thinking – a modality-specific maintenance function that is capable of preserving information over short periods of time and a manipulation or attentional control function that is capable

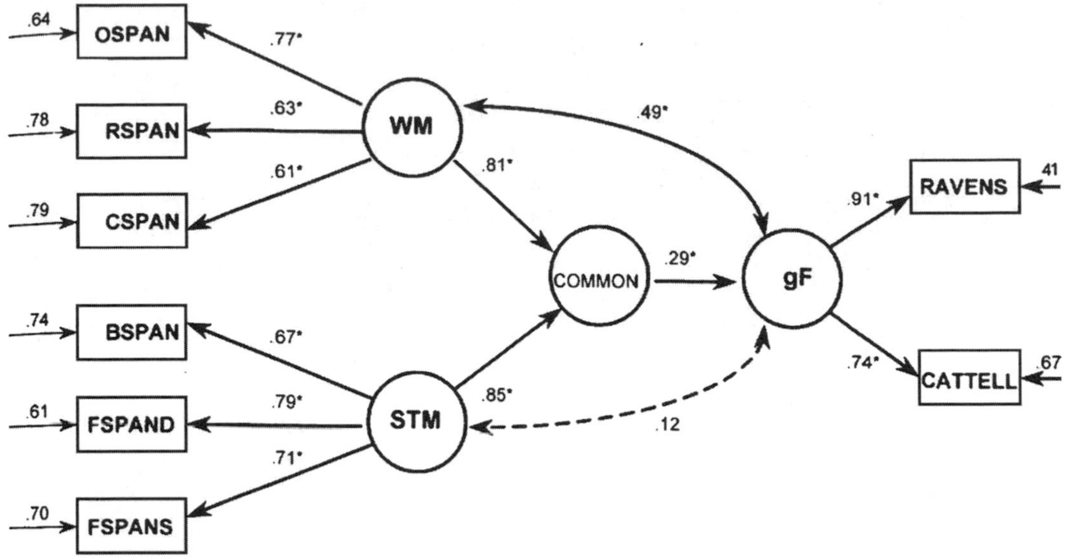

Figure 19.6. Structural Equation Model of the relationship of working memory and short-term memory and their role in analytic problem solving and intelligence. From Engle, Kane, and Tuholski (1999).

of activating, operating, and updating this information during conscious thought. Recently, cognitive neuroscientists have devoted much effort to answering the question of *where* in the brain these working memory mechanisms operate. This topic is beyond the scope of this chapter [see Goel, Chap. 20, for a more detailed treatment of the cognitive neuroscience of problem solving and Chein, Ravizza, and Fiez (2003) for a recent appraisal of the ability of Baddeley and Cowan's models to account for recent neuroimaging findings]; however, we know that at least several areas of the prefrontal and parietal corticies are critical for these functions. Although these areas may be specific to working memory, there is mounting evidence from both electrophysiology and functional magnetic resonance imaging (fMRI) that working memory is the result of activation of networks involving many brain regions.[2] A more interesting question than where, is *how* working memory operates thinking. Unfortunately, much less attention has been given to this question; however, several of the computational approaches outlined in this book begin to address this topic.[3]

It is the belief of many of the authors in this volume that high-level cognition is intrinsically relational in nature, a position long argued by many scientists (see Fodor and Pylyshyn, 1988; Spearman, 1923). In this account, one critical function for working memory to accomplish is the flexible binding of information stored in long-term memory. Working memory must also be able to nest relations to allow more complex knowledge structures to be used. Halford (Chap. 22) has referred to this factor as *relational complexity*. As the relational complexity of a particular problem increases, so do the demands placed on working memory. Goals are a particular subclass of relations that are especially important in deductive reasoning (see Goel, Chap. 20). Maintaining the complex goal hierarchies (high relational complexity) necessary for solving complex problems such as those encountered in chess or in tasks such as the Ravens Progressive Matrices or the Tower of Hanoi makes great demands on the working memory system (see Lovett & Anderson, Chap. 17; Carpenter, Just, & Shell, 1990; Newman et al., 2003). Most work directed at understanding how the brain implements working memory has focused on relatively simple tasks in which processing of relations is minimal.

The ways in which the brain's distributed architecture is used to process problems that require relation flexibility and relational complexity have just begun to be explored (see Christoff & Gabrieli, 2000; Christoff et al., 2001; Morrison et al., 2004; Prabhakaran et al., 2000; Waltz et al., 1999). Hummel and Holyoak's (1997, 2003; see also Doumas & Hummel, Chap. 4) LISA model solves the binding problem created by the need for the flexible use of information in a distributed architecture. The LISA model dynamically binds roles to their fillers in working memory by temporal synchrony of firing. This allows the distributed information in long-term memory to be flexibly bound in different relations and for the system to appreciate that the various entities can serve different functions in different relations and relational hierarchies. It is possible that one role of the prefrontal cortex is to control this synchrony process by firing the distributed network of neurons representing the actual fillers in long-term memory (see Doumas & Hummel Chap. 4, and Morrison et al., 2004, for a more detailed account of this approach). Although no direct evidence exists for synchrony of binding in high-level relational systems, several studies in animals (e.g., Gray et al., 1989) and in humans (e.g., Müller et al., 1996; Ruchkin et al., 2003) suggest that synchrony may be an important mechanism for other cognitive processes implemented in the brain. This type of system is also consistent with Baddeley's (2000) concept of an episodic buffer that binds information together in working memory.

Implicit in a working-memory system capable of handling relations is not only the ability to precisely activate information in long-term memory but also the ability to deactivate or inhibit it. Consider the simple analogy problem:

BLACK:WHITE::NOISY:_?_ (1) QUIET
(2) NOISIER

If the semantic association between NOISY and NOISIER is stronger than that between NOISY and QUIET, the correct relational response, QUIET, may initially be less active because of spreading activation in memory than the distractor item, NOISIER. Thus, during reasoning, it may be necessary to inhibit information that is highly related but inconsistent with the current goal (Morrison et al., 2004). This function of working memory has also been ascribed to the prefrontal cortex (see Kane & Engle, 2003b and 2003a; Miller & Cohen, 2001; and Shimamura, 2000, for reviews). Many complex executive tasks associated with frontal lobe functioning (e.g., Tower of Hanoi or London, Analogical Reasoning, Wisconsin Card Sorting) have important inhibitory components [Miyake et al., 2000; Morrison et al., 2004; Viskontas et al. (in press), and Welsh, Satterlee-Cartmell, & Stine, 1999]. Shimamura (2000) suggested that the role of prefrontal cortex is to filter information dynamically – a process that requires the use of both activation and inhibition to keep information in working memory relevant to the current goal. Miller and Cohen (2001) argued that "the ability to select a weaker, task-relevant response (or source of information) in the face of competition from an otherwise stronger, but task-irrelevant one [is one of the most] fundamental aspects of cognitive control and goal-directed behavior" (Ref. 48, p. 170) and is a property of prefrontal cortex. More generally, many researchers believed that inhibition is an important mechanism for complex cognition (see Dagenbach & Carr, 1994; Dempster & Brainerd, 1995; and Kane & Engle, 2003a, for reviews) and that changes in inhibitory control may explain important developmental trends (Bjorklund & Harnishfeger, 1990; Hasher & Zacks, 1988; Diamond, 1990) and individual differences (Dempster, 1991; Kane & Engle, 2003a, 2003b) in complex cognition.

Conclusions and Future Directions

Working memory is a set of central processes that makes conscious thought possible. It flexibly provides for the maintenance and manipulation of information through both activation and inhibition of information retrieved from long-term memory and newly accessed from perception. Relations are critical to thought and the working-memory system therefore must provide for the flexible binding of information. It also allows the problem solver to maintain goals that allow successful navigation of single problems but also allows for integration of various parts of larger problems. Working-memory capacity is limited, and this is an important individual difference that affects and perhaps even determines analytic intelligence. We know that working memory is critically dependent on prefrontal cortex functioning, but likely involves the successful activation and inhibition of large networks in the brain. Maintainence of information in working memory tends to be somewhat modality specific; however, attentional resources typically ascribed to a central executive tend to be more modality independent and allow for the connection of information from different modalities.

The future of working memory research resides in better understanding how these processes operate in the brain. Computational approaches allow researchers to make precise statements about functional processes necessary for a working-memory system to perform thinking and can provide useful predictions for evaluation with cognitive neuroscience methods. Whereas much effort has been placed on understanding where working memory resides in the cortex, much less attention has focused on how it functions. Understanding the neural processes underlying working memory will almost certainly require tight integration of methods that provide good spatial localization (e.g., fMRI) and good temporal information (e.g., electrophysiology) in the brain.

Acknowledgments

Preparation of this chapter was supported by grants from the Office of Naval Research, Xunesis (*www.xunesis.org*), and National Service Research Award (MH-064244) from the National Institute of Mental Health. Appreciation is due to Marsha Lovett and Keith Holyoak for comments on an earlier draft of this chapter.

Notes

1. The term "working memory" was originally used to describe rat behavior during radial arm maze learning [see Olton (1979) for a description of this literature). It was also used by Newell and Simon (1972)] to describe the component of their computational models that holds productions – that is, operations that the model must perform (see also Lovett and Anderson, Chap. 17).
2. Fuster (1997) has long argued for this approach to working memory based on electrophysiological and cortical cooling data from nonhuman primates. In Fuster's model, neurons in prefrontal cortex drive neurons in more posterior brain regions that code for the information to be activated in long-term memory. This perspective is also consistent with Cowan's (1988) Embedded-Processes model. See also Chein, Ravizza, and Fiez, 2003.
3. Both ACT (Lovett and Anderson, Chap. 17) and LISA (Doumas and Hummel, Chap. 4) provide accounts of how working memory may be involved in higher-level cognition. These theories and computational implementations provide excellent starting points for investigating how the brain actually accomplishes high-level thought. An excellent edited volume by Miyake and Shah (1999) reviews many of the traditional computational perspectives on working memory.

References

Atkinson, R. C. & Shiffrin, R. M. (1968). Human memory: A proposed system and its control processes. In K. W. Spence, & J. T. Spence (Eds.), *The Psychology of Learning and Motivation Vol. 2* (pp. 89–195). New York: Academic Press.

Baddeley, A. D. (1966). The capacity for generating information by randomization. *Quarterly Journal of Experimental Psychology*, 18, 119–29.

Baddeley, A. D. (1986). *Working Memory*. Oxford, UK: Oxford University Press.

Baddeley, A. D. (1996). Exploring the central executive. *Quarterly Journal of Experimental Psychology, 49A*, 5–28.

Baddeley, A. D. (2000). The episodic buffer: A new component of working memory? *Trends in Cognitive Sciences, 4*, 417–423.

Baddeley, A., Emslie, H., Kolodny, J., & Duncan, J. (1998). Random generation and the executive control of working memory. *Quarterly Journal of Experimental Psychology, 51A*, 819–852.

Baddeley, A., & Hitch, G. J. (1974). Working memory. In G. H. Bower (Ed.), *The Psychology of Learning and Motivation Vol. 8* (pp. 47–89). New York: Academic Press.

Bjorklund, D. F., & Harnishfeger, K. K. (1990). The resources construct in cognitive development: Diverse sources of evidence and a theory of inefficient inhibition. *Developmental Review, 10*, 48–71.

Brooks, L. R. (1968). Spatial and verbal components of the act of recall. *Canadian Journal of Psychology, 22*, 349–368.

Carpenter, P. A., Just, M. A., & Shell, P. (1990). What one intelligence test measures: A theoretical account of the processing in the raven progressive matrices test. *Psychological Review, 97*, 404–431.

Cattell Culture Fair Test (Institute for Personality and Ability Testing, 1973). Champaign, IL.

Chein, J. M., Ravizza, S. M., & Fiez, J. A. (2003). Using neuroimaging to evaluate models of working memory and their implications for language processing. *Journal of Neurolinguistics, 16*, 315–339.

Christoff, K., & Gabrieli, J. D. E. (2000). The frontopolar cortex and human cognition: Evidence for a rostrocaudal hierarchical organization within the human prefrontal cortex. *Psychobiology, 28*, 168–186.

Christoff, K., Prabhakaran, V., Dorfan, J., Zhao, Z., Kroger, J. K., Holyoak, K. J. et al. (2001). Rostrolateral prefrontal cortex involvement in relational integration during reasoning. *Neuroimage, 14*, 1136–1149.

Conrad, R. (1964). Acoustic confusion in immediate memory. *British Journal of Psychology, 55*, 75–84.

Conway, A. R. A., & Engle, R. W. (1994). Working memory and retrieval: A resource-dependent inhibition model. *Journal of Experimental Psychology: General, 123*, 354–373.

Cowan, N. (1988). Evolving conceptions of memory storage, selective attention, and their mutual constraints within the human information processing system. *Psychological Bulletin, 104*, 163–191.

Cowan, N. (1995). *Attention and Memory: An Integrated Framework*. New York: Oxford University Press.

Cowan, N. (1999). An embedded-processes model of working memory. In Akira Miyake & Priti Shad (Eds.) *Models of Working Memory: Mechanisms of Active Maintenance and Executive Control* (pp. 62–101). Cambridge, UK: Cambridge University Press.

Dagenbach, D. E., & Carr, T. H. (1994). *Inhibitory Processes in Attention, Memory, and Language*. San Diego, CA: Academic Press.

Daneman, M., & Carpenter, P. A. (1980). Individual differences in working memory and reading. *Journal of Verbal Learning and Verbal Behavior, 19*, 450–466.

Dempster, F. N. (1991). Inhibitory processes: A neglected dimension of intelligence. *Intelligence, 15*, 157–173.

Dempster, F. N., & Brainerd, C. J. (Eds.). (1995). *Interference and inhibition in cognition*. San Diego, CA: Academic Press.

de Renzi, E., & Nichelli, P. (1975). Verbal and non-verbal short-term memory impairment following hemispheric damage. *Cortex, 11*, 341–354.

Diamond, A. (1990). The development and neural bases of memory functions as indexed by the A-not-B and delayed response tasks in human infants and infant monkeys. In Diamond A. (Ed.), *The Development and Neural Bases of Higher Cognitive Functions* (pp. 267–317). New York: New York Academy of Sciences.

Engle, R. W., Carullo, J. J., & Collins, K. W. (1991). Individual differences in working memory for comprehension and following directions. *Journal of Educational Research, 84*, 253–262.

Engle, R. W., Kane, M. J., & Tuholski, S. W. (1999). Working memory and controlled attention. In Akira Miyake & Priti Shad (Eds.), *Models of Working Memory: Mechanisms of Active Maintenance and Executive Control* (pp. 102–134). Cambridge, UK: Cambridge University Press.

Ericsson, K. A. & Kintsch, W. (1995). Long-term working memory. *Psychological Review, 102*, 211–245.

Fodor, J. A., & Pylyshyn, Z. W. (1988). Connectionism and cognitive architecture: A critical analysis. In S. Pinker & J. Mehler (Eds.), *Connections and Symbols* (pp. 3–71). Cambridge, MA: MIT Press.

Fuster, J. M. & Alexander, G. E. (1971). Neuron activity related to short-term memory. *Science, 173*, 652–654.

Fuster, J. M. (1997). *The Prefrontal Cortex: Anatomy, Physiology, and Neuropsychology of the Frontal Lobe*. (3rd ed.). Philadelphia: Lippincott-Raven.

Fuster, J. M., Bodner, M., & Kroger, J. K. (2000). Cross-modal and cross-temporal association in neurons of frontal cortex. *Nature, 405*, 347–351.

Gilhooly, K. J., Logie, R. H., Wetherick, N. E., & Wynn, V. (1993). Working memory and strategies in syllogistic-reasoning tasks. *Memory and Cognition, 21*, 115–124.

Gray, C. M., Koenig, P., Engel, A. K., & Singer, W. (1989). Oscillatory responses in cat visual cortex exhibit inter-columnar synchronization which reflects global stimulus properties. *Nature*, 338: 334–337.

Hasher, L., & Zacks, R. T. (1988). Working memory, comprehension, and aging: A review and a new view. In G. Bower (Ed.), *The Psychology of Learning and Motivation: Advances in Research and Theory* (Vol. 22, pp. 193–225). San Diego, CA: Academic Press.

Hebb, D. O. (1949). *The Organization of Behavior*. New York: Wiley.

Hummel, J. E., & Holyoak, K. J. (1997). Distributed representations of structure: A theory of analogical access and mapping. *Psychological Review, 104*, 427–466.

Hummel, J. E., & Holyoak, K. J. (2003). A symbolic-connectionist theory of relational inference and generalization. *Psychological Review, 110*, 220–264.

James, W. (1890). *Principles of Psychology*. New York: Henry Holt & Co.

Johnson-Laird, P. N. (1983). *Mental Models*. Cambridge, UK: Cambridge University Press.

Just, M. A., & Carpenter, P. A. (1992). A capacity theory of comprehension: Individual differences in working memory. *Psychological Review*, 99, 122–149.

Kane, M. J., & Engle, R. W. (2003a). The role of prefrontal cortex in working-memory capacity, executive attention, and general fluid intelligence: An individual-differences perspective. *Psychonomic Bulletin and Review*, 9, 637–671.

Kane, M. J., & Engle, R. W. (2003b). Working-memory capacity and the control of attention: The contributions of goal neglect, response competition, and task set to Stroop interference. *Journal of Experimental Psychology: General, 132*, 47–70.

Kirby, K. N., & Kosslyn, S. M. (1992). Thinking visually. In G. W. Humphreys (Ed.), *Understanding Vision: An Interdisciplinary Perspective*. (pp. 71–86). Oxford, UK: Blackwell.

Klauer, K. C., Stegmaier, R., & Meiser, T. (1997). Working memory involvement in propositional and spatial reasoning. *Thinking and Reasoning*, 3, 9–47.

Kyllonen, P. C., & Christal, R. E. (1990). Reasoning ability is (little more than) working- memory capacity?! *Intelligence, 14*, 389–433.

Logie, R. H. (1995). *Visuo-spatial Working Memory*. Hillsdale, NJ: Erlbaum.

Markman, A. B., & Gentner, D. (1993). Structural alignment during similarity comparisons. *Cognitive Psychology, 25*, 431–467.

Miller, E. K., & Cohen, J. D. (2001). An integrative theory of prefrontal cortex function. *Annual Review of Neuroscience, 24*, 167–202.

Miller, G. A. (1956). The magical number seven, plus or minus two: Some limits on our capacity for processing information. *Psychological Review, 63*, 81–97.

Milner, B. (1966). Amnesia following operation on the temporal lobes. In C. W. M. Whitty & O. L. Zangwill (Eds.), *Amnesia* (pp. 109–133). London: Butterworths.

Miyake, A., Friedman, N. P., Emerson, M. J., Witzki, A. H., & Howerter, A. (2000). The unity and diversity of executive functions and their contributions to complex 'frontal lobe' tasks: A latent variable analysis. *Cognitive Psychology, 41*, 49–100.

Miyake, A. & Shah, P. (1999). *Models of working memory: Mechanisms of active maintenance and executive control*. New York: Cambridge University Press.

Morrison, R. G., Holyoak, K. J., & Truong, B. (2001). Working memory modularity in analogical reasoning. *Proceedings of the TwentyThird Annual Conference of the Cognitive*

Science Society (pp. 663–668). Mahwah, NJ: Erlbaum.

Morrison, R. G., Krawczyk, D. C., Holyoak, K. J., Hummel, J. E., Chow, T. W., Miller, B. L., et al. (2004). A neurocomputational model of analogical reasoning and its breakdown in Frontotemporal Lobar Degeneration. *Journal of Cognitive Neuroscience, 16*, 1–11.

Müller, M. M., Bosch, J., Elbert, T., Kreiter, A., Sosa, M. V., Sosa, P. V., et al. (1996). Visually induced gamma-band responses in human electroencephalographic activity: A link to animal studies. *Experimental Brain Research, 112*, 96–102.

Murdock, B. B., Jr. (1962). The retention of individual items. *Journal of Experimental Psychology, 64*, 482–488.

Newman, S. D., Carpenter, P. A., Varma, S. & Just, M. A. (2003). Frontal and parietal participation in problem solving in the Tower of London: fMRI and computational modeling of planning and high-level perception. *Neuropsychologia, 41*, 2003.

Newell, A., & Simon, H. A. (1972). *Human problem solving*. Englewood Cliffs, NJ: Prentice-Hall.

Norman, D. A., & Shallice, T. (1980). Attention to action: Willed and automatic control of behaviour. *University of California, San Diego CHIP Report* 99.

Norman, D. A., & Shallice, T. (1986). Attention to action: Willed and automatic control of behavior. In G. E. Schwartz & D. Shapiro (Eds.), *Consciousness and Self-Regulation*. New York: Plenum Press.

Olton, D. S. (1979). Mazes, maps and memory. *American Psychologist, 34*, 583–596.

Prabhakaran, V., Narayanan, K., Zhao, Z., & Gabrieli, J. D. E. (2000). Integration of diverse information in working memory within the frontal lobe. *Nature Neuroscience*, 3 (1), 85–90.

Raven, J. C. (1938). *Progressive Matrices: A Perceptual Test of Intelligence, Individual Form.* London: Lewis.

Ruchkin, D. S., Grafman, J., Cameron, K., & Berndt, R. (2003). Working memory retention systems: A state of activated long-term memory. *Behavioral and Brain Sciences, 26*, 709–777.

Shallice, T., & Warrington, E. K. (1970). Independent functioning of verbal memory store: A neuropsychological study. *Quarterly Journal of Experimental Psychology, 22*, 261–273.

Shimamura, A. P. (2000). The role of the prefrontal cortex in dynamic filtering. *Psychobiology, 28*, 207–218.

Smith, E. E., & Jonides, J. (1997). Working memory: A view from neuroimaging. *Cognitive Psychology, 33*, 5–42.

Spearman, C. (1923). *The Nature of Intelligence and the Principles of Cognition*. London, UK: MacMillian.

Sternberg, R. J. (1977). *Intelligence, Information Processing, and Analogical Reasoning: The Componential Analysis of Human Abilities*. Hillsdale, NJ: Erlbaum.

Toms, M., Morris, N., & Ward, D. (1993). Working memory and conditional reasoning. *Quarterly Journal of Experimental Psychology: Human Experimental Psychology, 46*, 679–699.

Turner, M. L. & Engle, R. W. (1989). Is working memory capacity task dependent? *Journal of Memory and Language, 28*, 127–154.

Viskontas, I. V., Morrison, R. G., Holyoak, K. J., Hummel, J. E., & Knowlton, B. J. (in press). Relational integration, inhibition and analogical reasoning in older adults. *Psychology and Aging.*

Waltz, J. A., Knowlton, B. J., Holyoak, K. J., Boone, K. B., Mishkin, F. S., de Menezes Santos, M., et al. (1999). A system for relational reasoning in human prefrontal cortex. *Psychological Science, 10*, 119–125.

Waltz, J. A., Lau, A., Grewal, S. K., & Holyoak, K. J. (2000). The role of working memory in analogical mapping. *Memory and Cognition, 28*, 1205–1212.

Waugh, N. C. & Norman, D. A. (1965). Primary memory. *Psychological Review, 72*, 89–104.

Welsh, M. C., Satterlee-Cartmell, T., & Stine, M. (1999). Towers of hanoi and london: Contribution of working memory and inhibition to performance. *Brain and Cognition, 41*, 231–242.

CHAPTER 20

Cognitive Neuroscience of Deductive Reasoning

Vinod Goel

Introduction

It is 4 P.M. and I hear the school bus pull up to the house. Soon there is the taunting of a 13-year-old boy followed by the exaggerated screams of an 8-year-old girl. My kids are home from school. Exasperated, I say to my son, "If you want dinner tonight, you better stop tormenting your sister." Given he doesn't want to go to bed hungry, he needs to draw the correct logical inference. Sure enough, peace is eventually restored. We are not surprised by his actions. His behavior is not a mystery (if he wants his dinner). It is just an example of the reasoning brain at work.

Reasoning is the cognitive activity of drawing inferences from given information. All reasoning involves the claim that one or more propositions (the premises) provide some grounds for accepting another proposition (the conclusion). The aforementioned example involves a deductive inference (see Evans, Chap. 8). A key feature of deduction is that conclusions are contained within the premises and are logically independent of the content of the propositions. Deductive arguments can be evaluated for *validity*, a relationship between premises and conclusion involving the claim that the premises provide absolute grounds for accepting the conclusion (i.e., if the premises are true, then the conclusion *must* be true).

Psychological Theories of Deductive Reasoning

Two theories of deductive reasoning (mental logic and mental models) dominate the cognitive literature. They differ with respect to the competence knowledge upon which they draw, the mental representations they postulate, the mechanisms they invoke, and the neuroanatomical predictions they make. Mental logic theories (Braine, 1978; Henle, 1962; Rips, 1994) postulate that reasoners have an underlying competence knowledge of the *inferential role* of the closed-form, or logical terms, of the language (e.g., "all, some, none, and," etc.). The internal representation of arguments preserve the structural properties of the propositional strings in which the premises are stated. A mechanism of inference is applied to these representations to draw conclusions from premises. Essentially, the claim is that deductive reasoning is a rule-governed process defined over syntactic strings.

By contrast, mental model theory (Johnson-Laird, 1983; Johnson-Laird & Byrne, 1991; see Johnson-Laird, Chap. 9) postulates that reasoners have an underlying competence knowledge of the *meaning* of the closed-form, or logical terms, of the language (e.g., "all, some, none, and," etc.)[1] and use this knowledge to construct and search alternative scenarios.[2] The internal representations of arguments preserve the structural properties of the world (e.g., spatial relations) that the propositional strings are about, rather than the structural properties of the propositional strings themselves. The basic claim is that deductive reasoning is a process requiring spatial manipulation and search.

A third alternative is provided by dual mechanism theories. At a very crude level, dual mechanism theories make a distinction between formal, deliberate, rule-based processes and implicit, unschooled, automatic processes. However, dual mechanism theories come in various flavors that differ on the exact nature and properties of these two systems. Theories differentially emphasize explicit and implicit processes (Evans & Over, 1996), conscious and preconscious processes (Stanovich & West, 2000), formal and heuristic processes (Newell & Simon, 1972; also see Kahneman & Frederick, Chap. 12), and associative and rule-based processes (Goel, 1995; Sloman, 1996). The relationship among these proposals has yet to be clarified.

Relevance and Role of Neurophysiological Data

The reader will note that these theories of reasoning are strictly cognitive theories uninformed by knowledge of the brain. This is not an oversight. Until recently, the central domains of human reasoning and problem solving have been largely cognitive and computational enterprises, with little input from neuroscience. In fact, an argument advanced by cognitive scientists – based on the independence of computational processes and the mechanism in which they are realized (i.e., the brain) – has led many to question the relevance of neuropsychological data to cognitive theories.

The "independence of computational level" argument is a general argument against the necessity of appealing to neurophysiology to capture the generalizations necessary to explain human mental life. The general idea is that liberation from neurophysiology is one of the great virtues of the cognitive/computational revolution. It gives us the best of both worlds. It allows us to use an intentional vocabulary in our psychological theories, and if this vocabulary meets certain (computational) constraints, we get a guarantee (via the Church–Turing hypothesis) that some mechanism will be able to instantiate the postulated process.[3] Beyond this, we don't have to worry about the physical. The psychological vocabulary will map onto the computational vocabulary, and it is, after all, cognitive/computational structure, not physical structure, that captures the psychologically interesting generalizations.

The argument can be articulated as follows:

(P1) There are good reasons to believe that the laws of psychology need to be stated in intentional vocabulary (Fodor, 1975; Pylyshyn, 1984).

(P2) Computation (sort of) gives us such a vocabulary (Cummins, 1989; Fodor, 1975; Goel, 1991, 1995; Newell, 1980a; Pylyshyn, 1984).

(P3) Our theory construction is motivated by computational concepts and constrained by behavioral data.

(P4) Computational processes are specified independently of physics and can be realized in any physical system.

(C1) Therefore, there is no way, in principle, that neurological data can constrain our computational/cognitive theories.

A closer examination will reveal at least two flaws in the argument. First, premise P4 is not strictly true. Computational processes cannot be realized in any and every system (Giunti, 1997; Goel, 1991, 1992, 1995). If it were true, then computational explanations would be vacuous (Searle, 1990) and our problems much more serious. Now, it is true that computational processes can be realized in multiple systems, but that is far removed from universal realizability. The former gives computational theorizing much of its power; the latter drains computational explanations of much of their substantive content.

Second, the conclusion C1 depends on what computational/cognitive theories seek to explain. It is true that the organization of a computing mechanism (for example, whether a Turing Machine has one head or two) *is irrelevant* when we are interested in specifying what function is being computed and are concerned only with the mappings of inputs to outputs. This is typically a concern for mathematicians and logicians. If cognitive theories will only enumerate the functions being computed, then the argument would seem to hold. However, cognitive scientists (and often computer scientists) have little interest in computation under the aspect of functions. Our primary concern is with the procedures that compute the functions (Marr, 1982). Real-time computation is a function of architectural considerations and resource availability and allocation. And it is real-time computation – the study of the behavioral consequences of different resource allocation and organization models – that must be of interest to cognitive science (Newell, 1980a; Newell & Simon, 1976), because it is only with respect to specific architectures that algorithms can be specified and compared (to the extent that they can be). If we are interested in the computational architecture of the mind – and we clearly are (Newell, 1990; Pylyshyn, 1984) – then the constraints provided by the mechanism that realizes the computational process become very relevant. Presumably neuroscience is where we will learn about the architectural constraints imposed on the human cognitive/computational system. As such, it can hardly be ignored.

But this whole line of argument and counterargument makes an unwarranted assumption. It assumes that the only contribution neuroscience can make is in terms of specifying mechanisms. However, a glance through any neuroscience text (e.g., Kandel, Schwartz, & Jessell, 1995) shows that neuroscience is still far from making substantive contributions to our understanding of the computational architecture of the central nervous system. This is many years in the future.

There are, however, two more immediate contributions – localization and dissociation – that cognitive neuroscience can make to our understanding of cognitive processes, including reasoning.

(1) Localization of brain functions: It is now generally accepted that Franz Joseph Gall (Forster, 1815) was largely right and Karl Lashley (1929) largely wrong about the organization of the brain. There is a degree of modularity in its overall organization. Over the years, neuropsychologists and neuroscientists have accumulated some knowledge of this organization. For example, we know some brain regions are involved in processing language and other regions process visual spatial information. Finding selective involvement of these regions in complex cognitive tasks such as reasoning can help us differentiate between competing cognitive theories that make different claims about linguistic and visuospatial processes in the complex task (as do mental logic and mental model theories of reasoning).

(2) Dissociation of brain functions: Brain lesions result in selective impairment of behavior. Such selective impairments are called dissociations. A *single* dissociation occurs when we find a case of a lesion in region x resulting in a deficit of function

> *a* but not function *b*. If we find another case, in which a lesion in region *y* results in a deficit in function *b* but not in function *a*, then we have a *double* dissociation. Recurrent patterns of dissociation provide an indication of causal joints in the cognitive system invisible in uninterrupted normal behavioral measures (Shallice, 1988). Lesion studies identify systems *necessary* for the cognitive processes under consideration. Neuroimaging studies identify cortical regions *sufficient* for various cognitive processes.[4] Both are sources of knowledge regarding dissociation of cognitive functions.

The identification of dissociations is the more important of these two contributions and warrants further discussion. Cognitive theories are functional theories. Functional theories are notoriously underconstrained. That is, they are "black box" theories. We usually use them when we do not know the underlying causal structure. This devalues the currency of functional distinctions. But if we can show that our functional distinctions map onto causally individuated neurophysiological structures, then we can have much greater confidence in the functional individuation.

By way of an example, suppose that we individuate the following three functions on the basis of behavioral data: (f1) raise left arm, (f2) raise left foot, (f3) wiggle right ear. If these functions could be mapped onto three causally differentiated structures in a one-to-one fashion, we would be justified in claiming to have discovered three distinct functions. If, however, all three of our behaviorally individuated functions map onto one causally differentiated structure, in a many-to-one fashion, we would say that our functional individuation was too fine-grained and collapse the distinctions until we achieved a one-to-one mapping. That is, raising the left arm does not constitute a distinct function from raising the left foot and wiggling the right ear, but the conjunction of the three does constitute a single function. If we encountered the reverse situation, in which one behavioral function mapped onto several causally distinct structures, we would conclude that our individuation was too coarse-grained and refine it until we achieved a one-to-one mapping. One final possibility is a many-to-many mapping between our functional individuation and casually individuated physiological structures. Here we would have a total cross-classification and would have to assume that our functional individuations (f1, f2, f3) were simply wrong and start over again.[5]

The most famous example of a dissociation comes from the domain of language. In the 1860s, Paul Broca described a patient with a lesion to the left posterior inferior frontal lobe who had difficulties in the production of speech but was quite capable of speech comprehension. This is a case of a single dissociation. In the 1870s, Carl Wernicke described two patients with lesions to the posterior regions of the superior temporal gyrus who had difficulty in speech comprehension but were quite fluent in speech production. Jointly, the two observations indicate a double dissociation and tell us something important about the causal independence of language production and comprehension systems. If this characterization is accurate (and there are now some questions about its accuracy), it tells us that any cognitive theory of speech production and comprehension needs to postulate two causally distinct functions or mechanisms.

Neuroanatomical Predictions of Cognitive Theories of Reasoning

Given that the relevance of neuroanatomical data to cognitive theories has not been fully appreciated, it is not surprising that there are few explicit neuroanatomical predictions made by these theories. The one exception is mental model theory. Johnson-Laird (1994) has predicted that if mental model theory is correct, then reasoning must occur in the right hemisphere. The rationale here presumably is that mental model theory offers a spatial hypothesis, and anecdotal neuropsychological evidence suggests that spatial processing occurs in the right hemisphere. A more accurate prediction for mental model theory would be that the neural structures for visuospatial processing contribute the basic representational building blocks used for logical reasoning (i.e., the visuospatial system is necessary and sufficient for reasoning). I will use the latter prediction.

By contrast, mental logic theory is a linguistic hypothesis (Rips, 1994) and needs to predict that the neuroanatomical mechanisms of language (syntactic) processing underwrite human reasoning processes [i.e., that the language (syntactic) system is both necessary and sufficient for deductive reasoning]. Both mental model and mental logic theories make explicit localization predictions (i.e., whether linguistic or visuospatial systems are involved) and implicit dissociation predictions – specifically, that the one system is necessary and sufficient for reasoning.

Dual mechanism theory needs to predict the involvement of two different brain systems in human reasoning, corresponding to and the formal, deliberate, rule-based system and the implicit, unschooled, automatic system. But it is difficult to make a prediction about localization without further specification of the nature of the two systems. Nonetheless, dual mechanism theory makes a substantive prediction about a dissociation in the neural mechanisms underlying the two different forms of reasoning.

Functional Anatomy of Reasoning

My colleagues and I have been carrying out a series of studies to investigate the neural basis of logical reasoning (Goel et al., 2000; Goel & Dolan, 2000, 2001, 2003; Goel et al., 1995, 1997, 1998). Our initial goal was to address the hypotheses made by the cognitive theories of reasoning and, in particular, differentiate between mental logic and mental model theories. We have made some progress along these lines (although with surprising results) and have also provided insights into the role of prefrontal cortex (PFC) in logical reasoning.

BASIC PARADIGM AND STRATEGY

We have been presenting subjects with syllogisms, each consisting of two premises and a conclusion (e.g., All dogs are pets; All poodles are dogs; All poodles are pets), while they undergo positron emission tomography or functional magnetic resonance imaging (fMRI) brain scans and asking them to exhibit knowledge of what logically follows from the premises by confirming or denying the given conclusion. Our strategy has been to (largely) stay with one type of argument (syllogisms), manipulate content (holding the logically relevant information constant), and see how the brain reacts. The specific content manipulations are described in the studies discussed subsequently.

Neuroimaging studies typically require a rest or baseline condition against which to compare the active condition. For our baseline tasks (in the fMRI studies) we used trials in which the first two sentences were related but the third sentence was unrelated (e.g., All dogs are pets; All poodles are dogs; All fish are scaly). Stimuli were presented one sentence at a time with each sentence staying up until the end of the trial. Trials appeared randomly in an event-related design (Figure 20.1). The task in all trials was the same. Subjects were required to determine whether the conclusion followed logically from the premises (i.e., whether the argument was valid). In baseline trials in which the first two sentences were related, subjects would begin to construct a representation of the problem, but when the third, unrelated, sentence appeared they would immediately disengage the task and respond "no." In reasoning condition trials in which the three sentences constituted an argument, subjects would continue with the reasoning component of the task after the presentation of the third sentence. The difference between completing the reasoning task and disengaging after the presentation of the third sentence isolates the reasoning components of interest. The data were modeled after the presentation of the third sentence. The presentation of the first two sentences and subjects' motor responses were modeled out as

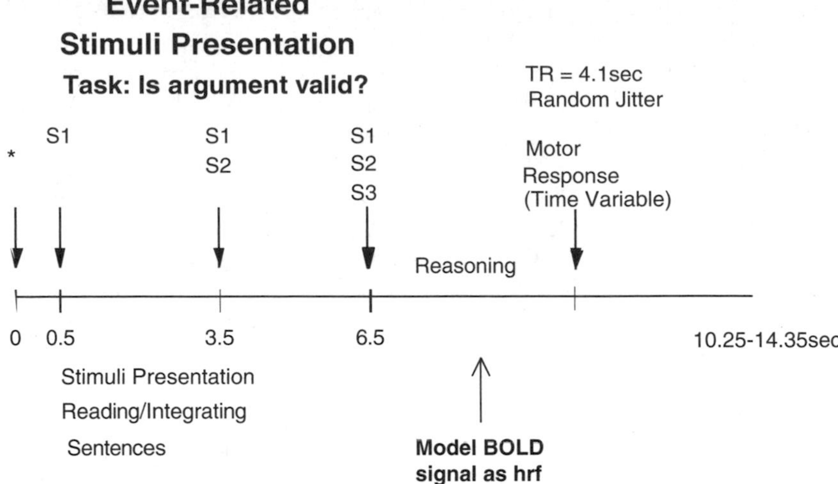

Figure 20.1. *Stimuli presentation:* Stimuli from all conditions were presented randomly in an event-related design. An "*" indicated the start of a trial at 0 milliseconds. The sentences appeared on the screen one at a time, with the first sentence appearing at 500 milliseconds, the second at 3500 milliseconds, and the last sentence at 6500 milliseconds. The duration of trials varied from 10.25 to 14.35 seconds, leaving subjects 3.75 to 7.85 seconds to respond.

events of no interest. This basic design was used in each of the imaging studies discussed subsequently.

We chose to use syllogisms (which test knowledge of quantification and negation) for technical reasons. Imaging studies require multiple presentations of stimuli to register a reliable neural signal. Syllogisms come in 64 different forms and therefore allow for multiple trial presentations with minimal or no repetition of form.

We chose to manipulate content because, logically, the content of an argument is irrelevant to the determination of its validity. For example, the argument

All men are mortal
Socrates is a man
Socrates is mortal

is valid by virtue of the fact it has the following form:

All A are B
C is A
C is B

It remains valid irrespective of whether it is about Socrates or elephants. Validity is a function of the logical structure of the argument as opposed to the content of the sentences.

However, it is well known that the semantic contents of arguments affect people's validity judgments. In a classic study, Wilkins (1928) showed that subjects performed better on syllogisms containing sentences with familiar semantic content (e.g., "All apples are red") than on syllogisms lacking semantic content (e.g., "All A are B"). When the semantic content of syllogisms was incongruent with beliefs (e.g., "All apples are poisonous"), performance suffered even more. These results have been explored and extended in more recent literature (Cherubini et al., 1998; Evans, Barston, & Pollard, 1983; Oakhill & Garnham, 1993; Oakhill, Johnson-Laird, & Garnham, 1989). The effect is very robust and has challenged all theories of reasoning.

We discuss our key findings subsequently. They include: (i) a dissociation between a frontal-temporal system and a parietal system as a function of the familiarity of the content of the reasoning material; (ii) asymmetrical involvement of right and left PFC, with the left PFC being necessary and sometimes sufficient, and the right PFC being

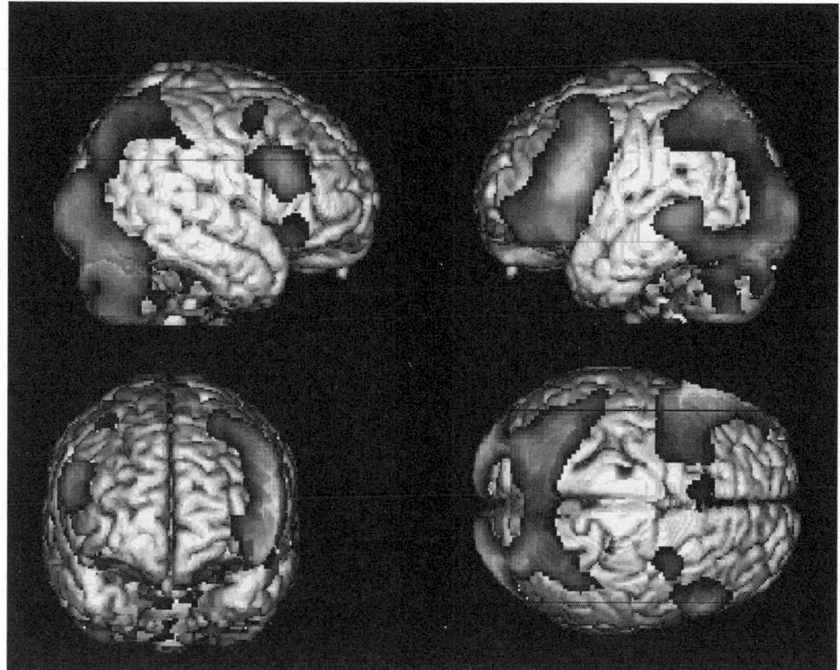

Figure 20.2. Main effect of reasoning [(content reasoning + no content reasoning) – (content preparation + no content preparation)] revealed activation of bilateral cerebellum (R > L), bilateral fusiform gyrus, left superior parietal lobe, left middle temporal gyrus, bilateral inferior frontal gyrus, bilateral basal ganglia nuclei (centered around the accumbens, caudate nucleus, and putamen), and brain stem. Reprinted with permission from Goel (2003).

sometimes necessary (in unfamiliar, incoherent, conflicting situations) but not sufficient for logical reasoning; and (iii) clarifying roles of right PFC and ventral medial PFC (VMPFC) in belief–logic conflict resolution.

BASIC FINDINGS

Dissociable neural networks. In Goel et al. (2000), we scanned eleven right-handed, normal subjects using event-related fMRI to measure task-related neural activity while they engaged in syllogistic reasoning. The study was designed to manipulate the presence of content in logical reasoning. Half the arguments contained content sentences, such as

All dogs are pets
All poodles are dogs
All poodles are pets

and the other half contained "no content" versions of these sentences, such as

All P are B
All C are P
All C are B

The logically relevant information in both conditions was identical. Half the arguments were valid, and the other half were invalid.

If mental model theory is correct, all reasoning trials should activate a visuospatial system (perhaps parietal cortex). If mental logic theory is correct, we would expect activation of the language system (left frontal and temporal lobe regions). Dual mechanism theory predicts engagement of two distinct (but unspecified) neural systems, as determined by whether subjects respond in a schooled, formal manner or an intuitive, implicit manner. What we actually found was that the main effect of reasoning implicated large areas of the brain (Figure 20.2), including regions predicted by both mental model and mental logic theories.

However, closer examination revealed this to be a composite activation consisting of two dissociable neural systems. The content reasoning trials compared with no-content reasoning trials revealed activation in left middle and superior temporal lobe (BA 21/22), left temporal pole (BA 21/38), and left inferior frontal lobe (BA 47) (Figure 20.3a). This is essentially a language and memory system. A similar network was activated in previous PET studies of deductive reasoning using contentful sentences (Goel et al., 1997, 1998).

The reverse comparison of no-content reasoning trials versus content reasoning trials resulted in activation of bilateral occipital (BA 19), bilateral superior and inferior parietal lobes (BA 7), and bilateral dorsal (BA 6) and inferior (BA 44) frontal lobes (Figure 20.3b). This pattern of activation is known to be involved in the internal representation and manipulation of spatial information (Jonides et al., 1993; Kosslyn et al., 1989) and is very similar to that reported for transitive inference involving geometrical shapes (Acuna et al., 2002) and certain types of mathematical reasoning involving approximation of numerical quantities (Dehaene et al., 1999).

It is possible to argue that the patterns of activation revealed by the direct comparison of content and no-content conditions are just a function of the presence or absence of content words, rather than being indicative of different reasoning mechanisms. To exclude this possibility, we examined the Content (content, no content) by Task (reasoning, baseline) interaction. The modulation of reasoning, by the addition of content ([content reasoning – content baseline] – [no-content reasoning – no-content baseline]) revealed activation in Wernicke's area. The reverse interaction, which examined the effect of the absence of semantic content ([no-content reasoning – no-content baseline] – [content reasoning – content baseline]), activated left parietal cortex. This interaction analysis eliminates the aforementioned possibility and confirms the involvement of these two systems in the reasoning process.

Contrary to mental logic theories that predict the language (syntactic) system is necessary and sufficient for deductive reasoning and mental model theories that predict the visuospatial system is necessary and sufficient for logical reasoning, Goel et al. (2000) found evidence for the engagement of both systems. The presence of semantic content engages the language and long-term memory systems in the reasoning process. The absence of semantic content engages the visuospatial system in the logically identical reasoning task. Before discussing the implications of these results for cognitive theories, let us consider some additional issues and data.

The Goel et al. (2000) study raises several interesting questions, one of which has to do with the involvement of a parietal visual-spatial system in the no-content or abstract syllogism condition. A second question has to do with the exact property of the stimuli that leads to the modulation of neural activity between frontal-temporal and parietal systems. Pursuing the first question led to a clarification of the second question.

The first question is whether argument forms involving three-term spatial relations such as:

The apples are in the barrel
The barrel is in the barn
The apples are in the barn

and

A are in B
B is in C
A are in C

are sufficient to engage the parietal system irrespective of the presence of content? One rationale for thinking this might be the case is subjects' reported phenomenological experience of using a visuospatial strategy during these tasks. Secondly, neuroimaging studies have also shown the involvement of the parietal system in the encoding of relational spatial information (Laeng, 1994; Mellet et al., 1996). To address this question, we carried out another fMRI study, this

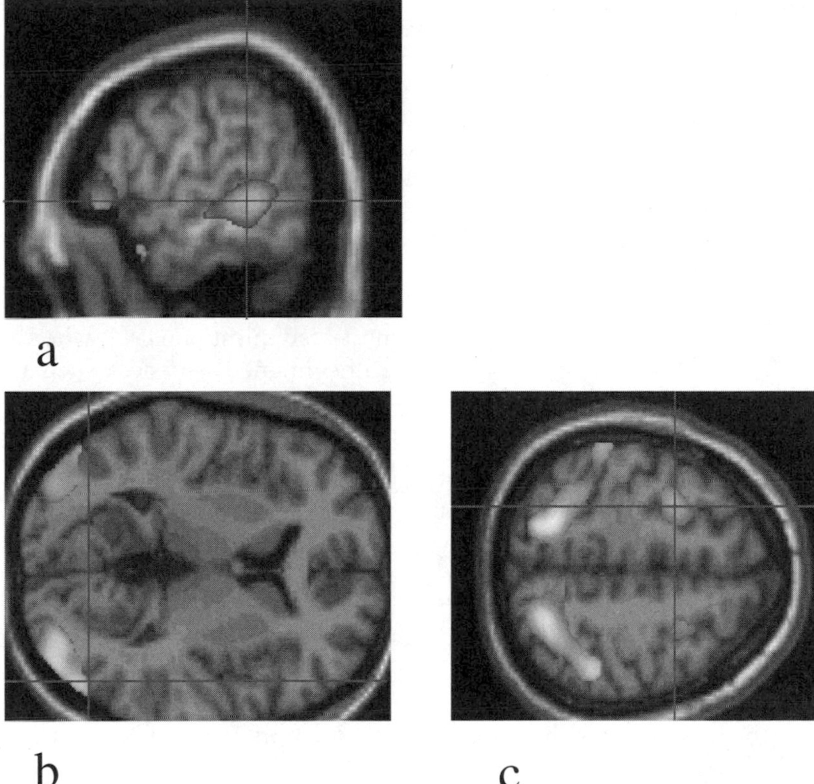

Figure 20.3. (a) The content reasoning–no-content reasoning comparison revealed activation of the left middle / superior temporal lobe (BA 21/22), the left inferior frontal lobe (BA 47), and bilateral (BA 17) and lingual gyri (BA 18). (b) The no-content reasoning–content reasoning comparison revealed activation of (a) bilateral occipital (BA 18, 19) and (c) bilateral superior and inferior parietal lobes (BA 7, 40), bilateral precentral gyrus (BA 6), and bilateral middle frontal gyrus (BA 6). Reprinted from Goel et al. (2000) with permission from Elsevier.

time using three-term relational arguments like those mentioned previously (Goel & Dolan, 2001).

Goel and Dolan (2001) found that reasoning about abstract and concrete three-term relations, as in the aforementioned examples, recruited a bilateral parietal-occipital system with greater involvement of parietal and occipital lobes in the abstract condition compared with the concrete condition. There was an absence of the two dissociable networks for concrete and abstract reasoning reported in the first study. In particular, the temporal lobe (BA 21/22) activation evident in concrete syllogistic reasoning in the first study was conspicuously absent in this study. One explanation for the lack of temporal lobe (BA 21/22) activation in Goel and Dolan (2001) might be the nature of the content used in the two studies. The concrete sentences in Goel et al. (2000) were of the form "All apples are poisonous" whereas the concrete sentences in Goel & Dolan (2001) were of the form "John is to the right of Mary." The former sentence types predicate known properties to known objects. We have beliefs about whether "all apples are poisonous." By contrast, the latter sentence types do not allow for such beliefs.[6] This leaves open the interesting possibility that involvement of BA 21/22 in reasoning may be specific to content processing involving belief networks rather than just concrete contents.

This hypothesis was tested in Goel and Dolan (2003) in which subjects were presented with arguments, such as

No reptiles are hairy
Some elephants are hairy
No elephants are reptiles

containing sentences that subjects could be expected to have beliefs about, and belief-neutral arguments, such as

No codes are highly complex
Some quipu are highly complex
No quipu are codes

containing sentences that subjects may not have beliefs about (because they may not know the meaning of one or more key terms). The referential terms in the two conditions were counterbalanced for abstract and concrete categories.

The results of this study replicated and clarified the results of Goel et al. (2000). Modulation of the reasoning task by absence of belief [(belief-neutral reasoning – belief-neutral baseline) – (belief-laden reasoning – belief-laden baseline)] revealed activation in the left superior parietal lobe (BA 7) unique to the belief-neutral condition. The reverse modulation [(belief-laden reasoning – belief-laden baseline) – (belief-neutral reasoning – belief-neutral baseline)] revealed activation of anterior left middle temporal gyrus (BA 21) unique to the belief-bias condition. These results confirm that a critical (sufficient) factor in the modulation of activity between these two neural systems is the presence of familiar or belief-laden content in the reasoning processes.

GENERALIZATION OF DISSOCIATION TO TRANSITIVE REASONING

We have demonstrated dual pathways for reasoning about categorical syllogisms. The question arises whether the results generalize to other forms of logical reasoning, particularly three-term spatial relations, where one might think the visuospatial system to be sufficient. To answer this question, Goel, Makale, and Grafman (2004) studied 14 volunteers using event-related fMRI, as they reasoned about landmarks in familiar and unfamiliar environments.

Half the arguments contained sentences, such as

Paris is south of London
London is south of Edinburgh
Paris is south of Edinburgh

describing environments with which subjects would be familiar (as confirmed by a post-scan questionnaire), whereas the other half contained sentences, such as

The AI lab is south of the Roth Centre
Roth Centre is south of Cedar Hall
AI lab is south of Cedar Hall

that subjects could not be familiar with because they describe a fictional, unknown environment.

Our main finding was an interaction between Task (reasoning and baseline) and Spatial Content (familiar and unfamiliar). Modulation of reasoning regarding unfamiliar landmarks resulted in bilateral activation of superior and inferior parietal lobule (BA 7, 40), dorsal superior frontal cortex (BA 6), and right superior and middle frontal gyri (BA 8) regions frequently implicated in visuospatial processing. By contrast, modulation of the reasoning task involving familiar landmarks engaged right inferior and orbital frontal gyrus (BA 11/47), bilateral occipital (BA 18, 19), and temporal lobes. The temporal lobe activation included right inferior temporal gyrus (BA 37), posterior hippocampus, and parahippocampal gyrus regions implicated in spatial memory and navigation tasks. These results provide support for the generalization of our dual mechanism account of transitive reasoning and highlight the importance of the hippocampal system in *reasoning* about landmarks in familiar spatial environments.

EVIDENCE FOR DISSOCIATION FROM PATIENT DATA

If we are correct that reasoning involving familiar situations engages a frontal-temporal lobe system and formally identical reasoning tasks involving unfamiliar situations recruit a frontal-parietal visuospatial network – with greater frontal lobe involvement in the former than the latter – then frontal lobe lesion patients should be more impaired on reasoning about familiar situations than on unfamiliar situations. To test this hypothesis, Goel et al. (2004) administered the Wason 4-Card Selection Task (Wason, 1966) to 19 frontal lobe patients and 19 age- and education-matched normal controls.

Wason 4-Card Selection Task (WST) (Wason, 1966) is the most widely used task to explore the role of content in reasoning. Subjects are shown four cards. They can see what is printed on one side of each card, but not the other side. They are given a rule of the form: if *p* then *q* (e.g., "If a card has a vowel on one side, it must have an even number on the other side.") and asked which cards they must turn over in order to verify the rule. The visible values on the cards correspond to the *p*, *not-p*, *q*, and *not-q* cases of the rule. According to standard propositional logic, the correct choices are *p* (to verify *q* is on the other side) and *not-q* (to verify *p* is not on the other side). Given an arbitrary rule like the above, typically fewer than 25% of normal subjects will turn over both the *p* and the *not-q* cards. However, the introduction of familiar, meaningful content in a rule (e.g., "If anyone is drinking beer, then that person must be over 21 years old.") greatly facilitates performance (Cheng & Holyoak, 1985; Cosmides, 1989; Cox & Griggs, 1982; Gigerenzer & Hug, 1992; Griggs & Cox, 1982; Wason & Shapiro, 1971).

Specifically, we manipulated the social knowledge involved in the task in the form of "permission schemas" (Cheng & Holyoak, 1985). Subjects performed the task with an arbitrary rule condition ("If a card has an A on one side, then it must have a 4 on the other side."), an abstract permission condition ("If one is to take action A, then one must first satisfy precondition P."), and a concrete permission condition ("If a person is to drink alcohol, he or she must be at least 21.").

The principal findings were that, in the purely logical (arbitrary rule) condition, frontal lobe patients performed just as well (or just as poorly) as normal controls. However, patient performance did not improve with the introduction of social knowledge in the form of abstract or concrete permission schemas as did normal control performance. Furthermore, there was no significant correlation between volume loss, IQ scores, memory scores, or years of education and performance in the abstract or concrete permission schema conditions. The failure of patients to benefit from social knowledge therefore cannot be explained in terms of volume loss, IQ scores, memory scores, or years of education.

Consistent with the neuroimaging data, our interpretation is that the arbitrary rule condition of the WST involves greater activation of the parietal lobe system, whereas the permission schema trials result in greater engagement of a frontal-temporal lobe system. The normal controls have both mechanisms intact and can take advantage of social knowledge cues to facilitate the reasoning process. The patients' parietal system is intact, and so their performance on the arbitrary rule trial is the same as that of normal controls. Their frontal lobe system is disrupted, preventing them from taking advantage of social knowledge cues in the permission schema trials.[7]

HEMISPHERIC ASYMMETRY

Our imaging studies have also revealed an asymmetry in frontal lobe involvement in logical reasoning. Reasoning about belief-laden material (e.g., All dogs are pets; All poodles are dogs; All poodles are pets) activates left prefrontal cortex (Figure 20.4a), whereas reasoning about belief-neutral material (e.g., All A are B; All C are A; All C are B) activates bilateral prefrontal cortex (Figure 20.4b) (Goel et al., 2000; Goel & Dolan, 2003). This asymmetry shows up consistently in patient data.

Caramazza et al. (1976) administered two-term problems such as the following: "Mike is taller than George. Who is taller?" to brain-damaged patients. They reported that left hemisphere lesion patients were impaired in all forms of the problem, but right hemisphere lesion patients were impaired only when the form of the question

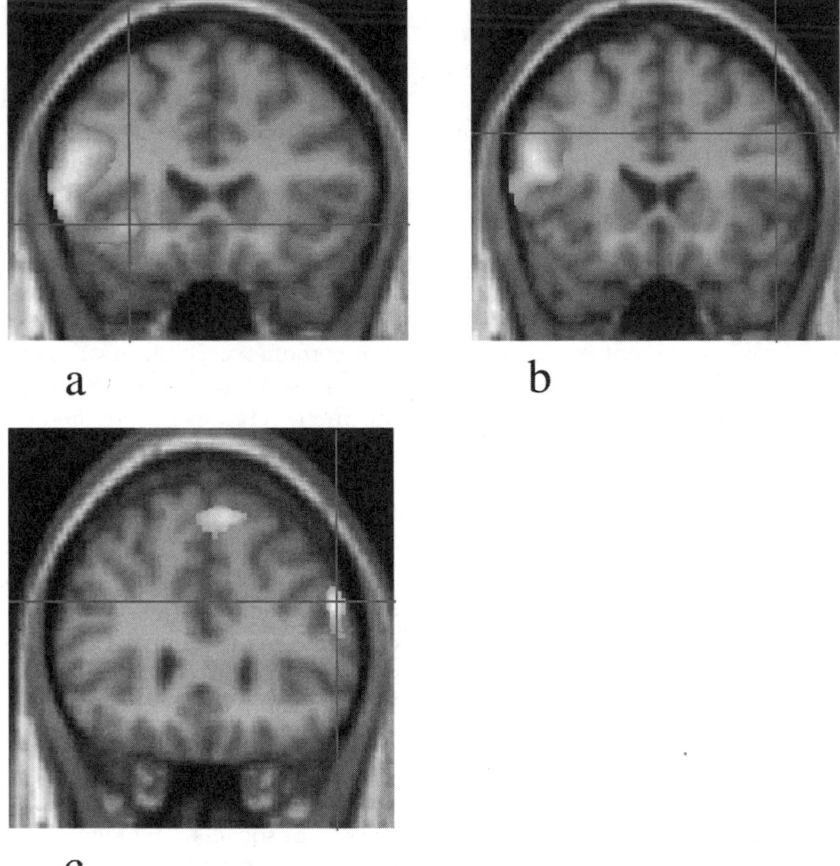

Figure 20.4. (a) Reasoning involving familiar conceptual content activates left inferior prefrontal cortex. (b) Reasoning involving unfamiliar content activates bilateral prefrontal cortex. (c) Right prefrontal cortex mediates belief–logic conflict detection and/or resolution. Reprinted from Goel et al. (2000) with permission from Elsevier.

was incongruent with the premise (e.g., Who is shorter?). Read (1981) tested temporal lobectomy patients on three-term relational problems with semantic content (e.g., George is taller than Mary; Mary is taller than Carol; Who is tallest?). Subjects were told that using a mental imagery strategy would help them to solve these problems. He reported that left temporal lobectomy patient performance was more impaired than right temporal lobectomy patient performance. In a more recent study using matched verbal and spatial reasoning tasks, Langdon and Warrington (2000) found that only left hemisphere lesion patients failed the verbal section, and both left and right hemisphere lesion patients failed the spatial sections. They concluded by emphasizing the critical role of the left hemisphere in both verbal and spatial logical reasoning.

In the WST patient study discussed previously (Goel et al., 2004), not only was it the case that frontal lobe patients failed to benefit from the introduction of familiar content into the task, but the result was driven by the poor performance of left hemisphere lesion patients. There was no difference in performance between right hemisphere lesion patients and normal controls but only between left hemisphere lesion patients and controls. These data show that the left hemisphere

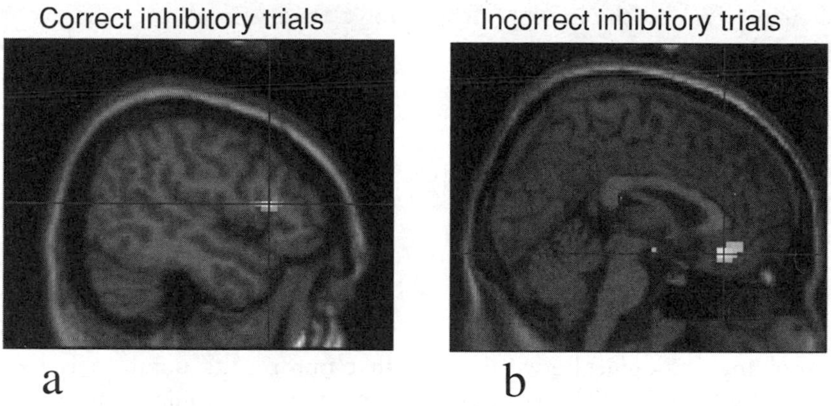

Figure 20.5. (a) Correct inhibitory trials activate right prefrontal cortex. (b) Incorrect inhibitory trials activate VMPFC cortex. Reprinted from Goel & Dolan (2003) with permission from Elsevier.

is necessary and often sufficient for reasoning whereas the right hemisphere is sometimes necessary but not sufficient. [This is of course contrary to the Johnson-Laird (1994) prediction for mental model theory, but, as noted previously, we chose to modify this prediction to make it consistent with basic neuropsychological knowledge.]

DEALING WITH BELIEF–LOGIC CONFLICTS

Although from a strictly logical point of view, deduction is a closed system, we have already mentioned that beliefs about the conclusion of an argument influence people's validity judgments (Wilkins, 1928). When arguments have familiar content, the truth value (or believability) of a given conclusion will be consistent or inconsistent with the logical judgment. Subjects perform better on syllogistic reasoning tasks when the truth value of a conclusion (true or false) coincides with the logical relationship between premises and conclusion (valid or invalid) (Evans, Barston, & Pollard, 1983). Such trials are facilitatory to the logical task and consist of valid arguments with believable conclusions (e.g., Some children are not Canadians; All children are people; Some people are not Canadians) and invalid arguments with unbelievable conclusions (e.g., Some violinists are not mutes; No opera singers are violinists; Some opera singers are mutes). When the logical conclusion is inconsistent with subjects' beliefs about the world, the beliefs are inhibitory to the logical task and decrease accuracy (Evans, Barston, & Pollard, 1983). Inhibitory belief trials consist of valid arguments with unbelievable conclusions (e.g., No harmful substances are natural; All poisons are natural; No poisons are harmful) and invalid arguments with believable conclusions (e.g., All calculators are machines; All computers are calculators; Some machines are not computers). Performance on arguments that are belief-neutral usually falls between these two extremes (Evans, Handley, & Harper, 2001).

Goel et al. (2000) noted that when logical arguments result in a belief-logic conflict, the nature of the reasoning process is changed by the recruitment of the right lateral prefrontal cortex (Figure 20.4c). Goel and Dolan (2003) further noted that, within the inhibitory belief trials, a comparison of correct items with incorrect items (correct inhibitory belief trials – incorrect inhibitory belief trials) revealed activation of right inferior prefrontal cortex (Figure 20.5a). The reverse comparison of incorrect response trials with correct response trials (incorrect inhibitory belief trials – correct inhibitory belief trials) revealed activation of VMPFC (Figure 20.5b).

Within the inhibitory belief trials, the prepotent response is associated with belief-bias. Correct responses (in inhibitory trials) indicate that subjects detected the conflict between their beliefs and the logical inference, inhibited the prepotent response associated with the belief bias, and engaged the reasoning mechanism. Incorrect responses in such trials indicate that subjects failed to detect the conflict between their beliefs and the logical inference and/or inhibit the prepotent response associated with the belief bias. Their response is biased by their beliefs. The involvement of right prefrontal cortex in correct response trials is critical in detecting and/or resolving the conflict between belief and logic. Such a role of the right lateral prefrontal cortex was also noted in Goel et al. (2000) and in a study of maintenance of an intention in the face of conflict between action and sensory feedback (Fink et al., 1999). A similar phenomenon has been noted in the Caramazza et al. (1976) study mentioned previously in which right hemisphere lesion patients were impaired only when there was an incongruency in the form of the question and the premises. By contrast, the activation of VMPFC in incorrect trials highlights its role in nonlogical, belief-based responses.

Conclusions and Future Directions

Consequences for Cognitive Theories of Reasoning

We now briefly address the question of how these data map onto the cognitive theories of reasoning with which we began our discussion. This is a complex question because the data do not fit neatly with any of the three theories. First and foremost, we show a dissociation in mechanisms involved in belief-neutral and belief-laden reasoning. The two systems we have identified are roughly the language system and the visuospatial system, which is what mental logic theory and mental model theory respectively predict. However, neither theory anticipates this dissociation. Each theory predicts that the system it postulates is necessary and sufficient for reasoning. This implies that the neuroanatomical data cross-classify these cognitive theories. A further complication is that mental logic theory implicates the syntactic component of language in logical reasoning. Our studies activate both the syntactic and semantic systems and components of long-term memory.

Our results do seem compatible with some form of dual mechanism theory, which explicitly predicts a dissociation. However, as noted, this theory comes in various flavors and some advocates may not be keen to accept our conclusions. The distinction that our results point to is between reasoning with familiar, conceptually coherent material versus unfamiliar, nonconceptual, or incoherent material. The former engages a left frontal-temporal system (language and long-term memory) whereas the latter engages a bilateral parietal (visuospatial) system. Given the primacy of belief bias over effortful thinking (Sloman, 1996), we believe that the frontal-temporal system is more "basic" and effortlessly engaged. It has temporal priority. By contrast, the parietal system is effortfully engaged when the frontal-temporal route is blocked because of a lack of familiar content, or when a conflict is detected between the logical response and belief bias.

This is very consistent with the dual mechanism account developed by Newell & Simon (1972) for the domain of problem solving. On this formulation, our frontal-temporal system corresponds to the "heuristic" system whereas the parietal system corresponds to the "universal" system. Reasoning about familiar situations automatically utilizes situation-specific heuristics that are based on background knowledge and experience. When no such heuristics are available (as in reasoning about unfamiliar situations), universal (formal) methods must be used to solve the problem. In the case of syllogistic reasoning, this may well involve a visuospatial system.

Our results go beyond addressing cognitive theories of reasoning and provide new insight into the role of the prefrontal cortex in human reasoning. In particular, the involvement of the prefrontal cortex in logical reasoning is selective and asymmetric. Its engagement is greater in reasoning about familiar, content-rich situations than unfamiliar, content-sparse situations. The left prefrontal cortex is necessary and often sufficient for reasoning. The right prefrontal cortex is sometimes necessary but not sufficient for reasoning. It is engaged in the absence of conceptual content and in the face of conflicting or conceptually incoherent content (as in the belief–logic conflicts discussed previously). Finally, the VMPFC is engaged by nonlogical, belief-biased responses.

Future Directions

Although some progress has been made over the past eight years, the cognitive neuroscience of reasoning is in its infancy. The next decade should be an exciting time of rapid development. There are a number of issues that we see as particularly compelling for further investigation. The first is how well the results can be generalized. Will the results regarding syllogisms, which are quite difficult, generalize to basic low-level inferences such as modus ponens and modus tollens? Second, all the imaging studies to date have utilized a paradigm involving the *recognition* of a given conclusion as valid or invalid. It remains to be seen whether the *generation* of a conclusion would involve the same mechanisms. Third, given the involvement of visuospatial processing systems in much of reasoning and the postulated differences between males and females in processing spatial information (Jones, Braithwaite, & Healy, 2003), one might expect neural-level differences in reasoning between the genders. Fourth, the issue of task difficulty has not been explored. As reasoning trials become more difficult, are additional neural resources recruited, or are the same structures activated more intensely? Fifth, what is the effect of learning on the neural mechanisms underlying reasoning? Sixth, most imaging studies to date have focused on deduction. Although deduction is interesting, much of human reasoning actually involves induction. The relationship between the two at the neural level is still an open question.

Finally, reasoning does not occur in a vacuum. Returning to the example of my children, with which I began, if I say to my son, "If you want dinner tonight, you better stop tormenting your sister" in a calm, unconcerned voice, it usually has an effect. However, if I state the same proposition in an angry, threatening voice, the impact is much more complete and immediate. Given that the logic of the inference is identical in the two cases, the emotions introduced into the situation through the modulation of my voice are clearly contributing to the resulting behavior. In fact, emotions can be introduced into the reasoning process in at least three ways: (i) in the content or substance of the reasoning material; (ii) in the presentation of the content of the reasoning material (as in voice intonation); and (iii) in the preexisting mood of the reasoning agent. We are currently channeling much of our research efforts to understanding the neural basis of the interaction between emotions and rational thought.

Acknowledgments

This research has been supported by a McDonnell-Pew Program in Cognitive Neuroscience Award, National Science and Engineering Research Council of Canada (NSERC) & Canadian Institutes of Health Research (CIHR) grants, and a Premier's Research Excellence Award to Vinod Goel.

Notes

1. Whether there is any substantive difference between "knowing the inferential role" and "knowing the meaning" of the closed-form terms is a moot point, debated in the literature.
2. See Newell (1980b) for a discussion of the relationship between search and inference.
3. The Church–Turing hypothesis makes the conjecture that all computable functions belong to the class of functions computable by a Turing Machine. So if we constrain the class of functions called for by our psychological theories to the class of computable functions, then there

will be some Turing Machine that can compute the function.

4. These are, of course, logical claims about neuroimaging and lesion studies. As in all empirical work, there are a number of complicating factors, including the relationship between statistical significance (or insignificance) and reality of an observed effect.
5. Again, I am making a logical point, independent of the usual complexities of mapping behavior onto causal mechanisms.
6. It is possible to generate relational sentences one can have beliefs about; for example, "London is north of Rome" or "Granite is harder than diamonds."
7. See also Bachman and Cannon, Chap. 21, for further discussion of disrupted thinking in patient populations.

References

Acuna, B. D., Eliassen, J. C., Donoghue, J. P., & Sanes, J. N. (2002). Frontal and parietal lobe activation during transitive inference in humans. *Cerebral Cortex, 12(12)*, 1312–1321.

Braine, M. D. S. (1978). On the relation between the natural logic of reasoning and standard logic. *Psychological Review, 85(1)*, 1–21.

Caramazza, A., Gordon, J., Zurif, E. B., & DeLuca, D. (1976). Right-hemispheric damage and verbal problem solving behavior. *Brain and Language, 3(1)*, 41–46.

Cheng, P. W., & Holyoak, K. J. (1985). Pragmatic reasoning schemas. *Cognitive Psychology, 17(4)*, 391–416.

Cherubini, P., Garnham, A., Oakhill, J., & Morley, E. (1998). Can any ostrich fly?: Some new data on belief bias in syllogistic reasoning. *Cognition, 69(2)*, 179–218.

Cosmides, L. (1989). The logic of social exchange: Has natural selection shaped how humans reason? Studies with the Wason selection task [see comments]. *Cognition, 31(3)*, 187–276.

Cox, J. R., & Griggs, R. A. (1982). The effects of experience on performance in Wason's selection task. *Memory and Cognition, 10(5)*, 496–502.

Cummins, R. (1989). *Meaning and Mental Representation*. Cambridge, MA: The MIT Press.

Dehaene, S., Spelke, E., Pinel, P., Stanescu, R., & Tsivkin, S. (1999). Sources of mathematical thinking: Behavioral and brain-imaging evidence. *Science, 284(5416)*, 970–974.

Evans, J. S., Handley, S. J., & Harper, C. N. (2001). Necessity, possibility and belief: A study of syllogistic reasoning. *The Quarterly Journal of Experimental Psychology A, 54(3)*, 935–958.

Evans, J. S. B. T., Barston, J., & Pollard, P. (1983). On the conflict between logic and belief in syllogistic reasoning. *Memory and Cognition, 11*, 295–306.

Evans, J. S. B. T., & Over, D. E. (1996). *Rationality and Reasoning*. New York: Psychology Press.

Fink, G. R., Marshall, J. C., Halligan, P. W., Frith, C. D., Driver, J., Frackowiak, R. S., & Dolan, R. J. (1999). The neural consequences of conflict between intention and the senses. *Brain, 122(3)*, 497–512.

Fodor, J. A. (1975). *The Language of Thought*. Cambridge, MA: Harvard University Press.

Forster, T. (1815). Sketch of the new anatomy and physiology of the brain and nervous system of Drs. Gall and Spurzheim: considered as comprehending a complete system of zoonomy. London: Law and Whittaker.

Gigerenzer, G., & Hug, K. (1992). Domain-specific reasoning: Social contracts, cheating, and perspective change. *Cognition, 43(2)*, 127–171.

Giunti, M. (1997). *Computation, Dynamics, and Cognition*. New York: Oxford University Press.

Goel, V. (1991). Notationality and the information processing mind. *Minds and Machines, 1(2)*, 129–165.

Goel, V. (1992). *Are Computational Explanations Vacuous?* Paper presented at the *Proceedings of the Fourteenth Annual Conference of the Cognitive Science Society*, Bloomington, Indiana.

Goel, V. (1995). *Sketches of Thought*. Cambridge, MA: MIT Press.

Goel, V. (2003). Evidence for dual neural pathways for syllogistic reasoning *Psychologica, 32*, 301–309.

Goel, V., Buchel, C., Frith, C., & Dolan, R. J. (2000). Dissociation of mechanisms underlying syllogistic reasoning. *NeuroImage, 12(5)*, 504–514.

Goel, V., & Dolan, R. J. (2000). Anatomical segregation of component processes in an inductive inference task. *Journal of Cognitive Neuroscience, 12(1)*, 1–10.

Goel, V., & Dolan, R. J. (2001). Functional neuroanatomy of three-term relational reasoning. *Neuropsychologia*, *39(9)*, 901–909.

Goel, V., & Dolan, R. J. (2003). Explaining modulation of reasoning by belief. *Cognition*, *87(1)*, B11–22.

Goel, V., Gold, B., Kapur, S., & Houle, S. (1997). The seats of reason: A localization study of deductive & inductive reasoning using PET (O15) blood flow technique. *NeuroReport*, *8(5)*, 1305–1310.

Goel, V., Gold, B., Kapur, S., & Houle, S. (1998). Neuroanatomical correlates of human reasoning. *Journal of Cognitive Neuroscience*, *10(3)*, 293–302.

Goel, V., Grafman, J., Sadato, N., & Hallet, M. (1995). Modelling other minds. *NeuroReport*, *6(13)*, 1741–1746.

Goel, V., Makale, M., & Grafman, J. (2004). The hippocampal system mediates logical reasoning about familiar spatial environments. *Journal of Cognitive Neuroscience*, *16(4)*, 654–664.

Goel, V., Shuren, J., Sheesley, L., & Grafman, J. (2004). Asymmetrical involvement of frontal lobes in social reasoning. *Brain*, *127*, 783–790.

Griggs, R. A., & Cox, J. R. (1982). The elusive thematic-materials effect in Wason's selection task. *British Journal of Psychology*, *73*, 407–420.

Henle, M. (1962). On the relation between logic and thinking. *Psychological Review*, *69(4)*, 366–378.

Johnson-Laird, P. N. (1983). *Mental Models: Towards a Cognitive Science of Language, Inference, and Consciousness*. Cambridge, MA.: Harvard University Press.

Johnson-Laird, P. N. (1994). Mental models, deductive reasoning, and the brain. In: M. S. Gazzaniga (Ed.), *The Cognitive Neurosciences* (pp. 999–1008). Cambridge, MA: MIT Press.

Johnson-Laird, P. N., & Byrne, R. M. J. (1991). *Deduction*. Hillsdale, NJ: Erlbaum.

Jones, C. M., Braithwaite, V. A., & Healy, S. D. (2003). The evolution of sex differences in spatial ability. *Behavioral Neuroscience*, *117(3)*, 403–411.

Jonides, J., Smith, E. E., Koeppe, R. A., Awh, E., & Minoshima, S. (1993). Spatial working memory in humans as revealed by PET. *Nature*, *363*, 623–625.

Kandel, E. R., Schwartz, J. H., & Jessell, T. M. (Eds.). (1995). *Essentials of Neural Science and Behaviour*. Norwalk, CT: Appleton & Lange.

Kosslyn, S. M., Koenig, O., Cave, C. B., Tang, J., & Gabrieli, J. D. E. (1989). Evidence for two types of spatial representations: Hemispheric specialization for categorical and coordinate relations. *Journal of Experimental Psychology: Human Perception and Performance*, *15(4)*, 723–735.

Laeng, B. (1994). Lateralization of categorical & coordinate spatial functions: A study of unilateral stroke patients. *Journal of Cognitive Neuroscience*, *6(3)*, 189–203.

Langdon, D., & Warrington, E. K. (2000). The role of the left hemisphere in verbal and spatial reasoning tasks. *Cortex*, *36(5)*, 691–702.

Lashley, K. S. (1929). *Brain Mechanisms and Intelligence: A Quantitative Study of Injuries to the Brain*. Chicago: University of Chicago Press.

Marr, D. (1982). *Vision: A Computational Investigation into the Human Representation and Processing of Visual Information*. San Francisco: Freeman.

Mellet, E., Tzourio, N., Crivello, F., Joliot, M., Denis, M., & Mazoyer, D. (1996). Functional anatomy of spatial mental imagery generated from verbal instructions. *The Journal of Neuroscience*, *16(20)*, 6504–6512.

Newell, A. (1980a). Physical symbol systems. *Cognitive Science*, *4*, 135–183.

Newell, A. (1980b). Reasoning, problem solving, and decision processes: The problem space as a fundamental category. In R. S. Nickerson (Ed.), *Attention and Performance VIII*. Hillsdale, NJ: Erlbaum.

Newell, A. (1990). *Unified Theories of Cognition*. Cambridge, MA: Harvard University Press.

Newell, A., & Simon, H. A. (1972). *Human Problem Solving*. Englewood Cliffs, NJ: Prentice-Hall.

Newell, A., & Simon, H. A. (1976). Computer science as empirical inquiry: symbols and search. *Communications of the ACM*, *19(March)*, 113–126.

Oakhill, J., & Garnham, A. (1993). On theories of belief bias in syllogistic reasoning. *Cognition*, *46(1)*, 87–92; discussion 93–87.

Oakhill, J., Johnson-Laird, P. N., & Garnham, A. (1989). Believability and syllogistic reasoning. *Cognition*, *31(2)*, 117–140.

Pylyshyn, Z. W. (1984). *Computation and Cognition: Toward a Foundation for Cognitive Science*. Cambridge, MA: MIT Press.

Read, D. E. (1981). Solving deductive-reasoning problems after unilateral temporal lobectomy. *Brain and Language*, 12, 116–127.

Rips, L. J. (1994). *The Psychology of Proof: Deductive Reasoning in Human Thinking*. Cambridge, MA: MIT Press.

Searle, J. R. (1990). *Is the Brain a Digital Computer?* Paper presented at the *Sixty-fourth Annual Pacific Division Meeting for the American Philosophical Association*, Los Angeles, CA, March 30, 1990.

Shallice, T. (1988). *From Neuropsychology to Mental Structure*. Cambridge, UK: Cambridge University Press.

Sloman, S. A. (1996). The empirical case for two systems of reasoning. *Psychological Bulletin, 119(1)*, 3–22.

Stanovich, K. E., & West, R. F. (2000). Individual differences in reasoning: Implications for the rationality debate. *Behavioral and Brain Sciences*, 22, 645–665.

Wason, P. C. (1966). Reasoning. In B. Foss (Ed.), *New Horizons in Psychology* (pp. 135–151). Baltimore: Penguin.

Wason, P. C., & Shapiro, D. A. (1971). Natural and contrived experience in a reasoning problem. *Quarterly Journal of Experimental Psychology*, 23, 63–71.

Wilkins, M. C. (1928). The effect of changed material on the ability to do formal syllogistic reasoning. *Archives of Psychology, 16(102)*, 5–83.

CHAPTER 21

Cognitive and Neuroscience Aspects of Thought Disorder

Peter Bachman
Tyrone D. Cannon

Introduction

During the course of assessments carried out at two clinical research centers, the following responses were provided to standardized questions intended to be open-ended and to elicit relatively abstract responses:

> [Examiner A] *"Can you explain the proverb, 'Speech is the picture of the mind'?"*
>
> [Subject A] *"You see the world through speech. Like my grandfather used to speak to me of Alaskans and Alsatians and blood getting thicker and thinner in the Eskimo. He was against the Kents in England. I can't smoke a Kent cigarette to this day" (Harrow & Quinlan, 1985, p. 44).*
>
> [Examiner B] *"Why should people pay taxes?"*
>
> [Subject B] *"Taxes is an obligation as citizens of our country. To our nation, to this country, the United States. As a citizen, I think we have an obligation. I think that's carried to an extreme. Within reason, taxes within reason. Taxation, we have representation, so therefore we have taxation. For we formed our constitution, it was taxation without representation is treason" (Johnston & Holzman, 1979, p. 263).*

Reading these two responses, and imagining hearing them aloud in conversation, almost surely evokes the feeling that something is not quite right – the statements are somehow disordered. For instance, the objects referred to in the first response seem to be related to each other only indirectly and along varying linguistic dimensions. Consequently, by the end of the statement, the response deviates dramatically from the content requested by the examiner. The reply to the second examiner's question does not follow such a rapidly digressing course but instead seems to fixate on an idea, or perhaps a phrase ("taxation without representation") indirectly related to the content of the question, seeming to repeat and elaborate on that phrase without offering additional ideas.

Apart from describing how these statements are disordered, understanding why the speakers produced them in such a manner is a daunting task. The process of comprehending and generating speech integrated into an ongoing conversation involves numerous interrelated cognitive mechanisms (Levelt, 1989), any or all of which could contribute to abnormal speech comprehension or production. Moreover, thought disorder tends to occur within the context of a more extensive psychopathology (Andreasen & Grove, 1986), including diagnoses as diverse as schizophrenia, mood disorders, certain personality disorders, and autism (American Psychiatric Association, 2000; Andreasen & Grove, 1986). In fact, the patient quoted in the first reply was diagnosed with schizophrenia, the condition perhaps most closely associated with the presence of thought disorder (e.g., Bleuler, 1911/1950). The second quote, however, was provided by a individual who was not herself diagnosed with a psychiatric disorder but who has a daughter diagnosed with schizoaffective disorder (a condition thought to be closely related to schizophrenia; American Psychiatric Association, 2000), highlighting the role of heritable factors contributing to significant symptom expression even in the absence of a clear diagnostic label.

Despite the prevalence of thought disorder across diagnostic populations, systematic efforts to study the pathology of thought disorder across diverse conditions, looking for common disease mechanisms, are rare. Rather, most investigators have chosen to study thought disorder strictly within the context of a particular disease entity such as schizophrenia. Unfortunately, the multitude of difficulties many schizophrenia patients face – including degraded information processing capabilities; presence of debilitating symptoms (including hallucinations and delusions); medication side-effects; social and occupational morbidity; stressful relationships with relatives, who may themselves be burdened by psychiatric disorders – defies models of etiology based on a single underlying deficit. In recognition of this complexity, psychopathology researchers have begun to dissect disorders whose manifestation coincides with the presentation of thought disorder into more fundamental neurocognitive traits that participate in symptom formation. Recent work adopting this approach has demonstrated, for instance, that certain neurocognitive disruptions in schizophrenia are associated with genetic vulnerability to the illness, whereas other traits are associated with disease expression (e.g., Cannon et al., 2000; Cannon et al., 2002).

This more complex, integrative view of the pathology of thought disorder endows the investigator with a more powerful heuristic for grappling with the multitude of intertwined cognitive domains and levels of analysis active in the study of thought and how thought might come to be disordered in particular disease states (Cannon & Rosso, 2002). Perhaps, for instance, the integration of behavioral genetic and experimental psychopathology approaches might yield the finding that deficits in two information processing systems may – on their own – be necessary but not sufficient for the phenotypic manifestation of thought disorder, whereas the coincidence of these deficits may result in its overt expression.

In applying this framework to a larger discussion of thought disorder, we attempt to elucidate a set of neurobiological and cognitive conditions that may participate in the generation of thought disorder through their collective action. More specifically, we focus first on the expression of thought disorder in psychopathology, highlighting descriptive approaches. Subsequently, we shift to discussion of a prominent model of speech production, as well as two models of disordered thinking in schizophrenia, to help us identify cognitive mechanisms likely disrupted in individuals displaying thought disorder. Finally, we attempt to integrate findings from distinct levels of analysis (e.g., behavioral and molecular genetics, structural and functional neuroanantomy, behavioral performance) to characterize diverse aspects of psychiatric disorder as traits specific to disease expression, which we characterize as involving abnormal activation of the brain's temporal lobe structures critical to the formation and retrieval of long-term memories and other types of concrete information and also involving traits specific to genetic vulnerability, which tend to involve more frontal lobe–mediated functions such as the online maintenance and manipulation of information (also see Morrison, Chap. 19).

Defining Thought Disorder

Perhaps the most common usage of the term "thought disorder," at least within clinical settings, is as shorthand for "formal thought disorder," which refers to a taxonomy of symptoms involving abnormal speech (Andreasen, 1979, 1982). In this usage, thought disorder is typically conceptualized as the product of a loosening of associations leading to a loss of continuity between ordered elements inferred to underlie a spoken utterance (Maher, 1991). The "formal" distinction, specifically with respect to schizophrenia, harkens back to the notion that pathologies of thought can be characterized as disorders of thought content or as disorders of thought form. The former of the two categories refers primarily to hallucinations, or well-defined percepts generated endogenously but experienced as, and attributed to, exogenous events and to delusions – objectively false and often bizarre beliefs held with a high level of conviction (i.e., the patient maintains the belief in the face of counter-evidence; American Psychiatric Association, 2000). A common example of a delusion is the belief that people in the patient's environment have the intention of monitoring and even harming the patient (i.e., a paranoid delusion).[1] The latter category, disorders of thought form, involves a disorganization of underlying thought processes indicated by abnormal speech such as that quoted at the outset of this chapter. Factor analytic studies of symptom prevalence in schizophrenia (e.g., Liddle, 1987) have generally supported this form-versus-content distinction, for ratings of formal thought disorder tend to covary with ratings of disorganized behavior on a factor including neither delusions nor hallucinations, suggesting that thought disorder symptoms indeed reflect a disorganization of ideational elements not necessarily specific to articulated speech.

Several clinical examples are pertinent to our description of formal thought disorder as a result of ideational disorganization. A thought-disordered individual might produce a neologism or a novel word formed by the unique integration of parts of other words. A neologism would therefore be conceptualized as the loosening of normal associative relationships between individual word parts (perhaps at the level of grammatical encoding, discussed subsequently). Johnston and Holzman (1979, p. 100) quoted one patient as responding to an examiner's request to define the word "remorse" by replying, "*Moisterous*, being *moistful*," combining legal word parts to form lexically invalid words.

Similarly, an affected individual's speech may be characterized by lexically valid but unrelated words strung together to make an unintelligible statement – a loosening of associations between words. An example of this type of disordered comment is, "If things turn by rotation of agriculture or levels or timed in regard to everything . . . " (Maher, 1966, p. 395). In its extreme form, clinicians sometimes refer to this type of disorganization as "word salad," indicating its highly jumbled presentation.

Formal thought disorder may also manifest itself in an abrupt shift between indirectly related topics, representing a loosened association between ideas or clauses within or between sentences. For example, when one patient with formal thought disorder was asked to explain why people who are born deaf are usually unable to talk, he replied, "When swallow in your throat like a key it comes out, but not as scissors. A robin, too, it means spring" (Harrow & Quinlan, 1985, p. 429). In this instance, the patient seems to have switched from employing one meaning of the word swallow (i.e., the verb) to an alternate meaning (i.e., the type of bird) and then articulating a concept (i.e., "robin") semantically related to the alternate meaning.

Perhaps even more salient in this last example than the abrupt shift is that the patient's response seems only very tangentially consistent with the interviewer's question.

In fact, disordered speech can involve statements that are overly vague or overly concrete, or otherwise do not seem congruent with the semantic or interpersonal demands implied by the comment or question posed by the other participant in the conversation.

In contrast to the taxonomy of speech abnormalities described previously, which resulted from application of the ideational confusion definition, Andreasen (1986) developed a descriptive system of assessing thought disorder intended to eschew theoretical assumptions regarding the pathology resulting in disordered speech, and to enhance clinical assessors' statistical reliability. In all, Andreasen (1986) identified eighteen classes of speech abnormality, most of which mapped loosely to more traditional clinical conventions. For instance, the notion of loosened associations was replaced by a set of five somewhat more technical categories, including "derailment," which the authors characterized as a consistent flow of ideas only tangentiality related to each other within the context of the spontaneous production of speech (sometimes referred to by clinicians as "flight of ideas"; Andreasen, 1986).

For our current purposes, the specific distinctions within Andreasen's (1986) catalog of categories are less important than some of the larger constructs that emerged from a factor analysis of observations of the prevalence of the abnormalities in a wide-ranging study of several psychiatric populations (Andreasen & Grove, 1986). Indeed, as mentioned previously, five of the eighteen types of abnormality clustered together to form a "loose associations" dimension that seemed to indicate the overall level of behavioral disorganization shown by patients with psychotic disorders (Andreasen & Grove, 1986). Another distinction appeared between what the authors characterized as aspects of "positive" and "negative" thought disorder (not to be confused with the analogous positive–negative schizophrenia symptom distinction) with the former involving aspects of loosened associations (e.g., derailment) in combination with a significant level of rapidity and volume of speech (sometimes referred to as "pressure" of speech) and the latter involving speech that is impoverished in terms of average number and length utterance or with respect to ideational content (as was the case in the second quote cited in the Introduction). Interestingly, this positive versus negative dimension seemed to effectively discriminate thought-disordered patients with mania from thought disordered patients with schizophrenia.

Levelt's Model of Normal Speech Production

To provide an organizing framework for our consideration of models relevant to formal thought disorder, we turn first to a model of normal speech production. Levelt (Levelt, 1989, 1999; Levelt, Roelofs, & Meyer, 1999) described such a model particularly useful here because of its comprehensive incorporation of diverse cognitive processes critical for effective interpersonal communication.

As shown in Figure 21.1, Levelt's model involves a serial process by which a message intended for communication moves through a succession of stages, each of which plays a unique role in transforming the message into an articulated sound wave. The first set of stages along this speech production sequence constitutes what Levelt refers to as a "rhetorical/semantic/syntactic system" responsible for filtering a given communicative intention through the speaker's model of how the listener will perceive and understand the message, which can be influenced by the speaker's mental model of the listener. This system also sequences ideas in a logical order and places that sequence in a propositional format (specific to linguistic expression) that includes the selection of lexical concepts, in turn triggering the retrieval of appropriate lemmas from the mental lexicon (for a discussion of computational evidence for the model's lexical selection mechanism, see Levelt, Roelofs, & Meyer, 1999; also see Medin & Rips, Chap. 3). The retrieval of the appropriate lemmas from the mental lexicon engages the

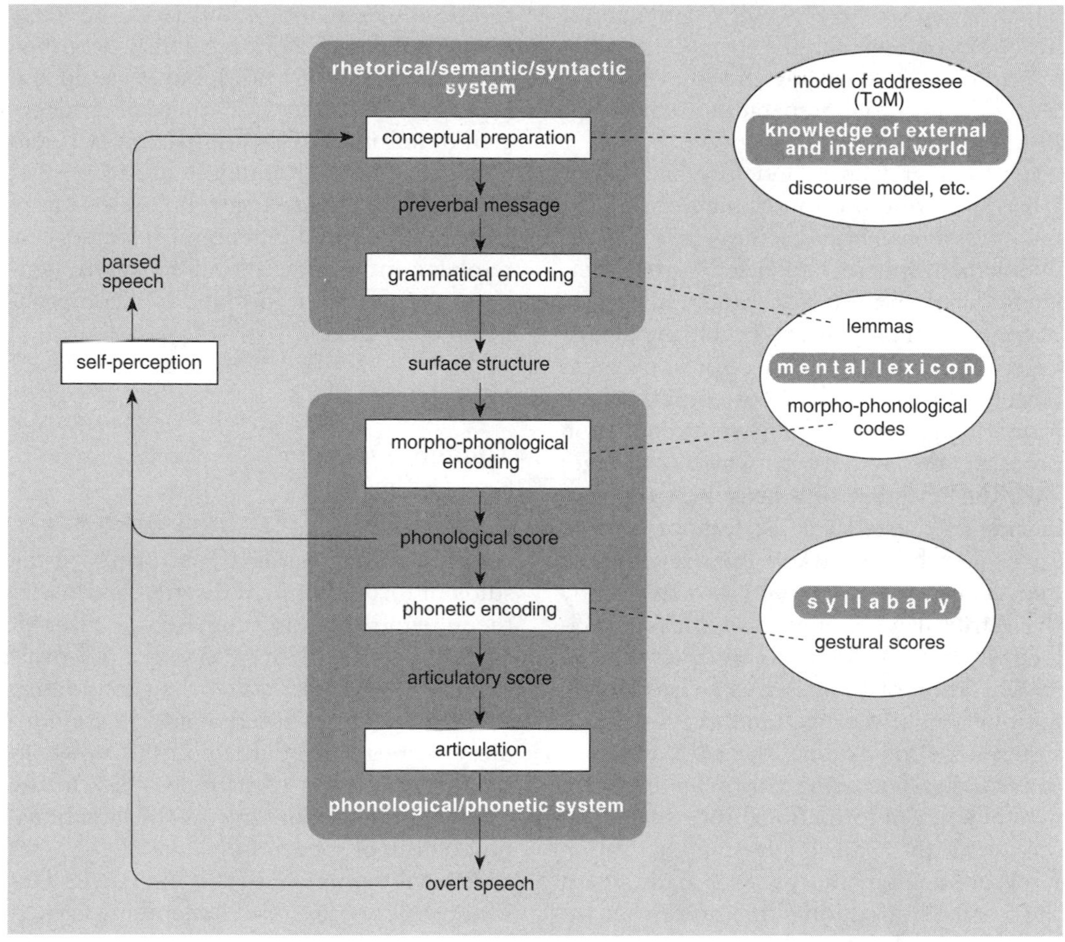

Figure 21.1. Levelt's model of normal speech production. Reprinted with permission from Levelt, 1999.

syntactic construction of the message, for lemmas must agree syntactically with each other and with the overall communicative intent of the speaker.

This retrieval of lemmas from the mental lexicon, which also entails retrieval of each lemma's inherent morpho-phonological code, serves as a transition out of the "rhetorical/semantic/syntactic system" and into the "phonological/phonetic system." Indeed, the lemmas' score in the mental lexicon represents the basic stage at which semantic and phonological information is bound together.

Accordingly, the phonological codes associated with each lemma's morphemes combine according to the predetermined sequence to form the syllabic structure of the message, a relative process, the product of which does not necessarily respect the boundaries of the superordinate lemmas. Next, during the process of phonetic encoding, the accumulation of the phonological syllables, or the phonological score, retrieves from a "mental syllabary" a gestural, or articulatory score, completing the process by which a fully formed syntactic and phonological message retrieves an appropriate articulatory motor plan. Subsequently, articulation, the generation of overt speech, is the physical realization of the selected motor plan.

The production of overt speech, however, does not represent the final stage in Levelt's model of speech production. In fact, the model also includes a feedback loop by which the speaker can perceive and monitor his or her own speech for errors or external interference, re-engaging the model at the level of conceptual preparation to make appropriate corrections if necessary.

On a neural level, Indefrey and Levelt (1999) describe the functioning of Levelt's model as being implemented in a primarily left-hemisphere–lateralized cortical network. They propose that the initial process of conceptual preparation occurs in range of heteromodal and cortical association areas (specific to the modality of contextual information preceding the present production process), the activity of which converges with the selection of a lexical concept occurring in the left middle temporal gyrus. Subsequently, Wernicke's area (roughly the temporal-parietal junction) is activated by the retrieval of phonological codes associated with retrieved lexical concepts followed by activation of Broca's area (posterior left inferior frontal cortex) and the left mid-superior temporal lobe, the sites at which phonological encoding continues independent of lexical information. Broca's area then remains active and is joined by activation in other supplementary motor areas and in the cerebellum during the process of articulation. Indefrey and Levelt (1999) further specify that self-monitoring, whether occurring covertly or overtly, activates regions of superior temporal lobe, as well as supplementary motor areas related to articulation.

Critically, the authors specify that this proposed speech production network is activated as such only during relatively automatic (i.e., seemingly without effort or conscious awareness and potentially occurring in parallel with other processes) speech production as opposed to the process of speech production specifically engaged during more controlled (effortful, conscious processing requiring capacity-limited attention and operating in a serial fashion; Schneider & Shiffrin, 1977) information processing, as would be more likely during the performance of an experimental cognitive task. Not only would speech production involving controlled selection, retrieval, and integration of semantic information be likely to activate the network previously described (Indefrey & Levelt, 1999), but it would also likely activate a relatively more anterior region of left inferior prefrontal cortex (Gold & Buckner, 2002; Kounios et al., 2003) that appears to facilitate controlled selection of information stored in long-term memory by resolving interference from activated, nontarget pieces of information (Thompson-Schill et al., 2002).

Thought Disorder or Speech Disorder?

An area of long-running controversy in the study of formal thought disorder is whether the phenomenon is ultimately a disorder of thought itself, or a disorder of overt speech. Specifically, rather than considering this markedly disrupted ability to communicate a speech production problem, we infer that the locus of pathology lies in the thought processes underlying the intentional production of speech (see Chaika, 1982, for additional discussion of this inference). Unfortunately, as discussed in depth by Critchley (1964) and Maher (1991), these thought processes themselves are not directly observable. Therefore, measurement of any putative disruption must necessarily occur indirectly – usually with the assumption that the psychomotor transformation from a thought to a spoken utterance occurs with a normal range of fidelity. It is certainly worthwhile considering whether this assumption is warranted.

Referring back to Levelt's model of normal speech production (Figure 20.1), we can consider each of the putative processing stages and attempt to infer what the observable product of "lesioning" each in isolation would sound like. Let us first examine the processing stage most closely affiliated with the actual act of speaking, the process of physical articulation. If an intact would-be utterance moves into the stage of physical articulation only to be compromised, one might expect the output to contain the intended words encoded grammatically but spoken in a manner that systematically distorts the articulatory score of the phrase. Such a spoken product would not resemble formally disordered thought but instead the product of conditions such as dysarthria or speech apraxia (Dick et al., 2001), two disorders familiar to neurologists and speech pathologists.

Similarly, if the lesion underlying formal thought disorder involved the process of phonetic encoding, one would expect spoken output to resemble speech characteristics of what Dodd and Crosbie (2002) refer to as "speech programming deficit disorder" in which speech is produced fluently, but the distorted phonological score would yield speech devoid of normal patterns of pitch and syllabification – perhaps sounding severely slurred – in the absence of dysarthria or speech apraxia.

The immediately preceding stage, morphophonological encoding, the first point in the process at which a word's phonological code is processed independent of semantic content, has also been shown to be compromised in isolation specifically in patients suffering from an anomic aphasia or a word-finding deficit (Indefrey & Levelt, 1999). Typically, such patients describe a sense of frustration over feeling that they have particular verbal concepts in mind but cannot retrieve the phonological code – cannot think of how to say the corresponding word. Certainly this condition is debilitating, but apart from the superficial similarity with thought blocking (sometimes considered a feature of negative formal thought disorder, but not a construct included in Andreasen's and Grove's system), anomic aphasia does not resemble formal thought disorder.

Finally, having ruled out deficits in the stages of speech production constituting Levelt's (1989, 1999) phonological/phonetic system, we work backward to the stage at which lemmas are selected and retrieved from the mental lexicon, initiating the grammatical encoding process. Agrammatic patients, such as patients suffering from Broca's aphasia, are characterized by speech in which words are selected and ordered appropriately, but the particular form of each word is not adjusted to accommodate the grammatical demands of nearby words or the phrase as a whole (e.g., verbs are not conjugated correctly; Indefrey & Levelt, 1999). Although, as apparent in the quotes at the beginning of the chapter, patients with formal thought disorder make grammatical mistakes in their speech, it is not necessarily clear that they make such mistakes more frequently than non–thought-disordered individuals do.

Evidence does exist (Andreasen & Grove, 1986; Berenbaum & Barch, 1995), however, that patients with formal thought disorder show a small but significant level of word substitution and approximation, which is the predictable consequence of faulty retrieval of lemmas from the mental lexicon, the initial process occurring under the heading of grammatical encoding. We therefore conclude that we can rule out lesions to all processing stages occurring after lemma retrieval up to and including the articulation of overt speech. The cause of formal thought disorder must therefore exist somewhere along the way through the rhetorical/semantic/syntactic system (including application of a mental model of the listener, the conceptual preparation, etc.) *or* in the self-monitoring feedback loop. Although where one draws the line between "thought" and "speech" is a somewhat of a philosophical issue, we propose that all processes underlying these two suspect components certainly warrant the label "thought," justifying the term "formal thought disorder" rather than "speech disorder."

Overview of Cognitive Models of Thought Disorder

The first major psychological discussion of the pathology of thought disorder was provided by Eugen Bleuler, a Swiss psychiatrist and theorist contemporary to both Sigmund Freud, founder of modern clinical psychology, and Wilhelm Wundt, often cited as the founder of modern experimental psychology. Based on his observation of patients with psychotic disorders (i.e., psychiatric disorders manifesting both severe reality distortion symptoms, such as hallucinations and delusions, and a significant level of behavioral disorganization), including schizophrenia, Bleuler (1911/1951) argued that the cause of psychosis involves a fundamental "loosening of associations" between ideational elements, which results in a conceptual confusion that manifests itself in disordered speech (in addition to other symptoms) – an idea preserved almost exactly in its original form in more contemporary definitions of thought disorder,[2] as discussed earlier.

Furthermore, Bleuler's conceptualization of the pathology of psychosis is analogous to more contemporary cognitive explanations of disordered information processing (e.g., Andreasen et al., 1999; Goldman-Rakic, 1995; Oltmanns & Neale, 1975; Silverstein et al., 2000) in that he proposed that a critical parameter of a fundamental *cognitive* mechanism is abnormal and that the consequences of this single defect account parsimoniously for the diverse phenomena observed in the behavior of many psychiatric patients. Like Bleuler, the proponents of these contemporary models identify the pathological cognitive mechanism and delineate how the functional consequences of the abnormality are propagated through subsequent processing stages, curtailing the normal integration of thought and behavior or, more specifically with respect to schizophrenia, the inability to use contextual information in the efficient guidance of ongoing, goal-directed behavior. We shall discuss at length two such models that were created in investigation of information processing abnormalities in schizophrenia and examine how these models might account for symptoms such as formal thought disorder.

Cohen's and Braver's Model

Cohen, Braver, and colleagues (Braver, Barch, & Cohen, 1999; Braver et al., 2001; Cohen et al., 1999; Cohen & Servan-Schreiber, 1992) have proposed a model of schizophrenic information processing (see Figure 21.2) in which at least a subset of information processing deficits observed in schizophrenia patients results from a disturbance in the interaction between a cognitive module specialized for the representation, active maintenance, and updating of information regarding stimulus context and a module responsible for the storage of learned behavioral contingencies. Given that an individual's repertoire of stimulus–response associations must be directly accessible to the behavioral selection process bridging the gap between the encoding of a stimulus and the execution of a response, the existence of a pathway allowing interaction between these stored behavioral contingencies (i.e., long-term memories, including motor plans) and the context processing module allows contextual information to influence the selection and execution of ongoing behavioral plans, ideally biasing behavior in a goal-appropriate manner (Braver, Barch, & Cohen, 1999). Context information therefore mediates the selection of learned associations, which otherwise would be dictated by environmental stimuli.

To serve this function, context information must be represented and maintained in a manner that leaves it both buffered against interference (from task-irrelevant stimuli) and available to be updated as required by changing task demands. In an extreme example, this system must be capable of exercising cognitive control: utilizing information from a previous stimulus to bias processing of other relevant information and to suppress processing of irrelevant information and then reflecting that critical information in the selection of appropriate goal-directed behavior even in the face of competition from more salient behavioral responses.[3]

Citing computational evidence (Braver, Barch, & Cohen, 1999), the investigators argue that variable efficiency of the interaction between the context processing module and the learned behavioral contingencies module could, in fact, account

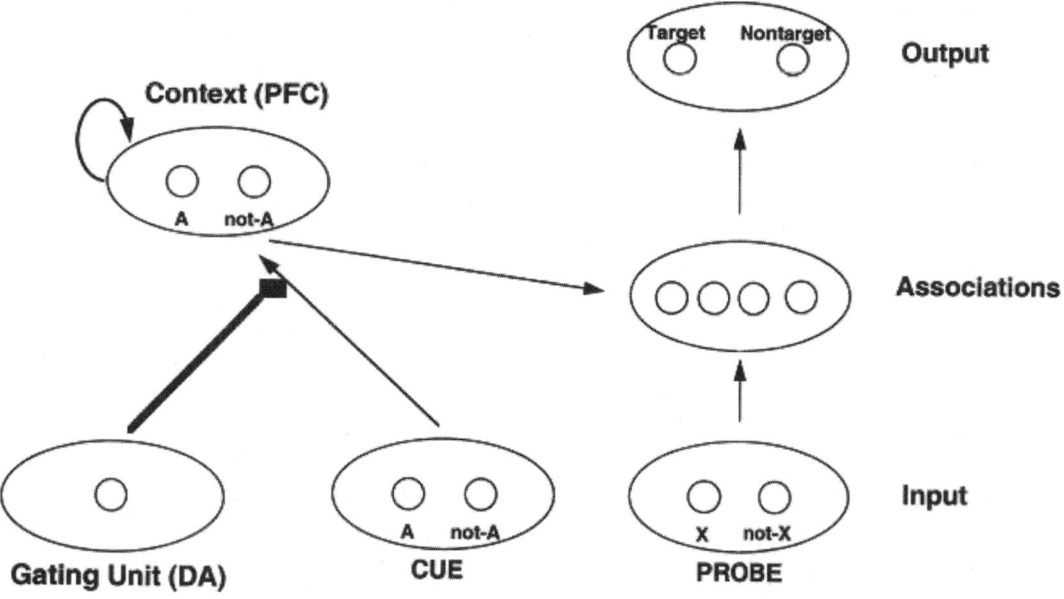

Figure 21.2. Cohen, Braver, and colleagues' model of information processing disruption in schizophrenia. Reprinted with permission from Braver, Barch, & Cohen, 1999.

for schizophrenia patients' apparent insensitivity to contextual information. They elaborate (Braver, Barch, & Cohen, 1999) that a gating mechanism must exist between the two modules, allowing contextual information to be encoded and maintained without interference from irrelevant perceptual information under certain circumstances and, at other times, making context information available for updating or to influence activation in the association storage module. Disrupted information processing in schizophrenia is therefore the consequence of failure of this "gate" between the association storage module and the context processing module to properly open and close, degrading the fidelity of encoding and maintenance of goal-related information, as well as the effectiveness of its biasing influence.

In support of their model, Cohen, Braver, and colleagues (Cohen et al., 1999) have presented data from schizophrenia patients and controls performing three tasks – a single-trial version of the Stroop task (Stroop, 1935), a lexical disambiguation task, and a "one-back" continuous performance task requiring subjects to continuously match each stimulus with the stimulus presented immediately prior (Cohen & Servan-Schreiber, 1992). In each task, the difficulty of maintaining context information and using it to select appropriate behavior was manipulated by varying the length of time during which context information must be maintained prior to response selection, as well as the salience of task-appropriate responses relative to task-inappropriate responses (i.e., the demand for cognitive control during the behavioral selection process). The investigators argue that, overall, schizophrenia patients display a differential insensitivity to contextual information, and this insensitivity interacts with variable information maintenance demands in two out of three experiments (Cohen et al., 1999). Additionally, the investigators report a significant negative correlation between context sensitivity and severity of disorganization symptoms (including formal thought disorder) among schizophrenia patients, suggesting that the ability to effectively and flexibly bind ideational elements to an appropriate context underlies both the production of organized speech and successful performance on these context-heavy tasks.

Cohen, Braver, and colleagues also bring to bear evidence that this contextual information is actively maintained, updated, and buffered against interference in the dorsolateral prefrontal cortex (Barch et al., 1997; Braver et al., 1997; Cohen et al., 1997; also see Goel, Chap. 20), which is also implicated in the exercise of cognitive control (Braver, Reynolds, & Donaldson, 2003). More recently, Miller and Cohen (2001; also, Kane and Engle, 2002, and Duncan, 2001) have reviewed evidence that the prefrontal cortex is not only capable of maintaining representations of context despite interference but is also critical in the modulation of activity in other regions of the brain thought to be associated with modality-specific buffers, with the ability to hold long-term memories at a high level of activation and the subsequent selection of goal-directed behavior. Incorporating an additional level of analysis, Cohen, Braver, and colleagues cite evidence that phasic dopamine activity modulates the gate between the prefrontal context processing module and the individual's repertoire of learned behavioral contingencies (Braver, Barch, & Cohen, 1999).

Although we agree that dopaminergic modulation of cortical activity certainly plays a role in the pathology of impaired information processing in psychosis (e.g., Abi-Dargham et al., 2002; Okubo et al., 1997), the particular mechanism Cohen and colleagues propose (i.e., increased tonic and decreased phasic dopamine activity; Braver, Barch, & Cohen, 1999), however, remains controversial (see, for example, Grace, 1991, or Laruelle, Kegeles, & Abi-Dargham, 2003).

In addition to being able to account qualitatively for the cognitive deficits the model was designed to simulate (Braver, Barch, & Cohen, 1999), the proposition that schizophrenia patients fail to appropriately use contextual information to guide ongoing behavior in a goal-directed manner certainly has face validity.[4] One might argue, however, that any behavior judged to be abnormal, or more specifically, deficient with respect to a given goal state, could be explained by a failure of this context processing mechanism.

Although perhaps an extreme argument, this proposition raises a question regarding how this model or any like it is distinct from one that simply predicts that schizophrenia patients will perform any given task incorrectly. The distinction indeed exists and highlights the reason why cognitive control is so critical to the model's successful implementation. Specifically, patients will perform a given task correctly when the correct behavioral response is somehow most salient or dominant with respect to other potential responses; in this case, the representation of context and the prepotency of the correct response are redundant mechanisms. When the correct response is less salient or less "prepotent" than an incorrect, distracter response, patients will tend to choose the distracter. Nonpsychotic subjects, conversely, will be more capable of using representations of context to inhibit the prepotent distracter and select the appropriate, less salient behavioral response – they will be more capable of exercising cognitive control.

This focus on cognitive control therefore represents a critical step in the development of this model – a process that should continue to advance, incorporating findings from studies of neural correlates of cognitive control (e.g., Braver et al., 2003), the cognitive mechanisms underlying recognition and resolution of response conflict (Botvinick et al., 2001), and the specificity of the findings to patients suffering from psychosis (Barch et al., 2003).

Finally, two additional issues awaiting resolution are also worthy of brief mention. The first area involves the mechanism by which particular behavioral responses acquire their levels of salience, or prepotency. Cohen, Braver, and colleagues refer to behavioral learning principles to account for how associations are formed between particular pieces of contextual information and specific outcomes (Braver, Barch, & Carter, 1999), linking contextual information to incentive salience, and therefore to behavioral response salience; however, they do not account for the initial identification and categorization of pieces of information (unless a stochastic process of sampling reward value

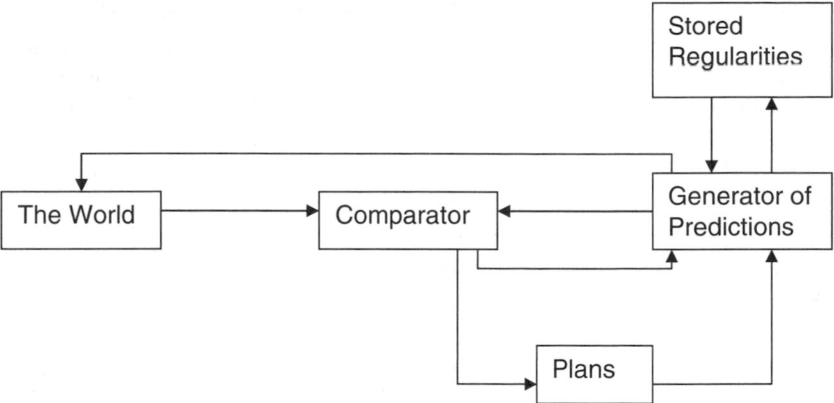

Figure 21.3. Hemsley's and Gray's model of disrupted information processing in schizophrenia. Reprinted with permission from Gray et al., 1991.

from among the set of available stimuli is assumed), nor do they argue that associations among behaviors, contextual information, and outcomes will generalize across situations.

Additionally, future discussion of contextual information, as defined by Cohen, Braver, and colleagues, might benefit from consideration of how this particular construct relates to definitions of context in other fields of research within cognitive psychology and neuroscience. Borrowing an example from the study of conditioning in nonhuman animals, investigators predictably define context as the aspects of the physical setting in which a particular conditioning trial takes place that are immediately observable by the animal (e.g., Fanselow, 2000; Goddard, 2001; Rudy & O'Reilly, 2001). This definition of context is relatively consistent and uniform across studies, facilitating the construct's incorporation into behavioral models and the subsequent generalization of those models to analogous, ecologically valid situations for which the model can generate behavioral predictions (such as the behavior of a recovered drug addict in a physical setting with which drug use is associated; e.g., Shaham et al., 2003). Cohen, Braver, and colleagues (Cohen et al., 1999) on the other hand, seem to define context purely in terms of performance an cognitive tasks. These ambiguities aside, as we will discuss, this and the following model provide critical theoretical traction in our attempt to understand how information processing abnormalities might contribute to the manifestation of thought disorder.

Hemsley's and Gray's Model

A model with properties analogous to aspects of the model developed by Cohen and colleagues, but with important incongruities as well, has developed in a body of publications authored by Hemsley, Gray, and colleagues over the past two decades (Gray, 1982; Gray, 1995; Gray, 1998; Gray et al., 1991; Hemsley, 1987; Hemsley, 1993; Hemsley, 1994; Weiner, 1990). As summarized most recently by Gray (1998), this model of disordered information processing in schizophrenia involves a disruption in the processes by which past regularities of experience are integrated with ongoing stimulus recognition and behavior selection and monitoring (see Figure 21.3). This failure to engage information fluidly from longer-term memory in the interpretation of the current perceptual state of the world and the prediction of subsequent states is essentially the failure of an information processing system to identify and utilize contextual information in the automatic guidance of goal-directed behavior. As delineated by Gray (1998), what should seem familiar to the patient and elicit automatic processing of information (seemingly without effort or conscious awareness and, potentially, in parallel with other processes) instead seems novel, engaging finite, controlled information processing resources (effortful, conscious processing requiring attentional focus and operating in a serial fashion; Schneider & Shiffrin, 1977). Consistent with an earlier proposal put forth by Nuechterlein and Dawson (1984), Hemsley (1994) and Gray (1998) argue that schizophrenia patients are significantly more likely to engage these controlled processes than are nonpsychotic subjects, resulting in patients' engaging information processing bottlenecks significantly more frequently, and, through physiological mechanisms discussed subsequently, this disparity leads to the conscious experience of psychosis.

Similar to the model discussed previously, Hemsley's and Gray's model accounts for the influence of contextual information on the goal-oriented direction of behavior. Unlike the previous model, however, Hemsley and Gray (Gray et al., 1991) mention explicitly that their model includes a dedicated comparator mechanism that examines the products of regular perceptual sampling of the environment within the context of a predicted model of the perceptual world (corrected for the influence of ongoing motor plans, as well as other dynamic aspects of the perceptual world stored in long-term memory). The results of this comparison are then abstracted according to the degree to which they match the prediction and transmitted to the motor programming system, which interprets a relative "match" signal as an indication that it should allow the current motor program to continue (i.e., "the behaviors executed are having the predicted effects") and a relative "mismatch" signal as an indication that it should interrupt the ongoing motor plan because something novel or unexpected has occurred.

However, the presence of a relative mismatch signal orients the individual's attention to the possibility of a meaningful change in the perceptual environment, increasing the intensity of sensory processing (Gray, 1998) – a proposition that converges with Sokolov's (1963) suggestion that the autonomic orienting response observed in humans and other animals occurs in order to increase the cognitive resources available for sensory processing.

For individuals suffering from schizophrenia, the fundamental deficit "... lies at the moment of integration of past experience with current information handling" (Gray, 1998, p. 261). Specifically, information about past regularities of experience is not integrated fluently with current perceptual information, preventing the system from making an appropriate prediction about the next state of the perceptual world and markedly decreasing the likelihood that a match signal will be generated. Consequently, the impaired individual experiences the detection of novelty in the perceptual environment much more frequently than would an individual generating more frequent match signals. In light of the increased sensory processing demands and the concomitantly increased demand placed on Gray's comparator mechanism, as well as the need to select and initiate a different motor program, the cognitive processing demands once fulfilled automatically now require capacity-limited, controlled processing.

This conjecture does seem to reflect subjective experiences reported by many schizophrenia patients, who describe feeling overwhelmed by a somehow foreign-seeming, disjointed perceptual landscape, unable to discern more meaningful features of the environment from less meaningful features (Davis & Cutting, 1994; McGhie & Chapman, 1961). Indeed, Hemsley's (1994) and Gray's (1998) proposal that actively psychotic schizophrenia patients engage their sensory environment in a much more attentionally intensive manner, all the while sensing endogenous indications that some aspect of that environment is novel or unexpected, appears to account for patients' reports of attributing increased significance to aspects of the environment that nonschizophrenic individuals would consider insignificant (Davis & Cutting, 1994), potentially participating in the development of delusional beliefs (e.g., Maher, 2002).

Moreover, Gray (1998) delineates a second consequence of the pathologically frequent interruption of ongoing motor programs in schizophrenia patients: disruption in the "labeling" of interrupted motor programs as internally generated – a consequence of impaired self-monitoring. That is, the patient recognizes the results of the (at least partial) execution of a motor program, but does not attach a sense of personally willed intention to the motor program – a mechanism first proposed by Frith (1987). Considering that speech – even covert or subvocal speech – essentially constitutes a complex motor program, a consequence of a failure to recognize that motor program as a behavior willfully enacted by oneself may lead to the conclusion that the speech experienced was generated by an agent other than the individual – the definition of an auditory hallucination (see Ford et al., 2002, for a possible fronto-temporal correlate of this phenomenon). In this manner, Gray (1998) and Frith and colleagues (1992) argue the failure to associate willed intention with the execution of a motor program can lead to the experience of a significant perceptual abnormality, such as a hallucination.

With respect to its neural implementation, Hemsley's and Gray's model (Gray, 1998) focuses on regulatory functions of dopamine, as does Cohen's and Braver's; unlike Cohen's and colleagues' model, however, it places greatest emphasis on the dopaminergic modulation of a structure other than the prefrontal cortex – namely, the nucleus accumbens, a site of great integration of disparate neural circuits, located in the basal ganglia. Gray (1998) posits that the comparison between predicted and observed perceptual information is carried out in the ventral portion of the frontal lobe,[5] and the results are transmitted through a medial temporal lobe pathway to the nucleus accumbens. Importantly, this excitatory, glutamatergic input to the nucleus accumbens is paired with an inhibitory efferent connection from the dopamine-releasing nuclei of the midbrain. Gray suggests that when the excitatory input is disrupted, the nucleus accumbens receives a relative overload of dopaminergic inhibition, effectively disrupting the ability of the ventral frontal lobe to communicate match signals and in turn setting off a chain reaction of inhibitory steps throughout the basal ganglia, eventually inhibiting the reticular nucleus of the thalamus. Once the reticular nucleus is inhibited, the excitatory, largely feed-forward loops comprising thalamocortical sensory information processing circuits are left relatively unchecked – a consequence possibly related to the subjective sense of increases in the degree of conscious sensory processing underway (also see Grace, Moore, & O'Donnell, 1998). Moreover, this thalamocortical disinhibition and concomitant sense of increased conscious processing of stimuli facilitates patients' and controls' differential engagement of highly controlled cognitive processes – a functional dissociation seen most strikingly in the prefrontal cortex (Jansma et al., 2001). Furthermore, this thalamic disinhibition disrupts the functioning of parietal and interconnected prefrontal areas active during the attribution of overt behavior as being self-generated (Frith et al., 1992) – an operation closely related to the functioning of the ventral prefrontal comparator.

Two areas of concern warrant brief mention. The first involves the possibility that the model's predictions might prove relatively nonspecific with respect to the primary locus of pathology: Any number of disruptions in the proposed information processing system would result in a marked drop in the number of match signals received, leading to a greater degree of controlled processing. In addition to this potential nonspecificity, one might argue that the behavioral evidence cited in support of the model does not easily map onto the clinical phenomena for which it attempts to account. Although Hemsley's and Gray's model seems to relate in meaningful ways to the subjective experiences of schizophrenia patients, much of the behavioral evidence supporting it (Gray et al., 1991; Gray, 1998) is drawn from studies of latent inhibition (Lubow, 1959) – a phenomenon of classical conditioning defined as the difference in amplitude or intensity of conditioned responses to conditioned stimuli of two types: stimuli to which the subject was already exposed prior to association with the present response and stimuli otherwise novel to the subject when first associated with the present response. An association usually occurs more readily between the "non–pre-exposed" stimulus and the response, which is a phenomenon believed to be associated with an inhibition of association formation caused by the persisting representation of the "pre-exposure" experience of the stimulus. The contextual information comprised by the representation of the pre-exposure therefore influences the efficiency with which a subsequent behavioral association is formed. Taken alone, evidence that schizophrenia patients do not show expected latent inhibition effects may be interpreted as a failure by patients to utilize contextual information in the behavioral conditioning domain. One might question, however, whether evidence taken primarily from classical conditioning serves as an adequate foundation for an information processing model as wide-ranging and complex as Gray's and Hemsley's and that carries implications for elusive aspects of cognition such as conscious awareness.

Studies of Information Processing Deficits Related to Formal Thought Disorder

To help us fill in the gap in available theory between mechanisms underlying a modality-nonspecific degradation in information processing ability and the mechanisms generating organized, goal-directed speech, we turn to the literature on (quasi) experimental approaches to studying the pathology of formal thought disorder. Thankfully, this work has been examined capably in a recent meta-analysis by Kerns and Berenbaum (2002), who organize the range of published hypotheses involving specific cognitive impairments associated with formal thought disorder into four general categories.

We have already discussed the first of these categories, involving investigations of cognitive mechanisms relatively proximal to speech production, such as those included in Levelt's phonological/phonetic system (e.g., Barch & Berenbaum, 1996, and Goldberg et al., 1998). In agreement with our conclusion, Kerns and Berenbaum (2002) report only a very minor relationship between phonological/phonetic system impairment and ratings of thought disorder and argue that this relationship is carried entirely by measures of anomia and word substitution and approximation, deficits likely related to the retrieval of lemmas from the mental lexicon (Indefrey & Levelt, 1999). The vast majority of clinical phenomena related to formal thought disorder (Andreasen & Grove, 1986), however, is left unaccounted for by deficient speech production.

Kerns' and Berenbaum's (2002) second category of hypothesized deficit involves increased amount of activation spreading automatically between nodes in semantic networks (assumed to operate like standard neural network models; Dell & O'Seaghdha, 1991), resulting in increased priming of nearby semantic associates of a target word, raising the probability that one of these nontarget words will be retrieved and integrated into ongoing speech. A relatively intense area of study in schizophrenia research (for a review, see Minzenberg et al., 2002), investigators looking for evidence of abnormal semantic network priming have reported seemingly contradictory findings, with some showing evidence of hyper-priming at tested nodes (suggesting increased amount of activation spreading throughout the network; Spitzer et al., 1993, 1994; Weisbrod et al., 1998) and others showing evidence of hypopriming at tested nodes (suggestive of a reduced amount of activation; Blum & Freides, 1995; Passerieux et al., 1997; Besche et al., 1997). This contradiction prompted the suggestion that thought-disordered patients actually experience an increase in *distance* of activation spread, while maintaining an overall level of activation comparable with controls, effectively yielding an increased number of nodes activated, with none activated to as high a degree as controls' nodes (Spitzer, 1997). In their analysis, Kerns and Berenbaum (2002) reject the hyperpriming hypothesis, and indeed report that a small amount of evidence exists supporting increased distance of activation spread and decreased amount of activation at any given node, suggesting that a thought-disordered patient should be slightly more likely than controls to retrieve a word relatively distantly related to the target word.

Aside from this evidence of a relatively minor contribution to the expression of formal thought disorder, the first deficit shown by Kerns and Berenbaum (2002) to contribute significantly to thought disorder involves semantic memory functioning relatively distinct from automatic spreading of activation, such as impairment of controlled retrieval of information from semantic memory, which may itself have an abnormal netware structure (because of the cumulative effects of a chronic inability to encode semantic information, for instance). Relevant studies (e.g., Allen et al., 1993; Goldberg et al., 1998; Kerns et al., 1999) tend to employ fluency tasks requiring retrieval of information from semantic memory by means such as a controlled implementation of retrieval strategy (Ruff et al., 1997). In agreement with conclusions offered by Minzenberg, Ober, & Vinogradov (2002) and by Baving and colleagues (2001), all of whom argue that semantic retrieval is most consistently and robustly impaired in schizophrenia patients when a high degree of controlled processing is required, Kerns and Berenbaum (2002) present evidence of a strong, consistent association between this type of semantic processing abnormality and presence of formal thought disorder. They argue additionally that the current literature does not offer evidence permitting a disambiguation between abnormal network structure and impaired information retrieval.

Evidence of impaired semantic retrieval associated with formal thought disorder is consistent with Hemsley's and Gray's (Gray et al., 1991; Gray, 1998) model's focus on the smooth integration of stored information with incoming information and response selection: Specifically, information from (long-term) semantic memory is continuously retrieved and integrated into comprehension and online production of verbal behavior. Failure of this fluid integration therefore has the ability to ultimately prevent a match signal from being generated, engaging (albeit indirectly) capacity-limited, controlled processing resources, and likely recruiting activation of left inferior prefrontal cortex to facilitate the otherwise automatic selection of semantic information mediated by activity in the left middle temporal gyrus (Gold & Buckner, 2002; Indefrey & Levelt, 1999).

This process of semantic memory retrieval and integration itself may be modulated by the subject of Kerns' and Berenbaum's (2002) fourth category of cognitive deficit contributing to formal thought disorder – namely, impaired executive functioning. As a composite construct, Kerns and Berenbaum (2002) demonstrate that executive function abnormality is strongly related to the presence of formal thought disorder. Of course, executive function itself entails a number of critical subsystems (Baddeley, 1986), including a mechanism for processing contextual information (and effectively inhibiting irrelevant, noncontextual information), a mechanism for allocation of attentional capacity serving to maintain information over a delay, and a mechanism for monitoring one's own behavior, including speech.

CONTEXT/SELECTIVE ATTENTION

Consistent with Cohen's and Braver's model, there is indeed considerable evidence that thought-disordered patients suffer from abnormal processing of contextual information. In fact, Levelt's model of speech production incorporates contextual information at numerous stages, such as during conceptual preparation (when interpersonal context is considered, for instance). Additionally, the process of lexical selection may be influenced by discourse context (Horn & Ward, 2001), which describes the representation of previously uttered verbal information one must hold in mind to ensure that subsequent utterances will show adequate structural continuity with and semantic and conceptual relevance to the overarching conversation. Numerous investigators have examined schizophrenia patients' capacity to use discourse context to guide selection of verbal behaviors. Studies using the traditional cloze procedure (Taylor, 1953), in which the subject reads a block of text missing every fourth or fifth word and must attempt to use the context preceding each blank to guess what word is required, have found that psychotic patients tend to show impaired performance (reviewed in Cozolino, 1983); however, several marked methodological limitations of the procedure (Maher, 1991) cast uncertainty on interpretation of those findings. A great number of studies have taken a different approach (Benjamin & Watt, 1969; Chapman & Chapman, 1973; Cohen & Servan-Schreiber, 1992; Kuperberg, McGuire, & David, 1998; Sitnikova et al., 2002) using various lexical disambiguation tasks that require the subject to use contextual information from preceding clauses to determine the relevant meaning of a homograph, or a word with multiple possible definitions.

These and other investigators have generally concluded that patients with psychotic disorders fail to demonstrate sensitivity to the biasing influence of preceding contextual information; however, Chapman and Chapman (1973) refined this conclusion, arguing that patients fail to demonstrate sensitivity to discourse context only when it suggests a homograph's nondominant meaning. They characterized this deficit as "excessive yielding to normal biases," or a tendency to utilize dominant meanings. For instance, when one patient was asked to interpret the proverb "One swallow does not make a summer," he responded, "When you swallow something, it could be all right, but the next minute you could be coughing, and dreariness and all kind of miserable things coming out of your throat" (Harrow & Quinlan, 1985, p. 436). The patient clearly demonstrated a bias toward the more dominant meaning of the word "swallow," despite the fact that the context of the question implied the nondominant meaning.

Of course, excessive yielding to normal biases is the logical complement of Cohen's and Braver's cognitive control mechanism, which is defined by its ability to overcome these normal biases. Accordingly, Cohen, Braver, and colleagues argue that an individual's representation of discourse context, as well as his or her goals for the interaction (e.g., make a particular point, communicate in a certain manner) constitute contextual information, guiding the ongoing implementation of related semantic concepts (Botvinick et al., 2001). Failure to encode, update, or maintain this contextual information therefore leads to a failure to utilize discourse context to constrain and select subsequent verbal output, appearing to the observer as a relative lack of association between units of language output.

Moreover, if failure to encode, maintain, or implement contextual information is, in fact, a mechanism underlying formal thought disorder, it may explain a long-held piece of clinical wisdom – specifically, disordered speech is more likely to be elicited by abstract, ambiguous, open-ended stimuli (such as the general question posed to the quoted subjects at the beginning of this chapter, or even Rorschach inkblots; Johnston & Holzman, 1979) than by specific, closed-ended prompts. In other words, the fewer structural demands and intermediate goal states provided explicitly, the more difficult it is to practice cognitive control. Under these circumstances, not only is specific contextual information either never encoded or lost from active maintenance, but the context processing module loses the concomitant ability to inhibit the activation of competing pieces of information, exposing the system to increased memory retrieval interference (Anderson & Spellman, 1995) and subsequent loss of goal orientation in produced speech.

CAPACITY ALLOCATION

Given this continued focus on controlled processing as critical to information processing abnormalities related to formal thought disorder, it is important to consider the allocation of working memory capacity, a process shown to involve activation of dorsolateral prefrontal cortex as well as more modality-specific regions of posterior cortex (e.g., Garavan et al., 2000), as well as availability of free capacity, which appears to be reflected in the activity of dorso- (Callicott et al., 1999) and ventrolateral prefrontal cortex (Rypma, Berger, & D'Espasito 2002). Numerous studies (e.g., Docherty & Gordinier, 1999; Harvey & Pedley, 1989; Nuechterlein et al., 1986) have found correlational evidence of a relationship between working-memory capacity and aspects of formal thought disorder. Attempting to clarify the direction of this relationship, Barch and Berenbaum (1994) report that, among nonill subjects, reduction in overall processing capacity (achieved through a dual-task manipulation) is associated with decreases in verbosity and syntactic complexity, which are verbal phenomena included in formal thought disorder – particularly "negative thought disorder" (Andreasen & Grove, 1986). Melinder and Barch (2003) extend this approach to include psychotic patients, showing that they, too, manifest increased negative thought disorder with decreasing availability of working-memory capacity. These results are particularly noteworthy because the investigators were able to demonstrate that reduced processing capacity can actually *cause* speech to become disordered rather than to show a correlation between reduced processing capacity and thought disorder. Indeed, this represents one instance out of many in which schizophrenia research has shown working-memory capacity to act as a bottleneck, limiting the production or implementation of abstract ideas (e.g., Glahn et al., 2000; Silver et al., 2003).

SELF-MONITORING

Additionally, inspired by Levelt's (1989) assertion that the production of nondisordered speech requires the speaker to monitor his or her own speech, and consistent with evidence that schizophrenia patients show an impairment in the ability to self-correct erroneous behaviors (e.g., Malenka, et al., 1982) and that patients with formal thought disorder demonstrate significant impairment in self-monitoring of motor behavior (e.g., Kircher & Leube, 2003), Barch and Berenbaum (1996) administered a task requiring patients to read separate word lists and then, later, to recall whether presented words were read aloud or silently or were novel to the testing phase of the study. Patients who demonstrated worse performance on this task tended to produce a greater number of verbal derailments (i.e., switching tangentially between topics of discussion) in the independent speech sample, suggesting that, whereas amount and content of disordered speech are strongly affected by working-memory capacity available, the coherence and goal directedness of speech are influenced to a great degree by contextual processing and self-monitoring ability.

INTEGRATION OF COGNITIVE DEFICITS CONTRIBUTING TO FORMAL THOUGHT DISORDER

Hemsley and Gray also argue for impairment in self-monitoring among schizophrenia patients, proposing that disruptions in this capability result in a failure to generate match signals and a consequential increase in the extent of controlled, effortful processing engaged. Given that this repeated failure results in a reduction in availability of online processing resources concomitant with the shift from automatic to more controlled functioning, it should lead to a change in the manner in which information is retrieved from semantic memory (Badre & Wagner, 2002). Specifically, the retrieval of target information should be biased by the activation as well as by the inhibition of nontarget information (Neely, 1977) consistent with the notion of cognitive control.

An investigation by Titone, Levy, and Holzman (2000) provides further empirical support for the presence and operation of these pathological semantic memory retrieval and executive functions contributing to formal thought disorder. The authors reported the results of a cross-modal semantic priming study in which particular meanings of otherwise semantically ambiguous words were biased either moderately or strongly by the context of a preceding sentence. Experimental parameters were optimized to increase the likelihood that more controlled retrieval of semantic information would be utilized. Schizophrenia patients showed a pattern of priming identical to controls in the strong contextual bias condition but exhibited a greater degree of priming in the moderate contextual bias condition (i.e., patients showed priming effects for both relatively dominant and relatively subordinate meanings, whereas controls showed priming facilitation only for subordinate meanings). The authors point out that retrieval of a particular meaning of a word requires not only activation of the word within a semantic network but also inhibition of nearby, less relevant meanings. Patients were able to perform this selection process normally when strong contextual bias was present, but when this influence was more subtle, the patients' degraded, retrieval-related inhibitory mechanism failed to filter out alternate meanings, creating interference with the most immediately relevant meaning.

Therefore, to the extent that the study indeed engaged controlled processing mechanisms (and consequently did not rely entirely on the automatic spread of activation in a semantic network), the results support the hypothesis that disordered speech results from disrupted executive-assisted semantic memory retrieval mechanisms involving both abnormal activation-based retrieval of information from semantic memory and impaired executive function involving reduced inhibition of irrelevant, noncontextual information. Additionally, recognizing this possibility, Kerns and Berenbaum (2002) call for more direct testing of hypotheses involving a primarily inhibitory deficit fundamental to formal thought disorder.

Ex cogito, Dementia

As the foregoing discussion illustrates, current cognitive models of thought disorder have many merits, not the least of which is the ability to predict patient performance data in a variety of experimental cognitive tasks. In addition, these models converge with descriptive analyses of the experience of thought disorder in patients with psychotic disorders. Yet the parsimony that these models gain in attributing context-processing deficits in thought-disordered patients to a disturbance in a particular processing component (i.e., either a disruption in short-term representations of stimulus context or in the integration of current contextual information with memories of prior stimulus contexts) also leaves them vulnerable to refutation inasmuch as disturbances in other (or multiple) processing components of the complex, integrated circuitry mediating willed behavior could account equally well for a wide variety of thought-disordered phenomena. That is to say, demonstrating that a particular neurocognitive impairment *could* account for a particular behavioral abnormality does not necessarily demonstrate that the impairment *does* cause the abnormal behavior to occur.

Indeed, as mentioned in the Introduction, more than four decades of intensive neuroscientific investigations have failed to identify conclusively a single defining lesion in patients with schizophrenia or other forms of psychosis. Rather, as discussed in more detail subsequently, these syndromes manifest with deficits to many neural systems (e.g., cortico-cortical, fronto-striatal, temporo-limbic) across several levels of analysis (e.g., alterations in gray matter volume, dendritic arborization in cortical neurons, and neurotransmitter receptor distributions). In light of this complexity, we attempt to apply a relatively new analytical framework that has become the dominant paradigm in psychopathology research – that is, the endophenotype approach (Gottesman & Gould, 2003) – to theoretical accounts of thought disorder. The basic premise of the endophenotype approach is that a given clinical syndrome such as schizophrenia is composed of multiple neurocognitive trait deficits, each of which may be determined by at least partially independent mechanisms. A major consequence of this model is that a certain trait deficit may be necessary but not sufficient for the phenotypic manifestation of a syndrome; thus, the trait deficit will be shared by individuals with a vulnerability to the syndrome regardless of whether they manifest the syndrome phenotypically. Other deficits may be specific to individuals who manifest the syndrome phenotypically; these latter deficits may thus potentiate the expression of a symptom in those who carry vulnerability (i.e., those who have deficits in other neurocognitive domains that are necessary but not sufficient for overt disease expression). To develop this framework further in the context of a discussion of thought disorder, it will first be useful to explicate a number of facts about the genetic epidemiology and clinical neuroscience of schizophrenia.

The Genetic Epidemiology of Schizophrenia

Although we are aware of only one study reporting on the heritability of formal thought disorder itself (Gambini et al., 1997), a great deal of evidence is available demonstrating that genetic factors contribute substantially to the development of schizophrenia, accounting for about 80% of the risk of developing the disorder. The transmission pattern, however, is complex, involving at least several different genes as well as environmental factors (Cannon et al., 1998; Tsuang, Stone, & Faraone, 1999; Tsuang & Faraone, 1999). One consequence of the complexity of the inheritance pattern in schizophrenia is that an individual may carry some degree of genetic predisposition to the illness without expressing it phenotypically – or at least without expressing it to a degree severe enough to meet diagnostic criteria. Stated differently, only a subset of genetically vulnerable individuals actually develops a psychotic disorder. For many with such a genetic predisposition, an environmental contribution (to which genetically predisposed individuals might be differentially sensitive) to development of a psychotic disorder is also required. Among the environmental factors that may be involved, prenatal and perinatal complications, particularly those associated with fetal hypoxia or oxygen deprivation, are robustly associated with an increased risk for schizophrenia. Complications associated with fetal hypoxia are also of interest because fetal oxygen deprivation represents a plausible mechanism for explaining much of the structural pathology of the brain detected in neuroimaging studies of adult schizophrenia patients (Cannon, 1997).

Applying the conclusion that such genetic and environmental influences combine (additively or interactively) to determine an individual's risk for expressing a psychotic disorder to the study of neurocognitive traits helps demonstrate which such traits are likely necessary, but not sufficient, for the expression of a psychosis phenotype (or to the expression of any phenotype, including specific symptoms, for example). Specifically, deficits related entirely to the genetic diathesis for developing the given phenotype may be necessary but clearly are not sufficient for the manifestation of that phenotype. This endophenotype should be present in any individual carrying the genetic vulnerability. Consequently, if one member of a set of monozygotic twins (who, by definition, have identical genomes) displays a vulnerability-specific trait, the other must as well. Additionally, any trait not shared by both monozygotic twins must result to some degree from the influence of unique environmental events.

Neural System Abnormalities in Schizophrenia

Although neither the specific neurobiological processes associated with the expression of formal thought disorder nor those associated with psychosis in general have been definitively isolated, disturbances in prefrontal and temporo-limbic systems and their interconnections are likely to play critical roles in both (Cohen & Servan-Schreiber, 1992; Grace & Moore, 1998; Gray et al., 1991). The prefrontal cortex is thought to support higher-order cognitive processes such as working memory, the strategic allocation of attention, reasoning, planning, and other forms of abstract thought (Goldman-Rakic, 1995; Kane & Engle, 2002; Miller & Cohen, 2001). The medial temporal lobe structures (i.e., hippocampus, amygdala) and adjacent temporal cortex are involved in learning and recall of episodic information, emotion (especially the amygdala), and certain aspects of language processing (Squire & Zola, 1996).

Neuropsychological studies have shown that, against a background of generalized information processing impairment, schizophrenia patients manifest profound deficits in the areas of long-term and working memory (Cannon et al., 2000; Saykin et al., 1994). These deficits appear not to be merely secondary effects of impaired attention, disease chronicity, or medication exposure (Cirillo & Seidman, 2003). Such findings have been corroborated by evidence of abnormal physiologic activity (i.e., altered blood flow) in prefrontal and temporal lobe regions in patients with schizophrenia during performance of tests assessing these same domains of functioning (Berman et al., 1992; Callicott et al., 1998; Heckers et al., 1998; Yurgelun-Todd et al., 1996). At the structural anatomical level, schizophrenia patients show a variety of volumetric changes throughout the brain, including reduced cortical, hippocampal, and thalamic volumes (Pfefferbaum & Marsh, 1995). Recent neuroimaging work indicates a relatively greater degree of reduction in frontal and temporal cortical volumes compared with posterior cortical volumes (Cannon et al., 1998).

Prefrontal Cortex and Working-Memory Deficits

Several lines of evidence suggest that working-memory deficits and associated abnormalities in prefrontal cortical structure and function are reflective of an inherited diathesis to schizophrenia. In a Finnish twin sample, we found that impaired performance on tests of spatial working-memory capacity and structural abnormalities in polar and dorsolateral prefrontal regions varied in a dose-dependent fashion with degree of genetic loading for schizophrenia (Cannon et al., 2000; Cannon et al., 2002; Glahn et al., 2002). Interestingly, global and dorsolateral prefrontal volumetric deficits have been found to correlate with performance deficits on tests sensitive to diverse working-memory processes (Maher et al., 1995; Seidman et al., 1994). The nature of the pathological mechanism underlying these correlations is not necessarily obvious, however. Rather than a loss of neurons or interneurons, it has been suggested that gross gray matter volume decrements reflect a reduction of interneuronal neuropil – the space between neural cells consisting largely of neurons, dendrites, and axons – in the prefrontal region in patients with schizophrenia and result in impaired working-memory functioning through hypoactive dopaminergic modulation of pyramidal cell activity (Goldman-Rakic & Selemon, 1997). Rather than subcortical dopaminergic dysregulation, in this case, dopamine would be acting within the cortex (although affecting a distinct set of receptors). This prediction has been supported by a position emission tomography investigation that found significantly decreased dopamine receptor binding in the prefrontal cortex of schizophrenia patients (Okubo et al., 1997). Notably, dopamine receptor reduction predicted certain types of symptoms, as well as working-memory impairment (but also see Abi-Dargham et al., 2002). It is also of interest in this context that treatment with medication modulating cortical dopamine levels is associated with normalization of blood flow in the prefrontal cortex and increased behavioral accuracy during performance of a working-memory test (Honey & Andrew, 1999).

Given that abnormalities of working memory and prefrontal structure and function are associated with genetic liability to schizophrenia, it should be possible to identify specific genes that underlie these disturbances, especially in light of accumulating evidence of physiological abnormality. Weinberger and colleagues have reported evidence of one such genetic influence – the *MET/VAL* polymorphism of the *COMT* gene (located on chromosome 22), with *VAL* alleles promoting more rapid breakdown of synaptic dopamine, leading to prefrontal hypofunction in patients with schizophrenia (Egan et al., 2001). We have been interested in another potential susceptibility locus that may affect prefrontal function in schizophrenia – this one on chromosome 1.

Inspired by independent reports of a locus of susceptibility within a specific region on chromosome 1 (Ekelund et al., 2000; Millar et al., 2000; St. Clair et al., 1990), we performed linkage and association analyses across the chromosome 1 region of interest using quantitative neuropsychological measures of liability in our sample of twins discordant for schizophrenia (Gasperoni et al., 2003). Analyses revealed that the Visual Span subtest of the Wechsler Memory Scale, an indicator of spatial working-memory function, was significantly and uniquely sensitive to allelic varation of a gene within a highly specific portion of the chromosome – very likely to be the *DISC1* gene. The DNA sequence of the *DISC1* gene is most homologous to proteins involved in axon guidance, synaptogenesis, and intracellular axonal and dendritic transport. Recently, the protein was shown to promote neurite outgrowth (Ozeki et al., 2003). This function may help explain the reductions in neuropil volume observed in postmortem studies of schizophrenia patients.

Together, these findings strongly implicate genetic factors as playing a role in the abnormalities of prefrontal cortex and working memory in schizophrenia. Because deficits on tests sensitive to working memory have also been observed in children at elevated genetic risk (Cosway et al., 2000), it is tempting to conclude that disturbances in the prefrontal cortex in schizophrenia are reflective of an inherited vulnerability to the disorder that is present from early in life. Nevertheless, patients with schizophrenia have been found to show even greater disturbances in dorsolateral prefrontal cortex function and structure than their nonill monozygotic twins (Cannon et al., 2002). Thus, although genetic factors may cause patients and some of their first-degree relatives to share a certain degree of compromise in prefrontal cortical systems, nongenetic, disease-specific influences cause the dorsolateral prefrontal cortex to be further deviant in the patients.

TEMPORAL LOBE AND EPISODIC MEMORY DEFICITS

Several microscopic abnormalities of the hippocampus have been documented in schizophrenia, including alterations in neuronal density (Falkai & Bogerts, 1986; Huttenlocher, 1979; Jeste & Lohr, 1989; Zaidel, Esiri, & Harrison, 1997), size (Arnold, 2000; Benes, Sorensen, & Bird, 1991), and orientation (Conrad et al., 1991; Conrad & Scheibel, 1987; Kovelman & Scheibel, 1984). These hippocampal volume decrements appear to be present at disease onset (Bilder et al., 1995; Velakoulis et al., 1999) and also appear to be present to some degree in healthy biological relatives of schizophrenia patients, suggesting hippocampal volume is related to the genetic diathesis for developing schizophrenia (Lawrie et al., 1999; Seidman et al., 1999; Seidman et al., 2002). Postmortem and magnetic resonance imaging (MRI) studies of schizophrenia patients, however, have reported positive correlations between hippocampal volume and age at onset (Bogerts et al., 1990; Dauphinais et al., 1990; Stefanis et al., 1999; Van Erp et al., 2002), suggesting a relationship between hippocampal volume and the disease process, which complicates any simple interpretation.

From a neurocognitive perspective, impaired declarative memory processes that depend on the integrity of the hippocampus (Faraone et al., 2000) have been reported in both high-risk adolescents (Byrne et al., 1999) and nonpsychotic relatives of schizophrenia patients (Cannon et al., 1994), suggesting they derive, in part, from an inherited genotype. However, because long-term memory deficits are specifically more pronounced in patients compared with their own healthy monozygotic twins, nongenetic, disease-specific factors must also be involved (Cannon et al., 2000). Importantly, two studies have shown a significant relationship between deficits in verbal declarative memory and smaller hippocampal volumes in relatives of schizophrenia patients (O'Driscoll et al., 2001; Seidman et al., 2002). Furthermore, initial evidence indicates that impairment in long-term verbal memory and, to a lesser extent, executive function is associated with the occurrence of psychotic symptoms in subjects thought to be at significantly elevated risk for eventually developing a diagnosable psychotic disorder such as schizophrenia, suggesting that these deficits may mark the pathophysiological processes underlying functional deterioration during the earliest phase of disease onset (Cosway et al., 2000).

Given the putative importance of the hippocampus to verbal and executive function and, therefore, its possible role in producing disordered speech, it is of interest to revisit the issue of genetic versus environmental contributions to hippocampal integrity. Compared with other parts of the brain, the hippocampus is acutely vulnerable to hypoxic–ischemic damage (Vargha-Khadem et al., 1997; Zola & Squire, 2001) – that is, insult temporarily depriving neural cells of oxygen. In monozygotic twins discordant for schizophrenia, relatively reduced hippocampal volume in the ill twin was significantly related to the presence of labor or delivery complications and to prolonged labor, which are both risk factors associated with fetal oxygen deprivation (McNeil et al., 2000). We have previously found, in a Helsinki birth cohort, that schizophrenia patients who experienced fetal hypoxia have smaller hippocampal volumes than in those who did not – a difference not noted within unaffected siblings and healthy comparison subjects (Van Erp et al., 2002). At the same time, hippocampal volume differences occurred in a stepwise fashion with increase in genetic vulnerability for developing schizophrenia (consistent with the findings of Seidman et al., 2002), suggesting that, in patients with schizophrenia spectrum disorders, hippocampal volume is influenced in part by schizophrenia susceptibility genes and an interaction of these genes with experience of fetal hypoxia. Together, these findings indicate that, whereas hippocampal volume in healthy subjects is under substantial genetic control, hippocampal volume in schizophrenia patients and their relatives appears to be influenced to a greater extent by unique and shared environmental factors (Van Erp et al., in press).

Integrating Cognitive Models and Endophenotypes

It appears possible to unify components of the two cognitive models of disrupted information processing in schizophrenia patients and the findings related specifically to formal thought disorder reviewed in the first part of this chapter with the research on neurocognitive endophenotypes in schizophrenia just summarized. At the cognitive level of analysis, two mechanisms appear to be necessary for the expression of formal thought disorder: an executive, online processing system responsible for encoding, maintaining, and updating of goal-related information (context information in Cohen's and Braver's model) and an integrated system involving the retrieval of information from semantic memory and its fluid integration into verbal behavior (i.e., the key component of Hemsley's and Gray's model).

In terms of the endophenotype framework described previously, individuals at elevated genetic risk but not expressing the schizophrenia phenotype show mildly impaired functioning of executive systems and related working memory and attention components. These executive processing deficits therefore appear to be associated with the diathesis necessary, but not sufficient, for the development of thought disorder. Beyond this diathesis, the abnormal interaction of executive and semantic memory systems – likely in service of controlled retrieval of information and its integration into ongoing speech – is associated with a psychosis-specific factor itself related to both genetic vulnerability and exposure to environmental risk factors. Individuals with schizophrenia and their unaffected twins show a qualitatively similar pattern of prefrontal structural and functional abnormality – somewhat greater in severity in the patients. Patients and their relatives additionally show temporal lobe abnormalities; however, the degree of difference in temporal lobe abnormality between schizophrenia patients and genetically vulnerable individuals is significantly larger than the corresponding difference in prefrontal abnormality.

Taken together, these results suggest that mild impairment in prefrontal cortex and associated impairment of the functioning of online cognitive processing systems (i.e., executive functions, including working memory and selective attention) constitute a necessary but not sufficient (i.e., contributing) cause of thought disorder, which itself derives from a genetic diathesis to developing a psychotic disorder such as schizophrenia. An additional factor related etiologically to exposure to an environmental insult interacting with genetic predisposition and also necessary but not sufficient for the expression of schizophrenia involves disrupted interaction between an executive, online processing system and a semantic memory storage and selection system loosely mapping onto schizophrenia patients' prefrontal and temporal lobe abnormalities, respectively. That is, abnormalities in both the prefrontal or executive-related circuitry and in the temporal lobe circuitry (i.e., medial temporal lobe for episodic memory and nearby middle temporal gyrus for semantic memory; Kircher et al., 2001) may be required to account for the full range of thought disorder observed in patients with schizophrenia, whereas only the former may be required to account for the subtler thought disturbances seen in genetically vulnerable individuals who do not manifest the full schizophrenia syndrome phenotypically (perhaps the case with the interviewee in the second quote at the beginning of this chapter). Of course, it is also possible that severity of phenotypic thought disorder scales with severity of compromise of both components of the system rather than to their conjunction per se. Further work is needed to segregate these two possibilities.

In summary, research related to the cognitive, genetic, and neural pathologies of thought disorder in general, and schizophrenia specifically, has necessarily taken on a complex, interactive structure. As we have seen, cognitive models designed to predict particular behavioral outcomes can, in fact, help researchers to understand the functional correlates of anatomical abnormalities measured between genetically defined risk groups. Similar permutations involving these and numerous other levels of analysis equip us with heuristics that guide our struggle to unravel the complexities of neuropsychiatric phenomena such as formal thought disorder. We have attempted to present such a heuristic framework based on links we have observed between bodies of research into the pathology of thought disorder; some of these links cross between levels of analysis, ideally helping us to map genetic, neurological, and cognitive systems onto each other.

Future Directions

Along the way to accomplishing this integrative goal, a great deal more work needs to be done. Ideally, the parsing of formal thought disorder into necessary and sufficient functional components – such as the work being carried out on the level of cognitive specification by Barch, Berenbaum, and colleagues – will be complemented by further study of the physiological and genetic variations associated with the production of abnormal speech.

This line of work will likely be facilitated by cognitive neuroscience's growing ability to study the activity of particular brain mechanisms during the production of speech, overcoming previously prohibitive practical obstacles caused by movement artifacts detrimental to work utilizing functional MRI (Barch et al., 1999) and EEG (e.g., Ford et al., 2002). Prior to these methodological advances, only speech production studies employing *covert* vocalization were practical; however, these investigations typically fall short of describing compellingly aspects of formal thought disorder itself – a phenomenon measured entirely in terms of *overt* speech production.

Additional progress in the study of thought disorder involves application of paradigms from the emerging field of social cognitive neuroscience (e.g., Adolphs, 2003; Wood, 2003) to the study of interpersonal deficits in schizophrenia (e.g., Penn et al., 2002; Pinkham et al., 2003), including the distinctly interpersonal task of verbal communication (Grossman & Harrow, 1996; Racenstein et al., 1999). For instance, the study of communication deviance (including aspects of formal thought disorder) within the families of patients with psychotic disorder diagnoses or patients thought to be at high risk for developing a psychotic disorder has been an area of active research for some time (e.g., Docherty, 1995; Sass et al., 1984; Wahlberg et al., 2000). Applying this established framework to the examination of neuronal correlates of receptive and productive aspects of intrafamily communication – potentially distinct from communication with nonfamily individuals because of the role of factors such as increased interpersonal familiarity and less predictable affective modulation of cognitive processes involved in communication – offers a novel perspective with the potential to reinvigorate this important line of thought disorder research.

Another area of thought disorder research deserving continued attention involves the study of formal thought disorder in populations other than those currently meeting diagnostic criteria for a major mental illness. Although modern antipsychotic medications appear to be relatively effective at helping psychotic patients organize their speech (e.g., Wirshing et al., 1999), significant levels of thought disorder often appear noticeable in groups of patients who would not typically be treated with therapeutic doses of such medications (Andreasen & Grove, 1986). For instance, in a sample of patients judged to be at significantly elevated risk for developing a psychotic disorder (in part because they were displaying some psychotic symptoms but at a level of intensity or frequency below diagnostic threshold), we found a significant level of formal thought disorder – interestingly, coupled with significant impairment of selective attention – which remitted with relatively low-dose antipsychotic pharmacotherapy (Cannon et al., 2002). These and similar findings raise interesting questions regarding the potential utility of formal thought disorder as a prodromal indicator of psychosis as well as the potential benefits of symptom-based treatment outside the context of a major psychiatric diagnosis.

Acknowledgments

Preparation of this manuscript was supported by grants MH52857, MH65079, and MH66286 from the National Institute of Mental Health; by grant RR00827 to the FIRST Biomedical Informatics Research Network (*http://www.nbirn.net*), which is funded by the National Center for Research Resources at the National Institutes of Health; and by a gift to the University of California, Los Angeles Foundation, from Garen and Shari Staglin.

Notes

1. Delusions and similar disorders of thought content are not the central focus of this chapter but might be of interest to cognitive psychologists. For instance, the study of development and maintenance of delusions is an area of active research. See Bermudez (2001), Garety and Freeman (1999), Gold and Hohwy (2000), and/or Maher (2002) for debate over whether or not delusions represent products of flawed inferential reasoning.
2. Bleuler is likely also the source of the distinction between thought form and content discussed earlier because he drew the distinction (Bleuler, 1911/1950) between what he labeled "fundamental symptoms," including, but not limited to, the loosening of ideational associations, and "accessory symptoms," including hallucinations and delusions.
3. Working in parallel with Cohen, Braver, and colleagues, Kane and Engle (2002) and their

collaborators have proposed a model of information maintenance and behavioral response selection entirely compatible with Cohen, Braver, and colleagues' model. Rather than referring to a context-processing module, however, Kane and Engle (2002) deem the same cognitive mechanism "controlled attention" and survey implications of applying the model to patients with frontal lobe lesions, although this mechanism is certainly relevant to psychosis.

4. In fact, Bleuler (1911/1951, as discussed in Chapman & Chapman, 1973), writing nearly one century ago, argued that formal thought disorder in schizophrenia patients involves a failure to utilize context information to bind ideational elements together in logical sequence. However he blamed this disorder on the breaking of the "associative thread" linking a given goal to the appropriate contextual influence, rather than considering the goal context itself.
5. See Andreasen et al. (1999) for the description of an alternate, circuit-based comparator mechanism.

References

Abi-Dargham, A., Mawlawi, O., Lombardo, I., Gil, R., Martinez, D., Huang, Y., et al. (2002). Prefrontal dopamine D1 receptors and working memory in schizophrenia. *Journal of Neuroscience*, *22*(9), 3708–3719.

Adolphs, R. (2003). Cognitive neuroscience of human social behavior. *Nature Reviews Neuroscience*, *4*(3), 165–178.

Allen, H. A., Liddle, P. F., & Frith, C. D. (1993). Negative features, retrieval processes and verbal fluency in schizophrenia. *British Journal of Psychiatry*, 163, 769–775.

American Psychiatric Association. (2000). *Diagnostic and Statistical Manual of Mental Disorders, Fourth Edition, Text Revision*. Washington, DC: American Psychiatric Association.

Anderson, M. C., & Spellman, B. A. (1995). On the status of inhibitory mechanisms in cognition: Memory retrieval as a model case. *Psychology Review*, *102*(1), 68–100.

Andreasen, N. C. (1979). Thought, language, and communication disorders. I. Clinical assessment, definition of terms, and evaluation of their reliability. *Archives of General Psychiatry*, *36*(12), 1315–1321.

Andreasen, N. C. (1982). Should the term "thought disorder" be revised? *Comprehensive Psychiatry*, *23*(4), 291–299.

Andreasen, N. C. (1986). Scale for the assessment of thought, language, and communication (TLC). *Schizophrenia Bulletin*, *12*(3), 473–482.

Andreasen, N. C., & Grove, W. M. (1986). Thought, language, and communication in schizophrenia: Diagnosis and prognosis. *Schizophrenia Bulletin*, *12*(3), 348–359

Andreasen, N. C., Nopoulos, P., O'Leary, D. S., Miller, D. D., Wassink, T., & Flaum, M. (1999). Defining the phenotype of schizophrenia: Cognitive dysmetria and its neural mechanisms. *Biological Psychiatry*, *46*(7), 908–920.

Arnold, S. E. (2000). Cellular and molecular neuropathology of the parahippocampal region in schizophrenia. *Annals of the New York Academy of Science*, *911*, 275–292.

Baddeley, A. D. (1986). *Working Memory*. New York: Oxford University Press.

Badre, D., & Wagner, A. D. (2004). Selection, integration, and conflict monitoring: Assessing the nature and generality of prefrontal cognitive control mechanisms. *Neuron*, *41*(3), 473–487.

Barch, D., & Berenbaum, H. (1994). The relationship between information processing and language production. *Journal of Abnormal Psychology*, *103*(2), 241–250.

Barch, D. M., & Berenbaum, H. (1996). Language production and thought disorder in schizophrenia. *Journal of Abnormal Psychology*, *105*(1), 81–88.

Barch, D. M., Braver, T. S., Nystrom, L. E., Forman, S. D., Noll, D. C., & Cohen, J. D. (1997). Dissociating working memory from task difficulty in human prefrontal cortex. *Neuropsychologia*, *35*(10), 1373–1380.

Barch, D. M., Carter, C. S., MacDonald, A. W., Braver, T. S., & Cohen, J. D. (2003). Context-processing deficits in schizophrenia: Diagnostic specificity, 4-week course, and relationships to clinical symptoms. *Journal of Abnormal Psychology*, *112*(1), 132–143.

Barch, D. M., Sabb, F. W., Carter, C. S., Braver, T. S., Noll, D. C., & Cohen, J. D. (1999). Overt verbal responding during fMRI scanning: Empirical investigations of problems and potential solutions. *Neuroimage*, *10*(6), 642–657.

Baving, L., Wagner, M., Cohen, R., & Rockstroch, B. (2001). Increased semantic and repetition priming in schizophrenic patients. *Journal of Abnormal Psychology, 110(1)*, 67–75.

Berenbaum, H., & Barch D. (1995). The categorization of thought disorder. *Journal of Psycholinguistic Research, 24(5)*, 349–376.

Benes, F. M., Sorensen, I., & Bird, E. D. (1991). Reduced neuronal size in posterior hippocampus of schizophrenic patients. *Schizophrenia Bulletin, 17(4)*, 597–608.

Benjamin, T. B., & Watt, N. F. (1969). Psychopathology and semantic interpretation of ambiguous words. *Journal of Abnormal Psychology*, 706–714.

Berman, K. F., Torrey, E. F., Daniel, D. G., & Weinberger, D. R. (1992). Regional cerebral blood flow in monozygotic twins discordant and concordant for schizophrenia. *Archives of General Psychiatry, 49(12)*, 927–934.

Bermudez, J. L. (2001). Normativity and rationality in delusional psychiatric disorders. *Mind and Language, 16(5)*, 457–493.

Besche, C., Passerieux, C., Segui, J., Sarfati, Y., Laurent, J. P., & Hardy-Bayle, M. C. (1997). Syntactic and semantic processing in schizophrenic patients evaluated by lexical-decision tasks. *Neuropsychology, 11(4)*, 498–505.

Bilder, R. M., Bogerts, B., Ashtari, M., Wu, H., Alvir, J. M., Jody, D., et al. (1995). Anterior hippocampal volume reductions predict frontal lobe dysfunction in first episode schizophrenia. *Schizophrenia Research, 17(1)*, 47–58.

Bleuler, E. (1911). *Dementia Praecox, or the Group of Schizophrenias*. Translated by J. Zinkin (1950). New York: International Universities Press.

Bleuler, E. (1911/1951). Autistic-undisciplined Thinking. Reprinted in D. Rapaport (Ed.), *Organization and Pathology of Thought*. New York: Columbia University Press.

Blum, N. A., & Freides, D. (1995). Investigating thought disorder in schizophrenia with the lexical decision task. *Schizophrenia Research, 16(3)*, 217–224.

Bogerts, B., Ashtari, M., Degreef, G., Alvir, J. M., Bilder, R. M., & Lieberman, J. A. (1990). Reduced temporal limbic structure volumes on magnetic resonance images in first episode schizophrenia. *Psychiatry Research, 35(1)*, 1–13.

Botvinick, M. M., Braver, T. S., Barch, D. M., Carter, C. S., & Cohen, J. D. (2001). Conflict monitoring and cognitive control. *Psychological Review, 108(3)*, 624–652.

Braver, T. S., Barch, D. M., & Cohen, J. D. (1999). Cognition and control in schizophrenia: A computational model of dopamine and prefrontal function. *Biological Psychiatry, 46(3)*, 312–328.

Braver, T. S., Barch, D. M., Keys, B. A., Carter, C. S., Cohen, J. D., Kaye, J. A., et al. (2001). Context processing in older adults: Evidence for a theory relating cognitive control to neurobiology in healthy aging. *Journal of Experimental Psychology: General, 130(4)*, 746–763.

Braver, T. S., Cohen, J. D., Nystrom, L. E., Jonides, J., Smith, E. E., & Noll, D. C. (1997). A parametric study of prefrontal cortex involvement in human working memory. *Neuroimage, 5(1)*, 49–62.

Braver, T. S., Reynolds, J. R., & Donaldson, D. I. (2003). Neural mechanisms of transient and sustained cognitive control during task switching. *Neuron, 39(4)*, 713–726.

Byrne, M., Hodges, A., Grant, E., Owens, D. C., & Johnstone, E. C. (1999). Neuropsychological assessment of young people at high genetic risk for developing schizophrenia compared with controls: Preliminary findings of the Edinburgh High Risk Study (EHRS). *Psychological Medicine, 29(5)*, 1161–1173.

Callicott, J. H., Ramsey, N. F., Tallent, K., Bertolino, A., Knable, M. B., Coppola, R., et al. (1998). Functional magnetic resonance imaging brain mapping in psychiatry: Methodological issues illustrated in a study of working memory in schizophrenia. *Neuropsychopharmacology, 18(3)*, 186–196.

Callicott, J. H., Mattay, V. S., Bertolino, A., Finn, K., Coppola, R., Frank, J. A., et al. (1999). Physiological characteristics of capacity constraints in working memory as revealed by functional MRI. *Cerebral Cortex, 9(1)*, 20–26.

Cannon, T. D. (1997). On the nature and mechanisms of obstetric influences in schizophrenia: A review and synthesis of epidemiologic studies. *International Review of Psychiatry, 9(4)*, 387–397.

Cannon, T. D., Huttunen, M.O, Dahlstróm, M., Larmo, I., Rásánen, P., & Juriloo, A. (2002). Antipsychotic drug treatment in the prodromal phase of schizophrenia. *Archives of General Psychiatry, 159(7)*, 1230–1232.

Cannon, T. D., Huttunen, M. O., Lonnqvist, J., Tuulio-Henriksson, A., Pirkola, T., Glahn, D., et al. (2000). The inheritance of neuropsychological dysfunction in twins discordant for schizophrenia. *American Journal of Human Genetics, 67(2)*, 369–382.

Cannon, T. D., Kaprio, J., Lonnqvist, J., Huttunen, M., & Koskenvuo, M. (1998). The genetic epidemiology of schizophrenia in a Finnish twin cohort. A population-based modeling study. *Archives of General Psychiatry, 55(1)*, 67–74.

Cannon, T. D., & Rosso, I. M. (2002). Levels of analysis in etiological research on schizophrenia. *Development and Psychopathology, 14(3)*, 653–666.

Cannon, T. D., Rosso, I. M., Hollister, J. M., Bearden, C. E., Sanchez, L. E., & Hadley, T. (2000). A prospective cohort study of genetic and perinatal influences in the etiology of schizophrenia. *Schizophrenia Bulletin, 26(2)*, 351–366.

Cannon, T. D., Thompson, P. M., van Erp, T. G., Toga, A. W., Poutanen, V. P., Huttunen, M., et al. (2002). Cortex mapping reveals regionally specific patterns of genetic and disease-specific gray-matter deficits in twins discordant for schizophrenia. *Proceedings of the National Academy of Sciences, U.S.A., 99(5)*, 3228–3233.

Cannon, T. D., van Erp, T. G., Huttunen, M., Lonnqvist, J., Salonen, O., Valanne, L., et al. (1998). Regional gray matter, white matter, and cerebrospinal fluid distributions in schizophrenic patients, their siblings, and controls. *Archives of General Psychiatry, 55(12)*, 1084–1091.

Cannon, T. D., Zorrilla, L. E., Shtasel, D., Gur, R. E., Gur, R. C., Marco, E. J., et al. (1994). Neuropsychological functioning in siblings discordant for schizophrenia and healthy volunteers. *Archives of General Psychiatry, 51(8)*, 651–661.

Chaika, E. (1982). Thought disorder or speech disorder in schizophrenia? *Schizophrenia Bulletin, 8(4)*, 587–594.

Chapman, L. J., & Chapman, J. P. (1973). *Disordered Thought in Schizophrenia*. New York: Appleton-Century-Crofts.

Cirillo, M. A., & Seidman, L. J. (2003). Verbal declarative memory dysfunction in schizophrenia: From clinical assessment to genetics and brain mechanisms. *Neuropsychology Review, 13(2)*, pp. 43–77.

Clark, H. H. (1996). *Using Language*. Cambridge, UK: Cambridge University Press.

Cohen, J. D., Barch, D. M., Carter, C., & Servan-Schreiber, D. (1999). Context-processing deficits in schizophrenia: Converging evidence from three theoretically motivated cognitive tasks. *Journal of Abnormal Psychology*, 108(1), 120–133.

Cohen, J. D., Perlstein, W. M., Braver, T. S., Nystrom, L. E., Noll, D. C., Jonides, J., et al. (1997). Temporal dynamics of brain activation during a working memory task. *Nature, 386(6625)*, 604–608.

Cohen, J. D., & Servan-Schreiber, D. (1992). Context, cortex, and dopamine: A connectionist approach to behavior and biology in schizophrenia. *Psychological Review, 99(1)*, 45–77.

Conrad, A. J., Abebe, T., Austin, R., Forsythe, S., & Scheibel, A. B. (1991). Hippocampal pyramidal cell disarray in schizophrenia as a bilateral phenomenon. *Archives of General Psychiatry, 48(5)*, 413–417.

Conrad, A. J., & Scheibel, A. B. (1987). Schizophrenia and the hippocampus: The embryological hypothesis extended. *Schizophrenia Bulletin, 13(4)*, 577–587.

Cosway, R., Byrne, M., Clafferty, R., Hodges, A., Grant, E., Abukmeil, S. S., et al. (2000). Neuropsychological change in young people at high risk for schizophrenia: Results from the first two neuropsychological assessments of the Edinburgh High Risk Study. *Psychological Medicine, 30(5)*, 1111–1121.

Cozolino, L. J. (1983). The oral and written productions of schizophrenic patients. *Progress in Experimental Personality Research*, 12, 101–152.

Critchley, M. (1964). The neurology of psychotic speech. *British Journal of Psychiatry*, 110, 353–364.

Dauphinais, I. D., DeLisi, L. E., Crow, T. J., Alexandropoulos, K., Colter, N., Tuma, I., et al. (1990). Reduction in temporal lobe size in siblings with schizophrenia: A magnetic resonance imaging study. *Psychiatry Research, 35(2)*, 137–147.

David, A. S., & Cutting, J. C. (1994). *The Neuropsychology of Schizophrenia*. Hove, UK: Psychology Press.

DeLisi, L. E. (2001). Speech disorder in schizophrenia: Review of the literature and exploration of its relation to the uniquely human capacity for language. *Schizophrenia Bulletin, 27(3)*, 481–496.

Dell, G. S., & O'Seaghdha, P. G. (1991). Mediated and convergent lexical priming in language production: A comment on Levelt et al. (1991). *Psychological Review, 98(4)*, 604–614.

Dell, G. S., Schwartz, M. F., Martin, N., Saffran, E. M., & Gagnon, D. A. (1997). Lexical access in aphasic and nonaphasic speakers. *Psychological Review, 104(4)*, 801–838.

Dick, F., Bates, E., Wulfeck, B., Utman, J. A., Dronkers, N., & Gernsbucher, M. A. (2001). Language deficits, localization, and grammer: Evidence for a distributive model of language breakdown in aphasic patrents and neurologically intact individuals. *Psychological Review, 108(4)*, 759–788.

Docherty, N. M. (1995). Expressed emotion and language disturbances in parents of stable schizophrenia patients. *Schizophrenia Bulletin, 21(3)*, 411–418.

Docherty, N. M., & Gordinier, S. W. (1999). Immediate memory, attention and communication disturbances in schizophrenia patients and their relatives. *Psychological Medicine, 29(1)*, 189–197.

Dodd, B., & Crosbie, S. (2002). Language and cognition: Evidence from disordered language. In Goswami, U. (Ed.), *Blackwell Handbook of Childhood Cognitive Development*. Malden, MA: Blackwell.

Dronkers, N. F., Redfern, B. A., & Knight, R. T. (1999). The neural architecture of language disorders. In M. S. Gazzaniga, (Ed.), *The New Cognitive Neurosciences, (2nd ed.)*. Cambridge, MA: MIT Press.

Duncan, J. (2001). An adaptive coding model of neural function in prefrontal cortex. *Nature Reviews Neuroscience, 2(11)*, 820–829.

Egan, M. F., Goldberg, T. E., Kolachana, B. S., Callicott, J. H., Mazzanti, C. M., et al. (2001). Effect of COMT Val108/158 Met genotype on frontal lobe function and risk for schizophrenia. *Proceedings of the National Academy of Sciences U.S.A., 98(12)*, 6917–6922.

Ekelund, J., Lichtermann, D., Hovatta, I., Ellonen, P., Suvisaari, J., Terwilliger, J. D., et al. (2000). Genome-wide scan for schizophrenia in the Finnish population: Evidence for a locus on chromosome 7q22. *Human Molecular Genetics, 9(7)*, 1049–1057.

Falkai, P., & Bogerts, B. (1986). Cell loss in the hippocampus of schizophrenics. *European Archives of Psychiatry and Neurological Science, 236(3)*, 154–161.

Fanselow, M. S. (2000). Contextual fear, Gestalt memories, and the hippocampus. *Behavioral Brain Research, 110(1–2)*, 73–81.

Faraone, S. V., Seidman, L. J., Kremen, W. S., Toomey, R., Pepple, J. R., & Tsuang, M. T. (2000). Neuropsychologic functioning among the nonpsychotic relatives of schizophrenic patients: The effect of genetic loading. *Biological Psychiatry, 48(2)*, 120–126.

Ford, J. M., Mathalon, D. H., Whitfield, S., Faustman, W. O., & Roth, W. T. (2002). Reduced communication between frontal and temporal lobes during talking in schizophrenia. *Biological Psychiatry, 51 (6)*, 485–492.

Frith, C. (2002). Attention to action and awareness of other minds. *Consciousness and Cognition, 11 (4)*, 481–487.

Frith, C. D. (1987). The positive and negative symptoms of schizophrenia reflect impairments in the perception and initiation of action. *Psychological Medicine, 17(3)*, 631–648.

Frith, C. D., Friston, K. J., Liddle, P. F., & Frackowiak, R. S. (1992). PET imaging and cognition in schizophrenia. *Journal of the Royal Society of Medicine, 85(4)*, 222–224.

Gambini, O., Campana, A., Macciardi, F., & Scarone, S. (1997). A preliminary report of a strong genetic component for thought disorder in normals: A twin study. *Neuropsychobiology, 36(1)*, 13–18.

Garety, P. A., & Freeman, D. (1999). Cognitive approaches to delusions: A critical review of theories and evidence. *British Journal of Clinical Psychology, 38(2)*, 113–154.

Garavan, H., Ross, T. J., Li, S. J., & Stein, E. A. (2000). A parametric manipulation of central executive functioning. *Cerebral Cortex, 10(6)*, 585–592.

Gasperoni, T. L., Ekelund, J., Huttunen, M., Palmer, C. G., Tuulio-Henriksson, A., Lonnqvist, J., Kaprio, J., Peltonen, L., & Cannon, T. D. (2003). Genetic linkage and association between chromosome 1q and working memory function in schizophrenia. *American Journal of Medical Genetics, 116B(1)*, 8–16.

Glahn, D. C., Cannon, T. D., Gur, R. E., Ragland, J. D., & Gur, R. C. (2000). Working memory constrains abstraction in schizophrenia. *Biological Psychiatry, 47(1)*, 34–42.

Glahn, D. C., Kim, J., Cohen, M. S., Poutanen, V. P., Therman, S., Bava, S., et al. (2002).

Maintenance and manipulation in spatial working memory: Dissociations in the prefrontal cortex. *Neuroimage, 17*(1), 201–213.

Goddard, M. J. (2001). Context modulation of US signal value following explicit and nonexplicit training. *Behavioral Processes, 56*(2), 67–74.

Gold, B. T., & Buckner, R. L. (2002). Common prefrontal regions coactivate with dissociable posterior regions during controlled semantic and phonological tasks. *Neuron, 35*(4), 803–812.

Gold, I., & Hohwy, J. (2000). Rationality and schizophrenic delusion. *Mind and Language, 15*(1), 146–167.

Goldberg, T. E., Aloia, M. S., Gourovitch, M. L., Missar, D., Pickar, D., & Weinberger, D. R. (1998). Cognitive substrates of thought disorder, I: The semantic system. *American Journal of Psychiatry, 155*(12), 1671–1676.

Goldman-Rakic, P. S. (1995). Architecture of the prefrontal cortex and the central executive. *Annals of the New York Academy of Science, 769*, 71–83.

Goldman-Rakic, P. S., & Selemon, L. D. (1997). Functional and anatomical aspects of prefrontal pathology in schizophrenia. *Schizophrenia Bulletin, 23*(3), 437–458.

Gottesman, II, & Gould, T. D. (2003). The endophenotype concept in psychiatry: Etymology and strategic intentions. *American Journal of Psychiatry, 160*(4), 636–645.

Grace, A. A. (1991). Phasic versus tonic dopamine release and the modulation of dopamine system responsivity: A hypothesis for the etiology of schizophrenia. *Neuroscience, 41* (1), 1–24.

Grace, A. A., & Moore, H., & O'Donnell, P. (1998). The modulation of corticoaccumbens transmission by limbic afferents and dopamine: A model for the pathophysiology of schizophrenia. *Advances in Pharmacology, 42*, 721–724.

Grace, A. A., & Moore, H. (1998). Regulation of information flow in the nucleus accumbens: A model for the pathophysiology of schizophrenia. In M. F. Lenzenweger & R. H. Dworkin (Eds). *Origins and Development of Schizophrenia: Advances in Experimental Psychopathology*. Washington, DC: American Psychological Association.

Gray, J. A. (1982). *The Neuropsychology of Anxiety: An Enquiry into the Functions of the Septo-Hippocampal System*. New York: Oxford University Press.

Gray, J. A. (1995). Dopamine release in the nucleus accumbens: The perspective from aberrations of consciousness in schizophrenia. *Neuropsychologia, 33*(9), 1143–1153.

Gray, J. A. (1998). Integrating schizophrenia. *Schizophrenia Bulletin, 24*(2), 249–266.

Gray, J. A., Feldon, J., Rawlins, J. N., Hemsley, D. R., Young, A. M. J., Warburton, E. C., et al. (1991). The neuropsychology of schizophrenia. *Behavioral and Brain Sciences, 14*(1), 1–84.

Grossman, L. S., & Harrow, M. (1996). Interactive behavior in bipolar manic and schizophrenic patients and its link to thought disorder. *Comprehensive Psychiatry, 37*(4), 245–252.

Harrow, M., & Quinlan, D. M. (1985). *Disordered Thinking and Schizophrenic Psychopathology*. New York: Gardner Press.

Harvey, P. D., & Pedley, M. (1989). Auditory and visual distractability in schizophrenia: Clinical and medication status correlates. *Schizophrenia Research*, 2 (3), 295–300.

Heckers, S., Rauch, S. L., Goff, D., Savage, C. R., Schacter, D. L., Fischman, A. J., et al. (1998). Impaired recruitment of the hippocampus during conscious recollection in schizophrenia. *Nature Neuroscience, 1* (4), 318–323.

Hemsley, D. R. (1987). An experimental psychological model for schizophrenia. In W. Janzavik (Ed.), *Search for the Causes of Schizophrenia* (pp. 179–188). Stuttgart: Springer-Verlag.

Hemsley, D. R. (1993). A simple (or simplistic?) cognitive model for schizophrenia. *Behavioral Research and Therapy, 31* (7), 633–645.

Hemsley, D. R. (1994). A cognitive model for schizophrenia and its possible neural basis. *Acta Psychiatrica Scandinavica, Suppl.* 384, 80–86.

Honey, R. C., & Watt, A. (1999). Acquired relational equivalence between contexts and features. *Journal of Experimental Psychology: Animal Behavior Processes, 25*(3), 324–333.

Honigfeld, G. (1963). Effect of an hallucinogenic agent on verbal behavior. *Psychological Reports, 13*(2), 383–385.

Horn, L., & Ward, G. (2001). Pragmatics. In F. C. Keil (Ed.), *The MIT Encyclopedia of the Cognitive Sciences (MITECS), (Vol. 1)*. Cambridge, MA: MIT Press.

Huttenlocher, P. R. (1979). Synaptic density in human frontal cortex - developmental changes and effects of aging. *Brain Research, 163(2)*, 195–205.

Indefrey, P., & Levelt, W. J. M. (1999). Chapter 59. The neural correlates of language production. In M. S. Gazzaniga (Ed.), *The New Cognitive Neurosciences* (2nd ed.), (pp. 845–866). Cambridge, MA: MIT Press.

Jansma, J. M., Ramsey, N. F., Slagter, H. A., & Kahn, R. S. (2001). Functional anatomical correlates of controlled and automatic processing. *Journal of Cognitive Neuroscience, 13(6)*, 730–743.

Jeste, D. V., & Lohr, J. B. (1989). Hippocampal pathologic findings in schizophrenia. A morphometric study. *Archives of General Psychiatry, 46(11)*, 1019–1024.

Johnston, M. H., & Holzman, P. S. (1979). *Assessing Schizophrenic Thinking*. San Francisco: Jossey-Bass.

Kane, M. J., & Engle, R. W. (2002). The role of prefrontal cortex in working-memory capacity, executive attention, and general fluid intelligence: An individual-differences perspective. *Psychonomic Bulletin and Review, 9(4)*, 637–671.

Kerns, J. G., Berenbaum, H., Barch D. M., Banick, M. T., & Stolar, N. (1999). Word production in schizophrenia and its relationship to positive symptoms. *Psychiatry Research, 87(1)*, 29–37.

Kerns, J. G., & Berenbaum, H. (2002). Cognitive impairments associated with formal thought disorder in people with schizophrenia. *Journal of Abnormal Psychology, 111 (2)*, 211–224.

Kircher, T. T., & Leube, D. T. (2003). Self-consciousness, self-agency, and schizophrenia. *Consciousness and Cognition, 12(4)*: 656–669.

Kircher, T. T., Liddle, P. F., Brammer, M. J., Williams, S. C., Murray, R. M., & McGuire, P. K. (2001). Neural correlates of formal thought disorder in schizophrenia: Preliminary findings from a functional magnetic resonance imaging study. *Archives of General Psychiatry, 58(8)*, 769–774.

Kolb, B., & Whishaw, I. Q. (1996) *Fundamentals of human neuropsychology, (fourth edition)*. New York: Freeman Press.

Kostova, M., Passerieux, C., Laurent, J. P., Hardy-Bayle, M. C. (2003). An electrophysiologic study: Can semantic context processes be mobilized in patients with thought-disordered schizophrenia?. *Canadian Journal of Psychiatry, 48(9)*, 615–623.

Kounios, J., Bachman, P., Casasanto, D., Grossman, M., Smith, R. W., & Yang, W. (2003). Novel concepts mediate word retrieval from human episodic associative memory: Evidence from event-related potentials. *Neuroscience Letters, 345(3)*, 157–160.

Kovelman, J. A., & Scheibel, A. B. (1984). A neurohistological correlate of schizophrenia. *Biological Psychiatry, 19(12)*, 1601–1621.

Kuperberg, G. R., McGuire, P. K., & David, A. S. (1998). Reduced sensitivity to linguistic context in schizophrenic thought disorder: Evidence from on-line monitoring for words in linguistically anomalous sentences. *Journal of Abnormal Psychology, 107(3)*, 423–434.

Landre, N. A., & Taylor, M. A. (1995). Formal thought disorder in schizophrenia. Linguistic, attentional, and intellectual correlates. *Journal of Nervous and Mental Disease, 183(11)*, 673–680.

Laruelle, M., Kegeles, L. S., & Abi-Dargham, A. (2003). Glutamate, dopamine, and schizophrenia: From pathophysiology to treatment. *Annals of the New York Academy of Sciences*, 1003, 138–158.

Lawrie, S. M., Whalley, H., Kestelman, J. N., Abukmeil, S. S., Byrne, M., Hodges, A., et al. (1999). Magnetic resonance imaging of brain in people at high risk of developing schizophrenia. *Lancet, 353(9146)*, 30–33.

Levelt, W. J. M. (1989). *Speaking: From Intention to Articulation*. Cambridge, MA: The MIT Press.

Levelt, W. J. M. (1999). Language production: A blueprint of the speaker. In C. Brown & P. Hagoort, (Eds.), *Neurocognition of Language*. Oxford, UK: Oxford University Press.

Levelt, W. J., Roelofs, A., Meyer, A. S. (1999). A theory of lexical access in speech production. *Behavioral and Brain Sciences, 22(1)*, 1–75.

Liddle, P. F. (1987). The symptoms of chronic schizophrenia. A re-examination of the positive-negative dichotomy. *British Journal of Psychiatry*, 151, 145–151.

Lubow, R. E. M. (1959). Latent inhibition: The effect of nonreinforced pre-exposure to the conditional stimulus. *Journal of Comparative and Physiological Psychology*, 52, 415–419.

Maher, B. A. (1966). *Principles of Psychopathology: An Experimental Approach*. New York: McGraw-Hill.

Maher, B. A. (1991). Language and schizophrenia. In J. H. Gruzelier (Ed.), *Neuropsychology, Psychophysiology, and Information Processing. Handbook of Schizophrenia, Vol. 5*, (pp. 437–464). New York: Elsevier Science.

Maher, B. A. (2002). Psychopathology and delusions: Reflections on methods and models. In M. F. Lenzenweger (Ed.), *Principles of Experimental Psychopathology: Essays in Honor of Brendan A. Maher, (1st ed.)*. Washington, DC: American Psychological Association.

Maher, B. A., Manschreck, T. C., Woods, B. T., Yurgelun-Todd, D. A., & Tsuang, M. T. (1995). Frontal brain volume and context effects in short-term recall in schizophrenia. *Biological Psychiatry, 37(3)*, 144–150.

Malenka, R. C., Angel, R. W., Hampton, B., & Berger, P. A. (1982). Impaired central error-correcting behavior in schizophrenia. *Archives of General Psychiatry, 39(1)*, 101–107.

Martin, A., Chao, L. L. (2001). Semantic memory and the brain: Structure and processes. *Current Opinion in Neurobiology, 11(2)*, 194–201.

Martin, R. C., & Freedman, M. L. (2001). Short-term retention of lexical-semantic representations: Implications for speech production. *Memory, 9(4)*, 261–280.

McGhie, A., & Chapman, J. (1961). Disorders of attention and perception in early schizophrenia. *British Journal of Medical Psychology, 34*: 103–116.

McNeil, T. F., Cantor-Graae, E., & Weinberger, D. R. (2000). Relationship of obstetric complications and differences in size of brain structures in monozygotic twin pairs discordant for schizophrenia. *American Journal of Psychiatry, 157(2)*, 203–212.

McNeill, D., & S. Duncan. (1999). Growth points in thinking for speaking. In E. D. McNeill (Ed.), *Language and Gesture: Window into Thought and Action*. Cambridge, UK: Cambridge University Press.

Millar, J. K., Wilson-Annan, J. C., Anderson, S., Christie, S., Taylor, M. S., Semple, C. A., et al. (2000). Disruption of two novel genes by a translocation co-segregating with schizophrenia. *Human Molecular Genetics, 9(9)*, 1415–1423.

Miller, E. K., & Cohen, J. D. (2001). An integrative theory of prefrontal cortex function. *Annual Review of Neuroscience, 24*, 167–202.

Minzenberg, M. J., Ober, B. A., & Vinogradov, S. (2002). Semantic priming in schizophrenia: A review and synthesis. *Journal of the International Neuropsychology Society, 8(5)*, 699–720.

Neely, J. H. (1977). Semantic priming and retrieval from lexical memory: Roles of inhibitionless spreading activation and limited-capacity attention. *Journal of Experimental Psychology: General, 106(3)*, 226–254.

Nestor, P. G., Kimble, M. O., O'Donnell, B. F., Smith, L., Niznikiewicz, M., Shenton, M. E., et al. (1997). Aberrant semantic activation in schizophrenia: A neurophysiological study. *American Journal of Psychiatry, 154(5)*, 640–646.

Nestor, P. G., Akdag, S. J., O'Donnell, B. F., Niznikiewicz, M., Law, S., Shenton, M. E., et al. (1998). Word recall in schizophrenia: A connectionist model. *American Journal of Psychiatry, 155(12)*, 1685–1690.

Nuechterlein, K. H., & Dawson, M. E. (1984). Information processing and attentional functioning in the developmental course of schizophrenic disorders. *Schizophrenia Bulletin, 10(2)*, 160–203.

Nuechterlein, K. H., Edell, W. S., Norris, M., & Dawson, M. E. (1986). Attentional vulnerability indicators, thought disorder, and negative symptoms. *Schizophrenia Bulletin, 12(3)*, 408–426.

O'Driscoll, G. A., Florencio, P. S., Gagnon, D., Wolff, A. V., Benkelfat, C., Mikula, L., et al. (2001). Amygdala-hippocampal volume and verbal memory in first-degree relatives of schizophrenic patients. *Psychiatry Research, 107(2)*, 75–85.

Okubo, Y., Suhara, T., Suzuki, K., Kobayashi, K., Inoue, O., et al. (1997). Decreased prefrontal dopamine D1 receptors in schizophrenia revealed by PET. *Nature, 385(6617)*, 634–636.

Oltmanns, T. F., & Neale, J. M. (1975). Schizophrenic performance when distractors are present: Attentional deficit or differential task difficulty? *Journal of Abnormal Psychology, 84(3)*, 205–209.

Ozeki, Y., Tomoda, T., Kleiderlein, J., Kamiya, A., Bord, L., Fujii, K., et al. (2003). Disrupted-in-Schizophrenia-1 (DISC-1): Mutant truncation prevents binding to NudE-like (NUDEL) and inhibits neurite outgrowth. *Proceedings of the National Academy of Sciences, U.S.A., 100(1)*, 289–294.

Passerieux, C., Sergui, J., Besche, C., Chevalier, J. F., Widlocher, D., & Hardy-Bayle, M. C.

(1997). Heterogeneity of cognitive functioning of schizophrenic patients evaluated by a lexical decision task. *Psychological Medicine, 27(6)*, 1295–1302.

Penn, D. L., Ritchie, M., Francis, J., Combs, D., & Martin, J. (2002). Social perception in schizophrenia: The role of context. *Psychiatry Research, 109(2)*, 149–159.

Pfefferbaum, A., & Marsh, L. (1995). Structural brain imaging in schizophrenia. *Clinical Neuroscience, 3(2)*, 105–111.

Pinkham, A. E., Penn, D. L., Perkins, D. O., & Lieberman, J. (2003). Implications for the neural basis of social cognition for the study of schizophrenia. *American Journal of Psychiatry, 160(5)*, 815–824.

Racenstein, J. M., Penn, D., Harrow, M., & Schleser, R. (1999). Thought disorder and psychosocial functioning in schizophrenia: The concurrent and predictive relationships. *Journal of Nervous and Mental Disease, 187(5)*, 281–289.

Rosso, I. M., Cannon, T. D., Huttunen, T., Huttunen, M. O., Lonnqvist, J., & Gasperoni, T. L. (2000). Obstetric risk factors for early-onset schizophrenia in a Finnish birth cohort. *American Journal of Psychiatry, 157(5)*, 801–807.

Rudy, J. W., & O'Reilly, R. C. (2001). Conjunctive representations, the hippocampus, and contextual fear conditioning. *Cognitive, Affective and Behavioral Neuroscience, 1(1)*, 66–82.

Ruff, R. M., Light, R. H., Parker, S. B., & Levin, H. S. (1997). The psychological construct of word fluency. *Brain and Language, 57(3)*, 394–405.

Rypma, B., Berger, J. S., & D'Esposito, M. (2002). The influence of working-memory demand and subject performance on prefrontal cortical activity. *Journal of Cognitive Neuroscience, 14(5)*, 721–731.

Sass, L. A., Gunderson, J. G., Singer, M. T., & Wynne, L. C. (1984). Parental communication deviance and forms of thinking in male schizophrenic offspring. *Journal of Nervous and Mental Disease, 172(9)*, 513–520.

Saykin, A. J., Shtasel, D. L., Gur, R. E., Kester, D. B., Mozley, L. H., Stafiniak, P., et al. (1994). Neuropsychological deficits in neuroleptic naive patients with first-episode schizophrenia. *Archives of General Psychiatry, 51(2)*, 124–131.

Schneider, W. S., & Shiffrin, R. M. (1977). Controlled and automatic human information processing: I. Detection, search, and attention. *Psychological Review, 84(1)*, 1–66.

Seidman, L. J., Faraone, S. V., Goldstein, J. M., Goodman, J. M., Kremen, W. S., Toomey, R., et al. (1999). Thalamic and amygdala-hippocampal volume reductions in first-degree relatives of patients with schizophrenia: An MRI-based morphometric analysis. *Biological Psychiatry, 46(7)*, 941–954.

Seidman, L. J., Faraone, S. V., Goldstein, J. M., Kremen, W. S., Horton, N. J., Makris, N., et al. (2002). Left hippocampal volume as a vulnerability indicator for schizophrenia: A magnetic resonance imaging morphometric study of nonpsychotic first-degree relatives. *Archives of General Psychiatry, 59(9)*, 839–849.

Seidman, L. J., Yurgelun-Todd, D., Kremen, W. S., Woods, B. T., Goldstein, J. M., Faraone, S. V., et al. (1994). Relationship of prefrontal and temporal lobe MRI measures to neuropsychological performance in chronic schizophrenia. *Biological Psychiatry, 35(4)*, 235–246.

Shaham, Y., Shalev, U., Lu, L., De Wit, H., & Stewart, J. (2003). The reinstatement model of drug relapse: History, methodology and major findings. *Psychopharmacology, 168(1–2)*, 3–20.

Silver, H., Feldman, P., Bilker, W., & Gur, R. C. (2003). Working memory deficit as a core neuropsychological dysfunction in schizophrenia. *American Journal of Psychiatry, 160(10)*, 1809–1816.

Silverstein, S. M., Kovacs, I., Corry, R., & Valone, C. (2000). Perceptual organization, the disorganization syndrome, and context processing in chronic schizophrenia. *Schizophrenia Research, 43(1)*, 11–20.

Sitnikova, T., Salisbury, D. F., Kuperberg, G., & Holcomb, P. I. (2002). Electrophysiological insights into language processing in schizophrenia. *Psychophysiology, 39(6)*, 851–860.

Sokolov, E. N. (1963). Orienting reflex as a cybernetic system/Orientirovochnyi refleks kak kiberneticheskaia sistema. *Zhurnal Vysshei Nervnoi Deyatel'nosti*, 816–830.

Spitzer, M., Braun, U., Hermle, L., & Maier, S. (1993). Associative semantic network dysfunction in thought-disordered schizophrenic patients: Direct evidence from indirect semantic priming. *Biological Psychiatry, 34(12)*, 864–877.

Spitzer, M., Weisker, I., Winter, M., Maier, S., Hermle, L., & Maher, B. A. (1994). Semantic and phonological priming in schizophrenia. *Journal of Abnormal Psychology, 103(3)*, 485–494.

Spitzer, M. (1997). A cognitive neuroscience view of schizophrenic thought disorder. *Schizophrenia Bulletin, 23(1)*, 29–50.

Squire, L. R., & Zola, S. M. (1996). Structure and function of declarative and nondeclarative memory systems. *Proceedings of the National Academy of Sciences, U.S.A., 93(24)*, 13515–13522.

St. Clair, D., Blackwood, D., Muir, W., Carothers, A., Walker, M., Spowart, G., et al. (1990). Association within a family of a balanced autosomal translocation with major mental illness. *Lancet, 336(8706)*, 13–16.

Stefanis, N., Frangou, S., Yakeley, J., Sharma, T., O'Connell, P., Morgan, K., et al. (1999). Hippocampal volume reduction in schizophrenia: Effects of genetic risk and pregnancy and birth complications. *Biological Psychiatry, 46(5)*, 697–702.

Stroop, J. R. (1935). Studies of interference in serial verbal reactions. *Journal of Experimental Psychology, 18*, 643–662.

Taylor, W. L. (1953). "Cloze procedure": A new tool for measuring readability. *Journalism Quarterly, 30*, 415–433.

Thompson-Schill, S. L., Jonides, J., Marshuetz, C., Smith, E. E., D'Esposito, M., Kan, I. P., et al. (2002). Effects of frontal lobe damage on interference effects in working memory. *Cognitive, Affective and Behavioral Neuroscience, 2(2)*, 109–120.

Titone, D., Levy, D. L., & Holzman, P. S. (2000). Contextual insensitivity in schizophrenic language processing: Evidence from lexical ambiguity. *Journal of Abnormal Psychology, 109(4)*, 761–767.

Tsuang, M. T., & Faraone, S. V. (1999). The concept of target features in schizophrenia research. *Acta Psychiatrica Scandinavica, Suppl. 99(395)*, 2–11.

Tsuang, M. T., Stone, W. S., & Faraone, S. V. (1999). Schizophrenia: A review of genetic studies. *Harvard Review of Psychiatry, 7(4)*, 185–207.

Van Erp, T. G., Saleh, P. A., Rosso, I. M., Huttunen, M., Lonnqvist, J., Pirkola, T., et al. (2002). Contributions of genetic risk and fetal hypoxia to hippocampal volume in patients with schizophrenia or schizoaffective disorder, their unaffected siblings, and healthy unrelated volunteers. *American Journal of Psychiatry, 159(9)*, 1514–1520.

Van Erp, T. G. W., Saleh, P., Huttunen, M. O., Lonnqvist, J., Kaprio, J., Salonen, O., et al. (in press). Hippocampal volumes in schizophrenic twins. *Archives of General Psychiatry*

Vargha-Khadem, F., Gadian, D. G., Watkins, K. E., Connelly, A., Van Paesschen, W., & Mishkin, M. (1997). Differential effects of early hippocampal pathology on episodic and semantic memory. *Science, 277(5324)*, 376–380.

Velakoulis, D., Pantelis, C., McGorry, P. D., Dudgeon, P., Brewer, W., Cook, M., et al. (1999). Hippocampal volume in first-episode psychoses and chronic schizophrenia: A high-resolution magnetic resonance imaging study. *Archives of General Psychiatry, 56(2)*, 133–141.

Wahlberg, K. E., Wynne, L. C., Oja, H., Keskitalo, P., Anais-Tanner, H., Koistinen, P., et al. (2000). Thought disorder index of Finnish adoptees and communication deviance of their adoptive parents. *Psychological Medicine, 30(1)*, 127–136.

Weisbrod, M., Maier, S., Harig, S., Himmelsbach, U., & Spitzer, M. (1998). Lateralised semantic and indirect semantic priming effects in people with schizophrenia. *British Journal of Psychiatry, 172*, 142–146.

Weiner, I. (1990). Neural substrates of latent inhibition: The switching model. *Psychological Bulletin, 108(3)*, 442–461.

Wirshing, D. A., Marshall, B. D., Green, M. F., Mintz, J., Marder, S. R., & Wirshing, W. C. (1999). Risperidone in treatment-refractory schizophrenia. *American Journal of Psychiatry, 156(9)*, 1374–1379.

Wood, J. N. (2003). Social cognition and the prefrontal cortex. *Behavioral and Cognitive Neuroscience Reviews, 2(2)*, 97–114.

Yurgelun-Todd, D. A., Waternaux, C. M., Cohen, B. M., Gruber, S. A., English, C. D., & Renshaw, P. F. (1996). Functional magnetic resonance imaging of schizophrenic patients and comparison subjects during word production.

American Journal of Psychiatry, 153(2), 200–205.

Zaidel, D. W., Esiri, M. M., & Harrison, P. J. (1997). Size, shape, and orientation of neurons in the left and right hippocampus: Investigation of normal asymmetries and alterations in schizophrenia. *American Journal of Psychiatry, 154*(6), 812–818.

Zola, S. M., & Squire, L. R. (2001). Relationship between magnitude of damage to the hippocampus and impaired recognition memory in monkeys. *Hippocampus, 11*(2), 92–98.

Part VI

ONTOGENY, PHYLOGENY, LANGUAGE, AND CULTURE

CHAPTER 22

Development of Thinking

Graeme S. Halford

It is appropriate to begin a review of research on cognitive development with the work of pioneering researchers such as Luria, Piaget, and Vygotsky, who provided much of the conceptual foundation on which later contributions were built. We will begin with a survey of this legacy, then proceed to more contemporary theories, and finally consider a number of key empirical research topics.

Early Influences

The single most powerful influence on past research into the development of thinking has been the work of Piaget and his collaborators (Inhelder & Piaget, 1958, 1964; Piaget, 1950, 1952, 1953, 1957, 1970), but the influence of Vygotsky (1962) appears to be increasing with time. The work of Luria (1976) deservedly had a major influence on early cognitive development research, but not primarily devoted to thinking. In this chapter, I consider Piaget first, followed by Vygotsky, and then the common ground between them.

Two ideas that were central to Piaget's conception of thought were structure and self-regulation, both of which were also held by the Gestalt school. However, a distinguishing feature of Piaget's theory was that it was based on logico-mathematical concepts, including function, operation, group, and lattice. Although he did not claim that logic defined the laws of thought (cf. Boole, 1854/1951), he used modified logics or "psycho-logics" to model thought.

Piaget's very extensive empirical investigations into the development of infants' and children's cognitions were conceptualized by a succession of distinct logics, which have come to be known as "stages" of cognitive development. The first was the sensorimotor stage, lasting from birth to about one-and-a-half to two years, characterized by structured, organized activity but not thought. During this stage, a structure of actions became elaborated into a mathematical group, meaning that an integrated, self-regulating system of actions developed. Piaget believed that the concept of objects as real and permanent emerged as this structure was elaborated. The preoperational stage lasted from approximately two to seven years, and during this time semiotic or symbolic functions were developed, including play, drawing, imagery, and language. Thought at this stage was conceptualized in terms of what Piaget called "function logic," the essential idea of which is a representation of a link between two variables. At the concrete operational stage, lasting from eight to about fourteen years, thought was conceptualized in terms of what Piaget called "groupings," which were equivalent to the mathematical concept of a groupoid, meaning a set with a single binary operation (Sheppard, 1978). The essential idea here is the ability to compose classes, sets, relations, or functions, into integrated systems (Halford, 1982). Concepts such as conservation (invariance of quantity, number, weight, and volume), seriation or ordering of objects, transitive inference, classification, and spatial perspectives emerge as a result of the more elaborate thought structures that develop during this time. At the formal operational stage, beginning in adolescence, the ability to compose concrete operations into higher-level structures emerges with the result that thought has greater autonomy and flexibility.

Cognitive development depended, according to Piaget, on *assimilation* of experience to cognitive structures with *accommodation* of the structure to the new information. The combination of assimilation and accommodation amounts to a process of self-regulation that Piaget termed "equilibration." He rejected the associationist learning theories of the time, although his conceptions in many ways anticipated modern conceptions of information processing and dynamic systems.

The work of the Piagetian school has been one of the most controversial topics in the field, and claims that Piaget was wrong in many important respects are not uncommon (Bjorklund, 1997; Gopnik, 1996). The following points are intended to help provide a balanced account of this issue. First, Piaget's empirical findings have been widely replicated (Modgil, 1974; Sigel & Hooper, 1968). That is, children have been found to perform as Piaget reported *on the tests he used*. The major challenges to his findings have been based on different methods of assessment, the claim being that his methods underestimated the cognitive capabilities of young children (Baillargeon, 1995; Bryant, 1972; Bryant & Trabasso, 1971; Donaldson, 1971; Gelman, 1972). However, these claims also have been subject to controversy. Miller (1976) showed that nonverbal assessments did not demonstrate improved reasoning if the cognitive skills employed were taken into account, and a similar point was made about subsequent research by Halford (1989). However, there were also some hundreds of training studies, reviewed by Field (1987) and Halford (1982), that were sometimes interpreted as showing that cognitive development could be accelerated and depended more on experience than on development of thought structures. The stage concept has also been heavily criticized for theoretical inadequacies (Brainerd, 1978) and for lack of empirical support (Bruner, Olver, & Greenfield, 1966). In particular, acquisition tends to be gradual and experience-based rather than sudden or "stage-like," and the concurrence between acquisitions at the same stage often has not been as close as Piagetian theory might be taken to imply. However, there have also been some spirited defenses of Piaget (Beilin, 1992; Lourenco & Machado, 1996), and Smith (2002) has given a contemporary account of Piagetian theory. See also the special issue of *Cognitive Development* edited by Bryant (2002) on "Constructivism Today."

The underlying problem here seems to have been that it is difficult to operationalize Piagetian concepts in the methodologies that evolved in Anglo-Saxon psychology to about 1970. His conceptions have been more compatible with methodologies that developed after the "cognitive revolution," including information processing and dynamic systems theories. In the next section I consider alternative ways of conceptualizing the development of children's thought.

The work of Vygotsky (1962) was the other major influence on research into the development of thinking, and his contribution is becoming increasingly influential even today (Lloyd & Fernyhough, 1999). Three of Vygotsky's most important contributions were his ideas on the relation between thought and language, his emphasis on the role of culture in the development of thinking, and the zone of proximal development. Early in the history of cognitive development research, there was considerable debate as to whether thought depends on language development, as implied by Bruner, Olver, & Greenfield. (1966), or the reverse, as implied by Slobin (1972). Vygotsky (1962) proposed that thought and language have different origins both in evolution and in development. Language was initially social in character, whereas problem solving was initially motor. Language and thought develop independently for some time after infancy; then the young child develops egocentric speech, the beginning of the representational function. Finally, children develop "inner speech," which serves the symbolic function of thought. Vygotsky emphasized the interaction between biological maturation and social experience. As the child matures, language becomes an increasingly important influence on the development of thought and is the chief means by which culture is absorbed by the child. Vygotsky's concept of the zone of proximal development, which means that new developments are close to existing cognitive abilities, is broadly consistent with Piaget's notion that new knowledge is assimilated to existing structure. This is part of a larger picture in which both Piaget and Vygotsky saw cognitive development as an active organizing process that tends toward an equilibrium with its own internal processes and with the external environment. Piaget's work had greater early influence, but the impact of Vygotsky's work is increasing at what appears to be an accelerating rate. Among the many areas in which it has been important are the development of education theory (Gallimore & Tharp, 1999) and research on collaborative problem solving (Garton, 2004; see also Greenfield, Chap. 27.)

Development of Theory

Theory of development of reasoning diversified in numerous directions in the latter half of the twentieth century and our conceptions of reasoning processes have undergone some fundamental changes. Perhaps one of the most important is that there is much less reliance on logic as a norm of reasoning and more emphasis on the interaction between reasoning processes and the child's experience. Information processing theories were one of the first lines of development following the impact of Piaget and Vygotsky, so it is appropriate to consider them first.

Information Processing Theories

An attempt to conceptualize development of thinking in terms of information processing concepts was made by what became known as the Neo-Piagetian school (Case, 1985, 1992a; Case et al., 1996; Chapman, 1987, 1990; Fischer, 1980; Halford, 1982, 1993; McLaughlin, 1963; Pascual-Leone, 1970; Pascual-Leone & Smith, 1969). These models, reviewed in detail by Halford (2002), reconceptualize Piaget's stages in terms of the information processing demands they make. All of them postulate that higher information processing capacity becomes available with development either through maturation (Halford, 1993) or increased processing efficiency that leaves more capacity available for working memory (Case, 1985). Note that these processes are not mutually exclusive. Chapman and Lindenberger (1989, p. 238) attempted to synthesize these theories under the principle that "the total capacity requirement of a given form of reasoning is equal to the number of operatory variables that are assigned values simultaneously in employing that form of reasoning in a particular task."

Other theoretical developments were more independent of the Piagetian tradition. An important class of theories was based on computer simulations first using symbolic architectures (Halford, Wilson, & McDonald, 1995; Klahr & Wallace, 1976;

Simon & Klahr, 1995) and later using neural nets (Elman, 1990; McClelland, 1995; Shultz, 1991; Shultz, et al, 1995). The model of Klahr and Wallace (1976) was concerned with quantification operators, including subitizing (direct estimation of small sets without counting), counting, and estimation (approximate quantification of large sets such as crowds). It was used to model conservation or understanding that a quantity remains invariant despite transformations of physical dimensions. In a typical simple number conservation task, two rows of beads are placed in one-to-one correspondence. Then one row is transformed (e.g., by spacing objects more widely and thus increasing the length of the row without adding any items); then the child is asked whether each row still contains the same number or whether they are different. Preconserving children cannot answer this question correctly because they have not learned that the transformation leaves number invariant. In the model of Klahr and Wallace (1976) the task is performed initially by quantifying first one row followed by the other in the pretransformed display and then comparing the results. The transformed row is quantified again after the transformation and found to be still the same as the other row. With repeated quantification before and after a transformation, the rule that pre- and post-transformed quantities are equal is learned, and the quantification operators are no longer employed. (See also Chap. 17 by Lovett & Anderson, on production system models of thinking.)

The Q-SOAR model of Simon and Klahr (1995) applied Newell's (1990) SOAR architecture to Gelman's (1982) study of number conservation acquisition. Children are shown two equal rows of objects, asked to count each row in turn and say how many each contains, then to say whether they are the same or different. Then one row is transformed and the preconserving child is unable to say whether they are the same or different. This is represented in Q-SOAR as an impasse. The model then searches for a solution to the problem using the quantification procedure of Klahr and Wallace (1976). With repeated experience, the model gradually learns to classify the action of spacing out the items as a conserving transformation, using the learning mechanism of the SOAR model, called "chunking," which has been shown to have considerable generality.

Acquisition of transitive inference was simulated by the self-modifying production system model of Halford, Smith, et al. (1995). Development of transitive inference strategies is guided by a concept of order based on any representation of an ordered set of at least three elements. When no production rule exists for a given problem, the model uses analogical mapping and means-end analysis to determine the correct answer; then a production rule is created to handle that case. Rules are strengthened or weakened by subsequent experiences with success or failure.

Neural Net Models

Neural net models of thinking are reviewed by Doumas and Hummel (Chap. 4), but the contribution of neural net models to cognitive development is considered here. A good way to illustrate neural net models of cognitive development is to examine McClelland's (1995) model of children's understanding of the balance scale. The net is shown schematically in Figure 22.1 together with a balance scale problem. It is a three-layered net, which means that activation is propagated from the input units to the hidden (middle) layer and then to the output layer. There are four sets of five input units representing one-to-five weights on pegs one to five steps from the fulcrum on both left and right sides. The units that are activated are shown as black. The activations in the input units represent the problem in the top of the figure. In the first set of input units, representing number of weights on the left, unit 3 is activated, coding the three weights on the left. Similarly, in the second set of input units, representing weights on the right, unit 4 is activating, coding four weights on the right. Distances are coded in a similar way by the two sets of input

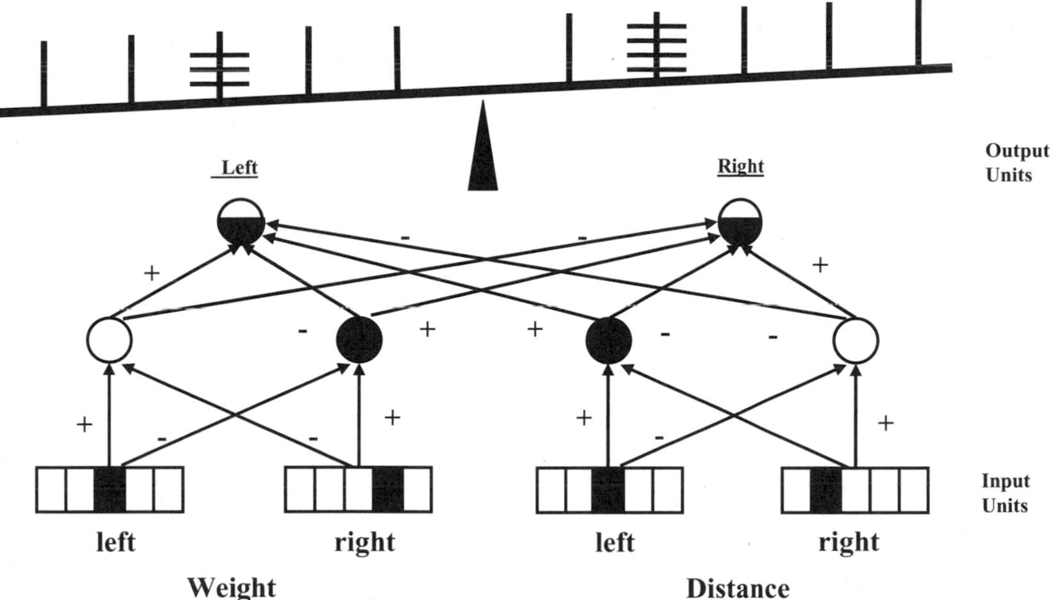

Figure 22.1. Balance scale model of McClelland (1995). By permission of the author and Oxford University Press.

units on the right. In the first set, unit 3 is activated, coding the weights on peg 3 on the left, whereas in the second set, unit 2 is activated, coding weights on peg 2 on the right.

There are four hidden units (shown in the middle of the net), two of which compare weights and two that compare distances. The units that are more highly activated are shown as black, although activations would be graded, rather than all-or-none. Finally, there are the output units that compute the balance state. Activation of an output unit represents the corresponding side of the balance beam going down. If the beam is balanced, the activations in the output units would be equal, which is defined as being within 0.3 of each other.

The operation of the unit can be understood from the connection weights between units, which are shown schematically in Figure 22.1 as +\−. The second hidden unit has positive connections to all input units representing weight on the right and negative connections to all input units representing weight on the left (although only a single arrow is shown in each case for simplicity). This unit is more strongly activated because weight on the right is greater than on the left. The first hidden unit has the opposite pattern of weights and will be more strongly activated if weight is greater on the left. The second hidden unit also has positive connections to the right output unit. Thus, greater weight on the right will tend to produce greater activation on the right output unit, representing a tendency for the right side going down. The second pair of hidden units compare distances in corresponding fashion. The activations of the output units depend on activations of hidden units comparing both weights and distances. In this case the greater weight on the right tends to make the right side go down, but this is countered by the greater distance on the left; thus, the predicted position of the beam will be approximately balanced, although, in fact, the left side would go down. The network does not compute the product of weight and distance but compares the influences of weights and distances on each side.

The network was trained by backpropagation; that is, comparing the network's output on each trial with the correct output and then adjusting the connection weights to reduce the discrepancy. The training would result in the units representing larger weights or larger distances having greater connection weights to the hidden units. Thus, metrics for weight and distance emerge as a result of training and are not predefined in the net. This is possibly the most important property of the model because it shows how a structured representation can emerge from the process of learning to compute input-output functions that match those in the environment.

The model also captures a number of crucial developmental results. Its progress through training corresponded with the course of development as defined by Siegler's (1981) rules. According to Rule I, judgments are based on weight, irrespective of distance. In Rule II states that distance is considered if the weights are first found to be equal. Rule III asserts that weight and distance are considered but difficulty is encountered when weight is greater on one side and distance is greater on the other. Rule IV (torque rule) involves comparing the product of weight and distance on the left side with the product of weight and distance on the right side. The model also captured the torque difference effect – that is, the difference between the product of weight and distance on the left ($W_l \times D_l$) and on the right ($W_r \times D_r$) affects children's performance, because they are more likely to recognize that one side will go down if torque difference is large even though there is no logical basis for this given that even a small torque difference will cause one side to go down. This is one of many ways in which neural net models capture psychological properties of task performance.

This model computes the balance state as a function of weight and distance on left and right sides of the balance beam. However, understanding the balance beam also entails determining weight or distance values that will make the beam balance. There are effectively five variables here: W_l, D_l, W_r, D_r, and *balance state*. Complete understanding of the balance scale would include being able to determine any variable given the other four; that is, compute all five functions implicated by the balance scale concept (Surber & Gzesh, 1984). Other restrictions are that, as Marcus (1998a, 1998b) has pointed out, if the model is trained on two or three weights on either side, it cannot generalize to problems with four or five weights. Again, however, it would be reasonable to expect that children would generalize in this way. The conclusions therefore are that the model can be trained to compute one function implicated by the balance scale, albeit under restricted conditions, and that it does not fully capture understanding of the concept but is nevertheless an important step forward in our understanding of cognitive development because it shows how structured representation can emerge.

The balance scale model by McClelland (1995) is a three-layered, or backpropagation, net. This type of architecture has been used in a great many models, in cognitive development and elsewhere. One reason is that it can, in principle, compute any input–output function. The simple recurrent net (Elman, 1990) is an important model in this class. In this type of net, activations in the hidden units are copied over into context units. On the next trial, activations in the hidden units are influenced by activations in both the input units and the context units. The result is that the output of the net is influenced by representations on previous trials as well as by the current input. The net therefore takes account of links between events in a sequence. The model was trained to predict the next word in a sentence. Training was based on a large corpus of sentences by representing each successive word in the input units, and the output units were trained to represent the next word. Feedback was given concerning the accuracy of the output, thereby adjusting the connection weights to improve the model's prediction. The model learned to predict the next word in a sentence and respected grammatical categories even when words in related categories spanned embedded clauses. Cluster analysis of the hidden unit activations showed that words in the same grammatical category, such as nouns or verbs, tended to have similar activations. Semantically similar words, such as those representing animals or foods, also tended to have similar hidden unit representations. Elman (1990) was careful not to predefine categories, and the inputs used were orthogonal; thus, no pre-existing similarities were supplied to the model. Similarities were created in the hidden unit activations that reflected the input–output functions the model was required to learn. Therefore, to the extent that categories developed, they are an emergent property of the model and one that reflects contingencies in the environment. This model, like that of McClelland (1995), offers a possible mechanism by which structured representation might be acquired.

The ability of simple recurrent nets to predict sequences has been utilized to model infants' expectations of the reappearance of occluded objects (Mareschal, Plunkett, & Harris, 1995; Munakata et al., 1997) thereby simulating infants' understanding of the object concept (Baillargeon et al., 1990). These models are basically consistent with the model of Smith et al. (1999). Again, however, there have been limitations. Marcus (1998a, 1998b) found that the model of Munakata et al. (1997) did not generalize to objects in new positions on the display.

The potential of models such as this to learn regularities in the environment and acquire concepts has inspired a whole new approach to cognitive development (Elman et al., 1996). Elman et al. (1996) see connectionism as giving more powerful means to analyze the gene–environment interactions that are the basis of development. They advocate a form of connectionism that is founded in biology, is influenced by developmental neuroscience, and that can produce neurologically plausible computational models. Although they see an undoubted role for innateness in cognitive development, they argue some nativist conceptions underestimate the potential for new cognitive forms to emerge from the interaction of neural processes. The simple recurrent net nicely illustrates how representations that respect distinctions between word categories emerge from the model's interaction with the environment.

Cascade Correlation Models

Cascade correlation models provide a mechanism by which the dimensionality of representations can be increased to handle increased dimensions in the task. They do this by adding units to the hidden layer. The initial net has minimal hidden units and sometimes starts with none. Training takes place in two modes. In the first mode, weights are adjusted to yield the appropriate output for each input. In the second mode, hidden units are recruited to increase the accuracy of the output. Recruitment is based on correlation between a candidate's activation and the existing error of the network. After recruitment of a hidden unit, training continues in the first mode and the system cycles between the modes until a learning criterion is reached.

Cascade correlation models have been used to model a number of developmental phenomena (Shultz, 1991; Shultz et al., 1995; Sirois & Shultz, 1998). Shultz and colleagues used cascade correlation to model the same balance scale problem modeled by McClelland (1995). The initial net was similar to that used by McClelland and shown in Figure 22.1, but without hidden units. Initial training was with problems varying only in weight, and the net performed consistent with Siegler's (1981) Rule 1. Once the distance variable was introduced, the net recruited a single hidden unit. It then progressed to Rule 2 and higher rules that take account of distance, effectively simulating the developmental progression in a manner similar to McClelland's model (1995).

Neural Net Models and Symbolic Processes

Concern that three-layered net models do not capture symbolic processes has been expressed by Fodor and Pylyshyn (1988). Properties that are considered essential by Fodor and Pylyshyn (1988) are compositionality and systematicity. The essential idea of compositionality is that symbols must retain their identity and their meaning when combined into more complex representations. Thus, the cognitive symbols for "dog" and "happy" must retain their identity when combined into the symbol for "happy dog." Prototypes are not necessarily compositional in this way (Fodor, 1995). One problem for three-layered net models is that the representations in the hidden units do not necessarily include the components of the input in a form that is recognizable to the performer. Any structure that exists in the hidden layer must be discovered by an external observer (the experimenter) using techniques such as cluster analysis (Elman, 1990). Representations in hidden units are not accessible to strategic processes. They are more like implicit knowledge (Karmiloff-Smith, 1994).

Systematicity, in essence, means that cognitive processes are subject to structural constraints independent of content. Three-layered nets lack strong systematicity (Marcus, 1998a, 1998b; Phillips, 1994), meaning they cannot generalize to an element that has not occurred in the same role before, even if the element is familiar. Thus, a net trained on "John loves Mary" and "Tom loves Jane" could generalize to "John loves Jane" but not to "Jane loves John" or even to "Mary loves John." Nets of this type learn representations that are needed to compute the input–output functions on which they are trained, but they do not learn abstract relations.

Although three-layered net models have real potential to advance research on cognitive development (Bray et al., 1997), it appears they lack the structural properties that have long been regarded as characteristic of higher cognition (Chomsky, 1980; Humphrey, 1951; Mandler & Mandler, 1964; Miller, Galanter, & Pribram, 1960; Newell, 1990; Piaget, 1950; Wertheimer, 1945). One response to this problem (Smolensky, 1988) is that neural net models seek to explain symbols as emergent properties of more basic processes, as was illustrated earlier. A second approach has been to develop symbolic neural net models of higher cognitive processes (Doumas & Hummel, Chap. 4; Shastri & Ajjanagadde, 1993; Smolensky, 1990; but see also Halford, Wilson, & Phillips, 1998). A symbolic connectionist account of cognitive development has been given by Halford and his collaborators (Halford, 1993; Halford, Wilson, & Phillips, 1998). See Halford (2002) for a summary of this approach.

Dynamic Systems Models

Dynamic systems models (Fischer & Bidell, 1998; Fischer & Pare-Blagoev, 2000; van Geert, 1991, 1998, 2000) have offered new ways to analyze developmental data. A dynamic system is a formal system, the state of which depends on its state at a previous point in time. The dynamic system model of van Geert (1998) was designed around principles derived from the work of Piaget and Vygotsky and has a number of interesting properties. It can account for different types of cognitive growth, such as slow linear increase and sudden discontinuities, within the same system. It can also show how a complex, self-regulating system can emerge from the interaction of a few variables. The model was fitted to a number of developmental data sets, and some important developmental phenomena, including conservation acquisition, were simulated. Links have also been made between dynamic systems models and neural net models.

Dynamic systems models have also been linked to other issues. Raijmakers, van Koten, and Molenaar (1996) analyzed McClelland's (1995) neural net model of the balance scale and found no evidence of the flags indicating discontinuities that are found in empirical data. They suggest that backpropagation models simulate the type of stimulus-response associations that are characteristic of animals and young children but do not simulate the rule-governed behavior characteristic of older children and adults. In many respects, this finding is consistent with the analysis of the model presented earlier. On the other hand, backpropagation models incorporate learning functions that have been missing from models of higher cognitive processes. As we have seen, they show how structured representations begin to emerge as a result of learning input-output functions.

Although there are acknowledged difficulties with dynamic systems models (van

Geert, 1998), they provide much more sophisticated implementations of important developmental theories, including that of Piaget and Vygotsky. This does not mean that Piaget and Vygotsky are fully vindicated by dynamic systems models, but concepts such as equilibration and self-regulation, which are at the core of their theories, do seem to have a new lease on life. Most importantly, dynamic systems models have potential to deepen our understanding of cognitive developmental processes. And, as Fischer and Pare-Blagoev (2000) point out, there are tools based on Lotus 123 or Microsoft Excel that make dynamic system modeling more accessible.

Links to Brain Development

The finding by Thatcher, Walker, and Giudice (1987) of brain growth spurts that appeared to correspond to stage transitions in cognitive development stimulated considerable interest in the explanatory potential of neural maturation. One of the important landmarks in infant development is the A not-B error: If infants are shown a toy hidden at A several times and allowed to retrieve it and then see it hidden at B, before approximately 12 months of age they tend to search for it at A. Studies by Diamond (1988) and Goldman-Rakic (1987) showing the link between frontal lobe function and the A not-B error were important stimuli to work on infant brain development. Case (1992a, 1992b) and Fischer (1987; Fischer & Rose, 1996) have drawn interesting parallels between cognitive development and the growth of connections between the frontal lobes and other brain regions. Robin and Holyoak (1995) and Waltz et al. (1999) have also drawn attention to the role of the frontal cortex in processing relations of the kind described by Halford and his collaborators (Halford, 1993; Halford, Bain et al., 1998; Halford, Wilson, & Phillips, 1998). In a different context, Rudy, Keith, and Georgen (1993) present evidence that configural learning (e.g., conditional discrimination, in which a cue-response link is reversed on change of background) depends on maturation of the hippocampus.

At a more general level, Quartz and Sejnowski (1997) have argued that synaptic growth, axonal arborization, and dendritic development play a role in processing capacity increase with age. They also point out that neural plasticity would cause capacity to increase as a function of experience. This implies that the issue of whether cognitive development depends on capacity, knowledge, or both may need to be redefined. It might be that cognitive development depends on growth of capacity, which is at least partly produced by experience.

Strategy Development

Problem-solving strategies are important to reasoning in children and adults, and much of the improvement in children's reasoning can be attributed to development of more powerful strategies. It is appropriate therefore that much research has been devoted to development of strategies. Following work on rule assessment (Briars & Siegler, 1984; Siegler, 1981), Siegler and his collaborators conducted an extensive study of strategy (Siegler, 1999; Siegler & Chen, 1998; Siegler & Jenkins, 1989; Siegler & Shipley, 1995; Siegler & Shrager, 1984). Two of the models were concerned with development of addition strategies in young children. When asked to add two single-digit numbers, they chose between a set of strategies including retrieving the answer from memory, decomposing the numbers (e.g., $3+5=4+4=8$), counting both sets (counting right through a set of three and a set of five, perhaps using fingers), and the *min strategy* of counting on from the top number in the larger set (e.g., 5, 6, 7, 8, so $3+5=8$).

Siegler and Shrager's early strategy choice model (1984) was based on distribution of associations. The idea is that each addition sum is associated with answers of varying strengths, and so for a given sample of children, $2+1$ might yield the answer "3" 80% of the time; "1" or "2," 4%; "4," 3%; and so on. The chance of an answer being chosen is a function of its associative strength relative to competing answers. The more peaked the distribution, the more likely it will be that a single answer will occur. However, it will be adopted only if it is above the confidence criterion. If not, alternative strategies, such as counting, are sought.

In their later work, Siegler and his collaborators developed the Adaptive Strategy Choice Model (ASCM, pronounced "Ask-em") which makes more active strategy choices. At the beginning, ASCM knows only the small set of strategies typically used by 4-year-olds, but it has general cognitive skills for choosing and evaluating strategies. The model is trained on a set of elementary addition facts; then the min strategy is added to the model's repertoire. This entails counting on from the larger number to be added, so if the sum is $5+3$, the procedure is to count 5, 6, 7, 8. The model chooses a strategy for each problem on the basis of the past speed and accuracy of the strategy and on similarity between the current problem and past problems in which a strategy has been used. Each time a strategy is used, the record of its success is updated, and the projected strength of the strategy for that problem is calculated. The strength of association between a problem and a specific answer is increased or decreased as determined by the success of the answer. One of the strengths of the model is that it can account for variability both between children and between different strategies used by the same child for a particular class of problems. Most importantly, it provides a reasonably accurate account of strategy development in children as they age.

Complexity

Children become capable of more complex reasoning with age, and it is therefore important to have some way of comparing the complexities of reasoning tasks. A conceptual complexity theory and accompanying metric that discriminate tasks of different difficulty and explain why they differ is essential to understanding cognitive development. It is also necessary to define *equivalence* in cognitive tasks. In the past, tasks have tended to be regarded as equivalent if they require the same knowledge domain and are similar methodologically, or if they have similar difficulties on a psychometric scale. Although these criteria have great utility, they have not led to an understanding of factors that underlie complexity, nor do they explain why tasks that differ in content or procedure can be of equivalent complexity whereas tasks that are superficially similar can be very different in complexity. Without a means of assigning cognitive tasks to equivalence classes with common properties and relating tasks in different classes to each other in an orderly way, psychology is in a position similar to that of chemistry without the periodic table (Frye & Zelazo, 1998). Two metrics for cognitive complexity have been developed in the past decade.

COGNITIVE COMPLEXITY AND CONTROL (CCC) THEORY

Frye, Zelazo, & Palfai (1995; Zelazo & Frye, 1998) analyze complexity according to the number of hierarchical levels of rules required for the task. A simple task entails rules that link an antecedent to a consequent, $a \rightarrow c$, whereas complex tasks have rules that are embedded in a higher-order rule that modifies the lower level rules; thus, another level is added to the hierarchy. The dimensional change card sort task has been a fruitful implementation of this theory. In a simple sorting task, a green circle might be assigned to the green category and a red triangle to the red category, where categories are indicated by templates comprising a green triangle and a red circle. In a complex task, sorting depends on whether the higher order rule specifies sorting by color, as just mentioned, or by shape. If sorting is by shape, the green circle is sorted with the red circle, and the red triangle is sorted with the green triangle. Normative data (e.g., Zelazo & Frye, 1998; Zelazo & Jacques, 1996) indicate that children typically process a single rule by two years of age, a pair of rules by three years, and a pair of rules embedded under a higher order rule by four years. The dimensional change card sort task has been a useful predictor of other cognitive performances such as concept of mind (Frye Zelazo, & Palfai, 1995).

THE RELATIONAL COMPLEXITY (RC) METRIC

Halford (Halford, Wilson, & Phillips, 1998) defines complexity as a function of the number of variables that can be related in a single cognitive representation. This corresponds to the arity, or number of arguments (slots) of a relation (an n-ary relation is a set of points in n-dimensional space). Normative data indicate that quaternary relations (four related variables) are the most complex that can be processed in parallel by most humans, although a minority can process quinary relations under optimal conditions. Children can process unary relations at one year, binary relations at two years, ternary relations at five years, and the adult level is reached at 11 years (median ages).

Complex tasks are *segmented* into components that do not overload capacity to process information in parallel. However, relations between variables in different segments become inaccessible (just as a three-way interaction would be inaccessible if two-way analyses were performed). Processing loads can also be reduced by *conceptual chunking*, which is equivalent to compressing variables (analogous to collapsing factors in a multivariate experimental design). For example, velocity = distance/time but can be recoded to a binding between a variable and a constant (e.g., speed = 80 kph) (Halford, Wilson, & Phillips, 1998. Section 3.4.1). Conceptual chunking reduces processing load, but chunked relations become inaccessible (e.g., if we think of velocity as a single variable, we cannot determine what happens to velocity if we travel the same distance in half the time). Complexity analyses are based on the principle that *variables can be chunked or segmented only if relations between them do not need to be processed*. Tasks that impose high loads are those in which chunking and segmentation are constrained.

CCC and RC theories have some common ground, but whereas CCC attributes complexity to the number of levels of a hierarchy, RC attributes it to the number of variables bound in a representation. Therefore RC theory is directly applicable both to hierarchical and nonhierarchical tasks. Also, the principles of segmentation and conceptual chunking imply that difficult tasks are those that cannot be decomposed into simpler tasks. In the sorting task discussed with respect to CCC theory, it is necessary to keep in mind that we are sorting by color in order to determine that the green circle is sorted with the green triangle. This means the task cannot be decomposed into two subtasks that are performed independently, because the conflicting dimension is always present.

Andrews and Halford (2002) showed that with four- to eight-year-old children, in the domains of transitivity, hierarchical classification, cardinality, comprehension of relative clause sentences, hypothesis testing, and class inclusion, a single relational complexity factor accounted for approximately 50% of variance and factor scores correlated with fluid intelligence ($r = .79$) and working memory ($r = .66$).

Increased Dimensionality

Taking account of extra dimensions is a fundamental requirement for cognitive development. For example, the progression from an undifferentiated concept of heat to a concept that distinguishes heat and temperature entails taking account of the dimensions of mass and specific heat: Heat = temperature × specific heat × mass. Similarly, the distinction between weight and density depends on taking into account volume and specific gravity: Weight = specific gravity × volume. Taking account of the extra dimensions enables children to progress from undifferentiated concepts of heat or weight to more sophisticated concepts that recognize the distinction between heat and temperature or between weight and specific gravity. Thus, they become capable of recognizing that a piece of aluminium weighs less than a similar volume of lead, but a sufficiently large piece of aluminium can weight more than a piece of lead. Arguably, the progression that children make here parallels the development of these concepts in the history of science (Carey & Gelman, 1991). In an entirely different context, acquisition of conservation of continuous quantity arguably entails taking account of height and width of containers, rather than fixating on height alone (Piaget, 1950). The essential point here is that cognitive representations must include sufficient dimensions to take account of the variations in a phenomenon, so children must represent volume and specific gravity to take account of variations in weight, and so on.

The importance of cascade correlation models, considered earlier, is that they offer a possible mechanism by which extra dimensions can be added to cognitive representations to take account of variations in the task. The model does not have to be told what dimensions to include. It creates dimensions in its own representations, contained in the hidden units, as required for input–output functions on which it is trained. This can be seen as modeling the increased dimensionality of children's cognitive representations as they learn to predict variations in the environment. This mechanism illustrates the potential for neural nets to provide the long-hoped-for basis of constructivism without postulating that all the dimensions children attend to are innately determined (Elman et al., 1996, but see also Marcus, 1998a, 1998b). Mareschal & Shultz (1996) suggest that cascade correlation models can provide a way to increase the computational power of a system, thereby overcoming a criticism by Fodor (1980) of constructivist models of cognitive development.

Knowledge and Expertise

The theories considered so far have placed major emphasis on development of reasoning processes, but acquisition and organization of knowledge is equally important. Furthermore, knowledge acquisition interacts with development of reasoning processes to determine how effectively children can reason and solve problems.

Several important lines of research have recognized acquisition of knowledge as a major factor in cognitive development (Carey & Gelman, 1991; Ceci & Howe, 1978; Keil, 1991). Cognitive development can also be seen as analogous to acquisition of expertise, so the reasoning of young children is analogous to that of the novice in a domain. The effect of domain expertise on even the most basic cognitive functions was demonstrated by Chi (1976), who showed that child chess experts outperformed adult chess novices on a simple recall test of chess pieces on a board. On recall of digits, the children performed according to age norms, and well below the level of adults. This experiment cannot be interpreted validly as showing that memory capacity does not change with age, because capacity is not measured and the experiment is quite consistent with an increase in capacity with age that is overridden by differences in domain expertise. The capacity question requires quite a different methodology. However, the study does show how powerful effects of domain knowledge can be. Carey (1991) argues that differentiation of heat and mass by young children is similarly attributable to knowledge acquisition. There is, of course, no logical reason to assume that explanations based on knowledge acquisition are necessarily incompatible with explanations based on growth in capacity. Most of the evidence suggests an interaction of these processes.

Although not in the mainstream of knowledge research in cognitive development, Halford and Wilson (1980) and Halford, Bain et al. (1998) investigated possible mechanisms for acquisition of structured knowledge along lines similar to the induction theory proposed by Holland et al. (1986). See also a special issue of *Human Development* (Kuhn, 1995) on reconceptualizing the intersection between development and learning.

Advances in our understanding of children's knowledge have had a pervasive influence on research in the field, and it would be hard to think of a domain that has not been touched by it. In this review, knowledge is considered in relation to children's expertise in specific domains, including conservation, transitivity, classification, prototype formation, theory of mind, and scientific and mathematical concepts. (See also Chap. 14 by Novick & Bassok on problem solving and expertise.)

Domain Specificity versus Generality

The view that cognitive processes are domain-specific rather than domain-general has developed in parallel with knowledge acquisition theories of cognitive development and has been reinforced by Fodor's proposal (1983) that many cognitive processes are performed by specialized modules. For example, it has been proposed that conditional reasoning (i.e., reasoning in which the major premise has the form "if-then") might depend on a module for cheater detection (Cheng & Holyoak, 1989; Cosmides & Tooby, 1992; but see Cosmides & Tooby, 1989), that understanding mathematics might depend on innate enumeration processes (Gelman, 1991), or that reasoning about cause might be facilitated by a module for processing causal information (Leslie & Keeble, 1987). One achievement has been to show that young children understand the distinction between artifacts and natural kinds (Keil, 1991) and have considerable knowledge of basic facts about the world. For example, they understand that animals move autonomously, have blood, and can die (Gelman, 1990; Keil, 1995). The distinction between animate and inanimate objects even seems to be appreciated in infancy (Gergely et al., 1995). One result of these developments has been an increasing biological perspective in theories of children's reasoning (Kenrick, 2001). Domain-specific knowledge must now be seen as having a major influence on the developing cognitions of children, but it does not displace domain-general knowledge entirely. Basic cognitive operations such as memory retrieval, and basic reasoning mechanisms such as analogy and means-end analysis, are applicable across domains. Furthermore, some higher reasoning processes such as transitive inference and classification are found to correspond across domains (Andrews & Halford, 2002). Theories such as that of Case (1985; Case et al., 1996) recognize the importance of both domain-specific and domain-general processes.

Reasoning Processes

Piaget based his theory of cognitive development on the child's progression through increasingly complex logics, but this approach has not been generally successful as a way of modeling children's reasoning (Halford, 1993; Osherson, 1974). Considerable success has been achieved in accounting for adult reasoning using mental models (Johnson-Laird & Byrne, 1991), analogies (Gentner & Markman, 1997; Hofstadter, 2001; Holyoak & Hummel, 2001; Holyoak & Thagard, 1995), schemas (Cheng et al., 1986), and heuristics (Kahneman, Slovic, & Tversky, 1982).

Analogical reasoning is reviewed by Holyoak (Chap. 6), but the implications for understanding cognitive development are considered here. An analogy is a structure-preserving map from a base or source to a target (Gentner, 1983; Holyoak & Thagard, 1989). The map is validated by structural correspondence rather than similar elements. Structural correspondence is defined by two principles; *uniqueness of mapping* implies that an element in the base is mapped to one and only one element in the target; *symbol-argument consistency* implies that if a relation symbol r in one structure is mapped to the relation symbol r' in the other structure, the arguments of r are mapped to the arguments of r' and vice versa. These principles operate as soft constraints and can be violated in small parts of the mapping if the overall mapping conforms to the criteria. Success in mapping depends on representation of the corresponding relations in the two structures and on ability to retrieve the relevant representations, which, in turn, depends on knowledge of the domain. Research on children's analogical reasoning is reviewed by Goswami (1998, 2002).

Numerous studies have assessed young children's ability to perform simple proportional analogy – that is, problems of the form A is to B as C is to D. Brown (1989) showed that children as young as three years could use analogies for both learning and problem solving if they understood the relevant relations, were able to retrieve them from memory, and understood the aims of the task. This was borne out by Goswami (1989), who showed that three-, four-, and six-year old children could perform analogies based on relations they understood, such as cutting or melting (e.g., chocolate:melted chocolate::snowman:melted snowman). In a less tightly structured context, Gentner (1977) showed that four- to six-year-old children could map human body parts to inanimate objects such as trees (e.g., if a tree had a knee it would be on the trunk a short distance above the ground). There appears to be consensus now that young children can perform analogies with simple relations if they have the relevant domain knowledge and if the test format is appropriate to the age of the children.

Young children can also use analogies for problem solving (Brown, Kane, & Echols, 1986; Crisafi & Brown, 1986; Holyoak, Junn, & Billman, 1984). In the study by Holyoak et al. (1984), children were told a story about a genie who transferred jewels from one bottle to another by rolling his magic carpet into a tube and rolling the jewels down it. Then they were given the problem of transferring gumballs from one jar to another using a tube made by rolling a sheet of heavy paper. Even four-year-olds showed evidence of analogical reasoning. Gholson et al. (1996) tested children from first to fifth grade on transfer from missionaries and cannibals problems to jealous husbands problems, both of which require a sequence of moves to be selected for transferring people from one place to another without violating constraints. In a second experiment they used similar problems that required a sequence of arithmetic steps to be chosen. The children showed evidence of analogical transfer, based on representation of common relations. Pauen and Wilkening (1997) found evidence that second- and fourth-grade children transferred selected aspects of balance scale problems to simple physical force problems.

Mental models have been found effective for providing explanations of human reasoning (Johnson-Laird & Byrne, 1991; Johnson-Laird, Chap. 9). A mental model is more content-specific than a logical rule and is used by analogy. Gentner and Gentner (1983) showed that high school and college students could use water flowing in pipes as mental models of electricity, so pipes were mapped to conductors, constrictions in pipes were mapped to resistors, water pressure to voltage, water flow to electric current, and reservoirs to batteries. Furthermore, reservoirs placed above one another were mapped into batteries in series, and the increase in water pressure was mapped to the increase in voltage, and so on.

It appears that mental models are also an effective way of accounting for development of reasoning in children (Barrouillet, Grosset, & Lecas, 2000; Barrouillet & Lecas, 1999; Halford, 1993; Markovits & Barrouillet, 2002). Marcovits and Barrouillet (2002) have developed a mental models theory that accounts for most of the data on children's conditional (if-then) reasoning. Conditionals may refer to classes (e.g., if X is a dog then X is an animal, or simply, all dogs are animals) or to causal relations (e.g., if it rains, the ground will get wet). For the problem, if p then q, p therefore q (modus ponens), construction of a mental model begins with the following representation:

p   q
     . . .

This represents the case in which p and q are both true. The model could now be fleshed out with other possibilities as follows (where ¬p is read as "not p"):

p   q
¬p   ¬q
¬p   q

The second premise "p" is processed by selecting those components of the model where p is true, in this case, the first line; then inference is made by examining these cases. In this model, in the only case in which p is true, q is also true; thus, the inference is "q." For example, if the major premise were "if an animal is a dog then it has legs," then the initial model would be

dog legs

This could be fleshed out with alternative cases such as

not dog no legs
not dog legs

Thus the premises are processed as relational propositions, referring to specific instances, and are fleshed out by retrieving relevant information from semantic memory. The accuracy of children's reasoning depends on the fleshing out process, which is influenced by availability of relevant information in memory and by working memory capacity. The minor premise "not dog" can produce the fallacious inference "no legs" (denial of the antecedent) if the second line of the mental model is missing. This could occur if the child failed to retrieve any cases of things that are not dogs but have legs. Similarly, the minor premise "legs" can produce the fallacious inference "dog" (affirmation of the consequent). Markovits (2000) has shown that children are more likely to recognize that these inferences are not justified if they can readily generate the alternative cases. In the aforementioned example, it is easy to generate instances of things that are not dogs but have legs. In a problem such as "if something is a cactus then it has thorns," generation of alternative cases is more difficult, and children are less likely to recognize the fallacies. The second major factor is processing (working memory) capacity. More complex problems entail representation of more relations. The example just given effectively entails three relations corresponding to the three lines of the mental model. A simpler problem would consist of only the first and second lines and corresponds to a biconditional interpretation of the major premise. This representation is simpler. Increase in effective capacity with age enables children to reason correctly on more complex problems. The model of Marcovits and Barrouillet (2002) can handle both content effects (Barrouillet & Lecas, 1998; Leevers & Harris, 1999) and complexity effects (Halford, Wilson, & Phillips, 1998).

Other studies of children's conditional reasoning have utilized the Wason selection task (Wason, 1966; see also Evans, Chap. 8). The task entails four cards containing (say) an A, B, 4, and 7, and participants are told that there is a letter on one side of each card and a number on the other. They are asked which cards must be turned over to test the proposition that if there is an A on one side there must be a 4 on the other. The correct answer, cards containing the A and 7, is rare even among adults. There are well-known content effects, and it has been shown that versions of the task based on permission (Cheng et al., 1986) or cheater detection (Cosmides & Tooby, 1992) are performed better. Similar improvements have been observed in children (Cummins, 1996; Light et al., 1989).

The literature supports the claim that conditional reasoning is possible for children, even as young as four, and improvements can be produced by more appropriate task presentation (Markovits et al., 1996) and by experience, but considerable development occurs throughout childhood (Muller, Overton, & Reene, 2001). Among the relatively late-developing competences are understanding of logical necessity (Falmagne, Mawby, & Pea, 1989; Kuhn, 1977; Morris & Sloutsky, 2002; Osherson & Markman, 1975) and reasoning that requires representation of complex relations.

Elementary Concepts

Conservation, transitivity, and classification are three concepts that have long been considered fundamental to children's reasoning. All have been controversial because Piaget's claim that they are concrete operational and unattainable before seven to eight years has been contested by many researchers. We briefly consider each in turn.

Conservation

Perhaps the most widely researched concept in the field, conservation, is still not well understood. The Q-SOAR model of conservation acquisition was briefly reviewed earlier, and other models exist (Caroff, 2002; Halford, 1970; Shultz, 1998; Siegler, 1995). However, the issues that have received most attention in the literature concern how conservation should be measured and the age at which children master it. A number of authors have argued that the Piagetian tests misled children and therefore underestimated their understanding. A common cause of the alleged misunderstanding is that an increase in the length of a row of objects (or an increase in the height of a column of liquid) makes the number (or amount) appear greater. This received substantial support from a study by Gelman (1969), who used an oddity training procedure to induce five-year-old children to attend to number rather than length and showed that they conserved number. This interpretation received further support from McGarrigle and Donaldson (1975), who improved conservation in children aged four to six years by having a "naughty teddy" perform the transformation, thereby making it accidental and removing any suggestion that an increase in amount was intended. These studies, like a host of others, showed improved performance in children about five to six years of age. However, Bryant (1972) eliminated length cues and showed that three- and four-year-old children carried a pretransformation judgment over into the posttransformation situation. However, his claim that this demonstrated conservation was disputed by Halford and Boyle (1985). Sophian (1995) also failed to replicate Bryant's finding of early conservation and showed that conservation was related to understanding of counting, suggesting that conservation reflects some aspects of children's quantitative concepts. From extensive reviews of the conservation literature (Halford, 1982, 1989), it seems there is clear evidence of conservation at approximately five years of age, which is earlier than Piaget claimed, but not as early as claimed by Bryant (1972).

Transitivity and Serial Order

A transitive inference has the form: aRb, bRc implies aRc, if R is a transitive relation. For example, a > b, b > c implies a > c. Piaget's claim of late attainment was challenged by Bryant and Trabasso (1971), who trained three- to six-year-old children to remember the relative lengths of adjacent sticks in a series (e.g., a < b, b < c, c < d, d < e). Then they were tested on all possible pairs. The crucial pair is b?d because this was not learned during training and must be inferred from b < c, c < d. Also, the bd pair avoids the end elements, which tend to be labeled as small (a) or large (e). Bryant and Trabasso found that three- and four-year-old children performed above chance on the bd pair, suggesting that they made a transitive inference. Riley and Trabasso (1974) showed that both children and adults performed the task by ordering the elements – that is, they formed the ordered set a,b,c,d,e. This in itself does not affect the validity of the test because an asymmetric, transitive binary relation is a defining property of an ordered set, so the children presumably utilized transitivity in some way while ordering the elements. The problem, however, was that, to facilitate acquisition, the premise pairs were presented initially in ascending or descending order (a < b, b < c, c < d, d < e, or the reverse). This clearly gave children undue help in ordering the elements. Furthermore, children who failed to learn the premise pairs were eliminated, and elimination rates were as high as 50% in some experiments. The problem with this is that children might have failed to learn the premises because they could not determine the correct order, which, in turn, might reflect lack of understanding of transitivity. When Kallio (1982) and Halford and Kelly (1984) eliminated these extraneous sources of help, success was not observed below five years of age. Subsequent research (Andrews & Halford, 1998; Pears & Bryant, 1990) has confirmed that transitive inference is understood by only a minority of four-year-olds, and the median age of attainment is about five years. For more extensive reviews and theoretical discussions, see Brainerd & Reyna (1993), Breslow (1981), Thayer & Collyer (1978), and Halford (1982, 1993).

A derivative of the Bryant and Trabasso (1971) paradigm, transitivity of choice, has found wide use in animal studies (Boysen et al., 1993; Chalmers & McGonigle, 1984; von Fersen et al., 1991; McGonigle & Chalmers, 1977; Terrace & McGonigle, 1994). Participants are trained to choose one member of each pair in a series. For example, they are rewarded for choosing A in preference to B, B in preference to C, C in preference to D, and D in preference to E. Transitivity of choice is indicated by choice of B in preference to D. However, whereas transitive inference implies an ordinal scale of premise elements, in transitivity of choice there is no such scale (Markovits & Dumas, 1992). Furthermore, whereas the transitive inference task is performed dynamically in working memory, following a single presentation of premises, the premise pairs in transitivity of choice are learned incrementally over many trials, and the task can be performed by associative processes (Wynne, 1995). Although both paradigms are important, transitive inference and transitivity of choice should not be regarded as equivalent tests of the transitivity concept.

Classification

Concepts and categories are reviewed by Medin and Rips (Chap. 3). Developmentally, categorization appears to progress from prototypes, arguably the most basic form of categorization, to more advanced categories, including those based on rules or theories. All advanced categories appear to have a label or symbol (e.g., "dog" for the dog category) so it will be convenient to deal with them under the heading of symbolic categories.

PROTOTYPE MODELS OF CLASSIFICATION

There is evidence that infants can form prototypic categories (Rosch & Mervis, 1975; Rosch et al., 1976) and can recognize that a set of objects with similar features, such as animals (dogs, cats), form categories (Quinn, 2002). They are also sensitive to the correlation between attributes (Younger & Fearing, 1999). However, prototypes are arguably subsymbolic because they are well simulated by three-layered nets (Quinn & Johnson, 1997) and do not have properties such as compositionality that are basic to symbolic processes (Fodor, 1995; Halford, Phillips, & Wilson, unpublished manuscript). Mandler (2000) argues that infants make the transition from perceptual categories, which enable objects to be recognized by their appearance, to conceptual categories, defined by the role objects play in events and that serve as a basis for inductive inference.

Neural nets are a very suitable basis for constructing models of prototype formation, and McClelland and Rumelhart (1985) produced an early prototype model that fundamentally changed the way we view categorization. Quinn and Johnson (1997) developed a three-layered net model of prototype formation in infants. There were thirteen input nodes that encoded attributes of pictorial instances of four animals (cats, dogs, elephants, rabbits) and four kinds of furniture (beds, chairs, dressers, tables). There were three hidden units and ten output units, two of which coded for category (animals, furniture) and the remainder coded for the eight instances. After the net was trained to recognize categories and instances, the representations in the hidden units were examined. Initially there was no differentiation, then the units differentiated mammals and furniture, then instances were distinguished within the categories. The study is important for showing how categories can be formed by a learning algorithm. As with the models of McClelland (1995) and Elman (1990) discussed earlier, the representations emerge from the learning process.

SYMBOLIC CATEGORIES

Even young children form categories based on, and draw inductive inferences about, essential or nonobvious properties (Gelman,

2000). This means that objects are categorized on the basis of hidden properties that cause their surface or observable features, so animals contain essential biological material that enable them to move, eat, make characteristic sounds, and reproduce animals of the same kind. Categorization by essential properties is sometimes interpreted as evidence that people have theories about the domain, such as theories about the nature of animals, although there are also interpretations based on causal laws rather than essences (Rehder & Hastie, 2001; Strevens, 2000). There is strong evidence that young children can make inductive inferences based on category membership. Gelman and Markman (1986) presented four-year-olds with a picture of a bird, told the children a property of the bird (feeds its young with mashed up food) and found that the children attributed the property to other, even dissimilar, birds but not to a different category such as bats. Young children appear to generalize even nonobservable properties on the basis of category membership, independent of appearance.

The ease with which young children make inductive inferences about categories contrasts with the difficulty they have in reasoning about hierarchically structured categories. For example, given twelve apples and three oranges, when asked whether there are more apples or more fruit, they tend to say there are more apples. This task is a derivative of class inclusion items originally used by Inhelder & Piaget (1964). The Piagetian hypothesis was that children lacked a concept of inclusion till they reached the concrete operations stage, but many alternative hypotheses have been proposed (McGarrigle, Grieve, & Hughes, 1978; Siegel et al., 1978; Winer, 1980). Misinterpretation of the question is the common feature in these proposals. That is, children interpret "more apples or more fruit" to mean "more apples or more *other kinds of* fruit," and because there are only three pieces of non-apple fruit (oranges), they say there are more apples. On the other hand Halford (1989) argued that many of the improved performances produced by alternative tests were no better than chance, or were amenable to alternative interpretations. Furthermore, techniques for estimating the number of answers attributable to misinterpretation or guessing have been developed (Hodkin, 1987; Thomas & Horton, 1997).

Alternative assessments have been devised, one based on a sorting task that was isomorphic to class inclusion but did not include potentially misleading questions (Halford & Leitch, 1989) and one based on property inference (Greene, 1994; Johnson, Scott, & Mervis, 1997). Understanding class inclusion entails recognition of the asymmetric relation between categories at different levels of the hierarchy. For example, properties of fruit apply to apples, but the reverse is not necessarily true, because apples may have properties not shared with other fruit. Halford, Andrews, & Jensen (2002) assessed category induction and class inclusion by equivalent methods, based on property inference. Relational complexity analysis showed that category induction is binary relational, because it entails a comparison of a class with its complement (e.g., birds and non-birds). Class inclusion is ternary relational because it necessarily entails an inclusive class (e.g., fruit), a subclass (e.g., apples), and a complementary subclass (non-apple fruit). When assessed by equivalent methods, class inclusion was found to be more difficult and performance on it was predicted by ternary relational tasks from other domains. This suggests that category induction and class inclusion are really the same paradigm at two levels of complexity.

Conservation, transitivity, and class inclusion are all ternary relational (Andrews & Halford, 1998; Andrews & Halford, 2002; Halford, Wilson, & Phillips, 1998) and this level of complexity is attainable by approximately twenty percent of four-year olds, 50% of five-year-olds, 70% of 6-year-olds, and 78% of seven- and eight-year-olds. There is no age at which children suddenly attain all these concepts, as implied by some interpretations of Piagetian stage theory. Rather, the proportion of children who succeed increases according to a biological growth function. We can conclude that all are attained at a median age of five years.

Concept of Mind

Children's ability to understand other people's mental states has been one of the most intensively researched topics in the past two decades. See Astington (1993) or Wellman, Cross, and Watson (2001) for reviews. Two main types of tasks have been employed – appearance-reality and false belief. Appearance-reality is tested by presenting children with an object that appears to be something else and asking them what it really is and what it appears to be. For example, Flavell, Green, and Flavell (1986) showed children a small white fish and then covered it with a blue filter and asked what color it was really and what color it appeared to their eyes. Children below about four years have difficulty recognizing both that the object is really white and that it appears blue. In a typical false-belief task (Wimmer & Perner, 1983), Person 1 hides an object in a box and leaves the room, then Person 2 shifts the object to a basket, and then Person 1 returns. Before age four, children have difficulty recognizing that Person 1 will look for the object in the box because he or she did not see it moved to the basket.

Numerous factors have been shown to influence children's concept of mind, including social-perceptual knowledge (Tager-Flusberg & Sullivan, 2000), understanding of mental states (Bretherton & Beeghly, 1982), and language (Astington & Jenkins, 1999). Astington & Gopnik (1991) proposed a theory-theory, meaning that children's concepts of belief, desire, and pretence are linked in an explanatory framework. The more neutral term "concept of mind" is used here, even though "theory of mind" is in common use, because there are still doubts that children's understanding of the mind amounts to a theory. For example, telling children that people's thoughts can be wrong or reminding them of their own false beliefs does not raise three-year-olds' performance above chance. Leslie (1987) proposed an innate theory of mind mechanism, or module, that is specialized for processing social cues indicating mood, interest, or attention.

There is growing evidence that concept of mind is related to executive function (Carlson & Moses, 2001; Perner, Lang, & Kloo, 2002) and is partly a function of ability to deal with the appropriate level of complexity. Halford (1993; Halford, Wilson, & Phillips, 1998) analyzed the complexity of concept of mind tasks and showed it entails integrating three variables – the environmental cue, the setting condition, and the person's representation. Appearance-reality requires processing the relation between object color (white), the color of the filter (blue), and the percept (white or blue). Evidence that complexity is a factor in concept of mind has been produced by several groups of researchers (Andrews et al., 2003; Davis & Pratt, 1995; Frye, Zelazo, & Palfai, 1995; Gordon & Olson, 1998; Halford, 1993; Keenan, Olson, & Marini, 1998).

The analysis showing that concept of mind requires processing ternary relations suggests this should not be possible for chimpanzees because the most complex relation they have been shown to process is binary (Halford, Wilson, & Phillips, 1998). Although the issue has been controversial, a well-controlled study by Call and Tomasello (1999) tends to support this prediction. (See also Tomasello & Call, Chap. 25.)

Scientific Thinking

The topics reviewed so far on children's understanding of conservation, transitive inference, serial order, classification, cause, and biological processes are all important to the development of scientific and mathematical thinking. In this section, we consider some of the more advanced forms of scientific and mathematical reasoning in children. (See also Chap. 5 on causal reasoning by Buehner & Cheng, Chap. 23 on mathematical thinking by Gallistel & Gelman, and Chap. 29 on reasoning in science by Dunbar & Fugelsang.)

Whether children think as young scientists has been a major question of interest motivated partly by evidence that categorization and concept of mind are driven by theories of the domain, as noted earlier. Kuhn et al. (1988) investigated how children assessed evidence in order to test hypotheses, and concluded that there was a considerable lack of scientific objectivity, especially among the younger children. Similarly, Klahr, Fay, and Dunbar (1993) found strong developmental effects in a study of ability to design experiments to determine rules underlying operation of a robot. On the other hand, Ruffman et al. (1993) found evidence that six-year-olds have some understanding of how covariation evidence has implications for hypotheses about factors responsible for an event. There is also evidence that children as young as five recognize the evidential diversity principle – that we can be more confident of a induction from a set of diverse premises than from a set of similar premises (Heit & Hahn, 2001; Lo et al., 2002; Sloman, Chap. 3, this volume). A theoretical account of the development of inductive reasoning is given by Kuhn (2001), and a review of the development of scientific reasoning skills is provided by Zimmerman (2000).

Time, Speed, Distance, and Area

Understanding time, speed, and distance is interesting because it entails relations among three variables; speed = distance − time^{-1}; and this relation should be accessible from other directions, so distance = speed × time, and so on. Matsuda (2001) found a progression from considering relations between two variables (e.g., between duration and distance or between distance and speed) at four years to integration of all three dimensions by age 11. Wilkening (1980) used an information integration theory approach in which the variance in children's judgments of distance was assessed as a function of speed and duration. In the information integration approach, reliance on a factor is indicated by a main effect, and reliance on the product of speed and duration is indicated by an interaction of these factors. Integration by an additive rule, speed + distance, is indicated by two main effects. Children from five years to adulthood showed evidence of the multiplicative rule. A similar assessment of children's understanding of area indicated gradual progression from additive rule (area = length + width) to a multiplicative rule (area = length × width) by adulthood. A cascade correlation model of time, distance, and velocity judgments is provided by Buckingham and Shultz (2000).

Causal Reasoning

Infants are able to perceive causal links between entities (Leslie & Keeble, 1987), but the causal reasoning of older children seems to be influenced by complexity (Brooks, Hanauer, & Frye, 2001; Frye et al., 1996) or by concept availability (Ackerman, Silver, & Glickman, 1990). The explanation may be that, as Leslie and Keeble (1987) suggest, the causal recognitions of infants are based on a modular process that is essentially perceptual. Modular processes are not typically influenced by cognitive complexity. The causal reasoning of older children probably depends on more conceptual or symbolic processes (Schlottman, 2001).

Balance Scale

Siegler (1981) applied the rule assessment approach to children's performance on the balance scale, yielding the four rules that were discussed in connection with McClelland's neural model (1995). Siegler's data showed Rule I (judgments based solely on weight) was used by five-year-olds, and they could also be taught to use Rule II (distance considered if weights are equal). Surber and Gzesh (1984) used an information integration approach and found that five-year-olds tended to favor the distance rule. Case (1985), Marini (1984), and Jansen and van der Maas (1997) generally supported Siegler's findings and saw little understanding of the balance scale before age five.

Relational complexity theory (Halford, 1993; Halford, Wilson, & Phillips, 1998) proposes that discrimination of weights with distance constant, or distances with weight constant, entails processing binary relations and should be possible for two-year olds. This prediction was contrary to previous theory (Case, 1985) and empirical observation (Siegler, 1981). Integration of weight and distance requires at least ternary relations and should emerge along with other ternary relational concepts at age five years. These predictions were confirmed by Halford et al. (2002).

Concept of the Earth

The development of children's concept of the earth (Hayes et al., 2003; Samarapungavan, Vosniadou, & Brewer, 1996; Vosniadou & Brewer, 1992) has special interest because it entails a conflict between the culturally transmitted conception that the Earth is a sphere and everyday experience that tends to make it appear flat. Resolution of this conflict entails recognition that the huge circumference of the earth makes it appear flat from the surface. There is also a conflict between gravity, naively considered as making objects fall down, and the notion that people can stand anywhere on the Earth's surface, including the southern hemisphere, which is conventionally regarded as "down under." This can be resolved by a concept of gravity as attraction between two masses, the Earth and the body (person) on the surface, but there is little basis for this concept in everyday life. The development of children's concept of the Earth provides an interesting study in the integration of complex relations into a coherent conception. Young children were found to attempt resolution of the conflicting ideas by, for example, drawing a circular earth with a horizontal platform inside for people to stand on, or as a flattened sphere to provide more standing room at the top. Nevertheless, there was a clear tendency for ideas to develop toward coherence.

Conclusions and Future Directions

Although acknowledging that predictions of future developments are inherently hazardous, it seems appropriate after an extensive assessment of the literature to try to identify some of the more promising developments. My bias is to look for developments that might provide a coherent body of theory because this is what the field of cognitive development, like the rest of psychology, needs most. I have identified four trends I feel deserve consideration in this respect.

Neuroscience and the Biological Perspective

The greatly increased knowledge of neuroscience and the use of brain imaging as a converging operation to help constrain theories of cognitive development represent major developments in the past two decades. Combined with the biological perspective, they do offer some hope of a coherent framework for viewing cognitive developmental data. The identification of changes in rates of neural and cognitive development is one example of what this field has achieved.

Dynamic Systems

Dynamic systems models have made considerable progress, and they are much more clearly linked to data than was the case a decade ago. They can provide new perspectives on important issues such as whether development is continuous or discontinuous or the fact that performance might be uneven across different indicators of the same task. The relative importance of different classes of observations might change fundamentally with this perspective.

Transition Mechanisms

Transition mechanisms and more advanced conceptions of learning have provided real conceptual advances and some of the most important empirical findings in the past decade. Neural net models have defined some potential mechanisms of concept acquisition that would almost certainly never have been recognized intuitively and would have been very difficult to discover using our contemporary empirical methods.

Analyses of Underlying Processes

Analyses of underlying processes using methods from general cognitive psychology and cognitive science can help bring order and clarity to the field. There are many examples of tasks that are superficially similar (such as transitive inference and transitivity of choice) yet entail fundamentally different processes, and it only creates confusion to categorize them together. Correspondingly, there are tasks that are superficially very different, yet may entail underlying cognitive processes with important common properties. An example would be the corresponding difficulties of the dimensional change card sort task, and ternary relational tasks such as transitivity, class inclusion, and the concept of mind. We cannot order tasks for difficulty, nor discover important equivalences, unless we look beneath surface properties. Cognitive psychology has progressed to the point at which we can do this with reasonable confidence.

References

Ackerman, B. P., Silver, D., & Glickman, I. (1990). Concept availability in the causal inferences of children and adults. *Child Development*, *61*, 230–246.

Andrews, G., & Halford, G. S. (1998). Children's ability to make transitive inferences: The importance of premise integration and structural complexity. *Cognitive Development*, 13, 479–513.

Andrews, G., & Halford, G. S. (2002). A complexity metric applied to cognitive development. *Cognitive Psychology*, 45, 153–219.

Andrews, G., Halford, G. S., Bunch, K.M, Bowden, D., Jones, T. (2003). Concept of mind and relational complexity. *Child Development*, 74(5), 1476–1499.

Astington, J. W. (1993). *The Child's Discovery of Mind*. Cambridge, MA: Harvard University Press.

Astington, J. W., & Gopnik, A. (1991). Theoretical explanations of children's understanding of the mind. *British Journal of Developmental Psychology*, 9, 7–31.

Astington, J. W., & Jenkins, J. M. (1999). A longitudinal study of the relation between language and theory-of-mind development. *Developmental Psychology*, 35, 1311–1320.

Baillargeon, R. (1995). A model of physical reasoning in infancy. In C. Rovee-Collier & L. P. Lipsitt (Eds.), *Advances in Infancy Research*, vol. 9 (pp. 305–371). Norwood, NJ: Ablex.

Baillargeon, R., Graber, M., DeVos, J., & Black, J. (1990). Why do young infants fail to search for hidden objects? *Cognition*, 36, 255–284.

Barrouillet, P., Grosset, N., & Lecas, J. (2000). Conditional reasoning by mental models: Chronometric and developmental evidence. *Cognition*, 75, 237–266.

Barrouillet, P., & Lecas, J. (1998). How can mental models theory account for content effects in conditional reasoning? A developmental perspective. *Cognition*, 67, 209–253.

Barrouillet, P., & Lecas, J. (1999). Mental models in conditional reasoning and working memory. *Thinking and Reasoning*, 5, 289–302.

Beilin, H. (1992). Piaget's enduring contribution to developmental psychology. *Developmental Psychology*, 28(2), 191–204.

Bjorklund, D. F. (1997). In search of a metatheory for cognitive development (or Piaget is dead and I don't feel so good myself). *Child Development*, 68, 144–148.

Boole, G. (1854/1951). *An Investigation of the Laws of Thought, on which are founded the Mathematical Theories of Logic and Probabilities*. New York: Dover.

Boysen, S. T., Berntson, G. G., Shreyer, T. A., & Quigley, K. S. (1993). Processing of ordinality and transitity by chimpanzees (pan troglodytes). *Journal of Comparative Psychology*, 107, 1–8.

Brainerd, C. J. (1978). The stage question in cognitive developmental theory. *The Behavioral and Brain Sciences*, 2, 173–213.

Brainerd, C. J., & Reyna, V. F. (1993). Memory independence and memory interference in cognitive development. *Psychological Review*, 100, 42–67.

Bray, N. W., Reilly, K. D., Villa, M. F., & Grupe, L. A. (1997). Neural network models and mechanisms of strategy development. *Developmental Review*, 17, 525–566.

Breslow, L. (1981). Reevaluation of the literature on the development of transitive inferences. *Psychological Bulletin*, 89, 325–351.

Bretherton, I., & Beeghly, M. (1982). Talking about internal states: The acquisition of an explicit theory of mind. *Developmental Psychology*, 18, 906–921.

Briars, D., & Siegler, R. S. (1984). A featural analysis of preschoolers' counting knowledge. *Developmental Psychology*, 20, 607–618.

Brooks, P. J., Hanauer, J. B., & Frye, D. (2001). Training 3-year-olds in rule-based causal reasoning. *British Journal of Developmental Psychology*, 19, 573–595.

Brown, A. L. (1989). Analogical learning and transfer: What develops? In S. Vosniadou & A. Ortony (Eds.), *Similarity and Analytical Reasoning* (pp. 369–412). New York: Cambridge University Press.

Brown, A. L., Kane, M. J., & Echols, C. H. (1986). Young children's mental models determine analogical transfer across problems with a common goal structure. *Cognitive Development*, 1, 103–121.

Bruner, J. S., Olver, R. R., & Greenfield, P. M. (1966). *Studies in cognitive growth*. New York: Wiley.

Bryant, P. (Ed.) (2002). Constructivism today. *Cognitive Development*, 17(3–4), 1283–1508.

Bryant, P. E. (1972). The understanding of invariance by very young children. *Canadian Journal of Psychology*, 26, 78–96.

Bryant, P. E., & Trabasso, T. (1971). Transitive inferences and memory in young children. *Nature*, 232, 456–458.

Buckingham, D., & Shultz, T. R. (2000). The developmental course of distance, time, and velocity concepts: A generative connectionist model. *Journal of Cognition and Development*, 1, 305–345.

Call, J., & Tomasello, M. (1999). A nonverbal false belief task: The performance of children and great apes. *Child Development*, 70, 381–395.

Carey, S. (1991). Knowledge acquisition: Enrichment or conceptual change? In S. Carey & R. Gelman (Eds.), *The Epigenesis of Mind: Essays on Biology and Cognition* (pp. 257–291). Hillsdale, NJ: Erlbaum.

Carey, S., & Gelman, R. (1991). *The Epigenesis of Mind: Essays on Biology and Cognition*. Hillsdale, NJ: Erlbaum.

Carlson, S. M., & Moses, L. J. (2001). Individual differences in inhibitory control and children's theory of mind. *Child Development*, 72, 1032–1053.

Caroff, X. (2002). What conservation anticipation reveals about cognitive change. *Cognitive Development*, 17, 1015–1035.

Case, R. (1985). *Intellectual Development: Birth to Adulthood*. New York: Academic Press.

Case, R. (1992a). *The Mind's Staircase: Exploring the Conceptual Underpinnings of Children's Thought and Knowledge*. Hillsdale, NJ: Erlbaum.

Case, R. (1992b). The role of the frontal lobes in the regulation of cognitive development. *Brain and Cognition*, 20, 51–73.

Case, R., Okamoto, Y., Griffin, S., McKeough, A., Bleiker, C., Henderson, B., et al. (1996). The role of central conceptual structures in the development of children's thought. *Monographs of the Society for Research in Child Development.*, 61.

Ceci, S. J., & Howe, M. J. (1978). Age-related differences in free recall as a function of retrieval flexibility. *Journal of Experimental Child Psychology*, 26, 432–442.

Chalmers, M., & McGonigle, B. (1984). Are children any more logical than monkeys on the five-term series problem? *Journal of Experimental Child Psychology*, 37, 355–377.

Chapman, M. (1987). Piaget, attentional capacity, and the functional limitations of formal structure. *Advances in Child Development and Behavior*, 20, 289–334.

Chapman, M. (1990). Cognitive development and the growth of capacity: Issues in NeoPiagetian theory. In J. T. Enns (Ed.), *The Development of Attention: Research and Theory* (pp. 263–287). Amsterdam: Elsevier Science Publishers.

Chapman, M., & Lindenberger, U. (1989). Concrete operations and attentional capacity. *Journal of Experimental Child Psychology*, 47, 236–258.

Cheng, P. W., & Holyoak, K. J. (1989). On the natural selection of reasoning theories. *Cognition*, 33, 285–313.

Cheng, P. W., Holyoak, K. J., Nisbett, R. E., & Oliver, L. M. (1986). Pragmatic versus syntactic approaches to training deductive reasoning. *Cognitive Psychology*, 18, 293–328.

Chi, M. T. H. (1976). Short-term memory limitations in children: Capacity or processing deficits? *Memory and Cognition*, 4, 559–572.

Chomsky, N. (1980). Rules and representations. *The Behavioral and Brain Sciences*, 3, 1–61.

Cosmides, L., & Tooby, J. (1989). Evolutionary Psychology and the generation of culture: II. Case study: A computational theory of social exchange. *Ethology and Sociobiology*, 10, 51–97.

Cosmides, L., & Tooby, J. (1992). Cognitive adaptations for social exchange. In J. H. Barkow & L. Cosmides & J. Tooby (Eds.), *The Adapted*

Mind: Evolutionary Psychology and the Generation of Culture (pp. 163–228). New York: Oxford University Press.

Crisafi, M. A., & Brown, A. L. (1986). Analogical transfer in very young children: Combining two separately learned solutions to reach a goal. *Child Development*, 57, 953–968.

Cummins, D. D. (1996). Evidence of deontic reasoning in 3- and 4-year-old children. *Memory and Cognition*, 24, 823–829.

Davis, H. L., & Pratt, C. (1995). The development of children's theory of mind: The working memory explanation. *Australian Journal of Psychology*, 47, 25–31.

Diamond, A. (1988). Abilities and neural mechanisms underlying A not-B performance. *Child Development*, 59, 523–527.

Donaldson, M. (1971). *Preconditions of inference*. Lincoln: University of Nebraska Press.

Elman, J. L. (1990). Finding structure in time. *Cognitive Science*, 14, 179–211.

Elman, J. L., Bates, E. A., Johnson, M. H., Karmiloff-Smith, A., Parisi, D., et al. (1996). *Rethinking Innateness: A Connectionist Perspective on Development*. London: The MIT Press.

Falmagne, R. J., Mawby, R. A., & Pea, R. D. (1989). Linguistic and logical factors in recognition of indeterminacy. *Cognitive Development*, 4, 141–176.

Field, D. (1987). A review of preschool conservation training: An analysis of analyses. *Developmental Review*, 7, 210–251.

Fischer, K. W. (1980). A theory of cognitive development: The control and construction of hierarchies of skills. *Psychological Review*, 87, 477–531.

Fischer, K. W. (1987). Relations between brain and cognitive development. *Child Development*, 58, 623–632.

Fischer, K. W., & Bidell, T. R. (1998). Dynamic development of psychological structures in action and thought. In W. Damon & R. M. Lerner (Eds.), *Handbook of Child Psychology. Vol. 1: Theoretical Models of Human Development* (5th ed., pp. 467–561). New York: Wiley.

Fischer, K. W., & Pare-Blagoev, J. (2000). From individual differences to dynamic pathways of development. *Child Development*, 71, 850–853.

Fischer, K. W., & Rose, S. P. (1996). Dynamic growth cycles of brain and cognitive development. In R. W. Thatcher & G. R. Lyon & J. Rumsey & N. Kresnegor (Eds.), *Developmental Neuroimaging: Mapping the Development of Brain and Behavior* (pp. 263–283). San Diego: Academic Press.

Flavell, J. H., Green, F. L., & Flavell, E. R. (1986). Development of knowledge about the appearance-reality distinction. *Monographs of the Society for Research in Child Development*, 51, 1–89.

Fodor, J. (1980). Fixation of belief and concept acquisition. In M. Piatelli-Palmarini (Ed.), *Language and Learning: The Debate between Chomsky and Piaget* (pp. 143–149). Cambridge, MA: Harvard University Press.

Fodor, J. (1994). Concepts: A potboiler. *Cognition*, 50, 95–113.

Fodor, J. A. (1983). *Modularity of Mind: An Essay on Faculty Psychology*. Cambridge, MA: MIT Press.

Fodor, J. A., & Pylyshyn, Z. W. (1988). Connectionism and cognitive architecture: A critical analysis. *Cognition*, 28, 3–71.

Frye, D., & Zelazo, P. D. (1998). Complexity: From formal analysis to final action. *Behavioral and Brain Sciences*, 21, 836–837.

Frye, D., Zelazo, P. D., Brooks, P. J., & Samuels, M. C. (1996). Inference and action in early causal reasoning. *Developmental Psychology*, 32, 120–131.

Frye, D., Zelazo, P. D., & Palfai, T. (1995). Theory of mind and rule-based reasoning. *Cognitive Development*, 10, 483–527.

Gallimore, R., & Tharp, R. (1999). Teaching mind in society: Teaching, schooling, and literate discourse. In P. Lloyd & C. Fernyhough (Eds.), *Lev Vygotsky Critical Assessments. Vol III.* (pp. 296–350). London: Routledge.

Garton, A. F. (2004) Exploring Cognitive Development: The Child as Problem Solver. Oxford, UK: Blackwell.

Gelman, R. (1969). Conservation acquisition: A problem of learning to attend to relevant attributes. *Journal of Experimental Child Psychology*, 7, 167–187.

Gelman, R. (1972). Logical capacity of very young children: Number invariance rules. *Child Development*, 43, 75–90.

Gelman, R. (1982). Accessing one-to-one correspondence: Still another paper about conservation. *British Journal of Psychology*, 73, 209–220.

Gelman, R. (1990). First principles organize attention to and learning about relevant data: Number and the animate-inanimate distinction. *Cognitive Science*, 14, 79–106.

Gelman, R. (1991). Epigenetic foundations of knowledge structures: Initial and transcendant constructions. In S. Carey & R. Gelman (Eds.), *The Epigenesis of Mind* (pp. 293–322). Hillsdale, NJ: Erlbaum.

Gelman, S. (2000). The role of essentialism in children's concepts. *Advances in Child Development and Behavior*, 27, 55–98.

Gelman, S. A., & Markman, E. M. (1986). Categories and induction in young children. *Cognition*, 23, 183–209.

Gentner, D. (1977). If a tree had a knee, where would it be? Children's performance on simple spatial metaphors. *Papers and Reports on Child Language Development*, 13, 157–164.

Gentner, D. (1983). Structure-mapping: A theoretical framework for analogy. *Cognitive Science*, 7, 155–170.

Gentner, D., & Gentner, D. R. (1983). Flowing waters or teeming crowds: Mental models of electricity. In D. Gentner & A. L. Stevens (Eds.), *Mental Models* (pp. 99–129). Hillsdale, NJ: Erlbaum.

Gentner, D., & Markman, A. B. (1997). Structure mapping in analogy and similarity. *American Psychologist*, 52, 45–56.

Gergely, G., Nadasky, Z., Csibra, G., & Biro, S. (1995). Taking the intentional stance at 12 months of age. *Cognition*, 56, 165–193.

Gholson, B., Smither, D., Buhrman, A., & Duncan, M. (1996). The sources of children's reasoning errors during analogical problem solving. *Applied Cognitive Psychology*, 10, s85–s97.

Goldman-Rakic, P. S. (1987). Development of cortical circuitry and cognitive function. *Child Development*, 58, 601–622.

Gopnik, A. (1996). The post-Piaget era. *Psychological Science*, 7, 221–225.

Gordon, A. C. L., & Olson, D. R. (1998). The relation between acquisition of a theory of mind and the capacity to hold in mind. *Journal of Experimental Child Psychology*, 68, 70–83.

Goswami, U. (1989). Relational complexity and the development of analogical reasoning. *Cognitive Development*, 4, 251–268.

Goswami, U. (1998). *Cognition in Children*. East Sussex, UK: Psychology Press.

Goswami, U. (2002). Inductive and deductive reasoning. In U. Goswami (Ed.), *Blackwell Handbook of Childhood Cognitive Development* (pp. 282–302). Oxford, UK: Blackwell.

Greene, T. R. (1994). What kindergartners know about class inclusion hierarchies. *Journal of Experimental Child Psychology*, 57, 72–88.

Halford, G. S. (1970). A theory of the acquisition of conservation. *Psychological Review*, 77, 302–316.

Halford, G. S. (1982). *The Development of Thought*. Hillsdale, NJ: Erlbaum.

Halford, G. S. (1989). Reflections on 25 years of Piagetian cognitive developmental psychology, 1963–1988. *Human Development*, 32, 325–387.

Halford, G. S. (1993). *Children's Understanding: The Development of Mental Models*. Hillsdale, NJ: Erlbaum.

Halford, G. S. (2002). Information processing models of cognitive development. In U. Goswami (Ed.), *Blackwell Handbook of Childhood Cognitive Development*. Oxford, UK: Blackwell.

Halford, G. S., Andrews, G., Dalton, C., Boag, C., & Zielinski, T. (2002). Young children's performance on the balance scale: The influence of relational complexity. *Journal of Experimental Child Psychology*, 81, 417–445.

Halford, G. S., Andrews, G., & Jensen, I. (2002). Integration of category induction and hierarchical classification: One paradigm at two levels of complexity. *Journal of Cognition and Development*, 3, 143–177.

Halford, G. S., Bain, J. D., Maybery, M., & Andrews, G. (1998). Induction of relational schemas: Common processes in reasoning and complex learning. *Cognitive Psychology*, 35, 201–245.

Halford, G. S., & Boyle, F. M. (1985). Do young children understand conservation of number? *Child Development*, 56, 165–176.

Halford, G. S., & Kelly, M. E. (1984). On the basis of early transitivity judgements. *Journal of Experimental Child Psychology*, 38, 42–63.

Halford, G. S., & Leitch, E. (1989). Processing load constraints: A structure-mapping approach. In M. A. Luszcz & T. Nettelbeck (Eds.), *Psychological Development: Perspectives Across the Life-Span* (pp. 151–159). Amsterdam: North-Holland.

Halford, G. S., Phillips, S., & Wilson, W. H. (under review). Structural complexity in cognitive processes: The concept of representational rank.

Halford, G. S., Smith, S. B., Dickson, J. C., Maybery, M. T., Kelly, M. E., et al. (1995). Modelling the development of reasoning strategies: The roles of analogy, knowledge, and capacity. In T. Simon & G. S. Halford (Eds.), *Developing Cognitive Competence: New Approaches to Cognitive Modelling* (pp. 77–156). Hillsdale, NJ: Erlbaum.

Halford, G. S., & Wilson, W. H. (1980). A category theory approach to cognitive development. *Cognitive Psychology, 12*, 356–411.

Halford, G. S., Wilson, W. H., & McDonald, M. (1995). *Complexity of structure mapping in human analogical reasoning: A PDP model.* Paper presented at the Proceedings of the Seventeenth Annual Conference of the Cognitive Science Society. Pittsburgh, PA.

Halford, G. S., Wilson, W. H., & Phillips, S. (1998). Processing capacity defined by relational complexity: Implications for comparative, developmental, and cognitive psychology. *Behavioral and Brain Sciences, 21*, 803–831.

Hayes, B. K., Heit, E., Goodhew, A., & Gillan, J. E. (2003). The role of diverse instruction in conceptual change. *Journal of Experimental Child Psychology, 86*, 253–276.

Heit, E., & Hahn, U. (2001). Diversity-based reasoning in children. *Cognitive Psychology, 43*, 243–273.

Hodkin, B. (1987). Performance model analysis in class inclusion: An illustration with two language conditions. *Developmental Psychology, 23*, 683–689.

Hofstadter, D. R. (2001). Analogy as the core of cognition. In D. Gentner, K. J. Holyoak, & B. N. Kokinov (Eds.), *The Analogical Mind: Perspectives from Cognitive Science* (pp. 499–538). Cambridge, MA: MIT Press.

Holland, J. H., Holyoak, K. J., Nisbett, R. E., & Thagard, P. R. (1986). *Induction: Processes of Inference, Learning and Discovery*. Cambridge, MA: Bradford Books/MIT Press.

Holyoak, K. J., & Hummel, J. E. (2001). Toward an understanding of analogy within a biological symbol system. In D. Gentner & K. J. Holyoak & B. N. Kokinov (Eds.), *The Analogical Mind: Perspectives from Cognitive Science* (pp. 161–195). Cambridge, MA: MIT Press.

Holyoak, K. J., Junn, E. N., & Billman, D. O. (1984). Development of analogical problem-solving skill. *Child Development, 55*, 2042–2055.

Holyoak, K. J., & Thagard, P. (1989). Analogical mapping by constraint satisfaction. *Cognitive Science, 13*, 295–355.

Holyoak, K. J., & Thagard, P. (1995). *Mental Leaps*. Cambridge, MA: MIT Press.

Humphrey, G. (1951). *Thinking: An Introduction to its Experimental Psychology*. London: Methuen.

Inhelder, B., & Piaget, J. (1958). *The Growth of Logical Thinking from Childhood to Adolescence*. A. Parsons (Trans.). London: Routledge & Kegan Paul. (Original work published 1955.)

Inhelder, B., & Piaget, J. (1964). *The Early Growth of Logic in the Child*. London: Routledge & Kegan Paul.

Jansen, B. R. J., & van der Maas, H. L. J. (1997). A statistical test of the rule assessment methodology by latent class analysis. *Developmental Review, 17*, 321–357.

Johnson, K. E., Scott, P., & Mervis, C. B. (1997). Development of children's understanding of basic-subordinate inclusion relations. *Developmental Psychology, 33*, 745–763.

Johnson-Laird, P. N., & Byrne, R. M. J. (1991). *Deduction*. Hillsdale, NJ: Erlbaum.

Kahneman, D., Slovic, P., & Tversky, A. E. (1982). *Judgment under Uncertainity: Heuristics and Biases*. Cambridge, UK: Cambridge University Press.

Kallio, K. D. (1982). Developmental change on a five-term transitive inference. *Journal of Experimental Child Psychology, 33*, 142–164.

Karmiloff-Smith, A. (1994). Precis of beyond modularity: A developmental perspective on cognitive science. *Behavioral and Brain Sciences, 17*, 693–745.

Keenan, T., Olson, D. R., & Marini, Z. (1998). Working memory and children's developing understanding of mind. *Australian Journal of Psychology, 50*, 76–82.

Keil, F. C. (1991). The emergence of theoretical beliefs as constraints on concepts. In S. Carey & R. Gelman (Eds.), *The Epigenesis of Mind: Essays on Biology and Cognition* (pp. 237–256). Hillsdale, NJ: Erlbaum.

Keil, F. C. (1995). An abstract to concrete shift in the development of biological thought: The insides story. *Cognition, 56*, 129–163.

Kenrick, D. T. (2001). Evolutionary psychology, cognitive science, and dynamical systems: Building an integrative paradigm. *Current Directions in Psychological Science, 10*, 13–17.

Klahr, D., Fay, A. L., & Dunbar, K. (1993). Heuristics for scientific experimentation: A developmental study. *Cognitive psychology, 24*(1), 111–146.

Klahr, D., & Wallace, J. G. (1976). *Cognitive Development: An Information Processing View.* Hillsdale, NJ: Erlbaum.

Kuhn, D. (1977). Conditional reasoning in children. *Developmental Psychology, 13*, 342–353.

Kuhn, D. (Ed.). (1995). Development and learning. Reconceptualizing the intersection [Special Issue]. *Human Development, 38*(6).

Kuhn, D. (2001). Why development does (and does not) occur: Evidence from the domain of inductive reasoning. In J. D. McClelland & R. S. Seigler (Eds.), *Mechanisms of Cognitive Development: Behavioral and Neural Perspectives.* London: Erlbaum.

Kuhn, D., Amsel, E., O'Loughlin, M., Schauble, L., Leadbeater, B., & Yotive, W. (1988). *The Development of Scientific Thinking Skills.* San Diego, CA: Academic Press.

Leevers, H. J., & Harris, P. L. (1999). Persisting effects of instruction on young children's syllogistic reasoning with incongruent and abstract premises. *Thinking and Reasoning, 5*, 145–173.

Leslie, A., & Keeble, S. (1987). Do six-month-old infants perceive causality? *Cognition, 25*, 265–288.

Leslie, A. M. (1987). Pretense and representation: The origins of "theory of mind." *Psychological Review, 94*, 412–426.

Light, P., Blaye, A., Gilly, M., & Girotto, V. (1989). Pragmatic schemas and logical reasoning in 6- to 8-year-old children. *Cognitive Development, 4*, 49–64.

Lloyd, P. & Fernyhough, C. (1999). *Lev Vygotsky Critical Assessments. Vol IV.* London: Routledge.

Lo, Y., Sides, A., Rozelle, J., & Osherson, D. (2002). Evidential diversity and premise probability in young children's inductive judgment. *Cognitive Science, 26*, 181–206.

Lourenco, O., & Machado, A. (1996). In defense of Piaget's theory: A reply to 10 common criticisms. *Psychological Review, 103*, 143–164.

Luria, A. R. (1976). *Cognitive Development: Its Cultural and Social Foundations.* Cambridge, MA: Harvard University Press.

Mandler, J. M. (2000). Perceptual and conceptual processes in infancy. *Journal of Cognition and Development, 1*, 3–36.

Mandler, J. M., & Mandler, G. (1964). *Thinking: From Association to Gestalt.* New York: Wiley.

Marcus, G. F. (1998a). Can connectionism save constructivism? *Cognition, 66*, 153–182.

Marcus, G. F. (1998b). Rethinking eliminative connectionism. *Cognitive Psychology, 37*, 243–282.

Mareschal, D., Plunkett, K., & Harris, P. (1995, July 22–25, 1995). *Developing Object Permanence: A Connectionist Model.* Paper presented at the Proceedings of the seventh annual conference of the Cognitive Science Society. Pittsburgh, PA.

Mareschal, D., & Shultz, T. R. (1996). Generative connectionist networks and constructivist cognitive development. *Cognitive Development, 11*, 571–603.

Marini, Z. (1984). *The Development of Social and Physical Cognition in Childhood and Adolescence.* Unpublished doctoral dissertation. University of Toronto (OISE), Toronto.

Markovits, H. (2000). A mental model analysis of young children's conditional reasoning with meaningful premises. *Thinking and Reasoning, 6*, 335–348.

Markovits, H., & Barrouillet, P. (2002). The development of conditional reasoning: A mental models account. *Developmental Review, 22*, 5–36.

Markovits, H., & Dumas, C. (1992). Can pigeons really make transitive inferences? *Journal of Experimental Psychology: Animal Behavior Processes, 18*, 311–312.

Markovits, H., Venet, M., Janveau-Brenman, G., Malfait, N., Pion, N., & Vadeboncoeur, I. (1996). Reasoning in young children: Fantasy and information retrieval. *Child Development, 67*, 2857–2872.

Matsuda, F. (2001). Development of concepts of interrelationship among duration, distance, and speed. *International Journal of Behavioral Development, 25*, 466–480.

McClelland, J. L. (1995). A connectionist perspective on knowledge and development. In T. Simon & G. S. Halford (Eds.), *Developing Cognitive Competence: New Approaches to Cognitive Modelling* (pp. 157–204). Hillsdale, NJ: Erlbaum.

McClelland, J. L., & Rumelhart, D. E. (1985). Distributed memory and the representation of general and specific information. *Journal of Experimental Psychology: General, 114*, 159–188.

McGarrigle, J., & Donaldson, M. (1975). Conservation accidents. *Cognition, 3*, 341–350.

McGarrigle, J., Grieve, R., & Hughes, M. (1978). Interpreting inclusion: A contribution to the study of the child's cognitive and linguistic development. *Journal of Experimental Child Psychology*, 26, 528–550.

McGonigle, B. O., & Chalmers, M. (1977). Are monkeys logical? *Nature*, 267, 355–377.

McLaughlin, G. H. (1963). Psycho-logic: A possible alternative to Piaget's formulation. *British Journal of Educational Psychology*, 33, 61–67.

Miller, G. A., Galanter, E., & Pribram, K. H. (1960). *Plans and the Structure of Behavior*. New York: Holt, Rinehart & Winston.

Miller, S. A. (1976). Nonverbal assessment of Piagetian concepts. *Psychological Bulletin*, 83, 405–430.

Modgil, S. (1974). *Piagetian Research: A Handbook of Recent Studies*. Windsor, Berkshire: NFER Publishing.

Morris, B. J., & Sloutsky, V. (2002). Children's solutions of logical versus empirical problems: What's missing and what develops? *Cognitive Development*, 16, 907–928.

Muller, U., Overton, W. F., & Reene, K. (2001). Development of conditional reasoning: A longitudinal study. *Journal of Cognition and development*, 2, 27–49.

Munakata, Y., McClelland, J. L., Johnson, M. H., & Siegler, R. S. (1997). Rethinking infant knowledge: Toward an adaptive process account of successes and failures in object permanence tasks. *Psychological Review*, 104, 686–713.

Newell, A. (1990). *Unified Theories of Cognition*. Cambridge, MA: Harvard University Press.

Osherson, D. N. (1974). *Logical Abilities in Children, Volume I: Organization of Length and Class Concept: Empirical Consequences of a Piagetian Formalism*. Potomac, MD: Erlbaum.

Osherson, D. N., & Markman, E. (1975). Language and the ability to evaluate contradictions and tautologies. *Cognition*, 3, 213–216.

Pascual-Leone, J. A. (1970). A mathematical model for the transition rule in Piaget's developmental stages. *Acta Psychologica*, 32, 301–345.

Pascual-Leone, J. A., & Smith, J. (1969). The encoding and decoding of symbols by children: A new experimental paradigm and a neo-Piagetian model. *Journal of Experimental Child Psychology*, 8, 328–355.

Pauen, S., & Wilkening, F. (1997). Children's analogical raesoning about natural phenomenon. *Journal of Experimental Child Psychology*, 67, 90–113.

Pears, R., & Bryant, P. (1990). Transitive inferences by young children about spatial position. *British Journal of Psychology*, 81, 497–510.

Perner, J., Lang, B., & Kloo, D. (2002). Theory of mind and self-control: More than a common problem of inhibition. *Child Development*, 73, 752–767.

Phillips, S. (1994). Connectionism and systematicity. In A. C. Tsoi & T. Downs (Eds.), *Proceedings of the Fifth Australian Conference on Neural Networks* (pp. 53–55). St. Lucia, Qld., Australia: University of Queensland Electrical and Computer Engineering.

Piaget, J. (1950). *The Psychology of Intelligence*. M. Piercy & D. E. Berlyne (Trans.). London: Routledge & Kegan Paul. (Original work published 1947).

Piaget, J. (1952). *The Child's Conception of Number*. C. Gattengo & F. M. Hodgson (Trans.). London: Routledge & Kegan Paul. (Original work published 1941).

Piaget, J. (1953). *The Origin of Intelligence in the Child*. London: Routledge & Kegan Paul.

Piaget, J. (1957). *Logic and Psychology* New York: Basic Books.

Piaget, J. (1970). *Structuralism*. C. Maschler (Trans.). New York: Basic Books, (Original work published 1968).

Quartz, S. R., & Sejnowski, T. J. (1997). The neural basis of cognitive development: A constructivist manifesto. *Behavioral and Brain Sciences*, 20, 537–596.

Quinn, P. C. (2002). Category representation in young infants. *Current Directions in Psychological Science*, 11, 66–70.

Quinn, P. C., & Johnson, M. H. (1997). The emergence of perceptual category representations in young infants: A connectionist analysis. *Journal of Experimental Child Psychology*, 66, 236–263.

Raijmakers, M. E. J., van Koten, S., & Molenaar, P. C. M. (1996). On the validity of simulating stagewise development by means of PDP networks: Application of catastrophe analysis and an experimental test of rule-like network performance. *Cognitive Science*, 20, 101–136.

Rehder, B., & Hastie, R. (2001). Causal knowledge and categories: The effects of causal beliefs on categorization, induction, and similarity. *Journal of Experimental Psychology: General*, 130, 323–360.

Riley, C. A., & Trabasso, T. (1974). Comparatives, logical structures and encoding in a transitive inference task. *Journal of Experimental Child Psychology*, 17, 187–203.

Robin, N., & Holyoak, K. J. (1995). Relational complexity and the functions of prefrontal cortex. In M. S. Gazzaniga (Ed.), *The Cognitive Neurosciences* (pp. 987–997). Cambridge, MA: MIT Press.

Rosch, E., & Mervis, C. B. (1975). Family resemblences: Studies in the internal structure of categories. *Cognitive Psychology*, 7, 573–605.

Rosch, E., Mervis, C. B., Gray, W. D., Johnson, M. D., & Boyes-Braem, P. (1976). Basic objects in natural categories. *Cognitive Psychology*, 8, 382–439.

Rudy, J. W., Keith, J. R., & Georgen, K. (1993). The effect of age on children's learning of problems that require a configural association solution. *Developmental Psychobiology*, 26, 171–184.

Ruffman, T., Perner, J., Olson, D. R., & Doherty, M. (1993). Reflecting on scientific thinking: Children's understanding of the hypothesis-evidence relation. *Child Development*, 64, 1617–1636.

Samarapungavan, A., Vosniadou, S., & Brewer, W. F. (1996). Mental models of the earth, sun and moon: Indian children's cosmologies. *Cognitive Development*, 11, 491–521.

Schlottman, A. (2001). Perception versus knowledge of cause and effect in children: When seeing is believing. *Current Directions in Psychological Science*, 10, 111–115.

Shastri, L., & Ajjanagadde, V. (1993). From simple associations to systematic reasoning: A connectionist representation of rules, variables, and dynamic bindings using temporal synchrony. *Behavioral and Brain Sciences*, 16, 417–494.

Sheppard, J. L. (1978). *A Structural Analysis of Concrete Operations*. London: Wiley.

Shultz, T. R. (1991). *Simulating Stages of Human Cognitive Development with Connectionist Models*. Paper presented at the 8th International Workshop of Machine Learning.

Shultz, T. R. (1998). A computational analysis of conservation. *Developmental Science*, 1, 103–126.

Shultz, T. R., Schmidt, W. C., Buckingham, D., & Mareschal, D. (1995). Modeling cognitive development with a generative connectionist algorithm. In T. J. Simon & G. S. Halford (Eds.), *Developing Cognitive Competence: New Approaches to Process Modeling* (pp. 205–261). Hillsdale, NJ: Erlbaum.

Siegel, L. S., McCabe, A. E., Brand, J., & Matthews, J. (1978). Evidence for the understanding of class inclusion in preschool children: Linguistic factors and training effects. *Child Development*, 49, 688–693.

Siegler, R. S. (1981). Developmental sequences within and between concepts. *Monographs of the Society for Research in Child Development*, 46, 1–84.

Siegler, R. S. (1995). How does change occur: A microgenetic study of number conservation. *Cognitive Psychology*, 28, 225–273.

Siegler, R. S. (1999). Strategic development. *Trends in Cognitive Science*, 3, 430–435.

Siegler, R. S., & Chen, Z. (1998). Developmental differences in rule learning: A microgenetic analysis. *Cognitive Psychology*, 36, 273–310.

Siegler, R. S., & Jenkins, E. A. (1989). *How Children Discover New Strategies*. Hillsdale, NJ: Erlbaum.

Siegler, R. S., & Shipley, C. (1995). Variation, selection, and cognitive change. In T. Simon & G. S. Halford (Eds.), *Developing Cognitive Competence: New Approaches to Process Modeling* (pp. 31–76). Hillsdale, NJ: Erlbaum.

Siegler, R. S., & Shrager, J. (1984). Strategy choices in addition and subtraction: How do children know what to do? In C. Sophian (Ed.), *Origins of Cognitive Skills* (pp. 229–293). Hillsdale, NJ: Erlbaum.

Sigel, I., & Hooper, F. H. E. (1968). *Logical Thinking in Children*. New York: Holt, Rinehart & Winston.

Simon, T., & Klahr, D. (1995). A computational theory of children's learning about number conservation. In T. Simon & G. S. Halford (Eds.), *Developing Cognitive Competence: New Approaches to Process Modeling* (pp. 315–353). Hillsdale, NJ: Erlbaum.

Sirois, S., & Shultz, T. R. (1998). Neural network modeling of developmental effects in discrimination shifts. *Journal of Experimental Child Psychology*, 71, 235–274.

Slobin, D. I. (1972). *Some Questions about Language Development*. Harmondsworth, UK: Penguin.

Smith, L. (2002). Piaget's model. In U. Goswami (Ed.), *Blackwell Handbook of Childhood Cognitive Development* (pp. 515–537). Oxford, UK: Blackwell.

Smith, L. B., Thelen, E., Titzer, R., & McLin, D. (1999). Knowing in the context of acting: The task dynamics of the a-not-b error. *Psychological Review*, 106, 235–260.

Smolensky, P. (1988). On the proper treatment of connectionism. *Behavioral and Brain Sciences*, 11, 1–74.

Smolensky, P. (1990). Tensor product variable binding and the representation of symbolic structures in connectionist systems. *Artificial Intelligence*, 46, 159–216.

Sophian, C. (1995). Representation and reasoning in early numerical development: Counting, conservation and comparison between sets. *Child Development*, 66, 559–577.

Strevens, M. (2000). The essentialist apect of naive theories. *Cognition*, 74, 149–175.

Surber, C. F., & Gzesh, S. M. (1984). Reversible operations in the balance scale task. *Journal of Experimental Child Psychology*, 38, 254–274.

Tager-Flusberg, H., & Sullivan, K. (2000). A componential view of theory of mind: Evidence from Williams syndrome. *Cognition*, 76, 59–89.

Terrace, H. S., & McGonigle, B. (1994). Memory and representation of serial order by children, monkeys, and pigeons. *Current Directions in Psychological Science*, 3, 180–185.

Thatcher, R. W., Walker, R. A., & Giudice, S. (1987). Human cerebral hemispheres develop at different rates and ages. *Science*, 236, 1110–1113.

Thayer, E. S., & Collyer, C. E. (1978). The development of transitive inference: A review of recent approaches. *Psychological Bulletin*, 85, 1327–1343.

Thomas, H., & Horton, J. J. (1997). Competency criteria and the class inclusion task: Modeling judgments and justifications. *Developmental Psychology*, 33, 1060–1073.

van Geert, P. (1991). A dynamic systems model of cognitive and language growth. *Psychological Review*, 98, 3–53.

van Geert, P. (1998). A dynamic systems model of basic developmental mechanisms: Piaget, Vygotsky, and beyond. *Psychological Review*, 105, 634–677.

van Geert, P. (2000). The dynamics of developmental mechanisms: From Piaget and Vygotsky to dynamic systems models. *Current Directions in Psychological Science*, 9, 64–68.

von Fersen, L., Wynne, C. D. L., Delius, J. D., & Staddon, J. E. R. (1991). Transitive inference in pigeons. *Journal of Experimental Psychology: Animal Behavior Processes*, 17, 334–341.

Vosniadou, S., & Brewer, W. F. (1992). Mental models of the earth: A study of conceptual change in childhood. *Cognitive Psychology*, 24, 535–585.

Vygotsky, L. S. (1962). *Thought and Language*. Cambridge, MA: MIT Press. (Original work published 1934).

Waltz, J. A., Knowlton, B. J., Holyoak, K. J., Boone, K. B., Mishkin, F. S., de Menezes Santos, M., et al. (1999). A system for relational reasoning in human prefrontal cortex. *Psychological Science*, 10, 119–125.

Wason, P. C. (1966). *Reasoning*. Harmondsworth, UK: Penguin.

Wellman, H. M., Cross, D., & Watson, J. (2001). Meta-analysis of theory-of-mind development: The truth about false belief. *Child Development*, 72, 655–684.

Wertheimer, M. (1945). *Productive Thinking*. New York: Harper.

Wilkening, F. (1980). Development of dimensional integration in children's perceptual judgment: Experiments with area, volume and velocity. In F. Wilkening, J. Becker, & T. Trabasso (Eds.), *Information Integration in Children* (pp. 47–69). Hillsdale, NJ: Erlbaum.

Wimmer, H., & Perner, J. (1983). Beliefs about beliefs: Representation and constraining function of wrong beliefs in young children's understanding of deception. *Cognition*, 13, 103–128.

Winer, G. A. (1980). Class-inclusion reasoning in children: A review of the empirical literature. *Child Development*, 51, 309–328.

Wynne, C. D. L. (1995). Reinforcement accounts for transitive inference performance. *Animal Learning and Behavior*, 23, 207–217.

Younger, B. A., & Fearing, D. D. (1999). Parsing items into separate categories: Developmental change in infant categorization. *Child Development*, 70, 291–303.

Zelazo, P. D., & Frye, D. (1998). Cognitive complexity and control: II. The development of executive function in childhood. *Current Directions in Psychological Science*, 7, 121–126.

Zelazo, P. D., & Jacques, S. (1996). Children's rule use: Representation, reflection and cognitive control. *Annals of Child Development*, 12, 119–176.

Zimmerman, C. (2000). The development of scientific reasoning skills. *Developmental Review*, 20, 99–149.

CHAPTER 23
Mathematical Cognition

C. R. Gallistel
Rochel Gelman

Mathematics is a system for representing and reasoning about quantities, with arithmetic as its foundation. Its deep interest for our understanding the psychological foundations of scientific thought comes from what Eugene Wigner called "the unreasonable efficacy of mathematics in the natural sciences." From a formalist perspective, arithmetic is a symbolic game, like tic-tac-toe. Its rules are more complicated, but not a great deal more complicated. Mathematics is the study of the properties of this game and of the systems that may be constructed on the foundation it provides. Why should this symbolic game be so powerful and resourceful when it comes to building models of the physical world? And on what psychological foundations does the human mastery of this game rest?

The first question is metaphysical – why is the world the way it is? We do not treat it, because it lies beyond the realm of experimental behavioral science. We review the answers to the second question suggested by experimental research on human and nonhuman animal cognition.

The general nature of the answer is that the foundations of mathematical cognition do not lie in language and the language faculty. The ability to estimate quantities and to reason arithmetically with those estimates exists in the brains of animals that have no language. The same or very similar nonverbal mechanisms appear to operate in parallel with verbal estimation and reasoning in adult humans. They also operate to some extent before children learn to speak and before they have had any tutoring in the elements of arithmetic. These findings suggest that the verbal expression of number and of arithmetic thinking is based on a nonverbal system for estimating and reasoning about discrete and continuous quantity, which we share with many nonverbal animals. A reasonable supposition is that the neural substrate for this system arose far back in the evolution of brains precisely because of the puzzle to which Wigner called attention: Arithmetic reasoning captures deeply important properties of the world, which the animal brain must represent in order to act effectively in it.

The recognition that there is a nonverbal system of arithmetic reasoning in human and many nonhuman animals is recent, but it influences most contemporary experimental work on mathematical cognition. This review is organized around the questions: (1) What are the properties of this nonverbal system? (2) How is it related to the verbal system and written numerical systems?

What Is a Number?

Arithmetic is one of the few domains of human thought that has been extensively formalized. This formalization did not begin in earnest until the middle of the nineteenth century (Boyer & Merzback, 1989). In the process of formalizing the arithmetic foundations of mathematics, mathematicians changed their minds about what a number is. Before formalization, an intuitive understanding of what a number is determined what could legitimately be done with it. Once the formal "games" about number were made explicit, anything that played by the rules was a number.

This formalist viewpoint is crucial to an understanding of issues in the current scientific literature on mathematical cognition. Many of them turn on questions of how we are to recognize and understand the properties of mental magnitudes. *Mental magnitude* refers to an inferred (but, one supposes, potentially observable and measurable) entity in the head that represents either numerosity (for example, the number of oranges in a case) or another magnitude (for example, the length, width, height, and weight of the case) and that has the formal properties of a real number.

For a mental magnitude to represent an objective magnitude, it must be causally related to that objective magnitude. It must also be shown that it is a player in a mental game (a functionally cohesive collection of brain processes) that operates according to at least some of the rules of arithmetic. When putative mental numbers do not validly enter into, at a minimum, mental addition, mental subtraction, and mental ordering, then they do not function as numbers.

Kinds of Numbers

The ancient Greeks had considerable success axiomatizing geometry, but mathematicians did not axiomatize the system of numbers until the nineteenth century, after it had undergone a large, historically documented expansion. Before this expansion, it was too messy and incomplete to be axiomatized, because it lacked *closure*. A system of numbers is closed under a combinatorial operation if, when you apply the operation to any pair of numbers, the result is a number. Adding or multiplying two positive integers always produces a positive integer, so the positive integers are closed under addition and multiplication. They are also closed under the operation of ordering. For any pair of numbers, $a \geq b = 1$ if a is greater or equal to than b, and 0 if not. These three operations – addition, multiplication, and ordering – are the core operations of arithmetic. They and their inverses make the system what it is.

The problem comes from the inverse operations of subtraction and division. When you subtract a bigger number from a smaller, the result is not a positive integer. Should one regard the result as a number? Until well into the nineteenth century, many professional mathematicians did not. Thus, subtracting a bigger number from a smaller number was not a legitimate mathematical operation. This was inconvenient, because it meant that in the course of algebraic reasoning (reasoning about unspecified numbers), one might unwittingly do something that was illegitimate. This purely practical consideration strongly motivated the admission of the negative numbers and zero to the set of numbers acknowledged to be legitimate.

When one divides one integer by another, the result, called a *rational number*, or, more colloquially, a *fraction*, is rarely an integer. From the earliest times from which we have written records, people who worked with written numbers included at least some rational numbers among the numbers, but, like school children to this day, they had extraordinary difficulties in figuring out how to do arithmetic with rational numbers in general. What is the sum of 1/3 and 11/17? That was a hard question in ancient Egypt and remains so today in classrooms all around the world.

The common notation for a fraction specifies a number not by giving it a unique name like *two* but rather by specifying a way of generating it (divide the number *one* by the number *two*). The practice of specifying a number by giving an arithmetic procedure that will generate it to whatever level of precision is required has grown stronger over the millenia. It is the key to a rigorous handling of both irrational and complex numbers and to the way in which digital computers operate with real numbers. But it is discomfiting, for several reasons. First, there are an infinity of different notations for the same number: 1/2, 2/4, 3/6, and so on, all specifying the same number. Moreover, for most rational numbers, there is no complete decimal representation. Carrying out the division gives a repeating decimal. In short, you cannot write down a symbol for most rational numbers that is both complete and unique.[1]

Finally, when fractions are allowed to be numbers, the *discrete* ordering of the numbers is lost. It no longer is possible to specify the next number in the sequence, because there are an infinite number of rational numbers between any two rational numbers. For all these reasons, admitting fractions to the system of numbers makes the system more difficult to work with in the concrete, albeit more powerful in the abstract, because the system of rational numbers is, with one exception, closed under division.

Allowing negative numbers and fractions to be numbers also creates problems with what otherwise seem to be sound principles for reasoning about numbers. For example, it seems to be sound to say that dividing the bigger of two numbers by the smaller gives a number that is bigger than the number one gets if one divides the smaller by the bigger. What then are we to make of the "fact" that $1/-1 = -1/1 = -1$?

Clearly, caution and clear thinking are going to be necessary if we want to treat as numbers entities that you do not get by counting. But, humans do want to do this, and they have wanted to since the beginning of recorded history. We measure quantities like lengths, weights, and volumes in order to represent them with numbers. What the measuring does – if it is done well – is give us "the right number" or at least one usable for our purposes. Measuring and the resulting representation of continuous quantities by numbers go back to the earliest written records. Indeed, it is often argued that writing evolved from a system for recording the results of measurements made in the course of commerce (bartering, buying, and selling), political economy (taxation), surveying, and construction (Menninger, 1969).

The ancient Greeks believed that, in principle, all measurable magnitudes could be represented by rational numbers. Everything was a matter of proportion, and any proportion could be expressed as the ratio of two integers. They were also the first to try to formalize mathematical thinking. In doing so, they discovered, to their horror, that fractions did not suffice to represent all possible proportions. They discovered that the proportion between the side of a square and its diagonal could not be represented by a fraction. The Pythagorean formula for calculating the diagonal of a square says that the diagonal is equal to the square root of the sum of the squares of the sides. In this case, the diagonal is equal to $\sqrt{(1^2 + 1^2)} = \sqrt{(1 + 1)} = \sqrt{2}$. The Greeks proved that there is no fraction that, when multiplied by itself, is equal to 2. If only integers and fractions are numbers, then the length of the diagonal of the unit square cannot be represented by a number. Put another way, you can measure the side of the square or you can measure its diagonal, but you cannot measure them both exactly within the same measuring system – unless you are willing to include among the numbers in that system numbers that are not integers (cannot be counted) and are not even the ratio of two integers. You must include what the Greeks called the irrational numbers. But if you do include the irrational numbers, how do you go about specifying them in the general case?

Many irrationals can be specified by the operation of extracting roots, which is the inverse of the operation of raising a number to a power. Raising any positive integer to the power of any other always produces a positive integer. Thus, the system of positive integers is closed under raising to a power. The problem, as usual, comes from the inverse operation – extracting roots. For most pairs of integers, *a* and *b*, the *a*th root of *b* is not a positive integer, nor even a rational number; it is an irrational number. The need within algebra to have an arithmetic that was closed under the extraction of roots was a powerful motivation for mathematicians to admit both irrational numbers and complex numbers to the set of numbers. By admitting irrational numbers, they created the system of so-called real numbers, which was essential to calculus. To this day, there are professional mathematicians who question the legitimacy of irrational numbers. Nonetheless, the real numbers, which include the irrationals (see Figure 23.1), are taken for granted by all but a very few contemporary mathematicians.

The notion of a real number and that of a magnitude (for example, the length of a line) are formally identical. This means, among other things, that for every line segment, there is a real number that uniquely represents the length of that segment (in a given system of measurement) and conversely, for every real number, there is a line segment that represents the magnitude of that number. Therefore, in what follows, when we mention a mental magnitude, we mean an entity in the mind (brain) that functions within a system with the formal properties of the real number system. Like the real number system, we assume that this system is a closed system: All of its combinatorial operations, when applied to any pair of mental magnitudes, generate another mental magnitude.

As this brief sketch indicates, the system of number recognized by almost all contemporary professional mathematicians as "*the* number system" – the ever more inclusive

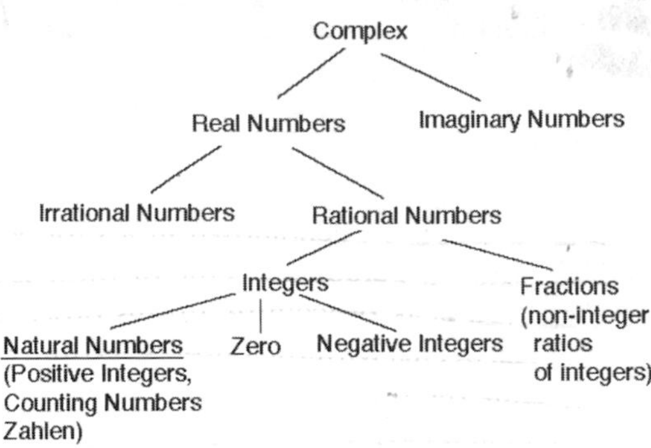

Figure 23.1. The number system on which modern mathematics is based. Not shown in this diagram are the algebraic numbers, which are the numbers that may be obtained through the extraction of roots (the solving of polynomial equations), nor the transcendental numbers, which may be obtained only by solving equations with trigonometric, exponential, or logarithmic terms. These are subcategories of the irrational numbers.

hierarchy of kinds of numbers shown in Figure 23.1 – has grown up over historical time with much of the growth culminating only in the preceding two centuries. The psychological question is, "What is it in the minds of humans (and perhaps also nonhuman animals) that has been driving this process?" And how and under what circumstances does this mental machinery enable educated modern humans to master the basics of formal mathematics, when, and to the extent that they do so?

Numerical Estimation and Reasoning in Animals

The development of verbalized and written reasoning about number that culminated in a formalized system of real numbers isomorphic to continuous magnitudes was driven by the fact that humans apply numerical reasoning to continuous quantity just as much as they do to discrete quantity. In considering the literature on numerical estimation and reasoning in animals, we begin by reviewing the evidence that they estimate and reason arithmetically about the quintessentially continuous quantity time.

Common laboratory animals, such as the pigeon, the rat, and the monkey, measure and remember continuous quantities, such as duration, as has been shown in a variety of experimental paradigms. One of these is the so-called peak procedure. In this procedure, a trial begins with the onset of a stimulus signaling the possible availability of food at the end of a fixed interval, called *the feeding latency*. Responses made at or after the interval has elapsed trigger the delivery of food. Responses prior to that time have no consequences. On twenty to fifty percent of the trials, food is not delivered. On these trials, the key remains illuminated, the lever remains extended, or the hopper remains illuminated for between four and six times longer than the feeding latency. On these trials, called *probe trials*, responding after the feeding latency has past is pointless.

Peak-procedure data come from these unrewarded trials. On such trials, the subject abruptly begins to respond some time before the expected end of the feeding latency and continues to peck or press or poke for some time after it has passed before abruptly stopping. The interval during which the subject responds brackets its subjective estimate of the feeding latency. Representative data are shown in Figure 23.2.

Figure 23.2A shows seemingly smooth increases and decreases in the probability that the mouse is making an anticipatory response (poking its head into the feeding hopper in anticipation of food delivery) on either side of the feeding latency. The smoothness is an averaging artifact. On any one trial, the onset and offset of anticipatory responding is abrupt, but the temporal locus of these onsets and offsets varies from trial to trial (Church, Meck, & Gibbon, 1994). The peak curves in Figure 23.2, like peak curves in general, are the cumulative start distributions minus the cumulative stop distributions, where start and stop refer to the onset and offset of sustained food anticipatory behavior.

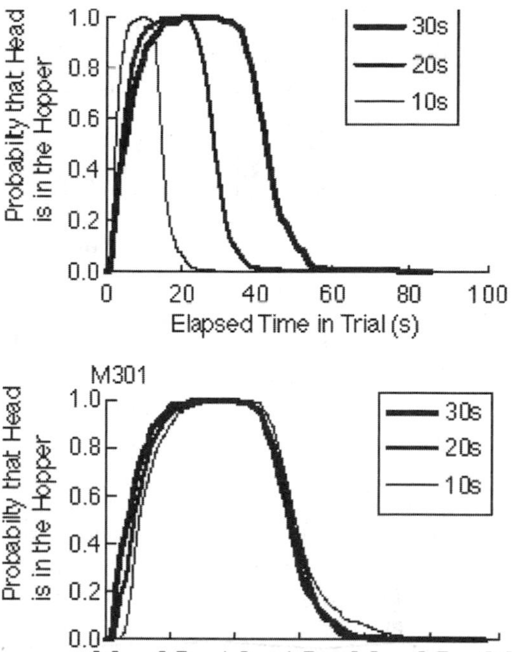

Figure 23.2. Representative peak procedure data: Probability that the mouse's head was in the feeding hopper as a function of the time elapsed since the beginning of a trial and the feeding latency. (The feeding latency varied between blocks of trials.) A. The original data. These peak curves are the cumulative distribution of start times (rising phase) minus cumulative distribution of stop times (falling phase). These are the raw distributions (no curve has been fitted.) B. Same data as in A, data replotted as a proportion of the feeding latency. Because the variability in the onsets and offsets of responding is proportional to the feeding latency, as are the location of the means of the distributions relative to the target times, the peak curves superpose when plotted as a proportion of this latency. Data originally published by King, McDonald, & Gallistel (2001).

When the data in Figure 23.2A are replotted against the proportion of the feeding latency elapsed, rather than against the latency itself, the curves superpose (Figure 23.2B). Thus, both the location of the distributions relative to the target latency and the trial-to-trial variability in the onsets and offsets of responding are proportional to the remembered latency. Put another way,

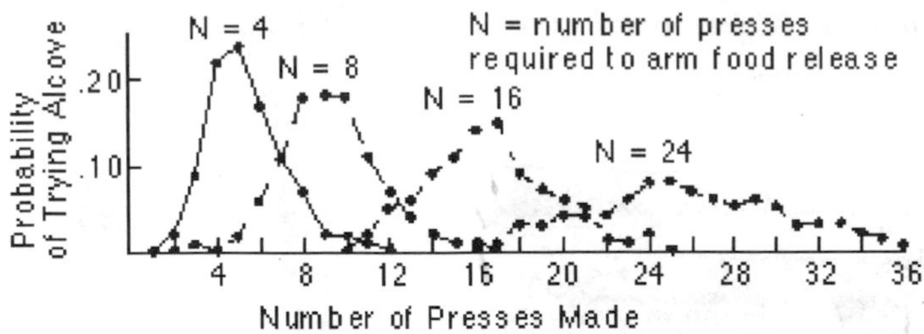

Figure 23.3. The probability of breaking off to try the feeding alcove as a function of the number of presses made on the arming lever and the number required to arm the food-release beam at the entrance to the feeding alcove. Subjects were rats. Redrawn from Platt & Johnson, 1971, with permission.

the probabilities that the subject will have begun to respond or will have stopped responding are determined by the proportion of the remembered feeding latency that has elapsed. This property of remembered durations is called *scalar variability.*

Rats, pigeons, and monkeys also count and remember numerosities (Brannon & Roitman, 2003; Church & Meck, 1984; Dehaene, 1997; Dehaene, Dehaene-Lambertz, & Cohen, 1998; Gallistel, 1990; Gallistel & Gelman, 2000). One of the early protocols for assessing counting and numerical memory was developed by Mechner (1958) and later used by Platt and Johnson (1971). The subject must press a lever some number of times (the target number) to arm the infrared beam at the entrance to a feeding alcove. When the beam is armed, interrupting it releases food. Pressing too many times before trying the alcove incurs no penalty beyond that of having made supernumerary presses. Trying the alcove prematurely incurs a 10-second time-out, which the subject must endure before returning to the lever to complete the requisite number of presses. Data from such an experiment are shown in Figure 23.3. They look strikingly like the temporal data. The number of presses at which subjects are maximally likely to break off pressing and try the alcove peaks at or slightly beyond the required number for required numbers ranging from four to twenty four. As the remembered target number gets larger, the variability in the break-off number also gets proportionately greater. Thus, behavior based on number also exhibits scalar variability.

The fact that behavior based on remembered numerosity exhibits scalar variability just like the scalar variability seen in behavior based on the remembered magnitude of continuous quantities such as duration suggests that numerosity is represented in the brains of nonverbal vertebrates by mental magnitudes; that is, by entities with the formal properties of the real numbers, rather than by discrete symbols such as words or bit patterns. When a device such as an analog computer represents numerosities by different voltage levels, noise in the voltages leads to confusions between nearby numbers. If, by contrast, a device represents countable quantity by countable (that is, discrete) symbols, as do digital computers and written number systems, then one does not expect to see the kind of variability seen in Figures 23.2 and 23.3. The bit-pattern symbol for fifteen is 01111, for example, and for sixteen it is 10000. Although the numbers are adjacent in the ordering of the integers, the discrete binary symbols for them differ in all five bits. Jitter in the bits (uncertainty about whether a given bit was 0 or 1) would make fourteen (01110), thirteen (01101), eleven (01011), and seven (00111) all equally and maximally likely to be confused with fifteen, because the confusion arises in each case from the misreading of one bit. These dispersed numbers should be confused with fifteen much more often than is the adjacent sixteen. (For an analysis of the error patterns to be expected in cascade counters, see Killeen & Taylor, 2001). Similarly, a scribe copying a handwritten English text is presumably more likely to confuse "seven" and "eleven" than "seven" and "eight." The nature of the variability in a remembered target number therefore suggests that what is being remembered is a magnitude – something that behaves like a continuous quantity, which is to say something with the formal properties of a real number.

Numerosity and Duration Are Represented by Comparable Mental Magnitudes

Meck and Church (1983) pointed out that the mental accumulator model that Gibbon (1977) had proposed to explain the generation of mental magnitudes representing durations could be modified to make it generate mental magnitudes representing numerosities. Gibbon had proposed that while a duration was being timed a stream of impulses fed an accumulator, so that the accumulation grew in proportion to the duration of the stream. When the stream ended (when timing ceased), the resulting accumulation was read into memory, where it represented the duration of the interval. Meck and Church postulated that to get magnitudes representing numerosity, the equivalent of a pulse former was inserted into the stream of impulses, so that for each count there was a discrete increment in the contents of the accumulator, as happens when a cup of liquid is poured into a graduated cylinder (Figure 23.4). At the end of the count, the resulting accumulation is read into memory, where it represents the numerosity.

The model in Figure 23.4 is the well-known accumulator model for nonverbal counting by the successive incrementation of mental magnitudes. It is also the origin of the hypothesis that the mental magnitudes representing duration and the mental magnitudes representing numerosity are essentially the same, differing only in the mapping process that generates them and, therefore, in what it is they refer to. Put another way, both numerosity and duration are represented mentally by real numbers. Meck and Church (1983) compared the psychophysics of number and time representation in the rat and concluded that the coefficient of variation, the ratio between the standard deviation and the mean, was the same, which is further evidence for the hypothesis that the same system of real numbers is used in both cases.

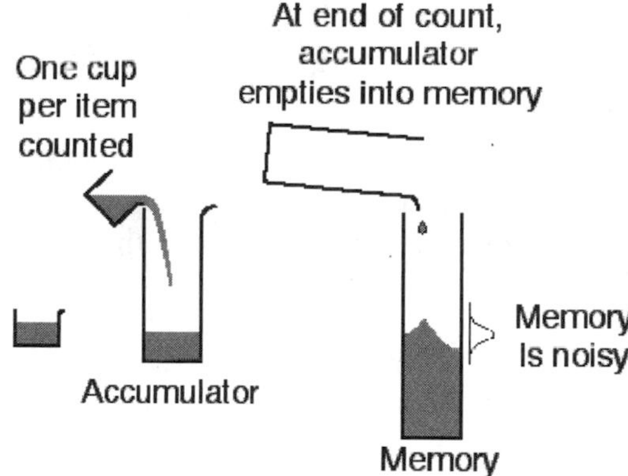

Figure 23.4. The accumulator model for the nonverbal counting process. At each count, the brain increments a quantity – an operation formally equivalent to pouring a cup into a graduate. The final magnitude (the contents of the graduate at the conclusion of the count) is stored in memory, where it represents the numerosity of the counted set. Memory is noisy (represented by the wave in the graduate), which is to say that the values read from memory on different occasions vary. The variability in the values read from memory is proportional to the mean value of the distribution (scalar variability).

The model in Figure 23.4 was originally proposed to explain behavior based on the numerosity of a set of serial events (for example, the number of responses made), but it may be generalized to the case in which the items to be counted are presented all at once – for example, as a to-be-enumerated visual array. In that case, each item in the array can be assigned a unit magnitude, and the unit magnitudes can then be summed (accumulated) across space, rather than over time. Dehaene and Changeux (1993) developed a neural net model based on this idea. In their model, the activity aroused by each item in the array is reduced to a unit amount of activity, so that it is no longer proportional to the size, contour, and so on, of the item. The units of activity corresponding to the entities in the array are summed across the visual field to yield a mental magnitude representing the numerosity of the array.

Nonhuman Animals Reason Arithmetically

We have repeatedly referred to the real number *system* because numbers (or magnitudes) are truly that only if they are arithmetically manipulated. Being causally connected to something that can be represented numerically does not make an entity in the brain or anywhere else a number. It also must be processed suitably. The defining features of a numerical representation are: (1) There is a causal mapping from discrete and continuous quantities in the world to the numbers. (2) The numbers are arithmetically processed. (3) The mapping is usefully (validly) invertible: The numbers obtained through arithmetic processing correctly refer through the inverse mapping back to the represented reality.

There is a considerable experimental literature demonstrating that laboratory animals reason arithmetically with mental magnitudes representing numerosity and duration. They add, subtract, divide, and order subjective durations and subjective numerosities; they divide subjective numerosities by subjective durations to obtain subjective rates of reward; and they multiply subjective rates of reward by the subjective magnitudes of the rewards to obtain subjective incomes. Moreover, the mapping between real magnitudes and their subjective counterparts is such that their mental operations on subjective quantities enable these animals to behave effectively. Here we summarize a few of the relevant studies. (For reviews, see Boysen & Hallberg, 2000; Brannon & Roitman, 2003; Dehaene, 1997; Gallistel, 1990; Spelke & Dehaene, 1999).

Adding Numerosities

Boysen and Berntson (1989) taught chimpanzees to pick the Arabic numeral corresponding to the number of items they observed. In the last of a series of tests of this ability, they had their subjects go around a room and observe either caches of actual oranges in two different locations or Arabic numerals that substituted for the caches themselves. When they returned from a trip, the chimps picked the Arabic numeral corresponding to the sum of the two numerosities they had seen, whether the numerosities had been directly observed (hence, possibly counted) or symbolically represented (hence not counted). In the latter case, the magnitudes corresponding to the numerals observed were presumably retrieved from a memory map relating the arbitrary symbols for number (the Arabic numerals) to the mental magnitudes that naturally represent those numbers. Once retrieved, they could be added very much like the magnitudes generated by the nonverbal counting of the caches. (For further evidence that nonverbal vertebrates sum numerical magnitudes, see Beran, 2001; Church & Meck, 1984; Hauser, 2001, and citations therein; Olthof, Iden, & Roberts, 1997; Olthof & Roberts, 2000; Rumbaugh, Savage-Rumbaugh, & Hegel, 1987.)

Subtracting Durations and Numerosities

On each trial of the time-left procedure (Gibbon & Church, 1981), subjects are offered an ongoing choice between a steadily diminishing delay on the one hand (the time-left option) and a fixed delay on the other hand (the standard option). At an unpredictable point in the course of a trial, the opportunity to choose ends. Before it gets its reward, the subject must then endure the delay associated with the option it was exercising at that moment. If it was responding at the so-called standard station, it must endure the standard delay; if it was responding at the time-left station, it must endure the time left. At the beginning of a trial, the time left is much longer than the standard delay, but it grows shorter as the trial goes on, because the time so far elapsed in a trial is subtracted from the initial value to yield the time left. When the subjective time left is less than the subjective standard, subjects switch from the standard option to the time-left option. The subjective time left is the subjective duration of a remembered initial duration (subjective initial duration) minus the subjective duration of the interval elapsed since the beginning of the trial. In this experiment, therefore, subjects' behavior depends on the subjective ordering of a subjective difference and a subjective standard (two of the basic arithmetic operations).

In the number-left procedure (Brannon, et al., 2001), pigeons peck a center key to generate flashes and to activate two choice keys. The flashes are generated on a variable ratio schedule, which means that the number of pecks required to generate each flash varies randomly between one and eight. When the choice keys are activated, the pigeons can get a reward by pecking either of them, but only after their pecking generates the requisite number of flashes. For one of the choice keys, the so-called standard key, the requisite number is fixed and independent of the number of flashes already generated. For the other choice, the number-left key, the requisite number is the difference between a fixed starting number and the tally of flashes already generated by pecking the center key. The flashes generated by pecking a choice key are also delivered on a variable ratio schedule.

The use of variable ratio schedules for flash generation partially dissociates time and number. The number of pecks required to generate any given number of flashes – and, hence, the amount of time spent pecking – varies greatly from trial to trial. This makes possible an analysis to determine whether subjects' choices are controlled by the time spent pecking the center key or by the number of flashes generated. The analysis shows that it was number, not duration, that controlled the pigeons' choices.

In this experiment, subjects chose the number-left key when the subjective number left was less than some fraction of the subjective number of flashes required on the standard key. Their behavior therefore was controlled by the subjective ordering of a subjective numerical difference and a subjective numerical standard. For an example of spontaneous subtraction in monkeys, see Sulkowski and Hauser (2001).

There also is evidence that the mental magnitudes representing duration and rates are signed – there are both positive and negative mental magnitudes (Gallistel & Gibbon, 2000; Savastano & Miller, 1998). In other words, there is evidence for subtraction and for the hypothesis that the system for arithmetic reasoning with mental magnitudes is closed under subtraction.

Dividing Numerosity by Duration

When vertebrates, from fish to humans, are free to forage in two different nearby locations, moving back and forth repeatedly between them, the ratio of the expected durations of the stays in the two locations matches the ratios of the numbers of rewards obtained per unit of time (Herrnstein, 1961). Until recently, it had been assumed that this matching behavior depended on the law of effect. When subjects do not match, they get more reward per unit of time invested in one patch than per unit of time invested in the other. Only when they match do they get equal returns on their investments. Matching therefore could be explained on the assumption that subjects try different ratios of investments (different ratios of expected stay durations) until they discover the ratio that equates the returns (Herrnstein & Vaughan, 1980).

Gallistel et al. (2001) showed that rats adjust to changes in the scheduled rates of reward as fast as it is in principle possible to do so; they are ideal detectors of such changes. They could not adjust so rapidly if they were discovering by trial and error the ratio of expected stay durations that equated their returns. The importance of this in the present context is that a rate is the number of events – a discrete or countable quantity, which is the kind of thing naturally represented by positive integers – divided by a continuous or (uncountable) quantity – the duration of the given interval, which is the kind of thing that can be represented only by a real number.

Gallistel and Gibbon (2000) review the evidence that both Pavlovian and instrumental conditioning depend on subjects' estimating rates of reward. They argue that rate of reward is the fundamental variable in conditioned behavior. The importance of this in the present context is twofold. First, it is evidence that subjects divide mental magnitudes. Second, it shows why it is essential that countable and uncountable quantity be represented by commensurable mental symbols – symbols that are part of the same system and can be combined arithmetically without regard to whether they represent countable or uncountable quantity. If countable quantity were represented by one system (say, a system of discretely ordered symbols, formally analogous to the list of counting words) and uncountable (continuous) quantity by a different system (a system of mental magnitudes), it would not be possible to estimate rates. The brain would have to divide mental apples by mental oranges.[2]

Multiplying Rate by Magnitude

When the magnitudes of the rewards obtained in two different locations differ, then the ratio of the expected stay durations is determined by the ratio of the incomes obtained from the two locations (Catania, 1963; Harper, 1982; Keller & Gollub, 1977; Leon & Gallistel, 1998). The income from a location is the product of the rate and the reward magnitude. This result implies that subjects multiply subjective rates by subjective magnitudes to obtain subjective incomes. The signature of multiplicative combination is that changing one variable by a given factor – for example, doubling the rate – changes the product by the same factor (doubles the income) regardless of the value of the other factor (the magnitude of the rewards). Leon and Gallistel (1998) showed that changing the ratio of the rates of reward by a given factor changed the ratio of the expected stay durations by that factor, regardless of the ratio of the reward magnitudes, thereby proving that subjective magnitudes combine multiplicatively with subjective rates to determine the ratio of expected stay durations.

Ordering Numerosities

Most of the paradigms that demonstrate mental addition, subtraction, multiplication, and division also demonstrate the ordering of mental magnitudes, because the subject's choice depends on this ordering. Brannon and Terrace (2000) demonstrated more directly that monkeys order numerosities by presenting simultaneously several arrays differing in the numerosity of the items constituting each array and requiring their macaque subjects to touch the arrays in the order of their numerosity. When subjects had learned to do this for numerosities between one and four, they generalized immediately to numerosities between five and nine.

The most interesting feature of Brannon and Terrace's results was that they found it impossible to teach subjects to touch the arrays in an order that did not conform to the order of the numerosities (either ascending or descending). This implies that the ordering of numerosities is highly salient for a monkey. It cannot ignore their natural ordering to learn an unnatural one. It also suggests that the natural ordering is not itself learned; it is inherent in the monkey's representation of numerosity. What is learned is to respond on the basis of numerical order, not the ordering itself.

For further evidence that nonverbal vertebrates order numerosities and durations, see Biro and Matsuzawa (2001), Brannon and Roitman (2003), Brannon and Terrace (2002), Carr and Wilkie (1997), Olthof, Iden, and Roberts (1997), Rumbaugh and Washburn (1993), and Washburn and Rumbaugh (1991).

In summary, research with vertebrates, some of which have not shared a common ancestor with humans since before the rise of the dinosaurs, implies that they represent both countable and uncountable quantity by means of mental magnitudes. The system of arithmetic reasoning with these mental magnitudes is closed under the basic operations of arithmetic; that is, mental magnitudes may be mentally added, subtracted, multiplied, divided, and ordered without restriction.

Humans Also Represent Numerosity with Mental Magnitudes

The Symbolic Size and Distance Effects

It would be odd if humans did not share with their remote vertebrate cousins (pigeons) and near vertebrate cousins (chimpanzees) the mental machinery for representing countable and uncountable quantity by means of a system of real numbers. That humans do represent integers with mental magnitudes was first suggested by Moyer and Landauer (1967; 1973) when they discovered what has come to be called *the symbolic distance effect* (Figure 23.5). When subjects are asked to judge the numerical order of Arabic numerals as rapidly as possible, their reaction time is determined by the relative numerical distance: The greater the distance between the two numbers, the more quickly their order may be judged. Subsequently, Parkman (1971) further showed that the greater the numerical value of the smaller digit, the longer it takes to judge their order (the size effect). The two effects together may be summarized under a single law, namely that the time to judge the numerical order of two numerals is a function of the ratio of the numerical magnitudes they represent. Weber's law that the ability of two magnitudes to be discriminated is a function of their ratio therefore applies to symbolically represented numerical magnitude.

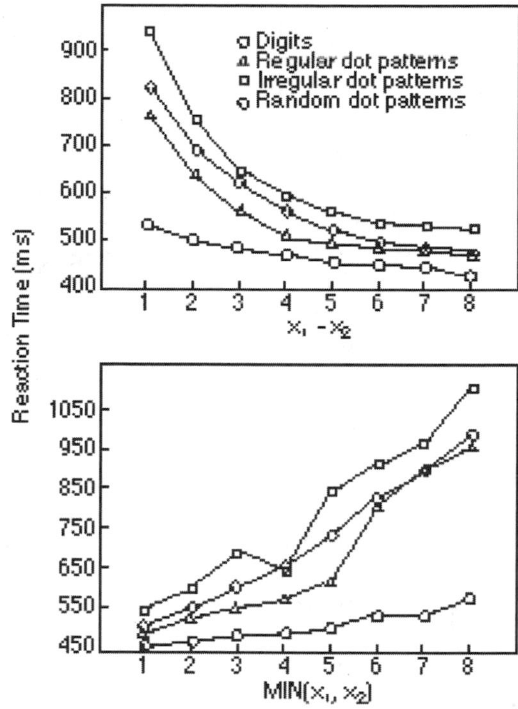

Figure 23.5. The symbolic and nonsymbolic size and distance effects on the human reaction time while judging numerical order in the range from 1 to 9. In three of the conditions, the numerosities to be judged were instantiated by two dot arrays (nonsymbolic numerical ordering). The dots within each array were in either a regular configuration, an irregular configuration that did not vary upon repeated presentation, or in randomly varying configurations. In the fourth condition, the numerosities were represented symbolically by Arabic numerals. The top panel plots mean reaction times as a function of the numerical difference. The bottom plots it as a function of the size of the smaller comparand. Replotted from Figures 23.1 and 23.2 in Buckley & Gillman, 1974.

The size and distance effects in human judgments of the ordering of discrete and continuous quantities are robust. They are observed when the numerosities being compared are actually instantiated (by visual arrays of dots) and when they are represented symbolically by Arabic numerals (Buckley & Gillman, 1974). The *symbolic* distance and size effects are observed in the single-digit range and in the double-digit range (Dehaene, Dupoux, & Mehler, 1990; Hinrichs, Yurko, & Hu, 1981). That this effect of numerical magnitude on the time to make an order judgment should appear for symbolically represented numerosities between 1

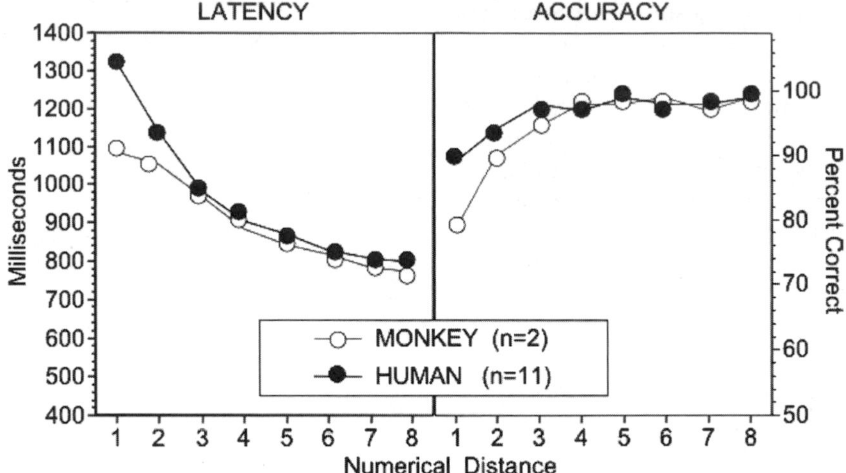

Figure 23.6. The reaction time and accuracy functions for monkey (Rhesus macaque) and human subjects in touching the more numerous of two random dot visual arrays presented side by side on a touch-screen video monitor. Reproduced from Brannon & Terrace, 2002 with permission.

and 100 is decidedly counterintuitive. If introspection were any guide to what one's brain was doing, one would think that the facts about which numbers are greater than which are stored in a table of some kind and simply looked up. In that case, why would it take longer to look up the ordering of 2 and 3 (or 65 and 62) than 2 and 5 (or 65 and 47)? It does, however, and this suggests that the comparison that underlies these judgments operates with noisy mental magnitudes. According to this hypothesis the brain maps the numerals to the noisy mental magnitudes that would be generated by the nonverbal numerical estimation system if it enumerated the corresponding numerosity. It then compares those two noisy mental magnitudes to decide which numeral represents the bigger numerosity.

On this hypothesis, the comparison that mediates the verbal judgment of the numerical ordering of two Arabic numerals uses the same mental magnitudes and the same comparison mechanism as that used by the nonverbal numerical reasoning system that we are assumed to share with many nonverbal animals. Consistent with this hypothesis is Brannon and Terrace's (2002) finding that reaction time functions from humans and monkeys for judgments of the numerical ordering of pairs of visually presented dot arrays are almost exactly the same (Figure 23.6).

Buckley and Gillman (1974) modeled the underlying comparison process. In their model, numbers are represented in the brain by noisy signals (mental magnitudes) with overlapping distributions. The closer two numerosities are in the ordering of numerosities, the more their corresponding signal distributions overlap. When the subject judges the ordering of two numerosities, the brain subtracts the signal representing the one numerosity from the signal representing the other, and puts the signed difference in an accumulator – a mechanism that adds up inputs over, in this case, time. The accumulator for the ordering operation has fixed positive and negative thresholds. When its positive threshold is exceeded, it reports the one number to be greater than the other and vice versa when its negative threshold is exceeded. If neither accumulator threshold is exceeded, the comparator resamples the two signals, computes a second difference, based on the two new samples, and adds it to the accumulator. The resampling explains why it takes longer (on average) to make the comparison when the numerosities being compared are closer. The closer they are, the more their corresponding signal distributions overlap. The more these distributions overlap, the more samples will have to be made and added together (accumulated) before (on average) a decision threshold is reached.

Nonverbal Counting in Humans

Given the evidence from the symbolic size and distance effects that humans represent number with mental magnitudes, it seems likely that they share with the nonverbal animals in the vertebrate clade a nonverbal counting mechanism that maps from numerosities to the mental magnitudes that represent them. If so, then it should be possible to demonstrate nonverbal counting in humans when verbal counting is suppressed. Whalen, Gallistel, and Gelman (1999) presented subjects with Arabic numerals on a computer screen and asked them to press a key as fast as they could without counting until it felt like they had pressed the number signified by the numeral. The results from humans looked very much like the results from pigeons and rats: The mean number of presses increased in proportion to the target number and the standard deviations of the distributions of presses increased in proportion to their mean, so that the coefficient of variation was constant.

This result suggests, first, that subjects could count nonverbally, and, second, that they could compare the mental magnitude thus generated to a magnitude obtained using a learned mapping from numerals to mental magnitudes. Finally, it implies that the mapping from numerals to mental magnitudes is such that the mental magnitude given by this mapping approximates the mental magnitude generated by counting the numerosity signified by a given numeral.

In a second task, subjects observed a dot flashing very rapidly but at irregular intervals. The rate of flashing (eight per second) was twice as fast as estimates of the maximum speed of verbal counting (Mandler & Shebo, 1982). Subjects were asked not to count but to say about how many times they thought the dot had flashed. As in the first experiment, the mean number estimated increased in proportion to the number of flashes and the standard deviation of the estimates increased in proportion to the mean estimate. This implies that the mapping between the mental magnitudes generated by nonverbal counting and the verbal symbols for numerosities is bidirectional; it can go from a symbol to a mental magnitude that is comparable to the one that would be generated by nonverbal counting, and it can go from the mental magnitude generated by a nonverbal count to a roughly corresponding verbal symbol. In both cases, the variability in the mapping is scalar.

Whalen et al. (1999) gave several reasons for believing that their subjects did not count subvocally. We will not review them here, because a subsequent experiment speaks more directly to this issue (Cordes et al., 2001).

Cordes et al. (2001) suppressed articulation by having their subjects repeat a common phrase ("Mary had a little lamb") while they attempted to press a target number of times, or by having subjects say "the" coincident with each press. In control experiments, subjects were asked to count their presses out loud. In all conditions, subjects were asked to press as fast as possible.

The variability data from the condition under which subjects were required to say "the" coincident with each press are shown in Figure 23.7 (filled squares). As in Whalen et al. (1999), the coefficient of variation was constant (scalar variability). The best-fitting line has a slope that does not differ significantly from zero. The contrasting results from the control conditions, in which subjects counted out loud, are the open squares. Here, the slope – on this log–log plot – does deviate very significantly from zero. In verbal counting, one would expect counting errors – double counts and skips – to be the most common source of variability. On the assumption that the probability of a counting error is approximately the same at successive steps in a count, the resulting variability in final counts should be binomial

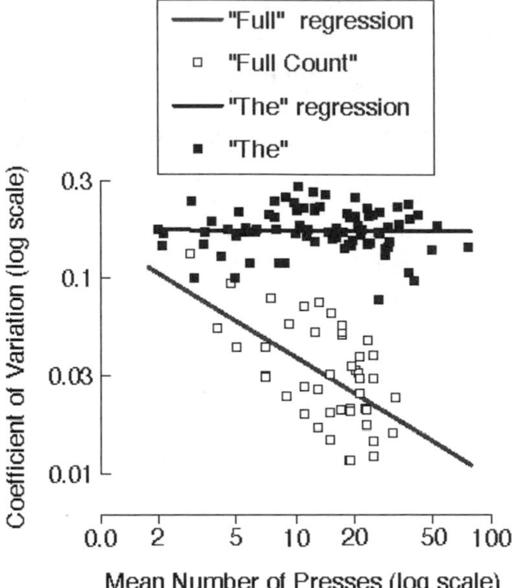

Figure 23.7. The coefficients of variation (σ/μ) are plotted against the numbers of presses for the conditions in which subjects counted nonverbally and for the condition in which they fully pronounced each count word (double logarithmic coordinates). In the former condition, there is scalar variability; that is, a constant coefficient of variation. The slope of the regression line relating the log of the coefficient of variation to the log of mean number of presses does not differ from zero. In the latter, the variability is much less and it is binomial; the coefficient of variation decreases in proportion to the square root of the target number. In the latter case, the slope of the regression line relating the log of the coefficient of variation to the log of the mean number of presses differs significantly from zero but does not differ significantly from −0.5, which is the slope predicted by the binomial variability hypothesis. Reproduced from Cordes et al., 2001, with permission.

rather than scalar. It should increase in proportion to the square root of the target value, rather than in proportion to the target value. If the variability is binomial rather than scalar, then when the coefficient of variation is plotted against the target number on a log–log plot, it should form a straight line with a slope of −0.5. This, in fact, is what was observed in the out-loud counting conditions: The variability was much less than in the nonverbal counting conditions and, more importantly, it was binomial rather than scalar. The mean slope of the subject-by-subject regression lines in the two control conditions was significantly less than zero and not significantly different from −0.5. The contrasting patterns of variability in the counting-out-loud and nonverbal counting conditions strengthen the evidence against the hypothesis that subjects in the nonverbal counting conditions were counting subvocally.

In sum, nonverbal counting may be demonstrated in humans, and it looks just like nonverbal counting in nonhumans. Moreover, mental magnitudes (real numbers) comparable to those generated by nonverbal counting appear to mediate judgments of the numerical ordering of symbolically presented integers. This suggests that the nonverbal counting system is what underlies and gives meaning to the linguistic representation of numerosity.

Nonverbal Arithmetic Reasoning in Humans

In humans, as in other animals, nonverbal counting would be pointless if they did not reason arithmetically with the resulting mental magnitudes. Recent experiments give evidence that they can.

Barth (2001; see also Barth et al., under review 2004) tested adults' performance on tasks that required the addition, subtraction, multiplication, and division of nonverbally estimated numerosities, under conditions in which verbally mediated arithmetic was unlikely. Subjects were given instances of two numerosities in rapid sequence, each instance presented too quickly to be countable verbally. Then, they were given an instance of a third numerosity, and they indicated by pressing one of two buttons whether the sum, or difference, or product, or quotient of the first two numerosities was greater or less than the third.

The numerosities were presented either as dot arrays (with dot density and area covered controlled) or as tone sequences. In some conditions, presentation modalities

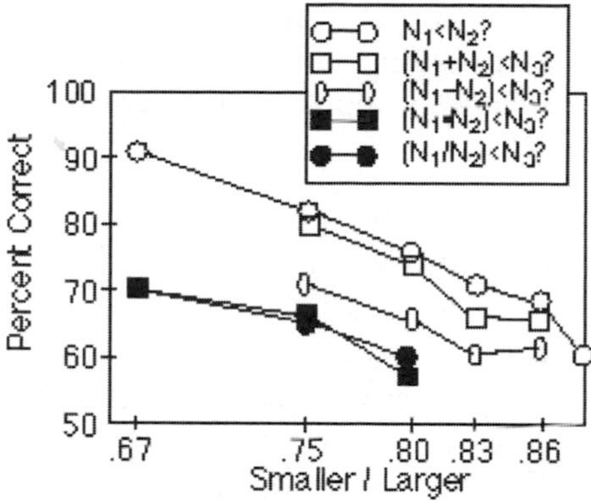

Figure 23.8. The accuracy of order judgments for two nonverbally estimated numerosities. The estimates of numerosity were based on direct instantiations in the first condition ($N_1 < N_2$). In the other conditions, one of them was derived from the composition of two other estimates. Data replotted from Barth, 2001, p. 109.

were mixed, so, for example, subjects compared the sum of a tone sequence and a dot array to either another tone sequence or another dot array.

In Barth's results, there was no effect of comparand magnitude on reaction time or accuracy, only an effect of their ratio. That is, it did not matter how big the two numerosities were; only the proportion of the smaller to the larger affected reaction time and accuracy. The same proved to be true in Barth's experiments involving mental magnitudes derived by arithmetic composition. This enables a comparison between the case in which the comparands are both given directly and the case in which one comparand is the estimated sum or difference of two estimated numerosities. As Figure 23.8 shows, the accuracy of comparisons involving a sum was only slightly less at each ratio of the comparands than the accuracy of a comparison between directly given comparands.

At a given comparand ratio, the accuracy of comparisons involving differences was less than the accuracy of a comparison between directly given comparands (Figure 23.8). This could hardly be otherwise. For addition, the sum increases as the magnitude of the pair of operands increases, but for subtraction, it does not; the difference between a billion and a billion and one is only one. The uncertainty (estimation noise) in the operands must propagate to the result of the operation, so the uncertainty about the true value of a difference must depend in no small measure on the magnitude of the operands from which it derived. If one looks only at the ratio of the difference to the other comparand, one fails to take account of the presumably inescapable impact of operand magnitude on the noise in the difference.

Barth's experiments establish by direct test the human ability to combine noisy nonverbal estimates of numerosity in accord with the combinatorial operations that define the system of arithmetic. In her data (Figure 23.8), as the proportion between the smaller and larger comparand increases toward unity, the accuracy of the comparisons degrades in a roughly parallel fashion regardless of the derivation of the first comparand. This suggests that the scalar variability in the nonverbal estimates of numerosity propagates to the mental magnitudes produced by the composition of those estimates.

Barth's data, however, do not directly demonstrate the variablity in the results of composition nor allow one to estimate the quantitative relation between the noise in the operands and the noise in the result. Cordes et al. (submitted 2004) used the previously described key-tapping paradigm to demonstrate the nonverbal addition and subtraction of nonverbal numerical estimates and the quantitative relation between the variability in the estimates of the sums and differences and the variability in the estimates of the operands.

In the baseline condition of the Cordes et al. (submitted 2004) experiment, subjects saw a sequence of rapid, arrhythmic, variable-duration dot flashes on a computer screen at the conclusion of which they attempted to make an equivalent number of taps on one button of a two-button response box, tapping as rapidly as they could while saying *the* out loud coincident with each tap. In the compositional conditions, subjects saw one sequence on the left side of the screen, a second sequence on the right side, and were asked to tap out either the sum or the difference. In the subtraction condition, they pressed the button on the side they believed to have had the fewer flashes as many times as they felt were required to make up the difference.

Sample results are shown in Figure 23.9. The numbers of responses subjects made, in all cases, were approximately linear functions of the numbers they were estimating, demonstrating the subjects' ability to add and subtract the mental magnitudes representing numerosities. In the baseline condition, the variability in the numbers tapped out was an approximately scalar function of the target number, although there was some additive and binomial variability.

The variability in the addition data was also, to a first approximation, a scalar function of the objective sum. Not surprisingly, however, the variability in the subtraction data was not. In addition, answer magnitude covaries with operand magnitude: The greater the magnitude of the operands, the greater the magnitude of their sum.[3] In subtraction, answer magnitude is poorly correlated with operand magnitude because large-magnitude operands often produce small differences. Insofar as the scalar variability in the estimates of operand magnitudes propagates to the variability in the results of the operations, there will be large variability in these small differences.

Cordes et al. (submitted 2004) fit regression models with additive, binomial, and scalar variance parameters to the baseline data, and to the addition and subtraction data. These fits enabled them to assess the extent to which the magnitude of the pair of operands predicted the variability in their sum and difference. On the assumption that there is no covariance in the operands, the variance in the results of both subtraction and addition should be equal to the sum of the variances for the two operands. When Cordes et al. plotted predicted variabilty against directly estimated variability (Figure 23.9D), they found that the subtraction data did conform approximately to expectations but that the addition data clearly fell above the line. In other words, the variability in results of subtraction was approximately what was expected from the sum of the estimated variances in the operands, but the variability in the addition results was greater than expected.

Retrieving Number Facts

There is an extensive literature on reaction times and error rates in adults doing single-digit arithmetic (Ashcraft, 1992; Campbell, 1999; Campbell & Fugelsang, 2001; Campbell & Gunter, 2002; Campbell, 2005; Campbell & Fugelsang, 2001; Noel, 2001). It resists easy summary. However, magnitude effects analogous to those found for order judgments are a salient and robust finding: The bigger the numerosities represented by a pair of digits, the longer it takes to recall their sum or product and the greater the likelihood of an erroneous recall. The same is true in children (Campbell & Graham, 1985). For both sets of number facts, there is a notable exception to this generalization. The sums and products of ties (for example, 4 + 4 or 9 × 9) are recalled much faster than is predicted by the regressions for non-ties, although ties, too, show a magnitude effect (Miller, Perlmutter, & Keating, 1984).

There is a striking similarity in the effect of operand magnitude on the reaction times for both addition and multiplication. The slopes of the regression lines (reaction time versus the sum or product of the numbers involved) are not statistically different (Geary, Widman, & Little, 1986). More importantly, Miller, Perlmutter, & Keating (1984) found that the best predictor of reaction times for digit multiplication problems was the reaction times for digit addition problems, and vice versa. In other words, the reaction-time data for these two different sets of facts, which are mastered at different ages, show very similar microstructure.

These findings suggest a critical role for mental magnitudes in the retrieval of the basic number facts (the addition and multiplication tables) upon which verbally mediated computation strategies depend. Whalen's (1997) diamond arithmetic

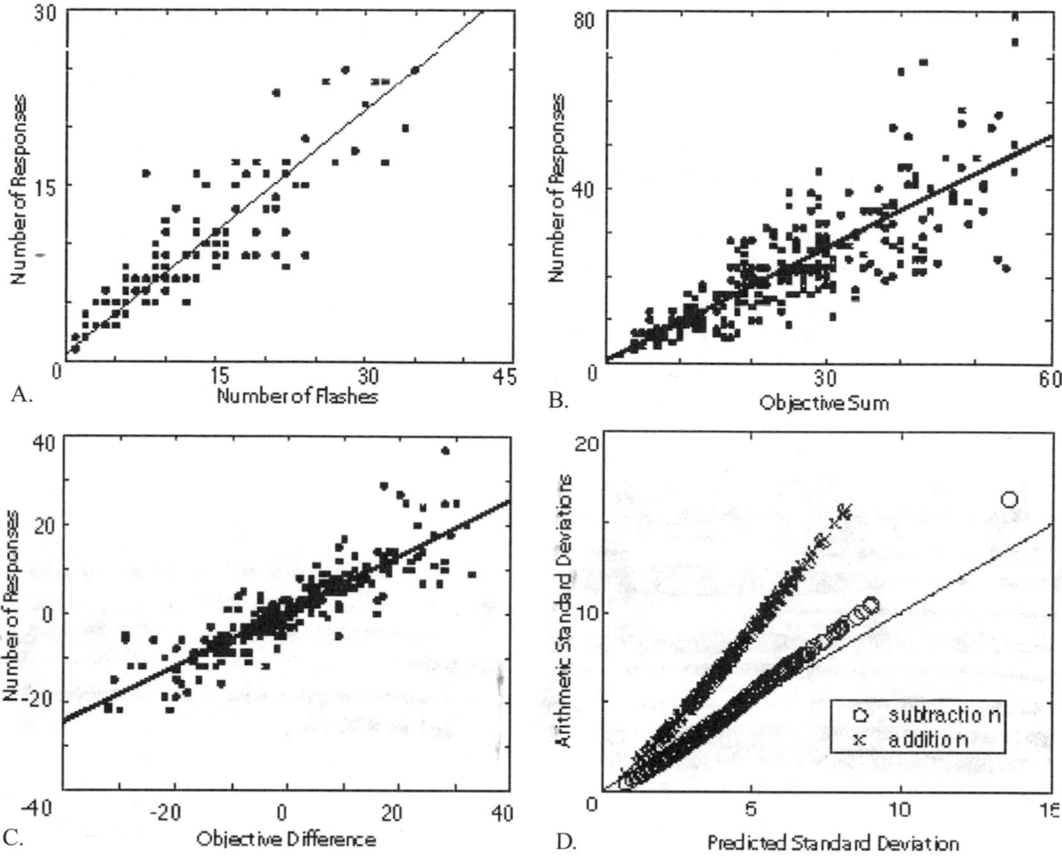

Figure 23.9. A. Number of responses (key taps) as a function of the number of flashes for one subject. B. Number of responses as a function of the sum of the numbers of flashes in two flash sequences. C. Number and sign (side) of the responses as a function of the difference between the numbers of flashes in two sequences of flashes. D. Predicting the variability in the sums and differences from the variability in the operands. Adapted from Cordes et al. (under review 2004) with permission.

experiment showed that these effects depend primarily on the magnitude of the operands, not on the magnitude of the answers, nor on the frequency with which different facts are retrieved (although these may also contribute). Whalen (1997) taught subjects a new arithmetic operation of his own devising, the diamond operation. It was such that there was no correlation between operand magnitude and answer magnitude. Subjects received equal practice on each fact, so explanations in terms of differential practice did not apply. When subjects had achieved a high level of proficiency at retrieving the diamond facts, Whalen measured their reaction times. He obtained the same pattern of results seen in the retrieval of the facts of addition and multiplication.

Two Issues

What is the Form of Mapping from Magnitudes to Mental Magnitudes?

Weber's law, that the discriminability of two magnitudes (two sound intensities or two light intensities) is a function of their ratio, is the oldest and best established quantitative law in experimental psychology. Its implications for the question of the quantitative relation between directly measurable magnitudes (hereafter called *objective magnitudes*) and the mental magnitudes by which they are represented (hereafter called *subjective magnitudes*) have been the subject of analysis and debate for more than a century. This line of investigation led to work on the mathematical foundations of measurement, work concerning the question of what it means to measure something (Krantz et al., 1971; Krantz, 1972; Luce, 1990; Stevens, 1951, 1970). The key insight from work on the foundations of measurement is that the quantitative form of the mapping from things to their numerical representives cannot be separated from the question of the arithmetic operations that are validly performed on the results of that mapping. The question of the form of the mapping is meaningful only at the point at which the numbers (magnitudes) produced by the mapping enter into arithmetic operations.

The discussion began when Fechner used Weber's results to argue that subjective magnitudes (for example, loudness and brightness) are logarithmically related to the corresponding objective magnitudes (sound and light intensity). Fechner's reasoning is echoed to the present day by authors who assume that Weber's law implies logarithmic compression in the mapping from objective numerosity to subjective numerosity. These conjectures are uninformed by the literature on the measurement of subjective quantities spawned by Fechner's assumption. In deriving logarithmic compression from Weber's law, Fechner assumed that equally discriminable differences in objective magnitude correspond to equal differences in subjective magnitude. When you directly ask subjects whether they think just discriminable differences in, for example, loudness, represent equal differences, however, they do not; they think a just discriminable difference between two loud sounds is greater than the just discriminable difference between two soft sounds (Stevens, 1951).

The reader will recognize that Barth performed both experiments – the discrimination experiment (Weber's experiment) and the difference judging experiment – but with numerosities instead of noises. In the discrimination experiment, she found that Weber's law applied: Two pairs of nonverbally estimated numerosities can be correctly ordered 75% of the time when $N_1/N_2 = N_3/N_4 = .83$, where N now refers to the (objective) numerosity of a set (Figure 23.8). From Moyer and Landauer (1967) to the present (Dehaene, 2002), this has been taken to imply that subjective numerosity is a logarithmic function of objective numerosity. If that were so, and if subjects estimated the arithmetic differences between objective magnitudes from the arithmetic differences in the corresponding subjective magnitudes, then the Barth (2001) and Cordes et al. (submitted 2004) subtraction experiments would have failed, and so would the experiments demonstrating subtraction of time and number in nonverbal animals, because the arithmetic difference between the logarithms of two magnitudes represents their quotient, not their arithmetic difference.

In short, when subjects respond appropriately to the arithmetic difference between two numerical magnitudes, their behavior is not based on the arithmetic difference between mental (subjective) magnitudes that are proportional to the logarithms of the objective magnitudes. That much is clear. Either (Model 1): The behavior is based on the arithmetic difference in mental magnitudes that are proportional to the objective magnitudes (a proportional rather than logarithmic mapping). Or (Model 2): Dehaene (2001) has suggested that mental magnitudes are proportional to the logarithms of objective magnitudes and that, to obtain from them the mental magnitude corresponding to the objective difference, the brain uses a look-up table, a procedure analogous to the procedure that Whalen's (1997) subjects used to retrieve the facts of diamond arithmetic. In this model, the arithmetic difference between two mental magnitudes is irrelevant; the two magnitudes serve only to specify where to enter the look-up table – where in memory the answer is to be found.

In summary, there are two intimately interrelated unknowns concerning the mapping from objective to subjective magnitudes – the form of the mapping and the formal character of the operations on the results of the mapping. Given the experimental evidence showing valid arithmetic processing, knowing either would fix the other.

In the absence of firm knowledge about either, can behavioral experimental evidence decide between the alternative models? Perhaps not definitively, but there are relevant considerations. The Cordes et al. (submitted 2004) experiment estimates the noise in the results of the mental subtraction operation at and around zero difference (Figure 23.9C). There is nothing unusual about the noise around answers of approximately zero. It is unclear what assumptions about noise would enable a logarithmic mapping model to explain this. The logarithm of a quantity goes to minus infinity as the quantity approaches zero, and there are no logarithms for negative quantities. On the assumption that realizable mental magnitudes, like realizable nonmental magnitudes, cannot be infinite, the model has to treat zero as a special case. How the treatment of that special case could exhibit noise characteristics of a piece with the noise well away from zero is unclear.

It is also unclear how the logarithmic-mapping-plus-table-lookup model can deal with the fact that the sign of a difference is not predictable a priori. In this model, a bigger magnitude (number) cannot be subtracted from a smaller, because the resulting negative number does not have a logarithm; there is no way to represent a negative magnitude in a scheme in which magnitudes are represented by their logarithms. Thus, this model is not closed under subtraction.

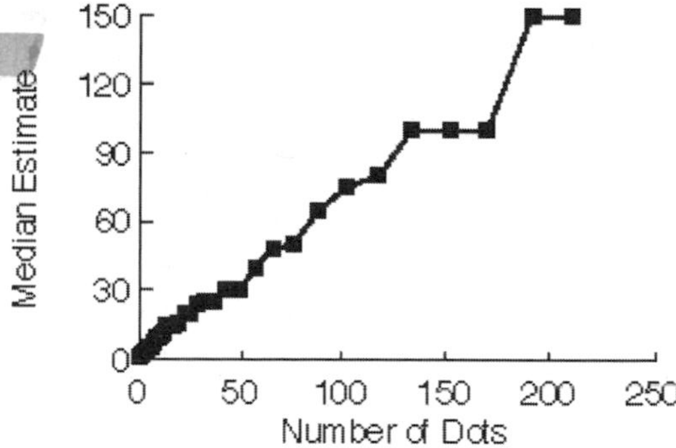

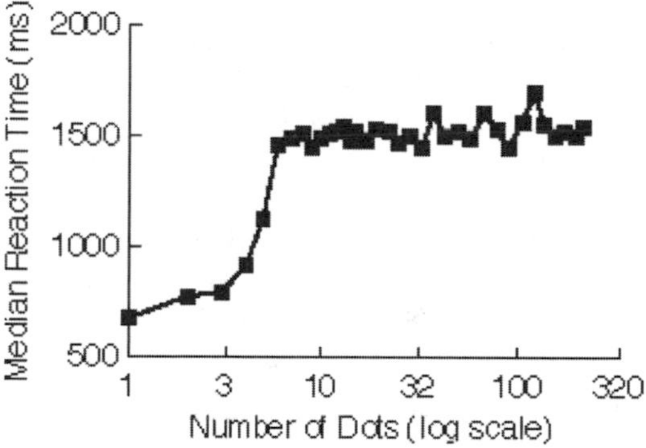

Figure 23.10. Estimates of dot numerosity (top) and time to make an estimate (bottom) as functions of the number of dots in tachistoscopically presented arrays of randomly positioned dots. Plotted from the data for the speeded instruction group in Table 1 of Kaufman et al., 1949, p. 510.

Is There a Distinct Representation for Small Numbers?

When instantiated as arrays of randomly arranged small dots, presented for a fraction of a second, small numerosities can be estimated more quickly than large ones, but only up to about six. Thereafter, the estimates increase more or less linearly with the number of dots, but the reaction time is flat (Figure 23.10).

Subjects' confidence in their estimates also falls off precipitously after six (Kaufman et al., 1949; Taves, 1941). This led Taves to argue that the processes by which subjects arrive at estimates for numerosities of five or fewer are distinct from the processes by which they arrive at estimates for numerosities of seven or more. Kaufman et al. (1949) coined the term *subitizing* to describe the process that operates in the range below six.

When the dot array to be enumerated is displayed until the subject responds, rather than very briefly by a tachistoscope, the reaction time function is superimposable on the one shown in Figure 23.10, up to and including numerosity six. It does not level off at six, however; rather, it continues with the same slope (about 325 ms/dot) indefinitely (Jensen, Reese, & Reese, 1950). This slope represents the time it takes to count subvocally. The discontinuity at six therefore represents the point at which a nonverbal numerosity–estimating mechanism or process takes over from the process of verbal counting, because, presumably, it is not possible to count verbally more than six items under tachistoscopic conditions.

The nonverbal numerosity-estimating process is probably the basis for the demonstrated capacity of humans to compare (order) large numerosities instantiated either visually or auditorily (Barth, Kanwisher, & Spelke, 2003). The reaction times and accuracies for these comparisons show the Weber law characteristic, which is a signature of the process that represents numerosities by mental magnitudes rather than by discrete wordlike symbols (Cordes et al., 2001). The assumption that the representation is by mental magnitudes regardless of the mode of presentation is consistent with the finding that there is no cost to cross-modal comparisons of large numerosities; these comparisons take no longer and are no more inaccurate than comparisons within presentation modes (Barth et al., 2003).

There is controversy about the implications of the reaction time function within the subitizing range below six. In this range, there is approximately a 30-ms increment in going from one to two dots, an 80-ms increment in going from two to three, and a 200-ms increment in going from three to four. These are large increments. The net increment from one to four is about 300 ms, half the total latency to respond to a one-item array (Jensen, Reese, & Reese 1950; Kaufman et al., 1949; Mandler & Shebo, 1982). Moreover, the increments increase at each step. In particular, the step from two to three is significantly greater than the step from one to two in almost every data set.

It is often claimed that there is a discontinuity in the reaction time function within the subitizing range (Davis & Pérusse, 1988; Klahr & Wallace, 1973; Piazza et al., 2003; Simon, 1999; Strauss & Curtis, 1984; Woodworth & Schlosberg, 1954); but it also often has been pointed out that there is no empirical support for this claim (Balakrishnan & Ashby, 1992). Because the reaction time function is neither flat nor linear in the range from one to three, it offers no support for the common theory that very small numbers are directly perceived, as was first pointed out by the authors who coined the term subitizing (Kaufman, et al., 1949).

Gallistel and Gelman (1992) and Dehaene and Cohen (1994) suggested that, in the subitizing range, there is a transition from a strategy based on mapping from nonverbally estimated mental magnitudes to a strategy based on verbal counting. This hypothesis has recently received important support from a paper by Whalen and West (2001). By strongly encouraging rapid, approximate estimates and taking measures to make verbal counting more difficult, Whalen & West (2001) obtained a reaction time function with a slope of 47 ms per item, from one to sixteen items.

The coefficient of variation in the estimated numbers was constant from 1 to 16, at about 14.5%, which is close to the value of 16% in the animal timing literature (Gallistel, King, & McDonald, 2004). The Whalen et al. data therefore show scalar variability in rapid number estimates all the way down to estimates of one and two, as do the data of Cordes et al. (2001). Whalen, & West (2001) show that with this level of noise in the mental magnitudes being mapped to number words, the expected percent errors in the resulting verbal estimates of numerosity are close to zero in the range one to three and increase rapidly thereafter – in close accord with the experimentally observed percent errors in their speeded condition (Figure 23.11). This explains why subjects in experiments in which it is not strongly discouraged switch to subvocal verbal counting somewhere between four and six, and why their confidence in their speeded estimates falls off rapidly after six (Kaufman et al., 1949; Taves, 1941). Whalen et al. (under review) attribute the constant slope of 47 ms/item in the speeded reaction time function to a serial nonverbal counting process. In short, the reaction time function does not support the hypothesis that there are percepts of twoness and threeness, constituting a representation of small numerosities incommensurable with the mental magnitudes that represent other numerosities.

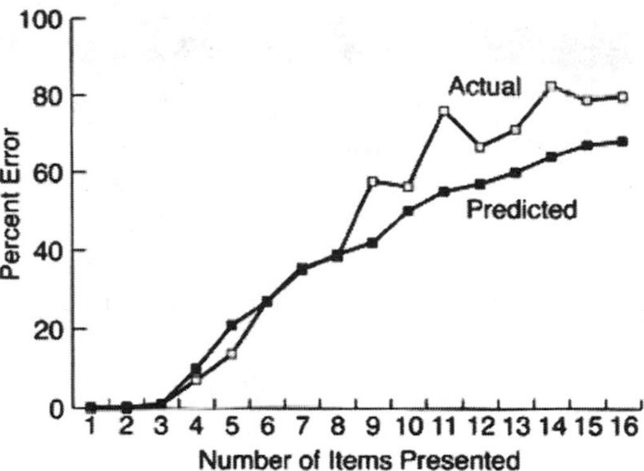

Figure 23.11. The observed percent errors as a function of number of dots in Whalen's speeded condition compared with the percent expected from the hypothesis that the estimates were obtained by way of a mapping from nonverbal mental magnitudes to the corresponding number words and that the mental magnitudes had scalar variability with a coefficient of variation of 0.145. Reproduced from Whalen et al. (under review) with permission.

The Development of Verbal Numerical Competence

It appears that the system of nonverbal mental magnitudes plays a fundamental role in verbal numerical behavior: When verbal counting is too slow to satisfy time constraints, it mediates the finding of a number word that specifies approximately the numerosity of a set. It mediates the ordering of the symbolic numbers and the numerosities they represent. And it mediates the retrieval of the verbal number facts (the addition and multiplication tables) upon which verbal computational procedures rest. All of these roles require a mapping between the mental magnitudes that represent numerosity and number words and written numerals. In the course of ordinary development, therefore, humans learn a bidirectional mapping between the mental magnitudes that represent numerosity and the words and numerals that represent numerosity (Gallistel & Gelman, 1992; Gelman & Cordes, 2001). They make use of this bidirectional mapping in talking about number and the effects of combinatorial operations with numbers. There is broad agreement on this conclusion within the literature on numerical cognition because of the abundant evidence for Weber-law characteristics in symbolic numerical behavior. The literature on the deficits in numerical reasoning seen in brain-injured patients is broadly consistent with this same conclusion (Dehaene, 1997; Noel, 2001).

It also seems plausible that the nonverbal system of numerical reasoning mediates verbally expressed numerical reasoning. It seems plausible, for example, that adults believe that $(2 + 1) > 2$ and *four minus two is less than four* because that is the behavior of the mental magnitudes to which they (unconsciously) refer those symbols to endow them with meaning and reference to the world.

Empiricists offer as an alternative the hypothesis that adults believe these symbolic propositions because they have repeatedly observed that the properties of the world to which the words or symbols refer behave in this way. Adults know, for example, that the word *two* refers to every set that can be placed in one–one correspondence with some foundational set of two and likewise, *mutatis mutandis*, for the word *one*, and that the phrase *plus* refers to the uniting of sets, and that the phrase *greater than* refers to the relation between a set and its proper subsets, and so on. From an empiricist's perspective, the words have these real world references only by virtue of the experiences adults have had, which are ubiquitous and universal.

Nativists or rationalists respond that reference to the world by verbal expressions is mediated by preverbal world-referring symbolic systems in the mind of the hearer and that the ubiquity and universality of the experiences that are supposed to have created world-reference for these expressions are grounds for supposing that symbolic systems with these properties are part of the innate furniture of the mind. We will not pursue this old debate further, except to note the possible relevance of the experiments previously reviewed demonstrating that nonverbal animals reason arithmetically about both numerosities (integer quantities) and magnitudes (continuous quantities).

We turn instead to the experimental literature on numerical competence in very young children. It is difficult to demonstrate conclusively behavior based on numerosity in infants because it is hard not to confound variation in one or more continuous quantities with variation in numerosity, and infants often respond on the basis of continuous dimensions of the stimulus (Clearfield & Mix, 1999; Feigenson, Carey, & Spelke, 2002; see Mix, Huttenlocher, & Levine, 2002, for review). Nonetheless, there are studies that appear to demonstrate sensitivity to numerical order in infants (Brannon, 2002). Moreover, the ability of infants to discriminate sets on the basis of numerosity extends to pairs as large as eight versus sixteen (Lipton & Spelke, 2003; Xu & Spelke, 2000). As a result, there is reason to suppose that preverbal children share with nonverbal animals a nonverbal representation of numerosity.

The assumption that preverbal children represent numerosities by a system of mental magnitudes homologous to the system found in nonverbal animals is the foundation of the account of the development of verbal numerical competence suggested by Gelman and her collaborators (Gelman & Brenneman, 1994; Gelman & Cordes, 2001; Gelman & Williams, 1998). They argue that the development of verbal numerical competence begins with learning to count, which is guided from the outset by the child's recognition that verbal counting is homomorphic to nonverbal counting. In nonverbal counting, the pouring of successive cups into the accumulator (the addition of successive unit magnitudes to a running sum) creates a one-to-one correspondence between the items in the enumerated set and a sequence of mental magnitudes. Although the mental magnitudes thus created have the formal properties of real numbers, the process that creates them generates a discretely ordered sequence of mental magnitudes, an ordering in which each magnitude has a next magnitude. The final magnitude represents the numerosity of the set. Verbal counting does the same thing; it assigns successive words from an ordered list to successive items in the set being enumerated, with the final word representing the cardinality of the set.

Gelman and her collaborators argue that the principles that govern nonverbal counting inform the child's counting behavior from its inception (Gelman & Gallistel, 1978). Children recognize that number words reference numerosities because they implicitly recognize that they are generated by a process homomorphic to the nonverbal counting of serially considered sets. Number words have meaning for the child, as for the adult, because it recognizes at an early age that they map to the mental magnitudes by which the nonverbal mind represents numerosities. On this account, the child's mind tries to apply from the outset the Gelman and Gallistel counting principles (Gelman & Gallistel, 1978) – that counting must involve a one–one assignment of words to items in the set, that the words must be taken from a stably ordered list, and that the last word represents the cardinality of the set. It takes a long time to learn the list and to implement the verbal counting procedure flawlessly, because list learning is hard, because the implementation of the procedure is challenging (Gelman & Greeno, 1989), and because the child is often confused about what the experimenter wants.

Critical to Gelman's account is evidence that during the period when they are learning to count children already understand that the last count word represents a property of the set about which it is appropriate to reason arithmetically. Without such evidence, there is no ground for believing that the child has a truly numerical representation. Evidence on this crucial point comes from the so-called magic experiments (Brannon & Van de Walle, 2001; Bullock & Gelman, 1977; Gelman, 1972, 1977, 1993). These experiments drew children into a game in which a winner and loser plate could be distinguished on the basis of the number of toy mice they contained. The task engaged children's attention and caused them to justify their judgments as to whether an uncovered plate was or was not the winner. Children as young as two and a half years indicated that the numerosity was the decisive dimension, and they spontaneously counted to justify their judgment that the plate with the correct numerosity was the winner. On magic trials, a mouse was surreptitiously added or subtracted from the winner plate during the shuffling, so that it had the same numerosity as the loser plate. Now, both plates when uncovered were revealed to be loser plates. In talking about what surprised them, children indicated that something must have been added or subtracted, and they counted to justify themselves. This is strong evidence that children as young as two and one half years of age understand that counting gives a representation of numerosity about which it is appropriate to reason arithmetically. This is well before they become good counters (Fuson, 1988; Gelman & Gallistel, 1978; Hartnett & Gelman, 1998). Surprised two-and-half-year-olds made frequent use of number words. They used them in idiosyncratic ways, but ways that nonetheless conformed to the counting principles (Gelman, 1993), including the cardinality principle.

A second account of the development of counting and numerical understanding grows, first, out of the conviction of many researchers that, although two-year-olds count, albeit badly, they do not understand what they are doing (Carey, 2001a, 2001b; Fuson, 1988; Mix, Huttenlocher, & Levine 2002; Wynn, 1990; Wynn, 1992b). It rests, secondly, on evidence suggesting that in the spontaneous processing of numerosities by infants and monkeys, there is a discontinuity between numbers of four or less and bigger numbers. In some experiments, the infant and monkey subjects discriminate all numerosity pairs in the range one to four but fail to discriminate pairs that include a numerosity outside that range (e.g., <3,6>), even when, as in the example, their ratio is greater than the ratio between discriminable pairs of four or less (Feigenson, Carey, & Hauser, 2002; Uller, et al., 1999; Uller, Hauser, & Carey, 2001).

How to reconcile these latter findings with the finding that infants do discriminate the pair <8,16> (Lipton & Spelke, 2003; Xu & Spelke, 2000) is unclear. Similarly, it is unclear how to reconcile the monkey findings with the literature showing the discrimination of numerosities small and large in nonverbal animals. Particularly to be borne in mind in this connection is the finding that monkeys cannot be taught to order numerosities in other than a numerical order (Brannon & Terrace, 2000), even though they can be taught to order things other than numerosities in an arbitrary, experimenter-imposed order (Terrace, Son, & Brannon, 2003). This implies that numerical order is spontaneously salient to a monkey.

The account offered by Carey (Carey, 2001a, 2001b) begins with the assumption that convincing cases of infant number discrimination involving numbers less than four may depend on the object tracking system. In Wynn's (1992a) experiment, for example, the infants saw an object appear to join or leave one or two objects behind an occluding screen. They were surprised when the screen was removed to reveal a number of objects different from the number that ought to have been there. This surprise may have arisen only from the infant's belief in object permanence.

When an infant sees an object move behind an occluding screen, the subsequent removal of which fails to reveal an object, the infant is surprised (Baillargeon, 1995; Baillargeon, Spelke, & Wasserman, 1985). The child's surprise presumably is mediated by a system for tracking objects, such as the object file system suggested by Kahneman, Treisman, and Gibbs (1992) or the FINST system suggested by Pylyshyn and Storm (1988). This system maintains a marker (object file or FINST) for each object it is tracking, but it can only track about four objects (Scholl & Pylyshyn, 1999). As a result, infants in experiments like Wynn's are surprised for the same reason as in original object-permanence experiments: An object is missing. The infant has an active mental marker or pointer that no longer points to an object. Alternatively, there is an object for which it has no marker.

Carey argues that sets of object files are the foundations on which the understanding of integers rests. The initial meaning of the words *one, two, three,* and *four* does not come from the corresponding mental magnitudes; rather, it comes from sets of object files. The child comes to recognize the ordering of the referents of *one, two, three,* and *four* because a set of two active object files has as a proper subset a set of one object file, and so on. The child comes to recognize that addition applies to the things referred to by these words because the union of two sets of object files yields another set of object files (provided the union does not create a set greater than four). This is the foundation of the child's belief in the successor principle: Every integer has a unique successor.

This account seems to ignore the basic function of a set of, for example, two object files (FINSTs, pointers), which is to point to two particular objects. If *two* referred to a particular set of two object files, it presumably would be usable only in connection with the two objects it pointed to. It would be a name for *that* pair of objects, not for all sets that share with that set the property of twoness.

A particular set of pointers cannot substitute for (is not equal to) another such set without loss of function, because its function is to point to one pair of objects, whereas the function of another such set is to point to a different pair. There is no reason to believe that there is any such thing as a general set of two pointers – a set that does not point to any particular set of two objects, but represents all the sets that do so point. Any set of two object files is an instance of a set with the twoness property (a token of twoness), but it can no more represent twoness than a name that picks out one particular dog (e.g., *Rover*) can represent the concept of a dog. A precondition of *Rover*'s serving the latter function is that it not serve the former. By contrast, any instance of the numeral 2 can be substituted for any other without loss of function, and so can a pair of hash marks.

A second problem with this account is that it is unclear how a system so lacking in closure could be the basis for inferring a system, the function of which depends so strongly on closure. The Carey suggestion is motivated by findings that the maximum numerosity of a set of active object files is at most four. There are only nine numerically distinct unordered pairs of sets of four or less (<1,1>, <1,2>, <1,3>, <1,4>, <2,2>, <2,3>, <2,4>, <3,3>, and <3,4>). Five of the nine pairs, when composed (united) yield a set too numerous to be a set of object files. From this foundation, the mind of the child is said to infer that the numbers may be extended indefinitely by addition. One wants to know what the inference rule is that ignores the many negative instances in the base data set.

Conclusions and Future Directions

There is a widespread consensus, backed by a large and diverse experimental literature, that adult humans share with nonverbal animals a nonverbal system for representing discrete and continuous quantity that has the formal properties of continuous magnitudes. Mental magnitudes represent quantities in the same sense that, given a proper measurement scheme, real numbers represent line lengths. That is, the brains of nonverbal animals perform arithmetic operations with mental magnitudes; they add, subtract, multiply, divide, and order them. The processes or mechanisms that map numerosities (discrete quantities) and magnitudes (continuous quantities) into mental magnitudes, and the operations that the brain performs on them, are together such that the results of the operations are approximately valid, albeit imprecise; the results of computations on mental magnitudes map appropriately back onto the world of discrete and continuous quantity.

Scalar variability is a signature of the mental magnitude system. Scalar variability and Weber's law are different sides of the same coin: Models that generate scalar variability also yield Weber's law. There are two such models. One assumes that the mapping from objective quantity to subjective quantity (mental magnitude) is logarithmic; the other assumes that it is scalar. Both assume noise. That is, they assume that the signal corresponding to a given objective quantity varies from occasion to occasion in a manner described by a Gaussian probability density function. The variation is on the order of 15% in both animal timing and human speeded number estimation.

The first model (logarithmic mapping) assumes that scalar behavioral variability reflects a constant level of noise in the signal distributions. This yields proportional (scalar) variability, because constant logarithmic intervals correspond to constant proportions in the corresponding nonlogarithmic magnitudes. The second model (scalar mapping) assumes scalar variability in the underlying signal distributions. The overlap in the two signal distributions is a function only of the ratio between the represented numerosities in both models, which is why they both predict Weber's law.

Both models assume there is only one mapping from objective quantities to subjective quantities (mental magnitudes), but there is no compelling reason to accept this assumption. The question of the quantitative form of the mapping makes sense only at the point at which the mental magnitudes enter into combinatorial operations. The form may differ for different combinatorial operations. In the future, the analysis of variability in the answers from nonverbal arithmetic may decide between the models. An important component of future models, therefore, must be the specification of how variability propagates from the operands to the answers.

The system of mental magnitudes plays many important roles in verbalized adult number behavior. For example, it mediates judgments of numerical order and the retrieval of the verbal number facts (addition and multiplication tables) upon which verbalized and written calculation procedures depend. It also mediates the finding of number words to represent large numerosities, presented too briefly to be verbally counted, and, more controversially, the rapid retrieval of number words to represent numerosities in the subitizing range (one through six).

Any account of the development of verbal numerical competence must explain how subjects learn the bidirectional mapping between number words and mental magnitudes, without which mental magnitudes could not play the roles just described. One account of the development of verbal numerical competence assumes that it is directed from the outset by the mental magnitude system. The homomorphism between serial nonverbal counting and verbal counting is what causes the child to appreciate the enumerative function of the count words. The child attends to these words because of the homomorphism. Learning their meaning is the process of learning their mapping to the mental magnitudes. Another account assumes that the count words from *one* to *four* are initially understood to refer to sets of object files – mental pointers that pick out particular objects. On this account, the learning of the mapping to mental magnitudes comes later, after the child has extensive counting experience.

Acknowledgments

Some of the research by the authors reported in this chapter was supported by NSF Grants SBR-9209741 and NSF DFS-920974 to Gelman, NIH Grant MH 63866 to Gallistel, and NSF No.SPR9720402 to both Gelman and Gallistel.

Notes

1. Technically, not really true, because Cantor discovered a way to assign a unique positive integer to every rational number. The integers his procedure assigns, however, are useless for computational purposes.
2. Fortran and C programmers, who have made the mistake of dividing an integer variable by a floating point variable will know whereof we speak.
3. The magnitude of a pair of numbers is the square root of the sum of their squares.

References

Ashcraft, M. H. (1992). Cognitive arithmetic: A review of data and theory. *Cognition*, 44(1–2), 75–106.

Baillargeon, R. (1995). Physical reasoning in infancy. In M. S. Gazzaniga (Ed.), *The Cognitive Neurosciences* (pp. 181–204). Cambridge, MA: MIT Press.

Baillargeon, R., Spelke, E., & Wasserman, E. (1985). Object permanence in 5-month-old infants. *Cognition*, 20, 191–208.

Balakrishnan, J. D., & Ashby, F. G. (1992). Subitizing: Magical numbers or mere superstition. *Psychological Research*, 54, 80–90.

Barth, H., Kanwisher, N., & Spelke, E. (2003). The construction of large number representations in adults. *Cognition*, 86(3), 201–221.

Barth, H., La Mont, K., Lipton, J., Dehaene, S., Kanwisher, N., & Spelke, E. (under review 2003). Nonsymbolic arithmetic in adults and young children.

Barth, H. C. (2001). *Numerical Cognition in Adults: Representation and Manipulation of Nonsymbolic Quantities*. Unpublished dissertation, MIT, Cambridge, MA.

Beran, M. J. (2001). Summation and numerousness judgments of sequentially presented sets of items by chimpanzees (*Pan troglodytes*). *Journal of Comparative Psychology*, 115, 181–191.

Biro, D., & Matsuzawa, T. (2001). Chimpanzee numerical competence: Cardinal and ordinal skills. In Matsuzawa, Tetsuro (Ed.), *Primate Origins of Human Cognition and Behavior* (pp. 199–225). New York: Springer-Verlag.

Boyer, C. B., & Merzback, U. C. (1989). *A History of Mathematics* (2nd Ed.) New York: Wiley.

Boysen, S. T., & Berntson, G. G. (1989). Numerical comptetence in a chimpanzee (*Pan troglodytes*). *Journal of Comparative Psychology*, 103, 23–31.

Boysen, S. T., & Hallberg, K. I. (2000). Primate numerical competence: Contributions toward understanding nonhuman cognition. *Cognitive Science*, 24(3), 423–443.

Brannon, E. M. (2002). The development of ordinal numerical knowledge in infancy. *Cognition*, 83(3), 223–240.

Brannon, E. M., & Roitman, J. D. (2003). Nonverbal representations of time and number in animals and human infants. In W. H. Meck (Ed.), *Functional and Neural Mechanisms of Interval Timing* (pp. 143–182). Boca Raton, FL: CRC Press.

Brannon, E. M., & Terrace, H. S. (2000). Representation of the numerosities 1–9 by rhesus macaques (*Macaca mulatta*). *Journal of Experimental Psychology: Animal Behavior Processes*, 26(1), 31–49.

Brannon, E. M., & Van de Walle, G. A. (2001). The development of ordinal numerical competence in young children. *Cognitive Psychology*, 43(1), 53–81.

Brannon, E. M. & Terrace, H. S. (2002). The evolution and ontogeny of ordinal numerical ability. In M. Bekoff, C. Allen, et al. (Eds.), *The Cognitive Animal: Empirical and Theoretical Perspectives on Animal Cognition* (pp. 197–204). Cambridge, MA: MIT Press.

Brannon, E. M., Wusthoff, C. J., Gallistel, C. R., & Gibbon, J. (2001). Numerical subtraction in thc pigeon: Evidence for a linear subjective number scale. *Psychological Science*, 12(3), 238–243.

Buckley, P. B., & Gillman, C. B. (1974). Comparisons of digits and dot patterns. *Journal of Experimental Psychology*, 103, 1131–1136.

Bullock, M., & Gelman, R. (1977). Numerical reasoning in young children: The ordering principle. *Child Development*, 48, 427–434.

Campbell, J. I. D. (1999). Division by multiplication. *Memory and Cognition*, 27(5), 791–802.

Campbell, J. I. D., & Fugelsang, J. (2001). Strategy choice for arithmetic verification: Effects of numerical surface form. *Cognition*, 80(3), B21–B30.

Campbell, J. I. D., & Epp, L. J. (2005). Architectures for arithmetic. In J. I. Campbell (Ed.), *Handbook of Mathematical Cognition*. (347–360) Psychology Press.

Campbell, J. I. D., & Fugelsang, J. (2001). Strategy choice for arithmetic verifcation: Effects of numerical surface form. *Cognition*, 80(3), B21–B30.

Campbell, J. I. D., & Graham, D. J. (1985). Mental multiplication skill: Structure, process, and acquisition. *Canadian Journal of Psychology*. 39, 338–366.

Campbell, J. I. D., & Gunter, R. (2002). Calculation, culture, and the repeated operand effect. *Cognition*, 86(1), 71–96.

Carey, S. (2001a). Cognitive foundations of arithmetic: Evolution and ontogenesis. *Mind and Language*, 16, 37–55.

Carey, S. (2001b). On the very possibility of discontinuities in conceptual development. In E. Dupoux (Ed.), *Language, Brain, and Cognitive Development* (pp. 304–324). Cambridge, MA: MIT Press.

Carr, J. A. R., & Wilkie, D. M. (1997). Rats use an ordinal timer in a daily time-place learning task. *Journal of Experimental Psychology: Animal Behavior Processes*, 23(2), 232–247.

Catania, A. C. (1963). Concurrent performances: A baseline for the study of reinforcement magnitude. *Journal of the Experimental Analysis of Behavior*, 6, 299–300.

Church, R. M., & Meck, W. H. (1984). The numerical attribute of stimuli. In H. L. Roitblatt, T. G. Bever, & H. S. Terrace (Eds.), *Animal Cognition* (pp. 445–464). Hillsdale, NJ: Erlbaum.

Church, R. M., Meck, W. H., & Gibbon, J. (1994). Application of scalar timing theory to individual trials. *Journal of Experimental Psychology: Animal Behavior Processes*, 20(2), 135–155.

Clearfield, M., & Mix, K. (1999). Number versus contour length in infants' discrimination of small visual sets. *Psychological Science*, 10, 408–411.

Cordes, S., Gallistel, C. R., Gelman, R., & Latham, P. E. (under review 2004). Nonverbal arithmetic in humans.

Cordes, S., Gelman, R., Gallistel, C. R., & Whalen, J. (2001). Variability signatures distinguish verbal from nonverbal counting for both large and small numbers. *Psychonomic Bulletin and Review*, 8(4), 698–707.

Davis, H., & Pérusse, R. (1988). Numerical competence in animals: Definitional issues, current evidence, and a new research agenda. *Behavioral and Brain Sciences.*, 11, 561–615.

Dehaene, S. (1997). *The Number Sense*. Oxford, UK: Oxford University Press.

Dehaene, S. (2001). Subtracting pigeons: Logarithmic or linear? *Psychological Science*, 12(3), 244–246.

Dehaene, S. (2002). Single neuron arithmetic. *Science*, 297, 1652–1653.

Dehaene, S., & Changeux, J. P. (1993). Development of elementary numerical abilities: A neuronal model. *Journal of Cognitive Neuroscience*, 5, 390–407.

Dehaene, S., & Cohen, L. (1994). Dissociable mechanisms of subitizing and counting: Neuropsychological evidence from simultanagnostic patients. *Psychological Review*, 20, 958–975.

Dehaene, S., Dehaene-Lambertz, G., & Cohen, L. (1998). Abstract representations of numbers in the animal and human brain. *Trends in Neurosciences*, 21, 355–361.

Dehaene, S., Dupoux, E., & Mehler, J. (1990). Is numerical comparison digital? Analogical and symbolic effects in two-digit number comparison. *Journal of Experimental Psychology: Human Perception and Performance*, 16, 626–641.

Feigenson, L., Carey, S., & Hauser, M. (2002). The representations underlying infants' choice of more: Object files versus analog magnitudes. *Psychological Science*, 13, 150–156.

Feigenson, L., Carey, S., & Spelke, E. (2002). Infants' discrimination of number vs. continuous extent. *Cognitive Psychology*, 44(1), 33–66.

Fuson, K. (1988). *Children's Counting and Concepts of Number*. New York: Springer Verlag.

Gallistel, C. R. (1990). *The Organization of Learning*. Cambridge, MA: Bradford Books/MIT Press.

Gallistel, C. R., & Gelman, R. (1992). Preverbal and verbal counting and computation. *Cognition*, 44, 43–74.

Gallistel, C. R., & Gelman, R. (2000). Non-verbal numerical cognition: From reals to integers. *Trends in Cognitive Sciences*, 4, 59–65.

Gallistel, C. R., & Gibbon, J. (2000). Time, rate and conditioning. *Psychological Review*, 107, 289–344.

Gallistel, C. R., King, A., & McDonald, R. (2004). Sources of variability and systematic error in mouse timing behavior. *Journal of Experimental Psychology: Animal Behavior Processes*, 30, 3–16.

Gallistel, C. R., Mark, T. A., King, A., & Latham, P. E. (2001). The rat approximates an ideal detector of changes in rates of reward: Implications for the law of effect. *Journal of Experimental Psychology: Animal Behavior Processes*, 27, 354–372.

Geary, D. C., Widman, K. F., & Little, T. D. (1986). Cognitive addition and mulitplication: Evidence for a single memory network. *Memory and Cognition*, 14, 478–487.

Gelman, R. (1972). Logical capacity of very young children: Number invariance rules. *Child Development*, 43, 75–90.

Gelman, R. (1977). How young children reason about small numbers. In N. J. Castellan, D. B. Pisoni & G. R. Potts (Eds.), *Cognitive Theory* (Vol. 2, pp. 27–61). Hillsdale, NJ: Erlbaum.

Gelman, R. (1993). A rational-constructivist account of early learning about numbers and objects. In D. Medin (Ed.), *Learning and Motivation*. (Vol. 30, pp. 61–96). New York: Academic Press.

Gelman, R., & Brenneman, K. (1994). First principles can support both universal and culture-specific learning about number and music. In L. Hirschfeld & S. Gelman (Eds.), *Mapping the Mind: Domains, Culture and Cognition* (pp. 369–390). Cambridge, UK: Cambridge University Press.

Gelman, R., & Cordes, S. A. (2001). Counting in animals and humans. In E. Dupoux (Ed.), *Language, Brain, and Cognitive Development: Essays in honor of Jacques Mehler* (pp. 279–301). Cambridge, MA: MIT Press.

Gelman, R., & Gallistel, C. R. (1978). *The Child's Understanding of Number*. Cambridge, MA: Harvard University Press.

Gelman, R., & Greeno, J. G. (1989). On the nature of competence: Principles for understanding in a domain. In L. B. Resnick (Ed.), *Knowing and Learning: Issues for a Cognitive Science of Instruction*. Hillsdale, NJ: Erlbaum.

Gelman, R., & Williams, E. (1998). Enabling constraints on cognitive development. In D. Kuhn & R. Siegler (Eds.), *Cognition, Perception and Language. Vol. 2. Handbook of Child Psychology. 5th ed.* (pp. 575–630). New York: Wiley.

Gibbon, J. (1977). Scalar expectancy theory and Weber's law in animal timing. *Psychological Review*, 84, 279–335.

Gibbon, J., & Church, R. M. (1981). Time left: Linear versus logarithmic subjective time. *Journal of Experimental Psychology: Animal Behavior Processes*, 7(2), 87–107.

Harper, D. G. C. (1982). Competitive foraging in mallards: Ideal free ducks. *Animal Behaviour*, 30, 575–584.

Hartnett, P., & Gelman, R. (1998). Early understandings of numbers: Paths or barriers to the construction of new understandings? *Learning and Instruction*, 8(4), 341–374.

Hauser, M. D. (2001). What do animals think about numbers? In P. Sherman, J. Alcock, (Eds.), Exploring Animal Behavior: Readings from American Scientist (3rd ed.) Research Triangle Park, NC: Sigma Xi.

Herrnstein, R. J. (1961). Relative and absolute strength of response as a function of frequency of reinforcement. *Journal of the Experimental Analysis of Behavior*, 4, 267–272.

Herrnstein, R. J., & Vaughan, W. J. (1980). Melioration and behavioral allocation. In J. E. R. Staddon (Ed.), *Limits to Action: The Allocation of Individual Behavior* (pp. 143–176). New York: Academic Press.

Hinrichs, J. V., Yurko, D. S., & Hu, J. M. (1981). Two-digit number comparison: Use of place information. *Journal of Experimental Psychology. Human Perception and Performance*, 7, 890–901.

Jensen, E. M., Reese, E. P., & Reese, T. W. (1950). The subitizing and counting of visually presented fields of dots. *The Journal of Psychology*, 30, 363–392.

Kahneman, D., Treisman, A., & Gibbs, B. J. (1992). The reviewing of object files: Object-specific integration of information. *Cognitive Psychology*, 24, 175–219.

Kaufman, E. L., Lord, M. W., Reese, T. W., & Volkman, J. (1949). The discrimination of visual number. *American Journal of Psychology*, 62, 498–525.

Keller, J. V., & Gollub, L. R. (1977). Duration and rate of reinforcement as determinants of concurrent responding. *Journal of the Experimental Analysis of Behavior*, 28, 145–153.

Killeen, P. R., & Taylor, T. (2001). How the propagation of error through stochastic counters affects time discrimination and other psychophysical judgments. *Psychological Review*, 107, 430–459.

King, A. S., McDonald, R., & Gallistel, C. R. (2001). Screening for mice that remember incorrectly. *International Journal of Comparative Psychology*, 14, 232–257.

Klahr, D., & Wallace, J. G. (1973). The role of quantification operators in the development of conservation. *Cognitive Pschology*, 4, 301–327.

Krantz, D., Luce, R. D., Suppes, P., & Tversky, A. (1971). *The Foundations of Measurement*. New York: Academic Press.

Krantz, D. H. (1972). Measurement structures and psychological laws. *Science*, 175, 1427–1435.

Leon, M. I., & Gallistel, C. R. (1998). Self-stimulating rats combine subjective reward magnitude and subjective reward rate multiplicatively. *Journal of Experimental Psychology: Animal Behavior Processes*, 24(3), 265–277.

Lipton, J. S., & Spelke, E. S. (2003). Origins of number sense: Large-number discrimination in human infants. *Psychological Science*, 14(5), 396–401.

Luce, R. D. (1990). What is a ratio in ratio scaling. In S. J. Bolanowski & G. A. Gescheider (Eds.), *Ratio Scaling of Psychological Magnitude: In Honor of the Memory of S. S. Stevens*. Hillsdale, NJ: Erlbaum.

Mandler, G., & Shebo, B. J. (1982). Subitizing: An analysis of its component processes. *Journal Experimental Psychology General, 11*, 1–22.

Mechner, F. (1958). Probability relations within response sequences under ratio reinforcement. *Journal of the Experimental Analysis of Behavior, 1*, 109–122.

Meck, W. H., & Church, R. M. (1983). A mode control model of counting and timing processes. *Journal of Experimental Psychology: Animal Behavior Processes, 9*, 320–334.

Menninger, K. (1969). *Number Words and Number Symbols*. Cambridge, MA: MIT Press.

Miller, K. F., Perlmutter, M., & Keating, D. (1984). Cognitive arithmetic: Comparison of operations. *Journal of Experimental Psychology. Learning, Memory, and Cognition, 10*, 46–60.

Mix, K. S., Huttenlocher, J., & Levine, S. C. (2002). *Quantitative Development in Infancy and Early Childhood*. Oxford, UK: Oxford University Press.

Moyer, R. S., & Landauer, T. K. (1967). Time required for judgments of numerical inequality. *Nature, 215*, 1519–1520.

Moyer, R. S., & Landauer, T. K. (1973). Determinants of reaction time for digit inequality judgments. *Bulletin of the Psychonomic Society, 1*, 167–168.

Noel, M. P. (2001). Numerical cognition. In B. Rapp (Ed.), *The Handbook of Cognitive Neuropsychology: What Deficits Reveal About the Human Mind* (pp 495–518). Philadelphia Psychology Press.

Olthof, A., Iden, C. M., & Roberts, W. A. (1997). Judgments of ordinality and summation of number symbols by squirrel monkeys. *Journal of Experimental Psychology: Animal Behavior Processes, 23*(3), 325–339.

Olthof, A., & Roberts, W. A. (2000). Summation of symbols by pigeons (*Columbia livia*): The importance of number and mass of reward items. *Journal of Comparative Psychology, 114*(2), 158–166.

Parkman, J. M. (1971). Temporal aspects of digit and letter inequality judgments. *Journal of Experimental Psychology, 91*, 191–205.

Piazza, M., Giacomini, E., Le Bihan, D., & Dehaene, S. (2003). Single-trial classification of parallel pre-attentive and serial attentive processes using functional magnetic resonance imaging. *Proceedings of the Royal Society (London) Series B, 270*, 1237–1245.

Platt, J. R., & Johnson, D. M. (1971). Localization of position within a homogeneous behavior chain: Effects of error contingencies. *Learning and Motivation, 2*, 386–414.

Pylyshyn, Z. W., & Storm, R. W. (1988). Tracking multiple independent targets: Evidence for a parallel tracking system. *Spatial Vision, 3*, 179–197.

Rumbaugh, D. M., Savage-Rumbaugh, S., & Hegel, M. T. (1987). Summation in the chimpanzee (*Pan troglodytes*). *Journal of Experimental Psychology: Animal Behavior Processes, 13*, 107–115.

Rumbaugh, D. M., & Washburn, D. A. (1993). Counting by chimpanzees and ordinality judgments by macaques in video-formatted tasks. In S. T. Boyesen & E. J. Capaldi (Eds.), *The Development of Numerical Competence: Animal and Human Models* (pp. 87–106). Hillsdale, NJ: Erlbaum.

Savastano, H. I., & Miller, R. R. (1998). Time as content in Pavlovian conditioning. *Behavioural Processes, 44*(2), 147–162.

Scholl, B. J., & Pylyshyn, Z. (1999). Tracking multiple items through occlusion: Clues to visual objecthood. *Cognitive Psychology, 38*, 259–290.

Simon, T. J. (1999). The foundations of numerical thinking in a brain without numbers. *Trends in Cognitive Sciences, 3*(10), 363–364.

Spelke, E., & Dehaene, S. (1999). Biological foundations of numerical thinking. *Trends in Cognitive Sciences, 3*(10), 365–366.

Stevens, S. S. (1951). Mathematics, measurement and psychophysics. In S. S. Stevens (Ed.), *Handbook of Experimental Psychology* (pp. 1–49). New York: Wiley.

Stevens, S. S. (1970). Neural events and the psychophysical law. *Science, 170*(3962), 1043–1050.

Strauss, M. S., & Curtis, L. E. (1984). Development of numerical concepts in infancy. In C. Sophian (Ed.), *Origins of Cognitive Skills* (pp. 131–155). Hillsdale, NJ: Erlbaum.

Sulkowski, G. M., & Hauser, M. D. (2001). Can rhesus monkeys spontaneously subtract? *Cognition, 79*(3), 239–262.

Taves, E. H. (1941). Two mechanisms for the perception of visual numerousness. *Archives of Psychology, 37*(No. 265).

Terrace, H. S., Son, L. K., & Brannon, E. M. (2003). Serial expertise of *Rhesus macaques*. *Psychological Science, 14*, 66–73.

Uller, C., Carey, S., Huntley-Fenner, G., & Klatt, L. (1999). What representations might underlie infant numerical knowledge? *Cognitive Development, 14*(1), 1–36.

Uller, C., Hauser, M., & Carey, S. (2001). Spontaneous representation of number in cotton-top tamarins (*Saguinus oedipus*). *Journal of Comparative Psychology*, 115(3), 248–257.

Washburn, D. A., & Rumbaugh, D. M. (1991). Ordinal judgments of numerical symbols by macaques (*Macaca mulatta*). *Psychological Science*, 2, 190–193.

Whalen, J. (1997). *The Influence of Semantic Representations of Number on Arithmetic Fact Retrieval*. Unpublished dissertation, Johns Hopkins, Baltimore.

Whalen, J., Gallistel, C., & Gelman, R. (1999). Nonverbal counting in humans: The psychophysics of number representation. *Psychological Science*, 10(2), 130–137.

Whalen, J., & West, V. (2001). Why you shouldn't count on subitizing: Evidence from counting and estimating. *Psychomics Society Abstracts*, 6, p. 66, No 453.

Woodworth, R. S., & Schlosberg, H. (1954). *Experimental Psychology: Revised Edition*. New York: Holt, Rinehart & Winston.

Wynn, K. (1990). Children's understanding of counting. *Cognition*, 36, 155–193.

Wynn, K. (1992a). Addition and subtraction by human infants. *Nature*, 358, 749–750.

Wynn, K. (1992b). Children's acquisition of the number words and the counting system. *Cognitive Psychology*, 24, 220–251.

Xu, F., & Spelke, E. S. (2000). Large number discrimination in 6-month-old infants. *Cognition*, 74(1), B1–B11.

CHAPTER 24

Effects of Aging on Reasoning

Timothy A. Salthouse

This chapter reviews empirical research on adult age differences in reasoning. It is important to begin with three disclaimers, however. First, although many types of reasoning have been identified (e.g., deductive, inductive, analogical, and visuospatial; see articles in this volume by Evans, Chap. 8; Sloman & Lagnado, Chap. 5; Buehner & Cheng, Chap. 7; Holyoak, Chap. 6; and Tversky, Chap. 10), few age-comparative studies have included more than two or three different reasoning variables and, as a result, there is little evidence for distinctions among various types of reasoning in studies of aging. Different reasoning tasks therefore are considered together in this chapter, although it is recognized that combining them in this manner may be obscuring potentially important distinctions. Second, the discussion is limited to reasoning tasks with minimal involvement of knowledge. Because knowledge is likely relevant in most everyday reasoning, the tasks discussed may refer to only a subset of real-life reasoning. The third disclaimer is that most of the discussion refers to research derived from my laboratory. This obviously represents only a portion of the relevant literature, but limitations of space preclude comprehensive coverage of all of the research related to the topic of aging and reasoning. A more inclusive review of the earlier literature on this topic can be found in Salthouse (1992a).

Some of the most convincing data on the relations between age and reasoning are those derived from standardized tests because the variables were designed to optimize psychometric properties such as sensitivity, reliability, and construct validity, and the normative samples have typically been moderately large and selected to be representative of the general population (see Sternberg, Chap. 31, for discussion of intelligence tests). Three recent cognitive test batteries have each included at least two measures of reasoning. The tests included in the Kaufman Adult Intelligence Test (Kaufman & Kaufman, 1993) were described on page 6 of the test manual in the following manner: Logical Steps – "Examinees attend to logical premises presented both visually and aurally, and then respond to a question making use of the logical premises;" and Mystery Codes – "Examinees study the identifying codes

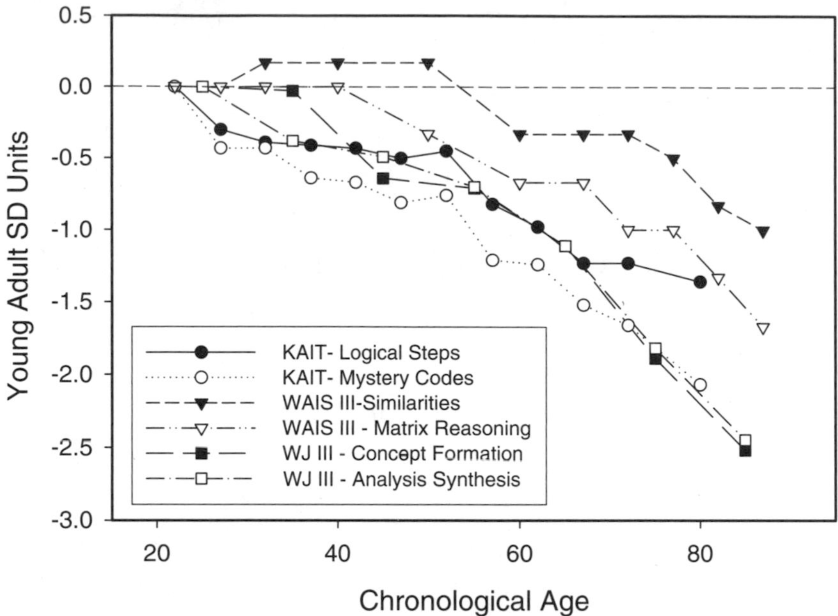

Figure 24.1. Relations of reasoning performance to age in variables from standardized tests. Sample sizes were 1,350 for the Kaufman Adolescent and Adult Intelligence Test (KAIT), 2,050 for the Wechsler Adult Intelligence Scale (WAIS) III, and 2,505 for the Woodcock Johnson (WJ) III.

associated with a set of pictorial stimuli and then figure out the code for a novel pictorial stimulus." Two reasoning tests included in the latest version of the Wechsler test battery, the Wechsler Adult Intelligence Scale III (Wechsler, 1997) were described in Table 24.1 of the Administration and Scoring Manual as follows: Similarities – "A series of orally presented pairs for which the examinee explains the similarity of the common objects or concepts they represent;" and Matrix Reasoning – "A series of incomplete gridded patterns that the examinee completes by pointing to or saying the number of the correct response from five possible choices." Finally, two reasoning tests included in the Woodcock–Johnson III (Woodcock, McGrew, & Mather, 2001) battery were described in Table 4.2 of the Examiner's Manual as follows: Concept Formation – "Identifying, categorizing, and determining rules;" and Analysis–Synthesis – "Analyzing puzzles (using symbolic formulations) to determine missing components."

To allow across-variable comparisons, the variables must be converted into the same scale, and a convenient scale for this purpose is standard deviation units. (These particular variables could have been expressed in units of percentage correct, but that scale is not as widely applicable because, for example, it is not meaningful when the variables are measured in units of time.) The manuals for these tests did not present the normative data in a form that would allow conversion of the scores to standard deviation units of the total sample. However, it was possible to express the scores in standard deviations of a young adult group, which has the advantage that the magnitude of the age-related effect can be expressed relative to the peak level of performance achieved across all ages. Age relations in the six reasoning tests just described therefore are portrayed in Figure 24.1 in standard deviation units of a reference group of young adults.

Examination of the figure reveals that all of the variables exhibit the same trend of lower performance with increased age. In particular, for most of the variables, the average seventy-year-old is performing about one standard deviation below the average

Matrix Reasoning

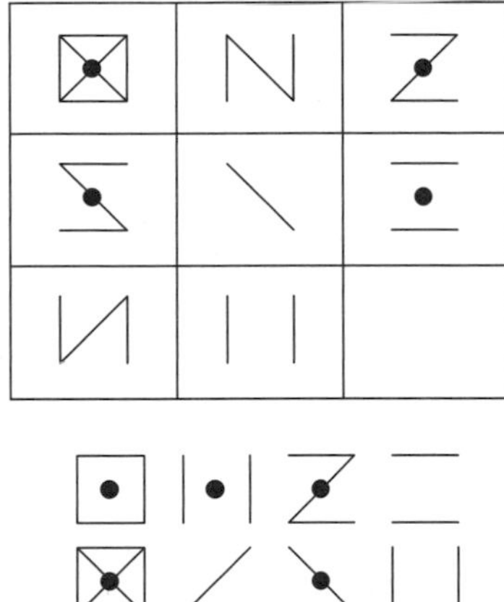

Analytical Reasoning

Jason and Jessica are planning a dinner party and have invited six guests: Mark and Meredith, Christopher and Courtney, and Shawn and Samantha. Their table seats three people on each side and one at each end. In planning the seating arrangements they need to: have Jason and Jessica sit at opposite ends of the table; place Christopher at a corner with no one on his left; not have Mark seated next to Samantha; and have Courtney seated next to Meredith.

Which of the following is an acceptable arrangement of diners along one side of the table?

- Jason, Samantha, Mark
- Christopher, Jessica, Shawn
- Mark, Courtney, Samantha
- Meredith, Shawn Courtney
- Shawn,Christopher,Meredith

Series Completion

13 – 15 – 20 – 28 – 39 - **???**

Integrative Reasoning

F and G do the SAME
E and F do the OPPOSITE
G and H do the OPPOSITE
If E increases will H decrease?

Figure 24.2. Examples of problems in four different reasoning tasks used in studies by Salthouse and colleagues. See text for details.

of the young adults. The age trends are not completely uniform because the age effects appear to be later and smaller for some variables (e.g., Similarities) than for other variables (e.g., Analysis–Synthesis). However, it is important to note that there is also considerable across-sample variation because the age gradients are shallower for both Wechsler subtests (i.e., Similarities and Matrix Reasoning) than for the subtests from the other batteries.

Relations between age and measures of reasoning can also be illustrated with four reasoning tasks used in several studies in my laboratory. Examples of problems in each type of task are portrayed in Figure 24.2. In matrix reasoning tasks (such as Raven's Progressive Matrices, Raven, 1962), the examinee attempts to select the best completion of the missing cell from the alternatives presented below the matrix. The goal in series completion tasks (such as the Shipley Abstraction Test, Zachary, 1986) is to determine the item that provides the best continuation of the sequence of items. In analytical reasoning tasks, the examinee uses the presented information to determine which of several alternatives best satisfies the specified constraints. Finally, examinees in integrative reasoning tasks use the information in the premises to answer a question about the relation between two of the variables. Although no formal evidence is available, it seems likely that these four tests represent somewhat different types of reasoning, and they certainly involve different requirements and types of material.

Because the tasks were each administered in two or more studies from my laboratory, the data have been combined across studies. The research participants in the studies were all similar in that they ranged from 18 to over 80 years of age, had an average of between 14 and 17 years of education, and generally reported themselves to be in good to excellent health.

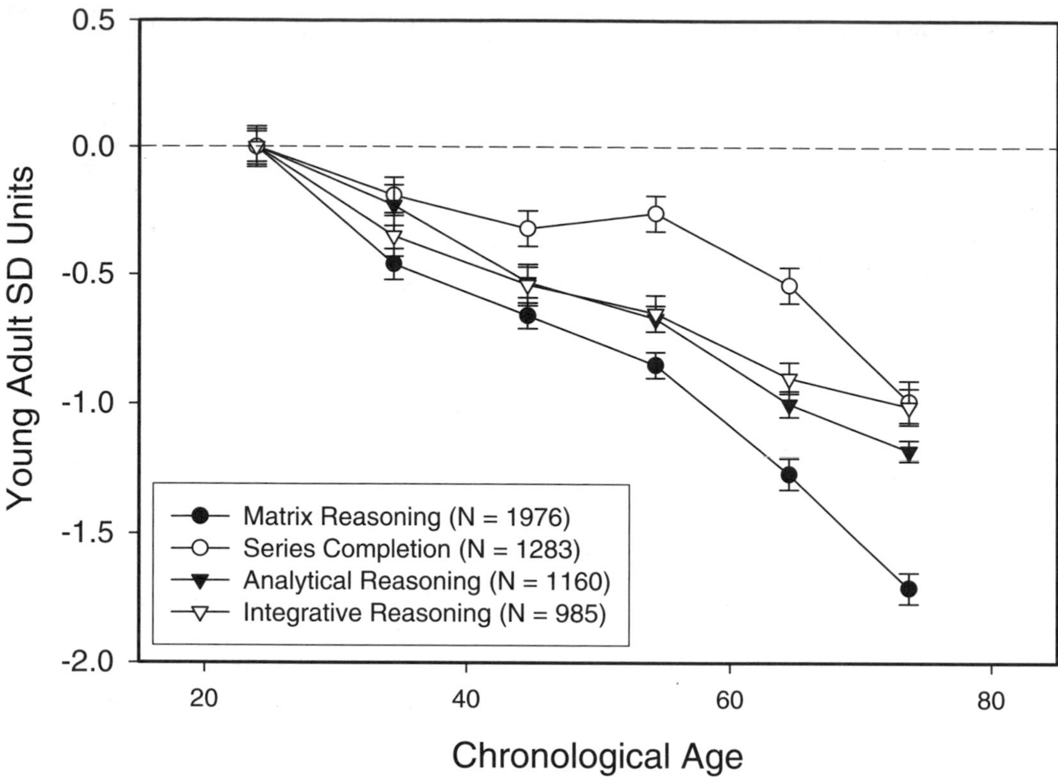

Figure 24.3. Means and standard errors of performance in four different reasoning tasks as a function of age. Data from various studies by Salthouse and colleagues.

Age relations in these four tasks are portrayed in Figure 24.3 in the same format used to display results of the tests from the psychometric test batteries. It can be seen that the pattern with these data closely resembles that from the normative samples in the standardized test batteries. In particular, there is an approximately linear decline in performance with increased age, such that the average at age seventy is about one standard deviation below the average of the reference group of young adults.

The age relations for three of the variables in Figure 24.3 were nearly identical, but the age function was shallower for the series completion variable. This may be because several items in the Shipley Abstraction series completion test (from which these data were derived) have considerable reliance on verbal knowledge, which tends to be relatively well preserved across this age range. For example, some of the items in that test involve determining relations among letters in reverse alphabetical sequence, or among words with particular semantic relations. Additional support for this differential-involvement-of-knowledge interpretation of the different age trends is provided by the correlations of the reasoning variables with a composite vocabulary variable, as the correlations were 0.37 for matrix reasoning, 0.23 for analytical reasoning, 0.24 for integrative reasoning, and 0.66 for series completion.

Although not apparent in Figures 24.1 and 24.3, other results indicate that the age relations on variables assessing reasoning are as large or, in some cases, even larger than the age relations on other types of cognitive variables. For example, Verhaeghen and Salthouse (1997) reported a meta-analysis in which the weighted correlation (based on 9,342 individuals across thirty-eight studies) between age and measures of reasoning was −.40, and the weighted correlation (based on 5,871 individuals across twenty-nine studies) between age and measures of episodic memory was −0.33. Furthermore, in analyses to be described later, the correlations between age and factor scores were very similar for factors based on memory (r = −0.48) and reasoning (r = −0.49) variables.

Despite their similar magnitude, age differences in reasoning are not as widely recognized as age differences in memory. A possible reason may be that considerable knowledge is required in many everyday situations that involve reasoning, such that any age effects might not be noticed either because of a large positive relation between age and knowledge, or because any deficiencies are attributed to lack of relevant knowledge instead of to problems of reasoning.

The primary question in light of age differences such as those apparent in Figures 24.1 and 24.3 is, "What is responsible for the large negative relations between age and performance on measures of reasoning?" Much of the research that has been conducted to address this question can be classified into one of two broad categories. One category consists of investigations of the influence of factors such as comprehension, speed, strategy, and working memory on the age differences in the performance of a particular reasoning task. The second category of research has involved examining age-related effects on measures of reasoning in the context of age-related effects on other cognitive abilities. In the remaining sections of this chapter, the two approaches are illustrated with research from my laboratory.

Process-Oriented Research

The majority of the empirical research in the area of cognitive aging has focused on a single cognitive variable (with different studies concentrating on different variables), and has attempted to determine the relative contribution of different processes to the age differences on that particular variable. Among the potential determinants of age differences in reasoning variables that have been investigated in this manner are comprehension, speed, strategy, and working memory. Empirical research relevant to each of these potential determinants is briefly summarized in this section.

Comprehension

It is conceivable that at least some of the age differences in reasoning are simply attributable to greater difficulties associated with increased age in understanding exactly what is required to perform the task successfully. This is an important possibility to consider because age differences in reasoning would probably not be of much theoretical interest if they merely reflected comprehension problems.

The primary means by which the comprehension interpretation has been investigated restricted comparisons to individuals for whom there is evidence that they understood the task requirements. For example, participants with accuracy less than some criterion value have been excluded from the analyses in integrative reasoning (Salthouse, 1992b, 1992c) and matrix reasoning (Salthouse & Skovronek, 1992) tasks, and analyses have been restricted to participants with correct responses on the first two items in the matrix reasoning (Salthouse, 1993) task. In each of these cases, strong negative age relations were evident among the participants who understood the tasks well enough to answer several problems correctly. These results therefore suggest that age differences in simple comprehension probably are not responsible for much, if any, of the age differences observed in measures of reasoning.

Speed

Another relatively uninteresting possibility is that age differences in measures of reasoning might merely reflect a slower rate of reading or of responding, without any detrimental effects on the quality of performance. Because effects of age-related slowing have been extensively documented (e.g., Salthouse, 1996a), it is important to consider whether age differences in reasoning might be attributable to slower peripheral processes associated with encoding or responding to the information.

One way in which the role of slower rates of input or output has been investigated involves examining age relations on reasoning tasks administered under untimed, or self-paced, conditions. Most of the comparisons have revealed significant age differences even when the participants are allowed to control the duration of the stimulus presentation, and take as long as they want to respond. Age differences in decision accuracy under these conditions have been found in geometric analogies (Salthouse, 1987), series completion (Salthouse & Prill, 1987), matrix reasoning (Salthouse, 1993; 1994; Salthouse & Skovronek, 1992), and integrative reasoning (Salthouse, 1992c; Salthouse et al., 1989; 1990) tasks, and in the Wisconsin Card Sorting Test (WCST; Salthouse et al., 1996; Fristoe, Salthouse, & Woodard, 1997; Salthouse et al., 2003).

The role of speed on age differences in matrix reasoning was examined more closely in two studies by Salthouse (1994) by obtaining separate measures of study time, decision time, and decision accuracy from each participant. Not only were significant age differences found on each measure, but analyses revealed that some of the age-related effects on the decision accuracy measure were statistically independent of the age-related effects on the study time and decision time measures. At least in this project, therefore, older adults took longer than younger adults to work on the problems and to communicate their decisions, and their decisions were less accurate.

A second method of investigating the role of limited time on age differences in reasoning involves examining age differences in the percentage of items answered correctly only for attempted items, as inferred by the presence of an overt response. Strong negative age relations have been found even when only attempted items were considered in integrative reasoning (Salthouse, 1992b), geometric analogies (Salthouse, 1992b), and matrix reasoning (Salthouse, 1991; 1993; 1994) tasks, and on the accuracy of early items in matrix reasoning and analytical reasoning tests that were attempted by everyone (Salthouse, 2000, 2001).

Taken in combination, the results just described suggest that adult age differences in reasoning are not simply attributable to slower rates of reading or responding. The speed of internal mental operations may be a factor in some of the performance differences (see Salthouse, 1996a), but because sizable age differences in accuracy are found when there are no external time constraints, the differences do not appear to be solely the result of slower rates of input or output.

Strategy

One of the most popular interpretations of age differences in cognitive functioning, at least in part because it implies that the age differences might be amenable to intervention, attributes them to the use of different strategies by adults of different ages. It is important to consider two issues when evaluating this distinction: whether or not adults of different ages actually do use different strategies when performing the task and, if so, what is responsible for those differences.

Information about the existence of possible strategy differences has been obtained by examining the distribution of study times across different parts of the reasoning problem. For example, the research participant could be instructed to press a key to view each element of the problem, and then the time between successive keystrokes could be recorded to determine the time devoted to inspecting or studying each element. Variants of this method have been used in a number of reasoning tasks with comparable outcomes. Specifically, the relative distribution of inspection or study times has been found to be similar in young and old adults in series completion (Salthouse & Prill, 1987), integrative reasoning (Salthouse et al., 1990), and geometric analogies (Salthouse 1987). To the extent that relative time allocation across different elements of a problem can be considered as evidence of a particular strategy, therefore, these results imply that young and old adults were using a similar strategy.

Additional evidence relevant to the strategy interpretation of age-related differences in reasoning is based on an examination of possible age differences in the pattern of incorrect alternatives selected when choosing a response. The rationale is that adults of different ages might be expected to differ in the frequency of selecting particular incorrect alternatives if they were relying on different rules or strategies to select their answers. However, no age differences in the relative percentages of different types of errors in a matrix reasoning task were found by Salthouse (1993; also see Babcock, 2002), which suggests that adults of different ages were probably using the same strategies but that the effectiveness of the strategies was lower with increased age.

Finally, a study by Fristoe, Salthouse, & Woodard (1997) was designed to investigate the manner in which young and old adults performed the WCST. The WCST is a concept identification test in which the stimuli consist of cards that vary in the number, color, and shape of objects. An unusual feature of the test is that the rule (i.e., number, color, or shape) used to determine the correct sorting of the cards changes after every 10 correct sorts without informing the participant. The participants in the Fristoe, Salthouse, & Woodard (1997) study were asked to indicate the dimension that they were using in making their decisions about how to sort stimulus cards. By combining this information with the responses selected and the feedback received after each response, it was possible to determine the percentage of times each participant maintained the same hypothesis after receiving positive feedback (i.e., "win–stay"), and the percentage of times he or she changed hypotheses after receiving negative feedback (i.e., "lose–shift").

Optimal performance in this type of feedback-based concept identification situation would be manifested in high percentages of "win–stay" and "lose–shift" behavior. Compared with young adults, older adults had lower percentages of both types of behavior, and statistical control of a composite measure of feedback usage reduced the age-related variance in a measure of WCST performance by 74%. These results clearly indicate that the young and old adults in this study performed the task in a somewhat different fashion and that the difference was related to success in the task. However, because there was no evidence that the older adults were as capable as the young adults of performing in the same optimal manner, it is questionable whether the differences observed in the way the task was performed should be considered evidence for differences in strategy, which has a voluntary or optional connotation.

Although only a limited amount of relevant evidence is currently available, it does not appear that much, if any, of the age-related differences in reasoning can be explained by differences in the strategies used to perform the task. Furthermore, it is important to recognize that, even if evidence of strategy differences were available, interpretations based on strategy differences are likely to be somewhat ambiguous unless an explanation is also provided for why people of different ages used different strategies. That is, if strategy differences were to be found, a critical question is whether the most effective or optimal strategy is still feasible for older adults but not used for some reason, or whether older adults are less able to use the more powerful or optimal strategy than young adults. As a result, a difference in strategy might be viewed merely as a different level of description, such that if age differences were to be found, they would still need to be explained, just as would age differences in measures of overall task performance.

Working Memory

An interpretation that has generated considerable interest, particularly since a provocative article by Kyllonen and Christal (1990) that reported a very strong relation between measures of working memory (WM) and measures of reasoning (see Morrison, Chap. 19), is that at least some of the age-related differences in reasoning might be attributable to age differences in WM. Because WM has been defined as the ability to preserve information while processing the same or other information, and because many reasoning tasks require that information be maintained in order for it to be operated upon, interpreting the age differences in reasoning as a function of WM has considerable intuitive plausibility.

One method used to investigate the role of WM in reasoning involves manipulation of the number of premises presented in integrative reasoning problems. The rationale that increasing the number of premises would increase the WM requirements, which might then be expected to increase the magnitude of the age differences in reasoning performance if at least some of those differences are attributable to WM limitations. Support for this expectation was provided in four independent studies (Salthouse, 1992b, 1992c; Salthouse et al., 1989; Salthouse et al., 1990). In each study, reasoning accuracy decreased as the number of premises increased, and the magnitude of this decrease was greater for older adults than for young adults.

Another manipulation incorporated in several integrative reasoning studies involved the presentation of trials in which only one of the premises was relevant to the decision. Consider the problem portrayed in the lower right panel of Figure 24.2, for example. In the version displayed, all of the premises are relevant to the decision and would need to be considered to reach a valid conclusion. If, instead of referring to variables E and H, the question referred to variables E and F, however, all of the information relevant to the decision would have been presented in a single premise. These "one-relevant" trials are interesting because no across-premise integration of information is required for a correct decision, and the major determinant of quality of performance therefore is presumably the ability to maintain the relevant information in memory until it is needed. (In these particular studies, the task was administered on a computer and only one premise was visible at a time.)

A consistent finding in each of these studies (i.e., Salthouse, 1992c; Salthouse et al., 1989; Salthouse et al., 1990) was that the relation of accuracy to the number of premises was nearly identical when only one premise was relevant and when two or more premises were relevant. Furthermore, this pattern was similar across adults of all ages. These results therefore suggest that the primary reason why accuracy was lower when the problems contained more premises was related to the availability of information and not to difficulties in integrating relevant information. The fact that the pattern was similar in adults of all ages further implies that the age differences in this task are largely attributable to differences in the availability of relevant information.

An additional expectation from the information-availability interpretation is that age differences should be evident in the shape of the serial position functions relating decision accuracy to sequential position of the relevant premise. In fact, Salthouse et al. (1990) did find that young adults exhibited a classical serial position function, with higher accuracy for the more recent premises, whereas the function for older adults was flat. However, for reasons that are not yet clear, this pattern was not replicated in a later study by Salthouse (1992c).

Manipulation of the number of problem elements has also been examined in geometric analogy and matrix reasoning tasks, with somewhat different patterns of results. To illustrate, three studies found that age differences in measures of decision time, decision accuracy, or both, were larger when there were more relevant elements in geometric analogy problems (Salthouse, 1987, 1988, 1992c). In several studies reported by Salthouse (1993) and in a study by Salthouse (1994), however, age differences in a matrix reasoning task were nearly constant across increases in the number of relations among elements, and in none of these studies was there a significant interaction between age and number of relations in the problem. Specific characteristics of the tasks may be responsible for the different patterns of results across integrative reasoning, geometric analogy, and matrix reasoning tasks, but the exact nature of those characteristics is not yet known.

Another method used to investigate the role of WM in reasoning involves assessing on-line availability of information during the performance of the task. For example, Salthouse (1993) and Salthouse and Skovronek (1992) presented a successive version of the matrix reasoning task in which each matrix cell was numbered. To view a cell in the matrix, the participant had to type the corresponding number. In three separate studies, older adults were found to examine the same cell more frequently than young adults, as though the information inspected earlier was no longer functionally available to them. Furthermore, when presented with probes of information examined earlier, older adults were less accurate than young adults in recognizing the contents of previously viewed cells (Salthouse, 1993).

A final piece of evidence relevant to the WM interpretation of age differences in reasoning is that Salthouse (1992c) found a qualitatively similar pattern of differences between young and old adults, and between young adults with and without a concurrent memory load (of five random digits). To the extent that a concurrent memory load is viewed as simulating reduced WM capacity, this finding is consistent with the hypothesis that at least some of the age differences in the integrative reasoning task are attributable to age differences in WM.

In summary, results from a number of different types of comparisons in a variety of reasoning tasks lend credibility to the interpretation that the ability to maintain relevant information during the performance of reasoning tasks likely contributes to at least some of the adult age differences in reasoning. Although the available evidence suggests that working memory is probably involved in the age differences in reasoning, the exact extent of that involvement, and the role of other factors in the age differences, remain to be determined.

Correlational Analyses

The second major approach to investigating adult age differences in cognition has relied upon correlational data to attempt to specify the number and nature of statistically distinct age-related influences operating on different types of cognitive variables. In this section, results relevant to understanding effects of aging on reasoning based on mediational, componential, correlated-factors, and hierarchical structure models are described briefly.

Mediational Models

The goal of mediational models is to examine the role of one or more constructs as potential mediators of the age differences in measures of reasoning by means of statistical adjustment. The rationale is that if age-related effects on variable Y are at least partially attributable to age-related effects on variable X, then statistical control of X should reduce the magnitude of the age-related effects on Y. For the purpose of these analyses, X could be a measure of any factor hypothesized to be important in the target variable, Y. Most of the mediational models applied to reasoning have used measures of WM in the role of X because of the assumption that reasoning tasks frequently require that earlier information be preserved when processing later information, and individuals who are better able to do that, as reflected by higher scores on WM tasks, therefore would be expected to perform at higher levels on reasoning tasks.

Several studies in my laboratory have relied upon two tasks to assess WM. Both require participants to remember information while simultaneously processing other information. In the computation span task, for example, arithmetic problems had to be answered while remembering the last digit in each problem, and in the listening span sk, questions about a sentence had to be answered while remembering the last word in each sentence. Measures of performance in these tasks have been found to exhibit good reliability, and to be negatively correlated with age.

Three sets of results are necessary to establish the plausibility of a mediational interpretation of age-related differences in reasoning. The first is the demonstration of age-related differences in the expected direction in measures of the hypothesized mediator, because a construct cannot mediate age differences in other variables or constructs if it is not related to age. The second necessary result is the existence of a moderate relation between the hypothesized mediator and the target variable it is presumed to explain, because no mediation is possible if the suspected mediator and the target variable are not related to one another. Third, age-related differences in the target variable should be reduced after statistical control of the mediator, with the magnitude of the reduction serving as an approximate index of the degree of mediation. This last result is critical because mediation is not plausible if the relations of age to the target variable are not at least moderately attenuated when the variability in the hypothesized mediator is eliminated.

A variety of procedures can be used to statistically control the hypothesized mediator, such as partial correlation, semipartial correlation (available from hierarchical regression), analysis of covariance, and so on. In each case, the goal is to eliminate the variance in the target variable that is related to the mediator such that relations between age and the target variable can be examined when differences in the level of the mediator no longer influence the target variable.

The most relevant comparisons from mediational analyses of WM on reasoning are those between the initial age relation on the reasoning variable and the age–reasoning relation after statistical control of the WM measure. A consistent finding across several different types of reasoning tasks has been a substantial reduction in the age-related variance after statistical control of WM, with reductions of 57% (Salthouse et al., 1989), 88% (Salthouse, 1992b; also see Salthouse, 1991), and 48% (Salthouse, 1992c) in integrative reasoning tasks, 65% in a geometric analogies task (Salthouse, 1992b), and 43% to 84% in matrix reasoning tasks (Salthouse, 1993). Similar findings have been reported by other researchers with matrix reasoning (Babcock, 1994) and syllogistic reasoning (Fisk & Sharp, 2002; Gilinsky & Judd, 1994) tasks. Sizable reductions in the age-related differences after control of WM have been found even with percentage correct measures (Salthouse, 1992b) and on the accuracy of individual items in a matrix reasoning task (Salthouse, 1993). A significant relation of WM on two-premise and three-premise integrative reasoning problems also has been found after control of the influence of one-premise problems (Salthouse, 1992b, 1996b), which implies that WM specifically contributes to the maintenance of information needed in more complex problems.

This pattern of results clearly is consistent with the hypothesized influence of WM on age-related differences in reasoning. However, it is important to recognize that comparable, and sometimes even larger, reductions in the age-related effects in reasoning have been found after statistical control of other theoretical constructs, such as perceptual speed (e.g., Salthouse, 1991, 1993, 1994, 1996a). Because most cognitive variables are positively correlated with one another, some attenuation of the age-related effects on one cognitive variable likely would be expected after statistical control of almost any other cognitive variable. A discovery of attenuated age-related variance after statistical control of a hypothesized mediator therefore should be considered only necessary, but not sufficient, evidence for the validity of mediational hypotheses.

Componential Models

Componential models are more complex than mediational models because they postulate that nearly every cognitive task involves multiple processes or components, and that performance of the task is influenced by the efficiency or effectiveness of each component. Componential models have been investigated by relying upon the pattern of correlations among measures of the components and a measure of performance on the target reasoning task to determine the relative contribution of each hypothesized component. For example, a researcher might postulate that components A, B, and C are required to perform a particular task, administer tasks to obtain variables that reflect A, B, and C as directly as possible, and then examine correlations among the variables based on the reasoning tasks and the component tasks. Componential models can be applied to research on aging by determining the degree to which age-related effects on the target reasoning task are altered when variability in measures of the components is statistically controlled.

Componential models of the matrix reasoning and analytical reasoning tasks were investigated by Salthouse (2001), and a somewhat different componential analysis of age differences in matrix reasoning was reported by Babcock (1994). Salthouse hypothesized three components were involved in each of the tasks: rule identification, rule application, and information integration in the matrix reasoning task; and simple comprehension, information integration, and condition verification in the analytical reasoning task. Primarily on the basis of intuition and judgments of face validity, two variables were selected to represent each hypothesized component. To illustrate, the rule identification component was assessed by a Figure Classification test, in which examinees determine the basis by which different figures are related to one another, and by a Location test, in which examinees determine the rule governing the position of a set of Xs in each row of a matrix. The rule application component was assessed with two tasks (i.e., Pattern Transformation and Geometric Transformation) in which the examinee views an initial line pattern or geometric figure, carries out a specified transformation (such as rotation, subtraction, or addition), and then decides whether the transformation applied to the initial figure would match a comparison figure.

A critical prerequisite for a componential analysis is that the pattern of correlations and, specifically, the results from a confirmatory factor analysis, should provide evidence for distinct constructs. That is, only if there is evidence that the variables represent separate constructs is it meaningful to examine their relative contributions to the age differences in the performance of the criterion reasoning task. The results of the two studies reported by Salthouse (2001) were not consistent with the existence of three separate factors because all of the variables had similar correlations with one another. To illustrate, the correlation between the two-rule identification variables was 0.50, and their correlations with variables hypothesized to reflect the rule application component ranged from 0.48 to 0.62. Because there was no evidence that the hypothesized components represented distinct dimensions of individual differences (i.e., exhibited construct validity), it was impossible in these studies to decompose the age differences in the target tasks into discrete components.

There are at least three possible interpretations of results such as those just described. First, the theoretical models may not have been valid because the designated components are not actually required to perform the tasks. Second, the models could have been valid and the components might have been relevant to performance on the target task, but the components were not accurately assessed with the selected tasks. And third, the models may not have been valid because the hypothesized components do not actually exist as distinct entities. Unfortunately, the available data do not allow these alternatives to be distinguished. However, it is worth considering whether a similar situation may exist in componential models of other cognitive tasks but has not been recognized because there have seldom been any attempts to investigate the construct validity of the hypothesized processes or components. Results of the Salthouse (2001) project therefore suggest that it is important to obtain empirical evidence of the construct validity of hypothesized components before investigating their role in cognitive tasks.

Correlated Factor Models

The variables included in mediational and componential models typically have been selected because of their presumed relevance to the target variable one is trying to explain. An alternative approach based on correlational data would be to consider the interrelations among a broad variety of cognitive variables in terms of some organizational structure and then examine relations of age to the target variable within the context of that structure.

The simplest organizational structure is one in which the variables are grouped into several first-order factors or abilities, with the factors allowed to correlate with one another. Age-related effects on specific reasoning variables can be investigated in this type of correlated-factors structure by determining the degree to which the age-related effects on the target reasoning variable are direct or are indirect and operate through one or more cognitive abilities.

The ideal data set for analyses involving cognitive abilities would involve a wide variety of cognitive variables, and as large and diverse a sample of participants as possible. No single study is likely to possess all of these characteristics, but an approximation to this ideal can be obtained by aggregating data across different studies involving different combinations of variables. Aggregation of the data in this way essentially treats the individuals as though they were participants in a single large study but with missing values for the variables that were not collected in the particular study in which an individual participated. Although data with a large proportion of missing values can be complicated to analyze, meaningful analyses can be conducted by relying on an algorithm such as the full information maximum likelihood procedure (e.g., Enders & Bandalos, 2001) to take advantage of all available information.

A combined data set of this type was created by aggregating data across 33 separate studies from my laboratory involving a total of 6,828 individuals. The major variables included in the aggregate data set are listed in Table 24.1 together with the respective sample sizes and age correlations. Entries in the right-most columns in Table 24.1 are the factor loadings from a confirmatory factor analysis in which factors corresponding to reasoning, spatial visualization, episodic memory, perceptual speed, and vocabulary abilities were postulated. As expected, the loadings of the variables on the factors all were high, with only four below 0.7, and the factors were moderately correlated with one another. A second model examined relations between age and each of the ability factors. These (standardized) relations were −0.49 for reasoning, −0.41 for space, −0.48 for episodic memory, 0.63 for speed, and 0.25 for vocabulary.

Inspection of the coefficients in the reasoning column reveals that the matrix reasoning and analytical reasoning variables both had high loadings on the reasoning factor and therefore can be considered prototypical reasoning tasks. The contributions of the five abilities to these two variables therefore were examined by modifying the analysis to specify relations of each of the five abilities to these variables. In effect, these analyses are asking what abilities contribute, and by how much, to the individual differences in performance of these tests. The top panel of Table 24.2 summarizes results of these analyses, where it can be seen that, as expected, the strongest relation of each variable was with the reasoning factor. However, it is important to note that each variable also had significant relations with factors representing other cognitive abilities. Both the matrix reasoning and the analytical reasoning variables were positively related to spatial visualization ability and negatively related to vocabulary ability. This latter relation is rather puzzling because it suggests that, when other relations are taken into consideration, people with higher levels of vocabulary tend to perform somewhat worse on these reasoning tasks than people with lower levels of vocabulary.

This simple structure can be used to estimate the indirect effects of age on reasoning

Table 24.1. Results of a Confirmatory Factor Analysis on Data Aggregated across Multiple Studies

			Factor Loading				
Variable	*N*	*Age r*	*Rea*	*Spc*	*Mem*	*Spd*	*Voc*
Matrix reasoning	1976	−.50	.87				
Analytical reasoning	1160	−.46	.76				
Shipley abstraction	1283	−.29	.87				
Integrative reasoning	985	−.35	.62				
Figure classification	458	−.60	.74				
Cattell matrices	420	−.48	.82				
Letter sets	1179	−.26	.80				
Geometric analogies	756	−.36	.78				
PMA reasoning	305	−.41	.86				
Grammatical reasoning	229	−.35	.80				
Series completion	150	−.37	.80				
Analysis synthesis	204	−.36	.79				
Power letter series	150	−.47	.93				
WCST number of categories	711	−.28	.56				
Diagramming relations	449	−.40	.76				
Locations	449	−.41	.60				
Spatial relations	1154	−.34		.91			
Paper folding	994	−.43		.81			
Form boards	847	−.38		.80			
Surface development	639	−.32		.72			
PMA space	305	−.39		.76			
Block design	463	−.39		.89			
Object assembly	259	−.41		.81			
Cube assembly	1272	−.17		.60			
Paired associates	1769	−.38			.72		
Free recall	1764	−.42			.84		
Logical memory	793	−.24			.72		
Free recall of transfer list	1054	−.35			.77		
Digit symbol	2041	−.57				.78	
Letter comparison	6082	−.43				.79	
Pattern comparison	6082	−.52				.82	
Cross out	204	−.71				.92	
Digit symbol reaction time	2417	−.56				.77	
WAIS vocabulary	795	.13					.86
WJ picture vocabulary	795	.30					.80
Antonym vocabulary	3509	.18					.90
Synonym vocabulary	3511	.27					.89
Shipley vocabulary	259	.22					.93
Factor correlations							
	Reasoning (Rea)		–	.88	.73	.79	.47
	Space (Spc)			–	.65	.67	.46
	Memory (Mem)				–	.70	.42
	Speed (Spd)					–	.28
	Vocabulary (Voc)						–

Notes: N = number, Age r = , Rea = reasoning, Spc = space, Mem = memory, Spd = speed, Voc = vocabulary, PMA = Primary Mental Abilities, WCST = Wisconsin Card Sorting Test, WAIS = Wechsler Adult Intelligence Scale, WJ = Woodcock–Johnson.

Table 24.2. Loadings of Matrix Reasoning and Analytical Reasoning Variables on Five Cognitive Abilities

	Rea	*Spc*	*Mem*	*Spd*	*Voc*
All					
Matrix reasoning	.86*	.25*	−.06	−.07	−.20*
Analytical reasoning	.76*	.25*	−.04	−.13	−.17*
Matrix reasoning					
Under age 50	.97*	.18	−.11	−.08	−.20*
Age 50 and over	.79*	.30*	−.02	−.02	−.21*
Analytical reasoning					
Under age 50	.91*	.01	−.04	−.04	−.10
Age 50 and over	.50*	.46*	−.04	−.09	−.17

*$p < .01$
Note: None of the coefficients for the under-age fifty group and the age-fifty-and-over group was significantly different from one another.
Rea = reasoning, Spc = space, Mem = memory, Spd = speed, Voc = vocabulary.

variables by incorporating information about the relations between age and each ability. To illustrate, because the standardized coefficient for the relation from age to the reasoning ability factor was −0.49, and that for the relation between the reasoning factor and the matrix reasoning variable was 0.87, it can be inferred that −0.43 (i.e., −0.49 × 0.87) of the total −0.50 age effect on matrix reasoning (cf. Table 24.1) is associated with influences through the reasoning ability factor.

The correlated-factors structure can also be used to investigate whether the variables represent the same constructs to the same degree at different ages (i.e., the issue of measurement equivalence). The preceding analyses therefore were repeated in samples of adults under and over the age of 50, with the results summarized in the bottom panels of Table 24.2. Inspection of the entries indicates that the pattern of ability relations for the matrix reasoning variable was very similar in the two age groups, consisting of a large positive relation with the reasoning factor, a small positive relation with the spatial visualization factor, and a small negative relation with the vocabulary factor. Although the pattern appears somewhat different across the two age groups for the analytical reasoning variable, a direct test in which the parameters were constrained to be equal in the two samples to determine if there was a significant loss of fit to the data indicated that the group differences were not statistically significant. It therefore appears from these results that the two reasoning variables represent nearly the same combination of abilities at different ages. These particular results should be replicated before reaching any strong conclusions, but they serve to illustrate how correlational results can be informative about the possibility of qualitative differences in performance at different ages.

Hierarchical Structure Models

The correlated-factors model can be considered relatively simple because, although the factors are allowed to correlate with one another, there is no attempt to explain the basis for those correlations in the context of the model. A somewhat more complicated model involves a hierarchical structure in which one or more higher-order factors are postulated to be responsible for the relations among the first-order factors (Carroll, 1993). An advantage of hierarchical models for the investigation of age-related effects is that they allow broad (on the higher-order common factor) and narrow (on the first-order ability factors) age-related influences to be examined simultaneously.

A hierarchical analysis was conducted on the combined data summarized in Table 24.1 by examining the relations of age

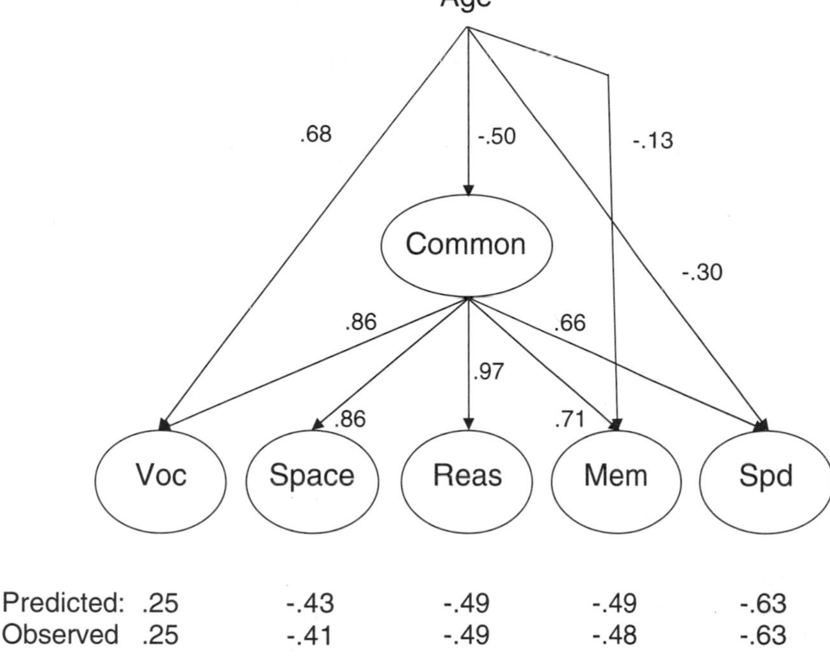

Figure 24.4. Hierarchical structural model of age relations on different cognitive abilities based on the data summarized in Table 24.1. Numbers adjacent to the arrows are standardized regression coefficients, and numbers in the bottom two rows are correlations between age and the latent construct directly above.

to a second-order factor representing variance common to the first-order factors and to each first-order factor, and then deleting all relations from age that were not significantly different from zero. Because the aggregation of data from samples with different combinations of variables results in a very high proportion of missing values for most variables, conventional measures of fit are not readily available in analyses with this type of data. However, the observed age-factor correlations can be compared with those predicted from the parameters of the model, and inspection of the entries at the bottom of Figure 24.4 indicates that the predicted age correlations were very close to the observed age correlations, implying that the model is plausible.

The coefficients provided from the hierarchical structure analysis on these data are portrayed in Figure 24.4, where it can be seen that four statistically independent age-related influences were identified. There was a large negative influence of age on the highest-order factor, a moderate positive influence on the vocabulary factor, and small to moderate negative influences on factors corresponding to speed and memory abilities. A very similar pattern recently was found by Salthouse and Ferrer-Caja (2003) in analyses of three separate data sets, so these results apparently are robust.

The hierarchical structure represented in Figure 24.4, together with the factor loadings presented in Table 24.1, can be used to estimate age-related influences on individual variables. Because the product of the standardized path coefficients provides an estimate of the expected correlation between the variables, the product of the age-common, common-reasoning, and reasoning-variable coefficients can be compared with the observed age-variable correlation to determine how accurately the model and its estimated parameters reproduce the actual relations in the data. The predicted age correlation for the matrix reasoning variable was −0.42, the observed correlation was −0.50, and corresponding predicted and observed values for the analytical reasoning variable were −0.37 and −0.46, respectively. With these particular variables, therefore, the age relations are underestimated by the model, which implies that additional paths, such as a direct negative relation from age to the variable, may be necessary to provide more accurate estimates of the true covariations in the data.

One of the most interesting results in Figure 24.4, which was also apparent in the analyses reported by Salthouse and Ferrer-Caja (2003), is that the reasoning factor was the first-order factor with the strongest relation to what is common to all variables. In fact, the standardized coefficient of 0.97 in Figure 24.4 indicates that there was almost complete overlap of the individual differences in the reasoning factor with the individual differences in what is common to several different cognitive abilities. This finding is intriguing because it suggests that an explanation of the age differences in reasoning likely also will explain much of the age-related influences on other cognitive abilities, and vice versa.

Conclusions and Future Directions

Large age differences have been found in many measures of reasoning, and in some cases the differences are as large as those found in measures of other cognitive abilities such as memory. There still is no convincing explanation of the causes of age-related effects on reasoning, although the available evidence suggests that aspects of WM likely contribute to at least some of these effects. Results of correlational analyses suggest that reasoning variables are central to what is common across a wide variety of cognitive abilities and to the age differences in different cognitive abilities. It therefore seems reasonable to expect that an understanding of age-related effects on reasoning may help explain much of the age-related differences in a broad variety of cognitive variables. Finally, because of the centrality of reasoning to the individual differences in much of cognitive functioning, future research likely will benefit from a broader, more multivariate, perspective than that typically employed in contemporary research and by considering the effects of aging on what is common to many different types of cognitive variables instead of focusing exclusively on the determinants of age-related differences in one particular task.

Acknowledgments

Research described in this chapter was supported by National Institute on Aging Grants R37-06826; RO1-06858, and RO1-19627.

References

Babcock, R. L. (1994). Analysis of the adult age differences on the Raven's Advanced Progressive Matrices Test. *Psychology and Aging*, 9, 303–314.

Babcock, R. L. (2002). Analysis of age differences in types of errors on the Raven's Advanced Progressive Matrices. *Intelligence*, 30, 485–503.

Carroll, J. B. (1993). *Human Cognitive Abilities: A Survey of Factor Analytic Studies*. New York: Cambridge University Press.

Enders, C. K., & Bandalos, D. L. (2001). The relative performance of full information maximum likelihood estimation for missing data in structural equation models. *Structural Equation Modeling*, 8, 430–437.

Fisk, J. E., & Sharp, C. (2002). Syllogistic reasoning and cognitive aging. *Quarterly Journal of Experimental Psychology*, 55, 1273–1293.

Fristoe, N. M., Salthouse, T. A., & Woodard, J. L. (1997). Examination of age-related deficits on the Wisconsin Card Sorting Test. *Neuropsychology*, 11, 428–436.

Gilinsky, A. S., & Judd, B. B. (1994). Working memory and bias in reasoning across the life span. *Psychology and Aging*, 9, 356–371.

Kaufman, A. S. & Kaufman, N. L. (1993). *Kaufman Adolescent and Adult Intelligence Test (KAIT)*. Circle Pines, MN: American Guidance Service.

Kyllonen, P. C., & Christal, R. E. (1990). Reasoning ability is (little more than) working-memory capacity?! *Intelligence*, 14, 389–433.

Raven, J. (1962). *Advanced Progressive Matrices, Set II*. London: H. K. Lewis.

Salthouse, T. A. (1987). The role of representations in age differences in analogical reasoning. *Psychology and Aging*, 2, 357–362.

Salthouse, T. A. (1988). The role of processing resources in cognitive aging. In M. L. Howe, & C. J. Brainerd (Eds.), *Cognitive Development in Adulthood*. New York: Springer-Verlag.

Salthouse, T. A. (1991). Mediation of adult age differences in cognition by reductions in working memory and speed of processing. *Psychological Science*, 2, 179–183.

Salthouse, T. A. (1992a). Reasoning and spatial abilities. In F. I. M. Craik & T. A. Salthouse (Eds.)., *Handbook of Aging and Cognition*. Hillsdale, N.J.: Erlbaum.

Salthouse, T. A. (1992b). Why do adult age differences increase with task complexity? *Developmental Psychology*, 28, 905–918.

Salthouse, T. A. (1992c). Working memory mediation of adult age differences in integrative reasoning. *Memory and Cognition*, 20, 413–423.

Salthouse, T. A. (1993). Influence of working memory on adult age differences in matrix reasoning. *British Journal of Psychology*, 84, 171–199.

Salthouse, T. A. (1994). The nature of the influence of speed on adult age differences in cognition. *Developmental Psychology*, 30, 240–259.

Salthouse, T. A. (1996a). The processing speed theory of adult age differences in cognition. *Psychological Review*, 103, 403–428.

Salthouse, T. A. (1996b) Where in an ordered sequence of variables do independent age-related effects occur? *Journal of Gerontology: Psychological Sciences*, 51 *B*, P166–P178.

Salthouse, T. A. (2000). Item analyses of age relations on reasoning tests. *Psychology and Aging*, 15, 3–8.

Salthouse, T. A. (2001). Attempted decomposition of age-related influences on two tests of reasoning. *Psychology and Aging*, 16, 251–263.

Salthouse, T. A., & Ferrer-Caja, E. (2003). What needs to be explained to account for age-related effects on multiple cognitive variables? *Psychology and Aging*, 18, 91–110.

Salthouse, T. A., Legg, S. E., Palmon, R., & Mitchell, D. R. D. (1990). Memory factors in age-related differences in simple reasoning. *Psychology and Aging*, 5, 9–15.

Salthouse, T. A., Mitchell, D. R. D., Skovronek, E., & Babcock, R. L. (1989). Effects of adult age and working memory on reasoning and spatial abilities. *Journal of Experimental Psychology: Learning, Memory, and Cognition*, 15, 507–516.

Salthouse, T. A., & Prill, K. A. (1987). Inferences about age impairments in inferential reasoning. *Psychology and Aging*, 2, 43–51.

Salthouse, T. A., Atkinson, T. M., & Berish, D. E. (2003). Executive functioning as a potential mediator of age-related cognitive decline in normal adults. *Journal of Experimental Psychology, General*, 132, 566–594.

Salthouse, T. A., Fristoe, N., & Rhee, S. H. (1996). How localized are age-related effects on neuropsychological measures? *Neuropsychology*, 10, 272–285.

Salthouse, T. A., & Skovronek, E. (1992). Within-context assessment of age differences in working memory. *Journal of Gerontology: Psychological Sciences*, 47, P110–P120.

Verhaeghen, P., & Salthouse, T. A. (1997). Meta-analyses of age-cognition relations in adulthood: Estimates of linear and non-linear age effects and structural models. *Psychological Bulletin*, 122, 231–249.

Wechsler, D. (1997). *Wechsler Adult Intelligence Scale – Third Edition*. San Antonio, TX: The Psychological Corp.

Woodcock, R. W., McGrew, K. S., & Mather, N. (2001). *Woodcock-Johnson III Tests of Cognitive Abilities*. Itasca, IL: Riverside.

Zachary, R. A. (1986). *Shipley Institute of Living Scale – Revised*. Los Angeles, CA: Western Psychological Services.

CHAPTER 25

Reasoning and Thinking in Nonhuman Primates

Josep Call
Michael Tomasello

Fifty years ago, a chapter with the title "Reasoning and Thinking in Nonhuman Primates" would have been a very short chapter. Behaviorists, of course, did not believe in reasoning and thinking, and people who studied animals in their natural habitats (eventually known as ethologists) were interested in other things. In the 1960s, the cognitive revolution transformed the way psychologists studied human behavior and cognition, but much of this research was about human symbolic, propositional representations ("the language of thought") and was not easily applied to research with nonhuman animals. The cognitive revolution thus came to the study of animal behavior only very slowly. But during the past two decades, it has arrived, and in the modern study of animal behavior, questions of cognition are among the most prominent.

Scientists who study animals typically have a background in biology, so everything flows from the theory of evolution. These behavioral biologists and psychobiologists are interested in how animals adapt to their environments – both physically and behaviorally. In this context, some behavioral adaptations may be considered cognitive in the sense that they involve the individual organism's learning and reasoning and thinking on the basis of its own individual experience before deciding on the best way to act in a given circumstance. There are specifiable ecological circumstances in which evolution favors the greater flexibility afforded by cognitive adaptations, as opposed to, for example, hardwiring specific behavioral responses to specific environmental stimuli (Boyd & Richerson, 1985).

In the case of nonhuman primates in particular, there were actually two pioneers in cognitive research in the early part of the twentieth century. In Germany, Wolfgang Köhler was a Gestalt psychologist interested in intelligence as something that took organisms beyond punctate sensations and blind trial-and-error learning. He studied a small group of chimpanzees in a variety of problem-solving situations, looking for cases of perceptual restructuring and insight (Köhler, 1925). In America, Robert Yerkes studied a variety of behavioral phenomena in a number of primate species. His work included studies in which animals had to solve complex cognitive problems. In the middle part of the century, behaviorists studied such things as the speed with which different species could be taught through reward-based training to make discriminations, form learning sets, and the like (Harlow, 1959; Rumbaugh, 1970) – phenomena which, today, could be given interesting cognitive interpretations.

The most exciting work in the modern context comes under the two titles "comparative cognition" and "cognitive ethology," however. The former often refers to experimental work in the laboratory, and the latter often refers to observational work in the natural environment. Ideally, for any given phenomenon, the two approaches provide complementary types of information.

Our aim in this chapter is to provide an up-to-date overview of research on thinking and reasoning in nonhuman primates (henceforth, simply "primates"). Thinking and reasoning, in our view, are characterized by mental transformations or leaps, not just direct perception or memory of particular stimuli; going "beyond the information given." We therefore focus on primates solving novel problems – that is, those that require them to do more than simply learn and remember. In terms of content, we focus on topics that constitute aspects of human cognition represented by other chapters in the current volume, focusing in each case on both selected classic studies and the latest research findings. Our main topics are spatial (Tversky, Chap. 10), relational, analogical (Holyoak, Chap. 6), inferential, quantitative (Gallistel & Gelman, Chap. 23), causal (Buehner & Cheng, Chap. 7), and social reasoning and thinking. Although the chapter is mainly about primates, readers interested in fuller accounts of animal cognition in general are referred to books published in the past few years (Pepperberg, 1999; Roberts, 1998; Shettleworth, 1998; Tomasello & Call, 1997; Vauclair, 1996).

Spatial Reasoning

The spatial behavior and cognition of primates and other animals is a very large field of research. Here we explore two aspects: (1) how individuals navigate in large-scale locomotor space while traveling and (2) how individuals search for objects more locally in small-scale manipulatory space. In both cases, the key skills involved in thinking and reasoning enable an individual to predict things – namely, the best path for its own locomotion or the likely future position of moving objects.

Travel Strategies

DETOURS

The use of detours was one of the main issues investigated by Köhler (1925) with chimpanzees. He found that they were capable of taking alternative routes to a goal when the direct route was blocked. Since then, little additional research has been done except in other animals species such as chickens or dogs. Recently, however, several researchers used computerized systems to present mazes. Here, the subject does not move, but it moves a cursor through the maze to get to a goal box. This is a good tool to investigate detours because mazes often involve the use of detours in which subjects have to move away from the direct approach to the goal box and use an indirect route to reach it. Iversen and Matsuzawa (2001) trained two chimpanzees to navigate through mazes presented on a computer touch screen. Chimpanzees gradually mastered a series of mazes of increasing difficulty. One of the chimpanzees learned to use detours when the route on a familiar maze was blocked and later was able to use detours on novel mazes. The authors indicated, however, that subjects did not fully develop a generalized ability to solve mazes, and some practice with the particular mazes seemed to be required to solve the problem.

SHORTCUTS

Fieldworkers often report that several species of primates travel from certain locations to others in an efficient manner – that is, taking the shortest routes possible (Garber, 1989; Sigg, 1986). Menzel (1973) tested the ability of four young captive chimpanzees to use least-distance strategies, traveling the least while obtaining the most food rewards in a large enclosure. He found that chimpanzees minimized the distance traveled. Similarly, Boesch and Boesch (1984) found that wild chimpanzees traveled efficiently when collecting stones needed to crack open nuts. They selected stones that were closer to their current location. Recently, a number of researchers have described the use of least-distance strategies in vervet monkeys, common marmosets, and yellow-nosed monkeys (Cramer & Gallistel, 1997; MacDonald, Pang, & Gibeault, 1994; MacDonald & Wilkie, 1990).

There also is a computerized version of the shortcut task. Washburn (1992; see also Washburn & Rumbaugh, 1992) presented rhesus monkeys with a moving target on a screen that they had to intercept with a cursor that subjects controlled with a joystick. To do so appropriately, subjects not only had to chase the target but on many occasions had to predict its location and use shortcuts to ambush it because the target speed was equal or superior to that of the cursor. In other words, they had to take shortcuts to intercept the moving target. This skill may be more demanding than using shortcuts when traveling between various food sources because subjects have to adapt to a moving target. This may be a useful skill in intercepting prey or competitors who hold valuable resources. These authors found that subjects again were more effective at intercepting targets when they followed predictable rather than unpredictable paths. Although subjects required some experience to learn the paths of the targets, results from presentation of novel target paths (e.g., the target disappearing on the top and reappearing on the bottom of the screen) suggested that monkeys had learned a general rule about the target's behavior rather than a set of stimulus–response associations. In a similar vein, Iversen and Matsuzawa (2001) indicated that when mazes had one short and a long route to get to the goal box, the chimpanzee selected the short one.

SEARCH FOR MOVING OBJECTS

Several studies investigated the ability of primates to retrieve objects after they have undergone different invisible displacements. In object permanence tasks, the experimenter places a piece of food under a small container that is displaced under several other containers and the food is left under one of them. To solve this problem effectively, subjects have to search under all and only boxes under which the food might have been deposited given the trajectory of the box that initially contained the food. Several apes pass this task but monkeys do not (Call, 2000; De Blois, Novak, & Bond, 1998; De Blois & Novak, 1994; Dumas & Brunet, 1994; Natale et al., 1986), although there are individual exceptions (Schino, Spinozzi, & Berlinguer, 1990). Apes also have problems if the two locations visited are not adjacent; that is, the experimenter visits the box on the right and the left, leaving the center box untouched (Call, 2000; De Blois, Novak, & Bond, 1998; Natale et al., 1986). This is interpreted as reconstructing the trajectory of the reward.

Other types of displacements recently have been investigated with apes. In rotational displacements, a reward is hidden under one of two cups and the platform is rotated circularly – for instance, 180 degrees. In transpositions, the reward is placed under one of various containers and their locations are swapped while the platform remains stationary. Results show that chimpanzees, orangutans, and bonobos are capable of solving these displacements (Beran & Minahan, 2000; Call, 2003). Taken together, this means that subjects can track a variety of displacements based on the movement of the object (object permanence), the containers (transpositions), or the substrate on which the object and containers rest (rotations). All these result in changes in the location of the object and subjects can infer its position.

In summary, primates are capable of travelling efficiently by using detours and shortcuts and they track the displacement of hidden objects and infer their new locations after various spatial transformations.

Relational Reasoning

In simple discrimination problems, subjects learn to respond to a single stimulus or to a stimulus category at some level of abstraction. Discrimination learning of relational categories, on the other hand, involves concepts that can be learned only by comparing stimuli to one another and inducing a relation (e.g., "same as" "larger than"). The three most studied instances of relational concepts are the identity relation as manifest in generalized match-to-sample problems, the oddity relation as manifest in generalized oddity problems, and the sameness–difference relation as manifest in generalized relation-matching problems. In all three cases, the basic idea is that the subject is given some problems in training that can be solved by attending to a relation and then is given transfer tests that use completely different objects that can be seen as instantiations of that same relation. If learning is relatively fast in the transfer phase, the inference is that the subject acquired a relational concept in the training phase and is now applying it in the transfer phase. If the learning is at the same basic rate in training and transfer (with some allowance for the formation of a learning set), the inference is that the subject has not learned a relational concept but is treating each new problem as a separate entity with its own particular stimulus characteristics.

Identity

Several studies have shown that monkeys and chimpanzees can solve identity problems based on generalized matching to sample (D'Amato & Salmon, 1984; D'Amato et al., 1986; Nissen, Blum, & Blum, 1948; Oden, Thompson, & Premack, 1988). In the only study of which we are aware in which human children were tested in this same type of procedure, they, like the chimpanzees, generalized immediately to new match-to-sample problems using only two sets of stimuli in training (Weinstein, 1941). It should be noted, however, that this successful performance with one stimulus dimension (e.g., shape) does not generalize in most studies across other stimulus dimensions (D'Amato & Colombo, 1985; Jackson & Pegram, 1970a, 1970b; Kojima; 1979; Fujita, 1982; but see Wright, Shyan, & Jitsumori, 1990). Monkeys trained with shapes and capable of solving identity problems with novel shapes, for instance, do not transfer their identity concept to other dimensions such as color (see Doumas & Hummel, Chap. 4, for a discussion of relational generalization). The rule that monkeys seem to learn is therefore better characterized as "pick the same shape" rather than "pick the same."

Oddity

Numerous studies demonstrate that many primate species can acquire the concept of oddity, as evidenced by their ability to solve novel problems after a period of training (King & Fobes, 1982; Rumbaugh & McCormack; 1967; Thomas & Boyd, 1973). Some primate species have also been able to solve dimension-abstracted oddity problems in which the odd object must be distinguished from four other alternatives that are not identical to one another (as in traditional oddity problems) but only resemble one another with respect to some dimensions (e.g., objects of different shapes that are all red, as opposed to the odd object, which is blue). Macaques, squirrel monkeys, chimpanzees, and gorillas were capable of solving this problem (Bernstein, 1961; Thomas & Frost, 1983). Human children have been presented with oddity problems in a number of studies and generally perform very well in the earliest trials of transfer (e.g., Lipsett & Serunian, 1963).

Sameness–Difference

In the previous two tasks, subjects have to respond either to similarity or difference. Some tasks have investigated whether subjects can decide whether a pair of stimuli are similar or different simultaneously. Several monkey species, chimpanzees, and orangutans were capable of judging whether two stimuli were "same" or "different" (Wright, Santiago, & Sands; 1984; Fujita, 1983; King & Fobes; 1975; Robinson, 1955, 1960; King, 1973). These studies invariably involved subjects making judgments at the perceptual level, not the functional level. Recently, however, Bovet and Vauclair (2001) investigated the ability of baboons to make same–different judgments based on the functional properties of the stimuli. They presented baboons with pairs of stimuli corresponding to two different categories (i.e., food vs. nonfood). The items belonging to these two categories varied in their perceptual features. Results indicated that baboons were capable of judging as "same" items belonging to the same category despite their perceptual dissimilarities and as "different" items belonging to different categories.

Analogical Reasoning

Premack (1983) argued that identity, oddity, and sameness–difference tasks as traditionally administered do not require the kind of relational concepts that investigators have claimed. Because the matching takes place across trials in all of these tasks, he claimed that "the animal simply reacts to whether it has experienced the item before. Old/new or familiar/unfamiliar would be better tags for this case than same/different" (Ref. 86, p. 354). Instead, he advocated use of a generalized match-to-sample procedure in which the matching to be accomplished involves the relations between items. Premack (1983) presented chimpanzees with a sample pair of stimuli that either matched (so-called AA pairs, such as two apples) or that did not match (so-called CD pairs, such as a pear and an orange). Their task was to pick which of two alternatives matched the relation exemplified in the sample – either a pair of new items that matched (a so-called BB pair, such as two bananas) or a pair of new items that did not match (a so-called EF pair, such as a plum and a grape). When the sample was AA, the subject was to choose BB (rather than EF) because the relation between items in both cases is one of "sameness." If the sample was CD, the subject should choose EF (rather than BB) because the relation between items in each case was one of "difference."

Gillan, Premack, and Woodruff (1981) presented the language-trained chimpanzee Sarah (Premack, 1976) with pairs of objects that had various relations; Sarah's job was to identify another pair that had an analogous relation. In so-called figural problems, Sarah was presented with an odd shape with a dot on it and that same shape without the dot; she was then presented with another shape with a dot and had to choose from a pair of alternatives that same shape without the dot (i.e., the analogous relation of two shapes with and without a dot). In so-called conceptual problems Sarah was presented with household items with which she was familiar and asked to draw analogies, for example, between a key and lock and a can opener and can. On figural items, Sarah performed correctly about three-quarters of the time and on conceptual items she was correct at a slightly higher rate. Having ruled out various possible alternative explanations, the investigators concluded that Sarah was able to understand the relation in the first pair of stimuli at a level of abstraction sufficient to allow her to identify it in subsequent stimulus pairs, both perceptually and conceptually.

Recently, Thompson, Oden, and Boysen (1997) found that language-naïve chimpanzees were also able to solve analogies if, prior to testing, they had been trained to associate a token of one shape with pairs of similar items and a different token for a pair of items that were not similar. Presented with the same token, they selected the similar pair, and presented with the different token, they selected the pair with unequal items (this is comparable to Burdyn and Thomas, 1984, in which squirrel monkeys used a figure to choose between the identical or the different objects in the pair). On the testing phase, subjects were presented with a pair of identical or different objects as a sample and two choices (one that bore the same the relation as the sample and another with a different relation). Chimpanzees performed above chance, indicating that they could identify the relation between relations. In contrast, rhesus monkeys presented with an analogous procedure were unable to solve this problem even though they were able to solve other kinds of relations such as correctly identifying the perceptual analogies (Washburn, Thompson, & Oden, cited in Thompson & Oden, 2000).

Several authors have indicated that only chimpanzees that had received some training that involved using tokens representing "same" and "different" were able to solve analogies (Premack, 1983; Thompson & Oden, 2000). They argued that learning a symbolic code such as language fundamentally changed the nature of the cognitive representations used by chimpanzees by providing them with an abstract propositional code (rather than a concrete imaginal code) in terms of which they might interpret their experience. This idea, however, has been challenged from two main directions. First, Oden, Thompson, and Premack (1990) used a different procedure and found that four infant chimpanzees (around one year of age with no language training) also engaged in the matching of relations. They simply presented the subject with a sample stimulus that consisted of a pair of objects mounted on a small board; the pair could either match (AA) or not match (CD). Subjects could play with this sample as desired, and their play time was recorded. They were then presented with two test pairs of objects, also mounted on board, that they might play with; one was a matching pair (BB) and one was a nonmatching pair (EF). Subjects' initial play with the sample affected their handling time with the new test pairs. If subjects had played with the sample pair that matched (AA) they were no longer interested in the matching relation and so played more with the nonmatching test pair (EF); if they had played with the nonmatching sample (CD), they played more with the matching test pair (BB). The conclusion of these investigators was that chimpanzees can understand relations among relations, even if they do not always show this competence in tasks in which they must actively choose stimuli. The modified conclusion of these authors was that, although chimpanzees understand second-order relations, language training helps them incorporate this into their instrumental behavior. Interestingly, children perform like chimpanzees and distinguish the relations, whereas monkeys do not (Thompson & Oden, 2000). Thompson and Oden (2000), however, have indicated that these represent implicit rather than explicit judgments of the kind shown in generalized relation-matching tasks (see Litman & Reber, Chap. 18 on implicit thinking).

Second, and more importantly, Vonk (2003) has recently shown that orangutans and a gorilla can solve analogies without any token experience or extensive training (see also Smith et al., 1975) using a delayed matching to sample (DMTS) task in which subjects had to match the relation represented by a pair of geometric figures to those of one of the two alternatives provided – the same method used by other authors to test analogical reasoning in chimpanzees. There is also a study with baboons that showed they can match a sample depicting a set of identical or different items to the corresponding alternative (Fagot, Wasserman, & Young, 2001). Unlike previous studies with apes, however, baboons reached high performance only when the sample and alternatives were formed by multiple items. When the number of items was reduced, there was a clear decrement in accuracy, particularly for the "different" samples. This effect, as well as the extensive training involved (baboons received thousands of trials before they mastered the initial task), opens the door to other interpretations based on the perception of perceptual entropy.

One area in analogical reasoning that has received some recent research attention from a comparative perspective is that of spatial analogy. Using a task pioneered by DeLoache and colleagues (DeLoache 1995), Kuhlmeier, Boysen, and Mukobi (1999) tested the ability of chimpanzees to make spatial analogies. Subjects were presented with a very accurate three-dimensional scale model of a room and subjects witnessed how the experimenter placed an object (e.g., soda can) in a particular location in the scale model (e.g., inside a cupboard). Subjects then moved to the real room and were allowed to search the room. Chimpanzees were capable of using the scale model to accurately predict the location of the object in the room and vice versa; they were able to point to a location in the scale model that corresponded to a location in the actual room. Initially, female chimpanzees were more proficient than males at this task. Male chimpanzees tended to search the room in a predetermined pattern until they eventually found the object rather than going to the specific places indicated in the scale model. When reward delivery was made contingent on visiting the specific location on their first try, however, males' performance became comparable to that of female chimpanzees (Kuhlmeier & Boysen, 2001).

In summary, primates are capable of perceiving various types of relations between objects. Moreover, apes can solve analogies regarding the similarity or difference between pairs of objects, and chimpanzees can also solve spatial analogies involving the use of scale models.

Inferential Reasoning

Transitivity

The use of transitive inference has received much research attention. Although human studies on transitivity (see Halford, Chap. 22) have often used stimuli that vary systematically and naturally along a quantitative dimension such as height (e.g., Piaget, 1952), most studies with primates have used so-called associative transitivity. This consists of presenting subjects with pairs of arbitrary stimuli and differentially reinforcing one of the stimulus of the pair, thereby creating different values. For instance, the red cup is always reinforced when presented with the blue cup, whereas the blue cup is always reinforced when presented with the yellow cup, and so on. Once the initial pairs are trained, subjects are presented with pairs of stimuli that have not been paired before, for instance, red versus yellow cup.

There is ample evidence showing that primates can make transitive inferences when subjects are presented with novel pairs (D'Amato et al., 1985; D'Amato & Colombo, 1988; Gillan 1981; Boysen et al., 1993). This includes cases in which subjects have been trained with more than three stimuli. This is important because the most interesting cases are those that involve intermediate stimuli – that is, stimuli that are not the first or the last of the sequence, because those are always or never reinforced, respectively. D'Amato and Colombo (1988) trained capuchin monkeys to touch five arbitrary items in a specified order (labeled A, B, C, D, and E). After they had mastered this task they were presented with novel pairs. Of particular importance were the internal pairs B–C, C–D, and B–D. The B–D comparison was especially important because these two items were both internal to the series and were nonadjacent to one another in the previous training. Subjects ordered these three internal pairs correctly 81% to 88% of the time, well above chance. When presented with triplets from which they were to choose the highest item, they ordered the internal triplet B-C-D correctly 94% of the time, also well above chance. This finding essentially replicates, with even stronger results, the findings of McGonigle and Chalmers (1977) with squirrel monkeys. These authors also found evidence for a symbolic distance effect – the farther apart two items, the more successful the subjects, presumably because the items were easier to distinguish.

One open question is, What is the mechanism responsible for this performance? Two mechanisms have been postulated – the associative mechanisms based on responding to the differential reinforcement and associative strength of the stimuli, and the relational or linear mechanism based on creating a mental order of the stimuli. Bond, Kamil, and Balda (2003) argued that, under an associative mechanism, errors increase at the end of the sequence, whereas latencies should be unaffected regardless of the position of the items. In contrast, the relational mechanism predicts that accuracy will remain unchanged, whereas the latency to respond will be affected. First, subjects' latency to respond to the first item of a pair increased as that item moved down the series: They responded most quickly to pairs in which the first item was A, then for pairs in which the first item was B, then C, then D. The implication is that each time they are presented with a pair, the subjects are mentally reconstructing the entire five-item series (D'Amato & Colombo, 1988). Second, animals responded most quickly to the second item of a pair for pairs with adjacent items (e.g., A–B, C–D, etc.), then for pairs separated by one gap (e.g., A–C, C–E, etc.), then for pairs separated by two gaps (i.e., A–D, B–E), and they were slowest on the second item when the gap was three (A–E). Again, the implication is that subjects are going through the entire series mentally on every trial. Swartz, Chen, and Terrace (1991) essentially replicated these results – both in terms of ordinal judgments and in terms of reaction times – for rhesus macaques.

Although these results are quite convincing, D'Amato and Colombo (1989) pointed out that the results of this study are compatible with an associative chain interpretation in which each item simply serves as a discriminative stimulus evoking the next item, obviating the need for some representation of serial order. To investigate whether capuchin monkeys were also associating a specific serial position with each item in the associative chain, D'Amato and Colombo (1989) used a procedure that essentially broke the chain. Using monkeys who had already learned the ABCDE sequence, on some trials they introduced a "wild card" item at a particular point in the sequence (e.g., ABCXE). This was a novel item that had never been used as part of the training and therefore had no associations with any other items. These investigators found that no matter the position in which the wild card item appeared, subjects treated it in a manner similar to the item it replaced at above-chance levels, touching it at the appropriate place in the sequence approximately 60% of the time. They performed just as well with sequences containing two wild card items. Consequently, D'Amato and Colombo argued that the monkeys in this study, and presumably in previous studies, were operating with something more than an associative chain; they were operating with some mentally represented sequence of items in which the ordinal position of each item was essential information.

Ordinality

Many of the studies on transitivity have already indicated that monkeys learn something about the linear representation in a series – they learn the order in which the items should appear. Some studies have pushed this argument a bit further and have substituted boxes by Arabic numerals representing different quantities. Boysen et al. (1993) found that after chimpanzees were trained with pairs of adjacent numerals in the same pairwise as used in the studies previously reported, they were then presented with the novel pair 2–4. In this study, after appropriate training with the initial pairs, subjects all were able to successfully choose the 4 over the 2 in the novel pairwise test. The investigators concluded that with appropriate training, chimpanzees can learn the serial order of symbolic stimuli. Washburn and Rumbaugh (1991) taught two rhesus macaques to associate Arabic numerals with the reception of a corresponding number of food pellets. Because monkeys try to maximize their food intake, they learned to select the larger quantity represented by the various numerals that were presented to them. The authors reserved some of the pairs for their transitivity tests. One of the two subjects was above chance in choosing the larger member of the novel pair in the very first set of trials. Similarly, presented with five numerals simultaneously, result of both were above chance immediately in choosing the largest one. These investigators interpret their results as indicating that the monkeys formed a representation of a "matrix of values" corresponding to the numerals.

Additional evidence for ordinality is provided by two studies not based on a transitivity paradigm. First, Brannon and Terrace (1998) trained rhesus macaques to touch a series of stimuli depicting different numerosities in ascending order. Initially, the monkeys were trained on sets of stimuli depicting numerosities ranging from 1 to 4. In transfer tests, monkeys were able to solve problems involving numerosities ranging 5 to 9. The authors argued that their results demonstrated that rhesus macaques can represent numerosities ranging from 1 to 9 in an ordinal manner. In a follow-up study, Brannon and Terrace (2000) trained monkeys to touch a series of stimuli in descending order. They failed to transfer the descending rule into new numerosities, however. Monkeys also failed to learn to select numerosities in a monotonic series despite extensive training. This suggests that ordinality may be an especially salient dimension for monkeys. The accuracy in responding and the latency indicated distance effects similar to those in other studies, including human studies (e.g., Moyer & Landaeur, 1967). Second, Kawai and Matsuzawa (2000) showed that the chimpanzee Ai was capable of selecting Arabic numerals presented on the computer screen in ascending order. She had 90% accuracy with four-numeral series and 65% accuracy with five-numeral series. The response latency was longest for the first item in the series compared with the remaining ones, which suggests the chimpanzee was planning the sequence before executing the entire sequence.

Conjunctive Negation

This refers to the ability to infer that if a given object can be located in one of two containers and, upon searching the first container, is not found there, then it must be in the other one. Premack and Premack (1994) presented chimpanzees with two boxes and two types of fruit, such as a banana and an apple. Chimpanzees were allowed to witness the experimenter deposit each fruit in one of the boxes so that both boxes were baited. Later, subjects saw the experimenter eating one of the fruits (e.g., banana) and the question was whether given the opportunity to select either box, they would select the one in which the experimenter had deposited the food he was not currently eating (i.e., apple), presumably because it still contained the fruit. Chimpanzees solved this problem quickly, without trial-and-error, showing that they were able to infer that if the experimenter was eating the banana, the box where the banana was deposited would be empty.

More recently, Call (2004) presented all four great apes with two cups (one baited) and gave visual or auditory information about the contents of one or both cups. Visual information consisted of removing the top of the cup so that subjects could look inside it. Auditory information consisted of shaking the cup so that it produced a rattling sound when the food was inside. Subjects correctly selected the baited cup both when they saw the food and when they heard it. More importantly, subjects also selected the correct cup when only the empty cup was either shown or shaken. This means that subjects chose correctly without having seen or heard the food. Control tests showed that, in general, subjects were not more attracted to noisy cups or avoided shaken noiseless cups. Also, subjects were unable to learn to use other comparable auditory cues such as tapping on the baited cup to find the food. The author argued that apes made inferences about the food location, rather than just associating an auditory cue with the reward. This suggests that subjects understood that the food caused the noise, not simply that the noise was associated with the food.

There are also two studies in which chimpanzees were able to solve inferential exclusion in a matching to sample paradigm. Hashiya and Kojima (2001) presented a chimpanzee with two pictures of people she knew and the voice of one of them. The chimpanzees successfully matched the voice with the correct picture. Then Hashiya and Kojima (2001) presented her with two pictures (one of someone she knew and the other of someone she did not know) and an unfamiliar voice. The chimpanzee correctly matched the unfamiliar voice to the unfamiliar picture. Beran and Washburn (2002) presented chimpanzees with pictures and lexigrams as samples and alternatives, respectively. Pictures and lexigrams could be either familiar or unfamiliar. Familiar samples and alternatives consisted of pictures and lexigrams, respectively, that subjects had learned to associate before the test. As expected, chimpanzees reliably selected the familiar appropriate lexigrams representing the sample pictures, but, in addition, chimpanzees also were able to select unfamiliar lexigrams when presented with familiar lexigrams and an unfamiliar picture. Their success in this task did not translate into the acquisition of the unfamiliar lexigram as a representation for the unfamiliar picture, however.

In summary, primates are capable of making inferences about pieces of missing information in transitivity and conjunctive negation problems of various types.

Quantitative Reasoning

Primates can perform operations on quantities by adapting to novel arrays when some quantities are added, subtracted, or simply change in appearance but remain constant. They also have some skills in counting, on which these more complex skills depend.

Counting

Rumbaugh and coalleagues (Beran & Rumbaugh, 2001; Rumbaugh et al., 1989) presented two chimpanzees with a computer task in which subjects had to collect the number of dots from the bottom of the screen specified by an Arabic numeral presented on the top of the screen. Subjects indicated when they had finished their selection with the use of the cursor. The chimpanzees performed above chance with the numerals up to six and seven, respectively. Rumbaugh et al. (1989) also indicated that the chimpanzee Lana could solve this task even if the squares disappeared as she touched them (with a tone sounding as they disappeared) – implying that she could keep track mentally of how many she had already touched. The authors ruled out some explanations such as subitizing or using the temporal pattern rather than the number of dots as the basis for their choices. Beran and Rumbaugh (2001) argued that chimpanzees' performance decreased proportionally to the magnitude of the numerals presented. The authors argued that the chimpanzees seemed to represent quantities in a continuous rather than a discrete fashion. This characterization differs in some way from that of Rumbaugh et al. (1989), who indicated that these subjects were counting in a way similar to human children in that they knew not only the ordinality but also the cardinality of the Arabic numerals involved.

Boysen and Berntson (1989) trained the chimpanzee Sheba to count objects using Arabic numerals using a different method. First, they administered a one-to-one correspondence task in which she had to place one and only one object in each of six compartments of a divided tray. Then, she was required to pick a card with the same number of dots as the number of food items (ranging from one to three pieces) presented on a tray. The researchers then replaced the cards with dots with cards having Arabic numerals and continued the training until Sheba was able to select the Arabic numeral corresponding to the number of dots on a card. Finally, the authors trained the subject in Arabic numeral comprehension so that, presented with an Arabic numeral, she had to select the card with the corresponding number of dots. After she mastered these tasks, Boysen and Berntson conducted two transfer tests. First, they presented her with one, two, or three common household items and asked her to pick the corresponding Arabic numeral, which she readily did. Second, they introduced the Arabic numerals 4, 5, and 0 directly (without first using cards with dots), and Sheba readily learned to associate these with the correct number of objects as well.

During this training of Sheba, Boysen and Bernston noticed that she often engaged in "indicating acts" as she counted. That is, she touched, displaced, or "pointed to" objects serially in attempting to determine the appropriate Arabic numeral – much as human children touch or otherwise indicate objects as they count them. In a follow-up study, therefore, Boysen et al. (1995) looked to see whether the number of indicating acts Sheba used as she engaged in these tasks correlated with the number of items in the array (by the time of this study, Sheba knew the numerals 0–7). They gave her some counting tasks, using the numerals 0 to 7, and found that she correctly counted 54% of the time (with errors distributed equally across the 1 to 7 range). They found further that whereas the absolute number of Sheba's indicating acts did not correspond to the number of items in the array precisely, typically being about twice as large, these did correlate significantly ($r = .74$). It is unclear whether this correlation is attributable to counting or to the fact that determining the numerosity of the larger numerals requires more time, so that a constant rate of indicating acts across all numerals would lead to the correlation. In any case, the investigators concluded that Sheba was counting objects in much the same way as human children, and that her indicating acts were serving a mediating function in the process.

Summation and Subtraction

Rumbaugh and colleagues (Perusse & Rumbaugh, 1990; Rumbaugh, Savage-Rumbaugh, & Hegel, 1987; Rumbaugh, Savage-Rumbaugh, & Pate, 1988) presented two language-trained chimpanzees (Sherman & Austin) with two unequal sets of candies (M&M) but presented as spatially distinct subsets. For instance, a trial consisted of presenting four and three candies compared with five and one candies. Chimpanzees were capable of comparing these two sets and combining the spatially distinct subsets (e.g., $4 + 3$ vs. $5 + 1$) to net the larger total array (up to a maximum of seven candies) on more than 90% of the trials. Although the investigators did not claim that their subjects "added" numbers in anything resembling the human method, they argued that the skills required for this task go beyond simple subitizing, because the items in each of the two quantities to be compared are separated into two spatially distinct subsets. This is far from summation understood as a mental operation, however, because subjects were not required to perform any mental operations. Directly perceiving the larger of the two overall quantities in either side would suffice to solve this task. In other words, this can be seen as a relative numerousness judgment over a large area, without any operation beyond perception being implicated.

In an attempt to solve this problem, Call (2000) presented orangutans with two quantities in two dishes and then added a third one into one of the dishes. In some trials, this resulted in the smaller of the two initial quantities having more and sometimes did not change. Call (2000) also subtracted quantities from the initial quantities and showed how much he had subtracted. The important point is that subjects never saw the final quantities directly, but they had to decide based on how much had been added to or subtracted from the quantities. Orangutans were capable of performing above chance in both addition and subtraction.

Sulkowski and Hauser (2001) also investigated subtraction in rhesus macaques. They showed subjects two quantities (up to three items each), hid each of them in two separate adjacent locations and then removed either one or no items from each location. Rhesus macaques selected the location with more items even when subtractions occurred from both locations and when some nonedible items rather than food were subtracted.

Beran (2001) found that two chimpanzees were also able to add quantities presented sequentially up to nine pieces of candy (M&M). Unlike the previous study, each piece of candy was added individually to one of two cups rather than presenting the array in its totality. In different experiments, subjects witnessed the experimenter placing different quantities into the cups in various steps. All candies may be added at one time in a given cup or the addition rounds could be alternated between the two cups. In the final experiment, subjects witnessed the experimenter removing one candy from one of the cups before being allowed to choose. Both chimpanzees performed above chance in the addition trials, whereas only one chimpanzee was above chance in the subtraction trials. These two studies suggest that orangutans and chimpanzees can represent quantities and mentally operate on those quantities to net the largest array.

Olthof, Iden, and Roberts (1997) raised the bar a bit further and replaced the actual quantities by Arabic numerals. First the monkeys were trained to identify the numerals corresponding to quantities that subjects knew. Then subjects were given a choice between different combinations of numerals involving two numerals in each pair, one numeral and two numerals, or three numerals in each pair. For instance (1 + 1 + 3) against (2 + 2 + 2). Squirrel monkeys were capable of selecting the larger total quantity. Additional tests indicated that this effect could not be explained by choosing the largest numeral available or avoiding the smallest number available.

Similarly, Boysen and Berntson (1989) also reported that Sheba was able to visit three locations in the room, look for hidden items that might be there and report the total number of items (up to four) at a different location by picking up a card depicting the arabic numeral corresponding to the total number of items available in the room. Sheba was able to do this by using either actual objects or Arabic numerals with an overall accuracy of 75% (chance = 25%). Given that Sheba also can make transitive inferences with an ordered series of items (Boysen et al., 1993) and uses indicating acts as she attempts to determine the numerical value of sets of objects (see previous section), the investigators hypothesize that she is actually counting, in a human-like way, in these foraging tasks, and that her number concept is very much like that of a young human child.

Conservation

Piaget and Inhelder (1941) considered the ability to understand that physical quantities remain constant after changing their perceptual appearance an important step toward the formation of logical thinking in children. Seven-year-old children and older understand that if two quantities were the same prior to a perceptual transformation (and nothing has been added or removed) they *must* be the same after the transformation has taken place. This logical necessity is the cornerstone of the conservation experiments (see also Halford, Chap. 22).

Although some studies on conservation in monkeys have been done (e.g.,Thomas & Peay, 1976), the lack of information about how subjects judge the two quantities prior to a transformation prevents us from drawing any conclusions. Two studies with chimpanzees collected this information and therefore can be interpreted more accurately. First, Woodruff, Premack, and Kennel (1978) presented Sarah with liquid, solid, and number conservation tasks. Before this test, Sarah had learned to use plastic tokens to indicate whether a pair of stimuli were "same" or "different." In the liquid conservation task, she was presented with a pair of equal or unequal liquid quantities in identical containers and asked to judge them with the tokens. One of the quantities was then poured into another container with a different shape, and she was asked to make a judgment on the novel stimuli. Results indicated that she correctly judged the quantities in liquid and solid but not in number conservation tasks. Additional tests also showed that Sarah was unable to judge correctly when she was prevented from seeing the quantities presented in identical containers first. This result led Woodruff, Premack, & Kennel (1978) to conclude that she based her judgments on logical necessity rather than perceptual estimation. Similarly, Muncer (1983) reported that a chimpanzee was capable of selecting the larger of two quantities after applying a transformation that changed the appearance of the liquid. As in the previous study, the chimpanzee was unable to select the larger quantity if she was prevented from seeing the pretransformation quantities displayed in identical containers.

Call and Rochat (1996) investigated the ability of four orangutans to solve liquid conservation using a modified version of Muncer's procedure. Subjects were presented with a pair of identical containers with unequal amounts of juice. Once subjects had indicated their choice by pointing (which invariably was to the larger quantity), the experimenter transferred the liquid quantities into a pair of unequal containers. In different experiments, the authors varied either the shape of the containers or the number of containers available (while keeping the shape constant). Although some apes still selected the larger quantity after a shape transformation, this performance deteriorated when the contrast between the shape of the containers was increased. In contrast, some of the six- to eight-year-old children they tested performed satisfactorily. Furthermore, none of the apes solved the task when the quantities were transferred into multiple containers. Call and Rochat (1996) concluded that orangutans depended upon perceptual information rather than logical necessity, thereby demonstrating "pseudoconservation." In a follow-up study, Call and Rochat (1997) investigated the use of perceptual strategies underlying the orangutans' pseudoconservation. The authors examined three possible perceptual strategies to identify the larger amount of liquid: visual estimation of the liquid in the container, the use of information about quantity based on pouring the liquid, and a tracking strategy that consisted of following the liquid that subjects had initially chosen. Results indicated that the visual estimation strategy best accounted for the orangutan's pseudoconservation. Overall, these investigators interpreted their results as indicating that orangutans are very good at estimating quantities and at tracking the quantity they prefer across various spatial displacements, but they do not conserve quantities across perceptual transformations in a humanlike manner.

The studies cited with chimpanzees suggest the use of logical reasoning, whereas studies with orangutans suggest the use of perceptual estimation in the solution of liquid conservation problems. Because both the species and methods employed in the studies were not comparable, it is difficult to know whether chimpanzees and orangutans truly differ in the mechanisms they use to solve conservation problems or the differences were a result of the methods used in each set of studies. Recently, Suda and Call (in press) set out to resolve this discrepancy by studying chimpanzees and orangutans with the same procedures. They presented apes with various liquid conservation problems in which the initial quantities were transferred into containers of different shapes or into multiple containers, dividing the total quantity. Results supported the notion that most apes relied on perceptual estimation rather than logical necessity with orangutans being slightly more proficient than chimpanzees.

In summary, primates can solve quantitative problems that require combining or dissociating quantities, and they can develop the notion of ordinality. In contrast, there is little evidence that primates use logical necessity when confronted with various Piagetian conservation problems.

Causal Reasoning

Causal reasoning is a complex topic, and much hinges on the chosen definition of causality. Some researchers interpret causality as the ability to form stimulus–stimulus or stimulus–response associations. In this broad sense there is no doubt that many animals are sensitive to causality. We concentrate more narrowly on the understanding of the underlying "structures" and "forces" that are responsible for certain effects. This has been most studied in the domain of tool use, but it has also been investigated in a variety of other types of physical events in which the subject does not manipulate but only observes.

Tool Use

Many introductory texts to psychology mention the experiments involving tool use by chimpanzees as groundbreaking studies. Since then, it has been shown that several primate species use tools in a variety of ways and for a variety of purposes (see Beck, 1980; Tomasello & Call, 1997, for reviews). We concentrate on three tasks that have been used to investigate causality.

SUPPORT PROBLEM

In this problem, a reward is placed on a cloth. The reward itself is outside the subject's reach, but one of the ends of the cloth is within reach. The solution to this problem consists of pulling the cloth to bring the reward within reach. Piaget (1952) studied this problem in human infants and indicated that by 12 months of age children not only readily pull in the cloth but, more importantly, they withhold pulling when the reward is not in contact with the cloth. This indicates that children at this age understand that spatial contact is necessary for the tool to act on the reward.

Spinozzi and Potì (1989) tested several infant primates (one Japanese macaque, two capuchin monkeys, two longtail macaques, and one gorilla) on this problem. In one condition, the reward was placed on the cloth, whereas in another condition the reward was placed off the cloth to the side. All primates responded appropriately by pulling in the cloth when the reward was on the cloth and withheld pulling when the reward was off the cloth. In a second experiment, Spinozzi and Potì (1989) tested the generality of these findings by modifying the conditions of the off-cloth condition by placing the reward near the end of the cloth rather than to the side of it. The authors reasoned that if subjects had simply learned to respond appropriately to a specific configuration of the cloth and the reward rather than a more general relation between them, they would respond inappropriately to this novel configuration. Results confirmed their previous findings: All subjects pulled in the on-cloth condition but not in the off-cloth condition. Recently, Spinozzi and Potì (1993) administered the same support problem to two infant chimpanzees and only one of them succeeded.

Hauser and colleagues recently investigated this problem in detail with cotton-top tamarins (Hauser, Kralik & Botto-Mahan, 1999). Their studies questioned whether these monkeys can distinguish between relevant and irrelevant features of tools – in this case, the cloth. They found that tamarins were able to master this problem. In particular, presented with two cloths and two rewards from which to choose, they pulled the cloth on which the reward rested. In another experiment, subjects selected the cloth that was connected somehow to the reward but avoided the cloth that was not connected to the reward. Once subjects had mastered these two problems, the authors presented monkeys with both relevant and irrelevant changes to the problem. Relevant changes included the position of the reward in relation to the reward or the connectedness between two pieces of cloth; irrelevant changes included variations in the color, texture, or shape of the cloth. The tamarins ignored irrelevant changes to the tool such as color or shape. They failed to solve some problems involving changes in the relevant features, although they mastered those problems with additional experience. The authors interpreted this as an ability to distinguish between relevant and irrelevant features.

Hauser et al. (2002) investigated whether experience with tool use played a role in deciding what constituted the relevant functional features of a tool. They presented monkeys with a number of cloth problems that varied along several parameters except that the correct alternative was always indicated by the same color. Subjects therefore could solve the various problems by either attending to the relevant features of the problem (e.g., connectedness) or the color of the cloth. Once animals had mastered the series of preliminary tests, they were presented with novel problems but with the color contingency reversed so that color always signaled the incorrect alternative. Results indicated that tool-experienced monkeys relied less on irrelevant cues such as color than tool-naïve individuals in solving the cloth problem. Nevertheless, all monkeys experienced a postreversal decrement performance, albeit performance of tool-experienced monkeys suffered less.

STICK AND HOOK PROBLEM

A more challenging task than the support problem consists of using a tool to bring in a reward that is not in direct contact with the tool. This situation entails putting the tool into contact with the reward and then sweeping the reward within reach. According to Natale (1989), solving this task demonstrates an ability to understand complex causal relations such as that the stick must be of the appropriate size and material (e.g., long and rigid) and that only certain kinds of contact (e.g., with a certain force and directionality) would be successful.

Natale (1989) presented eight subjects from the same four species tested by Spinozzi and Potì (1989) with an out-of-reach reward and a stick placed in different positions relative to the object in different experimental conditions. Three of the four capuchin monkeys and the gorilla were moderately successful in obtaining the reward in various tool-reward spatial arrangements. These results have been confirmed by other studies (see Beck, 1980; Tomasello & Call, 1997 for a review). Although none of the macaques tested by Natale (1989) was able to obtain the reward with the stick, other studies have shown that macaques and other primates, including baboons, orangutans, and chimpanzees, are capable of solving the stick problem (see Tomasello & Call, 1997 for a review).

A refinement of the stick problem consists of presenting a hook-shaped tool and a straight tool as alternatives for retrieving the reward. Hauser (1997) presented cotton-top tamarins with two hooked tools, only one of which had the reward inside the hook so that pulling it would bring the reward. Once tamarins consistently solved this problem – that is, they preferred the stick with the reward inside the hook – the authors presented novel problems in which they varied either relevant or irrelevant features of the task, as previously done with the cloth problem. Results mirrored those of the cloth problem and indicated that individuals selected tools most often based on relevant, as opposed to irrelevant, functional features. Hauser, Pearson, and Seelig (2002) recently investigated the role of experience in the ability to distinguish relevant from irrelevant features. They found that infant tamarins, without much experience with tools, also selected tools based on relevant features, reproducing the results of the adult subjects.

TUBE AND TRAP PROBLEM

In this problem, the reward is placed inside the middle portion of a transparent tube, and subjects have to use a stick to push the reward out the end opposite to which the reward was inserted. In a series of studies, Visalberghi and colleagues explored the ability of capuchin monkeys and apes (mainly chimpanzees) to solve this problem and to adjust to novel variations of this problem.

Visalberghi and Trinca (1989) found that three of four capuchin monkeys succeeded in the basic version of the problem, and then the authors administered three variations of the problem involving different types of tools that required different solutions. In the bundle task, subjects were given a bundle of sticks taped together that, as a whole, was too wide to fit in the tube; the solution consisted of breaking the sticks apart. In the short-sticks task, subjects were given three short sticks that, together, added up to the length required; the solution consisting of putting them all in the same end of the tube to displace the food out the other side. Finally, in the H-tool task, subjects were given a stick with transverse pieces on either end that prevented its insertion into the tube; the solution consisted of removing the blocking piece from the tool. Although all three subjects eventually solved these variations of the task, they made a number of errors such as attempting to insert the whole bundle or inserting one short stick in one end of the tube and another short stick in the other end. Moreover, these errors did not decrease significantly over trials, suggesting that capuchins understood little about the causal relations between the elements in the task. Visalberghi, Fragaszy, and Savage-Rumbaugh (1995) essentially replicated the results of the bundle and the H-tool tasks with six other capuchins.

One recent study, however, suggests that some capuchins may understand more about causal relations than previously thought. Anderson and Henneman (1995) tested the ability of two adult capuchin monkeys to anticipate (and solve) a variety of problems associated with using a stick to extract honey from a box with multiple holes. In a series of experiments of increasing complexity, subjects were required to select a stick of the appropriate diameter to fit the holes, rake in a stick of the appropriate diameter with the help of another tool, modify a stick that was too thick or too twisted to fit the holes, or construct a rake that would permit them to obtain a suitable stick to extract the honey. Results indicated that both capuchins (especially the male) readily selected sticks of a diameter suitable to fit the holes. This even included cases in which the box and the sticks available were not within the same visual field. This result contrasts with Visalberghi's (1993) findings in which capuchins failed to select appropriate tools to solve the tube task when the tools were left in a room adjacent to the tube with food in it. Moreover, Anderson and Henneman (1995) noted that one capuchin modified tools in a very purposeful manner without committing the sort of errors described by Visalberghi and Trinca (1989). The same capuchin also used a tool (itself not suitable for honey-dipping) to rake in appropriate sticks for honey-dipping. Neither of the subjects, however, was able to construct a rake to obtain honey-dipping sticks.

The tube task has also been administered to apes. First, Bard, Fragaszy, and Visalberghi (1995) administered this task to young chimpanzees (two to four years old) and found that in the two most difficult versions of the task (i.e., short-sticks and H-tool), the performance of the majority of subjects actually deteriorated over trials, indicating they may not have come to understand the causal relations involved, although their young age may have explained their poor performance. Visalberghi Fragaszy, & Savage-Rumbaugh (1995) presented the bundle and H-tool tasks to subadult and adult apes (four bonobos, five chimpanzees, and one orangutan). Eight of the ten apes solved the basic tube task on the first trial, and the other two were successful later. When given a bundle of sticks, all subjects immediately disassembled the bundle and, unlike capuchins, no ape attempted to insert the bundle as a whole. Apes proved less successful in the H-tool task, however, making some of the same mistakes as the capuchins. Indeed, a statistical comparison of the two species in this condition revealed no significant difference. Although there was an overall group tendency to decrease the number of errors across trials, some subjects increased their errors.

To examine further the understanding of causal relations in the tube task, Visalberghi and Limongelli (1994) presented a new tube problem that punished subjects who did not foresee the consequences of their behavior. The authors presented four capuchin monkeys with a tube that had a trap in its bottom center, and placed the food next to the trap. If subjects pushed the food in the direction of the trap, it would fall in it and they would lose it; to get the food out, they had to push the food away from the trap toward the other end of the tube. Visalberghi and Limongelli (1994) found that only one subject solved the task, systematically pushing the reward away from the trap. Although this subject seemed to be planning her moves in advance, the authors noted that in half the trials, she inserted the tool in the wrong side of the tube and, upon seeing that the reward was moving into the trap, withdrew the tool, reinserted it in the other end, and pushed out the reward. Visalberghi and Limongelli (1994) probed further her understanding of the relation between the trap and the reward by inverting the trap 180 degrees so that the trap was on top of the tube, where it was no longer effective. The subject, however, persisted in her strategy of pushing the food away from the trap, suggesting that she had apparently simply learned to push the food away from the trap side without understanding the causal relations between the trap and the reward.

Limongelli, Boysen, and Visalberghi (1995) presented the trap-tube task to five chimpanzees who behaved at chance levels for the first seventy trials, although two of them learned to avoid the trap during seventy additional trials. The authors administered an additional test to assess whether chimpanzees understood the relationship between the position of the reward with respect to the trap or whether they were simply using the simple rule of pushing the reward out the side to which it was closest, thus avoiding the trap. Limongelli, Boysen, and Visalberghi (1995) varied the location of the trap in the tube. In some cases, the trap was located very close to one end with the food just beyond it, so that subjects actually had to push the food out the end from which it was farthest. In other cases, the opposite arrangement was used. Both subjects solved these variations easily, with almost no errors, so the researchers concluded that these two chimpanzees understood the causal relations in this task better than the capuchin monkeys. It should be noted, however, that the variations used in this experiment could still be solved by the rule "push the food away from the trap," which could have been learned during the previous trials. Unfortunately, the authors did not invert the trap as was previously done with capuchins.

In summary, this section has shown that various primates have some knowledge about causal relations regarding what makes a tool effective. They know that objects have to be in contact for a tool to be effective, recognize the relevant and irrelevant functional features of a tool, and can choose the appropriate dimensions of an effective tool in a particular task. Nevertheless, these studies have also shown clear limitations, perhaps more clearly seen in the tube task and its variations.

Perceiving and Judging Physical Events

One area that has received considerable attention is that of object knowledge in infants. These studies present subjects with a series of events – some that follow the laws of physics such as solidity or gravity and others that violate those laws. Using looking measures, numerous studies have found that human infants respond selectively to the violation of physics laws (Baillargeon, 1995; Spelke et al., 1995). These authors have argued that even at this young age, children show object knowledge. Hauser and colleagues have been instrumental in introducing this area of research in nonhuman primates. They have concentrated on two topics: gravity and solidity.

In the gravity area, Hood et al. (1999) presented cotton-top tamarins with three containers arranged in a straight line. One of the containers was connected to an opaque tube through which the experimenter dropped food. Subjects consistently searched for the food in the container over which the food was dropped. They did this regardless of whether the tube was connected to the container or not. This indicates that monkeys failed to understand that the reward's straight-fall trajectory can be deviated by the tube. This bias persisted despite variations on the incentives offered to the subjects for successful performance. Children presented with the same task also show a gravity bias, although older children can eventually overcome it (Hood, Care, & Prasada, 2000). In a follow-up experiment, Hauser et al. (2001) reported that when the reward trajectory was horizontal rather than vertical (as in the original test), tamarins performed better and the biases observed previously disappeared. Also subjects with experience with the horizontal version of the task performed better in the original task (i.e., free-fall reward) than subjects without such experience, even though the gravity bias was still apparent. Taken together, these results suggest that tamarins have a pervasive gravity bias that impairs their search for hidden objects.

Hauser (2001) investigated the same topic with a different paradigm. He presented rhesus macaques with a table and two boxes. The first box was placed on top of the table and the second box was placed under the table right under the first box. The experimenter then raised a screen that occluded both boxes (and the table) and dropped a reward over the top box. Because of the screen, the monkeys never saw where the reward entered the box, they just saw it falling toward the table and disappearing behind the screen. Monkeys searched for the food in the bottom box, thus showing a gravity bias. Control tests indicated that subjects did not have a preference for the bottom box, nor did they avoid the top box in the absence of the reward drop. Interestingly, Santos and Hauser (2002) found that rhesus monkeys tested with the same paradigm but using a violation of expectation measures solved this problem. In other words, subjects looked longer in trials in which the reward appeared on the bottom (apparently going through a solid partition) than in trials in which the reward stayed on top of the partition.

Call (2004) recently investigated two other aspects of the object knowledge that subjects may use to find food. The first is whether apes know that food inside a container when shaken makes a noise. He found that apes are capable of using the noise made by shaking food to identify the correct container (see inferential reasoning section). Although one may argue that this simply involves detecting an association between the food and the cue rather than an understanding that the food causes the noise, there are several lines of evidence that suggest that this interpretation oversimplifies the phenomenon. First, subjects performed well from the beginning, with no evidence of gradual improvement over trials. If subjects had learned to associate a noise with food in the past, it is unclear why, in control tests, they failed to associate a noise made by tapping the baited cup, which was comparable to that made by shaking the food inside the cup, with the presence of food. This failure was especially striking because subjects were tested after they had solved the initial problem. Second, their performance in this tapping test was comparable to performance in learning novel stimuli with arbitrary relations – for instance, learning that a green cup has food and a yellow cup does not. Subjects responded correctly to the auditory cue when it held a causal connection to the food but failed to do so when the auditory cue held a noncausal connection to the food.

In a second study, Call (unpublished data) investigated the ability of apes to use the shape of objects to locate food. In the initial problem, he presented two rectangular trays on a platform and hid a piece of food under one of them. One of the trays therefore rested flat on the platform whereas the other rested in an inclined orientation (because of the food placed under it). Subjects selected preferentially the inclined tray but failed to do so in a control test in which the inclined tray was substituted by a wooden wedge that produced the same visual effect as the inclined tray. This result was important because it ruled out the possibility that subjects simply preferred the perceptual appearance of the inclined tray, perhaps because it had been reinforced in the past. More importantly, subjects failed to select the wedge, an arbitrary stimulus, after they were successful in the inclined tray test. This result is analogous to that of the previous study in which subjects failed to respond above chance to stimuli with noncausal connections to the food after they had succeeded with very similar stimuli with causal connections. It therefore is found again that when there are arbitrary (i.e., noncausal) relations between the food and the elements of the problem, subjects perform poorly compared with when the connection is nonarbitrary (i.e., causal). It is unlikely that these results are based solely on learning to associate a cue with a response without any insight into the structure of the problem. Instead, it is conceivable that subjects understood that it was the food that caused the noise or made the tray incline, not simply that the food was associated with the presence of the noise or the shape.

In summary, primates have some knowledge about the physical properties of objects, and they can use this knowledge to predict the location in which rewards can be found.

Social Reasoning

Primates' social cognition represents a large area of research in its own right. At the most basic level, it involves how individuals understand and predict the behavior and, perhaps, the perceptual activities of others. Of course, it also may involve how individuals understand the psychological states and activities of others, which are less directly observable. So the question is whether primates can reason about the psychological states and activities of others. Despite many richly interpreted anecdotes, until recently there was very little evidence that primates reasoned about what others were seeing, intending, wanting, and thinking (see Tomasello & Call, 1997, for a review). Some recent studies have demonstrated that primates can reason about some – although clearly not all – of the psychological states about which humans reason.

Hare et al. (2000) placed a subordinate and a dominant chimpanzee into rooms on opposite sides of a third room. Each had a guillotine door leading into the third room which, when cracked at the bottom, allowed them to observe two pieces of food at various locations within that room – and to see the other individual looking under her door. After the food had been placed, the doors for both individuals were opened and they were allowed to enter the third room. The basic problem for the subordinate in this situation is that the dominant will take all of the food it can see. In some cases, however, things were arranged so that the subordinate could see a piece of food that the dominant could not see – because it was on her side of a small barrier. The question in these cases was whether the subordinate knew that the dominant could not see a particular piece of food, so it was safe for her to go for it.

The basic finding was that subordinates did go for food only they could see much more often than they went for food that both they and the dominant could see. In some cases, the subordinate may have been monitoring the behavior of the dominant, but in other cases this possibility was ruled out by giving subordinates a small headstart, forcing them to make their choice (to go to the food that both competitors could see, or to go to the food that only they could see) before the dominant was released into the area. Moreover, we ran two other control conditions. In one, the dominant's door was lowered before the two competitors were let into the room (and again the subordinate got a small headstart), so that the subordinate could not see which piece the dominant was looking at under the door (i.e., it is possible that in the first studies the subordinate saw that the dominant was looking at the out-in-the-open food and so went for the other piece). The results were clear. Subordinates preferentially targeted the hidden piece. In the other control study, we followed the same basic procedure as before (one piece of food in the open, one on the subordinate's side of a barrier) but we used a transparent barrier that did not prevent the dominant from seeing the food behind it. In this case, chimpanzees chose equally between the two pieces of food, seeming to know that the transparent barrier was not serving to block the dominant's visual access (and so her "control" of the food). The findings of these studies suggest that chimpanzees know what conspecifics can and cannot see and, further, that they use this knowledge to make inferences about what their competitor is about to do next.

In a follow-up study, Hare, Call, and Tomasello (2001) investigated whether chimpanzees were also able to take into account past information such as whether the dominant had seen the baiting. For these experiments, two barriers and one piece of food were used, and what the dominant saw was manipulated. In experimental trials, dominants had not seen the food hidden, or food they had seen hidden was moved to a different location when they were not watching, whereas in control trials, they saw the food being hidden or moved. Subordinates, on the other hand, always saw the entire baiting procedure and could monitor the visual access of the dominant competitor. Subordinates preferentially retrieved and approached the food that dominants had not seen hidden or moved, which suggests that subordinates were sensitive to what dominants had or had not seen during baiting a few moments before. In this case, deciding which piece of food to approach depended on the subordinate's making inferences about what the dominant knew about the situation.

These studies of what may be called social problem solving demonstrate that some primates may make inferential leaps not just about directly perceivable things, but also about less observable things such as what others do and do not see, or even have or have not seen in the immediate past.

Conclusions and Future Directions

There was a time when the dominant view in the Western intellectual tradition was that human beings were rational and all other animals were simply preprogrammed brutes or automata. That view is demonstrably false. All the evidence reviewed in this chapter suggests that nonhuman primates interact with their worlds in many creative ways, relying on a variety of cognitive processes to do so. They reason and make inferences about space, causality, objects, quantities, and the psychological states of other individuals, and in some cases they can engage in relational and analogical reasoning concerning particular objects or even categories of objects.

The main pitfall to avoid in attempting to integrate our knowledge about the cognitive skills of other animals with our knowledge about human cognition is oversimplification. Asking dichotomously whether or not animals reason or think or have a theory of mind generally is not very useful (Tomasello, Call, & Hare, 2003a, 2003b). Nonhuman animals quite often have some components, or some aspects, of the human version, and in some cases they possess skills that humans do not have or do not have to the same degree (e.g., some of the memory skills demonstrated by food-caching birds; Shettleworth, 1998). We need to compare the skills in detail if we want to provide an anatomy of their structure from an evolutionary point of view.

Because this book is mainly about human reasoning and thinking, we should conclude with a word about what we believe makes human cognition different from that of other primates. The answer, in a word, is culture (Tomasello & Call, 1997; Tomasello, 1999). The thought experiment we use to demonstrate the point is to imagine a human child raised on a desert island without any social contacts. Our contention is that in adulthood this adult's cognitive skills would not differ very much – perhaps a little, but not very much – from those of other great apes. This person would certainly not invent by him or herself a natural language, or algebra or calculus, or science or government. The human cognitive skills that make the most difference are those that enable individuals of the species *Homo sapiens*, in a sense, to pool their cognitive resources – to create and participate in collective cultural activities and products. When viewed from the perspective of the individual mind, the cognitive skills necessary for cultural creation and learning may not differ so very much from those of other primate species.

In any case, much can be learned about human cognition by looking at how it is similar to and how it is different from that of closely related species. We hope to have shown in this chapter that, in many fundamental respects, human cognition is simply one form of primate cognition. The vast gulf that seems to separate what humans and other primates can do cognitively – in the domain of mathematics, as just one instance – in many, if not most, cases is the result of fairly small differences of individual psychology that enable humans to accumulate knowledge across generations and to use collective artifacts such as linguistic and mathematical symbols.

Acknowledgment

The authors wish to thank Keith Holyoak for comments made on an earlier draft of this chapter.

References

Anderson, J. R. & Henneman, M. C. (1995). Solutions to a tool-use problem in a pair of *Cebus apella*. *Mammalia*, 58, 351–361.

Baillargeon, R. (1995). Physical reasoning in infancy. In M. Gazzaniga (Ed.), *The Cognitive Neurosciences* (pp. 181–204) Cambridge, MA: MIT Press.

Bard, K. A., Fragaszy, D. M., & Visalberghi, E. (1995). Acquisition and comprehension of a tool-using behavior by young chimpanzees (*Pan troglodytes*): Effects of age and modelling. *International Journal of Comparative Psychology*, 8, 47–68.

Beck, B. B. (1980). *Animal Tool Behavior*. New York: Garland Press.

Beran, M. J. (2001). Summation and numerousness judgments of sequentially presented sets of items by chimpanzees (*Pan troglodytes*). *Journal of Comparative Psychology*, 115, 181–191.

Beran, M. J., & Minahan, M. F. (2000). Monitoring spatial transpositions by bonobos (*Pan paniscus*) and chimpanzees (*P. troglodytes*). *International Journal of Comparative Psychology*, 13, 1–15.

Beran, M. J., & Rumbaugh, D. M. (2001). "Constructive" enumeration by chimpanzees (*Pan troglodytes*) on a computerized task. *Animal Cognition*, 4, 81–89.

Beran, M. J., & Washburn, D. A. (2002) Chimpanzee responding during matching to sample: Control by exclusion. *Journal of the Experimental Analysis of Behavior*, 78, 497–508.

Bernstein, I. S. (1961). The utilization of visual cues in dimension-abstracted oddity by primates. *Journal of Comparative and Physiological Psychology*, 54, 243–247.

Boesch, C., & Boesch, H. (1984). Mental map in wild chimpanzees: An analysis of hammer transports for nut cracking. *Primates*, 25, 160–170.

Bond, A. B., Kamil, A. C., & Balda, R. P. (2003). Social complexity and transitive inference in Corvids. *Animal Behaviour*, 65, 479–487.

Bovet, D., & Vauclair, J. (2001). Judgment of conceptual identity in monkeys. *Psychonomic Bulletin and Review*, 8, 470–475.

Boyd, R., & Richerson, P. (1985). *Culture and the Evolutionary Process*. Chicago: The University of Chicago Press.

Boysen, S. T., & Berntson, G. G. (1989). Numerical competence in a chimpanzee (*Pan troglodytes*). *Journal of Comparative Psychology*, 103, 23–31.

Boysen, S. T., Berntson, G. G., Shreyer, T. A., & Hannan, M. B. (1995). Indicating acts during counting by a chimpanzee (*Pan troglodytes*). *Journal of Comparative Psychology*, 109, 47–51.

Boysen, S. T., Berntson, G. G., Shreyer, T. A., & Quigley, K. S. (1993). Processing of ordinality and transitivity by chimpanzees (*Pan troglodytes*). *Journal of Comparative Psychology*, 107, 208–215.

Brannon, E. M., & Terrace, H. S. (1998). Ordering of the numerosities 1 to 9 by monkeys. *Science*, 282, 746–749.

Brannon, E. M., & Terrace, H. S. (2000). Representation of the numerosities 1–9 by Rhesus macaques (*Macaca mulatta*). *Journal of Experimental Psychology: Animal Behavior Processes*, 26, 31–49.

Burdyn, L. E., & Thomas, R. K. (1984). Conditional discrimination with conceptual simultaneous and successive cues in the squirrel monkey (*Saimiri sciureus*). *Journal of Comparative Psychology*, 98, 405–413.

Call, J. (2000). Estimating and operating on discrete quantities in orangutans (*Pongo pygmaeus*). *Journal of Comparative Psychology*, 114, 136–147.

Call, J. (2001). Object permanence in orangutans (*Pongo pygmaeus*), chimpanzees (*Pan troglodytes*), and children (*Homo sapiens*). *Journal of Comparative Psychology*, 115, 159–171.

Call, J. (2003). Spatial rotations and transpositions in orangutans (*Pongo pygmaeus*) and *chimpanzees (Pan troglodytes)*. *Primates*, 44, 347–357.

Call, J. (2004). Inferences about the location of food in the great apes. *Journal of Comparative Psychology*, 118, 232–241.

Call, J., & Rochat, P. (1996). Liquid conservation in orangutans. Individual differences and perceptual strategies *Journal of Comparative Psychology*, 100, 219–232.

Call, J., & Rochat, P. (1997). Perceptual strategies in the estimation of physical quantities by orangutans (*Pongo pygmaeus*). *Journal of Comparative Psychology, 111*, 315–329.

Cramer, A. E., & Gallistel, C. R. (1997). Vervet monkeys as travelling salesmen. *Nature, 387*, 464.

D'Amato, M. R., & Colombo, M. (1985). Auditory matching-to-sample in monkeys (*Cebus apella*). *Animal Learning and Behavior, 13*, 375–382.

D'Amato, M. R., & Colombo, M. (1988). Representation of serial order in monkeys (*Cebus apella*). *Journal of Experimental Psychology: Animal Behavior Processes, 14*, 131–139.

D'Amato, M. R., & Colombo, M. (1989). Serial learning with wild card items by monkeys (*Cebus apella*): Implications for knowledge of ordinal position. *Journal of Comparative Psychology, 103*, 252–261.

D'Amato, M. R., & Salmon, D. P. (1984). Cognitive processes in cebus monkeys. In H. L. Roitblat, T. G. Bever, & H. S. Terrace (Eds.), *Animal Cognition* (pp. 149–168). Hillsdale, NJ: Erlbaum.

D'Amato, M. R., Salmon, D. P., Loukas, E., & Tomie, A. (1985). Symmetry and transitivity of conditional relations in monkeys (*Cebus apella*) and pigeons (*Columba livia*). *Journal of the Experimental Analysis of Behavior, 44*, 35–47.

D'Amato, M. R., Salmon, D. P., Loukas, E., & Tomie, A. (1986). Processing of identity and conditional relations in monkeys (*Cebus apella*) and pigeons (*Columba livia*). *Animal Learning and Behavior, 14*, 365–373.

De Blois, S. T., & Novak, M. A. (1994). Object permanence in rhesus monkeys (*Macaca mulatta*). *Journal of Comparative Psychology, 108*, 318–327.

De Blois, S. T., Novak, M. A., & Bond, M. (1998). Object permanence in orangutans (*Pongo pygmaeus*) and squirrel monkeys (*Saimiri sciureus*). *Journal of Comparative Psychology, 112*, 137–152.

DeLoache, J. S. (1995). Early understanding and use of symbols: The model model. *Currents Directions in Psychological Science, 4*, 109–113.

Dumas, C. & Brunet, C. (1994). Pernamence de l'objet chez le singe capucin (*Cebus apella*): Etude des desplacements invisibles. *Revue Canadienne de psychologie experimentale, 48*, 341–357.

Fagot, J., Wasserman, E. A. & Young, M. E. (2001). Discriminating the relation between relations: The role of entropy in abstract conceptualization by baboons (*Papio papio*) and humans (*Homo sapiens*). *Journal of Experimental Psychology: Animal Behavior Processes, 27*, 316–328.

Fujita, K. (1982). An analysis of stimulus control in two-color matching-to-sample behaviors of Japanese monkeys (*Macaca fuscata fuscata*). *Japanese Psychological Research, 24*, 124–135.

Fujita, K. (1983). Formation of the sameness-difference concept by Japanese monkeys from a small number of color stimuli. *Journal of the Experimental Analysis of Behavior, 40*, 289–300.

Garber, P. (1989). Role of spatial memory in primate foraging patterns: *Saguinus mystax* and *Saguinus fuscicollis*. *American Journal of Primatology, 19*, 203–216.

Gillan, D. J. (1981). Reasoning in the chimpanzee: II. Transitive inference. *Journal of Experimental Psychology: Animal Behavior Processes, 7*, 150–164.

Gillan, D. J., Premack, D., & Woodruff, G. (1981). Reasoning in the chimpanzee: I. Analogical reasoning. *Journal of Experimental Psychology: Animal Behavior Processes, 7*, 1–17.

Hare, B., Call, J., Agnetta, B., & Tomasello, M., (2000). Chimpanzees know what conspecifics do and do not see. *Animal Behaviour, 59*, 771–785.

Hare, B., Call, J., & Tomasello, M., (2001). Do chimpanzees know what conspecifics know and do not know? *Animal Behaviour, 61*, 139–151.

Harlow, H. F. (1959). The development of learning in the rhesus monkey. *American Scientist, 47*, 459–479.

Hashiya, K., & Kojima, S. (2001). Hearing and auditory-visual intermodal recognition in the chimpanzee. In T. Matsuzawa (Ed.). *Primate Origins of Human Cognition and Behavior* (pp. 155–189). Berlin: Springer-Verlag.

Hauser, M. D., Kralik, J., & Botto-Mahan, C. (1999). Problem solving and functional design features: Experiments on cotton-top tamarins, *Saguinus oedipus*. *Animal Behaviour, 57*, 565–582.

Hauser, M., Pearson, H., & Seelig, D. (2002). Ontogeny of tool use in cotton-top tamarins, *Saguinus oedipus*: Innate recognition of functionally relevant features. *Animal Behaviour*, 64, 299–311.

Hauser, M. D. (1997). Artifactual kinds and functional design features: What a primate understands without language. *Cognition*, 64, 285–308.

Hauser, M. D. (2001). Searching for food in the wild: A nonhuman primate's expectations about invisible displacement. *Developmental Science*, 4, 84–93.

Hauser, M. D., Santos, L. R., Spaepen, G. M., & Pearson, H. E. (2002). Problem solving, inhibition and domain-specific experience: Experiments on cotton-top tamarins, *Saguinus oedipus*. *Animal Behaviour*, 64, 387–396.

Hauser, M. D., Williams, T., Kralik, J. D., & Moskovitz, D. (2001). What guides a search for food that has disappeared? Experiments on cotton-top tamarins (*Saguinus oedipus*). *Journal of Comparative Psychology*, 115, 140–151.

Hood, B., Carey, S. & Prasada, S. (2000). Predicting the outcomes of physical events: Two-year-olds fail to reveal knowledge of solidity and support. *Child Development*, 71, 1540–1554.

Hood, B. M., Hauser, M. D., Anderson, L., & Santos, L. (1999). Gravity biases in a nonhuman primate? *Developmental Science*, 2, 35–41.

Iversen, I. H., & Matsuzawa, T. (2001). Acquisition of navigation by chimpanzees (*Pan troglodytes*) in an automated fingermaze task. *Animal Cognition*, 4, 179–192.

Jackson, W. J., & Pegram, G. V. (1970a). Acquisition, transfer and retention of matching by Rhesus monkeys. *Psychological Reports*, 27, 839–846.

Jackson, W. J., & Pegram, G. V. (1970b). Comparison of intra- vs. extradimensional transfer of matching by Rhesus monkeys. *Psychonomic Science*, 19, 162–163.

Kawai, N., & Matsuzawa, T. (2000). Numerical memory span in a chimpanzee. *Nature*, 403, 39–40.

King, J. E., & Fobes, J. L. (1975). Hypothesis analysis of sameness-difference learning-set by capuchin monkeys. *Learning and Motivation*, 6, 101–113.

King, J. E., & Fobes, J. L. (1982). Complex learning by primates. In J. L. Fobes, & J. E. King (Eds.), *Primate Behavior*. (pp. 327–360). New York: Academic Press.

King, J. E. (1973). Learning and generalization of a two-dimensional sameness-difference concept by chimpanzees and orangutans. *Journal of Comparative and Physiological Psychology*, 84, 140–148.

Köhler, W. (1925). *The Mentality of Apes*. London: Routledge & Kegan Paul.

Kojima, T. (1979). Discriminative stimulus context in matching-to-sample of Japanese monkeys. *Japanese Psychological Research*, 21, 189–194.

Kuhlmeier, V. A., Boysen, S. T., & Mukobi, K. L. (1999). Scale-model comprehension by chimpanzees (*Pan troglodytes*). *Journal of Comparative Psychology*, 113, 396–402.

Kuhlmeier, V. A., & Boysen, S. T. (2001). The effect of response contingencies on scale model task performance by chimpanzees (*Pan troglodytes*). *Journal of Comparative Psychology*, 115, 300–306.

Limongelli, L., Boysen, S. T., & Visalberghi, E. (1995). Comprehension of cause-effect relations in a tool-using task by chimpanzees (*Pan troglodytes*). *Journal of Comparative Psychology*, 109, 18–26.

Lipsett, L. P., & Serunian, S. A. (1963). Oddity-problem learning in young children. *Child Development*, 34, 201–206.

MacDonald, S. E., Pang, J. C., & Gibeault, S. (1994). Marmoset (*Callithrix jacchus jacchus*) spatial memory in a foraging task: Win-stay versus win-shift strategies. *Journal of Comparative Psychology*, 108, 328–334.

MacDonald, S. E., & Wilkie, D. M. (1990). Yellow-nosed monkeys' (*Cercopithecus ascanius whitesidei*) spatial memory in a simulated foraging environment. *Journal of Comparative Psychology*, 104, 382–387.

McGonigle, B. O., & Chalmers, M. (1977). Are monkeys logical?. *Nature*, 267, 694–696.

Menzel, E. W. Jr. (1973). Chimpanzee spatial memory organization. *Science*, 182, 943–945.

Muncer, S. J. (1983). "Conservations" with a chimpanzee. *Developmental Psychobiology*, 16, 1–11.

Natale, F. (1989). Causality II: The stick problem. In F. Antinucci (Ed.), *Cognitive Structure and Development in Nonhuman Primates* (pp. 121–133). Hilldsale, NJ: Erlbaum.

Natale, F., Antinucci, F., Spinozzi, G., & Potì, P. (1986). Stage 6 object concept in nonhuman primate cognition: A comparison between gorilla (*Gorilla gorilla gorilla*) and Japanese macaque (*Macaca fuscata*). *Journal of Comparative Psychology*, 100, 335–339.

Nissen, H. W., Blum, J. S., & Blum, R. A. (1948). Analysis of matching behavior in chimpanzee. *Journal of Comparative and Physiological Psychology*, 41, 62–74.

Oden, D. L., Thompson, R. K. R., & Premack, D. (1988). Spontaneous transfer of matching by infant chimpanzees (*Pan troglodytes*). *Journal of Experimental Psychology: Animal Behavior Processes*, 14, 140–145.

Oden, D. L., Thompson, R. K. R., & Premack, D. (1990). Infant chimpanzees spontaneously perceive both concrete and abstract same/different relations. *Child Development*, 61, 621–631.

Olthof, A., Iden, C. M., & Roberts, W. A. (1997). Judgments of ordinality and summation of number symbols by squirrel monkeys (*Saimiri sciureus*). *Journal of Experimental Psychology Animal Behavior Processes*, 23, 325–339.

Pepperberg, I. M. (1999). The Alex studies. Cognitive and communicative abilities of grey parrots. Cambridge, MA: Harvard University Press.

Perusse, R., & Rumbaugh, D. M. (1990). Summation in chimpanzees (*Pan troglodytes*): Effects of amounts, number of wells, and finer ratios. *International Journal of Primatology*, 11, 425–437.

Piaget, J. (1952). *The Origins of Intelligence in Children*. New York: Norton.

Piaget, J., & Inhelder, B. (1941). *Le développement des quantités physiques chez l'enfant*. Neuchâtel, Switzerland: Delachaux; and Paris: Niestlé.

Premack, D., & Premack, A. J. (1994). Levels of causal understanding in chimpanzees and children. *Cognition*, 50, 347–362.

Premack, D. (1976). *Intelligence in Ape and Man*. Hillsdale, NJ: Earlbaum.

Premack, D. (1983). The codes of man and beasts. *Behavioral and Brain Sciences*, 6, 125–167.

Roberts, W. A. (1998). *Principles of Animal Cognition*. Boston: McGraw-Hill.

Robinson, J. S. (1955). The sameness-difference discrimination problem in chimpanzee. *Journal of Comparative and Physiological Psychology*, 48, 195–197.

Robinson, J. S. (1960). The conceptual basis of the chimpanzee's performance on the sameness-difference discrimination problem. *Journal of Comparative and Physiological Psychology*, 53, 368–370.

Rumbaugh, D. M., & McCormack. (1967). The learning skills of primates: A comparative study of apes and monkeys. In D. Starck, R. Schheider, & H. J. Ruhn (Eds.), *Progress in Primatology* (pp. 289–306). Stuggart: Gustav Fischer Verlag.

Rumbaugh, D. M. (1970). Learning skills of anthropoids. In L. A. Rosenblum (Ed.), *Primate Behavior: Developments in Field and Laboratory Research* (pp. 1–70). New York: Academic Press.

Rumbaugh, D. M., Hopkins, W. D., Washburn, D. A., & Savage-Rumbaugh, E. S. (1989). Lana chimpanzee learns to count by "Numath": A summary of videotaped experimental report. *Psychological Record*, 39, 459–470.

Rumbaugh, D. M., Savage-Rumbaugh, E. S., & Hegel, M. T. (1987). Summation in the chimpanzee (*Pan troglodytes*). *Journal of Experimental Psychology: Animal Behavior Processes*, 13, 107–115.

Rumbaugh, D. M., Savage-Rumbaugh, E. S., & Pate, J. L. (1988). Addendum to "Summation in the chimpanzee (*Pan troglodytes*)". *Journal of Experimental Psychology: Animal Behavior Processes*, 14, 118–120.

Santos, L. R., & Hauser, M. D. (2002). A nonhuman primate's understanding of solidity: Dissociations between seeing and acting. *Developmental Science*, 5, 1–7.

Schino, G., Spinozzi, G., & Berlinguer, L. (1990). Object concept and mental representation in *Cebus apella* and *Macaca fascicularis*. *Primates*, 31, 537–544.

Shettleworth, S. J. (1998). *Cognition, Evolution, and Behavior*. New York: Oxford University Press.

Sigg, H. (1986). Ranging patterns in hamadryas baboons: Evidence for a mental map. In J. G. Else, & P. C. Lee (Eds.), *Primate Ontogeny, Cognition and Social Behaviour* (pp. 87–91). Cambridge, UK: Cambridge University Press.

Smith, H. J., King, J. E., Witt, E. D., & Rickel, J. E. (1975). Sameness–difference matching from sample by chimpanzees. *Bulletin of the Psychonomic Society*, 6, 469–471.

Spelke, E. S., Phillips, A., & Woodward, A. L. (1995). Infants' knowledge of object motion and human action. In D. Sperber, D. Premack & A. J. Premack (Eds.). *Causal Cognition*.

A Multidisciplinary Debate (pp. 44–78). New York: Oxford University Press.

Spinozzi, G. & Potì, P. (1989). Causality I: The support problem. In F. Antinucci (Ed.), *Cognitive Structure and Development in Nonhuman Primates* (pp. 113–119). Hilldsale, NJ: Erlbaum.

Spinozzi, G. & Potì, P. (1993). Piagetian Stage 5 in two infant chimpanzees (*Pan troglodytes*): The development of permanence of objects and the spatialization of causality. *International Journal of Primatology*, 14, 905–917.

Suda, C. & Call, J. (in press). Piagetian liquid conservation in the great apes. *Journal of Comparative Psychology*.

Sulkowski, G. M & Hauser, M. D. (2001). Can Rhesus monkeys spontaneously subtract? *Cognition*, 79, 239–262.

Swartz, K., Chen, S., & Terrace, H. (1991). Serial learning by rhesus monkeys I: Acquisition and retention of multiple four item lists. *Journal of Experimental Psychology: Animal Behavior Processes*, 17, 396–410.

Thomas, R. K., & Boyd, M. G. (1973). A comparison of *Cebus albifrons* and *Saimiri sciureus* on oddity performance. *Animal Learning and Behavior*, 1, 151–153.

Thomas, R. K., & Frost, T. (1983). Oddity and dimension-abstracted oddity (DAO) in squirrel monkeys. *American Journal of Psychology*, 96, 51–64.

Thomas, R. K., & Peay, L. (1976). Length judgments by squirrel monkeys: Evidence for conservation? *Developmental Psychology*, 12, 349–352.

Thompson, R. K. R., & Oden, D. L. (2000). Categorical perception and conceptual judgments by nonhuman primates: The paleological monkey and the analogical ape. *Cognitive Science*, 24, 363–396.

Thompson, R. K. R., Oden, D. L., & Boysen, S. T. (1997). Language-naive chimpanzees (Pan troglodytes) judge relations between relations in a conceptual matching-to-sample task. *Journal of Experimental Psychology: Animal Behavior Processes*, 23, 31–43.

Tomasello, M. (1999). *The cultural origins of human cognition*. Cambridge, MA: Harvard University Press.

Tomasello, M., & Call, J. (1997). *Primate Cognition*. New York: Oxford University Press.

Tomasello, M., Call, J. & Hare, B. (2003a). Chimpanzees understand psychological states – the question is which ones and to what extent. *Trends in Cognitive Sciences*, 7, 153–156.

Tomasello, M., Call, J. & Hare, B. (2003b). Chimpanzees versus humans: It's not that simple. *Trends in Cognitive Sciences*, 7, 239–240.

Vauclair, J. (1996). *Animal Cognition. An Introduction to Modern Comparative Cognition*. Cambridge, MA: Harvard University Press.

Visalberghi, E. (1993). Tool use in a South American monkey species: An overview of the characteristics and limits of tool use in *Cebus apella*. In A. Berthelet, & J. Chavaillon (Eds.), *The Use of Tools by Human and Non-Human Primates* (pp. 118–131). New York: Oxford University Press.

Visalberghi, E., Fragaszy, D. M., & Savage-Rumbaugh, E. S. (1995). Performance in a tool-using task by common chimpanzees (*Pan troglodytes*), bonobos (*Pan paniscus*), an orangutan (*Pongo pygmaeus*), and capuchin monkeys (*Cebus apella*). *Journal of Comparative Psychology*, 109, 52–60.

Visalberghi, E., & Limongelli, L. (1994). Lack of comprehension of cause-effect relations in tool-using capuchin monkeys (*Cebus apella*). *Journal of Comparative Psychology*, 108, 15–22.

Visalberghi, E., & Trinca, L. (1989). Tool use in capuchin monkeys: Distinguishing between performing and understanding. *Primates*, 30, 511–521.

Vonk, J. (2003). Gorilla (*Gorilla gorilla gorilla*) and orangutan (*Pongo abelii*) understanding of first- and second-order relations. *Animal Cognition*, 6, 77–86.

Washburn, D. A. (1992). Human factors with nonhumans: Factors that affect computer-task performance. *International Journal of Comparative Psychology*, 5, 191–204.

Washburn, D. A., & Rumbaugh, D. M. (1991). Ordinal judgements of numerical symbols by macaques (*Macaca mulatta*). *Psychological Science*, 2, 190–193.

Washburn, D. A., & Rumbaugh, D. M. (1992). Comparative assessment of psychomotor performance: Target prediction by humans and macaques (*Macaca mulatta*). *Journal of Experimental Psychology: General*, 121, 305–312.

Weinstein, B. (1941). Matching-from-sample by Rhesus monkeys and by children. *Journal of Comparative and Physiological Psychology*, 31, 195–213.

Woodruff, G., Premack, D., & Kennel, K. (1978). Conservation of liquid and solid quantity by the chimpanzee. *Science*, 202, 991–994.

Wright, A. A., Santiago, H. C., & Sands, S. F. (1984). Monkey memory: Same/different concept learning, serial probe acquisition, and probe delay effects. *Journal of Experimental Psychology: Animal Behavior Processes*, 10, 513–529.

Wright, A. A., Shyan, M., & Jitsumori, M. (1990). Auditory same/different concept learning by monkeys. *Animal Learning and Behavior*, 18, 287–294.

CHAPTER 26

Language and Thought

Lila Gleitman
Anna Papafragou

Possessing a language is one of the central features that distinguishes humans from other species. Many people share the intuition that they think in language and the absence of language therefore would be the absence of thought. One compelling version of this self-reflection is Helen Keller's (1955) report that her recognition of the signed symbol for 'water' triggered thought processes that had theretofore – and consequently – been utterly absent. Statements to the same or related effect come from the most diverse intellectual sources: "The limits of my language are the limits of my world" (Wittgenstein, 1922); and "The fact of the matter is that the 'real world' is to a large extent unconsciously built upon the language habits of the group" (Sapir, 1941, as cited in Whorf, 1956, p. 75).

The same intuition arises with regard to particular languages and dialects. Speaking the language of one's childhood seems to conjure up a host of social and cultural attitudes, beliefs, memories, and emotions, as though returning to the Casbah or to Avenue L and East 19th Street and conversing with the natives opens a window back into some prior state of one's nature. But do such states of mind arise because one is literally thinking in some new representational format by speaking in a different language? After all, many people experience the same or related changes in sociocultural orientation and sense of self when they are, say, wearing their battered old jeans versus some required business suit or military uniform; or even more poignantly when they reexperience a smell or color or sound associated with dimly recalled events. Many such experiences evoke other times, other places.

But according to many anthropological linguists, sociologists, and cognitive psychologists, speaking a particular language exerts vastly stronger and more pervasive influences than an old shoe or the smell of boiling cabbage. The idea of "linguistic relativity" is that having language, or having a particular language, crucially shapes mental life. Indeed, it may not be only that a specific language exerts its idiosyncratic effects as we speak or listen to it – that language might come to "be" our thought; we may have no way to think many thoughts, conceptualize many of our ideas, without this language, or outside of and independent of this language. From such a perspective, different communities of humans, speaking different languages, would think differently to the extent that languages differ from one another. But is this so? Could it be so? That depends on how we unpack the notions alluded to so informally thus far.

In one sense, it is obvious that language use has powerful and specific effects on thought. That's what it is for, or at least that is one of the things it is for – to transfer ideas from one mind to another mind. Imagine Eve telling Adam "Apples taste great." This fragment of linguistic information, as we know, caused Adam to entertain a new thought with profound effects on his world knowledge, inferencing, and subsequent behavior. Much of human communication is an intentional attempt to modify others' thoughts and attitudes in just this way. This information transmission function is crucial for the structure and survival of cultures and societies in all their known forms.

But the language-and-thought debate is not framed to query whether the content of conversation can influence one's attitudes and beliefs, for the answer to that question is too obvious for words. At issue, rather, is the degree to which natural languages provide the format in which thought is necessarily (or at least habitually) couched. Do formal aspects of a particular linguistic system (e.g., features of the grammar or the lexicon) organize the thought processes of its users? One famous "Aye" to this question appears in the writings of B. L. Whorf in the first half of the twentieth century. According to Whorf (1956, p. 214), the grammatical and lexical resources of individual languages heavily constrain the conceptual representations available to their speakers. To quote:

> *We are thus introduced to a new principle of relativity, which holds that all observers are not led by the same physical evidence to the same picture of the universe, unless their linguistic backgrounds are similar, or can in some way be calibrated.*

This relativistic view, in its strictest form, entails that linguistic categories will be the "program and guide for an individual's mental activity" (Ref. 143, p. 212), including categorization, memory, reasoning, and decision making. If this is right, then the study of different linguistic systems may throw light onto the diverse modes of thinking encouraged or imposed by such systems. Here is a recent formulation of this view (Pederson et al., 1998, p. 586):

> *We surmise that language structure . . . provides the individual with a system of representation, some isomorphic version of which becomes highly available for incorporation as a default conceptual representation. Far more than developing simple habituation, use of the linguistic system, we suggest, actually forces the speaker to make computations he or she might otherwise not make.*

Even more dramatically, according to stronger versions of this general position, we can newly understand much about the development of concepts in the child mind: One acquires concepts as a consequence of their being systematically instantiated in the exposure language (Bowerman & Levinson, 2001, p. 13):

> *Instead of language merely reflecting the cognitive development which permits and constrains its acquisition, language is thought of as potentially catalytic and transformative of cognition.*

The importance of this position cannot be underestimated: Language here becomes a vehicle for the growth of *new* concepts – those that were not theretofore in the mind, and perhaps could not have been there without the intercession of linguistic experience. It therefore poses a challenge to the venerable view that one could not acquire a concept that one could not antecedently entertain (Plato, 5th–4th B.C.E.; Descartes, 1662; Fodor, 1975, *inter alia*].

Quite a different position is that language, although being the central human conduit for thought in communication, memory, and planning, neither creates nor materially distorts conceptual life: Thought is first; language is its expression. This contrasting view of cause and effect leaves the link between language and mind as strong as ever and just as relevant for understanding mental life. From Noam Chomsky's universalist perspective (1975, p. 4), for example, the forms and contents of all particular languages derive, in large part, from an antecedently specified cognitive substance and architecture and therefore provide a rich diagnostic of human conceptual commonalities:

> *Language is a mirror of mind in a deep and significant sense. It is a product of human intelligence . . . By studying the properties of natural languages, their structure, organization, and use, we may hope to learn something about human nature; something significant, if it is true that human cognitive capacity is the truly distinctive and most remarkable characteristic of the species.*

This view of concepts as prior to and progenitive of language is not proprietary to the rationalist position for which Chomsky is speaking here. This commonsensical position is maintained – rather, presupposed – by students of the mind who differ among themselves in almost all other regards. The early empiricists, for example, took it for granted that our concepts derive from experience with properties, things, and events in the world and not, originally, from language (Hume, 1739; Book I):

> *To give a child an idea of scarlet or orange, of sweet or bitter, I present the objects, or in other words, convey to him these impressions; but proceed not so absurdly, as to endeavor to produce the impressions by exciting the ideas.*

And as a part of such experience of objects, language learning will come along for the ride (Locke, 1690, Book 3.IX.9; emphasis ours):

> *If we will observe how children learn languages, we shall find that, to make them understand what the names of simple ideas or substances for, people ordinarily* show them the thing whereof they would have them have the idea; *and then repeat to them the name that stands for it . . .*

Thus linguistic relativity, in the sense of Whorf and many recent commentators, is quite novel and, in its strongest interpretations, revolutionary. At the limit, it is a proposal for how new thoughts can arise in the mind as a result of experience with language rather than as a result of experience with the world of objects and events.

Before turning to the recent literature on language and thought, we want to emphasize that there are no ideologues ready to man the barricades at the absolute extremes of the debate just sketched. To our knowledge, none – well, very few – of those who are currently advancing linguistic–relativistic themes and explanations believe that infants enter into language acquisition in a state of complete conceptual nakedness later redressed (perhaps we should say "dressed") by linguistic information. Rather, by general acclaim, infants are believed to possess some "core knowledge" that enters into first categorization of objects, properties, and events in the world (e.g., Carey, 1982; Kellman, 1996; Baillargeon, 1993; Gelman & Spelke, 1981; Leslie & Keeble, 1987; Mandler, 1996; Quinn, 2001; Spelke et al., 1992). The general question is how richly specified this innate basis may be and how experience refines, enhances, and transforms the mind's original furnishings. The specific question is whether language knowledge may be one of these formative or transformative aspects of experience. To our knowledge, none – well, very few – of those who adopt a nativist position on these matters reject as a matter of a priori conviction the possibility that there could be salience effects of language on thought. For instance, some particular natural language might formally mark a category whereas another does not; two languages might draw a category boundary at different places; two languages might differ in the computational resources they require to make manifest a particular distinction or category.

We will try to draw out aspects of these issues within several domains in which commentators and investigators are trying to disentangle cause and effect in the interaction of language and thought. We cannot discuss it all, of course, or even very much of what is currently in print on this topic.

There is too much of it (for recent anthologies, see Gumperz & Levinson, 1996; Bowerman & Levinson, 2001; Gentner & Goldin-Meadow, 2003).

Do We Think In Language?

We begin with a very simple question: Do our thoughts take place in natural language? If so, it would immediately follow that Whorf was right all along, since speakers of Korean and Spanish, or Swahili and Hopi would have to think systematically different thoughts.

If language directly expresses our thought, it seems to make a poor job of it. Consider for example the final (nonparenthetical) sentence in the preceding section:

1. There is too much of it.

Leaving aside, for now, the problems of anaphoric reference (what is "it"?), the sentence still has at least two interpretations that are compatible with its discourse context:

1a. There is too much written on linguistic relativity to fit into this article.

1b. There is too much written on linguistic relativity. (*Period*!)

We authors had one of these two interpretations in mind (guess which one). We had a thought and expressed it as (1) but English failed to render that thought unambiguously, leaving doubt between (1a) and (1b). One way to think about what this example portends is that language cannot, or in practice does not, express all and only what we mean. Rather, language use offers hints and guideposts to hearers, such that they can usually reconstruct what the speaker had in mind by applying to the uttered words a good dose of common sense – *aka* thoughts, inferences, and plausibilities – in the world.

The question of just how to apportion the territory between the underlying semantics of sentences and the pragmatic interpretation of the sentential semantics, of course, is far from settled in linguistic and philosophical theorizing. Consider the sentence *It is raining*. Does this sentence directly – that is, as an interpretive consequence of the linguistic representation itself – convey an assertion about rain falling *here*, in the immediate geographical environment of the speaker? Or does the sentence – the linguistic representation – convey only that rain is falling, leaving it for the common sense of the listener to deduce that the speaker likely meant raining here and now rather than raining today in Bombay or on Mars; likely, too, that if the sentence was uttered indoors, the speaker more likely meant *here* to convey "just outside of here" than "right here, as the roof is leaking." The exact division of labor between linguistic semantics and pragmatics has implications for the language–thought issue, because the richer (one claims that) the linguistic semantics is, the more likely it is that language guides our mental life. Without going into detail, we will argue that linguistic semantics cannot fully envelop and substitute for inferential interpretation, and the representations that populate our mental life therefore cannot be identical to the representations that encode linguistic (semantic) meaning.

Language Is Sketchy, Thought Is Rich

There are several reasons to believe that thought processes are not definable over representations that are isomorphic to linguistic representations. One is the pervasive ambiguity of words and sentences. *Bat*, *bank*, and *bug* all have multiple meanings in English and are associated with multiple concepts, but these concepts themselves are clearly distinct in thought, as shown *inter alia* by the fact that one may consciously construct a pun. Moreover, several linguistic expressions including pronouns (*he*, *she*) and indexicals (*here*, *now*) crucially rely on context for their interpretation whereas the thoughts they are used to express are usually more specific. Our words are often semantically general – i.e., they fail to make distinctions that nevertheless are present in thought: *Uncle* in English does not semantically specify whether the individual comes from the mother's or the father's side, or whether he is a relative by blood or marriage, but usually the speaker who utters "my uncle . . . " possesses the relevant information. Indeed, lexical items typically take on different interpretations tuned to the occasion of use (*He has a square face. The room is hot.*) and depend on inference for their precise construal in different contexts (e.g., the implied action is systematically different when we *open an envelope/a can/an umbrella/a book*, or when an instance of that class of actions is performed to serve different purposes: *Open the window to let in the evening breeze/the cat*). Moreover, there are cases in which linguistic output does not even encode a complete thought or proposition (*tomorrow, maybe*). Finally, the presence of implicatures and other kinds of pragmatic inference ensures that – to steal a line from the Mad Hatter – although speakers generally mean what they say, they do not and could not say exactly what they mean.

From this and related evidence, it appears that linguistic representations underdetermine the conceptual contents they are used to convey: Language is *sketchy* compared with the richness of our thoughts (for a related discussion, see Fisher & Gleitman, 2002). In light of the limitations of language, time, and sheer patience, language users make reference by whatever catch-as-catch-can methods they find handy, including the waitress who famously told another that "The ham sandwich wants his check" (Nunberg, 1978). What chiefly matters to talkers and listeners is that successful reference be made, whatever the means at hand. If one tried to say all and exactly what one meant, conversation could not happen; speakers would be lost in thought. Instead, conversation involves a constant negotiation in which participants estimate and update each others' background knowledge as a basis for what needs to be said given what is mutually known and inferable (e.g., Grice, 1975; Sperber & Wilson, 1986; Clark, 1992; Bloom, 2002).

In limiting cases, competent listeners ignore linguistically encoded meaning if it patently differs from what the speaker intended – for instance, by smoothly and rapidly repairing slips of the tongue. Oxford undergraduates had the wit, if not the grace, to snicker when Reverend Spooner reputedly said, "Work is the curse of the drinking classes." Often, the misspeaking is not even consciously noticed but is repaired to fit the thought – evidence enough that the word and the thought are two different matters.[1] The same latitude for thought to range beyond established linguistic means holds for the speakers, too. Wherever the local linguistic devices and locutions seem insufficient or overly constraining, speakers invent or borrow words from another language, devise similes and metaphors, and sometimes make permanent additions and subtractions to the received tongue. It would be hard to understand how they do so if language were itself, and all at once, both the format and vehicle of thought.

All the cases just mentioned refer to particular tokenings of meanings in the idiosyncratic interactions between people. A different problem arises when languages categorize aspects of the world in ways that are complex and inconsistent. An example is reported by Malt et al. (1999). They examined the vocabulary used by English, Spanish, and Chinese subjects to label the various containers we bring home from the grocery store full of milk, juice, ice cream, bleach, or medicine (e.g., *jugs, bottles, cartons, boxes*). As the authors point out, containers share names based not only on some perceptual resemblances but also on very local and particular conditions with size, shape, substance, contents, and nature of the contents, not to speak of the commercial interests of the purveyor, all playing interacting and shifting roles. In present-day American English, for instance, a certain plastic container that looks like a bear with a straw stuck in its head is called *a juice box*, although it is not boxy either in shape (square or rectangular) or typical constitution (your prototypical American box is made of cardboard). The languages Malt et al. studied differ markedly in the set of terms available for this domain, and also in how their subjects extended these terms to describe diverse new containers. Speakers of the three languages differed in which objects (old and new) they classified together by name. For example, a set of objects distributed across the sets of *jugs*, *containers*, and *jars* by English speakers were unified by the single label *frasco* by Spanish speakers. Within and across languages, not everything square is a box, not everything glass is a bottle, not everything *not* glass is *not* a bottle, and so on. The naming, in short, is a complex mix resulting from perceptual resemblances, historical influences, and a generous dollop of arbitrariness. Yet Malt et al.'s subjects did not differ much (if at all) from each other in their classification of these containers by overall similarity rather than by name. Nor were the English and Spanish, as one might guess, more closely aligned than, say, the Chinese and Spanish. So here we have a case in which cross-linguistic practice groups objects in a domain in multiple ways that have only flimsy and sporadic correlations with perception without discernible effect on the nonlinguistic classificatory behaviors of users.[2]

So far, we have emphasized that language is a relatively impoverished and underspecified vehicle of expression that relies heavily on inferential processes outside the linguistic system for reconstructing the richness and specificity of thought. If correct, this seems to place rather stringent limitations on how language could serve as the original engine and sculptor of our conceptual life. Nevertheless, it is possible to maintain the idea that certain formal properties of language causally affect thought in more subtle, but still important, ways.

Use It or Lose It: Language Determines the Categories of Thought

We begin by mentioning the most famous and compelling case of a linguistic influence on perception: categorical perception of the phoneme (Liberman, 1970; Liberman et al., 1967; Kuhl et al., 1992). Children begin life with the capacity and inclination to discriminate among all of the acoustic–phonetic properties by which languages encode distinctions of meaning – a result famously documented by Peter Eimas (Eimas et al., 1971) using a dishabituation paradigm (for details and significant expansions of this basic result, see Jusczyk, 1985; and for extensions with neonates, Peña et al., 2003). These authors showed that an infant will work (e.g., turn its head or suck on a nipple) to hear a syllable such as *ba*. After some period of time, the infant habituates; that is, its sucking rate decreases to some base level. The high sucking rate can be reinstated if the syllable is switched to, say, *pa*, demonstrating that the infant detects the difference. These effects are heavily influenced by linguistic experience. Infants only a year or so of age – just when true language is making its appearance – have become insensitive to phonetic distinctions that are not phonemic (play no role at higher levels of linguistic organization) in the exposure language (Werker & Tees, 1984). Although these experience-driven effects are not totally irreversible in cases of long-term second-language immersion, they are pervasive and dramatic (for discussion, see Werker & Logan, 1985; Best, McRoberts, & Sithole, 1988). Without special training or unusual talent, the adult speaker–listener can effectively produce and discriminate the phonetic categories required in the native tongue, and little more. Not only that, these discriminations are categorical in the sense that sensitivity to within-category phonetic distinctions is poor and sensitivity at the phonemic boundaries is especially acute. Although the learning and use of a specific language has not created perceptual elements *de novo*, certainly it has refined, organized, and limited the set of categories at this level in radical ways. As we will discuss, several findings in the concept-learning literature have been interpreted analogously to this case.

An even more intriguing effect in this general domain is the reorganization of phonetic elements into higher-level phonological categories as a function of specific language spoken. For example, American English speech regularly lengthens vowels in syllables ending with a voiced consonant (e.g., *ride* and *write*) and neutralizes the *t/d* distinction in favor of a dental flap in certain unstressed syllables. The effect is that (in most dialects) the consonant sounds in the middle of *rider* and *writer* are physically the same. Yet the English-speaking listener seems to perceive a *d/t* difference in these words all the same, and – except when asked to reflect carefully – fails to notice the characteristic difference in vowel length that his or her own speech faithfully reflects. The complexity of this phonological reorganization is often understood as a reconciliation (interface) of the cross-cutting phonetic and morphological categories of a particular language. *Ride* ends with a *d* sound; *write* ends with a *t* sound; morphologically speaking, *rider* and *writer* are just *ride* and *write* with *er* added on; therefore, the phonetic entity between the syllables in these two words must be *d* in the first case and *t* in the second. Morphology trumps phonetics (for discussion see Bloch & Trager, 1942; Chomsky, 1964; Gleitman & Rozin, 1977).

When considering linguistic relativity, one might be tempted to write off the phonetic categorical perception effect as one that merely tweaks the boundaries of acoustic distinctions built into the mammalian species – a not-so-startling sensitizing effect of language on perception. But the phonological effect just discussed is no mere tweak. There has been a systemic reorganization creating a new set of lawfully recombinatorial elements – one that varies very significantly cross-linguistically.

Much of the literature on linguistic relativity can be understood as raising related issues in various perceptual and conceptual domains. Is it the case that distinctions of lexicon or grammar made regularly in one's language sensitize one to these distinctions and suppress or muffle others? Even to the extent of radically reorganizing the domain? An important literature has investigated this issue using the instance of color names and color perception. Languages differ in their terms for hue and brightness (Berlin & Kay, 1969; cf. Kay & Regier, 2002). Do psychophysical judgments differ accordingly? For instance, are adjacent hues that share a name in a particular language judged more similar by its speakers than equal-magnitude differences in wavelength and intensity that are consensually given different names in that language? And are the similarity spaces of speakers of other languages different in the requisite ways? Such language-caused distinctions have been measured in various ways – for example, discrimination across hue labeling boundaries (speed, accuracy, confusability), memory, and population comparisons. By and large, the results of such cross-linguistic studies suggest a remarkable independence of hue perception from labeling practice (e.g., Brown & Lenneberg, 1954; Heider & Oliver, 1972). One relevant finding comes from red–green color-blind individuals (Jameson & Hurwich, 1978). The perceptual similarity space of the hues for such individuals is systematically different from that of individuals of normal vision; that is what it means to be colorblind. Yet a large subpopulation of red–green colorblind individuals names hues, even of new things, consensually with normal-sighted individuals and orders these hue labels consensually. That is, these individuals do not perceptually order a set of color chips with the reds at one end, the greens at the other, and the oranges somewhere in between; yet they organize *the words* with *red* semantically at one end, *green* at the other, and *orange* somewhere in between. In short, the naming practices and perceptual organization of color mismatch in these individuals, which is a fact that they rarely notice until they enter the vision laboratory.

Overall, the language–thought relations for one perceptual domain (speech-sound perception) appear to be quite different from those in another perceptual domain (hue perception). Language influences acoustic phonetic perception much more than it influences hue perception. As a result, there is no deciding in advance that language does or does not influence perceptual life. Moreover, despite the prima facie relevance of these cases and the elegance of the literature that investigated them, the perception of relatively low-level perceptual categories, the organization of which we share with many nonhuman species, are less than ideal places to look for the linguistic malleability of thought.[3] However, these instances serve to scaffold discussion of language influences at higher levels and therefore for more elusive aspects of conceptual organization.

Do the Categories of Language Become the Categories of Thought?

A seminal figure in reawakening interest in linguistic relativity was Roger Brown, the great social and developmental psychologist who framed much of the field of language acquisition in the modern era. Brown (1957) performed a simple and elegant experiment that demonstrated an effect of lexical categorization on the inferred meaning of a new word. Young children were shown a picture, for example, of hands that seemed to be kneading confettilike stuff in an overflowing bowl. Some children were told *Show me the sib*. They pointed to the bowl (a solid rigid object). Others were told *Show me some sib*. They pointed to the confetti (an undifferentiated mass of stuff). Others were told *Show me sibbing*. They pointed to the hands and made kneading motions with their own hands (an action or event). Plainly, the same stimulus object was represented differently depending on the linguistic cues to the lexical categories count noun, mass noun, and verb. That is, the lexical categories themselves have notional correlates – at least in the minds of these young English speakers.

Some commentators have argued that the kinds of cues exemplified here – that persons, places, and things surface as nouns – are universal and can play causal roles in the acquisition of language – of course, by learners who are predisposed to find just these kinds of syntactic–semantic correlations natural (Pinker, 1984; Gleitman, 1990; Fisher, 1996; Bloom, 1994a; Lidz, Gleitman, & Gleitman, 2003; Baker, 2001, *inter alia*). Brown saw his result the other way around. He supposed that languages would vary arbitrarily in these mappings onto conceptual categories. If that is so, then language cannot play the causal role that Pinker and others envisaged for it – that is, as a cue to antecedently "prepared" correlations between linguistic and conceptual categories. Rather, those world properties yoked together by language would cause a (previously uncommitted) infant learner to conceive them as meaningfully related in some ways (Brown, 1957, p. 5):

> *In learning a language, therefore, it must be useful to discover the semantic correlates for the various parts of speech; for this discovery enables the learner to use the part-of-speech membership of a new word as a first cue to its meaning... Since [grammatical categories] are strikingly different in unrelated languages, the speakers [of these languages] may have quite different cognitive categories.*

As recent commentators have put this position, linguistic regularities are part of the correlational mix that creates ontologies, and language-specific properties therefore will bend psychological ontologies in language-specific ways (Smith, Colunga, & Yoshida, 2001). The forms of particular languages – or the habitual language usage of particular linguistic communities – by hypothesis, could yield different organizations of the fundamental nature of one's conceptual world: what it is to be a thing or some stuff, or a direction or place, or a state or event. We will discuss some research on these category types and their cross-linguistic investigation. But before doing so, we want to mention another useful framework for understanding potential relations between language and thought: that the tweakings and reorganizations language may accomplish happen under the dynamic control of communicative interaction, of "thinking for speaking."

Thinking for Speaking

It is natural to conceive conversation as beginning with a thought or mental message one wishes to convey. This thought is the first link in a chain of mental events that, on most accounts, gets translated into successively more languagelike representations, eventuating in a series of commands to the articulatory system to utter a word, phrase, or sentence (Levelt, 1989; Dell, 1995). As we have just described matters, there is a clear distinction at the two ends of this process – what you meant to say and how you express it linguistically. But this is not so clear. Several commentators, notably Dan Slobin (1996, 2003), have raised the possibility of a more dynamic and interactive process in which what one chooses to mean and the expressive options that one's language makes available are not so neatly divorced. It may not be that speakers of every language set out their messages identically all the way up to the time that they arrange the jaw, mouth, and tongue to utter *one two three* versus *un deux trois.* Instead, the language one has learned causes one to "intend to mean" in somewhat different ways. For instance, and as we will discuss in more detail, it may be that as a speaker of English, with its myriad verbs of *manner* of motion, one comes to inspect – and speak of – the world in terms of such manners, whereas a speaker of Greek or Spanish, with a vocabulary emphasizing verbs relating to *path* of motion, inspects – and speaks of – the world more directly in terms of the paths traversed. The organization of the thought, on this view, might be dynamically impacted along its course by specific organizational properties of the individual language.

Slobin (2001) and Levelt (1989) have pointed to some cases in which a distinction across languages in the resources devoted to different conceptual matters seems almost inevitable. This case is the closed-class functional vocabulary, the "grammatical" words such as modals, auxiliaries, tense and aspect markers, determiners, complementizers, case markers, prepositions, and so forth. These words play rather specific grammatical roles in marking the ways in which noun phrases relate to the verb and how the predications within a sentence relate to each other. These same grammatical words usually also have semantic content – for example, the directional properties of *from* in *John separated the wheat from the chaff.* Slobin has given a compendium of the semantic functions known to be expressed by such items and these number at least in the several hundreds, including not only tense, aspect, causativity, number, person, gender, mood, definiteness, and so on, found in English, but also first-hand versus inferred knowledge, social status of the addressee, existence–nonexistence, shape, and many others. Both Slobin and Levelt have argued as follows: As a condition of uttering a well-formed English sentence, the speaker of English must decide for example, whether the number of creatures being referred to is one or more in order to choose *the dog* or *the dogs*. Some modicum of mental resources, no matter how small, must be devoted to this issue repeatedly – hundreds of times a day every day, every week, every year – by English speakers. But speakers of Mandarin need not think about number, except when they particularly want to, because its expression is not grammaticized in their language. The same is true for all the hundreds of other properties. So either all speakers of languages covertly compute all these several hundred properties as part of their representations of the contents of their sent and received messages or they compute only some of them – primarily those that they *must* compute to speak and understand the language of their community. On information-handling grounds, one would suspect that not all these hundreds of conceptual interpretations and their possible combinations are computed at every instance. But if one computes only what one must for the combined purposes of linguistic intelligibility and present communicative purpose, then speakers of different languages, to this extent, must be thinking differently. As Slobin (2001, p. 442) puts it, "From this point of view, grammaticizable notions have a role in structuring language-specific mental spaces, rather than being there at the beginning, waiting for an input language to turn them on." On the basis of this reasoning, it is plausible to entertain the view of a language-based difference in the dynamics of converting thought to speech. How far such effects percolate downstream is the issue to which we now turn. Do differences in phraseology, grammatical morphology, and lexical semantics of different languages yield underlying disparities in their modes of thought?

Semantic Arenas of the Present Day Language–Thought Investigation

Objects and Substances

The problem of reference to *stuff* versus *objects* has attracted considerable attention because it starkly displays the indeterminacy in how language refers to the world (Chomsky, 1957; Quine, 1960). Whenever we indicate a physical object, we necessarily indicate some portion of a substance as well; the reverse is also true. Languages differ in their expression of this distinction (Lucy & Gaskins, 2001). Some languages make a grammatical distinction that roughly distinguishes object from substance. Count nouns in such languages denote individuated entities; such as, object kinds. These are marked in English with determiners and are subject to counting and pluralization (*a horse, horses, two horses*). Mass nouns typically denote nonindividuated entities – that is, substance rather than object kinds. These are marked in English with a different set of determiners (*more porridge*) and need an additional term that specifies quantity to be counted and pluralized (*a tube of toothpaste* rather than *a toothpaste*). Soja, Carey, and Spelke (1991) asked whether children approach this aspect of language learning already equipped with the ontological distinction between things and substance or whether they are led to make this distinction through learning count and mass syntax. Their subjects, English-speaking two-year-olds, did not yet make these distinctions in their speech. Soja et al. (1991) taught these children words in reference to various types of unfamiliar displays. Some were solid objects such as a T-shaped piece of wood, and others were nonsolid substances such as a pile of hand cream with sparkles in it. The children were shown such a sample, named with a term presented in a syntactically neutral frame that identified it neither as a count nor as a mass noun – for example, *This is my blicket* or *Do you see this blicket?* In extending these words to new displays, two-year-olds honored the distinction between object and substance. When the sample was a hard-edged solid object, they extended the new word to all objects of the same shape, even when made of a different material. When the sample was a nonsolid substance, they extended the word to other-shaped puddles of that same substance but not to shape matches made of different materials. Soja et al. took this finding as evidence of a conceptual distinction between objects and stuff, independent of and prior to the morphosyntactic distinction made in English.

This interpretation was put to stronger tests by extending such classificatory tasks to languages that differ from English in these regards: Either these languages do not grammaticize the distinction, or they organize it in different ways (see Lucy, 1992; Lucy & Gaskins, 2001, for findings from Yucatec Mayan; Mazuka & Friedman, 2000; Imai & Gentner, 1997, for Japanese). Essentially, nouns in these languages all start life as mass terms, requiring a special grammatical marker (called *a classifier*) to be counted. One might claim, then, that substance is in some sense linguistically basic for Japanese whereas objecthood is basic for English speakers because of the dominance of its count-noun morphology.[4] So if children are led to differentiate object and substance reference by the language forms themselves, the resulting abstract semantic distinction should differ cross-linguistically. To test this notion, Imai and Gentner replicated the tests of Soja et al. with Japanese and English children and adults. Some of their findings appear to strengthen the evidence for a universal prelinguistic ontology that permits us to think about both individual objects and portions of stuff because both American and Japanese children (even two-year-olds) extended names for complex hard-edged nonsense objects on the basis of shape rather than substance. The lack of separate grammatical marking did not put Japanese children at a disadvantage in this regard.

Another aspect of the results hints at a role for language in categorization, however. Japanese children tended to extend names for mushy hand cream displays according to their substance, for example, whereas American children were at chance for these items. There were also discernible language effects on word extension for certain very simple stimuli (e.g., a kidney bean–shaped piece of colored wax) that seemed to fall at the ontological midline between object and substance. Whereas the Japanese at ages two and four years were at chance on these items, English speakers showed a tendency to extend words for them by shape.

How are we to interpret these results? Several authors have concluded that ontological boundaries literally shift to where language makes its cuts; that the substance versus object distinction works much like the categorical perception effects we noticed for phonemes (and perhaps colors; for an important statement, see Gentner & Boroditsky, 2001). Lucy and Gaskins (2001) bolster this interpretation with evidence that populations speaking different languages differ increasingly in this regard with age. Whereas young Mayan speakers do not differ much from their English-speaking peers, by age nine years members of the two communities differ significantly in relevant classificatory and memorial tasks. The implication is that long-term use of a language influences ontology with growing conformance of concept grouping to linguistic grouping. Of course, the claim is not for a rampant Procrustean reorganization of thought; only for boundary shifting. For displays that blatantly fall to one side or the other of the object/substance boundary, therefore, the speakers of all the tested languages sort the displays in the same ways.

As usual, neither the findings nor the interpretations of such experiments are easy to attain at the present state of the art. For one, thing, Mazuka and Friedman (2000) failed to reproduce Lucy's effects for Mayan versus English-speaking subjects' classificatory performance in the predicted further case of Japanese. As these authors point out, the sameness in this regard between Japanese and English speakers, and the difference in this regard between Mayan and English speakers, may best be thought of as arising from cultural and educational differences between the populations rather than linguistic differences.

In light of all the findings so far reviewed, there is another interpretation of the results that does not implicate an effect of language on thought but only an effect of language on language: One's implicit understanding of the organization of a specific language can influence one's interpretation of conversation. Interpretations from this perspective have been offered by many commentators. Bowerman (1996), Brown (1958), Landau and Gleitman (1985), and Slobin (1996, 2001) propose that native speakers not only learn and use the individual lexical items their language offers but also learn the *kinds* of meanings typically expressed by a particular grammatical category in their language and come to expect new members of that category to have similar meanings. Slobin calls this "typological bootstrapping." Languages differ strikingly in their common forms and locutions – preferred fashions of speaking, to use Whorf's phrase. These probabilistic patterns could bias the interpretation of new words. Such effects occur in experiments when subjects are offered language input (usually nonsense words) under conditions in which implicitly known form-to-meaning patterns in the language might hint at how the new word is to be interpreted.

Let us reconsider the Imai and Gentner object–substance effects on this hypothesis. As we saw, when the displays themselves were of nonaccidental-looking hard-edged objects, subjects in both language groups opted for the object interpretation.

But when the world was uninformative (e.g., for softish waxy lima bean shapes), the listeners fell back upon linguistic cues, if available. No relevant morphosyntactic clues exist in Japanese, so Japanese subjects chose at random for these indeterminate stimuli. For English-speaking subjects, the linguistic stimulus in a formal sense also was interpretively neutral: *This blicket* is a template that accepts both mass and count nouns (*this horse/toothpaste*). But here principle and probability part company. Recent experimentation leaves no doubt that child and adult listeners incrementally exploit probabilistic facts about word use to guide the comprehension process on line (e.g., Snedeker, Thorpe, & Trueswell, 2001). In the present case, any English speaker equipped with even a rough subjective probability counter should take into account the massive preponderance of count nouns over mass nouns in English and conclude that a new word, *blicket*, used to refer to some indeterminate display, is probably a new count noun rather than a new mass noun. Count nouns, in turn, tend to denote individuals rather than stuff and so have shape predictivity (Smith, 2001; Landau, Smith, & Jones, 1998).

Applying this interpretation, it is not that speaking English leads one to tip the scales toward object representations of newly seen referents for perceptually ambiguous items, but that hearing English leads one to tip the scales toward count-noun representation of newly heard nominals in linguistically ambiguous structural environments. Derivatively, then, count syntax hints at object representation of the newly observed referent. Notice that such effects can be expected to increase with age as massive lexical–linguistic mental databases are built, consistent with the findings of Lucy and Gaskins (2001).[5]

Spatial Relationships

Choi and Bowerman (1991) studied the ways in which common motion verbs in Korean differ from their counterparts in English. First, Korean motion verbs often contain location or geometric information that is more typically specified by a spatial preposition in English. To describe a scene in which a cassette tape is placed into its case, for example, English speakers would say "We put the tape *in the case*." Korean speakers typically use the verb *kkita* to express the *put in* relation for this scene. *Kkita* does not have the same extension as *put in*. Both *put in* and *kkita* describe an act of putting an object in a location; but *put in* is used for all cases of containment (fruit in a bowl, flowers in a vase) whereas *kkita* is used only in case the outcome is a tight fit between two matching shapes (tape in its case, one Lego piece on another, glove on hand). Notice that there is a cross-classification here: Whereas English appears to collapse across tightnesses of fit, Korean makes this distinction but conflates across *putting in* versus *putting on*, which English regularly differentiates. Very young learners of these two languages have already worked out the language-specific classification of such motion relations and events in their language, as shown by both their usage and their comprehension (Choi & Bowerman, 1991).

Do such cross-linguistic differences have implications for spatial cognition? McDonough, Choi, and Mandler (2003) focused on spatial contrasts between relations of tight containment versus loose support (grammaticalized in English by the prepositions *in* and *on* and in Korean by the verbs *kkita* and *nohta*) and tight versus loose containment (both grammaticalized as *in* in English but separately as *kkita* and *nehta* in Korean). They showed that prelinguistic infants (nine to fourteen months old) in both English- and Korean-speaking environments are sensitive to such contrasts, and so are Korean-speaking adults (see also Hespos & Spelke, 2000, who show that five-month-olds are sensitive to this distinction). Their English-speaking adult subjects, however, showed sensitivity only to the tight containment versus loose support distinction, which is grammaticalized in English (*in* versus *on*). The conclusion drawn from these results was that some spatial relations that are salient during the prelinguistic stage become less salient for adult speakers if language does not systematically encode them: "Flexible infants become rigid adults."

This interpretation again resembles that for the perception of phoneme contrasts, but by no means as categorically. The fact that English speakers learn and readily use verbs such as *jam*, *pack*, and *wedge* weakens any claim that the lack of common terms seriously diminishes the availability of categorization in terms of tightness of fit. One possibility is that the observed language-specific effects with adults are attributable to verbal mediation: Unlike preverbal infants, adults may have turned the spatial classification task into a linguistic task. It therefore is useful to turn to studies that explicitly compare performance when subjects from each language group are instructed to classify objects or pictures by *name*, as opposed to when they are instructed to classify the same objects by *similarity*. In one such study, Li et al. (1997) showed Korean- and English-speaking subjects pictures of events such as putting a suitcase on a table (an example of "on" in English, and of "loose support" in Korean). For half the subjects from each language group (each tested fully in their own language), these training stimuli were labeled by a videotaped cartoon character who performed the events (*I am Miss Picky and I only like to put things on things. See?*), and for the other subjects, the stimuli were described more vaguely (*. . . and I only like to do things like this. See?*). Later categorization of new instances followed language in the labeling condition: English speakers identified new pictures showing tight fits (e.g., a cap put on a pen) as well as the original loose-fitting ones as belonging to the category that Miss Picky likes, but Korean speakers generalized only to new instances of loose fits. These language-driven differences radically diminished in the similarity sorting condition in which the word (*on* or *nohta*) was not invoked; in this case the categorization choices of the two language groups were essentially the same. The "language on language" interpretation we commended in discussing the object/substance distinction in this case, too, seems to encompass the various laboratory effects in dealing with spatial relations.

Motion

Talmy (1985) described two styles of motion expression characterizing different languages: Some languages, including English, typically use a verb plus a separate path expression to describe motion events. In such languages, manner of motion is encoded in the main verb (e.g., *walk, crawl, slide*, or *float*), and path information appears in nonverbal elements such as particles, adverbials, or prepositional phrases (e.g., *away, through the forest, out of the room*). In Greek or Spanish, the dominant pattern instead is to include path information within the verb itself (e.g., Greek *bjeno*, "exit" and *beno*, "enter"); the manner of motion often goes unmentioned or appears in gerunds, prepositional phrases, or adverbials (*trehontas*, "running"). These patterns are not absolute. Greek has motion verbs that express manner, and English has motion verbs that express path (*enter, exit, cross*). But several studies have shown that children and adults have learned these dominance patterns. Slobin (1996) showed that child and adult Spanish and English speakers vary in the terms they typically use to describe the same picture-book stories with English speakers displaying greater frequency and diversity of manner of motion verbs. Papafragou, Massey, and Gleitman (2002) showed the same effects for the description of motion scenes by Greek- versus English-speaking children and, much more strongly, for Greek-versus English-speaking adults.

Do such differences in event encoding affect the way speakers think about motion events? Papafragou et al. (2002) tested their English- and Greek-speaking subjects on either memory of path or manner details of motion scenes, or categorization of motion events on the basis of path or manner similarities. Even though speakers of the two languages exhibited an asymmetry in encoding manner and path information in their verbal descriptions, they did not differ in terms of classification or memory for path and manner.[6] Similar results have been obtained for Spanish versus English by Gennari et al. (2002). Corroborating evidence also comes from studies by Munnich, Landau, and Dosher (2001), who compared English, Japanese, and Korean speakers' naming of spatial locations and their spatial memory for the same set of locations. They found that, even in aspects in which languages differed (e.g., encoding spatial contact or support), there was no corresponding difference in memory performance across language groups.

Relatedly, the same set of studies suggests that the mental representation of motion and location is independent of linguistic naming *even within a single language.* Papafragou et al. (2002) divided their English- and Greek-speaking subjects' verbal descriptions of motion according to whether they included a path or manner verb, regardless of native language. Although English speakers usually chose manner verbs, sometimes they produced path verbs; the Greek speakers also varied but with the preponderances reversed. It was found that verb choice did not predict memory for path or manner aspects of motion scenes or choice of path or manner as a basis for categorizing motion scenes. In the memory task, subjects who had used a path verb to describe a scene were no more likely to detect later path changes to that scene than subjects who had used a manner verb (and vice versa for manner). In the classification task, subjects were not more likely to name two motion events they had earlier categorized as most similar by using the same verb. Naming and cognition, then, are distinct under these conditions: Even for speakers of a single language, the linguistic resources mobilized for labeling underrepresent the cognitive resources mobilized for cognitive processing (e.g., memorizing, classifying, reasoning, etc.).

An obvious conclusion from these studies of motion representation is that the conceptual organization of space and motion is robustly independent of language-specific labeling practices. Just as obvious, however, is that specific language usage influences listeners' interpretation of the speaker's intended meaning if the stimulus situation leaves such interpretation unresolved. In another important demonstration of this language-on-language effect, Naigles and Terrazas (1998) asked subjects to describe and categorize videotaped scenes – for example, of a girl skipping toward a tree. They found that Spanish- and English-speaking adults differed in their preferred interpretations of new (nonsense) motion verbs in manner-biasing (*She's kradding toward the tree* or *Ella está mecando hacia el árbol*) or path-biasing (*She's kradding the tree* or *Ella está mecando el árbol*) sentence structures. The interpretations were heavily influenced by syntactic structure. But judgments also reflected the preponderance of verbs in each language – Spanish speakers gave more path interpretations and English speakers gave more manner interpretations. Similar effects of language-specific lexical practices on presumed word extension have been found for adjectives (Waxman, Senghas, & Benveniste, 1997).

A fair conclusion from this and related evidence is that verbal descriptions are under the control of many factors related to accessibility, including the simple frequency of a word's use, as well as of faithfulness as a description of the scene. As several authors have argued, the dynamic process of expressing one's thoughts is subject to the exigencies of linguistic categories that can vary from language to language. Given the heavy information-processing demands of rapid conversation, faithfulness often is sacrificed to accessibility. For these and other reasons, verbal reports do not come anywhere near exhausting the observers' mental representations of events. Language use, in this sense, is "sketchy." Rather than "thinking in words," humans seem to make easy linguistic choices that, for competent listeners, serve as rough but usually effective pointers to those ideas.

Spatial Frames of Reference

Certain linguistic communities (e.g., Tenejapan Mayans) customarily use an externally referenced (absolute) spatial coordinate system to refer to nearby directions and positions ("to the north"); others (e.g., Dutch speakers) use a viewer-perspective (relative) system ("to the left"). Brown and Levinson (1993) and Pederson et al. (1998) recently suggested that these linguistic practices affect spatial reasoning in language-specific ways. In one of their experiments, Tenejapan Mayan and Dutch subjects were presented with an array of objects (toy animals) on a tabletop; after a brief delay, subjects were taken to the opposite side of a new table (they were effectively rotated 180 degrees), handed the toys, and asked to reproduce the array "in the same way as before." The overwhelming majority of Tenejapan (absolute) speakers rearranged the objects so they were heading in the same cardinal direction after rotation, whereas Dutch (relative) speakers massively preferred to rearrange the objects in terms of left–right directionality. This covariation of linguistic terminology and spatial reasoning seems to provide compelling evidence for linguistic influences on nonlinguistic cognition.

As so often is the case in this literature, however, it is quite hard to disentangle cause and effect. For instance, it is possible that the Tenejapan and Dutch groups think about space differently because their languages pattern differently; but it is just as possible that the two linguistic–cultural groups developed different spatial-orientational vocabulary to reflect (rather than cause) differences in their spatial reasoning strategies. Li and Gleitman (2002) investigated this second position. They noted that absolute spatial terminology is widely used in many English-speaking communities whose environment is geographically constrained and includes large stable landmarks such as oceans and looming mountains. The absolute terms *uptown*, *downtown*, and *crosstown* (referring to North, South, and East–West) are widely used to describe and navigate in the space of Manhattan Island, Chicagoans regularly make absolute reference to the lake, etc. It is quite possible, then, that the presence or absence of stable landmark information rather than language spoken influences the choice of absolute versus spatial coordinate frameworks. After all, the influence of such landmark information on spatial reasoning has been demonstrated with nonlinguistic (rats; Restle, 1957) and prelinguistic (infants; Acredolo & Evans, 1980) animals. To examine this possibility, Li and Gleitman replicated Brown and Levinson's rotation task with English speakers, but they manipulated the presence or absence of landmark cues in the testing area. The result, just as for the rats and the infants, was that English-speaking adults respond absolutely in the presence of landmark information (after rotation, they set up the animals going in the same cardinal direction) and relatively when it is withheld (they set up the animals going in the same relative – left or right – direction).

Flexibility in spatial reasoning in this regard should come as little surprise. The ability to navigate in space is hard-wired in the brain of moving creatures, including bees and ants. For all of these organisms, reliable orientation and navigation in space are crucial for survival (Gallistel, 1990). Accordingly, neurobiological evidence from humans and other species that the brain routinely uses a multiplicity of coordinate frameworks in coding for the position of objects to prepare for directed action (Gallistel, 2002). It would be quite amazing if, among all the creatures that walk, fly, and crawl on the earth, only humans, by virtue of acquiring a particular language, lose the ability to use both absolute and relative spatial coordinate frameworks flexibly. The case is by no means closed even on this issue, however, because successive probes of the rotation situation have continued to yield conflicting results both within and across languages (e.g., Levinson, Kita, & Haun, 2002; Li & Gleitman, in preparation]. One way of reconciling these findings and theories has to do with the level of analysis to which the Levinson groups' findings are thought to apply. Perhaps we are prisoners of language only in complex and highly derived tasks and only when behavior is partly under the control of verbal instructions that include vague expressions such as "make it the same." But it is fair to say that the jury is still out on this phenomenon.

Evidentiality

One of Whorf's most interesting conjectures concerned the possible effects of evidentials (linguistic markers of information source) on the nature of thought. Whorf pointed out that Hopi – unlike English – marked evidential distinctions in its complementizer system. Comparing the sentences *I see that it is red* vs. *I see that it is new*, he remarked (Whorf, 1956, p. 85):

> *We fuse two quite different types of relationship into a vague sort of connection expressed by 'that', whereas the Hopi indicates that in the first case seeing presents a sensation 'red,' and in the second that seeing presents unspecified evidence for which is drawn the inference of newness.*

Whorf concluded that this grammatical feature was bound to make certain conceptual distinctions easier to draw for the Hopi speaker because of the force of habitual linguistic practices.

Papafragou, Li, Choi, and Han (in preparation) sought to put this proposal to test. They compared English, which mainly marks evidentiality lexically (*I saw/heard/inferred that John left*), with Korean, in which evidentiality is encoded through a set of dedicated morphemes. Given evidence that such morphemes are produced early by children learning Korean (Choi, 1995), they asked whether Korean children develop the relevant conceptual distinctions earlier and with greater reliability than learners of English, in which evidentiality is not grammatically encoded. In a series of experiments, they compared the acquisition of nonlinguistic distinctions between sources of evidence in three- and four-year-olds learning English or Korean: No difference in nonlinguistic reasoning in these regards was found between the English and Korean group. For instance, children in both linguistic groups were equally good at reporting how they found out about the contents of a container (e.g., by looking inside or by being told); both groups were also able to attribute knowledge of the contents of a container to a character who had looked inside but not to another character who had had no visual access to its content. Furthermore, Korean learners were more advanced in their nonlinguistic knowledge of sources of information than in their knowledge of the meaning of linguistic evidentials. In this case, then, learned linguistic categories do not seem to serve as a guide for the individual's nonlinguistic categories in the way that Whorf conjectured. Rather, the acquisition of linguistically encoded distinctions seems to follow, and build upon, the conceptual understanding of evidential distinctions. The conceptual understanding itself appears to proceed similarly across diverse language-learning populations.

Time

Thus far, we have focused on grammatical and lexical properties of linguistic systems and their possible effects on conceptual structure. Here we consider another aspect of languages as expressive systems – their systematically differing use of certain networks of metaphor; specifically, metaphor for talking about time (Boroditsky, 2001). English speakers predominantly talk about time as if it were horizontal (one *pushes deadlines back, expects good times ahead*, or *moves meetings forward*), whereas Mandarin speakers more usually talk about time in terms of a vertical axis (they use the Mandarin equivalents of *up* and *down* to refer to the order of events, weeks, or months). Boroditsky showed that these differences predict aspects of temporal reasoning by speakers of these two languages. In one of her manipulations, subjects were shown two objects in vertical arrangement, say, one fish following another one downward, as they heard something like *The black fish is winning*. After this vertically oriented prime, Mandarin speakers were faster to confirm or disconfirm temporal propositions (e.g., *March comes earlier than April*) than if they were shown the fish in a horizontal array. The reverse was true for English speakers. Boroditsky concluded that spatiotemporal metaphors in language affect how people reason about time. She has suggested, more generally, that such systematic linguistic metaphors are important in shaping habitual patterns of thought.

However, these results are again more complex than they seem at first glance. For one thing, and as Boroditsky acknowledges, vertical metaphors of time are by no means absent from ordinary English speech (e.g., *I have a deadline coming up*), although they are more sporadic than in Mandarin. So again we have a cross-linguistic difference of degree, rather than a principled opposition. Moreover, Boroditsky briefly trained her English-speaking subjects to think about time vertically, as in Mandarin. After such training, the English speakers exhibited the vertical (rather than the former horizontal) priming effect. Apparently, fifteen minutes of training on the vertical overcame and completely reversed twenty-plus years of the habitual use of the horizontal in these speakers. The effects of metaphor, it seems, are transient and fluid without long-term influence on the nature of conceptualization or its implicit deployment to evaluate propositions in real time.

Number

Prelinguistic infants and nonhuman primates share an ability to represent both exact numerosities for very small sets (roughly up to three objects) and approximate numerosities for larger sets (Dehaene, 1997). Human adults possess a third system for representing number that allows for the representation of exact numerosities for large sets; in principle has no upper bound on set size; and can support the comparison of numerosities of different sets, as well as processes of addition and subtraction. Crucially, this system is *generative* because it possesses a rule for creating successive integers (the successor function) and therefore is characterized by discrete infinity (see Gallistel & Gelman, Chap. 23).

How do young children become capable of using this uniquely human number system? One powerful answer is that the basic principles underlying the adult number system are innate; gaining access to these principles gives children a way of grasping the infinitely discrete nature of natural numbers, as manifested by their ability to use verbal counting (Gelman & Gallistel, 1978; Gallistel & Gelman, Chap. 23). Other researchers propose that children come to acquire the adult number system by conjoining properties of the two prelinguistic number systems via natural language. Specifically, they propose that grasping the *linguistic* properties of number words (e.g., their role in verbal counting or their semantic relations to quantifiers such as *few, all, many, most*; see Spelke & Tsivkin, 2001a and Bloom, 1994b; Carey, 2001 respectively) enables children to put together elements of the two previously available number systems to create a new, generative number faculty. In Bloom's (1994b, p. 186) words, "in the course of development, children 'bootstrap' a generative understanding of number out of the productive syntactic and morphological structures available in the counting system."

Upon hearing the number words in a counting context, for instance, children realize that these words map onto both specific representations delivered by the exact-numerosities calculator and inexact representations delivered by the approximator device. By conjoining properties of these two systems, children gain insight into the properties of the adult conception of number (e.g., that each of the number words picks out an exact set of entities, that adding or subtracting exactly one object changes number, etc.). Ultimately, it is hypothesized that this process enables the child to compute exact numerosities even for large sets (such as *seven* or *twenty-three*) – an ability not afforded by either of the prelinguistic calculation systems.

Spelke and Tsivkin (2001a, b) experimentally investigated the thesis that language contributes to exact large-number calculations. In their studies, bilinguals who were trained on arithmetic problems in a single language and later tested on them were faster on large-number arithmetic if tested in the training language; however, no such advantage of the training language appeared with estimation problems. The conclusion from this and related experiments was that the particular natural language is the vehicle of thought concerning large exact numbers but not about approximate numerosities. Such findings, as Spelke and her collaborators have emphasized, can be part of the explanation of the special "smartness" of humans. Higher animals, like humans, can reason to some degree about approximate numerosity, but not about exact numbers. Beyond this shared core knowledge, however, humans have language. If language is a required causal factor in exact number knowledge, in principle this could explain the gulf between creatures like us and creatures like them.

How plausible is the view that the adult number faculty presupposes linguistic mediation? Recall that, on this view, children infer the generative structure of number from the generative structure of grammar when they hear others counting. However, counting systems vary cross-linguistically, and in a language like English, their recursive properties are not really obvious from the outset. Specifically, until number eleven, the English counting system presents no evidence of regularity, much less of generativity: A child hearing *one, two, three, four, five, six,* up to *eleven,* would have no reason to assume – based on properties of form – that the corresponding numbers are lawfully related (namely, that they successively increase by one). For larger numbers, the system is more regular, even though not fully recursive because of the presence of several idiosyncratic features (e.g., one can say *eighteen* or *nineteen* but not *tenteen* for twenty). In sum, it is not so clear how the "productive syntactic and morphological structures available in the counting system" will provide systematic examples of discrete infinity that can then be imported into number cognition (see Grinstead et al., 2003, for detailed discussion).

Can properties of other natural language expressions bootstrap a generative understanding of number? Quantifiers have been proposed as a possible candidate (Carey, 2001). However, familiar quantifiers lack the hallmark properties of the number system: They are not strictly ordered with respect to one another, and their generation is not governed by the successor function. In fact, several quantifiers presuppose the computation of cardinality of sets – for example, *neither* and *both* apply only to sets of two items (Keenan & Stavi, 1986; Barwise & Cooper, 1981). Moreover, quantifiers compose in quite different ways from numbers. For example, the expression *most men and women* cannot be interpreted to mean a large majority of the men and much less than half the women (A. Joshi, personal communication). In light of the semantic disparities between the quantifier and integer systems, it is hard to see how it is possible to bootstrap the semantics of one from the other.

Recent experimental findings suggest, moreover, that young children understand certain semantic properties of number words well before they know those of quantifiers. One case involves the scalar interpretation of these terms. In one experiment, Papafragou and Musolino (2003) had five-year-old children watch as three horses were shown jumping over a fence. The children would not accept *Two of the horses jumped over the fence* as an adequate description of that event (even though it is necessarily true that if three horses jumped, then certainly two did). But at the same age, they will accept *Some of the horses jumped over the fence* as an adequate description even though it is true that all of the horses jumped. In another experiment, Hurewitz, Papafragou, Gleitman, and Gelman (in review) found that three-year-olds understand certain semantic properties of number words such as *two* and *four* well before they know those of quantifiers such as *some* and *all*. It seems, then, that the linguistic systems of number and natural-language quantification are developing rather independently. If anything, the children seem more advanced in knowledge of the meaning of number words than quantifiers so it is hard to see how the semantics of the former lexical type is to be bootstrapped from the semantics of the latter.

Orientation

A final domain we discuss is spatial orientation. Cheng and Gallistel (1984) found that rats rely on geometric information to reorient themselves in a rectangular space, and seem incapable of integrating geometrical with nongeometrical properties (e.g., color, smell, etc.) in searching for a hidden object. If they see food hidden at the corner of a long and a short wall, they will search equally at either of the two such walls of a rectangular space after disorientation; this is true even if these corners are distinguishable by one of the long walls being painted blue or having a special smell, and so on. Hermer and Spelke (1994, 1996) reported a very similar difficulty in young children. Both animals and young children can navigate and reorient by the use of either geometric or nongeometric cues; it is integrating across the cue types that creates trouble. These difficulties are overcome by older children and adults, who are able, for instance, to go straight to the corner formed by a long wall to the left and a short blue wall to the right. Hermer and Spelke found that success in these tasks was significantly predicted by the spontaneous combination of spatial vocabulary and object properties such as color within a single phrase (e.g., *to the left of the blue wall*).[7] Later experiments (Hermer-Vasquez, Spelke, and Katsnelson, 1999) revealed that adults who were asked to shadow speech had more difficulty in these orientation tasks than adults who were asked to shadow a rhythm with their hands; however, verbal shadowing did not disrupt subjects' performance in tasks that required the use of nongeometric information only. The conclusion was that speech-shadowing, unlike rhythm-shadowing, by taking up linguistic resources, blocked the integration of geometrical and object properties, which is required to solve complex orientation tasks. In short, success at the task seems to require encoding of the relevant terms in a specifically linguistic format.

In a recent review article, Carruthers (2002) suggests even more strongly that in number, space, and perhaps other domains, language is the medium of intermodular communication, a format in which representations from different domains can be combined to create novel concepts. In standard assumptions about modularity, however, modules are characterized as computational systems with their own proprietary vocabulary and combinatorial rules. Because language itself is a module in this sense, its computations and properties (e.g., generativity, compositionality) cannot be transferred to other modules because they are defined over – and can only apply to – language-internal representations. One way out of this conundrum is to give up the assumption that language is – on the appropriate level – modular:

> *Language may serve as a medium for this conjunction . . . because it is a domain-general, combinatorial system to which the representations delivered by the child's . . . [domain-specific] nonverbal systems can be mapped. (Spelke & Tsivkin, 2001b, p. 84).*

> *Language is constitutively involved in (some kinds of) human thinking. Specifically, language is the vehicle of nonmodular, nondomain-specific, conceptual thinking which integrates the results of modular thinking (Carruthers, 2002, p. 666).*

On this view, the output of the linguistic system just *is* Mentalese: There is no other level of representation in which the information *to the left of the blue wall* can be entertained. This picture of language is novel in many respects. In the first place, replacing Mentalese with a linguistic representation challenges existing theories of language production and comprehension. Traditionally, and as discussed earlier, it is assumed the production of sentences begins by entertaining the corresponding thought, which then mobilizes the appropriate linguistic resources for its expression (e.g., Levelt, 1989).

On recent proposals, however, Carruthers, (2002, p. 668) observed:

> *We cannot accept that the production of a sentence 'The toy is to the left of the blue wall' begins with a tokening of the thought THE TOY IS TO THE LEFT OF THE BLUE WALL (in Mentalese), since our hypothesis is that such a thought cannot be entertained independently of being framed in a natural language.*

Inversely, language comprehension classically is taken to unpack linguistic representations into mental representations that then can trigger further inferences. But in Carruthers' proposal, after hearing *The toy is to the left of the blue wall*, the interpretive device cannot decode the message into the corresponding thought because there is no level of Mentalese independent of language in which the constituents are lawfully connected to each other. Interpretation can only dismantle the utterance and send its concepts back to the geometric and landmark modules to be processed. In this sense, understanding an utterance such as *The picture is to the right of the red wall* turns out to be a very different process than understanding superficially similar utterances such as *The picture is to the right of the wall*, or *The picture is on the red wall*, which do not, on this account, require cross-domain integration.

Furthermore, if language is to serve as a domain for cross-module integration, then the lexical resources of each language become crucial for conceptual combination. Lexical gaps in the language will block conceptual integration, for instance, because there would be no relevant words to insert into the linguistic string. We know that color terms vary across languages (Kay & Regier, 2002); more relevantly, not all languages have terms for *left* and *right* (Levinson, 1996). It follows that speakers of these languages should fail to combine geometric and object properties in the same way as do English speakers to recover from disorientation. In other words, depending on the spatial vocabulary available in their language, disoriented adults may behave either like Spelke and Tsivkin's English-speaking population or like prelinguistic infants and rats. This prediction, although merely carrying the original proposal to its apparent logical conclusion, is quite radical: It allows a striking discontinuity among members of the human species, contingent not upon the presence or absence of human language and its combinatorial powers (as the original experiments seem to suggest) or even upon cultural and educational differences, but on vagaries of the lexicon in individual linguistic systems.

Despite its radical entailments, there is a sense in which Spelke's proposal to interpret concept configurations on the basis of the combinatorics of natural language can be construed as decidedly nativist. In fact, we so construe it. Spelke's proposal requires that humans be equipped with the ability to construct novel structured syntactic representations, insert lexical concepts at the terminal nodes of such representations (*left*, *blue*, etc.), and interpret the outcome on the basis of familiar rules of semantic composition (*to the left of the blue wall*). In other words, humans are granted principled knowledge of how phrasal meaning is to be determined by lexical units and the way they are composed into structured configurations. That is, what is granted is the ability to read the semantics off of phrase structure trees. Further, the assumption is that this knowledge is not attained through learning but belongs to the in-built properties of the human language device. But notice that granting humans the core ability to build and interpret phrase structures is already granting them quite a lot. Exactly these presuppositions have been the hallmark of the nativist program in linguistics and language acquisition (Chomsky, 1957; Pinker, 1984; Gleitman, 1990; Lidz, Gleitman, & Gleitman, 2002; Jackendoff, 1990) and the target of vigorous dissent elsewhere (Tomasello, 2000; Goldberg, 1995). To the extent that Spelke and Tsivkin's arguments about language and cognition rely on the combinatorial and generative powers of language, they already make quite deep commitments to abstract (and unlearnable) syntactic principles and their semantic reflexes. Notice in this regard that because these authors hold that *any* natural language will serve as the source and vehicle for the required inferences, the principles at work here must be abstract enough to wash out the diverse surface-structural realizations of *to the left of the blue* wall in the languages of the world. Independently of particular experiences, an organism with such principles in place could generate and *systematically* comprehend novel linguistic strings with meanings predictable from the internal organization of those strings and, for different but related reasons, *just as systematically* fail to understand other strings such as *to the left of the blue idea*. We would be among the last to deny such a proposal in its general form. We agree that there are universal aspects of the syntax–semantics interface. Whether these derive from or augment the combinatorial powers of thought is the question at issue here. For the present commentators, it is hard to see how shifting the burden of the acquisition of compositional semantics from the conceptual system to the linguistic system diminishes the radical nativist flavor of the position.

Conclusions and Future Directions

We have just tried to review the burgeoning psychological and anthropological literature that attempts to relate language to thought. We began with the many difficulties involved in radical versions of the linguistic relativity position, including the fact that language seems to underspecify thought and to diverge from it regarding the treatment of ambiguity, paraphrase, and deictic reference. Moreover, there is ample evidence that several forms of cognitive organization are independent of language: Infants who have no language are able to entertain relatively complex thoughts; for that matter, they can learn languages or even invent them when the need arises (Goldin-Meadow, 2003; Senghas et al., 1997). Many bilinguals, as a matter of course, "code-switch" between their known languages even during the utterance of a single sentence (Joshi, 1985). Aphasics sometimes exhibit impressive propositional thinking (Varley & Siegal, 2000). Animals can form representations of space, artifacts, and perhaps even mental states without linguistic crutches (Hauser & Carey, 1998; Gallistel, 1990; Hare, Call, & Tomasello, 2001; and Call & Tomasello, Chap. 25). In light of all these language–thought disparities, it would seem perverse to take an equative position on relations between the two.

At the same time, compelling experimental studies again and again document intimate, seemingly organic, relationships among language, thought, and culture, of much the kind that Whorf and Sapir drew out of their field experiences. What is to explain these deep correlations between culturally divergent ways of thinking and culturally divergent ways of talking? In certain cases, we argued that cause and effect had simply been prematurely placed on one foot or another because of the crudeness of our investigative tools. Inconveniently enough, it is often hard to study language development apart from conceptual and cultural learning or to devise experiments in which these factors can be prevented from interacting, so it is hard to argue back to origins. On the other hand, the difficulty of even engineering such language–thought dissociations in the laboratory is one significant point in favor of a linguistic–relativistic view. Why should it be so hard to pry them apart if they are so separate?

Over the course of the discussion, our reading of the evidence provides source global support for what we take to be the "typological bootstrapping" and "thinking for speaking" positions articulated in various places by Slobin [1996; 2001; 2003, *inter alia*]. Language influences thought "on line" and in many ways. For the learner, the particular speech events that one experiences can and do provide cues to nonlinguistic categorization – that is, a new linguistic label "invites" the learner to attend to certain types of classification criteria over others. Markman and Hutchinson (1984) found that if one shows a two-year-old a new object and says *See this one; find another one*, the child typically reaches for something that has a spatial or encyclopedic relation to the original object (e.g., finding a bone to go with the dog). But if one uses a new word (*See this fendle, find another fendle*), the child typically looks for something from the same category (e.g., finding another dog to go with the first dog). Similar effects have been obtained with much younger children: Balaban and Waxman (1997) showed that labeling can facilitate categorization in infants as young as nine months (cf. Xu, 2002). Beyond categorization, labeling has been shown to guide infants' inductive inference (e.g., expectations about nonobvious properties of novel objects), even more so than perceptual similarity (Welder & Graham, 2001). Other recent experimentation shows that labeling may help children solve spatial tasks by pointing to specific systems of spatial relations (Loewenstein & Gentner, 2003). For learners, then, the presence of linguistic labels constrains criteria for categorization and serves to foreground a *codable* category out of all the possible categories to which a stimulus could be said to belong.

To what extent these linguistic influences result in mere tweaks – slight shifts in the boundaries between categories – or to more radical reorganizations of the learners' conceptual world (as in the reorganizational principles that stand between phonetics and phonology) is hard to say at the present time. For competent adult users, thinking for speaking effects arise again to coax the listener toward certain interpretations of the speech he or she is hearing as a function of probabilistic features of a particular language. The clearest example in the analysis we presented is the series of inferences that lead to different cross-linguistic categorizations of novel not-clearly-individuatable stimulus items with nonsense names: If it is an English noun, it is probably an English count-noun; if it is an English count-noun, it is probably naming an individuatable object.

It appears to us that much discussion about the relationship between language and thought has been colored by an underlying disagreement about the nature of language itself. Many commentators, struck by observed cross-linguistic diversity in semantic and syntactic categories, have taken this diversity as a possible source of deeper cognitive discontinuities among speakers of different languages. But other commentators see this cross-linguistic diversity as much more limited and superficial than the blooming, buzzing confusion coming out of the tower of Babel. For instance, many studies in morphosyntax show that apparently distinct surface configurations of linguistic elements in different languages can be analyzed in terms of underlying structural similarities (Chomsky, 2000; Baker, 2001). Studies in linguistic semantics suggest that the properties and meanings of syntactic entities (e.g., determiners) are severely constrained cross-linguistically (Keenan & Stavi, 1986). Many of these principles of language organization seem to map quite transparently from core knowledge of the kinds studied in infants (e.g., Quinn, 2001; Baillargeon, 1993; and other sources mentioned throughout). For instance, scenes of kangaroos jumping come apart into the kangaroo (argument) part and jumping (predicate) part in every natural language, but also in the prelinguistic parsing of events by children, including those learning language under circumstances of extreme linguistic and sensory deprivation (e.g., blind or isolated deaf children: Goldin-Meadow, 2003; Landau & Gleitman, 1985; Senghas et al., 1997). Focus on this kind of evidence suggests that cross-linguistic diversity is highly constrained by rich and deep underlying similarities in the nature of thought. Thus, rather than pointing to cognitive discontinuities among speakers of different languages, cross-linguistic diversity could reveal principled points of departure from an otherwise common linguistic–conceptual blueprint humans share as a consequence of their biological endowment.

Acknowledgments

We thank Jerry Fodor for a discussion of the semantics of raining, Ray Jackendoff for a discussion of phonology, as well as Dedre Gentner for her comments on this chapter. Much of our perspective derives from our collaborative work with Cynthia Fisher, Henry Gleitman, Christine Massey,

Kimberly Cassidy, Jeff Lidz, Peggy Li, and Barbara Landau. Writing of this chapter was supported by NIH Grant No. 1-R01-HD37507-02 to J. Trueswell and L. R. Gleitman and NIH Grant No. 1F32MH65020-01A2 to A. Papafragou.

Notes

1. In one experimental demonstration, subjects were asked: *When an airplane crashes, where should the survivors be buried?* They rarely noticed the meaning discrepancy in the question (Barton & Sanford, 1996).
2. The similarity test may not be decisive for this case, as Malt, Sloman, and Gennari (2003), as well as Smith, Colunga, and Yoshida (2001), among others, have pointed out. Similarity judgments applied as the measuring instrument could systematically mask various nonperceptual determinants of organization in a semantic–conceptual domain, some potentially language-caused. Over the course of this chapter, we will return to consider other domains and other psychological measures. For further discussion of the sometimes arbitrary and linguistically varying nature of the lexicon, even in languages that are typologically and historically closely related, see Kay (1996). He points out, for example, that English speakers use *screwdriver* whereas the Germans use *Schraubenzieher* (literally, "screwpuller"), and the French *tournevise* (literally, "screwturner") for the same purposes; our turnpike exit–entry points are marked *exit*, whereas the Brazilians have *entradas*; and so forth.
3. Categorical perception for speech sounds has been documented for other species, including chinchillas and macaques (e.g., Kuhl & Miller, 1978). Moreover, studies from Kay and Kempton (1984) and Roberson, Davies, and Davidoff (2000) suggest that even for hue perception, the relationship between linguistic and perceptual categorization is not so clear with categorical perception effects obtained or not obtained depending on very delicate choices of experimental procedure and particular characteristics of the stimulus. For an important review, see Munnich and Landau (2003).
4. This argument is not easy. One might argue that English is a classifier language much like Yucatec Mayan or Japanese – that is, that all its words start out as mass nouns and become countable entities only through adding the classifiers *the* and *a* (compare *brick* the substance to *a brick*, the object). Detailed linguistic analysis, however, suggests there is a genuine typological difference here (Slobin, 2001 and Lucy & Gaskins, 2001; Chierchia, 1998; Krifka, 1995, for discussion). The question is whether, because all languages formally mark the mass or count distinction in one way or another, the difference in particular linguistic means could plausibly rebound to impact ontology.
5. We should point out that this hint, at best, is a weak one, another reason why the observed interpretive difference for Japanese and English speakers, even at the perceptual midline, is also weak. Notoriously, English often violates the semantic generalization linking mass noun morphology with substancehood (compare, for example, *footwear, silverware, furniture*).
6. Subsequent analysis of the linguistic data revealed that Greek speakers were more likely to include manner of motion in their verbal descriptions when manner was unexpected or noninferable, whereas English speakers included manner information regardless of inferability (Papafragou, Massey, & Gleitman, 2003). This suggests that speakers may monitor harder-to-encode event components and choose to include them in their utterances when especially informative. This finding reinforces the conclusion that verbally encoded aspects of events vastly underdetermine the subtleties of event cognition.
7. Further studies show that success in this task among young children is sensitive to the size of the room: In a large room, more four-year-olds succeed in combining geometric and landmark information (Learmonth, Nadel, & Newcombe, in press). Moreover, it is claimed that other species (chickens, monkeys) can use both types of information when disoriented (Vallortigara, Zanforlin, & Pasti, 1990; Gouteux, Thinus-Blanc, & Vauclair, in press). For discussion, see Carruthers (2002).

References

Acredolo, L., & Evans, D. (1980). Developmental changes in the effects of landmarks on infant spatial behavior. *Developmental Psychology*, 16, 312–318.

Baillargeon, R. (1993). The object concept revisited: New directions in the investigation of infants' physical knowledge. In C. E. Granrud (Ed.), *Carnegie Mellon Symposia on Cognition, Vol. 23: Visual Perception and Cognition in Infancy* (pp. 265–315). Hillsdale, NJ: Erlbaum.

Baker, M. (2001). *The Atoms of Language*. New York: Basic Books.

Balaban, M. T., & Waxman, S. R. (1997). Do words facilitate object categorization in 9-month-old infants? *Journal of Experimental Child Psychology, 64*, 3–26.

Barton, S. B., & Sanford, A. J. (1993). A case study of anomaly detection: Shallow semantic processing and cohesion establishment. *Memory and Cognition, 21*, 477–487.

Barwise, J., & Cooper, R. (1981). Generalized quantifiers and natural language. *Linguistics and Philosophy, 4*, 159–219.

Berlin, B., & Kay, P. (1969). *Basic Color Terms: Their Universality and Evolution*. Berkeley: University of California Press.

Best, C., McRoberts, G., & Sithole, N. (1988). The phonological basis of perceptual loss for non-native contrasts: Maintenance of discrimination among Zulu clicks by English-speaking adults and infants. *Journal of Experimental Psychology: Human Perception and Performance, 14*, 345–360.

Bloch, B., & Trager, G. L. (1942). *Outline of Linguistic Analysis*. Baltimore: Waverly Press.

Bloom, P. (1994a). Possible names: The role of syntax-semantics mappings in the acquisition of nominals. *Lingua, 92*, 297–329.

Bloom, P. (1994b). Generativity within language and other cognitive domains. *Cognition, 51*, 177–189.

Bloom, P. (2000). *How Children Learn the Meaning of Words*. Cambridge, MA: MIT Press.

Boroditsky, L. (2001). Does language shape thought?: Mandarin and English speakers' conception of time. *Cognitive Psychology, 43*, 1–22.

Bowerman, M. & Choi, S. (2001). Shaping meanings for language: Universal and language-specific in the acquisition of spatial semantic categories. In M. Bowerman, & S. C. Levinson (Eds.), *Language Acquisition and Conceptual Development* (pp. 475–511). Cambridge, UK: Cambridge University Press.

Bowerman, M., & Levinson, S. C. (Eds.) (2001). *Language Acquisition and Conceptual Development*. Cambridge, UK: Cambridge University Press.

Bowerman, M. (1996). The origins of children's spatial semantic categories: Cognitive versus linguistic determinants. In J. Gumperz, & S. C. Levinson (Eds.), *Rethinking Linguistic Relativity* (pp. 145–176). Cambridge, UK: Cambridge University Press.

Bowerman, M., & Levinson, S. C. (2001). Introduction. In M. Bowerman and S. C. Levinson (Eds.), *Language Acquisition and Conceptual Development* (pp. 1–16). Cambridge, UK: Cambridge University Press.

Brown, P., & Levinson, S. C. (1993). "Uphill" and "downhill" in Tzeltal. *Journal of Linguistic Anthropology, 3*, 46–74.

Brown, R. (1957). Linguistic determinism and the parts of speech. *Journal of Abnormal and Social Psychology, 55*, 1–5.

Brown, R., & Lenneberg, E. (1954). A study of language and cognition. *Journal of Abnormal and Social Psychology, 49*, 454–462.

Carey, S. (1982). The child as word learner. In M. Halle, J. Bresnan, & G. Miller (Eds.), *Linguistic Theory and Psychological Reality* (pp. 264–293). Cambridge, MA: MIT Press.

Carey, S. (2001). Whorf versus continuity theorists: Bringing data to bear on the debate. In M. Bowerman, & S. Levinson (Eds.), *Language Acquisition and Conceptual Development* (pp. 185–214). Cambridge, UK: Cambridge University Press.

Carruthers, P. (2002). The cognitive functions of language. *Behavioral and Brain Sciences, 25*, 657–674.

Cheng, K., & Gallistel, C. R. (1984). Testing the geometric power of an animal's spatial representation. In H. Roitblat, T. G. Bever, & H. Terrace (Eds.), *Animal Cognition* (pp. 409–423). Hillsdale, NJ: Erlbaum.

Chierchia, G. (1998). Reference to kinds across languages. *Natural Language Semantics, 6*, 339–405.

Choi, S., & Bowerman, M. (1991). Learning to express motion events in English and Korean: The influence of language-specific lexicalization patterns. *Cognition, 41*, 83–121.

Choi, S. (1995). The development of epistemic sentence-ending modal forms and functions in Korean children. In J. Bybee, & S. Fleischman (Eds.), *Modality in Grammar and Discourse* (pp. 165–204). Amsterdam: Benjamins.

Chomsky, N. (1957). *Syntactic Structures*. The Hague: Mouton.

Chomsky, N. (1964) *Current Issues in Linguistic Theory*. The Hague: Mouton.

Chomsky, N. (1965). *Aspects of the Theory of Syntax*. Cambridge, MA: MIT Press.

Chomsky, N. (1975). *Reflections on Language*. New York: Pantheon.

Chomsky, N. (2000). *New Horizons in the Study of Language and Mind*. Cambridge, UK: Cambridge University Press.

Clark, H. (1992). *Arenas of Language Use*. Chicago: University of Chicago Press.

Dehaene, S. (1997). *The Number Sense*. New York: Oxford University Press.

Dell, G. (1995). Speaking and mispeaking. In L. Gleitman, & M. Liberman (Eds.), *Language: An Invitation to Cognitive Science*, (pp. 183–208). Cambridge, MA: MIT Press.

Descartes, R. (1662). *Trait de l'homme*. E. S. Haldane, & G. R. T. Ross (Trans). Cambridge, UK: Cambridge University Press.

Eimas, P., Siqueland, E., Jusczyk, P., & Vigorito, J. (1971). Speech perception in infants. *Science*, 171, 303–306.

Fisher, C. (1996). Structural limits on verb mapping: The role of analogy in children's interpretations of sentences. *Cognitive Psychology*, 31, 41–81.

Fisher, C., & Gleitman, L. R. (2002). Breaking the linguistic code: Current issues in early language learning. In H. F. Pashler (series Ed.), & R. Gallistel (vol. Ed.), *Steven's Handbook of Experimental Psychology, Vol. 1 : Learning and Motivation (3rd ed.)*. New York: Wiley.

Fodor, J. (1975). *The Language of Thought*. New York: Crowell.

Gallistel, C. R., & Gelman, R. (1992). Preverbal and verbal counting and computation. *Cognition*, 44, 43–74.

Gallistel, R. (1990). *The Organization of Learning*. Cambridge, MA: MIT Press.

Gallistel, R. (2002). Language and spatial frames of reference in mind and brain. *Trends in Cognitive Science*, 6, 321–322.

Gelman, R., & Spelke, E. (1981). The development of thoughts about animate and inanimate objects: Implications for research on social cognition. In J. H. Flavell, & L. Ross (Eds.), *Social Cognitive Development: Frontiers and Possible Futures* (pp. 43–66). Cambridge, UK: Cambridge University Press.

Gennari, S., Sloman, S., Malt, B., & Fitch, W. (2002). Motion events in language and cognition. *Cognition*, 83, 49–79.

Gentner, D., & Boroditksy, L. (2001). Individuation, relativity and early word learning. In M. Bowerman, & S. Levinson (Eds.), *Language Acquisition and Conceptual Development* (pp. 215–256). Cambridge, UK: Cambridge University Press.

Gentner, D., & Goldin-Meadow, S., (Eds.) (2003). *Language in Mind: Advances in the Study of Language and Thought*. Cambridge, MA: MIT Press.

Gleitman, L. (1990). The structural sources of verb meaning. *Language Acquisition*, 1, 1–55.

Glietman, L., Abarbanell, L., Gallistel, G. R., Lee, P., & Papafragou, A. (in preparation). *On the flip side: Spatial reasoning of Mayan and English speakers*.

Gleitman, L., & Rozin P. (1977). The structure and acquisition of reading I: Relations between orthographies and the structure of language. In A. Reber, & D. Scarborough (eds.), *Toward a Psychology of Reading*. Hillsdale, NJ: Erlbaum.

Goldberg, A. (1995). *Constructions: A Construction Grammar Approach to Argument Structure*. Chicago: University of Chicago Press.

Goldin-Meadow, S. (2003). Thought before language: Do we think ergative? In D. Gentner, & S. Goldin-Meadow (Eds.), *Language in Mind: Advances in the Study of Language and Thought*, (pp. 493–522). Cambridge, MA: MIT Press.

Gouteux, S., Thinus-Blanc, C., & Vauclair, S. (in press). Rhesus monkeys use geometric and non-geometric information during a reorientation task. *Journal of Experimental Psychology: General*, 130, 505–519.

Grice, P. (1975). Logic and conversation. In P. Cole, & J. Morgan (Eds.), *Syntax and Semantics, Vol. 3 : Speech Acts*. New York: Academic Press.

Grinstead, J., MacSwan, J., Curtiss, S., & Gelman, R. (2003). (under review) The independence of language and number.

Gumperz, J., & Levinson, S., (Eds.) (1996). *Rethinking Linguistic Relativity*. Cambridge, UK: Cambridge University Press.

Hare, B., Call, J., & Tomasello, M. (2001). Do chimpanzees know what conspecifics know? *Animal Behaviour*, 61, 139–151.

Hauser, M., & Carey, S. (1998). Building a cognitive creature from a set of primitives. In D. Cummins, & C. Allen (Eds.), *The Evolution of Mind*. Oxford, UK: Oxford University Press.

Heider, E., & Oliver, D. C. (1972). The structure of color space in naming and memory for two languages. *Cognitive Psychology*, 3, 337–354.

Hermer, L., & Spelke, E. (1994). A geometric process for spatial representation in young children. *Nature*, 370, 57–59.

Hermer, L., & Spelke, E. (1996). Modularity and development: The case of spatial reorientation. *Cognition, 61*, 195–232.

Hermer-Vasquez, L., Spelke, E., & Katsnelson, A. (1999). Sources of flexibility in human cognition: Dual-task studies of space and language. *Cognitive Psychology*, 39, 3–36.

Hespos, S., & Spelke, E. (2000). Conceptual precursors to spatial language: Categories of containment. Paper presented at the Meeting of the International Society on Infant Studies. Brighton, UK.

Hume, D. (1739). D. F. Norton, & M. Norton, (Ed.). *A Treatise on Human Nature*. New York: Oxford University Press, 2000.

Hurewitz, F., Papafragou, A., Gleitman, L., & Gelman, R. (in prep.). The acquisition of numbers and quantifiers. Rutgers University and University of Pennsylvania.

Imai, M., & Mazuka, R. (1997). A crosslinguistic study on the construal of individuation in linguistic and non-linguistic contexts. Paper presented at the Biannual Meeting of the Society for Research in Child Development. Washington, DC.

Imai, M. (2000). Universal ontological knowledge and a bias toward language-specific categories in the construal of individuation. In S. Niemeier, & R. Dirven (Eds.), *Evidence for Linguistic Relativity* (pp. 139–160). Amsterdam: Benjamins.

Imai, M., & Gentner, D. (1997). A crosslinguistic study of early word meaning: Universal ontology and linguistic influence. *Cognition*, 62, 169–200.

Imai, M., Gentner, D., & Uchida, N. (1994). Children's theories of word meaning: The role of shape similarity in early acquisition. *Cognitive Development*, 9, 45–76.

Jackendoff, R. (1990). *Semantic Structures*. Cambridge, MA: MIT Press.

Jameson, D., & Hurwich, L. M. (1978). Dichromatic color language: "reds" and "greens" do not look alike but their colors do. *Sensory Processes*, 2, 146–155.

Joshi, A. (1985). How much context-sensitivity is necessary for assigning structural descriptions: Tree adjoining grammars. In D. Dowty, L. Karttunen, & A. Zwicky (Eds.), *Natural Language Parsing*. Cambridge, UK: Cambridge University Press.

Jusczyk, P. (1985). On characterizing the development of speech perception. In J. Mehler, & R. Fox (Eds.), *Neonate Cognition: Beyond the Blooming Buzzing Confusion*. Hillsdale, NJ: Erlbaum.

Kay, P. & Regier, T. (2002). Resolving the question of color naming universals. *Proceedings of the National Academy of Sciences*, 100(15), 9085–9089.

Kay, P. (1996). Intra-speaker relativity. In J. Gumperz, & S. Levinson (Eds.), *Rethinking Linguistic Relativity* (pp. 97–114). Cambridge, UK: Cambridge University Press.

Kay, P., & Kempton, W. (1984). What is the Sapir-Whorf hypothesis? *American Anthropologist*, 86, 65–79.

Keenan, E., & Stavi, J. (1986). A semantic characterization of natural language determiners. *Linguistics and Philosophy*, 9, 253–326.

Keller, H. (1955). *Teacher: Anne Sullivan Macy*. Westport, CT: Greenwood Press.

Kellman, P. (1996). The origins of object perception. In R. Gelman, & T. Au (Eds.), *Perceptual and Cognitive Development* (pp. 3–48). San Diego: Academic Press.

Krifka, M. (1995). Common nouns: A contrastive analysis of Chinese and English. In G. Carlson, & F. J. Pelletier (Eds.), *The Generic Book* (pp. 398–411). Chicago & London: University of Chicago Press.

Kuhl, P. K., & Miller, J. D. (1978). Speech perception by the chinchilla: Identification functions for synthetic VOT stimuli. *Journal of the Acoustical Society of America*, 63, 905–917.

Kuhl, P., Williams, K., Lacerda, F., Stevens, K., & Lindblom, B. (1992). Linguistic experience alters phonetic perception in infants by six months of age. *Science*, 255, 606–608.

Landau, B., & Gleitman, L. (1985). *Language and Experience: Evidence from the Blind Child*. Cambridge, MA: Harvard University Press.

Landau, B., Smith, L., & Jones, S. (1998). The importance of shape in early lexical learning. *Cognitive Development*, 3, 299–321.

Learmonth, A., Nadel, L., & Newcombe, N. (in press). Children's use of landmarks: Implications for modularity theory. *Psychological Science*.

Leslie, A., & Keeble, S. (1987). Do six-month-old infants perceive causality? *Cognition*, 25, 265–288.

Levelt, W. (1989). *Speaking: From Intention to Articulation*. Cambridge, MA: MIT Press.

Levinson, S. C. (1996). Frames of reference and Molyneux's question: Crosslinguistic evidence. In P. Bloom, M.,Oederson, L. Nadel & M. Garrett, *Language and Space* (pp. 109–169). Cambridge, MA: MIT Press.

Levinson, S. C., Kita, S., & Haun, D. (2002). Returning the tables: Language affects spatial reasoning. *Cognition*, 84, 155–188.

Li, P. & Gleitman, L. (in prep.). Language and spatial reasoning.

Li, P., & Gleitman, L. (2002). Turning the tables: Spatial language and spatial cognition. *Cognition*, 83, 265–294.

Li, P., Gleitman, H., Gleitman, L., & Landau, B. (1997), Spatial language in Korean and English. Proceedings from the 19th Annual Boston University Conference on Language Development. Somerville: Cascadilla Press.

Liberman, A. M. (1970). The grammars of speech and language. *Cognitive Psychology*, 1, 301–323.

Liberman, A.M, Cooper, F. S., Shankweiler, D. P., & Studdert-Kennedy, M. (1967). Perception of the speech code. *Psychological Review*, 74, 431–461.

Lidz, J., Gleitman, H., & Gleitman, L. (2002). Understanding how input matters: Verb learning and the footprint of universal grammar. *Cognition*, 87, 151–178.

Locke, J. (1690/1964). A. D. Woozley (Ed.). *An Essay Concerning Human Understanding*. Cleveland: Meridian Books.

Loewenstein, J., & Gentner, D. (Submitted 2003). Relational language and the development of relational mapping. *Cognitive Psychology*.

Lucy, J. (1992). *Grammatical Categories and Cognition: A Case Study of the Linguistic Relativity Hypothesis*. Cambridge, UK: Cambridge University Press.

Lucy, J., & Gaskins, S. (2001). Grammatical categories and the development of classification preferences: A comparative approach. In M. Bowerman, & S. Levinson (Eds.), *Language Acquisition and Conceptual Development* (pp. 257–283). Cambridge, UK: Cambridge University Press.

Malt, B., Sloman, S., & Gennari, S. (2003). Universality and language specificity in object naming. *Journal of Memory and Language*, 49, 20–42.

Malt, B., Sloman, S., Gennari, S., Shi, M., & Wang, Y. (1999). Knowing versus naming: Similarity and the linguistic categorization of artifacts. *Journal of Memory and Language*, 40, 230–262.

Mandler, J. (1996). Preverbal representation and language. In P. Bloom, M. Peterson, L. Nadel, & M. Garrett (Eds.), *Language and Space* (pp. 365–384). Cambridge, MA: MIT Press.

Markman, E., & Hutchinson, J. (1984). Children's sensitivity to constraints on word meaning: Taxonomic versus thematic relations. *Cognitive Psychology*, 16, 1–27.

Mazuka, R., & Friedman, R. (2000). Linguistic relativity in Japanese and English: Is language the primary determinant in object classification? *Journal of East Asian Linguistics*, 9, 353–377.

McDonough, L., Choi, S., & Mandler, J. M. (2003). Understanding spatial relations: Flexible infants, lexical adults. *Cognitive Psychology*, 46, 229–259.

Munnich, E., & Landau, B. (2003). The effects of spatial language on spatial representation: Setting some boundaries. In D. Gentner, & S. Goldin-Meadow (Eds.), *Language in Mind*, (pp. 113–155). Cambridge, MA: MIT Press.

Munnich, E., Landau, B., & Dosher, B. A. (2001). Spatial language and spatial representation: A cross-linguistic comparison. *Cognition*, 81, 171–207.

Naigles, L., & Terrazas, P. (1998). Motion-verb generalizations in English and Spanish: Influences of language and syntax. *Psychological Science*, 9, 363–369.

Nunberg, G. (1978). *The Pragmatics of Reference*. Bloomington, IN: Indiana University Linguistics Club.

Papafragou, A, Li, P., Choi, Y., & Han, C. (in preparation). Evidentiality and the language/cognition interface.

Papafragou, A., & Musolino, J. (2003). Scalar implicatures: Experiments at the semantics-pragmatics interface. *Cognition*, 86, 153–182.

Papafragou, A., Massey, C., & Gleitman, L. (2002). Shake, rattle 'n' roll: the representation of motion in language and cognition. *Cognition*, 84, 189–219.

Papafragou, A., Massey, C., & Gleitman, L. (2003). Motion event conflation and clause structure. To appear, Proceedings of the 39th Annual Meeting of the Chicago Linguistics Society. University of Chicago.

Pederson, E., Danziger, E., Wilkins, D., Levinson, S., Kita, S. & Senft, G. (1998). Semantic typology and spatial conceptualization. *Language*, 74, 557–589.

Peña, M., Maki, A., Kovacic, D., Dehaene-Lambertz, G., Koizumi, H., Bouquet, F. et al. (2003). Sounds and silence: An optical topography study of language recognition at birth. *Proceedings of the National Academy of Science U S A*, 100(20), 11702–5.

Pinker, S. (1984). *Language Learnability and Language Development*. Cambridge, MA: Harvard University Press.

Quine, W. V. O. (1960). *Word and Object*. Cambridge, MA: MIT Press.

Quinn, P. (2001). Concepts are not just for objects: Categorization of spatial relational information by infants. In D. Rakison, & L. Oakes (Eds.), *Early Category and Object Development: Making Sense of the Blooming, Buzzing Confusion*. Oxford, UK: Oxford University Press.

Restle, F. (1957). Discrimination of cues in mazes: A resolution of the place-vs.-response question. *Psychological Review*, 64, 217–228.

Roberson, D., Davies, I., & Davidoff, J. (2000). Color categories are not universal: Replications and new evidence from a stone-age culture. *Journal of Experimental Psychology: General*, 129, 369–398.

Rosch, E., Mervis, C. B., Gray, W. D., Johnson, D. M., & Boyes-Braem, P. (1976). Basic objects in natural categories. *Cognitive Psychology*, 8, 382–439.

Sapir, E. (1941). In L. Spier, Language, culture and personality: Essays in memory of Edward Sapir. Menasha, WI: Memorial Publication Fund. Cited in Whorf (1956, Ref. 143, p. 134).

Senghas, A., Coppola, M., Newport, E., & Suppala, T. 1997. Argument structure in Nicaraguan Sign Language: The emergence of grammatical devices. In Proceedings of BUCLD 21. Somerville: Cascadilla Press.

Slobin, D. (1996). From 'thought and language' to 'thinking for speaking'. In J. Gumperz, & S. C. Levinson (Eds.), *Rethinking Linguistic Relativity* (pp. 70–96). Cambridge, UK: Cambridge University Press.

Slobin, D. (2001). Form-function relations: How do children find out what they are? In M. Bowerman, & S. Levinson (Eds.), *Language Acquisition and Conceptual Development* (pp. 406–449). Cambridge, UK: Cambridge University Press.

Slobin, D. (2003). Language and thought online: Cognitive consequences of linguistic relativity. In D. Gentner & S. Goldin-Meadow (Eds.), *Language in Mind: Advances in the Investigation of Language and Thought* (pp. 157–191). Cambridge, MA: MIT Press.

Smith, L. (2001). How domain-general processes may create domain-specific biases. In M. Bowerman, & S. C. Levinson (Eds.), *Language Acquisition and Conceptual Development* (pp. 101–131). Cambridge, UK: Cambridge University Press.

Smith, L., Colunga, E., & Yoshida (2001). Making an ontology: Cross-linguistic evidence. In D. Rakison, & L. Oakes (Eds.), *Early Category and Object Development: Making Sense of the Blooming, Buzzing Confusion* (pp. 275–302). Oxford, UK: Oxford University Press.

Snedeker, J., Thorpe, K., & Trueswell, J. (2001). On choosing the parse with the scene: The role of visual context and verb bias in ambiguity resolution. Proceedings of the 23rd Annual Conference of the Cognitive Science Society. Mahwah, NJ: Erlbaum.

Soja, N., Carey, S., & Spelke, E. (1991). Ontological categories guide young children's inductions of word meaning: Object terms and substance terms. *Cognition*, 38, 179–211.

Spelke, E., & Tsivkin, S. (2001a). Language and number: A bilingual training study. *Cognition*, 78, 45–88.

Spelke, E., & Tsivkin, S. (2001b). Initial knowledge and conceptual change: space and number. In M. Bowerman, & S. C. Levinson (Eds.), *Language Acquisition and Conceptual Development* (pp. 70–100). Cambridge, UK: Cambridge University Press.

Spelke, E., Breinliger, K., Macomber, J., & Jacobson, K. (1992). The origins of knowledge. *Psychological Review*, 99, 605–632.

Sperber, D., & Wilson, D. (1986). *Relevance: Communication and Cognition*. Cambridge, MA: Harvard University Press.

Talmy, L. (1985). Lexicalization patterns: Semantic structure in lexical forms. In T. Shopen (Ed.), *Language Typology and Syntactic Description* (pp. 57–149). New York: Cambridge University Press.

Tomasello, M. (2000). Do young children have adult syntactic competence? *Cognition*, 74, 209–253.

Vallortigara, G., Zanforlin, M., & Pasti, G. (1990). Geometric modules in animals' spatial representations: A test with chicks. *Journal of Comparative Psychology*, 104, 248–254.

Varley, R., & Siegal, M. (2000). Evidence for cognition without grammar from causal reasoning and 'theory of mind' in an agrammatic aphasic patient. *Current Biology*, 10, 723–726.

Waxman, S. R., Senghas, A., & Benveniste, S. (1997). A cross-linguistic examination of the noun-category bias: Its existence and specificity in French- and Spanish-speaking preschool-aged children. *Cognitive Psychology*, 43, 183–218.

Waxman, S., & Markow, D. (1995). Words as invitations to form categories: Evidence from 12- to 13-month-old infants. *Cognitive Psychology*, 29, 257–302.

Welder, A. N., & Graham, S. A. (2001). The influence of shape similarity and shared labels on infants' inductive inferences about nonobvious object properties. *Child Development*, 72, 1653–1673.

Werker, J., & Logan, J. (1985). Cross-language evidence for three factors in speech perception. *Perception and Psychophysics*, 37, 35–44.

Werker, J., & Tees, R. (1984). Cross-language speech perception: Evidence for perceptual reorganization during the first year of life. *Infant Behavior and Development*, 7, 49–63.

Whorf, B. L. (1956). J. Carroll (Ed.). *Language, Thought and Reality*. Cambridge, MA: MIT Press.

Wittgenstein, L. (1922). D. F. Pears (Ed.). *Tractatus Logico-Philosophicus*. London: Routledge, 1981.

Xu, F. (2002). The role of language in acquiring object kind concepts. *Cognition*, 85, 223–250.

CHAPTER 27
Paradigms of Cultural Thought

Patricia M. Greenfield

Two Paradigms of Thought: Phenomena, Theory, and Methodology

In 1963, Jerome Bruner gave me the chance of a lifetime – to go to Senegal to do my dissertation on relations between culture and the development of thought. While there I made an unexpected discovery, one that led me into two radically different paradigms of cultural thought. I found that unschooled Wolof children, participating in a classic Piagetian conservation task, were unable to reply to the question, "Why do you *think* (or *say*) this glass has more (or equal) water?"; yet they quickly answered an alternative form of the question: "Why *does* this glass have more (or equal) water?" (Greenfield, 1966). U.S. or Swiss children, of course, had no difficulty in understanding the first question. Neither did Wolof schoolchildren. What did this difference mean? At first this seemed to be a methodological problem. Later I realized it was a reflection of deep differences in cultural psychology: In providing a reason for their thoughts or words, Western and Wolof school children were displaying psychological mindedness; they distinguished between their own thought or statement about something and the thing itself. In contrast, the unschooled Wolof children were not making this distinction. They were assuming the world on one plane with thought and object of thought as one unified reality.

I am going to use this difference to provide some historical background for the theoretical theme of this chapter – that there are two major paradigms of cultural thought, an individualistic one and a collectivistic one, and that each is part of a larger pathway of development that encompasses the social as well as the cognitive (Greenfield et al., 2003). Although this theme leads to a very selective review of research on culture and thinking, it also provides theoretical coherence for a diverse body of literature.

I took the terminology of individualism and collectivism from anthropologists Florence Kluckhohn and Fred Strodtbeck's pathbreaking 1961 book, *Variations in Value Orientation*. For me, collectivism was a world view in which people were more connected both to each other and to the physical world than in the individualistic worldview. The terminology was not perfect and continues to be problematic (e.g., Oyserman, Coon, & Kemmelmeier, 2002). The important point for me, however, was that a worldview and a value system had significant cognitive implications.

The intrinsic connectedness of the physical and social worlds for our unschooled Wolof participants was substantiated by the distinctive causal reasoning of unschooled children who had not yet attained conservation. Children who believed the quantity of water had changed after the experimenter transfered it to a taller, thinner beaker (or divided it into several smaller beakers) would often say that the amount had changed because "you poured it." This justification contrasted with the more usual perceptual reasons I had seen in the United States – for example, the amount has changed because "the water is higher." At first, I thought that "a natural phenomenon was being explained by attributing special, magical powers to intervening human agents" (Greenfield & Bruner, 1966/69). But then we realized this was an ethnocentric interpretation. We drew upon Kohler (1937/1962), who points out that such phenomena are made possible by a worldview,

> *in which animate and inanimate phenomena occupy a single plane of reality. That is, the child in the conservation experiment is faced with the following sequence of events: (1) water a certain way, (2) experimenter's action, (3) water changed. When the child says the amount is not the same because the experimenter poured it, he is basing his causal inference on contiguity – the usual procedure even in our society. But under ordinary circumstances, we would accept an explanation in terms of contiguous physical events* or *contiguous social events, but not a causal chain that included* both *kinds of event. Thus "magic" only exists from the perspective of a dualistic ontology.*
> (Greenfield & Bruner, 1969, p. 639).

The presence of a school in the bush village where I worked, Taiba N'Diaye, made possible a natural experiment. Some children went to school; others, even from the same families, did not. There was no selection for school attendance on the basis of intelligence. We therefore could see what difference school made. Indeed, it suppressed the action reasons for inequality judgments with what we called at the time "astonishing absoluteness"; there was not one instance among all the school children, either in the village or in the capital city of Dakar (Greenfield & Bruner, 1966/1969). This was my second hint that school functions to create an individualistic psychology. One route to this effect might be that, in school, one is always being asked to give reasons for things. At the time, however, my best candidate was literacy, introduced into the oral Wolof culture by the school, of French colonial origin. In the written word, a thought clearly has a separate physical manifestation from its referents in the real world; this could be the beginning of understanding self as separate from world and thought as separate from its referent (Greenfield, 1972/1975). But the finding also shows that worldviews are not immutable; they are constructed by experience.

Finally, a learning experiment helped us analyze further the thought processes of the unschooled children. We devised a procedure in which the child, rather than the experimenter, first transfered the water from one beaker to a taller, thinner one, then to six tiny ones. We thought that the child might be willing to attribute powers to an authority figure that he was was not willing to attribute to himself. Indeed, at all ages (from six to thirteen), conservation performance was much better when the child poured than when the experimenter poured, and there was good transfer of the conservation judgment to posttests in which the experimenter did the pouring (Greenfield, 1966). We concluded that the experimenter as authority figure was considered to have causal power to change the amount of water. Once the child had a chance to "do-it-himself or herself," the powers of the experimenter were somehow diminished. Only recently have I come to realize that the action reason for inequality, reflecting the importance of social authority, is also part of the collectivistic worldview.

We connected these patterns of thought to early Wolof socialization on the one hand and to African philosophy on the other. First we reasoned as follows:

> *It may be that a collective, rather than individual, value orientation develops where the individual lacks power over the physical world. Lacking personal power, he has no notion of personal importance. In terms of his cognitive categories, now, he will be less likely to set himself apart from others and the physical world, he will be less self-conscious at the same time that he places less value on himself. Thus, mastery over the physical world and individualistic self-consciousness will appear together in a culture, in contrast to a collective orientation and a . . . world view in which people's attitudes and actions are not placed in separate conceptual pigeonholes from physical events.* (Greenfield & Bruner, 1969, p. 640).

Indeed, I had noted that the unschooled Wolof children had never spontaneously manipulated the materials in the conservation experiment. I saw this as indicative of the absence of a sense of power over the physical world.

The Importance of Ethnography

Was there a developmental reason in early socialization for this dichotomy between individual mastery over the physical world and a collectivistic value orientation? I turned to the anthropological method of ethnography to find out. Ethnography is often defined in anthropology as participant observation; in the course of developing an appropriate participant role or roles in a real-life cultural setting, the researcher is able to record, traditionally by means of in-depth field notes, everyday life and discourse relevant to a particular topic or multiple topics.

My colleague and friend in Senegal, Jacqueline Rabain, working on an ethnographic dissertation for the Sorbonne, found some clues to early socialization in the everyday life of children and their caregivers. She found clues, for example, in adult interpretations of the child's developing motor capacities. Whereas we, in the United States or France, would get excited about the child's first step as an index of developing skill and even independence, a Wolof mother would likely interpret it as signifying the child's desire in relation to a person in his surrounding; for example, she might say something like "Look, he's walking toward you!" (Rabain-Zempléni, 1965).

> *Thus, adult interpretation of the child's first actions would seem to be paradigmatic for the choice between an individualistic and a collective orientation; a social interpretation of an act not only relates the actor to the group but also relates the group, including the actor, to physical events. When on the other hand, acts are given an interpretation in terms of motoric competence, other people are irrelevan and, moreover, the act is separated from the motivations, interntions, and desires of the actor himself.*
> (Greenfield & Bruner, 1969, p. 641)

Such selective interpretations serve an important socializing function: They expose the child to what is considered important in a particular culture.

Rabain also found the first clues that collectivism was associated with de-emphasis of the world of objects. She noted that manipulation of objects was an occasional and secondary activity for the Wolof child from two to four years and that self-image rested more on power over people than power over objects. She noted further that verbal exchanges between adults and children often concerned valued relations between people but rarely concerned explanations of the physical world (Rabain-Zempléni, 1965). Because scientific thinking is so linked to the world of objects, this was a clue that collectivistic world view might privilege social thinking, thinking about people and their relations, over scientific thinking. Later research has confirmed this paradigm of early socialization for a world that emphasizes thinking about people rather than things (Greenfield et al., 2003). It contrasts greatly with a paradigm that emphasizes learning to manipulate and understand objects, in the form of toys, from early infancy on (Greenfield et al., 2003).

Most intriguing, because it related directly to my conservation experiment, was Rabain's observation that, in the everyday situation of sharing a quantity among several persons (a situation not too different from the second half of my conservation experiment, in which a quantity of water was divided among six breakers), Wolof bush children pay more attention to who receives what, when, than to the amount received (Rabain-Zempléni, 1965). It parallels the "magical" action reason for nonconservation: More attention is focused on the person pouring, the social aspect of the situation, than on the purely physical aspect, the amount of water. This observation could also explain why Wolof children in Senegal achieved conservation in the standard experiment later than children in the United States or Switzerland.

This work illustrates the way in which ethnography can complement experiments to deepen understanding of paradigms of cultural thought. Ethnography has a very special role to play because it introduces cultural interpretations of behavior – it reveals that the very same behavior can have an opposite meaning in two different cultural settings. In a sense, when we do experiments in the United States, we already have done our ethnography. Because we are members of the society, we have a good idea of the cultural meaning of our results. This is not the case when we study a culture different from our own. Ethnography also connects our findings in the laboratory to the real world phenomena of everyday life. Finally, because cultural values are implicit in the very design of our experiments, often without our realizing it, ethnography is required to design valid cross-cultural experiments. We omit this first ethnographic stage of cross-cultural research at our own peril, as the reader will see later in this chapter.

The Level of Social Ideology

Rabain's ethnography did not uncover only socialization antecedents to the thinking patterns found in my experiments. Equally fascinating were parallels on the broader cultural level of social ideology. Aimée Césaire had developed a concept of *négritude* or blackness, a worldview that distinguished Black values from White. In opposition to the individualism of European cultures, *négritude* emphasizes "solidarity, born of the cohesion of the . . . clan" (Kestelhoof, 1962). The poet and president of Senegal, Leopold Senghor, defined *négritude* as "participation of the subject in the object, participation of the man in cosmic forces, communion of man with all other men" (Monteil, 1964, p. 31, my translation). This formulation of social and cultural ideology looked like my experimental results in Senegal writ large!

It was therefore not surprising that cultural world view also permeated the second cognitive domain of my dissertation research in Senegal, the development of categorization. If unschooled Wolof children were assuming that the world exists on one plane, with thought and object of thought as one unified reality, then it followed that the notions of individual viewpoints and different points of view would also be meaningless. Data from a study of picture categorization were relevant to this implication (Greenfield, Reich, & Olver, 1966/1972). Children of different ages were given triads of pictures and asked to pick the pair that was most alike. After unschooled Wolof children had selected a pair, the pictures were replaced and the participants were asked to find two different pictures from the same set that were also alike. In fact, each set of three images had been designed to have three bases of similarity – form, function, and color. But unschooled Wolof children did not find a second basis of similarity; they saw the stimuli from only one point of view. Researchers working in other parts of the nonindustrial world found parallel results (Cole et al., 1971; Irwin & McLaughlin, 1970). Thus, categorization behavior also revealed indications of taking for granted a single perspective on the world. (See Goldstone & Son, Chap. 2, for a review of theories of similarity; and Medin & Rips, Chap. 3, for a review of studies of categorization.)

In their landmark 1974 book, *Culture and Thought*, Cole and Scribner noted the need for integrative theory "to pull together a variety of disconnected experiments" (Cole & Scribner, 1974, p. 172). I did not realize that the two paradigms of thought I had stumbled upon in Senegal formed the basis of such an integrative theory. Data on culture and thought that could later be inserted into this larger framework continued to accumulate. Like my problem in developing questions that were meaningful to elicit reasoning in a conservation experiment, many of the findings were initially seen as methodological barriers to be overcome rather than as deep cultural differences in cognitive functioning.

Let me give an example from Cole et al. (1971). These researchers took a categorization task to Liberia, where they presented it to their Kpelle participants. This task involved a set of 20 objects that divided evenly into the linguistic categories of foods, implements, food containers, and clothing. When asked to group objects that were similar, the Kpelle participants did not do the taxonomic sorts expected by the researchers. Instead participants consistently made functional pairings (Glick, 1968). For example, rather than sorting objects into groups of tools and foods, participants would put a potato and a knife together because "you take the knife and cut the potato" (Cole et al., 1971, p. 79). According to Glick, participants often justified their pairings by stating "that a wise man could only do such and such" (Glick, 1968, p. 13). In total exasperation, the researchers "finally said, 'How would a fool do it?' The result was a set of nice linguistically ordered categories – four of them with five items each" (Glick, 1968, p. 13).

From the methodological perspective of a cognitive psychologist, the researchers had failed to tap into the participants' obvious competence in categorization with their first procedure. This example illustrates what Cole and Scribner (1974) viewed as two general problems in the cross-cultural study of thought:

1. *There is a great readiness to assume that particular kinds of tests or experimental situations are diagnostic of particular kinds of cognitive capacities or processes.*
2. *Psychological processes are treated as "entities" which a person "has" or "does not have." In other words, they are considered a property of the person rather than the situation.*

(Cole & Scribner, 1974, p. 173).

There is another problem in this story that also can be considered methodological – the ethnocentrism of the criteria for "correct" sorting. Such methodological problems led Cole and Scribner (1974) to recommend that researchers take into account "knowledge about the culture and behavior of the people gained from the work of anthropologists, linguists, and other social scientists." (Ref. 8, p. 196). They went a step "further in suggesting that the *methods* of these relevant fields need to be integrated.... Field and laboratory, anthropological observation and psychological experimentation, can yield knowledge from different perspectives about the same function" (Ref. 8, p. 196). We already have seen this advice in action; collection of both qualitative and quantitative data is part of the methodological armoire of the cultural psychologist (Greenfield, 1997a).

But the problems of "wise" and "foolish" sorting also get to the substantive heart of the collectivistic paradigm of cognition. From the vantage point of a collectivistic worldview, I would submit that the "wise man's" pairings were of social utility, whereas the "foolish man's" taxonomic groupings of five items each were socially or pragmatically useless. I believe that is why, for the Kpelle, a wise man would make functional pairs, whereas only a fool would make taxonomic sorts.

This analysis leads us to an even deeper level of cultural definitions of intelligence: In the Kpelle example, the researchers' criterion for *intelligent* behavior was the participants' criterion for *foolish;* the participants' criterion for *wise* behavior was the researchers' criterion for *stupid* (Greenfield, 1997b). Underlying these interpretations of the experiment are different ethnotheories, that is, folk theories of intelligence. Most profoundly, our theories of what kind of thought is worth studying are very much influenced by our ethnotheories of what constitutes intelligent behavior. And what constitutes intelligent behavior depends on what is adaptive and valued in a particular ecocultural environment. The investigation of ethnotheories of intelligence proved to greatly deepen understanding of cultural paradigms of thought (see Sternberg, Chap. 31, for further discussion of intelligence).

Theories and Ethnotheories of Intelligence

Clearly, human intelligence and the brain structure that supports it are keys to our adaptation as a species. Yet within this broad rubric of human intelligence, different forms of intelligence are valued and adaptive in different ecocultural niches. Mundy-Castle (1974/1976) contrasted technological intelligence, which is more developed in the independent, individualist characteristic of Europe, and social intelligence, which is more developed in the interdependent, collectivist characteristic of Africa. Closely related to technological intelligence (and perhaps indistinguishable from it) is scientific intelligence. Indeed, underlying Piaget's theory of cognitive development is a theory of intelligence as scientific thinking (Greenfield, 1974). By his own admission, understanding the basis for Western scientific thought was Piaget's most fundamental theoretical concern (Piaget, 1963/1977). Under Inhelder's leadership, Piaget investigated the development of scientific thought (chemistry and physics) in a set of experimental studies (Inhelder & Piaget, 1958). This body of theory and research implies the importance of scientific intelligence as a developmental goal for processes of thinking. Scientific or technological intelligence as a folk theory supports thinking skills that relate to the world of things rather than people; this would include most of the items and subtests of standardized intelligence tests.

Following Mundy-Castle's depiction of technological and social intelligence, related explorations of intelligence concepts in different cultures began to appear (Dasen & de Ribeaupierre, 1987; Serpell, 1994; Sternberg et al., 1981; Wober, 1974); all challenged the assumption that technological or scientific intelligence was a universal endpoint of development (Greenfield, 1974). Indeed, social intelligence turned out to be the predominant ideal in Africa and Asia (e.g., Wober, 1974; Super, 1983; Dasen, 1984; Gill & Keats, 1980; Serpell, 1994; Nsamenang & Lamb, 1994; Grigorenko et al., 2001). Intelligence in all these investigations includes a concern with responsible ways of contributing to the social world. The central feature of the Baoulé concept of intelligence in Ivory Coast, West Africa, for example, is willingness to help others (Dasen 1984). In general, African cultures not only emphasize social intelligence but also see the role of technical skills as a means to social ends (Dasen 1984). This sort of ethnotheory of intelligence could explain why the taxonomic sorter was a foolish man in Kpelle eyes.

As a group, such conceptions can be seen as collectivistic conceptions of intelligence (Segall et al., 1999). Note that these conceptions are not all-or-none. Differences to a great extent, are a matter of differential priorities. At the same time, there is not one collectivistic conception of intelligence, nor a single individualistic conception of intelligence. There are cross-cultural surface variations for each underlying theme (Greenfield, 2000).

Who and What Are the Individualists and Collectivists?

This is perhaps the place to stop and define who are the individualists and who are the collectivists. In doing so, I will not present a simple picture. Instead, I will discuss ideal cases, in-between cases, culture change, biculturalism, and culture contact. These complexities take me beyond simple binary distinctions that have bothered some (Rogoff, 2003).

My nonbinary starting point is that all human beings are both individual and social.

What varies is the extent to which cultures try to maximize one or the other facet of the human experience. Correlated with this maximization are different forms that the social and the individual take within each paradigm. So, for example, social behavior tends to be more automatic in the collectivistic system and more by choice, providing individual autonomy, in the individualistic system. The other side of the maximization coin is the fact that the major mode of one cultural paradigm may be the minor mode of the other. For example, in the society of the United States, we might see religions as often emphasizing the communitarian in a primarily individualistic surround. The universal existence of both modes can be seen in priming studies in which the minor mode (individualism in the case of Asians, collectivism in the case of North Americans) can be elicited by a relevant prime (Gardner, Gabriel, & Lee, 1999).

It is also important to realize that we are talking about cultural *systems*, not isolated attributes (cf. Kitayama, 2002). The distribution of autonomy and obedience between men and women in a collectivistic culture has been used as an argument against the very concept of collectivistic culture and for the notion that autonomy and obedience are individual difference variables rather than culture-level characteristics (Turiel, 2000). In response to this argument, I note that one essence of a collectivistic culture is *relations* of obedience between women and men, clearly providing more autonomy for men than for women. Similarly, the *relation* of equality among individuals provides more autonomy for both women and men in an individualistic culture. It is not the *existence* of autonomy that is important in the characterization of a culture according to the present paradigm; it is the *patterning* that counts. Indeed, I would see the emphasis on individuals as separate rather than as interrelated (the hallmark of psychology founded upon the independent individual as the unit of analysis) as an individualistic perspective on social science itself. Culture as a system of relations, the patterning of attributes, the forms of individual and social behavior, and the system of priorities – these are the bottom line of this theoretical paradigm.

Who are the collectivists? Harry Triandis notes that they include 70% of the world's population – the populations of Africa, Asia, Latin America, and Native America (Triandis, 1989). Equally important, there are demographic, ecological, and historical factors that are inputs into the expressed value system. Some of the most important demographic factors are economic level [rich are more individualistic than poor (Segall et al., 1999)], the urban–rural contrast [large-scale urban more individualistic than small-scale rural (Kim & Choi, 1994)], formal education [which functions as an individualizer (Reykowski, 1994)], high technology [which functions as an individualizer (Mundy-Castle, 1974)], immigration and migration (making people more individualistic), agricultural subsistence versus commerce [the latter functioning as an individualizer (Greenfield, Maynard, & Childs, 2003; Greenfield, 2004)], and religion (some are more individualistic; e.g., Protestantism, others more collectivistic; e.g., Catholicism).

Indeed, it is useful to see the two paradigms as originating as adaptations to different ecologies. Demographic factors influence ecology and, through ecology, they form psychologies. Thus, rich people do not need to cooperate with a larger group for their survival; poor people do. The urban environment contains many strangers, and so community relations become less functional (Kim, 1994). In formal education, the irreducible unit of performance is the individual who must receive an individual grade and performance evaluation (Greenfield, 1994). Complex technology functions as an individualizer in multiple ways – through providing large dwellings and office buildings with the opportunity for private space and through substituting interaction with a machine for interaction with people (e.g., television replacing frequent face-to-face visits).

When you immigrate to a new country or migrate to a new location within a country, you often leave extended family behind. As a consequence, a high rate of geographical mobility should increase individualism. This might be a reason why Europeans are less individualistic than Americans. Note, too, that nation states composed primarily of immigrants at their founding – for example, the United States, Canada, and Australia – are generally among the most individualistic (Hofstede, 1980; Oyserman, Coon, & Kemmelmeier, 2002).

In subsistence agriculture settings, all must cooperate to produce mainly perishable goods. In a commercial setting, it is desirable to maximize the monetary resources of an individual to accumulate nonperishable consumer goods like cars or televisions (Collier, 2003). Catholicism emphasizes the communal, including a pathway to God through another human being, the priest; Protestantism emphasizes the independent individual with a direct pathway to God. It is interesting that, as commerce develops in Mexico and Central America and when immigrants come to the commercial environment of the United States from the more agricultural environment of Mexico, evangelical Protestantism has become much more popular whereas Catholicism has declined in popularity.

It is also important to note that, because of all these factors, individualism and collectivism are relative terms, their systematic nature notwithstanding. If one tests rural versus urban populations in the same country (e.g., Mexico), one will usually find the rural population to be more collectivistic (e.g., Madsen & Shapira, 1970). On the other hand, if you compare Latino immigrant families in Los Angeles, an urban setting, and Euro-American families in Los Angeles, the urban Latino families will respond more collectivistically than the Euro-Americans (Raeff, Greenfield, & Quiroz, 2000). In other words, the nature of these demographic variables is such as to make individualism and collectivism graded, rather than all-or-none systems. Because they are so central to adaptation, they are clearly very sensitive to environmental factors.

Multiple demographic factors create paradigmatic cases on the extremes (H. Keller, personal communication, June, 2003): The small, stable, poor, agrarian village with an oral culture and without advanced technology would be the paradigmatic case on the collectivistic end of the spectrum. The large, mobile, rich, urban neighborhood with a high level of formal schooling and advanced technology would be the paradigmatic case on the individualistic end of the spectrum. Clearly, all other cases would fall between these extremes.

A particular type of in-between case is the immigrant family who has come, most generally, from a poorer, more collectivistic society into a richer, more individualistic one. In general, such immigrants will be at a point between their compatriots in the ancestral country and natives of the host country on cognitive tasks that tap into individualistic and collectivistic paradigms of thought (Nisbett, 2003). In addition, we expect, as generations in the host country increase, the host country culture will make an increasingly large mark on patterns of thought.

Because of the development of the world in the direction of a dense urban, commercial, high-tech environment, there is a worldwide movement toward increasing individualism. Finally, because of high rates of immigration, there is also increasing contact between more individualistic and more collectivistic cultures in the world. This often leads to mismatches and misunderstandings. I will give an example of a cognitive mismatch and misunderstanding later in the chapter. But let me now turn to some additional thought processes in which the two paradigms manifest themselves, yielding interesting cross-cultural differences.

Thinking about People: Theory of Mind

Given what I had observed in Senegal concerning the absence of a notion of point-of-view, I became very skeptical when theory of mind became popular in cognitive development research. The claims for universality of the sort of calculus that requires a participant to know, for example, what someone knows a third party has said to a fourth party (e.g., Does Mary know the ice-cream man has talked to John?", Baron-Cohen,

1989) seemed to involve too much differentiation of viewpoints for children whose world view emphasized unity with the world and those around them. I wanted to think through the individualistic assumptions that might be being made in this line of research and to think about what a collectivistic alternative might look like. This search eventuated in one section of an article, "Cultural Pathways through Universal Development" (Greenfield, et al., 2003), which I present here.

Understanding self and others is part of our universal evolutionary heritage (Tomasello, 1999; Whiten, 2002). The mirror neuron system of the cerebral cortex reveals a common neuromuscular activation for acting oneself and for understanding the actions of others (Fadiga et al., 1995; Iacoboni et al., 1999). In ontogeny, the first step in understanding self and others occurs at birth, when infants discriminate people from things (Trevarthen, 1980). Comprehension of agency as the production of goal-directed action begins in early infancy (Gelman & Lucariello, 2002). An ability to distinguish between self and others as intentional agents develops at eight or nine months of age (Piaget, 1952; Tomasello, 1999; Trevarthen, 1980).

At the one-word stage of language development (between one and two years of age), infants code the intentional action not just of self but of others (Greenfield & Smith, 1976; Greenfield, 1980), and this encoding seems to have ancient phylogenetic roots (Greenfield & Savage-Rumbaugh, 1990; Greenfield & Lyn, in press). The linguistic encoding of intentional action becomes more complex with age and the acquisition of language (Bloom, Lightbown, & Hood, 1975). At the same time, there is very early understanding of the effects of action on other people. Script knowledge, which begins in the second year of life, involves the understanding of both intentions and effects of human action (Gelman & Lucariello, 2002). It also requires an understanding of the coordination of action by more than one person.

These two universal capacities – the capacity to encode the intentions of self and others and the capacity to encode the social effects of one's own and others' action – provide the groundwork for two distinct cultural emphases in the development of person knowledge. Some cultures emphasize the individual psyche, individual traits, and the individual intentions behind action (Vinden & Astington, 2000); other cultures emphasize the social effects and social context of a person's action (Duranti, 1988, 1993; Shweder & Bourne, 1984; Fiske et al., 1998). The latter also see mind and heart as integrated rather than separate (Lillard, 1998: Zambrano, 1999). We see the former as the individualistic emphasis and the latter as the collectivistic or sociocentric emphasis.

Most literature on theory of mind – the ability to think about other people's mental states – has assumed an emphasis on individual minds (Flavell, 1999). I, however, see theory of mind as a special culturally canalized case of person knowledge (cf. Hobson, 1993). I therefore review the literature indicating the existence of these two different cultural emphases – individual psyche versus social effects or context – in the development of social understanding or person knowledge.

Although it claims universality, I utilize the classical literature on theory of mind to complete the picture of the individualistic pathway to person knowledge. Early steps along this pathway have to do with the acquisition of mentalistic terms; children as young as twenty-two months first produce mentalistic terms such as *know* and *pretend* (Wellman, 1990). Later, the child is able to imagine a mental state of affairs in another person different from the information available to oneself (e.g., Perner, 1991). Similar trends occur in literate, developed countries, both Western and non-Western (Wellman, Cross, & Watson, 2001). The differentiation and individuation of people according to their states of mind is basic to this developmental pathway to social understanding.

In the other pathway, however, mentalistic terms are lacking in the lexicon, are not understood in the same way as the English equivalents, and are not applied to oneself. This phenomenon has been found in a number of subsistence ecologies (Greenfield & Bruner, 1966/1969; Vinden, 1996, 1999). As mentioned earlier, however, both schooling, with its demand for justifications, and literacy, with its separation of thought (on paper) from thinker, leads to an understanding of the mentalistic term *think* (Greenfield & Bruner, 1966/1969). (See Lillard (1998) for a cross-cultural review of the theory-of-mind literature).

In a nonliterate subsistence ecology in Africa, children between two and four years old were given a theory-of-mind task embedded into a context of social action. In addition, the task used the term *heart* rather than *thought* (Avis & Harris, 1991). Under these circumstances, Baka children in southeast Cameroon showed the development of social understanding that had been found in the United States and Europe. The results contrasted strongly with another study that (1) decontextualized the task, presenting it as a task involving only one actual person, the subject; (2) asked about the deceived's thought rather than action in reference to a hidden object; and (3) asked about mind rather than heart. Under these conditions, Quechua children between about four and eight performed at chance levels (Vinden, 1996). Somewhat more contextualized tasks led to somewhat improved performance in subsistence groups in Cameroon, West Africa (the Mofu), and Papua New Guinea (the Tainae and Tolai) (Vinden, 1999).

Meta-analysis indicates that, around the world, children from subsistence cultures solve theory-of-mind tasks better when these are presented in context (Wellman, Cross, & Watson, 2001). However, Vinden (1999) found a lag in age in all groups relative to children of European-derived cultures; false belief (the understanding that another person has been misled into believing that something is true that, in fact, is false) assessed using the word "think" was at chance levels at all ages in the two groups most isolated from the outside world of European culture.

Here we interpret a lag as indicating that the skill in question is not valued in a particular culture (LeVine, 1997). "With a collectivist or group orientation, personal, mental, and emotional states are relatively unimportant" (Vinden & Astington, 2000, p. 512). In line with the notion that school ecology favors the development of attention to the individual psyche, schooled children performed better on several of the tasks relating to predicting an individual's behavior or emotion in a nonsocial situation (Vinden, 1999).

On the other hand, in a culturally important situation involving social responsibility, young children from small, face-to-face societies with subsistence traditions show advanced understanding of the knowledge state and feelings of another person whose knowledge differs from one's own. In a successful apprenticeship situation, the expert must be aware of how much less the novice knows in comparison with self. The expert must also be aware of the novice's need for materials and the novice's motivations. In a video study of naturalistic teaching interactions, Zinacantec Maya children as young as four years old were able to supply necessary materials and model tasks for their younger siblings (Maynard, 2002). They were also able to provide useful verbal guidance in teaching, such as narrating a task they were demonstrating and giving commands to the younger child. By the age of eight, children were very adept at simplifying the task for younger children by giving them parts of tasks, one at a time, and at scaffolding the task by providing complex verbal information. These advanced thinking skills showed an understanding of the knowledge state, material needs, and motivation of the younger children. Sibling caregiving as an important social responsibility may have played a role in the young children's desire and skill in teaching their younger siblings. Similar sibling teaching practices were found in another sibling-caregiving culture – the Wolof of Senegal (Rabain-Jamin, Maynard, & Greenfield, 2003). Future research is needed to explore the relationship between the cognitive operations of person knowledge in sibling caregiving and in experimental tasks.

Indeed, it may be culturally significant that person knowledge has been measured so frequently by false belief, the dominant theory-of-mind task. In a false-belief task, the participant must understand that another person has a different perspective (the false belief) from his or her own. It is a task that requires individuation of one's perspective from that of another. Individuation is an important component of the development of the independent self. It may be that socialization in interdependent cultures emphasizes *shared* perspectives more than *different* perspectives. Only future research can tell us whether this may be another reason for relatively poor performance on false-belief tasks in collectivistic, subsistence cultures.

Ideally, cross-cultural comparison would involve a developmental analysis of tasks tapping into both of these cultural emphases within the context of universal developments. A pioneering study of social explanation in India and the United States by Joan Miller (1984) did exactly that: Children in both the United States and India improved at social explanation with age (the universal development). At the same time, children in the United States increasingly formulated their social explanations of events in terms of an individual's stable traits (emphasis on the individual psyche). Indian children, in contrast, increasingly formulated their social explanations in terms of contextual factors, particularly factors in the social surround (emphasis on social context).

Miller's findings were replicated in a real world situation by Morris and Peng (1994). They found that when a Chinese physics student at the University of Iowa shot his advisor and several other people after losing an award competition, the reasons given were quite different in U.S. and Chinese newspapers:

> *Michael Morris, a graduate student at Michigan at the time, noticed that the explanations for Gang Lu's behavior in the campus newpapers focused almost entirely on Lu's presumed qualities – the murderer's psychological foibles ("very bad temper," "sinister edge to his character"), attitudes ("personal belief that guns were an important means to redress grievances"), and psychological problems ("a darkly disturbed man who drove himself to success and destruction," "a psychological problem with being challenged"). He asked his fellow student Kaiping Peng what kinds of accounts of the murder were being given in Chinese newspapers. They could scarcely have been more different. Chinese reporters emphasized causes that had to do with the context in which Lu operated. Explanations centered on Lu's relationships ("did not get along with his advisor," "rivalry with slain student," "isolation from Chinese community"), pressures in Chinese society ("victim of Chinese 'Top Student' educational policy") and aspects of the American context ("availability of guns in the U.S.").* (Morris & Peng, pp. 111–112).

Morris and Peng found the same pattern of differences when the incident involved a student from the United States. The Chinese focused on the killer's relation to context, particularly social context, in explaining his behavior. U.S. reporters focused on qualities of the individual. A whole series of experiments on causal attribution led to the conclusion that "Westerners attend primarily to the focal . . . person and Asians attend more broadly to the field and to the relations between the object and the field" (Nisbett, 2003, p. 127). Thus, a pattern of cultural differnces found in the developing child by Miller also show up in adulthood, the endpoint or outcome of development.

Hong Kong is a setting in which two cultures, one more collectivistic (Chinese) and one more individualistic (British) coexist. Hong et al. (2000) showed the dynamism of the bicultural mind in the arena of social explanation. When primed with symbols of Western culture (e.g., Mickey Mouse) in an experiment concerning social explanation (participants had to explain why, in a picture, one fish was swimming in front of the other fish), participants constructed more explanations in terms of individual motivation. When primed with symbols of Chinese culture (e.g., with a dragon), participants constructed more explanations in terms of the other fish or the context.

These same differences in thinking about people can affect a sense of one's own continuity of self over time. Parallel to the two modes of social explanation discovered by Miller, researchers Lalonde, Chandler, and Sokol (1999) identify two cultural modes of addressing the problem of self-continuity over time in autobiographical narratives. This is the problem of how to experience and conceptualize a continuing self in the presence of dramatic changes over the course of development. They term the first model "an 'Essentialist' or 'Entity' notion of selfhood" (Ref. 55, 1999, p. 1); these narratives focus attention upon some aspect of the self "that is thought to remain untouched by time and change" (Lalonde, Ref. 55, 1999, p. 1). The pathway of the independent, autonomous self requires a source of self-continuity that is functional in the face of separation from parents, the modal adolescent identity formation in the United States and Canada. Internal essences or entities would fill this requirement; this is the way in which most non-Native Canadians explain self-continuity (Chandler et al., 2003). And, as we have seen from Miller's research, internal traits or essences are generally used in causal attribution in the individualistic paradigm.

They call the second model a "relationship-centered" notion of self. It uses narrative to connect the self across different time periods. The narratives often situate the speakers in family and community relationships that continue across various periods in the life cycle. This is the way most Native Canadians explain self-continuity (Lalonde, Chandler, & Sokol, 1999).

Thinking about Things: Categories, Physical Relations, and Social Relations

A more collectivistic ethnotheory of intelligence that values relationships and social utility can explain why the wise Kpelle person would make functional pairs in a categorization task, rather than sort by taxonomic categories. Taxonomic categories, in contrast, revolve around a defining trait or traits of its members. These defining traits are decontextualized from the social utility of the object or from other parts of the physical world. We saw this same contrast between an emphasis on inner traits that transcend context and contextualized explanation when we examined two paradigms of social reasoning (Miller, 1984).

If the Kpelle mode of categorization typifies a collectivistic worldview, then it should appear in other collectivistic cultures. Indeed, this is the case. Ji, Zhang, and Nisbett (2002) compared U.S. college students with students from China and Taiwan on a triadic test of categorization. In each triad (e.g., panda, monkey, banana), there were two pictures that could be paired on the basis of taxonomic similarity (in this triad, panda and monkey are both animals), and there were two that could be paired on the basis of functional relationships (in this triad, the monkey eats the banana). When asked which two of the three pictures were most closely related, U.S. college students preferred to group "on the basis of common category membership: Panda and monkey fit in to the animal category." The Chinese participants showed a preference for grouping on the basis of thematic relationships (e.g., monkey and banana) and justified their answers in terms of relationships: "Monkeys eat bananas" (Ji, Zhang, & Nisbett, 2002, p. 140–141). This same cross-cultural difference developed in childhood (Chiu, 1972). But, again, cultural preferences do not necessarily exclude the development of a minor mode. Illustrating this point, a study by Wisniewski and Bassok (1999) indicates that, in the absence of a forced choice between the taxonomic similarity and functional relationships, U.S. college students can and do use both modes of thought as an implicit basis for similarity judgments and other cognitive operations.

Perhaps the most basic difference between the two modes of thinking is the collectivistic tendency to contextualize the world of objects in a web of social relations versus the individualistic tendency to see the world of physical objects as operating in its own plane of reality. The former is what we saw in the causal reasoning among the unschooled Wolof children; the latter is what we expect in the world of physical science. These two modes of thinking about things are socialized very early (Bakeman et al., 1990; Clancy, 1986; Fernald & Morikawa, 1993; Rabain, 1979; Rabain-Jamin, 1994; Zempléni-Rabain, 1973).

Cross-Cultural Conflict in What Counts as Thinking

When families with a collectivistic cultural heritage emmigrate to an individualistic society, the two paradigms can come into sharp conflict, particularly at school. Cultural models not only have values attached to them – what counts as good and bad, what takes priority over what – but they also have epistemologies – what counts as knowledge. These cultural models are so basic they normally remain implicit. As long as everyone interacting in the same social world shares the same model, the implicit quality of the models does not cause a problem. In fact, it provides an underlying set of shared assumptions that makes social life – for example, life in school – run smoothly. The next example is about what happens in a bicultural classroom when teachers and learners have different implicit understandings of what counts as thinking.

> *In a pre-kindergarten class, the teacher held an actual chicken egg. She asked the children to describe eggs by thinking about the times they had cooked and eaten eggs. One of the children tried three times to talk about how she cooked eggs with her grandmother, but the teacher disregarded these comments in favor of a child who explained how eggs are white and yellow when they are cracked.* (Greenfield, Raeff, & Quiroz, 1996).

The two features of this incident – the first child's emphasis on a family-based story and the teacher's disregard and devaluation of the child's seemingly unscientific answer – occur frequently in classrooms with immigrant Latino students. But what is really happening here?

Our theoretical analysis rests on the following two points: What counts as thinking for the teacher is thinking about the physical world apart from the social world. It is the teacher's definition of scientific thinking, and, in her mind, this is a science lesson. Her focus is on one part of her instructions, "Describe eggs." The child, in contrast, is responding more to the other part of the teacher's instructions – "Think about the times you have cooked and eaten eggs" and, based on a different set of assumptions about what counts as thinking, focuses on the social aspect of her experience with eggs, in particular, a family experience. This is the first aspect of the misunderstanding and cultural mismatch between teacher and learner.

The second aspect of the mismatch is that the child who was passed over is providing a narrative, also valued in her home culture, whereas the teacher is expecting a simple statement of fact. Implicitly, the teacher is making Bruner's distinction between narrative thought and logical–scientific thought. Bruner's analysis is very relevant here:

> *There appear to be two broad ways in which human beings organize and manage their knowledge of the world, indeed structure even their immediate experience: One seems more specialized for treating of physical "things," the other for treating people and their plights. These are conventionally known as* logical–scientific *thinking and* narrative *thinking.* (Bruner, 1996, p. 39).

The child who talks about cooking and eating eggs with grandmother is responding in the narrative mode; but the teacher expects the logical–scientific mode: "What are the bare facts about eggs?" she wants to know. Narrative is, in the dominant culture, associated with the humanities, logical–scientific thought is associated with the sciences. As Bruner says, the value of logical–scientific thinking "is so implicit in our highly technological culture that its inclusion in school curricula is taken for granted" (Bruner, 1996,

p. 41). It is so taken for granted that, as the egg incident shows, the narrative mode becomes invisible to the teacher.

Logic

The same type of contrast applies to logical thought (see Evans, Chap. 8). Deductive logic is intrinsically decontextualized from its content (Nisbett et al., 2001; Nisbett, 2003). We therefore would expect it would be part of individualistic but not collectivistic habits of thought. Instead, a collectivist might recontextualize a deductive problem. This phenomenon was first identified by Luria in the 1930s with uneducated Soviet peasants in Central Asia (Luria, 1971). Inspired by Luria, Cole et al. (1971) gave such problems to nonliterate Kpelle adults in a rural area of Liberia. Here is an example of a deductive logic problem and how the participant refuses to deal with the decontextualized structure and, instead, recontextualizes it, first by asking more questions concerning context and then by applying his own experience to the problem:

> EXPERIMENTER: *At one time spider went to a feast. He was told to answer this question before he could eat any of the food. The question is: Spider and black deer always eat together. Spider is eating. Is black deer eating?*
> SUBJECT: *Were they in the bush?*
> EXPERIMENTER: *Yes.*
> SUBJECT: *They were eating together?*
> EXPERIMENTER: *Spider and black deer always eat together. Spider is eating. Is black deer eating?*
> SUBJECT: *But I was not there. How can I answer such a question?*
> EXPERIMENTER: *Can't you answer it? Even if you were not there you can answer it.*
> SUBJECT: *Ask the question again for me to hear.*
> EXPERIMENTER: *(repeats the question)*
> SUBJECT: *Oh, oh black deer was eating.*
> EXPERIMENTER: *Black deer was eating?*
> SUBJECT: *Yes.*
> EXPERIMENTER: *Black deer was eating?*
> SUBJECT: *Yes.*
> EXPERIMENTER: *What is your reason for saying that black deer was eating?*
> SUBJECT: *The reason is that black deer always walks about all day eating green leaves in the bush. When it rests for a while it gets up again and goes to eat.*
> (Cole et al., 1971, p. 187).

In essence, this participant rejects the abstract, decontextualized structure of the logical problem. This type of response was typical of a group of nonliterate Kpelle adults. In line with our notion of school as promoting an individualistic worldview, Kpelle high school students generally answered the logical problems in the way the researchers had in mind – as decontextualized logical deductive problems.

Again, if this distinction is typical of the two paradigms of thought, it should apply to other groups who might differ on the individualism–collectivism worldview. Using different methods, Nisbett and his colleagues showed that East Asians, like the Kpelle, rejected decontextualized abstract logic and preferred to reason on the basis of experience (Nisbett et al., 2001).

Visual Pattern Construction: A Case of Historical Change

The worldwide direction of change on all critical demographic variables – toward greater population density, formal education, technology, and commerce-based wealth – yields an historical push toward the pole of individualism. I will use the domain of visual representation to provide an example of how historical change can move cognition in the direction of the individualistic paradigm of thought. One of the marks of a collectivistic cultural system is respect for elders and their traditions. The individualistic side of this coin places a value on novelty and innovation. The typical economy in which respect for elders predominates is agricultural subsistence. Innovation, in turn, is an important value in commercial entrepreneurship. An experiment demonstrated how a shift from one economy to another affected the representation of culturally novel patterns.

In 1969 and 1970, I did a pattern representation experiment in a Zinacantec Maya community of Chiapas, Mexico (Greenfield & Childs, 1977) that involved, among other things, continuing both culturally novel and culturally familiar (from traditional weaving) striped patterns. The experimenter would place sticks of different colors in a rectangular wooden frame, providing three repetitions of the pattern (for example, green, green, green, yellow would be a single repetition of one of the patterns). She would then ask the subject to continue the same pattern. At that time, the dominant economy was agricultural subsistence with relatively little cash or commerce.

I returned to the community in 1991 after a period of economic development in which commercial entrepreneurship and a cash economy had grown greatly with a corresponding decline in agricultural subsistence. I predicted that skill in continuing novel (not familiar) patterns would have increased, and this is exactly what I found. Even more interesting, I was able to relate this skill with novel representations directly to participation in commerce. Change had been uneven, and children whose families were most involved in commercial activities in both their business dealings and as consumers showed the most skill in constructing the novel patterns. Structural equation modeling indicated a causal relationship between correct completion of the novel patterns and commercial involvement.

At the same time in this community, where weaving was the most important skill learned by all girls, there had been a shift in woven patterns from tradition to novelty. At the earlier period, there was a closed set of about four patterns that girls and women wove for clothing and other utilitarian purposes. By the time we went back in 1991, the basic patterns still existed, but they had been supplemented by an ongoing process of innovation through girls and women who created an infinite number of woven and embroidered designs. So skill in representing culturally novel patterns in our experiment was a reflection of change in the culture as a whole as it moved from subsistence agriculture to money and commerce.

In terms of the socialization processes that could develop these new cognitive styles, we found an historical change in weaving apprenticeship that also had moved toward a more individualistic model. In commercial families, weaving apprenticeship had, between 1970 and the early 1990s, moved from help and guidance from the teacher to a more independent trial-and-error learning process for the novice weaver. Moreover, we also found a correlation between the more independent, individualistic mode of weaving apprenticeship skill and continuing the novel patterns in our experiment.

So these basic cultural paradigms of thinking are not constant. They are adaptations to social conditions, including socialization processes, that change over time. As the world becomes more commercial, more dense, and more formally educated, the Zinacantecs illustrate this worldwide trend from a more collectivistic to a more individualistic paradigm of thought.

CONCLUSIONS AND FUTURE DIRECTIONS

Identifying two basically different paradigms of thought, value, and behavior has linked together phenomena in the domain of culture and thinking that were once considered unrelated. With this linking thread has come deeper understanding of basic cultural differences. Although providing theoretical coherence, it has also removed some of the ethnocentrism from earlier accounts of difference, in which, for example, collectivistic forms of categorization, reasoning, and logic were considered the absence of Western skills rather than as examples of a different set of values about the nature of intelligence.

The primary omission in the preceding account is probably the ecocultural approach to everyday cognition and particularly the role of cultural artifacts in thinking. For good reviews from these perspectives, I recommend *Everyday Cognition* by Schliemann, Carraher, and Ceci (1997) and *Culturally Situated Cognition* by Wang, Ceci,

Williams, and Kopko (2004). The empirical body of work generated by these approaches is not at all antithetical to the theoretical paradigm presented here. In the future, I believe further theoretical integration will take place.

References

Avis, J., & Harris, P. L. (1991). Belief-desire reasoning among Baka children: Evidence for a universal conception of mind. *Child Development, 62*, 460–467.

Bakeman, R., Adamson, L. B., Konner, M., & Barr, R. G. (1990). !Kung infancy: The social context of object exploration. *Child Development, 61*, 794–809.

Baron-Cohen, S. (1989). The autistic child's theory of mind: A case of specific developmental delay. *Journal of Child Psychology and Psychiatry, 30*, 285–297.

Bloom, L., Lightbown, P., & Hood, L. (1975). Structure and variation in child language. *Monographs of the Society for Research in Child Development*, 40–97.

Bruner., J. S. (1996). *The Culture of Education*. Cambridge, MA: Harvard University Press.

Chandler, M., Lalonde, C. E., Sokol, B., & Hallett, D. (2003). Personal persistence, identity, development, and suicide: A study of native and non-native North American adolescents. *Monographs of the Society for Research in Child Development, 68*, No. 2, Serial No. 273.

Chiu, L.-H. (1972). A cross-cultural comparison of cognitive styles in Chinese and American children. *International Journal of Psychology, 7*, 235–242.

Clancy, P. M. (1986). The acquisition of communicative style in Japanese. In B. B. Schieffelin & E. Ochs (Eds.), *Language socialization across cultures.* Cambridge, UK: Cambridge University Press.

Cole, M., Gay, J., Glick, J., & Sharp, J. (1971). *The Cultural Context of Learning and Thinking: An Exploration in Experimental Anthropology*. New York: Basic Books.

Cole, M., & Scribner, S. (1974). *Culture and Thought: A Psychological Introduction*. New York: Wiley.

Collier, J. F. (2003). Presentation at UCLA Sloan Center Workshop on Kinship and Family. January 31, 2003.

Dasen, P. (Ed.) (1977). *Piagetian Psychology: Cross-cultural Contributions*. New York: Gardner Press.

Dasen, P. R. (1984). The cross-cultural study of intelligence: Piaget and the Baoulé. *International Journal of Psychology, 19*, 407–34.

Dasen P. R. & de Ribeaupierre, A. (1987). Neo-Piagetian theories: Cross-cultural and differential perspectives. *International Journal of Psychology, 22*, 793–832.

Duranti, A. (1988). Intentions, language and social action in a Samoan context. *Journal of Pragmatics, 12*, 13–33.

Duranti, A. (1993). Intentions, self, and responsibility: An essay in Samoan ethnopragmatics. In J. H. Hill, & J. T. Irvine (Eds.), *Responsibility and Evidence in Oral Discourse* (pp. 24–47). Cambridge, UK: Cambridge University Press.

Fadiga, L., Fogassi, L., Pavesi, G., & Rizolatti, G. (1995). Motor facilitation during action observation: A magnetic stimulation study. *Journal of Neurophysiology, 73*, 2608–2611.

Fernald, A., & Morikawa, H. (1993). Common themes and cultural variation in Japanese and American mothers' speech to infants. *Child Development, 64*, 637–656.

Fiske, A. P., Kitayama, S., Markus, H., & Nisbett, D. (1998). The cultural matrix of social psychology. In D. Gilbert, S. Fiske, & G. Lindzey (Eds.), *Handbook of Social Psychology* (Fourth Edition) (pp. 915–981). New York: McGraw-Hill.

Flavell, J. (1999). Cognitive development: Children's knowledge about the mind. *Annual Review of Psychology, 50*, 21–45.

Gardner, W. L., Gabriel, S., & Lee, A. (1999). "I" value freedom, but "we' value relationships: Self-construal priming mimics cultural differences in judgment. *Psychological Science, 10*, 321–326.

Gelman, R., & Lucariello, J. (2002). Role of learning in cognitive development. In C. R. Gallistel (Ed.), *Stevens' Handbook of Experimental Psychology* (Third Edition). *Vol. 3, Learning, Motivation, and Emotion* (pp. 395–443). New York: Wiley.

Gill, R., & Keats, D. M. (1980). Elements of intellectual competence: Judgments by Australian and Malay university students. *Journal of Cross-Cutlural Psychology, 11*, 233–43.

Glick, J. (1968, February). Cognitive style among the Kpelle of Liberia. Paper presented at the meeting on Cross-Cultural Cognitive Studies,

American Educational Research Association, Chicago.

Greenfield, P. M. (1966). On culture and conservation. In J. S. Bruner, R. R. Olver, & P. M. Greenfield, *Studies in Cognitive Growth* (pp. 225–256). New York: Wiley.

Greenfield, P. M. (1972). Oral or written language: The consequences for cognitive development in Africa, the United States, and England. *Language and Speech*, 15, 169–178.

Greenfield, P. M. (1974). Cross-cultural research and Piagetian theory: Paradox and progress. *Dossiers Pedagogiques*, March–April, 34–39. French translation.

Greenfield, P. M., (1975). Oral or written language: The consequences for cognitive development in Africa, the United States, and England. Reprinted in M. Maer & W. M. Stallings (Eds.), *Culture, child, and school: Sociocultural influences on learning.* Brooks/Cole Publishing.

Greenfield, P. M. (1976). Cross-cultural research and Piagetian theory: Paradox and progress. In English in K. F. Riegel & J. A. Meacham (Ed.), *The developing individual in a changing world. Vol. 1. Historical and cultural issues.* The Hague: Mouton, pp. 322–333.

Greenfield, P. M. (1980). Towards an operational and logical analysis of intentionality: The use of discourse in early child language. In D. R. Olson (Ed.), *The Social Foundations of Language and Thought: Essays in Honor of J. S. Bruner* (pp. 254–279). New York: Norton.

Greenfield, P. M. (1994). Independence and interdependence as developmental scripts: Implications for theory, research, and practice. In P. M. Greenfield, & R. R. Cocking (Eds.), *Cross Cultural Roots of Minority Child Development* (pp. 1–37). Hillsdale, NJ: Erlbaum.

Greenfield, P. M. (1997a). Culture as process: Empirical methods for cultural psychology. In J. W. Berry, Y. Poortinga, & J. Pandey (Eds.), *Handbook of Cross-cultural Psychology: Vol. 1. Theory and Method* (pp. 301–346). Boston: Allyn & Bacon.

Greenfield, P. M. (1997b). You can't take it with you: Why ability assessments don't cross cultures. *American Psychologist*, 52, 1115–1124.

Greenfield, P. M. (2000). Three approaches to the psychology of culture: Where do they come from? Where can they go? *Asian Journal of Social Psychology*, 3, 223–240.

Greenfield, P. M. (2004). *Weaving generations together: Evolving creativity in the Zinacantec Maya.* Santa Fe, CA: SAR Press.

Greenfield, P. M., & Bruner, J. S. (1966). Culture and cognitive growth. *International Journal of Psychology*, 1, 89–107.

Greenfield, P. M., & Bruner, J. S. (1969). Culture and cognitive growth, revised. In D. Goslin (Ed.), *Handbook of Socialization Theory* (pp. 633–660). Chicago: Rand McNally.

Greenfield, P. M., & Childs, C. P. (1977). Understanding sibling concepts: A developmental study of kin terms in Zinacantan. In P. Dasen (Ed.), *Piagetian Psychology: Cross-cultural contributions* (pp. 335–358). New York: Gardner Press.

Greenfield, P. M., Keller, H., Fuligni, A., & Maynard, A. (2003). Cultural pathways through universal development. *Annual Review of Psychology*, 54, 461–490.

Greenfield, P. M. & Lyn, H. (in press). Symbol combination in *Pan:* Language, action, culture. In D. Washburn (Ed.), Emergents and Rational Behaviorism: Essays in Honor of Duane M. Rumbaush (working title). Washington, DC: American Psychological Association.

Greenfield, P. M., Maynard, A. E., & Childs, C. P. (2003). Historical change, cultural learning, and cognitive representation in Zinacantec Maya children. *Cognitive Development*, 18, 455–487.

Greenfield, P. M., Raeff, C., & Quiroz, B. (1996). Cultural values in learning and education. In B. Williams (Ed.), *Closing the Achievement Gap: A Vision for Changing Beliefs and Practices* (pp. 37–55). Alexandria, VA: Association for Supervision and Curriculum Development.

Greenfield, P. M., Reich, L. C., & Olver, R. R. (1966). On culture and equivalence–II. In J. S. Bruner, R. R. Olver, P. M. Greenfield, et al., *Studies in Cognitive Growth* (pp. 270–318). New York: Wiley.

Greenfield, P. M., Reich, L. C., & Olver, R. R. (1972). On culture and equivalence–II. Reprinted in P. Adams (Ed.), *Language in Thinking* (pp. 217–235). Baltimore: Penguin Books.

Greenfield, P. M., & Savage-Rumbaugh, E. S. (1990). Grammatical combination in *Pan Paniscus:* Processes of learning and invention in the evolution and development of language. In S. Parker, & K. Gibson (Eds.), *"Language" and Intelligence in Monkeys and Apes: Comparative Developmental Perspectives* (pp. 540–578). Cambridge, UK: Cambridge University Press.

Greenfield, P. M., & Smith, J. H. (1976). *The Structure of Communication in Early Language Development*. New York: Academic Press.

Grigorenko, E. L., Geissler P. W., Prince, R., Okatcha F., Nokes, C., Kenney, D. A., et al. (2001). The organisation of Luo conceptions of intelligence: A study of implicit theories in a Kenyan village. *International. Journal of Behavioral Development*, 25, 367–378.

Hobson, R. P. (1993). *Autism and the Development of Mind*. Hillsdale, NJ: Erlbaum.

Hofstede, G. (1980). *Culture's Consequences: International Differences in Work-related Values*. Beverly Hills, CA: Sage.

Hong, Y. Y., Morris, M., Chiu, C. Y., & Benet-Martinez, V. (2000). Multicultural minds: A dynamic constructivist approach to culture and cognition. *American Psychologist*, 55, 709–720.

Iacoboni, M., Woods, R. P., Brass, M., Bekkering, H., Mazziotta, J. C., & Rizzolatti, G. (1999). Cortical mechanisms of human imitation. *Science*, 286, 2526–2528.

Inhelder B., & Piaget J. (1958). *The Growth of Logical Thinking from Childhood to Adolescence: An Essay on the Construction of Formal Operational Structures*. New York: Basic Books.

Irwin, M. H., & McLaughlin, D. H. (1970). Ability and preference in category sorting by Mano schoolchildren and adults. *Journal of Social Psychology*, 82, 15–24.

Ji, L., Zhang, Z., & Nisbett, R. E. (2002). Culture, language, and categorization. Unpublished manuscript. Queens University, Kingston, Ontario.

Kestelhoof, L. (1962). *Aimée Césare*. Paris: Editions Presse Seghers.

Kim, U. (1994). Individualism and collectivism: Conceptual clarification and elaboration. In U. Kim, H. C. Triandis, C. Kagitcibasi, S. C. Choi, & Yoon, G., *Individualism and Collectivism: Theory, Method, and Applications* (pp. 19–40). Thousand Oaks, CA: Sage.

Kim, U., & Choi, S.-H. (1994). Individualism, collectivism, and child development: A Korean perspective. In P. M. Greenfield & R. R. Cocking (Eds.), *Cross-cultural roots of minority child development* (pp. 227–257). Hillsdale, NJ: Erlbaum.

Kitiyama, S. (2002). Culture and basic psychological processes. *Psychological Bulletin*, 128, 89–96.

Kluckhohn, F. R. & Strodtbeck, F. L. (1961). *Variations in Value Orientations*. Evanston, IL: Row, Peterson.

Kohler, W. (1937). Psychological remarks on some questions of anthropology. *American Journal of Psychology*, 58, 271–278.

Kohler, W. (1962). Psychological remarks on some questions of anthropology. Reprinted in M. Henle (Ed.), *Documents of Gestalt psychology* (pp. 203–221). Berkeley: University of California Press.

Lalonde, C., Chandler, M. J., & Sokol, B. (1999, June). Alternative solutions to the problem of self-continuity among Canada's culturally mainstream and aboriginal youth. Paper presented to the 29th annual meeting of the Jean Piaget Society. Mexico City.

LeVine, R. A. (1997). Mother–infant interaction in cross-cultural perspective. In N. L. Segall, G. E. Weisfeld, & C. C. Weisfeld (Eds.), *Uniting Psychology and Biology: Integrative Perspectives on Human Development* (pp. 339–354). Washington, DC: American Psychological Association.

Lillard, A. (1998). Ethnopsychologies: Cultural variations in theories of mind. *Psychological Bulletin*, 123, 3–32.

Luria, A. R. (1971). Towards the problem of the historical nature of psychological processes. *International Journal of Psychology*, 6, 259–272.

Madsen, M., & Shapira, A. (1970). Cooperative and competitive behavior of urban Afro-Americna, Anglo-American, Mexican American, and Mexican village children. *Developmental Psychology*, 3, 16–20.

Maynard, A. E. (2002). Cultural teaching: The development of teaching skills in Zinacantec Maya sibling interactions. *Child Development*, 73, 969–982.

Miller, J. G. (1984). Culture and the development of everyday social explanation. *Journal of Personality and Social Psychology*, 46, 961–978.

Monteil, V. (1964). *L'islam noir*. Paris: Editions du Seuil.

Morris, M. W., & Peng, K. (1994). Culture and cause: American and Chinese attributions for social and physical events. *Journal of Personality and Social Psychology*, 67, 949–971.

Mundy-Castle, A. C. (1974). Social and technological intelligence in Western and non-Western cultures. *Universitas* 4, 46–52.

Nisbett, R. E. (2003). *The Geography of Thought: How Asians and Westerners Think Differently... and Why*. New York: Free Press.

Nisbett, R. E., Peng, K., Choi, I., & Norenzayan, A. (2001). Culture and systems of thought: Holistic versus analytic cognition. *Psychological Review*, 108(2), 291–310.

Nsamenang, B. & Lamb, M. (1994). Socialization of Nso children in the Bamenda grassfields of Northwest Cameroon. In P. M. Greenfield, & R. R. Cocking (Eds.), *Cross-cultural Roots of Minority Child Development* (pp. 133–46). Hillsdale, NJ: Erlbaum.

Oyserman, D., Coon, H. M., & Kemmelmeier, M. (2002). Rethinking individualism and collectivism: Evaluation of theoretical assumptions and meta-analyses. *Psychological Bulletin*, 128, 3–72.

Perner, J. (1991). *Understanding the Representational Mind*. Cambridge, MA: MIT Press.

Piaget, J. (1952). *The Origins of Intelligence in Children*. New York: Basic Books.

Piaget J. (1963/1977). Intellectual operations and their development. Reprinted in H. E. Gruber, H. & J. J. Vonèche (Eds.), *The Essential Piaget: An Interpretive Reference and Guide* (pp. 342–58). New York: Basic Books

Price-Williams, D. R. (1961). A study concerning concepts of conservation of quantities among primitive children. *Acta Psychologica*, 18, 297–305.

Rabain, J. (1979). *L'enfant du lignage*. Paris: Payot.

Rabain-Jamin, J. (1994). Language and socialization of the child of African families living in France. In P. M. Greenfield, & R. R. Cocking (Eds.), *Cross-cultural Roots of Minority Child Development* (pp. 276–292). Hillsdale, NJ: Erlbaum.

Rabain-Jamin, J., Maynard, A. E., & Greenfield, P. M. (2003). Implications of sibling caregiving for sibling relations and teaching interactions in two cultures. *Ethos*, 31, 204–231.

Rabain-Zempléni, J. (1965). *Quelques réfléxions sur les modes fondamentaux de relations chez l'enfant wolof du sevrage à l'intégration dans la classe d'âge*. Paris: Association Universitaire pour le Développement de l'Enseignement et de la culture en Afrique et à Madagascar.

Raeff, C., Greenfield, P. M., & B. Quiroz (2000). Developing interpersonal relationships in the cultural contexts of individualism and collectivism. In S. Harkness, C. Raeff, & C. R. Super (Eds.), *Variability in the Social Construction of the Child, New Directions in Child Development*. San Francisco: Jossey-Bass.

Reykowski, J. (1994). Collectivism and individualism as dimensions of social change. In U. Kim, H. C. Triandis, C. Kagitcibasi, S. C. Choi, & Yoon, G., *Individualism and Collectivism: Theory, Method, and Applications* (pp. 19–40). Thousand Oaks, CA: Sage.

Rogoff, B. (2003). *The Cultural Nature of Human Development*. Oxford, UK: Oxford University Press.

Schliemann, A., Carraher, D., & Ceci, S. J. (1997). Everyday cognition. In J. W. Berry, P. R. Dasen, & T. S. Saraswathi (Eds.), *Handbook of Cross-cultural Psychology. Vol. 2: Basic Processes and Human Development* (pp. 177–216). Boston: Allyn & Bacon.

Scribner, S., & Cole, M. (1981). *The Psychology of Literacy*. Cambridge, MA: Harvard University Press.

Segall, M. H., Dasen, P. R., Berry, J. W., & Poortinga, Y. H. (1999). *Human Behavior in Global Perspective: An Introduction to Cross-cultural Psychology*, (2nd ed.). Boston: Allyn & Bacon.

Serpell, R. (1993). *The Significance of Schooling: Life Journeys in an African Society*. Cambridge, UK: Cambridge University Press.

Serpell, R. (1994). The cultural construction of intelligence. In W. L. Lonner, & R. S. Malpass (Eds.), *Psychology and Culture* (pp. 157–63). Boston: Allyn & Bacon.

Shweder, R. A., & Bourne, E. J. (1984). Does the concept of the person vary cross-culturally? In R. A. Shweder, & R. A. Levine, *Culture Theory: Essays on Mind, Self, and Emotion* (pp. 158–199). New York: Cambridge University Press.

Sternberg, R. J., Conway, B. E., Ketron, J. L., & Bernstein, M. (1981). People's conceptions of intelligence. *Journal of Personality and Social Psychology*, 4, 37–55.

Super, C. M. (1983). Cultural variation in the meaning and uses of children's "intelligence." In J. Deregowski, S. Dziurawiec, & R. Annis (Eds.), *Explorations in Cross-cultural Psychology* (pp. 199–212). Amsterdam: Swets & Zeitlinger.

Tomasello, M. (1999). *The Cultural Origins of Human Cognition*. Cambridge, MA: Harvard University Press.

Trevarthen, C. (1980). The foundations of intersubjectivity: Development of interpersonal and cooperative understanding in infants.

In D. Olson (Ed.), *The Social Foundations of Language and Thought* (pp. 316–342). New York: Norton.

Triandis, H. (1989). Cross-cultural studies of individualism and collectivism. *Nebraska Symposium on Motivation*, 37, 41–133.

Turiel, E. (2000). Conflict, social development, and cultural change. In E. Turiel (Ed.), *Development and Cultural Change: Reciprocal Processes. New Directions for Child and Adolescent Development*, 83, 77–92.

Vinden, P. (1996). Junin Quechua children's understanding of mind. *Child Development*, 67, 1701–1706.

Vinden, P. (1999). Children's understanding of mind and emotion: A multi-culture study. *Cognition and Emotion*, 13, 19–48.

Vinden, P., & Astington, J. (2000). Culture and understanding Other Minds. In S. Baron-Cohen (Ed.), *Understanding Other Minds: Perspectives from Developmental Cognitive Neuroscience* (pp. 503–519). Oxford, UK: Oxford University Press.

Wang, Q., Ceci, S. J., Williams, W. M., & Kopko, K. A. (2004). In R. Sternberg (Ed.), *Culture and Competence*. Washington: American Psychological Association.

Wellman, H. M. (1990). *The Child's Theory of Mind*. Cambridge, MA: MIT.

Wellman, H. M., Cross, D., & Watson, J. (2001). Meta-analysis of theory-of-mind development: The truth about false belief. *Child Development*, 72, 655–684.

Whiten, A. (2002). Chimpanzee cognition and the question of mental re-representation. In D. Sperber (Ed.), *Metarepresentation* (pp. 139–167). Oxford, UK: Oxford University Press.

Whiting, B. B. (1976). Unpackaging variables. In K. F. Riegel, & J. A. Meacham (Eds.), *The Changing Individual in a Changing World* (pp. 303–309). Chicago: Aldine.

Wisniewski, E. J., & Bassok, M. (1999). What makes a man similar to a tie? Stimulus compatibility with comparison and integration. *Cognitive Psychology*, 39, 208–238.

Wober, M. (1974). Toward an understanding of the Kiganda concept of intelligence. In J. W. Berry, & P. R. Dasen, *Culture and Cognition* (pp. 261–280). London: Methuen.

Zambrano, I. (1999). *From* na' *to know: Power, epistemology and the everyday forms of state formation in Mitontik, Chiapas (Mexico)*. Doctoral dissertation. Cambridge, MA: Harvard University.

Zempleni-Rabain, J. (1973). Food and the strategy involved in learning fraternal exchange studies. London: Oxford University Press.

Part VII

THINKING IN PRACTICE

CHAPTER 28

Legal Reasoning

Phoebe C. Ellsworth

For more than a century, lawyers have written about legal reasoning, and the flow of books and articles describing, analyzing, and reformulating the topic continues unabated. The volume and persistence of this "unrelenting discussion" (Simon, 1998, p. 4) suggests that there is no solid consensus about what legal reasoning *is*. Legal scholars have a tenacious intuition – or at least a strong hope – that legal reasoning is distinctive, that it is not the same as logic, or scientific reasoning, or ordinary decision making, and there have been dozens of attempts to describe what it is that sets it apart from these other forms of thinking. These attempts generate criticism, the critics devise new formulations that generate further criticism, and the process continues. In this chapter, I describe the primary forms of legal reasoning, the most important schools of thought about legal reasoning, and some of the major differences between legal reasoning and scientific reasoning.

The first question is, "Whose legal reasoning are we talking about?" Jurors are given instructions on the law at the end of every trial and are asked to apply that law to the evidence they've heard to reach a verdict. They are asked to engage in "legal reasoning." Clients approach their attorneys with rambling stories and a strong, if somewhat vague, sense of injustice, and it is the attorney's job to figure out the laws, precedents, and facts that most favor the client and to integrate them into a persuasive case. This task involves legal reasoning, but the reasoning is driven by the desired outcome. The goal is not to reach the right decision but to make the best argument for one side. The evidence, as orchestrated by the lawyers and the legal arguments they make, form the raw materials for the judge's decision, although judges (like juries) may also draw on their own background knowledge and experience and their own interpretations of the evidence and (unlike juries) their own understanding of the law.

When scholars write about "legal reasoning," they are writing about judges. The lawyer does not have to decide the case, but only to make the strongest appeal for one side; lawyers' reasoning is discussed in courses and writings on advocacy. Jurors interpret the evidence to decide what actually happened and apply the law given to them in the judge's instructions to reach a verdict. The judge must also seek out the appropriate legal authority, deciding which laws and previous cases are applicable. Jurors are not supposed to reason about the law itself; that is the task of the judge. Judges are trained in the law, they know the statutes and precedents, and they have the experience of judging many cases and reading the decisions of other judges. Jurors do not provide reasons for their verdicts; judges often do. Finally, much of what is written about legal reasoning is about appellate court decisions, in which judges are primarily concerned with legal procedure and the law itself, not about who wins and loses, and in which they almost always must provide legal explanations for their decisions.

In the subsequent historical section, I describe how basic visions of the nature of legal reasoning have changed over time. Most judges, if they thought about their thought processes at all, have probably accepted the commonsense background theory prevalent in the legal culture of their era. Some, however, including some of the greatest judges, have recognized that they really can't explain how they reach decisions (Holmes, 1897; and cf. Nisbett & Wilson, 1977). In 1921, Benjamin Cardozo began his classic work, *The Nature of the Judicial Process*, with the observation that "[A]ny judge, one might suppose, would find it easy to describe the process which he had followed a thousand times and more. Nothing could be farther from the truth" (1921, p. 9).

But that does not mean there are no commonly accepted characteristics of legal reasoning. There are. The problem that vexes legal scholars is that they are incomplete. Although they undoubtedly *influence* judicial reasoning, they are insufficient either to predict future outcomes or to provide a fully satisfactory account for past ones. The two most common reasoning strategies, taught in every law school course on legal reasoning and writing, are the deductive method (rule-based reasoning) and the analogical method (case-based reasoning). These strategies are not unique to legal reasoning. They are commonly described in relation to scientific reasoning as well. What is distinctive about these forms of reasoning in the legal context is not so much the process but the context, the raw materials to which the processes are applied, and the nature of the rules.

Deductive and Analogical Reasoning in Law

Deductive (Rule-Based) Reasoning

In deductive scientific reasoning (see Dunbar & Fugelsang, Chap. 29), there is a general law or theory, and the scientist uses that theory to infer what will happen in some particular fact situation, makes a prediction, and designs an experiment to test it. If the prediction is not confirmed, there are three possibilities: The deduction was flawed, the experiment was flawed, or the theory is flawed. In deductive legal reasoning, the decision maker begins with a specific set of facts, looks at the law that applies to those facts, and reaches a verdict. If Joe's Liquor Store sells beer to 16-year-old Richard, and there is a law prohibiting the sale of alcohol to anyone under the age of 21, then Joe's Liquor Store is guilty. The reasoning is basically syllogistic, and in many cases the application of the law is unproblematic (see Evans, Chap. 8). These are called easy cases.

In practice, there are many ways in which ambiguity can creep into this apparently clear logical process. First, the decision maker is faced with a specific set of facts. If he or she is a judge, there are almost always two versions of the facts. It is the attorneys' job to organize the facts in a way that fits the legal outcome they wish to achieve, and they do this by emphasizing different facts and, often, different legal precedents. "[T]he law determines which facts are relevant while at the same time, the facts determine which law is relevant" (Burton, 1995, p. 141). There may be more than one law that is potentially applicable. There may be several statutory provisions that might be relevant, and the two opposing counsel may argue that a different rule is the one that should control this case. The statute itself may violate a higher rule, such as the state or federal constitution. The rule may be ambiguous, as in a ban on "excessive noise," or the application of the "reasonable person" standard ("Would a reasonable person have believed that her life was in danger?").

In preparing a case, an attorney will go back and forth between developing a coherent version of the facts that fits the law and conducting legal research to find out which laws frame the facts in the best possible way. The judge, faced with two competing arguments, may choose one of them, or may bring in additional factual interpretations or legal considerations not mentioned by either of the parties. Thus, even the apparently simplest form of legal reasoning – deciding whether the law covers the specific fact situation – is often quite complicated in practice. The commonsense idea that there is a behavior, there is a law, and the question is "Does the behavior conform to the law?" is much too simple to apply to interesting cases.

Analogical (Case-Based) Reasoning

In the Anglo-American common law tradition,[1] cases are decided by examining the patterns of decisions in earlier, related cases. No case has meaning in isolation, and general rules and propositions are useless without "the heaping up of concrete instances" (Llewellyn, 1930, p. 2), except in very simple cases. A somewhat similar form of reasoning occurs in science when a scientist examines a series of studies with apparently inconsistent results and tries to come up with a general principle that will explain the inconsistencies. In research on social facilitation, for example, some researchers found that people performed better on a task when other people were around, but other researchers found that people performed better when they were alone. In 1965, Robert Zajonc resolved this controversy by showing that the emotional arousal caused by the presence of others enhanced performance on well-learned tasks but impaired performance on tasks that were less familiar. He applied a more general principle that explained the apparently contradictory results of past research and made sense of the field. He then went on to devise a situation in which the new principle could be tested.

The judge begins where the scientist ends, with a specific situation in which the outcome must be decided – not predicted and tested but decided by examining the similarities and differences between this new case and the previous cases and choosing an outcome that corresponds to the holdings of the cases it most resembles. In the adversarial system, the lawyers emphasize the prior cases that were decided the way they want this one to be decided, finding crucial differences in the prior cases that went the "wrong way" so as to argue that their holdings are inapplicable in the present context. The lawyers have a certain leeway in their selection of which facts to emphasize, in their interpretation of the facts, and in their description of the legal significance of those facts (Llewellyn, 1930, p. 70). Like the scientist, the lawyer may identify some principle that explains why the current case should be considered an example of the first group rather than the second. The judge examines the strengths and weaknesses of the arguments of the two parties and either chooses between them or develops a different principle for placing the present case in the context of the past ones.

When legal educators claim that the basic mission of the first year of law school is to train the student to "think like a lawyer," it is this sort of analogical reasoning they generally have in mind – the ability to spot the factual and legal similarities and (more important) differences between the case under study and related previous cases and to recognize which similarities and differences are relevant (e.g., the defendant's state of mind) and which are not (e.g., the defendant's name). This entails defining the universe of possibly applicable cases and deciding which ones match the current case most closely and which, although apparently similar, do not apply. The focus is on the particular cases, and the reasoning is more like feature matching than like the application of a general principle (Sunstein, 1996, p. 67; see Holyoak, Chap. 6, for further discussion of analogical reasoning).

Finally, as with deductive reasoning, the significance of a particular fact depends on its legal significance, and the significance of a particular law or previous holding depends on the exact fact pattern of the case. The legal reasoner must consider both simultaneously.

Theories of Legal Reasoning

Formalism[2]

That "legal reasoning" is considered to be a distinctive form of reasoning worthy of being included as a separate topic in the *Cambridge Handbook on Thinking and Reasoning* is attributable in large measure to Christopher Columbus Langdell, who became the first Dean of the Harvard Law School in 1870, and who revolutionized legal education. He introduced the case-based technique of teaching law; he created the image of the law faculty as a group of permanent scholars devoted to legal research, explicitly promoting the analogy to the faculty of a science department; and he advocated a view of legal reasoning known as "legal formalism."

The essence of legal formalism is the idea that "a few basic top-level categories and principles formed a conceptually ordered system above a large number of bottom-level rules. The rules themselves were, ideally, the holdings of established precedents, which upon analysis could be seen to be discovered from the principles" (Grey, 1983, p. 11). In other words, there is a pyramid of rules with a very few fundamental "first principles" at the top, from which mid-level and finally a large number of specific rules could be derived. The legal decision maker, faced with a case to be decided, would study the body of law and discover the rule that determined the correct result.

In 1870, science represented the pinnacle of human intellectual achievement, and in his effort to make law an academic discipline rather than a mere trade, Langdell embraced the idea that law is a science (Langdell, 1880). He did not originate this view, which can be found in Blackstone's Commentaries and earlier (Kennedy, 1973), but he promulgated it enthusiastically. An obvious problem with this analogy is that in law there is no means of experimentation, no access to previously unknown data. The "data" consisted of the writings of earlier judges: "We have constantly inculcated the idea that the *library* is the proper workshop of professors and students alike; that it is to us all that the laboratories of the university are to the chemists and physicists, the museum of natural history to the zoologists, and the botanical gardens to the botanists (Langdell, 1887, p. 124; emphasis added). The data were what judges had said, and new data were what new judges said, based on their readings of their predecessors. Langdell did not argue that law as it existed actually achieved the beautiful hierarchical organization from clear, highly abstract principles down to lower levels that would finally allow precise derivations that would fit any new set of particular facts; creating such an arrangement was a *goal* of legal science.

Of course this view of science as a closed deductive system strikes most modern scientists as unrealistic and simplistic – a view of science that we were taught in eighth grade but that rarely seems like a description of what we actually *do* or how we actually think. The behavioral sciences especially (and it seems natural to us that if law is to be considered a science at all it should be a behavioral science) seem a poor fit for such an abstract deductive model of reasoning. Even in 1870, the excitement of observation, empiricism, and induction were rapidly replacing earlier deductive views of science.

Langdell's model of science was more like the taxonomic system of Linnaeus than like empirical science. Families of plants and animals were organized under phyla (the fundamental principles), genera under families, and species under genera. During the explorations of the eighteenth and nineteenth centuries, an astonishing variety of new plant and animal species was discovered, and each one could be compared with others at the species level and classified appropriately in its place in the ruling structure. In the same way, each new legal case could be examined for its similarities and differences to previously decided cases, which in turn had been classified according to the general taxonomy, and so could be decided accurately. In law, "the fundamental principles of common law were discerned by induction from cases, rules of law were then derived from principles conceptually, and, finally, cases were decided, also conceptually, from rules" (Grey, 1983, 19).

There were critics of legal formalism from the very beginning. The alternative view is illustrated in two famous remarks by Oliver Wendell Homes, Jr.: "The life of the law has not been logic: It has been experience" (Holmes, 1881, p. 1), and "general principles do not decide concrete cases" (dissenting opinion in *Lochner v. New York*, 1905, p. 76). Holmes and, later, critics such as Pound, Llewellyn, and Cardozo argued that legal principles were not "discovered" by careful research into the rules and principles, and that such research, however diligent, would not yield definite and incontrovertible answers in any but the easiest cases. Instead of clear distinctions between the cases decided in one way and those decided in the other (for the plaintiff or the defendant in a medical malpractice case, for example), there is overlap and fuzziness at the boundary and, in the end, the judge *creates* the defining distinction rather than discovering it (Cardozo, 1921, p. 167). The distinctions were often arbitrary, not logical, and influenced by the judge's own sense of what the right outcome *should* be. The fundamental principles and legal rules were important and provided considerable guidance to the judge but, in most cases, they were insufficient to determine the outcome. The certainty and sense of inevitability expressed in judicial opinions was quite unjustified. As time goes by and the legal landscape becomes dense with more and more intermediate cases, the failures of formalism become increasingly apparent. As Holmes put it

> *Two widely different cases suggest a general distinction which is a clear one when stated broadly. But as new cases cluster around the opposite poles, and begin to approach each other, the distinction becomes more difficult to trace; the determinations are made one way or the other on a very slight preponderance of feeling, rather than articulate reason; and at last a mathematical line is arrived at by the contact of contrary decisions, which is so far arbitrary that it might equally well have been drawn a little further the one side or the other* (Holmes, 1873, p. 652).

Although the idealistic theory behind formalism has largely been abandoned (cf. Kennedy, 1973; Gordon, 1984; Grey, 1983; Simon, 1998), its categories and its analytic methods persist. Its classifications are still robust – substantive versus procedural law; contracts, torts, property. They determine how the first year of law school is structured. No comprehensive new organizational scheme has replaced the categories of formalism, and they therefore continue to "influence judgment much as the agenda for a meeting influences the results of its deliberations" (Grey, 1983, p. 50).

The tenets of legal formalism still exercise a strong influence on the way judicial opinions are written. Decisions typically are presented as the inevitable consequence of a careful analysis of the facts and the applicable law based on the classification of this case in relation to previous cases. The correct decision and the governing principles are described as discovered, not created, by the judge (Schauer, 1995, p. 642, note 23), and are expressed with great certainty, as though there were no room for doubt. "It seems that this neo-formalist form of jurisprudence – typified by a self-reported experience of constraint, high confidence and singular correctness, all couched in the rhetoric of closure – is the predominant, albeit unofficial, mode of judicial reasoning in current American legal culture" (Simon, 1998, p. 11). In part, this persistence is attributable to the strong belief that the law requires stability. For people to have faith in the legal system, judges' decisions must be predictable, and for judges to make predictable, logical decisions there must be a fixed framework from which those decisions are derived. A major difference between law and science, as discussed subsequently, is that uncertainty and change are a sign of a healthy scientific climate; they would definitely not signal a healthy legal climate.

Legal Realism

Legal realism arose in opposition to formalism and can be seen as an extension and elaboration of Holmes's early skepticism. Legal realists rejected the formalist ideas that the law was a self-contained logical system providing for the scientific, deductive derivation of the right answer in all new cases. They regarded this view as a vain daydream disconnected from the real world influences on legal decision makers – hence the label "legal realism."

In a strict formalist analysis, two different judges should always judge the same case in the same way unless one of them was mistaken in his[3] understanding of the facts or the law. Clearly this was not the case. In the nineteenth century, as now, courts were often divided. There were judges in the majority and there were dissenters, and no one seriously argued that the dissenters were incompetent or in need of retraining. Of course the formalists did not believe this was the way the world really worked, but they did believe that the legal system could approximate that ideal and that it was an ideal worth striving for. The legal realists believed that it was an impossible ideal and that it was a waste of time to strive for it.

According to the legal realists, instead of reflecting an abstract set of nearly immutable principles, the law reflects historical, social, cultural, political, economic, and psychological forces, and the behavior of individual legal decision makers is a product of these forces. It therefore is not surprising that different judges, with different goals and backgrounds, should decide cases differently, and contrary decisions do not imply that some judges must be "wrong."

The first move toward legal realism was "Sociological Jurisprudence," which was expounded most explicitly by Roscoe Pound (1912). Like Holmes, Pound felt that the "mechanical jurisprudence" of the formalists was out of touch with social reality and that legal scholarship and judicial norms were standing still, out of touch with exciting developments in philosophy and, particularly, the social sciences. "Jurisprudence," he argued, "is the last in the march of sciences away from the method of deduction from predetermined conceptions" (Pound, 1909, p. 464). The strict doctrinal approach blinded legal writers to two essential considerations: first, the *purposes* of the law – the goal of doing justice rather than following the letter of the law; and second, the social, cultural, and psychological factors that influenced behavior, including the behavior of lawmakers and judges. Blind adherence to the abstract law-on-the-books might make for greater certainty and predictability, but "reasonable and just solutions of individual cases" were "too often sacrificed" (Pound, 1912, p. 515). The law treated all individuals as equivalent regardless of their social background or position. Thus, for example, the right of an employee to quit was legally the same as the right of the employer to fire him. Both were free agents enjoying the "liberty of contract." But of course the employer could easily find another employee, but the employee would have lost his livelihood and might have a very hard time finding another job. The law's refusal to acknowledge these obvious social truths was a major stimulus to sociological jurisprudence.

Pound argued that legal scholarship and judicial decisions should "take more account, and more intelligent account, of the social facts upon which law must proceed and to which it is to be applied" (1912, p. 513). The focus should not be on the abstract content of the laws but on how they actually work. It is important to consider the purpose of laws and to modify them if these purposes are not being achieved. And judges should regard the law as suggestive rather than determinative of their decisions: If strict application of the law would result in an outcome that is unjust or contrary to the purpose of the law, then flexibility in the cause of justice is appropriate.

The basic views of Holmes and Pound were quite similar – pragmatic and open-minded. Pound, however, was a far stronger proponent of an interdisciplinary solution to the problems of formalism. The social sciences were very much on the rise at the beginning of the twentieth century and seemed "progressive" in a way that law was not. Their ideas stretched the imaginations of the more intellectually curious law professors and challenged some of the most fundamental assumptions of the law. The sociologists (the most influential group) suggested that the equality of all assumed by the law (e.g., the "liberty of contract") was a myth because status and power significantly affected a person's choices, the anthropologists revealed a wide range of peaceful societies with entirely different kinds of legal systems, and psychologists raised questions about the essential legal concepts of free will and responsibility, suggesting that behavior was determined by psychological and social factors beyond the control of the individual (Green, 1995).

The period identified as the flowering of legal realism was the period between the wars (Fisher, Horwitz, & Reed, 1993). Holmes and Pound were the inspirational figures from the past,[4] but now there were enough like-minded scholars so they could legitimately be called a "school" or a "movement," although never an organization. Like the cognitive psychologists who shook off the shackles of behaviorism in the 1960s and 1970s, they were an eclectic group united mainly by their opposition to the old ways. Some tried to do empirical research, some were political activists (and some eventually became part of the New Deal government), some continued as legal scholars but preaching a new faith, and some were articulate gadflies. Some were and are highly respected figures in the history of legal scholarship, some were but are no longer, and some were always seen as fringe elements.

As with their predecessors, their primary unifying theme was a rejection of the old ways and a passionate belief that legal doctrine played a limited role in legal decision making – and that that was how it should be. Karl Llewellyn, one of the most important figures in the group, argued that law was about "disputes to be settled and disputes to be prevented" (1930, p. 2), not about rules; about what legal decision makers *do*, not what they say. Legal rules were regarded as, at best, post hoc justifications and, at worst, criteria that could lead judges to unjust decisions. Advocates in a trial could usually describe the facts *and the law* so as to produce coherent, complete, persuasive arguments for two diametrically opposite conclusions. Llewellyn even wrote an article on statutory interpretation showing that each of 28 basic legal propositions could be argued either way: "A statute cannot go beyond its text"/"To effect a purpose a statute may be implemented beyond its text"; "Where design has been distinctly stated no place is left for construction"/"Courts have the power to inquire into real – as distinct from ostensible – purposes" (Llewellyn, 1950, pp. 401, 403).

The agenda of the legal realists was both descriptive and prescriptive. According to Felix Cohen, "Fundamentally, there are only two significant questions in the field of law. One is, 'How do courts actually decide cases of a given kind?' The other is, 'How ought they to decide cases of a given kind?'"(1935, p. 824). The answer to the descriptive question was that courts do not decide cases on the basis of laws because the law always allows for multiple answers. In considering what sort of forces *do* influence case outcomes, different scholars emphasized social and cultural forces (Cohen, 1935; Lasswell, 1930; Yntema, 1928), unconscious psychological drives (Frank, 1930), or just a process of intuition that eventually culminated in a Gestalt-like "Aha effect" after long rumination (Hutcheson, 1929). These influences affect the assessment of the actual facts of the case – the credibility of the witnesses, the plausibility of the stories, as well as the judge's "sense of how the law ought to respond to these facts" (Fisher, Horwitz, & Reed, 1993, p. 165). Legal realists were ridiculed as believing that judicial decisions depended on what the judge ate for breakfast. However, the realists generally did not believe that judicial decisions were idiosyncratic or unpredictable. "Law is not a mass of unrelated decisions nor a product of judicial bellyaches. Judges are human, but they are a particular breed of humans, selected to a type and held to service under a potent system of governmental controls" (Cohen, 1935, p. 843). Because most judges come from the same social class, receive the same legal education, and are subject to the same social and historical influences and the same role demands, their decisions will resemble each other.

The intellectual enterprise of legal scholarship, therefore, should be to describe the actual behavior of courts, taking account of the broader social context. The realists were confident that this behavior would not be predictable from written legal doctrine or statutes. Instead, the legal rules and concepts would turn out to be consequences, rather than causes, of judges' behavior. To understand how judges reach their decisions, it is important to analyze their social backgrounds, previous experience, and role demands and the general political, social, and economic pressures of the times. Because these same forces affected the behavior of the parties of the case, the relation between the judge's position in society and that of the litigants should also be explored. This general set of ideas was easy to demonstrate in particular cases. Then, as now, the opinions of individual judges on particular issues were often easy to predict. Defense lawyers "shop" for judges known to be sympathetic to offenders who resemble their client (judges who believe that drug laws are too harsh, for example). On some issues, it is easy to predict Supreme Court Justices' positions based on their previous opinions and their general ideology. Coming up with a more general mid-level theory, something between vague abstract statements about "social forces" and predictions of what a particular judge would say in a particular case, was a much greater challenge and one the realists never actually accomplished.

The description of what courts actually do was supposed to explore not only the causes of judicial decisions but also their consequences. A study of consequences is essential to answer the second question, "How ought [courts] to decide cases of a particular kind?" Judicial decisions affect human behavior, often favoring one group's interests over another, and they affect future judicial decisions. Careful study of these consequences would allow for better-informed judicial decisions and better laws.

Prescriptively, the realists argued first that in applying the law, judges ought to consider the *purpose* of the law and, second, that they should focus on the particulars of the case and compare it with the particulars of preceding cases, rather than looking for broad general principles. Consideration of the purposes of the law was supposed to enhance the fairness and the consistency of decisions, and blind application to the rule without considering its purpose would lead to bad decisions (Llewellyn, 1942). To facilitate this approach, legislators and judges should make the reasons for the law explicit; to provide appropriate guidance to future judges: "Only the rule which shows its reason on its face has ground to claim maximum chance of *continuing* effectiveness" (Llewellyn, 1942, p. 260). Because social conditions were constantly changing, however, judges should be free to revise and reject even rules with clearly stated purposes; the development of law, like the development of science, should be a never-ending process of examination and re-examination.

Specific comparisons of the particular case to be decided and the facts of related cases, through analogical reasoning, was the preferred method. Just as a case read by itself is meaningless (Llewellyn, 1930, p. 49), a case read with reference to the law and without reference to other cases was also meaningless. Close factual comparisons will reveal the empirically grounded rules and cultural beliefs that actually explain legal decisions because "legal rules are simply formulae describing uniformities of judicial decision" (Cohen, 1935, p. 848). Some of the realists believed that close examination of the prior body of cases required more than a reading of the cases alone. Some felt that an education in social science was necessary to fully understand the social forces influencing the parties and the judge. Others felt that legal researchers should create databases on the background of judges and their decisions, the frequency with which laws on the books were actually enforced, whether they are enforced against some groups more than others, whether patterns of enforcement have changed over time (e.g., obscenity laws), and so on.

The legal realists have been identified with a "social science" point of view, but this meant different things to different scholars. Most of them probably shared Pound's belief that, although other scientific disciplines were making huge progress, law was stagnating, backwards looking, and clinging to a static, deductive model that had been abandoned by other sciences. The law, because it deals with ever-changing values, opportunities, and norms of behavior should keep pace with these changes. Most also were somewhat shaken by the ways in which sociology and psychology were undermining the notion of free will central to the law (Green, 1995). Most of them agreed that the focus of attention should be on how judges think, not on the written rules. They were fairly unified in describing what was *wrong* with formalism but never fully agreed on the remedies and, indeed, proposed very few.

Beyond this general sense that the law should develop as society develops and take general account of progress in the social sciences, the realists followed different paths. Some more or less stopped there. For others, the "critical realists" in Horwitz's (1992) terminology, social science mainly meant a concern with social policy. Politically they were progressives, and flourished under the New Deal. Cardozo, Brandeis, Frankfurter, and Douglas followed Holmes to the Supreme Court, and several others moved to important positions in the New Deal administration. For them, the social science that mattered was the sociologists' emphasis on social class and a generally socialist view of what should guide the government and the courts. For them, as for many of the social scientists of the time, social science meant social activism.

Another group, the "constructive realists" (Horwitz, 1992), believed that legal scholars should collect detailed statistical information about the causes and consequences of various rules, conducting interdisciplinary empirical research, and that courts should consider social science data in deciding cases. The method of marshaling social scientific evidence in arguing a case was pioneered by Louis Brandeis and Josephine Goldmark in the famous "Brandeis brief" in *Muller v. Oregon* (208 U.S. 412). In arguing that it was constitutionally permissible to restrict women's working hours to ten hours a day, they presented hundreds of excerpts from various articles and reports claiming that long working hours were damaging to women's health. Most of these were not actually scientific reports, but they were an effort (successful) to force the court to consider the social facts involved in the legal question and the social consequences of the decision. The "Brandeis brief" is legendary, and the inclusion of social science research in legal arguments is now common. Modern trial and appellate courts routinely consider social science data, although their actual influence is probably less than most social scientists would like to believe (Ellsworth & Getman, 1986).

There were some efforts to compile databases (Pound and Frankfurter, 1922; and cf. Schlegel, 1980) and a few attempts to actually carry out systematic research projects. However, these attempts generally failed to achieve the grand purposes their authors had in mind. In writing a traditional law review article, the author typically knows what the conclusion is at the beginning; empirical research, as any honest scientist knows, often forces agonizing rethinking and sometimes produces data so ambiguous that nothing can be concluded. So, in 1928, the future Supreme Court Justice William O. Douglas conducted a study of business failures designed to produce revolutionary insights but ended up with two small, inconclusive articles (Fisher, Horwitz, & Reed, 1993, p. 233). Underhill Moore, a Yale law professor in one of the three experimental law and social science interdisciplinary programs, attempted a behaviorist (Hullian) analysis of the effects of parking tickets (Moore and Callahan, 1943) that provoked intense ridicule even from other realists [Llewellyn later called it "the nadir of idiocy" (1956, p. 400)]. Empirical research by legal scholars has slowly increased over the past 50 or 60 years, but at the time, the admonishments of the legal realists only produced a brief spate of attempts, nothing like a major change in orientation. It is still the case that some law professors regard empirical research as mindless and mechanical with data a crutch for those whose mental capacities are insufficient to reach the truth on their own.

Although the excesses of Legal Realism are still parodied in well-worn clichés (such as the "what the judge had for breakfast" cliché), in the main, it has been absorbed into American legal thought; thus, only the excesses stand out as distinctive. Close comparison of cases is the standard method of legal education, and consideration of the social context, purposes, and policy implications of the law is common. The challenge posed by the realists – the relative role of law versus social and personal considerations – still looms over the study of law and defines the questions. Databases are everywhere, especially in the criminal justice system, but also in the civil arena. The American Bar Association regularly proposes guidelines based on statistical data as do government commissions. No one still believes in strict Langdellian formalism, although many law courses are an uneasy blend of formalism and the considerations raised by the legal realists, and judicial opinions are written in formalist language. And the later developments of legal realism, although never quite mainstream, are thriving. In 1935, Felix Cohen wrote that "It is reasonable to expect that some day even the impudencies of Holmes and Llewellyn will appear sage and respectable" (1935, p. 847), and that prophecy has certainly come true.

Critical Legal Studies, Law and Economics, and the Law and Society Movement

Although many of the ideas of the legal realists have been incorporated into the mainstream of law, there are three direct descendants that persist as independent currents. One, called Critical Legal Studies, is a reincarnation of the Progressive political themes of Legal Realism, and the other two (the Law and Economics movement and the Law and Society movement) are developments of the interdisciplinary social science endeavor.

Law and Economics scholars are fairly traditional in terms of economic theory [e.g., Tversky, Kahneman, and the behavioral economists so far have had minimal influence (Kahneman & Tversky, 2000; Kahneman, Slovic, & Tversky, 1982; Thaler, 1992)], taking as given the assumption that people rationally assess their circumstances and do what will maximize their own welfare. The potential criminal calculates the probabilities of getting caught, being punished, and the potential severity of punishment and weighs these considerations against the beneficial consequences of the crime (money, the extermination of a goal-blocking person) and accordingly decides whether or not to commit the crime. They attempt to fit legal decisions into a standard economic framework and, if they do not fit, to argue that they should.[5] Although they are often described as descendants of the legal realists, in some ways the Law and Economics movement bears a closer resemblance to the formalists. It has a formal model with a set of first principles: "Behavior always takes the form of constrained maximization. The actor chooses from some specified set of options, selecting the option that maximizes some objective function. In orthodox theory, consumers have *preferences* that are represented by a *utility function*, and they choose in a way that maximizes their utility..." (Kreps, 1990, p. 4, cited in Hanson & Yosifon, 2003). Explanations and recommendations follow deductively from the basic premises. Law and Economics has little to say about what is distinctive about *legal* reasoning; it is primarily another example of the economic model of reasoning in general.

By contrast, the Law and Society scholars are open-minded, eclectic, and devoid of any theoretical mission. Instead, they are committed to the social science method of inquiry and to the idea that history, culture, and social context matter. Friedman (1986) has proposed that Law and Society is a field like "Area Studies" in which scholars from many disciplines study law the way scholars from many disciplines study Latin America or Southeast Asia. Their concern with context and actual behavior means that they are relatively uninterested in "purely *intellectual* forces – the role of legal thinkers, formal doctrine, philosophy and theory of law; the role of abstract *ideas*" (Friedman, 1986) because such forces are mainly epiphenomena, not fundamentally causal. A great deal of important and interesting work has come from this school, but it is not really about legal reasoning in general. In fact Law and Society scholars would reject the idea that there is such a thing as legal reasoning in general.

Critical Legal Studies is the bad boy of the bunch, and in this regard it is more obviously connected to the Legal Realists in their role as iconoclastic rebels. Like the realists, they argue that interpretation of the law is subjective, and they emphasize the role of power and political ideology more strongly than most of the realists. Like the realists, they have been more effective as critics than as authors of an alternative vision (Kennedy, 1997), and some of them have glorified "trashing" as a sufficient contribution (Tushnet, 1984). In some ways, they resemble the postmodernists of other disciplines, insisting that there is "no there there," that all legal concepts, like all other social concepts, are socially constructed (except of course for power and dominance).

However, some of their analyses of legal reasoning went beyond what the legal realists had produced. In arguing that the legal realists' decisions were based on personal and social values, not law, the legal realists didn't quite get at the process by which a judge's *preference* is turned into a legal justification. Is the judge's reference to the law or precedent a "noble lie" in Dworkin's (1986) terms, resorted to because personal preferences or partisan political preferences could never be publicly stated as good reasons for justifying a decision? Are judges simply unquestioningly following the requirement that all decisions must be justified by legal authority and precedent? Or are they totally unaware of their own biases?

Duncan Kennedy, one of the founders of Critical Legal Studies, draws on the psychology of Kohler, Lewin, and Piaget to explore the thought processes of judges in a way that is less fuzzy and more nuanced than the general realist point of view (Kennedy, 1986). His hypothetical judge is a political reformist, of course, who is faced with a conflict between what the law seems to require and "how I want it to come out": "imagine that I think the rule that seems to apply is bad because it strikes the wrong balance between two identifiable conflicting groups, and does so as part of a generally unjust overall arrangement that includes many similar rules, all of which ought in the name of justice to change" (Kennedy, 1986, p. 519). The judge may reinterpret the facts, reinterpret the legal precedents, reinterpret the basic purpose of the law in the light of social policy, or make other moves. Judges will *also* consider how the public and other judges will view their decision, and finally, they really do care about the law and precedent; thus, the dilemma is a real cognitive dilemma, not just a matter of imposing their personal political motives. The decision will become part of the law that other judges must consider when they decide cases, so the judge also must worry about its future ramifications. "Legal argument is the process of creating the field of law through restatement rather than rule application" (Kennedy, 1986, p. 562). The thought process evolves in time, beginning as a conflict and ending as certainty. Once a strategy is chosen, the judge no longer can imagine any compelling counterargument. Simon recently updated this analysis in the light of more recent research in social and cognitive psychology and showed that it has considerable power even in cases in which the judge has no particular political motivation: An incoherent mass of contradictions develops into a coherent decision in which *no* opposing argument carries any weight, but *all* turn out upon close examination to support the decision (Simon, 1998).

Of course these biases – hindsight, hypothesis confirmation, motivated information processing, ultimate overconfidence, and others – are not unique to legal reasoners. They are true of us all, including scientists. Still, there are several important differences between legal reasoning and scientific reasoning.

Differences Between Scientific Reasoning and Legal Reasoning

As Llewellyn said, legal reasoning is not scientific reasoning, although it shares some analytic strategies, most notably the "method of comparison and difference" (Llewellyn, 1930, p. 43) or, as we might say, "convergent and discriminant validity" (Campbell & Fiske, 1959) and the technique of simultaneously considering alternative explanations or "multiple working hypotheses" (Chamberlin, 1890; Campbell & Stanley, 1966). In fact, the legal decision maker in an adversarial system is *forced* to consider at least two competing hypotheses proposed by the parties. In this sense, the judge has some marginal protection against the thoughtless hypothesis confirmation to which scientists occasionally fall prey. This is not to say that judges are immune from hypothesis-confirming biases, only that at the *beginning* of the process they are forced to consider at least two rival hypotheses.

Nonetheless, the judge and the scientist have different tools available to them, different constraints, and different goals. Science demands no final decisions; it is an ongoing process. If the evidence is murky, scientists can wait, can reserve judgment until they can conduct further research. And they can figure out what further research needs to be done to answer the question, and do it. Judges can neither reserve judgment nor go beyond the data presented in court, however ambiguous those data might be. They cannot carry out further research, nor wait until others have done so; they must decide.

And the judge's decision, whether the evidence is conclusive or completely inadequate, has the same precedential force. It is final. The scientist's conclusions are never final, always tentative.

The judge must also decide for one side or the other; the scientist's decision that the truth lies somewhere between the extreme points of view is typically not available to the judge. As I will argue, these role constraints in legal reasoning encourage categorical thinking and a corresponding distrust of probabilistic reasoning, overconfidence, and a strong dispositional bias in which situational factors and attributional biases are overlooked, and the idea of free will is preserved.

Lack of Opportunity for Empirical Testing

Scientists and judges must both decide between competing explanations. But when scientists are trying to decide among rival hypotheses, or even when testing a single hypothesis, sooner or later they put the question to nature. They design a study that will create new information, information that is not already in the system, that will help them to answer the question and to move forward in the way they think about the issues. In legal reasoning, there is no empirical option. Judges must work with the information given to them, and that information consists entirely of what other people have said and the judge's own knowledge. Judges listen to testimony and arguments and read the law, scholarly works, and the opinions of other judges; they arrange and rearrange these elements, selecting, interpreting, and looking for a rule that "holds good for the matter at hand" (Llewellyn, 1930, p. 72). The conclusion that the judge finally reaches is not empirically tested and cannot be disconfirmed.

Of course, the judge may consider empirical data as part of the factual evidence in a case. Most cases involve experts of one sort or another – some who present the results of diagnostic tests (e.g., of bullets, blood, dangerousness, mental illness, almost anything you can think of), some who present the results of empirical work specifically related to the case (e.g., contamination of the jury pool through pretrial publicity, evidence of racial discrimination in a company's promotion policies), some who describe the results of general research that is germane to the issue (e.g., evidence that some substance increases the risk of cancer, or of factors affecting the reliability of eyewitness testimony). The legal realists would be pleased about this increasing prevalence of social science evidence in legal decision making, but the judge does not collect new evidence.

The scientist is searching for truth. The judge wants to get the facts right, but that is not the whole task. The judge also wants to settle the dispute in a way that is consistent with the law and the decisions in previous disputes and that is just. So it could be argued that the whole concept of an empirical test of the final decision is irrelevant, that there is no empirical test of justice. If two scientists make opposite predictions, someone will do a study to try to choose between them or otherwise clarify the question. If a judge makes a decision, it is final unless it is appealed. If it is appealed, the appellate court rarely re-examines the facts and certainly does not invite new evidence but decides whether the lower court made a legal (procedural) error (Mathieson & Gross, 2004). The final decision is the decision of the majority, and a five to four decision in the Supreme Court has the same precedential authority as a unanimous decision. When the Court is split four to four, the views of the ninth, "swing" Justice decide the case and can have precedential force – even if those views are quite idiosyncratic (e.g., *Johnson v. Louisiana*, 1972; *Regents of the University of California v. Bakke*, 1978).

Need for an Immediate, Final Decision

Unlike the judge, the scientist can reserve judgment and can say that, given the muddled state of the current evidence, there are many questions that we can't answer yet and that further research is necessary. The judge has to decide, and usually he has to decide one way or the other, without the range of compromise solutions that are often available to the scientist. Just as judges cannot create new information by conducting empirical research, they cannot wait for new information before making a decision.

When the courts use available scientific data in reaching a decision, this finality can be a source of frustration to scientific researchers. In 1970, the Supreme Court held that the size of a jury (six versus twelve members) does not affect its functioning (*Williams v. Florida*, 1970), and in 1972, it held that deliberation would be just as thorough in juries that were not required to reach a unanimous verdict as in those that were (*Johnson v. Louisiana*, 1972; *Apodaca et al. v. Oregon*, 1972). In the early 1970s, when these decisions were handed down, there was almost no research on the effects of group size or the unanimity requirement. Social scientists were stunned that such important decisions could be made on the basis of so little information, and a flood of studies and commentaries quickly followed, many of them suggesting that twelve-person, unanimous juries deliberate more thoroughly than six-person or nonunanimous juries (Lempert, 1975; Saks & Ostrum, 1975; Zeisel, 1971, on jury size; Hastie, Penrod, & Pennington, 1983, on unanimity). However, the Court had *already held* that neither the size of the jury nor the unanimity requirement affected deliberations, and that six-person and nonunanimous juries were constitutional. Although it is certainly true that in science bad research can exert a baleful influence on the field for far longer than it should (because the finding is exciting, or because it is what people want to believe, or because the researcher is very famous, or for various other reasons), it doesn't have the same force as legal precedent. It is more acceptable and less costly for a scientist to reject a theory than for a judge to overturn a previous precedent. Authority matters in law; in science nothing enhances a career more than a convincing refutation of authority.

Still, there have been cases in which the Supreme Court has expressed a more provisional, scientific point of view. In *Witherspoon v. Illinois* (1968) the Court had before it sketchy evidence based on three unpublished studies suggesting that excluding opponents of the death penalty from juries in capital cases (the common practice known as "death qualification") biased the jury toward a guilty verdict, and so when a defendant's life was at stake he would face a greater risk of conviction than he would if the prosecutor had not asked for the death penalty. The Court decided that the research was, as yet, "too tentative and fragmentary" to reject death-qualification as unconstitutional but that future data might justify such a move. From a scientific point of view, such a holding is far more acceptable than a holding that said, "We have reviewed the evidence and we conclude that death-qualification does not create a bias and therefore is constitutional," which would be analogous to the *Williams* holding on jury size. From a practical point of view, however, leaving a question open invites more litigation, and if the practice later *is* found to be unconstitutional, there is the problem of retroactivity – that is of what to do about all those people who were convicted by biased, death-qualified juries.

Categorical Thinking, Lack of Compromise, and Certainty

The need to decide the particular case one way or the other also pushes legal reasoning toward categorical thinking: A person is either sane (guilty) or insane (not guilty); an unfit parent (someone else gets the child) or fit (he or she *may* get the child); a future danger to society (execution permitted) or not (execution not permitted, barring other aggravating factors). Psychologists consider sanity, fitness, and dangerousness to be continuous variables with no great gulf between the sane and the insane, the fit and the unfit, the safe and the dangerous, and many intermediate cases. But a legal case has to be decided for one party or the other, and so variables that are continuous are forced to become dichotomous. Sometimes there are more than two categories (first-degree murder, second-degree murder, and manslaughter), but a line must always be drawn.

The fact that the decision must be categorical very likely exercises an influence on the process of legal reasoning itself. Compromise decisions are usually impossible, and in an adversary system, the judge is faced with two attorneys, each making the strongest possible case for diametrically opposed outcomes and thus minimizing any ambiguities.[6] Experts may agree on most of the data in their field, but those are not the data that make for effective adversarial persuasion; thus, they are not likely to be presented in court, and the judge or jury is not likely to get a sense of how much consensus actually exists. The attorneys do their best to make every fact and every precedent fit their argument, trying to make it look as though the field is "impacted" (Kennedy, 1986), with little room for doubt, and that everything about this case places it clearly on one side of the line. The combination of adversarial presentation and the need for a dichotomous decision may eventually make the legal reasoning of judges resemble that of advocates. The facts and law may begin by seeming to be a mass of contradictions, and the judge may be plagued by "the doubts and misgivings, the hope and fears" (Cardozo, 1921, p. 167) common in significant enterprises that are fraught with uncertainty and ambiguity; however, judicial opinions almost never suggest that there was *ever* any uncertainty. Once the judge realizes which way he will probably decide the case and the rudiments of the justifications, "one of the effects . . . is a kind of tunnel vision: One is inside the strategy, sensitive to its internal economy, its history of trade-offs, attuned to developing it further but at least temporarily unable to imagine any other way to go" (Kennedy, 1986, p. 543). As in normal memory processes, strong pressures toward consistency and coherence arise, and the arguments and evidence that initially seemed to favor the other side evaporate. "This sense of unequivocal support for the one decision generates a sense of inevitability, of singular correctness" (Simon, 1998, p. 84), and judicial opinions are generally written as though *all* arguments support the conclusion, and there is no uncertainty whatever. Simon attributes this movement toward certainty to basic cognitive processes, and certainly this form of thinking is not unique to law; it is however exaggerated, I think, by the adversarial presentation of evidence (with little or no attention to the ambiguous, in-between facts and law) and by the necessity of always having to choose one side.

The feeling that there must be a certain outcome, and that expressions of uncertainty by a judge are a sign of weakness or incompetence (Simon, 1998, p. 12) seem quite bizarre in a world in which the basic insights of the legal realists are widely accepted. But it is real. Despite the fact that majority and dissenting justices are perfectly certain (so presumably either one side is dead wrong or there *is* some uncertainty), and despite the fact that everyone knows that as soon as the next case comes along "the legal materials lose their recently acquired character, and return to their ambiguous existence within the world of multiple meanings" (Simon, 1998, p. 127), nonetheless certainty is still valued as some sort of mastery and uncertainty as a sign of indecisiveness at best and incompetence at worst. The decision must be justified in terms of the law, and it would be dangerous, in law as in chess or sports, to suggest that the law itself is ambiguous.

Mistrust of Probabilistic Thinking and Aggregate Data

This concern with certainty and the need to make dichotomous judgments may help explain why judges and legal scholars are often uncomfortable with probabilistic statements and probabilistic data. Scientists regularly make explicit quantified probability judgments; lawyers and judges do not – certainly not about the ultimate issues. For example, they strongly resist placing a numerical value on the "reasonable doubt" standard: Is it 95% certainty, 99% certainty? Jurors are generally just given the stock phrase, sometimes supplemented by other phrases, such as "to a moral certainty" or "firmly convinced."

This hesitation to consider probabilities is not unreasonable given that the judge has to make a yes or no decision about a particular individual. The judge's task is more analogous to that of a doctor or clinical psychologist than to that of a research scientist, and it is no accident that psychiatrists and clinical psychologists had close ties to the legal system long before research psychologists did. Explaining (or predicting) the behavior of a specific individual in a specific set of circumstances is not what most scientists do and not what statistics are designed for. Experts willing to testify to the exact probability that a given defendant will commit a future crime are viewed as charlatans by the scientific community. However, statistical probabilistic data may be quite useful in illuminating other questions that judges must consider, such as whether a company is guilty of discrimination in hiring or whether a particular drug causes birth defects. These questions are typically addressed with aggregate data in which the results of many different studies involving many different people are provided by an expert. Judges have become far more receptive to statistical, empirical, aggregate studies over the past fifty years, but there is still a core reluctance. Experts who testify about the factors affecting eyewitness reliability often have to overcome a certain judicial skepticism about the value of their testimony because they have not examined *this particular* eyewitness but are only talking about the circumstances that affect most eyewitnesses most of the time. Large-scale studies of pervasive racial discrimination in capital sentencing (Baldus, Woodworth, & Pulaski, 1990; Gross & Mauro, 1989) were rejected by the Supreme Court in *McCleskey vs. Kemp* (1987) in part because the appellant had not shown that the particular jury that tried McCleskey was influenced by racial bias. The Court held that in order to succeed with a claim of racial discrimination, an appellant must prove either (1) "that the decision makers in *his* case acted with discriminatory purpose" [emphasis in original], or (2) "that the Georgia legislature enacted or maintained the death penalty statute *because of* an anticipated racially discriminatory effect" [emphasis in original] (*McCleskey vs. Kemp*, 1987, p. 1769).

Free Will and the Dispositional Bias

Aggregate data are threatening in another way; they imply that many people in the same circumstances would behave in the same way and thereby threaten the notion of autonomy and free will so deeply rooted in the minds of legal thinkers. The law sees behavior as caused by people's beliefs, desires, and preferences. Ideas of free choice and free will are still fundamental to legal thinking and largely unquestioned. This emphasis creates another source of tension between law and the social sciences because social science takes a much more deterministic point of view, emphasizing cultural, sociological, psychological, biological, and, especially in psychology, situational forces on behavior (Ross and Nisbett, 1991). The fact that economics is the social science that has been most successful in law schools is not surprising given this model; of all the social sciences, economics is the one most wedded to a free choice theory of behavior.

The law has developed a highly elaborate set of definitions of various degrees of personal responsibility, including deliberation, intention, knowledge, recklessness, and negligence, but has been relatively untouched by psychological research on attributional biases and particularly by the research on the dispositional bias (fundamental attribution error) or by social psychological research demonstrating that situations play a far greater role than personal preferences and dispositions in determining people's behavior (Ross & Nisbett, 1991). When situational forces *are* considered, such as in the concepts of necessity and duress, the situations are generally so extreme as to be irrelevant to everyday life – a person breaks into a lonely cabin in a blizzard because he is freezing to death or signs a contract because someone is holding a gun to her head – and can be taken as the exceptions that prove the rule that the pervasive power of the situation in *all* aspects of our lives is largely ignored by the law (Hanson & Yosifon, 2003; Ross & Shestowsky, 2003). The validity of the concept of free will has in fact troubled a sprinkling of legal scholars for a century (Pound, Green, Hanson), and these doubts have occasionally influenced sentencing practices but have rarely affected the basic attribution of guilt or liability. Even when exceptions are made, they generally are made on the basis of internal, dispositional factors (e.g., insanity, youth) and rarely on the basis of situational forces.

Conclusions and Future Directions

Legal reasoning is a form of expert reasoning. Einstein argued that expert reasoning – in particular, scientific reasoning – is "nothing but a refinement of our everyday thinking" (1936, in Bargmann [trans.] 1954, p. 290). Like everyday problem solving and scientific reasoning, legal reasoning begins by examining a set of facts and figuring out what happened and why. Of course, some of the "facts" may be fictions, and the judge must decide which to believe and which to reject, but that is true of all natural problem solving. Information is selected and rejected as part of the process of creating a coherent story.

It is the "refinements" that make one form of expert reasoning different from another. Like other forms of expert reasoning, the law has its own terminology, its own universe of acceptable data, and its own rules. In law, the rules are more flexible than they are in some domains and more central than they are in most. They are more flexible than the rules of chess, for example, because in complex cases there are often many possible rules and precedents from which to choose, and both the facts and the rules can be interpreted and reinterpreted in relation to each other until the judge is satisfied with the total combination – satisfied with the fitness or coherence of the overall picture, and satisfied that the decision is just.

The rules are more central in that every decision *must* be justified by explicit discussion of the relevant rules: The rules are not just a framework for decision making; they are an essential part of the process. The *sine qua non* of empirical scientific research is a clear description of the research method. The judge has a mass of materials to work with, ranging from the incoherent, self-serving blabbering of a witness to the decisions of other judges to the Constitution itself, and the *sine qua non* of legal reasoning is the explanation of why this decision is the right one (Schauer, 1995), an explanation ultimately expressed as argument. This explanation "is meant not only to justify the judgment in terms of an authoritative past but to constitute an authority to be referred to in the future" (White, 1985, p. 240).

Despite the major developments in legal scholars' *interpretations* of legal reasoning over the past century and a half, legal reasoning itself has not changed substantially, and it is unlikely to do so in the near future. Law is a socially defined and socially constructed system that is generally seen as serving its purposes well. Undoubtedly there will be further changes in the nature of the factual evidence judges consider relevant with increasing attention to general scientific research, but the form of legal reasoning, the rules of the game, cannot change without major changes in the system itself, and there is no indication of any such changes in the near future.

Acknowledgments

Research for this chapter was supported by the Cook Fund of the University of Michigan. I am grateful to Hanoch Dagan, Thomas A. Green, Sallyanne Payton, and Grace Tonner for guidance in the initial stages of this work, to Samuel Gross, Don Herzog, and Dan Molden for extremely useful comments on an earlier draft, and to Barbara Zezulka Brown for turning it into a readable manuscript.

Notes

1. European civil law systems differ from common law systems in many respects, such as a more active role for the trial court judge, less emphasis on precedent, and reconsideration of the facts at the appellate level. They are beyond the scope of this chapter.
2. This section owes much to the work of Robert Gordon (1984), Duncan Kennedy (1973), and, especially, Thomas C. Grey (1983).
3. In the era of formalism, judges were men, so I refer to them as "he." For the sake of balance, I refer to scientists as she.
4. By this time, Holmes had been on the Supreme Court for many years, and Pound had become more conservative and more prosaic.
5. Of course there are exceptions, and a brief description like this one must always be, in some ways, a caricature.
6. In actuality, compromise is pervasive in the legal system, because most civil cases are resolved by settlement and most criminal cases by plea bargain. The study of legal reasoning, however, focuses on the small minority of cases that are litigated and decided by judges.

References

Apodaca et al. v. Oregon, (1972) 406 U.S. 408.

Baldus, D., Woodworth, G., & Pulaski, C. (1990). *Equal Justice and the Death Penalty: A Legal Empirical Analysis*. Boston: Northeastern University Press.

Burton, S. J. (1995). *Law and Legal Reasoning* (2nd ed.). Aspen, CO: Aspen Publishers.

Campbell, D. T., & Fiske, D. W. (1959). Convergent and discriminant validation by the multitrait–multimethod matrix. *Psychological Bulletin*, 56, 81–105.

Campbell, D. T., & Stanley, J. C. (1966). *Experimental and Quasi-experimental Designs for Research.*Chicago: Rand McNally.

Cardozo, B. N. (1921). *The Nature of the Judicial Process*. New Haven, CT: Yale University Press.

Chamberlin, T. C. (1890). The method of multiple working hypotheses. *Science*, 15, 92 (old series); reprinted in *Science*, 148, 754–759 (1965).

Cohen, F. S. (1935). Transcendental nonsense and the functionalist approach. *Columbia Law Review*, 35, 809–849.

Dworkin, R. (1986). *Law's Empire*. Cambridge, MA: Harvard University Press.

Einstein, A. (1936). Physics and reality. In S. Bargmann (Trans.) (1954) (p. 290). *Ideas and Opinions of Albert Einstein*. New York: Crown Publishers.

Ellsworth, P. C., & Getman, J. G. (1986). Social science in legal decision-making. In L. Lipson & S. Wheeler (Eds.). *Law and the Social Sciences*. New York: Russell Sage.

Fisher, W. W. III, Horwitz, M. J., & Reed, T. A. (1993). *American Legal Realism*. New York and Oxford, UK: Oxford University Press.

Frank, J. (1930). *Law and the Modern Mind*. New York: Bretano's.

Friedman, L. M. (1986). The law and society movement. *Stanford Law Review*, 38, 763–780.

Gordon, R. W. (1984). Critical legal histories. *Stanford Law Review*, 38, 37–125

Green, T. A. (1995). Freedom and criminal responsibility in the age of Pound: An essay on criminal justice. *Michigan Law Review*, 93, 1915–2053.

Grey, T. C. (1983). Langdell's orthodoxy. *University of Pittsburgh Law Review*, 45, 1–53.

Gross, S., & Mauro, R. (1989) *Death and Discrimination: Racial Disparities in Capital Sentencing*. Boston: Northeastern University Press.

Hanson, J., & Yosifon, D. (2003). The situation: An introduction to the situational character, critical realism, power economics, and deep capture. *University of Pennsylvania Law Review*, 152, pp. 129–346.

Hastie, R., Penrod, S. D., & Pennington, N. (1983). *Inside the Jury*. Cambridge, MA: Harvard University Press.

Holmes, O. W. (1873). The theory of torts. *American Law Review*, 7, 652–663.

Holmes, O. W. (1881). *The Common Law*. Boston: Little, Brown.

Holmes, O. W. (1897). The path of the law. *Harvard Law Review*, 10, 457–478.

Horwitz, M. (1992). *The Transformation of American Law: 1870–1960: The Crisis of Legal Orthodoxy*. New York: Oxford University Press.

Hutcheson, J. C., Jr. (1929). The judgment intuitive: The function of the 'hunch' in judicial decision. *Cornell Law Quarterly*, 14, 274–288.

Johnson v. Louisiana (1972) 406 U.S. 356.

Kahneman, D., & Tversky, A. (Eds.) (2000). *Choices, Values, and Frames*. New York: Russell Sage Foundation; Cambridge, UK: Cambridge University Press.

Kahneman, D., Slovic, P., & Tversky, A. (Eds.) (1982). *Judgment Under Uncertainty: Heuristics and Biases*. Cambridge, UK: Cambridge University Press.

Kennedy, D. (1973). Legal formality. *Journal of Legal Studies*, 11, 351–398.

Kennedy, D. (1986). Freedom and constraint in adjudication: A critical phenomenology. *Journal of Legal Education*, 36, 518–562.

Kennedy, D. (1997). *A Critique of Adjudication (fin de siecle)*. Cambridge, MA: Harvard University Press.

Kreps, D. M. (1990). *A Course in Macroeconomic Theory*. Princeton, NJ: Princeton University Press.

Langdell, C. C. (1880). *Summary of the Law of Contracts*. Boston: Little, Brown.

Langdell, C. C. (1887). Speech delivered by C. C. Langdell at the quarter-millennial celebration of Harvard University, 5 November, 1887. Reprinted in *The Law Quarterly Review*, 3, 123–125 (1887).

Lasswell, H. (1930). Self-analysis and judicial thinking. *International Journal of Ethics*, 40, 354–362.

Lempert, R. O. (1975). Uncovering "nondiscernable" differences: Empirical research and the jury-size cases. *Michigan Law Review*, 73, 643–708.

Llewellyn, K. N. (1930). *The Bramble Bush*. Columbia Law School. Later published as *The Bramble Bush, or, Our Law and Its Study*. New York: Oceana, 1960.

Llewellyn, K. N. (1942). On the good, the true, the beautiful, in law. *University of Chicago Law Review*, 9, 224–265.

Llewellyn, K. N. (1950). Remarks on the theory of appellate decision and the rules or canons about how statutes are to be construed. *Vanderbilt Law Review*, 3, 395–406.

Llewellyn, K. N. (1956). On what makes legal research worthwhile. *Journal of Legal Education*, 8, 399–421.

Lochner v. New York (1905), 198 U.S. 45.

Mathieson, A., & Gross, S. R. (2004). Review for error, *Law, Probability and Risk*, 2, pp. 259–268.

McCleskey v. Kemp (1987). 481 U.S. 279.

Moore, U., & Callahan, C. C. (1943). Law and learning theory: A study in legal control. *Yale Law Journal*, 53, 1–136.

Muller v. Oregon (1908) 208 U.S. 412.

Nisbett, R. E., & Wilson, T. (1977). Telling more than we can know: Verbal reports on mental processes. *Psychological Review, 84*, 231–259.

Pound, R. (1909). Liberty of contract. *The Yale Law Journal, 18*, 454–487.

Pound, R. (1912). The scope and purpose of sociological jurisprudence. *Harvard Law Review, 25*, 489–516.

Pound, R., & Frankfurter, F. (1922). *Criminal Justice in Cleveland*. Cleveland, OH: The Cleveland Foundation.

Regents of the University of California v. Bakke (1978) 438 U.S. 265.

Ross, L. D., & Nisbett, R. E. (1991). *The Person and the Situation*. Boston: McGraw-Hill.

Ross, L., & Shestowsky, D. (2003). Contemporary psychology's challenges to legal theory and practice. *Northwestern University Law Review, 97*, pp. 1081–1114.

Saks, M. J., & Ostrum, T. M. (1975). Jury size and consensus requirements: The laws of probability vs. the law of the land. *Journal of Contemporary Law, 1*, 163–173.

Schauer, F. (1995). Giving reasons. *Stanford Law Review, 47*, 633–659.

Schlegel, J. (1980). American legal realism and empirical social science: From the Yale experience. *Buffalo Law Review, 28*, 459–586.

Simon, D. (1998). A psychological model of judicial decision making. *Rutgers Law Journal, 30*, 1–142.

Sunstein, C. R. (1996). *Legal Reasoning and Political Conflict*. New York: Oxford University Press.

Thaler, R. H. (1992). *The Winner's Curse: Paradoxes and Anomalies of Economic Life.* New York: Free Press.

Tushnet, M. (1984). Trashing. *Stanford Law Review, 36*, 293–348.

White, J. B. (1985). *Heracles' bow: Essays on the Rhetoric and Poetics of the Law*. Madison: University of Wisconsin Press.

Williams v. Florida (1970) 399 U.S. 78.

Witherspoon v. Illinois (1968) 391 U.S. 510.

Yntema, H. (1928). The hornbook method and the conflict of laws. *Yale Law Journal, 37*, 468–483.

Zajonc, R. B. (1965). Social facilitation. *Science, 149*, 269–274.

Zeisel, H. (1971). And then there were none: The diminution of the federal jury. *University of Chicago Law Review, 38*, 710–724.

CHAPTER 29

Scientific Thinking and Reasoning

Kevin Dunbar
Jonathan Fugelsang

What Is Scientific Thinking and Reasoning?

Scientific thinking refers to the mental processes used when reasoning about the content of science (e.g., force in physics), engaged in typical scientific activities (e.g., designing experiments), or specific types of reasoning that are frequently used in science (e.g., deducing that there is a planet beyond Pluto). Scientific thinking involves many general-purpose cognitive operations that human beings apply in nonscientific domains such as induction, deduction, analogy, problem solving, and causal reasoning. These cognitive processes are covered in many chapters of this handbook (see Sloman & Lagnado, Chap. 5 on induction; Holyoak, Chap. 6 on analogy; Buehner and Cheng, Chap. 7 on causality; Evans, Chap. 8 on deduction; Novick and Bassok, Chap. 14 on problem solving; Chi and Ohllson, Chap. 16 on conceptual change). What distinguishes research on scientific thinking from general research on cognition is that research on scientific thinking typically involves investigating thinking that has scientific content. A number of overlapping research traditions have been used to investigate scientific thinking. We cover the history of research on scientific thinking and the different approaches that have been used, highlighting common themes that have emerged over the past fifty years of research.

A Brief History of Research on Scientific Thinking

Science is often considered one of the hallmarks of the human species, along with art, music, and literature. Illuminating the thought processes used in science therefore reveals key aspects of the human mind. The thought processes underlying scientific thinking have fascinated both scientists and nonscientists because the products of science have transformed our world and because the process of discovery is shrouded in mystery. Scientists talk of the chance discovery, the flash of insight, the years of perspiration, and the voyage of discovery. These images of science have helped make the mental processes underlying the discovery process intriguing to cognitive scientists as they attempt to uncover what really goes on inside the scientific mind and how scientists really think. Furthermore, the questions, "Can scientists be taught to think better, avoiding mistakes of scientific thinking?" and "Could the scientific process be automated such that scientists are no longer necessary?" make scientific thinking a topic of enduring interest. One of the most compelling accounts of science that makes the reader want to understand science and why science is interesting recently appeared in the journal *Popular Science*. In this article, Charles Hirshberg discusses his mother, scientist Joan Feynman, and her scientific contributions as well as the difficulties of being a woman scientist. The following excerpt captures the excitement and thrill that even a household encounter with science can generate and that is thought to be at the root of many scientists' desire to conduct science (Hirschberg, 2003).

> *My introduction to chemistry came in 1970, on a day when my mom was baking challah bread for the Jewish New Year. I was about ten, and though I felt cooking was unmanly for a guy who played shortstop for Village Host Pizza in the Menlo Park, California, Little League, she had persuaded me to help. When the bread was in the oven, she gave me a plastic pill bottle and a cork. She told me to sprinkle a little baking soda into the bottle, then a little vinegar, and cork the bottle as fast as I could. There followed a violent and completely unexpected pop as the cork flew off and walloped me in the forehead. Exploding food: I was ecstatic! "That's called a chemical reaction," she said, rubbing my shirt clean. "The vinegar is an acid and the soda is a base, and that's what happens when you mix the two." After that, I never understood what other kids meant when they said that science was boring.*

The cognitive processes underlying scientific discovery and day-to-day scientific thinking have been a topic of intense scrutiny and speculation for almost 400 years (e.g., Bacon, 1620; Galilei, 1638; Klahr, 2000; Tweney, Doherty, & Mynatt, 1981). Understanding the nature of scientific thinking has been an important and central issue not only for our understanding of science, but also for our understating of what it is to be human. Bacon's *Novumm Organum*, in 1620, sketched out some of the key features of the ways that experiments are designed and data interpreted. Over the ensuing 400 years, philosophers and scientists vigorously debated the appropriate methods that scientists should use (see Giere, 1993). These debates over the appropriate methods for science typically resulted in the espousal of a particular type of reasoning method such as induction or deduction. It was not until the Gestalt psychologists began working on the nature of human problem solving during the 1940s that experimental psychologists began to investigate the cognitive processes underlying scientific thinking and reasoning.

The Gestalt Psychologist Max Wertheimer initiated the first investigations of scientific thinking in his landmark book, *Productive Thinking* (Wertheimer, 1945; see Novick & Bassok, Chap. 14). Wertheimer spent a considerable amount of time corresponding with Albert Einstein, attempting to discover how Einstein generated the concept of relativity. Wertheimer argued that Einstein had to overcome the structure of Newtonian physics at each step in his theorizing and the ways that Einstein actually achieved this restructuring were articulated in terms of Gestalt theories. For a recent and different account of how Einstein made his discovery, see Galison (2003). We will see later how this process of overcoming alternative theories is an obstacle with which both scientists and nonscientists need to deal when evaluating and theorizing about the world.

One of the first investigations of the cognitive abilities underlying scientific thinking was the work of Jerome Bruner and his colleagues at Harvard (Bruner, Goodnow, & Austin, 1956). They argued that a key activity in which scientists engage is to determine whether or not a particular instance is a member of a category. For example, a scientist might want to discover which substances undergo fission when bombarded by neutrons and which substances do not. Here, scientists have to discover the attributes that make a substance undergo fission. Bruner et al. (1956) saw scientific thinking as the testing of hypotheses and collecting of data with the end goal of determining whether something is a member of a category or not. They invented a paradigm in which people were required to formulate hypotheses and collect data that test their hypotheses. Using this approach, Bruner et al. identified a number of strategies people use to formulate and test hypotheses. They found that a key factor determining which hypothesis testing strategy people use is the amount of memory capacity the strategy takes up (see also Morrison, Chap. 19, on working memory). Another key factor they discovered was that it is much more difficult for people to discover negative concepts (e.g., not blue) than positive concepts (e.g., blue). Although the Bruner et al. research is most commonly thought of as work on concepts, they saw their work as uncovering a key component of scientific thinking.

A second early line of research on scientific thinking was developed by Peter Wason and his colleagues. Like Bruner et al., Wason (1968) saw a key component of scientific thinking as being the testing of hypotheses. Whereas Bruner et al. focused on the different types of strategies people use to formulate hypotheses, Wason focused on whether people adopt a strategy of trying to confirm or disconfirm their hypotheses. Using Popper's (1959) theory that scientists should try and falsify rather than confirm their hypotheses, Wason devised a deceptively simple task in which participants were given three numbers, such as 2-4-6, and were asked to discover the rule underlying the three numbers. Participants were asked to generate other triads of numbers, and the experimenter would tell the participant whether the triad was consistent or inconsistent with the rule. They were told that when they were sure they knew what the rule was they should state it. Most participants began the experiment by thinking that the rule was even numbers increasing by two. They then attempted to confirm their hypothesis by generating a triad like 8-10-12, then 14-16-18. These triads are consistent with the rule and the participants were told yes, that the triads were indeed consistent with the rule. However, when they proposed the rule, even numbers increasing by two, they were told that the rule was incorrect. The correct rule was numbers of increasing magnitude. From this research Wason concluded that people try and confirm their hypotheses, whereas normatively speaking, they should try and disconfirm their hypotheses. One implication of this research is that confirmation bias is not just restricted to scientists but is a general human tendency.

It was not until the 1970s that a general account of scientific reasoning was proposed. Herbert Simon, often in collaboration with Allan Newell (e.g., Newell & Simon, 1972), proposed that scientific thinking is a form of problem solving. He proposed that problem solving is a search in a problem space. Newell and Simon's (1972) theory of problem solving is discussed in many places in this volume, usually in the context of specific problems (see especially Novick & Bassok, Chap. 14, on problem solving). Herbert Simon (1977), however, devoted considerable time to understanding many different scientific discoveries and scientific reasoning processes. The common thread in his research was that scientific thinking and discovery is not a mysterious magical process but a process of problem solving in which clear heuristics are used. Simon's goal was to articulate the heuristics that scientists use in their research at a fine-grained level. He built many programs that simulated the process of scientific discovery and articulated the specific computations that scientists use in their research (see subsequent section on computational approaches to scientific thinking). Particularly important was Simon and Lea's (1974) work demonstrating that concept formation and induction consist of a search in two problem spaces: a space of instances and a space of rules. This idea has been highly influential on problem-solving accounts of scientific thinking that will be discussed in the next section.

Overall, the work of Bruner, Wason, and Simon laid the foundations for contemporary research on scientific thinking. Early research on scientific thinking is conveniently summarized in Tweney, Doherty, and Mynatt's 1981 book, *On Scientific Thinking*, in which they sketched out many of the themes that have dominated research on scientific thinking over the past few decades. Other more recent books, such as Ronald Giere's *Cognitive Models of Science* (1993); David Klahr's *Explaining Science* (2000); Peter Carruthers, Steven Stich, and Michael Siegal's *Cognitive Basis of Science* (2002); and Gorman and colleagues' *Scientific and Technical Thinking* (2005) provide detailed analyses of different aspects of scientific discovery. In this chapter, we discuss the main approaches that have been used to investigate scientific thinking.

One of the main features of investigations of research on the scientific mind has been to take one aspect of scientific thinking that is thought to be important and investigate it in isolation. How does one go about investigating the many different aspects of scientific thinking? Numerous methodologies have been used to analyze the genesis of scientific concepts, theories, hypotheses, and experiments. Researchers have used experiments, verbal protocols, computer programs, and analysis of particular scientific discoveries. A recent development has been to investigate scientists as they reason "live" (in vivo studies of scientific thinking) in their own laboratories (Dunbar, 1995, 2002). From a "thinking and reasoning" standpoint, the major aspects of scientific thinking that have been most actively investigated are problem solving, analogical reasoning, hypothesis testing, conceptual change, collaborative reasoning, inductive reasoning, and deductive reasoning.

Scientific Thinking as Problem Solving

One important goal for accounts of scientific thinking has been to provide an overarching framework to understand the scientific mind. One framework that has had a great influence in cognitive science is that scientific thinking and scientific discovery can be conceived as a form of problem solving. Simon (1977) argued that both scientific thinking in general and problem solving in particular could be thought of as a search in a problem space (see Chapter 11). A problem space consists of all the possible states of a problem and all the operations that a problem solver can use to get from one state to the next (see problem solving entry). According to this view, by characterizing the types of representations and procedures people use to get from one state to another, it is possible to understand scientific thinking. Scientific thinking therefore can be characterized as a search in various problem spaces (Simon, 1977). Simon investigated a number of scientific discoveries by bringing participants into the laboratory, providing the participants with the data to which a scientist had access, and getting the participants to reason about the data and rediscover a scientific concept. He then analyzed the verbal protocols participants generated and mapped out the types of problem spaces in which the participants searched (e.g., Qin & Simon, 1990). Kulkarni and Simon (1988) used a more historical approach to uncover the problem-solving heuristics that Krebs used in his discovery of the urea cycle. Kulkarni and Simon analyzed Krebs's diaries and proposed a set of problem-solving heuristics that he used in his research. They then built a computer program incorporating the heuristics and biological knowledge that Krebs had before he made his discoveries. Of particular importance are the search heuristics the program uses such as the experimental proposal heuristics and the data interpretation heuristics built into the program. A key heuristic was an unusualness heuristic that focused on unusual findings and guided the search through a space of theories and a space of experiments.

Klahr and Dunbar (1988) extended the search in a problem space approach and proposed that scientific thinking can be thought of as a search through two related spaces – an hypothesis space and an experiment space. Each problem space that a scientist uses will have its own types of representations and operators used to change the representations. Search in the hypothesis space constrains search in the experiment space. Klahr and Dunbar found that some participants move from the hypothesis space to the experiment space, whereas others move from the experiment space to the hypothesis space. These different types of searches lead to the proposal of different types of hypotheses and experiments. More recent work has extended the dual-space approach to include alternative problem-solving spaces, including those for data, instrumentation, and domain-specific knowledge (Schunn & Klahr, 1995, 1996; Klahr & Simon, 1999).

Scientific Thinking as Hypothesis Testing

Many researchers have regarded testing specific hypotheses predicted by theories as one of the key attributes of scientific thinking. Hypothesis testing is the process of evaluating a proposition by collecting evidence regarding its truth. Experimental cognitive research on scientific thinking that specifically examines this issue has tended to fall into two broad classes of investigations. The first class is concerned with the types of reasoning that lead scientists astray, blocking scientific ingenuity (see also Sternberg, Chap. 15 on creativity). A large amount of research has been conducted on the potentially faulty reasoning strategies that both participants in experiments and scientists use such as considering only one favored hypothesis at a time and how this prevents scientists from making discoveries. The second class is concerned with uncovering the mental processes underlying the generation of new scientific hypotheses and concepts. This research has tended to focus on the use of analogy and imagery in science as well as the use of specific types of problem-solving heuristics (see also Holyoak, Chapter 6 on analogy).

Turning first to investigations of what diminishes scientific creativity, philosophers, historians, and experimental psychologists have devoted a considerable amount of research to "confirmation bias." This occurs when scientists consider only one hypothesis (typically the favored hypothesis) and ignore alternative hypotheses or other potentially relevant hypotheses. This important phenomenon can distort the design of experiments, formulation of theories, and interpretation of data. Beginning with the work of Wason (1968) and as discussed previously, researchers have repeatedly shown that when participants are asked to design an experiment to test a hypothesis, they predominantly design experiments they think will yield results consistent with the hypothesis. Using the 2-4-6 task mentioned earlier, Klayman and Ha (1987) showed that in situations in which one's hypothesis is likely to be confirmed, seeking confirmation is a normatively incorrect strategy, whereas when the probability of confirming one's hypothesis is low, then attempting to confirm ones hypothesis can be an appropriate strategy. Historical analyses by Tweney (1989) on the way that Faraday made his discoveries and experiments investigating people testing hypotheses have revealed that people use a confirm early–disconfirm late strategy: When people initially generate or are given hypotheses, they try to gather evidence that is consistent with the hypothesis. Once enough evidence has been gathered, people attempt to find the boundaries of their hypothesis and often try to disconfirm their hypotheses.

In an interesting variant on the confirmation bias paradigm, Gorman (1989) has shown that when participants are told there is the possibility of error in the data they receive, they assume any data inconsistent with their favored hypothesis are attributable to error. The possibility of error therefore insulates hypotheses against disconfirmation. This hypothesis has not been confirmed by other researchers (Penner & Klahr, 1996) but is an intriguing one that warrants further investigation.

Confirmation bias is very difficult to overcome. Even when participants are asked to consider alternate hypotheses, they often fail to conduct experiments that could potentially disconfirm their hypothesis. Tweney and his colleagues provide an excellent overview of this phenomenon in their classic monograph "On Scientific Thinking" (1981). The precise reasons for this type of block are still widely debated. Researchers such as Michael Doherty have argued that limitations in working memory make it difficult for people to consider more than one hypothesis. Consistent with this view, Dunbar and Sussman (1995) showed that when participants are asked to hold irrelevant items in working memory while testing hypotheses, participants are unable to switch hypotheses in the face of inconsistent evidence (see also Morrison, Chap. 19, on working memory). Although limitations of working memory are involved in the phenomenon of confirmation bias, even groups of scientists can display confirmation bias. The recent controversies over cold fusion are an example of confirmation bias. Here, large groups of scientists had other hypotheses available to explain their data but yet maintained their hypotheses in the face of other, more standard alternative hypotheses. Mitroff (1974) provides some interesting examples of scientists at the National Aeronautical and Space Administration demonstrating confirmation bias that highlights the roles of commitment and motivation in this process.

Causal Thinking in Science

Much of scientific thinking and scientific theory building pertains to the development of causal models between variables of interest. For example, does smoking cause cancer, Prozac relieve depression, or aerosol spray deplete the ozone layer? (See also Buehner & Cheng, Chap. 7, on causality.) Scientists and nonscientists alike are constantly bombarded with statements regarding the causal relationship between such variables. How does one evaluate the status of such claims? What kinds of data are informative? How do scientists and nonscientists deal with data that are inconsistent with their theory?

One important issue in the causal reasoning literature that is directly relevant to scientific thinking is the extent to which scientists and nonscientists are governed by the search for causal mechanisms (i.e., the chain of events that lead from a cause to an effect) versus the search for statistical data (i.e., how often variables co-occur). This dichotomy can be boiled down to the search for qualitative versus quantitative information about the paradigm the scientist is investigating. Researchers from a number of cognitive psychology laboratories have found that people prefer to gather more information about an underlying mechanism than covariation between a cause and an effect (e.g., Ahn et al., 1995). That is, the predominant strategy that students in scientific thinking simulations use is to gather as much information as possible about how the objects under investigation work rather than collecting large amounts of quantitative data to determine whether the observations hold across multiple samples. These findings suggest that a central component of scientific thinking may be to formulate explicit mechanistic causal models of scientific events.

One place where causal reasoning has been observed extensively is when scientists obtain unexpected findings. Both historical and naturalistic research has revealed that reasoning causally about unexpected findings has a central role in science. Indeed, scientists themselves frequently state that a finding was attributable to chance or was unexpected. Given that claims of unexpected findings are such a frequent component of scientists' autobiographies and interviews in the media, Dunbar (1995, 1997, 1999; Dunbar & Fugelsang, 2004; Fugelsang et al., 2004) decided to investigate the ways that scientists deal with unexpected findings. In 1991–1992 Dunbar spent one year in three molecular biology laboratories and one immunology laboratory at a prestigious U.S. university. He used the weekly laboratory meeting as a source of data on scientific discovery and scientific reasoning. (This type of study he has called *InVivo cognition*). When he examined the types of findings the scientists made, he found that more than 50%

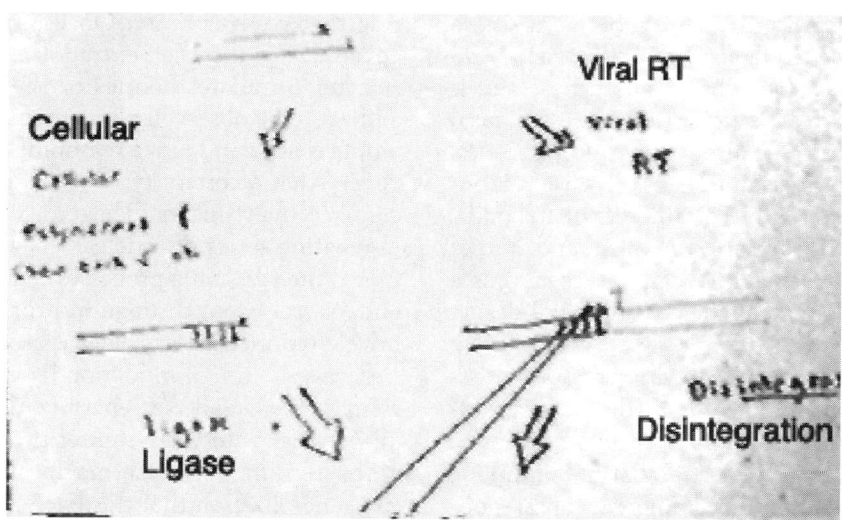

Figure 29.1. Causal thinking in science. Potential mechanisms of human immunodeficiency virus integration into host DNA. The diagram shows two potential causal mechanisms – cellular (left branch) and viral (right branch).

were unexpected and that these scientists had evolved a number of important strategies for dealing with such findings. One clear strategy was to reason causally about the findings: Scientists attempted to build causal models of their unexpected findings. This causal model building resulted in the extensive use of collaborative reasoning, analogical reasoning, and problem-solving heuristics (Dunbar, 1997; 2001).

Many of the key unexpected findings that scientists reasoned about in the *InVivo* studies of scientific thinking were inconsistent with the scientists' pre-existing causal models. A laboratory equivalent of the biology labs therefore was to create a situation in which students obtained unexpected findings that were inconsistent with their pre-existing theories. Dunbar and Fugelsang (2005; see also Fugelsang et al., 2004) examined this issue by creating a scientific causal thinking simulation in which experimental outcomes were either expected or unexpected. (Dunbar [1995] called this type of study of people reasoning in a cognitive laboratory *InVitro cognition*). They found that students spent considerably more time reasoning about unexpected findings than expected findings. Second, when assessing the overall degree to which their hypothesis was supported or refuted, participants spent the majority of their time considering unexpected findings. An analysis of participants' verbal protocols indicates that much of this extra time is spent formulating causal models for the unexpected findings.

Scientists are not merely the victims of unexpected findings but plan for unexpected events to occur. An example of the ways that scientists plan for unexpected contingencies in their day-to-day research is shown in Figure 29.1. Figure 29.1 is an example of a diagram in which the scientist is building causal models about the ways that human immunodeficiency virus (HIV) integrates itself into the host deoxyribonucleic acid (DNA) taken from a presentation at a lab meeting. The scientist proposes two main causal mechanisms by which HIV integrates into the host DNA. The main event that must occur is that gaps in the DNA must be filled. In the left-hand branch of Diagram 2, he proposes a cellular mechanism whereby cellular polymerase fills in gaps as the two sources of DNA integrate. In the right-hand branch, he proposes that instead of cellular mechanisms filling in the gaps, viral enzymes fill in the gap and join the two pieces of DNA. He then designs an experiment to distinguish between these two causal mechanisms. Clearly, visual and diagrammatic reasoning is used here and is a useful way of representing different causal mechanisms (see also Tversky, Chap. 10 on visuospatial reasoning). In this case, the visual representations of different causal paths are used to design an experiment and predict possible results. Thus, causal reasoning is a key component of the experimental design process.

When designing experiments, scientists know that unexpected findings occur often and have developed many strategies to take advantage of them (Baker & Dunbar, 2000). Scientists build different causal models of their experiments incorporating many conditions and controls. These multiple conditions and controls allow unknown mechanisms to manifest themselves. Rather than being the victims of the unexpected, the scientists create opportunities for unexpected events to occur, and once these events do occur, they have causal models that allow them to determine exactly where in the causal chain their unexpected finding arose. The results of these InVivo and InVitro studies all point to a more complex and nuanced account of how scientists and nonscientists test and evaluate hypotheses.

The Roles of Inductive and Deductive Thinking in the Scientific Mind

One of the most basic characteristics of science is that scientists assume that the universe that we live in follows predictable rules. Very few scientists in this century would refute the claim that the earth rotates around the sun, for example. Scientists reason from these rules using a variety of different strategies to make new scientific discoveries. Two frequently used types of reasoning strategies are inductive (see Sloman & Lagnado, Chap. 5) and deductive reasoning (see Evans, Chap. 8). In the case of inductive reasoning, a scientist may observe a series of events and try to discover a rule that governs them. Once a rule is discovered, scientists can extrapolate from the rule to formulate theories of the observed and yet to be observed phenomena. One example is using inductive reasoning in the discovery that a certain type of bacterium is a cause of many ulcers (Thagard, 1999). In a fascinating series of articles, Thagard documents the reasoning processes that Marshall and Warren went through in proposing this novel hypothesis. One key reasoning process was the use of induction by generalization. Marshall and Warren noted that almost all patients with gastric enteritis had a spiral bacterium in their stomachs and formed the generalization that this bacterium is the cause of many stomach ulcers. There are numerous other examples of induction by generalization in science, such as Tycho Brahe induction about the motion of planets from his observations, Dalton's use of induction in chemistry, and the discovery of prions as the source of mad cow disease. Many theories of induction have used scientific discovery and reasoning as examples of this important reasoning process.

Another common type of inductive reasoning is to map a feature of one member of a category to another member of a category. This is called *categorical induction*. This type of induction projects a known property of one item onto another item from the same category. Thus, knowing that the Rous Sarcoma virus is a retrovirus that uses RNA rather than DNA, a biologist might assume that another virus that is thought to be a retrovirus also uses RNA rather than DNA. Although research on this type of induction typically has not been discussed in accounts of scientific thinking, this type of induction is common in science. For an important contribution to this literature see Smith, Shafir, and Osherson (1993), and for a review of this literature see Heit (2000).

Turning now to deductive thinking, many thinking processes to which scientists adhere follow traditional rules of deductive logic. These processes correspond to conditions in which a hypothesis may lead to, or is deducible to, a conclusion. Although they are not always phrased in syllogistic form, deductive arguments can usually be phrased as "syllogisms," or as brief mathematical statements in which the premises lead to the conclusion. Deductive reasoning is an extremely important aspect of scientific thinking because it underlies a large component of how scientists conduct their research. By looking at many scientific discoveries, we can often see that deductive reasoning is at work. Deductive reasoning statements all contain information or rules that state an assumption about how the world works and a conclusion that would necessarily follow from the rule. A classic example that is still receiving much scientific investigation today is the case of Planet X. In the early twentieth century, Percival Lowell coined the term "Planet X" when referring to any planet yet to be discovered. Around that time and continuing to this day, based on rather large residual orbital perturbations of Uranus and Neptune, many scientists are convinced there exists a yet to be discovered planet in our solar system. Because it is assumed as fact that only large objects that possess a strong gravitational force can cause such perturbations, the search for such an object ensued. Given Pluto's rather meager stature, it has been dismissed as a candidate for these perturbations. We can apply these statements to deductive logic as follows:

Premise 1: The gravitational force of large planetary bodies causes perturbations in orbits of planetary bodies
Premise 2: Uranus and Neptune have perturbations in their orbits
Conclusion: The gravitational force of a large planetary body influences the orbits of Uranus and Neptune

Of course, the soundness of the logical deduction is completely dependent on the accuracy of the premises. If the premises are correct, then the conclusion will be correct.

Inductive and deductive reasoning, even by successful scientists, is not immune to error. Two classes of errors commonly found in deductive reasoning are context and content errors. A common context error that people often make is to assume that conditional relationships are, in fact, biconditional. The conditional statement "if someone has AIDS then they also have HIV," for example, does not necessarily imply that "if someone has HIV then they also have AIDS." This is a common error in deductive reasoning that can result in logically incorrect conclusions being drawn. A common content error people often make is to modify the interpretation of a conclusion based on the degree to which the conclusion is plausible. Here, scientists may be more likely to accept a scientific discovery as valid if the outcome is plausible. You can see how this second class of errors in deductive logic can have profound implications for theory development. Indeed, if scientists are overly blinded by the plausibility of an outcome, they may fail to objectively evaluate the steps in their deductive process.

The Roles of Analogy in Scientific Thinking

One of the most widely mentioned reasoning processes used in science is analogy. Scientists use analogies to form a bridge between what they already know and what they are trying to explain, understand, or discover. In fact, many scientists have claimed that the use of certain analogies was instrumental in their making a scientific discovery, and almost all scientific autobiographies and biographies feature an important analogy that is discussed in depth. Coupled with the fact that there has been an enormous research program on analogical thinking and reasoning (see Holyoak, Chap. 6), we now have a number of models and theories of analogical reasoning that show exactly how analogy can play a role in scientific discovery (see Gentner, Holyoak, & Kokinov, 2001). By analyzing the use of analogies in science, Thagard and Croft (1999), Nersessian (1999), Gentner and Jeziorski (1993), and Dunbar and Blanchette (2001) all have shown that analogical reasoning is a key aspect of scientific discovery.

Traditional accounts of analogy distinguish between two components of analogical reasoning – the target and the source. The target is the concept or problem that a scientist is attempting to explain or solve. The source is another piece of knowledge that the scientist uses to understand the target, or to explain the target to others. What the scientist does when he or she makes an analogy is to map features of the source onto features of the target. By mapping the features of the source onto the target, new features of the target may be discovered, or the features of the target can be rearranged so that a new concept is invented and a scientific discovery is made. A common analogy used with computers is to describe a harmful piece of software as a computer virus. Once a piece of software is called a virus, people can map features of biological viruses, such as they are small, spread easily, self-replicate using a host, and cause damage. Not only do people map a single feature of the source onto the target but also the systems of relations between features from the source to the target. They also make analogical inferences. If a computer virus is similar to a biological virus, for example, an immune system can be created on computers that can protect computers from future variants of a virus. One of the reasons scientific analogy is so powerful is that it can generate new knowledge such as the creation of a computational immune system having many of the features of a real biological immune system. This also leads to predictions that there will be newer computer viruses that are the computational equivalent of retroviruses, which lack DNA or standard instructions that will elude the computational immune system.

The process of making an analogy involves a number of key steps – retrieval of a source from memory, aligning the features of the source with those of the target, mapping features of the source onto those of the target, and possibly making of new inferences about the target. Scientific discoveries are made when the source highlights a hitherto unknown feature of the target or restructures the target into a new set of relations. Interestingly, research on analogy has shown that participants do not easily use analogy (see Gentner et al., 1997; Holyoak & Thagard, 1995). Participants tend to focus on the sharing of a superficial feature between the source and the target, rather than the relations among features. In his *InVivo* studies of science, Dunbar (1995, 2001, 2002) investigated the ways that scientists use analogies while they are conducting their research and found that scientists use both relational and superficial features when they make analogies. The choice of whether to use superficial or relational features depends on their goals. If their goal is to fix a problem in an experiment, their analogies are based upon superficial features. If their goal is to formulate hypotheses, they focus on analogies based upon sets of relations. One important difference between scientists and participants in experiments is that the scientists have deep relational knowledge of the processes they are investigating and can use that relational knowledge to make analogies.

Analogies sometimes lead scientists and students astray. Evelyn Fox-Keller (1985) shows how an analogy between the pulsing of a lighthouse and the activity of the slime mold dictyostelium led researchers astray for a number of years. Likewise, the analogy between the solar system (the source) and the structure of the atom (the target) has been shown to be potentially misleading to students taking more advanced courses in physics or chemistry. The solar system analogy has a number of misalignments to the structure of the atom, such as electrons being repelled rather than attracted by each other and that electrons do not have individual orbits like planets, but have orbit clouds of electron density. Furthermore, students have serious misconceptions about the nature of the solar system, which can compound their misunderstanding of the nature of the atom (Fischler & Lichtfield, 1992). Although analogy is a powerful tool in science, as is the case with all forms of induction, incorrect conclusions can be reached.

Conceptual Change in the Scientific Mind

Many researchers have noted that an important component of science is the generation of new concepts and modification of existing ones. Scientific concepts, like all concepts, can be characterized as containing representations of words, thoughts, actions, objects, and processes. How does one's knowledge of scientific concepts change over time? The large-scale changes that occur in conceptual structures have been labeled *conceptual change* (see Chi & Ohlsson, Chap. 16; Nersessian, 2002; Thagard, 1992). Theories of conceptual change focus on two main types of shifts. One is the addition of knowledge to a pre-existing conceptual structure. Here, there is no conflict between the pre-existing conceptual knowledge and the new information the student is acquiring. Such minor conceptual shifts are relatively easy to acquire and do not demand restructuring of the underlying representations of scientific knowledge. The second type of conceptual shift is what is known as "radical conceptual change" (see Keil, 1999, and Nersessian, 1998, for reviews of this literature). In this type of situation, it is necessary for a new conceptual system to be acquired that organizes knowledge in new ways, adds new knowledge, and results in a very different conceptual structure. This radical conceptual change is thought to be necessary for acquiring many new concepts in physics and is regarded as the major source of difficulty for students. The factors at the root of this conceptual shift view have been difficult to determine, although a number of studies in human development (Carey, 1985; Chi, 1992; Chi & Roscoe 2002), in the history of science (Nersessian, 1998; Thagard, 1992), and in physics education (Clement, 1982; Mestre, 1991) give detailed accounts of the changes in knowledge representation that occur when people switch from one way of representing scientific knowledge to another. A beautiful example of conceptual change is shown in Figure 29.2. This illustration is taken from the first edition of Isaac Newton's *Fluxions* (1736). It displays the ancient Greeks looking on in amazement at an English hunter who shoots at a bird using Newton's new method of fluxions. Clearly they had not undergone the conceptual change needed to understand Newtonian physics.

One area in which students show great difficulty in understanding scientific concepts is in physics. Analyses of students changing conceptions, using interviews, verbal protocols, and behavioral outcome measures indicate that large-scale changes in students' concepts occur in physics education (see McDermott and Redish 1999 for a review of this literature). Following Kuhn (1962), researchers have noted that students' changing conceptions are similar to the sequences of conceptual changes in physics that have occurred in the history of science. These notions of radical paradigm shifts and ensuing incompatibility with past knowledge states have drawn interesting parallels between the development of particular scientific concepts in children and in the history of physics.

Investigations of naïve people's understanding of motion indicate that students have extensive misunderstandings of motion. This naïve physics research indicates that many people hold erroneous beliefs about motion similar to a medieval "Impetus" theory (McCloskey, Caramazza, & Green, 1980). Furthermore, students appear to maintain "Impetus" notions even after one or two courses in physics. In fact, some authors have noted that students who have taken one or two courses in physics may perform worse on physics problems than naïve students (Mestre, 1991). It is only after extensive learning that we see a conceptual shift from "Impetus" theories of motion to Newtonian scientific theories. How one's conceptual representation shifts from "naïve" to Newtonian is a matter of contention because some have argued that the shift involves a radical conceptual change, whereas others have argued that the conceptual change is not really complete. Kozhevnikov and Hegarty (2001) argue that much of the naïve "Impetus" notions of motion are maintained at the expense of Newtonian principles even with extensive training in physics. They argue that such "Impetus" principles are maintained at an implicit level. Thus, although students can give the correct Newtonian answer to problems, their reaction times to respond indicate they are also using impetus theories.

Although conceptual changes are thought to be large-scale changes in concepts that occur over extensive periods of time, it has been possible to observe conceptual change using *InVivo* methodologies. Dunbar (1995) reported a major conceptual shift that occurred in immunologists, in which they obtained a series of unexpected findings that forced the scientists to propose a new concept in immunology that, in turn, forced the change in other concepts. The drive behind this conceptual change was the discovery of a series of different unexpected findings or anomalies that required the scientists to revise and reorganize their conceptual knowledge. Interestingly, this conceptual change was achieved by a group of scientists reasoning collaboratively, rather than by one scientist working alone. Different scientists tend to work on different aspects of concepts, and also different concepts, that, when put together, lead to a rapid change in entire conceptual structures.

Overall, accounts of conceptual change in individuals indicate it is, indeed, similar to that of conceptual change in entire scientific fields. Individuals need to be confronted with anomalies that their pre-existing theories cannot explain before entire conceptual structures are overthrown. However, replacement conceptual structures have to be generated before the old conceptual structure can be discarded. Often, people do not overthrow their naïve conceptual theories and have misconceptions in many fundamental scientific concepts that are maintained across the lifespan.

The Scientific Brain

In this chapter, we have provided an overview of research into the workings of the scientific mind. In particular, we have shown how the scientific mind possesses many cognitive tools that are applied differently depending on the task at hand. Research in thinking and reasoning has recently been extended to include a systematic analysis of the brain areas associated with scientific reasoning using techniques such as functional magnetic resonance imaging (fMRI), positron emission topography, and event related potentials. There are two main reasons for taking this approach. First, these approaches allow the researcher to look at the entire human brain, making it possible to see the many different sites involved in scientific thinking and to gain a more complete understanding of the entire range of mechanisms involved in scientific thinking. Second, these brain-imaging approaches allow researchers to address fundamental questions in research on scientific thinking. One important question concerns the extent to which ordinary thinking in nonscientific contexts and scientific thinking recruit similar versus disparate neural structures of the brain. Dunbar (2002) proposed that scientific thinking uses the same cognitive mechanisms all human beings possess, rather than being an entirely different type of thinking. He has proposed that in scientific thinking, standard cognitive processes are used, but are combined in ways that are specific to a particular aspect of science or a specific discipline of science. By comparing the results of brain imaging investigations of scientific thinking with brain imaging studies of nonscientific thinking, we can see both whether and when common versus dissociated brain sites are invoked during different cognitive tasks. This approach will make it possible to articulate more clearly what scientific thinking is and how it is both similar to and different from the nonscientific thinking typically examined in the cognitive laboratory (also see Goel, Chap. 20).

Considering the large arsenal of cognitive tools researchers have at their disposal, determining the neurological underpinning of scientific thinking becomes mainly a matter of dissecting the processes thought to be involved in the reasoning process and

Figure 29.2. Conceptual change in science: The ancient Greeks look on in amazement as a hunter uses Newtonian principles to shoot down a bird. This figure is taken from the frontispiece of his *Method of Fluxions and Infinite Series; with its Application to the Geometry of Curve Lines*. Frontispiece in Bodelian Library.

conducting systematic experiments on these subprocesses. What might these subprocesses be? As the previous sections of this chapter show, scientific thinking involves many cognitive capabilities including, but not limited to, analogical reasoning, casual reasoning, induction, deduction, and problem solving: These subprocesses undoubtedly possess common and distinct neural signatures. A number of cognitive neuroscientists recently examined problem solving (Fincham et al., 2002; Goel & Grafman, 1995; Colvin, Dunbar, & Grafman, 2001), analogical reasoning (Wharton et al., 2000; Kroger et al., 2002), hypothesis testing (Fugelsang & Dunbar, in press), inductive reasoning (Goel & Dolan, 2000; Seger et al., 2000), and deductive reasoning (Parsons & Osherson, 2001; Osherson et al., 1998). They all pointed to the role of the dorsolateral prefrontal/parietal network for tasks requiring these higher level cognitive capacities. It is important to note that this brain network has been implicated in tasks that are highly demanding on attention and working-memory.

One question cognitive neuroscience investigations of scientific thinking are beginning to address is the neurological underpinnings of conceptual change. Using fMRI to investigate students who have and who have not undergone conceptual change in scientific areas, it is possible to uncover the neural changes that accompany conceptual change. Fugelsang and Dunbar (submitted) have found shifts from ventral pathways to dorsal pathways in the brain when students shift from naïve impetus theories of motion to Newtonian theories of motion. These cognitive neuroscience investigations reveal the ways that knowledge is organized in the scientific brain and provide detailed accounts of the nature of the representation of scientific knowledge.

The extent to which these processes are lateralized in the right or left hemisphere is a matter of recent debate, especially as it pertains to inductive and deductive reasoning. Hemispheric differences in scientific deductive thinking potentially can be quite revealing about the nature of the representations of the scientific mind. For example, recent cognitive neuroscience research can provide important new insights into one of the most fundamental questions that has perplexed many scientists for decades – namely, whether complex scientific thinking processes, such as deductive and inductive reasoning, are represented in terms of linguistic or visual–spatial representations. Anecdotal claims are equivocal as to the nature of such representations. When thinking about scientific concepts and devising theoretical explanations for phenomena, for example, scientists may verbally represent their theories in text or visually represent theories in graphical models. More often than not, scientific theories are represented in both modalities to some degree.

Based on what we know about hemispheric differences in the brain, there are several clear predictions about how spatial and verbal thinking styles would be represented in the brain. If scientific thinking were predominantly based on verbal or linguistic representations, for example, we would expect activations of the basic language neural structures such as the frontal and inferior temporal regions in the left hemisphere. If scientific thinking were predominately based on visual-spatial representations, one would expect activation of the basic perception and motor control neural structures such as those found in the parietal and occipital lobes, particularly in the right hemisphere. To date, findings from research on this issue have been quite mixed. Goel and colleagues (e.g., Goel et al., 1998; Goel Chap. 20) have found significant activations for deductive reasoning to occur predominantly in the left hemisphere. Parsons and Osherson (2001) using a similar, but different, task of deductive reasoning, found that such tasks recruited resources predominantly from the right hemisphere.

Much research has been conducted to determine the cause of these different results and Goel (Chap. 20) provides a detailed account of recent research on the brain and deductive reasoning. One result regarding hemispheric differences important for studies of scientific thinking is that of Roser et al., (in press). They conducted experimental examinations of hemispheric differences in scientific causal thinking in a split-brain patient. They found that the patient's right hemisphere was uniquely able to detect causality in perceptually salient events (i.e., colliding balls), whereas his left hemisphere was uniquely able to infer causality based on a more complex, not directly perceivable, chain of events. These data add to our growing understanding of how the brain contains specialized neural structures that contribute to the interpretation of data obtained from the environment. The obvious experiments that need to be done would involve allowing scientists to think and reason naturally about their own theories versus theories from different domains while being imaged. This would allow one to decompose the effects of scientific thinking and familiarity. Clearly, research on the scientific brain is about to begin.

Computational Approaches to Scientific Thinking

Along with recent brain imaging studies, computational approaches have provided a more complete account of the scientific mind. Computational models provide specific detailed accounts of the cognitive processes underlying scientific thinking. Early computational work consisted of taking a scientific discovery and building computational models of the reasoning processes involved in the discovery. Langley et al. (1987) built a series of programs that simulated discoveries such as those of Copernicus and Stahl. These programs have various inductive reasoning algorithms built into them and, when given the data the scientists used, were able to propose the same rules. Computational models make it possible to propose detailed models of the cognitive subcomponents of scientific thinking that specify exactly how scientific theories are generated, tested, and amended (see Darden 1997; Shrager & Langley, 1990, for accounts of this branch of research). More recently, the incorporation of scientific knowledge into the computer programs resulted in a shift in emphasis from using programs to simulate discoveries to building programs that help scientists make discoveries. A number of these computer programs have made novel discoveries. For example, Valdes-Perez (1994) built systems for discoveries in chemistry, and Fajtlowicz has done this in mathematics (Erdos, Fajtlowicz, & Staton, 1991).

These advances in the fields of computer discovery have led to new fields, conferences, journals, and even departments that specialize in the development of programs devised to search large databases in the hope of making new scientific discoveries (Langley, 2000, 2002). This process is commonly known as "data mining." Not until relatively recently has this technique proven viable because of recent advances in computer technology. An even more recent development in the area of data mining is the use of distributed computer networks that take advantage of thousands, or even millions, of computers worldwide to jointly mine data in the hope of making significant scientific discoveries. This approach has shown much promise because of its relative cost effectiveness. The most powerful supercomputers currently cost over 100 million dollars, whereas a distributed network server may cost only tens of thousands of dollars for roughly the same computational power.

Another recent shift in the use of computers in scientific discovery is to have computers and people make discoveries together, rather than expecting computers to make an entire scientific discovery. Now, instead of using computers to mimic the entire scientific discovery process used by humans, computers can use powerful algorithms that search for patterns on large databases and provide the patterns to humans who can then use the output of these computers to make discoveries from the human genome to the structure of the universe.

Scientific Thinking and Science Education

Science education has undergone many changes over the past hundred years that mirrored wider changes in both education and society. In the early 1900s, science education was seen as a form of nature study – particularly in the kindergarten through eight grades. Each decade has seen a report on the need to improve science education. Starting in the 1930s, proponents of the progressive education movement began a movement that continues to this day. They argued that children should be taught more than just facts and should be taught methods and general principles, as well as ways in which science relate to the child's world. In 1938, a report by the Progressive Education Association noted that the psychology of the learner should be at the core of science education, as well as making a link to children's everyday lives. Various reports on science education appeared over the ensuing years, but it was the launch of the Sputnik satellite in 1957 that transformed science education in the United States. Seeing the Soviets launch a rocket before the United States galvanized the nation into training better scientists and identifying the brightest students. The net result for science education was that textbooks were updated, a factually based curriculum was maintained, and the notion of science as a voyage of discovery entered the popular imagination. By the 1980s, however, many cultural changes had occurred, and science students in the United States appeared to be falling behind those in other countries. Numerous reports by science teachers and scientists recommended widespread changes in the ways that science is taught. Most important in these changes was the move to a constructivist view of education. According to this view, students construct their knowledge rather than being the passive recipients of scientific knowledge (see also Ritchhart & Perkins, Chap. 32, on teaching thinking).

Beginning in the 1980s, a number of reports, often constructivist, stressed the need for teaching scientific thinking skills and not just methods and content. The addition of scientific thinking skills to the science curriculum from kindergarten through adulthood was a major shift in focus. Many of the particular scientific thinking skills emphasized were covered in previous sections of this chapter, such as deductive and inductive thinking strategies. Rather than focusing on one particular skill, such as induction, researchers in education have focused on how the different components of scientific thinking are put together in science. Furthermore, science educators have focused on situations in which science is conducted collaboratively, rather than being the product of one person thinking alone. These changes in science education parallel changes in methodologies used to investigate science, such as analyzing the ways that scientists think and reason in their laboratories.

By looking at science as a complex, multilayered, and group activity, many researchers in science education have adopted a constructivist approach. This approach sees learning as an active rather than a passive process and proposes that students learn through constructing their scientific knowledge. The goal of constructivist science education often is to produce conceptual change through guided instruction in which the teacher or professor acts as a guide to discovery rather than the keeper of all the facts. One recent and influential approach to science education is the inquiry-based learning approach. Inquiry-based learning focuses on posing a problem or a puzzling event to students and asking them to propose a hypothesis that can be used to explain the event. Next, students are asked to collect data that test the hypotheses, reach conclusions, and then reflect upon both the original problem and the thought processes they used to solve the problem. Students often use computers that aid in their construction of new knowledge. The computers allow students to learn many of the different components of scientific thinking. For example, Reiser and his colleagues have developed a learning environment for biology in which students are encouraged to develop hypotheses in groups, codify the hypotheses, and search databases to test them (Reiser et al., 2001).

One of the myths of science is the lone scientist toiling under a naked lightbulb, suddenly shouting "Eureka, I have made a discovery!" Instead, *InVivo* studies of scientists (e.g., Dunbar, 1995, 2002), historical analyses of scientific discoveries (Nersessian, 1999), and *InVivo* studies of children learning science at museums all point to collaborative scientific discovery mechanisms as being one of the driving forces of science (Crowley et al., 2001). What happens during collaborative scientific thinking is that there is usually a triggering event, such as an unexpected result or situation that a student does not understand. This results in other members of the group adding new information to the person's representation of knowledge, often adding new inductions and deductions that both challenge and transform the reasoner's old representations of knowledge (Dunbar, 1998). This means that social mechanisms play a key component in fostering changes in concepts that have been ignored in traditional cognitive research but are crucial for both science and science education. In science education, there has been a shift to collaborative learning, particularly at the elementary level, but in university education, the emphasis is still on the individual scientist. Because many domains of science now involve collaborations across scientific disciplines, we expect the explicit teaching of collaborative science heuristics to increase.

What is the best way to teach and learn science? Surprisingly, the answer to this question has been difficult to uncover. Although there has been considerable research on the benefits of using a particular way of learning science, few comparative studies of different methods have been conducted. Following Seymour Papert's book *MindStorms*, for example, (1980) many schools moved to discovery learning in which children discover aspects of programming and mathematics through writing their own computer programs in the LOGO programming language. This discovery learning approach, which thousands of schools have adopted, has been presented as an alternative to more didactic approaches to teaching and learning. By allowing students to discover principles on their own and to set their own goals, students are purported to have deeper knowledge that transfers more appropriately. Although there is much anecdotal evidence on the benefits of discovery learning, only recently has a direct comparison of discovery learning with more traditional methods been conducted. Klahr and Nigam (2004) conducted a study of third and fourth grade children learning about experimental design. They found that many more children learned from direct instruction than from discovery learning. Furthermore, they found that discovery learning children did not have richer or deeper knowledge than direct instruction children. This type of finding suggests that pure discovery learning, although intuitively appealing, benefits only a few children and that guided discovery coupled with explicit instruction is one of the most effective educational strategies in science.

Conclusions and Future Directions

Although much is known regarding certain components of scientific thinking, much remains to be discovered. In particular, there has been little contact among cognitive, neuroscience, social, personality, and motivational accounts of scientific thinking. Clearly, the relations among these different aspects of scientific thinking need to be combined to produce a comprehensive picture of the scientific mind. One way to achieve this is by using converging multiple methodologies as outlined previously, such as naturalistic observation, controlled experiments in the cognitive laboratory, and functional brain imaging techniques. Theoretical developments into the workings of the scientific mind would greatly benefit from more unconstrained analyses of the neuroanatomical correlates of the scientific reasoning process. We, as scientists, are beginning to get a reasonable grasp of the inner workings of the subcomponents of the scientific mind (i.e., problem solving, analogy, induction) and scientific thought. However, great advances remain to be made concerning how these processes interact so scientific discoveries can be made. Future research will focus on both the collaborative aspects of scientific thinking and the neural underpinnings of the scientific mind.

Acknowledgments

The authors would like to thank the following organizations: Dartmouth College, McGill University, The Spencer Foundation, The National Science Foundation, and the

Engineering Research Council of Canada for funding research discussed in this chapter. The comments of Keith Holyoak, Vimla Patel, and an anonymous reviewer were all helpful in making this a better chapter.

References

Ahn, W., Kalish, C. W., Medin, D. L., & Gelman, S. A. (1995). The role of covariation versus mechanism information in causal attribution, *Cognition*, 54, 299–352.

Azmitia, M. A. & Crowley, K. (2001). The rhythms of scientific thinking: A study of collaboration in an earthquake microworld. In K. Crowley, C. Schunn, & T. Okada (Eds.) *Designing for Science: Implications from Everyday, Classroom, and Professional Settings*. Mawah, NJ: Erlbaum.

Bacon, F. (1620/1854). *Novum Organum*. (B. Monatgue, Trans.). Philadelphia: Parry & McMillan.

Baker, L. M., & Dunbar, K. (2000). Experimental design heuristics for scientific discovery: The use of baseline and known controls. *International Journal of Human Computer Studies*, 53, 335–349.

Bruner, J. S., Goodnow, J. J., & Austin, G. A. (1956). *A Study of Thinking*. New York: Science Editions.

Carey, S. (1985). *Conceptual Change in Childhood*. Cambridge, MA: MIT Press.

Carruthers, P., Stich, S., & Siegal, M. (2002). *The Cognitive Basis of Science*. New York: Cambridge University Press.

Chi, M. (1992). Conceptual change within and across ontological categories: Examples from learning and discovery in science. In R. Giere (Ed.), *Cognitive Models of Science*. Minneapolis: University of Minnesota Press.

Chi, M. T. H., & Roscoe, R. D. (2002). The processes and challenges of conceptual change. In M. Limon, & L. Mason (Eds.), *Reconsidering Conceptual Change: Issues in Theory and Practice* (pp 3–27). The Netherlands: Kluwer Academic Publishers.

Clement, J. (1982). Students' preconceptions in introductory mechanics. *American Journal of Physics*, 50, 66–71.

Colvin, M. K., Dunbar, K., & Grafman, J. (2001). The effects of frontal lobe lesions on goal achievement in the water jug task. *Journal of Cognitive Neuroscience*, 13, 1129–1147.

Darden, L. (1997). Strategies for discovering mechanisms: Schema instantiation, modular subassembly, forward chaining/backtracking. *Proceedings of the 1997 Biennial Meeting of the Philosophy of Science Association*.

Dunbar, K. (1995). How scientists really reason: Scientific reasoning in real-world laboratories. In R. J. Sternberg, & J. Davidson (Eds.), *Mechanisms of Insight*. Cambridge, MA: MIT Press.

Dunbar, K. (1997). How scientists think: Online creativity and conceptual change in science. In T. B. Ward, S. M. Smith, & S. Vaid (Eds.), *Conceptual Structures and Processes: Emergence, Discovery and Change*. Washington, DC: APA Press.

Dunbar, K. (1998). Problem solving. In W. Bechtel, & G. Graham (Eds.). *A Companion to Cognitive Science*. London, UK: Blackwell.

Dunbar, K. (1999). The scientist *InVivo*: How scientists think and reason in the laboratory. In L. Magnani, N. Nersessian, & P. Thagard (Eds.), *Model-based Reasoning in Scientific Discovery*. New York Plenum.

Dunbar, K. (2001). The analogical paradox: Why analogy is so easy in naturalistic settings, yet so difficult in the psychology laboratory. In D. Gentner, K. J. Holyoak, & B. Kokinov, *Analogy: Perspectives from Cognitive Science*. Cambridge, MA: MIT Press.

Dunbar, K. & Blanchette, I. (2001). The invivo/invitro approach to cognition: the case of analogy. *Trends in Cognitive Sciences*, 5, 334–339.

Dunbar, K. (2002). Science as category: Implications of *InVivo* science for theories of cognitive development, scientific discovery, and the nature of science. In P. Caruthers, S. Stich, & M. Siegel (Eds.), *Cognitive Models of Science*. New York: Cambridge University Press.

Dunbar, K., & Fugelsang, J. (2004). Causal thinking in science: How scientists and students interpret the unexpected. To appear in M. E. Gorman, A. Kincannon, D. Gooding, & R. D. Tweney (Eds.), *New Directions in Scientific and Technical Thinking*. Hillsdale, NJ: Erlbaum.

Dunbar, K. & Sussman, D. (1995). Toward a cognitive account of frontal lobe function: Simulating frontal lobe deficits in normal subjects. *Annals of the New York Academy of Sciences*, 769, 289–304.

Erdos, P., Fajtlowicz, S., & Staton, W. (1991). Degree sequences in the triangle-free graphs. *Discrete Mathematics*, 92 (91), 85–88.

Fincham, J. M., Carter, C. S., van Veen, V., Stenger, V. A., & Anderson, J. R. (2002). Neural mechanisms of planning: A computational analysis using event-related fMRI. *Proclamations of the National Academy of Science*, 99, 3346–3351.

Fischler, H., & Lichtfeldt, M. (1992). Modern physics and students conceptions. *International Journal of Science Education*, 14, 181–190.

Fox-Keller, E. (1985). *Reflections on Gender and Science*. New Haven, CT: Yale University Press.

Fugelsang, J., & Dunbar, K. (submitted). *How the brain uses theory to interpret data*.

Fugelsang, J., & Dunbar, K. (in preparation). *How the brain learns physics*.

Fugelsang, J., Stein, C., Green, A., & Dunbar, K. (2004). Theory and data interactions of the scientific mind: Evidence from the molecular and the cognitive laboratory. *Canadian Journal of Experimental Psychology*, 58, 132–141.

Galilei, G. (1638/1991). A. de Salvio, & H. Crew trans. *Dialogues Concerning Two New Sciences*. Amherst, NY: Prometheus Books.

Galison, P. (2003). *Einstein's Clocks, Poincaré's Maps: Empires of Time*. New York, NY: W. W. Norton.

Gentner, D., Brem, S., Ferguson, R. W., Markman, A. B., Levidow, B. B., Wolff, P., et al. (1997). Analogical reasoning and conceptual change: A case study of Johannes Kepler. *The Journal of the Learning Sciences*, 6(1), 3–40.

Gentner, D., Holyoak, K. J., & Kokinov, B. (2001). *The Analogical Mind: Perspectives from Cognitive Science*. Cambridge, MA: MIT Press.

Gentner, D., & Jeziorski, M. (1993). The shift from metaphor to analogy in western science. In A. Ortony (Ed.), *Metaphor and Thought* (2nd ed., pp. 447–480). Cambridge, England: Cambridge University Press.

Giere, R. (1993). *Cognitive Models of Science*. Minneapolis, MN: University of Minnesota Press.

Goel, V., & Dolan, R. J. (2000). Anatomical segregation of component processes in an inductive inference task. *Journal of Cognitive Neuroscience*, 12, 110–119.

Goel, V., Gold, B., Kapur, S., & Houle, S. (1998). Neuroanatomical correlates of human reasoning. *Journal of Cognitive Neuroscience*, 10, 293–302.

Goel, V., & Grafman, J. (1995). Are the frontal lobes implicated in "planning" functions? Interpreting data from the Tower of Hanoi. *Neuropsychologia*, 33, 623–642.

Gorman, M. E. (1989). Error, falsification and scientific inference: An experimental investigation. *Quarterly Journal of Experimental Psychology: Human Experimental Psychology*, 41A, 385–412.

Gorman, M. E., Kincannon, A., Gooding, D., & Tweney, R. D. (2004). *New Directions in Scientific and Technical Thinking*. Lawrence Erlbaum. Hillsdale, NJ.

Heit, E. (2000). Properties of inductive reasoning. *Psychonomic Bulletin & Review*, 7, 569–592.

Hirschberg, C. (2003). My mother, the scientist. In R. Dawkins, & T. Folger (Eds.), *The Best American Science and Nature Writing 2003*. New York: Houghton Mifflin.

Holyoak, K. J., & Thagard, P. (1995). *Mental Leaps*. Cambridge, MA: MIT Press.

Keil, F. C. (1999). Conceptual change. In R. Wilson., & F. Keil (Eds.) *The MIT Encyclopedia of Cognitive Science*, Cambridge, MA: MIT press.

Klahr, D. (2000). *Exploring Science: The Cognition and Development of Discovery Processes*. Cambridge, MA: MIT Press.

Klahr, D., & Dunbar, K. (1988). Dual space search during scientific reasoning. *Cognitive Science*, 12, 1–48.

Klahr, D., & Nigam, M. (2004). The equivalence of learning paths in early science instruction: Effects of direct instruction and discovery learning *Psychological Science*, 15, 661–667.

Klahr, D., & Simon, H. (1999). Studies of scientific discovery: Complementary approaches and convergent findings. *Psychological Bulletin*, 125, 524–543.

Klayman, J., & Ha, Y. (1987). Confirmation, disconfirmation, and information in hypothesis testing. *Psychological Review*, 94, 211–228.

Kozhevnikov, M., & Hegarty, M. (2001). Impetus beliefs as default heuristic: Dissociation between explicit and implicit knowledge about motion. *Psychonomic Bulletin and Review*, 8, 439–453.

Kroger, J. K., Sabb, F. W., Fales, C. L., Bookheimer, S. Y., Cohen, M. S., & Holyoak, K. J. (2002). Recruitment of anterior dorsolateral prefrontal cortex in human reasoning: A parametric study of relational complexity. *Cerebral Cortex*, 12, 477–485.

Kuhn, T. (1962). *The Structure of Scientific Revolutions*. Chicago: University of Chicago Press.

Kulkarni, D., & Simon, H. A. (1988). The processes of scientific discovery: The strategy of experimentation. *Cognitive Science, 12*, 139–176.

Langley, P. (2000). Computational support of scientific discovery. *International Journal of Human-Computer Studies, 53*, 393–410.

Langley, P. (2002). Lessons for the computational discovery of scientific knowledge. In the *Proceedings of the First International Workshop on Data Mining Lessons Learned.*

Langley, P., Simon, H. A., Bradshaw, G. L., & Zytkow, J. M. (1987). *Scientific Discovery: Computational Explorations of the Creative Processes*. Cambridge, MA: MIT Press.

McCloskey, M., Caramazza, A., & Green, B. (1980). Curvilinear motion in the absence of external forces: Naive beliefs about the motion of objects. *Science, 210*, 1139–1141.

McDermott, L. C., & Redish, L. (1999). Research letter on physics education research. *American Journal of Psychics, 67*, 755.

Mestre, J. P. (1991). Learning and instruction in pre-college physical science. *Physics Today, 44*, 56–62.

Mitroff, I. (1974). *The Subjective Side of Science*. Amsterdam: Elsevier.

Nersessian, N. (1998). Conceptual change. In W. Bechtel, & G. Graham (Eds.). *A Companion to Cognitive Science*. London, UK: Blackwell.

Nersessian, N. (1999). Models, mental models, and representations: Model-based reasoning in conceptual change. In L. Magnani, N. Nersessian, & P. Thagard (Eds.). *Model-based Reasoning in Scientific Discovery*. New York: Plenum.

Nersessian, N. J. (2002). The cognitive basis of model-based reasoning in science In P. Carruthers, S. Stich, & M. Siegal (Eds). *The Cognitive Basis of Science*. New York: Cambridge University Press.

Newton, I. (1736). *Method of Fluxions and Infinite Series; with its Application to the Geometry of Curve Lines*. Frontispiece in Bodleian Library.

Newell, A., & Simon, H. A. (1972). *Human Problem Solving.* Oxford, UK: Prentice-Hall.

Osherson, D., Perani, D., Cappa, S., Schnur, T., Grassi, F., & Fazio, F. (1998). Distinct brain loci in deductive versus probabilistic reasoning. *Neuropsychologia, 36*, 369–376.

Papert, S. (1980). *Mindstorms: Children Computers and Powerful ideas*. New York: Basic Books.

Parsons, L. M., & Osherson, D. (2001). New evidence for distinct right and left brain systems for deductive versus probabilistic reasoning. *Cerebral Cortex, 11*, 954–965.

Penner, D. E., & Klahr, D. (1996). When to trust the data: Further investigations of system error in a scientific reasoning task. *Memory and Cognition*, 24(5), 655–668.

Popper, K. R. (1959). *The Logic of Scientific Discovery*. London, UK: Hutchinson.

Qin, Y., & Simon, H. A. (1990). Laboratory replication of scientific discovery processes. *Cognitive Science, 14*, 281–312.

Reiser, B. J., Tabak, I., Sandoval, W. A., Smith, B., Steinmuller, F., & Leone, T. J., (2001). BGuILE: Stategic and conceptual scaffolds for scientific inquiry in biology classrooms. In S. M. Carver, & D. Klahr (Eds.). *Cognition and Instruction: Twenty Five Years of Progress*. Mahwah, NJ: Erlbaum.

Roser, M., Fugelsang, J., Dunbar, K., Corballis, P., & Gazzaniga, M. (Submitted). *Causality perception and inference in the split-brain.*

Schunn, C. D., & Klahr, D. (1995). A 4-space model of scientific discovery. In the *Proceedings of the 17th Annual Conference of the Cognitive Science Society*. Pittsburgh, PA.

Schunn, C. D., & Klahr, D. (1996). The problem of problem spaces: When and how to go beyond a 2-space model of scientific discovery. Part of symposium on building a theory of problem solving and scientific discovery: How big is N in N-space search? In the *Proceedings of the 18th Annual Conference of the Cognitive Science Society*. San Diego, CA.

Seger, C., Poldrack, R., Prabhakaran, V., Zhao, M., Glover, G., & Gabrieli, J. (2000). Hemispheric asymmetries and individual differences in visual concept learning as measured by functional MRI. *Neuropsychologia, 38*, 1316–1324.

Shrager, J., & Langley, P. (1990). *Computational Models of Scientific Discovery and Theory Formation*. San Mateo, CA: Morgan Kaufmann.

Simon, H. A. (1977). *Models of Discovery*. Dordrecht, The Netherlands: D. Reidel.

Simon, H. A., & Lea, G. (1974). Problem solving and rule induction. In H. Simon (Ed.), *Models of Thought* (pp. 329 – 346). New Haven, CT: Yale University Press.

Smith, E. E., Shafir, E., & Osherson, D. (1993). Similarity, plausibility, and judgments of probability. *Cognition. Special Issue: Reasoning and Decision Making*, 49, 67–96.

Thagard, P. (1992). *Conceptual Revolutions*. Cambridge, MA: MIT Press.

Thagard, P. (1999). *How Scientists Explain Disease*. Princeton: Princeton University Press.

Thagard, P., & Croft, D. (1999). Scientific discovery and technological innovation: Ulcers, dinosaur extinction, and the programming language Java. In L. Magnani, N. Nersessian, & P. Thagard (Eds.). *Model-based Reasoning in Scientific Discovery*. New York: Plenum.

Tweney, R. D. (1989). A framework for the cognitive psychology of science. In B. Gholson, A. Houts, R. A. Neimeyer, & W. Shadish (Eds.), *Psychology of Science and Metascience*. Cambridge, MA: Cambridge University Press.

Tweney, R. D., Doherty, M. E., & Mynatt, C. R. (1981). *On Scientific Thinking*. New York: Columbia University Press.

Valdes-Perez, R. E. (1994). Conjecturing hidden entities via simplicity and conservation laws: Machine discovery in chemistry. *Artificial Intelligence*, 65(2), 247–280.

Wason, P. C. (1968). Reasoning about a rule. *Quarterly Journal of Experimental Psychology*, 20, 273–281.

Wertheimer, M. (1945). *Productive Thinking*. New York: Harper.

Wharton, C., & Grafman, J. (1998). Reasoning and the human brain. *Trends in Cognitive Science*. 2, 54–59.

Wharton, C. M., Grafman, J., Flitman, S. S., Hansen, E. K., Brauner, J., Marks, A., et al. (2000). Toward neuroanatomical models of analogy: A positron emission tomography study of analogical mapping. *Cognitive Psychology*, 40, 173–197.

CHAPTER 30

Thinking and Reasoning in Medicine

Vimla L. Patel
José F. Arocha
Jiajie Zhang

What Is Medical Reasoning?

Medical reasoning describes a form of qualitative inquiry that examines the cognitive (thought) processes involved in making medical decisions. Clinical reasoning, medical problem solving, diagnostic reasoning, and decision making are all terms used in a growing body of literature that examines how clinicians make clinical decisions. Medical cognition refers to studies of cognitive processes, such as perception, comprehension, decision making (see LeBoeuf & Shafir, Chap. 11), and problem solving (see Novick & Bassok, Chap. 14) in medical practice itself or in tasks representative of medical practice. These studies use subjects who work in medicine, including medical students, physicians, and biomedical scientists. The study of medical reasoning has been the focus of much research in cognitive science and artificial intelligence in medicine. Medical reasoning involves an inferential process for making diagnostic or therapeutic decisions or understanding the pathology of a disease process. On the one hand, medical reasoning is basic to all higher-level cognitive processes in medicine such as problem solving and medical text comprehension. On the other hand, the structure of medical reasoning itself is the subject of considerable scrutiny. For example, the directionality of reasoning in medicine has been an issue of considerable controversy in medical cognition, medical education, and artificial intelligence (AI) in medicine. Conventionally, we can partition medical reasoning into clinical and biomedical or basic science reasoning. These are some of the central themes that constitute this chapter.

Early Research on Medical Problem Solving and Reasoning

Medical cognition is a subfield of cognitive science devoted to the study of cognitive processes in medical tasks. Studies of medical cognition include analyses of performance in "real world" clinical tasks as well as in experimental tasks. Understanding the thought processes involved in clinical reasoning in order to promote more effective practices has been the subject of concern for nearly a century (Osler, 1906).

Human information processing research typically has focused on the individual. The dual focus on in-depth task analysis and on the study of human performance is a central feature of a cognitive science approach.

There have been two primary approaches to research investigating clinical reasoning in medicine – the decision – analytic approach and the information-processing or problem-solving approach. Decision analysis uses a formal quantitative model of inference and decision making as the standard of comparison (Dowie & Elstein, 1988). It compares the performance of a physician with the mathematical model by focusing on reasoning "fallacies" and biases inherent in human clinical decision making (Leaper et al., 1972). In contrast, the information-processing approach focuses on the description of cognitive processes in reasoning tasks and the development of cognitive models of performance, typically relying on protocol analysis (Ericsson and Simon, 1993) and other observational techniques.

Systematic investigations of medical expertise began more than forty years ago with the research by Ledley and Lusted (1959) on clinical inquiries. They proposed a two-stage model of clinical reasoning involving a hypothesis-generation stage followed by a hypothesis-evaluation stage in which the latter stage was amenable to formal decision analytic techniques. Probably the earliest empirical studies of medical reasoning can be traced to the work of Rimoldi (1961), who conducted experimental studies of diagnostic reasoning contrasting students with medical experts in simulated problem-solving tasks. The results emphasized the greater ability of expert physicians to selectively attend to relevant information and to narrow the set of diagnostic possibilities (i.e., consider fewer hypotheses). As cognitive science came into prominence in the early 1970s spearheaded by the immensely influential work of Newell and Simon (1972) on problem solving, research in information-processing psychology accelerated dramatically. Problem solving was conceived of as a search in a problem space in which a problem solver was viewed as selecting an option (e.g., a hypothesis or an inference) or performing an operation (from a set of possible operations) in moving toward a solution or a goal state (e.g., diagnosis or treatment plan). (See Novick & Bassok, Chap. 14, for a discussion of problem solving.) This conceptualization had an enormous impact in both cognitive psychology and artificial intelligence research. It also led to rapid advances in medical reasoning and problem-solving research, as exemplified by the seminal work of Elstein, Shulman, & Sprafka (1978). They were the first to use experimental methods and theories of cognitive science to investigate clinical competency. Their extensive empirical research led to the development of an elaborated model of hypothetico-deductive reasoning, which proposed that physicians reason by first generating and then testing a set of hypotheses to account for clinical data (i.e., reasoning from hypothesis to data). This model of problem solving had a substantial influence on studies of both medical cognition and medical education.

In the late 1970s and early 1980s, advances into the nature of human expertise were paralleled by developments in medical AI – particularly expert systems technology. Artificial intelligence in medicine and medical cognition mutually influenced each other in a number of ways, including (1) providing a basis for developing formal models of competence in problem-solving tasks, (2) elucidating the structure of medical knowledge and providing important epistemological distinctions, and (3) characterizing productive and less-productive lines of reasoning in diagnostic and therapeutic tasks. Gorry (1973) conducted a series of studies comparing a computational model of medical problem solving with the actual problem-solving behavior of physicians. This analysis provided a basis for characterizing a sequential process of medical decision-making – one that differs in important respects from early diagnostic computational systems based on Bayes' theorem. Pauker and colleagues (1976) capitalized on some of the insights of Gorry's earlier work and developed the Present Illness Program, a program designed to take the history of a patient with edema. Several of the questions guiding this research, including the nature and organization of expert knowledge, were of central concern to both developers of medical expert systems and researchers in medical cognition. The development and refinement of the program was partially based on studies of clinical problem solving.

Medical expert consultation systems such as Internist (Miller, Pople, & Myers, 1984) and MYCIN (Shortliffe, 1976) introduced the ideas about knowledge-based reasoning strategies across a range of cognitive tasks. MYCIN, in particular, had a substantial influence on cognitive science. It contributed several advances (e.g., representing reasoning under uncertainty) in the use of production systems as a representation scheme in a complex knowledge-based domain. MYCIN also highlighted the difference between medical problem solving and the cognitive dimensions of medical explanation. Clancey's work (Clancey & Lefsinger, 1984, 1985) in GUIDON and NEOMYCIN was particularly influential in the evolution of models of medical cognition. Clancey endeavored to reconfigure MYCIN to employ the system to teach medical students about meningitis and related disorders. NEOMYCIN was based on a more psychologically plausible model of medical diagnosis. This model differentiated data-directed and hypothesis-directed reasoning and separated control knowledge from the facts upon which it operates.

Feltovich and colleagues (Feltovich et al., 1984), drawing on models of knowledge representation from medical AI, characterized fine-grained differences in knowledge organization between subjects with different levels of expertise in the domain of pediatric cardiology. These differences accounted for subjects' inferences about diagnostic cues and evaluation of competing hypotheses. Patel and Groen (1986), incorporating distinctions introduced by Clancey, studied the knowledge-based solution strategies of expert cardiologists as evidenced by their pathophysiological explanations of a complex clinical problem. The results indicated that subjects who accurately diagnosed the problem employed a forward-oriented reasoning strategy – using patient data to lead toward a complete diagnosis (i.e., reasoning from data to hypothesis). In contrast, subjects who misdiagnosed or partially diagnosed the patient problem used a backward reasoning strategy. These research findings presented a challenge to the hypothetico-deductive model of reasoning as espoused by Elstein, Shulman, & Sprafka (1978), which did not differentiate expert from nonexpert reasoning strategies.

Much of the early research in the study of reasoning in domains such as medicine was carried out in laboratory or experimental settings. In more recent times, a shift occurred toward examining cognitive issues in naturalistic medical settings, such as medical teams in intensive care units (Patel, Kaufman, & Magder, 1996), anesthesiologists working in surgery (Gaba, 1992), nurses providing emergency telephone triage (Leprohon & Patel, 1995), and reasoning with technology by patients in the health care system (Patel et al., 2002). This research was informed by work in the area of dynamic decision making (Salas & Klein, 2001), complex problem solving (Frensch & Funke, 1995), human factors (Hoffman & Deffenbacher, 1993; Vicente & Rasmussen, 1990), and cognitive engineering (Rasmussen, Pejtersen, & Goodstein, 1994). Such studies, conducted in the workplace, reshaped our views of human thinking by shifting the onus of cognition from being the unique province of the individual to being distributed across social and technological contexts.

Models of Medical Reasoning

The traditional view of medical reasoning has been to treat diagnosis as similar to the scientist's task of making a discovery or engaging in scientific experimentation (see

Dunbar & Fugelsang, Chap. 29). Coherent with this view of science is the assumption that diagnostic inference follows a hypothetico-deductive process of reaching conclusions by testing hypothesis based on clinical evidence. From a cognitive perspective, as we saw previously, this view of the diagnostic process in medicine was first proposed in the influential work of Elstein, Shulman, and Sprafka (1978). The view of medical reasoning as hypothetico-deductive has been challenged from various points, empirical research, and philosophical discourse, as we will see in the following section.

Toward a Model of Reasoning in Medicine: Induction, Deduction, and Abduction

It generally is agreed that there are two basic forms of reasoning. One is deductive reasoning (see Evans, Chap. 8), which consists of deriving a particular valid conclusion from a set of general premises, and the other is inductive reasoning (see Sloman & Lagnado, Chap. 5), which consists of deriving a likely general conclusion from a set of particular statements. However, reasoning in the "real world" does not appear to fit neatly into these basic types. For this reason, a third form of reasoning has been recognized in which deduction and induction are combined. This was termed *abductive reasoning* by Peirce (1955).

Basically, all theories of medical reasoning characterize diagnosis as an abductive, cyclical process of generating possible explanations (i.e., identification of a set of hypotheses that are able to account for the clinical case on the basis of the available data) and testing those explanations (i.e., evaluation of each generated hypothesis on the basis of its expected consequences) for the abnormal state of the patient at hand (Elstein, Shulman, & Sprafka, 1978; Kassirer, 1989; Joseph & Patel, 1990; Ramoni et al., 1992). Traditional accounts of medical reasoning described the diagnostic process in a way that is independent of the underlying structure of the domain knowledge. These accounts simply make the assumption that some domain of knowledge exists and that all of the hypotheses needed to explain a problem are available when the diagnostic process begins.

Within this generic framework, various models of diagnostic reasoning may be constructed. Following Patel and Ramoni (1997), we could distinguish between two major models of diagnostic reasoning: *heuristic classification* (Clancey, 1985) and *cover and differentiate* (Eshelman, 1988). However, these models can be seen as special cases of a more general model: the *select and test* model, in which the processes of hypothesis generation and testing can be characterized in terms of four types of inferences (Peirce, 1955) – abstraction, abduction, deduction, and induction. The first two inference types drive hypothesis generation whereas the latter two types drive hypothesis testing. During *abstraction*, data are filtered according to their relevance for the problem solution and chunked in schemas representing an abstract description of the problem at hand (e.g., abstracting that an adult male with hemoglobin concentration less than 14 d/gl is an anemic patient). Following this, hypotheses that could account for the current situation are related through a process of *abduction* characterized by a "backward flow" of inferences across a chain of directed relations that identify initial conditions from which the current abstract representation of the problem originates. This provides tentative solutions to the problem at hand by way of hypotheses. For example, knowing that disease *A* will cause symptom *b*, abduction will try to identify the explanation for *b*, and deduction will forecast that a patient affected by disease *A* will manifest symptom *b*: Both inferences are using the same relation along two different directions. These three types of reasoning in medicine are described in a paper by Patel and Ramoni (1997).

In the testing phase, hypotheses are tested incrementally according to their ability to account for the whole problem, and *deduction* serves to build up the possible world described by the consequences of each hypothesis. This kind of reasoning is customarily regarded as a common way to evaluate diagnostic hypotheses (Kassirer, 1989; Patel, Evans, & Kaufman, 1989; Joseph & Patel, 1990; Patel, Arocha, & Kaufman, 1994, 2001). As predictions are derived from hypotheses, they are matched to the case through a process of *induction* in which a prediction generated from a hypothesis can be matched with one specific aspect of the patient problem. The major feature of induction, therefore, is the ability to rule out hypotheses, the expected consequences of which turn out to be not in agreement with the patient's problem. This is because there is no way to logically confirm a hypothesis, but we can only disconfirm or refute it in the presence of contrary evidence. This evaluation process closes the testing phase of the diagnostic cycle. Moreover, it determines which information is needed to discriminate among hypotheses and, therefore, which information has to be collected.

Hypothesis Testing and Clinical Reasoning

Although a model such as the one just presented can be used to account for a large part of the medical diagnostic process, empirical literature points to various strategies of diagnostic reasoning that underscore the relative importance of deduction, induction, or abduction. In their seminal work, Elstein and colleagues (1978) studied the problem-solving processes of physicians by drawing on then-contemporary methods and theories of cognition. Their view of problem solving had a substantial influence on both studies of medical reasoning and medical education. They were the first to use experimental methods and theories of cognitive science to investigate clinical competency. Their research findings led to the development of an elaborated model of hypothetico-deductive reasoning, which proposed that physicians reasoned by first generating and then testing a set of hypotheses to account for clinical data (i.e., reasoning from hypothesis to data). Physicians first generated a small set of hypotheses very early in the case, as soon as the first pieces of data became available. Second, they were selective in the data they collected, focusing only on the relevant data. Third, physicians made use of the hypothetico-deductive process, which consists of four stages – cue acquisition, hypothesis generation, cue interpretation, and hypothesis evaluation. Cues in the clinical case led to the generation of a few selected hypotheses, and each cue was interpreted as positive, negative, or noncontributory to each hypothesis generated. Then each hypothesis was evaluated for consistency with the cues. Using this framework, these investigators were unable to find differences between superior physicians (as judged by their peers) and other physicians (Elstein, Shulman, & Sprafka, 1978).

Forward-Driven and Backward-Driven Reasoning

Later, Patel and Groen (1986) studied knowledge-based solution strategies of expert cardiologists as evidenced by their pathophysiological explanations of a complex clinical problem. The results indicated that subjects who accurately diagnosed the problem employed a forward-oriented (data-driven) reasoning strategy – using patient data to lead toward a complete diagnosis (i.e., reasoning from data to hypothesis). This was in contrast to subjects who misdiagnosed or partially diagnosed the patient problem, who tended to use a backward or hypothesis-driven reasoning strategy. The results of this study presented a challenge to the hypothetico-deductive model of reasoning as espoused by Elstein and colleagues (1978), which did not differentiate expert from nonexpert reasoning strategies.

A hypothesis for reconciling these seemingly contradictory results is that forward reasoning is used in clinical problems in which the physician has ample experience. When reasoning through unfamiliar or difficult cases, however, physicians resort to backward reasoning because their knowledge base does not support a pattern-matching process. To support this explanation, Patel, Groen, and Arocha (1990) looked for the conditions under which forward reasoning breaks down. Cardiologists and endocrinologists were asked to solve diagnostic problems in both fields. They showed that under conditions of case complexity and uncertainty, the pattern of forward reasoning was disrupted. More specifically, the breakdown occurred when nonsalient cues in the case were tested for consistency against the main hypothesis, even in subjects who had generated the correct diagnosis. Otherwise, the results supported previous studies in that subjects with accurate diagnoses used pure forward reasoning.

If forward reasoning breaks down when case complexity is introduced, then experts and novices should reason differently because routine cases for experts would not be so for less-than-expert subjects. Investigating clinical reasoning in a range of contexts of varying complexity (Patel & Groen, 1991; Patel, Arocha, Kaufman, 1994), the authors found that novices and experts have different patterns of data-driven and hypothesis-driven reasoning. As before, experts used data-driven reasoning, which depends on the physician's possessing a highly organized knowledge base about the patient's disease, including sets of signs and symptoms. Furthermore, because of their extensive knowledge base and the high-level inferences they make, experts typically skip steps in their reasoning. In contrast, because of their lack of substantive knowledge or their inability to distinguish relevant from irrelevant knowledge, less-than-expert subjects (novices and intermediates) used more hypothesis-driven reasoning, resulting often in very complex reasoning patterns. Similar patterns of reasoning have been found in other domains (Larkin et al., 1980).

The fact that experts and novices reason differently suggests that they might reach different conclusions (e.g., decisions or understandings) when solving medical problems. Although data-driven reasoning is highly efficient, it often is error prone in the absence of adequate domain knowledge because there are no built-in checks on the legitimacy of the inferences that a person makes. Pure data-driven reasoning is successful only in constrained situations in which one's knowledge of a problem can result in a complete chain of inferences from the initial problem statement to the problem solution. In contrast, hypothesis-driven reasoning is slower and requires high memory load, because one has to keep track of goals and hypotheses. It therefore is most likely to be used when domain knowledge is inadequate or the problem is complex. Hypothesis-driven reasoning is an exemplar of a weak method of problem solving in the sense that it is used in the absence of relevant prior knowledge and when there is uncertainty about problem solution. In problem-solving terms, strong methods engage knowledge, whereas weak methods refer to general strategies. Weak does not necessarily imply ineffectual in this context.

Studies also showed that data-driven reasoning can break down because of uncertainty (Patel, Groen, & Arocha, 1990). These conditions include the presence of "loose ends" in explanations in which some piece of information remains unaccounted for and isolated from the overall explanation. Loose ends trigger explanatory processes that work by hypothesizing a disease, for instance, and trying to fit the loose ends within it in a hypothesis-driven reasoning fashion. The presence of loose ends may foster learning as the person searches for an explanation for them. A medical student or a physician may encounter a sign or a symptom in a patient problem, for instance, and look for information that may account for the finding by searching for similar cases seen in the past, reading a specialized medical book, or consulting a domain expert. (See Chi & Ohlsson, Chap. 16, for a discussion of such complex forms of learning.)

In some circumstances, however, the use of data-driven reasoning may lead to a heavy cognitive load. When students are given problems to solve while they are being trained in the use of problem-solving strategies, for instance, the situation produces a heavy load on cognitive resources, which may diminish students' ability to focus on the task. The reason is that students have to share cognitive resources (e.g., attention, memory) between learning the problem-solving method and learning the content of the material. Research (Sweller, 1988) suggests that when subjects use a strategy based on data-driven reasoning, they are more able to acquire a schema for the problem. In addition, other characteristics associated with expert performance were observed, such as a reduced number of moves to the solution. When subjects used a hypothesis-driven reasoning strategy, their problem-solving performance suffered. The study of medical reasoning has been summarized in a series of articles (e.g. Patel et al., 1994; Patel, Kaufman, & Arocha, 2002) and papers in edited volumes (Clancey & Shortliffe, 1984; Szolovits, 1982).

The Role of Similarity in Diagnostic Reasoning

The fact that physicians make use of forward reasoning in routine cases suggests a type of processing that is fast enough to be able to lead to the recognition of a set of signs and symptoms in a patient and generate a diagnosis based on such recognition. Most often this has been interpreted as a type of specific-to-general reasoning (e.g., reasoning from an individual case to a clinical schema or prototype). However, consistent with the model of abductive reasoning, some philosophers (Schaffner, 1986) and empirical researchers (Norman & Brooks, 1997) have supported an alternative hypothesis that consists of specific-to-specific reasoning. That is, experts also use knowledge of specific instances (e.g., particular patients with specific disease presentations) to interpret particular cases, rather than relying only on general clinical knowledge (Kassirer & Kopelman, 1990).

Brooks and colleagues (Brooks, Norman, & Allen, 1991; Norman & Brooks, 1997) argued that clinicians make use of specific instances to compare and interpret a current clinical case. In such studies, mainly involving visual diagnosis – based on data sources such as radiographs, dermatological slides, and electrocardiograms – specific similarity to previous cases accounts for about 30% of diagnoses made (see Goldstone & Son, Chap. 2; Medin & Rips, Chap. 3). Furthermore, errors made by experts in identifying abnormalities in images are affected by the prior history of the patient. That is, if the prior history of the patient mentioned a possible abnormality, expert physicians more often identified abnormalities in the images even when none existed, which also supports the effect of specific past cases on the interpretation of a current case.

In pursuing their explanation, Norman and colleagues (Norman and Brooks, 1997) argued against the hypothesis that expert physicians diagnose clinical cases by "analyzing" signs and symptoms and developing correspondences among those signs, symptoms, and diagnoses, as traditional cognitive research in medical reasoning suggests. They suggest instead the "nonanalytic" basis for medical diagnosis, in which diagnostic reasoning is characterized by the unanalyzed retrieval of a similar case previously seen in medical practice to interpret the current case – a kind of exemplar-based or case-based reasoning. This discussion has its counterpart in the psychology of categorization, in which two accounts have been proposed – categorization works either by a reliance on prototypes or by exemplars (Medin & Rips, Chap. 3).

Exemplar-based thinking is certainly a fundamental aspect of human cognition. There is ample evidence of the conditions under which reasoning by analogy to previous cases is used (Gentner & Holyoak, 1997; Holyoak & Thagard, 1997; see Holyoak, Chap. 6). Furthermore, given the complexity of natural reasoning in a highly dense knowledge domain such as medicine, it is highly likely that more than one type of reasoning is actually employed. Seen in this light, the search for a single manner in which clinicians diagnose clinical problems may not be a reasonable goal. The inherent adaptability of humans to different kinds of knowledge domains, situations, problems, and cases may call for the use of a variety of reasoning strategies, which is what, after all, the notion of abductive medical reasoning tries to formalize (Patel & Ramoni, 1997). Alongside rule-based and prototype reasoning, a model of clinical reasoning may allow for case-based, nonanalytical reasoning, in which recognizing similarity between particulars may be the main cognitive mechanism. A reason for the variety of strategies used in actual diagnostic problems may be found in the inherent organization of medical knowledge.

Reasoning and the Nature of Medical Knowledge

Although a motivation for looking at medical reasoning was to establish its relationship with reasoning in other fields, such as science, the prevalent view in the philosophy of medicine (Blois, 1990) has been that medical knowledge has an extremely complex organization, requiring the use of different reasoning strategies than those used in other more formal scientific disciplines, such as physics. Disciplines such as physics, chemistry, and some subfields of biology, are said to be horizontally organized, which means these domains are characterized by the construction of causal relations among concepts and by the application of general principles to specific instances (Blois, 1990). By this, it is meant that such scientific fields are organized in a hypothetico-deductive manner in which particular statements are generated from general statements and causality plays a major role. This type of reasoning, in which one connects one concept to another by forming causal networks, has been called *horizontal* reasoning (Blois, 1990). These philosophers argued that causal reasoning does not play such an important role in the medical domain. They argue, instead, that reasoning in medicine requires *vertical* thinking. This kind of reasoning makes more use of the analogy than the reasoning typically found in other scientific domains. In this view, the medical disciplines, notably clinical medicine, are organized vertically, and reasoning by analogy (see Holyoak, Chapter 6) plays a more important role than causal reasoning. Based on such a distinction, it has been argued that reasoning in the physical sciences and reasoning in the biomedical sciences are of different types.

In particular, it has been argued that reasoning in the physical sciences, to some extent, can be conceptualized as a "deductive systematization of a broad class of generalizations under a small number of axioms," but this characterization cannot be applied to the biomedical sciences. The latter are characterized by what Shaffner (1986, p. 68) calls "a series of overlapping interleaved temporal models" that are based on familiarity with shared exemplars to a much greater degree than is necessary in the physical sciences. Shaffner's characterization, unlike that of Blois, applies to both biomedical research and clinical medicine. In biomedical research, an organism such as a *Drosophila*, for instance, is used as an exemplar embodying a given disease mechanism that, by analogy, applies to other organisms, including humans. In the clinical sciences, the patient is seen as an exemplar to which generalizations based on multiple overlapping models are applied from diseases and the population of similar patients.

In the empirical research on medical reasoning, the distinction between reasoning from cases versus reasoning from prototypes has not been established. Medical knowledge consists of two categories of knowledge – clinical knowledge, including knowledge of disease processes and associated findings; and basic science knowledge, incorporating subject matter such as biochemistry, anatomy, and physiology. Basic science or biomedical knowledge is supposed to provide a scientific foundation for clinical reasoning. The conventional view is that basic science knowledge can be seamlessly integrated into clinical knowledge analogous to the way that learning the rules of the road can contribute to one's mastery of driving a car. In this capacity,

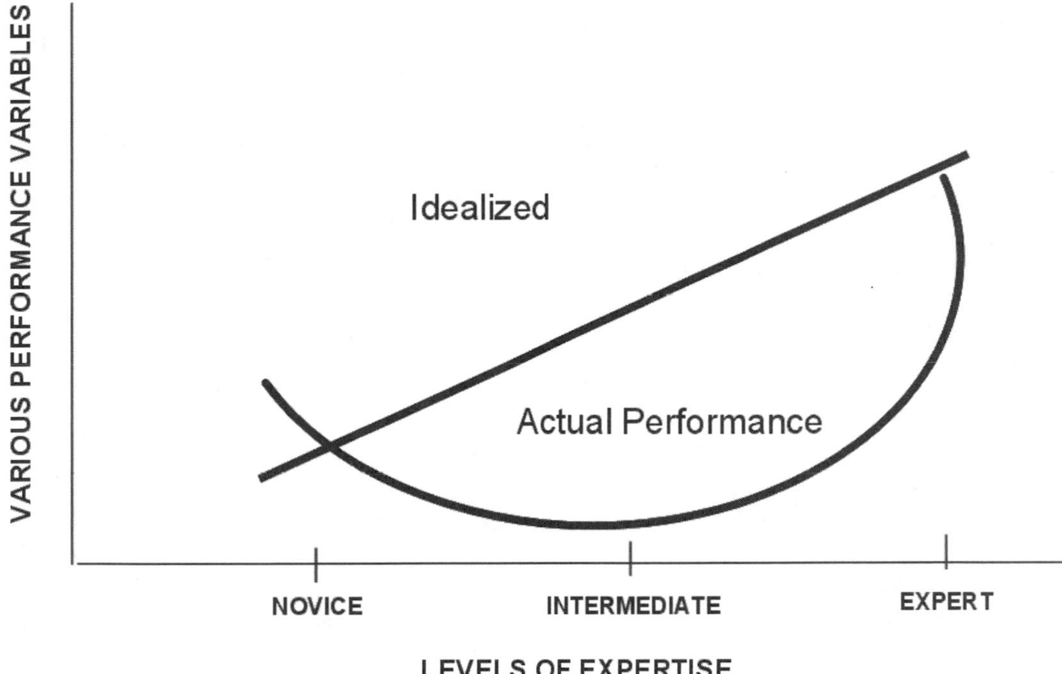

Figure 30.1. Idealized representation of the "intermediate effect." The straight line gives a commonly assumed representation of performance development by level of expertise. The curved, U-shaped, line represents the actual development from novice to expert. The *y*-axis may represent performance variables, such as the number of errors made, irrelevant concepts recalled, conceptual elaborations, or number of extraneous hypotheses generated in a variety of tasks.

a particular piece of biomedical knowledge could be automatically elicited in a range of clinical contexts and tasks in more or less the same fashion.

Knowledge Organization and Changes in Directionality

Following Blois (1988) and Schaffner (1986), it can be argued that the way medical knowledge is organized can be a determinant factor explaining why experts do not use the hypothetico-deductive method of reasoning. Maybe the medical domain is too messy to allow its neat partitioning and deductive use of reasoning strategies. Although the theory of reasoning in medicine is basically a theory of expert knowledge, reaching the level of efficient reasoning of the expert clinician reflects the extended continuum of training and levels of reasoning performance (Thibodeau et al., 1989; Chi et al., 1989). This continuum also points to the particular nature of medical knowledge and its acquisition.

Changes have been described in this process that serve to characterize the various phases medical trainees go through to become expert clinicians. An important characteristic of this process is the *intermediate effect*. This refers to the fact that, although it seems reasonable to assume that performance improves with training or time on task, there appear to be particular transitions in which subjects exhibit a certain drop in performance. This is an example of what is referred to as *nonmonotonicity* in the developmental literature (Strauss & Stavy, 1982) and is also observed in skill acquisition. The symptom is a learning curve or developmental pattern that is shaped like a U or an inverted U, as illustrated in Figure 30.1. In medical expertise development, intermediates' performance reflects the degradation in reasoning that results from the acquisition of knowledge through a time during which such knowledge is not well-organized and irrelevant associations abound in the intermediate's knowledge base. In contrast, the novice's knowledge base is too sparse, containing very few associations, whereas the expert's knowledge base is well pruned of the irrelevancies that characterize intermediates. It should be noted that not all intermediate performance is nonmonotonic; for example, on some global criteria such as diagnostic accuracy, there appears to be a steady improvement.

The intermediate effect occurs with many tasks and at various levels of expertise. The tasks vary from comprehension of clinical cases and explanation of clinical problems to problem solving to generating laboratory data. The phenomenon may be attributable to the fact that intermediates have acquired an extensive body of knowledge but have not yet reorganized this knowledge in a functional manner. Intermediate knowledge therefore has a sort of network structure that results in considerable search, which makes it more difficult for intermediates to set up structures for rapid encoding and selective retrieval of information (Patel & Groen, 1991). In contrast, expert knowledge is finely tuned to perform various tasks, and experts can readily filter out irrelevant information using their hierarchically organized schemata. The difference is reflected in the structural organization of knowledge and the extent to which it is proceduralized to perform different tasks.

Schmidt and Boshuizen (1993) reported that intermediate nonmonotonicity recall effects disappear by using short exposure times (about thirty seconds), which suggests that under time-restricted conditions, intermediates cannot engage in extraneous search. Whereas a novice's knowledge base is likely to be sparse and an expert's knowledge base is intricately interconnected, the knowledge base of an intermediate possesses many of the pieces of knowledge but lacks the extensive connectedness of an expert. Until this knowledge becomes further consolidated, the intermediate is more likely to engage in unnecessary search. Whether this knowledge, painfully acquired during medical training, is really necessary for clinical reasoning has been a focus of intensive research and great debate. If expert clinicians do not explicitly use underlying biomedical knowledge, does that mean that it is not necessary? Or could it be simply that this knowledge remains "dormant" until is really needed? This raises an important question of whether expert medical knowledge is deep or shallow.

Causal Reasoning in Medicine

The differential role of basic science knowledge (e.g., physiology and biochemistry) in solving problems of varying complexity and the differences between subjects at different levels of expertise (Patel et al., 1994) have been a source of controversy in the study of medical cognition (Patel & Kaufman, 1995) as well as in medical education and AI. As expertise develops, the disease knowledge of a clinician becomes more dependent on clinical experience, and clinical problem solving is increasingly guided by the use of exemplars and analogy and becomes less dependent on a functional understanding of the system in question. However, an in-depth conceptual understanding of basic science plays a central role in reasoning about complex problems and is also important in generating explanations and justifications for decisions.

Researchers in AI were confronted with similar problems in extending the utility of systems beyond their immediate knowledge base. Biomedical knowledge can serve different functional roles depending on the goals of the system. Most models of diagnostic reasoning in medicine can be characterized as being shallow. A shallow medical expert system (e.g., MYCIN and INTERNIST) reasons by relating observations to intermediate hypotheses that partition the problem space and further by associating intermediate hypotheses with diagnostic hypotheses. This is consistent with the way physicians appear to reason.

There are other medical reasoning system models that propose a "deep" mode of reasoning as a main mechanism. Chandrasekeran, Smith, & Sticklen, (1989) characterize a deep system as one that embodies a causal mental model of bodily function and malfunction, similar to the models used in qualitative physics (Bobrow, 1985). Systems such as MDX-2 (Chandrasekeran et al., 1989) or QSIM (Kuipers, 1987) have explicit representations of structural components and their relations, the functions of these components (in essence their purpose), and their relationship to behavioral states.

To become licensed physicians, medical trainees undergo a lengthy training process that entails the learning of biomedical sciences, including biochemistry, physiology, anatomy, and others. The apparent contradiction between this type of training and the absence of deep biomedical knowledge during expert medical reasoning has been pointed out. To account for such apparent inconsistency, Boshuizen and Schmidt (1992) proposed a learning mechanism – *knowledge encapsulation*. Knowledge encapsulation is a learning process that involves the subsumption of biomedical propositions and their interrelations in associative clusters under a small number of higher-level clinical propositions with the same explanatory power. Through exposure to clinical training, biomedical knowledge presumably becomes integrated with clinical knowledge. Biomedical knowledge can be "unpacked" when needed but is not used as a first line of explanation.

Boshuizen and Schmidt (1992) cite a wide range of clinical reasoning and recall studies that support this kind of learning process. Of particular importance is the well-documented finding that with increasing levels of expertise, physicians produce explanations at higher levels of generality, using fewer and fewer biomedical concepts while producing consistently accurate responses. The intermediate effect can also be accounted for as a stage in the encapsulation process in which a trainee's network of knowledge has not yet become sufficiently differentiated, resulting in more extensive processing of information.

Knowledge encapsulation provides an appealing account of a range of developmental phenomena in the course of acquiring medical expertise. The integration of basic science in clinical knowledge is a rather complex process, however, and encapsulation is likely to be only part of the knowledge development process. Basic science knowledge plays a different role in different clinical domains. For example, clinical expertise in perceptual domains, such as dermatology and radiology, necessitates a relatively robust model of anatomical structures that is the primary source of knowledge for diagnostic classification. In other domains, such as cardiology and endocrinology, basic science knowledge has a more distant relationship with clinical knowledge. The misconceptions evident in physicians' biomedical explanations would argue against their having well-developed encapsulated knowledge structures in which basic science knowledge can easily be retrieved and applied when necessary.

The results of research into medical problem solving are consistent with the idea that clinical medicine and biomedical sciences constitute two distinct and not completely compatible worlds with distinct modes of reasoning and quite different ways of structuring knowledge (Patel, Arocha, & Kaufman, 1994). Clinical knowledge is based on a complex taxonomy that relates disease symptoms to underlying pathology. In contrast, biomedical sciences are based on general principles defining chains of causal mechanisms. Learning to explain how a set of symptoms is consistent with a diagnosis therefore may be very different from learning how to explain what causes a disease. (See Buehner & Cheng, Chap. 7, for a discussion of causal learning.)

The notion of the progression of mental models (White & Frederiksen, 1990) has been used as an alternative framework for characterizing the development of conceptual understanding in biomedical contexts. Mental models are dynamic knowledge structures composed to make sense of experience and to reason across spatial or temporal dimensions (see Johnson-Laird, Chap. 9). An individual's mental models provide predictive and explanatory capabilities of the function of a given system. The authors employed the progression of mental models to explain the process of understanding increasingly sophisticated electrical circuits. This notion can be used to account for differences between novices and experts in understanding circulatory physiology, describing misconceptions (Patel, Arocha, & Kaufman, 1994), and explaining the generation of spontaneous analogies in causal reasoning.

Running a mental model is a potentially powerful form of reasoning but it is also cognitively demanding. It may require an extended chain of reasoning and the use of complex representations. It is apparent that skilled individuals learn to circumvent long chains of reasoning and chunk or compile knowledge across intermediate states of inference (Chandrasekaran, 1994; Newell, 1990). This results in shorter, more direct, inferences that are stored in long-term memory and are directly available to be retrieved in the appropriate contexts. Chandrasekaran (1994) refers to this sort of knowledge as *compiled causal knowledge*. This term refers to knowledge of causal expectations that people compile directly from experience and partly by chunking results from previous problem-solving endeavors. The goals of the individual and the demands of recurring situations largely determine which pieces of knowledge get stored and used. When physicians are confronted with a similar situation, they can employ this compiled knowledge in an efficient and effective manner. The development of compiled knowledge is an integral part of the acquisition of expertise.

The idea of compiling declarative knowledge bears a certain resemblance to the idea of knowledge encapsulation, but the claim differs in two important senses. The process of compiling knowledge is not one of subsumption or abstraction, and the original knowledge (uncompiled mental model) may no longer be available in a similar form (Kuipers & Kassirer, 1984). The second difference is that mental models are composed dynamically out of constituent pieces of knowledge rather than prestored unitary structures. The use of mental models is somewhat opportunistic and the learning process is less predictable. The compilation process can work in reverse as well. That is to say, discrete cause-and-effect relationships can be integrated into a mental model as a student reasons about complex physiological processes.

Errors and Medical Reasoning

According to the report from the Institute of Medicine (Kohn, Corrigan, & Donaldson, 1999), medical error is the eighth leading cause of death in the United States ahead of deaths attributable to motor vehicle accidents, breast cancer, or acquired immunodeficiency syndrome. Cognitive mechanisms, such as mistakes of reasoning and decision making and action slips of skilled performance, are the major factors contributing to medical errors. A cognitive taxonomy is essential to understanding, explaining, and predicting medical errors and to developing interventions to reduce medical errors. Based on the definition and preliminary taxonomy by Reason (1990) and the action theory by Norman (1986), Zhang et al. (2004, in review) developed a cognitive taxonomy for human errors in medicine.

A Cognitive Taxonomy of Medical Errors

One critical step toward understanding the cognitive mechanisms of various errors in medical reasoning is to categorize the errors along cognitively meaningful dimensions. Reason (1990) defines human error as a failure to achieve the intended outcome in a planned sequence of mental or physical activities. He divides human errors into two major categories: (1) slips that result from the incorrect execution of a correct action sequence and (2) mistakes that result from the correct execution of an incorrect action sequence. Norman's theory of action (Norman, 1986) decomposes a human activity into seven stages.

Based on Reason's definition of human error and Norman's action theory, Zhang and colleagues developed a cognitive taxonomy. Under this taxonomy, errors are divided into slips and mistakes, just like Reason's two main categories. Then slips are divided into execution slips and evaluation slips. Execution slips include goal, intention, action specification, and action execution slips, whereas evaluation slips include perception, interpretation, and evaluation slips. Similarly, mistakes can be divided into execution mistakes that include goal, intention, action specification, and action execution mistakes and evaluation mistakes that include perception, interpretation, and evaluation mistakes. This taxonomy can cover major types of medical errors, because a medical error is a human error in an action and any action goes through the seven stages of the action cycle. Most reasoning and decision-making errors in medicine are under the category of mistakes in the taxonomy. They are attributable to incorrect or incomplete knowledge.

Reasoning and Decision-Making Mistakes in Medicine

In the cognitive taxonomy, goal and intention mistakes are mistakes about declarative knowledge – knowledge about factual statements and propositions, such as "Motrin is a pain reliever and fever reducer." Action specification mistakes and action execution mistakes are mistakes about procedural knowledge – knowledge about procedures and rules, such as "give 1 tsp Motrin to a child per dosage up to 4 times a day if the child has fever or toothache and the weight of the child is 24–35 lbs."

Goal mistakes and intention mistakes are caused by many complex factors such as incorrect knowledge, incomplete knowledge, and misuse of knowledge; biases; faulty heuristics; and information overload. For example, neglect of base rate information could result in incorrect diagnosis of a disease. This is a well-documented finding in human decision making (Tversky & Kahneman, 1974; Kahneman & Frederick, Chap. 12). As another example, the goal of "treating the disease as pneumonia" could be a mistake if it is a misdiagnosis based on incomplete knowledge (e.g., without radiographic images). Intention mistakes can be caused by similar factors, such as the following example: A physician treating a patient with oxygen set the flow control knob between one and two liters per minute, not realizing that the scale numbers represented discrete, rather than continuous, settings. As a result, the patient did not receive any oxygen. This is a mistake caused by incomplete knowledge. The use of heuristics is another common source of goal and intention mistakes. A heuristic often used is the reliance on disease schemata during clinical diagnosis. Disease schemata are knowledge structures that have been formed from previous experience with diagnosing diseases and contain information about relevant and irrelevant signs and symptoms. When physicians and medical students diagnose patients, they tend to rely on their schemata and base their reasoning on the apparent similarity of patient information with these schemata instead of a more objective analysis of patient data. The schemata used in diagnosis often guide future reasoning about the patient, affecting what tests are run and how data are interpreted. Arocha and Patel (1995) found that medical students and trainees maintained their initial hypotheses, even if subsequent data were contradictory. Therefore, if the initial hypothesis is wrong, errors in diagnosis and treatment are likely to occur. Preliminary presentation of the patient (e.g., signs and symptoms), then, becomes very important because it can suggest strongly held hypotheses (i.e., lead to the use of schemata).

Action specification and action execution mistakes are procedural mistakes that can be caused by many factors, such as lack of correct rules, overgeneralized application of good rules, misapplication of good rules, encoding deficiencies in rules, and dissociation between knowledge and rules. Overgeneralized application of good rules, for example, can cause an error because the condition part of a condition-action rule could be misidentified and mismatched, causing the firing of the action part of the rule. Procedural mistakes caused by encoding efficiencies of action rules are usually attributable to the evolving nature of the rules and unforeseeable conditions that cannot be encoded in the rules. A good rule may be misused because the user may have incorrect or incomplete knowledge about the condition of the rule in a specific context. The knowledge of a rule and the knowledge of how to use a rule are not always automatically linked without extensive practice. This dissociation, attributable to the lack of experience and practiced skills, may also lead to action execution mistakes.

Perception mistakes can be caused by expectation-driven processing. What we perceive is a function of the input and our expectations. This mechanism is what allows us to read sloppy handwriting or recognize degraded images. However, our expectations can also lead to misperceptions. Interpretation mistakes are the incorrect interpretation of feedback caused by incorrect or incomplete knowledge. Suppose, for instance, that an intravenous infusion pump, a device often used in critical care environments to give medications, indicates readiness to begin infusing medications using a steady green light and indicates the infusion is in progress by flashing the green light. If the device user does not know the meaning of the steady green light, he or she may incorrectly interpret it as an indication that the infusion has begun. Generating different interpretations and treatment procedures from the same evidence is another source of interpretation mistake. An action evaluation mistake occurs when incorrect or incomplete knowledge leads a person to judge the completion or incompletion of a goal erroneously.

Medical Reasoning and Decision Research

Decision making is central to medical activity. Although health-care professionals are generally highly proficient decision makers, their erroneous decisions have become the source of considerable public scrutiny (Kohn, Corrigan, & Donaldson, 1999).

Decisions involve the application of reasoning to select some course of action that achieves the desired goal (see LeBoeuf & Shafir, Chap. 11). Hastie (2001) identified three components of decision making: (1) choice options and courses of actions; (2) beliefs about objective states, processes, and events in the world, including outcome states and means to achieve them; and (3) desires, values, or utilities that describe the consequences associated with the outcomes of each action–event combination. Reasoning plays a major role in this process. In this context, a major thrust of research has been the study of hypothesis testing, which has been studied widely in the medical domain. Such research has shown the pervasiveness of confirmation bias, evidenced by the generation of a hypothesis and the subsequent search for evidence consistent with the hypothesis, often leading to failure to adequately consider alternative diagnostic possibilities. This bias may result in a less-than-thorough investigation with possible adverse consequences for the patient. A desire to confirm one's preferred hypothesis, moreover, may contribute to increased inefficiency and costs by ordering additional laboratory tests that will do little to revise one's opinion, providing largely redundant data (Chapman & Elstein, 2000).

Health-care team decision making is the rule rather than the exception in medicine. Naturalistic decision-making (NDM) is concerned with the study of cognition in real world work environments that are often dynamic (i.e., rapidly changing) (Klein, 1993). The majority of this research combines conventional protocol analytic methods with innovative methods designed to investigate reasoning and behavior in realistic settings (Woods, 1993; Rasmussen, Pejtersen, & Goodstein, 1994). The study of decision making in the work context necessitates an extended cognitive science framework beyond typical characterizations of knowledge structures, processes, and skills to include modulating variables such as stress, time pressure, and fatigue, as well as communication patterns in team performance.

Among the issues investigated in NDM are understanding how decisions are jointly negotiated and updated by participants differing substantially in their areas of expertise (e.g., pharmacology, respiratory medicine), how the complex communication process in these settings occurs, what role technology plays in mediating decisions and how it affects reasoning, and what sources of error exist in the decision making process.

Patel, Kaufman, and Magder (1996) studied decision-making in a medical intensive care unit with the particular objective of describing jointly negotiated decisions, communication processes, and the development of expertise. Intensive care decision-making is characterized by a rapid serial evaluation of options leading to immediate action in which reasoning is schema-driven in a forward direction toward action with minimal inference or justification. When patients do not respond in a manner consistent with the original hypothesis, however, the original decision comes under scrutiny. This strategy can result in a brainstorming session in which the team retrospectively evaluates and reconsiders the decision and considers possible alternatives. In such circumstances, various patterns of reasoning are used to evaluate alternatives in these brainstorming sessions. These include probabilistic reasoning, diagnostic reasoning, and biomedical causal reasoning. Supporting decision making in clinical settings necessitates an understanding of communication patterns.

In summary, although traditional approaches to decision making looked at decisions as choosing among known alternatives, real-world decision-making is best investigated by a naturalistic approach in which reasoning is constrained by dynamic factors, such as stress, time pressure, risk, and team interactions. Looking at medical reasoning in social and collaborative settings is even more important when information technologies are part of the ebb and flow of clinical work.

Reasoning and Medical Education

The failures and successes of reasoning strategies and skills can be traced back to their sources – education. There is evidence suggesting that the way physicians reason follows from the way they were educated. Medical education in North America as well as in the rest of the world has followed a similar path – from practice-based training to an increasingly scientific type of training.

Motivated by the increasing importance of basic scientific knowledge in the context of clinical practice, problem-based learning (PBL) was developed on the premise that not only should physicians possess the ordered and systematic knowledge of science, but they should *think* like scientists during their practices. Consistent with this idea, an attempt was made to teach hypothetico-deductive reasoning to medical students to provide an adequate structure to medical problem solving. After all, this was the way scientists were supposed to make discoveries.

Based on cognitive research in other knowledge domains, some researchers argued, however, that the hypothetico-deductive method might not be the most efficient way of solving clinical problems. To investigate how the kind of training medical students received affected their reasoning patterns, Patel, Groen, and Norman (1993) looked at the problem-solving processes of students in two medical schools with different modes of instruction – classical and problem-based. They found that students in the problem-based curriculum reasoned in a way that was consistent with their training methods, showing a preponderance of hypothetico-deductive reasoning and extensive elaborations of biomedical information. The PBL students have been shown to use hypothesis-driven reasoning – from the hypothesis to explain the patient data – whereas non-PBL students use mainly data-driven reasoning – from data toward the hypothesis. In explaining clinical cases, PBL students produce extensive elaborations using detailed biomedical information, which is relatively absent from non-PBL students' explanations. However, these elaborations result in the generation of errors. Problem-based learning promotes the activation and elaboration of prior knowledge.

Patel and colleagues (Patel, Arocha, & Lecissi, 2001) also investigated the effects of non-PBL curricula on the use and integration of basic science and clinical knowledge and their relationship to reasoning in diagnostic explanation. The results showed that biomedical and clinical knowledge are not integrated and that very little biomedical information is used in routine problem-solving situations. There is significant use of expert-like, data-driven strategies, however, in non-PBL students' explanations. The use of biomedical information increases when the clinical problems are complex; at the same time, hypothesis-driven strategies replace the data-driven strategies.

Students from a PBL school integrated the two types of knowledge and, in contrast to the non-PBL students, they spontaneously used biomedical information in solving even routine problems. We concluded that, for students in the non-PBL curriculum, the clinical components of problems are treated separately from the biomedical science components. The two components of problem analysis seem to be viewed as serving different functions. When needed, however, biomedical knowledge is and seems to act as a "glue" that ties the two kinds of information together.

In the PBL curriculum, the integration of basic science and clinical knowledge is so tight that students appear unable to separate the two. As a result, PBL students generate unnecessarily elaborate explanations, leading to errors of reasoning. Problem-based learning seems to promote a type of learning in which basic biomedical knowledge becomes so tightly tied to specific clinical problem types that it becomes difficult to decouple this knowledge in context to transfer to a new situation (Anderson, Reder, & Simon, 1996; Holyoak, 1984).

This outcome is consistent with how biomedical information is taught in the classroom in PBL schools – by encouraging use of the hypothetico-deductive method, resulting in a predominantly backward-directed mode of reasoning. Elaborations are accompanied by a tendency to generate errors of scientific fact and flawed patterns of explanation, such as circular reasoning. Even though a student's explanation may be riddled with bugs and misconceptions, their harmful effects may be dependent on the direction of reasoning. If they reason forward, then they are likely to view their existing knowledge as adequate. In this case, misconceptions may be long lasting and difficult to eradicate. If they reason backward, misconceptions might best be viewed as transient hypotheses that, in the light of experience, are refuted or modified to form the kernel of a more adequate explanation. Interestingly, differences in the patterns of reasoning acquired in both PBL and non-PBL medical curricula are found to be quite stable, even after the students have completed medical school and are in residency training programs (Patel, Arocha, Lecissi, 2001; Patel & Kaufman, 2001).

Instruction that emphasizes decontextualized abstracted models of phenomena has not yielded much success in medicine or in other spheres of science education. It is widely believed that the amount of transfer will be a function of the overlap between the original domain of learning and the target domain (Holyoak, 1984). Problem-based learning's emphasis on real-world problems represents a very good source of transfer to clinical situations. However, it is very challenging to create a problem set that most effectively embodies certain biomedical concepts while maximizing transfer. Knowledge that is overly contextualized actually can reduce transfer.

Technology-Mediated Reasoning

All technologies mediate human performance. Technologies, whether they be computer-based or in some other form, transform the ways individuals and groups behave. They do not merely augment, enhance, or expedite performance, although a given technology may do all of these things. The difference is not one of quantitative change but one that is qualitative in nature. Technology, tools, and artifacts enhance people's ability to perform tasks and change the way they perform tasks. In cognitive science, this ubiquitous phenomenon is called the *representational effect*, which refers to the phenomenon that different representations of a common abstract structure can generate dramatically different representational efficiencies, task complexities, and behavioral outcomes (Zhang & Norman, 1994).

Technology as External Representations

One approach to the study of how technology mediates thinking and reasoning is to consider technology as external representations (Zhang & Norman, 1994, 1995; Zhang, 1997). External representations are the knowledge and structure in the environment as physical symbols, objects, or dimensions (e.g., written symbols, beads of an abacus, dimensions of a graph), and as external rules, constraints, or relations embedded in physical configurations (e.g., spatial relations of written digits, visual and spatial layouts of diagrams, physical constraints in abacuses). The information in external representations can be picked up, analyzed, and processed by perceptual systems alone, although the top-down participation of conceptual knowledge from internal representations sometimes facilitates or inhibits the perceptual processes. External representations are more than inputs and stimuli to the internal mind. For many tasks, they are intrinsic components without which the tasks cease to exist or completely change in nature.

Diagrams, graphs, pictures, and information displays are typical external representations. They are used in many cognitive tasks such as problem solving, reasoning, and decision making. In studies of the relationship between mental images and external pictures, Chambers and Reisberg (1985; Reisberg, 1987) showed that external representations could give people access to knowledge and skills that are unavailable from internal representations. This advantage typically arises because internal representations are already interpreted and difficult to change, whereas external representations are subject to interpretations and can lead to different understandings under different conditions. In their studies of diagrammatic problem solving, Larkin & Simon (1987; Larkin, 1989) show that diagrammatic representations help reasoning and problem solving because they support operators that can recognize features easily and make inferences directly. In studies of logical reasoning with diagrams, Stenning and Oberlander (1994) demonstrated that diagrammatic representations such as Euler circles limit abstraction and thereby ease processing effort. It is well known that different forms of graphic displays have different representational efficiencies for different tasks and can cause different cognitive behaviors. For example, Kleinmuntz and Schkade (1993) showed that different representations (graphs, tables, and lists) of the same information can dramatically change decision-making strategies: With a tabular display, people made one decision, but with a graph display of the same information, people made a different decision.

The Impact of Technology on Thinking in Medicine

The mediating role of technology can be evaluated at several levels. For example, electronic medical records alter the practice of individual clinicians in significant ways, as discussed subsequently. Changes to an information system substantially impact organizational and institutional practices, from research to billing to quality assurance. Even the introduction of patient-centered medical records early in the twentieth century necessitated changes in hospital architecture and considerably affected work practices in clinical settings. Salomon, Perkins, and Globerson (1991) introduced a useful distinction in considering the mediating role of technology on individual performance – the effects *with* technology and the effects *of* technology. The former is concerned with the changes in performance displayed by users while equipped with the technology. For example, when using an effective medical information system, physicians should be able to gather information more systematically and efficiently. In this capacity, medical information technologies may alleviate some of the cognitive load associated with a given task and permit physicians to focus on higher-order thinking skills, such as hypothesis generation and evaluation. The effects of technology refer to enduring changes in general cognitive capacities (knowledge and skills) as a consequence of interaction with a technology. For example, frequent use of information technologies may result in lasting changes in medical decision-making practices even in the absence of the system.

In several studies involving the mediating role of technology in clinical practice, Patel and colleagues (Patel et al., 2000) observed the change in thinking and reasoning patterns caused by the change in methods of writing patient records, from paper records to electronic medical records (EMR). They found that before using EMR, physicians focused on exploration and discovery, used complex propositions, and tended to use data-driven reasoning. With EMR, which structures data, physicians focus on problem solving, use simple propositions, and tend to use problem-directed and hypothesis-driven reasoning. The change of behavior caused by the use of EMR remains when physicians go back to paper records, showing the enduring effects of technology on human reasoning in medicine.

As the basis for many medical decisions, diagnostic reasoning requires collecting, understanding, and using many types of patient information, such as history, laboratory results, symptoms, prescriptions, images, and so on. It is affected by the expertise of the clinicians and the way the information is acquired, stored, processed, and presented. If we consider clinicians as rational decision makers, the format of a display, as long as it contains the same information, should not affect the outcome of the reasoning and decision-making process. But the formats of displays do affect many aspects of clinicians' task performance. Several recent studies examined how different displays of information in EMR affect clinicians' behavior. Three major types of displays have been studied – source-based, time-based, and concept-based. Source-based displays organize medical data by the sources of the data, such as encounter notes, laboratory results and reports, medications, radiology imaging and reports, physical examinations, and so on. Time-based displays organize medical data as a temporal history. Concept-based displays organize medical data by clinically meaningful concepts or problems. In this case, all data related to each specific problem are displayed together. For example, if a patient has symptoms such as coughing, chest pain, and fever, the laboratory results, imaging reports, prescriptions, assessments, and plans are displayed together. A study by Zeng, Cimino, & Zou, (2002) found that different displays were good for different tasks. Source-based displays are good for clinicians to retrieve information for a specific test or procedure from a specific department, for example, whereas concept-based displays are good for searching for information related to a specific disease.

With the rapid growth of computer-based information systems, we are interacting more and more with computer-generated health information displays. If these displays are to generate the information people need for informed reasoning effectively and accurately, good design is necessary.

Conclusions and Future Directions

The process of medical reasoning is one area in which advances in cognitive science have made significant contributions to investigation. In particular, reasoning in medical contexts involving a dense population and a high degree of uncertainty (such as critical care environments), compounded with constraints imposed by resource availability, leads to increased use of heuristic strategies. The utility of heuristics lies in limiting the extent of purposeful search through data sets, which have substantial practical value by reducing redundancy. A significant part of a physician's cognitive effort is based on heuristic thinking, but its use introduces considerable bias in medical reasoning, often resulting in a number of conceptual and procedural errors. These include misconceptions about laws governing probability, instantiation of general rules to a specific patient at the point of care, prior probabilities and actions, and false validation. Much of physicians' reasoning is inductive with attached probability. Human thought is fallible and we cannot appreciate the fallibility of our thinking unless we draw on understanding of how physicians' thinking processes operate in the real working environment.

Cognitive studies are increasingly moving toward investigations of real-world phenomena. The constraints of laboratory-based work prevent capturing the dynamics of real-world problems. This problem is particularly salient in high-velocity critical care environments. In the best-case scenarios, this is creating the potential for great synergy between laboratory-based research and cognitive studies in the "wild." As discussed in this chapter, studies of thinking and reasoning in medicine, including a focus on medical errors and technology-mediated cognition, are increasingly paying attention to dimensions of medical work in clinical settings. The recent concern with understanding and reducing medical errors provides an opportunity for cognitive scientists to apply cognitive theories and methodologies to a pressing practical problem. A trend in health care, spurred partly by the advent of information technologies that foster communication, is the shift in health-care systems to become increasingly multidisciplinary, collaborative, and geographically spanning regions. In addition, increasing costs of health care and rapid knowledge growth have accelerated the trend toward collaboration of health-care professionals in sharing knowledge and skills. Comprehensive patient care necessitates the communication of health-care providers in different medical domains, thereby optimizing the use of their expertise. Research on reasoning will need to continue to move toward a distributed model of cognition. This model will include a focus on both socially shared and technology-mediated reasoning.

Acknowledgment

This chapter is dedicated to the memory of the late Yogesh C. Patel, who devoted his life to the advancement of biomedical science. Through his deeds and words, he inspired us to devote ourselves to superior pursuits and to aspire to higher scientific standards.

References

Anderson, J. R., Reder, L. M., & Simon, H. A. (1996). Situated learning and education. *Educational Researcher*, 25(4), 5–11.

Arocha, J. F., & Patel, V. L. (1995). Construction-integration theory and clinical reasoning. In C. A. I. Weaver, C. R. Fletche, & S. Mannes (Eds.), *Discourse Comprehension: Essays in Honor of Walter Kintsch* (pp. 359–381). Hillsdale, NJ: Erlbaum.

Blois, M. S. (1990). Medicine and the nature of vertical reasoning. *New England Journal of Medicine*, 318, 847–851.

Bobrow, D. G. (Ed.). (1985). *Qualitative Reasoning about Physical Systems* (1st MIT Press ed.). Cambridge, MA: MIT Press.

Boshuizen, H. P. A., & Schmidt, H. G. (1992). On the role of biomedical knowledge in clinical reasoning by experts, intermediates, and novices. *Cognitive Science*, 16(2), 153–184.

Brooks, L. R., Norman, G. R., & Allen, S. W. (1991). Role of specific similarity in a medical diagnostic task. *Journal of Experimental Psychology: General*, *120(3)*, 278–287.

Chambers, D., & Reisberg, D. (1985). Can mental images be ambiguous? *Journal of Experimental Psychology: Human Perception and Performance*, *11(3)*, 317–328.

Chandrasekaran, B. (1994). The functional representation and causal process. In M. Yovitz (Ed.), *Advances in Computing*. New York: Academic Press.

Chandrasekaran, B., Smith, J. W., & Sticklen, J. (1989). Deep models and their relation to diagnosis. *Artificial Intelligence in Medicine*, 1, 29–40.

Chapman, G. B., & Elstein, A. S. (2000). Cognitive processes and biases in medical decision making. In G. B. Chapman & A. Frank (Eds.), *Decision Making in Health Care: Theory, Psychology, and Applications* (pp. 183–210). Cambridge, UK: Cambridge University Press.

Chi, M. T. H., Bassok, M., Lewis, M. W., Reiman, P., & Glaser, R. (1989). Self explanations: How students study and use examples in learning to solve problems. *Cognitive Science*, 13, 145–182.

Chi, M. T. H., & Glaser, R. (1981). Categorization and representation of physics problems by experts and novices. *Cognitive Science*, 5, 121–152.

Clancey, W. J. (1985). Heuristic classification. *Artificial Intelligence*, 27, 289–350.

Clancey, W. J., & Letsinger, R. (1984). NEOMYCIN: Reconfiguring a rule-based expert system for application to teaching. In W. J. Clancey, & E. H. Shortliffe (Eds.), *Readings in medical artificial intelligence: The first decade* (pp. 361–81). Reading, MA: Addison-Wesley.

Clancey, W. J., & Shortliffe, E. H. (1984). Readings in medical artificial intelligence: The first decade. Reading, MA: Addison-Wesley.

Coiera, E. (2000). When conversation is better than computation. *Journal of the American Medical Informatics Association*, 7(3), 277–286.

Dowie, J., & Elstein, A. S. (Eds.). (1988). *Professional Judgment: A Reader in Clinical Decision Making*. Cambridge, UK: Cambridge University Press.

Elstein, A. S., Kleinmuntz, B., Rabinowitz, M., McAuley, R., Murakami, J., et al. (1993). Diagnostic reasoning of high- and low-domain-knowledge clinicians: A reanalysis. *Medical Decision Making*, *13(1)*, 21–29.

Elstein, A. S., Shulman, L. S., & Sprafka, S. A. (1978). *Medical Problem Solving: An Analysis of Clinical Reasoning*. Cambridge, MA: Harvard University Press.

Ericsson, K. A., & Simon, H. A. (1993). *Protocol Analysis: Verbal Reports as Data* (Revised ed.). Cambridge, MA: MIT Press.

Ericsson, K. A., & Smith, J. (1991). *Toward a General Theory of Expertise: Prospects and Limits*. New York: Cambridge University Press.

Eshelman, L. (1988). MOLE: A knowledge acquisition tool for Cover-and-Differentiatiate systems. In S. C. Marcus (Ed.), *Automating Knowledge Acquistion for Expert Systems* (pp. 37–80). Boston: Kluwer Academic.

Feltovich, P. J., Johnson, P. E., Moller, J. H., & Swanson, D. B. (1984). LCS: The role and development of medical knowledge in diagnostic expertise. In W. J. Clancey, & E. H. Shortliffe (Eds.), *Readings in Medical Artificial Intelligence: The First Decade* (pp. 275–319). Reading, MA: Addison-Wesley.

Flexner, A. (1910). *Medical Education in the United States and Canada. A Report to the Carnegie Foundation for the Advancement of Teaching*. Boston: Updyke.

Fordyce, J., Blank, F. S., Pekow, P., Smithline, H. A., Ritter, G., Gehlbach, S., et al. (2003). Errors in a busy emergency department. *Annals of Emergency Medicine*, 42(3), 324–333.

Frensch, P. A., & Funke, J. (1995). *Complex Problem Solving: The European Perspective*. Hillsdale, NJ: Erlbaum.

Frijda, N. H., & Elshout, J. J. (1979). Problem solving and thinking. In J. A. Michon, E. G. J. Eijkman, & L. F. W. De Klerk (Eds.), *Handbook of Psychonomics* (Vol. 2). Amsterdam: North-Holland.

Gaba, D. M. (1992). Dynamic decision-making in anesthesiology: Cognitive models and training approaches. In D. A. Evans, & V. L. Patel (Eds.), *Advanced Models of Cognition for Medical Training and Practice* (pp. 123–147). New York: Springer-Verlag.

Gentner, D., & Holyoak, K. J. (1997). Reasoning and learning by analogy: Introduction. *American Psychologist*, 52(1), 32–34.

Gorowitz, S., & McIntyre, A. (1978). Toward a theory of medical fallibility. *Journal of Medicine and Philosophy*, 1, 51–71.

Gorry, G. A. (1973). Computer-assisted clinical decision-making. *Methods of Information in Medicine*, 12(1), 45–51.

Hardiman, P. T., Dufresne, R., & Mestre, J. P. (1989). The relation between problem categorization and problem solving among experts and novices. *Memory and Cognition*, 17(5), 627–638.

Hastie, R. (2001). Problems for judgment and decision making. *Annual Review of Psychology*, 52, 653–683.

Hoffman, R. R., & Deffenbacher, K. A. (1993). An analysis of the relations of basic and applied science. *Ecological Psychology*, 5, 315–52.

Holland, J. H. (1986). *Induction : Processes of Inference, Learning, and Discovery*. Cambridge, MA: MIT Press.

Holyoak, K. J. (1985). The pragmatics of analogical transfer. *The Psychology of Learning and Motivation*, 19, 59–87.

Holyoak, K. J., & Thagard, P. (1997). The analogical mind. *American Psychologist*, 52(1), 35–44.

Joseph, G. M., & Patel, V. L. (1990). Domain knowledge and hypothesis generation in diagnostic reasoning. *Medical Decision Making*, 10(1), 31–46.

Kassirer, J. P. (1989). Diagnostic reasoning. *Annals of Internal Medicine*, 110(11), 893–900.

Kassirer, J. P., & Kopelman, R. I. (1990). Diagnosis and the structure of memory. 2. Exemplars, scripts, and simulation. *Hospital Practice (Office Edition)*, 25(11), 29–33, 36.

Klein, G. A. (1993). *Decision Making in Action: Models and Methods*. Norwood, NJ: Ablex.

Kleinmuntz, D. N., & Schkade, D. A. (1993). Information displays and decision processes. *Psychological Science*, 4(4), 221–227.

Kohn, L. T., Corrigan, J., & Donaldson, M. S. (1999). *To Err Is Human: Building a Safer Health System*. Washington, DC: National Academy Press.

Kuhn, D. (1995). Scientific thinking and knowledge acquisition. *Monographs of the Society for Research in Child Development*, 60(4), 152–157.

Kuipers, B. (1987). Qualitative simulation as causal explanation. *IEEE Transactions on Systems, Man, and Cybernetics*, 17, 432–444.

Kuipers, B., & Kassirer, J. P. (1984). Causal reasoning in medicine: Analysis of a protocol. *Cognitive Science*, 8(4), 363–385.

Larkin, J. H., McDermott, J., Simon, H. A., & Simon, D. P. (1980). Expert and novice performances in solving physics problems. *Science*, 208, 1335–42.

Larkin, J., & Simon, H. A. (1987). Why a diagram is (sometimes) worth ten thousand words. *Cognitive Science*, 11(1), 65–99.

Leaper, D. J., Horrocks, J. C., Staniland, J. R., & De Dombal, F. T. (1972). Computer-assisted diagnosis of abdominal pain using "estimates" provided by clinicians. *British Medical Journal*, 4(836), 350–354.

Ledley, R. S., & Lusted, L. B. (1959). Reasoning foundations of medical diagnosis. *Science*, 130, 9–21.

Leprohon, J., & Patel, V. L. (1995). Decision-making strategies for telephone triage in emergency medical services. *Medical Decision Making: An International Journal of the Society of Medical Decision Making*, 15(3), 240–253.

Lin, L., Isla, R., Doniz, K., Harkness, H., Vicente, K. J., & Doyle, D. J. (1998). Applying human factors to the design of medical equipment: Patient-controlled analgesia. *Journal of Clinical Monitoring, and Computing*, 14(4), 253–263.

Miller, R. A., Pople, H. E., & Myers, J. D. (1984). Internist-I, an experimental computer-based diagnostic for general internal medicine. In W. J. Clancey, & E. H. Shortliffe (Eds.), *Readings in Medical Artificial Intelligence: The First Decade* (pp. xvi, 512 p). Reading, MA: Addison-Wesley.

Newell, A. (1990). *Unified Theories of Cognition*. Cambridge, MA: Harvard University Press.

Newell, A., & Simon, H. A. (1972). *Human Problem Solving*. Englewood Cliffs, NJ: Prentice-Hall.

Norman, D. A. (1986). Cognitive engineering. In D. A. Norman, & S. W. Draper (Eds.), *User Centered System Design: New Perspectives on Human-computer Interaction* (pp. 31–61). Hillsdale, NJ: Erlbaum.

Norman, D. A. (1988). *The Psychology of Everyday Things*. New York: Basic Books.

Norman, G. R., & Brooks, L. R. (1997). The non-analytical basis of clinical reasoning. *Advances in Health Sciences Education*, 2(2), 173–184.

Norman, G. R., Brooks, L. R., & Allen, S. W. (1989). Recall by expert medical practitioners and novices as a record of processing attention. *Journal of Experimental Psychology: Learning, Memory, and Cognition*, 15(6), 1166–1174.

Osler, W. (1906). *Aequanimitas. With other addresses to medical students, nurses and practitioners of medicine*. Philadelphia: Blakiston's Son & Co.

Patel, V. L., Arocha, & Kaufman, D. R. (1994). Diagnostic reasoning and expertise. *Psychology of Learning and Motivation*, 31, 137–252.

Patel, V. L., Kaufman, D. R., & Magder, S. A. (1996). The acquisition of medical expertise in complex dynamic environments. In Ericsson, K. A. (Ed.), *The road to excellence: The acquisition of expert performance in the arts and sciences, sports and games*. (pp. 126–65). Hillsdale, NJ: Erlbaum.

Patel, V. L., & Arocha, J. F. (2001). The nature of constraints on collaborative decision making in health care settings. In E. Salas, & G. Klein (Eds.), *Linking Expertise and Naturalistic Decision Making* (pp. 383–405). Mahwah, NJ: Erlbaum.

Patel, V. L., Arocha, J. F., & Kaufman, D. R. (2001). A primer on aspects of cognition for medical informatics. *Journal of the American Medical Informatics Association*, 8(4), 324–343.

Patel, V. L. Arocha, J., & Lecissi, M. (2001). Impact of undergraduate medical training on housestaff problem solving performance, implications for health education in problem-based curricula. *Journal of Dental Education*. 65(11) 1199–1218.

Patel, V. L., Evans, D. A., & Kaufman, D. R. (1989). Cognitive framework for doctor-patient communication. In D. A. Evans, & V. L. Patel (Eds.), *Cognitive Science in Medicine: Biomedical Modeling* (pp. 257–312). Cambridge, MA: MIT Press.

Patel, V. L., & Groen, G. J. (1986). Knowledge-based solution strategies in medical reasoning. *Cognitive Science*, 10, 91–116.

Patel, V. L., & Groen, G. J. (1991). The general and specific nature of medical expertise: A critical look. In K. A. Ericsson, & J. Smith (Eds.), *Toward a General Theory of Expertise: Prospects and Limits* (pp. 93–125). New York: Cambridge University Press.

Patel, V. L., Groen, G. J., & Arocha, J. F. (1990). Medical expertise as a function of task difficulty. *Memory and Cognition*, 18(4), 394–406.

Patel, V. L., Groen, G. J., & Norman, G. R. (1993). Reasoning and instruction in medical curricula. *Cognition and Instruction*, 10(4), 335–378.

Patel, V. L., & Kaufman, D. R. (1995). Clinical reasoning and biomedical knowledge: Implications for teaching. In J. Higgs, & M. Jones (Eds.), *Clinical Reasoning in the Health Professions* (pp. 117–128). Oxford, UK: Butterworth Heinemenn.

Patel, V. L., & Kaufman, D. R. (2001, Feb 02). Medical education isn't just about solving problems. *The Chronicle of Higher Education*, B12.

Patel, V. L., Kaufman, D. R., Allen, V. G., Shortliffe, E. H., Cimino, J. J., & Greenes, R. A. (1999). Toward a framework for computer-mediated collaborative design in medical informatics. *Methods of Information in Medicine*, 38(3), 158–176.

Patel, V. L., Kaufman, D. R., & Arocha, J. F. (2002). Emerging paradigms of cognition in medical decision-making. *Journal of Biomedical Informatics*, 35, 52–75.

Patel, V. L., Kaufman, D. R., & Magder, S. A. (1991). Causal reasoning about complex physiological concepts in cardiovascular physiology by medical students. *International Journal of Science Education*, 13, 171–185.

Patel, V. L., Kushniruk, A. W., Yang, S., & Yale, J. F. (2000). Impact of a computer-based patient record system on data collection, knowledge organization, and reasoning. *Journal of the American Medical Informatics Association*, 7(6), 569–585.

Patel, V. L., & Ramoni, M. F. (1997). Cognitive models of directional inference in expert medical reasoning. In P. J. Feltovich, & K. M. Ford (Eds.), *Expertise in Context: Human and Machine* (pp. 67–99): Cambridge, MA: MIT Press.

Patil, R. S., Szolovits, P., & Schwartz, W. B. (1985). Causal understanding of patient illness in medical diagnosis. In J. A. Reggia, & S. Tuhrim (Eds.), *Computer-assisted Medical Decision Making* (Vol. 2, pp. 272–292). New York: Springer-Verlag.

Peirce, C. S. (1955). Abduction and induction. In C. S. Peirce, & J. Buchler (Eds.), *Philosophical Writings of Peirce* (pp. 150–156). New York: Dover.

Perkins, D. N., & Simmons, R. (1988). An integrative model of misconceptions. *Review of Educational Research*, 58, 303–326.

Ramoni, M. F., Stefanelli, M., Magnani, L., & Barosi, G. (1992). An epistemological framework for medical knowledge based system. *IEEE Transactions on Systems, Man, and Cybernetics*, 22, 1361–1375.

Rasmussen, J., Pejtersen, A. M., & Goodstein, L. P. (1994). *Cognitive Systems Engineering*. New York: Wiley.

Reason, J. T. (1990). *Human Error*. Cambridge, UK: Cambridge University Press.

Reisberg, D. (1987). External representations and the advantages of externalizing one's thoughts. In *Proceedings of the Eighth Annual Conference of the Cognitive Science Society*. Hillsdale, NJ: Erlbaum.

Rimoldi, H. J. A. (1961). The test of diagnostic skills. *Journal of Medical Education*, 36, 73–79.

Rogoff, B., & Lave, J. (1984). *Everyday Cognition: Its Development in Social Context*. Cambridge, MA: Harvard University Press.

Salas, E., & Klein, G. A. (2001). *Linking Expertise and Naturalistic Decision Making*. Mahwah, NJ: Erlbaum.

Salomon, G., & Perkins, D. N. (1989). Rocky roads to transfer: Rethinking mechanisms of a neglected phenomenon. *Educational Psychologist*, 24, 113–142.

Salomon, G., Perkins, D. N., & Globerson, T. (1991). Partners in cognition: Extending human intelligence with intelligent technologies. *Educational Researcher*, 20(3), 2–9.

Schaffner, K. F. (1986). Exemplar reasoning about biological models and diseases: A relation between the philosophy of medicine and philosophy of science. *Journal of Medicine and Philosophy*, 11, 63–80.

Schauble, L. (1996). The development of scientific reasoning in knowledge-rich contexts. *Developmental Psychology*, 32(1), 102–119.

Schmidt, H. G., & Boshuizen, H. P. A. (1993). On the origin of intermediate effects in clinical case recall. *Memory and Cognition*, 21, 338–351.

Shortliffe, E. H. (1976). *Computer-based Medical Consultations, MYCIN*. New York: Elsevier.

Simon, D. P., & Simon, H. A. (1978). Individual differences in solving physics problems. In R. Siegler (Ed.), *Children's Thinking: What Develops?* Hillsdale, NJ: Erlbaum.

Stefanelli, M., & Ramoni, M. F. (1992). Epistemological constraints on medical knowledge-based systems. In D. A. Evans, & V. L. Patel (Eds.), *Advanced Models of Cognition for Medical Training and Practice* (Vol. 97, pp. 3–20). Heidelberg: Springer-Verlag.

Stenning, K., & Oberlander, J. (1994). A cognitive theory of graphical and linguistic reasoning: Logic and implementation. *Cognitive Science*, 19, 97–140.

Strauss, S., & Stavy, R. (1982). *U-shaped Behavioral Growth*. New York: Academic Press.

Sweller, J. (1988). Cognitive load during problem solving: Effects on learning. *Cognitive Science*, 12, 257–85.

Szolovits, P. (Ed.) (1982). *Artificial Intelligence in Medicine* (Vol. 51). Boulder, CO: Published by Westview Press for the American Association for the Advancement of Science.

Thibodeau, P., Hardiman, P. T., Dufresne, R., & Mestre, J. P. (1989). The relation between problem categorization and problem-solving among experts and novices. *Memory and Cognition*, 17, 627–38.

Tversky, A., & Kahneman, D. (1974). Judgment under uncertainty: Heuristics and biases. *Science*, 185(4157), 1124–1131.

Vicente, K. J., & Rasmussen, J. (1990). The ecology of human-machine systems. II: Mediating "direct perception" in complex work domains. *Ecological Psychology*, 2, 207–250.

White, B. Y., & Frederiksen, J. R. (1990). Causal model progressions as a foundation for intelligent learning environments. In W. J. Clancey & E. Soloway (Eds.), *Artificial Intelligence and Learning Environments, Special Issues of Artificial Intelligence: An International Journal* (pp. 99–157). Cambridge, MA: MIT Press.

Woods, D. D. (1993). Process-tracing methods for the study of cognition outside of the experimental psychology laboratory. In G. A. Klein, & J. Orasanu (Eds.), *Decision Making in Action: Models and Methods* (pp. 228–251). Norwood, NJ: Ablex.

Woods, D. D., & Cook, R. (1998). *A tale of two stories, contrasting views of patient safety*. National Health Care Safety Council of the National Patient Safety Foundation at the AMA.

Zeng, Q., Cimino, J. J., & Zou, K. H. (2002). Providing concept-oriented views for clinical data using a knowledge-based system: An evaluation. *Journal of the American Medical Informatics Association*, 9(3), 294–305.

Zhang, J. (1996). A representational analysis of relational information displays. *International Journal of Human-Computer Studies*, 45(1), 59–74.

Zhang, J. (1997). The nature of external representations in problem solving. *Cognitive Science*, 21(2), 179–217.

Zhang, J., & Norman, D. A. (1994). Representations in distributed cognitive tasks. *Cognitive Science*, 18, 87–122.

Zhang, J., & Norman, D. A. (1995). *A representational analysis of numeration systems. Cognition*, 57, 271–295.

Zhang J., Patel VL, Johnson TR, Shortliffe EH (2004). A cognitive taxonomy of medical errors. *Journal of Biomedical Informatics*, 37, 193–204.

CHAPTER 31
Intelligence

Robert J. Sternberg

What is intelligence? This chapter discusses the nature of intelligence and related issues. The chapter is divided into several major parts: The first discusses people's conceptions of intelligence, also referred to as implicit theories of intelligence; the second presents a brief discussion of intelligence testing; the third offers a review of major approaches to understanding intelligence; the fourth discusses how intelligence can be improved; and the last part briefly draws some conclusions. The chapter does not discuss artificial intelligence and computer simulation (see Lovett & Anderson, Chap. 17), neural networks, or parallel distributed processing (see Doumas & Hummel, Chap. 4).

Implicit Theories of Intelligence

What do people believe intelligence to be? In 1921, when the editors of the *Journal of Educational Psychology* asked 14 famous psychologists that question, the responses varied but generally embraced two themes: Intelligence involves the capacity to learn from experience and the ability to adapt to the surrounding environment. Sixty-five years later, Sternberg and Detterman (1986) asked twenty-four cognitive psychologists with expertise in intelligence research the same question. They, too, underscored the importance of learning from experience and adapting to the environment. They also broadened the definition to emphasize the importance of metacognition – people's understanding and control of their own thinking processes. Contemporary experts also more heavily emphasized the role of culture, pointing out that what is considered intelligent in one culture may be considered stupid in another (Serpell, 2000). Intelligence, then, is the capacity to learn from experience, using metacognitive processes to enhance learning, and the ability to adapt to the surrounding environment, which may require different adaptations within different social and cultural contexts.

According to the *Oxford English Dictionary*, the word *intelligence* entered our language in about the twelfth century. Today, we can look up intelligence in numerous dictionaries, but most of us still have our own implicit (unstated) ideas about what it means to be smart; that is, we have our own implicit theories of intelligence. We use our implicit theories in many social situations, such as when we meet people or when we describe people we know as being very smart or not so smart.

Within our implicit theories of intelligence, we also recognize that it has different meanings in different contexts. A smart salesperson may show a different kind of intelligence than a smart neurosurgeon or a smart accountant, each of whom may show a different kind of intelligence than a smart choreographer, composer, athlete, or sculptor (see Sternberg et al., Chap. 15, for a discussion of the related concept of creativity). We often, use our implicit and context-relevant definitions of intelligence to make assessments of intelligence. Is your mechanic smart enough to find and fix the problem in your car? Is your physician smart enough to find and treat your health problem? Is this attractive person smart enough to hold your interest in a conversation?

Western notions about intelligence are not always shared by other cultures (Sternberg & Kaufman, 1998). For example the Western emphasis on speed of mental processing (Sternberg et al., 1981) is not shared in many cultures. Other cultures may even be suspicious of the quality of work that is done very quickly. Indeed, other cultures emphasize depth rather than speed of processing. Even in the West, some prominent theorists have pointed out the importance of depth of processing for full command of material (e.g., Craik & Lockhart, 1972).

Even within the United States, many people have started viewing as important not only the cognitive aspects but also the emotional aspects of intelligence. Mayer, Salovey, and Caruso (2000, p. 396) defined emotional intelligence as "the ability to perceive and express emotion, assimilate emotion in thought, understand and reason with emotion, and regulate emotion in the self and others." There is good evidence for the existence of some kind of emotional intelligence (Ciarrochi, Forgas, & Mayer, 2001; Mayer & Salovey, 1997; Mayer, Salovey, & Caruso, 2000; Salovey & Sluyter, 1997), although the evidence is mixed (Davies, Stankov, & Roberts, 1998).

A related concept is that of social intelligence, the ability to understand and interact with other people (Kihlstrom & Cantor, 2000). Research also shows that personality variables are related to intelligence (Ackerman, 1996).

Explicit definitions of intelligence frequently take on an assessment-oriented focus. In fact, some psychologists, such as Edwin Boring (1923), have defined intelligence as whatever it is that the tests measure. This definition, unfortunately, is circular and, moreover, what different tests of intelligence measure is not always the same. Different tests measure somewhat different constructs (Daniel, 1997, 2000; Embretson & McCollam, 2000; Kaufman, 2000; Kaufman & Lichtenberger, 1998), so it is not feasible to define intelligence by what tests test, as though they all measured the same thing. Although most cognitive psychologists do not go to that extreme, the tradition of attempting to understand intelligence by measuring various aspects of it has a long history (Brody, 2000).

Intelligence Testing

History

Contemporary measurements of intelligence usually can be traced to one of two very different historical traditions. One tradition concentrated on lower level, psychophysical abilities (such as sensory acuity, physical strength, and motor coordination); the other focused on higher level, judgment abilities (which we traditionally describe as related to thinking).

Francis Galton (1822–1911) believed that intelligence was a function of psychophysical abilities and, for several years, Galton maintained a well-equipped laboratory where visitors could have themselves measured on a variety of psychophysical tests. These tests measured a broad range of psychophysical skills and sensitivities, such as weight discrimination (the ability to notice small differences in the weights of objects), pitch sensitivity (the ability to hear small differences between musical notes), and physical strength (Galton, 1883). One of the many enthusiastic followers of Galton, Clark Wissler (1901), attempted to detect links among the assorted tests, which would unify the various dimensions of psychophysically based intelligence. Much to Wissler's dismay, no unifying association could be detected. Moreover, the psychophysical tests did not predict college grades. The psychophysical approach to assessing intelligence soon faded almost into oblivion, although it would reappear many years later.

An alternative to the psychophysical approach was developed by Alfred Binet (1857–1911). He and his collaborator, Theodore Simon, also attempted to assess intelligence, but their goal was much more practical. Binet had been asked to devise a procedure to distinguish normal from mentally retarded learners in an academic setting (Binet & Simon, 1916). In Binet's view, judgment not psychophysical acuity, strength, or skill, is the key to intelligence. For Binet (Binet & Simon, 1916), intelligent thought – mental judgment – comprises three distinct elements: direction, adaptation, and criticism. The importance of direction and adaptation certainly fits with contemporary views of intelligence, and Binet's notion of criticism actually seems prescient, considering the current appreciation of metacognitive processes as a key aspect of intelligence. Binet viewed intelligence as a broad potpourri of cognitive and other abilities and as highly modifiable.

Major Intelligence Scales

Lewis Terman of Stanford University built on Binet and Simon's work in Europe and constructed the earliest version of what has come to be called the *Stanford–Binet Intelligence Scales* (Terman & Merrill, 1937, 1973; Thorndike, Hagen, & Sattler, 1986). For years, the Stanford-Binet test was the standard for intelligence tests, and it is still widely used, as are the competitive Wechsler scales. The Wechsler tests yield three scores – a verbal score, a performance score, and an overall score. The verbal score is based on tests such as vocabulary and verbal similarities in which the test-taker has to say how two things are similar. The performance score is based on tests such as picture completion, which requires identification of a missing part in a picture of an object; and picture arrangement, which requires rearrangement of a scrambled set of cartoon-like pictures into an order that tells a coherent story. The overall score is a combination of the verbal and performance scores.

Although Wechsler clearly believed in the worth of attempting to measure intelligence, he did not limit his conception of intelligence to test scores. Wechsler believed that intelligence is not represented just by a test score or even by what we do in school. We use our intelligence not just in taking tests and in doing homework, but also in relating to people, in performing our jobs effectively, and in managing our lives in general.

Approaches to Intelligence

Psychometric Approaches to Intelligence

Psychologists interested in the structure of intelligence have relied on factor analysis as an indispensable tool for their research. Factor analysis is a statistical method for separating a construct – intelligence in this case – into a number of hypothetical factors or abilities the researchers believe to form the basis of individual differences in test performance. The specific factors derived, of course, still depend on the specific questions being asked and the tasks being evaluated.

Factor analysis is based on studies of correlation. The idea is that the more highly two tests are correlated the more likely they are to measure the same thing. In research on intelligence, a factor analysis might involve these steps: (1) Give a large number of people several different tests of ability. (2) Determine the correlations among all those tests. (3) Statistically analyze those correlations to simplify them into a relatively small number of factors that summarize people's performance on the tests. The investigators in this area have generally agreed on and followed this procedure, yet the resulting factorial structures of intelligence have differed among theorists such as Spearman, Thurstone, Guilford, Cattell, Vernon, and Carroll.

SPEARMAN: THEORY OF G

Charles Spearman is usually credited with inventing factor analysis (Spearman, 1927). Using factor-analytic studies, Spearman concluded that intelligence can be understood in terms of both a single general factor that pervades performance on all tests of mental ability and a set of specific factors, each of which is involved in performance on only a single type of mental-ability test (e.g., arithmetic computations). In Spearman's view, the specific factors are of only casual interest because of their narrow applicability. To Spearman, the general factor, which he labeled "*g*," provides the key to understanding intelligence. Spearman believed *g* to be attributable to "mental energy." Many psychologists still believe Spearman's theory to be essentially correct (e.g., Jensen, 1998; see essays in Sternberg & Grigorenko, 2002). The theory is useful in part because *g* accounts for a sizable, although not fixed, percentage of variance in school and job performance, usually somewhere between 5% and 40% (Jensen, 1998). Spearman (1923) provided a cognitive theory of intelligence. He suggested that intelligence comprises apprehension of experience (encoding of stimuli), eduction of relations (inference of relations), and eduction of correlates (application of what is learned). He therefore may have been the earliest serious cognitive theorist of intelligence.

THURSTONE: PRIMARY MENTAL ABILITIES

In contrast to Spearman, Louis Thurstone (1887–1955) concluded (Thurstone, 1938) that the core of intelligence resides not in one single factor but in seven such factors, which he referred to as *primary mental abilities*: verbal comprehension, measured by vocabulary tests; verbal fluency, measured by time-limited tests requiring the test-taker to think of as many words as possible that begin with a given letter; inductive reasoning, measured by tests such as analogies and number-series completion tasks; spatial visualization, measured by tests requiring mental rotation of pictures of objects, number, measured by computation and simple mathematical problem-solving tests; memory, measured by picture and word-recall tests; and perceptual speed, measured by tests that require the test-taker to recognize small differences in pictures or to cross out a "each time it appear in a string" of varied letters.

GUILFORD: THE STRUCTURE OF INTELLECT

At the opposite extreme from Spearman's single *g*-factor model is J. P. Guilford's (1967, 1982, 1988) structure-of-intellect model, which includes up to 150 factors of the mind in one version of the theory. According to Guilford, intelligence can be understood in terms of a cube that represents the intersection of three dimensions – operations, contents, and products. Operations are simply mental processes, such as memory and evaluation (making judgments, such as determining whether a particular statement is a fact or opinion). Contents are the kinds of terms that appear in a problem, such as semantic (words) and visual (pictures). Products are the kinds of responses required, such as units (single words, numbers, or pictures), classes (hierarchies), and implications. Thus, Guilford's theory, like Spearman's, had an explicit cognitive component.

CATTELL, VERNON, AND CARROLL: HIERARCHICAL MODELS

A more parsimonious way of handling a number of factors of the mind is through a hierarchical model of intelligence. One such model, developed by Raymond Cattell (1971), proposed that general intelligence comprises two major subfactors – fluid ability (speed and accuracy of abstract reasoning, especially for novel problems) and crystallized ability (accumulated knowledge and vocabulary). Subsumed within these two major subfactors are other, more specific factors. A similar view was proposed by Philip E. Vernon (1971), who made a general division between practical-mechanical and verbal-educational abilities.

More recently, John B. Carroll (1993) proposed a hierarchical model of intelligence based on his analysis of more than 460 data sets obtained between 1927 and 1987. His analysis encompasses more than 130,000 people from diverse walks of life and even countries of origin (although non–English-speaking countries are poorly represented among his data sets). The model Carroll proposed, based on his monumental undertaking, is a hierarchy comprising three strata – Stratum I, which includes many narrow, specific abilities (e.g., spelling ability, speed of reasoning); Stratum II, which includes various broad abilities (e.g., fluid intelligence, crystallized intelligence); and Stratum III, a single general intelligence, much like Spearman's *g*.

In addition to fluid intelligence and crystallized intelligence, Carroll includes in the middle stratum learning and memory processes, visual perception, auditory perception, facile production of ideas (similar to verbal fluency), and speed (which includes both sheer speed of response and speed of accurate response). Although Carroll does not break new ground in that many of the abilities in his model have been mentioned in other theories, he does masterfully integrate a large and diverse factor-analytic literature, thereby giving great authority to his model. Whereas the factor-analytic approach has tended to emphasize the structures of intelligence, the cognitive approach has tended to emphasize the operations of intelligence.

Cognitive Approaches to Intelligence

Cognitive theorists are interested in studying how people (or other organisms; Zentall, 2000) mentally represent and process what they learn and know about the world. The ways in which various cognitive investigators study intelligence differ primarily in terms of the complexity of the processes being studied. Among the advocates of this approach have been Ted Nettelbeck, Arthur Jensen, Earl Hunt, Herbert Simon, and myself. Each of these researchers has considered both the speed and the accuracy of information processing to be important factors in intelligence. In addition to speed and accuracy of processing, Hunt considered verbal versus spatial skill, as well as attentional ability.

INSPECTION TIME

Nettelbeck (e.g., 1987; Nettelbeck & Lally, 1976; Nettelbeck & Rabbitt, 1992; see also Deary, 2000, 2002; Deary & Stough, 1996) suggested a speed-related indicator of intelligence involving the encoding of visual information for brief storage in working memory. But what is critical in this view is not speed of response but rather the length of time a stimulus must be presented for the subject to be able to process that stimulus. The shorter the presentation length, the higher the score. The key variable is the length of time for the presentation of the target stimulus, not the speed of responding by pressing the button. Nettelbeck operationally defined inspection time as the length of time for presentation of the target stimulus after which the participant still responds with at least 90% success. Nettelbeck (1987) found that shorter inspection times correlate with higher scores on intelligence tests [e.g., various subscales of the Wechsler Adult Intelligence Scale (WAIS)] among differing populations of participants. Other investigators have confirmed this finding (e.g., Deary & Stough, 1996).

CHOICE REACTION TIME

Arthur Jensen (1979, 1998, 2002) emphasized a different aspect of information-processing speed; specifically, he proposed that intelligence can be understood in terms of speed of neuronal conduction. In other words, the smart person is someone whose neural circuits conduct information rapidly. When Jensen proposed this notion, direct measures of neural-conduction velocity were not readily available, so Jensen primarily studied a proposed proxy for measuring neural-processing speed – choice reaction time, the time it takes to select one answer from among several possibilities. For example, suppose that you are one of Jensen's participants. You might be seated in front of a set of lights on a board. When one of the lights flashed, you would be expected to extinguish it by pressing as rapidly as possible a button beneath the correct light. The experimenter would then measure your speed in performing this task. Jensen (1982) found that participants with higher intelligence quotients (IQs) are faster than participants with lower IQs in their reaction time (RT), the time between when a light comes on and the finger leaves the home (central) button. In some studies, participants with higher IQs also showed a faster movement time, the time between letting the finger leave the home button and hitting the button under the light. Based on such tasks, Reed and Jensen (1991, 1993) propose that their findings may be attributable to increased central nerve-conduction velocity, although at present this proposal remains speculative.

More recently, researchers have suggested that various findings regarding choice RT may be influenced by the number of response alternatives and the visual-scanning requirements of Jensen's apparatus rather than being attributable to the speed of RT alone (Bors, MacLeod, & Forrin, 1993). In particular, Bors and colleagues found that manipulating the number of buttons and the size of the visual angle of the display could reduce the correlation between IQ and RT. Thus, the relation between reaction time and intelligence is unclear.

LEXICAL ACCESS SPEED AND SPEED OF SIMULTANEOUS PROCESSING

Like Jensen, Earl Hunt (1978) suggested that intelligence be measured in terms of speed. However, Hunt has been particularly interested in verbal intelligence and has focused on lexical-access speed – the speed with which we can retrieve information about words (e.g., letter names) stored in our long-term memories. To measure this speed, Hunt proposed a letter-matching RT task (Posner & Mitchell, 1967).

For example, suppose that you are one of Hunt's participants. You would be shown pairs of letters, such as "A A," "A a," or "A b." For each pair, you would be asked to indicate whether the letters constitute a match in name (e.g., "A a" match in name of letter of the alphabet but "A b" do not). You would also be given a simpler task, in which you would be asked to indicate whether the letters match physically (e.g., "A A" are physically identical, whereas "A a" are not). Hunt would be particularly interested in discerning the difference between your speed for the first set of tasks, involving name matching, and your speed for the second set, involving matching of physical characteristics. Hunt would consider the difference in your reaction time for each task to indicate a measure of your speed of lexical access. Thus, he would subtract from his equation the physical-match reaction time. For Hunt, the response time in indicating that "A A" is a physical match is unimportant. What interests him is a more complex reaction time – that for recognizing names of letters. He and his colleagues have found that students with lower verbal ability take longer to gain access to lexical information than do students with higher verbal ability.

Earl Hunt and Marcy Lansman (1982) also studied people's ability to divide their attention as a function of intelligence. For example, suppose that you are asked to solve mathematical problems and simultaneously to listen for a tone and press a button as soon as you hear it. We can expect that you would both solve the math problems effectively and respond quickly to hearing the tone. According to Hunt and Lansman, one thing that makes people more intelligent is that they are better able to timeshare between two tasks and to perform both effectively.

In sum, process timing theories attempt to account for differences in intelligence by appealing to differences in the speed of various forms of information processing; inspection time, choice RT, and lexical access timing all have been found to correlate with measures of intelligence. These findings suggest that higher intelligence may be related to the speed of various information-processing abilities, including encoding information more rapidly into working memory, accessing information in long-term memory more rapidly, and responding more rapidly.

Why would more rapid encoding, retrieval, and responding be associated with higher intelligence test scores? Do rapid information processors learn more? Other research on learning in aged persons investigated whether there is a link between age-related slowing of information processing and (1) initial encoding and recall of information and (2) long-term retention (Nettelbeck et al., 1996; Bors & Forrin, 1995). The findings suggest that the relation between inspection time and intelligence may not be related to learning. In particular, Nettelbeck et al. found there is a difference between initial recall and actual long-term learning – whereas initial recall performance is mediated by processing speed (older, slower participants showed deficits), longer-term retention of new information (preserved in older participants) is mediated by cognitive processes other than speed of processing, including rehearsal strategies. This implies speed of information processing may influence initial performance on recall and inspection time tasks, but speed is not related to long-term learning. Perhaps faster information processing aids participants in performance aspects of intelligence test tasks, rather than contributing to actual learning and intelligence (see also Salthouse, Chap. 24). Clearly, this area requires more research to determine how information-processing speed relates to intelligence.

WORKING MEMORY

Recent work suggests that a critical component of intelligence may be working memory (see Morrison, Chap. 19 for a discussion of working memory in thinking). Indeed, Kyllonen (2002) and Kyllonen and Christal (1990) have argued that intelligence may be little more than working memory! Daneman and Carpenter (1983) had participants read sets of passages and, after they had read the passages, try to remember the last word of each passage. Recall was highly correlated with verbal ability. Turner and Engle (1989) had participants perform a variety of working-memory tasks. In one task, for example, the participants saw a set of simple arithmetic problems, each of which was followed by a word or a digit. An example would be "Is $((3 \times 5) - 6 = 7$?" TABLE. The participants saw sets of from two to six such problems and solved each one. After solving the problems in the set, they tried to recall the words that followed the problems. The number of words recalled was highly correlated with measured intelligence. It therefore appears that the ability to store and manipulate information in working memory may be an important aspect of intelligence, although probably not all there is to intelligence (see Morrison, Chap. 19 for discussion of working memory and thinking).

THE COMPONENTIAL THEORY AND COMPLEX PROBLEM SOLVING

In my early work on intelligence, I (Sternberg, 1977) began using cognitive approaches to study information processing in more complex tasks, such as analogies, series problems (e.g., completing a numerical or figural series), and syllogisms (Sternberg, 1977, 1983, 1985). The goal was to find out just what made some people more intelligent processors of information than others. The idea was to take the kinds of tasks used on conventional intelligence tests and to isolate the components of intelligence – the mental processes used in performing these tasks, such as translating a sensory input into a mental representation, transforming one conceptual representation into another, or translating a conceptual representation into a motor output (Sternberg, 1982). Since then, many people have elaborated upon and expanded this basic approach (Lohman, 2000).

Componential analysis breaks down people's reaction times and error rates on these tasks in terms of the processes that make up the tasks. This kind of analysis revealed that people may solve analogies and similar tasks by using several component processes including encoding the terms of the problem, inferring relations among at least some of the terms, mapping the inferred relations to other terms that would be presumed to show similar relations, and applying the previously inferred relations to the new situations.

Consider the analogy, LAWYER : CLIENT :: DOCTOR : (a. PATIENT b. MEDICINE). To solve this analogy, you need to encode each term of the problem, which includes perceiving a term and retrieving information about it from memory. You then infer the relationship between lawyer and client – that the former provides professional services to the latter. You then map the relationship in the first half of the analogy to the second half of the analogy, noting that it will involve that same relationship. Finally, you apply that inferred relationship to generate the final term of the analogy, leading to the appropriate response of PATIENT. Studying these components of information processing reveals more than measuring mental speed alone (see Holyoak, Chapter 6, for a detailed discussion of analogical reasoning).

When measuring speed alone, I found significant correlations between speed in executing these processes and performance on other traditional intelligence tests. However, a more intriguing discovery is that participants who score higher on traditional intelligence tests take longer to encode the terms of the problem than do less intelligent participants, but they make up for the extra time by taking less time to perform the remaining components of the task. In general, more intelligent participants take longer during global planning – encoding the problem and formulating a general strategy for attacking the problem (or set of problems) – but they take less time for local planning – forming and implementing strategies for the details of the task (Sternberg, 1981).

The advantage of spending more time on global planning is the increased likelihood that the overall strategy will be correct. Thus, brighter people may take longer to do something than will less bright people when taking more time is advantageous. For example, the brighter person might spend more time researching and planning a term paper but less time in actually writing it. This same differential in time allocation has been shown in other tasks as well (e.g., in solving physics problems; Larkin et al., 1980; Sternberg, 1979, 1985); that is, more intelligent people seem to spend more time planning for and encoding the problems they face but less time in the other components of task performance. This may relate to the previously mentioned metacognitive attribute many include in their notions of intelligence. The bottom line, then, is that intelligence may reside as much in how people allocate time as it does in the amount of time it takes them to perform cognitive tasks.

In a similarly cognitive approach, Simon studied the information processing of people engaged in complex problem-solving situations, such as when playing chess and performing logical derivations (Newell & Simon, 1972; Simon, 1976). A simple, brief task might require the participant to view an arithmetic or geometric series, figure out the rule underlying the progression, and guess what numeral or geometric figure might come next; for example, more complex tasks might include some problem-solving tasks (e.g., the water jugs problems; see Estes, 1982). These problems were similar or identical to those used on intelligence tests.

Biological Approaches to Intelligence

Although the human brain is clearly the organ responsible for human intelligence, early studies (e.g., those by Karl Lashley and others) seeking to find biological indices of intelligence and other aspects of mental processes were a resounding failure despite great efforts. As tools for studying the brain have become more sophisticated, however, we are beginning to see the possibility of finding physiological indicators of intelligence. Some investigators (e.g., Matarazzo, 1992) believe that we will have clinically useful psychophysiological indices of intelligence very early in the current millennium, although widely applicable indices will be much longer in coming. In the meantime, the biological studies we now have are largely correlational, showing statistical associations between biological and psychometric or other measures of intelligence. The studies do not establish causal relations (see Goel, Chapter 20, for a description of the neural basis of deductive reasoning).

BRAIN SIZE

One line of research looks at the relationship of brain size to intelligence (see Jerison, 2000; Vernon et al., 2000). The evidence suggests that, for humans, there is a modest but significant statistical relationship between brain size and intelligence. It is difficult to know what to make of this relationship, however, because greater brain size may cause greater intelligence, greater intelligence may cause greater brain size, or both may depend on some third factor. Moreover, it probably is more important how efficiently the brain is used than what size it is. On average, for example, men have larger brains than women, but women have better connections of the two hemispheres of the brain through the corpus callosum. So it is not clear which gender, on average, would be at an advantage, and probably neither would be. It is important to note that the relationship between brain size and intelligence does not hold across species (Jerison, 2000). Rather, what holds seems to be a relationship between intelligence and brain size relative to the rough general size of the organism.

SPEED OF NEURAL CONDUCTION

Complex patterns of electrical activity in the brain, which are prompted by specific stimuli, appear to correlate with scores on IQ tests (Barrett & Eysenck, 1992). Several studies (e.g., McGarry-Roberts, Stelmack, & Campbell, 1992; Vernon & Mori, 1992) initially suggested that speed of conduction of neural impulses correlates with intelligence as measured by IQ tests. A follow-up study (Wickett & Vernon, 1994), however, failed to find a strong relation between neural-conduction velocity (as measured by neural-conduction speeds in a main nerve of the arm) and intelligence (as measured on the Multidimensional Aptitude Battery). Surprisingly, neural-conduction velocity appears to be a more powerful predictor of IQ scores for men than for women, so gender differences may account for some of the differences in the data (Wickett & Vernon, 1994). Additional studies on both males and females are needed.

POSITRON EMISSION TOMOGRAPHY, FUNCTIONAL MAGNETIC RESONANCE IMAGING

An alternative approach to studying the brain suggests that neural efficiency may be related to intelligence; such an approach is based on studies of how the brain metabolizes glucose (simple sugar required for brain activity) during mental activities. Richard Haier and colleagues (Haier et al., 1992) cited several other researchers who support their own findings that higher intelligence correlates with reduced levels of glucose metabolism during problem-solving tasks – that is, smarter brains consume less sugar (and hence expend less effort) than do less smart brains doing the same task. Furthermore, Haier and colleagues found that cerebral efficiency increases as a result of learning on a relatively complex task involving visuospatial manipulations (the computer game Tetris). As a result of practice, more intelligent participants show not only lower cerebral glucose metabolism overall but also more specifically localized metabolism of glucose. In most areas of their brains, smarter participants show less glucose metabolism, but in selected areas of their brains (believed to be important to the task at hand), they show higher levels of glucose metabolism. Thus, more intelligent participants may have learned how to use their brains more efficiently to focus their thought processes on a given task.

More recent research by Haier and colleagues suggests that the relationship between glucose metabolism and intelligence may be more complex (Haier et al., 1995; Larson et al., 1995). Whereas Haier's group

(1995) confirmed the earlier findings of increased glucose metabolism in less smart participants (in this case, mildly retarded participants), the study by Larson et al. (1995) found, contrary to the earlier findings, that smarter participants had increased glucose metabolism relative to their average comparison group.

One problem with earlier studies is that the tasks used were not matched for difficulty level across groups of smart and average individuals. The Larson et al. study used tasks that were matched to the ability levels of the smarter and average participants and found that the smarter participants used more glucose. Moreover, the glucose metabolism was highest in the right hemisphere of the more intelligent participants performing the hard task – again suggesting selectivity of brain areas. What could be driving the increases in glucose metabolism? Currently, the key factor appears to be subjective task difficulty with smarter participants in earlier studies simply finding the tasks too easy. Matching task difficulty to participants' abilities seems to indicate that smarter participants increase glucose metabolism when the task demands it. The preliminary findings in this area need to be investigated further before any conclusive answers are reached.

Some neuropsychological research (e.g., Dempster, 1991) suggests that performance on intelligence tests may not indicate a crucial aspect of intelligence – the ability to set goals, to plan how to meet them, and to execute those plans. Specifically, persons with lesions in the frontal lobe of the brain frequently perform quite well on standardized IQ tests, which require responses to questions within a highly structured situation, but do not require much in the way of goal setting or planning. If intelligence involves the ability to learn from experience and to adapt to the surrounding environment, the ability to set goals and to design and implement plans cannot be ignored. An essential aspect of goal setting and planning is the ability to attend appropriately to relevant stimuli and to ignore or discount irrelevant stimuli.

Evolutionary Theory

Some theorists have tried to understand intelligence in terms of how it has evolved over the eons (e.g., Bjorklund & Kipp, 2002; Bradshaw, 2002; Byrne, 2002; Calvin, 2002; Corballis, 2002; Cosmides & Tooby, 2002; Flanagan, Hardcastle, & Nahmias, 2002; Grossman & Kaufman, 2002; Pinker, 1997). The basic idea in these models is that we are intelligent in the ways we are because it was important for our distant ancestors to acquire certain sets of skills. According to Cosmides and Tooby (2002), for example, we are particularly sensitive at detecting cheating because people in the past who were not sensitive to cheaters did not live to have children, or had fewer children. Evolutionary approaches stress the continuity of the nature of intelligence over long stretches of time, and in some theories, across species. However, during evolution, the frontal lobe increased in size, so it is difficult to know whether changes in intelligence are just a manifestation of physiological changes or the other way around.

Contextual Approaches to Intelligence

According to contextualists, intelligence cannot be understood outside its real-world context. The context of intelligence may be viewed at any level of analysis, focusing narrowly, on the home and family environment, or extending broadly, on entire cultures (see Greenfield, Chap. 27). Even cross-community differences have been correlated with differences in performance on intelligence tests; such context-related differences include those of rural versus urban communities, low versus high proportions of teenagers to adults within communities, and low versus high socioeconomic status of communities (see Coon, Carey, & Fulker, 1992). Contextualists are particularly intrigued by the effects of cultural context on intelligence.

In fact, contextualists consider intelligence so inextricably linked to culture that they view intelligence as something that a culture creates to define the nature of adaptive performance in that culture and to account for why some people perform better than others on the tasks that the culture happens to value (Sternberg, 1985). Theorists who endorse this model study just how intelligence relates to the external world in which the model is being applied and evaluated. In general, definitions and theories of intelligence will more effectively encompass cultural diversity by broadening in scope. Before exploring some of the contextual theories of intelligence, we will look at what prompted psychologists to believe that culture might play a role in how we define and assess intelligence.

People in different cultures may have quite different ideas of what it means to be smart. One of the more interesting cross-cultural studies of intelligence was performed by Michael Cole and colleagues (Cole et al., 1971). These investigators asked adult members of the Kpelle tribe in Africa to sort concept terms. In Western culture, when adults are given a sorting task on an intelligence test, more intelligent people typically sort hierarchically. For example, they may sort names of different kinds of fish together, and then the word fish over that, with the name animal over fish and over birds, and so on. Less intelligent people typically sort functionally. They may sort fish with eat, for example, because we eat fish, or clothes with wear, because we wear clothes. The Kpelle sorted functionally – even after investigators unsuccessfully tried to get the Kpelle spontaneously to sort hierarchically. Finally, in desperation, one of the experimenters (Glick) asked a Kpelle to sort as a foolish person would sort. In response, the Kpelle quickly and easily sorted hierarchically. The Kpelle had been able to sort this way all along; they just hadn't done it because they viewed it as foolish – and they probably considered the questioners rather unintelligent for asking such stupid questions.

The Kpelle people are not the only ones who might question Western understandings of intelligence. In the Puluwat culture of the Pacific Ocean, for example, sailors navigate incredibly long distances, using none of the navigational aids that sailors from technologically advanced countries would need to get from one place to another (Gladwin, 1970). Were Puluwat sailors to devise intelligence tests for us and our fellow Americans, we might not seem very intelligent. Similarly, the highly skilled Puluwat sailors might not do well on American-crafted tests of intelligence. These and other observations have prompted quite a few theoreticians to recognize the importance of considering cultural context when assessing intelligence.

The preceding arguments may make it clear why it is so difficult to come up with a test that everyone would consider culture-fair – equally appropriate and fair for members of all cultures. If members of different cultures have different ideas of what it means to be intelligent, then the very behaviors that may be considered intelligent in one culture may be considered unintelligent in another. Take, for example, the concept of mental quickness. In mainstream American culture, quickness is usually associated with intelligence. To say someone is "quick" is to say that the person is intelligent and, indeed, most group tests of intelligence are quite strictly timed. Even on individual tests of intelligence, the test-giver times some responses of the test-taker. Many information-processing theorists and even psychophysiological theorists focus on the study of intelligence as a function of mental speed.

In many cultures of the world, people believe that more intelligent people do not rush into things. Even in our own culture, no one will view you as brilliant if you decide on a marital partner, a job, or a place to live in the 20 to 30 seconds you might normally have to solve an intelligence-test problem. Thus, given that there exist no perfectly culture-fair tests of intelligence, at least at present, how should we consider context when assessing and understanding intelligence?

Several researchers have suggested that providing culture-relevant tests is possible (e.g., Baltes, Dittmann-Kohli, & Dixon, 1984; Jenkins, 1979; Keating, 1984); that is, tests that employ skills and knowledge that relate to the cultural experiences of the test-takers. Baltes and his colleagues, for example, designed tests measuring skill in dealing with the pragmatic aspects of everyday life. Designing culture-relevant tests requires creativity and effort but probably is not impossible. A study by Daniel Wagner (1978), for example, investigated memory abilities – one aspect of intelligence as our culture defines it – in our culture versus the Moroccan culture. Wagner found that level of recall depended on the content that was being remembered, with culture-relevant content being remembered more effectively than irrelevant content (e.g., compared with Westerners, Moroccan rug merchants were better able to recall complex visual patterns on black-and-white photos of Oriental rugs). Wagner further suggested that when tests are not designed to minimize the effects of cultural differences, the key to culture-specific differences in memory might be the knowledge and use of metamemory strategies, rather than actual structural differences in memory (e.g., memory span and rates of forgetting).

In Kenya, research has shown that rural Kenyan school children have substantial knowledge about natural herbal medicines they believe fight infection; Western children, of course, would not be able to identify any of these medicines (Sternberg et al., 2001; Sternberg & Grigorenko, 1997). In short, making a test culturally relevant appears to involve much more than just removing specific linguistic barriers to understanding.

Stephen Ceci (Ceci & Roazzi, 1994) found similar context effects in childrens' and adults' performance on a variety of tasks. Ceci suggests that the social context (e.g., whether a task is considered masculine or feminine), the mental context (e.g., whether a visuo-spatial task involves buying a home or burgling it), and the physical context (e.g., whether a task is presented at the beach or in a laboratory) all affect performance. For example, fourteen-year-old boys performed poorly on a task when it was couched as a cupcake-baking task but performed well when it was framed as a battery-charging task (Ceci & Bronfenbrenner, 1985). Brazilian maids had no difficulty with proportional reasoning when hypothetically purchasing food but had great difficulty with it when hypothetically purchasing medicinal herbs (Schliemann & Magalhües, 1990). Brazilian children whose poverty had forced them to become street vendors showed no difficulty in performing complex arithmetic computations when selling things but had great difficulty performing similar calculations in a classroom (Carraher, Carraher, & Schliemann, 1985). Thus, test performance may be affected by the context in which the test terms are presented. In this study, the investigators looked at the interaction of cognition and context. Several investigators have proposed theories that seek explicitly to examine this interaction within an integrated model of many aspects of intelligence. Such theories view intelligence as a complex system.

Systems Approaches to Intelligence

GARDNER: MULTIPLE INTELLIGENCES

Howard Gardner (1983, 1993) proposed a theory of multiple intelligences, in which intelligence is not just a single, unitary construct. Instead of speaking of multiple abilities that together constitute intelligence (e.g., Thurstone, 1938), Gardner (1999) speaks of eight distinct intelligences that are relatively independent of each other. Each is a separate system of functioning, although these systems can interact to produce what we see as intelligent performance.

In some respects, Gardner's theory sounds like a factorial one because it specifies several abilities that are construed to reflect intelligence of some sort. However, Gardner views each ability as a separate intelligence, not just as a part of a single whole. Moreover, a crucial difference between Gardner's theory and factorial ones is in the sources of evidence Gardner used for identifying the eight intelligences. Gardner used converging operations, gathering evidence from multiple sources and types of data.

Gardner's view of the mind is modular, Because as a major task of existing and future research on intelligence is to isolate the portions of the brain responsible for each of the intelligences. Gardner has speculated regarding at least some of these locales, but hard evidence for the existence of these separate intelligences has yet to be produced. Furthermore, Nettelbeck and Young (1996) question the strict modularity of Gardner's theory. Specifically, the phenomenon of preserved specific cognitive functioning in autistic savants (persons with severe social and cognitive deficits, but with corresponding high ability in a narrow domain) as evidence for modular intelligences may not be justified. According to Nettelbeck and Young, the narrow long-term memory and specific aptitudes of savants is not really intelligent. As a result, there may be reason to question the intelligence of inflexible modules.

STERNBERG: THE TRIARCHIC THEORY OF SUCCESSFUL INTELLIGENCE

Whereas Gardner emphasizes the separateness of the various aspects of intelligence, I tend to emphasize the extent to which they work together in the triarchic theory of successful intelligence (Sternberg, 1985, 1988, 1996, 1999). According to the triarchic (tri-, "three"; -archic, "governed") theory, intelligence comprises three aspects, dealing with the relation of intelligence (1) to the internal world of the person, (2) to experience, and (3) to the external world.

How intelligence relates to the internal world. This part of the theory emphasizes the processing of information, which can be viewed in terms of three different kinds of components: (1) metacomponents – executive processes (i.e., metacognition) used to plan, monitor, and evaluate problem solving; (2) performance components – lower order processes used to implement the commands of the metacomponents; and (3) knowledge-acquisition components – the processes used to learn how to solve the problems in the first place. The components are highly interdependent.

How intelligence relates to experience. The theory also considers how prior experience may interact with all three kinds of information-processing components. That is, each of us faces tasks and situations with which we have varying levels of experience, ranging from a completely novel task, with which we have no previous experience, to a completely familiar task, with which we have vast, extensive experience. As a task becomes increasingly familiar, many aspects of the task may become automatic, requiring little conscious effort to determine what step to take next and how to implement that next step. A novel task makes demands on intelligence different from those of a task for which automatic procedures have been developed.

According to the triarchic theory, relatively novel tasks – such as visiting a foreign country, mastering a new subject, or acquiring a foreign language – demand more of a person's intelligence. In fact, a completely unfamiliar task may demand so much of the person as to be overwhelming.

How intelligence relates to the external world. The triarchic theory also proposes that the various components of intelligence are applied to experience to serve three functions in real-world contexts – adapting ourselves to our existing environments, shaping our existing environments to create new environments, and selecting new environments.

According to the triarchic theory, people may apply their intelligence to many different kinds of problems. Some people may be more intelligent in the face of abstract, academic problems, for example, whereas others may be more intelligent in the face of concrete, practical problems. The theory does not define an intelligent person as someone who necessarily excels in all aspects of intelligence. Rather, intelligent persons know their own strengths and weaknesses and find ways in which to capitalize on their strengths and either to compensate for or to correct their weaknesses.

In a recent comprehensive study testing the validity of the triarchic theory and its usefulness in improving performance, we predicted that matching students' instruction and assessment to their abilities would lead to improved performance (Sternberg et al., 1996, 1999). Students were selected for one of five ability patterns: high only in analytical ability, high only in creative ability, high only in practical ability, high in all three abilities, or not high in any of the three abilities. Then students were assigned at random to one of four instructional groups that emphasized memory-based, analytical, creative, or practical learning followed by subsequent assessment. We found that students who were placed in an instructional condition that matched their strength in terms of ability pattern (e.g., a high-analytical student being placed in an instructional condition that emphasized analytical thinking) outperformed students who were mismatched (e.g., a high-analytical student being placed in an instructional condition that emphasized practical thinking).

Teaching all students to use all of their analytic, creative, and practical abilities has resulted in improved school achievement for all students, whatever their ability pattern (Grigorenko, Jarvin, & Sternberg, 2002; Sternberg, Torff, & Grigorenko, 1998). One important consideration in light of such findings is the need for changes in the assessment of intelligence (Sternberg & Kaufman, 1996). Current measures of intelligence are somewhat one-sided, measuring mostly analytic abilities with little or no assessment of creative and practical aspects of intelligence (Sternberg et al., 2000; Wagner, 2000). A well-rounded assessment and instruction system could lead to greater benefits of education for a wider variety of students – a nominal goal of education.

TRUE INTELLIGENCE

Perkins (1995) proposed a theory of what he refers to as *true intelligence*, which he believes synthesizes classic views as well as new ones. According to Perkins, there are three basic aspects of intelligence – neural, experiential, and reflective.

Neural intelligence concerns what Perkins believes to be the fact that some people's neurological systems function better than do the neurological systems of others, running faster and with more precision. He mentions "more finely tuned voltages" and "more exquisitely adapted chemical catalysts" as well as a "better pattern of connecticity in the labyrinth of neurons" (Perkins, 1995, p. 497), although it is not entirely clear what any of these terms means. Perkins believes this aspect of intelligence to be largely genetically determined and unlearnable. This kind of intelligence seems to be somewhat similar to Cattell's (1971) idea of fluid intelligence.

The experiential aspect of intelligence is what has been learned from experience. It is the extent and organization of the knowledge base and thus is similar to Cattell's (1971) notion of crystallized intelligence.

The reflective aspect of intelligence refers to the role of strategies in memory and problem solving, and appears to be similar to the construct of metacognition or cognitive monitoring (Brown & DeLoache, 1978; Flavell, 1981).

No empirical test of the theory of true intelligence has been published, so it is difficult to evaluate the theory at this time. Like Gardner's (1983) theory, Perkins's theory is based on literature review, and, as noted previously, such literature reviews often tend to be selective and then interpreted in a way that maximizes the fit of the theory to the available data.

THE BIOECOLOGICAL MODEL OF INTELLIGENCE

Ceci (1996) proposed a bioecological model of intelligence, according to which multiple cognitive potentials, context, and knowledge all are essential bases of individual differences in performance. Each of the multiple cognitive potentials enables relationships to be discovered, thoughts to be monitored, and knowledge to be acquired within a given domain. Although these potentials are biologically based, their development is closely linked to environmental context, and it is difficult, if not impossible, to cleanly separate biological from environmental contributions to intelligence. Moreover, abilities may express themselves very differently in different contexts. For example, children given essentially the same task in the context of a video game versus a laboratory cognitive task performed much better when the task was presented in the video game context.

The bioecological model appears in many ways more to be a framework than a theory. At some level, the theory must be right. Certainly, both biological and ecological factors contribute to the development and manifestation of intelligence. Perhaps what the theory needs most at this time are specific and clearly falsifiable predictions that would set it apart from other theories.

Improving Intelligence

Although designers of artificial intelligence have made great strides in creating programs that simulate knowledge and skill acquisition, no existing program even approaches the ability of the human brain to enhance its own intelligence. Human intelligence is highly malleable and can be shaped and even increased through various kinds of interventions (Detterman & Sternberg, 1982; Grotzer & Perkins, 2000; Perkins & Grotzer, 1997; Sternberg et al., 1996; Sternberg et al., 1997; see Ritchhart & Perkins, Chap. 32, for a review of work on teaching thinking skills). Moreover, the malleability of intelligence has nothing to do with the extent to which intelligence has a genetic basis (Sternberg, 1997). An attribute (such as height) can be partly or even largely genetically based and yet be environmentally malleable.

The Head Start program was initiated in the 1960s to provide preschoolers with an edge on intellectual abilities and accomplishments when they started school. Long-term follow-ups have indicated that by mid-adolescence, children who participated in the program were more than a grade ahead of matched controls who did not receive the program (Lazar & Darlington, 1982; Zigler & Berman, 1983). The children in the program also scored higher on a variety of tests of scholastic achievement, were less likely to need remedial attention, and were less likely to show behavioral problems. Although such measures are not truly measures of intelligence, they show strong positive correlations with intelligence tests.

An alternative to intellectual enrichment outside the home may be to provide an enriched home environment. A particularly successful project has been the Abecedarian Project, which showed that the cognitive skills and achievements of lower socioeconomic status children could be increased through carefully planned and executed interventions (Ramey & Ramey, 2000).

Bradley and Caldwell (1984) found support for the importance of home environment with regard to the development of intelligence in young children. These researchers found that several factors in the early (preschool) home environment were correlated with high IQ scores – emotional and verbal responsivity of the primary caregiver and the caregiver's involvement with the child, avoidance of restriction and punishment, organization of the physical environment and activity schedule, provision of appropriate play materials, and opportunities for variety in daily stimulation. Further, Bradley and Caldwell found that these factors more effectively predicted IQ scores than did socioeconomic status or family-structure variables. It should be noted, however, that the Bradley–Caldwell study is correlational and therefore cannot be interpreted as indicating causality. Furthermore, their study pertained to preschool children, and children's IQ scores do not begin to predict adult IQ scores well until age four years. Moreover, before age seven years, the scores are not very stable (Bloom, 1964). More recent work (e.g., Pianta & Egeland, 1994) suggested that factors such as maternal social support and interactive behavior may play a key role in the instability of scores on tests of intellectual ability between ages two and eight years.

The Bradley and Caldwell data should not be taken to indicate that demographic variables have little effect on IQ scores. To the contrary, throughout history and across cultures, many groups of people have been assigned pariah status as inferior members of the social order. Across cultures, these disadvantaged groups (e.g., native Maoris vs. European New Zealanders) have shown differences in tests of intelligence and aptitude (Steele, 1990; Zeidner, 1990). Such was the case of the Burakumin tanners in Japan, who, in 1871, were granted emancipation but not full acceptance into Japanese society. Despite their poor performance and underprivileged status in Japan, those who immigrate to America and are treated like other Japanese immigrants – perform on IQ tests and in school achievement at a level comparable to that of their fellow Japanese Americans (Ogbu, 1986).

Similar positive effects of integration were shown on the other side of the world. In Israel, the children of European Jews score much higher on IQ tests than do children of Arabic Jews – except when the children are reared on kibbutzim in which the children of all national ancestries are raised by specially trained caregivers in a dwelling separate from their parents. When these children shared the same child-rearing environments, there were no national-ancestry-related differences in IQ.

Altogether, there is now abundant evidence that people's environments (e.g., Ceci, Nightingale, & Baker, 1992; Reed, 1993; Sternberg & Wagner, 1994; Wagner, 2000), their motivation (e.g., Collier, 1994; Sternberg & Ruzgis, 1994), and their training (e.g., Feuerstein, 1980; Sternberg, 1987) can profoundly affect their intellectual skills. Thus, the controversial claims made by Herrnstein and Murray (1994) in their book, *The Bell Curve*, regarding the futility of intervention programs, are unfounded when one considers the evidence in favor of the possibility of improving cognitive skills. Likewise, Herrnstein and Murray's appeal to "a genetic factor in cognitive ethnic differences" (Herrnstein & Murray, 1994, p. 270) falls apart in light of the direct evidence against such genetic differences (Sternberg, 1996) and results from a misunderstanding of the heritability of traits in general.

Heredity certainly plays a role in individual differences in intelligence (Loehlin, 2000; Loehlin, Horn, & Willerman, 1997; Plomin, 1997), as does the environment (Grigorenko, 2000, 2002; Sternberg & Grigorenko, 1999; Wahlsten & Gottlieb, 1997). Genetic inheritance may set some kind of upper limit on how intelligent a person may become. However, we now know that for any attribute that is partly genetic, there is a reaction range – that is, the attribute can be expressed in various ways within broad limits of possibilities. Thus, each person's intelligence can be developed further within this broad range of potential intelligence (Grigorenko, 2000). We have no reason to believe that people now reach their upper limits in the development of their intellectual skills. To the contrary, the evidence suggests that we can do quite a bit to help people become more intelligent (for further discussion of these issues, see R. Mayer, 2000, and Neisser et al., 1996).

Environmental as well as hereditary factors may contribute to retardation in intelligence (Grigorenko, 2000; Sternberg & Grigorenko, 1997). Environmental influences before birth may cause permanent retardation, which may result from a mother's inadequate nutrition or ingestion of toxins such as alcohol during the infant's prenatal development (Grantham-McGregor, Ani, & Fernald, 2002; Mayes & Fahy, 2001; Olson, 1994), for example. Among the other environmental factors that can negatively impact intelligence are low social and economic status (Ogbu & Stern, 2001; Seifer, 2001), high levels of pollutants (Bellinger & Adams, 2001), inadequate care in the family or divorce (Fiese, 2001; Guidubaldi & Duckworth, 2001), infectious diseases (Alcock & Bundy, 2001), high levels of radiation (Grigorenko, 2001), and inadequate schooling (Christian, Bachnan, & Morrison, 2001). Physical trauma can injure the brain, causing mental retardation.

Conclusions and Future Directions

In conclusion, many approaches have been taken to improve understanding of the nature of intelligence. Great progress has been made in elaborating the construct but much less progress in converging upon either a definition or a universally accepted theory. Much of current debate revolves around trying to figure out what the construct is and how it relates to other constructs, such as learning, memory, and reasoning. Intelligence can be measured, to some extent, and it can be improved. Improvements are not likely to eliminate individual differences, however, because attempts to improve intelligence can help people at all levels and with diverse kinds of intelligence. No matter how high one's intelligence, there is always room for improvement; and no matter how low, there are always measures that can be taken to help raise it.

Acknowledgments

Preparation of this article was supported by Grant REC-9979843 from the National Science Foundation and by a grant under the Javits Act Program (Grant No. R206R000001) as administered by the Institute of Education Sciences, U.S. Department of Education. Grantees undertaking such projects are encouraged to express freely their professional judgment. This article, therefore, does not necessarily represent the position or policies of the National Science Foundation, Office of Educational Research and Improvement, or the U.S. Department of Education, and no official endorsement should be inferred.

References

Ackerman, P. L. (1996). A theory of adult intellectual development: Process, personality, interests, and knowledge. *Intelligence*, 22, 229–259.

Alcock, K. J., Bundy, D. A. P. (2001). The impact of infectious disease on cognitive development. In R. J. Sternberg, & E. L. Grigorenko (Eds.), *Environmental Effects on Cognitive Abilities* (pp. 221–253). Mahwah, NJ: Erlbaum.

Baltes, P. B., Dittmann-Kohli, F., & Dixon, R. A. (1984). New Perspectives on the development of intelligence in adulthood: Toward a dual-process conception and a model of selective optimization with compensation. In P. B. Baltes, & O. G. Brim, Jr. (Eds.), *Life-span Development and Behavior* (Vol. 6, pp. 33–76). New York: Academic Press.

Barrett, P. T., & Eysenck, H. J. (1992). Brain evoked potentials and intelligence: The Hendrickson Paradigm. *Intelligence*, 16, 361–381.

Bellinger, D. C., & Adams, H. F. (2001) Environmental pollutant exposures and children's cognitive ability. In R. J. Sternberg, & E. L. Grigorenko (Eds.), *Environmental Effects on Cognitive Abilities* (pp. 157–188). Mahwah, NJ: Erlbaum.

Binet, A., & Simon, T. (1916). *The Development of Intelligence in Children*. Baltimore: Williams & Wilkins. (Originally published in 1905).

Bjorklund, D. F., & Kipp, K. (2002). Social cognition, inhibition, and theory of mind: The evolution of human intelligence. In R. J. Sternberg, & J. C. Kaufman, (Eds.), *The Evolution of Intelligence* (pp. 27–54). Mahwah, NJ: Erlbaum.

Bloom, B. S. (1964). *Stability and Change in Human Characteristics*. New York: Wiley.

Boring, E. G. (1923, June 6). Intelligence as the tests test it. *New Republic*, 35–37.

Bors, D. A., Forrin, B. (1995). Age, speed of information processing, recall, and fluid intelligence. *Intelligence*, 20(3), 229–248.

Bors, D. A., MacLeod, C. M., & Forrin, B. (1993). Eliminating the IQT correlation by eliminating an experimental confound. *Intelligence*, 17(4), 475–500.

Bradley, R. H., & Caldwell, B. M. (1984). 174 Children: A study of the relationship between home environment and cognitive development during the first 5 years. In A. W. Gottfried (Ed.), *Home Environment and Early Cognitive Development : Longitudinal Research*. San Diego, CA: Academic Press.

Bradshaw, J. L. (2002). The evolution of intellect: Cognitive, neurological, and primatological aspects and hominid culture. In R. J. Sternberg, & J. C. Kaufman, (Eds.), *The Evolution of Intelligence* (pp. 57–58). Mahwah, NJ: Erlbaum.

Brody, N. (2000). History of theories and measurements of intelligence. In R. J. Sternberg (Ed.), *Handbook of Intelligence* (pp. 16–33). New York: Cambridge University Press.

Brown, A. L., & DeLoache, J. S. (1978). Skills, plans, and self-regulation. In R. Siegler (Ed.), *Children's Thinking: What Develops?* Hillsdale, NJ: Erlbaum.

Byrne, R. W. (2002). The primate origins of human intelligence. In R. J. Sternberg & J. C. Kaufman, (Eds.), *The Evolution of Intelligence* (pp. 79–96). Mahwah, NJ: Erlbaum.

Calvin, W. H. (2002). Pumping up intelligence: Abrupt climate jumps and the evolution of higher intellectual functions during the Ice Ages. In R. J. Sternberg, & J. C. Kaufman, (Eds.), *The Evolution of Intelligence* (pp. 97–116). Mahwah, NJ: Erlbaum.

Carraher, T. N., Carraher, D., & Schliemann, A. D. (1985). Mathematics in the streets and in schools. *British Journal of Developmental Psychology*, 3, 21–29.

Carroll, J. B. (1993). *Human Cognitive Abilities: A Survey of Factor-analytic Studies*. New York: Cambridge University Press.

Cattell, R. B. (1971). *Abilities: Their Structure, Growth and Action*. Boston: Houghton Mifflin.

Ceci, S. J. (1996). *On Intelligence . . . More or Less* (expanded ed.). Cambridge, MA: Harvard University Press.

Ceci, S. J., & Bronfenbrenner, U. (1985). Don't forget to take the cupcakes out of the oven: Strategic time-monitoring, prospective memory and context. *Child Development*, 56, 175–190.

Ceci, S. J., Nightingale, N. N., & Baker, J. G. (1992). The ecologies of intelligence: Challenges to traditional views. In D. K. Detterman (Ed.), *Current Topics in Human Intelligence (Vol. 2). Is Mind Modular or Unitary?* (pp. 61–82). Norwood, NJ: Ablex.

Ceci, S. J., & Roazzi, A. (1994). The effects of context on cognition: Postcards from Brazil. In R. J. Sternberg, & R. K. Wagner (Eds.), *Mind in Context: Interactionist Perspectives on Human Intelligence* (pp. 74–101). New York: Cambridge University Press.

Christian, K., Bachnan, H. J., & Morrison, F. J. (2001). Schooling and cognitive development. In R. J. Sternberg, & E. L. Grigorenko (Eds.), *Environmental Effects on Cognitive Abilities* (pp. 287–335). Mahwah, NJ: Erlbaum.

Ciarrochi, J., Forgas, J. P., & Mayer, J. D. (Eds.) (2001). *Emotional Intelligence in Everyday Life: A Scientific Inquiry*. Philadelphia: Psychology Press.

Cole, M., Gay, J., Glick, J., & Sharp, D. W. (1971). *The Cultural Context of Learning and Thinking*. New York: Basic Books.

Collier, G. (1994). *Social Origins of Mental Ability*. New York: Wiley.

Coon, H., Carey, G., & Fulker, D. W. (1992). Community influences on cognitive ability. *Intelligence*, 16(2), 169–188.

Corballis, M. C. (2002). Evolution of the generative mind. In R. J. Sternberg, & J. C. Kaufman, (Eds.), *The Evolution of Intelligence* (pp. 117–144). Mahwah, NJ: Erlbaum.

Cosmides, L., & Tooby, J. (2002). Unraveling the enigma of human intelligence: Evolutionary psychology and the multimodular mind. In R. J. Sternberg, & J. C. Kaufman, (Eds.), *The Evolution of Intelligence* (pp. 145–198). Mahwah, NJ: Erlbaum.

Craik, F. I. M., & Lockhart R. S. (1972). Levels of processing: A framework for memory research. *Journal of Verbal Learning and Verbal Behavior*, 11, 671–684.

Daneman, M., & Carpenter, P. A. (1983). Individual differences in integrating information between and within sentences. *Journal of Experimental Psychology: Learning, Memory, and Cognition*, 9(4), 561–584.

Daniel, M. H. (1997). Intelligence testing: Status and trends. *American Psychologist*, 52, 1038–1045.

Daniel, M. H. (2000). Interpretation of intelligence test scores. In R. J. Sternberg (Ed.), *Handbook of Intelligence* (pp. 477–491). New York: Cambridge University Press.

Davies, M., Stankov, L., & Roberts, R. D. (1998). Emotional intelligence: In search of an elusive construct. *Journal of Personality and Social Psychology*, 75, 989–1015.

Deary, I. J. (2000). Simple information processing. In R. J. Sternberg (Ed.), *Handbook of Intelligence* (pp. 267–284). New York: Cambridge University Press.

Deary, I. J. (2002). *g* and cognitive elements of information processing: An agnostic view. In R. J. Sternberg, & E. L. Grigorenko (Eds.), *The General Factor of Intelligence: How General Is It?* (pp. 151–181). Mahwah, NJ: Erlbaum.

Deary, I. J., & Stough, C. (1996). Intelligence and inspection time: Achievements, prospects, and problems. *American Psychologist*, 51, 599–608.

Dempster, F. N. (1991). Inhibitory processes: A neglected dimension of intelligence. *Intelligence*, 15, 157–173.

Detterman, D. K., & Sternberg, R. J. (Eds.) (1982). *How and How Much Can Intelligence Be Increased?* Norwood, NJ: Erlbaum.

Embretson, S., & McCollam, K. (2000). Psychometric approaches to the understanding and measurement of intelligence. In R. J. Sternberg

(Ed.), *Handbook of Intelligence* (pp. 423–444). New York: Cambridge University Press.

Estes, W. K. (1982). Similarity-related channel interactions in visual processing. *Journal of Experimental Psychology: Human Perception and Performance*, 8(3), 353–382.

Feuerstein, R. (1980). *Instrumental Enrichment: An Intervention Program for Cognitive Modifiability*. Baltimore: University Park Press.

Fiese, B. H. (2001). Family matters: A systems view of family effects on children's cognitive health. In R. J. Sternberg, & E. L. Grigorenko (Eds.), *Environmental Effects on Cognitive Abilities* (pp. 39–57). Mahwah, NJ: Erlbaum.

Flanagan, O., Hardcastle, V. G., & Nahmias, E. (2002). Is human intelligence an adaptation? Cautionary observations from the philosophy of biology. In R. J. Sternberg, & J. C. Kaufman, (Eds.), *The Evolution of Intelligence* (pp. 199–222). Mahwah, NJ: Erlbaum.

Flavell, J. H. (1981). Cognitive monitoring. In W. P. Dickson (Ed.), *Children's Oral Communication Skills* (pp. 35–60). New York: Academic Press.

Galton, F. (1883). *Inquiry into Human Faculty and Its Development*. London: Macmillan.

Gardner, H. (1983). *Frames of Mind: The Theory of Multiple Intelligences*. New York: Basic Books.

Gardner, H. (1993). *Multiple Intelligences: The Theory in Practice*. New York: Basic Books.

Gardner, H. (1999). Are there additional intelligences? The case for naturalist, spiritual, and existential intelligences. In J. Kane (Ed.), *Education, Information, and Transformation* (pp. 111–131). Upper Saddle River, NJ: Prentice-Hall.

Gladwin, T. (1970). *East Is a Big Bird*. Cambridge, MA: Harvard University Press.

Grantham-McGregor, S., Ani, C., & Fernald, L. (2002). The role of nutrition in intellectual development. In R. J. Sternberg, & E. L. Grigorenko (Eds.), *Environmental Effects on Cognitive Abilities* (pp. 119–155). Mahwah, NJ: Erlbaum.

Grigorenko, E. L. (2000). Heritability and intelligence. In R. J. Sternberg (Ed.), *Handbook of Intelligence* (pp. 53–91). New York: Cambridge University Press.

Grigorenko, E. L. (2001). The invisible danger: The impact of ionizing radiation on cognitive development and functioning. In R. J. Sternberg, & E. L. Grigorenko (Eds.), *Environmental Effects on Intellectual Functioning* (pp. 255–286). Mahwah, NJ: Erlbaum.

Grigorenko, E. L. (2002). Other than *g*: The value of persistence. In R. J. Sternberg, & E. L. Grigorenko (Eds.), *The General Factor of Intelligence: Fact or Fiction* (pp. 299–327). Mahwah, NJ: Erlbaum.

Grigorenko, E. L., Jarvin, L., & Sternberg, R. J. (2002). School-based tests of the triarchic theory of intelligence: Three settings, three samples, three syllabi. *Contemporary Educational Psychology*, 27, 167–208.

Grossman, J. B., & Kaufman, J. C. (2002). Evolutionary psychology: Promise and perils. In R. J. Sternberg, & J. C. Kaufman, (Eds.), *The Evolution of Intelligence* (pp. 9–25). Mahwah, NJ: Erlbaum.

Grotzer, T. A., & Perkins, D. A. (2000). Teaching of intelligence: A performance conception. In R. J. Sternberg (Ed.), *Handbook of Intelligence* (pp. 492–515). New York: Cambridge University Press.

Guidubaldi, J., & Duckworth, J. (2001). Divorce and children's cognitive ability. In E. L. Grigorenko, & R. J. Sternberg (Eds.), *Family Environment and Intellectual Functioning* (pp. 97–118). Mahwah, NJ: Erlbaum.

Guilford, J. P. (1967). *The Nature of Human Intelligence*. New York: McGraw-Hill.

Guilford, J. P. (1982). Cognitive psychology's ambiguities: Some suggested remedies. *Psychological Review*, 89, 48–59.

Guilford, J. P. (1988). Some changes in the structure-of-intellect model. *Educational and Psychological Measurement*, 48, 1–4.

Haier, R. J., Chueh, D., Touchette, R., Lott, I., et al. (1995). Brain size and cerebral glucose metabolic rate in nonspecific mental retardation and Down's syndrome. *Intelligence*, 20, 191–210.

Haier, R. J., Siegel, B., Tang, C., Abel, L., & Buchsbaum, M. S. (1992). Intelligence and changes in regional cerebral glucose metabolic rate following learning. *Intelligence*, 16, 415–426.

Herrnstein, R. J, & Murray, C. (1994). *The Bell Curve*. New York: Free Press.

Hunt, E. B. (1978). Mechanics of verbal ability. *Psychological Review*, 85, 109–130.

Hunt, E. B., & Lansman, M. (1982). Individual differences in attention. In R. J. Sternberg (Ed.), *Advances in the Psychology of Human*

Intelligence (Vol. 1, pp. 207–254). Hillsdale, NJ: Erlbaum.

Jenkins, J. J. (1979). Four points to remember: A tetrahedral model of memory experiments. In L. S. Cermak, & F. I. M. Craik (Eds.), *Levels of Processing in Human Memory* (pp. 429–446). Hillsdale, NJ: Erlbaum.

Jensen, A. R. (1979). *g:* Outmoded theory or unconquered frontier? *Creative Science and Technology*, 2, 16–29.

Jensen, A. R. (1982). Reaction time and psychometric g. In H. J. Eysenck (Ed.), *A Model for Intelligence*. Heidelberg: Springer-Verlag.

Jensen, A. R. (1998). *The g Factor: The Science of Mental Ability*. Westport, CT: Praeger/Greenwood.

Jensen, A. R. (2002). Psychometric *g*: Definition and substantiation. In R. J. Sternberg, & E. L. Grigorenko (Eds.), *The General Factor of Intelligence: How General Is It?* (pp. 39–53). Mahwah, NJ: Erlbaum.

Jerison, H. J. (2000). The evolution of Intelligence. In R. J. Sternberg (Ed.), *Handbook of Intelligence* (pp. 216–244). New York: Cambridge University Press.

Kaufman, A. S. (2000). Tests of intelligence. In R. J. Sternberg (Ed.), *Handbook of Intelligence* (pp. 445–476). New York: Cambridge University Press.

Kaufman, A. S., & Lichtenberger, E. O. (1998). Intellectual assessment. In C. R. Reynolds (Ed.), *Comprehensive Clinical Psychology. Vol. 4: Assessment* (pp. 203–238). Tarrytown, NY: Elsevier Science.

Keating, D. P. (1984). The emperor's new clothes: The "new look" in intelligence research. In R. J. Sternberg (Ed.), *Advances in the Psychology of Human Intelligence* (Vol. 2, pp. 1–45). Hillsdale, NJ: Erlbaum.

Kihlstrom, J., & Cantor, N. (2000). Social intelligence. In R. J. Sternberg (Ed.), *Handbook of Intelligence* (pp. 359–379). New York: Cambridge University Press.

Kyllonen, P. C. (2002). *g*: Knowledge, speed, strategies, or working-memory capacity? A systems perspective. In R. J. Sternberg, & E. L. Grigorenko (Eds.), *The General Factor of Intelligence: How General Is It?* (pp. 415–445). Mahwah, NJ: Erlbaum.

Kyllonen, P., & Christal, R. (1990). Reasoning ability is (little more than) working-memory capacity? *Intelligence*, 14, 389–433.

Larkin, J. H., McDermott, J., Simon, D. P., & Simon, H. A. (1980). Expert and novice performance in solving physics problems. *Science*, 208, 1335–1342.

Larson, G. E., Haier, R. J., LaCasse, L., & Hazen, K. (1995). Evaluation of a "mental effort" hypothesis for correlation between cortical metabolism and intelligence. *Intelligence*, 21, 267–278.

Laughon, P. (1990). The dynamic assessment of intelligence: A review of three approaches. *School Psychology Review*, 19, 459–470.

Lazar, I., & Darlington, R. (1982). Lasting effects of early education: A report from the consortium for longitudinal studies. *Monographs of the Society for Research in Child Development*, 47, (Serial No. 195, 2–3).

Loehlin, J. C. (2000). Group differences in intelligence. In R. J. Sternberg (Ed.), *Handbook of Intelligence* (pp. 176–193). New York: Cambridge University Press.

Loehlin, J. C., Horn, J. M., & Willerman, L. (1997). Heredity, environment, and IQ in the Texas adoption project. In R. J. Sternberg, & E. L. Grigorenko (Eds.), *Intelligence, Heredity, and Environment* (pp. 105–125). New York: Cambridge University Press.

Lohman, D. F. (2000). Complex information processing and intelligence. In R. J. Sternberg (Ed.), *Handbook of Intelligence* (pp. 285–340). New York: Cambridge University Press.

Matarazzo, J. D. (1992). Psychological testing and assessment in the 21st century. *American Psychologist*, 47(8), 1007–1018.

Mayer, R. E. (2000). Intelligence and education. In R. J. Sternberg (Ed.), *Handbook of Intelligence* (pp. 519–533). New York: Cambridge University Press.

Mayer, J. D., & Salovey, P. (1997). What is emotional intelligence? In P. Salovey, & D. J. Sluyter (Eds.), *Emotional Development and Emotional Intelligence: Educational Implications* (pp. 3–34). New York: Basic Books.

Mayer, J. D., Salovey, P., & Caruso, D. (2000). Emotional intelligence. In R. J. Sternberg (Ed.), *Handbook of Intelligence* (pp. 396–421). New York: Cambridge University Press.

Mayes, L. C., & Fahy, T. (2001). Prenatal drug exposure and cognitive development. In R. J. Sternberg, & E. L. Grigorenko (Eds.), *Environmental Effects on Cognitive Abilities* (pp. 189–219). Mahwah, NJ: Erlbaum.

McGarry-Roberts, P. A., Stelmack, R. M., & Campbell, K. B. (1992). Intelligence, reaction time, and event-related potentials. *Intelligence*, 16(3, 4), 289–313.

Neisser, U., Boodoo, G., Bouchard T. J., Boykin, W. A., Brody, N., Ceci, S. J., et al. (1996). Intelligence: Knowns and unknowns. *American Psychologist*, 51 (2), 77–101.

Nettelbeck, T. (1987). Inspection time and intelligence. In P. A. Vernon (Ed.), *Speed of Information-processing and Intelligence* (pp. 295–346). Norwood, NJ: Ablex.

Nettelbeck, T., & Lally, M. (1976). Inspection time and measured intelligence. *British Journal of Psychology*, 67(1), 17–22.

Nettelbeck, T., & Rabbitt, P. M. (1992). Aging, cognitive performance, and mental speed. *Intelligence*, 16(2), 189–205.

Nettelbeck, T., Rabbitt, P. M. A., Wilson, C., & Batt, R. (1996). Uncoupling learning from initial recall: The relationship between speed and memory deficits in old age. *British Journal of Psychology*, 87, 593–607.

Nettelbeck, T., & Young, R. (1996). Intelligence and savant syndrome: Is the whole greater than the sum of the fragments? *Intelligence*, 22, 49–67.

Newell, A., & Simon, H. A. (1972). *Human Problem Solving*. Englewood Cliffs, NJ: Prentice-Hall.

Ogbu, J. U. (1986). The consequences of the American caste system. In U. Neisser (Ed.), *The School Achievement of Minority Children*. Hillsdale, NJ: Erlbaum.

Ogbu, J. U., & Stern, P. (2001). Caste status and intellectual development. In R. S. Sternberg, & E. L. Grigorenko (Eds.), *Environmental Effects on Intellectual Functioning*. Hillsdale, NJ: Erlbaum.

Olson, H. C. (1994). Fetal alcohol syndrome. In R. J. Sternberg (Ed.), *Encyclopedia of Human Intelligence* (Vol. 1, pp. 439–443). New York: Macmillan.

Perkins, D. N. (1995). Insight in minds and genes. In R. J. Sternberg, & J. E. Davidson (Eds.), *The Nature of Insight* (pp. 495–534). Cambridge, MA: MIT Press.

Perkins, D. N., & Grotzer, T. A. (1997). Teaching intelligence. *American Psychologist*, 52, 1125–1133.

Pianta, R. C., & Egeland, B. (1994). Predictors of instability in children's mental test performance at 24, 48, and 96 months. *Intelligence*, 18(2), 145–163.

Pinker, S. (1997). *How the Mind Works*. New York: Norton.

Plomin, R. (1997). Identifying genes for cognitive abilities and disabilities. In R. J. Sternberg, & E. L. Grigorenko (Eds.), *Intelligence, Heredity, and Environment* (pp. 89–104). New York: Cambridge University Press.

Posner, M. I., & Mitchell, R. F. (1967). Chronometric analysis of classification. *Psychological Review*, 74, 392–409.

Ramey, C. T., & Ramey, S. L. (2000). Intelligence and public policy. R. J. Sternberg (Ed.), *Handbook of Intelligence* (pp. 534–548). New York: Cambridge University Press.

Reed, T. E. (1993). Effect of enriched (complex) environment on nerve conduction velocity: New data and review of implications for the speed of information processing. *Intelligence*, 17(4), 533–540.

Reed, T. E., & Jensen, A. R. (1991). Arm nerve conduction velocity (NCV), brain NCV, reaction time, and intelligence. *Intelligence*, 15, 33–47.

Reed, T. E., & Jensen, R. (1993). A somatosensory latency between the thalamus and cortex also correlates with level of intelligence. *Intelligence*, 17, 443–450.

Salovey, P., & Sluyter, D. J. (Eds.) (1997). *Emotional Development and Emotional Intelligence: Educational Implications*. New York: Basic Books.

Schliemann, A. D., & Magalhües, V. P. (1990). Proportional reasoning: From shops, to kitchens, laboratories, and, hopefully, schools. Proceedings of the 14th International Conference for the Psychology of Mathematics Education. Oaxtepec, Mexico.

Seifer, R. (2001). Socioeconomic status, multiple risks, and development of intelligence. In R. J. Sternberg, & E. L. Grigorenko (Eds.), *Environmental Effects on Cognitive Abilities* (pp. 59–81). Mahwah, NJ: Erlbaum.

Serpell, R. (2000). Intelligence and culture. In R. J. Sternberg (Ed.), *Handbook of Intelligence* (pp. 549–580). New York: Cambridge University Press.

Simon, H. A. (1976). Identifying basic abilities underlying intelligent performance of complex tasks. In L. B. Resnick (Ed.), *The Nature of Intelligence* (pp. 65–98). Hillsdale, NJ: Erlbaum.

Spearman, C. (1923). *The Nature of 'Intelligence' and the Principles of Cognition* (2nd ed.). London: Macmillan. (1923 edition reprinted in 1973 by Arno Press, New York).

Spearman, C. (1927). *The Abilities of Man*. London: Macmillan.

Steele, C. (1990, May). A conversation with Claude Steele. *APS Observer*, pp. 11–17.

Sternberg, R. J. (1977). *Intelligence, Information Processing, and Analogical Reasoning: The Componential Analysis of Human Abilities*. Hillsdale, NJ: Erlbaum.

Sternberg, R. J. (1979). Is absolute time relatively interesting? *Behavioral and Brain Sciences*, 2, 281–282.

Sternberg, R. J. (1981). Intelligence and nonentrenchment. *Journal of Educational Psychology*, 73, 1–16.

Sternberg, R. J. (1982). Natural, unnatural, and supernatural concepts. *Cognitive Psychology*, 14, 451–488.

Sternberg, R. J. (1983). Components of human intelligence. *Cognition*, 15, 1–48.

Sternberg, R. J. (1985). *Beyond IQ: A Triarchic Theory of Human Intelligence*. New York: Cambridge University Press.

Sternberg, R. J. (1987). Teaching intelligence: The application of cognitive psychology to the improvement of intellectual skills. In J. B. Baron, & R. J. Sternberg (Eds.), *Teaching Thinking Skills: Theory and Practice* (pp. 182–218). New York: Freeman Press.

Sternberg, R. J. (1988). *The Triarchic Mind: A New Theory of Human Intelligence*. New York: Viking.

Sternberg, R. J. (1996). For whom does the Bell Curve toll? It tolls for you. *Journal of Quality Learning*, 6(1), 9–27.

Sternberg, R. J. (1997). *Successful Intelligence*. New York: Plume.

Sternberg, R. J. (1999). A triarchic approach to the understanding and assessment of intelligence in multicultural populations. *Journal of School Psychology*, 37, 145–159.

Sternberg, R. J., Conway, B. E., Ketron, J. L., & Bernstein, M. (1981). People's conceptions of intelligence. *Journal of Personality and Social Psychology*, 41, 37–55.

Sternberg, R. J., & Detterman, D. K. (1986). *What Is Intelligence?* Norwood, NJ: Ablex.

Sternberg, R. J., Ferrari, M., Clinkenbeard, P. R., & Grigorenko, E. L. (1996). Identification, instruction, and assessment of gifted children: A construct validation of a triarchic model. *Gifted Child Quarterly*, 40(3), 129–137.

Sternberg, R. J., Forsythe, G. B., Hedlund, J., Horvath, J., Snook, S., Williams, W. M., et al. (2000). *Practical Intelligence in Everyday Life*. New York: Cambridge University Press.

Sternberg, R. J., & Grigorenko, E. L. (Eds.) (1997). *Intelligence, Heredity, and Environment*. New York: Cambridge University Press.

Sternberg, R. J., & Grigorenko, E. L. (1999). *Our Labeled Children: What Every Parent and Teacher Needs to Know About Learning Disabilities*. Reading, MA: Perseus.

Sternberg, R. J., & Grigorenko E. L. (Eds.) (2002). *The General Factor of Intelligence: How General Is It?*. Mahwah, NJ: Erlbaum.

Sternberg, R. J., Grigorenko, E. L., Ferrari, M., & Clinkenbeard, P. (1999). The triarchic model applied to gifted identification, instruction, and assessment. In N. Colangelo, & S. G. Assouline (Eds.), *Talent Development III: Proceedings from the 1995 Henry B. and Jocelyn Wallace National Research Symposium on Talent Development* (pp. 71–80). Scottsdale, AZ: Gifted Psychology Press.

Sternberg, R. J., & Kaufman, J. C. (1996). Innovation and intelligence testing: The curious case of the dog that didn't bark. *European Journal of Psychological Assessment*, 12(3), 175–182.

Sternberg, R. J., & Kaufman J. C. (1998). Human abilities. *Annual Review of Psychology*, 49, 479–502.

Sternberg, R. J., Nokes, K., Geissler, P. W., Prince, R., Okatcha, F., Bundy, D. A., et al. (2001). The relationship between academic and practical intelligence: A case study in Kenya. *Intelligence*, 29, 401–418.

Sternberg, R. J., Powell, C., McGrane, P. A., & McGregor, S. (1997). Effects of a parasitic infection on cognitive functioning. *Journal of Experimental Psychology: Applied*, 3, 67–76.

Sternberg, R. J., & Ruzgis, P. (Eds.) (1994). *Personality and Intelligence*. New York: Cambridge University Press.

Sternberg, R. J., Torff, B., & Grigorenko, E. L. (1998). Teaching triarchically improves school achievement. *Journal of Educational Psychology*, 90, 374–384.

Sternberg, R. J., & Wagner, R. K. (Eds.) (1994). *Mind in Context*. New York: Cambridge University Press.

Terman, L. M., & Merrill, M. A. (1937). *Measuring Intelligence*. Boston: Houghton Mifflin.

Terman, L. M., & Merrill, M. A. (1973). *Stanford–Binet Intelligence Scale: Manual for the Third Revision*. Boston: Houghton Mifflin.

Thorndike, R. L., Hagen, E. P., & Sattler, J. M. (1986). *Technical Manual for the Stanford–Binet Intelligence Scale: 4th Edition*. Chicago: Riverside.

Thurstone, L. L. (1938). *Primary Mental Abilities*. Chicago: University of Chicago Press.

Turner, M. L., & Engle, R. W. (1989). Is working memory capacity task dependent? *Journal of Memory and Language*, 28(2), 127–154.

Vernon, P. E. (1971). *The Structure of Human Abilities*. London: Methuen.

Vernon, P. A., & Mori, M. (1992). Intelligence, reaction times, and peripheral nerve conduction velocity. *Intelligence*, 8, 273–288.

Vernon, P. A., Wickett, J. C., Bazana, P. G., & Stelmack, R. M. (2000). The neuropsychology and psycholophysiology of human intelligence. In R. J. Sternberg (Ed.), *Handbook of Intelligence* (pp. 245–264). New York: Cambridge University Press.

Wagner, D. A. (1978). Memories of Morocco: The influence of age, schooling and environment on memory. *Cognitive Psychology*, 10, 1–28.

Wagner, R. K. (2000). Practical intelligence. In R. J. Sternberg (Ed.), *Handbook of Human Intelligence* (pp. 380–395). New York: Cambridge University Press.

Wahlsten, D. & Gottlieb, G. (1997). The invalid separation of effects of nature and nurture: Lessons from animal experimentation. In R. J. Sternberg, & E. L. Grigorenko (Eds.), *Intelligence, Heredity, and Environment* (pp. 163–192). New York: Cambridge University Press.

Wechsler, D. (1980). *Wechsler Preschool and Primary Scale of Intelligence – Revised*. (WPPSI). San Antonio, TX: Psychological Corporation.

Wechsler, D. (1991). *Manual for the Wechsler Intelligence Scales for Children (3rd ed.)* (WISC-III). San Antonio, TX: Psychological Corporation.

Wechsler, D. (1997). *Manual for the Wechsler Adult Intelligence Scales* (WAIS-III). San Antonio, TX: Psychological Corporation.

Wickett, J. C., & Vernon, P. A. (1994). Peripheral nerve conduction velocity, reaction time, and intelligence: An attempt to replicate Vernon and Mori. *Intelligence*, 18, 127–132.

Wissler, C. (1901). The correlation of mental and physical tests. *Psychological Review, Monograph Supplement*, 3(6).

Zeidner, M. (1990). Perceptions of ethnic group modal intelligence: Reflections of cultural stereotypes or intelligence test scores? *Journal of Cross-Cultural Psychology*, 21(2), 214–231.

Zentall, T. R. (2000). Animal intelligence. In R. J. Sternberg (Ed.), *Handbook of Intelligence* (pp. 197–215). New York: Cambridge University Press.

Zigler, E., & Berman, W. (1983). Discerning the future of early childhood intervention. *American Psychologist*, 38, 894–906.

CHAPTER 32

Learning to Think: The Challenges of Teaching Thinking

Ron Ritchhart
David N. Perkins

The idea that thinking can be taught, or at least productively nurtured along its way, is ancient. Beginning with the efforts of Plato and the introduction of Socratic dialog, we see attention to improving intelligence and promoting effective thinking as a recurring educational trend throughout the ages. Early in the twentieth century, Dewey (1933) again focused North American's attention on the importance of thinking as an educational aim. At the same time, Selz (1935) was advocating the idea of learnable intelligence in Europe. In the 1970s and 1980s, specific programs designed to teach thinking took shape, many of which continue in schools today. Efforts to teach thinking have proliferated in the new millennium, often becoming less programmatic in nature and more integrated within the fabric of schools.

Despite this long history of concern with thinking, one reasonably might ask: Why do we need to "teach" thinking anyway? After all, given reasonable access to a rich cultural surround, individuals readily engage in situated problem solving, observing, classifying, organizing, informal theory building and testing, and so on, without much prompting or even support. Indeed, neurological findings suggest that the brain is hard-wired for just such activities as a basic mechanism for facilitating language development, socialization, and general environmental survival. Furthermore, it might be assumed that these basic thinking skills are already enhanced through the regular processes of schooling, as students encounter the work of past thinkers, engage in some debate, write essays, and so on. Why, then, should we concern ourselves with the teaching and learning of thinking? Addressing these issues entails looking more closely at a fuller range of thinking, particularly what might be called high-end thinking, as well as examining the role education plays in promoting thinking.

Although it is true that the human mind comes readily equipped for a wide variety of thinking tasks, it is equally true that some kinds of thinking run against these natural tendencies. For example, probabilistic thinking is often counterintuitive in nature or doesn't fit well with our experience (Tversky & Kahneman,1993; also see Kahneman & Frederick, Chap. 12). We have a natural tendency toward favoring our own position and interests – my-side bias (Molden & Higgins, Chap. 13) – that can lead to poor conclusions in decision making and discernments of truth (Baron, et al. 1993). We frequently draw conclusions and inferences based on limited evidence (Perkins, 1989, 1995). The fundamental attribution error (Harvey, Town, & Yarkin, 1981) names the tendency, particularly in Westerners, to ascribe characterological traits to others based on limited but highly salient encounters.

Furthermore, sometimes our natural ways of making sense of the world actually stand in the way of more effective ways of thinking. For instance, our ability to focus attention can lead to narrowness of vision and insight. Our natural tendency to detect familiar patterns and classify the world can lock us into rigid patterns of action and trap us in the categories we invent (Langer, 1989). Relatedly, already developed understandings constitute systems of knowledge that are much more readily extended than displaced: We tend to dismiss or recast challenges rather than rethinking our understandings, which is a deep and general problem of learning (see Chi and Ohlsson, Chap. 16). Our emotional responses to situations can easily override more deliberative thinking (Goleman, 1995). The phenomenon of groupthink, in which the dominant views of the group are readily adopted by group members, can lead to limited processing and discernment of information (Janis, 1972). These are just a few thinking shortfalls suggesting that truly good thinking does not automatically develop in the natural course of events.

Even when our native tendencies do not lead us astray, they can usually benefit from development. The curiosity of the child for discovering and making sense of the world does not automatically evolve into an intellectual curiosity for ideas, knowledge, and problem solving (Dewey, 1933), for example. Our ability to see patterns and relationships forms the basis for inductive reasoning (see Sloman & Lagnado, Chap. 5), but the latter requires a level of precision and articulation that must be learned. Our natural ability to make inferences becomes much more sophisticated through systematized processes of reasoning with evidence, weighing evidentiary sources, and drawing justifiable conclusions. Indeed, for most thinking abilities that might be considered naturally occurring, one can usually identify a more sophisticated form that such thinking might take with some deliberate nurturing. This type of thinking is what is often referred to as high-end thinking or critical and creative thinking. Such thinking extends beyond a natural processing of the world into the realm of deliberative thinking acts aimed at solving problems, making decisions (see LeBoeuf & Shafir, Chap. 11), and forming conclusions.

The contribution of schooling to the development of thinking is a vexed matter (see Greenfield, Chap. 27, for a cross-cultural perspective on the impact of schooling). On the one hand, it is clear that schooling enhances performance of various kinds on formal tasks and IQ-like instruments (Grotzer & Perkins, 2000; Perkins, 1985; see Sternberg, Chap. 31, for a discussion of intelligence). For the most part, however, schools have addressed knowledge and skill acquisition. The narrowness of this focus and absence of strong efforts to nurture thinking were criticized by Dewey at the turn of the century. Such critiques have continued until today from a variety of sources. In a series of empirical investigations, Perkins and colleagues (Perkins, Allen, & Hafner, 1983; Perkins, Faraday & Busheq, 1991) investigated the impact of conventional education at the high school, university, and graduate school levels on informal reasoning about everyday issues. Cross-sectional studies examining the impact of three years of high school, college, and graduate school revealed only marginal gains (Perkins, 1985). Several national reports on schooling in the 1980s discussed how schools were dominated by rote work and involved very little thinking (Boyer, 1983; National Commission on Excellence in Education, 1983; Goodlad, 1983).

The problems of overcoming thinking shortfalls while enhancing native thinking processes through education therefore constitute an important rationale for the explicit teaching of thinking. Furthermore, as knowledge and information become at the same time more complex and more accessible, critics argue that teaching thinking should be considered even more of a priority (Resnick, 1987). In this setting, it is not enough to simply consume predigested knowledge, one must also become a knowledge builder (Scardamalia, Bereiter, & Lamon, 1994) and problem solver (Polya, 1957; Schoenfeld, 1982; Selz, 1935).

This need for thinking instruction has led to a rapid increase in efforts to teach thinking over the past thirty years. During this time, a few well-established thinking programs have taken hold in schools and sustained their development, while a plethora of new programs, often small interventions based on current cognitive theory, have flourished. In addition, an increasing array of subject-based programs and designed learning environments aimed at developing students' thinking also have emerged. These programs deal with many different aspects of thinking, including critical and creative thinking (for more on creative thinking, see Sternberg et al. Chap. 15), reflective and metacognitive thinking, self-regulation, decision-making, and problem solving, as well as disciplinary forms of thinking.

All of these programs – whether aimed at developing thinking as part of a standalone course within the context of teaching a particular subject or as part of a larger design of the instructional environment – confront at least five important challenges in their efforts to develop thinking. We use these as the basis for the present review. The first challenge relates to the bottom line: Can thinking be taught with some reasonable signs of success? The second challenge concerns what is meant when one talks about good thinking. Programs and efforts to teach thinking are shaped largely by the answer to this question. The third challenge deals with the dispositional side of thinking, not just skills and processes but attitudes and intellectual character (Ritchhart 2002; Tishman 1994). The fourth challenge is that of transfer, a pivotal concern within the teaching of thinking. We conclude with a fifth challenge, that of creating cultures of thinking, in which we examine the social context and environment in which thinking is being promoted. Each of these challenges involves key philosophical and practical issues that all efforts to teach thinking, whether undertaken by a single teacher or a major research university, must confront. We review the ways in which various efforts to teach thinking address these challenges to clarify just what is involved in teaching thinking.

The Challenge of Attaining Results

As is the case with any class of educational interventions, one of the most fundamental questions to be asked is: Do they work – at least with some populations under some circumstances? This is especially important for an area like the teaching of thinking, which is haunted by skepticism on the part of lay people and some scholars.

It may seem premature to turn to findings without discussing details about background theories and issues in the field, but letting the question of impact hover for many pages while we deal with such matters also seems troublesome. After all, if there isn't at least some indication that thinking can be taught, then the remaining challenges become academic. Accordingly, we turn to this ultimate challenge first, asking whether, at least sometimes, coordinated efforts to teach thinking work in a reasonable sense, also taking it as an opportunity to put quick profiles of several interventions on the table to give readers a feel for the range of approaches.

In looking for success, it is helpful to bear in mind three broad criteria – *magnitude, persistence,* and *transfer* (Grotzer & Perkins, 2000). An intervention appears successful to the extent that it shows some magnitude of impact on learners' thinking with effects that persist well beyond the period of instruction and with transfer to other contexts and occasions. Previous reviewers of thinking programs pointed out that the empirical evidence needed to assess program effectiveness is often hard to come by in the research literature (e.g., Adams, 1989; Nickerson, Perkins, & Smith, 1985; Sternberg, 1986), often because of the lack of funding for careful long-term program evaluation. We emphatically do not limit this article only to those programs receiving extensive evaluation, but we do focus this section on a few such programs. The good news is that the history of efforts to teach thinking provides proofs for achieving all three criteria, at least to some extent.

Programs designed to teach thinking come in many different styles. For instance, some programs are designed to develop discrete skills and processes such as classification and sequencing as means of developing the building blocks for thinking. Paul (1984) refers to these programs as "micrological" in nature. They often find their theoretical justification in theories of intelligence (see next section for more on how various programs define good thinking), and they often use decontextualized and abstract materials similar to those one might find on standardized psychometric tests.

Perhaps the best-known program of this type is Instrumental Enrichment (IE) (Feuerstein, 1980). It uses very abstract, test-like activities to develop skills in areas such as comparisons, categorization, syllogisms, and numerical progressions, among others. Instructors are encouraged to "bridge" the abstract exercises by relating the skills to world problem solving. Instrumental enrichment was designed to bring students who show marked ability deficits into mainstream culture, although it can be used with other students as well.

In one study, matched samples of low functioning, low socio-economic status (SES) twelve- to fifteen-year-olds participated in IE or general enrichment (GE) programs providing direct help, such as math or science tutoring. Instrumental enrichment subjects made greater pre- to posttest gains on tests of interpersonal conduct, self-sufficiency, and adaptation to work demands. Instrumental enrichment subjects scored slightly above normal, far better than would have been expected, and significantly better than GE subjects by about a third of a standard deviation on incidental follow-up testing on an Army Intelligence test (DAPAR) two years later (Feuerstein et al., 1981; Rand, Tannenbaum, & Feuerstein, 1979). These findings show both magnitude and persistence of effects, with some transfer. The program uses testlike activities, so the transfer to a nonverbal intelligence test might be considered a case of near transfer (Perkins & Salomon, 1988). Evidence of transfer to school tasks – far transfer – seems to depend on the individual teacher or instructor, who is responsible for providing the bridging (Savell, Twohig, & Rachford, 1986; Sternberg, 1986).

These findings have proved less easily replicated with students of average or above-average ability. What is consistent, however, is the change in behavior and attitude students experience, generally in terms of increased confidence in abilities and a more positive attitude toward school work (Blagg, 1991; Kriegler, 1993).

Another type of program to teach thinking tends to be more "macrological" in nature (Paul, 1984), being contextualized and real world oriented, focusing on more broad-based skills such as considering multiple points of view, dealing with complex information or creative problem solving. Philosophy for Children (Lipman, 1976), and CoRT (Cognitive Research Trust) (de Bono, 1973), are examples of this approach. The Philosophy for Children program engages students in philosophical discussions around a shared book to cultivate students' ability to draw inferences, make analogies, form hypotheses, and so forth. The CoRT program teaches a collection of thinking "operations," defined by acronyms for creative and critical thinking; operations these aim to broaden and organize thinking and facilitate dealing with information. Through a developed set of practice problems, for instance, students learn to apply the PMI operation (plus, minus, interesting), identifying the pluses, minuses, and interesting but otherwise neutral points about a matter at hand.

Both of these programs have been around long enough to develop a strong base and avid followers, resulting in a wealth of anecdotal evidence and reports of effectiveness. Indeed, observers of these programs tend to be impressed with the involvement of students and the level of thinking demonstrated (Adams, 1989). Furthermore, some evidence can be found to support both programs. Edwards (1994) reports that twelve-year-olds taught all sixty lessons of the *CoRT* program showed improved scores on quantitative as well as qualitative measures. Compared with other seventh grade students, scores of CoRT students ranged from 48% to 62% above the national mean on standardized tests, whereas other seventh graders' scores ranged from 25% to 43% above the national norm of 31%, indicating a magnitude effect. Teachers reported improvements in student thinking and confidence. Although students reported using the skills in other areas of their lives, there was no formal measure of transfer on this evaluation. Other evaluations revealed mixed results on transfer (Edwards & Baldauf, 1983, 1987). The program produces an interesting finding with respect to persistence that should be noted. Although reviews of research on CoRT suggest that the effects were short-term (Edwards, 1991a, 1991b), it was found that a small amount of follow-up reinforcement given in the two years after the intervention resulted in increased persistence of effects with scores that were one-third better than controls three years after the intervention (Edwards, 1994).

With respect to Philosophy for Children, evaluations have shown that children in grades four to eight display significant gains in reading comprehension or logical thinking (Lipman, 1983). Transfer is built into the program because the discussions are text-based and consequently deepen comprehension while teaching and modeling thinking strategies within the real world contexts of the stories. As Adams (1989, p. 37) points out, the texts give "Lipman the freedom to introduce, reintroduce, and elaborate each logical process across a diversity of real-world situations."

Another program worth mentioning is a unique hybrid. The Odyssey (Adams, 1986) program developed through a collaboration between Harvard Project Zero, Bolt Beranek and Newman, Inc., and the Venezuela Ministry of Education was specifically designed to systematically build macrological skills upon micrological skills. The first lessons of the program deal with micrological skills, or what the program developers call first-order processes of classification, hierarchical classification, sequencing, and analogical reasoning, to build the foundation for the macrological process of dimensional analysis. Processes often are introduced in the abstract, but then application is made to varied contexts. The program takes the form of a separate course with 100 lessons, but it seeks to connect directly to the scholastic activities of students and provide links to everyday life as well. The Odyssey program has been evaluated only in Venezuela. In a relatively large evaluation of the program involving roughly 900 students in control and experimental groups across twenty-two seventh grade classes, the group gains of the experimental group were 117 percent more than that of the control group on course-designed pre- and postmeasurements – a strong indicator of magnitude of effects. A battery of tests were used to assess for transfer, including those of general ability, word problems, and nonverbal reasoning. All showed significant gains for the experimental group, indicating both magnitude and transfer of effects (Herrnstein, et al., 1986).

The abovementioned programs, whether focusing on micrological or macrological skills, were stand-alone interventions with perhaps a modest degree of integration. A number of programs are fully integrated and connected to the curriculum. A few of these are Intuitive Math (Burke, 1971) and *Problem Solving and Comprehension* (Whimbey and Lochhead, 1979), both focused on mathematics, and *Think* (Adams, 1971) and *Reciprocal Teaching* (Brown & Palincsar, 1982), which are focused on language arts and reading. All of these programs are designed to connect thinking processes to specific school content to enhance student understanding and thinking. Think and Intuitive Math focus on skills such as classification, structure analysis, and seeing analogies. Problem Solving and Comprehension uses a technique called "paired problem solving" to develop metacognitive awareness of one's thinking during problem solving. Reciprocal Teaching is not so much a program as an approach to teaching reading comprehension. Through a dialog with the teacher, students engage in cycles of summarizing, question generating, clarifying, and predicting. All of these interventions have been shown to produce impressive results for their target populations, generally low-achieving students, within the domains of their focus. In addition, transfer effects have been documented for Intuitive Math and Think (Worsham & Austin, 1983; Zenke & Alexander, 1984).

As promised, these examples – and others discussed later – offer a kind of existence proof regarding the challenge of attaining results (more reviews of these and other thinking programs can be found in Adams, 1989; Grotzer & Perkins, 2000; Hamers & Overtoom, 1997; Idol, 1991; McGuinness & Nisbet, 1991; Nickerson et al., 1985; Perkins, 1995; Sternberg, 1986). They give evidence that instruction designed to improve learners' thinking can advance it, with persistent impact, and with some degree of transfer to other contexts and occasions. Along the way, they also illustrate how rather different approaches can serve this purpose.

This is not to say that such results demonstrate overwhelming success. Impacts on learners' thinking are typically moderate rather than huge. The persistence of effects tapers off after a period of months or years, particularly when learners return to settings that do not support the kind of development in question. Transfer effects are often spotty rather than sweeping. These limitations are signs that the grandest ambitions regarding the teaching of thinking are yet to be realized. That said, enough evidence is at hand to show that the prospects of teaching thinking cannot simply be dismissed on theoretical or empirical grounds. This opens the way for a deeper consideration of the challenges of doing so in the upcoming sections.

The Challenge of Defining Good Thinking

Any program that aspires to teach thinking needs to face the challenge of defining good thinking, not necessarily in any ultimate and comprehensive sense but at least in some practical, operational sense. With the foregoing examples of programs in mind, it will come as no surprise that many different approaches have been taken to answer this challenge.

To begin, it is useful to examine some general notions about the nature of good thinking. There are a number of very broad characterizations. Folk notions of intelligence, in contrast with technical notions, boil down to good thinking. A number of years ago, Sternberg et al. (1981) reported research synthesizing the characteristics people envision when they think of someone as intelligent. Intelligent individuals reason systematically, solve problems well, think in a logical way, deploy a good vocabulary, make use of a rich stock of information, remain focused on their goals, and display intelligence in practical as well as academic ways. Perkins (1995) summed up a range of research on difficulties of thinking by noting the human tendency to think in ways that are *hasty* (impulsive, insufficient investment in deep processing and examining alternatives), *narrow* (failure to challenge assumptions, examine other points of view), *fuzzy* (careless, imprecise, full of conflations), and *sprawling* (general disorganization, failure to advance or conclude). Baron (1985) advanced a search-and-inference framework that emphasized effective search and inference around forming beliefs, making decisions, and choosing goals. Ennis (1986) offered a list of critical thinking abilities and dispositions, including traits such as seeking and offering reasons, seeking alternatives, and being open-minded. There are many others as well.

The overlap among such conceptions is apparent. They can be very useful for a broad overview and for the top level of program design, but they are not virtues of thinking that learners can straightforwardly learn or teachers teach. They do not constitute a good theory of action (e.g., Argyris, 1993; Argyris & Schön, 1996) that would guide and advise learners about how to improve their thinking, or guide and advise teachers and program designers about how to cultivate thinking. With this general challenge in mind, we turn to describing three approaches through which researchers and educators have constructed theories of action that characterize good thinking – by way of norms and heuristics, models of intelligence, and models of human development.

Norms and Heuristics

One common approach to defining good thinking is to characterize concepts, standards, and cognitive strategies that serve a particular kind of thinking well. These guide performance as norms and heuristics. When people know the norms and heuristics, they can strive to improve their practice accordingly. The result is a kind of "craft" conception: Good thinking is a matter of mastering knowledge, skills, and habits appropriate to the kind of thinking in question as guided by the norms and heuristics.

Norms provide criteria of adequacy for products of thinking such as arguments or grounded decisions. Examples of norms include suitable conditions for formal deduction or statistical adequacy, formal (e.g., affirming the consequent) or informal (e.g., ad hominem argument) fallacies to be avoided, or maximized payoffs in game theory (Hamblin, 1970; Nisbett, 1993; Voss, Perkins, & Segal, 1991). Heuristics guide the process of thinking, but without the guarantees of success that an algorithm provides. For instance, mathematical problem solvers often do well to examine specific cases before attempting a general proof or to solve a simpler related problem before tackling the principal problem (Polya, 1954, 1957).

The norms and heuristics approach figures widely in educational endeavors. Training in norms of argument goes back at least to the Greek rhetoriticians (Hamblin, 1970) and continues in numerous settings of formal education today with many available texts. Heuristic analyses have been devised and taught for many generic thinking practices – everyday decision making, problem solving, evaluating of claims, creative thinking, and so on.

Looking to programs mentioned earlier for examples, we note that the CoRT program teaches "operations" such as PMI (consider plus, minus, and interesting factors in a situation) and OPV (consider other points of view) (de Bono, 1973). The Odyssey program teaches strategies for decision-making, problem solving, and creative design, among others, foregrounding familiar strategies such as looking for options beyond the obvious, trial and error, and articulation of purposes (Adams, 1986). Polya (1954, 1957) offered a well-known analysis of strategies for mathematical problem solving, including examining special cases, addressing a simplified form of the problem first, and many others. This led to a number of efforts to teach mathematical problem solving, with unimpressive results, until Schoenfeld (1982; Schoenfeld & Herrmann, 1982) demonstrated a very effective intervention that included the instructor's working problems while commenting on strategies as they were deployed, plus emphasis on the students' self-management of the problem-solving process. Many simple reading strategies have been shown to improve student retention and understanding when systematically applied, including, for example, the previously mentioned "reciprocal teaching" framework in which young readers interact conversationally in small groups around a text to question, clarify, summarize, and predict (Brown & Palincsar, 1982).

Nisbett (1993) reported a series of studies conducted by himself and colleagues about the effectiveness of teaching norms and heuristics of statistical, if-then, cost-benefit, and other sorts of reasoning, mainly to college students. Nisbett concluded that instruction in rules of reasoning was considerably more effective than critics of general, context-free rules for reasoning had claimed. To be sure, student performance displayed a range of lapses and could have been better. Nonetheless, students often applied the patterns of reasoning that they were studying quite widely, well beyond the content foregrounded in the instruction. Relatively abstract and concise formulations of principle alone led to some practical use of rules for reasoning, and this improved when instruction included rich exploration of examples. Nisbett emphasized that we could certainly teach rules for reasoning much better than we do. Nonetheless, the basic enterprise appeared to be sound.

To summarize, the characteristic pedagogy of the approach through norms and heuristics follows from its emphasis on thinkers' theories of action. Programs of this sort typically introduce norms and heuristics directly, demonstrate their application, and engage learners in practice with a range of problems, often with an emphasis on metacognitive awareness, self-management, and reflection on the strategies, general character, and challenges of thinking.

Readily grasped concepts and standards, strategies with three or four steps, and the like characterize the majority of norms and heuristics approaches. One objection to such simplicity is that it can seem simpleminded. "Everyone knows" that people should consider both sides of the case in reasoning or look for options beyond the obvious. However, as emphasized in the introduction to this article, such lapses are commonplace. Everyone does not know, and those who do know often fail to do so. The point of norms and heuristics most often is not to reveal novel or startling secrets of a particular kind of thinking but to articulate some basics and help bridge from inert knowledge to active practice.

Models of Intelligence

The norms and heuristics approach to defining and cultivating good thinking may be the most common, but another avenue looks directly to models of intelligence (see Sternberg, Chap. 31). Not so often encountered in the teaching of thinking is good thinking defined through classic intelligence quotient (IQ) theory. On the one hand, many, although by no means all, scholars consider general intelligence in the sense of Spearman's *g* factor to be unmodifiable by direct instructional interventions (Brody, 1992; Jensen, 1980, 1998). On the other hand, a single factor does not afford much of a theory of action, because it does not break down the learning problem into components that can be addressed systematically.

Models of intelligence with components offer more toward a theory of action. J. P. Guilford's 1967 (Guilford & Hoepfner, 1971) *Structure of Intellect* (SOI) model, for example, proposes that intelligence involves no fewer than 150 different components generated by a three-dimensional analysis involving several cognitive operations (cognition, memory, evaluation, convergent production, divergent production) crossed with several kinds of content (behavioral, visual figural, and more) and cognitive products (units, classes, relations, and more). An intervention developed by Meeker (1969) aims to enhance the functioning of a key subset of these components. Feuerstein (1980) argues that intelligence is modifiable through mediated learning (with a mediator scaffolding learners on the right kinds of tasks). His Instrumental Enrichment program offers a broad range of mediated activities organized around three broad categories of cognitive process – information input, elaboration, and output – to work against problems such as blurred and sweeping perception, impulsiveness, unsystematic hypothesis testing, and egocentric communication.

Sternberg (1985) developed the triarchic theory of intelligence over a number of years, featuring three dimensions of intelligence – analytic (as in typical IQ tests), practical (expert "streetwise" behavior in particular domains), and creative (invention, innovation). Sternberg, et al. (1996) report an intervention based on Sternberg's (1985) triarchic theory of intelligence: High school students taking an intensive summer college course were grouped by their strengths according to Sternberg's three dimensions and taught the same content in ways building on their strengths. The study included other groups not matched with their strengths. Matched students exhibited superior performance.

The typical pedagogy of interventions based on models of intelligence emphasizes not teaching norms and heuristics but rather providing abundant experience with the thinking processes in question in motivated contexts with strong emphasis on attention and self-regulation. Often, although by no means always – the Sternberg intervention is an exception here, for example – the tasks have a rather abstract character on the theory that the learning activities are enhancing the functioning of fundamental cognitive operations and content is best selected for minimal dependence on background knowledge. That said, it is important to recognize that no matter what the underlying theory – norms and heuristics, intelligence-based, or developmental, as in the following section – interventions often pragmatically combine a variety of methods rather than proceeding in a purist manner.

Models of Human Development

Another approach to defining good thinking looks to models of human development that outline how cognitive development normally advances, often through some sequence of stages that represent plateaus in the complexity of cognition, as with the classic concrete and formal operational stages of Inhelder and Piaget (1958; see Halford, Chap. 22). For example, the program called Cognitive Acceleration through Science Education (CASE) (Adey & Shayer, 1993, 1994) teaches patterns of thinking in science – for instance the isolation and control of variables – based on Piagetian principles of uncovering students' prior conceptions and creating opportunities for them to reorganize their thinking. Lessons introduce cognitive dissonance around particular puzzles so students are led to examine their assumptions and rethink their prior conceptions. In addition to the thinking skills, the program focuses explicitly on fostering metacognition and transferring knowledge and strategies between contexts. A formal evaluation compared CASE students with control students on school science achievement tests with delayed posttesting. For some groups, substantial and statistically significant differences emerged for science, mathematics, and English performance two years after participation in CASE, demonstrating magnitude, persistence, and transfer of impact, the criteria used in the foregoing results section (Adey & Shayer, 1994, p. 92).

Although this example takes a stage-like view of human development, another tradition looks to the work of Vygotsky and his followers, seeing development more as a process of internalization from social situations that scaffold for the thinking of the participant (1978). In addition to its Piagetian emphasis, the work of Adey and Shayer draws upon social scaffolding. Scardamalia and colleagues developed an initiative initially called CSILE (Computer Supported Intentional Learning Environments) and now Knowledge Forum, that engages students in the collaborative construction of knowledge through an online environment that permits building complex knowledge structures and labels for many important epistemic elements such as hypotheses and evidence (Scardamalia, et al., 1989). The social character of the enterprise and the forms of discourse it externalizes through the online environment create conditions for Vygotskian internalization of patterns of thinking. Studies of impact have shown gains in students' depth of explanation and knowledge representation, capability in dealing with difficult texts, recall of more information from texts, and deeper conceptions of the nature of learning with more of a mastery emphasis (Scardamalia, Bereiter, & Lamon, 1994).

Of course, developmental psychology has evolved greatly since the days of Vygotsky and Piaget. For example, the past half century has seen development explained in terms of expansion in, and more efficient use of, working memory (e.g., Case, 1985; Fischer, 1980; Pascual-Leone, 1978); semi-independent courses of development traced in different domains (e.g., Case, 1992; Fischer, 1980; Carey, 1985); strands of development attributed to the modularity of mind, with innate mental structures anticipating certain kinds of knowledge (e.g., Detterman, 1992; Hirschfeld & Gelman, 1994), and so on.

It is not the role of this chapter to review the complexities of contemporary developmental psychology, especially because as far as we know, few approaches to the teaching of thinking have based themselves on recent developmental theory. Quite likely, there are substantial opportunities that have not been taken. To give a sense of the promise, Case (1992) advanced the idea of *central conceptual structures*, which are core structures in broad domains such as quantity, narrative, and intentionality that lie at the foundations of development in these domains and enable further learning. Working from this notion, Griffin, Case, and Capodilupo (1995) designed and assessed an intervention called Rightstart to develop the central conceptual structure for number and advance kindergarteners' preparation for learning basic arithmetic operations through formal instruction. Testing demonstrated that the children in the treatment group indeed acquired a more fully developed central conceptual structure for number, displayed greater understanding of number in content areas not included in the training, and responded with substantially greater gains to later formal instruction in the basics of arithmetic as well as showing far transfer to sight reading in music and to the notion of distributive justice, areas related to the central conceptual structure for number.

As these examples illustrate, the general pedagogical style of the developmental approach is to harness "natural" footholds and mechanisms of development to accelerate and perhaps reach levels that the learner otherwise would not attain. As theories of action, models of human development, like models of intelligence, do not so much offer strategic advice to learners as they address teachers and especially designers, suggesting how they might arrange activities and experiences that will push development forward. Indeed, a common, although questionable, tenet of much developmental theory is that you cannot teach directly the underlying logical structures. Learners must attain them by wrestling with the right kinds of problems under appropriately reflective and supportive conditions.

What Effect Does a Theory of Good Thinking Have?

With approaches to defining good thinking through heuristic analysis, intelligence, and human development on the table, perhaps the most natural question to ask is which approach is "right" and therefore would lead to the most powerful interventions. Unfortunately, the matter is far too complex to declare a winner. One complication is that all programs, despite their theoretical differences, share key features. All programs engage learners in challenging thinking tasks that stretch beyond what they normally undertake. All programs place some emphasis on focused attention and metacognitive self-regulation. It may be that these demand characteristics are the factors that influence an intervention's success more than the underlying theory. Furthermore, as underscored earlier, programs are often eclectic in their means: Their methods overlap more than their philosophies.

To further complicate declaring a winner, different programs speak to the distinctive needs of different audiences – children of marked disabilities with unsystematic and impulsive ways of thinking, students of elementary science conceptually confused about themes such as control of variables, math students in college struggling with strategies of proof, and so on.

Another confounding factor is that a technically well-grounded theory may not be that helpful as a theory of action. As noted earlier, this is a problem with classic *g* theory. Finally, and somewhat paradoxically, a theory, that is, in some ways suspect may lead to an intervention that proves quite effective. For example, Piagetian theory has been challenged in a number of compelling ways (e.g., Brainerd, 1983; Case, 1984, 1985), yet applying certain key aspects of it appears to serve the demonstrably effective CASE program very well (Adey & Shayer, 1993, 1994), perhaps because the kinds of thinking it foregrounds are important to complex cognition of the sort targeted, putting aside the standing of Piagetian theory as a whole.

In summary, although approaches based on norms and heuristics, theories of intelligence, and models of development can be identified, it is difficult at present to dismiss any of them as misguided. As with much of human enterprise, the devil is in the details – here, the details of particular programs' agendas, the learners they mean to serve, and the extent to which their conceptions of good thinking provide helpful theories of action.

That said, there is a general limitation to all three approaches: They all concern what it is to think well *when you are thinking*. Such criteria are certainly important, but this leaves room to ask: What if you don't feel moved to think about the matter at hand, or what if you don't even notice that the circumstances invite thinking? This brings us to the next fundamental challenge of teaching thinking – the role of dispositions.

The Challenge of Attending to Thinking Dispositions

We discussed earlier how approaches to teaching thinking needed to address the question: What is good thinking? In a sense, that question was incomplete. Good thinkers, after all, are more than people who simply think well when they think: They also think at the right times with the right commitments – to truth and evidence, creativity and perspective taking, sound decisions, and apt solutions. Views of thinking that bring this to the fore are often called *dispositional* because they look not just to how well people think when trying hard but what kinds of thinking they are *disposed* to undertake.

Most views of thinking are abilities-centered, but several scholars have developed dispositional perspectives – for instance Dewey (1922), who wrote of habits of mind; Baron (1985) as part of his search-inference framework; Ennis (1986) and Norris (1995) as part of analyses of critical thinking; Langer (1989, p. 44), with the notion of mindfulness, which she defined as "an open, creative, and probabilistic state of mind"; and Facione et al. (1995). Models of self-regulation have emphasized volitional aspects of thinking and individuals' motivation to engage thoughtfully (Schunk & Zimmerman, 1994). We and our colleagues have done extensive work in this area, referring to intellectual character as a particular perspective on dispositions (Ritchhart, 2002; Tishman, 1994, 1995) and to dispositions themselves (Perkins, Jay, & Tishman, 1993; Perkins et al., 2000; Perkins & Tishman, 2001; Perkins & Ritchhart, 2004).

Accordingly, it is important to examine the dispositional side of the story and appraise its importance in the teaching of thinking.

The Logical Case for Dispositions

One line of argument for the importance of dispositions looks to logic and common experience. There is a natural tendency to associate thinking with blatant occasions – the test item, the crossword puzzle, the choice of colleges, the investment decision. Plainly, however, many situations call for thinking with a softer voice all too easily unheard – the politician's subtle neglect of an alternative viewpoint, your own and others' reasoning from ethnic stereotypes, the comfort of "good enough" solutions that are not all that good. Even when we sense opportunities for deeper thinking in principle, there are many reasons why we often shun them – blinding confidence in one's own view, obliviousness to the possibilities for seeing things differently, aversion to complexities and ambiguities, and the like. Such lapses seem all too common, which is why, for example, Dewey (1922) emphasizes the importance of good *habits of mind* that can carry people past moments of distraction and reluctance. Scheffler (1991, p. 4), writing about cognitive emotions, put the point eloquently in stating that "emotion without cognition is blind, and... cognition without emotion is vacuous."

It also is notable that the everyday language of thinking includes a range of terms for positive and negative dispositional traits considered to be important: A person may be open-minded or closed-minded, curious or indifferent, judicious or impulsive, systematic or careless, rational or irrational, gullible or skeptical. Such contrasts have more to do with how well people actually use their minds than how well their minds work.

The Empirical Case for Dispositions

The foregoing arguments from logic and common sense give some reason to view the dispositional side of thinking as important. Beyond that, a number of researchers have investigated a range of dispositional constructs and provided empirical evidence of their influence on thinking, their trait-like character, and their distinctness from abilities.

Research on dispositional constructs such as the need for cognitive closure (Kruglanski, 1990) and the need for cognition (describing an individual's tendency to seek, engage in, and enjoy cognitively effortful activity; Cacioppo & Petty, 1982) has shown that they influence when and to what extent individuals engage in thinking and has demonstrated test–retest reliability (Kruglanski, 1990; Cacioppo et al., 1996). Measures of an individual's need for cognition developed by Cacioppo and colleagues show that it is a construct distinguishable from ability (Cacioppo et al., 1996).

Dweck and colleagues investigated another dispositional construct for a number of years – the contrast between entity learners and incremental learners (Dweck, 1975, 2000). Broadly speaking, learners with an entity mindset believe that "you either get it or you don't," and if you don't, you probably are not smart enough. As a result, they tend to quit in the face of intellectual challenges. In contrast, learners with an incremental mindset believe their abilities can be extended through step-by-step effort, so they persist. An extended program of research has shown that these traits are independent of cognitive abilities but often affect cognitive performance greatly. Also, teaching style and classroom culture can shape the extent to which students adopt entity versus incremental mindsets.

Using self-report measures of dogmatism, categorical thinking, openness, counterfactual thinking, superstitious thinking, and actively open-minded thinking, Stanovich and West (1997) found these measures predicted performance on tests of argument evaluation even after controlling for cognitive capacities.

These studies support the notion that dispositional constructs do influence behavior and can be useful in predicting performance, although perhaps not in any absolute sense. One can be curious in one situation and not in another, for instance. Likewise with dispositions such as friendliness or skepticism. Although there is evidence for cross-situational stability for some dispositional constructs (Webster & Kruglanski, 1994), the value of the dispositional perspective does not rest on an assumed cross-situational character. Indeed, rather than acting in a top-down, trait-like fashion, dispositions offer a more bottom-up explanation of patterns of behavior consistent with emerging social-cognitive theories of personality (Cervone, 1999; Cervone & Shoda, 1999). A dispositional perspective takes into account both the situational context and individual motivational factors, positing that patterns of behavior are emergent and not merely automatic. To better understand how such behavior emerges and how dispositions differ from traits, it is necessary to break apart dispositional behavior into its distinct components.

For a number of years, the authors and their colleagues have sustained a line of research on the nature of dispositions, as cited earlier. Although most scholars view dispositions as motivating thinking, we have analyzed the dispositional side of thinking into two components – sensitivity and inclination. Sensitivity does not motivate thinking as such but concerns whether a person notices occasions in the ongoing flow of events that might call for thinking, such as noticing a hasty causal inference, a sweeping generalization, a limiting assumption to be challenged, or a provocative problem to be solved. Inclination concerns whether a person is inclined to invest effort in thinking the matter through because of curiosity, personal relevance, and so on.

Our empirical research argues that sensitivity is supremely important. We used stories that portrayed people thinking through various problems and decisions with embedded shortfalls in their thinking, such as not going beyond the obvious options or not examining the other side of the case (Perkins et al., 2000; Perkins & Tishman, 2001). In multiple studies, we found that subjects detected only about 10% of the thinking problems, although, when prompted, they showed good ability, readily brainstorming further options or generating arguments on the other side of the case. Inclinations played an intermediate role in their engagement in thinking.

In one study, we examined test–retest correlations on sensitivity scores for detecting thinking shortfalls and found correlations of about 0.8 for a ninth grade sample and 0.6 for a fifth grade sample. The findings provide evidence that sensitivity to the sorts of shortfalls examined is a somewhat stable characteristic of the person. In several studies, we examined correlations between our dispositional measures and various measures of cognitive ability with results ranging from no to moderate correlation but lower than correlations within ability measures (Perkins et al., 2000; Perkins & Tishman, 2001). The findings suggest that sensitivity and inclination are not simply reflections of cognitive ability as usually conceived: Dispositions are truly another side of the story of thinking.

Cultivating Thinking Dispositions

These lines of evidence support the fundamental importance of dispositions in understanding what it is to be a good thinker. The question remains what role attention to dispositions does – and should – play in the teaching of thinking. Most programs do not attend directly and systematically to dispositional aspects of thinking, although they may foster dispositions as a side-effect. Indeed, it is inconvenient to address dispositions through programs that focus on direct instruction and regimens of practice. The dispositional side of thinking concerns noticing when to engage thinking seriously, which inherently does not come up in abilities-centered instruction that point-blank directs students to think about this or that problem using this or that strategy.

One solution to this suggests that culture is the best teacher of dispositions (cf. Dewey, 1922, 1933; Ritchhart, 2002; Tishman, Jay, & Perkins, 1993; Tishman, Perkins, & Jay, 1995; Vygotsky, 1978). A culture in the classroom, the family, or the workplace that foregrounds values of thinking and encourages attention to thinking would plausibly instill the attitudes and patterns of alertness called for.

Interventions that wrap learners in a culture include the *Philosophy for Children* program developed by Lipman and colleagues (Lipman, 1988; Lipman, Sharp, & Oscanyon, 1980), which foregrounds Socratic discussion, and the online collaborative knowledge-building environment CSILE (Scardamalia & Bereiter, 1996; Scardamalia et al., 1989, 1994), both of which were discussed earlier. Instrumental Enrichment (Feuerstein, 1980) involves a strong culture of support between mediator and learners. We have also worked on programs with a cultural emphasis, including *Keys to Thinking* (Perkins, Tishman, & Goodrich, 1994; Cilliers et al., 1994) and one now under development (Perkins & Ritchhart, 2004), and have published a book for teachers with this emphasis – *The Thinking Classroom* (Tishman, Perkins, & Jay, 1995). The theme of cultures of thinking is important in other ways as well, so, rather than elaborating further, we will return to it in a later section.

It is reasonable to ask whether such interventions have been shown to enhance learners' thinking dispositions. Unfortunately, evidence on this question is sparse. Although most of these programs have been formally evaluated, the assessments by and large are abilities-oriented. Their performance-on-demand character does not estimate what students are disposed to do in the absence of explicit demands, which is what dispositions are all about. That acknowledged, it is worth recalling that CSILE students revealed deeper conceptions of the nature of learning, a tendency to make mastery-oriented choices in their learning, and an avowed valuing of deep thinking (Scardamalia, Bereiter, & Lamon, 1994). Low-ability students responding to IE show marked increases in self-confidence (Feuerstein et al., 1981; Rand, Tannenbaum, & Feuerstein, 1979). The authors think it likely that many programs have at least some impact on learners' dispositions, but an extensive empirical case remains to be made.

In summary, both folk psychology and a good deal of academic psychology give abilities center stage in explaining good and not-so-good thinking and thinkers. Along with this abilities-centered view of thinking comes a concomitant view of what it is to teach thinking: To get people to think better and improve their abilities, teach problem-solving skills, learning skills, self-management skills, and so on. All this certainly has value as far as it goes. However, the arguments advanced here question the completeness of the storyline. They challenge whether performance-on-demand tasks are a good model of how thinking works in everyday life and urge that well-rounded efforts to teach thinking attend to dispositional development as well as the development of abilities.

As is the case with abilities development, dispositions need to be considered from the standpoint of transfer of learning. Not only skills, but dispositions need to be generalized broadly from their initial contexts of learning for them to develop a robust nature. This brings us to our next challenge, that of teaching transfer.

The Challenge of Transfer

Like education in general, efforts to teach thinking do not simply target the here and now: They mean to serve the there and then. What learners acquire today in the way of thinking skills, strategies, cognitive schemata, underlying cognitive operations, dispositions, metacognitive capabilities, and the like aims to help them there and then make a difficult personal decision or study quantum physics or manage a business or draft and deliver a compelling political statement. In other words, the teaching of thinking reaches for transfer of learning. Sometimes the ambition for transfer is modest – experiences with reading for understanding or mathematical problem solving here and now should improve performance for the same activities later in other contexts. Not uncommonly, however, the ambition is far more grand – fundamental and far-reaching transformation of the person as a thinker.

Some have charged that such ambitions are overwrought. Although thinking may be cultivated in particular contexts for particular purposes, far-reaching transformation may be impossible. Relatedly, some have argued that it may be impossible to teach thinking in an abstract way – say, with puzzle-like problems and through stepwise strategies – with gains that will spread far and wide.

Empirical research shows us that the prospects of transfer cannot be utterly bleak. In the second section of this article, we offered a number of existence proofs for magnitude, persistence, and transfer of impact, and more appeared in the subsequent section. Before looking further at such results, let us hear the case for meager transfer. At least three lines of scholarship pose a challenge to transfer – research on transfer itself, research on expertise and the role of knowledge in cognition, and research on situated cognition. We will look briefly at each in turn.

Transfer of learning has a vexed history, particularly with respect to far transfer, a somewhat informal term for transfer to contexts very different from that of the initial learning (see Holyoak, Chap. 6, for a review of work on transfer by use of analogies). We can touch only briefly on this complex literature. The classic studies are Thorndike's (1923, Thorndike & Woodworth, 1901) demonstrations that the intellectual rigor of studying Latin did not lead to improved performance on other fronts. Since that time, numerous reviews and compilations have shown that far transfer is hard to come by (e.g., Detterman, 1992; Detterman & Sternberg, 1992; Salomon & Perkins, 1989). For an interesting echo of Thorndike's era, a number of efforts in the 1980s to teach various versions of computer programming as, it might be said, "the new Latin," generally showed no cognitive gains beyond the programming skills themselves (Salomon & Perkins, 1987). Thorndike's view that transfer depended on "identical elements" and is less likely to apply to domains far removed from one another remains a tempting explanation of the difficulties.

A more recent view in a somewhat similar spirit, Transfer Appropriate Processing, holds that the prospects of transfer depend on a match between the features foregrounded during initial encoding and the kinds of features called for in the target context. Initial encoding may tie the learning to extraneous or unnecessarily narrow features of the situation, limiting the prospects of transfer to other situations that happen to share the same profile (Morris, Bransford, & Franks, 1977). Another rather different barrier reflects the position held by many IQ theorists that there is nothing to train and transfer: Very general cognitive capabilities simply are not subject to improvement by direct training, although genetics, nutrition, long-term enculturation by schooling, and other factors may influence general cognitive capability.

Research directly on transfer aside, more damage to the prospects comes from studies of expertise and the importance of domain-specific knowledge. Although it might be thought that skilled cognition reflects general cognitive capabilities, an extensive body of research has shown the fundamental importance of familiarity with the knowledge, strategies, values, challenges, and other features of particular disciplines and endeavors (e.g., Bereiter & Scardamalia, 1993; Ericsson & Smith, 1991; Ericsson, 1996). For a classic example, de Groot (1965) and, building on his work, Chase and Simon (1973) demonstrated that skillful chess play depends on a large repertoire of strategic patterns about chess specifically accessed in a perception-like way (see Novick & Bassok, Chap. 14).

Evidence from a range of professions argues that naturalistic decision-making depends on quick typing of situations to link them to prototypical solutions that can be adjusted to the immediate circumstances (Klein, 1999). In the same spirit, path analyses of performance in practical job contexts has shown specific knowledge to be a much more direct predictor of performance than general intelligence (Hunter, 1986). Several scholars have argued that intelligent behavior is deeply context bound (e.g. Ceci, 1990; Detterman, 1992b; Glaser, 1984; Lave, 1988). Effective thinking depends so much on a large repertoire of reflexively activated, context-specific schemata that substantial transfer of expert thinking from one domain to another is impossible. Everyday support for this comes from the informal observation that people rarely manage to display high-level thinking in more than one field.

Interventions consistent with this view include programs in mathematics and science education that focus on a particular domain and try to advance learners' expertise. For example, Schoenfeld and Herrmann (1982) documented how subjects in a previously mentioned experimental intervention based on heuristics became more expert-like in their mathematical problem solving, coding problems more in terms of their deep structure than surface features.

Further skepticism about the prospects for far transfer derives from studies of the situated character of cognition and learning (Brown, Collins, & Duguid, 1989; Kishner & Whitson, 1997; Lave, 1988; Lave & Wenger,

1991). The general point here is that skilled activity is socially and physically situated in particular contexts, depending for its fluency and depth on a web of interactions with peers, mentors, physical and symbolic tools, and so on. Skill and knowledge do not so much sit in the heads of individuals as they are distributed through the social and physical setting (Salomon, 1993) and constituted through that setting. Individuals off-load certain thinking tasks onto the environment by use of note-taking, organizational mechanisms, fellow collaborators, and other technological tools to free up mental space for more complex forms of thinking (Pea, 1993).

Accordingly, complex cognition is more likely to develop through "cognitive apprenticeship" (Collins, Brown, & Newman, 1989) in the context of rich social and physical support than through instruction that attempts to teach abstract schemas. Within such environments, individuals may first participate on the periphery of the group or with high-levels of support and gradually progress to more independent and central forms of operation as their expertise and comfort level increases (Lave & Wenger, 1991). Because cognition is so situated, the story goes, it is hard to uproot patterns of cognition and transplant them into very different contexts where they can still thrive. Interventions consistent with this view include, for example, the CSILE collaborative online knowledge building environment mentioned earlier (Scardamalia, Bereiter, & Lamon, 1994) and the Jasper Woodbury program, which helps youngsters build mathematical skills and insights through situating problem solving within compelling narratives and by making it a social endeavor (Van Haneghan et al., 1992).

This triple challenge to the prospects of transfer seems daunting indeed. However, it is important to emphasize that these critiques by and large address the prospects of *far* transfer. They allow ample room for CSILE, the Jasper Woodbury program, writers' workshops, design studios, philosophy classes and the like, where the aim is to get better at a particular kind of thinking.

Second, the positions on transfer, expertise, and situated cognition just outlined have their critics as well as their proponents. Many moderate positions take the most severe implications of these views with a large grain of salt. For example, Salomon and Perkins (1989) outlined a two-channel model of transfer specifying conditions for transfer by way of reflective abstraction and by way of automatization of routines, pointing out that there certainly were some successes reported in the transfer literature, and explaining a range of failures by the absence of conditions that would support transfer along one channel or the other. In similar spirit, Gick and Holyoak (1980, 1983) (see Holyoak, Chap. 6) demonstrated effective transfer between quite different problem-solving contexts when subjects spontaneously or upon prompting reflectively abstracted underlying principles. Bassok and Holyoak (1993) summarize experiments by making the case that superficial content context was not as limiting as some had argued. In many cases, learners bridged quite effectively from one content context to another quite different, although mismatches in the character of key variables in source and target sometimes induced considerable interference. Bransford and Schwartz (1999) urged reframing the problem of transfer in terms of readier learning in the future, not of direct gains in performance, arguing that this afforded ample opportunity for far transfer.

Turning to the theme of expertise, it can be acknowledged that a rich collection of schemata constitutes an essential engine for high-level thinking in a domain. Although necessary in itself this engine is not sufficient. Expert status does not protect a person from blind spots such as failure to examine the other side of the case (Perkins, Farady, & Bushey, 1991). Indeed, people who "ought to know better" can behave with remarkable obtuseness (Sternberg, 2002). In keeping with this, many norms and heuristics for good thinking address not the complex knowledge characteristic of domain mastery but broad patterns of processing, such as engaging anomalies seriously, examining other perspectives, or questioning assumptions, the neglect of which commonly entraps even those with well-developed knowledge in a domain (see Chi and Ohlsson, Chap. 16).

Moreover, expert thinking is misleading as a gold standard. Producing expert thinking by no means is the sole aim of the teaching of thinking. In many contexts, good thinking needs to be understood not as good-for-an-expert but good-for-a-learner or good-for-an-amateur. Some scholars have observed that there seems to be such a thing as "expert novices," and "expert learners" who bring to learning situations a range of attitudes and strategies highly conducive to developing expertise more quickly (Bereiter & Scardamalia, 1993; Brown, Ferrera, & Campione, 1983; Bruer, 1993). Moreover, in many facets of complex modern life – consider filing income taxes, functioning as responsible citizens, purchasing a new car or home – most of us operate as perpetual amateurs. We do not engage in such activities enough to build deep expertise. The question is less whether good general thinking enables us to behave like an expert – it does not – and more whether good general thinking enables us to perform better than we otherwise would by leveraging more effectively what knowledge we do have and helping us to acquire more as we go.

Turning to the related theme of situated knowledge, Anderson, Reder, and Simon (1996) identified four core claims characteristic of the situated position – that action is grounded in concrete situations, knowledge does not transfer between tasks, training by abstraction is of little use, and instruction must be done in complex social environments – and proceeded to summarize empirical evidence contrary to all of them as universal generalizations. Bereiter (1997) and Salomon and Perkins (1998) underscored how learners productively learn under many degrees and kinds of social relations and situatedness. Greeno, Smith, and Moore (1992) offered an account of transfer from the perspective of situated cognition, explaining how people sometimes export systems of activity to other superficially quite different contexts. The point of all this is certainly not to argue the opposite – that transfer comes easily, expertise depends largely on general cognitive capabilities, and learning is not somewhat entangled in its particular contexts – but rather to point out that the most dire readings of the prospects of transfer do not seem to be warranted.

Although the foregoing treats the general debate, the evidence on transfer from efforts to teach thinking also warrants consideration. As cited earlier, Nisbett (1993) summarized a number of studies in which efforts to teach statistical, if–then, cost–benefit, and other sorts of reasoning had led to transfer across content domains. As emphasized under the first challenge we addressed, there is considerable evidence for persistent far transfer of improvements in thinking from a number of studies. The signs of such transfer include impact on general reading skills, IQ-like measures, thinking in various subject matters, the general cognitive competence of retarded people, and more. It will be recalled that the philosophies and methods of these programs are quite diverse, with some using rather abstract tasks well removed from any particular subject matter or natural community.

In summary, we suggest that the debate around transfer, expertise, and situated learning has been overly polarized and ideological, leading to sweeping declarations on both sides regarding what is possible or impossible that do not stand up to empirical examination. The relationship between general cognitive structures and particular situations perhaps needs to be understood as more complex and dynamic. Perkins and Salomon (1989) offer the analogy of the human hand gripping something. The human hand plainly is a very flexible general instrument, but it always functions in context, gripping different things in different ways. Moreover, we need to learn to grasp objects according to their affordances: You don't hold a baby the same way you hold a brick. Likewise, one can acknowledge a broad range of general strategies, cognitive operations, and schemata without naïvely holding that they operate in context-neutral ways. Adjustments are always made – sometimes easily, sometimes with difficulty. Skilled cognition involves complex interarticulations of the general and the specific.

So the prospects of transfer escape these skirmishes with skepticism – but not unscathed! Indeed, there are pointed lessons to be drawn. We can learn from research on the difficulties of transfer that transfer is nothing to take for granted. Well-designed efforts to cultivate thinking will face up to the challenge, for instance by incorporating episodes of reflective abstraction to help learners to decontextualize patterns of thinking and by providing practice across multiple distinct contexts. Well-designed efforts to cultivate thinking will look closely at the behavior of experts to construct their heuristic analyses, and will not expect general norms and heuristics to do the job of norms and heuristics tailored to particular endeavors such as writing or mathematical problem solving. Well-designed efforts to cultivate thinking will recognize the distributed nature of cognition, and take advantage of social and physical support systems to advance individual and collective thinking.

The Challenge of Creating Cultures of Thinking

Thus far, we've examined four challenges that efforts to teach thinking traditionally have faced. As teachers and program developers seek to meet those challenges, a host of additional concerns arise; for example; How do we provide enough time, context, and diverse applications so that new patterns of thinking actually take hold? How can we best take into account that school learning happens in a social context within a classroom among a group of individuals? Is the development of individual thinking best served and supported by the development of group learning practices? How do we uncover the thinking that is going on in individuals and within the group so we can respond to it and learn from it? These questions connect us to our last and final challenge, the challenge of creating cultures of thinking.

Culture has been mentioned briefly in previous sections, but one still might ask: What is it about culture, and cultures of thinking in particular, that demands attention (see Greenfield, Chap. 27, for further discussions on the role of culture)? Three important motives are worthy of attention: First, the supporting structures of culture are needed to sustain gains and actualize intelligent behavior over time, as opposed to merely building short-term capacity (Brown & Campione, 1994; Scardamalia et al., 1994; Tishman, Perkins, & Jay, 1993). It is through the culture of the classroom that strategies and practices take on meaning and become connected to the work of learning. Second, culture helps to shape what we attend to, care about, and focus our energies upon (Bruner, Olver, & Greenfield, 1966; Dasen, 1977; Super, 1980). Thus, culture is integrally linked to the dispositional side of thinking and to the cultivation of inclination and sensitivity. Third, researchers and program developers increasingly have recognized that thinking programs are not merely implemented but are enacted, developed, and sustained in a social context. As a result, they have found it necessary to move away from teacher-proof materials, which view learning as an isolated individual process, and toward approaches that pay more attention to the underlying conditions of learning.

As a result of the awareness of the role culture plays in learning, the past two decades have seen efforts to teach thinking shift from programmed strategy instruction aimed at students as individuals to broad-based approaches aimed at building classroom cultures supportive of the active social construction of knowledge among groups. These approaches take a variety of forms, such as cognitive apprenticeship (Collins, Brown, & Newman, 1989), fostering a community of learners (Brown & Campione, 1994), group knowledge building (Bereiter & Scardamalia, 1996; Scardamalia & Bereiter, 1996), inquiry-based teaching (Lipman, 1983), and the development of patterns of thinking (Tishman, Perkins, & Jay, 1995) and habits of mind (Costa & Kallick, 2002). Several programs associated with these approaches were mentioned previously – CISLE/Knowledge Forum, Philosophy for Children, and Keys to Thinking among them. We'll examine a few additional ones subsequently. Before doing so, however, it may be useful to take a closer look at just what is meant by culture in the cultural approach.

Culture, construed broadly, refers to the context and general surround in which we operate. This doesn't tell us much about what it means to become enculturated, however. To illuminate this issue it is helpful to look at particular intellectual subcultures or communities of practice, say of mathematicians or writers or even mechanics. What does it mean to be a part of these cultures? A frame that we have found useful is based on two top-level conceptions: *resources* and *practice* (Roth, 1995). Resources are the things upon which members of the culture of practice draw when they do their work. Resources can be physical in nature: computers, books, instruments, tools, and the like. There are also social resources such as colleagues, coworkers, editors, peer-review boards, and so on. These types of resources help distribute cognition outside the individual thinker's mind (Salomon, 1993). In addition, there are conceptual resources consisting of the conceptual, knowledge, and belief systems in which the subculture readily traffics. Also included in the conceptual resources are the symbol systems and notational structures evolved to support abstract thought (Gardner, 1983; Goodman, 1976; Olson, 1974).

Practice captures the constructive acts engaged in by the cultural group – what it is they do, the kind of work that is valued and rewarded, the methods they employ. This connects the group to the socio-historically valued ways of knowing and thinking, such as the epistemic forms of the disciplines that are part of the group's heritage (Collins & Ferguson, 1993; Perkins, 1994, 1997). Resources and practice interact dialectically in that individual and group practice transform resources that, in turn, have an effect on practice. At the same time, resources and practice provide supports for distributed intelligence, scaffolding intelligent behavior beyond that which can be displayed by an individual mind (Salomon, 1993).

This dialectical interplay between practice and resources informs our understanding of just what the "it" is in which individuals become enculturated. But, how does this enculturation happen? How are a culture's practice and resources conveyed and learned by group members? In a study of thoughtful classrooms, Ritchhart (Ritchhart, 2002) identified seven cultural forces at work in classrooms that facilitated the process of enculturation in thinking: (1) messages from the physical environment about thinking, (2) teacher modeling of thinking and dispositions, (3) the use of language of thinking, (4) routines and structures for thinking, (5) opportunities created for thinking, (6) conveyance of expectations for thinking, and (7) interactions and relationships supportive of thinking.

These cultural forces act as direct and indirect vehicles for teaching. For example, the use of routines and structures for thinking, which connects to the idea of norms and heuristics mentioned previously, is a highly integrated but still direct form of teaching. By introducing "thinking routines" (Ritchhart, 2002), teachers provide students with highly transportable tools for thinking that they learn in one context and then transfer to other situations over time until the strategy has become a routine of the classroom. We and our colleagues are currently capitalizing on this approach in the design of a new thinking program. The use of the language of thinking (Tishman & Perkins, 1997; Ritchart, 2002) – which includes *process* (justifying, questioning, analyzing), *product* (theory, conjecture, summation), *stance* (challenge, agree, concur), and *state* (confused, puzzled, intrigued) words – is a much more indirect method of promoting thinking that gives students the vocabulary for talking about thinking. By combining the direct (routines and structures, and opportunities) and the indirect (modeling, language, relationships and interactions, environment, expectations), a culture of thinking is built and sustained.

One can see these cultural forces at play in the Community of Learners approach (Brown & Campione, 1994). In this approach, a premium is placed on research, knowledge-building, and critical thinking, thus communicating expectations for thinking to students through the types of opportunities provided. In this environment, individual responsibility is coupled with the communal sharing of expertise. Discourse (constructive discussion, questioning, and criticism) is the norm, making use of the language of thinking and interactions and relationships supportive of thinking. Ritual, familiar participant structures, and routines are introduced to help students navigate and work within the new culture. All of this is accomplished within an environment that makes thinking visible for students.

Research suggests that, at least in this particular case, a broad-based cultural approach was superior to one based on teaching heuristics. Approximately ninety fifth and sixth graders in the Community of Learners (CL) group outperformed a group using only a reciprocal teaching technique in which students led the learning in reading discussions on criterion-referenced tests of reading comprehension (and this result occurred even though the group was given twice as much practice as the CL group). There was no improvement in a reading-only control group. Scores on questions dealing with inference, gist, and analogy improved dramatically. The results show magnitude of effects but require further study to assess the generality and persistence of effects. Further research is needed to determine whether the effects are sustaining in the sense of ongoing repertoire, the ultimate goal of a cultural approach, or whether their impact is limited to behaviors in the immediate environment.

A common thread running through cultural approaches to teaching thinking is the effort to make thinking visible, often through the various cultural forces. This occurs as teachers model their thought processes before the class, students are asked to share their thinking and discuss the processes they went through in solving problems or coming to conclusions, group ideas and conjectures are recorded and reviewed, the artifacts of thinking are put on display in the classroom, and so on. At the heart of these efforts lies reflection on one's thinking and cognitive monitoring, the core processes of metacognition. Ultimately, teaching students to be more metacognitive and reflective, providing rich opportunities for thinking across various contexts, setting up an environment that values thinking, and making the thinking of group members visible contribute a great deal to the formation of a culture of thinking. The cultural forces can be leveraged toward this end. Within such a culture of thinking, other efforts to teach thinking, both formal and informal, have a greater likelihood of taking hold because they will be reinforced through the culture and opportunities for transfer and reflection will increase.

In summary, in some sense, a fully developed culture of thinking in the classroom or, indeed, in other settings such as the home or the workplace, represents the cohesive culmination of the separate challenges of achieving results, defining the thinking, attaining transfer, and attending to thinking dispositions. A thoroughgoing culture of thinking attends to all of these. Unfortunately, the converse is certainly not so. It is possible to attend assiduously to the first four – say, every Tuesday and Thursday from 11 to 12, or when we do math projects for a day at the end of each unit – and still fall far short of a pervasive culture of thinking. Results reviewed earlier in this article suggest that even limited treatments may well benefit students' thinking. However, one has to ask about the rest of their learning. In the end, the point of a culture of thinking is not just to serve the development of thinking but to serve the breadth and depth of students' learning on all fronts.

Conclusions and Future Directions

This review of the teaching of thinking has cast a wide net to look at programs for which adequate data exist for examination and discussion. These programs address a great variety of thinking – creative and critical thinking, problem solving, decision making, and metacognition as well as subject-specific types of thinking. Even so, we have only scratched the surface of the ongoing efforts to teach thinking. Why does the teaching of thinking continue to be such a central question in education? Why do we even need to teach thinking? As discussed earlier, efforts to teach thinking deal with both amplifying native tendencies and addressing problems of thinking shortfalls. In addition, a major goal of most thinking interventions is to enhance learning and promote deeper understanding. The idea that deep and lasting learning is a product of thinking provides a powerful case for the teaching of thinking. Indeed, we venture that the true promise of the teaching of thinking will not be realized until learning to think and thinking to learn merge seamlessly.

Toward this end, we singled out five challenges that must be dealt with along the way. The first addressed the question of whether or not thinking can be taught with some reasonable signs of success. We reviewed several programs as a kind of existence proof that, indeed, it is possible to produce impacts with substantial magnitude, persistence, and transfer. These programs spanned a variety of philosophical and methodological approaches while sharing the common characteristics of increasing the demand for thinking, developing thinking processes, and paying attention to metacognitive self-regulation. These common demand characteristics appear to be key elements in the teaching of thinking.

The second challenge concerned what one means when talking about good thinking. We showed how efforts to teach thinking are shaped largely by how they answer this question. Thus, the content, sequence, and methods of instruction for a particular intervention arise from a single or collective set of grounding theories, be they linked to norms and heuristics, intelligence, or human development. Interestingly, programs with quite different theories seem to have achieved substantial success. Why should this be? Does theory matter at all? As with the first challenge, the answer to effectiveness may lie more with certain demand characteristics of programs than with any single theoretical approach. Increased explicit involvement with thinking and systematic attention to managing one's thinking may be the most critical conditions. To untangle this issue empirically, one would need to compare the effectiveness of programs with different theoretical bases but with the same demands for thinking and reflection. Unfortunately, it is rare in the literature on the teaching of thinking to find alternative approaches addressing the same kinds of thinking and the same sorts of learners pitted against one another.

The third challenge dealt with the dispositional side of thinking. We showed how the effective teaching of thinking is more than just the development of ability, demanding the development of awareness and inclination as well. In particular, the lack of a sensitivity to occasions for thinking appears to be a major bottleneck when it comes to putting one's abilities into action. It is our belief that some programs accomplish this. Although most data focus on abilities, leaving impact on sensitivity and inclination unassessed, there are a few indications of impact on dispositions. Certainly, more work is needed in this area.

Transfer, a pivotal concern within the teaching of thinking, constituted our fourth challenge. Although some have argued that transfer cannot be obtained because all knowledge is bound to context, the empirical record of successful programs has shown clearly that some degree of transfer is possible across domains of content knowledge. This is by no means automatic, however. Transfer must be designed deliberately into interventions by highlighting key features of the situation that need attention, promoting reflective abstraction of underlying principles, and providing practice across multiple contexts. Even then, one is more likely to see near transfer of thinking to similar contexts than far transfer.

Our fifth challenge, that of creating cultures of thinking, examined the social context and environment in which thinking is fostered. Efforts to teach thinking cannot be removed from their social context. Context provides important avenues for the development of supporting inclinations toward thinking, learning from more accomplished peers, focusing attention, and access to the resources and practices of the group. In classrooms, a set of cultural forces directs and shapes students' learning experiences both directly and indirectly. These cultural forces convey to students how much and what kinds of thinking are valued, what methods the group uses to go about thinking, and what expectations there are regarding thinking. Furthermore, the thinking of individuals and groups is made visible through these forces.

Our review of these five challenges suggests several fronts for further investigation:

- The questions of transfer and sustained impact need to be better understood. In particular, little is known about the impact of extended interventions. One might expect that broad multi-year interventions would yield wide impact sustained for many years, but the empirical work has not been done to our knowledge. Relatedly, what would be the effect of a cross-subject thinking intervention in which students encounter the same practices concurrently in multiple disciplines?
- An exploration of the trade-offs among the norms and heuristics, models of intelligence, and developmental approaches is needed to better understand the role of theory in successful interventions. How and where does the underlying theory of thinking matter? When demands for thinking are held constant, does one theoretical approach work better than another? What is it that makes successful programs work? What characteristics and practices are most pivotal to success?
- Within the realm of thinking dispositions, there is much to be learned. How successful are existing programs at developing the dispositional side of thinking? What kinds of practices and interventions effectively foster students' inclination and sensitivity? Are dispositions bound to the social context in which they are developed or do they transfer to new settings? How does attention to the development of sensitivity to occasions affect transfer of thinking skills? Efforts to teaching thinking skills are sometimes done in a limited time frame, raising the question: What is the appropriate time frame for the development of dispositions?

Perhaps the biggest question about the teaching of thinking concerns how to integrate it with other practices, in school and out of school, in an effective way. We already know enough about the teaching of thinking to have a substantial impact, and yet the reality of collective practice falls short. We must ask ourselves: How can thinking initiatives be sustained and integrated with the many other agendas faced by schools, museums, clubs, corporate cultures, and other settings in which thinking might thrive? Only when we understand how to foster cultures of thinking not just within individual families or classrooms but across entire schools, communities, and, indeed, societies, will scholarly insights and the practical craft of teaching thinking achieve their mutual promise.

Acknowledgments

Some of the ideas and research reported here were developed with much-appreciated support from the Stiftelsen Carpe Vitam Foundation and the John D. and Catherine T. MacArthur Foundation. The positions taken by the authors, of course, are not necessarily those of the foundations. The authors would like to thank Stellan Ohlsson and Keith Holyoak for their thoughtful editorial suggestions in response to the first draft and Nicole Weiss for her research assistance.

References

Adams, C. (Ed.) (1971). *Think*, Stanford, CT: Innovative Sciences.

Adams, M. J. (1989). Thinking skills curricula: Their promise and progress. *Educational Psychologist*, 24(1), 25–77.

Adams, M. J. (Ed.) (1986). *Odyssey: A Curriculum for Thinking*. Watertown, MA: Charlesbridge.

Adey, P., & Shayer, M. (1993). An exploration of long-term far-transfer effects following an extended intervention program in the high school science curriculum. *Cognition and Instruction*, 11(1), 1–29.

Adey, P., & Shayer, M. (1994). *Really Raising Standards: Cognitive Intervention and Academic Achievement*. London: Routledge.

Anderson, J. R., Reder, L. M., & Simon, H. A. (1996). Situated learning and education. *Educational Researcher*, 25(4), 5–11.

Argyris, C. (1993). *On Organizational Learning*. Cambridge, MA: Blackwell.

Argyris, C., & Schön, D. A. (1996). *Organizational Learning II: Theory, Method, and Practice*. New York: Addison-Wesley.

Bassok, M., & Holyoak, K. J. (1993). Pragmatic knowledge and conceptual structure: Determinants of transfer between quantitative domains. In D. K. Detterman, & R. J. Sternberg (Eds.), *Transfer on Trial: Intelligence, Cognition, and Instruction*. Norwood, NJ: Ablex.

Baron, J. (1985). *Rationality and Intelligence*. New York: Cambridge University Press.

Baron, J. B., Granato, L., Spranca, M., & Teubel, E. (1993). Decision-making biases in children and early adolescents: Exploratory studies. *Merrill-Palmer Quarterly*, 39(1), 22–46.

Bereiter, C. (1997). Situated cognition and how to overcome it. In D. Kishner, & J. A. Whitson (Eds.), *Situated Cognition: Social, Semiotic, and Psychological Perspectives* (pp. 281–300). Hillsdale, NJ: Erlbaum.

Bereiter, C., & Scardamalia, M. (1993). *Surpassing Ourselves: An Inquiry into the Nature and Implications of Expertise*. Chicago: Open Court.

Bereiter, C., & Scardamalia, M. (1996). Rethinking learning. In D. R. Olson, & N. Torrance (Eds.), *The Handbook of Education and Human Development: New Models of Learning, Teaching and Schooling* (pp. 485–413). Cambridge, MA: Basil Blackwell.

Blagg, N. (1991). *Can We Teach Intelligence? A Comprehensive Evaluation of Feuerstein's Instructional Enrichment Program*. Hillsdale, NJ: Erlbaum.

Boyer, E. (1983). *High School: A Report on Secondary Education in America*. New York: Harper & Row.

Brainerd, C. J. (1983). Working-memory systems and cognitive development. In C. J. Brainerd (Ed.), *Recent Advances in Cognitive-developmental Theory: Progress in Cognitive Development Research* (pp. 167–236). New York: Springer-Verlag.

Bransford, J. D., & Schwartz, D. L. (1999). Rethinking transfer: A simple proposal with interesting implications. In A. Iran-Nejad, & P. D. Pearson (Eds.), *Review of Research in Education* (Vol. 24, pp. 61–101). Washington, DC: American Educational Research Association.

Brody, N. (1992). *Intelligence*. New York: Academic Press.

Brown, A. L., Bransford, J. D., Ferrara, R. A., & Campione, J. C. (1983). Learning, remembering, and understanding. In P. H. Mussen (ED.) *Handbook of Child Psychology. Vol. 3: Cognitive Development*. New York: Wiley.

Brown, J. S., Collins, A., & Duguid, P. (1989). Situated cognition and the culture of learning. *Educational Researcher*, 18(1), 32–42.

Brown, A. L., & Campione, J. C. (1994). Guided discovery in a community of learners. In K. McGilly (Ed.), *Classroom Lessons: Integrating Cognitive Theory and Classroom Practice*. Cambridge, MA: MIT Press/Bradford Books.

Brown, A. L., & Palincsar, A. S. (1982). Introducing strategic learning from text by means of informed, self-control training. *Topic in Learning and Learning Disabilities*, 2(1), 1–17.

Bruner, J. S., Olver, R., & Greenfield, P. (1966). *Studies in Cognitive Growth*. New York: Wiley.

Burke, T. (Ed.) (1971). *Intuitive Math*. Stanford, CT: Innovative Sciences.

Cacioppo, J. T., & Petty, R. E. (1982). The need for cognition. *Journal of Personality and Social Psychology*, 42, 116–131.

Cacioppo, J. T., Petty, R. E., Feinstein, J. A., & Jarvis, W. B. G. (1996). Dispositional differences in cognitive motivation: The life and times of individuals varying in need for cognition. *Psychological Bulletin*, 119(2), 197–253.

Carey, S. (1985). *Conceptual Change in Childhood*. Cambridge, MA: MIT Press.

Carey, S. (1985b). *Conceptual Change in Childhood*. Cambridge, MA: MIT Press.

Case, R. (1984). The process of stage transition: A neo-Piagetian viewpoint. In R. J. Sternberg (Ed.), *Mechanisms of Cognitive Development* (pp. 19–44). New York: Freeman.

Case, R. (1985). *Intellectual Development: Birth to Adulthood*. New York: Academic Press.

Case, R. (1992). *The Mind's Staircase: Exploring the Conceptual Underpinnings of Children's Thought and Knowledge*. Hillsdale, NJ: Erlbaum.

Ceci, S. J. (1990). *On Intelligence . . . More or Less: A Bio-ecological Treatise on Intellectual Development*. Englewood Cliffs, NJ: Prentice-Hall.

Cervone, D. (1999). Bottom-up explanation in personality psychology: The case of cross-situational coherence. In D. Cervone, & Y. Shoda (Eds.), *The Coherence of Personality: Social-cognitive Bases of Consistency* (pp. 303–341). New York: Guilford Press.

Cervone, D., & Shoda, Y. (1999). Beyond traits in the study of personality coherence. *Current Directions in Psychological Science*, 8(1), 27–32.

Chase, W. C., & Simon, H. A. (1973). Perception in chess. *Cognitive Psychology*, 4, 55–81.

Cilliers, C., Botha, L., Capdevielle, B., Perkins, D. N., & van der Vyver, D. (1994). The development of a curriculum for thinking skills. *International Journal of Special Education*, 9,(3), 257–270.

Collins, A., & Ferguson, W. (1993). Epistemic forms and epistemic games: Structures and strategies to guide inquiry. *Educational Psychologist*, 28(1), 25–42.

Collins, A., Brown, J. S., & Newman, S. F. (1989). Cognitive apprenticeship: Teaching the craft of reading, writing, and mathematics. In L. B. Resnick (Ed.), *Knowing, Learning, and Instruction: Essays in Honor of Robert Glase* (pp. 453–494). Hillsdale, NJ: Erlbaum.

Costa, A. L., & Kallick, B. (2002). *Habits of Mind* (Vol. I–IV). Alexandria, VA: Association for Supervision and Curriculum Development.

Dasen, P. R. (Ed.) (1977). *Piagetian Psychology: Cross-cultural Contributions*. New York: Gardner Press.

de Bono, E. (1973). *CoRT Thinking Program: Workcards and Teacher Notes*. Sydney: Direct Educational Services.

de Groot, A. D. (1965). *Thought and Choice in Chess*. The Hague: Mouton.

Detterman, D. K. (Ed.) (1992a). *Current Topics in Human Intelligence. Vol. 2 : Is Mind Modular or Unitary?* Norwood, NJ: Ablex.

Detterman, D. K. (1992). The case for the prosecution: Transfer as an epiphenomenon. In D. K. Detterman, & R. J. Sternberg (Eds.), *Transfer on Trial* (pp. 1–24). Norwood, NJ: Ablex.

Detterman, D., & Sternberg, R. (Eds.) (1992). *Transfer on Trial*. Norwood, NJ: Ablex.

Dewey, J. (1922). *Human Nature and Conduct*. New York: Holt.

Dewey, J. (1933). *How We Think: A Restatement of the Relation of Reflective Thinking to the Educative Process*. Boston: Heath.

Dweck, C. S. (1975). The role of expectations and attributions in the alleviation of learned helplessness. *Journal of Personality and Social Psychology*, 31, 674–685.

Dweck, C. S. (2000). *Self-theories: Their Role in Motivation, Personality, and Development*. Philadelphia: Psychology Press.

Edwards, J., & Baldauf, R. B. (1983). Teaching thinking in secondary science. In W. Maxwell (Ed.), *Thinking: The Expanding Frontier*. Philadelphia: Franklin Institute Press.

Edwards, J., & Baldauf, R. B. (1987). The effects of the CoRT-1 thinking skills program on students. In D. N. Perkins, J. Lochhead & J. C. Bishop (Eds.), *Thinking: The Second International Conference*. Hillsdale: Erlbaum.

Edwards, J. (1991a). The direct teaching of thinking skills. In G. Evans (Ed.), *Learning and Teaching Cognitive Skills* (pp. 87–106). Melbourne: Australian Council for Educational Research.

Edwards, J. (1991b). Research work on the CoRT method. In S. Maclure, & P. Davies (Eds.), *Learning to Think: Thinking to Learn* (pp. 19–30). Oxford, UK: Pergamon.

Edwards, J. (1994). Thinking, education, and human potential. In J. Edwards (Ed.), *Thinking: International Interdisciplinary Perspectives* (pp. 6–15). Melbourne: Hawker Brownlow Education.

Ennis, R. H. (1986). A taxonomy of critical thinking dispositions and abilities. In J. B. Baron, & R. S. Sternberg (Eds.). *Teaching Thinking Skills: Theory and Practice* (pp. 9–26). New York: Freeman.

Ericsson, K. A. (Ed.) (1996). *The Road to Excellence: The Acquisition of Expert Performance in the Arts and Sciences, Sports, and Game*. Mahwah, NJ: Erlbaum.

Ericsson, K. A., & Smith, J. (Eds.) (1991). *Toward a General Theory of Expertise: Prospects and Limits*. Cambridge, UK: Cambridge University Press.

Facione, P. A., Sanchez, C. A., Facione, N. C., & Gainen, J. (1995). The disposition toward critical thinking. *Journal of General Education*, 44(1), 1–25.

Feuerstein, R. (1980). *Instrumental Enrichment: An Intervention Program for Cognitive Modifiability*. Baltimore: University Park Press.

Feuerstein, R., Miller, R., Hoffman, M. B., Rand, Y., Mintzker, Y., & Jensen, M. R. (1981). Cognitive modifiability in adolescence: Cognitive structure and the effects of intervention. *The Journal of Special Education*, 15, 269–286.

Fischer, K. W. (1980). A theory of cognitive development: The control and construction of hierarchies of skills. *Psychological Review*, 87(6), 477–531.

Gardner, H. (1983). *Frames of Mind*. New York: Basic Books.

Gick, M. L., & Holyoak, K. J. (1980). Analogical problem solving. *Cognitive Psychology*, 12, 306–365.

Gick, M. L., & Holyoak, K. J. (1983). Schema induction and analogical transfer. *Cognitive Psychology*, 15, 1–38.

Glaser, R. (1984). Education and thinking: The role of knowledge. *American Psychologist*, 39, 93–104.

Goleman, D. (1995). *Emotional Intelligence*. New York: Bantam Books.

Goodlad, J. I. (1983). *A Place Called School: Prospects for the Future*. New York: McGraw-Hill.

Goodman, N. A. (1976). *Languages of Art*. Indianapolis: Hackett.

Greeno, J. G., Smith, D. R., & Moore, J. L. (1992). Transfer of situated learning. In D. Detterman, & R. Sternberg (Eds.), *Transfer on Trial* (pp, 99–167). Norwood, NJ: Ablex.

Griffin, S. A., Case, R., & Capodilupo, S. (1995). Teaching for understanding: The importance of central conceptual structures in the elementary school mathematics curriculum. In A. McKeough, J. Lupart, & A. Marini (Eds.), *Teaching for Transfer: Fostering Generalization in Learning*. Hillsdale, NJ: Erlbaum.

Grotzer, T., & Perkins, D. N. (2000). Teaching intelligence: A performance conception. In R. J. Sternberg (Ed.), *Handbook of Intelligence*. New York: Cambridge University Press.

Guilford, J. P. (1967). *The Nature of Human Intelligence*. New York: McGraw-Hill.

Guilford, J. P., & Hoepfner, R. (1971). *The Analysis of Intelligence*. New York: McGraw-Hill.

Hamblin, C. L. (1970). *Fallacies*. London: Methuen.

Hamers, J. H. M., & Overtoom, M. (Eds.) (1997). *Teaching Thinking in Europe: Inventory of European Programmes*. Utrecht: Sardes.

Harvey, J. H., Town, J. P., & Yarkin, K. L. (1981). How fundamental is "the fundamental attribution error"? *Journal of Personality and Social Psychology*, 40(2), 346–349.

Herrnstein, R. J., Nickerson, R. S., Sanchez, M., & Swets, J. A. (1986). Teaching thinking skills. *American Psychologist*, 41, 1279–1289.

Hirschfeld, L. A., & Gelman, L. A. (Eds.) (1994). *Domain Specificity in Cognition and Culture*. Cambridge, UK: Cambridge University Press.

Hunter, J. E. (1986). Cognitive ability, cognitive aptitudes, job knowledge, and job performance. *Journal of Vocational Behavior*, 29, 340–362.

Idol, L., Jones, B. F. (Ed.) (1991). *Educational Values and Cognitive Instruction: Implications for Reform*. Hillsdale, NJ: Erlbaum.

Inhelder, B., & Piaget, J. (1958). *The Growth of Logical Thinking from Childhood to Adolescence*. New York: Basic Books.

Janis, I. (1972). *Victims of Groupthink: Psychological Study of Foreign-Policy Decisions and Fiascoes (2nd ed.)*. Boston: Houghton Mifflin.

Jensen, A. R. (1980). *Bias in Mental Testing*. New York: Free Press.

Jensen, A. R. (1998). *The* g *Factor: The Science of Mental Ability*. Westport, CT: Praeger.

Kishner, D., & Whitson, J. A. (Eds.)(1997). *Situated Cognition: Social, Semiotic, and Psychological Perspectives*. Hillsdale, NJ: Erlbaum.

Klein, G. (1999). *Sources of Power: How People Make Decisions*. Cambridge, MA: MIT Press.

Kriegler, S., van Niekerk, H. (1993). IE: A contribution to cultivating a culture of learning? *International Journal of Cognitive Education and Mediated Learning*, 3(1), 21–26.

Kruglanski, A. W. (1990). Motivations for judging and knowing: Implications for causal attribution. In E. T. Higgins, & R. M. Sorrentino

(Eds.), *The Handbook of Motivation and Cognition: Foundation of Social Behavior* (Vol. 2, pp. 333–368). New York: Guilford Press.

Langer, E. (1989). *Mindfulness*. Reading, MA: Addison-Wesley.

Lave, J. (1988). *Cognition in Practice: Mind, Mathematics and Culture in Everyday Life*. Cambridge, UK: Cambridge University Press.

Lave, J., & Wenger, E. (1991). *Situated Learning: Legitimate Peripheral Participation*. New York: Cambridge University Press.

Lipman, M. (1976). Philosophy for children. *Metaphilosophy*, 7, 17–19.

Lipman, M. (1983). *Thinking Skills Fostered by Philosophy for Children*. Montclair, NJ: Institute for the Advancement of Philosophy for Children.

Lipman, M. (1988). *Philosophy Goes to School*. Philadelphia: Temple University.

Lipman, M., Sharp, A., & Oscanyon, F. (1980). *Philosophy in the Classroom*. Philadelphia: Temple University.

McGuinness, C., & Nisbet, J. (1991). Teaching thinking in Europe. *British Journal of Educational Psychology*, 61, 174–186.

Meeker, M. N. (1969). *The Structure of Intellect: Its Interpretation and Uses*. Columbus, OH: Charles E. Merrill.

Morris, C. D., Bransford, J. D., & Franks, J. J. (1977). Levels of processing versus transfer appropriate processing. *Journal of Verbal Learning and Verbal Behavior*, 16, 519–533.

National Commission on Excellence in Education (1983). *A Nation at Risk: The Imperative for Educational Reform*. Washington, DC: U.S. Department of Education.

Nickerson, R. S., Perkins, D. N., & Smith, E. E. (1985). *The Teaching of Thinking*. Hillsdale, NJ: Erlbaum.

Nisbett, R. E. (Ed.) (1993). *Rules for Reasoning*. Hillsdale, NJ: Erlbaum.

Norris, S. P. (1995). The meaning of critical thinking test performance: The effects of abilities and dispositions on scores. In D. Fasko, Jr. (Ed.), *Critical Thinking: Current Research, Theory, and Practice*. Dordect, The Netherlands: Kluwer Academic.

Olson, D. (Ed.) (1974). *Media and Symbols: The Forms of Expression, Communication, and Education*. Chicago: University of Chicago Press.

Pascual-Leone, J., Goodman, D., Ammon, P., & Subelman, I. (1978). Piagetian theory and neo-Piagetian analysis as psychological guides in education. In J. M. Gallagher (Ed.), *Knowledge and Development* (Vol. 2). New York: Plenum.

Paul, R. W. (1984). Critical thinking: Fundamental to education for a free society. *Educational Leadership*, 42(1), 4–14.

Pea, R. D. (1993). Practices of distributed intelligence and designs for education. In G. Salomon (Ed.), *Distributed Cognitions* (pp. 47–87). New York: Cambridge University Press.

Perkins, D. N. (1985). Postprimary education has little impact on informal reasoning. *Journal of Education Psychology*, 77(5), 562–571.

Perkins, D. N. (1994). The hidden order of open-ended thinking. In J. Edwards (Ed.), *Thinking: Interdisciplinary Perspectives*. Victoria, Australia: Hawker Brownlow Education.

Perkins, D. N. (1995). *Outsmarting IQ: The Emerging Science of Learnable Intelligence*. New York: Free Press.

Perkins, D. N. (1989). Reasoning as it is and could be. In D. Topping, D. Crowell, & V. Kobayashi (Eds.), *Thinking: The Third International Conference*. Hillsdale, NJ: Erlbaum.

Perkins, D. N. (1995). *Outsmarting IQ*. New York: Free Press.

Perkins, D. N. (1997). Epistemic games. *International Journal of Educational Research*, 27(1), 49–61.

Perkins, D. N., Allen, R., & Hafner, J. (1983). Difficulties in everyday reasoning. In W. Maxwell (Ed.), *Thinking: The Frontier Expands* (pp. 117–189). Hillsdale, NJ: Erlbaum.

Perkins, D. N., Farady, M., & Bushey, B. (1991). Everyday reasoning and the roots of intelligence. In J. Voss, D. N. Perkins & J. Segal (Eds.), *Informal Reasoning* (pp. 83–105). Hillsdale, NJ: Erlbaum.

Perkins, D. N., & Goodrich-Andrade, H. (1998). Learnable intelligence and intelligent learning. In R. J. Sternberg, & W. M. Williams (Eds.), *Intelligence, Instruction, and Assessment* (67–94). Hillsdale, NJ: Erlbaum.

Perkins, D. N., & Ritchhart, R. (2004). When is good thinking? In D. Y. Dai & R. J. Sternberg (Eds.), *Motivation, Emotion, and Cognition: Integrative Perspectives on Intellectual Functioning and Development*. Mahwah, NJ: Erlbaum.

Perkins, D. N., & Salomon, G. (1988). Teaching for transfer. *Educational Leadership*, Sept., 22–32.

Perkins, D. N., & Salomon, G. (1989). Are cognitive skills context bound? *Educational Researcher*, 18(1), 16–25.

Perkins, D. N., Jay, E., & Tishman, S. (1993). Beyond abilities: A dispositional theory of thinking. *The Merrill-Palmer Quarterly*, 39(1), 1–21.

Perkins, D. N., Tishman, S., & Goodrich, H. (1994). *Keys to Thinking*. Johannesburg: UPTTRAIL Trust.

Perkins, D. N., Tishman, S., Ritchhart, R., Donis, K., & Andrade. A. (2000). Intelligence in the wild: A dispositional view of intellectual traits. *Educational Psychology Review*, 12(3), 269–293.

Perkins. D. N., & Tishman, S. (2001). Dispositional aspects of intelligence. In S. Messick, & J. M. Collis (Eds.), *Intelligence and Personality: Bridging the Gap in Theory and Measurement* (pp. 233–257). Mahwah, NJ: Erlbaum.

Polya, G. (1954). *Mathematics and Plausible Reasoning* (2 vols.). Princeton, NJ: Princeton University Press.

Polya, G. (1957). *How to Solve It: A New Aspect of Mathematical Method*. Garden City, NY: Doubleday.

Rand, Y., Tannenbaum, A. J., & Feuerstein, R. (1979). Effects of instrumental enrichment on the psychoeducational development of low-functioning adolescents. *Journal of Educational Psychology*, 71, 751–763.

Resnick, L. B. (1987). *Education and Learning to Think*. Washington, DC: National Academy Press.

Ritchhart, R. (2002). *Intellectual Character: What It Is, Why It Matters, and How to Get It*. San Francisco: Jossey-Bass.

Roth, W.-M. B., Michael, G. (1995). Knowing and interacting: A study of culture, practices, and resources in a Grade 8 open-inquiry science classroom guided by a cognitive apprenticeship metaphor. *Cognition and Instruction*, 13(1), 73–128.

Salomon, G. (Ed.) (1993). *Distributed Cognitions*. New York: Cambridge University Press.

Salomon, G., & Perkins, D. N. (1987). Transfer of cognitive skills from programming: When and how? *Journal of Educational Computing Research*, 3, 149–169.

Salomon, G., & Perkins, D. N. (1989). Rocky roads to transfer: Rethinking mechanisms of a neglected phenomenon. *Educational Psychologist*, 24(2), 113–142.

Salomon, G., & Perkins, D. N. (1998). Individual and social aspects of learning. In P. D. Pearson, & A. Iran-Nejad (Eds.), *Review of Research in Education: Vol. 23*. (pp. 1–24). Washington, DC: AERA.

Savell, J. M., Twohig, P. T., & Rachford, D. L. (1986). *Empirical Status of Feuerstein's "Instrumental Enrichment" (FIE) as a Method of Teaching Thinking Skills* (No. 699). Arlington, VA: U.S. Army Research Institute.

Scardamalia, M., & Bereiter, C. (1996). Engaging students in a knowledge building society. *Educational Leadership, November*, 6–10.

Scardamalia, M., & Bereiter, C. (1996). Adaptation and understanding: A case for new cultures of schooling. In S. Vosniadou, E. DeCorte, R. Glaser, & H. Mandl (Eds.), *International Perspectives on the Design of Technology-supported Learning Environments* (pp 149–163). Mahwah, NJ: Erlbaum.

Scardamalia, M., Bereiter, C., & Lamon, M. (1994). The CSILE Project: Trying to bring the classroom into world 3. In K. McGilly (Ed.), *Classroom Lessons: Integrating Cognitive Theory and Classroom Practice* (pp. 201–228). Cambridge, MA: MIT Press.

Scardamalia, M., Bereiter, C., McLean, R. S., Swallow, J., & Woodruff, E. (1989). Computer-supported intentional learning environments. *Journal of Educational Computing Research*, 5(1), 51–68.

Scheffler, I. (1991). In praise of cognitive emotions. In I. Scheffler (Ed.), *In Praise of Cognitive Emotions* (pp. 3–17). New York: Routledge.

Schoenfeld, A. H. (1982). Measures of problem-solving performance and of problem-solving instruction. *Journal of Research in Mathematics Teaching*, 13, 31–49.

Schoenfeld, A. H., & Herrmann, D. J. (1982). Problem perception and knowledge structure in expert and novice mathematical problem solvers. *Journal of Experimental Psychology: Learning, Memory, and Cognition*, 8, 484–494.

Schunk, D. H., & Zimmerman, B. J. (Eds.) (1994). *Self-regulation of Learning and Performance: Issues and Educational Applications*. Hillsdale, NJ: Erlbaum.

Selz, O. (1935). Attempt to raise the level of intelligence. *Zeitschrift für Psychologie*, 134, 236–301.

Stanovich, K. E., & West, R. F. (1997). Reasoning independently of prior belief and individual differences in actively open-minded thinking. *Journal of Educational Psychology*, 89(2), 342–357.

Sternberg, R. J. (1985). *Beyond IQ: A Triarchic Theory of Human Intelligence*. Cambridge, UK: Cambridge University Press.

Sternberg, R. J., Ferrari, M., Clinkenbeard, P., & Grigorenko, E. L. (1996). Identification, instruction, and assessment of gifted children: A construct validation of a triarchic model. *Gifted Child Quarterly*, 40(3), 129–137.

Sternberg, R. J. (Ed.) (2002). *Why Smart People Can Be So Stupid*. New Haven, CT: Yale University Press.

Sternberg, R. J., Conway, B. E., Ketron, J. L., & Bernstein, M. (1981). People's conceptions of intelligence. *Journal of Personality and Social Psychology*, 41(1), 37–55.

Sternberg, R. J., & Bhana, K. (1986). Synthesis of research on the effectiveness of intellectual skills programs: Snake-oil remedies or miracle cures? *Educational Leadership*, 44(2), 60–67.

Super, C. (1980). Cognitive development: Looking across at growing up. In C. Super, & S. Harkness (Eds.), *New Directions for Child Development: Anthropological Perspectives on Child Development* (pp. 59–69). San Francisco, Jossey-Bass.

Swartz, R. J., & Parks, S. (1994). *Infusing the Teaching of Critical and Creative Thinking into Elementary Instruction: A Lesson Design Handbook*. Pacific Grove, CA: Critical Thinking Press and Software.

Swartz, R. J., & Perkins, D. N. (1989). *Teaching Thinking: Issues and Approaches*. Pacific Grove, CA: Midwest Publications.

Thorndike, E. L. (1923). The influence of first year Latin upon the ability to read English. *School Sociology*, 17, 165–168.

Thorndike, E. L., & Woodworth, R. S. (1901). The influence of improvement in one mental function upon the efficiency of other functions. *Psychological Review*, 8, 247–261.

Tishman, S. (1994) *Thinking Dispositions and Intellectual Character*. Paper presented at the 1994 Annual Meeting of the American Educational Research Association, April 4–8. New Orleans, LA.

Tishman, S. (1995). High-level thinking, ethics, and intellectual character. *Think: The Magazine on Critical and Creative Thinking*, October, 9–14.

Tishman, S., & Perkins, D. N. (1997). The language of thinking. *Phi Delta Kappan*, 78(5), 368–374.

Tishman, S., Perkins, D. N., & Jay, E. (1993). Teaching thinking dispositions: From transmission to enculturation. *Theory into Practice*, 3, 147–153.

Tishman, S., Perkins, D. N., & Jay, E. (1995). *The Thinking Classroom: Learning and Teaching in a Culture of Thinking*. Needham Heights, MA: Allyn & Bacon.

Tversky, A., & Kahneman, D. (1993). Probabilistic reasoning. In A. I. Goldman (Ed.), *Readings in Philosophy and Cognitive Science* (pp. 43–68). Cambridge, MA: MIT Press.

Van Haneghan, J., Barron, L., Young, M., Williams, S., Vye, N., & Bransford, J. (1992). The Jasper series: An experiment with new ways to enhance mathematical thinking. In D. Halpern (Ed.), *Enhancing Thinking Skills in the Sciences and Mathematics* (pp. 15–38). Hillsdale, NJ: Erlbaum.

Voss, J. F., Perkins, D. N., & Segal, J. W. (1991). *Informal Reasoning and Education*. Hillsdale, NJ: Erlbaum.

Vygotsky, L. S. (1978). *Mind in Society: The Development of Higher Psychological Processes*. Cambridge, MA: Harvard University Press.

Webster, D. M., & Kruglanski, A. W. (1994). Individual differences in need for cognitive closure. *Journal of Personality and Social Psychology*, 67(6), 1049–1062.

Whimbey, A., & Lochhead, J. (1986). *Problem Solving and Comprehension*. Hillsdale, NJ: Erlbaum.

Worsham, A. W., & Austin, G. R. (1983). Effects of teaching thinking skills on SAT scores. *Educational Leadership*, 41(3), 50–51.

Zenke, L., & Alexander, L. (1984). Teaching thinking skills in Tulsa. *Educational Leadership*, 42(1), 81–84.

Author Index

Subject Index